The SAGE Handbook of
Media Processes
and Effects

To my parents, Rhona and Saleh Nabi, for being just who they are.
And to Cam and Mia—just because.

R. L. N.

To John, with love, for being my partner in all journeys.

M. B. O.

The SAGE Handbook of
Media Processes and Effects

Edited by
Robin L. Nabi
University of California, Santa Barbara

Mary Beth Oliver
Pennsylvania State University

Los Angeles | London | New Delhi
Singapore | Washington DC

For information:

SAGE Publications, Inc.
2455 Teller Road
Thousand Oaks, California 91320
E-mail: order@sagepub.com

SAGE Publications Ltd.
1 Oliver's Yard
55 City Road
London EC1Y 1SP
United Kingdom

SAGE Publications India Pvt. Ltd.
B 1/I 1 Mohan Cooperative Industrial Area
Mathura Road, New Delhi 110 044
India

SAGE Publications Asia-Pacific Pte. Ltd.
33 Pekin Street #02-01
Far East Square
Singapore 048763

Printed in the United States of America

Library of Congress Cataloging-in-Publication Data

The SAGE handbook of media processes and effects / Robin L. Nabi, Mary Beth Oliver [editors].
    p. cm.
Includes bibliographical references and index.
ISBN 978-1-4129-5996-4 (cloth)
  1. Mass media—Influence. 2. Mass media—Influence—Research—Methodology. 3. Mass media—Social aspects. 4. Mass media—Psychological aspects. I. Nabi, Robin L. II. Oliver, Mary Beth.
P94.S24 2009
302.23—dc22   2009010772

This book is printed on acid-free paper.

09   10   11   12   13   10   9   8   7   6   5   4   3   2   1

Acquisitions Editor:	Todd R. Armstrong
Editorial Assistant:	Aja Baker
Production Editor:	Astrid Virding
Copy Editor:	Brenda Weight
Typesetter:	C&M Digitals (P) Ltd.
Proofreader:	Scott Oney
Indexer:	Molly Hall
Cover Designer:	Candice Harman
Marketing Manager:	Jennifer Reed Banando

CONTENTS

Introduction   1
    Robin L. Nabi and Mary Beth Oliver

PART I: CONCEPTUAL AND METHODOLOGICAL ISSUES

1. A Retrospective and Prospective Look at Media Effects   9
   Jennings Bryant and Dolf Zillmann

2. Conceptualizing the Audience   19
   W. James Potter

3. Quantitative Methods and Causal Inference in Media Effects Research   35
   Itzhak Yanovitzky and Kathryn Greene

4. Qualitative Methods   53
   Thomas R. Lindlof

PART II: SOCIETY, POLITICS, AND CULTURE

5. Cultivation Analysis and Media Effects   69
   Michael Morgan

6. Framing and Agenda Setting   83
   Dhavan V. Shah, Douglas M. McLeod,
   Melissa R. Gotlieb, and Nam-Jin Lee

7. The Influence of Presumed Media Influence: Origins and Implications of the Third-Person Perception   99
   Nurit Tal-Or, Yariv Tsfati, and Albert C. Gunther

8. News and Politics 113
Vincent Price and Lauren Feldman

9. Media Effects and Cultural Studies:
A Contentious Relationship 131
Toby Miller

PART III: MESSAGE SELECTION AND PROCESSING

10. Uses and Gratifications: An Evolving
Perspective of Media Effects 147
Alan M. Rubin

11. Entertainment 161
Mary Beth Oliver

12. Current Research in Media Priming 177
David R. Roskos-Ewoldsen
and Beverly Roskos-Ewoldsen

13. The Limited Capacity Model
of Motivated Mediated Message Processing 193
Annie Lang

14. Emotion and Media Effects 205
Robin L. Nabi

15. Mediated Relationships and Media Effects:
Parasocial Interaction and Identification 223
Jonathan Cohen

16. Individual Differences in Media Effects 237
Marina Krcmar

17. Media Use and the Social Environment 251
Daniel G. McDonald

PART IV: PERSUASION AND LEARNING

18. Theories of Persuasion 269
Daniel J. O'Keefe

19. Social Cognitive Theory and Media Effects 283
Frank Pajares, Abby Prestin,
Jason Chen, and Robin L. Nabi

20. Emerging Issues in Advertising Research 299
L. J. Shrum, Tina M. Lowrey, and Yuping Liu

21. Media Effects and Population Health 313
K. Viswanath, Sherrie Flynt Wallington,
and Kelly D. Blake

22. Educational Television 331
Marie-Louise Mares

23. Media Literacy 345
W. James Potter and Sahara Byrne

PART V: CONTENT AND AUDIENCES

24. Violent Media Effects 361
    Brad J. Bushman, L. Rowell Huesmann,
    and Jodi L. Whitaker

25. Racial/Ethnic Stereotyping and the Media 377
    Dana E. Mastro

26. Media and the Body 393
    Kristen Harrison

27. Media and Sexuality 409
    Jane D. Brown

28. Perceptions of Media Realism and Reality TV 423
    Alice E. Hall

29. The Effects of Viewing Televised Sports 439
    Arthur A. Raney

30. Digital Games 455
    Peter Vorderer and Ute Ritterfeld

31. Children and Adolescents: Distinctive
    Audiences of Media Content 469
    Barbara J. Wilson and Kristin L. Drogos

PART VI: MEDIUM ISSUES

32. Diffusion of Innovations: Theoretical Extensions 489
    Ronald E. Rice

33. Displacement Effects 505
    Jennings Bryant and Wes Fondren

34. Medium Theory: An Alternative
    to the Dominant Paradigm of Media Effects 517
    Joshua Meyrowitz

35. The Evolution of Media System Dependency Theory 531
    Sandra J. Ball-Rokeach and Joo-Young Jung

36. Media Effects 2.0: Social and Psychological Effects
    of Communication Technologies 545
    S. Shyam Sundar

37. The Study of Media Effects in the Era
    of Internet Communication 561
    Miriam J. Metzger

Author Index 577

Subject Index 605

About the Contributors 635

INTRODUCTION

◆ Robin L. Nabi and Mary Beth Oliver

The study of media effects is one of the most central to the discipline of communication and encompasses a vast array of theoretical perspectives, methodological tools, and applications to important social contexts. However, in light of the extraordinarily rapid changes in the media environment over the last 20 years, media effects research is at a point where the innovations in content and technology have outpaced the theories typically applied to them. Thus, the timing seems right to reflect on and critically evaluate not only where the field of media effects has been over the past several decades, but more important, where it would be most fruitful to go in the years ahead. These are the underlying motivations and goals of this volume.

In recent years, a subtle (and sometimes not so subtle) malaise seems to have cast a pall over a large contingent of media researchers, due to what we argue are a series of theoretical, methodological, and conceptual crossroads facing the field. Focusing first on theory, recent content analyses (Bryant & Miron, 2004; Potter & Riddle, 2007) paint a somewhat discouraging picture of the media effects research landscape—one that is at best as likely to mention any theory as not, one that uses theory as a framework only a quarter of the time, and one with little attention to theoretical development. Even for the most commonly studied theories, there is often little systematic attention and critical examination. The concern that scholars are chasing effects rather than reflecting on the processes that underlie the outcomes of media exposure has exacerbated this dissatisfaction with the theoretical state of the field.

Added to this discontent are concerns about the methods used to evaluate media processes and effects, including issues regarding the determination of content categories, the measurement of media exposure and use, the samples used and threats to generalizability, and the lack of realistic social environments in which media use is studied. Moreover, a range of conceptual issues faces the field, the most critical of which is arguably this: What do we mean by "media effects"? If one had thought the field was on a smooth course, one only had to attend the 2008 International Communication Association panel "The Future of Media Effects Theory: Charting a Course for the 21st Century" to find passionate discussion and debate regarding where we are at present and where we need to go. Although no consensus was reached, participants (and there were many) seemed united in the sense that the field is in need of reorientation (Nabi, Cappella, Wartella, & Roskos-Ewoldsen, 2008).

As we reflect on why the study of media effects has reached this crossroads, we suggest that it may be that one of the strongest motivations for studying the media—its great practical appeal—may also serve as its greatest stumbling block in that the concern over (usually) harmful effects generates excitement to pursue problem-based research. Once effects are demonstrated, the lure of issues of application often becomes stronger than those related to illumination of process. Exacerbating this problem, we believe, are structural issues within academe in which the pressures to publish as junior scholars and to pursue grant opportunities result in the development of habits (and perhaps realities) in which replication-based and applied work is more adaptive to pursue, and often at the expense of the more sophisticated, theoretically rich work that we value as a discipline.

However, the new media environment, with its associated innovations in technology and content, offers the ideal catalyst to encourage scholars to reassess the state of media effects research and how we might proceed so that we can meet our dual goals of producing scholarship that is both theoretically insightful and socially relevant. As we reflected on the state of the field, several observations shaped our vision for this volume. First, numerous theoretical paradigms that seemed to have served the field well (e.g., cultivation, uses and gratifications), though still frequently referenced, have been increasingly maligned in print and conversation. Have such paradigms exceeded their "sell by" date, or might efforts to reflect on such theories in light of the new media age engender a renewal of their relevance to modern media study? Second, there appear to be a number of topics that—though seemingly central to issues of media consumption and effects—have been, if not ignored, then sorely overlooked (e.g., emotion, social context of consumption). Consideration of a range of media phenomena in light of these and other concepts has the potential to breathe new life into more fatigued areas of media research. Further, the new media environment itself, especially to the extent it introduces issues related to time and place (e.g., DVR technology, portable media) and allows for greater user involvement (e.g., interactivity, user-generated content), raises a host of questions and highlights the increasingly complex process of conceptualizing media consumption and effects.

In light of these thoughts, our goal with the *Handbook* has been to address key theoretical, methodological, and conceptual issues within a range of areas central to media research such that each chapter may offer both a comprehensive orientation to that area and an agenda for future thinking and research. With this in mind, each chapter is designed to address the area's historical context, relevant theory, and conceptual developments; to provide an assessment of what conclusions can be drawn from the extant research; to highlight notable methodological issues; to discuss criticisms and controversies that have been raised; to consider the impact of the new media environment for research in the area; and to outline critical directions for future research.

Given the scope and diversity of the field of media effects, finding an organization scheme for the range of chapters was one of the more challenging aspects of this project. Our thinking on this front was guided by an attempt to group material based on critical issues related to the study of media: conceptualization of key process elements, the societal and individual factors involved in the process of media consumption, the processes and outcomes related to intentional influence, and finally the content and medium issues of prominence and import. Surely there are other ways to organize the vast landscape of media effects scholarship, but our hope is that this presentation will conceptually cohere both within and across sections.

The *Handbook*, then, is divided into six sections. In Part I, we begin with an overview of the field, conceptualizations of media effects and audiences, and the key methodological issues most relevant to the study of media effects. As the extent and validity of the knowledge we gain is contingent on our methods of knowledge acquisition, we consider this to be an essential component to the value of this volume.

In Part II, we focus on dominant theoretical approaches in the media effects arena from more societal, political, and cultural perspectives. Here we include some of the central theoretical paradigms in the media effects realm (i.e., cultivation, framing, perceived influence) that relate to the broad-reaching effects of media with macrolevel implications.

In Part III, we focus on the themes of message selection and processing that are central to the mass media literature. These chapters range in the scope of their theoretical development in that some of the chapters focus on specific theoretical perspectives and models (e.g., uses and gratifications, limited capacity model), whereas other chapters examine selection, processing, and response variables that can be examined from a host of theoretical vantage points (e.g., emotion, identification, individual differences). Regardless, these processes all cut across and thus are relevant to the full complement of media content domains.

In Part IV, the volume turns to a dominant trend in media effects literature—its relation to persuasion and learning—and traces its theoretical perspectives, including major theories of persuasion and especially social cognitive theory, through the various contexts in which media have such effects, including health, advertising, and media literacy.

Part V then takes us to the contexts and audiences that have been traditional foci of media effects research—violence, children, body image, video games, sports, and the like. In each chapter, the authors take broad and integrative perspectives, addressing the theories most applicable to those contexts and the current state of knowledge, while also reflecting on the critical issues that remain unresolved.

Part VI moves the *Handbook* from more specific forms of content to a concern central and unique to the communication discipline—message medium. These chapters examine how the medium of the message influences processing and effects ranging from what messages are attended to (e.g., media dependency), to how we spend our time (e.g., displacement effects), and even to how we interact as a society (e.g., medium theory).

We recognize that there are several volumes that currently review the domain of media effects quite well. Our hope is that this volume will complement those offerings in several ways. First, we believe the bird's eye view of the field taken by these chapters, including addressing the relevant historical and methodological issues and providing integrative summaries of the state of the research in that area, will help give readers unique perspective and context to these research domains. Second, this volume emphasizes process in ways that we hope highlight the importance of issues related to viewer selection, interpretation, understanding, and engagement. Finally, we have encouraged authors—all top experts in their fields—to offer their insights and reflections on their own domains of research, with particular attention to new media, with the hope that their ideas will generate discussion and collaboration and thus provide media effects research with more direction and traction than the field may have had in recent years.

There is just one final point we wish to make. Throughout this introduction and the volume, you will note that the term *media effects* is frequently used, often as a shorthand not simply to reflect the outcomes of media consumption but to capture the full range of media effects processes, which are often quite complicated, fluid, and interactive. Unfortunately, use of this shorthand within the field can lead to the misperception that media scholars are not interested in process but only in outcome. As it is unlikely that use of the truncated term *media effects* to reflect our interest in the full range of media consumption processes will wane, we chose to title this volume *The SAGE Handbook of Media Processes and Effects* to highlight the increasing emphasis and interest of media effects scholars on the processes of effects resulting from media exposure.

Finally, before we leave you to this volume, we wish to offer our most sincere thanks to those who have made this project possible. The authors of these chapters are exceptional scholars who,

given their dedication to this field, made remarkable efforts to produce chapters that we believe will truly help advance the study of media effects, and for this we extend our eternal thanks. We also wish to thank Todd Armstrong, Aja Baker, and the SAGE team for their unwavering support of this project, as well as the reviewers of the initial prospectus (Brad J. Bushman, University of Michigan; David R. Ewoldsen, The Ohio State University; Ken Lachlan, Boston College; W. James Potter, University of California, Santa Barbara; Alan M. Rubin, Kent State University; Dietram A. Scheufele, University of Wisconsin—Madison; Michael Slater, The Ohio State University; and Glenn G. Sparks; Purdue University) and our colleagues whose advice and guidance have been indispensable, especially in the early stages of this work.

There are, of course, no words to express our gratitude to and for our spouses, Bob Kennedy and John Christman, for their unconditional patience and support throughout this journey. We can only imagine that they are as happy as we are to see this volume in print—and for all the right reasons. And finally, we thank you—our readers—for your interest in this work, and we hope you find that it delivers on its promise to illuminate the processes and effects of the media embedded within our personal and social worlds and that it inspires you to undertake the next generation of research in this most important and worthy pursuit.

◆ References

Bryant, J., & Miron, D. (2004). Theory and research in mass communication. *Journal of Communication, 54,* 662–704.

Nabi, R. L., Cappella, J. N., Wartella, E., & Roskos-Ewoldsen, D. (2008). *The future of media effects theory? Charting a course for the 21st century.* Panel presentation at the International Communication Association, Montreal, Quebec, Canada.

Potter, W. J., & Riddle, K. (2007). A content analysis of the media effects literature. *Journalism & Mass Communication Quarterly, 84,* 90–104.

PART I

CONCEPTUAL AND METHODOLOGICAL ISSUES

A RETROSPECTIVE AND PROSPECTIVE LOOK AT MEDIA EFFECTS

◆ Jennings Bryant and Dolf Zillmann

◆ *Roots of Concerns About Communication Effects*

It has been suggested that considerations of communication effects date back at least to ancient Greece, when Socrates was criticized for corrupting the youth of Athens by creatively enhancing the persuasive potency of speech. When such a claim for the antiquity of concern with communication effects is coupled with considerations of Plato's fear that the ascendancy of the written word would surpass and suppress the power of the spoken word, the case could be made that concern with potentially harmful media effects can be traced back to as early as the fifth century BCE (Perloff, 2002).

With the advent of printing (in China around 220 CE), movable type (in China around 1040 CE), metal movable type (in Korea around 1230 CE), and finally the printing press (in Germany around 1450 CE), the technological prerequisites for the earliest forms of mass media were in place. When the spread of literacy began in earnest in the 19th century, the technological revolution in publishing joined with it, and what resulted was the development of newspapers, novels, and other forms of print media that soon were designed and produced for and disseminated to everyday folk. Thus, mass communication was born. This development spawned our first major communication revolution, which rapidly changed the nature of the communication equation by putting entertainment, information, and commercial content in the hands of the people.

These developments also upped the ante in terms of concerns about seriously harmful media effects. Shadowing Plato's fear, society's elite increasingly recognized the potential social upheaval that could result from widespread exposure to the printed word. Suddenly, critics began to decry the potency of novels that could cause "the entire destruction of the powers of the mind" (Starker, 1989, p. 8), as well as "annuals, brochures, and family newspapers [that can sow] a seed of corruption which will bring disgrace and wretchedness upon thousands, if not lay the foundation of that sensual and selfish spirit which will contaminate the nation at large, and threaten the downfall of its free institutions" ("Pernicious Literature," 1847, p. 46).

Numerous European attempts to thwart the free flow of information emanating from these foundling mass media bear testimony to the desire of those in authority to suppress the written word. For example, in 1559, Pope Paul IV began disseminating an *Index of Prohibited Books,* which included Protestant books, pornography, occult books, and opposition political works. When Martin Luther and his Protestant compatriots defied the pope and found creative ways to use the printing press to spread Reformation literature to the masses, those rebels who used media without authority were often severely punished by those in power, including being imprisoned, beheaded, or burned at the stake. Later, King Henry VIII was so concerned about the impact of the printed word that he formed the Court of the Star Chamber to prosecute those who printed material hostile to the Crown. He also instituted a licensing system to control the English press (Bryant & Thompson, 2002).

Although the American colonists celebrated their successful fight for independence by incorporating press freedoms into the Bill of Rights of their governing Constitution, a critical look at U.S. history reveals numerous efforts to throttle press freedoms and institute various forms of censorship, again because of obvious fear of media effects. Notable efforts of suppression include the Sedition Act of 1798, designed to muffle pro-French voices in American newspapers during the French Revolution, and the Espionage Act of 1917 and the Sedition Act of 1918 during World War I, which made it illegal to publish information critical of the U.S. government or overtly supportive of enemy powers. Implicit in these and other attempts at censorship and suppression, which continued into the present day with the USA Patriot Act of 2001, were models that assume potent effects from giving the press and public unbridled tongues. As Judge Alexander Addison wrote in 1799 in the *Columbian Centinel,* "Give to any set of men the command of the press and you give them the command of the country, for you give them the command of public opinion, which commands everything" (Sloan, 1998, p. 119).

To be candid, media were in part responsible for these efforts at restriction because the popular press often chronicled and irresponsibly sensationalized instances of powerful media effects, fanning the flames of public concern about propaganda, violence, and indecent material. But concern with powerful media effects also was owed, in part, to the development and increased prominence of stimulus-response models in psychology and the other social sciences, which focused attention on the impact of powerful stimuli, including media messages (e.g., Perse, 2001). Even more intense concern was expressed because of widespread uncertainty about the social and psychological impact of the earliest generation of those newfangled electronic mass media, especially on children and adolescents.

◆ *Early Scientific Study of Media Effects*

The scientific study of media effects began during World War I, in large part in response to concerns about propaganda spread by the military at home and abroad. Critics also expressed similar concerns about what were perceived to be incredibly potent advertising and public relations efforts being employed by rapidly expanding and often ruthless and inhumane corporations.

Initially, many social scientists, as well as the general public, tended to believe that mass media produced uniformly powerful (and negative) effects on their unsuspecting and largely helpless audiences. This supreme and presumably subversive power of media messages on vulnerable audiences was often described using colorful metaphors: Mass media supposedly *fired* messages like dangerous bullets, or *injected* messages like strong drugs propelled through hypodermic needles. Such potent metaphors gave rise to the "bullet" or "hypodermic needle" theories of powerful media effects. Other scholars have labeled these early theoretical models "the theory of uniform media influences" (e.g., Harris, 1994).

The traditional history of media effects research typically attributes the rise of these powerful effects theories to the development of a worldview of a mass society of fragmented individuals who served as the hapless consumers of mass media messages. Several early media theorists (e.g., Bruntz, 1938; Lasswell, 1927; Lippmann, 1922) focused on the marked changes taking place in society during the late 19th and early 20th centuries. They emphasized the concept of mass behavior, which typically was attributed to the urbanization and industrialization of society, which, in turn, allegedly was due primarily to the social and economic pressures that uprooted people from their local cultures and familial and peer group settings, which seemingly led to feelings of isolation and increased vulnerability.

Several influential early books on mass media were written with an apparent underlying acceptance of the bullet or hypodermic needle theories. These included Lippmann's *Public Opinion* (1922), Lasswell's *Propaganda Technique in the World War* (1927), and Bruntz's *Allied Propaganda and the Collapse of the German Empire in 1918* (1938). The powerful effects model also stimulated and helped shape the creation of the influential Institute for Propaganda Analysis (IPA, 1937–1942), which was devoted to informing the public about propaganda. A collaborative, nonprofit organization of professors at Princeton, Columbia, and several other organizations, but headquartered in New York City, the IPA was one of the first major attempts at "media education," or, more specifically, in preventing harmful media effects through "inoculation." The Institute received considerable public attention because of the widespread fear that without critical education about propaganda, citizens of the emerging unstable mass society could not withstand the onslaught of subversive mass media messages.

Journalist Walter Lippmann's *Public Opinion* (1922) was an especially important catalyst in the history of media effects research. In this classic work, Lippmann relied heavily on his experiences with propaganda during World War I, and he stressed the role of the news media in robustly influencing audiences' perceptions about important issues. Lippmann's poignant prose (e.g., "the world outside and the pictures in our head") framed public opinion research for future generations of communication scholars, for better or for worse.

The powerful effects model is frequently alleged to have served as the conceptual basis for a series of early empirical media effects investigations into media violence sponsored by the Payne Fund in the 1920s, but in fact those principal investigators routinely considered factors such as age, cognitive abilities, and peer influence that could mitigate potentially powerful media effects. Although these investigators examined the influence of motion pictures on children—and typically found movies to be powerful instruments of education, attitude change, emotional impact, health, and behaviors—such effects were not found to be uniform for all children and youth.

◆ A Shift in Effects Models

With few exceptions, the powerful effects model (or theory of uniform media influences) seems to have remained the dominant paradigm of media effects until the mid-1940s, when empirical studies began to suggest that effects from mass media were neither as uniform nor as powerful as originally thought. The prevalent worldview of scholars shifted also. Rather than a society of fragmented souls who received omnipotent messages from mass media, the public began to be viewed as a loose collective of somewhat interconnected individuals who typically were neither alienated nor isolated, and who were active in selecting, discarding, and even resisting media messages. This active audience was perceived as limiting the effects of media messages and as having considerable self-determination and influence.

Moreover, studies by Paul Lazarsfeld and associates at Columbia University's Bureau of Applied Social Research, especially the voting studies reported in *The People's Choice* (Lazarsfeld, Berelsen, & Gaudet, 1944/1948), revealed the important role of individual opinion leaders, who discussed and interpreted media messages for their peers, a process that sometimes mitigated media impact. Other social scientists, such as Carl Hovland, then working for the U.S. War Department, confirmed empirically that mass media had only limited effects on individuals in their audiences. Hovland conducted relatively sophisticated controlled experiments that assessed attitude change among soldiers who viewed training or motivational films. He found that many of the films had little or no effect on the soldiers' attitudes or motivations, and that individual-difference factors were very important in determining who was persuaded and who was not.

The limited effects model received enhanced visibility when Joseph Klapper published *The Effects of Mass Communication* (1960). This classic work reviewed hundreds of media effects studies from the 1920s through the 1950s and offered numerous generalizations and conclusions about mass media effects. Klapper called for a new, "phenomenistic" approach to research in the field, which emphasized several factors that seemingly limited the effects of mass media messages on individuals. In Klapper's view, audience members were typically perceived as selecting and utilizing media messages that reinforced existing opinions, abilities, and beliefs, rendering the role of media more typically that of a sustainer and supporter than an agent of change.

◆ Yet Another Shift: Moderate-to-Powerful Effects

In the decades following the 1960s, mass media research thrived. The discipline of mass communication became firmly established at research universities throughout the United States, and it began to gain credibility and a foothold in academic institutions worldwide. As new approaches to studying media effects emerged, especially in areas other than public opinion, voting, and marketing, many new theories and research findings did not fit neatly into the limited effects paradigm. Rather quickly, the media effects portfolio was expanded to include new studies that indicated moderate-to-powerful media effects under certain conditions.

Perhaps the most widely discussed theory of the time to assert more robust media effects, although one rarely attempting to demonstrate such empirically, was Marshall McLuhan's sense extension theory, presented in *Understanding Media* (1964). This theory claimed that media effects do not result from exposure to media *content* per se, but from using the essential *form* of a medium that is routinely and almost universally consumed. In other words, media effects are often medium specific and may be cultural—rather than essentially individual—in scope. Such medium effects were depicted as altering basic patterns of information processing, perception, and cognition among an entire population of users. As previously suggested, compelling empirical evidence that would support or refute such claims about culturally universal effects of using one medium versus another is largely lacking, but McLuhan's ideas were prominently featured in the popular press, as well as in trade books authored or coauthored by McLuhan, and they captured the public's imagination. Not only did such publicity elevate the public's interests in McLuhan's notions: it also garnered increased attention for other types of media effects research.

For roughly a quarter of a century, from the latter 1960s through the early 1990s, the study of media effects thrived, progressing in a relatively linear manner, and emerging as the dominant perspective for studying the media (Harris, 1994). A number of well-developed theories and models of media uses and effects emerged (e.g., agenda setting, uses and gratifications, excitation transfer) and were tested via programmatic research efforts, through which they were refined and canonized. In retrospect, this may well have been the Golden Age of media effects research, in which our scholarly journals bulged with increasingly more sophisticated and relatively uniform approaches to theory construction in this popular area of mass communication inquiry. Although some dissenting voices were raised, most notably in the "Ferment in the Field" issue of *Journal of Communication* in 1983, a bird's eye view of this era undoubtedly would reveal a rapidly accumulating and maturing, relatively cohesive body of knowledge about media effects (e.g., Bryant & Miron, 2004).

◆ Conceptualizations of Media Effects

One of the several issues raised in the "ferment debate" had to do with conceptualizations of media effects. As Perse (2001) noted, "one of the first and most important assumptions of the study of mass communication has been the presumption that media and their content have significant and substantial effects" (p. 3).

WHAT ARE MEDIA EFFECTS?

This notion of *media effects* warrants further explication. In general, when scholars talk about media effects, they are considering the social or psychological changes that occur in consumers of media message systems—or in their social milieu or cultural values—as a result of being exposed to, processing, or acting on those mediated messages. Five classes of media effects on individuals are often considered: behavioral, attitudinal, cognitive, emotional, and physiological. *Behavioral* effects result when a media message consumer performs some action presented via media. *Attitudinal* effects occur when media shape message consumers' opinions, beliefs, and values. *Cognitive* effects are those that result when media change what consumers think or know. *Emotional* effects occur when media produce certain feelings, such as fear, anxiety, or euphoria, in message consumers. And *physiological* effects are those changes in arousal or other physical bodily reactions that are derived from media consumption. Numerous other typologies of media effects (e.g., immediate vs. long-term, beneficial vs. detrimental, intentional vs. accidental) are also employed by scholars who investigate media effects.

DETERMINING CAUSALITY WITH MEDIA EFFECTS

All of these presumptions of effects of various types from consuming media messages transport us into one of the thorniest areas of philosophy: the analysis of cause and effect, or causality. Causality denotes a necessary relationship between one event and another, of which the second event (the effect) is the direct result of the first (the cause). For centuries, this straightforward concept of causality was the foundation of scientific theory. That is, the prevailing notion in science was that a specific event caused a predictable reaction. It was this purview that was the foundling epistemological cradle for the study of media effects. For example, Lippmann (1922) argued that mass media messages created pictures of the world that shaped the images in the minds of message consumers, a classic example of the notion of cause and effect.

However, although such early conceptualizations of media effects were born in the context of this prevailing linear, mechanistic model, soon thereafter, Max Born (1949) shook up the scientific world by introducing the notion that cause and effect could not be determined exactly, only probabilistically. In Born's probabilitistic

view, three assumptions reshaped the notion of causality from its deterministic roots: (1) the occurrence of an entity B (the effect) of a certain class depends on the occurrence of an entity A (the cause) of another class; (2) the cause must be prior to, or at least simultaneous with, the effect; and (3) contiguity postulates that cause and effects must be in spatial contact or connected by a chain of intermediate things in contact.

Such reasoning soon became normative in media effects models, although many critics of media effects research continued to identify it with more simplistic, strictly deterministic philosophies. However, the majority view of media effects seems better represented by Perry's (1996) application of the probabilistic-causality perspective to mass communication:

> Any discussion of media effects requires a concern with causation. Before a researcher can conclude that one concept is a cause of another, the research must establish three things. First, the presumed cause and the presumed effect must *covary,* or go together. For example, people who are heavily exposed to mediated violence should tend, on the average, to be either more or less aggressive than those who are less exposed. If aggressiveness increases along with exposure, the two variables are positively correlated or associated. If aggressiveness tends to decline as exposure increases, the two are negatively correlated. Second, the presumed cause must precede the presumed effect. Finally, a researcher must eliminate plausible rival (i.e., third variable) explanations for the observed covariation of the presumed cause and effect. (pp. 25–26)

This interpretation reflects Born's (1949) probabilitistic causation, rather than the purely deterministic model, and undoubtedly reflects the epistemological underpinnings of most contemporary media effects research.

◆ Recent Trends

Accompanying this shift in dominant perceptions of causation have been a number of recent trends in media effects research that also rely on evolving epistemological notions. For example, media reception theory emphasized the role of social constraints and audience interpretations of media texts (or message systems), which began to receive widespread credence as mediating or mitigating factors in media effects. Most of this theory and research originated from Europe or Australia during the 1970s and 1980s, but it took more than a decade to receive widespread recognition and limited adoption in the United States, often in the form of critical or cultural studies approaches to the study of media effects (e.g., De Certeau, 1988; Hayward, 2000; Morley, 1980; Staiger, 2002; see also Miller, Chapter 9, this volume).

Another critical change—one that often yielded more pronounced effect sizes than in prior media effects research—was a shift toward examining dimensions of media effects other than their behavioral impact. In fact, studies assessing cognitive, affective, physiological effects often revealed that changes in knowledge, attitude, or affect were important in their own right, even if they did not necessarily lead to immediate and overt changes in behaviors.

Several prominent models of media effects—the so-called stalactite/stalagmite or drip (as opposed to drench) theories—such as the cultivation hypothesis, along with several epidemiological health communication models (e.g., Centerwall, 1989; Eron & Huesmann, 1984; cf. Perry, 2007), proposed that some of the most culturally important media effects could only be observed over time, because they were inherently iterative in nature. Novel research protocols (e.g., long-term treatment, delayed assessment) and statistical models (e.g., path analysis) were adopted

to help guide and interpret findings from such new effects models.

Moreover, in the latter two decades of the 20th century and into the 21st century, many investigators began to focus on the *process* of effects, including precursors of effects (e.g., selective exposure, attention, comprehension, information acquisition) and reception processes per se (e.g., disposition, empathy). As with the "drip" theories, these new approaches required new theories (e.g., elaboration likelihood model, mood management) and measurement approaches (e.g., physiological research, reaction time), along with refined statistical procedures (e.g., structural equation modeling).

New procedures for aggregating research evidence across numerous studies that had investigated the same topic (e.g., meta-analysis) also helped give communication scholars more accurate and holistic models of media effects (e.g., Preiss, Gayle, Burrell, Allen, & Bryant, 2007). When used in conjunction with more sophistical longitudinal designs and field experiments, findings often revealed that many of the most robust sorts of media effects accumulate over time and with continued media use (i.e., cumulative effects).

As a result of this burgeoning body of increasingly coherent, cohesive, and consensual evidence, a number of professional associations (e.g., American Medical Association, American Academy of Pediatrics, American Psychological Association, Parent-Teachers Association) have issued public policy statements regarding the place of media consumption in the personal and public health of societies and their citizens, especially young people. The vast majority of these statements have implicitly or explicitly adopted moderate-to-powerful media effects models and have taken a decidedly negatively valenced view of media effects. A typical resultant statement might be that under certain social and ecological conditions (e.g., media use pattern, family structure, mediation style), regular and prolonged exposure to certain types of media fare (e.g., violence, pornography, commercials for fast foods) contributes to mental or physical health problems (e.g., increased aggression or hostility, ADHD, obesity), especially among children and adolescents. Such claims for moderate and even powerful negative media effects have often become truisms in postmodern information societies, occasionally influencing public policy. However, in reality many of the most important media effects questions remain unanswered, at least to the satisfaction of many communication scholars, and the numerous studies revealing positive media effects (e.g., Mares & Woodard, 2007) rarely gain the public eye, much less the attention and use of policymakers.

◆ The Future

Without question, the nature of today's mediated communication has shifted dramatically. Among many other changes, traditional mass media have become less important in everyday life compared with even the recent past, and they have been replaced in terms of use, perceived value, and credibility by more interactive, personalized, mobile media that allow user agency and even user-generated production of messages. Little, if any, question remains that models and theories of media effects are in for a sea change, if they are to remain viable and veridical.

Moreover, today's new media (e.g., the Internet, video and computer games) undoubtedly will not be tomorrow's new media. For example, one of our oldest forms of media, wireless communication, has been reinvented and repurposed into the early 21st century's media darling and the fastest growing communication technology of all times (Castells, Fernandez-Ardevol, Qiu, & Sey, 2007). With its ascendancy, we are moving into new

phases of "the network society" (Castells, 2000), in which many of the educational, information, social, and entertainment functions of communication, especially for younger, more affluent citizens, are being delivered by mobile communications, creating a "mobile network society" (Castells et al., 2007).

As this new communication revolution alters the fundamental nature of traditional media functions (e.g., news gathering, editorialization, education, entertainment), and as the market adjusts and even newer technologies emerge to better serve media's newer functions (e.g., social networking, user-generated communication), not only will new models and theories of media effects be essential, but the essential nature of our research methodologies must change. Indeed, the fundamental discussion of the nature of media effects must be renegotiated.

◆ References

Born, M. (1949). *Natural philosophy of cause and chance.* Oxford: Clarendon Press.

Bruntz, G. G. (1938). *Allied propaganda and the collapse of the German empire in 1918.* Stanford, CA: Stanford University Press.

Bryant, J., & Miron, D. (2004). Theory and research in mass communication. *Journal of Communication, 54,* 662–704.

Bryant, J., & Thompson, S. (2002). *Fundamentals of media effects.* New York: McGraw-Hill.

Castells, M. (2000). *The rise of network society* (2nd ed.). Oxford: Blackwell.

Castells, M., Fernandez-Ardevol, M., Qiu, J., & Sey, A. (2007). *Mobile communication and society: A global perspective.* Cambridge, MA: MIT Press.

Centerwall, B. S. (1989). Exposure to television as a risk factor for violence. *American Journal of Epidemiology, 129,* 643–652.

De Certeau, M. (1988). *The practice of everyday life.* Berkeley: University of California Press.

Eron, L. D., & Huesmann, L. R. (1984). The control of aggressive behavior by changes in attitudes, values, and the conditions of learning. In R. J. Blanchard & D. C. Blanchard (Eds.), *Advances in the study of aggression* (pp. 139–171). Orlando: Academic Press.

Harris, R. J. (1994). *A cognitive psychology of mass communication* (2nd ed.). Hillsdale, NJ: Erlbaum.

Hayward, S. (2000). *Cinema studies: The key concepts.* London: Routledge.

Klapper, J. T. (1960). *The effects of mass communication.* New York: Free Press.

Lasswell, H. D. (1927). *Propaganda technique in the World War.* New York: Knopf.

Lazarsfeld, P. F., Berelsen, B., & Gaudet, H. (1948). *The people's choice.* New York: Duell, Sloan, and Pearce. (Original work published 1944)

Lippmann, W. (1922). *Public opinion.* New York: Harcourt Brace.

Mares, M.-L., & Woodard, E. H. (2007). Positive effects of television on children's social interaction: A meta-analysis. In R. W. Preiss, B. M. Gayle, N. Burrell, M. Allen, & J. Bryant (Eds.), *Mass media effects research: Advances through meta-analysis* (pp. 281–300). Mahwah, NJ: Erlbaum.

McLuhan, M. (1964). *Understanding media: The extensions of man.* New York: McGraw-Hill.

Morley, D. (1980). *The nationwide audience.* London: British Film Institute.

Perloff, R. M. (2002). The third-person effect. In J. Bryant & D. Zillmann (Eds.), *Media effects: Advances in theory and research* (2nd ed., pp. 489–506). Mahwah, NJ: Erlbaum.

Pernicious literature: No. 1. (1847). *United States Catholic Magazine and Monthly Review, 6,* 46–48.

Perry, D. K. (1996). *Theory and research in mass communication: Contexts and consequences.* Mahwah, NJ: Erlbaum.

Perry, D. K. (2007). Does television kill? Testing a period-characteristic model. *Media Psychology, 9,* 567–594.

Perse, E. M. (2001). *Media effects and society.* Mahwah, NJ: Erlbaum.

Preiss, R. W., Gayle, B. M., Burrell, N., Allen, M., & Bryant, J. (Eds.). (2007). *Mass media effects research: Advances through meta-analysis.* Mahwah, NJ: Erlbaum.

Sloan, W. D. (1998). The partisan press/ 1783–1833. In W. D. Sloan (Ed.), *The age of mass communication* (pp. 119–146). Northport, AL: Vision Press.

Staiger, J. (2002). Reception studies in film and television. In G. Turner (Ed.), *The film culture reader* (pp. 46–72). London: Routledge.

Starker, S. (1989). *Evil influences: Crusade against the mass media.* New Brunswick, NJ: Transaction.

2

CONCEPTUALIZING
THE AUDIENCE

◆ W. James Potter

◆ *Conceptualizing the Audience*

This chapter analyzes how conceptualizations of "audience" are related to mass media effects. The chapter begins with an overview of changes in those scholarly conceptualizations over the past century and then builds to a critical analysis of current thinking about audiences. From that critical analysis, the chapter moves into a synthesis of the main ideas and then into a media exposure model that is presented as a way of organizing thinking about the variety of ways audiences experience media messages and how those messages may—or may not—be influencing them.

◆ *Changes in Thinking About Audience*

When scholars write about mass media audiences, they typically take an historical approach and show how thinking about the nature of mass media audiences has changed (for example, see Bauer, 1973; Ettema & Whitney, 1994; Freidson, 1971; Kitzinger, 2004; Lowery & DeFleur, 1988; McQuail, 2005; Schramm, 1973; Webster & Phalen, 1997; Wright, 1986). Such thinking generally reflects five different ideas about how the audience is influenced by media messages: (1) mass audience and powerful propaganda, (2) limited effects and complex sets of factors, (3) social context, (4) individual differences in selection and use, and (5) multiple meanings from personal interpretations.

1. *Mass audience and powerful propaganda.* Scholars in the early part of the 20th century regarded media audiences as a "mass" audience, defined as an undifferentiated collection of anonymous, widely dispersed, interchangeable people who were relatively defenseless from the power of media influence (see Blumer, 1939). Propaganda was seen as being a successful shaper of public opinion in a uniform and widespread manner. Because audience members were regarded as passive isolates, they simply accepted the meaning presented in the media messages. Therefore, the mass media were believed to be very powerful, as illustrated by the use of the mixed metaphors of the media being hypodermic needles and their messages being magic bullets.

2. *Limited effects and complex sets of factors.* By the middle of the 20th century, scholars changed their belief to one of the mass media exerting a relatively weak or even nonexistent influence on audience members. The evidence for powerful effects was then regarded as anecdotal and suspect (for example, see Cantril, 1940). After reviewing the empirical literature on media effects up until 1958, Klapper (1960) concluded that mass media messages were associated with only relatively weak effects on audiences. Further, when researchers did find evidence of effects, there was no basis for cause-and-effect conclusions because the media messages were only one factor in a complex set of interacting influences. This came to be known as the limited effects model.

3. *Social context.* Supporting Klapper's conclusions were studies that showed audience members were typically part of social networks where they interacted with people on a continual basis (see Merton, 1949). The mass media had a stronger influence on some people than on others; that is, some people got their information and attitudes directly from the mass media, whereas other people got their information indirectly through opinion leaders (Katz & Lazarsfeld, 1955). This conception of audience influence became known as the two-step flow model.

4. *Individual differences in selection and use.* In the 1960s, scholars began regarding audience members as taking an active role in making medium and message exposure choices. People selectively exposed themselves to messages and selectively perceived certain bits of information within those messages such that most media messages and hence the potential for media influence was filtered out (Freedman & Sears, 1965; also see Zillmann & Bryant, 1985). Audience members actively make selections in order to solve personal problems, to satisfy preferences, to please other people, and to defend their egos (Bauer, 1973). This idea of an active audience that makes conscious decisions in selecting and using information from media messages spawned an approach to mass media studies called uses and gratifications (Katz, 1959; Katz, Blumler, & Gurevitch, 1974; Lazarsfeld & Stanton, 1949; Rosengren, Wenner, & Palmgreen, 1985; Rubin, Chapter 10, this volume). In this conceptualization, the audience is viewed as active and individual; people make rational informed choices based on preferences and needs.

5. *Multiple meanings from personal interpretations.* Not only do people make their own exposure choices; they also interpret their own meaning from media messages. Rarely do messages present a single meaning. Rather, media messages are polysemic (Hall, 1980), which means they are open to more than one reading. However, this does not mean that every person has his or her own personal meaning. Scholars who argued for the polysemic nature of

messages (e.g., Morley, 1980; Radway, 1984) regarded the audience as being composed of different groupings of people along social and cultural dimensions. Readings of a given media text differed across these groupings. Thus, people within a social or cultural group formed social networks where they learned particular sets of values and interpretations that shaped their readings of media texts.

◆ Current Thinking

This literature has left us with many ideas about how audiences should be conceptualized and how audiences are affected by mass media messages. When reviewing these ideas, scholars typically regard the current situation as being very complicated (Biocca, 1988; Butsch, 2000; Nightingale, 2004), with the notion of the audience becoming, as McQuail (2005) has said, "an increasingly diverse and complex reality, open to alternative and competing formulations" (p. 396). To help make sense of this complexity, I will highlight what I believe are the three most important themes in this scholarly thinking about mass media audiences. Then I will review the typologies that have been presented to organize this thinking. Given these typologies do not capture well the complexity of audiences as they tend to accept one side of a debate and ignore other positions, I will present an alternative perspective that synthesizes as many of these ideas as possible in a more complementary fashion.

THEMES IN AUDIENCE CONCEPTUALIZATIONS

Arguably, the three most important themes in the audience literature involve conceptions of exposure, audience activeness, and locus of meaning, each of which is discussed in the following paragraphs.

Exposure. Underlying all conceptions of audience is the idea of exposure to mass media messages. Without exposure, there can be no audience. But what is exposure? Most scholars treat this as a given and do not address it, but the few who have addressed it often equate it with some kind of attention to a message. In an oblique reference to exposure, Butsch (2000) argued that it is the text that gives meaning to the idea of audience when he says, "The 'television audience' exists only with the text of a program. Beyond that, 'the audience' does not exist; rather the individuals or households exist as entities unrelated to each other" (p. 289). In essence, Butsch is not only saying that without texts we can have no audiences; he is also implying that individuals must expose themselves to the text in order for them to be included in the audience.

A more direct treatment of exposure was offered by Salomon and Cohen (1978), who argued that physical exposure to a television set is a necessary—but not sufficient—condition for television viewing. They said, "Viewing-as-perception of messages entails more than the sheer number of hours spent in front of the screen. It may entail factors such as attention, motivation, and the like" (p. 268). They argue that unless viewers pay attention to messages, those messages can have no effect on them and therefore should not be considered exposure. "If televised content is to have an effect on behaviors, interests, attitudes, inclinations or cognitive skills, it must somehow be perceived by the viewer. Messages which are not perceived, that is, are not even noticed by a viewer, can hardly be expected to be influential" (p. 267).

In contrast to this position, Geiger and Newhagen (1993) argue that exposure can require attention but that it need not. They divide exposure into two kinds: controlled and automatic. "Controlled attention is synonymous with mental effort and is dictated by the goals of the individual processor. Automatic attention does not require the use of limited resources, and is determined by attributes of the information" (p. 44). Other cognitive psychologists explain that there is a range of consciousness about individual acts of cognition, that is, they fall along a continuum from automatic processing to controlled processing (Shiffrin, 1988). The positioning along this continuum is determined by the amount of cognitive resources required to execute it, which in turn is determined by the person's abilities and familiarity with a task (Pashler, 1998).

In sum, many scholars treat exposure as a primitive concept and do not define it. Those who do define exposure all require some sort of physical contact with messages. However, there is a disagreement as to whether attention is required for exposure or not. Some scholars require attention and even memory of the message in order to stipulate exposure; they argue that media influence cannot take place without attention. Other scholars argue that while exposure is often associated with attention, it can also take place unconsciously.

Audience activeness. There is a long-standing debate about the degree to which the audience is active. Recall the initial conception of mass audience and powerful propaganda where individuals were thought to be passive and therefore vulnerable to any and all mass media messages. Over the past 70 years, there has been a shift in thinking, from the view that the mass media audience is largely passive to the view that it is active. This does not mean that the idea of passive audience has disappeared. For example, Gauntlett (2005) has observed, "The notion of direct media effects on behaviour, rather than seeming absurd, is commonly recognised as entirely viable, and a cause for concern. It is likely that this is a result of the ever-recurrent moral panics in the press and other media, and the sheer persistence with which the question has been investigated by the academic community" (p. 5).

The debate about whether the audience is active or passive continues. Power, Kubey, and Kiousis (2002), however, are critical of scholarship on this point,

arguing that most researchers now accept either position, and then design their studies based on that one view—either active or passive. Yet, it is more likely that there are times when the audience is active and other times when it is passive.

Locus of meaning. There continues to be scholarly debate over the extent to which meaning resides in the media messages or is constructed by audiences. If meaning is in the messages, then the function of the audience is to analyze the messages to identify that denoted, or intended, meaning. That denoted meaning is cleanly conveyed when people are skilled in extracting the meaning from the messages. If some audience members do not extract the correct denoted meaning, their resulting meaning is faulty. This is the position typically taken by communication researchers who design experiments to test media influence. Experimental designs rely on the assumption that a different denoted meaning is conveyed by each of their treatments; participants are asked for the denoted meaning in manipulation checks to ensure that they have extracted the correct—or researcher-expected—denoted meanings.

On the other side of the debate are scholars who argue that media messages merely stimulate the meaning construction process. Media messages are multilayered and so rich in images, sounds, and words that they always suggest a variety of meanings (see Corner, 1991; Gray, 1999; Hall, 1980; Miller & Philo, 2001). In addition, these scholars argue that people's language is culturally influenced; that is, the way people interpret cultural symbols (such as the elements in all media messages) is shaped by how they have come to learn the meaning of these symbols in interactions with other people in their culture. Furthermore, each audience member brings to the exposure situation a complex array of personal experiences and needs; this complexity substantially shapes the meaning construction process. Thus, the meaning that the sender thinks he or she has built into the message is not always the meaning that is received by audience members.

TYPOLOGIES

To help make sense of this complexity, scholars have presented several typologies to organize thinking about audiences and try to show the main dimensions of differences among them. For example, Nightingale (2004) says audiences are often referred to as publics, markets, and communities. She offers a four-part typology of audience as people assembled, audience as people addressed, audience as happening, and audience as hearing or audition. McQuail says audiences can be delineated by place (local, national), by people (gender, age), by medium or channel (print, television), by content (genres), or by time (day parts). Webster and Phalen (1994) argue that there are four audience models, or distinct notions of what a mass media audience is: audience as victim, citizens, consumers, and commodity.

Although many of the categories in these typologies are relevant to how audiences are affected by the mass media, the categories are largely descriptive, rather than explanatory. That is, they suggest differences across groupings, but they do not specify the differing natures of their meaning processing. Also, though they are useful in organizing the salient differences in thinking about audiences across the conceptualizations, they are not useful in organizing the types of experiences audience members have during media exposures. Further, these typologies do little to help resolve any of the major debates about the nature of mass media audiences.

NEED FOR A COMPLEMENTARY APPROACH

There are powerful, valid arguments on both sides of these three debates. One way for an individual to resolve a debate is to accept one side and ignore the arguments from the other side. This simplifies things considerably, but it also requires one to ignore a lot of good ideas. A better way to resolve these debates is to invest effort into synthesizing the ideas of both sides into a construction that allows for both polar opposites as well as the many middle positions that lie between them. Livingstone (1990) makes this argument by pointing out the danger in taking a polar view of the audience being either passive or active when she says, "If we see the media or life events as all-powerful creators of meaning, we neglect the role of audiences; if we see people as all-powerful creators of meaning, we neglect the structure of that which people interpret" (p. 23; see also Power et al., 2002, for a similar argument.)

It is important to recognize that exposure can be unconscious as well as conscious. A person can be influenced by media messages in both states. We need to recognize that people are often active in their media choices and processing of meaning, but that there are many times when people are passive. We need to recognize that people are capable of interpretation, and they exhibit idiosyncratic personal interpretations of media messages frequently. This makes for great variety, and it generates a good deal of variation on most measures used in any social scientific study. However, there is also a significant degree of processing of denoted meaning from messages. Without this function, there could be no clear communication. The task lies not in evaluating which side of an argument is stronger. Instead, the task lies in finding value in each side, then blending all elements of value together into a system of explanation that both recognizes the complexity of the phenomenon and organizes scholarly thinking in a way that increases our understanding of that phenomenon.

The rest of this chapter will orient toward this task. The purpose driving the rest of this chapter is to synthesize such a typology—called the media exposure model—from the ideas about exposure states and message processing tasks. This typology does not separate individuals out into different audiences as other typologies do. Instead, the media exposure model focuses on the commonalities we share in our everyday experiences with mass media messages, and structures those experiences by states. Thus, the typology is based not on types of people but rather on types of exposure states and exposure tasks.

◆ Exposure States

As mentioned previously, there are scholars who argue that membership in an audience requires conscious exposure to media messages and that without attention, there is no exposure (Salomon & Cohen, 1978). However, other scholars point out that exposure to media messages is a mundane activity where attention is split or very low. For example, Kubey and Csikszentmihalyi (1991) found that television viewing typically was an uninvolving, secondary activity. During television exposures, people were reading, doing household chores, or talking to people. The same was found more recently by Schmitt, Woolf, and Anderson (2003).

In contrast, there are scholars who suggest that there are exposure states that require a very high degree of concentration. For example, scholars who write about techniques of media literacy suggest a high degree of message analysis and critical awareness is necessary (for a more complete discussion of this, see Potter, 2004). Also, another kind of hyperconcentration state suggested by scholars who highlight the way audiences can be "swept away" with media messages has been elaborated as flow (Csikszentmihalyi, 1988), presence (Lombard, Reich, Grabe, Bracken, & Ditton, 2000), transportation (Burke, 1969), and strong identification with characters in stories (Noble, 1975).

These are all important perspectives on the experience audience members have during exposure to mass media messages. These perspectives suggest that there is more than just a variation in the degree of attention during exposure, but that there are also *qualitatively* different kinds of exposure experiences. Elements from messages can enter our minds either when we are not paying conscious attention to those messages or when we are. Further, at the high end of attention, there appear to be several exposure states that are qualitatively different in terms of the exposure experience for audience members. These differences in exposure states have profound implications for how we conceptualize audience experience. Therefore, I suggest that there are four exposure states when it comes to media exposure: (1) attentional, (2) automatic, (3) transported, and (4) self-reflexive. The states are separated from one another by liminal thresholds such that the experience of crossing over a threshold from one state to the next is not simply a matter of changing the degree of cognitive effort; instead, crossing the line from one state into another results in a qualitatively different experience with the message.

ATTENTIONAL STATE

Attentional exposure refers to people being aware of the messages and actively interacting with their elements. This does not mean they must have a high level of concentration, although that is possible. The key is conscious awareness of the messages during exposures. Within the attentional state, there is a range of attention depending on how much of a person's mental resources are devoted to the exposure. At a minimum, the person must be aware of the message and consciously track it, but there is a fair degree of elasticity in the degree of concentration, which can range from partial to quite extensive processing depending on the number of elements handled and the depth of analysis employed.

Almost all experimental designs that test media effects have assumed that their participants are in the attentional state while being exposed to the treatment materials. Without this assumption, most measures used in this research would not have face validity. For example, media effects researchers frequently ask their participants to express their reactions to message elements and to engage cognitive processes required to make judgments about characters, plot points, credibility of information, persuasiveness of arguments, emotional reactions, and the like. All of these measures require participants to have paid attention to the stimulus materials and to consciously engage in cognitive processes of induction, inference, or evaluation. Also, because these researchers, in writing up their results, generalize their findings to everyday media exposure situations outside their laboratories, much of the mass media effects literature is based on the assumption that audiences are in the attentional state most of the time.

AUTOMATIC STATE

In the automatic processing state, message elements are physically perceived but processed automatically in an unconscious manner. This exposure state resides above the threshold of human sense perception but below the threshold of conscious awareness. The person is in a perceptual flow that continues until an interruption stops the exposure or "bumps" the person's perceptual processing into a different state of exposure, or until the media message moves outside of the person's physical or perceptual ability to be exposed to it.

In the automatic state, people can look active to outside observers (e.g., flipping through the pages of a magazine or clicking through the channels on a TV),

but they are not thinking about what they are doing. Although there is evidence of exposure behavior, this does not necessarily mean that people's minds are engaged and that they are "making" decisions. Rather, their minds are "running on automatic pilot" where they are following standard routines. Exposure to much of the media, especially radio and television, is likely in the automatic state. People have no conscious awareness of the exposure when it is taking place, nor do they have a recollection of the details in the experience later. Therefore, what happens in this exposure state cannot be reliably measured on self-report questionnaires, such as viewing diaries.

This is one of the more overlooked conditions in media scholarship. As Thompson (1995) said, one of the shortcomings of mass media research has been the neglect of describing the mundane character of how people encounter media messages in their everyday life. He says that "the reception of media products is a routine, practical activity which individuals carry out as an integral part of their everyday lives. If we wish to understand the nature of reception, then we must develop an approach which is sensitive to the routine and practical aspects of receptive activity" (p. 38).

Cultivation is one theory, for example, that is based on an assumption that much of media exposure takes place in an automatic state. Although Gerbner (1969) did not address exposure states explicitly, his arguments suggest that television viewers typically are not paying much attention to the particulars of the messages, and they do not actively process those messages by keeping running tabulations of numbers of occurrences of violent acts, sexual acts, types of characters, and so forth. Also, scholars who test for cognitive processes that explain the cultivation effect typically find that people generally use heuristics when providing their responses to cultivation indicator questions (for example, see Shrum, 1996). Thus, the cultivation literature suggests that people are typically in an automatic state during much of their exposures to the media.

TRANSPORTED STATE

When people are in the attentional state but then are pulled into the message so strongly that they lose awareness of being apart from the message, they cross over into the transported state. In the transported state, audience members lose their sense of separateness from the message, that is, they are swept away into the world of the message, and lose track of their own social world surroundings. As Green, Garst, and Brock (2004) note, a "transported individual is cognitively and emotionally involved in the story and may experience vivid mental images tied to the story's plot" (p. 168). My view of the transported state differs from that of Green et al., however, in that whereas Green et al. argue that transportation may aid in suspension of disbelief, which reduces a person's motivation to counterargue the issues raised in the story, I argue that suspension of disbelief is a process that is required in order for the transportation state to be entered and maintained. For example, producers of media messages will meet audience members in their real-world experience in terms of settings, plots, and characters. They then gradually pull the audience away from their world and transport them into another experience with more attractive, glamorous, and intriguing settings; faster and more intense plots; and bigger-than-life characters. Audience members must accept each step away from their mundane everyday real-world existence by willingly accepting each sweetened setting, plot point, and character alteration until they are transported into an experience.

The transported state is similar to the idea of flow as expressed by Csikszentmihalyi (1988), who defines flow as a state of high concentration and internally generated pleasure. Often, people are producing something during times of flow, such as an artist working on a painting, but there are other times when people are engaging in flow activities, such as sports and games, to avoid boredom. During flow, there is a distortion of time; hours can pass like minutes and conversely, a few seconds can seem to last a long time. Also, the person temporarily loses self-awareness that in normal life often intrudes in consciousness and causes psychic energy to be diverted from what needs to be done. According to Csikszentmihalyi, there are two key requirements for flow. First, there needs to be a challenge in a task so that it absorbs people, that is, it challenges their level of skill. Second, there needs to be a set of rules known to the person.

The transported state is similar, I argue, but not identical to flow. It is similar in that people are swept away by the experience and lose track of time as well as their real-world surroundings. It is different in that the transported state is triggered and maintained by media messages that intensely resonate with the audience member whereas flow is triggered and heightened by a challenge that slightly exceeds the person's skill level. In the transported state, people project themselves deeply into the media story; in flow, people project themselves into a challenge, and continually monitor their progress as they work hard to meet that challenge.

The transported state is not regarded in this media exposure model as the high end of the attentional state. Instead, the transported state is qualitatively different from the attentional state. Although attention is very high in the transported state, it is also very narrow. People are swept into the message (Green & Brock, 2000). In this sense, it is the opposite of the automatic state where people stay grounded in their social world and are unaware of the media messages in their perceptual environment. In the transported state, people have tunnel vision and focus on the media message in a way that eliminates the barrier between them and the message. Media scholars who design research to test the effects of repeated exposure to video games and virtual worlds through the Internet typically assume that their participants are in a transported state while playing. Thus, these designs cannot rely on self-reports of time and actions and instead must employ observations of behaviors and electronic recordings of actions.

SELF-REFLEXIVE STATE

In the self-reflexive state, people are hyperaware of the message *and of their processing of the message*. It is as if they are sitting on their own shoulder, monitoring their own reactions as they experience the message. In the self-reflexive state, people are not only consciously aware of the elements in the message; they are also aware of their processing of those elements. This represents the fullest degree of awareness: that is, people are aware of the media message, their own social world, and their position in the social world while they process the media message. In the self-reflexive exposure state, the viewer exercises the greatest control over perceptions by reflecting on questions such as, Why am I exposing myself to this message? What am I getting out of this exposure and why? and Why am I making these interpretations of meaning? Not only is there analysis, but there is meta-analysis. Although the self-reflexive and transported states might appear similar in that they are both characterized by high involvement, the two exposure states are very different. In the transported state, people are highly involved emotionally, and they lose themselves in the action. In contrast, the self-reflexive state is characterized by people being highly involved cognitively and very much aware of themselves as they

analytically process messages. The self-reflexive state is what is envisioned by scholars interested in media literacy. The goal of much media literacy research is to test which treatments are most successful in getting audiences to think more critically about their media exposures while they are being exposed.

In order to appreciate the value of considering exposure states in media effects research, we need to examine them in relation to what people do with the messages during exposures. Thus, I outline the sequence of three major tasks of exposure in the following section.

◆ Exposure Tasks

Regardless of exposure state, the experience of exposure is structured by a sequence of three information-processing tasks: filtering, meaning matching, and meaning construction (see Table 2.1). People encounter the filtering task as they are constantly confronted with exposure choices, and they must decide what to filter out and what gets their attention. The important questions governing the filtering task are, How can we make good decisions about filtering messages in a way that, on the one hand, helps us take advantage of the positive effects and, on the other hand, protects us from the negative effects of being overwhelmed or having our minds shaped by forces outside our control? And furthermore, how can we achieve this in a relatively efficient manner? The audience member can ask these questions consciously, but typically, these questions are posed in automatic, unconscious routines.

Once we have filtered in messages, we need to determine their meaning. I break this meaning assessment task into two separate processes of meaning matching and meaning construction. This distinction is based partially on the idea of closed codes and open codes as expressed by

Table 2.1 Summary of Three Tasks of Information Processing

Filtering Message

Task:	To decide which messages to filter out (ignore) and which to filter in (pay attention to)
Goal:	To attend to only those messages that have the highest utility and avoid all others
Focus:	Messages in the environment
Problem Type:	Frequently partially specified

Meaning Matching

Task:	To use basic competencies to recognize symbols and locate definitions for each
Goal:	To access previously learned meanings efficiently
Focus:	Referents in messages
Problem Type:	Frequently fully specified

Meaning Construction

Task:	To use skills to construct meaning for one's self in order to get more out of a message
Goal:	To interpret messages from more than one perspective as a means of identifying the range of meaning options, then choose one or synthesize across several
Focus:	One's own knowledge structures
Problem Type:	Almost always partially specified

Note: The three tasks are usually posed in sequence beginning with filtering; then moving to meaning matching; and then, if needed, moving to meaning construction. If a message is filtered out, then meaning matching and meaning construction are not encountered for that message. If a message is filtered in and meaning matching is sufficient, then meaning construction is not needed.

Stuart Hall (1980). Closed codes are those that direct people to particular denoted meanings that are commonly accepted, whereas open codes allow for divergence in meaning. Hall uses these terms to focus on choices made by message designers, that is, when people encode meaning into their messages. As for the decoding of the meaning by individuals, Hall says that messages are open to more than one meaning, that is, the codes in media messages are polysemic. However, he does not believe the codes are "pluralistic." For a code to be pluralistic, all readings must be given equal status. Hall says that there is one dominant reading of a code; this is usually the reading that is preferred by the encoder of the message. There are also oppositional and negotiated readings possible. An oppositional reading is one in contrast to the dominant one, and a negotiated reading is one that is created when a reader constructs a new interpretation somewhere between the writer's intention and the reader's natural position. Hall says that when audiences decode messages, they need to know the codes or meaning system. People in a given culture share the same meanings for particular codes. Thus, communicators use the codes to design messages, and receivers use the codes to decode them.

My distinction between meaning matching and meaning construction builds from Hall's (1980) ideas of open and closed codes. With meaning matching, meaning is assumed to reside outside the person in an authority, such as a teacher, an expert, a dictionary, a textbook, or the like. The task for the person is to find those meanings and memorize them. Thus, parents and educational institutions are primarily responsible for housing the authoritative information and passing it on to the next generation. The media are also a major source of information, and for many people, the media have attained the status of an authoritative source, so people accept the meanings presented there. Thus, the meaning-matching task involves working with closed codes. In contrast, the process of meaning construction deals with open codes, thus requiring people to select from among several possible meanings.

Another way to elaborate this distinction between meaning matching and meaning construction is to point out that meaning matching typically deals with fully specified problems, whereas meaning construction typically forces audiences to confront partially specified problems. Fully specified problems are those that give us enough information to guide us to one and only one solution, such as solving for X when $6 + X = 10$. In contrast, partially specified problems do not give us enough information to arrive at one and only one solution, such as solving for two unknowns of X and Y when we are only given the equation $X + Y = 10$. Dealing with partially specified problems is a much more challenging task because it requires reasoning, which in turn requires insight (Evans, 1998; Evans, Legrenzi, & Firotto, 1999; see also Potter, 2009).

Meaning construction, then, is a process wherein people transform messages they take in and create meaning for themselves. There are many meanings that can be constructed from any media message, and further, there are many ways to go about constructing that meaning. Thus, people cannot learn a complete set of rules to accomplish this task; instead, they need to be guided by their own information goals and use well-developed skills to creatively construct a path to reach their goals.

The two processes of meaning matching and meaning construction are not discrete. Meaning matching is more fundamental, and it is often sufficient. That is, the person is satisfied with making a quick connection to the denoted meaning and is not motivated to expend the additional effort to construct meaning. However, there are many times when people are motivated to move beyond the simple denoted meaning to construct additional meaning for themselves. In order to construct meaning, a person has to first recognize key elements in media messages and understand the sense in which those elements are being used in the message. Thus, the meaning-matching process is a precursor to the meaning construction task because its product is the necessary springboard for the construction process.

◆ *The Media Exposure Model*

Now that I have laid out the fundamental ideas involved with mass media audiences, exposure, and attention, I present a media exposure model (see Table 2.2) that can be used as a guide to help us move beyond the use of attribute variables and self-reported motives to explain the differences across audience experiences with media messages and focus instead on more fundamental characteristics as a foundation to build more useful explanations of media effects.

First, not all exposure experiences are the same; they differ from one another in many ways, and among those differences, the exposure state is one of the most

Table 2.2 Exposure and Information-Processing Model

Exposure State	Information-Processing Tasks		
	Filtering	*Meaning Matching*	*Meaning Construction*
Automatic	Screening	Highly Automatic	Highly Automatic Construction
Attentional	Scanning	Automatic	Typical Construction
Transported	Swept	Personal & Highly Automatic	Highly Emotional Construction
Self-Reflexive	Searching Actively	Personal & Highly Conscious	Highly Personalized Construction

fundamental to our understanding of media influence. Audience members who experience a particular message in an automatic state are likely to have their experience governed by automatic routines running unconsciously in their minds and therefore are likely to have those routines reinforced. Audience members who experience the same message in the attentional state are likely to expend more mental energy evaluating the message or inferring a pattern from the elements in that message with elements in remembered messages. Audience members who experience the same message in a self-reflexive state are likely to expend much mental energy in processing the message and evaluating their processes in order to alter them consciously to make them more useful. And audience members who experience the message in a transported state are likely to be awash in emotions and encode the information they experience in a highly intuitive, personal manner.

These differences in exposure states can lead to a greater degree of explanation for media effects. To illustrate this point, consider an experiment conducted by Pool, Koolstra, and van der Voort (2003) to find out if background use of media influenced adolescents' performance on homework. They found that

background music left homework performance unaffected. Also, there was no indication that background media influenced the amount of time spent to complete homework assignments. However, watching soap operas during homework reduced student performance. These are interesting results, but they appear equivocal. Also, they do not explain why exposure to one type of media message could reduce homework performance while another form of message would leave it unaffected. In their results, the focus is on type of message or medium. However, if we used the media exposure model, we would shift the focus of explanation to the experience of the audience member during the exposure, and this could help explain the pattern of results. It is likely that background music was experienced by most students in the automatic exposure state where they did not need to expend any mental energy, saving their full cognitive capacity for the homework. In contrast, it is likely that many, but not all, students watching soap operas were in a transported exposure state, thus having no cognitive resources left over for studying during that time. Furthermore, it is likely that students who were in a transported exposure state for the soap operas or music had the lowest performance on homework. Therefore, exposure state would seem to be a much better predictor of audience cognitive allocations than would genre of media message.

Second, there is a difference between meaning matching and meaning construction. Human beings are capable of constructing an idiosyncratic meaning special to them from almost any given message. However, in the course of everyday life while people are encountering thousands of media messages, they typically default to a state of automaticity in which previously learned (and frequently reinforced) mental routines screen out almost all messages. Furthermore, when these automatic routines allow messages through the filter, those messages are processed with quick associations to denoted meanings. This is very efficient and allows people to get through the flood of messages in their mundane lives. However, there are also times when people may need to create a meaning that is more conducive to their existing belief system or emotional state, so they engage in meaning construction. People are constantly doing both. Thus, researchers need to make the distinction carefully between meaning matching and meaning construction in the design of their measures and analyses. If researchers intend to measure meaning matching–type information, they can use a criterion of accuracy, that is, they can compare participants' responses to a consistent standard to assess how accurate each of those responses is. In contrast, if researchers intend to measure responses generated through a meaning construction process, then it is important for them to allow for individual interpretations and focus attention on that variation as a useful finding rather than treating it as an indication of error.

Third, there are important interactions between exposure states and information processing tasks. For example, the experience of filtering media messages is very different when one is in an automatic state, where schemata are running in a person's mind unconsciously, and when one is in an attentional state, where a person is actively scanning for a particular message. Also, meaning matching is different when one is in a transported state, and thus more vulnerable to the denoted message meaning, than when one is in a self-reflexive state, where one is second-guessing assumed meanings. Taking these interactions into account when designing research studies will help scholars generate more useful explanations about the experiences audience members have during exposures to media messages and eventually about how those experiences influence media effects.

Finally, it is important to note that these states suggest limits on how those exposure experiences have been measured. For example, participants who experience a media message in an attentional state are likely able to provide information about that exposure experience, but if those same participants encountered a media message while in an automatic state, they would likely have no conscious recollection of that experience. Likewise, when researchers are focusing on meaning matching, their measures and analyses should be very different than when they are focusing on meaning construction. With meaning matching, convergence of thinking is valued, and divergence can be regarded as error. But with meaning construction, divergence of thinking should be the focus.

◆ Summary

In this chapter, I have attempted a synthesis of a wide range of ideas in the conceptualization of mass media audiences. The key debates over exposure, degree of audience activity, and locus of meaning were analyzed to identify key scholarly ideas about media audiences. The synthesis takes the form of a media exposure model, which is a typology crossing four exposure states (automatic, attentional, transported, and self-reflexive) with three fundamental exposure tasks (filtering, meaning matching, and meaning construction). The media exposure model is intended to encourage researchers to consider carefully the experience states their participants are in when they encounter media treatments in experiments as well as media exposures in everyday life and to translate this understanding into more useful measures of exposure and attention and more probing analyses of their data.

◆ References

Bauer, R. (1973). *The audience*. In I. De Sola Pool, F. W. Frey, W. Schramm, N. Maccoby, & E. B. Parker (Eds.), *Handbook of communication* (pp. 141–152). Chicago: Rand McNally.

Biocca, F. A. (1988). Opposing conceptions of the audience. In J. A. Anderson (Ed.), *Communication yearbook 11* (pp. 51–80). Newbury Park, CA: Sage.

Blumer, H. (1939). The mass, the public and public opinion. In A. M. Lee (Ed.), *New outlines in the principles of sociology*. New York: Barnes & Noble.

Burke, K. (1969). *A rhetoric of motives*. Berkeley: University of California Press.

Butsch, R. (2000). *The making of American audiences: From stage to television, 1750–1990*. Cambridge, UK: Cambridge University Press.

Cantril, H. (1940). *The invasion from Mars: A study of the psychology of panic*. Princeton, NJ: Princeton University Press.

Corner, J. (1991). Meaning, genre and context: The problematics of "public knowledge" in the new audience studies. In J. Curran & M. Gurevitch (Eds.), *Mass media and society* (pp. 267–285). London: Edward Arnold.

Csikszentmihalyi, M. (1988). The flow experience and its significance for human psychology. In M. Csikszentmihalyi & I. S. Csikszentmihalyi (Eds.), *Optimal experience: Psychological studies of flow in consciousness* (pp. 15–35). New York: Cambridge University Press.

Ettema, J. S., & Whitney, D. C. (1994). The money arrow: An introduction to audience-making. In J. S. Ettema & D. C. Whitney (Eds.), *Audiencemaking: How the media create the audience* (pp. 1–18). Thousand Oaks, CA: Sage.

Evans, J. St B. T. (1998). Matching bias in conditional reasoning: Do we understand it after 25 years? *Thinking and Reasoning, 4,* 45–82.

Evans, J. St B. T., Legrenzi, P., & Firotto, V. (1999). The influence of linguistic form on reasoning: The case of matching bias. *Quarterly Journal of Experimental Psychology, 52A,* 185–216.

Freedman, J. L., & Sears, D. (1965). Selective exposure. In L. Berkowitz (Ed.), *Advances in experimental social psychology* (pp. 58–98). New York: Academic Press.

Freidson, E. (1971). Communications research and the concept of the mass. In W. Shramm & D. F. Roberts (Eds.), *The process and effects of mass communication, revised edition* (pp. 197–208). Urbana: University of Illinois Press.

Gauntlett, D. (2005). *Moving experiences: Media effects and beyond* (2nd ed.). Eastleight, UK: John Libbery.

Geiger, S., & Newhagen, J. (1993). Revealing the black box: Information processing and media effects. *Journal of Communication, 43*(4), 42–50.

Gerbner, G. (1969). Toward "cultural indicators": The analysis of mass mediated public message systems. *AV Communication Review, 17*(2), 137–148.

Gray, A. (1999). Audience and reception research in retrospect: The trouble with audience. In P. Alasuutari (Ed.), *Rethinking the media audience* (pp. 22–37). London: Sage.

Green, M. C., & Brock, T. C. (2000). The role of transportation in the persuasiveness of public narratives. *Journal of Personality and Social Psychology, 79,* 701–721.

Green, M. C., Garst, J., & Brock, T. C. (2004). The power of fiction: Determinants and boundaries. In L. J. Shrum (Ed.), *The psychology of entertainment media: Blurring the lines between entertainment and persuasion* (pp. 161–176). Mahwah, NJ: Erlbaum.

Hall, S. (1980). Encoding and decoding in the television discourse. In S. Hall, D. Hobson, A. Lowe, & P. Willis (Eds.), *Culture, media, language*. London: Hutchinson.

Katz, E. (1959). Mass communication research and the study of popular culture. *Studies in Public Communication, 2*, 1–6.

Katz, E., Blumler, J. G., & Gurevitch, M. (1974). Utilization of mass communication by the individual. In J. G. Blumler & E. Katz (Eds.), *The uses of mass communication* (pp. 19–32). Beverly Hills, CA: Sage.

Katz, E., & Lazarsfeld, P. F. (1955). *Personal influence: The part played by people in the flow of mass communications*. Glencoe, IL: Free Press.

Kitzinger, J. (2004). Audience and readership research. In J. D. H. Downing, D. McQuail, P. Schlesinger, & E. Wartella (Eds.), *The Sage handbook of media studies* (pp. 167–181). Thousand Oaks, CA: Sage.

Klapper, J. T. (1960). *The effects of mass communication*. Glencoe, IL: Free Press.

Kubey, R. W., & Csikszentmihalyi, M. (1991). *Television and the quality of life*. Hillsdale, NJ: Erlbaum.

Lazarsfeld, P. F., & Stanton, F. (1949). *Communication research 1948–49*. New York: Harper & Row.

Livingstone, S. M. (1990). *Making sense of television: The psychology of audience interpretation*. New York: Pergamon Press.

Lombard, M., Reich, R. D., Grabe, M. E., Bracken, C. C., & Ditton, T. B. (2000). Presence and television: The role of screen size. *Human Communication Research, 26*, 75–98.

Lowery, S. A., & DeFleur, M. L. (1988). *Milestones in mass communication research* (2nd ed.). White Plains, NY: Longman.

McQuail, D. (2005). *McQuail's mass communication theory* (5th ed.). London: Sage.

Merton, R. K. (1949). *Social theory and social structure*. Glencoe, IL: Free Press.

Miller, D., & Philo, G. (2001). The active audience and wrong terms in media studies: Rescuing media power. Soundscape, 4. Retrieved January 2009 from http://www.icce.rug.nl/~soundscapes/VOLUME04/Active_audience.shtml

Morley, D. (1980). *The Nationwide audience*. London: British Film Institute.

Nightingale, V. (2004). Contemporary television audiences. In J. D. H. Downing, D. McQuail, P. Schlesinger, & E. Wartella (Eds.), *The Sage handbook of media studies* (pp. 227–249). Thousand Oaks, CA: Sage.

Noble, G. (1975). *Children in front of the small screen*. London: Constable.

Pashler, H. E. (1998). *The psychology of attention*. Cambridge, MA: MIT Press.

Pool, M. M., Koolstra, C. M., & van der Voort, T. H. A. (2003). The impact of background radio and television on high school students' homework performance. *Journal of Communication, 53*, 74–87.

Potter, W. J. (2004). *Theory of media literacy: A cognitive approach*. Thousand Oaks, CA: Sage.

Potter, W. J. (2009). *Arguing for a general framework for mass media scholarship*. Thousand Oaks, CA: Sage.

Power, P., Kubey, R., & Kiousis, S. (2002). Audience activity and passivity. In W. B. Gudykunst (Ed.), *Communication yearbook 26* (pp. 116–159). Mahwah, NJ: Erlbaum.

Radway, D. J. (1984). *Reading the romance*. Chapel Hill: University of North Carolina Press.

Rosengren, K. E., Wenner, L. A., & Palmgreen, P. (Eds.). (1985). *Media gratifications research: Current perspectives*. Beverly Hills, CA: Sage.

Salomon, G., & Cohen, A. A. (1978). On the meaning and validity of television viewing. *Human Communication Research, 4*, 265–270.

Schmitt, K. L., Woolf, K. D., & Anderson, D. R. (2003). Viewing the viewers: Viewing behaviors by children and adults during television programs and commercials. *Journal of Communication, 53*, 265–281.

Schramm, W. (1973). Channels and audiences. In I. De Sola Pool, F. W. Frey, W. Schramm, N. Maccoby, & E. B. Parker (Eds.), *Handbook of communication* (pp. 116–140). Chicago: Rand McNally.

Shiffrin, R. M. (1988). Attention. In R. A. Atkinson, R. J. Hernstein, G. Lindzey, & R. D. Luce (Eds.), *Stevens' handbook of experimental psychology: Vol. 2. Learning and cognition* (pp. 739–811). New York: John Wiley.

Shrum, L. J. (1996). Psychological processes underlying cultivation effects: Further tests of construct accessibility. *Human Communication Research, 22,* 482–509.

Thompson, J. B. (1995). *The media and modernity: A social theory of the media.* Stanford, CA: Stanford University Press.

Webster, J. G., & Phalen, P. F. (1994). Victim, consumer, or commodity? Audience models in communication policy. In J. S. Ettema & D. C. Whitney (Eds.), *Audiencemaking: How the media create the audience* (pp. 19–37). Thousand Oaks, CA: Sage.

Webster, J. G., & Phalen, P. F. (1997). *The mass audience: Rediscovering the dominant model.* Mahwah, NJ: Erlbaum.

Wright, C. R. (1986). *Mass communication: A sociological perspective* (3rd ed.). New York: Random House.

Zillmann, D., & Bryant, J. (1985). Affect, mood and emotion as determinants of selective exposure. In D. Zillmann & J. Bryant (Eds.), *Selective exposure to communication* (pp. 157–190). Hillsdale, NJ: Erlbaum.

3

QUANTITATIVE METHODS AND CAUSAL INFERENCE IN MEDIA EFFECTS RESEARCH

◆ Itzhak Yanovitzky and Kathryn Greene

Although media effects can be (and are) studied from a variety of methodological perspectives, the application of quantitative methods has dominated media effects research since Schramm's (1957) early investigation into journalism research (see also Kamhawi & Weaver, 2003; Lowry, 1979). A recent systematic review of methods used by media effects scholars (Potter & Riddle, 2007) found that 71% of all studies published in 16 prominent mass communication journals between 1993 and 2005 used quantitative methodologies, with in-class surveys (32%) and laboratory experiments (29%) being the most popular methods to study media effects. Other quantitative methods frequently used by media effects scholars include field experiments, quantitative content analysis, and the analysis of archival (secondary) data (Frey, Botan, & Kreps, 2000). This bias toward the use of quantitative methods in media effects research continues to be debated in the field (see Bryant & Cummins, 2007, for a discussion), and it is not our purpose to resolve this debate. Nor is it our purpose to review each of the quantitative methods used to study media effects, and their relative strengths and weaknesses, as others have already produced excellent such reviews (e.g., Bryant & Thompson, 2002; Preiss, Gayle, Burrell, Allen, & Bryant, 2007; Wimmer & Dominick, 2000). Rather, we turn our attention to the issue most central to the pursuit of media effects research from a quantitative research perspective, that of causal inference.

The basic conception of a cause-effect relationship between media stimuli and audience-related outcomes is the defining feature of theories that fall into the "effects tradition" within mass communication research (Littlejohn & Foss, 2008). Indeed, there is a strong expectation from various stakeholders—policymakers, educators, parents, journalists, external funders, scientists in other disciplines, and media consumers themselves—that research findings about media effects be articulated in clear causal terms to the extent possible (Hornik, 2002; Nabi, 2007). Further, in recent years, with the mathematical advances in the modeling of causal relationships, the study of causation and causal inference has seemingly matured in many related fields (psychology, sociology, political science, and epidemiology; Pearl, 2000), developing into an integrative force that has the potential to bring together diverse fields of scientific inquiry.

However, despite the centrality of causation to media effects research, little systematic attention to causation considerations has been given in the field beyond the standard treatment of causation in basic research methods textbooks. This is not to say that media effects scholars have not been concerned with issues of causal inference. Work critical of current research practices that limit causal inference in media effects research, whether focusing on issues of sampling (e.g., Long, Slater, Boiarsky, Stapel, & Keefe, 2005), measurement of key constructs (e.g., Fishbein & Hornik, 2008), or hypothesis testing (e.g., Holbert & Stephenson, 2003; Levine & Hullett, 2002), has been published periodically in communication journals. But such sporadic efforts have been for the most part geared toward increasing the degree of rigor with which media effects researchers engage questions about causal relationships rather than a concentrated, systematic effort to tackle this important

issue. Therefore, our primary goal is to begin conceptualizing some analytical tools for guiding the design and evaluation of causally valid media effects research. We do so with an eye toward the key challenges inherent in the study of media effects as we understand them and with the intention of stimulating a much-needed disciplinary conversation about ways to rise to these fundamental challenges in order to take media effects research to the next level.

We begin this chapter with a brief discussion of causation and explanation from a social scientific perspective and describe the traditional approach to causal inference from quantitative data. We then explain why this traditional approach is largely inadequate for addressing causality considerations in media effects research. Next, we provide a short overview of the key challenges to causal inference in media effects research: (1) the multilevel nature of media effects, (2) the dynamic nature of media effects, (3) the complexity of causal chains, (4) the measurement of key constructs, and (5) audience activity. We conceptualize potential threats to causal inference posed by each challenge in terms of logical fallacies and, where appropriate, point to some useful research procedures and/or quantitative applications that may mitigate them. We conclude that (1) more careful explication of mechanisms and processes of media effects and (2) better matching of the methods employed to the complexity of the phenomena under investigation will greatly enhance researchers' ability to address issues of causal inference and facilitate better integration of theory and research on media effects.

◆ Causation and Causal Inference

CAUSATION AND EXPLANATION IN THE SOCIAL SCIENCES

Although most people possess an intuitive understanding of causality as it appears in everyday life, scholars and philosophers, at least as far back as Aristotle, have been debating the notion of causation and the best ways to describe and assess it. Classic conceptions of causation identified agency and manipulation as the forces underlying causal relationships between phenomena (e.g., the earthquake was caused by God). This approach is best exemplified by the logic and language of experiments, where the researcher (agent) creates an intervention in order to produce (manipulate) a certain outcome. The key features of causation in this perspective are contiguity (observed covariation of cause and effect) and temporal precedence (the cause preceding the effect in time). In contrast, modern theories of causation, dating back to Scottish philosopher David Hume, understand causal relationships in terms of mechanisms and capacities that exist naturally (e.g., earthquakes are caused by plate tectonics). For Hume, the *regularity* of the association between causes and their effects is a key feature of causation. This rationale suggests that causal laws can be discovered through empirical observations, and thus justifies the observational (or nonexperimental) approach to research in which the researcher observes (rather than manipulates) naturally occurring relationships among variables (Pearl, 2000).

Hume's widely accepted idea that logical causal claims are empirical rather than analytical (that is, they stem from people's sensory experience with the world rather than from abstract ideas) gave rise to a concern about the type of evidence needed to make legitimate claims about cause-effect relationships. Some, like the 19th-century philosopher John Stuart Mill, were concerned about drawing causal inference from accidental (or chance) regularities, emphasizing that causation is not the same as correlation. Mill's thought in particular popularized three requirements for inferring cause-effect relationships: (1) evidence of covariation between the presumed cause and effect; (2) evidence of the temporal precedence of the cause; and (3) evidence

ruling out alternative interpretations for a possible cause-and-effect connection (Cook & Campbell, 1979). Mill's approach to dealing with possible spuriousness of causal relationships emphasized the importance of multiple different replications (i.e., observing the same causal relationship for different people, in different places, and at different times) and the design of crucial experiments that can offer a decisive empirical test of two or more alternative causal explanations (see also Popper, 1959; Stinchcombe, 1968). In their authoritative text on the topic, Cook and Campbell (1979) categorized the universe of alternative causal explanations into four threats to the validity of causal inference: internal validity, external validity, construct validity, and statistical conclusion validity. Simply put, one may infer a cause-effect relationship if he or she can demonstrate that (1) no other causal mechanism accounts for this relationship (internal validity); (2) the observed causal relationships can be generalized to and across alternate measures of cause and effect, and across different types of units, settings, and times (external validity); (3) the way variables are observed (measured) empirically fits tightly with their theoretical meaning (construct validity); and (4) conclusions about causal relationships in a population are drawn from representative and unbiased samples (statistical conclusion validity). Their framework suggests that a potentially large number of alternative hypotheses must be falsified before a causal claim can be considered valid.

David Lewis's counterfactual approach to causation (see Winship & Morgan, 1999) greatly simplified the task of eliminating alternative causal explanations. The counterfactual logic asks what would have happened if a certain premise were true. For example, what would have been the effect on a person had that person received a treatment for cancer rather than being denied one. The counterfactual claim assumes a causal relationship between the treatment and effect (if X, then Y). Hence, evidence supporting the counterfactual claim (if no X, then no Y) also supports that causal claim. The key to this approach is the ability of the researcher to create a counterfactual condition that is identical (or at least very similar) to the condition under which the actual effect is observed, with the exception that X is not present. This is achieved through controlled experiments (where subjects are randomized to either an experimental or control group) or by statistical means such as the use of propensity scores (see Yanovitzky, Hornik, & Zanutto, 2008). Accordingly, classic experimental designs (or more specifically, the use of a control group and random assignment to treatment or control) became the gold standard for establishing causation whereas observational studies are perceived to be more vulnerable to spurious causal inference because temporal precedence is difficult to establish (as nothing is manipulated) and there is no way to know whether those cases that get the treatment and those that do not differ from one another in other ways (the problem of selection bias).

In summary, the traditional approach to causation in the social sciences is inherently deterministic in that it assumes a lawlike relationship between causes and effects where the same initial conditions inevitably produce the same outcome. Further, it views causal inference as contingent upon sound research design choices, such as experiments incorporating a control group and random assignment of units to conditions, a probability sampling scheme, reliable and valid measures, and statistical guards against chance occurrences of relationships in the population (see Cook & Campbell, 1979).

CAUSATION AND EXPLANATION IN MEDIA EFFECTS RESEARCH

With one notable exception, media effects researchers' understanding of causal inference conforms to the traditional approach to causation described in the preceding paragraphs. This is evidenced by the fact that controlled experiments are frequently used in the field and that researchers employing observational studies typically limit themselves to correlational (rather than causal) hypotheses. The notable exception is the tendency of many to confuse causal inference with statistical inference. As demonstrated previously, causal inference is inherently a function of the research design; it cannot be derived or inferred from statistical claims alone. Thus, when researchers claim to have supported their causal hypotheses simply by virtue of rejecting the null statistical hypothesis (which is, following Cook and Campbell, only one type of possible threat to the validity of causal claims), they are stepping beyond the bounds of their own evidence.

Beyond that, however, lies the far more fundamental question about the extent to which the traditional social scientific approach to causation and causal inference is adequate for making legitimate causal claims about media effects. We believe it is not, for several reasons. First, getting a grip on causality requires researchers to have a detailed understanding of the kinds of mechanisms that could link one event with another. Most psychological theories, with their emphasis on stimulus-response relationships between causes and effects, understand causation in terms of agency and manipulation, leading psychologists to prefer evidence from experimental studies when making legitimate (or valid) causal claims. Most sociological theories, in contrast, understand causation in terms of naturally occurring regularities, and this notion imposes an effort to uncover mechanisms and capacities that enable causal relationships through the use of observational studies. Theories of media effects are not equally single-minded in this respect. They tend to combine the agency and manipulation conception of causation with that of the "regularities" conception of causation. As a result, it is unlikely that a single research method can produce the empirical evidence needed for making legitimate causal claims about media effects.

Second, whereas the traditional model of causation is deterministic, empirical findings about media effects suggest overwhelmingly that the *same* initial conditions (or stimuli) produce *different* audience outcomes (i.e., some media outputs influence some people, under some circumstances). Put differently, media effects research has produced many examples where causal relationships appear to be probabilistic. Therefore, it may be unrealistic for media effects researchers to produce legitimate evidence of causation from a deterministic perspective. Rather, causation in media effects research may be better expressed and evaluated in probabilistic terms.

Last, it is important to recognize that media effects research encompasses a set of rather complex phenomena. As Bryant and Thompson (2002) note, media effects may be cognitive, behavioral, or affective; direct or indirect; short term, long term, or delayed; self-contained or cumulative. No doubt, this complexity makes the task of drawing causal inference about media effects ever more difficult and unlikely to be resolved simply by the choice of a research design, as the traditional approach to causation leads us to believe. Rather, we believe that the field is better served by a conception of threats to causal inference that is more directly derived from (but also more directly responsive to) the key theoretical and methodological challenges to media effects research: (1) the multilevel nature of media effects, (2) the dynamic nature of media effects, (3) the complexity of causal chains, (4) the measurement of key constructs, and (5) audience activity. We review each of these challenges in the next section and discuss the threats they pose to causal inference in media effects research. Where appropriate, we also point to some useful research procedures or quantitative applications that may mitigate such potential threats.

◆ **Challenges to Causal Inference in Media Effects Research**

THE MULTILEVEL NATURE OF MEDIA EFFECTS

An important factor contributing to the complexity of media effects as a subject of investigation is that such effects occur simultaneously at multiple levels of analysis. At the most basic level of abstraction, this means that media effects occur *independently* at different levels of analysis: individuals, groups, organizations, and social institutions (Bryant & Thompson, 2002). A more common interpretation of media effects as a set of multilevel phenomena (e.g., Slater, Snyder, & Hayes, 2006) is grounded in the recognition that characteristics or processes that occur at a higher level of analysis (e.g., groups) are bound to influence media effects at a lower level (e.g., individuals). Thus, some similarities and differences in the way individuals respond to or learn from information in the media can be explained by the characteristics of the groups or the organizations to which they belong. In essence, the source of complexity in this conception of media effects as multilevel phenomena is the *structural or relational context* in which media effects take place. But by far the most challenging notion of media effects as multilevel phenomena recognizes that the effect that media stimuli have at one level of analysis is often confounded with (or rarely independent of) the effect they have at another level of analysis (Pan & McLeod, 1991). For example, news coverage of drunk driving over time likely influences individuals' drunk driving–related attitudes and behaviors, but it also simultaneously affects group norms and public policy on the issue, which themselves are an important source of influence on individuals' attitudes and behaviors (Yanovitzky, 2002; Yanovitzky & Bennett, 1999; Yanovitzky & Stryker, 2001). We return to this issue in our discussion that follows of the complexity of causal chains in media effects.

As others have already noted (Pan & McLeod, 1991; Slater et al., 2006), by virtue of limiting their focus of investigation to a particular (usually the individual) level of analysis, media effects researchers appear to have settled (conceptually and methodologically) on a single-level view of media effects, thus ignoring, for the most part, the cross-level linkages suggested by the multilevel view of effects. Consequently, such researchers likely expose themselves to at least three types of threats to causal inference (see Dansereau, Cho, & Yammarino, 2006; Price, Ritchie, & Eulau, 1991): fallacy of composition, ecological fallacy, and fallacy of the wrong level. *Fallacy of composition* (or atomistic fallacy) refers to cases in which an erroneous conclusion is drawn about a whole based on the features of its parts, such as when data collected from individuals is aggregated to represent the groups to which those individuals belong. The source of error here is that individual-level properties (e.g., personal attitudes, beliefs, or behavior) or relationships between such variables that are observed for individual members of the group are considered to be analytically equivalent to group-level properties (e.g., public opinion, norms) or to relationships between the same variables at the group level, when in fact they are not. For example, members' perceptions of group norms (an individual property) are conceptually different from group norms themselves, which are a property of the group (Yanovitzky & Rimal, 2006). Therefore, inferring group norms from aggregate measures of members'

perceptions of norms is inappropriate. To mitigate concerns about the fallacy of composition, researchers should take care to select units that are comparable and representative of the whole (e.g., using information obtained from regular group members rather than from opinion leaders) and to offer empirical evidence that the same mechanism or process that causes one unit to change in response to a media stimulus (for example, information processing) can be generalized to all other units.

Ecological fallacy (or fallacy of division) is the inverse of the fallacy of composition. It pertains to cases when an erroneous conclusion is drawn from the characteristics of a whole to those of its parts. That is, group-level properties (or relationships observed among group-level variables) are mistakenly assumed to hold for individual members of the group. For example, in the context of the debate about the effects of media violence (see Bushman, Huesmann, & Whitaker, Chapter 24, this volume), some have proposed that links between levels of media violence and levels of societal violence support claims about the causal effect of media violence on individuals' aggression (Centerwall, 1989). However, this proposition has been challenged on the grounds of the ecological fallacy, as evidence indicates that violent criminals tend to be exposed to less (rather than more) media violence compared with their noncriminal counterparts (e.g., Freedman, 2002). Generally, then, one ought to avoid making causal claims about relationships between variables measured at a lower level of analysis from relationships observed among these variables (or their proxies) at a higher level of analysis. One exception to this is when the researcher is using data aggregated from lower-level units, such as when the percentage of women obtaining a mammogram each month is estimated from aggregated survey responses of women who answered a question about this behavior. In these cases (which are quite characteristic of data used in media effects research), a researcher interested in making causal claims about individual units based on aggregated data may choose to test for the same effect in subsamples representing relatively homogeneous subgroups and to demonstrate that relationships among variables that exist at the higher or population level are also present at the levels of subgroups.

Finally, ignoring cross-level linkages may cause researchers to look for media effects at the wrong level of analysis. This potential error is termed *fallacy of the wrong level* and encompasses cases in which an effect is attributed to a variable, relationship, or process that exists at one level of analysis when it should in fact be attributed to a variable, relationship, or process that exists at another level. For example, while the majority of studies that have tested the effects of anti–drunk driving campaigns on drivers' drunk driving–related cognitions and behavior failed to find evidence of an effect at the individual level, there is credible evidence that these campaigns have been effective in generating anti–drunk driving legislation, which, in turn, influences drivers' behaviors (Yanovitzky, 2002). Thus, the conclusion that these campaigns failed to decrease drunk driving behavior is at best premature (if not simply erroneous) since effects at other levels of analysis were ignored. The only way to avoid an erroneous causal inference in this case is to test causal hypotheses at multiple levels of analysis, provided that there is a good logical or theoretical reason to expect relationships between variables to exist at multiple levels of analysis.

It is worth noting that all three types of fallacies involve a problem of inference, not of measurement or misspecification of statistical models. That is, these fallacies are largely outcomes of inadequate theorizing about the nature of cross-level relationships rather than a problem of using inadequate analytical tools. Whereas

many of the media effects theories covered in this volume (e.g., agenda setting, cultivation, and knowledge gap) conceptualize effects at multiple levels of analysis, they fail to offer logical cross-level links (Pan & McLeod, 1991). To illustrate, how may cultivation effects on individuals help us explain cultivation effects that occur at the societal level (such as mainstreaming), and vice versa? If we assume that all members of society are similarly influenced to cultivate a certain perception of the world following exposure to media content, then the societal-level effect of cultivation is simply the aggregate effect of media on individuals, and causal inference is straightforward. However, if other processes of effects are involved in the transition from the individual to the societal level of cultivation (for example, diffusion of information among members of a social group through interpersonal communication), then drawing causal inference about cultivation effects is likely more problematic. Therefore, the first line of defense against these fallacies is more careful cross-level theorizing and clearly explicating plausible mechanisms and processes that logically link effects that are observed at different levels. Perhaps the best-known example of such theorizing is the two-step-flow hypothesis (Katz & Lazarsfeld, 1955): a macrolevel variable (media content) is linked to a microlevel variable (a person's political attitudes and behavior) through a process of interpersonal influence that employs a mechanism of interpersonal communication. Similarly, diffusion of innovation theory provides a logical link between information processing and behavior change at the individual level to processes of social change (see Rogers, 1962). The bottom line is that causal inference about multilevel effects can only be as rigorous as the theory and logical assumptions on which it is based.

The other key to drawing valid causal inference from multilevel relationships between variables is the use of appropriate methodology. Such methodology necessarily requires sampling of units from multiple levels (e.g., multistage probability sampling) and taking appropriate measures at each level of analysis. Unfortunately, the samples typically used in media effects research are far from meeting this requirement. Furthermore, when aggregated data is used, it is usually collected without regard for the fact that individual-level variations (for example, in political attitudes) are confounded with the characteristics of the groups to which individuals belong (e.g., shared values and norms). Consequently, evidence of causal relationships obtained in these studies may be spurious unless estimates of effects are corrected for bias due to group-level effects. Here it is important to recognize that the standard data analytical tools used in media effects research (e.g., analysis of variance and regression analysis) are not designed to handle multilevel data. Such statistical tools can serve causal inference well, particularly when randomized experiments are used, only as long as higher-level variables or processes are deemed irrelevant to the relationship of interest. If the potential confounding of levels of analysis cannot be logically dismissed, researchers who are interested in making causal claims should consider using more advanced data analytic methods that can handle multilevel relationships, such as multilevel modeling (see Hayes, 2006, for an excellent discussion of the potential use of multilevel modeling in communication research).

THE DYNAMIC NATURE OF MEDIA EFFECTS

A second major source of complexity in studying media effects involves the conception of media effects as a *process*—causal relationships between variables that are dynamically situated in a temporal context, such that time is a central

dimension of media effects (see Yanovitzky & VanLear, 2008). Rarely, however, do media effects researchers use quantitative methodology to model processes of media effects (Watt & VanLear, 1996). The methodological approach used in these studies typically seeks to correlate effects (the beginning of a process) with outcomes (the end of the process), treating everything in between as a "black box" or making unverifiable assumptions about the unobserved process that links effects and outcomes. To illustrate, consider information processing from the perspective of the elaboration likelihood model (Petty & Cacioppo, 1986). According to this model, two inherently different routes of information processing (one that involves elaboration of, or thinking about, the claims made in a message and another that does not) can end up causing the same observed outcome (attitude change). A researcher who is primarily concerned with causation would need to trace the process of attitude change over time (short as it may be) to determine or verify which of the two routes was used. Ignoring the process and focusing on the relationship between the stimulus and the outcome could lead to erroneous conclusions about the way the effect came to be. In other words, taking the process of effect into account in the analysis of quantitative data allow us to move from simply saying *what* works to being able to explicate *how* it works, which is a crucial element for making causal claims.

The inclusion of time in the analysis of media effects has four important implications to drawing causal inference. The most obvious of these relates to the *fallacy of confusing cause and effect*. While a theory can (and should) be used to logically justify the expectation that one variable causes another, the task of determining the causal direction between two variables usually depends on knowledge of a time sequence between the effect and the outcome. This is typically a problem in cross-sectional studies, though the temporal order between variables can be retrospectively constructed in many cases. When longitudinal data is available to the researcher (such as when data on the same variables is collected at multiple time points), the causal direction between two variables can be determined via a Granger causality test (Granger, 1969). The test is predicated on the assumption that past behavior of a variable is the best predictor of this variable's current behavior. According to Granger, X is said to cause Y when the previous (or lagged) values of X significantly predict Y after controlling for the effect of lagged values of Y on Y itself (operationally, this means including the lagged values of Y as an additional predictor of Y in a regression model estimating the effect of the lagged values of X on Y). In the next step, the order of variables is reversed such that X is being predicted from lagged values of Y. If X cannot be predicted from the lagged values of Y, then X is determined to be a cause of Y.

The second implication of time in media effects research relates to the history and future of the phenomena studied. By ignoring the time dimension in the analysis of media effects, we ignore an important source of variation in the relationship between media stimuli and audiences' reactions to these stimuli. Focusing on the conceptualization and operationalization of the effect (namely, exposure), it seems safe to argue that many media effects studies ignore the effect of past cumulative exposure (and its likely interaction with current exposure) on audiences' outcomes. For example, by the time they reach adulthood, most individuals in most parts of the world have been exposed numerous times to fear appeals in persuasive messages. It is only logical to assume that repeated exposure to fear appeals will influence the way they react to yet another use of fear appeal in a message (effects like priming, fatigue, or even reactance come to mind). Yet, studies of fear appeal almost always assume implicitly that subjects were

exposed to fear appeals for the first time. This is the *fallacy of ignoring the past*. The *fallacy of ignoring the future* focuses on the outcome itself, where too often the possibility of delayed media effects is ignored (Hornik, 2002; Hornik & Yanovitzky, 2003). Because experimental and cross-sectional designs are limited to the investigation of instantaneous media effects, researchers may commit a Type II error (i.e., claiming to find no media effects when, in fact, effects do exist but are delayed) or a Type I error (i.e., claiming media effects when, in fact, they do not last much beyond exposure to the stimulus). Thus, planning to study variables in relation to their past and future can greatly reduce the potential for errors of causal inference in media effects research.

The third problem associated with ignoring the time dimension in media effects research is the *fallacy of the secular trend*. By "secular trend," we mean natural, long-term change in the characteristics of a phenomenon over time. People, groups, organizations, and societies are in a constant state of change. Therefore, even an ineffective media stimulus (e.g., a social marketing campaign) may appear to cause change in audiences, leading the researcher to erroneously claim campaign effects (Snyder & Hamilton, 2002). It may also be that the effect of the campaign is confounded with that of the secular trend such that a positive secular trend may cause researchers to falsely overestimate the effect of the campaign, whereas a negative secular trend may lead them to underestimate the effect of the campaign. However, this is more a problem of estimation than a problem of causal inference. Interrupted time-series designs (see Cook & Campbell, 1979) are generally considered an effective tool for partitioning the true effect of programs, such as communication campaigns, from the effect of the secular trend.

Finally, it is possible for a process or an outcome variable to assume a cyclical pattern (change in direction) over the study period, thus changing the dynamics of the relationship between media stimuli and their hypothesized outcomes. Consider, for example, the issue-attention cycle in media coverage of issues (Downs, 1972). Now suppose you want to link media attention to HIV/AIDS to the public's perceived salience of this issue (see Rogers, Dearing, & Chang, 1991). Your conclusion about the power of media coverage to set the public's agenda on this issue is contingent almost entirely upon the time frame chosen for analysis. If you observe the relationship during the time frame in which media attention to the issue is at its peak, you may conclude that the effect of this coverage is positive and strong. However, if you are observing this relationship during the time frame in which media attention to the issue is declining, you may conclude that there is little or no evidence of an agenda-setting effect. We term this potential threat to causal inference the *fallacy of the wrong timing*. Avoiding this fallacy may require researchers to conduct a sort of sensitivity analysis, where relationships between two or more phenomena over time are compared for time periods of different lengths.

In general, then, the most efficient way to avoid potential threats to causal inference due to the dynamic nature of media effects phenomena is to employ longitudinal designs (e.g., panel, cohort, and time-series designs) and specialized data analysis tools that can handle time-sequenced data. Different approaches to modeling longitudinal media effects have been employed by media effects researchers (see Yanovitzky & VanLear, 2008, for a review), but the use of these methods remains infrequent despite the continued vitality of theories that conceptualize media effects as a process.

THE COMPLEXITY
OF CAUSAL CHAINS

The question of *how exactly* media stimuli influence audiences is as crucial to media effects theory and research as it is to causal inference about media effects. Specifically, while the initial conception of media effects was based on a simple stimulus-response model, empirical findings demonstrating variations in how members of the audience responded to the same media stimuli undermined this basic conception, replacing it with the growing recognition that "(a) communication involves multiple, substantively distinct processes; (b) these processes may be redundant, complementary or contradictory; and (c) processes may mediate or moderate other processes" (Babrow, 1993, p. 110).

This statement suggests a nontrivial potential for misspecification of causal relationships in media effects research. In particular, each of three general types of causal modeling errors is relevant. The first is the *fallacy of the wrong causal process*. That is, the phenomenon of interest is being caused by a different mechanism or process than the one hypothesized. There are several variations of this fallacy. An immediately familiar example is understanding a media effect as either an outcome of learning from media messages (Fishbein & Ajzen, 1975) or an outcome of activation of preexisting knowledge following media exposure (Roskos-Ewoldsen & Fazio, 1992). Both may produce the same observed effect, but they involve very different cognitive processes. Another variation of this is the failure to match constructs' level of analysis with processes' level of analysis. For example, Scheufele (2000) notes that agenda-setting, priming, and framing effects have been examined under the broad category of cognitive effects, using similar research designs, where, in fact, conceptual differences or differences in level of analysis exist among these three types of media effects—framing and priming effects are appropriately conceptualized and tested at the individual level, whereas the agenda-setting effect is appropriately conceptualized and tested at the societal level. One final variation of this fallacy is the general tendency in media effects research to focus on cognitive (psychological) processes as plausible causes of outcomes while ignoring social (sociological) or biological processes that may cause the same outcomes. For example, both exposure to information in the mass media and a social diffusion process can cause change in health-related attitudes and behaviors (see Yanovitzky & Stryker, 2001, for an example of a study that models both processes), though they may interact in different ways to influence audiences (see Yanovitzky & Blitz, 2000, for an example of a study comparing five plausible models of interaction). An effective strategy to avoid the fallacy of the wrong causal process is to appropriately conceptualize multiple causal mechanisms or processes of media effects and to devise empirical tests that directly compare the fit of two or more alternative causal processes to the data.

A second type of possible causal modeling error is the *fallacy of nonreciprocal causation.* The common hypotheses-testing procedure in media effects research relies on statistical tools that can only estimate recursive (or unidirectional) models of effect. A unidirectional model assumes that no two variables in the model are reciprocally related, with each affecting the other. This is unfortunate, since many theories employed by media effects scholars imply complex processes of effects that contain reciprocal causation and feedback loops (i.e., nonrecursive models). For example, there has been considerable debate in the persuasion literature about the causal relationship involved in the attitude-behavior or the intention-behavior link, with most researchers recognizing that some sort of reciprocal relationship exists between the two such that people's newly formed attitudes influence their behavior but also that people's current behavior is used to infer their attitude (O'Keefe, 2002; see also Eveland, Shah, & Kwak, 2003, for additional empirical evidence of nonrecursive relationships

among media-related variables). Although several data analytical methods for estimating nonrecursive causal models exist (Berry, 1984), Stephenson, Holbert, and Zimmerman (2006) note that many nonrecursive models of media effects can be quite easily and efficiently estimated through the use of structural equation modeling (SEM).

The final type of possible causal modeling errors, the *third variable fallacy,* is assumed to be the most common in media effects research (Holbert & Stephenson, 2003). The third variable problem refers to confounding relationships in which a third variable intervenes in (causes, mediates, or moderates) the observed causal relationship between two others. Since randomized experiments and statistical control in observational studies provide reasonable guards against potential spuriousness (i.e., a situation in which the existence of a misleading correlation between two variables is produced through the operation of a third causal variable), mediation poses the greatest potential for misspecified causal relationships in media effects research.

The notion of mediation is explicitly integrated into theories and models that are frequently used in the field, such as the theory of reasoned action (Fishbein & Ajzen, 1975) and the extended parallel processing model (Witte, 1994). However, though tests of mediation are somewhat common in media effects research, tests of more sophisticated, theory-driven hypotheses about processes of media effects are far less common (Preacher & Hayes, 2008; Stephenson et al., 2006). When data are collected from an observational study, the recommendation is to use SEM to test for mediation (Stephenson et al., 2006), though many other alternative approaches exist, including techniques specifically for longitudinal and multilevel data (for a comprehensive review, see MacKinnon, Fairchild, & Fritz, 2007). However, mediation is not only an issue in observational studies. As O'Keefe

(2003) argued convincingly, it is equally crucial to consider mediation relationships in experimental settings to gain more clarity about causal chains.

In summary, the misspecification of causal chains linking media stimuli to their observed effects on audiences presents significant threats to causal inference in media effects research. The most effective way to mitigate these threats is through careful conceptualization and rigorous testing of causal chains, which of course serves as a golden opportunity for researchers to provide more accurate theoretical accounts of the causal mechanisms and processes underlying media effects.

MEASUREMENT OF KEY CONSTRUCTS

Problems with construct measurement are linked to causal inference through the notion of *construct validity,* or the degree of fit between the conceptual definition of the construct and the means by which it is observed. Specifically, Chaffee (1991) identified the explication of communication constructs as one of the main challenges to communication research. Concept explication, he explained, "is about a way of thinking; it is concerned with the disciplined use of words, with observation of human behavior, and especially with the connection between the two" (p. 1). The explication of theoretical constructs has proven to be a difficult task for media effects researchers, not only due to the complexity of these constructs but also because contextual factors such as the rapid evolution of communication technologies and the illusive nature of the audience effectively transform the meaning of constructs from time to time.

Consider the case of media exposure. Despite the centrality of this variable to media effects research as the primary independent variable, "systematic research about measuring exposure is remarkably thin" (Fishbein & Hornik, 2008, p. 1),

and little has been published about the stability, reliability, or validity of most exposure measures. The two most common approaches for assessing variations in media exposure are through the use of experimental manipulations and individual self-reports (Rubin, Palmgreen, & Sypher, 1994). Another common approach involves content analysis of archival data (typically news stories appearing in the *New York Times* and the *Washington Post*) to infer exposure potential for members of the audience (Fishbein & Hornik, 2008). Less common are efforts to assess media exposure based on spending or media buys (Southwell, Barmada, Hornik, & Maklan, 2002). Each approach offers a radically different way of conceptualizing and measuring exposure, and each has some notable strengths and weaknesses. For example, experimental manipulations afford researchers control over the timing and dose of exposure to a particular media stimulus, but they raise legitimate concerns about the validity of this measure in real, uncontrolled environments. Self-reported measures of exposure are externally valid but are prone to recall errors (Potter, 2008), and estimating exposure from archival data is plagued with potential inference errors involving flaws in the sampling of sources and units for inclusion in the study, the coding of content units, and inferring the likelihood of exposure (see Stryker, 2008).

One crucial aspect of measuring exposure (and, we would argue, other variables) in media effects research is the lack of conceptual clarity (or clear explication) about what exactly constitutes exposure (see Potter, Chapter 2, this volume). Some focus on the media exposure act itself, equating exposure with time spent with the medium or content (Rubin et al., 1994). Others (Krugman, Cameron, & McKearney White, 1995; Slater, Hayes, & Ford, 2007) conceptualize media exposure in terms of attention to media stimuli, either self-reported or as measured by tracking eye movements. Still others (e.g., Southwell, 2005) conceptualize exposure in terms of its expected outcomes, such as recall, reception, or encoded exposure (i.e., a minimal memory trace of the message content). There are also proxy measures of exposure, such as measures obtained based on content analysis (e.g., Gonzenbach, 1996), and measures of exposure that are conceptualized in terms of experimental manipulation. The fact that no agreed-on method for measuring exposure has emerged in the field most certainly influences the quality of conclusions drawn from research integrations, such as meta-analysis (Preiss et al., 2007). Different measures have different theoretical implications and yield different results. So what exactly can we claim, with confidence, about the effect of exposure to, for example, media violence on audiences' behavior if our key independent variable is measured in so many different ways?

There are two lines of defense against the threat of construct validity. The primary one involves careful explication of constructs and their meaning. For example, a careful explication of exposure ought to define this act while distinguishing it from its antecedents (the experimental manipulation), its outcomes (e.g., arousal, storage of information in memory), and its proxies (e.g., recall of information), as well as from related terms (e.g., scanning of information). It is also reasonable to expect that, depending on the particular context in which measures are taken, one way of measuring a construct will be superior to other ways of measuring the same construct. The way subjects experience exposure in laboratory experiments may be different than the way they experience it in natural settings; children may experience exposure differently than adults; the hearing-impaired may experience it differently than the vision-impaired. Only by capturing similarities and differences in the ways exposure is experienced by different people and under different circumstances can we begin to achieve clarity about the meaning of this construct and the most valid way to observe it.

The other way to improve construct validity is to seek rigorous, unbiased measures of key variables. One goal to pursue in this respect is the development of measures that are independent of person factors, such as differential capacities or motivations to engage with the measurement instrument. Item response theory (see Embretson & Reise, 2000) provides the framework and statistical tools needed to achieve this goal, and the time is ripe for media effects researchers to take advantage of procedures developed in other fields for improving measurement in this way. Combined with cross-validation of measures through triangulation (DeVellis, 2003), this approach can greatly simplify the construction of valid measures of variables in media effects research.

THE ACTIVE AUDIENCE

As the initial conception of audiences as passive receivers of information from the mass media has all but dissipated in favor of the active audience conception (see Potter, Chapter 2, this volume), an additional set of challenges to causal inference was introduced into media effects research. Specifically, audience activity introduces a significant potential for *selection bias* into the study of media effects. Selection bias is associated with the researcher's lack of control over the assignment of units to different levels of the independent variable because the units self-select into these levels based on factors such as personal relevance and opportunity to participate. In the context of media effects research, selection bias is actually a function of three documented forms of audience activity. First is selective exposure, or people's tendency to expose themselves predominately and preferentially to information that is consistent with their own beliefs, attitudes, and prior experience (Zillmann & Bryant, 1985). The second form of audience activity is selective processing (or interpretation) of information received from the media (Hall, 1980; Kunda, 1990). The third form of audience activity involves message production by the audience as an alternative to consuming information produced by mass media organizations (Riegner, 2007).

The first form of audience activity (selective exposure) fits neatly into the traditional definition of selection bias in that audiences (and not the researcher) control their exposure to the media stimuli. The second (selective processing) involves lack of researchers' control over the mechanism of effect (information processing). The third form of audience activity undermines researchers' control over the direction of effect. Importantly, there is a reason to believe that these three forms of audience activity are not independent of one another, and their likely interaction makes the task of controlling for selection bias in media effects research ever more complicated. The potential threat of audience activity to causal inference relates to both internal and external validity. Correcting for potential selection bias under these circumstances inevitably means controlling for an ever-growing number of audience-centered variables in statistical models that estimate media effects (Nabi, 2007). This also means collecting data from larger and more heterogeneous samples to ensure sufficient power and representativeness. Methods for bias correction, such as propensity score models (see Yanovitzky et al., 2008), make this task more manageable and facilitate causal inference about media effects through a matching procedure that closely approximates random assignment to experimental conditions.

◆ Conclusion

We agree with Nabi (2007) that "it is this diversity—in outcomes assessed, stimuli considered, and methods employed—that makes conclusions about the psychological and social effects of the media so difficult to pin down" (p. 137). At the same time, we also recognize that the field's engagement with the issue of causal inference has been less than optimal and believe that more attention to causation consideration has the potential for promoting greater integration and synthesis of empirical findings in media effects research. Throughout this chapter, we made three central claims about causal inference in media effects research. First, we claim that the traditional social scientific approach to causation is largely inadequate as a framework for studying causal relationships in media effects research and should be replaced with a framework that is more directly derived from and responsive to the challenges inherent in studying media effects phenomena (the multilevel nature of media effects, the dynamic nature of media effects, the complexity of causal chains, the measurement of key constructs, and audience activity). In all, we identified 13 unique threats to causal inference in media effects research, but there are likely others that we missed and that we count on others to point out.

Our second central claim is that getting a grip on causality in media effects research requires researchers to have a detailed understanding of the kinds of mechanisms and processes that could link one event with another. Researchers must think about what these processes might be and how they operate before they test causal propositions. Existing theories of media effects (particularly those that were refined over time) can provide important guidance in terms of the conceptualization of key constructs and relationships, but only if researchers engage them fully and more frequently than they have done in the past (Bryant & Cummins, 2007). Better explication of causal relationships is also directly linked to more compelling and less abstract theorizing of media effects (Hornik & Yanovitzky, 2003), which is necessary for translating scientific knowledge about media effects into practical, real-world applications.

Our third claim is that researchers interested in causal inference ought to make a concerted effort to match their method of investigation with the relative complexity of the phenomenon they study. Standard research designs and methods are reasonably equipped to handle basic research on causal relationships and causal mechanisms. More complex causal phenomena require more sophisticated designs and data analysis tools. Both kinds of studies have a role in advancing the science of media effects, providing that causation considerations are no longer secondary to statistical inference. This leaves much room for the legitimate use of methods, ranging from basic laboratory experiments to complex evaluations of public communication campaigns, to test causal relationships in media effects research. A greater attention to causation considerations implies that media effects researchers spend more of their time designing causally valid research and less time acquiring advanced statistical skills that they can easily tap by calling on the statistician next door.

As media effects research continues to produce evidence about the significance of media effects phenomena to the everyday lives of people, communities, and institutions, media effects scholars ought to take more responsibility for the implications of the theories they use and of the findings they generate. The path to greater accountability must go through serious discussion among scholars about issues of causation in media effects research. The task is not easy, but the potential payoff in terms of integration and synthesis of media effects research makes this a worthwhile investment in the field's future.

♦ References

Babrow, A. S. (1993). The advent of multiple-process theories of communication. *Journal of Communication, 43*(3), 110–118.

Berry, W. D. (1984). *Nonrecursive causal models.* Newbury Park, CA: Sage.

Bryant, J., & Cummins, R. G. (2007). Traditions of mass media theory and research. In R. W. Preiss, B. M. Gayle, N. Burrell, M. Allen, & J. Bryant (Eds.), *Mass media effects research: Advances through meta-analysis* (pp. 2001–2013). Mahwah, NJ: Erlbaum.

Bryant, J., & Thompson, S. (2002). *Fundamentals of media effects* (1st ed.). Boston: McGraw-Hill.

Centerwall, B. S. (1989). Exposure to television as a risk factor for violence. *American Journal of Epidemiology, 129*(4), 643–652.

Chaffee, S. H. (1991). *Explication.* Newbury Park, CA: Sage.

Cook, T. D., & Campbell, D. T. (1979). *Quasi-experimentation: Design and analysis issues for field settings.* Boston: Houghton Mifflin.

Dansereau, F., Cho, J., & Yammarino, F. J. (2006). Avoiding the "fallacy of the wrong level": A within and between analysis (WABA) approach. *Group Organization Management, 31*(5), 536–577.

DeVellis, R. F. (2003). *Scale development: Theory and applications* (2nd ed.). Thousand Oaks, CA: Sage.

Downs, A. (1972). Up and down with ecology: The issue-attention cycle. *Public Interest, 28,* 38–50.

Embretson, S. E., & Reise, S. P. (2000). *Item response theory for psychologists.* Mahwah, NJ: Erlbaum.

Eveland, W. P., Jr., Shah, D. V., & Kwak, N. (2003). Assessing causality in the cognitive mediation model: A panel study of motivations, information processing, and learning during Campaign 2000. *Communication Research, 30*(4), 359–386.

Fishbein, M., & Ajzen, I. (1975). *Belief, attitude, intention and behavior: An introduction to theory and research.* Reading, MA: Addison-Wesley.

Fishbein, M., & Hornik, R. (2008). Measuring media exposure: An introduction to the special issue. *Communication Methods and Measures, 2*(1), 1–5.

Freedman, J. L. (2002). *Media violence and its effect on aggression: Assessing the scientific evidence.* Toronto, ON: University of Toronto Press.

Frey, L. R., Botan, C. H., & Kreps, G. L. (2000). *Investigating communication: An introduction to research methods* (2nd ed.). Boston: Allyn & Bacon.

Gonzenbach, W. J. (1996). *The media, the president, and public opinion: A longitudinal analysis of the drug issue, 1984–1991.* Mahwah, NJ: Erlbaum.

Granger, C. W. J. (1969). Investigating causal relations by econometric models and cross-spectral methods. *Econometrica, 37,* 424–438.

Hall, S. (1980). Encoding/decoding. In S. Hall, D. Hobson, A. Lowe, & P. Willis (Eds.), *Culture, media, language* (pp. 197–208). London, UK: Hutchinson.

Hayes, A. F. (2006). A primer on multilevel modeling. *Human Communication Research, 32*(4), 385–410.

Holbert, R. L., & Stephenson, M. T. (2003). The importance of indirect effects in media effects research: Testing for mediation in structural equation modeling. *Journal of Broadcasting & Electronic Media, 47*(4), 556–572.

Hornik, R. (2002). *Public health communication: Evidence for behavior change.* Mahwah, NJ: Erlbaum.

Hornik, R., & Yanovitzky, I. (2003). Using theory to design evaluations of communication campaigns: The case of the National Youth Anti-Drug Media Campaign. *Communication Theory, 13*(2), 204–224.

Kamhawi, R., & Weaver, D. (2003). Mass communication research trends from 1980 to 1991. *Journalism & Mass Communication Quarterly, 80*(1), 7–27.

Katz, E., & Lazarsfeld, P. F. (1955). *Personal influence: The part played by people in the flow of mass communications.* New York: Free Press.

Krugman, D. M., Cameron, G. T., & McKearney White, C. (1995). Visual attention to programming and commercials: The use of in-home observations. *Journal of Advertising, 24*(1), 1–12.

Kunda, Z. (1990). The case for motivated reasoning. *Psychological Bulletin, 108,* 480–498.

Levine, T. R., & Hullett, C. R. (2002). Eta squared, partial squared, and misreporting of effect size in communication research. *Human Communication Research, 28*(4), 612–625.

Littlejohn, S. W., & Foss, K. A. (2008). *Theories of human communication* (9th ed.). Belmont, CA: Wadsworth/Thomson Learning.

Long, M., Slater, M. D., Boiarsky, G., Stapel, L., & Keefe, T. (2005). Obtaining nationally representative samples of local news media outlets. *Mass Communication & Society, 8*(4), 299–322.

Lowry, D. T. (1979). An evaluation of empirical studies reported in seven journals in the '70s. *Journalism Quarterly, 56*(2), 262–282.

MacKinnon, D. P., Fairchild, A. J., & Fritz, M. S. (2007). Mediation analysis. *Annual Review of Psychology, 58,* 593–614.

Nabi, R. I. (2007). "And miles to go . . .": Reflections on the past and future of mass media effects research. In R. W. Preiss, B. M. Gayle, N. Burrell, M. Allen, & J. Bryant (Eds.), *Mass media effects research: Advances through meta-analysis* (pp. 137–144). Mahwah, NJ: Erlbaum.

O'Keefe, D. J. (2002). *Persuasion: Theory and research* (2nd ed.). Thousand Oaks, CA: Sage.

O'Keefe, D. J. (2003). Massage properties, mediating states, and manipulation checks: Claims, evidence, and data analysis in experimental persuasive message effects research. *Communication Theory, 13*(3), 251–274.

Pan, Z., & McLeod, J. M. (1991). Multilevel analysis in mass communication research. *Communication Research, 18*(2), 140–173.

Pearl, J. (2000). *Causality: Models, reasoning, and inference.* New York: Cambridge University Press.

Petty, R. E., & Cacioppo, J. T. (1986). *Communication and persuasion: Central and peripheral routes to attitude change.* New York: Springer-Verlag.

Popper, K. R. (1959). *The logic of scientific discovery.* New York: Harper & Row.

Potter, J. W. (2008). The importance of considering exposure states when designing survey research studies. *Communication Methods and Measures, 2*(1), 152–166.

Potter, W. J., & Riddle, K. (2007). A content analysis of the media effects literature. *Journalism & Mass Communication Quarterly, 84*(1), 90–104.

Preacher, K. J., & Hayes, A. F. (2008). Contemporary approaches to assessing mediation in communication research. In A. F. Hayes, M. D. Slater, & L. B. Snyder (Eds.), *The Sage sourcebook of advanced data analysis methods for communication research* (pp. 13–54). Thousand Oaks, CA: Sage.

Preiss, R. W., Gayle, B. M., Burrell, N., Allen, M., & Bryant, J. (2007). *Mass media effects research: Advances through meta-analysis.* Mahwah, NJ: Erlbaum.

Price, V., Ritchie, L. D., & Eulau, H. (1991). Cross-level challenges for communication research: Epilogue. *Communication Research, 18*(2), 262–271.

Riegner, C. (2007). Word of mouth on the Web: The impact of Web 2.0 on consumer purchase decisions. *Journal of Advertising Research, 47*(4), 436–447.

Rogers, E. M. (1962). *Diffusion of innovations.* New York: Free Press of Glencoe.

Rogers, E. M., Dearing, J. W., & Chang, S. (1991). AIDS in the 1980s: The agenda setting process for a public issue. *Journalism Monographs, 126,* 1–82.

Roskos-Ewoldsen, D. R., & Fazio, R. H. (1992). On the orienting value of attitudes: Attitude accessibility as a determinant of an object's attraction of visual attention. *Journal of Personality & Social Psychology, 63*(2), 198–211.

Rubin, R. B., Palmgreen, P., & Sypher, H. E. (1994). *Communication research measure: A sourcebook.* New York: Guilford Press.

Scheufele, D. A. (2000). Agenda-setting, priming, and framing revisited: Another look at cognitive effects of political communication. *Mass Communication and Society, 3*(2), 297–316.

Schramm, W. (1957). Twenty years of journalism research. *Public Opinion Quarterly, 21,* 91–107.

Slater, M. D., Hayes, A. F., & Ford, V. L. (2007). Examining the moderating and mediating roles of news exposure and attention on adolescent judgments of alcohol-related risks. *Communication Research, 34*(4), 355–381.

Slater, M. D., Snyder, L., & Hayes, A. F. (2006). Thinking and modeling at multiple levels: The potential contribution of multilevel modeling to communication theory and research. *Human Communication Research, 32*(4), 375–384.

Snyder, L. B., & Hamilton, M. A. (2002). Meta-analysis of U.S. health campaign effects on behavior: Emphasize enforcement, exposure, and new information, and beware the secular trend. In R. Hornik (Ed.), *Public health communication: Evidence for behavior change* (pp. 357–383). Hillsdale, NJ: Erlbaum.

Southwell, B. G. (2005). Between messages and people: A multilevel model of memory for television content. *Communication Research, 32*(1), 112–140.

Southwell, B. G., Barmada, C. H., Hornik, R. C., & Maklan, D. M. (2002). Can we measure encoded exposure? Validation evidence from a national campaign. *Journal of Health Communication, 7*(5), 445–453.

Stephenson, M. T., Holbert, R. L., & Zimmerman, R. S. (2006). On the use of structural equation modeling in health communication research. *Health Communication, 20*(2), 159–167.

Stinchcombe, A. L. (1968). *Constructing social theories.* New York: Harcourt.

Stryker, J. E. (2008). Measuring aggregate media exposure: A construct validity test of indicators of the national news environment. *Communication Methods and Measures, 2*(1), 115–133.

Watt, J. H., & VanLear, C. A. (1996). *Dynamic patterns in communication processes.* Thousand Oaks, CA: Sage.

Wimmer, R. D., & Dominick, J. R. (2000). *Mass media research: An introduction* (6th ed.). Belmont, CA: Wadsworth.

Winship, C., & Morgan, S. L. (1999). The estimation of causal effects from observational data. *Annual Review of Sociology, 25,* 659–706.

Witte, K. (1994). Fear control and danger control: A test of the extended parallel process model (EPPM). *Communication Monographs, 61*(2), 113–134.

Yanovitzky, I. (2002). Effect of news coverage on the prevalence of drunk-driving behavior: Evidence from a longitudinal study. *Journal of Studies on Alcohol, 63*(3), 342–351.

Yanovitzky, I., & Bennett, C. (1999). Media attention, institutional response, and health behavior change: The case of drunk driving, 1978–1996. *Communication Research, 26*(4), 429–453.

Yanovitzky, I., & Blitz, C. L. (2000). Effect of media coverage and physician advice on utilization of breast cancer screening by women 40 years and older. *Journal of Health Communication, 5*(2), 117–134.

Yanovitzky, I., Hornik, R., & Zanutto, E. (2008). Estimating causal effects in observational studies: The propensity score approach. In A. F. Hayes, M. D. Slater, & L. B. Snyder (Eds.), *The Sage sourcebook of advanced data analysis methods for communication research* (pp. 159–184). Thousand Oaks, CA: Sage.

Yanovitzky, I., & Rimal, R. N. (2006). Communication and normative influence. *Communication Theory, 16*(1), 1–6.

Yanovitzky, I., & Stryker, J. E. (2001). Mass media, social norms, and health promotion efforts: A longitudinal study of media effects on youth binge drinking. *Communication Research, 28*(2), 208–239.

Yanovitzky, I., & VanLear, A. (2008). Time series analysis: Traditional and contemporary approaches. In A. F. Hayes, M. D. Slater, & L. B. Snyder (Eds.), *The Sage sourcebook of advanced data analysis methods for communication research* (pp. 89–124). Thousand Oaks, CA: Sage.

Zillmann, D., & Bryant, J. (1985). *Selective exposure to communication.* Hillsdale, NJ: Erlbaum.

4

QUALITATIVE METHODS

◆ Thomas R. Lindlof

◆ *Qualitative Methods*

During the past three decades, qualitative methods have gained a central place in the toolkit of communication research. Considering their former status of suspect scientific value and legitimacy, it is significant that these methods are now recognized as a disciplined form of inquiry with their own standards of quality. More important, the rising use of qualitative methods helped spur the growth of cultural media studies, contributing important findings and theoretic dialogue about all stages of the circuit of mediated communication—from the institutions that produce symbolic goods, to the products themselves, to their circulation in the audience. They have proven to be particularly well suited for studying the audience reception of media, where such reception is viewed as *a situated activity* (carried out in sociohistorical contexts), *a routine activity* (integrated into daily life), *a skilled accomplishment* (enacted through learned codes and competencies), and *a hermeneutic process* (interpreted with reference to existing meanings; Thompson, 1995, pp. 38–43). Among the major questions that audience scholars have opened up for investigation over this 30-year period are the following: What are the multiple meanings that people construct from attending to media texts, and what aspects of the text-reader interaction are responsible for producing those meanings? How do the structural features of society—e.g., unequal distributions of power, resources, and social capital—make themselves felt in the microlevel settings of reception? How do people use media to negotiate their interpersonal relationships as well as to fashion their identities as members of families, peer groups, subcultures, and national communities?

The thread running through the questions is one of studying the "audience-as-agent," rather than the "audience-as-outcome" of exposure to content (Webster, 1998). In other words, audiences are seen as knowledgeable, creative agents, constantly interpreting the meanings of media technologies and content within the scope of their collective understandings and individual subjectivities. This perspective, White (1994) points out,

> does not deny that, in some degree, media have behavioral effects nor does it deny that motivations for uses and gratifications come into play, but these perspectives [of the "creative audience"] must now be *seen in the light of what we know about the audience's construction of the meaning that often is different and independent from* the interpretative meaning that the program producers may have placed on their product. (p. 25; emphasis in original)

These constructions of meaning are fruitfully studied through qualitative "methods of intimacy" (Anderson, 1996) that enable one to enter the semiotic domain of media usage.

This chapter reviews the role of qualitative *methodology* (as a set of epistemological arguments) and qualitative *methods* (as a set of research practices) as they have been applied to the study of media audiences. The chapter begins by considering the purview of qualitative methodology, including its major features and assumptions. Next, a methodological history of qualitative audience research is presented, highlighting some of the major accomplishments, turning points, and critical issues of

research practice. The chapter concludes with a view of the future of qualitative methods in media studies.

◆ Qualitative Methodology

In a recent review of qualitative research in organizational communication, Taylor and Trujillo (2001) claim that it is "futile" to attempt to write a universally accepted definition of qualitative research. To illustrate their point, Taylor and Trujillo quote from several definitions in the sociology and communication literature—putting on display a tangle of semantic nuances and inconsistencies—before opting themselves out of the business of defining qualitative research, "because it is so large and amorphous, and because it is growing and changing even as you read this chapter" (p. 162).

For most dedicated qualitative researchers— a breed of scholar who prizes his or her ability to tolerate (or tease out) ambiguity—this lack of a clear definition is neither surprising nor particularly embarrassing. Still, a set of common features and assumptions of qualitative methodology can be sketched out, even if complete agreement on all the details remains elusive. We begin with a plank on which almost everyone is willing to stand. According to Atkinson and Hammersley (1994), a key feature of ethnography—and fieldwork methods in general—is ethnographers' use of "unstructured data, that is, data that have not been coded at the point of data collection in terms of a closed set of analytic categories" (p. 248). Lindlof and Taylor (2002) build upon that idea, stating that qualitative researchers "seek to preserve and analyze the situated form, content, and experience of social action, rather than subject it to mathematical or other formal relationships" (p. 18). Thus, qualitative researchers try to faithfully represent the observable qualities of social action from the point of data capture all the way through data analysis. This is arguably what makes a qualitative study recognizably "qualitative."

At the same time, it is important to resist categorizing qualitative and quantitative methodologies as Manichean opposites, a view that has probably outlived whatever usefulness it once had. Bavelas (1995) blames this binary thinking for promoting "a series of concatenated false dichotomies" (p. 50)—empirical versus nonempirical, objective versus subjective, inductive versus deductive, generalizable versus nongeneralizable, and so forth. In her view, qualitative and quantitative approaches are joined at the hip by a shared model of scientific logic, even if they pursue different aims and create different kinds of data. Moreover, each tradition needs the insights and procedures of the other if both are to thrive. Thus, it is perforce impossible to develop a research argument, construct a hypothesis, or interpret statistical findings without at least some interpretive (qualitative) license on the part of the analyst. It is equally impossible for qualitative researchers, who are inclined to move inductively from observing particulars to crafting general concepts, to avoid deductive reasoning at various moments and stages of a study. The qualitative/quantitative divide also breaks down at the tactical level. For example, experimentalists sometimes turn to qualitative techniques like focus group interviews when it is necessary to assess what subjects think of different versions of a stimulus. And ethnographers sometimes turn to quantitative measures when they want to track the frequency of certain social phenomena in a bounded setting. Even qualitative researchers who eschew variables and measures have been known to indulge in quasi-quantitative locutions like "in many families," "in several cases," and "in most of the cases."

Ultimately, most qualitative researchers are not agnostic in matters of epistemology. What is most distinctive about qualitative research is not that it deals in unstructured data—although that aspect is essential to the methods used—but that it is typically put to *interpretive* purposes. This type of explanation is closely associated with the method of empathetic understanding called *verstehen*. *Verstehen* is put into motion by aligning closely with the subject:

> Only by "reliving" a person's line of action can scholars gain knowledge of the contents and qualities of meaningful experience. . . . The investigator enters the life world of the subject by whatever means available—for example, texts, conversation, and social participation—and tries to reconstruct the totality of what the subject believes, values, and desires. (Lindlof, 2008, p. 5259)

In ethnography, *verstehen* is executed by taking up residence with the group under study. To quote the pioneering anthropologist Bronislaw Malinowski (1922/1961), the ethnographer's goal is "to grasp the native's point of view, his relation to life, to realize his vision of his world" (p. 25). The practice of ethnography has changed in many ways since Malinowski's day, but qualitative researchers still study what Geertz (1973, p. 5) has called the "webs of significance" that form the basis of people's social worlds and cultural practices. These webs of significance—beliefs, ideologies, values, social rules, and any and all truth claims about reality—lend a sense of coherence, security, and direction to the ways in which we act.

Almost all interpretive research, therefore, subscribes to the doctrine of constructivism, which holds that reality is an ongoing production of our own efforts as socialized human beings. Two assumptions of constructivism are very important in characterizing qualitative research. First, everything that human beings experience is subject to variable interpretations, from sense data like color, movement, and air pressure, to social data like artifacts, language, and ritual. Even science is a reality production, not a value-free pursuit for recording "brute data" in a point-to-point correspondence with the material world. Following from this assumption, qualitative researchers take seriously the idea that their own interpretive activity contributes to the creation of the social realities they set out to study. It is therefore incumbent on researchers to note the relational aspects of their participation with human subjects and consider the political and ethical implications of their fieldwork and published accounts. Second, the reality we speak of in constructivism is the everyday world of commonly held understandings. A valid claim of any kind—scientific, religious, juridical, moral, and so on—depends on some level of intersubjective agreement about the object of reference. These understandings are not held by people in the abstract, but are embodied in "the iconic, discursive, and performative practices which are the resources for our communicative efforts" (Anderson, 1996, p. 46). It is in fact a hallmark of qualitative inquiry that it can reveal the artful, complex nature of the most mundane human act. But to do that, the investigator must be able to see the mundane through the eyes of the stranger and question the foundations of this taken-for-granted knowledge. Of course, the mass media and popular culture are quintessentially mundane features of life in modernity. Much of what passes for "common sense"—for example, the social rules of TV viewing—is opaque to analysis until we begin asking questions about the forms it takes and why it is so widely trusted.

The methods deployed in qualitative research—participant observation, extensive interviews, focus group interviews, protocol analysis, material culture analysis, and so on—place us in the frontier of commonly held understandings so that we can start to unpack this tacit knowledge. Through a process of tacking between social actors' understandings of what they are doing and the formalized conceptualizations of the academic discipline, we gradually learn to grasp a person's (or group's) experience of media. Because meanings are always elusive and ever changing, we can never do more than write a partial account of these experiences. Moreover, theoretical inferences always have a sociohistorical particularity: these are the interpretations of this group, at this place and time, living in these social, economic, and political conditions. However, even interpretive analysts can generalize findings to some degree, due to the cultural consistency of the social worlds they study (Williams, 2000).

◆ Qualitative Audience Studies: A Methodological History

Qualitative methods made sporadic appearances during the formative years of mass communication research. Some prominent examples of their use include the oral histories of young people's engagement with movies that Herbert Blumer collected and analyzed in the early 1930s for the Payne Fund Studies; Herta Herzog's celebrated study of women's uses of 1940s radio serials; and Kurt Lang and Gladys Lang's 1953 observational study of the perceptual effects of television's live news coverage. In Great Britain in the 1930s and 1940s, mass observation studies of everyday life, including moviegoing and other domestic media uses, were carried out. Individually, these studies yielded intriguing descriptions of midcentury media culture, but none of them led to programmatic lines of theory-driven research. From the 1940s through the 1970s, positivist, effects-focused media research held sway as the dominant research paradigm and qualitative work was generally consigned to a prescientific, or exploratory role.

By the late 1970s, opinion about the value of qualitative research—especially in the service of ideas of audience agency and activity—began to shift decisively. Seminal studies were under way in the United States and Great Britain that soon helped elevate questions of interpretation in the mass communication agenda. Yet, even at this early juncture, it was evident that the methodological pathways were diverging. In the United States, media researchers were developing a social action approach to studying television, grounded in the logic and practice of participant observation. James Lull (1980) advocated the use of ethnography in family settings, and James A. Anderson, Timothy P. Meyer, and their colleagues (Meyer, Traudt, & Anderson, 1980) proposed a similar agenda for ethnographic case studies of family life. They were commonly dissatisfied with how media use had been defined—or ignored altogether—by survey and experimental approaches to audience measurement. Meyer et al. (1980), for example, argued that television viewing is not a static, isolatable behavior, but a dynamic social process that assumes many forms. Lull (1980) characterized television as an expedient, practical resource that social actors use to pursue daily routines and goals *in their own terms and on their own grounds* (p. 198; emphasis in original). Uses and gratifications shared this premise of an active audience, but its roots in functionalism limited the theory's ability to explain people's actions in natural contexts. Taking inspiration from the interpretive sociologies of ethnomethodology and symbolic interactionism, Lull and Anderson and his colleagues argued that ethnographic research is uniquely capable of registering the context-sensitive, taken-for-granted character of ordinary media use. Notably, Lull's ethnography of more than 200 families suggested that people use television as a regulator of time and space in the home and also as a rich source of exemplars for managing interpersonal relations.

Ethnography situates researchers in the middle of the social action. (Ontologically, social action has no beginning or ending; but as a practical matter, researchers must choose where they will intervene in the ongoing stream.) By entering a living unit for a period of time, the participant observer gains an insider's perspective on the significance of family members' media use. In an early methodological guide, Lull (1985) described some of the key considerations for doing this: an observational period of 3 to 7 days with a family; the rapid establishment of rapport with family members so that the researcher could observe more or less inconspicuously; the researcher's involvement in family routines (e.g., chores, leisure activity) in order to gain acceptance and be able to engage in informal questioning; and, in the final stage of fieldwork, as a check on validity and reliability, the use of interviews with family members "regarding the issues raised by the observer and to report their beliefs and opinions about other family members" (p. 84). Meyer et al. (1980) also proposed that observations be augmented with an array of measures (questionnaires, biographical sketches, time use logs, etc.) for achieving both a global portrait of the family and a fine-grained look at how media use plays out over longer periods.

The early media ethnographies were largely unconcerned with subjective responses to media content. According to social action media theory (Schoening & Anderson, 1995), content becomes meaningful only when it is appropriated in social routines; thus, shifting contexts of usage produce moment-by-moment differences in what a segment of content actually means for the involved social actor. Exposure to content is not even necessary for "uses" and "effects" to occur. The pervasive penetration of media signifiers in everyday life is sufficient to permit people to use and interpret them without ever having seen (or heard) the original texts. Participant observation offered a means for studying the myriad circumstances in which content choice is ambiguous, accidental, or negotiated (e.g., public TV viewing; Lemish, 1982), or where media usage consists of discursive routines (conversations, jokes, etc.) in which content is referenced for supporting identity claims (e.g., police culture; Pacanowsky & Anderson, 1982).

This radical break from the variable-analytic orthodoxy of audience research prompted questions about the reactivity effects that occur when a researcher inserts himself or herself in intimate settings. Media ethnographers countered that family members cannot suppress, delay, or modify their routines for very long, even with a stranger present. According to Lull (1985), by the 3rd day of a 7-day fieldwork model, "the researcher begins to feel that the interpersonal dramas unfolding are normal" (p. 83). Survey data collected by Lull's trained observers seemed to support this claim, showing that relatively few family members, children included, act differently or alter typical patterns of television use while being studied in their homes. A more consequential question concerned the observational period: Can the role of media in a complex system like the family be understood in only a few days? Lull and others contended that the brief time frame was adequate for inferring a family's social rules and role structures vis-á-vis the television medium. However, other early audience ethnographies did employ longer contact periods with family members (e.g., Wolf, Meyer, & White, 1982).

The first audience ethnographies were heavily influenced by a naturalistic field-work style that stressed observation over participation. As a consequence, these ethnographies were characterized by an attitude of neutral detachment from the scenes being observed as well as a benign neglect of the larger ideological forces at play in local settings. Eventually, media ethnographers realized that this posture was at odds with the actual process of engaging in mutual recognition and

adaptation with others in the field—a process known as reflexivity. By the late 1980s, anthropological innovations in dialogical, politically engaged forms of ethnography (Marcus & Fischer, 1986) filtered into the other social sciences, including communication and media studies. An "I-thou" dialectic of field relations began to replace the objectifying gaze of the realist ethnography.

Meanwhile, in Great Britain, David Morley, a researcher affiliated with the University of Birmingham's Centre for Contemporary Cultural Studies, was involved in a 4-year study of a British current affairs program, *Nationwide*. Investigation of audience decodings of the program constituted a major part of the study. Morley's project was motivated in part by a critique of the then-influential screen theory of text-spectator relations. "At the root of these objections," noted Moores (1990), "was the assertion that 'screen theory' failed to distinguish between the reader implied by or inscribed in the text and the actual social subjects who interpret or decode texts" (p. 14). Stuart Hall's recently articulated model of media communication as a series of "moments" of encoding and decoding (Hall, 1980) provided a justification for pushing the uses and gratifications approach into the semiotic realm. Morley found that *Nationwide*'s production and ideological codes, while setting limits on the kinds of meanings that could be generated (nobody, for example, called it a comedy), did not drive the viewers' own decodings. Rather, the social positionings of the viewer groups he studied—particularly, their class, occupation, and ethnicity—were highly related to the meanings they made of *Nationwide*. The study suggested that the discourses circulating in a person's social groups have a strong influence on how he or she reads a media text. Some of the viewers' evaluations were even aberrant, or "subversive," with respect to the program's preferred meaning. As

Morley (1992) remarked about his findings, "the 'meaning' of a text or message must be understood as being produced through an interaction of the codes embedded in the text with the codes inhabited by the different sections of the audience" (p. 118).

Another study from this period, Janice Radway's *Reading the Romance* (1984), played a major role in the newly emerging focus on audience consciousness. Radway found that the female devotees of romance novels, a lowbrow genre that carried putatively patriarchal themes, read them as empowering stories and used the books in stolen moments to escape from their family responsibilities. The study successfully integrated a number of elements—narrative analysis, feminist criticism, and analysis of audience discourse—for understanding how a popular media product fits into a social context. She also introduced a concept from literary studies—the interpretive community—that suggested a process by which people collectively define a media genre and establish their own standards of literacy.

The appearance of Morley's and Radway's studies, along with others conducted in the 1980s, inaugurated a new kind of audience research: reception analysis (or reception study). Reception analysis addressed some key problems in a number of fields and conceptual frameworks, from British cultural studies to social semiotics, feminist theory, and postmodernism. More than anything, it provided a warrant for exploring the semiotic fecundity of cultural objects—the idea that the meanings of media content come alive through its reception. Instead of assuming that people "read off" the hegemonic meanings already inscribed in content, researchers explored how social subjects of different backgrounds interpret the aesthetic and politicized discourses of contemporary media. They began to study the multiple "pleasures" that people derive from engaging with the polysemic qualities of media texts—including their ironic, playful, self-referential signs. In a more sociological vein, reception analysts began to look seriously at the productive cultural activity of fans and other audience formations that display a high commitment to, and specialized tastes for, certain symbolic goods. In sum, reception analysis offered critical and cultural scholars a bridge between the humanistic and social scientific views of media influence (Jensen, 1987). Although few of them crossed all the way over to the social scientific side, they borrowed concepts and methods that proved useful in studying audiences empirically.

In methodological terms, reception analysis is characterized by "an insistence that studies include a comparative empirical analysis of media discourses with audience discourses—content structures with the structure of audience responses regarding content" (Jensen & Rosengren, 1990, p. 218). The textual analysis phase of a reception study establishes the relevant content structures that will be used for comparisons with the audience decodings. Some of these encoded features operate at the level of manifest (or denotative) content, whereas others operate at the connotative level of signification and are subject to greater variance of interpretations at the decoding stage. Selection of content for a reception study depends on the underlying theoretical rationale as well its relevance to trends in consumption, politics, or media policy. The text one selects may exemplify a social problem; or a unique relationship to its audience; or a popular genre, because genres are "the best estimate of where the producers last had a sense of the moving identities of the audience" (White, 1994, p. 26).

The audience component is carried out through an interview protocol that aims to elicit "viewers' interpretations, decodings, readings, meaning productions, perceptions or comprehension of programmes" (Hoijer, 1990, p. 29). The sample of audience members is usually chosen to align with the actual (or intended) audience of the content. For example, if a genre's modal audience is a highly committed fan base, respondents may be drawn from a similarly cohesive group, as in the case of Radway's romance readers. Morley, on the other hand, opted for a more variegated sample for the *Nationwide* study because the program itself reached a broad national audience. Reception studies also employ samples that are structured demographically to "test" for differences in interpretation. For example, Press (1991) conducted interviews of working-class and middle-class women after showing them a television program featuring the issue of abortion; Liebes and Katz (1990) assembled viewing groups on four continents to study cross-cultural differences in meanings of the 1980s TV series *Dallas*.

Reception analysts took a particular view of the functions and uses of interviews. In sociology, folklore, and other fields, qualitative researchers often use long interviews to produce narratives (or oral histories) about cultural practices, key life events, or other personal matters. Reception studies, however, rarely treat a respondent's speech as the expression of a biographical self. Rather, it is assumed that people construct their subjectivity in relation to a media text by means of the discourses they routinely speak in their social worlds. The researcher thus conceives of study participants as "speaking subjects," whose identities are already formed in terms of constructions like class, race, and gender, and whose linguistic performance in the study setting reveals the influence of these subject positions on the decoding of media (Seiter, 1999, pp. 28–31). Ideally, the semistructured interviews or focus group discussions yield evidence of the meanings that already circulate in society.

One of the chief criticisms leveled at the first generation of reception studies concerned the media-centric character of the interviews, especially those using focus group discussions. The study conditions seemed to encourage participants to view programs with a seriousness of purpose that is alien to their everyday experience and then discuss them with a group of strangers. Morley (1987) understood that these interviews differed from the customary social rhythms and textures of watching television:

> In the absence of any significant element of participant observation of actual behavior beyond the interview situation, I am left only with the stories that respondents chose to tell me. These stories are, however, themselves both limited by, and indexical of, the cultural and linguistic frames of reference which respondents have available to them, through which to articulate their responses, though . . . these are limited to the level of conscious experience. (p. 24)

Still, it was not uncommon for reception analysts to infer, or otherwise imagine, the home environment from interview data alone (e.g., Morley, 1986).

The period from the mid-1980s through the early 1990s witnessed a surge of research activity about the audience. Much of this work was theoretical or polemical in nature, but empirical studies were also published in greater numbers. The interview-based reception studies done under the rubrics of cultural studies far outpaced social action ethnography, due in part to the latter's demanding requirements of time, logistics, and social engagement. *Reception* even gained currency as a covering term for all audience phenomena—not just content-decoding processes, but also the social contexts and consequences of media use (Jensen, 1987, 2002).

Ironically, this blossoming of research activity occurred just as critiques of the enterprise began to intrude from several directions. The more exuberant claims of a "semiotic democracy," in which audience members enjoy wide-ranging freedoms to resist, oppose, and refashion the floating signifiers of commercial media, were regarded by some skeptics as overblown. Critical theorists in particular asserted that the interpretive turn in studying audiences ignored the power of the text and lost sight of the historical and material conditions that shape the media landscape (e.g., Carragee, 1988). Some audience researchers asked searching questions of their own about how, or whether, audience studies could contribute usefully to macrolevel analyses of the public sphere (Livingstone, 1998; Morley, 1993). Reception study was also confronted with arguments, mostly coming from a poststructuralist point of view, that the "audience" itself is a reification of media industry discourse. According to this view, real audiences exist only in the traces of social activity in which media play a part. Only ethnographies, wrote Ang (1991), are capable of tracking "the dispersed, indefinitely proliferating chain of situations in which television audiencehood is practiced and experienced" (p. 164). Even the meaning of *ethnography* was hotly contested. A number of scholars, many of them belonging to disciplines that have different concepts of the rigors and standards of ethnography, questioned the appropriation of the term for describing all qualitative audience studies and dismissed many of the reception study findings as narrow and banal (e.g., Abu-Lughod, 1997; Gillespie, 1995).

Finally, there was the gnawing sense that the accumulation of reception studies of various audience groups, texts, and contexts was not moving the field forward, and certainly not advancing a general theory of reception. Some perceived a reinventing-the-wheel syndrome at work as studies spun out new names for interpretative strategies that had been described previously (e.g., Michelle, 2007). By the end of the 1990s, Livingstone (1998) was moved to write that "audience studies is losing its direction," an apparent casualty of "a closing down of the theoretical

diversity that was so exciting and productive 10 or 15 years ago" (p. 194).

Despite these difficulties, the turn of the 21st century was marked by new beginnings for qualitative audience studies—developments that had as much to do with an influx of new scholars in media studies as it did with the onrushing trends of economic globalization; transnational flows of people and information (creating an almost endless profusion of hybridized cultures); the explosive growth of digital technologies; and new relationships among content creators, marketers, and audiences. A second generation of audience researchers, many of them from non-Western backgrounds, rediscovered ethnography as an approach that combines theoretical, strategic, and personal interests in cultural self-expression and social change. Gillespie's (1995) ethnography of the mediated culture of an immigrant Indian community in London is often credited as a key study in this renewal. Unlike their predecessors, this cohort of media ethnographers typically spend more time in the field; get to know informants on deeper levels; and adopt dispersed, multisited research strategies by studying participants on the move or in locales beyond the home (e.g., Ritson & Elliott, 1999). Interests in the reception of genres or individual media texts have not been forsaken. However, the media-centric character of the earlier interview-based designs has been replaced by projects with a more ethnographic flavor. Increasingly, as demonstrated in Mayer's (2003) and La Pastina's (2004) ethnographies of social engagement with telenovelas, the scope of investigation encompasses an entire social community or geographic area and situates the interpretation of media content within a matrix of historical traditions, economic and political conditions, and native linguistic and other signifying systems. As La Pastina aptly notes, referring to the issue of gender roles in his study, "In order to comprehend the reception process, there is a need to understand how different contextual factors influence viewers' interpretations and how the contextual factors, in concert with the telenovelas, might reproduce patriarchal power structures that traditionally privilege men over women" (p. 165). Such contextualization results in more thickly described cases that can allow multiple voices and perspectives to be incorporated in the ethnographic text.

Another sign of the growing maturity of audience ethnography is seen in the appearance of more sophisticated discussions of reflexivity. Few of the early reception studies or social action ethnographies showed much consideration of the power differences between researcher and participants, or the motives and identity constructions that each brings to a project. By turning their attention to the specific ways in which relationships with ethnographic subjects develop—especially at the intersections of gender, education, class, race, and other markers of cultural difference—researchers gain greater awareness of the situated, partial, and contingent nature of the knowledge they are producing. Explicit discussions of fieldwork practices can also help audience ethnographers think in more considered ways about developing mutually constructive and ethical ways of engaging with the people they study. Jordan (2006), for example, interrogated her own experiences as a participant observer of family life in terms of the "social constructions" she adopted or that her participants ascribed to her: the researcher as student, the researcher as person, the researcher as guest, and the researcher as negative agent. Murphy and Kraidy (2003) suggest the possibility of negotiating more coequal relationships, even to the extent of encouraging subjects to think of themselves as a "cultural interlocutor" or "coresearcher." Clearly, cross-cultural encounters in the field call for media researchers to take note of the effects of their own ethnic identity—a matter of special concern for White academics

(Mayer, 2005). However, being the same ethnicity as one's subjects does not guarantee acceptance or privileged knowledge of their interests, as Parameswaran (2001) discovered in traveling back to her native India to study romance reading among young women in India. As these self-reflexive accounts suggest, qualitative audience research is moving toward fieldwork models that emphasize personal accountability and respect for the integrity of others' life worlds.

Transformations in the media landscape have also rejuvenated qualitative audience studies. The media industries are rapidly shifting away from the mass delivery of manufactured content units according to rigid schedules, and toward on-demand accessibility of digital content via multiple platforms. The implications of this shift for audience behavior are dramatic and well documented. People in technologically advanced societies have grown accustomed to accessing a variety of media devices on the go. They now expect to acquire content tailored to their situational needs, and increasingly they combine the roles of content creator, content aggregator, and content consumer. These developments enable people to talk to (and with) producing entities as never before and to influence the dialogue and interpretations of others sharing the same networked systems (Jenkins, 2006). For more than 15 years, audience researchers have been conducting expeditions into this complex semiotic terrain of fan groups, diasporic cultures, and mobile media users. The methodological implications, however, are dimly understood at this point. Due to the multifunctional, user-controlled nature of digital technologies, and the specialized (and ephemeral) qualities of the content they offer, researchers confront daunting challenges in gaining access to the sites of usage. The Internet, writes Livingstone (2004), "is at times highly personal, even transgressive—including intimate conversations, pornography, personal concerns, etc., making observation or interviews difficult. Even if we get close to the experience of Internet use, it is unclear how to record this" (p. 82).

Qualitative researchers often deal with these issues by relying on observations of public postings, chat rooms, blogs, podcasts, Web pages, and simulations—an approach that transforms "fieldwork" into an exercise in textual analysis. Such strategies can disclose the "what" of public users' practices, but they are not as successful at coping with "how" and "why" questions— to say nothing of investigating the more private precincts of the Internet. The latter goals often cannot be achieved without some degree of participation in the actions of online users. The means of participation in virtual worlds are always available to researchers—for example, taking on the roles of chat room confidant or fellow gamer—but these methods carry special risks in the areas of identity disclosure, privacy infringement, and informed consent (Lotz & Ross, 2004). There are also differences of opinion about whether online scenes such as Second Life should be treated as a complete, self-justifying social world, or whether researchers should contextualize them in the social and psychological circumstances of the people "pulling the strings" of avatars.

Finally, as traditional meanings of "audience" have come to seem obsolete, "community" has resurfaced as a way of thinking about social formations characterized by negotiated strategies for classifying, reading, and using texts. The empirical validity of the older construct, interpretive community, has been called into question by, among others, Jensen (2002), who favors "interpretive repertoires" for describing audience decoding. Nevertheless, qualitative researchers have recently found new applications for the construct in mediated communication, from the moral-religious communities that engage in dialogue about appropriate uses of media (Stout, 2004); to the virtual communities

that coalesce on the Internet along lines of affinity (Jenkins, 2006); to the brand communities of people who identify with certain branded products, purchase or create artifacts that extend a brand's cultural reach, and even organize aspects of their social lives around the brand image (Kates, 2006). As media technologies and content forms continue to adopt social networking capabilities (a trend that shows no signs of slowing), they make it possible for people to connect with each other in socially useful ways and display a sense of mutual obligation not unlike that of the sociologically dense features of "real" communities. Qualitative research will undoubtedly play a major role in studying the sense making, values, and performances that support the development of these communities.

◆ Future Directions

Predicting the future is always perilous. Of course, one popular way of playing it safe is simply to extrapolate from presently evolving trends (while ignoring the possibility that these trends will not be able to sustain themselves when unforeseen events occur). Another way to play the futures game, the one chosen to end this chapter, is to simply state one's own preferences for how things *should* turn out, a gambit that at least holds out the chance that the future can be influenced by a persuasive argument.

One major development that should occur in the next decade—and probably will, at least on a limited, experimental basis—is growth in the collaborative nature of audience studies. Although ethnography has traditionally been a solitary pursuit, team research has become more common in the other social sciences, particularly when community stakeholders become involved in the articulation of research goals. And in the spirit of an earlier part of this chapter, qualitative and quantitative scholars would be well served by dismantling the barriers between them and forging alliances on selected projects. The differences in skill sets and philosophical orientations will not vanish, but certain problems in media effects could be profitably attacked by a greater emphasis on interpretative processes, and certain problems in cultural studies could be examined anew through quantitative analyses and the application of theories and concepts from areas like media psychology. Qualitative researchers should also be willing to collaborate with content providers, technology developers, and others in the private and public sectors, when their interests converge. (One such area of common interest is alleviating the digital divide.) It is instructive in this regard to see the appearance of studies of new technology usage conducted by in-house teams of ethnographers from Intel Corporation and other companies; indeed, examples of this corporate-sponsored research feature highly innovative fieldwork techniques not seen in the scholarly literature (e.g., Hindus, Mainwaring, Leduc, Hagstrom, & Bayley, 2001).

While participant observation and interviewing will continue to serve as primary methods of studying media use and interpretation, they are not the only ones. Audience researchers should expand the scope of their data-gathering methods. For example, the wealth of popular culture artifacts that people ordinarily buy, produce, collect, trade, and give away can be utilized as "found" data. Analysis of these artifacts can tell us much about what people truly value in their media environment, and when combined with other qualitative techniques, provide insights into their identities, beliefs, and relationships. Brown, Dykers, Steele, and White (1994) studied teenage girls' bedrooms as a private place that they adorned with posters of sports figures and movie stars, magazine art, stuffed animals, and other objects; the researchers' tours of this "room culture," augmented by the girls' own commentary, enabled them to see patterns in the expression of self. Qualitative researchers should also avail themselves of communication technologies, such as e-mail (Hessler et al., 2003) and digital video (Shrum, Duque, & Brown, 2005), for involving participants in the documentation of their own activity. The payoff of resourceful new methods consists in richer data—and research texts—that can capture the experience of living in media-suffused social worlds.

◆ References

Abu-Lughod, L. (1997). The interpretation of culture(s) after television. *Representations, 59,* 110–134.

Anderson, J. A. (1996). Thinking qualitatively: Hermeneutics in science. In M. B. Salwen & D. W. Stacks (Eds.), *An integrated approach to communication theory and research* (pp. 45–59). Mahwah, NJ: Erlbaum.

Ang, I. (1991). *Desperately seeking the audience.* London: Routledge.

Atkinson, P., & Hammersley, M. (1994). Ethnography and participant observation. In N. K. Denzin & Y. Lincoln (Eds.), *Handbook of qualitative research* (pp. 248–261). Thousand Oaks, CA: Sage.

Bavelas, J. B. (1995). Quantitative versus qualitative? In W. Leeds-Hurwitz (Ed.), *Social approaches to communication* (pp. 49–62). New York: Guilford.

Brown, J. D., Dykers, C. R., Steele, J. R., & White, A. B. (1994). Teenage room culture: Where media and identities intersect. *Communication Research, 21,* 813–827.

Carragee, K. M. (1988). Interpretive media study and interpretive social science. *Critical Studies in Mass Communication, 7,* 81–96.

Geertz, C. (1973). *The interpretation of cultures: Selected essays.* New York: Basic Books.

Gillespie, M. (1995). *Television, ethnicity and cultural change.* London: Routledge.

Hall, S. (1980). Encoding/decoding. In S. Hall, D. Hobson, A. Lowe, & P. Willis (Eds.), *Culture, media, language* (pp. 128–139). London: Hutchinson.

Hessler, R. M., Downing, J., Beltz, C., Pelliccio, A., Powell, M., & Vale, W. (2003). Qualitative research on adolescent risk using e-mail: A methodological assessment. *Qualitative Sociology, 26,* 111–124.

Hindus, D., Mainwaring, S. D., Leduc, N., Hagstrom, A. E., & Bayley, O. (2001, March 31–April 5). *Casablanca: Designing social communication devices for the home.* In the proceedings of the SIGCHI Conference of Human Factors in Computing Systems, Seattle. Retrieved January 29, 2008, from http://courses.media.mit.edu/2006spring/mas963/papers/awareness/casablanca.pdf

Hoijer, B. (1990). Studying viewers' reception of television programmes: Theoretical and methodological considerations. *European Journal of Communication, 5,* 29–56.

Jenkins, H. (2006). *Convergence culture.* New York: New York University Press.

Jensen, K. B. (1987). Qualitative audience research: Toward an integrative approach to reception. *Critical Studies in Mass Communication, 4,* 21–36.

Jensen, K. B. (2002). Media reception: Qualitative traditions. In K. B. Jensen (Ed.), *A handbook of media and communication research: Qualitative and quantitative methodologies* (pp. 156–170). London: Routledge.

Jensen, K. B., & Rosengren, K. E. (1990). Five traditions in search of the audience. *European Journal of Communication, 5,* 207–238.

Jordan, A. B. (2006). Make yourself at home: The social construction of research roles in family studies. *Qualitative Research, 6,* 169–185.

Kates, S. M. (2006). Researching brands ethnographically: An interpretive community approach. In R. Belk (Ed.), *Handbook of qualitative research methods in marketing* (pp. 94–105). Northampton, MA: Edward Elgar.

La Pastina, A. C. (2004). Telenovela reception in rural Brazil: Gendered readings and sexual mores. *Critical Studies in Media Communication, 21,* 162–181.

Lemish, D. (1982). The rules of viewing television in public places. *Journal of Broadcasting, 26,* 757–791.

Liebes, T., & Katz, E. (1990). *The export of meaning: Cross cultural readings of Dallas.* New York: Oxford University Press.

Lindlof, T. R. (2008). Verstehen vs. erklaren. In W. Donsbach (Ed.), *The international encyclopedia of communication* (Vol. 11, pp. 5257–5261). Malden, MA: Blackwell.

Lindlof, T. R., & Taylor, B. C. (2002). *Qualitative communication research methods* (2nd ed.). Thousand Oaks, CA: Sage.

Livingstone, S. (1998). Audience research at the crossroads: The "implied audience" in media and cultural theory. *European Journal of Cultural Studies, 1,* 193–217.

Livingstone, S. (2004). The challenge of changing audiences: Or, what is the audience researcher to do in the age of the Internet? *European Journal of Communication, 19,* 75–86.

Lotz, A. D., & Ross, S. M. (2004). Toward ethical cyberspace audience research: Strategies for using the Internet for television audience studies. *Journal of Broadcasting & Electronic Media, 48,* 501–512.

Lull, J. (1980). The social uses of television. *Human Communication Research, 6,* 197–209.

Lull, J. (1985). Ethnographic studies of broadcast media audiences. In J. R. Dominick & J. E. Fletcher (Eds.), *Broadcasting research methods* (pp. 80–88). Boston: Allyn & Bacon.

Malinowski, B. (1961). *Argonauts of the Western Pacific.* Prospect Heights, IL: Waveland Press. (Original work printed 1922)

Marcus, G. E., & Fischer, M. M. J. (1986). *Anthropology as cultural critique: An experimental moment in the human sciences.* Chicago: University of Chicago Press.

Mayer, V. (2003). Living telenovelas/telenovelizing life: Mexican American girls' identities and transnational telenovelas. *Journal of Communication, 53,* 479–495.

Mayer, V. (2005). Research beyond the pale: Whiteness in audience studies and media ethnography. *Communication Theory, 15,* 148–167.

Meyer, T. P., Traudt, P. J., & Anderson, J. A. (1980). Non-traditional mass communication research methods: Observational case studies of media use in natural settings. In D. Nimmo (Ed.), *Communication yearbook 4* (pp. 261–275). New Brunswick, NJ: Transaction.

Michelle, C. (2007). Modes of reception: A consolidated analytical framework. *Communication Review, 10,* 181–222.

Moores, S. (1990). Texts, readers and contexts of meaning: Developments in the study of media audiences. *Media, Culture and Society, 12,* 9–29.

Morley, D. (1986). *Family television: Cultural power and domestic leisure.* London: Comedia.

Morley, D. (1987). Changing paradigms in family studies. In E. Seiter, H. Borchers, G. Kreutzner, & E.-M. Warth (Eds.), *Remote control: Television, audiences, and cultural power* (pp. 16–43). London: Routledge.

Morley, D. (1992). *Television, audiences and cultural studies.* New York: Routledge.

Morley, D. (1993). Active audience theory: Pendulums and pitfalls. *Journal of Communication, 43*(4), 13–19.

Murphy, P. D., & Kraidy, M. M. (2003). *Global media studies: Ethnographic perspectives.* New York: Routledge.

Pacanowsky, M., & Anderson, J. A. (1982). Cop talk and media use. *Journal of Broadcasting, 26,* 741–755.

Parameswaran, R. (2001). Feminist media ethnography in India: Exploring power, gender, and culture in the field. *Qualitative Inquiry, 7,* 69–103.

Press, A. L. (1991). Working-class women in a middle-class world. *Critical Studies in Mass Communication, 8,* 421–441.

Radway, J. (1984). *Reading the romance.* Chapel Hill: University of North Carolina Press.

Ritson, M., & Elliott, R. (1999). The social uses of advertising: An ethnographic study of adolescent advertising audiences. *Journal of Consumer Research, 26,* 260–277.

Schoening, G. T., & Anderson, J. A. (1995). Social action media studies: Foundational arguments and common premises. *Communication Theory, 5,* 93–116.

Seiter, E. (1999). *Television and new media audiences.* New York: Oxford University Press.

Shrum, W., Duque, R., & Brown, T. (2005). Digital video as research practice: Methodology for the millennium. *Journal of Research Practice, 1*(1). Retrieved July 8, 2007, from http://jrp.icaap.org/index.php/jrp/article/viewFile/6/11

Stout, D. A. (2004). Secularization and the religious audience: A study of Mormons and Las Vegas media. *Mass Communication & Society, 7,* 61–75.

Taylor, B. C., & Trujillo, N. (2001). Qualitative research methods. In F. M. Jablin & L. L. Putnam (Eds.), *The new handbook of organizational communication* (pp. 161–194). Thousand Oaks, CA: Sage.

Thompson, J. B. (1995). *The media and modernity: A social theory of the media.* Stanford, CA: Stanford University Press.

Webster, J. G. (1998). The audience. *Journal of Broadcasting & Electronic Media, 42,* 190–207.

White, R. A. (1994). Audience "interpretations" of media: Emerging perspectives. *Communication Research Trends, 14*(3), 3–40.

Williams, M. (2000). Interpretivism and generalization. *Sociology, 34,* 209–224.

Wolf, M. A., Meyer, T. P., & White, C. (1982). A rules-based study of television's role in the construction of social reality. *Journal of Broadcasting, 26,* 813–829.

PART II

SOCIETY, POLITICS, AND CULTURE

5

CULTIVATION ANALYSIS AND MEDIA EFFECTS

◆ Michael Morgan

In the 1960s, George Gerbner (1919–2005) devised a way of thinking about media effects that he called *cultivation*. The theoretical framework and methodological techniques of cultivation have evolved in many ways over the years since his original formulations, and it has become one of the most widely known and influential approaches to studying the consequences of growing up and living with television. According to Bryant and Miron (2004), cultivation, agenda setting, and uses and gratifications were by far the three most-cited theories in mass communication research published in key scholarly journals from 1956 to 2000.

Cultivation analysis explores television's independent contribution to viewers' conceptions of social reality. In practice, cultivation research typically uses survey methods to assess the difference (if any) that amount of television viewing makes to a broad variety of opinions, images, and attitudes, across a variety of samples, types of measures, topical areas, and intervening variables (Gerbner, Gross, Morgan, Signorielli, & Shanahan, 2002). Stated most simply, the central hypothesis explored in cultivation research is that those who spend more time watching television are more likely to perceive the real world in ways that reflect the most common and recurrent messages of the television world, compared with people who watch less television but are otherwise comparable in terms of important demographic characteristics.

Gerbner conceived of cultivation analysis as one part of a three-pronged research strategy for a larger project, called Cultural Indicators (Gerbner, 1973). The first, known as institutional process analysis, investigates how the flow of media messages is produced and managed, how decisions are made, and how media organizations function. The second, message system analysis, has been used since 1967 to track the most stable, pervasive, and recurrent images in media content, in terms of the portrayal of violence, race and ethnicity, gender roles, occupations, and many other topics and aspects of life. The third is cultivation analysis, which is the study of how exposure to the world of television contributes to viewers' conceptions about the real world.

Cultural Indicators research has been prolific. As of 2008, nearly 500 relevant studies have been published (two thirds of which are extensions, replications, reviews, and critiques conducted by independent researchers not associated with Gerbner and the original research team).[1] Cultivation studies have been carried out in Argentina, Australia, Belgium, Brazil, China, England, Germany, Hungary, Israel, Japan, Mexico, Russia, South Korea, Sweden, Thailand, and elsewhere. Clearly, such a large body of work—and all the complex issues and implications it raises—cannot be exhaustively treated here, so this chapter attempts to provide only a general introduction to this area of research. (For an extensive examination of the cultivation literature, see Shanahan and Morgan, 1999.)

◆ Conceptual Framework

From a theoretical perspective, Gerbner was especially interested in the role of *messages,* both in everyday social interaction and at the larger sociocultural level, where they are mass produced and widely shared. He defined communication as "interaction through messages," and he saw culture as "a system of messages and images that regulates and reproduces social relations" (Gerbner, 1990, p. 250). On the cultural level, he argued that message systems "provide many of the raw materials of our consciousness (and of the terms of our perceptions)" (Gerbner, 1963, p. 39). In other words, culture is a system of mass-produced stories "that mediates between existence and consciousness of existence, and thereby contributes to both" (Gerbner, 1990, p. 251). As a result, the messages and images that surround us both reflect and reproduce the ways we think about the world.

Our everyday lives are now so flooded with mass-produced messages and images that we tend to forget that this is a relatively recent historical development. It has created a new symbolic cultural environment, and this environment shapes the way we perceive and interpret the world. These messages are not "neutral," but instead reflect the values and priorities of the institutions that create them. The key question, then, is this: What assumptions, outlooks, ways of perceiving, and general worldviews do dominant systems of messages cultivate?

But that is not the only question. Gerbner envisioned the Cultural Indicators paradigm as a means to address a broad range of interrelated questions, such as,

- What perspectives and relationships are expressed in message systems produced for large and diverse communities?

- How do these systems vary over time, across cultures, and in different societies?

- How is the mass production and distribution of messages organized, controlled, and managed?

- What common assumptions do message systems cultivate over and above those apparent in single or selected messages or individual and selective responses?

- How does the cultivation of these collective assumptions shape the conduct of public affairs (and, of course, vice versa)? (Gerbner, 1970, p. 71)

The insistence on keeping the focus on all three "prongs"—the media institutions, the message systems they produce, and the shared assumptions they cultivate—is what distinguished cultivation analysis from earlier ways of thinking about media effects, which usually "stemmed from theoretical perspectives that did not consider relevance to the mass-cultural process a principal criterion" (Gerbner, 1970, p. 71). So, studies looking at whether a given television program might instigate aggressive behavior, or whether a specific commercial might change attitudes toward some politician or brand of toothpaste, rarely if ever took into account the historically distinct *institutional* and *cultural* qualities of mass communication. These include concentrated control over the production of pervasive cultural images by private commercial interests and the fact that otherwise heterogeneous audiences are massively exposed to common images and messages over long periods of time.

Prior to the development of cultivation analysis, most researchers in mass communication were interested in knowing how specific messages, channels, and sources could produce *changes* in attitudes or behaviors. Early research on television's impacts had typically focused on the effects of single programs or messages, usually measured immediately after exposure in a relatively artificial context.

Cultivation was an attempt to go beyond the then-dominant paradigm of persuasion and propaganda research and to escape the positivism of the "effects" tradition. This required setting aside formal aesthetic categories along with conventional concerns about style, artistic quality, high culture versus low culture,

and selective exposure, as well as idiosyncratic judgments, selective "readings," or interpretations of specific media messages. It was not that Gerbner denied the importance of these concerns and phenomena, but rather that he sought to bracket them, in order to address issues that could not be explained in such terms. (As discussed in the following, it also required a reworking of the traditional tactics that had been used to assess media "effects.") As noted previously, the idea was to ask about the *common assumptions* cultivated by message systems "over and above those apparent in single or selected messages or individual and selective responses" (Gerbner, 1970, p. 71).

◆ Storytelling

The concept of storytelling is central to the theory of cultivation. Gerbner argued that the basic difference between human beings and other species is that we live in a world that is created by the stories we tell. Humans uniquely live in a world experienced and constructed largely through many forms and modes of storytelling. We have neither personally nor directly experienced great portions of what we know or think we know; we "know" about many things based on the stories we hear and the stories we tell (see Morgan, 2002).

Although storytelling has been the hallmark of all human societies since the dawn of time, television has transformed the cultural process of storytelling into a centralized, standardized, market-driven, advertiser-sponsored system. In earlier times, the stories of a culture were told face-to-face by members of a community, parents, teachers, or the clergy. Today, television tells most of the stories to most of the people, most of the time. The cultural process of storytelling is now in the hands of global commercial interests who have something to sell; in effect, they operate outside the reach of democratic decision making, and have little incentive to be interested in the content of their stories beyond their ability to attract specific, well-defined, profitable audiences, with a minimum of public objections. Thus, the symbolic world we are inhabiting and (re)creating is designed according to the specifications of marketing strategies and commercial interests, as opposed to, say, public service, education, democratic negotiation, or other potential driving principles.

The research focuses on television because for over 50 years it has been the dominant source and distributor of our most pervasive and widely shared cultural message systems. Again, cultivation analysis is not concerned with the "impact" of any particular television program, genre, or episode, but with the *system* of messages, the aggregate and repetitive patterns of images and representations to which entire communities are exposed over long periods of time. All television is not the same—*American Idol* is a far cry from *The Sopranos,* which in turn bears little resemblance to *Grey's Anatomy* or to *The Daily Show.* But there are persistent cultural themes, images, lessons, and values that cut across many dramatic genres and that emerge within many programs that seem on the surface to have little in common. In the aggregate, these interlocking and complementary patterns constitute the system of messages on which cultivation focuses.

What is most likely to cultivate stable and common conceptions of reality is the overall pattern of programming to which total communities are regularly exposed over long periods of time. That is the pattern of settings, casting, social typing, actions, and related outcomes that cuts across program types and viewing modes and defines the world of television. No matter what they watch, most heavy viewers cannot easily avoid being exposed to those recurrent patterns, usually many times a day. Therefore, cultivation analysis

interrogates the contribution of amount of exposure to that total pattern rather than to specific genres or programs.

There may well be some heavy viewers who watch nothing but shopping channels, travel documentaries, golf tournaments, or weather forecasts (and current technologies make these sorts of viewing patterns possible now). But cultivation simply assumes that most regular and heavy viewers will, over time, watch "more of everything." With few exceptions, most of the programs that attract large, heterogeneous groups of viewers are narrative in nature. As narratives, different genres of fictional programs tend to manifest complementary—although, of course, not invariant—basic features. One will certainly see more representations of police, crime, and violence on action/adventure shows than on game shows or a cooking channel; but potential lessons about safety, vulnerability, victimization, and the legal system are not limited to cop shows, and it is precisely the overall contribution of these lessons with which cultivation is concerned.

In sum, cultivation wants to know how long-term exposure to television's most recurrent and unambiguous patterns of messages and images contributes to our shared cultural assumptions about the world. Whether or not genre X has an effect on attitude Y or belief Z, and how people differ in the way they "read" various media texts, are other, distinct, questions. Cultivation does not deny the fact that some programs may contain some messages more than others, or that messages themselves may change somewhat over time. But these variations are seen as "drops," while cultivation is concerned with "the bucket." It thus attempts to say something at a more global and organic level about the broad-based, ideological consequences of a commercially supported cultural industry celebrating consumption, materialism, individualism, power, and the status quo along lines of gender, race, class, and age.

◆ Cultivation Analysis Methods

Cultivation analysis should always begin by identifying the most common and stable patterns in television content, emphasizing the consistent images, portrayals, and values that cut across program genres. This is accomplished either by conducting a message system analysis or by examining existing content studies. In general, message system analysis illuminates four dimensions of content: existence (what *is* in the symbolic world?), priorities (what is important?), values (what is right or wrong, good or bad, etc.?), and relationships (what is related to what else, and how?). These dimensions illuminate the symbolic functions of how things work in the world of storytelling.

Once those patterns are identified, the goal is to ascertain if those who spend more time watching television are more likely to perceive the real world in ways that reflect those particular messages and lessons. That is, cultivation analysts develop hypotheses about what heavy viewers would be expected to think about some topic or issue, if they think about it in terms of the way it is presented on television.

Cultivation typically uses survey procedures to examine relationships between amount of television viewing and conceptions of social reality. The questions are of several types. Some juxtapose answers reflecting the statistical "facts" of the television world with those more in line with reality; others examine symbolic transformations and more general implications of the message system data. Some of the questions are "semiprojective" (e.g., asking respondents to estimate some aspect of reality relative to their own situation), and some simply ask about beliefs, opinions, attitudes, or behaviors. The questions are posed to samples (national probability, regional, convenience) of children, adolescents, or adults. Secondary analyses of large-scale national surveys (for example, the General Social Surveys) have often been conducted when the data sets include questions that relate to relevant aspects of the television world as well as measures of television viewing.

The substantive survey questions do not mention television in any way, to avoid contaminating responses. The respondents' awareness of the source of their information is irrelevant; cultivation is not about what people "think about" television either in general or in terms of any specific programs.

Amount of viewing is usually assessed by asking how much time the respondent spends watching on an "average day." These data may be used in their original form (a ratio scale) or may be grouped by level of exposure ("light," "medium," and "heavy" viewing). Viewing is seen in relative terms, and the determination of what constitutes light, medium, and heavy is made on a sample-by-sample basis, using as close to an even three-way split of hours of self-reported daily television viewing as possible. These measures are not assumed to be perfectly accurate; they simply assume that, for example, most of those who say they watch "four hours a day" do, on balance, watch more than those who say "two hours a day." Of course, more precise measures would add greater specificity to the analysis.

People who regularly consume a great deal of television differ from light viewers in many ways besides simply how much time they spend watching. In general, lighter and heavier viewers differ by age, sex, income, education, race, leisure time, religion, social isolation, political orientation, and a host of other demographic, social, and psychological variables. But they also differ in the extent to which television dominates their sources of consciousness. Light viewers tend to be exposed to more varied and diverse information sources (both mediated and interpersonal), whereas heavy viewers, by definition, tend to rely more on television.

To deal with this, differences among the responses of light, medium, and heavy viewers are examined within specific demographic subgroups, and the effects of other variables are statistically controlled. Differences associated with amount of viewing are sometimes independent of, but usually interact with, the many social, cultural, and personal factors that differentiate light and heavy viewers. In other words, the strength, shape, and even direction of cultivation relationships may all vary considerably for different types of people and groups at different social locations. In addition, the analysis should always examine associations between amount of viewing and attitudes while applying simultaneous controls, as in partial correlation and multiple regression, although this was not always done in the early days of the research.

◆ Early Results

In the first published cultivation study, Gerbner and Gross (1976) reported that heavy viewers were more likely than light viewers to give "television answers" to questions about law enforcement, crime, danger, and mistrust. Message system analysis had shown that television greatly exaggerates the amount of violence in society and overrepresents the number of police, detectives, criminal lawyers, and so on, in the workforce.

Respondents were asked if they thought the number of people working in law enforcement and crime detection was 1% (closer to the real-world figure) or 5% (referred to as the "TV answer," since it is closer to the ways things are in the world of television). The data showed that 50% of the light viewers, compared with 59% of the heavy viewers, said 5%—that is, heavy viewers were more likely to give the TV answer. This difference (here, nine percentage points) was referred to as the "cultivation differential" and was interpreted

as indicating the difference that greater television viewing makes to a particular attitude, outlook, or belief.

Message system data also showed that almost two thirds (64.4%) of the characters in network dramatic programs were involved in violence each week. In contrast, FBI and police data at the time indicated that there were between .32 and .41 violent crimes per 100 persons per *year*. Clearly, one's chances of actually encountering violence in the United States are vastly lower than the risks faced by characters in the world of fictional television. Respondents were asked if they thought the number of people involved in violence each week was "closer to 1 in 10" (the TV answer) or "closer to 1 in 100." In this case, 39% of light viewers but 52% of heavy viewers gave the TV answer (1 in 10), a cultivation differential of +13. Thus, the earliest cultivation research suggested that heavier exposure to the pervasively violent TV world was related to how people see the real world.

Other analyses involved more than the comparison of real-world and TV-world statistics. Some of the most interesting and important issues for cultivation analysis have involved the symbolic transformation of message system data into more general issues and assumptions.

For example, when asked if "most people can be trusted," 48% of light viewers but 65% of heavy viewers responded that "you can't be too careful." From these patterns, the notion of the "mean world syndrome" emerged, suggesting that television viewing cultivates a complex of outlooks that includes an exaggerated sense of victimization, apprehension, insecurity, anxiety, and mistrust.

These early findings were elaborated in a series of annual *Violence Profiles* (e.g., Gerbner, Gross, Jackson-Beeck, Jeffries-Fox, & Signorielli, 1978; Gerbner, Gross, Signorielli, Morgan, & Jackson-Beeck, 1979). The research not only turned conventional thinking about television violence on its head; it also argued that symbolic violence is a demonstration of power and a mechanism of social control. In showing who can get away with what against whom, television violence perpetuates a social hierarchy of power, vulnerability, and control (Morgan, 1983). Cultivating a sense of insecurity and risk can intensify dependence on authority and promote a willingness to accept repressive measures that promise greater security.

Although the earliest studies focused on violence, the Cultural Indicators project was intended from the start to be broadly based, and cultivation studies have focused on an increasingly wide range of issues and topics. Studies have examined the cultivation of sex-role stereotypes; political orientations and behavior; images of aging; health-related beliefs and behaviors; opinions about science; attitudes toward marriage, the family, and work; and beliefs about the environment, religion, and many other issues, along with an increasing emphasis on international extensions and cross-cultural comparisons (see Shanahan & Morgan, 1999; Signorielli & Morgan, 1990).

◆ *Critiques and Refinements*

Few theories of media effects (and perhaps few areas of social research in general) have been critiqued as heavily and fiercely as cultivation. (For some examples, see Hirsch, 1980; Hughes, 1980; Potter, 1993, 1994; see also Shanahan & Morgan, 1999.) These critiques have focused on many diverse issues, including cultivation's emphasis on overall exposure (as opposed to specific types of programs), the way television viewing is measured and divided into categories, justifications for interpreting television-world answers, the linearity of cultivation associations, and much more. Although nearly every aspect of conceptualization, measurement, coding, sampling, question wording, reliability, data analysis,

and more has come under intense scrutiny, some of the most heated issues of contention have revolved around questions of spuriousness and the proper use of statistical controls.

Powerful predictors of social beliefs and attitudes, such as race, education, income, gender, and so on, are also typically closely associated with amount of television viewing. For instance, higher-income respondents and those with more education tend to watch less TV. Therefore, comparisons of light and heavy viewers are always carried out under controls—that is, within important demographic subgroups. Cultivation differentials are compared for, say, those with and without a college education, males and females, and those under and over 30 years old. From the start, it was clear that cultivation patterns were not uniform across demographic subgroups. Associations were stronger in some groups and weaker or nonexistent in others.

Yet, early on, cultivation researchers had typically applied a single control variable at a time. In contrast, various critics—reanalyzing the same data—argued that when multiple controls were applied *at the same time,* the relationships between television viewing and attitudes mostly disappeared (i.e., were rendered spurious). This led them to conclude that there was essentially no meaningful evidence to support the cultivation hypothesis.

Gerbner and his colleagues countered that even if a relationship disappears under multiple controls, significant patterns may still exist within specific subgroups, a pattern they called "mainstreaming" (Gerbner, Gross, Morgan, & Signorielli, 1980). Among light viewers, people who differ in terms of background factors such as age, education, social class, political orientations, and region of residence tend to have sharply different conceptions of social reality regarding violence, interpersonal mistrust, gender-role stereotypes, and a broad range of political and social outlooks.

Yet, among heavy viewers across those same groups, those differences tend to be much smaller or even to disappear entirely.

For example, Gerbner et al. (1980) found that low-income respondents were more likely than those with higher incomes to say that "fear of crime is a very serious personal problem." Among low-income respondents, amount of television viewing was not related at all to perceptions of crime. In contrast, although higher-income respondents as a group were less likely to think of crime as a serious personal problem, the heavy viewers with higher incomes were much more likely than the light viewers to be especially worried about crime. In other words, heavy viewers with higher incomes had the same perception as all of those with lower incomes; among heavy viewers, the difference stemming from income was sharply diminished. Similarly, among lighter viewers, those with more education have been found to express more "progressive" attitudes about gender roles, but this difference disappears among heavy viewers; more educated heavy viewers express the same "traditional" beliefs as do those with less education. Figure 5.1 illustrates the typical mainstreaming pattern found between counterpart subgroups.

Many cultivation studies explored the political implications of mainstreaming. As television seeks to attract large and heterogeneous audiences, its messages are intended to disturb as few as possible. Therefore, television programs tend to "balance" opposing perspectives, and to steer a "middle course" along the supposedly nonideological mainstream. Heavy viewers are substantially more likely to call themselves "moderate" and to avoid labeling themselves as either "liberal" or "conservative." The mainstream is not "the middle of the road," however, in

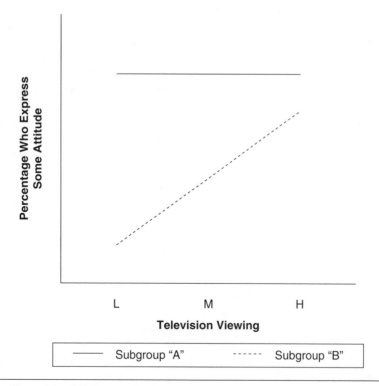

Figure 5.1 Illustration of Mainstreaming

terms of the specific political attitudes that people take. Looking at such topics as racial segregation, homosexuality, abortion, minority rights, and other "wedge" issues, the expected differences between liberals and conservatives are mainly evident among those who watch little television. Among heavy viewers, liberals and conservatives are much closer to each other than among light viewers.

These patterns suggest that cultivation is like a gravitational process, in which the angle and direction of the "pull" depends on where groups of viewers and their styles of life are with reference to the center of gravity, the mainstream of the world ovision. Mainstreaming thus means that heavy television viewing contributes to an erosion of differences in people's perspectives that stem from other factors and influences (Morgan, 1986). People who otherwise have little in common besides television are brought into the same dominant mainstream by cumulative heavy viewing. Cultivation researchers contend that television contributes to a blurring of cultural, political, social, regional, and class-based distinctions, the blending of attitudes into the television mainstream, and the bending of the direction of that mainstream to serve the political and economic tasks of the medium and the institutions that subsidize it.

◆ *Cultivation and the Audience*

Cultivation has frequently been criticized for taking a "passive" view of the audience. It is often claimed that cultivation assumes that viewers take messages at their face value and that all audience members pretty much interpret all messages in pretty much the same way. Yet, Gerbner and his colleagues have not said much of anything about the presumed activity or passivity of the audience one way or the other. That is because the entire active/ passive debate is not seen as especially relevant to cultivation.

Of course different viewers interpret different programs differently. Of course different programs engage us at different levels; sometimes we feel like just "vegging out," and sometimes we get intensely wrapped up in what we are watching (and, in any case, we know from neuroscience that television viewing does spark immensely complex activities in our brains; see Anderson, 2007). Sometimes we barely pay any conscious attention to what's on, and sometimes we are transfixed by it. It is clear that there is a multidimensional continuum of audience "activity." It is just as clear that we do learn from our environments, sometimes with and sometimes without a great deal of conscious processing.

As viewers encounter particular messages, they will interpret them in a variety of ways, and this is an important topic for theory and research. But the question of audience activity must be completely reframed when the focus is on the *system* of messages. It is one thing to have divergent "readings" of, say, a particular depiction of violence—how severe was it, how justified was it, how effective was it, how disturbing or exciting was it, what were its consequences, and so on. There are very useful models for studying how people make sense of individual messages, but it is not clear how these models might apply to the massive floods of images that wash over us over long periods of time. A given instance of violence may produce myriad interpretations and responses; but when we are talking about exposures to violent images that occur several times an hour over weeks and months and years, those individual differences tend to wash out, cultivating among heavy viewers the simple assumption that "violence is common."

Audiences are neither cultural dupes nor all-powerful. The enormous variation in cultivation associations across different demographic subgroups itself shows that there is indeed a broad and diverse range of readings and interpretations to be enacted. Rather than assume anything about audience activity, cultivation simply *tests* whether or not heavy viewers are more likely to show evidence of having absorbed television's dominant messages, and leaves activity as a question for others to study. Whether or not audiences "resist" these messages is seen in the extent of the congruity between the television worldview and audience belief systems. Audience activity is a relevant question when it comes to persuasive messages or attitude change, but less so when the focus is on cultivation—the process by which mass communication creates publics and defines the perspectives and assumptions which are most broadly shared among those publics.

The point is not so much that cultivation occurs (it is, after all, the historic and universal function of all sociocultural institutions and the stories they tell), but that the cultivation of collective consciousness is now institutionalized and corporately managed to an unprecedented degree.

◆ Cultivation in the New Media Environment

The theory of cultivation was developed when "television" in the United States meant three national broadcast networks, plus a small handful of independent and public/educational stations. The three networks attracted well over 90% of the viewing audience, night after night. Program shares of 50% were not uncommon. Fledgling cable systems mainly extended the reach of the networks, providing little competitive programming. Most people were watching the same shows, at the same time.

Those days are long gone. Technological developments such as digital cable, satellite, VCRs, DVDs, VOD, DVRs, and the Internet have drastically cut the audience share for the old "Big Three" networks. Today, the *top* network shows may achieve ratings and shares that reflect what was barely the *minimum* required to stay on the air in the 1970s. Overall television viewing levels continue to reach historic new heights, but now the audience is chopped up among hundreds of cable/satellite channels and other alternatives.

On the other hand, there is little evidence that the proliferation of channels has led to any substantially greater diversity of content. As the number of channels has grown, ownership and control of production have actually become more concentrated, as the traditional barriers between and among networks, studios, MSOs, and cable networks have dissolved.

Newer technologies give viewers a previously unimaginable degree of control over *when* and *where* they watch television. If you missed *The Ed Sullivan Show* at 8:00 p.m. on Sunday on CBS, you were out of luck. Now, you can tape it on a VCR (if you still have one of those) or, more likely, record it on your TiVo, or call it up on-demand through your digital cable, or go to the Internet and stream or download it. Then you can watch it on your wide-screen HDTV with surround sound, or pop it onto your cell phone or iPod and watch it wherever you wish.

The remarkable proliferation of DVDs, pay-per-view (PPV), on-demand, and streaming gives viewers an unprecedented range of *potential* choices. And digital signal compression will soon flood viewers with even more broadcast-originated channels. But it would be a mistake to conclude that this means that viewers are now no longer exposed to the dominant message system of television. In fact, as channels proliferate, sources of original dramatic programming and diverse perspectives decline, and channels often rely on programs previously broadcast on network prime time (or programs produced by the same studios) to fill their programming needs. Most people watch a small number of the channels that are available, while much of the content that heavy television viewers consume most often presents worldviews and values that are fundamentally comparable to network-type programs.

In particular, the Internet and digital downloading seem to threaten the stability of the traditional media landscape. They certainly challenge the traditional business model of the media. But Nielsen/ NetRatings reports that average Web usage amounts to just a fraction of the time most people spend watching television (Nielsen, 2007). Figuring prominently among top sites are those with strong connections to dominant television networks, including Disney (owner of ABC), Time Warner, and News Corporation. Networks and cable channels work feverishly to drive their viewers to their Web sites, to obtain more personal information from them, and to create additional platforms for advertising. Although the Internet may provide access to alternative channels of information, it can also deepen and sharpen the reach of dominant media corporations—and it is actually turning out to be a popular and effective way to increase the viewing of actual network programs. (It is estimated that advertising on streaming programs will bring the broadcast networks over $4 billion by 2010.)

Channels will continue to proliferate, by cable, satellite, and digital transmission. New developments such as digital video recorders will spread, allowing viewers to more easily indulge their own personal programming tastes (and, maybe, to ignore commercials, causing advertisers to respond with such strategies as product placement). There will be more options for direct, on-demand delivery of programs through set-top boxes, DVRs, and high-speed Internet connections. The broadcast network audience share will therefore continue to shrivel (despite the occasional blockbuster series) and be divided among an ever-increasing number of competing channels. Yet, changes in the modes of distribution may make little difference if the messages do not change. Given that, there is little evidence to date that the dominant patterns of image cultivation will show any corresponding fragmentation.

◆ The Future of Cultivation Research

The future offers a wealth of complex and challenging questions for cultivation research. One key area (excluded from this chapter due to space limitations) is the exploration of the cognitive processes that can illuminate how it is that cultivation "works" in psychological terms. Although cultivation was conceived as a broad cultural theory, many have argued that it raises cognitive questions about how the symbolic content of television finds its way into the heads of the audience, and then becomes transformed into conceptions of social reality that may be elicited in response to questions from survey interviewers (and, presumably, in other contexts as well).

In an extensive series of experiments and surveys, Shrum (e.g., 1995, 1999, 2001, 2007) has shown that for heavy viewers, TV-derived images are more readily accessible and are more likely to spring quickly to mind. As a result, heavy viewers are more likely to furnish TV-influenced responses when a situation requires them to formulate a belief—such as when they are asked for their perceptions of society on surveys. This work has many implications consistent with cultivation; among other things, it suggests that television viewing does not necessarily *change* attitudes, but that it makes them *stronger*. Elucidation of the underlying cognitive mechanisms does boost the case for the internal validity of cultivation, but there is much more exciting work in this area to be done.

A meta-analysis of all cultivation studies was presented by Shanahan and

Morgan (1999), showing a small but persistent pattern of cultivation across different variables and populations. But the study was not able to detect clear evidence as to what factors might be moderating the observed effects and producing variations across the body of cultivation work. Perhaps enough additional studies have been conducted in the decade since to allow for a clearer answer to that question. Similarly, there are now areas of cultivation research that span 30 years in some data sets (e.g., the General Social Survey), encompassing issues that have seen dramatic social change (such as women's roles). Long-term trend analysis of cultivation patterns is a very appealing area for future research.

Cross-cultural and international comparative cultivation analysis will continue to offer tantalizing research opportunities. Dozens of countries that used to have tightly controlled, government-owned media systems have turned things over to private, commercial (often multinational) interests. Local production has boomed, but imported U.S. programs are still prominent. Theoretical and empirical work that addresses cultivation in the context of globalization (as well as "glocalization" and processes of cultural hybridity) would be highly useful.

The emergence of new channels and delivery systems will raise new challenges for cultivation, especially as we make the transition to digital. Although cultivation clearly focuses on overall exposure to the entire system of messages, it is not yet well understood how some new forms and genres fit into that message system or contribute to the cultivation of common assumptions. What is the role of the various kinds of newer "reality" shows—elimination dating shows, game shows, makeovers, competitions of humiliation, and singing and dancing contests, many with audience participation (e.g., voting), and so forth—within the overall message system? (Interestingly, the emergence of

these genres is due more to the economic struggles of the industry—these kinds of shows are vastly cheaper to produce—than to technological innovations.)

Without overromanticizing what the new technologies of the future will bring, the question must be asked: At some point, will new channels and delivery systems inject significant diversity into the message system, in a way that meaningfully diversifies what most heavy viewers consume? Will the continued fragmentation of the audience (for marketing purposes) and the vanishing of the everyday mass ritual of television viewing diminish what we "know in common"? That is, will television become less of a force for homogenization (mainstreaming) when we are not watching the same shows at the same time? The spread of VCRs and cable did not disrupt the cultivation process, as many assumed they would; the mere availability of more channels does not fundamentally change the socioeconomic dynamics that drive the production and distribution of programs or the nature of their messages. The upcoming technologies of today and tomorrow may not change those dynamics either, but instead just give us more of the same (with storytelling still controlled by a relatively small number of elite institutions). Either way, cultivation research will continually need to take these and other developments into account.

As we have seen, cultivation means that the dominant modes of cultural production tend to generate messages and representations that nourish and sustain the ideologies, perspectives, and practices of the institutions and cultural contexts from which they arise. Changes in those modes of production, institutions, or cultural contexts should by definition lead to changes in cultivation. Tracking, analyzing, and interpreting such changes, and paying attention to their policy implications, will be a continuing task for cultivation research in the years ahead.

◆ Note

1. The complete "Bibliography of Publications Related to the Cultural Indicators Project" is available at http://people.umass.edu/mmorgan/CulturalIndicatorsBibliography.pdf

◆ References

Anderson, D. R. (2007). A neuroscience of children and media? *Journal of Children and Media, 1*(1), 77–85.

Bryant, J., & Miron, D. (2004). Theory and research in mass communication. *Journal of Communication, 54,* 662–704.

Gerbner, G. (1963). A theory of communication and its implications for teaching. In *The nature of teaching: Implications for the education of teachers* (pp. 33–46). Milwaukee: University of Wisconsin–Milwaukee, School of Education.

Gerbner, G. (1970). Cultural Indicators: The case of violence in television drama. *The Annals of the American Academy of Political and Social Science, 388,* 69–81.

Gerbner, G. (1973). Cultural Indicators: The third voice. In G. Gerbner, L. Gross, & W. H. Melody (Eds.), *Communications technology and social policy* (pp. 555–573). New York: John Wiley & Sons.

Gerbner, G. (1990). Epilogue: Advancing on the path of righteousness (maybe). In N. Signorielli & M. Morgan (Eds.), *Cultivation analysis: New directions in media effects research* (pp. 249–262). Newbury Park, CA: Sage.

Gerbner, G., & Gross, L. (1976). Living with television: The violence profile. *Journal of Communication, 26*(2), 173–199.

Gerbner, G., Gross, L., Jackson-Beeck, M., Jeffries-Fox, S., & Signorielli, N. (1978). Cultural Indicators: Violence profile No. 9. *Journal of Communication, 28*(3), 176–207.

Gerbner, G., Gross, L., Morgan, M., & Signorielli, N. (1980). The "mainstreaming" of America: Violence profile No. 11. *Journal of Communication, 30*(3), 10–29.

Gerbner, G., Gross, L., Morgan, M., Signorielli, N., & Shanahan, J. (2002). Growing up with television: Cultivation processes. In J. Bryant & D. Zillmann (Eds.), *Media effects: Advances in theory and research* (2nd ed., pp. 43–67). Hillsdale, NJ: Erlbaum.

Gerbner, G., Gross, L., Signorielli, N., Morgan, M., & Jackson-Beeck, M. (1979). The demonstration of power: Violence profile No. 10. *Journal of Communication, 29*(3), 177–196.

Hirsch, P. (1980). The "scary world" of the non-viewer and other anomalies: A reanalysis of Gerbner et al.'s findings of cultivation analysis. *Communication Research, 7,* 403–456.

Hughes, M. (1980). The fruits of cultivation analysis: A re-examination of the effects of television watching on fear of victimization, alienation, and the approval of violence. *Public Opinion Quarterly, 44,* 287–302.

Morgan, M. (1983). Symbolic victimization and real-world fear. *Human Communication Research, 9,* 146–157.

Morgan, M. (1986). Television and the erosion of regional diversity. *Journal of Broadcasting and Electronic Media, 30,* 123–139.

Morgan, M. (Ed.). (2002). *Against the mainstream: Selected writings of George Gerbner.* New York: Peter Lang.

Nielsen. (2007). *Internet audience metrics.* Retrieved August 24, 2007, from http://www.nielsen-netratings.com/resources.jsp?section=pr_netv&nav=1

Potter, W. J. (1993). Cultivation theory and research: A conceptual critique. *Human Communication Research, 19,* 564–601.

Potter, W. J. (1994). Cultivation theory and research: A methodological critique. *Journalism Monographs, 147,* 1–35.

Shanahan, J., & Morgan, M. (1999). *Television and its viewers: Cultivation theory and research.* Cambridge/New York: Cambridge University Press.

Shrum, L. J. (1995). Assessing the social influence of television: A social cognition perspective on cultivation effects. *Communication Research, 22,* 402–429.

Shrum, L. J. (1999). The relationship of television viewing with attitude strength and extremity: Implications for the cultivation effect. *Media Psychology, 1,* 3–25.

Shrum, L. J. (2001). Processing strategy moderates the cultivation effect. *Human Communication Research, 27,* 94–120.

Shrum, L. J. (2007). The implications of survey method for measuring cultivation effects. *Human Communication Research, 33,* 64–80.

Signorielli, N., & Morgan, M. (Eds.). (1990). *Cultivation analysis: New directions in media effects research.* Newbury Park, CA: Sage.

6

FRAMING AND AGENDA SETTING

◆ Dhavan V. Shah, Douglas M. McLeod,
Melissa R. Gotlieb, and Nam-Jin Lee

Research on agenda setting and framing has dominated over four decades of empirical communication science inquiry on the interface of media and politics. By some accounts, agenda setting and framing are part of the same broad tradition of research on how news can influence audiences through the choice of what stories to feature and how much prominence to give particular elements within these reports. These news reports and their internal features are thought to shape the nature of cognitive responses, the mechanism through which agenda-setting and framing effects occur. It is through this shared history of understanding communication influence as contingent on the nature of cognitive responses—a history that can be traced back to McGuire (1968a, 1968b)—along with later attempts to situate framing as an aspect or extension of agenda setting (Iyengar & Simon, 1994; McCombs & Ghanem, 2001; McCombs, Shaw, & Weaver, 1997) that have resulted in these two distinct approaches to understanding political communication becoming blended, some would say unnecessarily so.

Indeed, those who assert that framing is an extension of agenda setting have encountered considerable opposition, with scholars long contending that framing is conceptually and procedurally distinct from agenda setting (Kosicki, 1993; Maher, 2001). These scholars argue that while framing and agenda setting involve a similar set of psychological mechanisms, the specific cognitive processes underlying them differ considerably (Price & Tewksbury, 1997). More important, those who take this latter position also trace framing back to a broader set of sociological and cultural theories of news production (see Pan & Kosicki, 1993; Shah, Domke, & Wackman, 1996). From this perspective, framing is understood through the process of message construction, with the focus on journalists, their construction of news texts, and the related implications for audience understanding (Entman, 1993; Gitlin, 1980). We explore these critiques of situating framing under agenda setting in the pages that follow.

This chapter has multiple goals: (1) to explicate first- and second-level agenda setting; (2) to differentiate framing from agenda setting, including second-level agenda setting; (3) to situate framing within its family of sociological and cultural theories of news production; (4) to locate framing and priming within a set of cognitive accounts of media effects; (5) to trace the historical development and central distinctions of framing and framing effects theory; (6) to discuss recent efforts to integrate approaches to framing and examine the processes underlying these effects; and (7) to suggest models for advancing future study on these phenomena. Our goal here is not to engage in a conventional literature review, but rather to synthesize extant research in novel ways to arrive at new possibilities for agenda-setting and framing theory.

◆ First- and Second-Level Agenda Setting

The long tradition of agenda-setting research began with McCombs and Shaw's (1972) seminal research on the 1968 presidential election. By connecting the issue priorities of the press to those of the public, they proposed that press attention to issues during campaigns influences voters' evaluations of issue importance. This conjecture about an "agenda-setting" function of the press established a subfield of activity, with many researchers examining the sources of the media agenda, contingent conditions, and new domains of influence beyond issue salience (Kiousis & McCombs, 2004; Rogers, Hart, & Dearing, 1997).

The early work on agenda setting documented the parameters of the phenomenon along with the factors that amplified and attenuated it. Factors such as need for cognition, need for orientation, and political involvement were found to increase agenda-setting effects through media surveillance (Rogers et al., 1997). Likewise, abstract issues such as the budget deficit, for which the public lacks direct, concrete experience, were observed to have more pronounced influence when present on the media agenda, as were issues consistent with personal orientations (McCombs et al., 1997). Across all of this work, the central assumption of agenda-setting theory, and the presumed psychological process explaining the effect, is salience transfer, the ability of media to convey the importance of items as indicated by their placement on news agendas.

Nonetheless, much of this research left unexamined the psychological processes that accounted for agenda-setting effects in the first place (Kosicki, 1993). As a result, the development of a theoretical account of these effects would need to wait nearly a decade (Iyengar, Peters, & Kinder, 1982). Proposing a cognitive explanation for media's ability to shape the public agenda, Iyengar and Kinder (1987) relied on experimental methods to advance their individual-level account of agenda setting and a related form of media influence: priming. The publication of their book contributed to a shift in media effects research, which began to understand media influence as the product of an interaction with individuals' cognitive systems.

The original formulation of agenda setting—in recent years referred to as the "first level" of agenda setting (McCombs & Bell, 1996)—broadly explores how the degree of attention to an issue is related to its salience among the public, but does not focus on the nuances of coverage *within* an issue. This approach, some argue, "strips away almost everything worth knowing about how the media cover an issue and leaves only the shell of the topic" (Kosicki, 1993, p. 112), and in so doing, "overlooks the idea that *controversy* is the underlying basis of any issue that becomes a topic of media coverage" (Jasperson, Shah, Watts, Faber, & Fan, 1998, p. 206). That is, although agenda setting highlights the media's impact on the perceived salience of a particular issue, the model's failure to look within controversies means it cannot account for the significant role media play in shaping public opinion. In contrast, Entman (1989) emphasizes "an interaction between media messages and what audiences make of them" (p. 349), concluding that media do not just tell us "what to think about," but "what to think."

In response to these critiques, some have sought to extend the agenda-setting framework to consider how the variations within coverage of an issue influence public opinion beyond issue salience (McCombs, 1992). McCombs and Estrada (1997) assert that it is through the selection of particular issue attributes—the second level of agenda setting—that news affects public opinion. That is, elites shape issue conceptions by the transmission of particular attributes. As such, second-level agenda setting borrows heavily from the definition of framing as making some aspects of reality more salient in a text in order to promote a particular "problem definition, causal interpretation, moral evaluation and/or treatment recommendation for the item described" (Entman, 1993, p. 52). Politicians and journalists characterize an issue in ways that help shape its reality for an audience, creating

the acceptable range of meaning (Gitlin, 1980). This understanding of framing and its influence predates second-level agenda setting and provides a way of describing the power of media to direct individual thoughts toward an interpretation of a situation or object, telling audiences what to think, not just what to think about.

◆ Framing and Priming

Framing, as a process by which the emphasis or construction of a message affects the interpretation of the receiver, has a long tradition that transcends its application to mass communication research (Goffman, 1974). The term *framing* itself reflects early analogies that were used to describe this process. In the field of sociology, for example, Bateson (1972) adopted the metaphor of a picture frame to describe the way that frames organize information and provide a perspective through which message receivers come to understand the subject matter. Implicit in many of the sociological studies from which the concept of media framing originated, textual and visual devices order and organize the perception of audience members by including and excluding certain elements, and turn "unrecognizable happenings or amorphous talk into a discernible event" (Tuchman, 1978, p. 192; see also Gitlin, 1980; Graber, 1988; Hall, Critcher, Jefferson, Clarke, & Roberts, 1978; Shah et al., 1996).

Of course, analogies are not limited to the notion of a picture frame. From the field of psychology, Bock and Loebell (1990) refer to the frame of a building that shapes the form the structure will ultimately take. Just as a building frame includes doors and windows—openings through which the visitor will experience the interior—media frames may activate particular existing cognitions in the mind of the viewer. According to this perspective, the ordering or framing of textual materials activates certain considerations, which interact with a person's political predispositions to guide subsequent reactions (Krosnick, 1991; Zaller, 1992). Much of this psychologically grounded work on framing can be traced back, implicitly or explicitly, to Kahneman and Tversky's (1979, 1984) classic prospect theory studies examining how cognitive frames structure interpretations of the consequences and contingencies associated with a particular choice. In experiments in which available choices were numerically equivalent but the explanatory rationale was formulated differently, they found that the frame in which identical facts are presented shapes choice process (Tversky & Kahneman, 1981).

In blending these sociological and psychological accounts, framing in the field of mass communication generally refers to the process by which meaning is given to an account of a political issue or event. It is the result of the complex interplay among political elites, individual journalists, news organizations, professional norms and practices, and the broader culture or ideology (see Shoemaker & Reese, 1996). By structuring press accounts around certain frames, or themes, journalists shape audience interpretations of the issue or event (Pan & Kosicki, 1993). As such, experimental research has focused on the effect of news frames on cognitive, attitudinal, and behavioral outcomes such as knowledge, public opinion, and decision making (Cappella & Jamieson, 1997; Shah et al., 1996).

Although more from a distinct set of theoretical moorings than agenda setting, framing is often related to agenda setting through priming, another example of media effects that emerged as part of the cognitive revolution in the social sciences (see Roskos-Ewoldsen & Roskos-Ewoldsen, Chapter 12, this volume). As cognitive effects of mass media, framing and priming share much in common. At the most basic level, they describe how the structure of a stimulus

message interacts with the cognitive structure of audience members to affect subsequent judgments. Noting this similarity, Iyengar and Kinder (1987) identify both framing and priming as accessibility effects whereby characteristics of the stimulus message render certain cognitions more likely to be used in making judgments at some point after exposure. In fact, Chong and Druckman (2007b) refer to framing and priming processes as "interchangeable."

We argue that framing and priming, although not interchangeable, are related processes. In fact, these media effects can be located within a common cognitive processing model. Whereas framing effects tend to apply to immediate responses shaped by a message, priming effects may refer more generally to when messages render certain schemas more accessible for activation and use in subsequent tasks. As Price and Tewksbury (1997) argue, framing effects are expressed directly following message exposure, whereas priming effects are a product of both recency and chronicity of exposure to stimuli. As such, we view these as related but distinguishable phenomena resulting from differing patterns of message exposure.

◆ Approaches to Studying Framing Effects

Reflecting what Entman (1993) referred to as a "fractured paradigm," the assessment of the nature of framing effects has taken a variety of forms, with no two approaches exactly alike. Nevertheless, we are able to classify these approaches based on two important dimensions: precision versus realism in frame construction, and context-specific versus context-transcendent frame scope. The former distinction refers to the chosen approach to conceptualize framing effects; that is, whether researchers stress internal validity in terms of isolating the effects of news story frames, or whether they emphasize external validity by trying to use realistic story manipulations in which the facts of news stories are allowed to vary along with the framing manipulations. The latter dimension refers to whether researchers examine the effects of framing distinctions that are specific to the topical context of the news story in which they are embedded or whether they adopt framing distinctions that transcend the topic of the news story such that they can be applied to a variety of different news story topics/issues.

PRECISION VERSUS REALISM

An approach emphasizing precision adopts a strict experimentalist orientation to studying framing effects. That is, it seeks to experimentally isolate the frame by holding all other content material constant. In this way, researchers can identify and assess the effect of the frame, eliminating the possibility that the effect is caused by something other than the frame. The prime example of this approach is Kahneman and Tversky's (1979) prospect theory research. Their messages presented participants with one of two choices, one framed in terms of losses and the other in terms of gains. In all other respects, the two versions were logically equivalent. The researchers could then be confident that the observed results—risk aversion in the gain condition, risk seeking in the loss condition— were attributable to frame shifts.

This precision approach to isolating the pure effects of message frames, however, does have some significant limitations. The events and issues that are the subject of most news stories do not lend themselves to setting up mathematically equivalent frames. Rather, they are qualitatively different alternatives for how to assemble events, facts, and other information into a news story. Attempts to limit framing manipulations to logically equivalent frames

or to shifts in the emphasis of lead paragraphs may produce stories that don't correspond to the news stories that are produced by working journalists, who may alter the selection of textual packages, the facts, sources, and targets that correspond with the frame.

This critique is driven by the concern that researchers interested in studying framing effects should seek to inform society about the consequences of the framing choices that actual journalists make. This is not possible when frames are neutered. This also raises conceptual questions about what is a frame and how one should manipulate it. That is, is the frame of the news an observable content feature that one can identify (i.e., the headline or lead of a news story) or something that permeates the story in ways that are not easily tangible? These are conceptual and methodological questions that confront advocates of the precision approach.

The limitations associated with the strict experimental control of the precision perspective have led some researchers to adopt a more lenient, realism approach to studying framing effects. Often, such researchers adapt actual news stories for experimental manipulations (e.g., McLeod & Detenber, 1999; Rhee, 1997), sacrificing the ability to experimentally isolate which element of the shifting text—the frame, the facts, the source, or the target—is producing the observed effect. This is done in the interest of estimating the effects of story differences as they occur in actual news texts. As a result, in experimental studies of this sort, news stories with different frames may contain additional facts and information that are not equivalent across conditions. In studies examining news and public opinion outside of the laboratory, frames shift with attendant supporting facts (Shah, Watts, Domke, & Fan, 2002), which may exhibit their full potential influence. Regardless of the method, the internal validity of this approach suffers considerably as a result of the fact that the influence of the frame has not been isolated.

CONTEXT-SPECIFIC VERSUS CONTEXT-TRANSCENDENT FRAMES

The second distinction in framing effects research pertains to whether the frames used in experimental manipulations are specific to the issue context of the study or whether they can be applied to a variety of different issue contexts. Chong and Druckman (2007a) challenge the importance of this distinction, arguing that frames are never transcendent. They contend that they are inherently tied to their issue context. For example, an economic frame applied to the issue of health care policy is qualitatively different from an economic frame applied to political election coverage. In the former context, an economically framed story might evaluate the economic viability and implications of various health care proposals, whereas in the context of a political election, an economically framed story might address how the current state of the economy might affect the election outcome or how the election outcome might affect the economy. In other words, the meaning of an economic frame changes across story contexts.

We argue that some frames may be context specific, but there are other frames that have common elements that make them applicable across different issues. Certain frames have been repeatedly tested in different contexts and shown to have consistent effects. This is true of gain versus loss frames (Kahneman & Tversky, 1979), ethical versus material frames (Domke, Shah, & Wackman, 1998b; Shah et al., 1996), strategy versus issue frames (Cappella & Jamieson, 1997; Rhee, 1997), and episodic versus thematic frames (Iyengar, 1991). As this shows, it is important to identify transcendent frames to generate theories of framing effects that are generalizable across multiple issues and various contexts.

EXAMPLES OF FRAMING EFFECTS RESEARCH

By combining the dimensions of precision versus realism and context specific versus context transcendent, framing effects research can be organized into four categories. Representing the *precision-specific* approach, Shen and Edwards (2005) examined the framing effects of constructed news stories about welfare reform presented alternatively within the "public aid" frame (emphasizing the need for assistance programs on humanitarian grounds) or the "strict work" frame (emphasizing the importance of self-reliance). The news story itself was standardized across experimental conditions with only the material necessary to convey the frame (i.e., the headline, lead, and concluding paragraph) differing between the two articles. Results of this study demonstrated that the frames had expected effects on cognitions and attitudes about welfare (see also Druckman & Nelson, 2003; Nelson & Kinder, 1996).

Following in the tradition of the message framing experiments of Tversky and Kahneman (1981), *precision-transcendent* studies are typified by Shah et al. (1996), who presented participants with constructed news stories about the issue positions of political candidates on health care. In the precision tradition, the information about candidate stands on the health care issue and their policy implications were consistent across conditions; however, the stories were framed in either ethical or material terms—transcendent frames that were applied to stories about a wide variety of issues. Ethical frames increased noncompensatory decision making (the use of a single, dominant criterion) rather than compensatory decision making (a more complicated mental calculus using multiple, weighted criteria; see also Green & Blair; 1995; Price, Tewksbury, & Powers, 1997; Shah, Kwak, Schmierbach, & Zubric, 2004).

Studies that fit the *realism-specific* approach are illustrated by Nelson, Clawson, and Oxley (1997), who examined framing effects on tolerance judgments regarding a KKK rally in Ohio. Study participants exhibited more tolerance when they viewed a television news story framed around the issue of free speech than when they saw a story framed in terms of public order values. This study used real news stories to represent the two news frames. The stories had different themes, used different quotes, presented different images, and interviewed different sources. These differences reinforced the distinction between the free speech and the public order frames, which affected tolerance judgments (see also Iyengar & Simon, 1994; McLeod & Detenber, 1999; Richardson, 2005; Shah et al., 2002).

Finally, research in the *realism-transcendent* tradition has been the most prolific. As an example of this approach, Rhee (1997) began with real newspaper and television stories about the 1991 Philadelphia mayoral election that were recomposed to conform to either an issue or a strategy frame. More emphasis was put on making the stories reflect actual news stories than on isolating the framing manipulation. Issue and strategy frames can be applied to a wide variety of contexts, from political elections to various issue conflicts. Results showed that the news story frames influenced cognitions about the election, as indicated by the fact that participants who saw the issue frame described the election in terms of issues and those who saw the strategy frame described the election in strategic terms (see also Brewer, 2002; Cappella & Jamieson, 1997; Gamson, 1992; Iyengar, 1991; Rhee, 1997; Shen, 2004a).

BLENDING APPROACHES

Although it is clear that research on framing effects has benefited from the variety of research designs and different approaches to gathering empirical evidence, recent research has begun to develop hybrid research designs that avoid some of the limitations noted previously. For example, Shah et al. (2004) considered how different frames about the environment work in combination to produce effects by experimentally crossing gain-loss frames with individual-societal frames. They found that frame competition and correspondence can attenuate or amplify effects, respectively, with the combination of individual-gain and societal-loss frames producing the greatest effects on cognitive complexity. As this work demonstrated, it may be the interplay of frames that is responsible for observed framing effects.

Similarly, when individuals are exposed to competing frames representing opposing positions of an issue debate, research suggests that frames tend to cancel each other out, resulting in muted framing effects (e.g., Brewer, 2003; Sniderman & Theriault, 2004). Extending this idea of multiple frames competing against each other for influence, Chong and Druckman (2007a) examined the relative importance of the frequency (dosage) of frame exposure and the strength (potency) of frames (as assessed by a pretest panel of judges). Their results suggest that frame potency matters more than dosage, as frames previously found to be strong dominated those previously found to be weak, regardless of the number of repeated frame exposures. This study also indicated that frame competition generally fosters more deliberative opinion responses as competing frames expose individuals to diverging perspectives of an issue conflict.

Along these same lines, research has shown the benefits of systematically manipulating a wider range of textual elements in a single research design, with respondents encountering news reports that cross frame shifts with alterations of facts, sources, and subjects of stories (see Boyle et al., 2006; Cho, Gil de Zuniga, Shah, & McLeod, 2006; Keum et al., 2005; McLeod & Shah, 2008). This work isolates frame effects while also examining whether the power of these frames is contingent on particular source cues, story targets, or other factors that correspond or conflict with the resonant frame. All of these designs extend framing research beyond the manipulation of a single frame, thus avoiding the implicit assumption that news stories use only one frame, or that facts, sources, and targets remain constant even as frames change.

◆ Processes and Effects

FRAMING MODERATORS

Despite a wide range of framing distinctions and the potential interplay of these different textual elements on likely outcomes, there is a growing consensus that framing effects are not direct, uniform effects, but involve complicated interactions between audience characteristics, the message, and other contextual factors. In order to untangle the complex interaction patterns, framing research has examined a host of moderating variables (Druckman, 2001a; Iyengar, 1991; Nelson et al., 1997; Shen & Edwards, 2005; Slothuus, 2008). Moderators are factors that affect the direction/strength of framing effects, or define the conditions under which framing effects will or will not occur (Baron & Kenny, 1986). Although there are limitless numbers of potential moderators, framing research has largely focused on three factors: (1) audience characteristics, such as predispositions and motivations; (2) message features and their resonance with existing cognitions; and (3) situational contexts in which individuals receive these news frames.

First, framing research has identified numerous individual factors that regulate the impact of media frames. For instance, evidence suggests that media frames have a limited effect for those individuals who are strong partisans or for those who already have strong opinions on the issue in question (e.g., Gross & Brewer, 2007; Iyengar, 1991; Keum et al., 2005). This suggests that both strong political orientations and preexisting opinions provide individuals with resources with which to resist the influence of media frames. Evidence is mixed for the moderating effects of political knowledge, however. Some studies suggest that more knowledgeable individuals are less susceptible to framing effects because they are equipped to evaluate framed messages more critically, relying on their prior knowledge base (Kinder & Sanders, 1990; Valentino, Beckmann, & Buhr, 2001). Other studies indicate that knowledge may produce greater motivation and ability to process messages, thereby accentuating framing effects (Nelson et al., 1997; Slothuus, 2008). In an effort to resolve these conflicting research findings about the moderating effects of political knowledge, Druckman and Nelson (2003) explored the possibility that inconsistent findings may be due to a failure to control for prior opinions, as knowledgeable individuals tend to possess strong preexisting opinions, which may create resistance to framing effects, as is the case for those high in need for cognition (Smith & Levin, 1996). When individual tendency to have prior opinions was controlled, those with high levels of knowledge exhibited more susceptibility to framing.

Second, a growing body of research locates framing moderators in the intersection of frame features and audience cognitions. Shen and Edwards (2005) illustrate that framing effects are dependent not only on the featured frames themselves but also on whether those frames resonate with individuals' core values.

Using welfare reform as an issue context, these authors found that individuals who are humanitarian in their value orientations are more responsive to a "public aid" frame (emphasizing the need to assist those in need), whereas those who hold individualistic value orientations are more responsive to a "work requirement" frame (highlighting the importance of strict work requirement and self-reliance). Brewer (2001) also found that framing effects are dependent on the favorability of (cognitive and emotional) responses to the featured frame. Additionally, Druckman (2001a) found that individuals take into account the source credibility. That is, frames have a stronger effect when they are conveyed by a credible source (e.g., *New York Times*) than by a noncredible source (e.g., *National Enquirer*). This accumulated evidence that framing effects are highly contingent on how individuals process frames implies that individuals respond to frames in a relatively active and deliberate manner (Druckman, 2001b; Pan & Kosicki, 2005).

Finally, in addition to message features and individual cognitions, some situational factors have been shown to play moderating roles. As mentioned previously, the presence of counterframes tends to reduce framing effects as counterframes promote alternative interpretations (Brewer, 2002; Sniderman & Theriault, 2004). Likewise, interpersonal discussion, particularly when opposing viewpoints are represented, has been shown to dampen framing effects (Druckman & Nelson, 2003). Thus, dispositional and situational factors can condition framing.

FRAMING OUTCOMES

A growing number of framing effects studies examine cognitive process outcomes. For example, studies have examined the effects of frames on the activation of relevant cognitions (e.g.,

Price et al., 1997; Shen, 2004b), as well as the complexity of activated thoughts (e.g., Shah et al., 2004). These studies focus on the implication of cognitive processing for issue interpretation and meaning making. However, examination of the cognitive effects of news frames includes more strictly cognitive consequences including the ability to recall information (e.g., Valkenburg, Semetko, & de Vreese, 1999), the processing of surrounding information (Hwang, Gotlieb, Nah, & McLeod, 2007), and learning from news (Veenstra, Sayre, Shah, & McLeod, 2008).

A sizable body of existing experimental research also considers the attitudinal effects of message frames, with cognitive processing variables theorized but unmeasured. For example, studies have examined the effects of news frames on public opinion regarding controversial issues, such as support for welfare and health care reform, gay rights, affirmative action, and stem cell research (e.g., Brewer, 2001, 2003; Kinder & Sanders, 1990; Price et al., 1997; Shah et al., 1996; Shen, 2004b). They have also examined effects of news frames on tolerance for protesters and hate groups (e.g., Boyle et al., 2006; Keum et al., 2005; McLeod, 1995; McLeod & Detenber, 1999; Nelson et al., 1997), attributions of responsibility (e.g., Iyengar, 1990), and political cynicism (e.g., Cappella & Jamieson, 1997).

Affective and behavioral outcomes have also been considered, though these distal consequences are often explored in relation to more proximate mediating factors, such as cognitions. Studies have examined effects on general feelings toward various groups and individuals (Price et al., 1997), as well as specific emotions such as anger and disgust (Gross & Brewer, 2007; Nabi, 2003). With respect to behavioral outcomes, studies have focused on decision making, especially voting (Barker, 2005; Domke et al., 1998b; Valentino et al., 2001).

◆ *An Integrated Model of Effects*

Recognizing the related nature of these processes and outcomes, we draw on past research to provide an integrated model of message processing to guide future research (see Figure 6.1). The effects of message frames in shaping outcomes, such as issue interpretation and the processing of subsequent or previously encoded information, can be understood in terms of traditional cognitive-processing models. Accordingly, McLeod and Shah (2008) derived an integrated model of message processing that draws on prior research to predict how message frames interact with audience members' orientations and memory store to influence their thoughts, feelings, and behaviors. This model highlights six primary components of message processing: availability, applicability, accessibility, activation, association, and usability.

First, message processing and effects are influenced by the *availability* of relevant knowledge, beliefs, and expectations contained within the structure of an audience member's existing memory store (Anderson, 1983; Higgins, 1996). The likelihood that a particular message will trigger activation of available schemas into working memory, however, will depend on their *applicability* and *accessibility*. Applicability concerns the degree to which individuals hold relevant schemas and scripts suggested by the message frame. The resonance between the content of available schemas and that of the message (Bruner, 1957; Higgins, 1996) will influence the power of the frame in guiding message processing.

If applicable constructs are unavailable, the accessibility, or the ease with which

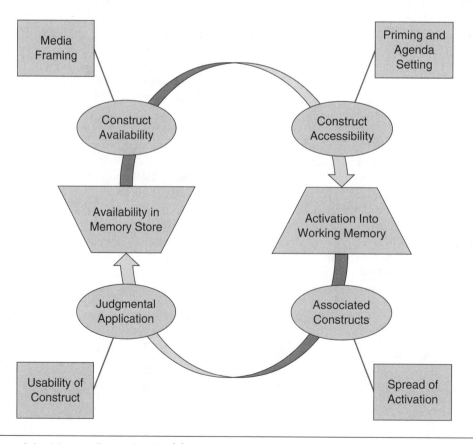

Figure 6.1 Message Processing Model

other available schemas may be activated into working memory, will determine which cognitions are used. This is largely influenced by the recency and chronicity of that memory node. Schemas that have been recently activated are likely to remain accessible for subsequent judgments (Higgins, 1996; Price & Tewksbury, 1997). Such temporary accessibility is at the heart of experimental priming effects, as a schema activated for one purpose remains accessible for evaluation of other objects. Similarly, schemas that have been frequently activated become chronically accessible (Roskos-Ewoldsen, 1997; Shen, 2004a). This helps explain priming and agenda-setting effects as they occur over time through the repeated emphasis by media on certain issues, which become persistent in their accessibility for judgments of issue salience, presidential support, and other evaluations (Krosnick & Brannon, 1993; Krosnick & Kinder, 1990).

However, several other individual-level differences will also influence schema activation. As alluded to previously, these include the orientations that individuals bring with them to the message processing experience, as well as their motivations and predispositions. Although motivation may influence the depth of message processing, predispositions, such as ideological preferences, have been shown to influence reliance on recently activated or chronically accessible schemas (Keum et al., 2005). Discussion has also proven to attenuate or amplify priming and framing effects along these same lines, possibly by altering patterns of message processing and thereby limiting elite and media influence (Druckman & Nelson, 2003; Mendelsohn, 1996).

Once available and relevant schemas are activated and brought into working memory, there is also a potential for this activation to spread to other associated schemas. As the strength of the linkages forged among associated schemas increases through recent and repeated activation, so

does the likelihood that a particular schema contained in this network will be activated through this cascading process (Judd & Krosnick, 1989). This spread of activation speaks to the importance of associative ties for priming and framing effects, which are often a function of the links between the initially activated and related constructs (Domke, Shah, & Wackman, 1998a; Cho et al., 2006).

Last, although the frame of a message is likely to influence activation, this does not necessarily mean that activated schemas will be judged as relevant for use in the judgment task (Higgins, 1989; Pan & Kosicki, 2005). That is, activated schemas are not automatically applied; rather, the *usability* of these thoughts regulates the impact they have on audience outcomes. For example, activation may spread to strongly linked but seemingly irrelevant schemas, which are consciously discounted in subsequent judgments. Those schemas that are deemed usable, and are applied in judgmental tasks, become more central in the memory store for subsequent use. It is through this complex process that most framing and priming effects are thought to occur.

◆ Future Directions in Framing Research

Our review of the expanding body of research on framing leads us to a number of observations and conclusions that will help guide future research. Indeed, as we lay out these observations, the implicit agenda for future research may seem distressingly vast.

First, rather than merely expressing dismay at the fractured nature of the framing paradigm, perhaps researchers should celebrate the diversity of knowledge provided by contrasting approaches. That is, researchers operating from both the psychological and sociological traditions, and from approaches emphasizing precision and realism, all contribute to our understanding of frames and their effects. It is up to theorists to understand differences in approaches and how they impact empirical findings. Still, attempts to standardize conceptual and operational definitions, and to enhance theoretical clarity and coherence, should be applauded.

Second, it is essential to broaden theoretical conceptions of framing. Our recommendation stems from observed commonalities between frames and *cues,* the labels used to identify policy issues, characterize social groups, and define public figures in the news (Shah et al., 2002). Although frames and cues differ in terms of the textual unit involved (i.e., the entirety of the story versus the specificity of the concept), they both operate by activating applicable cognitive schemas that, when deemed usable, are used to make subsequent judgments. By viewing framing as the imputation of meaning, we could say that a given message contains a range of frame devices, from concept labels to narrative themes (Pan & Kosicki, 1993). Framing research should consider all of these textual elements, as well as their interactions.

Third, framing and agenda-setting research needs to expand its focus. In particular, a majority of framing effects research has focused on print news accounts even though most people receive their news through broadcast reports (Fowler, Goldstein, Hale, & Kaplan, 2007). In the mixed-media environment of the Internet, the need to understand how text and video intersect to produce effects becomes more important. Veenstra et al. (2008) have explored how the textual features that often lead into video clips in online settings can substantially alter how this content is processed. As news audiences shift to the Internet, researchers will need to revisit earlier studies of framing that used video rather than textual manipulations (e.g., Iyengar, 1991).

Fourth, the additional recognition that framing effects are complex, indirect, and nonuniform further expands the potential for future research. It is crucial to identify the situational contexts under which various types of framing effects occur, along with the affective and motivational triggers (see Lee, McLeod, & Shah, 2008; Nabi, 2003; Shen & Dillard, 2007). Researchers should continue to identify and specify moderating variables and the role they play in shaping the nature of framing effects, as well as how their impact differs across contexts.

Fifth, this paradigm-wide research agenda is made even more ambitious when the message processing model described earlier is applied. As researchers continue to develop and refine such cognitive models, new research questions emerge. It is important for framing effects researchers to develop a more comprehensive understanding of how processes such as availability, accessibility, activation, applicability, association, and usability affect judgments made in response to message frames. Innovative, multicell designs will be required to allow researchers to understand the nature of these processes and the factors that regulate them. Measures of response latency are one example of this sort of work (Nelson et al., 1997).

Thus, as research on agenda setting has slowed, the opposite is true for framing effects inquiries. As our relative emphasis on these two traditions illustrates, the scope for future research on framing is vast, with many of the central questions revisiting core issues from the early days of agenda setting: How are frames built? What are the contingencies for their influence? Do they affect elites as well as the public? What kinds of issues are most readily framed, and why? This is not to say that research on agenda setting is moribund. Rather, scholars are charting new paths in agenda-setting research, examining it in novel contexts such as the power of political bloggers (Delwiche,

2005) and prime-time entertainment television (Holbrook & Hill, 2005) to set the news and public agenda. Clearly, more research on framing and agenda setting is necessary to map this expansive and expanding terrain.

◆ References

Anderson, J. R. (1983). A spreading activation theory of memory. *Journal of Verbal Learning and Verbal Behavior, 22,* 261–295.

Barker, D. (2005). Values, frames, and persuasion in presidential nomination campaigns. *Political Behavior, 27,* 375–394.

Baron, R. M., & Kenny, D. A. (1986). The moderator-mediator variable distinction in social psychological research: Conceptual, strategic, and statistical considerations. *Journal of Personality and Social Psychology, 51,* 1173–1182.

Bateson, G. (1972). *Steps to an ecology of mind.* New York: Ballantine.

Bock, K., & Loebell, H. (1990). Framing sentences. *Cognition, 35,* 1–39.

Boyle, M. P., Schmierbach, M. G., Armstrong, C. L., Cho, J., McLeod, D. M., & Shah, D. V. (2006). Expressive responses to news stories about extremist groups: A framing experiment. *Journal of Communication, 56,* 271–288.

Brewer, P. R. (2001). Value words and lizard brains: Do citizens deliberate about appeals to their core values? *Political Psychology, 22,* 45–64.

Brewer, P. R. (2002). Framing, value words, and citizens' explanations of their issue opinions. *Political Communication, 19,* 303–316.

Brewer, P. R. (2003). Values, political knowledge, and public opinion about gay rights: A framing-based account. *Public Opinion Quarterly, 67,* 173–201.

Bruner, J. (1957). On perceptual readiness. *Psychological Review, 64,* 123–152.

Cappella, J. N., & Jamieson, K. H. (1997). *Spiral of cynicism: The press and public good.* New York: Oxford University Press.

Cho, J., Gil de Zuniga, H., Shah, D. V., & McLeod, D. M. (2006). Cue convergence: Associative effects on social intolerance. *Communication Research, 33,* 136–154.

Chong, D., & Druckman, J. N. (2007a). Framing public opinion in competitive democracies. *American Political Science Review, 101,* 637–655.

Chong, D., & Druckman, J. N. (2007b). Framing theory. *Annual Review of Political Science, 10,* 103–126.

Delwiche, A. (2005). Agenda-setting, opinion leadership, and the world of Web logs. *First Monday, 10,* 12–5.

Domke, D., Shah, D. V., & Wackman, D. B. (1998a). Media priming effects: Accessibility, association, and activation. *International Journal of Public Opinion Research, 10,* 51–74.

Domke, D., Shah, D. V., & Wackman, D. B. (1998b). "Moral referendums": Values, news media, and the process of candidate choice. *Political Communication, 15,* 301–321.

Druckman, J. N. (2001a). On the limits of framing effects: Who can frame? *Journal of Politics, 63,* 1041–1066.

Druckman, J. N. (2001b). The implications of framing effects for citizen competence. *Political Behavior, 23,* 225–256.

Druckman, J. N., & Nelson, K. R. (2003). Framing and deliberation: How citizens' conversations limit elite influence. *American Journal of Political Science, 47,* 729–745.

Entman, R. M. (1989). How the media affect what people think: An information processing approach. *Journal of Politics, 51,* 347–370.

Entman, R. M. (1993). Framing: Toward the clarification of a fractured paradigm. *Journal of Communication, 43,* 51–58.

Fowler, E. F., Goldstein, K. M., Hale, M., & Kaplan, M. (2007). Does local news measure up? *Stanford Law and Policy Review, 18,* 410–431.

Gamson, W. A. (1992). *Talking politics.* New York: Cambridge University Press.

Gitlin, T. (1980). *The whole world is watching: Mass media in the making and unmaking of the new left.* Berkeley: University of California Press.

Goffman, E. (1974). *Frame analysis: An essay on the organization of experience*. Boston: Northeastern University Press.

Graber, D. A. (1988). *Processing the news: How people tame the information tide* (2nd ed.). New York: Longman.

Green, D. P., & Blair, I. V. (1995). Framing and the price elasticity of private and public goods. *Journal of Consumer Psychology, 4*, 1–32.

Gross, K., & Brewer, P. R. (2007). Sore losers: News frames, policy debates, and emotions. *Harvard Journal of Press/Politics, 12*, 122–130.

Hall, S., Critcher, C., Jefferson, T., Clarke, J., & Roberts, B. (1978). *Policing the crisis: Mugging, the state, and law and order*. New York: Holmes & Meier.

Higgins, E. T. (1989). Knowledge accessibility and activation: Subjectivity and suffering from unconscious sources. In J. S. Uleman & J. A. Bargh (Eds.), *Unintended thought* (pp. 75–123). New York: Guilford.

Higgins, E. T. (1996). Knowledge activation: Accessibility, applicability, and salience. In E. T. Higgins & A. W. Kruglanski (Eds.), *Social psychology: Handbook of basic principles* (pp. 133–168). New York: Guilford.

Holbrook, R. A., & Hill, T. G. (2005). Agenda-setting and priming in prime time television: Crime dramas as political cues. *Political Communication, 22*, 277–295.

Hwang, H., Gotlieb, M. R., Nah, S., & McLeod, D. M. (2007). Applying a cognitive processing model to presidential debate effects: Post-debate news analysis and primed reflection. *Journal of Communication, 57*, 40–59.

Iyengar, S. (1990). Framing responsibility for political issues: The case of poverty. *Political Behavior, 2*, 19–40.

Iyengar, S. (1991). *Is anyone responsible? How television frames political issues*. Chicago: University of Chicago Press.

Iyengar, S., & Kinder, D. (1987). *News that matters*. Chicago: University of Chicago Press.

Iyengar, S., Peters, M. D., & Kinder, D. R. (1982). Experimental demonstrations of the not-so-minimal political consequences of mass media. *American Political Science Review, 76*, 848–858.

Iyengar, S., & Simon, A. (1994). News coverage of the Gulf crisis and public opinion: A study of agenda-setting, priming, and framing. In W. L. Bennett & D. Paletz (Eds.), *Taken by storm* (pp. 167–185). Chicago: University of Chicago Press.

Jasperson, A. E., Shah, D. V., Watts, M., Faber, R. J., & Fan, D. P. (1998). Framing and the public agenda: Media effects on the importance of the federal budget deficit. *Political Communication, 15*, 205–224.

Judd, C. M., & Krosnick, J. A. (1989). The structural bases of consistency among political attitudes: Effects of political expertise and attitude importance. In A. Pratkanis, S. Beckler, & A. Greenwald (Eds.), *Attitude structure and function* (pp. 99–128). Hillsdale, NJ: Erlbaum.

Kahneman, D., & Tversky, A. (1979). Prospect theory: An analysis of decision under risk. *Econometrica, 47*, 263–291.

Kahneman, D., & Tversky, A. (1984). Choice, values, and frames. *American Psychologist, 39*, 341–350.

Keum, H., Hillback, E., Rojas, H., Gil de Zuniga, H., Shah, D. V., & McLeod, D. M. (2005). Personifying the radical: How news framing polarizes security concerns and tolerance judgments. *Human Communication Research, 33*, 337–364.

Kinder, D. R., & Sanders, L. M. (1990). Mimicking political debate with survey questions. *Social Cognition, 8*, 73–103.

Kiousis, S., & McCombs, M. (2004). Agenda-setting effects and attitude strength: Political figures during the 1996 presidential election. *Communication Research, 31*, 36–57.

Kosicki, G. M. (1993). Problems and opportunities in agenda-setting research. *Journal of Communication, 43*, 100–127.

Krosnick, J. A. (1991). Response strategies for coping with the cognitive demands of attitude measures in surveys. *Applied Cognitive Psychology, 5*, 231–236.

Krosnick, J. A., & Brannon, L. (1993). The media and the foundations of presidential support: George Bush and the Persian Gulf conflict. *Journal of Social Issues, 49*, 167–182.

Krosnick, J. A., & Kinder, D. R. (1990). Altering the foundations of support for the president through priming. *American Political Science Review, 84,* 497–512.

Lee, N. J., McLeod, D. M., & Shah, D. V. (2008). Framing policy debates: Issue dualism, journalistic frames, and opinions on controversial policy issues. *Communication Research, 35,* 695–718.

Maher, T. M. (2001). Framing: An emerging paradigm or a phase of agenda setting? In S. D. Reese, O. H. Gandy, Jr., & A. E. Grant (Eds.), *Framing public life: Perspectives on media and our understanding of the social world* (pp. 83–94). Mahwah, NJ: Erlbaum.

McCombs, M. (1992). Explorers and surveyors: Expanding strategies for agenda-setting research. *Journalism Quarterly, 69,* 813–824.

McCombs, M., & Bell, T. (1996). The agenda-setting role of mass communication. In M. B. Salwen & D. W. Stacks (Eds.), *An integrated approach to communication theory and research* (pp. 93–110). Mahwah, NJ: Erlbaum.

McCombs, M., & Estrada, G. (1997). The news media and the pictures in our heads. In S. Iyengar & R. Reeves (Eds.), *Do the media govern? Politicians, voters and reporters in America* (pp. 237–247). Thousand Oaks, CA: Sage.

McCombs, M., & Ghanem, S. I. (2001). The convergence of agenda setting and framing. In S. D. Reese, O. H. Gandy, Jr., & A. E. Grant (Eds.), *Framing public life: Perspectives on media and our understanding of the social world* (pp. 67–82). Mahwah, NJ: Erlbaum.

McCombs, M. E., & Shaw, D. L. (1972). The agenda-setting function of mass media. *Public Opinion Quarterly, 36,* 176–187.

McCombs, M. E., Shaw, D. L., & Weaver, D. L. (1997). *Communication and democracy: Exploring the intellectual frontiers in agenda-setting theory.* Mahwah, NJ: Erlbaum.

McGuire, W. J. (1968a). Personality and susceptibility to social influence. In E. Borgatta & L. Lambert (Eds.), *Handbook of personality theory and research* (pp. 1130–1188). Chicago: Rand McNally.

McGuire, W. J. (1968b). Theory of the structure of human thought. In R. P. Abelson, E. Aronson, W. J. McGuire, T. M. Newcomb, M. J. Rosenberg, & R. H. Tannenbaum (Eds.), *Theories of cognitive consistency: A sourcebook* (pp. 140–162). Chicago: Rand McNally.

McLeod, D. M. (1995). Communicating deviance: The effects of television news coverage of social protest. *Journal of Broadcasting and Electronic Media, 39,* 4–19.

McLeod, D. M., & Detenber, B. H. (1999). Framing effects of television news coverage of social protest. *Journal of Communication, 49,* 3–23.

McLeod, D. M., & Shah, D. V. (2008). *Framing the Patriot Act: News values and media effects.* Unpublished manuscript.

Mendelsohn, M. (1996). The media and interpersonal communications: The priming of issues, leaders, and party identification. *Journal of Politics, 58,* 112–125.

Nabi, R. L. (2003). Exploring the framing effects of emotion: Do discrete emotions differentially influence information accessibility, information seeking, and policy preference? *Communication Research, 30,* 224–247.

Nelson, T. E., Clawson, R. A., & Oxley, Z. M. (1997). Media framing of a civil liberties conflict and its effect on tolerance. *American Political Science Review, 91,* 567–583.

Nelson, T. E., & Kinder, D. R. (1996). Issue frames and group-centrism in American public opinion. *Journal of Politics, 58,* 1055–1078.

Pan, Z., & Kosicki, G. M. (1993). Framing analysis: An approach to news discourse. *Political Communication, 10,* 55–76.

Pan, Z., & Kosicki, G. M. (2005). Framing and the understanding of citizenship. In S. Dunwoody, L. B. Becker, G. M. Kosicki, & D. M. McLeod (Eds.), *The evolution of key mass communication concepts: Honoring Jack M. McLeod* (pp. 165–204). Cresskill, NJ: Hampton Press.

Price, V., & Tewksbury, D. (1997). News values and public opinion: A theoretical account of media priming and framing. In G. Barnett & F. Boster (Eds.), *Progress in communication sciences* (pp. 173–212). Norwood, NJ: Ablex.

Price, V., Tewksbury, D., & Powers, E. (1997). Switching trains of thought: The impact of news frames on readers' cognitive responses. *Communication Research, 24,* 481–506.

Rhee, J. W. (1997). Strategy and issue frames in election campaign coverage: A social cognitive account of framing effects. *Journal of Communication, 47,* 26–48.

Richardson, J. D. (2005). Switching social identities: The influence of editorial framing on reader attitudes toward affirmative action and African Americans. *Communication Research, 32,* 503–528.

Rogers, E. M., Hart, W. B., & Dearing, J.W. (1997). A paradigmatic history of agenda-setting research. In S. Iyengar & R. Reeves (Eds.), *Do the media govern? Politicians, voters, and reporters in America* (pp. 225–236). Thousand Oaks, CA: Sage.

Roskos-Ewoldsen, D. R. (1997). Attitude accessibility and persuasion: Review and a transactive model. In B. Burleson (Ed.), *Communication yearbook 20* (pp. 185–225). Beverly Hills, CA: Sage.

Shah, D. V., Domke, D., & Wackman, D. B. (1996). "To thine own self be true": Values, framing and voter decision-making strategies. *Communication Research, 23,* 509–560.

Shah, D. V., Kwak, N., Schmierbach, M., & Zubric, J. (2004). The interplay of news frames on cognitive complexity. *Human Communication Research, 30,* 102–120.

Shah, D. V., Watts, M. D., Domke, D., & Fan, D. P. (2002). News framing and cueing of issue regimes: Explaining Clinton's public approval in spite of scandal. *Public Opinion Quarterly, 66,* 339–370.

Shen, F. (2004a). Chronic accessibility and individual cognitions: Examining the effects of message frames in political advertisements. *Journal of Communication, 54,* 123–137.

Shen, F. (2004b). Effects of news frames and schemas on individuals' issue interpretations and attitudes. *Journalism and Mass Communication Quarterly, 81,* 400–416.

Shen, F., & Edwards, H. H. (2005). Economic individualism, humanitarianism, and welfare reform: A value-based account of framing effects. *Journal of Communication, 55,* 795–809.

Shen, L., & Dillard, J. P. (2007). The influence of behavioral inhibition/approach systems and message framing on the processing of persuasive health messages. *Communication Research, 34,* 433–467.

Shoemaker, P. J., & Reese, S. D. (1996). *Mediating the message: Theories of influence on mass media content* (2nd ed.). New York: Longman.

Slothuus, R. (2008). More than weighting cognitive importance: A dual-process model of issue framing effects. *Political Psychology, 29,* 1–28.

Smith, S. M., & Levin, I. P. (1996). Need for cognition and choice framing effects. *Journal of Behavioral Decision Making, 9,* 283–290.

Sniderman, P. M., & Theriault, S. M. (2004). The structure of political argument and the logic of issue framing. In W. E. Saris & P. M. Sniderman (Eds.), *Studies in public opinion* (pp. 133–165). Princeton, NJ: Princeton University Press.

Tuchman, G. (1978). *Making news: A study in the construction of reality.* New York: Free Press.

Tversky, A., & Kahneman, D. (1981). The framing of decisions and the psychology of choice. *Science, 211,* 453–458.

Valentino, N. A., Beckmann, N. M., & Buhr, T. A. (2001). A spiral of cynicism for some: The contingent effects of campaign news frames on participation and confidence in government. *Political Communication, 18,* 347–367.

Valkenburg, P. M., Semetko, H. A., & de Vreese, C. H. (1999). The effects of news frames and readers' thoughts and recall. *Communication Research, 26,* 550–569.

Veenstra, A. S., Sayre, B., Shah, D. V., & McLeod, D. M. (2008). Frames and knowledge in mixed media: How activation changes information intake. *Cyber-Psychology & Behavior, 11,* 443–450.

Zaller, J. (1992). *The nature and origins of mass opinion.* Cambridge, UK: Cambridge University Press.

7

THE INFLUENCE OF PRESUMED MEDIA INFLUENCE

Origins and Implications of the Third-Person Perception

◆ Nurit Tal-Or, Yariv Tsfati, and
Albert C. Gunther

Some of the most interesting effects of media on society take place because people think media are influential. A parent thinking that watching *The Simpsons* would negatively affect his or her child's behavior may limit the child's exposure to the presumably detrimental show. A teenager, thinking that positive depictions of smokers would influence his or her friends to think that smoking is cool, may start smoking as a result. Gays, believing that media portrayals create negative stereotypes about gays, may be less inclined to "come out" to their friends, family, and coworkers. And in the interpersonal context, a suitor, noticing a valentine with an unfamiliar return address in his girlfriend's mailbox and expecting that this card may have an impact on her feelings or expectations, may hastily buy her roses. All of these examples convey indirect but very real effects of perceived influence that take place even if people's expectations regarding the impact of communication are exaggerated or erroneous.

The idea that people act on their perceptions of media impact, regardless of whether or not these perceptions are accurate, dates back to Plato (Noelle-Neumann & Peterson, 2004). But in modern communication research, Lazarsfeld and Merton (1948/1971) were the first to claim that the influence and perceived importance of media are related to the "almost magical belief in their enormous power" (p. 555). Part of their argument mentions "the enforcement of social norms" as a central function of mass media (pp. 562–564). Media depictions of deviant behaviors are influential, they imply, not necessarily because they directly convince people that certain behaviors are immoral. Instead, public exposure to deviant behaviors may reinforce social norms because audiences think that such content shapes what *other* people will think is acceptable or unacceptable behavior.

The most influential statement of "the influence of presumed media influence" to date was published in 1983 by W. Phillips Davison. In a landmark article titled "The Third-Person Effect in Communication," Davison noted that, first, people exposed to persuasive communication in the mass media see it as having a greater effect on others than on themselves, and second, that this perceived media impact may lead them to take some action. These two steps are often referred to in current literature, respectively, as the perceptual and behavioral components of the third-person effect. Davison's brilliantly written paper contained intriguing anecdotes and examples, but the empirical evidence was based only on very small student samples and was focused on the perceptual component. He speculated about consequences, but Davison did not offer an examination or evidence supporting the idea that this perceptual gap matters for individual attitudes or behaviors.

Despite its empirical limitations, Davison's article has had a tremendous impact on communication research. At the time of this writing, it has been cited 186 times, according to the Social Sciences Citation Index, and a Google Scholar search yielded 246 articles, book chapters, and conference papers with the third-person effect (sometimes called the third-person perception) in the title. The third-person effect was recently ranked fifth on a list of "most popular theories" in 21st-century communication research (Bryant & Miron, 2004). A meta-analysis (Paul, Salwen, & Dupagne, 2000) investigating 121 separate findings established robust empirical support for the perceptual component of the third-person effect, with an average effect size of $r = .50$. This is, ironically, much larger than the observed effects of media on such outcomes as antisocial behaviors (Perse, 2001).

Whereas the third-person perception (TPP) has been documented in numerous studies as a robust perceptual gap, the causes of this phenomenon are not yet fully agreed on. We begin this chapter by reviewing research on the underlying mechanism accounting for people's perceptions of media influence and then move on to review and organize the literature on the consequences of such perceptions. These are two steps, perhaps unrelated. But we take this approach because we believe the reasons for people's perceptions may be theoretically linked to the consequences of these perceptions.

◆ Mechanisms Underlying People's Perceptions of Media Influence

There are generally two types of explanations for the TPP—cognitive and motivational mechanisms. The cognitive explanations view people as naive scientists who strive to form accurate perceptions of the social world (Eveland, Nathanson, Detenber, & McLeod, 1999). The motivational explanations, on the other hand, claim that social perceptions are biased by the personal needs of the perceiver (Heider, 1958; Tyler & Devinitz, 1981).

Motivational explanations. Motivational explanations for the TPP typically view it as related to other self-serving perceptions. It is well known that people tend to hold unrealistically positive self-perceptions. People believe they are better than others in areas ranging from personality traits to driving abilities (Taylor & Brown, 1988). People also tend to have an illusion of control in situations in which no such control exists. Finally, people tend to be unrealistically optimistic, believing that compared with others, they have a smaller chance of experiencing negative events and a larger chance of experiencing positive events.

The most common explanation for the TPP is the motivation for self-enhancement. According to this explanation, perceiving ourselves as immune to negative or undesirable persuasion, but others as not, helps to preserve and enhance our self-esteem (e.g., Duck & Mullin, 1995). This explanation might be seen as a specific case of the aforementioned self-serving perceptions, or as stemming from them. As suggested by Salwen and Dupagne (2003), because people tend to think that they are cleverer than others, they might conclude that they are less influenced by media compared with others.

The evidence for the self-enhancement account for the TPP focuses mainly on the conditions in which the TPP increases and decreases. For example, the TPP is usually documented in response to media messages that are perceived to be harmful and undesirable (e.g., Gunther & Mundy, 1993). When messages are perceived as positive, such as safe-sex advertisements (Duck, Terry, & Hogg, 1996), the effect is attenuated or even reversed, a phenomenon called the first-person perception (FPP; see also Duck & Mullin, 1995; Gunther & Hwa, 1996). Moreover, the TPP tends to decrease in response to high-quality messages (Duck et al., 1996) with strong arguments (White, 1997), and in response to messages whose source is perceived in a positive light (Gunther, 1991), presumably because more credible messages increase perceived influence on the self and therefore reduce the self-other difference. All of these findings

are congruent with the self-enhancement account of the TPP, as they refer to the motivation of people to perceive themselves positively.

Similarly, many studies have found that the TPP tends to increase as the social distance between oneself and a comparison group increases, a phenomenon termed the "social distance corollary" (Perloff, 2002). For example, Cohen, Mutz, Price, and Gunther (1988) compared the perceived effects of media materials on "other Stanford students" with "other Californians" and "public opinion at large," and found larger effects as the object of influence became more general and more remote from the respondents. Again, this tendency was explained by the self-enhancement bias—the self benefits from enhancing the value or virtue of the in-groups (the groups to which the person belongs) and diminishing the value of the out-groups.

Other researchers have used a different approach in attempting to support the self-enhancement account for the TPP. Abundant research in social psychology has documented the interchangeability between self-enhancement mechanisms. After people use one self-enhancing mechanism, their need to use another self-enhancing mechanism is reduced. On the other hand, people can compensate for a failure to enhance the self using one mechanism by using another mechanism (Tesser, Martin, & Cornell, 1996). According to this logic, if the TPP is indeed a self-enhancing mechanism, it should show interchangeability with other such mechanisms. In line with this idea, research has found that participants reported a smaller TPP after having had an opportunity to affirm themselves (Meirick, 2005), and also reported less self-affirming attitudes after having had an opportunity to report their TPPs (Tal-Or & Tsfati, 2007).

Most other motivational explanations, beyond self-enhancement, focus also on people's attempt to protect their inner self. For example, some researchers have suggested that the TPP reflects the motivation to control life events (Perloff, 2002). By perceiving themselves as invulnerable to media control, people can continue to enjoy consuming media content without being afraid of the implications of their media consumption. Likewise, another self-protecting explanation claims that people project the negatively viewed media influence from the self onto others in order to protect the self (Perloff, 2002). According to this explanation, people are, in fact, influenced by the media, but they are not inclined to admit this self-threatening influence and instead attribute this influence to others.

A recent study suggests an alternative explanation for the TPP that is based on impression management motives (Tal-Or & Drukman, 2008). This research suggests that people report being less influenced by the media compared with others in order to present themselves positively to their audience. If impression management underlies the TPP, then we should expect TPPs to be larger in public compared with private conditions. This reasoning was supported in an experiment that asked participants to report in public or in private on their perceptions of how an undesirable message affected themselves and others.

To conclude, motivational explanations for the TPP view it as a perception aimed at maintaining and enhancing the inner and outer self. However, people are also motivated to hold accurate perceptions of the world. This second motivation is covered by the cognitive explanations for the TPP.

Cognitive explanations. Cognitive accounts of the TPP assume that people are naive social scientists (Eveland et al., 1999; Peterson & Beach, 1967) who are motivated to make accurate estimations about how the world operates. When they observe the world and try to figure it out, they intuitively create theories about the effects of media on society and on specific people, and utilize these theories when responding to survey questions about media influence.

One of the most-studied intuitive theories of media impact regards perceived exposure. According to the exposure hypothesis, people take into account the perceived exposure of various groups to particular media content when estimating media influence on these groups. The higher the perceived exposure, the stronger the influence they assume (Eveland et al., 1999). The lay theory of influence in this case is a "magic bullet"—more exposure leads to more influence.

Similarly, other researchers have suggested that respondents take into account the perceived relevance of the media content to the group in question (e.g., Jensen & Hurley, 2005). The relevance of the message can have two contradictory impacts. On the one hand, if the group is perceived as close to the subject of a negative media message, its members are perceived as less influenced by it (Tsfati & Cohen, 2004). For example, residents of peripheral towns in Israel (which are generally portrayed negatively in the media) were perceived to be less influenced by media messages about peripheral towns compared with residents of more central parts of the country. On the other hand, if the group is perceived as the target of the media message, or is portrayed positively by the message, its members are perceived to be more influenced by it (Elder, Douglas, & Sutton, 2006; McLeod, Eveland, & Nathanson, 1997). For example, adults perceived other adults to be more influenced than children by ads featuring news broadcasters, which are presumably directed toward adults (Tal-Or, 2007).

Other cognitive explanations focus on additional perceived audience characteristics relating to the message at hand (aside from perceived exposure and relevance). According to one of these explanations based on self-categorization theory (Turner, Hogg, Oakes, Reicher, & Wetherell, 1987), when people estimate media influence, they take into account the norms of the in-group and those of the out-group (Reid,

Byrne, Brundidge, Shoham, & Marlow, 2007). Other cognitive explanations argue that people assess factors such as the susceptibility of the audience to influence and the severity of the effect (Shah, Faber, & Youn, 1999). According to this perspective, explanations that account for perceived susceptibility and severity incorporate the general expectancy-value principle, noting that people factor in likelihood assessments with appraisals of potential benefit and harm when making judgments about prospective events.

Likewise, much evidence shows that when estimating media impact, people use prior knowledge of the world organized as schemata and stereotypes. For example, Scharrer (2002) found that when estimating the influence of violent content on others, people used their schemata regarding susceptibility of younger audiences to media influence, and consequently assessed that children would be more affected than would adults. When assessing the susceptibility of males versus females to influence by media violence, people take into account the fact that "physical aggression is more socially accepted and therefore more often manifested among men than women" (Scharrer, 2002, pp. 696–697), and hence guess that males are more likely to be influenced by TV violence than are females. Actually, as Scharrer noted, when assessing the impact of media violence, individuals' expectations were generally consistent with the results of scientific research about media effects, at least when it comes to mapping out the more heavily influenced groups.

Reality constraints underlie another cognitive explanation, which views the TPP as resulting from causal attribution biases (e.g., Rojas, Shah, & Faber, 1996; Rucinski & Salmon, 1990). One of these approaches suggests the actor-observer attribution bias as an explanation for the TPP (Gunther, 1991). Perceptual constraints, such as the salience of other people when we perceive them and the salience of the situation when we perceive ourselves, influence the attributions we make for our behavior and for the behavior of others. According to this explanation, people acknowledge the impact of external factors such as persuasive intent when they estimate the (potentially undesirable) impact of media on themselves. However, when estimating that same effect on others, they concentrate on the innate characteristics of other people, such as gullibility.

Cognitive versus motivational explanations. With these explanations in mind, a major question remains: Do people estimate larger effects on others in order to protect their self- (or public) image, or is it their best (though flawed) attempt at accurately guessing the real impact of communication? Is the mechanism underlying the TPP cognitive or motivational? Or some of both? Unfortunately, there is almost no research testing the alternative hypotheses against each other. An aggregate reading of the literature leads to the conclusion that probably both hypotheses are partly correct. Arguably, self-protection mechanisms operate so long that they do not contradict people's reality perceptions. When it comes to self-perceptions, self-enhancement is typically congruent with people's perceived reality (given decades of psychological research documenting that people think their positively biased judgments about themselves are accurate), but this is not the case when it comes to perceptions of others.

Thus, it seems likely that different explanations for the TPP play differing roles in different parts of the phenomenon: We have several reasons to suspect that motivational mechanisms play a more substantial role in people's estimation, or underestimation, of media influences on the self, whereas cognitive mechanisms are more heavily related to perceptions of impact on others (and especially differing types of others).

This assertion follows from several research findings. The first set of evidence comes from the previously mentioned interchangeability studies (Tal-Or & Tsfati, 2007). In those studies, state self-esteem was manipulated prior to TPP measurement in order to examine whether or not the TPP (like other ego defense mechanisms) diminishes after the self has been affirmed. Results from this study showed that the self-influence items were much more strongly influenced by the affirmation manipulation, as compared with the items measuring perceived effects on others. Another set of evidence comes from the impression management study mentioned earlier (Tal-Or & Druckman, 2008) that examined whether the TPP takes place only in public compared with private contexts. In that study, people reported they were more influenced by media in a private compared with a public setting, but the publicity manipulation had no effect on the items measuring perceived influence on others.

In contrast, there are several findings suggesting that cognitive processes, such as perceived relevance and perceived exposure, are more strongly related to people's estimates of media effects on others than on the self. For example, research has documented that perceived exposure impacts perceived media influence on others but not on the self (McLeod, Detenber, & Eveland, 2001). Likewise, perceived relevance appears to have a stronger effect on perceived influence on others versus the self. Of particular importance here are studies comparing perceptions of media effects on different types of others (Scharrer, 2002). For example, when asking respondents to estimate the effects of exposure to pictures of fashion models on others' ideal body images, David, Morrison, Johnson, and Ross (2002) found that (in contrast to the social distance corollary) White participants perceived other Whites (but not themselves) to be *more* influenced than Black women when the race of the model was White. This finding may be accounted for by the perceived relevance of White models to other White women.

Summary. Research on TPPs has provided robust evidence for the tendency for individuals to believe that media have more harmful effects on others than on the self. A host of explanatory mechanisms have been provided to account for these differences, with motivational and cognitive explanations both garnering support. In general, this body of research suggests that these two explanations may play important roles in accounting for self-other differences, with estimates of influence on the self best accounted for in terms of motivation, and estimates of influence on others best accounted for in terms of cognitive mechanisms.

Thus far, our chapter has focused on the perceptual component of the third-person effect—reflecting that most research on the third-person effect to date has examined this component and the causes and mechanisms underlying it. Yet the reason for Davison's enthusiasm about TPPs was that he recognized the enormous ways in which these perceptions might impact the real world. However, only in recent years have scholars turned their attention to the behavioral consequences of people's biased perceptions of media coverage.

◆ The Behavioral Component: The Influence of Presumed Media Influence

The second component of the third-person effect, and possibly the reason it is called an "effect," suggests that people's perceptions of media influence may lead them to react in some way in response to their perceptions. These reactions, although often described as a behavioral component, can involve cognitive, perceptual, attitudinal, and other responses. This avenue of research received little attention to begin with, but in recent years, more and more research has been conducted that suggests that perceptions of media influence matter in a variety of contexts, from political communication, through parental mediation of harmful content, to health communication contexts. Taken together, these studies suggest that perceptions and beliefs about the effects of communication are sometimes very influential. This process is now also referred to as "the influence of presumed media influence" (Gunther & Storey, 2003).

The consequences of TPPs could be categorized in a variety of different ways. Our current perspective on these reactions leads us to propose three large categories: prevention, coordination, and normative influences.[1]

Prevention. Prevention reactions relate to the impulse to stop or limit the dissemination of an apparently harmful message. As Davison (1983) noted in his seminal piece, censorship offers what is perhaps the most interesting field for speculation about the role of the third-person effect in our lives:

> Insofar that faith and morals are concerned, at least, it is difficult to find a censor who will admit to having been adversely affected by the information whose dissemination is to be prohibited. Even the censor's friends are usually safe from pollution. It is the general public that must be protected. (p. 14)

Davison then provided an anecdote describing the abolition of censorship in the state of Maryland, accompanied by warnings by members of the Maryland State Board of Censors about the future morals of Maryland and the nation. The censors themselves, working on the Board for years, reported little or no influence personally despite watching large amounts of sexual and violent materials.

Consistent with Davison's predictions, research has documented that the more people perceive a strong negative influence of media on others, the more they support censorship. Support for message restrictions

as a result of perceived negative effects has been documented in various contexts, including pornography (Gunther, 1995), violence (Rojas, Shah, & Faber, 1996), and misogynic rap music (McLeod et al., 1997), and in particular when behavioral effects are considered (Hoffner et al., 1999). This set of findings has social implications, since it demonstrates that people may form their attitudes toward censorship and freedom of speech based on biased perceptions of negative media impact on others.

Although prevention reactions have by far received the most attention, it should be noted that what is typically measured is not "behavior" or even "behavioral intention," but rather an attitudinal construct—"support for restrictions." Moreover, it is noteworthy that TPPs are not as likely to predict support for censoring news (e.g., Salwen & Driscoll, 1997), perhaps because news effects are seen as less harmful or because Americans' attitudes toward freedom of speech are stronger in the political domain. Finally, it should be noted that a variety of individual traits (such as paternalism, conservatism, and source distrust) that are related to support for censorship may also underlie the perceptual component of the third-person effect (Andsager & White, 2007). Thus, more careful research needs to be conducted in order to rule out the possibility that the association between TPPs and support for message restrictions is, in fact, spurious.

Coordination. Whereas prevention reactions relate to situations in which future dissemination of a harmful message could possibly be prevented, the other two categories of behavioral responses relate to situations in which a message has already been disseminated. In these situations, the question then arises as to how to react to the fact that others have already been influenced. In the second category—coordination—the underlying principle is that information and accompanying inferences about others' behaviors or intentions are used to calculate how one's actions will interact with what others will do, and affect the chances of achieving one's goals. Sometimes it is advisable to avoid what others will do (e.g., not wearing what others will wear to an event). In other cases it is advisable to anticipate what others will do and preempt them (e.g., when investing in a stock whose value is anticipated to rise if others also decide to buy the same stock). In any case, anticipating how others will behave (as a result of media impact) provides a useful piece of information when people consider how their decisions will interact with the decisions of others.

Davison's (1983) article contained two examples of such coordination reactions. In the first, Davison noted that rumors and news reports cause fluctuations in the stock market because it is assumed that these reports "will cause others to sell (or buy) certain categories of shares; therefore, I will sell (or buy) in order to anticipate their actions" (p. 13). In the second example, Davison asserted that when media report of irregular supplies of consumer goods, people rush to the stores to get those goods the moment they hear about the anticipated shortage. According to Davison, as a result of assumed media impact, these people "want to stock up before the hoarders remove all goods from the shelves" (p. 13).

One empirical test examined the latter coordination hypothesis in the context of media reports of the millennium bug (Y2K) panic (Tewksbury, Moy, & Weis, 2004). This research found, in contrast to Davison's expectation, that respondents who perceived larger effects of media coverage on others compared with self were *less* (not more) likely to stockpile supplies of food, water, gasoline, and cash. Similarly, people who believed others to be more affected by newspaper coverage of earthquake predictions were somewhat *less* likely to report having taken steps to prepare their homes for the earthquake

(Atwood, 1994). Although several explanations for the contradictory findings were offered in each of the studies, it is again possible that some mechanism, such as biased optimism or some other self-serving mechanism, underlies both respondents' TPPs and their reports that they were not preparing for Y2K or the earthquake.

Coordination reactions have also been tested in the context of voting decisions (Tsfati & Cohen, 2007). Voters' perceptions regarding the influence of media on others were found to be related to their intention to vote strategically—that is, to vote for a party they favored less than their most preferred option. Namely, if news media are perceived to persuade other voters to switch their vote, it may be necessary to switch one's own vote to counterbalance the effects of media on others. The main explanation for this finding has to do with candidate or party viability: If media are seen to influence others by favoring the leading parties (or candidates), either through a positive tone or through providing those parties (or candidates) extensive and prominent coverage, voters supporting smaller parties may feel as if they are wasting their vote and may therefore switch their support to one of the leading parties.

It is possible to argue that those who are most prone to coordination reactions are politicians. As Gunther and Storey (2003) claim, "political figures, who are arguably more attentive to the drift of public sentiment than most people, may presume public opinion will follow from press coverage and may therefore take actions merely in anticipation of such media influence" (p. 213). In support of their claim, these authors cited evidence that some politicians started organizing public hearings about home health care fraud in Chicago when they heard the press was about to publish the story because they assumed the coverage would be influential on the public (Protess et al., 1991).

Normative influence. Whereas coordination reactions involve temporarily changing one's behavior for utility maximization processes, normative influences involve an active acceptance or defiance of deeper and more stable social norms. Perceiving that media promote, inadvertently or otherwise, the adoption of a social norm may cause individuals to *comply* with, and in other cases to act in *defiance* of, that norm. This assertion is consistent with psychological theories about group dynamics (Turner, 1991), social identity theory (Tajfel & Turner, 1986), and the theory of reasoned action (Ajzen & Fishbein, 1980). Each of these lines of research argues (at least in part) that our behavior is strongly influenced by the way we think others behave (descriptive norms), or by the way others expect us to behave (prescriptive norms), and our motivation to comply with these specific others. If perceptions of media influence shape our perception of social norms, then by definition, they indirectly shape any potential resulting compliance.

Compliance reactions have been documented in several settings. For example, the perceived influence of pro- and anti-smoking messages was found to be indirectly related to smoking initiation through perceived peer norms (Gunther, Bolt, Borzekowski, Liebhart, & Dillard, 2006). Studies of body image suggest that young people may change eating behaviors because of their perceptions of media influence on normative attitudes toward the ideal body type (Milkie, 1999). Likewise, adolescents perceiving that sexual messages on TV make their peers more permissive toward sex are significantly more likely to hold more permissive sexual attitudes themselves (presumably to comply with the perceived social norm), with these attitudes affecting their behavioral intentions to engage in sexual activities (Chia, 2006).

The most well-known work relating to normative influences resulting from perceptions of media impact is no doubt

Noelle-Neumann's (e.g., 1993) spiral of silence theory. Noelle-Neumann's model implies that people may not express their personal opinions because they feel that news media cause *other* people to hold *contrary* opinions (for a discussion and evidence about the spiral of silence in the third-person effect context, see Mutz, 1989). In this case, presumed media influence is the underlying cause of a normative reaction called "withdrawal" (Gunther, Perloff, & Tsfati, 2008), referring to situations in which compliance with a social norm causes people *not* to do something they would have done otherwise. Withdrawal reactions were documented in an Israeli study about residents of peripheral towns (Tsfati & Cohen, 2003). The more the residents thought that media coverage would cause other people to think negatively of their community, the more they considered relocation. This was the case even when controlling for a variety of social, demographic, and life satisfaction factors. In a related study that considered the reactions to the perceived influence of negative coverage when mobility was not an option, minority members (Arab Israeli citizens) who believed in the strong influence of biased majority (Jewish-Israeli) media coverage felt stigmatized and alienated from mainstream society (Tsfati, 2007), a reaction that could also be categorized as a type of (perhaps involuntary) withdrawal.

In contrast to withdrawal, at other times, individuals who believe that media influence the norms and opinions of others will react in *defiance* of those perceived trends. For example, the more that right-wing Jewish settlers in the Gaza Strip believed that Israeli public opinion toward the settlements was heavily influenced by unfavorably biased media coverage, the more likely they were to report they would forcefully resist government efforts to evacuate them from their homes (Tsfati & Cohen, 2005). Likewise, in a sharply different context, doctors were more likely to refuse to prescribe certain drugs when they perceived that DTC prescription drug advertising had negative effects on their clients (Huh & Langteau, 2007). These doctors were probably defying what they saw as inappropriate media influence on patient expectations, or the norm (cultivated by the growing visibility of DTC ads) that advertising helps patients in making health-related decisions.

Factors determining behavioral reactions. When do people comply with the norms apparently fostered by media, and when do they defy these norms? These questions have not yet received an answer in current research. Still, it is probable that the variables explaining normative influence include the degree of ideological commitment for or against the norm, and self-efficacy—that is, the perception that an individual reaction to the norm will bear fruit. Whether defiance or compliance are even options for the individual is also part of the answer. After all, sometimes people cannot easily change their behaviors (e.g., quit smoking or establish antimedia protest groups), let alone their demographic affiliation, in response to perceptions of media impact. For example, it is clearly not an option to change one's racial affiliation in response to perceptions of media influence on racial stereotypes.

And what about the more general categories of prevention, coordination, and normative influence? What gives rise to these general types of reactions? It might be that the consequences of presumed media influence are dependent on their antecedents. Most research on the behavioral component finds that it is perceived influence on others, rather than the perceptual difference between self and others, that is related to the outcome variables (perhaps with the exception of prevention reactions). Integrating this observation with our earlier conclusion that people's perceptions of media influence on others are accounted for more strongly by cognitive explanations (compared with motivational

mechanisms for self-perceptions) may imply that the behavioral component is grounded more strongly in cognitive processes than perceptual biases. If this view is correct, then the "effect" in the third-person effect should be viewed as stemming from people's best attempts to get an accurate grasp on reality, and their accommodating responses, and not from an irrational set of self-protective biases.

◆ Lingering Questions and Future Directions

Research on the TPP has revealed robust findings across a variety of issues and for a diversity of populations. Further, explorations of the mechanisms that lead to these perceptions and the outcomes these perceptions have on individuals' attitudes and behaviors have drawn from and complemented many theories in the discipline. At the same time, however, numerous questions remain that call for additional investigation.

For example, a major threat to the validity of findings in the current literature on the behavioral component may be that they stem from spurious correlations. It is possible that, as argued earlier, the motivational causes of the TPP independently contribute to the outcome variables, especially in the case of prevention. For example, paternalism can cause both TPPs and a willingness to espouse censorship; self-enhancing motivations may underlie both TPPs and reporting that one does not intend to prepare for Y2K, and so forth.

Questions about causal order also linger in many TPP studies. It is possible that the outcome variable is the cause, and not the outcome, of people's perceptions of media influence. For example, a recent study found that legislators' perceptions of media influence are related to the amount of effort they spend on obtaining coverage, and consequently on their actual coverage, as documented by content analysis (Cohen, Tsfati, & Sheafer, 2008). However, politicians may assign media little or no importance or influence because they do not appear in media (and not the other way around). Consistent with the reasoning of TPP research, some recent evidence has convincingly demonstrated that perceived effectiveness causes actual effectiveness (rather than the reverse) in the related domain of persuasion (Dillard, Shen, & Vail, 2007). However, experimental investigations manipulating people's perceptions of media influence, followed by measurement of their consequent behaviors, will be pivotal in establishing the causal mechanism behind the association between presumed media influence and behavioral intentions and attitudes.

Future studies in the area should thus focus on establishing causality between the perceptual component and the behavioral outcome, and on addressing the possibility of spuriousness by using tighter controls. Equally important, given that attitudes and perceptions are not always strong predictors of behaviors, are studies using more direct measures of actual behavior that will increase our confidence that perceptions of media impact really matter. Twenty-five years after the publication of Davison's original piece, it is important to keep in mind that the essence of his argument lies with the notion that TPPs shape people's actions.

Virtually all of the hundreds of studies of the TPP and its consequences occur in the context of traditional media channels. Another provocative question for further research is how this model will play on the contemporary stage of new electronic forms of communication. In traditional media formats—film, television, newspapers, and magazines—perceptions of influence were necessarily and largely based on mere inference. But new electronic technologies introduce a new element to this process. When a student clicks on a book purchase at Amazon.com, or rearranges her queue of Netflix movies, these clicks instantly produce additional information—information about what "other people" or "other people like you" thought about the selection. Similar information about the choices, thoughts, and attitudes of others is a by-product of many online transactions—from reactions to blog posts to the purchase of virtually any online product, to voting for the next American Idol. Hence, the online individual has new and different kinds of information from which to infer the thoughts, opinions, and behaviors of others. These are still inferences, to be sure—inferences vulnerable to errors like the law-of-small-numbers bias. But they are inferences potentially shaped by a technology that gives us all a new and far more interactive connection to the public sphere. And this connection may have significant effects on the perception of others that forms the critical fulcrum point in the TPP process.

After years of focusing on the construct of attitudes in psychological research on persuasion, social psychologists have realized that the utility of attitude rests largely on its ability to predict and explain behaviors, and that the attitude-behavior link is not self-evident (Stiff & Mongeau, 2003). Consequently, social-psychological research has shifted attention to deciphering under what conditions attitudes do matter for behavior. This is exactly the kind of shift we think would be most fruitful for future TPP research. TPP studies, many of which replicate a set of robust effects, have proliferated in recent years (Bryant & Miron, 2004). Among these many scores of studies are some with tantalizing hints of important consequences. The challenge for future research is to provide a clearer understanding, and more decisive causal evidence, of behavioral effects of presumed influence in various communication technologies. Facing this challenge may more fully realize the potential of Davison's idea as a sophisticated but also substantial theory of media effects.

◆ Note

1. In earlier reviews, we have proposed alternative categories of outcomes (see Gunther, Perloff, & Tsfati, 2008). In these attempts, we have found categorization to be a fickle exercise, sometimes faithful but more often capricious and imprecise. Even imperfect categorization, however, can be useful for conceptual and theoretical purposes.

◆ References

Andsager, J., & White, H. A. (2007). *Self versus others: Media, messages, and the third-person effect.* Mahwah, NJ: Erlbaum.

Ajzen, I., & Fishbein, M. (1980). *Understanding attitudes and predicting social behavior.* Englewood Cliffs, NJ: Prentice Hall.

Atwood, L. E. (1994). Illusions of power: The third-person effect. *Journalism Quarterly, 71,* 269–281.

Bryant, J., & Miron, D. (2004). Theory and research in mass communication. *Journal of Communication, 54,* 662–704.

Chia, S. (2006). How peers mediate media influence on adolescents' sexual attitudes and sexual behavior. *Journal of Communication, 56,* 585–606.

Cohen, J., Mutz, D., Price, V., & Gunther, A. (1988). Perceived impact of defamation. *Public Opinion Quarterly, 52,* 161–173.

Cohen, J., Tsfati, Y., & Sheafer, T. (2008). The influence of presumed media influence in politics: Do politicians' perceptions of media impact matter? *Public Opinion Quarterly, 72,* 331–344.

David, P., Morrison, G., Johnson, M. A., & Ross, F. (2002). Body image, race and fashion models: Social distance and social identification in third-person effects. *Communication Research, 29,* 270–294.

Davison, W. P. (1983). The third-person effect in communication. *Public Opinion Quarterly, 47,* 1–15.

Dillard, J. P., Shen, L., & Vail, R. G. (2007). Does perceived message effectiveness cause persuasion or vice versa? *Human Communication Research, 33,* 467–488.

Duck, J. M., & Mullin, B. (1995). The perceived impact of the mass media: Reconsidering the third-person effect. *European Journal of Social Psychology, 25,* 77–93.

Duck, J. M., Terry, D. J., & Hogg, M. A. (1996). The perceived influence of AIDS advertising: Third-person effects in the context of positive media content. *Basic & Applied Social Psychology, 17,* 305–325.

Elder, T. Y., Douglas, K. M., & Sutton, R. M. (2006). Perceptions of social influence when messages favor "us" versus "them": A closer look at the social distance effect. *European Journal of Social Psychology, 36,* 353–365.

Eveland, W. P., Jr., Nathanson, A. I., Detenber, B. H., & McLeod, D. M. (1999). Rethinking the social distance corollary: Perceived likelihood of exposure and the third-person effect. *Communication Research, 26,* 275–302.

Gunther, A. C. (1991). What we think others think: Cause and consequence in the third-person effect. *Communication Research, 18,* 355–372.

Gunther, A. C. (1995). Overrating the X-rating: The third-person perception and support for censorship of pornography. *Journal of Communication, 45*(1), 27–38.

Gunther, A. C., Bolt, D., Borzekowski, D. L. B., Liebhart, J. L., & Dillard, J. P. (2006). Presumed influence on peer norms: How mass media indirectly affect adolescent smoking. *Journal of Communication, 56,* 52–68.

Gunther, A. C., & Hwa, A. P. (1996). Public perceptions of television influence and opinions about censorship in Singapore. *International Journal of Public Opinion Research, 8,* 248–265.

Gunther, A. C., & Mundy, P. (1993). Biased optimism and the third-person effect. *Journalism Quarterly, 70,* 58–67.

Gunther, A. C., Perloff, R. M., & Tsfati, Y. (2008). Public opinion and the third-person effect. In W. Donsbach & M. Traugott (Eds.), *Handbook of public opinion research* (pp. 184–191). Thousand Oaks, CA: Sage.

Gunther, A. C., & Storey, J. D. (2003). The influence of presumed influence. *Journal of Communication, 53,* 199–215.

Heider, F. (1958). *The psychology of interpersonal relations.* New York: Wiley.

Hoffner, C., Buchanan, M., Anderson, J. D., Hubbs, L. A., Kamigaki, S. K., Kowalczyk, L., et al. (1999). Support for censorship of television violence: The role of third-person effect and news exposure. *Communication Research, 26,* 726–742.

Huh, J., & Langteau, R. (2007). Presumed influence of DTC prescription drug advertising on patients: Physicians' perspective. *Journal of Advertising, 36*(3), 151–172.

Jensen, J. D., & Hurley, R. J. (2005). Third-person effects and the environment: Social distance, social desirability and presumed behavior. *Journal of Communication, 55,* 242–256.

Lazarsfeld, P. F., & Merton, R. K. (1971). Mass communication, social taste and organized social action. In W. Schramm & D. F. Roberts (Eds.), *The process and effects of mass communication* (Rev. ed., pp. 554–578). New York: Harper & Row. (Original work published 1948)

McLeod, D. M., Detenber, B. H., & Eveland, W. P., Jr. (2001). Behind the third-person effect: Differentiating perceptual processes for self and others. *Journal of Communication, 51,* 678–695.

McLeod, D. M., Eveland, W. P., Jr., & Nathanson, A. I. (1997). Support for censorship of violent and misogynic rap lyrics. *Communication Research, 24,* 153–174.

Meirick, P. C. (2005). Self-enhancement motivation as a third variable in the relationship between first- and third-person effects. *International Journal of Public Opinion Research, 17,* 473–483.

Milkie, M. A. (1999). Social comparisons, reflected appraisals, and mass media: The impact of pervasive beauty images on Black and White girls' self-concepts. *Social Psychology Quarterly, 62,* 190–210.

Mutz, D. C. (1989). The influence of perceptions of media influence: Third-person effects and public expression of opinions. *International Journal of Public Opinion Research, 1,* 3–23.

Noelle-Neumann, E. (1993). *The spiral of silence: Public opinion—Our social skin.* (2nd ed.). Chicago: University of Chicago Press.

Noelle-Neumann, E., & Peterson, T. (2004). The spiral of silence and the social nature of man. In L. L. Kaid (Ed.), *Political communication research* (pp. 339–356). Mahwah, NJ: Erlbaum.

Paul, B., Salwen, M. B., & Dupagne, M. (2000). The third-person effect: A meta-analysis of the perceptual hypothesis. *Mass Communication & Society, 3,* 57–85.

Perloff, R. M. (2002). The third-person effect. In J. Bryant & D. Zillmann (Eds.), *Media effects: Advances in theory and research* (2nd ed., pp. 489–506). Mahwah, NJ: Erlbaum.

Perse, E. (2001). *Media effects and society.* Mahwah, NJ: Erlbaum.

Peterson, C. R., & Beach, L. R. (1967). Man as an intuitive statistician. *Psychological Bulletin, 68,* 29–45.

Protess, D. L., Cook, F. L., Doppelt, J. C., Ettema, J. S., Gordon, M. T., Leff, D. R., et al. (1991). *The journalism of outrage: Investigative reporting and agenda building in America.* New York: Guilford Press.

Reid, S. A., Byrne, S., Brundidge, J. S., Shoham, M. D., & Marlow, M. L. (2007). A critical test of self-enhancement, exposure, and self-categorization explanations for first- and third-person perceptions. *Human Communication Research, 33,* 143–162.

Rojas, H., Shah, D. V., & Faber, R. J. (1996). For the good of others: Censorship and the third-person effect. *International Journal of Public Opinion Research, 8,* 163–186.

Rucinski, D., & Salmon, C. T. (1990). The "other" as the vulnerable voter: A study of the third person effect in the 1988 U.S. presidential campaign. *International Journal of Public Opinion Research, 2,* 345–368.

Salwen, M. B., & Driscoll, P. D. (1997). Consequences of third-person perception in support of press restrictions in the O. J. Simpson trial. *Journal of Communication, 47*(2), 60–75.

Salwen, M. B., & Dupagne, M. (2003). News of Y2K and experiencing Y2K: Exploring the relationship between the third-person effect and optimistic bias. *Media Psychology, 5,* 57–82.

Scharrer, E. (2002). Third-person perception and television violence: The role of outgroup stereotyping in perceptions of susceptibility to effect. *Communication Research, 29,* 681–704.

Shah, D. V., Faber, R. J., & Youn, S. (1999). Susceptibility and severity: Perceptual dimensions underlying the third-person effect. *Communication Research, 26,* 240–267.

Stiff, J. B., & Mongeau, P. A. (2003). *Persuasive communication.* New York: Guilford.

Tajfel, H., & Turner, J. C. (1986). The social identity theory of intergroup behavior. In S. W. Worchel & W. Austin (Eds.), *Psychology of intergroup relations* (pp. 7–24). Chicago: Nelson-Hall.

Tal-Or, N. (2007). Age and third person perception in response to positive product advertisements. *Mass Communication & Society, 10,* 403–422.

Tal-Or, N., & Drukman, D. (2008). *Third person perception as an impression management tactic.* Paper presented at the annual conference of the International Communication Association, Montreal, Canada.

Tal-Or, N., & Tsfati, Y. (2007). On the substitutability of third-person perceptions. *Media Psychology, 10,* 231–249.

Taylor, S. E., & Brown, J. D. (1988). Illusion and well-being: A social psychological perspective on mental health. *Psychological Bulletin, 103,* 193–210.

Tesser, A., Martin, L. L., & Cornell, D. P. (1996). On the substitutability of self-protective mechanisms. In P. M. Gollwitzer & J. A. Bargh (Eds.), *The psychology of action* (pp. 48–68). New York: Guilford.

Tewksbury, D., Moy, P., & Weis, D. S. (2004). Preparations for Y2K: Revisiting the behavioral component of the third-person effect. *Journal of Communication, 54,* 138–155.

Tsfati, Y. (2007). Hostile media perceptions, presumed media influence, and minority alienation: The case of Arabs in Israel. *Journal of Communication, 57,* 632–651.

Tsfati, Y., & Cohen, J. (2003). On the effect of the "third-person effect": Perceived influence of media coverage and residential mobility intentions. *Journal of Communication, 53,* 711–727.

Tsfati, Y., & Cohen, J. (2004). Object-subject distance and the third-person perception. *Media Psychology, 6,* 335–362.

Tsfati, Y., & Cohen, J. (2005). The influence of presumed media influence on democratic legitimacy: The case of Gaza settlers. *Communication Research, 32,* 794–821.

Tsfati, Y., & Cohen, J. (2007, November). *The influence of presumed media influence on strategic voting: Evidence from the Israeli 2003 and 2006 elections.* Paper presented at the annual convention of the National Communication Association, Chicago.

Turner, J. C. (1991). *Social influence.* Pacific Grove, CA: Brooks/Cole.

Turner, J. C., Hogg, M. A., Oakes, P. J., Reicher, S. D., & Wetherell, M. S. (1987). *Rediscovering the social group: A self-categorization.* Oxford, UK: Blackwell.

Tyler, T. R., & Devinitz, V. (1981). Self-serving bias in attribution of responsibility: Cognitive versus motivational explanation. *Journal of Experimental Social Psychology, 17,* 408–416.

White, H. A. (1997). Considering interacting factors in the third-person effect: Argument strength and social distance. *Journalism & Mass Communication Quarterly, 74,* 557–564.

8

NEWS AND POLITICS

◆ Vincent Price and Lauren Feldman

Since their inception, theories of democracy have placed a premium on open systems of communication to and among citizens. The ideal system is generally framed as one capable of delivering news and fostering public debate that is open to popular participation, free flowing and uncensored, and well informed (e.g., Habermas, 1962/1989). How successfully the press measures up to these ideals is a matter of continuing concern and has motivated much of the research on the effects of news, particularly as related to politics. Does the press offer citizens a "truthful, comprehensive, and intelligent account of the day's events," as urged by the Commission of Freedom of the Press more than a half-century ago (Hutchins, 1947, p. 21)? What do people learn from the news? How do the news media alter audience perceptions of political issues, candidates, or other political figures or movements? What role does the news play in shaping the public agenda, or more pointedly, in persuading citizens to support particular political parties, candidates, or policy proposals?

Despite more than a century of empirical study of news and politics (e.g., Wilcox, 1900), most related insights are a product of the last four decades. Although the research terrain is vast and dotted with numerous interesting landscapes, our aim in this chapter is to give readers a sense of the key questions addressed by scholars, some of their general conclusions to date, and where research is headed given recent and dramatic changes in the news media environment flowing from the digital revolution in communication technologies. We begin with research on the content of news—politics and public affairs content in particular—and the forces that shape its presentation. Next, we turn to the effects of news in terms of both persuasion and learning. We then consider some of the central methodological and conceptual issues confronting scholars of news and politics, highlighting the key theoretical models used to guide empirical inquiry. We conclude by taking stock of the rapidly changing contemporary media environment and its impact on the news, and weigh some of the principal implications of these changes for future research.

◆ Constructing the News

Scholars have examined a wide array of phenomena that shape the construction of "news" as a media product (see Bennett, 2005), including journalists' values, ethics, and backgrounds; organizational influences, principally news-gathering routines; economic pressures (e.g., cost, efficiency, and advertising potential); cultural and ideological perspectives; and information and communication technologies that influence the speed and nature of news production and distribution (see Shoemaker & Reese, 1996, for a review). With this in mind, many analysts agree that news stories reflect a relatively small but well-defined set of "news values," or characteristics of events—conflict, drama, personalization, local interest, timeliness, and novelty—that are thought to be particularly appealing to audiences (see Bennett, 2005; Patterson, 1993).

NEWS BIASES

Most scholars operate from the assumption that news is socially constructed as a (usually commercial) product, and as such does not reflect a veridical presentation of an objective reality. Out of the constant flow of events and actions available as potential news, only certain items can be selected for treatment, and these are unavoidably framed—understood and reported—in distinctive ways. The study of news content is thus an effort to understand the particular biases reflected in the packaging of news, and the forces that underlie those biases.

Political partisan bias. One of the most persistent and long-standing concerns about the news is that it reflects either a politically liberal or conservative bias. Despite the popularity of monikers such as "the liberal media," there is little empirical evidence of systematic partisan bias in mainstream news outlets (e.g., Hofstetter, 1976; Niven, 2002; though, as noted in the following paragraphs, recent changes in the news marketplace may be calling this into question). Still, research has found ample evidence that audiences commonly *perceive* the news as biased and hostile to their personal views (Tal-Or, Tsfati, & Gunther, Chapter 7, this volume; Vallone, Ross, & Lepper, 1985).

Structural information biases. More typical than partisan bias and, in the eyes of many analysts, more far-reaching in their effects are various subtle biases in the structure of news, often rooted in news values or organizational practices. As Bennett (2005) has argued, the news typically displays inordinate *personalization, fragmentation,* and *dramatization.* For example, Iyengar's (1991) analysis of television news revealed that it tends to disproportionately depict issues as discrete, concrete instances or events ("episodic frame") as opposed to providing broader context in terms of historical background, policy debates, or collective outcomes ("thematic frame"). Relatedly, Cappella and Jamieson (1997) demonstrated that news about elections routinely emphasizes self-interested motivations of politicians and horse-race aspects of political contests ("strategy frame") as opposed to focusing on problems and solutions that stress mutual interest ("issue frame;" see also Patterson, 1993).

Bennett (2005) also identifies a fourth characteristic of the news, *normalization,* in which a somewhat narrow set of middle-of-the-road viewpoints tends to dominate discourse around most political issues. This tendency stems in part from the journalistic ideal of objectivity, which in practice tends to equate objectivity with balance, operationally defined as finding sources to speak for "both sides" of issues. The speakers most readily available to journalists are official sources. Thus, the range of voices and viewpoints in the news are "indexed" to the range of views prominent in government debate. In fact, Livingston and Bennett (2003) examined 8 years of international stories on CNN and found that, despite technological advancements that theoretically permit greater flexibility and editorial independence, news coverage nevertheless tends to incorporate an official response, even for unscripted, spontaneous events.

◆ The Impact of the News

From the earliest studies of news content, the effects of news exposure—usually of some problematic feature of the news in particular—has been of particular interest. At the turn of the 20th century, analyses of newspapers often focused on sensationalism, motivated primarily by worries about whether news might inadvertently foster crime, delinquency, or other antisocial behaviors (e.g., Fenton, 1910). In the realm of politics, the overriding concern has been whether news biases might, through more or less subtle means, persuade citizens to support particular viewpoints or candidates. Indeed, scholars have demonstrated that the persuasive effects of the news media often operate indirectly via the structuring or restructuring of cognitions and perceptions. Thus, outcomes like learning, issue perceptions, and engagement have also occupied a central place in research on the political impact of the news. At the

same time, scholars have recognized that the interpersonal contexts within which news exposure takes place are critical determinants of the media's influence and, accordingly, have incorporated measures of discussion into studies of news impact. This section reviews these various strands of research, highlighting what we believe to be the key findings and insights in each area.

POLITICAL PERSUASION

Some of the landmark studies of American mass media and their effects were carried out in connection with presidential election campaigns at midcentury (e.g., Berelson, Lazarsfeld, & McPhee, 1954; Lazarsfeld, Berelson, & Gaudet, 1944). These studies figure prominently in the historical development of media studies generally due to their unprecedented scope and scale, their deployment of the survey method and longitudinal designs in the context of ongoing campaigns, and, perhaps most of all, their suggestion that political decision making was driven by prior beliefs, not by media. A variety of factors—most notably the tendency of political messages to reach a limited audience of people already heavily engaged in the campaign (and hence already predisposed to particular candidates), the tendency of people to be exposed selectively to congenial communications, and the fact that people are generally embedded in supportive social networks and follow the lead of a small number of "opinion leaders" in those networks—all worked in tandem to limit the media's persuasive impact. Results from these early studies, as synthesized by Klapper (1960), indicated that the media functioned more as "an agent of reinforcement than an agent of change" (p. 15).

Limited or powerful effects? Klapper's (1960) synthesis, which became widely known as the limited effects model, was subsequently accepted by many and received further empirical support over the years (e.g., Finkel, 1993). However, Lazarsfeld and Merton (1948) argued that the media could indeed prove quite persuasive when conditions produced a shared, dominant message in the news (what they called *monopolization*), when this message resonates with other existing popular views or underlying dispositions (*canalization*), and when it meets with largely supportive face-to-face encounters (*supplementation*). The fact that the news media often carry conflicting messages that tend to be "heard" only by the more sophisticated audience members may naturally limit effects; however, under the right conditions, a more coherent and consistent message may be distributed to a larger and less resistant audience, thereby magnifying effects. Along these lines, Zaller (1992) demonstrated powerful media effects in instances when the message of one candidate is "louder" or more intense than the other. Identifying such effects, argued Zaller (1996), requires strong measures of news message reception, and an analytical model capable of capturing nonlinear effects of news messages, given that those most susceptible to effects are those sufficiently aware of politics to be interested but not so strongly engaged that they are resistant to change. Thus, as Bartels (1993, p. 267) put it, "the persuasive effects of the mass media may be more fugitive than minimal."

LEARNING FROM NEWS

Even more basic than attitudinal effects of news exposure are "simple" effects on knowledge—that is, recall and recognition of factual information from political news stories. How much do audiences learn (or fail to learn) from the news and public affairs information they consume? Given the value placed by many democratic theories on an informed citizenry, research on learning from the news has long held a central place in the study of journalism.

Knowledge gaps. Consistent with the early findings from election studies that the diffusion of political information is often shallow and restricted to those with strong interests in public affairs, Tichenor, Donohue, and Olien (1970) found persistent "knowledge gaps" in information distribution, such that the more advantaged segments of the population—those of higher socioeconomic status (SES) and who are better educated than their peers—tend to acquire news at a faster rate. As a result, any influx of new information into a social system will tend to exacerbate existing status-based differences in knowledge. Even sharper evidence of such widening gaps in news acquisition is obtained when prior public affairs knowledge is considered in place of education or SES (Price & Zaller, 1993). Although prior knowledge and social location regularly predict success in learning from the news, audience motivations also matter. Eveland (2001) found that surveillance motivations increase knowledge gain, and Kwak (1999) found that knowledge gap effects are mitigated in the presence of strong interest in the topics covered.

Differences across media. Given the array of news media available to the public, differences in learning across alternative media have been carefully examined. In general, newspaper reading has emerged as a better predictor of learning than TV news viewing (e.g., Robinson & Levy, 1986). However, when attention is considered in addition to exposure, TV performs on par with or better than newspapers (e.g., Chaffee & Schleuder, 1986; Price & Zaller, 1993). The rise of online news consumption has encouraged scholars to consider its impact on learning. Here, experimental studies suggest that news recognition and recall are higher for print than for online versions of newspapers (e.g., Althaus & Tewksbury, 2002; Tewksbury & Althaus, 2000), and survey research suggests a negligible role for Internet news use in political learning (e.g., Weaver & Drew, 2001).

As to "soft" news outlets that focus on entertainment and human interest (e.g., talk shows, infotainment programs, late-night comedy), available evidence suggests that these may not contribute much to public affairs knowledge as conventionally conceived, although exposure to soft news does appear to increase knowledge of topics prominently featured in such programming (Baum, 2003). Recent research has begun to more carefully differentiate between types of soft news programming. Among late-night comedy programs, Comedy Central's news satire, *The Daily Show With Jon Stewart,* has been found to rival traditional network and cable news in terms of its political substance (Fox, Koloen, & Sahin, 2007; Jones, 2007). Whether this translates into knowledge gain remains unclear: Experimental research indicates that while audiences do absorb some factual political content from *The Daily Show,* the learning benefits offered by traditional television news programs are significantly greater (Kim & Vishak, 2008).

Story features. The characteristics of a story, and the ways in which it is told, can also influence how much people learn from news. The amount of coverage given to a news story predicts how broadly it will be recognized and recalled (Price & Czilli, 1996). However, controlling for coverage, domestic news tends to be better remembered than foreign news (Gunter, 1985; Price & Czilli, 1996), as are stories that are personality based (Price & Czilli, 1996), and news that is psychologically close or personally relevant (Findahl & Hoijer, 1985).

The journalistic frame used to report a story can also affect learning. Strategic framing of candidate news stories appears to reduce story recognition (Valentino, Buhr, & Beckmann, 2001), and some evidence suggests that use of a human-interest frame reduces story recall relative to other types of news frames (Valkenburg, Semetko, & de Vreese, 1999). These effects presumably stem from variations in cognitive responses to a news story, which tend to mirror the frame used in that news story (e.g., Price, Tewksbury, & Powers, 1997; Valkenburg et al., 1999).

Finally, production features employed in news reporting can influence learning outcomes. Tabloid-style production features (e.g., sound effects, flash frame transitions, dramatic reporter voice tone) increase arousal and attention but do not necessarily improve learning (e.g., Grabe, Lang, & Zhao, 2003). Rapid pacing decreases recognition and recall, relative to slow or medium pacing (Lang, Bolls, Potter, & Kawahara, 1999). On the other hand, audio-video redundancy—a match between what is pictured and what is reported verbally—improves learning (e.g., Zhou, 2004). Interactivity—one of the hallmarks of the new media environment—may produce confusion (Bucy, 2004) and interfere with learning from online news (e.g., Eveland, Cortese, Park, & Dunwoody, 2004).

PERCEPTIONS OF ISSUES

Situated between basic learning effects and persuasion are a variety of other cognitive effects of news, many of which have proven to be politically consequential. As Price and Tewksbury (1997) noted, a cognitive turn in the social sciences in the 1980s produced within communication research a burgeoning interest in information-processing approaches to the news, highlighting various indirect influences of the news on public opinion operating through basic perceptions of issues shaped by patterns of coverage.

Agenda setting. Cohen (1963, p. 16) argued that, even if the media are not successful in telling people what to think, they are "stunningly" successful in telling people "what to think about." This ability of the news media to set the public agenda became the subject of systematic empirical scrutiny with the work of McCombs and Shaw (1972), who found that the salience of topics presented in the news was strongly correlated with the importance accorded those issues among the electorate. Research has subsequently demonstrated the agenda-setting effect of news media through both experiments (e.g., Iyengar & Kinder, 1987) and surveys, including time-series studies (e.g., Brosius & Kepplinger, 1990; Zhu, Watt, Snyder, & Yan, 1993).

While many agenda-setting studies focus on influences flowing from news media to the general public, some research has examined the ways in which political agendas are constructed through the interaction of political leaders, policymakers, and journalists (e.g., Lang & Lang, 1983) and, in some instances, their active collaboration (e.g., Cook et al., 1983). These studies, usually more sociological than psychological in orientation, conceive of the process as one of "agenda building" over time, flowing through institutional channels of political power, and mediating among myriad interests of politicians, interest groups, journalists, and news audiences.

Issue priming. Agenda setting is politically consequential because public concern over issues can facilitate or stymie elite political action; and for this reason, desire for control of the public agenda often engenders a hotly contested battle waged through and with the news media. It is further consequential because perceptions of issue importance can, in turn, shape citizens' evaluations. Iyengar and Kinder (1987) proposed that media coverage, by affecting the importance people attach to various issues, exerts a priming effect on political judgments by increasing accessibility of certain issues, and thoughts about those issues, in memory. A series of experiments by Iyengar and Kinder confirmed this proposition, as have a number of subsequent investigations. Recently, Althaus and Kim (2006) provided quasi-experimental evidence that news issue priming in complex information environments is a function not only of construct accessibility but also of construct applicability (that is, a judgment that a particular idea is applicable to the issue at hand), and that priming effects can stem from cumulative as well as recent exposure to news (see Roskos-Ewoldsen & Roskos-Ewoldsen, Chapter 12, this volume).

Issue framing. A third consequential impact that news can have on the public perception of issues has been called *framing,* which refers to the ability of news frames to direct attention to certain aspects of an issue, thereby increasing the likelihood that those aspects will enter into considerations and evaluations of the issue at hand (Cappella & Jamieson, 1997; Price & Tewksbury, 1997). Animated by concern over information biases in the structure of news, scholars have coupled content analyses of news frames with careful, usually experimental, studies of the way audiences respond to differently framed news stories. For example, Iyengar (1991) found that episodic framing, which highlights discrete events and individuals and often emphasizes human interest, induced news audiences to attribute responsibility for problems, like crime and poverty, to individuals, whereas thematic framing led audiences to attribute responsibility to societal factors. Cappella and Jamieson (1997) found that strategic news frames, which focus on the self-interested motivations of politicians and the horse-race aspects of political races, activated, and contributed to, political cynicism. Research has also shown that framing issues in terms of conflict between identifiable social groups can trigger social identification with those groups, in some cases polarizing audience opinions on those matters (e.g., Price, 1989; Valentino, Hutchings, & White, 2002). Still, the impact of news frames is unlikely to be uniform, and a host of individual characteristics, message features, and contextual factors have been identified to help explain the conditional nature of framing effects (see Shah, McLeod, Gotlieb, & Lee, Chapter 6, this volume).

Perceived climate of public opinion. In covering public affairs, journalists often convey not only details about events and political actors but also information about how the public responds to those events. Scholars have thus devoted considerable attention to examining popular perceptions of public opinion surrounding political issues, the ways these perceptions are affected by news, and the ways they might be implicated in opinion formation or change. Most notably, Noelle-Neumann (1974, 1993) proposed that people naturally monitor the surrounding climate of public opinion and use their sense of what other people think to guide their interpersonal interactions (e.g., whether or not to speak their mind on a controversial matter in a social setting). The media, Noelle-Neumann proposed, subtly convey impressions of which side is winning debates over public issues, or which candidate is gaining or losing ground in an election, and through these media representations, people form their perceptions of whether they are in the majority or on the winning side, or not. The general proposition that people learn about collective opinion from the media has been amply confirmed (e.g., Mutz, 1998), even though Noelle-Neumann's more distinctive proposition that these perceptions can trigger a withdrawal of the minority from asserting their views and trigger a "spiral of silence" has met with less consistent support (see Glynn, Hayes, & Shanahan, 1997, for a review).

POLITICAL ENGAGEMENT

Journalists often aspire not merely to inform but to engage audiences in politics. This goal has proven challenging, however, both because wide swaths of the population are typically neither attentive to nor active in politics and public affairs (Converse, 1964) and also because, critics argue, news gathering and production practices can work at cross-purposes with engaging typical citizens (e.g., Entman, 1989). Television news—with its tendencies toward superficial, "sound-bite" coverage of politics (Hallin, 1992)—has been singled out for its potential to breed cynicism and undermine political trust. For example, M. J. Robinson (1976) proposed that reliance on TV for political affairs information leads to greater mistrust of government, what has been dubbed the "videomalaise" hypothesis. Findings to date have been mixed. Some research has found that television exposure and public affairs media use are unrelated to political trust (e.g., Bennett, Rhine, Flickinger, & Bennett, 1999). However, specific types of news coverage—in particular, the strategic framing of issues (Cappella & Jamieson, 1997)—have indeed been found to contribute to political cynicism.

More generally, scholars have probed the possible connections between media use, social trust, and civic activity. Most prominently, Putnam (1995) marshaled a variety of survey data to show that America had seen a steady erosion of social capital in the final decades of the 20th century (reflected in decreasing social trust, interpersonal networks, and civic engagement); and he argued that these trends stemmed, at least in large part, from the introduction and diffusion of television. Putnam's thesis has been greeted with considerable debate, however; and whether or not lower social capital is linked to overall consumption of television, it does not seem to apply to citizens who consume televised public affairs programming (see Norris, 1996). Further, others argue that it is the motivations behind media use that determine its influence on trust. For example, Shah, Kwak, and Holbert (2001) found that the use of newspapers for hard news and the use of the Internet for information exchange were positively associated with trust.

THE INTERPLAY OF MASS AND INTERPERSONAL COMMUNICATION

Throughout the history of research on news and politics, scholars have recognized that media use does not occur in a vacuum and that a proper accounting of the effects of news must consider the interplay of interpersonal and mass-mediated influences. With the advent of newer, interactive communication technologies, these connections have become all the more relevant. Early studies, particularly those in electoral contexts, tended to frame face-to-face discussions as obstacles to media influence, constituting strong social filters through which media messages must flow. However, discussion networks can be complementary as well. Chaffee (1986) has argued that the relationship between discussion and media use is cyclical and reciprocal, and that "the most likely 'effect' of communication . . . is further communication" (p. 76).

Opinion leadership by centrally placed individuals in social networks has long been recognized in research, with the diffusion of news conceptualized as a two-step flow—from the news media to attentive "opinion leaders," and then from these leaders to the less active members of society (Katz & Lazarsfeld, 1955). Although widely broadcast messages can certainly flow directly to mass audiences without such intermediation (J. P. Robinson, 1976), often the news is indeed filtered through and interpreted by an influential minority, identifiable empirically through "strength of personality" scales and other means. Brosius and Weimann (1996) demonstrate, for instance, that the agenda-setting process is mediated by a two-step flow. In addition, recent research on learning from the news suggests that interpersonal discussion can sometimes bolster learning through supplementation and elaboration of news messages (Scheufele, 2002), or lead to countervailing messages and confusion, thus interfering with learning (Lenart, 1994).

Along these lines, Feldman and Price (2008) found that disagreement in discussion networks moderated the relationship between discussion and media use in predicting learning, and Druckman and Nelson (2003) showed experimentally that conversations including conflicting perspectives can undermine news-framing effects.

The political impact of the news is, then, far-reaching and varied, and is often contingent on characteristics of the audience, the news message, and the social environment. Whereas initial theorizing about media effects suggested that the power of the media necessarily resided in their ability to persuade audiences directly, the last several decades of political communication research have introduced a more nuanced view of how news influences citizens (i.e., by shaping the public's issue agenda, changing the standards by which citizens evaluate political actors, influencing popular perceptions of public opinion, etc.). Unfortunately, much of this research also indicates that the normative potential of the news media is not always realized. Learning from the news, for instance, is challenged by audience deficits in motivation and prior knowledge, as well as by editorial decisions that serve more to tantalize than inform. Likewise, structural biases in the news—such as focus on conflict, strategy, drama, and personal angles—can restrict citizens' interpretation of and engagement with political issues. To more clearly contextualize these myriad effects, we turn now to a consideration of the theoretical frameworks that have proven central to understanding the role of news in politics.

◆ Frameworks for Studying News and Politics

To a large extent, empirical study of news and politics has mirrored—and some might say has been central to establishing—the main trends in theory and conceptualization in the field of media effects generally (see Bryant & Zillmann, Chapter 1, this volume). Here we highlight just a few of the key frameworks that have characterized scholarship on news and politics over the years.

CONCEPTUALIZING THE NEWS AUDIENCE

Claims that a "hypodermic model" of communication dominated early studies of media effects—conceiving of messages as being "injected" into audiences without any interpretation on their part—are often overstated. Similarly, claims of a subsequent trend toward increasingly audience-centered and "active" conceptualizations of news readers and viewers have probably been overstated as well. Many contemporary experimental studies of news priming and framing, for example, implicitly cast news recipients in a passive role with their thinking directed, often without conscious knowledge, along certain lines promulgated by the media.

Regardless of historical fluctuations in the degree to which researchers have deployed relatively more passive or more active conceptualizations of the news audience, the latter models are generally more prominent. One long-recognized and consequential form of audience activity stems from established political attitudes, which can produce partisan selective exposure (e.g., Lazarsfeld & Merton, 1948; Stroud, 2008), perceptions of the media as hostile (Vallone et al., 1985), and processing of the news in line with prior predispositions—for instance, by actively counterarguing attitudinally incongruent information, while accepting without scrutiny attitudinally consistent information (a "disconfirmation bias," e.g., Lord, Ross, & Lepper, 1979).

Beyond such partisan motivations, people can be drawn to news media for a wide number of reasons, which may have much to do with the particular sorts of effects observed. Katz, Blumler, and Gurevitch (1974) argued that audiences are active in using media to satisfy their needs and achieve their goals, and that these must be properly understood to correctly identify likely outcomes. In line with this "uses and gratification" model (see Rubin, Chapter 10, this volume), Tewksbury (1999) demonstrated experimentally that people's processing goals (whether they were trying to evaluate candidates or merely pass the time) influence how they use and interpret information presented in the news. Though less invested in identifying motivations and needs, researchers who adopt a "constructivist" approach to the study of news and politics posit that news messages and their frames are only one contributor to popular understandings of politics as citizens actively construct political meaning from the news, drawing from their personal experience, peer influences, and cultural understandings (e.g., Gamson, 1992; Just et al., 1996).

THEORETICAL APPROACHES TO NEWS PROCESSING

Research on the effects of news has been heavily influenced by social-psychological models of persuasion, which it has adapted to political communication contexts. Evident in many contemporary writings on the news and its influence, for example, is McGuire's (e.g., 1985) notion of the "compensatory principal"—the idea that particular message inputs (e.g., the nature of the source or medium, the structure of the story, etc.) may have different and offsetting effects on various outputs (e.g., message exposure, attention, comprehension, or attitude change). A clear and well-documented instance of such offsetting effects appears in connection with the sophistication of the news viewer. For example, several studies have found that better-informed news consumers are more likely to be exposed to and understand a news message, but are less likely to alter their well-established opinions (e.g., Zaller, 1992).

Judgmental heuristics. Information-processing models have been influential in research on news and politics, most of them drawing from limited capacity theory (see Lang, Chapter 13, this volume) and its focus on the way people encode, store, and retrieve political messages. Particularly germane to politics are models positing that, to conserve cognitive resources in responding to news and forming opinions, most people—given their limited interest in public affairs—resort to using simplifying heuristics to make political judgments (Mondak, 1994). Using decision-making heuristics—principally following partisan cues or other elite signaling of group interests—affords ordinary citizens a means of achieving low-information rationality (Popkin, 1991) without the considerable investment of cognitive resources that would be required for careful, fulsome consideration of the pros and cons of various issue positions or candidates for office.

However, such judgmental heuristics are not without their biases, a number of which have been extensively researched. Among the best documented are biases toward readily available or easily accessible information. For instance, Zillmann and Brosius (2000) demonstrated that salient exemplars in news stories, such as anecdotes, photographs, and other particulars highlighted in news stories, are more influential than statistical base-rate information in shaping opinions on the issues reported. Relatedly, frequent repetition of issues in the news, or of particular themes in coverage of issues, has the effect of increasing the accessibility of those issues or themes in memory, thereby increasing the likelihood that these pieces of information will shape judgments. The accessibility bias has been one of the key explanations offered for agenda-setting, issue-priming, and issue-framing effects (e.g., Iyengar, 1991; Price & Tewksbury, 1997; but see Chong & Druckman, 2007, for alternative interpretations).

Dual-processing models. Given the long-documented presence of a minority of attentive, knowledgeable, and politically engaged citizens set against a large majority of far less interested and less well-informed audiences for news (Converse, 1964), it is perhaps natural that "dual-processing" models of information processing and persuasion would prove highly useful to scholars of political communication. The elaboration likelihood model (Petty & Cacioppo, 1986) and the heuristic-systematic model (Eagly & Chaiken, 1993), while they differ in their particulars, both posit that audiences who are motivated to follow public affairs will pay close attention to messages and their arguments, cognitively elaborate these messages with self-generated arguments and counterarguments, and systematically weigh all of these considerations; on the other hand, less interested news consumers will apply the sorts of cognitive shortcuts or heuristics described earlier in a relatively thoughtless manner. This is not to say that systematic processors are unbiased, however, as they will often apply a partisan schema in order to make sense of the news they receive (Graber, 1984).

Online versus memory-based processing. Another important distinction in the study of news and politics is between memory-based and online processing (e.g., Lavine, 2002). The former model, implicit in much of the literature on judgmental heuristics, assumes that when asked to make a political evaluation, people search their memories for relevant information, and whatever they call to mind directly contributes to their evaluation. Online processing (Lodge, McGraw, & Stroh, 1989) posits instead that people make political evaluations at the moment of exposure, store these evaluations as a kind of ongoing tally, and call up the tally—not message information per se—when making political decisions. If people recall global assessments of political actors and issues, and not the specific considerations that factored into those assessments, this would suggest that most people, who perform so poorly on tests of political knowledge (Delli Carpini & Keeter, 1996), can still make reasonably informed decisions.

◆ The Contemporary News Environment

Our understanding of news and politics rests today on an extraordinarily large and diverse body of empirical findings gathered over many decades. Nearly all of this research, however, reflects a world of political communication that may be rapidly becoming a thing of the past. The news media, as with mass media generally, have arguably undergone more profound transitions in the past 5 years than in the prior 50. In concluding this review, then, we consider recent changes in the news environment and their implications for research.

With the advent of digital signal transmission and storage technologies, expanded cable networks, and broadband Internet access, audiences today enjoy access to a much wider array of news and entertainment options than they did just a decade ago. The increased availability of consumer options has led to several quite striking trends in news audiences: newspaper readership declining at a steady rate, combined with dramatic losses of advertising revenues; growth in cable news at the expense of traditional broadcast news; burgeoning use of the Internet for obtaining news online; and the rise of many "soft news" alternatives drawing off sizable portions of the audience for traditional news formats (e.g., Pew Center, 2008; Project for Excellence in Journalism, 2008). As a result, news audiences are increasingly stratified by age, with older viewers and readers staying with the printed newspaper and broadcast news while younger cohorts splinter into myriad audiences for cable programming and online news and, increasingly, seek news through social networking sites (Pew Center, 2008).

Audiences are also becoming stratified by partisanship, with Republicans and conservatives migrating to conservatively oriented programming on radio and cable (e.g., Fox News), and the audiences for other outlets, such as MSNBC, becoming increasingly more Democratic and liberal (Pew Center, 2007a). Trust in news media has generally declined, and it has also become more partisan, with conservatives trusting like-minded outlets and distrusting those perceived as liberal, and the reverse pattern seen among liberals (Pew Center, 2007a). Despite the plethora of news outlets, however, one thing that has not changed is the overall level of public knowledge of public affairs, which remains low on average with high variability across segments of the audience (Pew Center, 2007b).

IMPLICATIONS FOR RESEARCH

While our basic models for understanding how news is processed remain unchanged, these profound shifts in the news environment have a number of important implications that will need to be addressed as we go forward. First, the multiplication of news outlets and myriad points of access to them leaves us with the basic problem of conceptualizing "news," which is no longer a homogeneous or clearly definable genre of communication. Which alternative sources of political information—late-night comedy, talk radio, blogs, cable punditry—count as "news"? Analysts increasingly question traditional distinctions between "soft" and "hard" news, and between "news" and "entertainment" (Delli Carpini & Williams, 2001; Holbert, 2005). For example, Comedy Central's *The Daily Show,* a comedic hybrid of news and entertainment, attracts a very knowledgeable audience and offers considerable information (Baym, 2005; Jones, 2007). It is thus essential that future research conceptualizes "news" more broadly, while also being careful to differentiate between the many political information sources available to citizens today.

Second, the study of news-consuming behavior has become far more complicated. In the increasingly complex communication environment, how do we measure "news" use? Implicit in many models of aggregate political effects (e.g., agenda setting, priming) are assumptions that consumers are exposed to a largely homogeneous news stream. Growth in media options and the availability of specialized content, however, lead to significantly greater opportunities for selective exposure based on audience motivations and gratification seeking. Mutz and Martin (2001) have demonstrated that when adequate choices are available, people tend to selectively expose themselves to media that are consonant with their political views, leading to concern about—and mounting evidence for—a political polarization of news audiences (e.g., Bimber & Davis, 2003; Jones, 2002). More fundamentally, audiences can more easily selectively expose themselves to different media as a function of political interest, such that those with minimal interest can avoid news altogether, leading to widening gaps in public affairs knowledge and political engagement (Prior, 2005). Thus, the "diet" of news consumed by any given individual becomes increasingly distinctive (Tewksbury, 2005) and difficult to detect. Just how specialized and fragmented such diets will become, however, remains the subject of research and debate (e.g., Lee, 2008; Reese, Rutigliano, Hyun, & Jeong, 2007). In any event, future research must strive to develop new measures of news use that appropriately capture the ways in which citizens are now engaging with political information in the contemporary media environment. Moreover, as traditional boundaries between information and entertainment continue to blur and news—particularly on cable and online—is infused with increasing amounts of opinion and ideology, audience motivations should be more carefully considered as a moderator of news effects. Whether political content is being used to inform or to entertain, to validate existing partisan predispositions or to open one's eyes to diverse viewpoints, is apt to have important implications for how audiences will be impacted by news and political information.

Last, the proliferation of alternative news outlets and blogs, along with various experiments in "citizen journalism" on the Web that draw upon ordinary people as amateur reporters, may presage a reduction in the traditional gatekeeping role of mainstream news media (Kovach & Rosenstiel, 2001; Rosen, 1999). Althaus and Tewksbury (2002) found that readers of the paper and online versions of the *New York Times* developed different issue agendas, likely due to the heightened selectivity permitted by the online version. Alternative news filters are emerging on the Internet, such as Slashdot.org and Indymedia.org (Bennett, 2004), and the rise of dialogic news on cable constitutes a threat to journalists' authority while reducing accountability for what is said on the airwaves (Ben-Porath, 2007). Again, however, the extent to which blogs or citizen-generated news outlets present news consumers with a new and distinctive form of editorial independence is unclear. Accordingly, future research should probe the ways in which online and especially user-created media are reconfiguring traditional gatekeeping roles, as well as examine the impact of these media on public knowledge, engagement, and opinion.

In sum, with a fertile and ever-changing modern media landscape, understanding the evolving character of news and how successfully it, as well as the citizens it serves, measures up to democratic ideals has arguably never been more critical. Fortunately, the scientific study of news, which blossomed in the latter half of the last century, is alive and well and poised to continue to illuminate our understanding of the effects of news on the electorate in the upcoming years.

◆ References

Althaus, S. L., & Kim, Y. M. (2006). Priming effects in complex information environments: Reassessing the impact of news discourse on presidential approval. *The Journal of Politics, 68*, 960–976.

Althaus, S. L., & Tewksbury, D. (2002). Agenda setting and the "new" news: Patterns of issue importance among readers of the paper and online versions of the *New York Times. Communication Research, 29*(2), 1180–1207.

Bartels, L. M. (1993). Messages received: The political impact of media exposure. *American Political Science Review, 87*, 267–285.

Baum, M. A. (2003). Soft news and political knowledge? Evidence of absence or absence of evidence? *Political Communication, 20*(2), 173–190.

Baym, G. (2005). *The Daily Show:* Discursive integration and the reinvention of political journalism. *Political Communication, 22*(3), 259–276.

Bennett, S. E., Rhine, S. E., Flickinger, R. S., & Bennett, L. L. M. (1999). "Video malaise" revisited: Public trust in the media and government. *Harvard International Journal of Press/Politics, 4*, 8–23.

Bennett, W. L. (2004). Gatekeeping and press-government relations: A multi-gated model of news construction. In L. L. Kaid (Ed.), *Handbook of political communication research* (pp. 283–314). Mahwah, NJ: Erlbaum.

Bennett, W. L. (2005). *News: The politics of illusion* (6th ed.). New York: Longman.

Ben-Porath, E. (2007). Internal fragmentation of the news: Television news is dialogical format and its consequences for journalism. *Journalism Studies, 8*, 414–431.

Berelson, B., Lazarsfeld, P. F., & McPhee, W. N. (1954). *Voting: A study of opinion formation in a presidential campaign.* Chicago: University of Chicago Press.

Bimber, B., & Davis, R. (2003). *Campaigning online: The Internet in U.S. elections.* New York: Oxford University Press.

Brosius, H. B., & Kepplinger, H. M. (1990). The agenda-setting function of television news. *Communication Research, 17*, 183–211.

Brosius, H. B., & Weimann, G. (1996). Who sets the agenda? Agenda-setting as a two-step flow. *Communication Research, 23*, 561–580.

Bucy, E. P. (2004). The interactivity paradox: Closer to the news but confused. In E. P. Bucy & J. E. Newhagen (Eds.), *Media access: Social and psychological dimensions of new technology use* (pp. 47–72). Mahwah, NJ: Erlbaum.

Cappella, J. N., & Jamieson, K. H. (1997). *Spiral of cynicism: The press and the public good.* New York: Oxford University Press.

Chaffee, S. H. (1986). Mass media and interpersonal channels: Competitive, convergent, or complementary? In G. Gumpert & R. Cathcart (Eds.), *Inter/media: Interpersonal communication in a media world* (3rd ed., pp. 62–80). New York: Oxford University Press.

Chaffee, S. H., & Schleuder, J. (1986). Measurement and effects of attention to media news. *Human Communication Research, 13*, 76–107.

Chong, D., & Druckman, J. N. (2007). A theory of framing and opinion formation in competitive elite environments. *Journal of Communication, 57*, 99–118.

Cohen, B. (1963). *The press and foreign policy.* Princeton, NJ: Princeton University Press.

Converse, P. E. (1964). The nature of belief systems in mass publics. In D. E. Apter (Ed.), *Ideology and discontent* (pp. 206–261). New York: Free Press.

Cook, F. L., Tyler, T. R., Goetz, E. G., Gordon, M. T., Protess, D., Leff, D. R., et al. (1983). Media and agenda setting: Effects on the public, interest group leaders, policy makers, and policy. *Public Opinion Quarterly, 47*, 16–35.

Delli Carpini, M. X., & Keeter, S. (1996). *What Americans know about politics and why it matters.* New Haven, CT: Yale University Press.

Delli Carpini, M. X. D., & Williams, B. A. (2001). Let us infotain you: Politics in the news media environment. In L. Bennett & R. Entman (Eds.), *Mediated politics: Communication in the future of democracy* (pp. 160–191). New York: Cambridge University Press.

Druckman, J. N., & Nelson, K. R. (2003). Framing and deliberation: How citizens' conversations limit elite influence. *American Journal of Political Science, 97*, 729–745.

Eagly, A., & Chaiken, S. (1993). *The psychology of attitudes.* Fort Worth, TX: Harcourt Brace Jovanovich.

Entman, R. M. (1989). *Democracy without citizens: Media and the decay of American politics.* Oxford: Oxford University Press.

Eveland, W. P. (2001). The cognitive mediation model of learning from the news: Evidence from nonelection, off-year election, and presidential election contexts. *Communication Research, 28*(5), 571–601.

Eveland, W., Cortese, J., Park, H., & Dunwoody, S. (2004). How Web site organization influences free recall, factual knowledge, and knowledge structure density. *Human Communication Research, 30*(2), 208–233.

Feldman, L., & Price, V. (2008). Confusion or enlightenment? How exposure to disagreement moderates the effects of political discussion and media use on candidate knowledge. *Communication Research, 35*(1), 61–87.

Fenton, F. (1910). The influence of newspaper presentations upon the growth of crime and other anti-social activity. *The American Journal of Sociology, 16*, 342–371.

Findahl, O., & Hoijer, B. (1985). Some characteristics of news memory and comprehension. *Journal of Broadcasting and Electronic Media, 29*(4), 379–396.

Finkel, S. E. (1993). Re-examining the "minimal effects" model in recent presidential campaigns. *Journal of Politics, 55*, 1–21.

Fox, J. A., Koloen, G., & Sahin, V. (2007). No joke: A comparison of substance in *The Daily Show* with Jon Stewart and broadcast network television coverage of the 2004 presidential election campaign. *Journal of Broadcasting & Electronic Media, 51*, 213–227.

Gamson, W. (1992). *Talking politics.* New York: Cambridge University Press.

Glynn, C. J., Hayes, A. F., & Shanahan, J. (1997). Perceived support for one's opinions and willingness to speak out: A meta-analysis of survey studies on the "Spiral of Silence." *Public Opinion Quarterly, 61*, 452–463.

Grabe, M. E., Lang, A., & Zhao, X. (2003). News content and form: Implications for memory and audience evaluations. *Communication Research, 30*(4), 387–413.

Graber, D. A. (1984). *Processing the news: How people tame the information tide.* White Plains, NY: Longman.

Gunter, B. (1985). News sources and news awareness: A British survey. *Journal of Broadcasting and Electronic Media, 29*(4), 397–406.

Habermas, J. (1989). *The structural transformation of the public sphere: An inquiry into a category of bourgeois society* (T. Burger, Trans.). Cambridge, MA: MIT Press. (Original work published 1962)

Hallin, D. (1992). Sound-bite news: Television coverage of elections, 1968–1988. *Journal of Communication, 45*, 5–24.

Hofstetter, C. R. (1976). *Bias in the news: Network television coverage of the 1972 election campaign.* Columbus: Ohio State University Press.

Holbert, R. L. (2005). A typology for the study of entertainment television and politics. *American Behavioral Scientist, 49*, 436–453.

Hutchins, R. M. (1947). *Commission on Freedom of the Press: Toward a free and responsible press.* Chicago: University of Chicago Press.

Iyengar, S. (1991). *Is anyone responsible? How television frames political issues.* Chicago: University of Chicago Press.

Iyengar, S., & Kinder, D. (1987). *News that matters: Television and American public opinion.* Chicago: University of Chicago Press.

Jones, D. A. (2002). The polarizing effect of new media messages. *International Journal of Public Opinion Research, 14*, 158–174.

Jones, J. (2007). "Fake" news versus "real" news as sources of political information: *The Daily Show* and postmodern political reality. In K. Reigert (Ed.), *Politcotainment: Television's take on the real* (pp. 129–149). New York: Peter Lang.

Just, M. R., Crigler, A. N., Alger, D. E., Cook, T. E., Kern, M., & West, D. M. (1996). *Crosstalk: Citizens, candidates, and the media in a presidential campaign.* Chicago: University of Chicago Press.

Katz, E., Blumler, J., & Gurevitch, M. (1974). Utilization of mass communication by the individual. In J. G. Blumler & E. Katz (Eds.), *The uses of mass communications* (pp. 19–32). Newbury Park, CA: Sage.

Katz, E., & Lazarsfeld, P. (1955). *Personal influence: The part played by people in the flow of mass communications.* New York: Free Press.

Kim, Y. M., & Vishak, J. (2008). Just laugh! You don't need to remember: The effects of entertainment media on political information acquisition and information processing in political judgment. *Journal of Communication, 58*(2), 338–360.

Klapper, J. T. (1960). *The effects of mass communication.* Glencoe, IL: Free Press.

Kovach, B., & Rosenstiel, T. (2001). *The elements of journalism: What newspeople should know and the public should expect.* New York: Three Rivers Press.

Kwak, N. (1999). Revisiting the knowledge gap hypothesis: Education, motivation, and media use. *Communication Research, 26*(4), 385–413.

Lang, A., Bolls, P., Potter, R. F., & Kawahara, K. (1999). The effects of production pacing and arousing content on the information processing of television messages. *Journal of Broadcasting & Electronic Media, 43*(4), 451–475.

Lang, G. E., & Lang, K. (1983). *The battle for public opinion: The president, the press, and the polls during Watergate.* New York: Columbia University Press.

Lavine, H. (2002). On-line versus memory-based process models of political evaluation. In K. R. Monroe (Ed.), *Political psychology* (pp. 225–274). Mahwah, NJ: Erlbaum.

Lazarsfeld, P. F., Berelson, B., & Gaudet, H. (1944). *The people's choice.* New York: Duell, Sloan & Pearce.

Lazarsfeld, P. F., & Merton, R. K. (1948). Mass communication, popular taste, and organized social action. In L. Bryson (Ed.), *The communication of ideas* (pp. 95–118). New York: Harper.

Lee, J. K. (2008). The effect of the Internet on homogeneity of the media agenda: A test of the fragmentation thesis. *Journalism and Mass Communication Quarterly, 84,* 745–760.

Lenart, S. (1994). *Shaping political attitudes: The impact of interpersonal communication and mass media.* Thousand Oaks, CA: Sage.

Livingston, S., & Bennett, W. L. (2003). Gatekeeping, indexing, and live-event news: Is technology altering the construction of news? *Political Communication, 20,* 363–380.

Lodge, M., McGraw, K., & Stroh, P. (1989). An impression-driven model of candidate evaluation. *American Political Science Review, 83,* 399–419.

Lord, C. G., Ross, L., & Lepper, M. R. (1979). Biased assimilation and attitude polarization: The effects of prior theories on subsequently considered evidence. *Journal of Personality & Social Psychology, 37,* 2098–2109.

McCombs, M. E., & Shaw, D. L. (1972). The agenda-setting function of mass media. *Public Opinion Quarterly, 36,* 176–187.

McGuire, W. J. (1985). Attitudes and attitude change. In G. Lindzey & E. Aronson (Eds.), *Handbook of social psychology* (Vol. 2, 3rd ed., pp. 233–346). New York: Random House.

Mondak, J. (1994). Cognitive heuristics, heuristic processing, and efficiency in political decision making. In M. X. Delli Carpini, L. Huddy, & R. Y. Shapiro (Eds.), *Research in micropolitics: New directions in political psychology* (pp. 117–142). Greenwich, CT: JAI Press.

Mutz, D. C. (1998). *Impersonal influence: How perceptions of mass collectives affect political attitudes.* Cambridge, UK: Cambridge University Press.

Mutz, D. C., & Martin, P. S. (2001). Facilitating communication across lines of political difference: The role of mass media. *American Political Science Review, 95,* 97–114.

Niven, D. (2002). *Tilt? The search for media bias.* Westport, CT: Praeger.

Noelle-Neumann, E. (1974). The spiral of silence. *Journal of Communication, 24,* 43–51.

Noelle-Neumann, E. (1993). *The spiral of silence: Public opinion—our social skin* (2nd rev. ed.). Chicago: University of Chicago Press.

Norris, P. (1996). Does television erode social capital? A reply to Putnam. *PS: Political Science & Politics, 29*, 474–479.

Patterson, T. E. (1993). *Out of order.* New York: Knopf.

Petty, R. E., & Cacioppo, J. T. (1986). The elaboration likelihood model of persuasion. In L. Berkowitz (Ed.), *Advances in experimental social psychology* (Vol. 19, pp. 123–205). New York: Academic Press.

Pew Center for the People and the Press. (2007a, August 9). *Internet news audience highly critical of news organizations: Views of press values and performance: 1985–2007.* Retrieved April 24, 2008, from http://people-press .org/reports/display.php3?ReportID=348

Pew Center for the People and the Press. (2007b, April 15). *Public knowledge of current affairs little changed by news and information revolutions: What Americans know: 1989–2007.* Retrieved April 24, 2008, from http://people-press.org/report/319/public-knowledge-of-current-affairs-little-changed-by-news-and-information-revolutions

Pew Center for the People and the Press. (2008, January 11). *Internet's broader role in campaign 2008: Social networking and online videos take off.* Retrieved April 24, 2008, from http://people-press.org/reports/display.php3?ReportID=384

Popkin, S. L. (1991). *The reasoning voter: Communication and persuasion in presidential campaigns.* Chicago: University of Chicago Press.

Price, V. (1989). Social identification and public opinion: Effects of communicating group conflict. *Public Opinion Quarterly, 53*, 197–224.

Price, V., & Czilli, E. J. (1996). Modeling patterns of news recognition and recall. *Journal of Communication, 46*(2), 55–78.

Price, V., & Tewksbury, D. (1997). News values and public opinion: A theoretical account of media priming and framing. In G. A. Barnett & F. J. Boster (Eds.), *Progress in the communication sciences* (Vol. 13, pp. 173–212). New York: Ablex.

Price, V., Tewksbury, D., & Powers, E. (1997). Switching trains of thought: The impact of news frames on readers' cognitive responses. *Communication Research, 24*(5), 481–506.

Price, V., & Zaller, J. (1993). Who gets the news? Alternative measures of news reception and their implications for research. *Public Opinion Quarterly, 57*(2), 133–164.

Prior, M. (2005). News v. entertainment: How increasing media choice widens gaps in political knowledge and turnout. *American Journal of Political Science, 49*, 577–592.

Project for Excellence in Journalism. (2008). *The state of the news media 2008: An annual report on American journalism.* Retrieved April 28, 2008, from http://www.state ofthenewsmedia.com/2008/index.php

Putnam, R. (1995). Bowling alone: America's declining social capital. *Journal of Democracy, 6*, 65–78.

Reese, S. D., Rutigliano, L., Hyun, K., & Jeong, J. (2007). Mapping the blogosphere. *Journalism, 8*, 235–261.

Robinson, J. P. (1976). Interpersonal influence in election campaigns: Two step-flow hypotheses. *Public Opinion Quarterly, 40*, 304–320.

Robinson, J. P., & Levy, M. R. (1986). *The main source: Learning from television news.* Beverly Hills, CA: Sage.

Robinson, M. J. (1976). Public affairs television and the growth of political malaise. *American Political Science Review, 70*, 409–442.

Rosen, J. (1999). *What are journalists for?* New Haven, CT: Yale University Press.

Scheufele, D. A. (2002). Examining differential gains from mass media and their implications for participatory behavior. *Communication Research, 29*, 46–65.

Shah, D. V., Kwak, N., & Holbert, R. L. (2001). "Connecting" and "disconnecting" with civic life: Patterns of Internet use and the production of social capital. *Political Communication, 18*, 141–162.

Shoemaker, P. J., & Reese, S. D. (1996). *Mediating the message: Theories of influences on mass media content* (2nd ed.). White Plains, NY: Longman.

Stroud, N. J. (2008). Media use and political predispositions: Revisiting the concept of selective exposure. *Political Behavior, 30,* 341–366.

Tewksbury, D. (1999). Differences in how we watch the news: The impact of processing goals and expertise on evaluations of political actors. *Communication Research, 26,* 4–29.

Tewksbury, D. (2005). The seeds of audience fragmentation: Specialization in the use of online news sites. *Journal of Broadcasting & Electronic Media, 49,* 332–348.

Tewksbury, D., & Althaus, S. L. (2000). Differences in knowledge acquisition among readers of the paper and online versions of a national newspaper. *Journalism & Mass Communication Quarterly, 77*(3), 457–479.

Tichenor, P. J., Donohue, G. A., & Olien, C. N. (1970). Mass media flow and differential growth in knowledge. *Public Opinion Quarterly, 34,* 159–170.

Valentino, N. A., Buhr, T. A., & Beckmann, M. N. (2001). When the frame is gone: Revisiting the impact of "strategic" campaign coverage on citizens' information retention. *Journalism and Mass Communication Quarterly, 78*(1), 93–112.

Valentino, N. A., Hutchings, V. L., & White, I. K. (2002). Cues that matter: How political ads prime racial attitudes during campaigns. *American Political Science Review, 96,* 75–90.

Valkenburg, P. M., Semetko, H. A., & de Vreese, C. H. (1999). The effects of news frames on readers' thoughts and recall. *Communication Research, 26*(5), 550–569.

Vallone, R. P., Ross, L., & Lepper, M. R. (1985). The hostile media phenomenon: Biased perception and perceptions of media bias in coverage of the Beirut massacre. *Journal of Personality & Social Psychology, 40,* 577–585.

Weaver, D., & Drew, D. (2001). Voter learning and interest in the 2000 presidential election: Did the media matter? *Journalism & Mass Communication Quarterly, 78*(4), 787–798.

Wilcox, D. F. (1900). The American newspaper: A study in social psychology. *Annals of the American Academy of Political & Social Science, 16,* 56–92.

Zaller, J. (1992). *The nature and origins of mass opinion.* Cambridge, UK: Cambridge University Press.

Zaller, J. (1996). The myth of massive media impact revived: New support for a discredited idea. In D. Mutz, P. M. Sniderman, & R. A. Brody (Eds.), *Political persuasion and attitude change* (pp. 17–62). Ann Arbor: University of Michigan Press.

Zhou, S. (2004). Effects of visual intensity and audiovisual redundancy in bad news. *Media Psychology, 6,* 237–256.

Zhu, J., Watt, J. H., Snyder, L. B., & Yan, J. (1993). Public issue priority formation: Media agenda setting and social interaction. *Journal of Communication, 43,* 8–29.

Zillmann, D., & Brosius, H. (2000). *Exemplification in communication: The influence of case reports on the perceptions of issues.* Mahwah, NJ: Erlbaum.

9

MEDIA EFFECTS AND CULTURAL STUDIES

A Contentious Relationship

◆ Toby Miller

C ultural studies is rather suspicious of effects research. It associates such work with a long tradition of seeking to control the popular classes, most recently manifested in contemporary moral panics about audiences. This chapter offers a meta-critical survey of media effects from a cultural studies point of view, summarizes how cultural studies itself undertakes audience research, engages criticisms from within and beyond the tradition, and outlines best practices for the future. To explain cultural studies' skepticism, I use Michel Foucault's concept of the *psy-function* to describe the shifting field of knowledge and power over the body that is composed of psychoanalysis, psychology, psycho-therapy, psychiatry, social psychology, criminology, and psychophar-macology, and their success in various disciplinary sites—educational, military, industrial, and carceral (Foucault, 2006, pp. 85–86, 189–190). The psy-function is particularly powerful in the home of effects research, the United States, where effects studies do crucial work on

Author's Note: Thanks to Robin Nabi, Justin Lewis, and Rick Maxwell for their comments.

behalf of reactionary politics to explain how an advanced economy can produce unprecedented levels of violence. This explanation generally declines to account for economic, social, and cultural inequality as causes of violence, so wedded is it to the behavioral *données* of the psy-function.

◆ Meta-Criticism of Media Effects

Cultural studies is troubled by the way that contemporary effects research un-self-consciously incarnates conservative concerns that arch over millennia, wrongly claiming positivism as a new truth when in reality it rehearses old anxieties for the umpteenth time. Drama, for example, has long been plagued with the reputation of being an ungodly public sphere of make-believe that dupes its audience. Writing in the first century AD, Plutarch recounts the following story about Solon. Having enjoyed what later became known as a tragedy, Solon asked the play's author, Thespis,

> whether he was not ashamed to tell such lies in front of so many people. When Thespis replied that there was no harm in speaking or acting in this way in make-believe, Solon struck the ground angrily with his staff and exclaimed, "Yes, but if we allow ourselves to praise and honour make-believe like this, the next thing will be to find it creeping into our serious business." (Plutarch, 1976, p. 73)

Is this so different from today's panics over the media? I think not. And there are other harbingers of the "modern" effects tradition. The emergence of private, silent reading in the 9th century, which ended religion's monopoly on textuality, was criticized as an invitation to idleness. In the 12th century, John of Salisbury warned of the negative impact of juggling, mime, and acting on "unoccupied minds . . . pampered

by the solace of some pleasure . . . to their greater harm" (quoted in Zyvatkauskas, 2007). As printed books began to proliferate in the early 18th century, critics feared a return to the "barbarism" of the post–Roman Empire; erudition would be overwhelmed by popular texts, just as it had been by war (Chartier, 2004). When Goethe's *The Sorrows of Young Man Werther* came out in 1774, its suiciding hero was deemed to have caused numerous mimetic suicides among readers, and the book was banned in many cities (Stack, 2003).

The Industrial Revolution brought new communications technologies, new democratic urges, new class anxieties, and new knowledges. By the early 20th century, academic experts had decreed media audiences to be passive consumers, thanks to the missions of literary criticism (distinguishing the cultivated from others) and the psy-function (distinguishing the competent from others; Butsch, 2000, p. 3). The origins of social psychology can be traced to anxieties about "the crowd" in suddenly urbanized and educated countries that raised the prospect of a long-feared "ochlocracy" of "the worthless mob" (Pufendorf, 2000, p. 144) able to share popular texts. Elite theorists emerged from both right and left, notably Vilfredo Pareto (1976), Gaetano Mosca (1939), Gustave Le Bon (1899), and Robert Michels (1915), arguing that newly literate publics were vulnerable to manipulation by demagogues. James Truslow Adams, the Latino founder of the "American Dream," saw "the mob mentality of the city crowd" as "one of the menaces to modern civilization." He was especially exercised by "the prostitution of the moving-picture industry" (1941, pp. 404, 413). These critics were frightened of socialism, democracy, and popular reason (Wallas, 1967, p. 137). With civil society growing restive, the wealth of radical civic associations was explained away in social-psychological terms rather than political-economic ones thanks to "new" scholarship. The psy-function warmed itself by campus fires in departments of psychology, sociology, and education. Scholars at Harvard took charge of the theory; faculty at Chicago the task of meeting and greeting the great unwashed; and those at Columbia the statistical manipulation (Staiger, 2005, pp. 21–22).

The extension through societies of the capacity to read had as its corollary the possibility of a public that transcended people physically gathered together, with obvious implications—mass literacy could inform industrial and political turmoil. When unionists in the Cuban cigar industry organized readings of news and current affairs to workers on the line, management and the state responded brutally. In the United States, slave owners terrorized African Americans who taught themselves and their colleagues to read; Nat Turner's 1831 Rebellion was attributed by many to his literacy. The advent of reading outdoors and the arrival of the train as a new site of public culture generated anxieties about open knowledge and debate. The telegraph's capacity to spread information from the eastern states to 19th-century Californians before they had finished breakfast was accused of exhausting emotional energies at the wrong time of day, while its presence in saloons expanded working-class betting on sporting events. Neurological experts attributed their increased business to telegraphy, alongside the expansion of steam, periodical literature, science, and educated women. Nineteenth-century U.S. society saw spirited debates over whether new popular media and genres, such as newspapers, crime stories, and novels, would breed anarchic readers lacking respect for the traditionally literate classes. The media posed a threat to established élites, because they enabled working people to become independently minded and informed, distracting them from servitude (Miller, 1998).

Specifically, gendered reactions against mass literacy became the heart of numerous campaigns against public sex and its representation, most notably the Comstock Law, which policed U.S. sex from the late 19th century. The law was named after the founder of the New York Society for the Suppression of Vice, the noted Post Office moralist Anthony Comstock. Much exercised by "evil reading," Comstock avowed that before Adam and Eve, reading was unknown. In the early 20th century, opera, Shakespeare, and romance fiction were censored for their immodest impact on the young. Many effects studies since that time have been colored by their links to governments and courts policing sexual material because of its alleged impact on young people, all the way from the uptake of Britain's 1868 *Regina v. Hicklin* decision and its anxieties about vulnerable youth through to the U.S. Supreme Court's 1978 *Federal Communications Commission v. Pacifica* (Heins, 2002, pp. 9, 29–32, 23; Manguel, 1996, pp. 110–111, 141, 280, 284; Stearns, 2006, p. 65).

Such tendencies moved into high scholarly gear with the Payne Fund studies of the 1930s, which juxtaposed the impact of films on "'superior' adults—young college professors, graduate students and their wives"—with children in juvenile correction centers, who were easily corralled due to their "regular régimes of living." These studies inaugurated mass social science panic about young people at the cinema through the collection of "authoritative and impersonal data which would make possible a more complete evaluation of motion pictures and their social potentialities" to answer "what effect do motion pictures have upon children of different ages?" especially on the many young people who were "retarded" (Charters, 1933, pp. 8, iv–v, 12–13, 31; see Blumer, 1933; Blumer & Hauser, 1933; Dale, 1933; Forman, 1933; May & Shuttleworth, 1933; Mitchell, 1929). Pioneering scholars boldly set out to see whether "the onset of puberty is or is not affected by motion pictures" in the light of "The Big Three" narrative themes: love, crime, and sex. They gauged reactions through autobiographical case studies that asked questions like whether "all, most, many, some, few, or no Chinese are cunning and underhand" and investigated cinematic "demonstrations of satisfying love techniques" for fear that "sexual passions are aroused and amateur prostitution . . . aggravated." This was done, *inter alia*, by assessing a viewer's skin response. Laboratory techniques used such sensational machinery as the psychogalvanometer and beds wired with hypnographs and polygraphs (Charters, 1933, pp. 4, 10, 15, 25, 32, 49, 54, 60; Staiger, 2005, p. 25; Wartella, 1996, p. 173).

Meanwhile, the field of communication studies was spreading across midwestern public universities in the United States. It emerged in the early 20th century to further the ability of White non-English-speaking migrants to assimilate into the workforce, then accidentally became the first home of media education because the engineering professors who founded radio stations in colleges during the 1920s needed program content, and drew volunteers from speech communication. As radio stations became laboratories, research was undertaken into technology, content, and reception (Kittross, 1999). The example of the Payne Fund studies, the development of communication studies, and the massive growth of the psy-function have led to seven more decades of attempts to correlate youthful consumption of popular culture with antisocial conduct, emphasizing the size and conduct of audiences to audiovisual entertainment: where they came from, how many there were, and what they did as a consequence of being present. Worries over the media's indexical and incarnate power underpin a wealth of research that questions, tests, and measures people and their texts. Not all this work assumes a strong relationship between social conduct and audience conduct, but that premise underpins it nevertheless.

Cultural studies regards these practices as reactions to the fact that audiences participate in the most global (but local), communal (yet individual), and time-consuming meaning making in world history—the concept and occasion of being an audience are links between society and person because viewing and listening involve solitary interpretation as well as collective behavior. Not surprisingly, effects research appeals to multiple materially interested constituencies. Production executives invoke the audience to measure success and claim knowledge of what people want; regulators to intervene in programming; psychologists to publish learned articles; and lobby groups to change content because of its putatively deleterious impact on those who are supposedly less intelligent and cultivated than they. Violence, politics, ignorance, apathy, and sales supposedly engendered by the media are routinely investigated by the psy-function. The audience as consumer, student, felon, voter, and idiot engages these institutional actors. Moral panics and the psy-function combine to create what Harold Garfinkel, writing in the 1960s, named a "cultural dope," a mythic figure who "produces the stable features of the society by acting in compliance with preestablished and legitimate alternatives of action that the common culture provides." The "common sense rationalities . . . of here and now situations" used by ordinary people are obscured and derided by such categorizations (1992, p. 68).

The pattern is that whenever new communications technologies emerge, young audiences in particular are immediately identified as both pioneers and victims, simultaneously endowed by manufacturers and critics with immense power and immense vulnerability—early adopters/early *naïfs*. They are held to be the first to know and the last to understand the media—the grand paradox of youth, latterly on display in the "digital sublime" of technological determinism, as always with the super-added valence of a future citizenship in peril (Mosco, 2004, p. 80). New technologies and genres have brought with them marketing techniques focused on young people, even as concerns about supposedly unprecedented and unholy new risks also recur: cheap novels during the 1900s; silent, then sound film during the 1920s; radio in the 1930s; comic books of the 1940s and '50s; pop music and television from the 1950s and '60s; satanic rock as per the 1970s and '80s; videocassette recorders in the 1980s; and rap music, video games, and the Internet since the 1990s. Recent studies totalize 8- to 18-year-olds as "Generation M" (for media). The satirical paper *The Onion* cleverly mocked the interdependent phenomena of the psy-function, panic, and commodification via a *faux* 2005 study of the impact on U.S. youth of seeing Janet Jackson's breast in a Super Bowl broadcast the year before (Kline, 1993, p. 57; Mazzarella, 2003, p. 228; Roberts, Foehr, & Rideout, 2005; "U.S. Children," 2005).

For those of us in cultural studies, effects research suffers the disadvantages of ideal-typical psychological reasoning. Scholars rely on methodological individualism, failing to account for cultural norms and politics, let alone the arcs of history and waves of geography that situate texts and responses to them inside politics, war, ideology, and discourse. Abundant tests of media effects are based on, as the refrain goes, "undergraduates at a large university in the Midwest." As politicians, grant givers, and pundits call for more and more research to prove that the media make you stupid, violent, and apathetic (or the opposite), the psy-function responds, rarely if ever interrogating its own conditions of existence—namely, that governments, religious groups, and the media themselves use it to account for social problems and engage in surveillance of popular culture.

Effects research is frequently complicit with what it professes to investigate. As jobs emerged from the 1950s for U.S. marketers trained in the psy-function, it even infiltrated the very genres it drew strength from denouncing. Since that time,

while some parts of the psy-function have aided consumer targeting, others feed anxieties about lost innocence via a raft of literature denouncing child commerce, promoted by media panickers like Action for Children's Television ("Children's Television," 2004; Cook, 2007; Cook & Kaiser, 2004, p. 215; DeFao, 2006). Right-wing front organizations like the Parents Television Council adore such analyses: the Council's Entertainment Tracking System (2005) is designed to "ensure that children are not constantly assaulted by sex, violence and profanity on television and in other media . . . along with stories and dialogue that create disdain for authority figures, patriotism, and religion." This complex mosaic of effects research fandom encompasses state, church, commerce, and academia, which may simultaneously governmentalize, demonize, and commodify youth culture (Hartley, 1998, p. 14).

◆ Cultural Studies' Conceptualization of the Audience

Of course, there have always been counters to the notion that audiences are influenced by the media. In the fifth century BC, Socrates may have been the first to argue that what we'd now call media effects could only occur by touching on already-extant proclivities in audiences. In the 18th century, Denis Diderot asked, "Who shall be the master? The writer or the reader?" Up to the early 19th century, it was mostly taken for granted that audiences were active interpreters, given their unruly and overtly engaged conduct at cultural events (Kline, 1993, pp. 52–53, 55; Manguel, 1996, pp. 51, 63, 71, 86). Within the effects tradition itself, some powerful tendencies have argued against the media's impact (Lewis, 2008).

By contrast with psy-function attempts to corral or control spectators, more populist, qualitative theories—articulated to progressive social change based on the insights of ordinary people—fed into cultural studies (see Miller, 2006, for further discussion of cultural studies). This perspective has offered a way in to research via cultural studies' love affair with the all-powerful interpreter—the audience. Umberto Eco's (1972) mid-1960s development of a notion of encoding-decoding, open texts, and aberrant readings—developed as a consultancy on audiences for Italian television—was a key paper. His insights were picked up by Frank Parkin (1971), then by Stuart Hall (1980), and applied to current-affairs television by David Morley (1980, 1992). The methods these scholars and their followers used included ethnographies of audiences and studies of cultural memory. They focused on resistance to dominant norms and expressions of cultural politics rather than the *bourgeois*-individualist norms of the psy-function's investment in "behavior," which was as much about ideological *idées fixes* as aggression or learning.

Dick Hebdige's *Subculture* (1979) is a foundational work of cultural studies within this tradition. A pathbreaking tour of the depressed, recessed, repressed Britain of the 1970s, *Subculture* focuses on resistance and reaction to workaday norms and cultures enacted by marginalized youth through the use of spectacle—audiences who have turned effects and reception into refusal and resignification. Hebdige shows that subordinate groups adopt and adapt signs and objects of the dominant culture, reorganizing them to manufacture new meanings. He demonstrates how their *bricolage* subverts achievement-oriented, materialistic corporate and state culture. Paradoxically, consumption reverses the status of such consumers: the oppressed become producers of new fashions, inscribing alienation, difference, and powerlessness on their bodies, be it via punk dress or Rasta dreads.

In the case of children and television—one of the most politically charged areas

of audience study—anxieties from the effects tradition about turning Edenic innocents into rabid monsters are challenged by research into how children distinguish between fact and fiction; the generic features and intertexts of children's news, drama, action-adventure, education, cartooning, and play; and how talking about TV makes for social interaction (Buckingham, 2005; Hodge & Tripp, 1986). Against claims that soap operas see women identify with maternal, policing functions, cultural studies suggests that female viewers may empathize with villainous characters because of their power, arguing that the genre appeals because it offers a world of glamour and joy in contradistinction to the workaday suburban *ennui* of patriarchy (Ang, 1982; Seiter, Borchers, Kreutzner, & Wrath, 1989). Similar findings have emerged from observing romance-fiction readers (Radway, 1991). And in accounting for cult cinema, Eco suggests viewers can "own" a text, psychologically if not legally, by quoting characters' escapades and proclivities. References to segments of an episode or the typical behavior of an actant catalyze collective memory, regardless of their significance for individual plotlines (1987, p. 198). In the early days of the Web, I used a snowball method to mobilize these insights. I identified and contacted latter-day followers of *The Avengers*, a 1960s British television program, from across the world to juxtapose popular memories of the program with the cultural politics of the time, especially gender relations and the Cold War (Miller, 1997). This was in keeping with studies undertaken in Latin America under the aegis of Néstor García Canclini and his collaborators, which disclose that the interrelationship between audiences and reality must be understood as a "process by which subjects construct and undergo the facts, transform them, and experience the resistance provided by the real" (2001, p. 62).

This idea that the audience is active and powerful has been elevated to a virtual *nostrum* in some cultural studies research into fans, who are thought to construct parasocial or imagined social connections to celebrities and actants in ways that fulfill the function of friendship and make sense of human interaction. Picking up on Garfinkel's (1992) cultural-dope insight to counter the psy-function, some cultural studies audience research claims that the public is so active that it makes its own meanings, outwitting institutions of the state, academia, and capitalism that seek to measure and control it. This critique asserts that media audiences routinely subvert patriarchy, capitalism, and other forms of oppression because they decode texts in keeping with their social situations. The audience is said to be weak at the level of cultural production, but strong as an interpretative community, especially via imagined links to stars. All this is supposedly evident to scholars from their perusal of audience conventions, Web pages, discussion groups, quizzes, and rankings, or by watching television with their children (Baym, 2000; Fiske, 1987; Jenkins, 1992).

◆ Criticisms

But can fans be said to resist labor exploitation, patriarchy, racism, and U.S. neoimperialism, or in some specifiable way make a difference to politics beyond their own selves when they interpret texts unusually, dress up in public as men from outer space, or chat about their romantic frustrations? Why have such practices become popular in the First World at the very moment when media policy fetishizes deregulation and consumer sovereignty? And are cultural studies' favored methods and samples so self-directed and self-regarding that they amount to narcissography? The *Wall Street Journal* welcomes such work as "deeply threatening to traditional leftist views of commerce." The *Journal* suggests that "cultural-studies mavens are betraying the leftist cause, lending support to the corporate

enemy and even training graduate students who wind up doing market research" (Postrel, 1999). It is certainly true that cultural studies frequently generates utopic pronouncements, such as the assertion that *America's Army,* an electronic game designed to recruit young people to the U.S. military via simulated first-person shooting, stimulates a vibrant counterpublic sphere in which veterans dispute the bona fides of nonmilitary players. *America's Army* is allegedly a contested site; what began as a recruitment device has transmogrified into "a place where civilians and service folk . . . discuss the serious experience of real-life war" (Jenkins, 2006, pp. 214–215). Such claims fail to account for other aspects of the game. Its online fora, such as Americasarmy.com/community, take full advantage of cybertarian fantasies about the new media as civil society; across the gamut of Internet chat, fan sites, and virtual competition, they enlist participants in a militaristic agenda. Studies of young people who have positive attitudes to the U.S. military indicate that 30% of them formed their views by playing the game—a game that forbids role reversal via modifications, thereby preventing players from experiencing the pain of the other (Craig, 2006; Gaudiosi, 2005; Lenoir 2003; Nieborg, 2004; Power, 2007, pp. 279–280; Thompson, 2004; Turse, 2008, pp. 117–118, 123–124, 157).

Marketing likes nothing better than active audiences who are bursting with knowledge about media texts; nothing better than diverse groups with easily identified cultural politics and practices; nothing better than fine-grained ethnographic and focus group work to supplement large-scale surveys that provide broad-based demographic data. For instance, digital interactive television is a key innovation for spying on the U.S. public via a set-top box that can provide masses of information about viewers to marketers and advertisers, from their use of mute buttons to their psychographic profiles. This "research" can be done at the behest of the state, which has already ordered such firms to share their data (Chmielewiski, 2002). The Internet also provides cheap market testing. TV producers leak information or request audience input about planned changes to programming to capture opinion without paying for it, keeping their attention on such noted TV-critic Web sites as Television Without Pity, TV Squad, and Futon Critic. Television Without Pity is even owned by NBC Universal (Kushner, 2007). And the idea that audiences are especially independent of media influence when using several different communications technologies at the same time as watching TV is not sustainable. For example, no fewer than a third of U.S. sports audiences who communicate electronically at the same time as viewing refer to the commercials they have seen, and almost two thirds have greater recognition of them than those who simply watch the TV without reaching out in these other ways to friends and fellow spectators (Loechner, 2007). Resistive interpreters? Active audiences? Perhaps not.

The problem with U.S. cultural studies of audiences is that many of them derive from a very specific uptake of venerable U.K. critiques of public broadcasting. Those critiques originated from a heavily regulated, duopolistic broadcasting system—1950s–70s Britain—in which the BBC represented a high-culture snobbery that many leftists associated with an oppressive class structure. Hence the desire for a playful, commercial, anticitizen address as a counter. When cultural studies made its Atlantic crossing, there was no public broadcasting behemoth in need of critique—more a squibby amoeba. And there were lots of not-very-leftist professors and students seemingly aching to hear that U.S. audiences' learning about parts of the world that their country bombs, invades, owns, misrepresents, or otherwise exploits was less important, and less political, than those audiences' interpretations of actually existing local soap operas, wrestling bouts,

or science fiction series. The outcome was rarely radical—for example, when cultural studies scholars intervened in policy matters, they supported video game industrialists against a commercial ordinance that required manufacturers to advise parents their products were risky for young people ("Brief," 2003; see Kline, 2003).

◆ Directions for Future Research

These criticisms should not obscure the fact that cultural studies has inspired some remarkable work that transcends the limitations I have identified by blending audience studies with cultural materialism. The direct opposition that is frequently drawn between active-audience theory (interpretation matters) and political economy (production matters) assumes that the variety of audience niches and responses nullifies the concentration and reach of economic power in mass culture—that pluralism ensures diversity (Schiller, 1989, pp. 147–148, 153). And it is often alleged that political economists have not accounted for the ability of audiences to interpret what they receive. But if we look back at the scholars who created that tradition, it is evident that they were well aware of this capacity. In the 1950s, Dallas Smythe wrote that "audience members act on the program content. They take it and mold it in the image of their individual needs and values" (1954, p. 143). He took it as read that soap opera *habituées* sometimes viewed the genre as fictional and sometimes as a guide for dealing with problems (Smythe, 1954, p. 148). At the height of his 1970s policy interventions in revolutionary societies, from Latin America to Africa, Armand Mattelart recognized the relative autonomy of audiences and their capacity and desire to generate cultural meanings (1980, p. 111). And in the classic 1960s text *Mass Communications and American Empire*, Herb Schiller stressed the need to build on the creativity of audiences by offering them entertaining and informative media (1992). Their example resonates in the best cultural studies.

Political-economic/cultural approaches that track the material lives of commodity signs bring attention to the fact that cultural texts change their meaning and value depending on where, when, and how they are experienced. Consider contemporary research into Mexican *tele-novelas*. Now seen in more than a hundred countries, these serials have been studied through *análisis semántico basado en imagines* (semantic analysis based on the imaginary), which uses viewer interviews about cultural responses to stories as they unfold (Clifford, 2005; Slade & Beckenham, 2005, p. 341, n. 1). Similar methods have shown that diasporic communities frequently create syncretic cultures of reception. Marie Gillespie illustrates how elderly Punjabi expatriates in London take the viewing of Hindi films with their children and grandchildren as opportunities to reminisce and educate family members about India (1995). There was controversy and even violence among exiled audiences in Los Angeles in 1990 when their image of Iran was challenged during a film festival devoted to post-revolutionary cinema (Naficy, 1993). Gay Asian-Caribbean-Canadian video maker Richard Fung (1991) talks about "searching" for Asian genitals in the much-demonized genre of pornography, an account not available in conventional denunciations of porn and its impact on minorities. And when JoEllen Shively (1992) returned as a researcher to the reservation where she grew up, her fellow Native Americans were reading Western films as they had done during her childhood, in an actantial rather than a political way that found them cheering for "cowboys" over "Indians," because heroic narrativization had overdetermined racial identification. Jacqueline Bobo's analysis of Black U.S. women viewers of *The Color Purple* shows how watching the movie, discussing it, and reading the novel drew

them back to Alice Walker's writing, with all three processes invoking their historical experience. These women "sifted through the incongruent parts of the film and reacted favorably to elements with which they could identify" (1995, p. 3). We see similar findings in the TV work of Karen Riggs (1998) on elderly U.S. audiences, Purnima Mankekar (1999) on South Asian women viewers, and Eric Kit-Wai Ma (1999) on Hong Kong focus groups.

At a policy level, Stuart Cunningham (1992) had an impact on public inquiries into the representation of violence and the impact of commercials with his survey of political-economic and cultural studies approaches to television audiences, and Justin Lewis's (2001) study of U.S. public opinion was a significant intervention. Rosalía Winocur (2002) produced a major account of the part played by audiences to talk-back radio in Latin American democracies newly freed from U.S.-backed dictators, while Ellen Seiter's (2005) ethnography of young Californians and new media is compelling. García Canclini and his associates have mobilized a *mélange* of field observations, interviews, surveys, and textual analyses to examine the reception of cultural events in Mexico (2001). At a conceptual level, several theorists have explained the essentially constructed nature of the audience, its ontology forever scarred by the way it is brought into being through the psy-function to perform specific tasks of surveillance and sales (Ang, 1991; Hartley, 1987; Lewis, 1991; Maxwell, 1991, 2000). Future research can follow their fine examples.

Cultural historian Roger Chartier proposes a tripartite approach to media analysis, namely, reconstruction of "the diversity of older readings from their sparse and multiple traces"; a focus on "the text itself, the object that conveys it, and the act that grasps it"; and an identification of "the strategies by which authors and publishers tried to impose an orthodoxy or a prescribed reading on the text" (1989, pp. 157, 161–163, 166). This grid directs us beyond behavioralism's individual focus, which paradoxically yet inexorably returns to a conservative collective politics. Because texts accrete and attenuate meanings on their travels as they rub up against, trope, and are troped by other media and the social, we must consider all the shifts and shocks that characterize their existence as cultural commodities—their ongoing renewal as the temporary "property" of varied, productive workers and publics, and the perennial "property" of businesspeople.

That may be the abiding contribution of cultural studies to "knowing" the audience. It is reductive to understand the media via methods that are fundamentally textual, fundamentally social, or fundamentally scientific. The media and their audiences are not just things to be read; they are not just coefficients of political and economic power; and they are not just outcomes of the psy-function. Rather, they are all these things. The media are hybrid monsters, coevally subject to rhetoric, status, and technology—to text, power, and science—all at once, but in contingent ways (Latour, 1993). To think otherwise is to diminish the material histories of media texts and their consumption, to reduce commodity signs with complex careers to business-as-usual attempts by the U.S. psy-function to blame them for high national levels of interpersonal violence and low levels of educational attainment, those obsessions ever more troubled by electronic texts' extraordinarily open, malleable, polyphonic qualities (Chartier, 2005). If nothing else, cultural studies will provide early warning whenever such research is packaged anew.

◆ References

Adams, J. T. (1941). *The epic of America*. New York: Triangle Books.

Ang, I. (1982). *Het geval Dallas*. Amsterdam: Uitgeverij SUA.

Ang, I. (1991). *Desperately seeking the audience*. London: Routledge.

Baym, N. K. (2000). *Tune in, log on: Soaps, fandom, and online community*. Thousand Oaks, CA: Sage.

Blumer, H. (1933). *Movies and conduct*. New York: Macmillan.

Blumer, H., & Hauser, P. M. (1933). *Movies, delinquency and crime*. New York: Macmillan.

Bobo, J. (1995). *Black women as cultural readers*. New York: Columbia University Press.

Brief *amici curiae* of thirty-three media scholars in interactive digital software association et al. v. St. Louis County et al. (2003). *Particip@tions: International Journal of Audience Research, 1*(1).

Buckingham, D. (2005). A special audience? Children and television. In J. Wasko (Ed.), *A companion to television* (pp. 468–486). Malden, MA: Blackwell.

Butsch, R. (2000). *The making of American audiences: From stage to television, 1750–1990*. Cambridge, UK: Cambridge University Press.

Charters, W. W. (1933). *Motion pictures and youth*. New York: Macmillan.

Chartier, R. (1989). Texts, printings, readings. In L. Hunt (Ed.), *The new cultural history* (pp. 154–175). Berkeley: University of California Press.

Chartier, R. (2004). Languages, books and reading from the printed word to the digital text (T. L. Fagan, Trans.). *Critical Inquiry, 31*.

Chartier, R. (2005, December 17). Le droit d'auteur est-il une parenthèse dans l'histoire? *Le Monde*.

Children's television: Too much of a good thing? (2004, December 18). *Economist*: 97–98.

Chmielewiski, D. C. (2002, May 2). SonicBlue ordered to track digital video recorder users. *Mercury News*.

Clifford, R. (2005). Engaging the audience: The social imaginary of the *novela*. *Television & New Media, 6*(4), 360–369.

Cook, D. T. (2007). Children's consumer culture. In G. Ritzer (Ed.), *Encyclopedia of sociology*. Malden, MA: Blackwell.

Cook, D. T., & Kaiser, S. B. (2004). Betwixt and be tween. *Journal of Consumer Culture, 4*(2), 203–227.

Craig, K. (2006, June 6). Dead in Iraq: It's no game. *Wired*.

Cunningham, S. (1992). *Framing culture: Criticism and policy in Australia*. Sydney: Allen & Unwin.

Dale, E. (1933). *The content of motion pictures*. New York: Macmillan.

DeFao, J. (2006, September 11). TV channel for babies? Pediatricians say turn it off. *San Francisco Chronicle*.

Eco, U. (1972). Towards a semiotic inquiry into the television message (P. Splendore, Trans.). *Working Papers in Cultural Studies, 3*, 103–121.

Eco, U. (1987). *Travels in hyperreality: Essays* (W. Weaver, Trans.). London: Picador.

Fiske, J. (1987). *Television culture*. London: Routledge.

Forman, H. J. (1933). *Our movie made children*. New York: Macmillan.

Foucault, M. (2006). *Psychiatric power: Lectures at the Collège de France, 1973–74* (G. Burchell, Trans., J. Lagrange, Ed.). Basingstoke, UK: Palgrave Macmillan.

Fung, R. (1991). Looking for my penis: The eroticized Asian in gay video porn. In Bad Object-Choices (Ed.), *How do I look? Queer film and video* (pp. 145–168). Seattle, WA: Bay Press.

García Canclini, N. (2001). *Consumers and citizens: Multicultural conflicts in the process of globalization* (G. Yúdice, Trans.). Minneapolis: University of Minnesota Press.

Garfinkel, H. (1992). *Studies in ethnomethodology*. Cambridge, UK: Polity Press.

Gaudiosi, J. (2005, July 13). PLAY. *Wired*.

Gillespie, M. (1995). *Television, ethnicity and cultural change*. London: Routledge.

Hall, S. (1980). Encoding/decoding. In S. Hall, D. Hobson, A. Lowe, & P. Willis (Eds.), *Culture, media, language* (pp. 128–139). London: Hutchinson.

Hartley, J. (1987). Invisible fictions: Television audiences, paedocracy, pleasure. *Textual Practice, 1*(2), 121–138.

Hartley, J. (1998). When your child grows up too fast: Juvenation and the boundaries of the social in the news media. *Continuum: Journal of Media & Cultural Studies, 12*(1), 9–30.

Hebdige, D. (1979). *Subculture: The meaning of style*. London: Methuen.

Heins, M. (2002). *Not in front of the children: "Indecency," censorship, and the innocence of youth*. New York: Hill & Wang.

Hodge, B., & Tripp, D. (1986). *Children and television*. Cambridge, UK: Polity Press.

Jenkins, H. (1992). *Textual poachers: Television fans & participatory culture*. New York: Routledge.

Jenkins, H. (2006). *Fans, bloggers, and gamers: Exploring participatory culture*. New York: New York University Press.

Kittross, J. M. (1999). A history of the BEA. *Feedback, 40*(2).

Kline, S. (1993). *Out of the garden: Toys, TV, and children's culture in the age of marketing*. London: Verso.

Kline, S. (2003). Media effects: Redux or reductive? *Particip@tions: International Journal of Audience Research, 1*(1).

Kushner, D. (2007, September 20). TV enters the blog world. *Rolling Stone*, 48.

Latour, B. (1993). *We have never been modern* (C. Porter, Trans.). Cambridge, MA: Harvard University Press.

Le Bon, G. (1899). *Psychologie des foules*. Paris: Alcan.

Lenoir, T. (2003). Programming theaters of war: Gamemakers as soldiers. In R. Latham (Ed.), *Bombs and bandwidth: The emerging relationship between information technology and security* (pp. 175–198). New York: New Press.

Lewis, J. (1991). *The ideological octopus: An exploration of television and its audience*. New York: Routledge.

Lewis, J. (2001). *Constructing public opinion: How political elites do what they like and why we seem to go along with it*. New York: Columbia University Press.

Lewis, J. (2008). Thinking by numbers: Cultural analysis and the use of data. In T. Bennett & J. Frow (Eds.), *The Sage handbook of cultural analysis* (pp. 654–673). London: Sage.

Loechner, J. (2007, September 5). Multi-tasking sports fans see more ads. *MediaPost*.

Ma, E. K. (1999). *Culture, politics, and television in Hong Kong*. London: Routledge.

Manguel, A. (1996). *A history of reading*. New York: Viking.

Mankekar, P. (1999). *Screening culture, viewing politics: An ethnography of television, womanhood, and nation in postcolonial India*. Durham, NC: Duke University Press.

Mattelart, A. (1980). *Mass media, ideologies and the revolutionary movement* (M. Coad, Trans.). Brighton, UK: Harvester Press; Atlantic Highlands, NJ: Humanities Press.

Maxwell, R. (1991). The image is gold: Value, the audience commodity, and fetishism. *Journal of Film and Video, 43*(1–2), 29–45.

Maxwell, R. (2000). Picturing the audience. *Television & New Media, 1*(2), 135–157.

May, M. A., & Shuttleworth, F. K. (1933). *The social conduct and attitudes of movie fans*. New York: Macmillan.

Mazzarella, S. R. (2003). Constructing youth: Media, youth, and the politics of representation. In A. N. Valdivia (Ed.), *A companion to media studies* (pp. 227–246). Malden, MA: Blackwell.

Michels, R. (1915). *Political parties: A sociological study of the oligarchical tendencies of modern democracy* (E. & C. Paul, Trans.). London: Jarrold & Sons.

Miller, T. (1997). *The Avengers*. London: British Film Institute.

Miller, T. (1998). *Technologies of truth: Cultural citizenship and the popular media*. Minneapolis: University of Minnesota Press.

Miller, T. (Ed.). (2006). *A companion to cultural studies*. Oxford: Blackwell.

Mitchell, A. M. (1929). *Children and the movies*. Chicago: University of Chicago Press.

Morley, D. (1980). *The Nationwide audience*. London: British Film Institute.

Morley, D. (1992). *Television, audiences and cultural studies*. London: Routledge.

Mosca, G. (1939). *The ruling class* (H. D. Kahn, Trans., A. Livingston, Ed.). New York: McGraw-Hill.

Mosco, V. (2004). *The digital sublime: Myth, power, and cyberspace*. Cambridge, MA: MIT Press.

Naficy, H. (1993). *The making of exile cultures: Iranian television in Los Angeles*. Minneapolis: University of Minnesota Press.

Nieborg, D. B. (2004). America's army: More than a game. In T. Eberle & W. C. Kriz (Eds.), *Transforming knowledge into action through gaming and simulation*. Munich: SAGSAGA.

Parents Television Council. (2005). Retrieved April 2008 from www.parentstv.org

Pareto, V. (1976). *Sociological writings* (D. Mirfin, Trans., S. E. Finer, Ed.). Oxford: Basil Blackwell.

Parkin, F. (1971). *Class inequality and political order*. London: MacGibbon & Kee.

Plutarch. (1976). *The rise and fall of Athens: Nine Greek lives by Plutarch* (I. Scott-Kilvert, Trans.). Harmondsworth, UK: Penguin.

Postrel, V. (1999, August 2). The pleasures of persuasion. *Wall Street Journal*.

Power, M. (2007). Digitized virtuosity: Video war games and post-9/11 cyber-deterrence. *Security Dialogue, 38*(2), 271–288.

Pufendorf, S. (2000). *On the duty of man and citizen according to natural law* (M. Silverthorne, Trans., J. Tully, Ed.). Cambridge, UK: Cambridge University Press.

Radway, J. (1991). *Reading the romance*. Chapel Hill: University of North Carolina Press.

Riggs, K. E. (1998). *Mature audiences: Television in the lives of elders*. New Brunswick, NJ: Rutgers University Press.

Roberts, D. F., Foehr, U. G., & Rideout, V. (2005). *Generation M: Media in the lives of 8–18 year-olds*. Kaiser Family Foundation.

Schiller, H. I. (1989). *Culture, Inc.: The corporate takeover of public expression*. New York: Oxford University Press.

Schiller, H. I. (1992). *Mass communications and American empire* (2nd ed.). Boulder, CO: Westview Press.

Seiter, E. (2005). *The Internet playground: Children's access, entertainment, and miseducation*. New York: Peter Lang.

Seiter, E., Borchers, H., Kreutzner, G., & Wrath, E.-M. (Eds.). (1989). *Remote control: Television, audiences and cultural power*. London: Routledge.

Shively, J. (1992). Cowboys and Indians: Perceptions of Western films among American Indians and Anglos. *American Sociological Review, 57*(6), 725–734.

Slade, C., & Beckenham, A. (2005). Introduction: Telenovelas and soap operas: Negotiating reality. *Television & New Media, 6*(4), 337–341.

Smythe, D. (1954). Reality as presented by television. *Public Opinion Quarterly, 18*(2), 143–156.

Stack, S. (2003). Media coverage as a risk factor in suicide. *Journal of Epidemiology and Community Health, 57,* 238–240.

Staiger, J. (2005). *Media reception studies.* New York: New York University Press.

Stearns, P. N. (2006). *American fear: The causes and consequences of high anxiety.* New York: Routledge.

Thompson, C. (2004, August 22). The making of an X Box warrior. *New York Times Magazine.*

Turse, N. (2008). *The complex: How the military invades our everyday lives.* New York: Metropolitan Books.

U.S. children still traumatized one year after seeing partially exposed breast on TV. (2005, January 26). *The Onion.*

Wallas, G. (1967). *The great society: A psychological analysis.* Lincoln: University of Nebraska Press.

Wartella, E. (1996). The history reconsidered. In E. E. Dennis & E. Wartella (Eds.), *American communication research—The remembered history* (pp. 169–180). Mahwah, NJ: Erlbaum.

Winocur, R. (2002). *Ciudadanos mediáticos: La construcción de lo publico en la radio.* Barcelona: Editorial Gedisa.

Zyvatkauskas, C. (2007, February 3). Theatre critic. *Economist,* 18.

PART III

MESSAGE SELECTION AND PROCESSING

USES AND GRATIFICATIONS

An Evolving Perspective of Media Effects

◆ Alan M. Rubin

◆ *The Perspective*

Since the middle of the 20th century, many communication scholars have adopted an alternative perspective to address communication processes from the vantage point of the individual communicator, rather than from that of the undue influence of the medium. *Uses and gratifications* is an alternative to traditional media effects approaches for studying media processes (McLeod & Becker, 1974). It has evolved and matured as a perspective highlighting the role of audience initiative to explain channel choice and message selection, interpretation, response, and impact.

According to uses and gratifications, the media and their content are sources of influence among other potential sources. Audience members take the initiative in selecting these media and are not simply passive targets of media messages. Besides individual motivation and choice, uses and gratifications highlights the role of background characteristics of individuals so that communication influence is socially and psychologically constrained (Rosengren, 1974). Individual differences and motivation, societal structure, and individual attitudes, initiative, and involvement, then, mediate the potential effects of the media. Therefore, if we seek to explain media effects, we must first understand media audiences. Uses and gratifications, then, is a psychological communication perspective (Fisher, 1978), shifting the focus from the direct and undue influence of the media on passive and isolated individuals to active audience members selecting and using the media.

Several assumptions underpin uses and gratifications (Katz, Blumler, & Gurevitch, 1974; Palmgreen, 1984; Palmgreen, Wenner, & Rosengren, 1985; Rubin, 2002). First, communication behavior is purposive and motivated. Second, people are relatively active participants who select media and their content. Third, social and psychological characteristics, societal structure, social groups and relationships, and personal involvement mediate communication behavior and effects. Fourth, media compete with other channels—that is, functional alternatives—for selection, attention, and use. Fifth, people are usually more influential than the media in the media effects process.

Katz et al. (1974) suggested an additional methodological assumption: People can articulate their own reasons to communicate and provide accurate information about media use. In fact, self-report questionnaires have been the primary method for data collection in uses and gratifications. Although some critics have questioned the validity of this assumption (e.g., Elliott, 1974), this method of data collection, which has been supplemented by ethnographic, diary, and experimental methods, has usually been shown to be valid and reliable (Rubin, 1981, 2002).

Uses-and-gratifications researchers have examined (a) a variety of traditional media, primarily television, but also radio, print media, music, and movies; (b) different media content such as news, soap operas, and sports; and (c) emerging media, including videocassette recorders, television remote controls, personal computers, and the Internet. Consistent with the philosophy of uses and gratifications, these newer media have enhanced people's choices and selectivity of channels and content when

they seek to gratify needs and desires, and have emphasized the role of individual initiative, motivation, and involvement.

When focusing on the various media and their content, uses-and-gratifications researchers have explored basic constructs of the perspective, especially motivation; audience initiative and involvement; and functional alternatives to the media, including links to interpersonal communication. They have examined social, psychological, and communication mediators in the uses-and-effects process, such as locus of control, loneliness, and unwillingness to communicate. When trying to understand media effects, research applications have followed a path from traditional to newer media, especially computer-mediated communication (CMC) and the Internet. We have learned that uses and gratifications is a most compatible approach to the study of uses and effects of the newer electronic media at the beginning of the 21st century.

◆ *Background and Development*

AUDIENCE CHOICE AND INITIATIVE

In its early years, uses and gratifications emerged from a shift in the focus of media researchers from the classical effects question "what do media do to people?" to a different query, "what do people do with media?" (Katz, 1959, p. 2). Katz argued that even powerful media usually cannot influence people who have no use for these media or their messages because "people's values, their interests, their associations, their social roles, are pre-potent" and "people selectively 'fashion' what they see and hear to these interests" (p. 3).

Closely following this argument, Klapper (1960) questioned the validity of mechanistic approaches to studying media effects and offered a phenomenistic view of mass communication. He proposed that several elements—including individual predispositions, selective perception, and interpersonal dissemination of messages—intervene between message and response so that media messages intended to persuade usually reinforce people's attitudes and behavior. Klapper stated two important points. First, the media, alone, are usually not necessary or sufficient causes of effects. Second, a medium might be an important source, but it is only one source of influence in our environment. Three years later, Klapper (1963) endorsed uses and gratifications for studying media effects. In addition, Bauer (1963) argued that we should consider the audience's initiative in "getting the information it wants and avoiding what it does not want" (p. 7).

According to uses and gratifications, media are sources of influence working within a context of other possible influences. Media audiences are largely purposive, motivated, goal-directed, and variably active communicators who take the initiative when communicating. People select and use communication vehicles to satisfy their felt needs or desires. Social and psychological factors generate expectations and desires about communication settings, partners, and media, and are important factors to address in the process. These individual differences filter behavior and socially and psychologically constrain mediated communication. We need to understand motives and individual differences to explain media effects.

Uses and gratifications emphasizes individual choice. People choose among available communication or functional alternatives. They make their choices based on their wants, interests, and expectations. These choices affect the process and outcomes of communication (Katz et al., 1974; Rubin, 2002). To understand communication processes and outcomes, we need to understand people's background, motives, and involvement (Rosengren, 1974). In particular, people are variably motivated and involved when they communicate.

RESEARCH PROGRESSION

The roots of uses-and-gratifications research lie in the 1940s. The early research formulated typologies of motives rather than explaining media processes or effects. These typologies include the appeal of radio programs and newspapers. For example, Lazarsfeld (1940) considered the appeals of radio programs. Herzog (1940) suggested that four types of appeals motivated listeners of a radio quiz program: competition, education, self-rating, and sporting. Herzog (1944) also suggested that women sought distinct gratifications when listening to radio daytime serials: emotional release, wishful thinking, and seeking advice. When examining why people missed a newspaper during a strike, Berelson (1949) identified five motives for reading newspapers: to be informed about and to interpret public affairs, as a tool for daily living, for relief and escape from personal problems, for social prestige, and to feel connected to people in the news. In addition, Lasswell (1948) suggested media are functional for people and societies because they perform discrete activities: surveillance of the environment, correlation of parts of that environment, and transmission of our heritage. Later, Wright (1960) added entertainment as a fourth media activity. The research of this era preceded more conceptual descriptions of media use identified in subsequent studies and writings.

Later, for instance, McQuail, Blumler, and Brown (1972) suggested people watch television for four reasons: diversion (e.g., escaping problems, relaxing, releasing emotions, filling time); personal relationships (e.g., seeking companionship, social empathy, and social utility when talking with others); personal identity (e.g., reinforcing values, self-understanding, exploring reality); and surveillance (e.g., learning, seeking advice, finding information). Similarly, Katz, Gurevitch, and Haas (1973) argued that people take the initiative for using the media to satisfy their cognitive needs (e.g., knowledge and understanding), affective needs (e.g., pleasure and emotion), social integrative needs (e.g., contact with family and friends), and tension-release needs (e.g., escape and disconnecting from others). From this foundation, Katz et al. (1974) synthesized the uses-and-gratifications approach, emphasizing an active audience, the initiative of motivated audience members in linking media choice and need gratification, and media competing with other functional alternatives for selection and use.

Over the years, uses-and-gratifications researchers have pursued a variety of tasks (Rubin, 2002). They have established typologies of media motives and linked these motives with people's attitudes such as affinity and perceived reality and behaviors. They have compared people's motives for using various media. They have examined people's psychological and social circumstances such as personality, lifestyle, and life position when using the media. They have analyzed links between gratifications sought and obtained when using media such as television. They have assessed how individual differences, motives, media orientations, and exposure affect outcomes such as learning, cultivation, and parasocial interaction. They have considered the measurement of motives and gratifications. Moreover, they have extended uses-and-gratifications study to a myriad of emerging communication technologies, including videocassette recorders, remote controls, personal computers, and the Internet. Researchers have accentuated the validity of emphasizing the role of individual initiative in selecting media and messages as communication alternatives have evolved and expanded.

◆ Core Elements of Uses and Gratifications

MOTIVATION, ACTIVITY, AND INVOLVEMENT

Across these studies, motivated behavior and involvement have been central to uses and gratifications' focus on active audiences choosing from available communication alternatives. How motivated, active, and involved people are affects whether someone might select and attend to a message, and whether a message has the opportunity to affect people (Rubin, 1993). *Motivation* is a key component because it influences the selective and active manner in which we participate in communication and the possible outcomes of the encounters. We are motivated to communicate, we anticipate, and we form expectations about a communication setting or relationship to coincide with our interests and desires.

Motivation and audience activity are central to uses and gratifications (Rubin, 1993). According to Blumler (1979), *audience activity* includes utility (i.e., people use the media), intentionality (i.e., motivation directs media exposure), selectivity (i.e., individual interests and preferences lead to media choice and behavior), and imperviousness (i.e., media are less likely to influence obstinate audiences). The social context also affects activity. For example, Lin (1994) observed that a more diversified home-media environment—including cable, satellite, and computer opportunities—encourages increased activity because it provides more options for audience members' choice and selectivity.

Lin (1993) also observed that audience activity actually describes the involvement of audience members when using the media. To understand activity and involvement, we need to understand audiences, because involvement is crucial for explaining the "role of active interactants in communication" (Rubin, 1998, p. 257).

Involvement mediates how we acquire, process, and share information (Salmon, 1986). It is a motivated state of anticipation and engagement (e.g., Zaichkowsky, 1986). Being involved suggests participation with, attention to, and emotional connection to salient media messages (Krugman, 1966). Involvement is "the extent to which audience members attend to and reflect on content" (Rubin & Perse, 1987, p. 59). It is cognitive and emotional participation when receiving and processing messages (Perse, 1990b, 1990c; Roser, 1990). Being motivated and involved, then, should result in robust outcomes such as learning, modeling, and attitude formation.

We have learned, though, that motivation and involvement are variable when communicating. We are not always fully or equally motivated and engaged. Our purpose, intent, and desire vary. As Windahl (1981) argued, the media audience is not always superrational or overly selective. People, though, are capable of cognitive thought and reason, and of purposive and selective action. They are, more or less, active participants in communication.

An appropriate and contemporary view suggests we are motivated to communicate. We anticipate and form expectations to meet our interests and desires. We are not, though, always equally or fully motivated and engaged. Our purpose, intent, and desire vary. Uses-and-gratifications researchers, then, have learned that motivation, activity, and involvement are *variable*.

Since Blumler's (1979) and Windahl's (1981) argument, researchers have sought to understand how this variability in motivation, activity, and involvement affect how we communicate and the outcomes of our behavior (Rubin, 1993). For example, Lin (1993) noted that gratifications obtained link to viewing involvement. Perse and Rubin (1988) reported that more involved viewers experience greater satisfaction with media content.

COMMUNICATION ORIENTATIONS

Variability in motivation and involvement is central to the notion of *communication orientations*. Media audience members can be distinguished based on whether they orient themselves to a medium or its content (Hearn, 1989). By conceptually and methodologically treating motives as interrelated structures or orientations rather than isolated entities, researchers have described media use as being primarily *ritualized* (i.e., diversionary) or *instrumental* (i.e., utilitarian) in nature (Rubin, 1984). A ritualized orientation suggests using a *medium* more habitually to consume time and for diversion. An instrumental orientation suggests seeking media *content* for goal-directed reasons. It relates to greater exposure to selected content and perceiving the content to be realistic. Instrumental use is more active and purposive than ritualized use and suggests greater audience utility, intention, selectivity, involvement, and potential influence.

Motivated and involved participants are often instrumental communicators. Being cognitively involved, for instance, means being more aware of and knowledgeable about characters, plots, and information (Lemish, 1985; Shoemaker, Schooler, & Danielson, 1989). Instrumental television use is linked to greater cognitive, affective, or behavioral involvement with media content (Perse, 1990a; Rubin & Perse, 1987).

Communicating instrumentally or ritualistically produces different *outcomes*, and activity and involvement play important mediating roles in this process. Variations in motivation, activity, and involvement, then, influence the outcomes of communication encounters. Because it denotes a more goal-directed, selective, attentive, and involved state of media use, instrumental media use is a catalyst of media effects. Selectivity, attention, and involvement—as indicative of an instrumental orientation—facilitate outcomes such as parasocial interaction, cultivation, and communication satisfaction; avoidance, distraction, and skepticism inhibit such outcomes (Kim & Rubin, 1997).

More motivated television viewers are more active when viewing and experience higher levels of satisfaction (Lin, 1993). In addition, cultivation effects are stronger when people perceive media content to be realistic (Potter, 1986; Rubin, Perse, & Taylor, 1988). Perceived realism has also been a key attitudinal element in explaining the enjoyment of reality-based versus fictional programming (Nabi, Stitt, Halford, & Finnerty, 2006).

PERSONAL INVOLVEMENT WITH THE MEDIA

Uses and gratifications sees communication influence as being socially and psychologically constrained and affected by individual differences and choice. Variations in personality, social context, motivation, and involvement lead to variations in communication behavior and effects. As suggested in the dependency model (Ball-Rokeach & DeFleur, 1976) and the uses and dependency model (Rubin & Windahl, 1986), differences in social, cultural, and political structure, as well as technological fragmentation, constrain individual choice and initiative and influence potential media effects.

One fruitful path in uses-and-gratifications study has been examining the interface of personal and mediated communication. This has included investigations of the role of interpersonal interaction and personal involvement in media uses and effects. For example, Perse and Courtright (1993) found interpersonal channels such as conversation and the telephone had more social presence and better met people's personal needs when compared with channels such as the computer.

Parasocial interaction has been an important affective and emotional involvement construct linking personal and mediated communication. Horton and Wohl (1956) originally proposed that broadcast personalities foster an illusionary relationship with viewers and listeners. Interpersonal notions of attraction, perceived similarity, homophily, empathy, and friendship form the foundation of parasocial interaction (Rubin, Perse, & Powell, 1985). Stated succinctly, audience members often feel a sense of camaraderie with media personalities, and this affects their communication choices, behavior, and outcomes.

According to researchers, involved and instrumental media users appear to form parasocial relationships with newscasters, soap opera characters, talk show hosts, or other media personalities. Parasocial relationships, for instance, affect attitudes and behavior of talk radio audience members, including planned and frequent listening, regarding the host as an important source of information, and feeling the host influences how listeners feel about and act upon issues (Rubin & Step, 2000). Such relationships could lead to divergent consequences. For example, Brown and Basil (1995) observed that emotional involvement with a media celebrity increases personal concern about health messages and risky sexual behavior. Harrison (1997), though, noted that interpersonal attraction to thin media characters promotes eating disorders in women college students.

INDIVIDUAL DIFFERENCES

Besides motivation, involvement, and orientations, researchers have examined *individual differences* of media participants to prevent a biased assessment of media effects (Oliver, 2002). Social and psychological circumstances affect the potential for interaction and the degree of communication and media involvement. Lifestyle, life position, and personality influence media behavior. Factors such as mobility, life satisfaction, and loneliness are important.

Researchers have examined how several individual differences or psychological and social circumstances affect media use (e.g., Finn & Gorr, 1988). Rubin et al. (1985), for example, examined how loneliness might affect the development of parasocial relationships with newscasters. In addition, researchers have observed that the social context and the potential for interaction influence the degree of audience motivation and media involvement. For instance, restricted mobility and poorer health lead to greater reliance on television (Rubin & Rubin, 1982, 1985). Loneliness leads to more reliance on electronic media and more passive television viewing to occupy one's time (Perse & Rubin, 1990). Reduced life satisfaction and anxiety contribute to escapist television viewing (Conway & Rubin, 1991; Rubin, 1985). In addition, personality factors, including neuroticism, extraversion, openness, and agreeableness, relate in different ways to watching or liking violent television content (Krcmar & Kean, 2005).

These individual, background differences play an important role in media uses and effects because lifestyle and life position, including social and psychological dispositions, affect communication motivation, the availability of communication alternatives, and media reliance or dependency. People can only choose from among the channels that are available to them. The importance of individual differences in media effects, then, has been observed in research surrounding traditional media and has been even more evident in the evolving digital age.

◆ The Newer Media Environment

Proceeding from studies of social antecedents of using videocassette recorders (Rubin & Rubin, 1989), development of personal relationships online (Parks & Roberts, 1998), and Internet use as a potential functional alternative to interpersonal interaction (Flaherty, Pearce, & Rubin, 1998), there has been an explosive growth in uses-and-gratifications research in the newer media environment during the early part of the 21st century.

COMMUNICATION MOTIVATION

Researchers in the newer media environment have explored communication motivation, and, similar to those examining the impact of individual differences in traditional media use, they have observed associations with the use of an array of newer media. For example, Morahan-Martin and Schumacher (2000) and LaRose, Lin, and Eastin (2003) examined addictive and pathological use of the Internet. Papacharissi (2002) explored the utility of personal home pages. In addition, Kaye and Johnson (2002) found that people who acquire political information online use the Internet for guidance, information seeking/surveillance, entertainment, and social utility reasons.

Evolving from studies of media and interpersonal communication motives, researchers have produced typologies of Internet motives. For example, Papacharissi and Rubin (2000) identified five motives for using the Internet: interpersonal utility, passing time, information seeking, convenience, and entertainment. Similarly, Kaye (1998) reported six motives for using the Internet: entertainment, social interaction, passing time, escape, information, and Web site preference. Sjoberg (1999) identified four reasons for Internet use by Swedish teenagers: surfing the Internet, searching for information, chatting with others, and downloading programs. In addition, Farquhar and Meeds (2007) used Q-methodology and identified online fantasy sports users as being casual, skilled, and isolationist thrill-seeking players.

Researchers have also identified motivational links to different functions of the Internet such as Web browsing and e-mailing. Wolfradt and Doll (2001), for instance, found chat room visits positively relate to interpersonal communication motives, but negatively relate to information motives. Sun, Rubin, and Haridakis (2008) found information-seeking motives relate to Internet Web browsing, but convenience and interpersonal control motives relate to Internet e-mailing. Ko, Cho, and Roberts (2005) found that those with stronger social interaction motives engage in human-to-human interaction on a Web site, whereas those with stronger information-seeking motives engage in human-message interaction.

INDIVIDUAL DISPOSITIONS

Such motives relate to individual dispositions for using CMC. As in studies of talk radio (e.g., Armstrong & Rubin, 1989), researchers have found that those who feel less valued in face-to-face encounters and tend to avoid face-to-face interaction use CMC to compensate for those interpersonal deficiencies (Papacharissi & Rubin, 2000). Scealy, Phillips, and Stevenson (2002) found that those who feel shy and anxious in face-to-face interpersonal encounters do not experience the same difficulties with CMC communication; those who avoid face-to-face communication use CMC for leisure and recreational purposes.

Investigators have also observed links between preferences for online interaction and such individual differences as loneliness, self-disclosure, and dependency. Caplan (2003) and Morahan-Martin and Schumacher (2003), for instance, found lonely people prefer online interaction to face-to-face interaction, feeling that online interactions are less threatening and more rewarding. Parks and Floyd (1996) found CMC users reveal moderate to high levels of depth and breadth disclosure of

personal information to others online. Tidwell and Walther (2002) found that partners during CMC exhibit greater self-disclosure and in-depth questioning than do face-to-face partners. Pornsakulvanich, Haridakis, and Rubin (2008) found that those who feel close to their online partners view their face-to-face interactions as rewarding, use CMC for self-fulfillment, and disclose their feelings to others online.

MEDIA DEPENDENCY

The availability and use of functional alternatives form the basis for *media dependency* (Rosengren & Windahl, 1972), which enhances the opportunity for the media to achieve effects (Miller & Reese, 1982). However, individual media dependency relationships vary according to intensity, goal scope, and referent scope (Ball-Rokeach, 1998).

Dependency on a medium results from an uncertain societal and media environment, narrow strategies for seeking and obtaining gratifications, and restricted access to functional alternatives. Resourceful communicators have "a wider availability of alternative channels, a broader conception of the potential channels, and the capacity for using more diversified message- and interaction-seeking strategies" (Rubin & Rubin, 1985, p. 39). Such resourceful communicators will less likely be dependent on any given person or medium. Effects should be stronger for those who depend on a particular medium such as television or the Internet or a media personality such as a talk radio host.

Media dependency, then, is an outcome that is contingent on available channels and audience involvement with and people's motivational investment in media and their content (Ball-Rokeach, 1998; Rubin & Windahl, 1986). Different media have "different potential for boosting involvement" (Greenwald & Levitt, 1984, p. 590). The Internet, for example, has unique attributes in integrating personal and mediated communication, which may help enhance or mitigate the effects on involvement (Eveland, 2003). Involvement mediates the relationship between using media for surveillance and information reasons (Eveland, 2001). Adapting Grant's (1996) Television Dependency Scale to measure Internet dependency, Sun et al. (2008) found stronger motivation predicts Internet dependency, but cognitive and affective involvement mediates the relationship between motivation to use the Internet and Internet dependency.

◆ Conclusion

As societies evolve, so do their communication media. As media evolve, so does research attention. Uses and gratifications has been "a cutting-edge theoretical approach" in the early stages of newer communication media (Ruggiero, 2000). Uses-and-gratifications research has demonstrated the importance of considering the interface of personal and mediated contexts. It also has pointed to the need to continue to expand our inquiries of media uses and effects into the newer media that have assumed a larger role in our lives. Uses and gratifications will continue to be an invaluable approach as we seek to understand the evolving, interactive digital environment.

The nature of the newer media—such as cell phones, blackberries, Wi-Fi, and high-definition audio and video—compels us to keep in constant contact with others, to be less patient in our communication, to feel more involved in the media experience, and to be frustrated when people do not acknowledge or respond to us in a timely fashion. These technologies are continually altering how people, organizations, and societies function, individually and collectively. Uses and gratifications is well positioned as a perspective for discerning our relationships with these newer technologies in a variety of communication and cultural settings.

The evolving study of media uses and effects must recognize the expanding role of newer media and the influence of cultural expectations in our research. Changes in technology alter how we communicate. Newer media pose challenges and opportunities, as do cultural nuances.

Rogers (2002) observed that the Internet has altered the nature of international communication. It provides inexpensive and quick access to participants from other countries in our research and raises new issues for the conduct of research. Chen and Kim (1998) suggested that because thinking patterns and expression styles differ between high- and low-context cultures, e-mail messages and electronic questionnaires should be designed differently for participants in those cultures. In addition, Nwosu, Taylor, and Onwumechili (1995) observed that research methods and measures might not be universally applicable. We need to consider revising our methods and measures or creating methods that are sensitive to the evolving media and the cultures in which we conduct our research. These are all continuing challenges to studying media uses and effects.

◆ References

Armstrong, C. B., & Rubin, A. M. (1989). Talk radio as interpersonal communication. *Journal of Communication, 39*(2), 84–94.

Ball-Rokeach, S. J. (1998). A theory of media power and a theory of media use: Different stories, questions, and ways of thinking. *Mass Communication & Society, 1*, 5–40.

Ball-Rokeach, S. J., & DeFleur, M. L. (1976). A dependency model of mass media effects. *Communication Research, 3*, 3–21.

Bauer, R. A. (1963). The initiative of the audience. *Journal of Advertising Research, 3*, 2–7.

Berelson, B. (1949). What "missing the newspaper" means. In P. F. Lazarsfeld & F. N. Stanton (Eds.), *Communications research 1948–1949* (pp. 111–129). New York: Harper.

Blumler, J. G. (1979). The role of theory in uses and gratifications studies. *Communication Research, 6,* 9–36.

Brown, W. J., & Basil, M. D. (1995). Media celebrities and public health: Responses to "Magic" Johnson's HIV disclosure and its impact on AIDS risk and high-risk behaviors. *Health Communication, 7,* 345–370.

Caplan, S. E. (2003). Preference for online social interaction: A theory of problematic Internet use and psychological well-being. *Communication Research, 30,* 625–648.

Chen, G. M., & Kim, C. (1998). *Intercultural communication via e-mail debate.* Retrieved November 24, 2004, from http://www.interculturalrelations.com/v1i4Fall1998/f98chen.htm

Conway, J. C., & Rubin, A. M. (1991). Psychological predictors of television viewing motivation. *Communication Research, 18,* 443–464.

Elliott, P. (1974). Uses and gratifications research: A critique and a sociological alternative. In J. G. Blumler & E. Katz (Eds.), *The uses of mass communications: Current perspectives on gratifications research* (pp. 249–268). Beverly Hills, CA: Sage.

Eveland, W. P. (2001). The cognitive mediation model of learning from the news: Evidence from nonelection, off-year election, and presidential election contexts. *Communication Research, 28,* 571–601.

Eveland, W. P. (2003). A "mix of attributes" approach to the study of media effects and new communication technologies. *Journal of Communication, 53,* 395–410.

Farquhar, L. K., & Meeds, R. (2007). Types of fantasy sports users and their motivations. *Journal of Computer-Mediated Communication, 12,* 1208–1228.

Finn, S., & Gorr, M. B. (1988). Social isolation and social support as correlates of television viewing motivations. *Communication Research, 15,* 135–158.

Fisher, B. A. (1978). *Perspectives on human communication.* New York: Macmillan.

Flaherty, L. M., Pearce, K. J., & Rubin, R. B. (1998). Internet and face-to-face communication: Not functional alternatives. *Communication Quarterly, 46,* 250–268.

Grant, A. E. (1996). Media dependency and multiple media sources. In A. Crigler (Ed.), *The psychology of political communication* (pp. 199–210). Ann Arbor: University of Michigan Press.

Greenwald, A. G., & Levitt, C. (1984). Audience involvement in advertising: Four levels. *Journal of Consumer Research, 11,* 581–592.

Harrison, K. (1997). Does interpersonal attraction to thin media personalities promote eating disorders? *Journal of Broadcasting & Electronic Media, 41,* 478–500.

Hearn, G. (1989). Active and passive conceptions of the television audience: Effects of a change in a viewing routine. *Human Relations, 42,* 857–875.

Herzog, H. (1940). Professor quiz: A gratification study. In P. F. Lazarsfeld, *Radio and the printed page* (pp. 64–93). New York: Duell, Sloan & Pearce.

Herzog, H. (1944). What do we really know about daytime serial listeners? In P. F. Lazarsfeld & F. N. Stanton (Eds.), *Radio research 1942–1943* (pp. 3–33). New York: Duell, Sloan & Pearce.

Horton, D., & Wohl, R. R. (1956). Mass communication and para-social interaction. *Psychiatry, 19,* 215–229.

Katz, E. (1959). Mass communication research and the study of popular culture. *Studies in Public Communication, 2,* 1–6.

Katz, E., Blumler, J. G., & Gurevitch, M. (1974). Utilization of mass communication by the individual. In J. G. Blumler & E. Katz (Eds.), *The uses of mass communications: Current perspectives on gratifications research* (pp. 19–32). Beverly Hills, CA: Sage.

Katz, E., Gurevitch, M., & Haas, H. (1973). On the use of the mass media for important things. *American Sociological Review, 38,* 164–181.

Kaye, B. K. (1998). Uses and gratifications of the World Wide Web: From couch potato to Web potato. *New Jersey Journal of Communication, 6*(1), 21–40.

Kaye, B. K., & Johnson, T. J. (2002). Online and in the know: Uses and gratifications of the Web for political information. *Journal of Broadcasting & Electronic Media, 46,* 54–71.

Kim, J., & Rubin, A. M. (1997). The variable influence of audience activity on media effects. *Communication Research, 24,* 107–135.

Klapper, J. T. (1960). *The effects of mass communication.* New York: Free Press.

Klapper, J. T. (1963). Mass communication research: An old road resurveyed. *Public Opinion Quarterly, 27,* 515–527.

Ko, H., Cho, C., & Roberts, M. S. (2005). Internet uses and gratifications. *Journal of Advertising, 34*(2), 57–70.

Krcmar, M., & Kean, L. G. (2005). Uses and gratifications of media violence: Personality correlates of viewing and liking violent genres. *Media Psychology, 7,* 399–420.

Krugman, H. E. (1966). The measurement of advertising involvement. *Public Opinion Quarterly, 30,* 583–596.

LaRose, R., Lin, C. A., & Eastin, M. S. (2003). Unregulated Internet usage: Addiction, habit, or deficient self regulation? *Media Psychology, 5,* 225–253.

Lasswell, H. D. (1948). The structure and function of communication in society. In L. Bryson (Ed.), *The communication of ideas* (pp. 37–51). New York: Harper.

Lazarsfeld, P. F. (1940). *Radio and the printed page.* New York: Duell, Sloan & Pearce.

Lemish, D. (1985). Soap opera viewing in college: A naturalistic inquiry. *Journal of Broadcasting & Electronic Media, 29,* 275–293.

Lin, C. A. (1993). Modeling the gratification-seeking process of television viewing. *Human Communication Research, 20,* 224–244.

Lin, C. A. (1994). Audience fragmentation in a competitive video marketplace. *Journal of Advertising Research, 34*(6), 30–38.

McLeod, J. M., & Becker, L. B. (1974). Testing the validity of gratification measures through political effects analysis. In J. G. Blumler & E. Katz (Eds.), *The uses of mass communications: Current perspectives on gratifications research* (pp. 137–164). Beverly Hills, CA: Sage.

McQuail, D., Blumler, J. G., & Brown, J. R. (1972). The television audience: A revised perspective. In D. McQuail (Ed.), *Sociology of mass communications* (pp. 135–165). Middlesex, UK: Penguin.

Miller, M. M., & Reese, S. D. (1982). Media dependency as interaction: Effects of exposure

and reliance on political activity and efficacy. *Communication Research, 9,* 227–248.

Morahan-Martin, J., & Schumacher, P. (2000). Incidence and correlates of pathological Internet use among college students. *Computers in Human Behavior, 16,* 13–29.

Morahan-Martin, J., & Schumacher, P. (2003). Loneliness and social uses of the Internet. *Computers in Human Behavior, 19,* 659–671.

Nabi, R. L., Stitt, C. R., Halford, J., & Finnerty, K. L. (2006). Emotional and cognitive predictors of the enjoyment of reality-based and fictional television programming: An elaboration of the uses-and-gratifications perspective. *Media Psychology, 8,* 421–447.

Nwosu, P., Taylor, D., & Onwumechili, C. (1995). Search for appropriate research methods in the African context. In P. Nwosu, C. Onwumechili, & R. M'Bayo (Eds.), *Communication and the transformation of society: A developing region's perspectives* (pp. 397–426). Lanham, MD: University Press of America.

Oliver, M. B. (2002). Individual differences in media effects. In J. Bryant & D. Zillmann (Eds.), *Media effects: Advances in theory and research* (2nd ed., pp. 507–524). Mahwah, NJ: Erlbaum.

Palmgreen, P. (1984). Uses and gratifications: A theoretical perspective. *Communication Yearbook, 8,* 20–55.

Palmgreen, P., Wenner, L. A., & Rosengren, K. E. (1985). Uses and gratifications research: The past ten years. In K. E. Rosengren, L. A. Wenner, & P. Palmgreen (Eds.), *Media gratifications research: Current perspectives* (pp. 11–37). Beverly Hills, CA: Sage.

Papacharissi, Z. (2002). The self online: The utility of personal home pages. *Journal of Broadcasting & Electronic Media, 46,* 346–368.

Papacharissi, Z., & Rubin, A. M. (2000). Predictors of Internet use. *Journal of Broadcasting & Electronic Media, 44,* 175–196.

Parks, M. R., & Floyd, K. (1996). Making friends in cyberspace. *Journal of Communication, 46*(1), 80–97.

Parks, M. R., & Roberts, L. D. (1998). "Making MOOsic": The development of personal relationships on-line and a comparison to their off-line counterparts. *Journal of Social and Personal Relationships, 15,* 517–537.

Perse, E. M. (1990a). Audience selectivity and involvement in the newer media environment. *Communication Research, 17,* 675–697.

Perse, E. M. (1990b). Involvement with local television news: Cognitive and emotional dimensions. *Human Communication Research, 16,* 556–581.

Perse, E. M. (1990c). Media involvement and local news effects. *Journal of Broadcasting & Electronic Media, 34,* 17–36.

Perse, E. M., & Courtright, J. A. (1993). Normative images of communication media: Mass and interpersonal channels in the new media environment. *Human Communication Research, 19,* 485–503.

Perse, E. M., & Rubin, A. M. (1988). Audience activity and satisfaction with favorite television soap opera. *Journalism Quarterly, 65,* 368–375.

Perse, E. M., & Rubin, A. M. (1990). Chronic loneliness and television use. *Journal of Broadcasting & Electronic Media, 34,* 37–53.

Pornsakulvanich, V., Haridakis, P., & Rubin, A. M. (2008). The influence of dispositions and Internet motivation on online communication satisfaction and relationship closeness. *Computers in Human Behavior, 24,* 2292–2310.

Potter, W. J. (1986). Perceived reality and the cultivation hypothesis. *Journal of Broadcasting & Electronic Media, 30,* 159–174.

Rogers, E. M. (2002). Funding international communication research. *Journal of Applied Communication Research, 30,* 341–349.

Rosengren, K. E. (1974). Uses and gratifications: A paradigm outlined. In J. G. Blumler & E. Katz (Eds.), *The uses of mass communications: Current perspectives on gratifications research* (pp. 269–286). Beverly Hills, CA: Sage.

Rosengren, K. E., & Windahl, S. (1972). Mass media consumption as a functional alternative. In D. McQuail (Ed.), *Sociology of mass communications* (pp. 166–194). Middlesex, UK: Penguin.

Roser, C. (1990). Involvement, attention, and perceptions of message relevance in the response to persuasive appeals. *Communication Research, 17,* 571–600.

Rubin, A. M. (1981). An examination of television viewing motivations. *Communication Research, 8,* 141–165.

Rubin, A. M. (1984). Ritualized and instrumental television viewing. *Journal of Communication, 34*(3), 67–77.

Rubin, A. M. (1985). Media gratifications through the life cycle. In K. E. Rosengren, L. A. Wenner, & P. Palmgreen (Eds.), *Media gratifications research: Current perspectives* (pp. 195–208). Beverly Hills, CA: Sage.

Rubin, A. M. (1993). Audience activity and media use. *Communication Monographs, 60,* 98–105.

Rubin, A. M. (1998). Personal involvement with the media. In J. S. Trent (Ed.), *Communication: Views from the helm for the 21st century* (pp. 257–263). Boston: Allyn & Bacon.

Rubin, A. M. (2002). The uses-and-gratifications perspective of media effects. In J. Bryant & D. Zillmann (Eds.), *Media effects: Advances in theory and research* (2nd ed., pp. 525–548). Mahwah, NJ: Erlbaum.

Rubin, A. M., & Perse, E. M. (1987). Audience activity and television news gratifications. *Communication Research, 14,* 58–84.

Rubin, A. M., Perse, E. M., & Powell, R. A. (1985). Loneliness, parasocial interaction, and local television news viewing. *Human Communication Research, 12,* 155–180.

Rubin, A. M., Perse, E. M., & Taylor, D. S. (1988). A methodological examination of cultivation. *Communication Research, 15,* 107–134.

Rubin, A. M., & Rubin, R. B. (1982). Contextual age and television use. *Human Communication Research, 8,* 228–244.

Rubin, A. M., & Rubin, R. B. (1985). Interface of personal and mediated communication: A research agenda. *Critical Studies in Mass Communication, 2,* 36–53.

Rubin, A. M., & Rubin, R. B. (1989). Social and psychological antecedents of VCR use. In M. R. Levy (Ed.), *The VCR age: Home video and mass communication* (pp. 92–111). Newbury Park, CA: Sage.

Rubin, A. M., & Step, M. M. (2000). Impact of motivation, attraction, and parasocial interaction on talk radio listening. *Journal of Broadcasting & Electronic Media, 44,* 635–654.

Rubin, A. M., & Windahl, S. (1986). The uses and dependency model of mass communication. *Critical Studies in Mass Communication, 3,* 184–199.

Ruggiero, T. E. (2000). Uses and gratifications theory in the 21st century. *Mass Communication & Society, 3*(1), 3–37.

Salmon, C. T. (1986). Perspectives on involvement in consumer and communication research. In B. Dervin & M. J. Voigt (Eds.), *Progress in communication sciences* (Vol. 7, pp. 243–268). Norwood, NJ: Ablex.

Scealy, M., Phillips, J. G., & Stevenson, R. (2002). Shyness and anxiety as predictors of patterns of Internet usage. *CyberPsychology & Behavior, 6,* 507–515.

Shoemaker, P., Schooler, C., & Danielson, W. A. (1989). Involvement with the media: Recall versus recognition of election information. *Communication Research, 16,* 78–103.

Sjoberg, U. (1999). The rise of electronic individual: A study of how young Swedish teenagers use and perceive Internet. *Telematics & Informatics, 16,* 113–133.

Sun, S., Rubin, A. M., & Haridakis, P. M. (2008). The role of motivation and media involvement in explaining Internet dependency. *Journal of Broadcasting & Electronic Media, 52,* 408–431.

Tidwell, L. C., & Walther, J. B. (2002). Computer-mediated communication effects on disclosure, impressions, and interpersonal evaluations: Getting to know one another a bit at a time. *Human Communication Research, 28,* 317–348.

Windahl, S. (1981). Uses and gratifications at the crossroads. *Mass Communication Review Yearbook, 2,* 174–185.

Wolfradt, U., & Doll, J. (2001). Motives for adolescents to use the Internet as a function of personality traits, personal and social factors. *Journal of Educational Computing Research, 24,* 13–27.

Wright, C. R. (1960). Functional analysis and mass communication. *Public Opinion Quarterly, 24,* 605–620.

Zaichkowsky, J. L. (1986). Conceptualizing involvement. *Journal of Advertising, 15*(2), 4–14, 34.

11

ENTERTAINMENT

◆ Mary Beth Oliver

Human beings appear to have an innate need for entertainment, as illustrated via a variety of venues and formats throughout history, including gladiator fights, storytelling, interpretative dance, and theatrical performance. Of course, contemporary media venues are no different, as entertainment arguably accounts for the largest amount of "acreage" in the media landscape (e.g., Lin, 1995). Although content such as news, political media, or educational programming accounts for an important part of the media diet, some scholars have suggested that even these more serious forms of media are largely entertainment-like in a world in which television (and now the Internet) are the dominant modes of public discourse (Postman, 1986).

Given the centrality of entertainment in the lives of most people, it is somewhat surprising that compared with research on other aspects of media, such as news or persuasion, most of the theorizing on entertainment media specifically has occurred relatively recently (Bryant, 2004). Within a short time span, though, scholarship on the psychology of entertainment has increased tremendously, with professional organizations now including specific divisions and interest groups on topics such as entertainment studies and gaming research.

Almost any type of content (e.g., advertising), any medium of communication (e.g., books, television), or any format of presentation (e.g., dance, painting) could be considered "entertainment" in the broadest sense of the word. This chapter narrows the focus of inquiry by conceptualizing "entertainment" as media content designed to be consumed for purposes of leisure (rather than specifically for information gain, learning, or persuasion). Further, given the focus of inquiry typical in most entertainment research, this chapter will also focus on electronic media (e.g., television shows, films), though noting that some scholarship has certainly employed alternative mediums (e.g., narrative text) to inform theorizing.

With this focus in mind, this chapter provides an overview of media entertainment theory and research that has formed the scholarly foundation for understanding individuals' responses to and gratifications derived from entertainment consumption. An assessment and critique of existing scholarship is then presented as a means of encouraging a broader conceptualization of the entertainment experience. Finally, avenues for future scholarship are considered, particularly in light of what newer technologies imply for media entertainment.

◆ Selection and Enjoyment of Media Entertainment

In considering the myriad of ways that individuals interact with media entertainment, the vast majority of research has focused on two particular questions: (a) What variables predict viewers' entertainment selections and preferences? and (b) What variables and concepts play pivotal roles in viewers' *enjoyment* of entertainment?

ENTERTAINMENT USES, PREFERENCES, AND SELECTION

Uses and gratifications. Perhaps one of the most basic and widely used approaches to studying media entertainment is via uses and gratifications (see Rubin, Chapter 10, this volume). In brief, uses and gratifications (U&G) conceives of audience members as "active" media users, with individuals

choosing to consume media on the basis of their felt needs and the degree to which the media can successfully address these needs (Katz, Blumler, & Gurevitch, 1973). A wide variety of needs exist, including instrumental needs, such as information seeking; needs related to social connection; and needs related to social status, among others (Rubin, 2002). With the breadth of possible media gratifications in mind, however, this section focuses on gratifications related to media entertainment specifically.

Some of the earliest studies on entertainment specifically employed what might arguably be characterized as a U&G approach. For example, Herzog's (1944) research on radio soap operas discussed listeners' gratifications related to problem solving, escape, and emotional release. Likewise, Lazarsfeld's (1940) analysis of a radio quiz show found that listeners enjoyed the program for testing self-knowledge, for engaging in competition, and for the perception that the shows were educational. Subsequently, Katz, Gurevitch, and Haas (1973) highlighted the importance of media for purposes of entertainment in their study in which approximately a quarter of their respondents reported that media consumption was better able than all other means to address needs relating to overcoming loneliness, escaping from reality of everyday life, killing time, and being entertained.

Since these earlier studies, a large body of research has examined the variety of uses and gratifications that individuals have for a diversity of entertainment forms. Some of these analyses have examined the uses of given mediums or channels of communication in general (e.g., why people use television, the Internet, or motion pictures overall). Here, the uses and gratifications of television viewing have arguably garnered the greatest amount of attention, with some of the more common uses (e.g., amusement, relaxation, passing the time) clearly pertinent to entertainment-related behaviors (Rubin, 1983). Likewise, studies of the Internet per se reveal similar entertainment-like gratifications, including pleasure, amusement, and thrill, among others (Ferguson & Perse, 2000).

In addition to examining gratifications across different mediums, a large body of research has also examined specific entertainment genres or content characteristics. Typically, studies with this focus provide insights into the types of individual differences that may be useful predictors for variation in entertainment selection and gratifications. For example, research on consumption of media violence generally suggests such content is more frequently viewed by individuals higher on such traits as aggressiveness, sensation seeking, or psychoticism (Aluja-Fabregat & Torrubia-Beltri, 1998; Zuckerman & Litle, 1986). Likewise, one study of horror films revealed gratifications such as thrill seeking and gore watching, with these motivations associated with higher levels of sensation seeking and lower levels of empathy, respectively (Johnston, 1995). Similar findings were also revealed in Reiss and Wiltz's (2004) study of reality-show viewing, with higher levels of viewing more evident among individuals with greater needs for social status and for vengeance.

Clearly, U&G has been a fruitful avenue for many theorists interested in media entertainment. At the same time, though, this perspective has received a fair amount of criticism. For example, scholars have questioned the broad characterization of the audience as necessarily "active," have suggested that the theory is more descriptive than predictive or explanatory, and have argued that U&G conceptualizations are often only vaguely defined (for an overview, see Ruggiero, 2000). In terms of methodology, scholars have also criticized U&G's assumption that individuals are aware of or are willing to articulate their motivations for media consumption, thereby questioning the validity of the self-report measurements typically employed (Zillmann, 1985;

Zillmann & Bryant, 1985). In part as a result of these criticisms, additional models of entertainment—namely mood management—have focused on more narrow and testable models that employ experimental methods and that make use of behavioral measures in addition to self-reports.

Mood management. As the name implies, mood management argues that one factor influencing entertainment selection is individuals' tendencies to arrange their environment to manage their moods or affective states (Oliver, 2003; Zillmann, 1988, 2000). Insofar as this theory presumes that hedonistic concerns are important motivations for many behaviors, individuals are predicted to select media entertainment that is successful in prolonging or intensifying positive moods, and (perhaps more important) diminishing or terminating negative moods. Further, this theory does not assume that individuals are necessarily aware of the motivations for their behaviors, but rather that they act in accordance with behaviors that were successful in the past. Consequently, as mentioned previously, this theory has often been tested via experimental procedures in which positive and negative mood states (including boredom and stress) are first induced, and measures of media selection are then assessed.

There are a host of media characteristics that are thought to aid in individuals' attempts to regulate their moods (Zillmann, 1988). For example, the *arousing potential* of media portrayals is predicted to assist individuals in avoiding unpleasant states of overarousal (stress) and underarousal (boredom). Likewise, individuals who are in negative moods are predicted to avoid content that has a negative *hedonic valence* (sad, negative content) or that is high in *behavioral affinity* (is similar to the context or reason for the individual's state). At the same time, negative mood states may lead to greater attraction to media content high in its *absorbing potential*, as such content may successfully distract the individual from his or her negative mood.

Support for mood management's basic assumptions has been obtained for a variety of content and in a diversity of settings. For example, in one earlier test of this theory, Bryant and Zillmann (1984) found that overaroused individuals were less likely than underaroused individuals to choose "calming" content, such as nature shows and soothing musical concerts, over more exciting fare such as a sporting event or a game show playoff. Likewise, Meadowcroft and Zillmann (1987) found that women in the premenstrual phase of their menstrual cycles were more likely than women in other phases to report preferences for viewing comedies. More recently, mood management has been tested in the context of online musical selections (Knobloch & Zillmann, 2002), with individuals in negative moods more likely than individuals in positive moods to select upbeat and joyful music over more somber selections.

With these supportive studies in mind, though, refinements to mood management have been made to help accommodate some findings that appear at odds with the basic assumptions of the theory. For example, in one early study, Zillmann, Hezel, and Medoff (1980) found that contrary to expectations, individuals in negative moods actually avoided television comedies. However, a closer examination of the *nature* of the comedic presentations revealed that they focused on hostile humor—a characteristic that may have been too similar to the context of the participants' bad moods (e.g., high on behavioral affinity). Likewise, other studies have often reported gender differences in entertainment selections as a function of mood, leading scholars to suggest that under some circumstances (e.g., when retaliation against the source of the negative mood is possible), individuals may opt to prolong rather than diminish their negative affect (Biswas, Riffe, & Zillmann, 1994; Knobloch-Westerwick

& Alter, 2006). Indeed, Knobloch (2003) has expanded upon this idea to suggest that rather than using media to necessarily engage in mood *management*, individuals may use media as a means of *adjusting* their moods to be appropriate for the context or situation, even if those moods are not necessarily positive (see also Erber & Erber, 2000, for a similar argument). Likewise, Nabi, Finnerty, Domschke, and Hull (2006) recently argued that under some circumstances, individuals may select negatively valenced content that is high on behavioral affinity because it ultimately serves their coping needs.

These refinements and additions to mood management are important developments to a theory that has enjoyed a great deal of empirical support. At the same time, though, additional "counter-evidence" has presented challenges that have yet to be fully resolved. Namely, a number of studies have reported that contrary to predictions, individuals in negative or sad affective states often appear to have a preference for somber or mournful entertainment, including both movies (Strizhakova & Krcmar, 2007) and music (Gibson, Aust, & Zillmann, 2000). A variety of different explanations have been suggested for these findings, including the idea that such preferences reflect information seeking, needs for feeling "understood" (Zillmann, 2000), or downward social comparison (Mares & Cantor, 1992). Ultimately, these explanations appear to adhere to conceptualizations of the audience as hedonistic, as these explanations suggest that individuals use media as a means of "feeling better," albeit via the temporary experience of negatively valenced content. In contrast, as I will suggest in a later section of this chapter, perhaps one way to "resolve" or address these paradoxical preferences is by considering additional motivations that reflect seeking involvement, greater insight, or meaningfulness (in addition to only pleasure) that may be orthogonal to hedonic concerns.

ENJOYMENT OF
MEDIA ENTERTAINMENT

Thus far, I have focused my attention on the selection of entertainment media and the predictors of entertainment preferences. Certainly, the selection of media entertainment *implies* that what is selected is enjoyed. Yet, the experience of enjoyment, its defining characteristics, and the types of entertainment portrayals that are most predictive of enjoyment are clearly distinct questions. Consequently, in this section I review scholarship that has focused on the experience of enjoyment specifically.

What is "enjoyment"? At first glance, it is tempting to suggest that enjoyment necessarily involves merriment, laughter, or pleasantness, as "enjoyment" is based on the root word *joy*. At the same time, though, a number of scholars have pointed out that enjoyment is a much more complex concept.

For example, Vorderer, Klimmt, and Ritterfeld (2004) provided a model of media entertainment that situated enjoyment as the "core" experience. This experience, though, was not conceptualized as only the experience of happiness or joy, but as a pleasant state resulting from such experiences as serenity, sensory delight, achievement, or suspense, among others. Further, the experience of enjoyment in response to media entertainment was argued to be the result of a number of antecedent conditions, including "user prerequisites" (e.g., suspension of disbelief, empathy), "motives" (e.g., escapism, competition) and "media prerequisites" (e.g., aesthetics, technology).

Bartsch, Vorderer, Mangold, and Viehoff (2008) recently discussed the utility of conceptualizing the entertainment experience (including enjoyment of entertainment) in terms of meta-emotions—one's emotions *about* one's emotions. Namely, these authors used an appraisal framework to suggest that users' experiences of and enjoyment of entertainment reflect their appraisal of emotions experienced during entertainment (including positive and negative emotions), and the emotional responses that result from that appraisal. From within this framework, then, media entertainment that elicits joy *or* sadness (for example) may result in favorable appraisals and hence favorable affective reactions—including enjoyment—at the metalevel.

As a final example illustrating the complexity and breadth of the enjoyment experience, Nabi and Krcmar (2004) argued that enjoyment may be best conceptualized as an attitude, noting that such a conceptualization accommodates affective, cognitive, and behavioral responses to the "attitude object" (media entertainment, in this instance). Further, such a conceptualization not only accounts for responses *during* the viewing experience (that is, attitudes may fluctuate in the face of new or changing stimuli), but also accounts for responses *after* the viewing experience (e.g., assessments of media entertainment upon reflection). Finally, Nabi and Krcmar also discussed the implications of their "tripartite" model of media enjoyment on the effects of entertainment on viewers, suggesting that the conceptualization of enjoyment as attitude may help clarify both the selection of entertainment, as it may be planned or spontaneous, but also the effects that such exposure may have on viewers.

Narrative depictions associated with enjoyment. The previous discussion of the different approaches for understanding the concept of "enjoyment" highlights that it is a multifaceted, nuanced, and fluctuating experience. As such, the specific characteristics that give rise to the experience of enjoyment may be difficult to identify. At the same time, however, common themes or plots in entertainment (e.g., "happily ever after," "boy gets girl") suggest that enjoyment may be more universally common for some types of portrayals or content over others. Consequently, some entertainment scholarship has attempted to identify the narrative elements in media entertainment that are most likely to give rise to viewer enjoyment.

Disposition theory is arguably the most notable example of scholarship in this area (Raney, 2003; Zillmann & Bryant, 1975; Zillmann & Cantor, 1977). In short, dispositional approaches suggest that viewers typically use moral considerations in forming judgments about the "goodness" or "badness" of characters (though the liking of certain characters can certainly be based on other factors such as fanship in the case of sports; see Raney, Chapter 29, this volume). Once these dispositional judgments are formed, viewers' enjoyment is predicted to be maximized when good (and therefore liked) characters experience positive outcomes and bad (and therefore disliked) characters experience negative (or at least "just") outcomes. Likewise, great disappointment is expected when disliked characters experience reward or liked characters suffer misfortunes. Consequently, disposition theory provides a coherent framework not only for understanding viewers' great enjoyment when the entertainment content is consistent with moral concerns, but also for explaining the dysphoria that can also happen when the entertainment deviates from hoped-for outcomes.

Dispositional approaches to understanding the enjoyment of media content have garnered widespread empirical support across a variety of genres, including humorous content (Zillmann & Bryant, 1991), sporting events (Zillmann, Bryant, & Sapolsky, 1989), crime drama (Raney & Bryant, 2002), and soap operas (Weber, Tamborini, Lee, & Stipp, 2008), among other types of programming. At the same time, though, a number of refinements to and extensions of the basic dispositional model have been made to help account for the enjoyment of content that appears at odds with the overarching predictions (i.e., content in which "good" characters appear to suffer). For example, in considering the enjoyment of suspenseful films that often feature the anguished and horrific experiences of presumably liked characters, Zillmann (1980, 1991) noted that many such films ultimately end with the victim escaping from her or his tormentor. As a consequence, via the process of excitation transfer (Bryant & Miron, 2003; Zillmann, 1971), viewers not only experience happiness when the desired outcome accrues, but they experience *heightened* levels of joy that are intensified by the arousal caused by the previously experienced anxiety.

Raney (2004) also recently offered an extension of dispositional approaches to entertainment enjoyment in his consideration of the seemingly contradictory situation in which viewers apparently enjoy portrayals in which presumably "liked" characters are shown performing arguably morally corrupt or reprehensible actions (e.g., acts of torture in the television program 24). Specifically, Raney suggested that although viewers *typically* form dispositional judgments on the basis of characters' actions, at other times, viewers' expectations, media story plots, or narrative schemas provide a dispositional framework that leads viewers to judge characters as "good" or "bad" prior to witnessing any behaviors that the characters may perform. Raney argued that when such judgments are made prior to our witnessing the character's actions, viewers are then likely to interpret subsequent character behaviors (including "bad" behaviors) through this lens, being more forgiving of bad or reprehensible behaviors that would otherwise disrupt the enjoyment of our beloved protagonist. As a result, Raney suggested that in order to experience enjoyment of entertainment that involves immoral behaviors on the part of otherwise liked characters (e.g., Tony Soprano on *The Sopranos*, Jack Bauer on 24, etc.), individuals may ultimately have to resort to forms of moral disengagement in which reprehensible acts are "recast" by viewers as acceptable or justified.

SUMMARY OF SELECTION AND ENJOYMENT

The landscape of media entertainment is vast and diverse, as is its history, its viewership, and the gratifications it affords. Much of the literature in this regard has tended to draw parallels between entertainment and exposure/enjoyment in terms of the positive affective experiences. This is understandable given that most entertainment is, indeed, a leisurely pastime that is undertaken in the pursuit of pleasure. Yet in looking more closely at the concept of "enjoyment," scholars are now more frequently recognizing the complexity of the experience as well as the importance of expanding our conceptualizations to account for entertainment and audience response that is broader than pleasure-as-positive-affect (Oliver & Nabi, 2004).

◆ Entertainment as More Than Pleasure Seeking

It is evident that the landscape of media entertainment includes content that appears seemingly contradictory to upbeat, joyous, or even affectively pleasant experiences. Indeed, tragedy as a form of entertainment is as old as storytelling itself, and tragic films, mournful love songs, tearjerker movies, and suffering heroines continue to enjoy wide-scale popularity. Further, as noted previously, some research has found that under some circumstances, viewers may be particularly drawn to this form of entertainment when they are feeling sad or blue themselves—a pattern of selection that appears to contradict the notion of individuals as pleasure seekers (Knobloch, Weisbach, & Zillmann, 2004; Strizhakova & Krcmar, 2007; Zillmann, 2000). With these challenges in mind, it becomes clear that additional considerations beyond pleasure defined in terms of positive affect may be useful in capturing the breadth of gratifications that viewers may derive from media entertainment.

TRANSPORTATION AND ENGAGEMENT

One example of pleasure that is conceptually distinct from positive affect is engagement or involvement. The idea of being absorbed by a good book, engrossed in a movie, or swept up in a musical performance is undoubtedly familiar to most people. These sorts of feelings are clearly important components of the entertainment experience and are ones that are studied in various forms, by a variety of names, for a variety of genres (see Cohen, Chapter 15, this volume; Vorderer & Ritterfeld, Chapter 30, this volume).

In terms of narrative entertainment specifically, perhaps one of the most widely discussed concepts in this regard is *transportation* (Green & Brock, 2000). Although transportation is conceptually similar to concepts such as *flow, absorption,* or *presence,* one distinction is that it is focused specifically on narrative content or stories. The concept of transportation refers to engagement in a story or plot in a narrative world to such an extent that the reader (or viewer) becomes lost in the story and is unaware of his or her immediate surroundings. As Green and Brock (2002) describe, transportation is "a convergent process, where all of the person's mental systems and capacities become focused on the events occurring in the narrative" (p. 324). More recently, Busselle and Bilandzic (2008) expanded on the notion of transportation, reformulating the concept as the flow-like state that one experiences while comprehending and making sense of a fictional world, its characters, and its events (i.e., while building mental models of the narrative world).

It seems intuitively evident that the experience of transportation into some entertainment offering and enjoyment of that fare would be positively related. For example, saying that we really "got into" a movie, that we found a play "engaging," or that we let ourselves "get lost" in a drama typically means that we enjoyed the experience. Yet Green, Brock, and Kaufman (2004) argued that although transportation may be empirically correlated with the experience of enjoyment, transportation is not necessarily related to positive affect: "The enjoyment of a transportation experience . . . does not necessarily lie in the valence of the emotions evoked by a narrative, but in the process of temporarily leaving one's reality behind" (p. 315). As a consequence, enjoyment of sad films, horrific films, or even disgusting films may be plausible from within this framework, provided there is a high level of engagement with the narrative. Although these authors provided a number of possible reasons *why* engagement with such materials may be gratifying (e.g., escaping the self, connecting with characters), such explanations await further empirical investigation.

MEANINGFULNESS AS GRATIFICATION

The idea that entertainment selection and enjoyment govern many other media-related behaviors is understandable. Yet conceptualizing humans (and their happiness or fulfillment) primarily in hedonistic terms may obscure additional motivations and concerns that may be as (if not more) important in overall life satisfaction. Current research on psychological and subjective well-being (Ryan & Deci, 2001; Waterman, 1993) draws from Aristotelian writings and highlights a distinction between *hedonic happiness* (associated with positive affect) and *eudaimonic happiness* (associated with greater meaningfulness, insight, and purpose). Such distinctions applied to media entertainment imply that whereas individuals may often be motivated to view entertainment

for the hedonic purposes of pleasure seeking (as studied in much extant research), there may be other individuals (or other times for a given individual) when entertainment consumption is more aptly described in terms of *eudaimonic* motivations—as "truth seeking" or "meaningfulness seeking" (Oliver, 2008; Oliver & Raney, 2008). In contrast to hedonic motivations, eudaimonic motivations are conceptualized in terms of cognitive and mixed affective blends associated with greater contemplativeness, reflectiveness, insight, or poignancy. Further, eudaimonic motivations may be associated with preferences for content that may elicit negative affect insofar as the entertainment is also associated with greater levels of meaningfulness or contemplation. Consequently, eudaimonia as a concept may be useful in terms of understanding both the selection of media content (as discussed at the beginning of this chapter) and the enjoyment of media content (as discussed subsequently).

In considering the idea that greater insight or meaningfulness may represent a motivation for viewing media entertainment or for guiding entertainment selections, it is important to note that eudaimonic considerations may function as both a trait (as an enduring preference) and as a state (as a transient or salient need that fluctuates from one moment to the next). Recently, Oliver and Raney (2008) provided evidence of the validity of trait-like eudaimonic motivations by showing that these motivations (unlike hedonic motivations) were predicted by individual differences, such as need for cognition (Cacioppo, Petty, & Kao, 1984), self-reflectiveness (Trapnell & Campbell, 1999), and search for meaning in life (Steger, Frazier, Oishi, & Kaler, 2006). Further, these motivations were associated with naming a favorite film that was reported to have elicited higher levels of contemplative and tender feelings, as measured by such items as *introspective, intrigued, contemplative, moved,* and *inspired.*

The investigation of eudaimonic motivations as state-like preferences has only begun to garner empirical investigation. However, recent research suggests that it may be a viable explanation that could help to account for situations in which seemingly sad or melancholy individuals appear to prefer sad or tragic entertainment. Namely, I recently reported a series of studies in which I argued that rather than suggesting that "sad people prefer sad films," the more apt description may be that people seeking meaningfulness or insight (and who may therefore be experiencing mixed affective states) may prefer entertainment that focuses on the human condition, including both its joys and its tragedies (Oliver, 2008). These studies supported the idea that tender affective states (characterized by feelings of tenderness, warmth, kindness, and sympathy) were associated with greater interest in consuming content focused on human relationships, including sad films, dramas, and romantic films, whereas feelings of sadness specifically were largely unrelated to these preferences. These results imply that prior research suggesting "paradoxical" findings that appear to contradict mood management predictions may have actually been pointing to an additional (and perhaps orthogonal) motivation of eudaimonia (in addition to hedonism that has been largely assumed and therefore assessed thus far).

If the notion of eudaimonia is an apt descriptor of an entertainment consumption motivation, then numerous questions remain concerning the nature of the *experience* of such entertainment. For example, films such as *Schindler's List*, *Sophie's Choice*, or *Hotel Rwanda* undoubtedly grapple with poignant and tragic human drama and may well provide feelings of meaningfulness and greater insight into the human condition. But to characterize the experience of such forms of entertainment in terms of "enjoyment" seems decidedly odd, if not offensive. As such, the recognition that entertainment can provide both positive affect *and* greater insight highlights the utility of taking note of the nuanced differences in the types of gratifications that viewers may experience. For example, in discussing the redeeming qualities of tragedy, Zillmann (1998) noted,

> It may be considered ill-advised, in fact, to focus on enjoyment as a redeeming value of tragedy. Perhaps we should return to Aristotle's (Poetica) declaration of tragedy's object, namely the evocation of pity, and grant redeeming value to tragic drama's capacity for honing our empathic sensitivities and for making us cognizant of our vulnerabilities, compassions, and needs for emotional wellness. (p. 1)

With Zillmann's (1998) advice in mind, one fruitful direction of research that has begun to garner additional scholarly interest is the exploration of the multidimensionality of gratifications that media entertainment may afford, including distinctions between *enjoyment* and *appreciation* (Oliver & Bartsch, in press; Raney, 2006). Likewise, as new technologies are introduced that allow for entertainment experiences not imaginable with traditional mediums such as television or film (e.g., video gaming, virtual reality), additional forms of gratification such as challenge, flow, presence, or competition will undoubtedly continue to emerge (Sherry, 2004; Vorderer & Ritterfeld, Chapter 30, this volume; Witmer & Singer, 1998).

◆ The Future of Media Entertainment Research

In the preface to the 2000 volume on media entertainment, Zillmann and Vorderer (2000) noted, "Never before in human history has so much media entertainment been so readily accessible to so many, for so much of their leisure time as is now, primarily because of the media of communication" (p. vii). In many respects, this observation now seems like an understatement when considering the overwhelming growth and change that has occurred in the entertainment industry since even that time. For example, the Entertainment Software Association reports that from 2003 to 2006, the growth of the entertainment software industry was approximately 17% (compared with 4% for the entire U.S. economy; see Entertainment Software Association, n.d.). Likewise, social networking sites, such as MySpace and Facebook, enroll millions of users, with hundreds of thousands of new users enrolling each day (Raacke & Bonds-Raacke, 2008). Mobile communication, the Internet, and computer software have radically and unalterably changed the media entertainment landscape in ways that theorists are just beginning to grapple with and that will, undoubtedly, lead to the creation of new theoretical approaches, the modification of existing frameworks, and the development of new methodological tools that will be necessary to fully capture what entertainment holds in store.

It is beyond the scope of this chapter to overview the phenomenal body of literature that has already developed in entertainment psychology on such topics as gaming or virtual reality (though see Vorderer & Ritterfeld, Chapter 30, this volume). Rather, the purpose of this brief conclusion is to highlight three sets of variables that may be particularly consequential to future research in the psychology of entertainment— causing us to rethink, revise, and create new forms of media entertainment theory.

First, the new and evolving media landscape offers greater opportunities for *selectivity* than has ever been imagined. Video-on-demand, TIVO, and streaming video are but a few examples of ways in which viewers may select any type of content in any way at any time that they want. In some respects, this greater opportunity for selection opens up many new avenues to explore existing theories. For example, Mastro, Eastin, and Tamborini (2002)

employed mood management theory to examine Internet surfing behavior, finding that stressed individuals surfed significantly more slowly (had fewer "hits") than did bored participants. At the same time that greater selectivity affords new ways of looking at existing theories, it also means that existing measures of media exposure become increasingly out of step with current usage. Gone are the days of a "mass audience" where global measures of time spent with a medium give us an indicator of entertainment exposure. Further, with the exception of some notable media events (the Super Bowl or the Academy Awards), we can also no longer assume that individuals necessarily share common media entertainment experiences that involve the simultaneous consumption of content.

Related to increases in entertainment selection, research in media entertainment now must also grapple with implications associated with *interactivity* (see also Metzger, Chapter 37, this volume; Sundar, Chapter 36, this volume). In current forms of entertainment, and particularly in gaming, users not only routinely have the opportunity to control and alter potential outcomes of narratives; they also have the opportunity to select, create, and alter themselves as characters *within* the narratives. Likewise, the development of YouTube and analogous image- and video-sharing sites has shifted individuals from being only viewers and audience members to being artists and creators of content in their own right. Shao's (2008) overview of user-generated media demonstrated that the growth of this form of media entertainment has vastly outpaced other types of Internet sites and is now generating substantially more visits than more "traditional" information sites such as those affiliated with media networks (e.g., ABC, NBC, CBS, and Fox).

This greater opportunity for increased interactivity and creativity abounds with implications concerning user engagement and control, though its implications in terms of entertainment experiences are far from being fully understood at this point. For example, Vorderer, Knobloch, and Schramm (2001) found that greater interactive control of the storyline in a movie increased suspense and movie evaluations among viewers with higher cognitive capacity (i.e., high school graduates), but decreased favorable evaluations among viewers with lower cognitive capacities. Such findings suggest great opportunities for exploring additional mediators and moderators afforded by increasing technologies on a host of potential affective and cognitive outcomes.

A third change worthy of note brought about by newer technologies concerns *mobility*. Users no longer gather together in their living rooms to watch television, but rather carry their entertainment with them on their cell phones, on their portable DVD players, and on their iPods. A recent report from the Pew Internet & American Life Project (Horrigan, 2008) reported that cell phones have now surpassed almost all other technologies (including television, the Internet, and e-mail) as the one technology that would be hardest to give up. Further, among cell phone or PDA users, a large percentage of younger respondents (18–29 years) report using the technology on a typical day for many nonvoice (and entertainment-like) activities, including taking pictures (31%), playing games (16%), playing music (16%), or watching video (6%). Research on what these changes mean for the entertainment experience is only beginning to emerge. Not only are there undoubtedly unique and important effects of context and locale on user responses, but individuals' uses of entertainment in "nonentertainment" settings (e.g., classrooms, public transportation) undoubtedly impact social interaction, notions of public-private space, and behaviors related to multitasking.

All of these changes in the entertainment landscape afford great opportunity for expansion of existing theorizing. At the same time, they present conceptual and methodological challenges that will undoubtedly require considerable care and creativity. For example, Klimmt, Vorderer, and Ritterfeld (2007) noted that greater interactivity poses substantial challenges to scholars who wish to build models with predictive power, as interactivity makes it difficult to control and replicate experimental stimuli. Likewise, when we consider that users are now the *creators* as well as the consumers of media content, we need to broaden our conceptualization of "*uses and gratifications*" to consider the implications of "*expressions and gratifications.*" And finally, insofar as theories such as mood management assume that we arrange our environments to effectively regulate our moods, the increasing mobility of media entertainment implies an even broader reach of media in the affective lives of most individuals. These are but a few of the undoubtedly countless ways in which entertainment is being transformed, and addressing these changes will require careful methodological innovation and conceptual clarification.

◆ Concluding Thoughts

This chapter began with an observation that entertainment has arguably always been integral to human life. We seem to be natural storytellers, and we seem to be enthused audience members. We also seem to have a need to express our creativity and identities to willing listeners and viewers, and we appear to gravitate toward many leisurely diversions that enthrall, delight, inspire, and even disturb us. The limits of entertainment seemingly have no bounds, yet the changing media landscape brought on by technological developments forces us to see that our boundaries need to be widened even further. There is no more exciting time to be a scholar of media entertainment than now, as the questions and challenges that face us are causing us to develop new theories and to augment existing ones. Rising to such an occasion will undoubtedly be entertaining, enjoyable, and, ultimately, deeply gratifying.

◆ References

Aluja-Fabregat, A., & Torrubia-Beltri, R. (1998). Viewing of mass media violence, perception of violence, personality and academic achievement. *Personality and Individual Differences, 25,* 973–989.

Bartsch, A., Vorderer, P., Mangold, R., & Viehoff, R. (2008). Appraisal of emotions in media use: Toward a process model of meta-emotion and emotion regulation. *Media Psychology, 11,* 7–27.

Biswas, R., Riffe, D., & Zillmann, D. (1994). Mood influence on the appeal of bad news. *Journalism Quarterly, 71,* 689–696.

Bryant, J. (2004). Critical communication challenges for the new century. *Journal of Communication, 54,* 389–401.

Bryant, J., & Miron, D. (2003). Excitation-transfer theory and three-factor theory of emotion. In J. Bryant, D. Roskos-Ewoldsen, & J. Cantor (Eds.), *Communication and emotion: Essays in honor of Dolf Zillmann* (pp. 31–59). Mahwah, NJ: Erlbaum.

Bryant, J., & Zillmann, D. (1984). Using television to alleviate boredom and stress: Selective exposure as a function of induced excitational states. *Journal of Broadcasting, 28,* 1–20.

Busselle, R., & Bilandzic, H. (2008). Fictionality and perceived realism in experiencing stories: A model of narrative comprehension and engagement. *Communication Theory, 18,* 255–280.

Cacioppo, J. T., Petty, R. E., & Kao, C. F. (1984). The efficient assessment of need for cognition. *Journal of Personality Assessment, 48,* 306–307.

Entertainment Software Association. (n.d.). Economic data. Retrieved January 2009 from http://www.theesa.com/facts/econdata.asp

Erber, R., & Erber, M. W. (2000). The self-regulation of moods: Second thoughts on the importance of happiness in everyday life. *Psychological Inquiry, 11,* 142–148.

Ferguson, D. A., & Perse, E. M. (2000). The World Wide Web as a functional alternative to television. *Journal of Broadcasting & Electronic Media, 44,* 155–174.

Gibson, R., Aust, C. F., & Zillmann, D. (2000). Loneliness of adolescents and their choice and enjoyment of love-celebrating versus love-lamenting popular music. *Empirical Studies of the Arts, 18,* 43–48.

Green, M. C., & Brock, T. C. (2000). The role of transportation in the persuasiveness of public narratives. *Journal of Personality and Social Psychology, 79,* 701–721.

Green, M. C., & Brock, T. C. (2002). In the mind's eye: Transportation-imagery model of narrative persuasion. In M. C. Green, J. J. Strange, & T. C. Brock (Eds.), *Narrative impact: Social and cognitive foundations.* Mahwah, NJ: Erlbaum.

Green, M. C., Brock, T. C., & Kaufman, G. E. (2004). Understanding media enjoyment: The role of transportation into narrative worlds. *Communication Theory, 14,* 311–327.

Herzog, H. (1944). What do we really know about daytime serial listeners? In P. F. Lazarsfeld & F. N. Stanton (Eds.), *Radio research 1942–1943* (pp. 3–33). New York: Duell, Sloan & Pearce.

Horrigan, J. (2008). *Mobile access to data and information: Pew Internet & American Life Project.* Retrieved June 13, 2008, from http://www.pewinternet.org/pdfs/PIP_Mobile.Data.Access.pdf

Johnston, D. D. (1995). Adolescents' motivations for viewing graphic horror. *Human Communication Research, 21,* 522–552.

Katz, E., Blumler, J. G., & Gurevitch, M. (1973). Uses and gratifications research. *Public Opinion Quarterly, 37,* 509–523.

Katz, E., Gurevitch, M., & Haas, H. (1973). Use of mass media for important things. *American Sociological Review, 38,* 164–181.

Klimmt, C., Vorderer, P., & Ritterfeld, U. (2007). Interactivity and generalizability: New media, new challenges. *Communication Methods and Measures, 1,* 169–179.

Knobloch, S. (2003). Mood adjustment via mass communication. *Journal of Communication, 53,* 233–250.

Knobloch, S., Weisbach, K., & Zillmann, D. (2004). Love lamentation in pop songs: Music for unhappy lovers? *Zeitschrift für Medienpsychologie, 16,* 116–124.

Knobloch, S., & Zillmann, D. (2002). Mood management via the digital jukebox. *Journal of Communication, 52,* 351–366.

Knobloch-Westerwick, S., & Alter, S. (2006). Mood adjustment to social situations through mass media use: How men ruminate and women dissipate angry moods. *Human Communication Research, 32,* 58–73.

Lazarsfeld, P. F. (1940). *Radio and the printed page.* New York: Duell, Sloan & Pearce.

Lin, C. A. (1995). Diversity of network prime-time program formats during the 1980s. *Journal of Media Economics, 8*(4), 17–28.

Mares, M. L., & Cantor, J. (1992). Elderly viewers' responses to televised portrayals of old age: Empathy and mood management versus social comparison. *Communication Research, 19,* 459–478.

Mastro, D. E., Eastin, M. S., & Tamborini, R. (2002). Internet search behaviors and mood alterations: A selective exposure approach. *Media Psychology, 4,* 157–172.

Meadowcroft, J. M., & Zillmann, D. (1987). Women's comedy preferences during the menstrual cycle. *Communication Research, 14,* 204–218.

Nabi, R. L., Finnerty, K., Domschke, T., & Hull, S. (2006). Does misery love company? Exploring the therapeutic effects of TV viewing on regretted experiences. *Journal of Communication, 56,* 689–706.

Nabi, R. L., & Krcmar, M. (2004). Conceptualizing media enjoyment as attitude: Implications for mass media effects research. *Communication Theory, 14*(4), 288–310.

Oliver, M. B. (2003). Mood management and selective exposure. In J. Bryant, D. Roskos-Ewoldsen, & J. Cantor (Eds.), *Communication and emotion: Essays in honor of Dolf Zillmann* (pp. 85–106). Mahwah, NJ: Erlbaum.

Oliver, M. B. (2008). Tender affective states as predictors of entertainment preference. *Journal of Communication, 58,* 40–61.

Oliver, M. B., & Bartsch, A. (in press). Appreciation as audience response: Exploring entertainment gratifications beyond hedonism *Human Communication Research.*

Oliver, M. B., & Nabi, R. L. (2004). Exploring the concept of media enjoyment: An introduction to the special issue. *Communication Theory, 14,* 285–287.

Oliver, M. B., & Raney, A. A. (2008, May). *Development of hedonic and eudaimonic measures of entertainment motivations: The role of affective and cognitive gratifications.* Paper presented at the annual convention of the International Communication Association, Montreal, Canada.

Postman, N. (1986). *Amusing ourselves to death.* New York: Penguin Books.

Raacke, J., & Bonds-Raacke, J. (2008). MySpace and Facebook: Applying the uses and gratifications theory to exploring friend-networking sites. *CyberPsychology & Behavior, 11,* 169–174.

Raney, A. A. (2003). Dispositon-based theories of enjoyment. In J. Bryant, D. Roskos-Ewoldsen, & J. Cantor (Eds.), *Communication and emotion: Essays in honor of Dolf Zillmann* (pp. 61–84). Mahwah, NJ: Erlbaum.

Raney, A. A. (2004). Expanding disposition theory: Reconsidering character liking, moral evaluations, and enjoyment. *Communication Theory, 14,* 348–369.

Raney, A. A. (2006). The psychology of disposition-based theories of media enjoyment. In J. Bryant & P. Vorderer (Eds.), *Psychology of entertainment* (pp. 137–150). Mahwah, NJ: Erlbaum.

Raney, A. A., & Bryant, J. (2002). Moral judgment and crime drama: An integrated theory of enjoyment. *Journal of Communication, 52,* 402–415.

Reiss, S., & Wiltz, J. (2004). Why people watch reality TV. *Media Psychology, 6,* 363–378.

Rubin, A. M. (1983). Television uses and gratifications: The interactions of viewing patterns and motivations. *Journal of Broadcasting, 27,* 37–51.

Rubin, A. M. (2002). The uses-and-gratifications perspective of media effects. In J. Bryant & D. Zillmann (Eds.), *Media effects: Advances in theory and research* (2nd ed., pp. 525–548). Mahwah, NJ: Erlbaum.

Ruggiero, T. E. (2000). Uses and gratifications theory in the 21st century. *Mass Communication & Society, 3,* 3–37.

Ryan, R. M., & Deci, E. L. (2001). On happiness and human potentials: A review of research on hedonic and eudaimonic well-being. *Annual Review of Psychology, 52,* 141–166.

Shao, G. (2008, June). *The emergence of user-generated media: Understanding their appeal from a uses and gratifications perspective.* Paper presented at the NCA Doctoral Honors Seminar, Tuscaloosa, AL.

Sherry, J. L. (2004). Flow and media enjoyment. *Communication Theory, 14,* 328–347.

Steger, M. F., Frazier, P., Oishi, S., & Kaler, M. (2006). The meaning in life questionnaire: Assessing the presence of and search for meaning in life. *Journal of Counseling Psychology, 53,* 80–93.

Strizhakova, Y., & Krcmar, M. (2007). Mood management and video rental choices. *Media Psychology, 10,* 91–112.

Trapnell, P. D., & Campbell, J. D. (1999). Private self-consciousness and the five-factor model of personality: Distinguishing rumination from reflection. *Journal of Personality and Social Psychology, 76,* 284–304.

Vorderer, P., Klimmt, C., & Ritterfeld, U. (2004). Enjoyment: At the heart of media entertainment. *Communication Theory, 14,* 388–408.

Vorderer, P., Knobloch, S., & Schramm, H. (2001). Does entertainment suffer from interactivity? The impact of watching an interactive TV movie on viewers' experience of entertainment. *Media Psychology, 3,* 343–363.

Waterman, A. S. (1993). Two conceptions of happiness: Contrasts of personal expressiveness (eudaimonia) and hedonic enjoyment. *Journal of Personality and Social Psychology, 64,* 678–691.

Weber, R., Tamborini, R., Lee, H. E., & Stipp, H. (2008). Enjoyment of daytime soap operas: A longitudinal test of affective disposition theory. *Media Psychology, 11,* 462-487.

Witmer, B. G., & Singer, M. J. (1998). Measuring presence in virtual environments: A presence questionnaire. *Presence, 7,* 225–240.

Zillmann, D. (1971). Excitation transfer in communication-mediated aggressive behavior. *Journal of Experimental Social Psychology, 7,* 419–434.

Zillmann, D. (1980). Anatomy of suspense. In P. Tannenbaum (Ed.), *The entertainment functions of television* (pp. 133–163). Hillsdale, NJ: Erlbaum.

Zillmann, D. (1985). The experimental exploration of gratifications from media entertainment. In K. E. Rosengren, L. A. Wenner, & P. Palmgreen (Eds.), *Media gratifications research: Current perspectives* (pp. 225–239). Beverly Hills, CA: Sage.

Zillmann, D. (1988). Mood management through communication choices. *American Behavioral Scientist, 31,* 327–340.

Zillmann, D. (1991). The logic of suspense and mystery. In J. Bryant & D. Zillmann (Eds.), *Responding to the screen: Reception and reaction processes* (pp. 281–303). Hillsdale, NJ: Erlbaum.

Zillmann, D. (1998). Does tragic drama have redeeming value? *Siegener Periodikum für Internationale Literaturwissenschaft, 16,* 1–11.

Zillmann, D. (2000). Mood management in the context of selective exposure theory. In M. E. Roloff (Ed.), *Communication yearbook* (Vol. 23, pp. 103–123). Thousand Oaks, CA: Sage.

Zillmann, D., & Bryant, J. (1975). Viewer's moral sanction of retribution in the appreciation of dramatic presentations. *Journal of Experimental Social Psychology, 11,* 572–582.

Zillmann, D., & Bryant, J. (1985). Affect, mood, and emotion as determinants of selective exposure. In D. Zillmann & J. Bryant (Eds.), *Selective exposure to communication* (pp. 157–190). Hillsdale, NJ: Erlbaum.

Zillmann, D., & Bryant, J. (1991). Responding to comedy: The sense and nonsense in humor. In J. Bryant & D. Zillmann (Eds.), *Responding to the screen: Reception and reaction processes.* Hillsdale, NJ: Erlbaum.

Zillmann, D., Bryant, J., & Sapolsky, B. S. (1989). Enjoyment from sports spectatorship. In J. H. Goldstein (Ed.), *Sports, games, and play: Social and psychological viewpoints* (2nd ed., pp. 241–278). Hillsdale, NJ: Erlbaum.

Zillmann, D., & Cantor, J. R. (1977). Affective responses to the emotions of a protagonist. *Journal of Experimental Social Psychology, 13,* 155–165.

Zillmann, D., Hezel, R. T., & Medoff, N. J. (1980). The effect of affective states on selective exposure to televised entertainment fare. *Journal of Applied Social Psychology, 10,* 323–339.

Zillmann, D., & Vorderer, P. (2000). Preface. In D. Zillmann & P. Vorderer (Eds.), *Media entertainment: The psychology of its appeal.* Mahwah, NJ: Erlbaum.

Zuckerman, M., & Litle, P. (1986). Personality and curiosity about morbid and sexual events. *Personality and Individual Differences, 7,* 49–56.

12

CURRENT RESEARCH IN MEDIA PRIMING

◆ David R. Roskos-Ewoldsen and
Beverly Roskos-Ewoldsen

A recent commercial made by the insurance company Liberty Mutual shows a women helping out another person by holding him back from a rush of traffic. A man happens to see the act. Later, that man helps an elderly woman with her grocery bag, and the exchange is again noticed by another, who, when getting on a roller-coaster ride, notices that the couple leaving it had left their photos, and she hands them to the couple, and so on. The tag line is "Responsibility. What's your policy?" The implication of the commercial is that people who are responsible help one another. However, was it really a sense of responsibility that led to subsequent behaviors? Perhaps it was simply that seeing the act of kindness primed thoughts of kindness, which in turn increased the likelihood of helping out another person. Taking this a step further, would a person who watched the commercial be more likely to help another, or even think about helping another, compared with someone who did not? That is, will the media message prime thoughts, beliefs, and behaviors? This is the crux of media priming.

This chapter reviews the extant theorizing and research on media priming. The first section describes priming, how it is measured, and general theories of priming. The next section presents three lines of research: violence-related priming in the media, political priming, and stereotyping. The final section compares each type of priming, describes how new media environments may affect the study of media priming, and contemplates the focus of the next 10 years of media priming research.

◆ *What Is Priming?*

Priming refers to the effect of some preceding stimulus or event on how we react, broadly defined, to some subsequent event or person (Roskos-Ewoldsen, Roskos-Ewoldsen, & Carpentier, 2009). The effect is analogous to that which happens when a water well is primed. The act of priming the well enables the well to produce water when it is pumped afterward. Cognitive and social psychologists have used priming paradigms since the early 1970s to study how humans process information and how that processed information affects our behavior. As applied to the media, priming refers to the effects of the content in the media on people's later behavior, thoughts, or judgments. Priming has been used extensively to study the short-term effects of media violence, the long-term effects of political coverage on evaluations of a candidate, and stereotyped portrayals of minorities (Roskos-Ewoldsen, Klinger, & Roskos-Ewoldsen, 2007).

The cognitive origins of priming, however, are much more focused. Priming was not a theory or explanation; rather, it was a procedure used to understand how information was represented in and retrieved from memory. Some theories of memory, such as network models of memory (Roskos-Ewoldsen, 1997), assume that information is stored in memory in the form of nodes and that each node represents a unique concept (e.g., "human being"). Furthermore, these nodes are connected to related nodes in memory by associative pathways (e.g., "human being" is linked to "family" or "community" or even "responsibility," but probably not directly linked to "President Herbert Hoover"). Also, it is believed that each node has an "activation threshold." If the node's level of activation exceeds its threshold, the node fires, and energy flows down network pathways from the activated node to other related nodes. Activation of nodes primarily comes from two sources: environmental input or the spread of activation from related nodes. For example, if the "human being" node fires (e.g., due to hearing the phrase), activation spreads from the "human being" node to related nodes such as "family." Once a related node is activated (in this example, "family"), it then requires less additional activation to reach its threshold and subsequently fire. In other words, the related node has been primed by the firing of the original node. Of course, it is functional for related concepts to be primed because it means that the cognitive system will be more efficient in processing information that is likely to be needed. If one is watching the Liberty Mutual commercial, that person is more likely to interpret an ambiguous situation as needing responsible action than, say, situations that involve President Herbert Hoover, so the fact that activation spreads to "responsibility" is likely to increase the efficiency of the cognitive processes.

Social and developmental psychologists have used priming procedures as a way to identify the types of cognitive processes that may play a role in person perception, stereotyping, and attitude activation. For example, Graham and Hudley (1994) had middle school boys read a paragraph that portrayed interpersonal situations with negative outcomes. For half of the boys, the paragraph described outcomes that were under the control of the perpetrator (e.g., deliberately splashing water on the boy), whereas for the other boys, the perpetrator was not responsible for the outcome (e.g., accidentally bumping into the boy). After completing this priming task, participants completed a second, seemingly unrelated study in which they were to imagine themselves drinking at a water fountain when another student knocked into them, causing them to spill water all over their shirt. The boys who had read the "responsible for outcome" sentences were more likely to judge that the child intentionally bumped into them than were the boys who read the "not responsible for outcome" sentences. This finding suggests a process whereby the negative outcome situations in the sentences activated related concepts in memory, such as the idea that negative outcomes are intentional. If a negative outcome situation were to occur again, the concept that negative outcomes are intentional would fire more quickly than the concept that negative outcomes are unintentional. The reverse would be true for sentences in which negative outcomes are unintentional. In other words, the sentences primed the judgment of intentionality.

CHARACTERISTICS OF PRIMING EFFECTS

Research utilizing priming methodologies soon demonstrated that not all primes are the same. Consequently, the properties of priming itself have been investigated. Research on priming has demonstrated three important characteristics of priming. First, the effect of a prime dissipates with time. Cognitive psychologists have shown that the activation level of a node will dissipate over time if no additional source of activation is present. Recent primes have more effect on judgments or behaviors than temporally distant primes (Higgins, Bargh, & Lombardi, 1985). *Recency* simply refers to the time lag between the prime and the target (e.g., the time between seeing a gun on TV and seeing an ambiguous behavior that could be interpreted as hostile). Returning to the metaphor of a water pump, if the pump has not been used for a while, it will no longer pump water without being primed again. Eventually, given no more activation, the activation level of the node returns to its resting state and is no longer considered to

be primed. With cognitive tasks such as lexical decision tasks, which involve judgments of whether a string of letters is a word, or attitude priming tasks, which involve judgments of whether a word has positive or negative connotations, the priming effect dissipates in less than a minute (Higgins et al., 1985). However, in tasks that involve social judgments or evaluations of a social stimulus, the priming effect can last up to 15 to 20 minutes and possibly up to one hour (Roskos-Ewoldsen et al., 2007).

Second, primes that are stronger will tend to have stronger effects on people's judgments and behavior. A stronger prime will result in higher activation levels in the target item, which will take more time to dissipate than a target item whose activation level is lower due to a weaker prime (Higgins et al., 1985). One of the problems with discussions of prime strength involves exactly what makes a prime stronger. Typically, the strength or intensity of a prime is manipulated either through the *frequency* of the priming event (e.g., a single exposure to a gun vs. five exposures to a gun in quick succession) or the duration of the priming event (e.g., 15 minutes of exposure versus 1 minute).

Third, as mentioned earlier, primes tend to have stronger effects on situations that are ambiguous (Otten & Stapel, 2007). Recall the Graham and Hudley (1994) study described earlier regarding intentionality judgments of an ambiguous shove after being primed with related sentences. Compare these ambiguous situations with one that is not ambiguous, such as a driver making a rude gesture at you and then cutting you off in traffic. The latter situation is perceived as hostile regardless of the presence of earlier primes.

A final point about the nature of priming is the accessibility of a concept when it is at rest, or prior to its being primed. Earlier it was noted that each concept is hypothesized to have an activation threshold, and a concept is activated in memory when its activation threshold is exceeded. Concepts can vary in how high their resting level of activity is compared with their thresholds. This means that concepts vary in how much additional activity is needed for them to fire. Those constructs that have "low activation thresholds" (i.e., high resting levels of activity relative to the threshold) are said to be highly accessible in memory. These concepts come to mind easily. Conversely, concepts with "high activation thresholds" (i.e., low activity levels relative to the threshold) take more energy to activate in memory; these concepts have low accessibility. These concepts come to mind with difficulty. For example, the name of the person who leads Al-Qaeda (Osama bin Laden) is probably highly accessible for most people in the United States. However, the name of the person who leads the United Nations (Ban Ki-moon) is probably either not very accessible or not available in memory.

At some point, the accessibility of a concept can become so high that it has chronically high activity (see research by Bargh, Bond, Lombardi, & Tota, 1986). In the attitudinal domain, someone's attitude toward cockroaches is probably chronically highly accessible from memory. When people see a cockroach, they do not have to think about whether they like cockroaches. Instead, their attitude toward cockroaches is activated from memory without conscious effort. On the other hand, someone's attitude toward Tibetan food is probably not chronically accessible. If asked what their attitude is toward Tibetan food, people may have to actively retrieve that attitude from memory or create the attitude on the spot (Roskos-Ewoldsen & Fazio, 1997). Chronically accessible concepts can be primed so that they are temporarily even more accessible from memory (Roskos-Ewoldsen et al., 2007). Nevertheless, without some form of reinforcement, even chronically accessible concepts eventually become less accessible across time (Grant & Logan, 1993).

MEASURING THE EFFECTS OF PRIMES

Priming effects are typically measured in three ways. First, as just discussed, priming can be studied by looking at the effects of different operationalizations of priming on people's judgments of ambiguous events. For example, in the Graham and Hudley (1994) study, the effect of priming was measured simply by comparing the ratings of intentionality by the two groups, where each group had a different prime (i.e., intentional or unintentional). When comparing two operationalizations of priming, it is crucial that the test scenario be ambiguous, as in the study by Graham and Hudley, who deliberately set up the drinking fountain scenario so that it was unclear whether or not the bump was intentional, and then measured participants' judgments of intentionality.

Second, one could measure the effect of priming on behaviors, such as the increase of aggressive behaviors for a group that saw a violent media program compared with another group that had not, as in Josephson's (1987) study in which adolescent boys were exposed to violent or nonviolent programming and then played field hockey. The critical question involved whether boys who were primed with violent programming engaged in more aggressive behaviors when they later played field hockey.

A third way to measure the effects of priming requires technology that can measure the time it takes to respond to some prompt with millisecond accuracy (i.e., reaction time, or RT). Examples of this type of research are found in Fazio, Sanbonmatsu, Powell, and Kardes's (1986) studies of attitude priming or Higgins et al.'s (1985) research testing various priming models. Primes are typically presented on a computer monitor. Participants may or may not have to respond to the primes, as long as it is clear that they attended to them. After the primes, a target appears about which participants make a judgment, such as like/dislike, good/bad, or even word/nonword. RT is measured as the time elapsed between the presentation of the target and the participant's response. The shorter the RT, the bigger the priming effect. Usually, RT for two different types of primes is compared. As with the other measures, it is crucial that the targets be ambiguous. Because RTs for a given type of prime often form skewed distributions, they are typically transformed to their inverses before analysis. This has the advantage of pulling in the extremes and making the distribution more normal (Arpan, Rhodes, & Roskos-Ewoldsen, 2007).

◆ TV Violence and Priming

An examination of media research involving priming reveals three primary domains of study: media violence, political judgments, and stereotyping. Extensive research has been conducted on the relationship between TV violence and aggressive thoughts, feelings, and behaviors (Anderson, Deuser, & DeNeve, 1995; see also Bushman, Huesmann, & Whitaker, Chapter 24, this volume). The available research indicates that TV violence can influence people's behavior in both the short and the long term, and these effects can range from decreased sensitization to violent behavior to increases in violent behavior (Potter, 2003). Meta-analysis suggests that the link between exposure to TV violence and aggressive behaviors is almost as strong as the link between smoking two packs of cigarettes a day and developing lung cancer (Bushman & Anderson, 2001).

Consistent with a priming explanation for media violence, many studies have demonstrated that people who are exposed to a violent TV clip or play a violent video game are more likely to think aggressive thoughts (see Anderson, 2004). However, does the priming of aggressive thoughts translate into aggressive behavior? The answer seems to

be, "it depends." For example, Josephson (1987) investigated the role of trait aggression, frustration, and violence-related cues in the priming effects of violent media on children's behavior. In this study, first, teachers indicated how aggressive the boys in their classes were, both in class and on the playground. Later, the boys saw either a violent or a nonviolent TV program. The violent TV segment showed the characters using walkie-talkies, but no walkie-talkies were seen in the nonviolent show. After watching the TV program, half the boys were purposefully frustrated by watching a nonviolent cartoon that became increasingly static-ridden. Next, all boys were mock interviewed, where either a walkie-talkie (violence-related prime) or a microphone was used. Finally, the boys played hockey and were observed both on and off the court for signs of aggressive behavior. The researchers found an interaction between aggressiveness and exposure to the violence-related prime such that boys who were high in trait aggressiveness acted more violently. This effect on aggressive boys was heightened both when violent programming was coupled with the violence-related cue and when violent programming was followed by frustration. However, as predicted by research on priming, the effect of TV violence on aggressive behaviors dissipated over time.

◆ Models of Aggression Priming

There are two major models of aggression priming. The first is Berkowitz's (1984) neoassociationistic model, which draws heavily from network models of priming. The model hypothesizes that depictions of violence in the media activate hostility- and aggression-related concepts in memory. The activation of these concepts increases the likelihood that others' behavior will be interpreted as aggressive or hostile and increases the likelihood that one will engage in aggressive behaviors. Without further input, however, the activity levels of these hostile and aggressive concepts fade with time, as does their associated likelihood of influencing aggressive behavior.

The second model is the general affective aggression model (GAAM), which is an extensive elaboration of the neoassociationistic model (Anderson et al., 1995; see also Bushman et al., Chapter 24, this volume). This model incorporates affect and arousal into a network framework, and introduces a three-stage process by which situations influence aggressive affect and behavior. In the first stage of the GAAM, situational variables, such as pain, frustration, or depictions of violence, prime aggressive cognitions (e.g., hostile thoughts and memories) and affect (e.g., hostility, anger), which results in increased arousal. This first stage involves relatively automatic processes that are outside the control of the individual. In the second stage, the primed cognitions and affect, in conjunction with the increased arousal, influence *primary appraisal*. Primary appraisal involves the interpretation of the situation, including the attribution of one's arousal in that situation, and tends to be more automatic than effortful in nature. The study in which boys with high trait aggression were influenced by violence cues or frustration represents primary appraisal. The final stage of the model involves *secondary appraisals,* which are more effortful, controlled appraisals of the situation, and involve more thoughtful consideration of various behavioral alternatives to the situation. This final stage can override the primary appraisal (Gilbert, 1991). For example, a person may have aggressive thoughts and affect primed or activated by playing a violent first-person shooter game. The activation of these thoughts leads to an increased likelihood of making hostile attributions when, for example, someone cuts the person off in traffic. However, the person can override these attributions and choose

not to respond in a hostile manner toward the other driver.

Berkowitz's (1997) neoassociationistic model and Anderson et al.'s (1995) GAAM explain many of the findings of the research on priming and media violence. Both models predict that media violence will temporarily increase aggressive thoughts (Anderson, 1997; Bushman, 1998), and sometimes aggressive behaviors (Bushman, 1995). Furthermore, both models predict that individuals who are high in trait aggressiveness are more likely to react aggressively than individuals who are low in trait aggressiveness (Bushman, 1996). Finally, both models specifically predict that the effects of media priming will fade with time (see Josephson, 1987).

LIMITATIONS AND FUTURE DIRECTIONS FOR AGGRESSION PRIMING

While numerous studies have supported both of these models of aggression, they have their limitations. First, several studies have failed to find the predicted effects of exposure to aggression on indirect measures of aggression, such as the accessibility of aggressive concepts. Recall that the second state of the GAAM predicts that exposure to aggression-related stimuli should increase the accessibility of violence-related concepts, which in turn will influence primary appraisals. To investigate this, Roskos-Ewoldsen, Eno, Okdie, Guadano, and DeCoster (2008) had two participants play a violent video game (Halo) simultaneously. Participants engaged in a direct competition condition in which they killed each other, an indirect competition condition in which they played separately with the goal of getting farther through the game than their opponent, a cooperative play condition in which they worked together against the aliens, or a no play control condition. After playing the game (or not), participants completed a lexical decision task (i.e., "Is a string of letters a word or not?"). For those targets that were words, people should make lexical decisions regarding a concept faster when the concept has been primed by a related, compared with an unrelated, concept. Across the four conditions, the accessibility of aggression-related targets was expected to be highest for the killing condition, with decreasing accessibility for the other conditions. Contrary to the predictions of the GAAM, however, there were no differences across the conditions in RTs for primed, aggression-related target words. There was enough power to detect a difference, so this null result suggests that the accessibility of the concepts may not be the mechanism by which this type of priming occurs. Bluemke and Zumbach (2007) provide another example that contradicts the predictions of the GAAM. Clearly, more research that tests the early stages of the GAAM is needed.

A second limitation of the models and their accompanying research is that they do not address variables that may influence the types of thoughts and behaviors that result from media priming. Violent portrayals in the media can evoke many different emotional responses beyond aggression, one being fear. In fact, regular TV programming, such as the local news or crime dramas that take place in a nearby city, elicit fear responses. Likewise, extensive research on cultivation theory has demonstrated that one of the long-term consequences of exposure to extensive violence in the media is fear (Roskos-Ewoldsen, Davies, & Roskos-Ewoldsen, 2004). These findings lead to several questions, such as, What are the circumstances under which aggression on TV primes fear? How do these circumstances prime the different responses? What other responses may be primed by aggression on TV? More research is required to address these questions.

A third limitation of the research in this area is the inadequate study of moderators of the priming effects of violent TV programming. Several possible moderators

exist, such as genre of the TV program. For example, sitcoms that contain a lot of verbal aggression do not prime aggression (Chory-Assad & Tamborini, 2004). Other moderators of violence priming include personality variables, like trait aggressiveness (Josephson, 1987; Roskos-Ewoldsen et al., 2007). Recent research suggests that, at least for the early stages of the GAAM, people low in trait aggression may show stronger priming effects (i.e., greater increases in the accessibility of aggressive thoughts) than people higher in trait aggression (Meier, Robinson, & Wilkowski, 2007). This finding probably reflects the impoverished aggression-related cognitive networks that characterize people who are lower in trait aggression (Bushman, 1996), as impoverished networks are more susceptible to priming effects of aggression-related thoughts and actions (Bartholow, Anderson, Carnagey, & Benjamin, 2005). However, the increased accessibility of aggression-related thoughts in low trait aggression people may not translate into aggressive behavior because they may inhibit their aggressive tendencies during the secondary appraisal stage of the GAAM. Conversely, people high in trait aggression may not show substantial changes in the accessibility of aggression-related thoughts, but the increase may be enough to put them over the threshold for behaving aggressively. Another personality trait—agreeableness—also appears to moderate the priming effects of violence: People who are high in agreeableness are less likely to show priming effects than people who are low in agreeableness (Meier, Robinson, & Wilkowski, 2006). Again, more research is needed in this area.

◆ Political Coverage and Presidential Evaluations

Another major line of research is political priming. *Political priming* focuses on the idea that the issues that the media are covering influence the information that people use to judge the president (Iyengar & Kinder, 1987). When judging how well the president is doing his or her job, people have a lot of different pieces of information they can use to make that judgment. For example, they could use the president's performance on the economy, civil rights, international affairs, or how well he or she dresses. The idea behind political priming is that the media doesn't influence what you think, but rather what information you use to make your judgments. Specifically, if the media are focusing primarily on international affairs, international affairs are made salient, and people will use their impressions of how well the president is doing in international affairs to judge how well he or she is doing overall. However, if the media are focusing on domestic affairs, domestic issues are made salient and people will use their impressions of how well the president is doing on domestic issues to judge how well the president is doing overall. During President George H. W. Bush's presidency (1988–1992), the media focused on the Gulf War and its success, and President Bush enjoyed very high approval ratings. Indeed, many political pundits did not think the Democratic Party would be able to field a candidate who could beat President Bush in 1992. However, after the Gulf War, the media turned its attention away from the Middle East and focused on domestic issues, and people started using their negative evaluations of President Bush's handling of domestic affairs to judge his overall performance. Consequently, President Bush's job performance ratings plummeted, despite the fact that people still thought he did a good job of handling international affairs (Iyengar & Simon, 1993).

MODELS OF POLITICAL PRIMING

Early theorizing on political priming used the availability heuristic to explain the effects of media coverage on political

priming (Iyengar & Simon, 1993). According to this explanation, media coverage of an issue influences which exemplars are accessed from memory when people make judgments of the president. However, the availability explanation has not been well developed or subjected to empirical tests within the political priming domain.

Only one model of political priming has been developed sufficiently to explain the political priming results (Scheufele & Tewksbury, 2007). Similar to Berkowitz's (1984) neoassociationistic model, Price and Tewksbury's (1997) model of political priming is based on network models of memory and the role the media play in increasing the accessibility of information from memory. As discussed earlier, network models maintain that both chronic and temporary accessibility of concepts influence their likelihood of activation. In addition, Price and Tewksbury incorporate the notion of *applicability* of information into their model. Applicability refers to deliberate judgments of the relevance of information to the current situation. Clearly, if primed information is not relevant, it will not be used when making political judgments. Within Price and Tewksbury's model, concepts that are activated by the media *and* judged as applicable to the current situation influence how the message is perceived or interpreted. On the other hand, those concepts that are activated by the media and judged as not applicable do not influence how the message is perceived.

Miller and Krosnick (2000) rigorously tested the accessibility component of political priming by manipulating media exposure to current issues (e.g., drugs and immigration). They gathered measures of participants' beliefs about the most important problems in the nation and approval of the current president's performance, and they found the basic priming effect. Participants who were exposed to the media coverage weighed those issues more heavily when judging the president's performance than those not exposed to the media coverage. To test whether the accessibility of these issues mediated this relationship, accessibility toward the issues was measured via RT. Contrary to expectations, however, those participants who were quicker at the reaction time task did not weigh the accessible information more heavily than those who were slower. Thus, the researchers concluded that network models of spreading activation, which rely on the accessibility of concepts, could not be the direct cause of political priming. Rather, the researchers argued that when the concepts that are highly accessible are activated, the activation causes a second, deliberative process. However, Miller and Krosnick (2001) incorrectly interpret the role of deliberative processing as meaning that accessibility was not an important component of the political priming effect. Recent research on automaticity has demonstrated that automatic processing can lead to deliberative processing (Roskos-Ewoldsen, 1997; Roskos-Ewoldsen, Bischel, Hill, & Hoffman, 2002; Roskos-Ewoldsen, Yu, & Rhodes, 2004). Thus, the deliberative processing that they found evidence for may well be a consequence of increases in the accessibility of the constructs primed by the manipulated media coverage.

LIMITATIONS AND FUTURE DIRECTIONS FOR POLITICAL PRIMING

Although there are clearly some unresolved issues that arise in the context of political priming, one point that is particularly puzzling is its time course, which is much longer than that found in cognitive priming tasks discussed earlier in this chapter. Consistent with the research from cognitive and social psychology, Carpentier, Roskos-Ewoldsen, and Roskos-Ewoldsen (2008) found that the effect of a news column about a political figure on judgments of that political figure faded

within 30 minutes after exposure. Likewise, Althaus and Kim (2006) demonstrated that media coverage of the Gulf War impacted opinions for hours afterward. However, these effects seemed to dissipate within 24 hours of the media exposure. On the other hand, contrary to the research in cognitive and social psychology and network models of memory, much of the political priming literature finds effects of exposure that last for several weeks (Roskos-Ewoldsen et al., 2007). Price and Tewksbury's (1997) network model might be able to explain these long-term priming effects by assuming that continued media coverage makes the concepts chronically accessible. However, whether long-term coverage creates chronically accessible concepts has not been demonstrated empirically.

Despite the ambiguities involving the time course of political priming, a rich outgrowth of research on political priming has recently occurred along several fronts. A significant focus is on whether different genres of media can produce political priming effects. For example, research has demonstrated that movies (Holbert & Hansen, 2006), crime dramas (Holbook & Hill, 2005), and late-night talk shows (Moy, Xenos, & Hess, 2005) can operate as political primes for judgments of the president's performance. Further, simpler or familiar topics (such as general economic trends or issues of character) were more likely to prime evaluations of the president than more complex issues (such as domestic or international policies). In addition to priming effects on presidential performance, there are priming effects for other political and policy issues (e.g., Sheafer & Weimann, 2005; cf. McGraw & Ling, 2003).

Second, there is a growing focus on the types of information that are primed by news coverage (Kim, 2005; Kim, Scheufele, & Shanahan, 2002). Political priming has generally been presented as a "hydraulic model" where the media primes people to use certain information at the expense of competing information. In a study of political priming resulting from coverage of the first Gulf War, Kim (2005) found that news coverage did not narrow the types of information used in the judgment as predicted by the hydraulic model. Rather, Kim found news coverage primed an increase in the variety of information that was used by people who pay careful attention to the media.

These very different aspects of political priming have provided a fruitful line of research. However, there are questions yet to be addressed fully. One question involves the circumstances under which political priming may be moderated. For example, political party identity can moderate the political priming effect (Holbert & Hansen, 2006), as can personality variables, like need for closure (Hansen & Hansen, 1988), and possibly authoritarianism, or political expertise.

Another aspect of political priming to be explored is one's dependence on the media as one's source of information. People who are dependent on the news media as their source of information (e.g., in China), may demonstrate a larger priming effect than people who are less dependent on the news media (e.g., in the United States). Finally, more effort needs to be directed toward the cognitive and affective mechanisms through which the political priming effect occurs. Perhaps consideration of a more global model of cognition, such as the interacting cognitive subsystems approach (e.g., Barnard, 1985; Teasdale & Barnard, 1993), would be a worthwhile place to explore. As one can see, there is much conceptual and empirical work that still remains to be done in the realm of political priming.

◆ Media Priming and Stereotyping

As in the domains of violence and political priming, research in the stereotype domain indicates that the media can prime thoughts,

judgments, and perhaps behaviors. This area has grown remarkably since 2000, with a focus on the potential for the media to prime various stereotypes, including those related to gender (Hansen & Krygowski, 1994) and ethnicity (Oliver, Ramasubramanian, & Kim, 2007; see Mastro, Chapter 25, this volume). As in the other lines of research discussed, priming is typically manipulated through exposure to a media message that portrays a stereotypic interaction between two people, a still shot of a stereotypic behavior, or even words that are associated with a stereotype. Afterward, participants are exposed to an ambiguous situation about which they are asked to make Likert-scale judgments, including positive and negative impressions, internal and external attributions of behavior, dominance of one person relative to another, and credibility.

As an example, one study investigated the priming effects of rock music videos on perceptions of men and women (Hansen & Hansen, 1988). Participants in the study watched a rock video that portrayed a stereotypic interaction between a man and a woman where the woman was portrayed as a sex object, or they watched an unrelated rock video. Then they watched a scripted videotape that depicted a "boy meets girl" situation, and finally, they completed a survey of their impressions of the man and woman interacting in the scripted video. Participants who viewed the stereotypical video had more stereotypic impressions of the scripted interaction compared with those who watched the neutral rock video. In particular, the man was perceived as more dominant and the woman more submissive than in the neutral group.

This research relates to the several studies that found the media can prime rape myths (e.g., Intons-Peterson, Roskos-Ewoldsen, Thomas, Shirley, & Blut, 1989). Rape myths involve stereotypes of women, such as that women enjoy being raped. Rape myths can influence later perceptions of the plaintiff and defendant in an acquaintance rape trial. In this particular study, male participants watched a scripted trial of an alleged acquaintance rape case after viewing either a sexually violent video, a sexual video, or a neutral video. Then, the men made judgments about the trial, such as the extent of guilt and, assuming guilt, what the recommended sentence should be. Men who saw the sexually violent video were more likely to accept rape myths of women and less likely to believe that the man was guilty of the alleged rape, and if they believed he was guilty, suggested less time in jail, compared with those who saw either of the other two videos.

Another interesting take on this area of research involves how representations of African Americans in the news influence people's attitudes toward various political issues that relate to racial stereotypes, such as crime or education (Dixon, 2006). Critically, in these studies, there was no information provided in the story connecting race to the target political issue. Yet, depictions of Blacks in pictures or simple mentions of the race of a person within the story influenced people's judgments of the racialized political issues. For example, Dixon found that participants supported the death penalty more strongly after viewing a newscast with African American suspects as compared with a newscast involving the same crimes but with the race of the criminal unspecified. Likewise, Abraham and Appiah (2006) found that pictures of African Americans in news articles about school vouchers or three-strikes crime laws resulted in White participants' perception that Blacks are more affected by the issues than Whites. When the pictures were of White Americans, there were no differences in which group was seen as affected more. Again, it is critical to note that there were no explicit references to the photo or to race, and the photos were nonstereotypical of Blacks. In addition, Domke, McCoy, and Torres (1999) found that how a news story about a political issue (immigration) was framed (focused on the economic effects vs. the ethics of immigration) could influence subsequent political judgments, such as the effects of immigration on the economy. Specifically, when news coverage of a policy issue, such as immigration, emphasizes jobs and resources, a material view of the issue is fostered, resulting in one being more likely to draw upon stereotypes of immigrants when judging the impact of immigration on the health of the U.S. economy. In contrast, when an ethical view is fostered, focusing on the humanitarian issues, one is less likely to draw upon stereotypes when making that same judgment.

MODELS OF STEREOTYPE PRIMING

In all of these studies, the main theoretical explanation for the priming effects found is that the media coverage activates stereotypes in memory, which in turn influence judgments of others and of policy issues. What is striking about these studies is that the stimuli are designed so that there is no explicit reference to these stereotypes. There is no reason why these stereotypes should be influencing thoughts and judgments, but they do. In other words, unlike the other lines of research, there is not a direct priming effect of the media. Rather, the media implicitly prime stereotypes, which directly influence thoughts, beliefs, and judgments. Nevertheless, the research on media priming of stereotypes increases our confidence in the generality of the media as a prime because this research provides validation that the media can act as a prime in a unique research domain, and that a variety of media (e.g., advertisements, rock music videos, newsletters) can serve this function.

LIMITATIONS AND FUTURE DIRECTIONS FOR STEREOTYPE PRIMING

As a unique research domain, stereotype priming has only recently been brought under the umbrella of media priming.

Therefore, it has not been as fully developed as violence priming and political priming. Some ideas for future research include investigating whether stereotype priming has the same characteristics of priming as outlined earlier in the chapter: priming dissipates with time, primes that are stronger will tend to have stronger effects, and primes tend to have stronger effects on situations that are ambiguous. Another future direction involves the comparison group for stereotype priming. Usually it is assumed that stereotypes are negative, whereas the counterstereotype is positive. However, these counterstereotypes often have the same effect as a nonstereotype neutral condition. In other words, stereotype primes do prime negative depictions but do not appear to prime positive ones. Why is this so? When and under which conditions is this so? It may be that the judgments used in this research tend to be at the negative end of the spectrum of political issues. Perhaps differences would be found if the judgments were about issues that people felt more positive about, in line with the positive psychology approach to understanding thoughts, judgments, and behavior (Roskos-Ewoldsen, 2006). Regarding behavior, unfortunately, no research in this area has yet focused on behavioral manifestations of the media's priming of stereotypes.

◆ Concluding Remarks on Media Priming

Media priming is a robust phenomenon that occurs across different domains and different media ranging from news coverage to rap lyrics to TV dramas to documentaries. The information people use when making judgments of the president or interpreting an ambiguous act as hostile can be influenced by the content of the media. Likewise, stereotypic depictions in the media can play a role in whether people use gender or ethnic stereotypes when making judgments of people and policy issues.

Priming is typically considered a "limited effects" model of media effects. As Rogers (2004) argues, political priming research grew out of the research on agenda setting, which is a classic limited effects model. In addition, the time course of priming—being rather brief—has typically set it up as a limited effects theory. Consequently, one might imagine an argument being made that as a limited effects theory, media priming may not be particularly consequential. More research is surely needed on the behavioral consequences of media priming.

Further, as this chapter has tried to demonstrate and somewhat counter to the notion of a limited effects model, media priming can have potentially large effects. As argued earlier, analysis of the 1992 election suggests that shifting media coverage from international to domestic issues played perhaps a limited role, in the shift from an overwhelmingly popular President Bush in 1991 to an unseated President Bush in 1992. Likewise, with the right configuration of environmental events, media priming may have profound effects, as suggested by the Mercury Theatre's *War of the Worlds* broadcast in 1938. The media's coverage of the looming war in Europe and Asia made the idea of an invasion highly salient to media users. The media's priming of invasion clearly played a role in many people's reactions to the broadcast. In addition, the Great Depression had been going on for nearly a decade, which increased people's reliance on the media. Cantril, Gaudet, and Herzog (1940) argued that this confluence of events played a clear role in the effects of the *War of the Worlds* broadcast. We believe this highlights the growing need to study the dynamic relations between the media, the larger culture, and the individual media user. The larger dynamic can play a critical role in explaining when a limited media effect can have profound consequences.

Given the many changes going on with the media, future research also needs to explore how new technologies influence media priming. Clearly, new technologies will not change the mechanisms by which media priming occurs—accessibility will continue to play a pivotal role in theorizing about media priming. However, given that new technologies allow messages to be more effectively tailored to the individual, will this result in stronger primes that have stronger effects on people's judgments and behavior? Likewise, very little is understood about the effects of interactivity on priming. Types of media that need to be explored are online news, Facebook, chat rooms, and Second Life, which vary in their degree of interactiveness. Does the extent of interaction with the information source increase or decrease the priming effect? The argument could be made that interactivity could increase priming effects because involvement with creating the priming event via interactivity may result in a stronger priming event. Conversely, interactivity may decrease priming because interactivity may result in more careful processing of information, which may decrease the impact of the prime because the priming event is relatively automatic (Olson & Fazio, 2009).

Finally, as we consider the next decade of priming research, we believe, first, that much of this future research will focus on examining moderators of priming effects. For example, there has been an increase in research on the impact of personality variables on aggressive priming (Meier et al., 2006, 2007). Second, more research is going to explore the generality of priming effects. Research on political priming has expanded to include research on the ability of different types of programming to prime evaluations of the president. Within the research on aggression and priming, research is exploring the impact of video games and is beginning to look at the effects of online gaming with its greater immersive environment. More specifically regarding media violence and priming, we believe that more research is needed to explore how people's interpretations of the depicted violence influence their reactions to that violence. Why do some depictions of violence increase fear and others aggression? But we believe that the most critical task facing priming researchers in the future is to more carefully test and refine the theories of political priming. As we have tried to note throughout this chapter, the current theories of priming have difficulties accounting for many of the existing results in the literature—most notably the time frame for priming effects. Future research needs to focus on developing dynamic models that bring together the exciting research that is being conducted on media priming across the different domains of study. Undoubtedly, such research will greatly enhance our understanding of the media and its influence on human behavior.

◆ References

Abraham, L., & Appiah, O. (2006). Framing news stories: The role of visual imagery in priming racial stereotypes. *Howard Journal of Communications, 17,* 183–203.

Althaus, S. L., & Kim, Y. M. (2006). Priming effects in complex information environments: Reassessing the impact of news discourse on presidential approval. *Journal of Politics, 68,* 960–976.

Anderson, C. A. (1997). Effects of violent movies and trait hostility on hostile feelings and aggressive thoughts. *Aggressive Behavior, 23,* 161–178.

Anderson, C. A. (2004). An update on the effects of playing violent video games. *Journal of Adolescence, 27,* 113–122.

Anderson, C. A., Deuser, W. E., & DeNeve, K. M. (1995). Hot temperatures, hostile affect, hostile cognition, and arousal: Tests of a general model of affective aggression. *Personality and Social Psychology Bulletin, 21,* 434–448.

Arpan, L., Rhodes, N., & Roskos-Ewoldsen, D. R. (2007). Accessibility, persuasion, and behavior. In D. R. Roskos-Ewoldsen & J. Monahan (Eds.), *Communication and social cognition: Theories and methods.* Mahwah, NJ: Erlbaum.

Bargh, J. A., Bond, R. N., Lombardi, W. J., & Tota, M. E. (1986). The additive nature of chronic and temporary sources of construct accessibility. *Journal of Personality and Social Psychology, 50,* 869–878.

Barnard, P. J. (1985). Interacting cognitive subsystems: A psycholinguistic approach to short-term memory. In A. Ellis (Ed.), *Progress in the psychology of language* (Vol. 2, pp. 197–258). Mahwah, NJ: Erlbaum.

Bartholow, B. D., Anderson, C. A., Carnagey, N. L., & Benjamin, A. J., Jr. (2005). Interactive effects of real life experience and situational cues on aggression: The weapons priming effect in hunters and nonhunters. *Journal of Experimental Social Psychology, 41,* 48–60.

Berkowitz, L. (1984). Some effects of thoughts on anti- and prosocial influences of media events: A cognitive-neoassociationistic analysis. *Psychological Bulletin, 95,* 410–427.

Berkowitz, L. (1997). Some thoughts extending Bargh's argument. In R. S. Wyer (Ed.), *The automaticity of everyday life: Advances in social cognition* (Vol. 10, pp. 83–92). Mahwah, NJ: Erlbaum.

Bluemke, M., & Zumbach, J. (2007). Implicit and explicit measures for analyzing the aggressiveness of computer games. In G. Steffgen & M. Gollwitzer (Eds.), *Emotions and aggressive behavior* (pp. 38–57). Ashland, OH: Hogrefe & Huber.

Bushman, B. J. (1995). Moderating role of trait aggressiveness in the effects of violent media on aggression. *Journal of Personality and Social Psychology, 69,* 950–960.

Bushman, B. J. (1996). Individual differences in the extent and development of aggressive cognitive associative networks. *Personality and Social Psychology Bulletin, 22,* 811–820.

Bushman, B. J. (1998). Priming effects of media violence on the accessibility of aggressive constructs in memory. *Personality and Social Psychology Bulletin, 24,* 537–545.

Bushman, B. J., & Anderson, C. A. (2001). Media violence and the American public: Scientific facts vs. media misinformation. *American Psychologist, 56,* 477–489.

Cantril, H., Gaudet, H., & Herzog, H. (1940). *The invasion from Mars: A study in the psychology of panic.* Princeton, NJ: Princeton University Press.

Carpentier, F. R. D., Roskos-Ewoldsen, D. R., & Roskos-Ewoldsen, B. B. (2008). A test of network models of political priming. *Media Psychology, 11,* 186–206.

Chory-Assad, R. M., & Tamborini, R. (2004). Television sit-com exposure and aggressive communication: A priming perspective. *North American Journal of Psychology, 6,* 415–422.

Dixon, T. L. (2006). Psychological reactions to crime news portrayals of Black criminals: Understanding the moderating roles of prior news viewing and stereotype endorsement. *Communication Monographs, 73,* 162–187.

Domke, D., McCoy, K., & Torres, M. (1999). News media, racial perceptions, and political cognition. *Communication Research, 26,* 570–607.

Fazio, R. H., Sanbonmatsu, D. M., Powell, M. C., & Kardes, F. F. (1986). On the automatic activation of attitudes. *Journal of Personality and Social Psychology, 50,* 229–238.

Gilbert, D. T. (1991). How mental systems believe. *American Psychologist, 46,* 107–119.

Graham, S., & Hudley, C. (1994). Attributions of aggressive and nonaggressive African-American male early adolescents: A study of construct accessibility. *Developmental Psychology, 30,* 365–373.

Grant, S. C., & Logan, G. D. (1993). The loss of repetition priming and automaticity over time as a function of degree of initial learning. *Memory & Cognition, 21,* 611–618.

Hansen, C. H., & Hansen, R. D. (1988). How rock music videos can change what is seen when boy meets girl: Priming stereotypic appraisal of social interaction. *Sex Roles, 19,* 287–316.

Hansen, C. H., & Krygowski, W. (1994). Arousal augmented priming effects: Rock music videos and sex object schemas. *Communication Research, 21,* 24–47.

Higgins, E. T., Bargh, J. A., & Lombardi, W. (1985). Nature of priming effects on categorization. *Journal of Experimental Psychology: Learning, Memory, & Cognition, 11*, 59–69.

Holbert, R. L., & Hansen, G. J. (2006). *Fahrenheit 9/11*, need for closure and the priming of affective ambivalence. *Human Communication Research, 32*, 109–129.

Holbrook, R. A., & Hill, T. G. (2005). Agenda-setting and priming in prime time television: Crime dramas as political cues. *Political Communication, 22*, 277–295.

Intons-Peterson, M. J., Roskos-Ewoldsen, B., Thomas, L., Shirley, M., & Blut, D. (1989). Will educational materials reduce negative effects of exposure to sexual violence? *Journal of Social and Clinical Psychology, 8*, 256–275.

Iyengar, S., & Kinder, D. R. (1987). *News that matters: Television and American opinion.* Chicago: The University of Chicago Press.

Iyengar, S., & Simon, A. (1993). News coverage of the Gulf Crisis and public opinion: A study of agenda-setting, priming, and framing. *Communication Research, 20*, 365–383.

Josephson, W. L. (1987). Television violence and children's aggression: Testing the priming, social script, and disinhibition predictions. *Journal of Personality and Social Psychology, 53*, 882–890.

Kim, S., Scheufele, D. A., & Shanahan, J. (2002). Think about it this way: Attribute agenda-setting function of the press and the public's evaluation of a local issue. *Journalism & Mass Communication Quarterly, 79*, 7–25.

Kim, Y. M. (2005). Use and disuse of contextual primes in dynamic news environments. *Journal of Communication, 55*, 737–755.

McGraw, K. M., & Ling, C. (2003). Media priming of president and group evaluations. *Political Communication, 20*, 23–40.

Meier, B. P., Robinson, M. D., & Wilkowski, B. M. (2006). Turning the other cheek: Agreeableness and the regulation of aggression-related primes. *Psychological Science, 17*, 136–142.

Meier, B. P., Robinson, M. D., & Wilkowski, B. M. (2007). Aggressive primes activate hostile information in memory: Who is most susceptible? *Basic and Applied Social Psychology, 29*, 23–34.

Miller, J. M., & Krosnick, J. A. (2000). News media impact on the ingredients of presidential evaluations: Politically knowledgeable citizens are guided by a trusted source. *American Journal of Political Science, 44*, 295–309.

Moy, P., Xenos, M. A., & Hess, V. K. (2005). Priming effects of late-night comedy. *International Journal of Public Opinion, 18*, 198–210.

Oliver, M. B., Ramasubramanian, S., & Kim, J. (2007). Media and racism. In D. R. Roskos-Ewoldsen & J. Monahan (Eds.), *Communication and social cognition: Theories and methods* (pp. 273–292). Mahwah, NJ: Erlbaum.

Olson, M. A., & Fazio, R. H. (2009). Implicit and explicit measures of attitudes: The perspective of the MODE model. In R. E. Petty, R. H. Fazio, & P. Brinol (Eds.), *Attitudes: Insights from the new implicit measures* (pp. 19–64). New York: Psychology Press.

Otten, S., & Stapel, D. A. (2007). Who is this Donald? How social categorization affects aggressive-priming effects. *European Journal of Social Psychology, 37*, 1000–1015.

Potter, W. J. (2003). *The 11 myths of media violence.* Thousand Oaks, CA: Sage.

Price, V., & Tewksbury, D. (1997). New values and public opinion: A theoretical account of media priming and framing. In G. A. Barnett & F. J. Boster (Eds.), *Progress in communication sciences: Vol. 13. Advances in persuasion* (pp. 173–212). Greenwich, CT: Ablex.

Rogers, E. M. (2004). Theoretical diversity in political communication. In L. L. Kaid (Ed.), *Handbook of political communication research* (pp. 3–16). Mahwah, NJ: Erlbaum.

Roskos-Ewoldsen, B. (2006). Converging on a richer understanding of human behavior and experience through a blending of cognitive and clinical psychology. *Journal of Clinical Psychology, 62*, 367–371.

Roskos-Ewoldsen, B., Davies, J., & Roskos-Ewoldsen, D. R. (2004). Implications of the mental models approach for cultivation theory. *Communications, 29*, 345–363.

Roskos-Ewoldsen, D. R. (1997). Attitude accessibility and persuasion: Review and a transactive model. In B. Burleson (Ed.), *Communication yearbook 20* (pp. 185–225). Beverly Hills, CA: Sage.

Roskos-Ewoldsen, D. R., Bischel, J., Hill, J., & Hoffman, K. (2002). The influence of accessibility of source likeability on persuasion. *Journal of Experimental Social Psychology, 38,* 137–143.

Roskos-Ewoldsen, D. R., Eno, C., Okdie, B., Guadano, R., & DeCoster, J. (2008). Unpublished data.

Roskos-Ewoldsen, D. R., & Fazio, R. H. (1997). The role of belief accessibility in attitude formation. *Southern Communication Journal, 62,* 107–116.

Roskos-Ewoldsen, D. R., Klinger, M., & Roskos-Ewoldsen, B. (2007). Media priming. In R. W. Preiss, B. M. Gayle, N. Burrell, M. Allen, & J. Bryant (Eds.), *Mass media theories and processes: Advances through meta-analysis* (pp. 53–80). Mahwah, NJ: Erlbaum.

Roskos-Ewoldsen, D. R., Roskos-Ewoldsen, B., & Carpentier, F. R. D. (2009). Media priming: An updated synthesis. In J. Bryant & M. B. Oliver (Eds.), *Media effects: Advances in theory and research* (3rd ed., pp. 74–93). New York: Routledge/Taylor & Francis.

Roskos-Ewoldsen, D. R., Yu, H. J., & Rhodes, N. (2004). Fear appeal messages affect accessibility of attitudes toward the threat and adaptive behaviors. *Communication Monographs, 71,* 49–69.

Scheufele, D. A., & Tewksbury, D. (2007). Models of media effects. *Journal of Communication, 57,* 9–20.

Sheafer, T., & Weimann, G. (2005). Agenda-building, agenda-setting, priming, individual voting intentions, and the aggregate results: An analysis of four Israeli elections. *Journal of Communication, 55,* 347–365.

Teasdale, J. D., & Barnard, P. J. (1993). *Affect, cognition, and change.* Mahwah, NJ: Erlbaum.

13

THE LIMITED CAPACITY MODEL OF MOTIVATED MEDIATED MESSAGE PROCESSING

◆ Annie Lang

The limited capacity model of motivated mediated message processing (LC4MP) is a data-driven model developed to investigate the real-time processing of mediated messages (Lang, 2006a, 2006b). The LC4MP provides a basic theoretical conceptualization of human information processing, a psychologically driven conceptualization of media, and a toolbox of measures that allow the researcher to track the over time interactions occurring between a message, a medium, and a user. The strengths of the model are that it is applicable to all types of media (including those not yet invented), all types of messages, and all types of situations and users. It is a model because the basic empirical work that must be done to generate an understanding of these interactions for any given medium or class of messages may not yet have been done. In some areas, for example, the processing of television messages and audio-only (or radio) messages, a great deal of the empirical work has been done, and the LC4MP provides a strong theoretical explanation for how such messages are attended to, encoded, processed, stored, and recalled. For other types of media, like the Web, early work using the LC4MP approach has only just begun to yield an understanding of how the human information processing system interacts with Web-based messages.

The LC4MP is unique in that it applies a small number of basic cognitive and motivational mechanisms to understanding and predicting the real-time interactions between any mediated message and the human information processing system. Rather than standing in opposition to other theories of effects or processing, it seeks to reveal the underlying mechanisms of message processing that can be used to understand what people attend to and take away from a message. This knowledge can then be used to better understand subsequent effects of messages, types of messages, and media. The first section of this chapter will lay out the basic assumptions underlying the LC4MP, followed by a description of the model. The second section will describe the operational toolbox associated with the model. The final section will discuss future directions for LC4MP.

◆ *The Model*

ASSUMPTIONS

The LC4MP has five basic assumptions. First, humans are assumed to be limited capacity information processors. Cognitive resources are required to process information, and humans have only a finite and limited supply of cognitive resources available for use at any given time. Second, humans have two evolutionarily old motivational systems, the appetitive and the aversive systems, which are designed to promote survival and protect from harm. Third, media are conceptualized as continuous and continuously varying streams of sensory information occurring in one or multiple modalities with variable levels of redundancy among the modalities. Fourth, human activity is conceived of as occurring over time. People act, react, and interact continuously as they move through time. Their behaviors, processing, emotional

experiences, and so forth, are all constrained or facilitated by what happened just before and what will happen just after any time period of interest. Fifth, communication is the ongoing, dynamic, continuous interaction between a message or medium and a message recipient or user. It is worth noting that the LC4MP does not distinguish between interpersonal and mediated communication. Interpersonal communication is simply the case where the medium is a human located physically in the same place as the message recipient.

MOTIVATED COGNITION— THE HUMAN MOTIVATED INFORMATION PROCESSING SYSTEM

The basic model of the motivational systems and information processing system used here comes out of theoretical work in psychology, psychophysiology, and cognitive science. *Information processing* is defined as the simultaneous, continuous, over time operation of at least (but not necessarily only) three basic subprocesses— encoding, storage, and retrieval. Information is thoroughly processed when it has been encoded, has been stored, and can be retrieved. Each of these subprocesses requires cognitive resources to operate. The amount of information that can be thoroughly processed is constrained by the system's finite capacity (Lang, 2000).

Encoding is conceptualized as the continuous, nonveridical, idiosyncratic process of selecting information from the environment and creating a mental representation of that information. This process is continuous because humans are constantly scanning and encoding information. It is nonveridical because mental representations are not exact representations of the stimulus. Rather, they are a mental approximation of what actually existed. It is idiosyncratic because both the mental representations and the selection of which information to encode are dependent not only on characteristics of the environment and the stimulus, but also on the previous experiences of the perceiver. Thus, no two individuals, because of their differing life experiences, perceiving the same mediated message will create exactly the same mental representation of the message. However, because encoding is also driven, to some extent, by characteristics of the stimuli, some stimuli will be encoded by most people whereas others will be encoded by only a few.

Storage is the process of creating a long-term representation of the encoded information. LC4MP uses a basic spreading activation associative network model of memory. As new information is encoded, links or associations are formed between the new information and previously held information. Generally, links are assumed to be formed between pieces of information that are simultaneously active. Thus, all incoming information is initially linked together, along with previously known information that has been activated in order to understand the incoming stimulus.

Retrieval is the process by which previously stored information is activated. Information can be retrieved in response to questions following message processing, but it is also a dynamic process occurring during message processing. People are constantly retrieving old information in order to understand, contextualize, think about, and respond to incoming information.

It is worth stressing that the relationship among encoding, storage, and retrieval is not thought to be strictly linear. Certainly, an incoming piece of information must be encoded before it can be stored; however, all incoming information is not new. Thus an incoming piece of information may be encoded at the same time that it is being retrieved from long-term storage. Similarly, only a subset of encoded information is ever stored at all and the degree to which any given piece of information is stored varies. As people interact with an incoming message, they are encoding new information, retrieving old information, and linking old and new information. All of these subprocesses are occurring at the same time.

The thoroughness with which each of these subprocesses is carried out depends on the level of resources required to carry out the subprocess and the level of resources allocated to carrying out the subprocess. LC4MP posits that resources are allocated through automatic and through controlled processing mechanisms independently to the subprocesses of encoding, storage, and retrieval. *Controlled resource allocation* is defined as the allocation of resources that are under the control of the media user. Users intentionally allocate resources when they try to pay attention, remember, relax, or engage with media in the pursuit of some goal.

Automatic allocation mechanisms are not under the control of the media user. Resources are allocated automatically either as a result of stimulus properties or in unconscious support of the conscious goals of the user. One of the mechanisms through which resources are allocated automatically is the *orienting response* (Lang, 1990). The orienting response is elicited by two classes of stimuli, those that are new to the environment and those that a person has learned signal relevant or important information. The existence of the orienting response allows humans to automatically, without conscious effort or thought, scan the environment for new or relevant information.

Many aspects of mediated messages elicit orienting due to their stimulus or signal properties. When orienting responses are elicited, it is theorized that resources are automatically allocated to the encoding subprocess (Ohman, 1979). Once encoded, the stimulus that elicited the orienting response can be identified and selected for further processing, or not. A great deal of research has been done in radio (Potter,

Lang, & Bolls, 1998), television (Lang, 1990), and Web-based (Diao & Sundar, 2004; Lang, Borse, Wise, & David, 2002) messages to identify stimulus properties of each medium that elicit orienting responses (e.g., radio: voice changes, music onsets; TV: camera changes, sudden movement; Web: animation, emotional pictures, and warnings). Although these lists are not yet complete, they provide us with a basic knowledge of both content and structural elements of these media that can be used to increase the automatic allocation of resources to message encoding as well as a list of those that can't (e.g., TV: pans, zooms; Web: onset of text, onset of non-emotional pictures).

Stimuli that are motivationally relevant also elicit automatic resource allocation. LC4MP posits that the motivational and cognitive systems are interconnected and constantly influencing one another. The motivational system consists of the appetitive, or approach, system and the aversive, or avoid, system. The theoretical model of the motivational system incorporated in the LC4MP comes primarily from work by Cacioppo and P. J. Lang that conceptualizes these systems as separate and independent (Bradley, 2000; Bradley & Lang, 2000; Cacioppo & Gardner, 1999; Cacioppo, Gardner, & Berntson, 1997). Motivationally relevant stimuli are those that activate one or both of these motivational systems. Positive stimuli activate the appetitive system. Negative stimuli activate the aversive system. Stimuli can be motivationally relevant because of physical characteristics (e.g., speed of onset, size, intensity, etc.) or because they have been learned (e.g., birthday cakes and guns). Some types of motivationally relevant stimuli are primary motivational stimuli; that is, their motivational relevance is likely inborn, rather than learned (e.g., potential mates, food, snakes, etc.).

The ability to perceive, encode, and identify motivationally relevant stimuli automatically promotes survival. The LC4MP posits that motivationally relevant stimuli result in resources being automatically allocated to both encoding and storage. Resources are allocated to encoding to facilitate identification and to storage because facilitating memory for motivationally relevant stimuli (e.g., the existence of food and danger) promotes long-term survival.

The extent to which activation of the motivational systems results in the automatic allocation of resources to encoding and storage is thought to be related to the level of activation in the motivational systems. Cacioppo's (Cacioppo et al., 1997) dual-system theory lays out different activation functions for the appetitive and aversive systems. At low levels of activation, that is, in a neutral environment, the appetitive system is thought to be more active than the aversive system. This difference in resting activation is called the positivity offset. As activation in the systems increases, the aversive system is theorized to activate more quickly than the appetitive system, since responding quickly to possible danger has great survival value. This quicker aversive system activation is called the negativity bias.

LC4MP posits that the level of cognitive resources allocated to processing a motivationally relevant stimulus is related to the level of activation in the motivational systems (Lang, 2006a, 2006b). For messages that activate the appetitive system, relatively more resources are thought to be allocated to encoding and storage as the level of activation increases. However, for messages that activate the aversive system, it is thought that there is an increase followed by a slight decrease at high levels of activation in the relationship between resources allocated to encoding and aversive activation. This is because, initially, as aversive activation increases, many resources are allocated to encoding in order to identify the potentially dangerous stimuli. However, once that stimulus has been identified, if that identification results in continued activation of the aversive system, then resources are shifted away from encoding toward problem solving and decision making (e.g., figuring out what to do, how to get away, etc.).

Empirical research to date has shown that positive emotional messages appear to activate the appetitive motivational system and negative emotional messages activate the aversive system. In addition, messages that contain both positive and negative material appear to activate both systems simultaneously. The level of activation in the motivational systems seems to be related to the level of arousing content in the messages. In addition, studies have begun to test the predicted relationship between level of activation in the motivational systems and resources allocated to encoding and storage (Lang, Yegiyan, & Bradley, 2006a; Shin & Lang, 2006a, 2006b).

To review, then, LC4MP posits that media users allocate some level of resources to processing the medium they have chosen to use. Once engaged in that activity, additional resources are automatically allocated to encoding and storing the message as a result of stimulus characteristics, signal properties, and motivational relevance. Signal properties likely vary from one individual to another. Stimulus characteristics are likely fairly consistent across individuals. Some aspects of motivational relevance will be consistent across individuals (food, sex, predators, etc.) whereas others will be cultural (colors of mourning, music, expressions, etc.) or individual (my mother).

During mediated message processing, all of these things are constantly changing. Resource allocation varies continuously in response to the changing stimulus characteristics, information load, and motivational relevance, as well as the level of activation in the user's motivational systems, goals, and intentions. If, at a given moment, sufficient resources are available to allow the user to understand, encode, and store the message, it will be

thoroughly processed. However, if any one of the subprocesses has insufficient resources to completely carry out its task, then performance on that task will suffer. This has been referred to as *cognitive overload.*

It is important to understand that cognitive overload is not a complete collapse or inability to process, comprehend, enjoy, or interact with the message. Rather, it is a state of relative insufficiency in one or more subprocesses lasting for some amount of time. That amount of time could be as brief as a second or as long as an hour. The insufficiency is relative because it does not mean that the task has ceased to function, but simply that it is not being completed as well as it was previously or as well as it could be. The insufficiency of resources could be confined to a single subprocess or spread across subprocesses. The resultant decrement in task performance may be extremely severe or extremely slight.

A second point to remember is that cognitive overload is not solely determined by the level of resources allocated to processing the message but that it is codetermined by the number of resources required by the message. Some messages require few resources whereas others require many. Further, the same message may require few resources for an expert in the topic and many for the novice. This interaction between the resources required to process the message and the resources allocated to processing it determines, ultimately, whether cognitive overload occurs.

Research using the LC4MP model has demonstrated that many aspects of mediated messages elicit both brief and longer-term periods of cognitive overload at various stages of processing. For example, a cut to a new visual scene during a television message elicits an orienting response resulting in additional resources being allocated to encoding. If the information following the camera change is easy to process, then the encoding of information immediately following the camera change improves. If the information is difficult to process, encoding gets worse for about 2 to 3 seconds. This is an example of brief cognitive overload (Lang, Geiger, Strickwerda, & Sumner, 1993; Thorson & Lang, 1992).

A longer-term example of cognitive overload is seen in research that varies the rate of structural features in a television message. This research shows that in messages that have frequent orienting-eliciting structural features and high information density, the level of encoding decreases across the course of the message as the encoding subprocess becomes more and more overloaded (Lang, Bolls, Potter, & Kawahara, 1999).

It is also important to recognize that different media place different constraints on the various subprocesses and, therefore, on the availability of resources across the subprocesses. For example, television and radio usually occur in real time. The continuous nature of the stimulus puts a strain on the information processing system, in particular, the encoding process, to keep up with message presentation. Once a piece of information has left the screen, or ceased to be heard, it is no longer available to be encoded. As a result, many resources may be allocated to encoding. Similarly, concurrent retrieval of information needed to understand the ongoing message must also occur in real time as the message unfolds. Thus, the demands of concurrent retrieval and encoding may leave very few resources available for storage, hence the oft-reported fact that people recall very little of what they see on TV.

◆ *The Toolbox*

There are three primary categories of variables in the LC4MP, those related to motivated cognition, those related to message structure and content, and those related to the media user. The relevant variables identified to date and operational definitions developed to index them are presented in the next three sections.

MEASURING THE BLACK BOX

The primary motivated cognition variables that must be measurable are resource allocation, motivational activation, encoding, storage, and retrieval. Again, it is worth remembering that all of these things are theorized to be changing continuously over time during media use; therefore, each of the measures we use must be collectable in real time indexed to message time.

Resource allocation. Resource allocation is at the heart of the LC4MP, and there are several types of resource allocation to be considered. Resources are thought to be allocated through controlled and automatic processes, and they are thought to be allocated independently to the various subprocesses. It is worthwhile considering the conceptual differences between these different types of resource allocation. First, controlled resource allocation is related to a user's goals, intentions, and experiences. Within a single period of media use, the user's goals, intentions, and experiences are relatively unchanging. For this reason, controlled resource allocation is conceptualized as a fairly long-term (or tonic) activity. Automatic resource allocation, on the other hand, is thought to be a short-term (or phasic), continuously changing process, which is responding to various aspects of the message. Given that cognitive resources and resource allocation are both abstract concepts and not necessarily specifically related to flesh-and-blood body parts, one must be careful not to reify these measures. The goal of these measures is not to actually measure the flow of resources, but rather to infer the availability of these resources to the various subprocesses.

Phasic, or short-term, resource allocation has been assessed in the LC4MP in two ways: first, through the use of secondary task reaction time (STRT) methodology (Basil, 1994), and second, through phasic analysis of heart rate (Lang, 1990). STRT is a method borrowed from cognitive psychology. The basic idea behind the methodology is that when a person is engaged in what is called the primary task, the speed with which he or she can do a very simple secondary task is indicative of how many resources are being consumed by the primary task. In the media laboratory, media use is the primary task, and pressing a button in response to an auditory or visual probe is the secondary task. The fewer resources available to do the primary task, the slower the responses on the secondary task. In the media laboratory, STRT probes can be placed at points of interest throughout the media stimulus to measure momentary changes in resource availability. LC4MP argues that in the media use context, the STRT probe is essentially indexing the resources available to the encoding subprocess since the secondary task is essentially an encoding task. In the future, research should attempt to develop similar measures for resources allocated to retrieval and storage. Research by Tom Grimes using cognitive preloads may provide a model for developing these types of measures (Grimes, 1991).

The second measure of short-term resource allocation is the measure of the characteristic 5- to 6-second slowdown in heart rate associated with an orienting response. The occurrence of the orienting response indicates a brief increase in resources allocated to encoding.

In the LC4MP, overall resource allocation, that is, the total resources allocated to message processing through controlled and automatic mechanisms, is referred to as *cognitive effort*. The level of cognitive effort expended by a media user over the course of the message is measured using a tonic analysis of heart rate (Lang, 1994). In general, the speed with which the heart beats is determined jointly by activation in the sympathetic and parasympathetic nervous systems. Parasympathetic activation is associated with attention to external stimuli and causes the heart rate to slow. Sympathetic activation is associated with arousal, emotion, and motivational activation, and causes an increase in heart rate. Empirical research suggests that, because media are external stimuli and because they are not actually dangerous, parasympathetic activation tends to dominate sympathetic activation in heart rate measure during media use. Therefore, increases in cognitive effort are seen as decreases in heart rate, even when messages are extremely emotional and arousing. Recent research has begun to use heart rate variability analysis to separate the sympathetic and parasympathetic contributions to changes in heart rate during media use (Koruth, Potter, Bolls, & Lang, 2007).

Thus, one can assess moment-by-moment changes in the level of resources allocated to encoding using STRTs, or phasic heart rate analysis. One can assess the relatively slow-changing variation in total resources allocated to the message, or cognitive effort, by looking at variations over time in heart rate time locked to media use.

Motivational Activation

The LC4MP argues that motivational activation underlies and enables emotional experience. Thus, activation in the aversive system leads to negative emotional experience, and activation in the appetitive system leads to positive emotional experiences. Simultaneous activation of both systems, called coactivation, leads to mixed emotional experiences. Thus, one way of inferring motivational activation is through measurements of emotional experience. A great deal of research suggests that there are three primary categories of data that are relevant to emotional experience: self-report, physiological, and behavioral (Bradley, 2000). The LC4MP uses self-reports of emotional experience and physiological measures to assess motivational experience. The measures used in the LC4MP come from dimensional emotion theory. In this approach, emotions are thought to be distributed across an emotional space defined by two primary dimensions: valence (positive or negative) and arousal (calm or excited). Self-reports of arousal are used as an indicator of the level of activation in the motivational systems. Because the motivational systems are thought to be independent, valence is assessed by two separate scales, one asking users how negative they feel and the other how positive. Their self-report of negative feelings is an indicator of aversive activation, and their self-report of positive feelings is an indicator of appetitive activation.

In addition, physiological measures are used. First, facial electromyography is used to index positive and negative emotional experiences, and by extension, appetitive and aversive activation (Bolls, Lang, & Potter, 2001). Increased corrugator activation is used an indicator of negative emotional experience and aversive activation. Increased zygomatic activation is used as an indicator of positive emotional experience and appetitive activation. Both of these measures can be collected in real time and time locked to changes in the motivationally relevant content (e.g., emotional content) of the message.

In addition to these measures of emotion, LC4MP also uses two probe methodologies, eyeblink startle (Bradley, 2007b) and the postauricular response (PAR, measured behind the ear; Sparks & Lang, 2007), which are thought to be more direct measures of aversive and appetitive activation respectively. The magnitude of the eyeblink associated with the startle response elicited by a probe embedded in a media message has been shown to be modulated by emotional experience. Specifically, the magnitude of the eyeblink is larger in negative compared with neutral compared with positive messages. The magnitude is thought to be an indicator of the level of activation in the aversive motivational system. Similarly, the size of the PAR (e.g., activation of the postauricular muscle located behind the ears), following a probe embedded in messages, appears to be related to appetitive activation. PAR magnitude is larger during positive compared with either negative or neutral messages. Inserting probes at particular times during media use allows for a measurement of appetitive and aversive activation at any given moment in time.

Encoding, Storage, and Retrieval

Finally, encoding, storage, and retrieval are assessed using memory measures (Lang, 2000). Encoding is assessed using recognition tests. Recognition measures show participants the exact stimulus they saw and ask, yes or no, did you see this before? Techniques for measuring recognition include paper-and-pencil multiple-choice questions about either audio or video information, forced choice yes/no audio and visual recognition tests, and signal detection measures and analysis. These techniques can be combined to separately measure audio and visual information over time as a function of change in the message.

Storage has been assessed using cued recall measures. In general, LC4MP studies have used fill-in-the-blank-type questions that cue respondents to specific parts of a message and ask them to retrieve a specific piece of audio or visual information in order to correctly complete a sentence. Post-viewing retrieval of information presented in the message has been assessed using free recall techniques. To date, no measure of concurrent retrieval has been developed for use during message processing.

MEASURING THE MESSAGE

The second class of variables to be measured in LC4MP relates to the message. Any number of message characteristics could be assessed over time and used as a variable in the LC4MP perspective. Because message processing is constrained by available resources, of particular importance are variables that measure the resources required to process the message and those that measure stimulus characteristics that elicit automatic resource allocation. Many different types of measurement have been used over the years, and there is insufficient space here to cover all of them. Instead, here we will present two measures that have been developed for use with television and radio messages which, when used together, seem to assess both resources required and resources automatically allocated to a message. The measures are called orienting-eliciting structural features (OESF) and information introduced (II) (Lang, Park, Sanders-Jackson, Wilson, & Wang, 2007; Potter et al., 2006). OESF is coded by viewing a message and counting the number of structural features that have been shown to elicit orienting responses. These can be coded over time for a real-time measure or summed and divided by the number of seconds in the message for a global assessment of resource allocation. II is then coded to determine the information introduced by each of the structural features. To do this, content immediately before and after the structural feature is compared to determine whether new information has been introduced along seven video or six audio dimensions. The video dimensions are object change, new object, unrelated, perspective change, distance change, form change, and emotion change. The audio dimensions are voice change, new voice, unrelated, form change,

natural sound, and emotion change. Again, this information can produce an over time record of resources required or be divided by seconds for a global measure.

The other type of information that needs to be assessed is motivationally relevant information. Again, this can be done globally or locally. Global indications of the amount of motivationally relevant information can be obtained by having coders or research participants rate how they felt emotionally after viewing messages. A more precise, over time indicator of motivationally relevant content can be obtained by having participants rate messages continuously on various motivationally relevant dimensions such as negativity, positivity, arousal, sexual attraction, humor, fear, threat, and so forth.

MEASURING THE MEDIA USER

Individual differences among media users present another potentially endless category of variables. However, LC4MP suggests types of individual difference variables that will be particularly relevant to message processing. For example, any individual difference variable that is related to resource allocation or resources required to process the message will be an important variable in LC4MP. Among the variables that have been looked at in this category are expertise and familiarity. Another class of variables that are important are those related to motivational activation. Recent work in LC4MP has developed an individual difference measure of resting activation in the appetitive and aversive systems (Lang, Bradley, Sparks, & Lee, 2007; Lang, Shin, & Lee, 2005). The measure called the Motivational Activation Measure (MAM) has participants rate their emotional responses on three scales (positivity, negativity, and arousal) to 32 previously selected emotional pictures. These ratings are used to create two variables called positivity offset and negativity bias, which indicate an individual's overall tendency to approach and avoid. Research suggests that those high in positivity offset show greater appetitive activation in response to many types of mediated messages. Similarly, those high in negativity bias show larger aversive activation in response to mediated messages. These individual differences influence the ongoing motivational activation elicited by mediated messages and, as a result, influence how those messages are processed (Lang, Yegiyan, & Bradley, 2006a, 2006b).

◆ A Little Future Music

The LC4MP is a broad framework that provides a way of thinking about message processing in all media (old, new, and not yet invented) and a set of tools to help investigate how those messages and media are processed. The theoretical foundation is based on what we know about the human information processing system (which changes only slowly over millions of years), while the fast-changing media are represented by variables in the framework. The approach focuses on the actual time period when messages are being processed by individuals within an environment. Environments—which also can change rapidly—also represent a class of variables in the model. It recognizes that things about individuals, things about environments, things about media, and things about messages all influence what information is taken away from a media use session. However, while recognizing the complexity of the over time interaction, it begins the process of explicating how those variables interact with one another and argues that it is indeed possible to understand, explain, and eventually predict those interactions. The most recent work in the perspective is beginning the process of trying to model the over-time interactions among motivational activation, message change, and cognitive processing (Bradley,

2007a; Wang, 2007). It is hoped that this work will lead to the development of complex cognitive models that will successfully predict the emotional response and overall memory for mediated messages as a function of message structure and content. In the meantime, a great deal of work remains to be done assessing which structural features of which media elicit automatic resource allocation and which types of media content are motivationally relevant, assessing more exactly the relationship between motivational activation and cognitive processing, and developing better measures of all of these variables.

◆ References

Basil, M. (1994). Secondary reaction-time measures. In A. Lang (Ed.), *Measuring psychological responses to media* (pp. 85–98). Hillsdale, NJ: Erlbaum.

Bolls, P. D., Lang, A., & Potter, R. F. (2001). The effects of message valence and listener arousal on attention, memory, and facial muscular responses to radio advertisements. *Communication Research, 28*(5), 627–651.

Bradley, M. (2000). Emotion and motivation. In J. T. Cacioppo, L. G. Tassinary, & G. G. Berntson (Eds.), *Handbook of psychophysiology* (pp. 602–642). Cambridge, UK: Cambridge University Press.

Bradley, M. M., & Lang, P. J. (2000). Measuring emotion: Behavior, feeling, and physiology. In R. D. Lane & L. Nadel (Eds.), *Cognitive neuroscience of emotion* (pp. 242–276). New York: Oxford University Press.

Bradley, S. D. (2007a). Dynamic, embodied, limited-capacity attention and memory: Modeling cognitive processing of mediated stimuli. *Media Psychology, 9*(1), 211–239.

Bradley, S. D. (2007b). Examining the eyeblink startle reflex as a measure of emotion and motivation to television programming. *Communication Methods and Measures, 1*(1), 7–30.

Cacioppo, J. T., & Gardner, W. L. (1999). Emotion. *Annual Review of Psychology, 50*, 191–214.

Cacioppo, J. T., Gardner, W. L., & Berntson, G. G. (1997). Beyond bipolar conceptualizations and measures: The case of attitudes and evaluative space. *Personality & Social Psychology Review, 1*(1), 3–25.

Diao, F., & Sundar, S. S. (2004). Orienting response and memory for Web advertisements: Exploring effects of pop-up window and animation. *Communication Research, 31*(5), 537–567.

Grimes, T. (1991). Mild auditory-visual dissonance in television news may exceed viewer attentional capacity. *Human Communication Research, 18*(2), 268–298.

Koruth, J., Potter, R. F., Bolls, P. D., & Lang, A. (2007). An examination of heart rate variability during positive and negative radio messages. *Psychophysiology, 44*(Suppl. 1), S60.

Lang, A. (1990). Involuntary attention and physiological arousal evoked by structural features and emotional content in TV commercials. *Communication Research, 17*(3), 275–299.

Lang, A. (1994). What can the heart tell us about thinking? In A. Lang (Ed.), *Measuring Psychological Responses to Media* (pp. 99–112). Hillsdale, NJ: Erlbaum.

Lang, A. (2000). The limited capacity model of mediated message processing. *Journal of Communication, 50*(1), 46–71.

Lang, A. (2006a). Motivated cognition (LC4MP): The influence of appetitive and aversive activation on the processing of video games. In P. Messaris & L. Humphries (Eds.), *Digital media: Transformation in human communication* (pp. 237–256). New York: Peter Lang.

Lang, A. (2006b). Using the limited capacity model of motivated mediated message processing to design effective cancer communication messages. *Journal of Communication, 56*(Suppl. 1), S57–S80.

Lang, A., Bolls, P., Potter, R. F., & Kawahara, K. (1999). The effects of production pacing and arousing content on the information processing of television messages. *Journal of Broadcasting & Electronic Media, 43*(4), 451–475.

Lang, A., Borse, J., Wise, K., & David, P. (2002). Captured by the World Wide Web: Orienting to structural and content features of computer presented information. *Communication Research, 29*(3), 215–245.

Lang, A., Bradley, S. D., Sparks, J. V., Jr., & Lee, S. (2007). The Motivation Activation Measure (MAM): How well does MAM predict individual differences in physiological indicators of appetitive and aversive activation? *Communication Methods and Measures, 1*(2), 113–136.

Lang, A., Geiger, S., Strickwerda, M., & Sumner, J. (1993). The effects of related and unrelated cuts on viewers' memory for television: A limited capacity theory of television viewing. *Communication Research, 20*, 4–29.

Lang, A., Park, B., Sanders-Jackson, A. N., Wilson, B. D., & Wang, Z. (2007). Cognition and emotion in TV message processing: How valence, arousing content, structural complexity, and information density affect the availability of cognitive resources. *Media Psychology, 10*(3), 317–338.

Lang, A., Shin, M., & Lee, S. (2005). Sensation seeking, motivation, and substance use: A dual system approach. *Media Psychology, 7*(1), 1–29.

Lang, A., Yegiyan, N., & Bradley, S. D. (2006a). Effects of motivational activation on processing health messages. *Psychophysiology, 43*(Suppl. 1), S56.

Lang, A., Yegiyan, N. S., & Bradley, S. D. (2006b). Reactivity to risky products: Is motivational activation appetitive or aversive? *Psychophysiology, 43(Suppl. 1)*, S56–S57.

Ohman, A. (1979). The orienting response, attention, and learning: An information-processing perspective. In H. D. Kimmel, E. H. Van Olst, & J. F. Orlebeke (Eds.), *The orienting reflex in humans* (pp. 443–471). Hillsdale, NJ: Erlbaum.

Potter, R. F., Lang, A., & Bolls, P. D. (1998). Orienting to structural features in auditory media messages. *Psychophysiology, Supplement* (S66).

Potter, R. F., Wang, Z., Angelini, J. R., Sanders-Jackson, A., Kurita, S., Koruth, J., et al. (2006). The effect of structural complexity and information density on cognitive effort and arousal during audio message processing. *Psychophysiology, 43*(Suppl. 1), S79.

Shin, M., & Lang, A. (2006a). The impact of positivity offset and negativity bias on emotional message processing. *Psychophysiology, 43*(Suppl. 1), S91.

Shin, M., & Lang, A. (2006b). The role of motivation activation in processing emotional media messages. *Psychophysiology, 43*(Suppl. 1), S90–S91.

Sparks, J. V., Jr., & Lang, A. (2007). *A validation of the post auricular response as a physiological indicator of appetitive activation during television viewing.* Paper presented at the National Communication Association, Chicago.

Thorson, E., & Lang, A. (1992). The effects of television videographics and lecture familiarity on adult cardiac orienting responses and memory. *Communication Research, 19*(3), 346–369.

Wang, Z. (2007). *Motivational processing and choice behavior during television viewing: An integrative dynamic approach.* Unpublished doctoral dissertation, Indiana University, Bloomington.

14

EMOTION AND MEDIA EFFECTS

◆ Robin L. Nabi

The role of emotion in media processes and effects is without question a very broad and exciting line of inquiry, holding promise for a vast array of communicative contexts, such as health, politics, advertising, entertainment, educational programming, online communication, and so on. Yet, given the cognitive bias pervading media effects theorizing, there has been relatively little systematic attention to the role of emotion in effects processes. The purpose of this chapter is to offer a critical examination of the ways in which emotion has been integrated into media effects research with the ultimate goal of determining how future research might benefit from more systematic inclusion of emotion-related constructs.

With this in mind, this chapter focuses first on defining the concept of emotion and examining its history in the context of media effects research. Next, it examines the various threads of research that have considered emotion as (a) an impetus for message selection, (b) an outcome of message exposure, and (c) a mechanism by which other media effects emerge. After some discussion of methodological issues, the chapter concludes with possible directions for future research, focusing specifically on the critical role emotion plays in directing cognition and action within particular media effects processes and contexts, and keeping in mind the ever-changing media environment in which we now live.

◆ Defining Emotion

Although a clear definition of emotion has proven elusive (Izard, 2007), in general, emotions are viewed as internal, mental states representing evaluative, valenced reactions to events, agents, or objects that vary in intensity (e.g., Ortony, Clore, & Collins, 1988). They are generally short-lived, intense, and directed at some external stimulus. This is in contrast to moods, which are untargeted and more enduring experiences (see Fiske & Taylor, 1991, for a review). Although different theorists define emotion by emphasizing different physiological, subjective, or motivational factors, general consensus suggests that emotion is a psychological construct consisting of five components: (1) cognitive appraisal or evaluation of a situation; (2) the physiological component of arousal; (3) a subjective feeling state; (4) a motivational component, including behavior intentions or readiness; and (5) motor expression (Scherer, 1984; see Plutchik, 1980, and Fiske & Taylor, 1991, for reviews of emotion).

Building from this foundation, there are two basic models of emotion that guide the vast majority of the extant research: dimensional and discrete. Dimensional views focus on emotion as a motivational state generally characterized by two broad affective dimensions: arousal and valence (e.g., Lang, Greenwald, Bradley, & Hamm, 1993; Russell, 1980). Research from this perspective focuses on how the degree of positive or negative feeling evoked by a stimulus affects various physiological, cognitive, and behavioral outcomes. Discrete emotion perspectives, on the other hand, focus on individual emotional states identified by the unique set of cognitive appraisals, or thought patterns, underlying them (e.g., Frijda, 1986; Izard, 1977; Lazarus, 1991; Plutchik, 1980). The discrete emotion perspective holds that particular patterns of appraisals lead to certain states of action readiness. The associated physiological changes, together with the emotions' particular action tendencies (e.g., flight for fear, retaliation for anger), influence perceptions, cognitions, and behaviors in ways consistent with each particular emotion's adaptive goal. Only states with unique appraisal patterns, subjective experiences, and action tendencies are considered discrete emotions.

◆ Historical Roots of Emotion in Media Research

To appreciate the history and landscape of emotion and media effects research, it might help to contextualize them in the broader psychological literature. One can trace modern interest in the psychological construct of emotion to the late 19th- and early 20th-century work of preeminent scholars, like Darwin (1872/1965), James (1884), and Cannon (1927), yet given the more dominant focus on behaviorism in the early decades of the 20th century, emotion research was relatively quiet during this time frame. It wasn't until the mid-20th century, when the discipline of psychology experienced somewhat of a paradigm shift from behaviorism to cognitivism, that more systematic attention was paid to emotion, largely through the cognitive appraisal perspective (e.g., Arnold, 1960; Schacter & Singer, 1962). Still, this line of research was far from central to the discipline. Only in the past 20 years has emotion research slowly gained respect, perhaps due in part to the greater technological developments in the 1990s that have allowed for more precise scientific examination of emotion and brain functioning (e.g., Damasio, 1994; see Davidson, 2000), and it is only in the past decade or so that emotion research has arguably become not only mainstream but on the cutting edge of intellectual thought in a host of different psychologically-based research domains.

Given the strong ties between the disciplines of psychology and communication, it should come as no surprise that the corpus of media effects research reveals a similar pattern of neglect of emotion constructs. One might argue that early research in film and radio demonstrated some interest in emotional reactions to media (see Nabi & Wirth, 2008), but it was not until the 1950s and Carl Hovland's research on fear and persuasion that one could point to a program of research that demonstrated systematic attention to a context linking emotion with media effects (Hovland, Janis, & Kelley, 1953). In subsequent decades and in the shadow of cognitivism, investigation into emotion-related constructs in media research slowly continued to develop, largely through the efforts of Dolf Zillmann. Based on his three-factor theory of emotion, Zillmann laid out the foundation for several models of effects that continue to inspire research endeavors today (e.g., excitation-transfer theory, Zillmann, 1983, and mood management theory, Zillmann, 1988; see Bryant, Roskos-Ewoldsen, & Cantor, 2003, for a festschrift in his honor). Through the 1980s and 1990s, as emotion became an increasingly "hot topic" in psychology, media researchers seemed to take greater interest in emotion-related constructs. The extensive literature on fright reactions (Cantor, 2002), the growing literature on the role of emotion in limited capacity message processing (see Lang, 2000), and the increasing attention to emotions' role in persuasion (Nabi, 1999) are examples of domains of research inspired by these early scholarly efforts.

Today, one would likely be hard-pressed to find a scholar who would disagree that emotion is of central concern in the media effects arena. However, though there is growing evidence of its import, the state of the literature is such that much is still left to learn about its role in the exposure to media and the processing and outcomes of this exposure. The following sections outline the extant theories and research within these categories of media effects research, and offer suggestions for future related research directions. Throughout these discussions, dimensional and discrete views of emotion will be discussed as appropriate.

◆ Emotion as the Impetus for Media Selection

One of the more long-standing and important questions posed by media effects scholars is: Why do audiences select the media messages that they do? Although extant media theory has a history of recognizing the important role that emotional needs play in media consumption (see Rubin, Chapter 10, this volume), the most well-developed line of research in this area stems from Zillmann's (1988, 2000) mood management theory (MMT). MMT in essence asserts that people use media to modulate their affective states. More specifically, Zillmann argues that people, driven by hedonistic desires, strive to alter negative moods as well as maintain and prolong positive ones. Consequently, they will arrange their environments to adjust a full range of moods, using any genre or specific type of communication available. He further argues that because mood management processes are based on operant conditioning, people may, but need not, be cognizant of the reasons for their choices. Zillmann goes on to note four message features that might impact mood-based message selection: excitatory potential, absorption potential, semantic affinity, and hedonic valence. For each, the underlying principle is the same. If a message reflects one or more features that might perpetuate the negative state, the message is likely to be avoided in favor of one that would interrupt the negative state.

Much research supports mood management theory's predictions (see Oliver, 2003, for a recent review). However, its boundaries have been challenged by paradoxes of media selection, like the enjoyment of watching horror movies or tearjerkers that are designed to evoke negative affect, seemingly in contradiction to MMT's assumption of hedonistic motivation (e.g., Oliver, 2003). Thus, recent research has examined alternative motivations linking affect to media selection. For example, Knobloch's (2003) mood adjustment theory asserts that when anticipating a future activity, people might use media to achieve the mood they believe will be most conducive to completing that task. Thus, the focus is on mood optimization, which Knobloch argues is a more specific goal than mood regulation. Most recently, Oliver (2008) argued that media consumers are at times driven not by hedonism, but by *eudaimonia*, or happiness rooted in greater insight and connection to the human experience. This motivation, she argues, explains viewers' desires to consume more poignant or tragic fare (see also Oliver, Chapter 11, this volume).

Although the extant research on media message selection overwhelmingly emphasizes mood, rather than discrete emotions, some research has considered the unique role that discrete emotions might play in this process. For example, Boyanowsky (1977) found that women under threat (i.e., who believed an attack to have recently occurred on campus) preferred more arousing content (i.e., male-on-male violence and sexual content) than those not primed with the notion of attack. Most recently, Nabi, Finnerty, Domschke, and Hull (2006) examined the effects of regret on media message preference and found, counter to MMT predictions, that people with lingering regret over a past experience were more, not less, likely to want to see programming on the topic of their regret. These studies suggest that discrete emotions may function differently than moods in that media selection may be driven by coping, rather than simple regulation, needs.

Clearly, moods and emotions impact media message selection, and given the necessity of message exposure to media effects (see Potter, Chapter 2, this volume), it is critical that we more fully explore emotion's role in selection processes. Future research would do well to conceptually distinguish moods from emotions, and to consider how a range of different discrete emotions (e.g., fear, anger, jealousy, grief, pride) result in the selection of different forms of content such that regulation, optimization, and coping needs are met.

◆ Emotion as the Outcome of Media Exposure

Another dominant focus of media effects and emotion research has been on the emotions that *result* from message exposure—both specific emotions, like fear, and more general affective-based constructs, like enjoyment. Both of these lines of research are discussed in the following section, along with theories that relate to the intensity of emotional responses generated by media exposure.

AFFECT-BASED RESPONSES TO THE MEDIA

Without question, media messages have the capacity to evoke a wide range of emotions. Indeed, MMT is based on the premise that media messages have the capacity to alter affective states. Perhaps the most specific line of research in which the emotional response itself is of primary interest (as opposed to the subsequent effects of those emotional reactions, as discussed later in this chapter) involves children's fright reactions to media fare (see Cantor, 2002; see also Wilson & Drogos, Chapter 31, this volume). In essence, this line of research documents that children experience fear in response to the programs they view and examines the conditions under which such reactions emerge. Specific content that frightens children of different ages (e.g., monsters vs. abstract threats), the individual differences that moderate fright reactions (e.g., empathy and gender), and the effectiveness of coping strategies to manage potentially fright-inducing media exposure have all been explored. To explain why people have emotional responses to what are not immediate threats to the viewer, Cantor draws from the notion of stimulus generalization, arguing that because what we see in the media approximates reality, we respond to the media content as though it is real.

At a more general level, we can consider the research on media enjoyment as a form of affective response to media exposure. Although the notion of media enjoyment has been conceptualized in a variety of ways (see Oliver & Nabi, 2004, for a series of articles on this issue), and likely derives from a collection of affective, cognitive, and even behavioral elements (Nabi & Krcmar, 2004), it has primarily been considered an affectively driven construct that largely represents the degree of liking for media fare (Raney & Bryant, 2002). Given the importance of liking to continued media message exposure, understanding why people enjoy what they do is an important line of inquiry. Apart from the examination of personality traits in media enjoyment (see Krcmar, Chapter 16, this volume; Weaver, 2000), the most systematic line of research in this domain focuses on the disposition theory of drama, which in essence suggests that viewers' enjoyment of media fare is based on their affective dispositions, or feelings, toward media characters, and the outcomes the characters experience (e.g., Raney & Bryant, 2002; Zillmann, 1980, 1991). More specifically, viewers enjoy seeing good things happen to liked characters, and bad things happen to disliked characters. It is less enjoyable, however, to watch bad things happen to good guys, and good things happen to bad guys (see Raney, 2003). The role of moral judgments and empathy have traditionally been considered integral to this process, though recently the role of schemas in setting expectations for various characters has been explored (Raney, 2004) such that the type of character (protagonist or antagonist) may

influence character liking first and assessment of behavior morality second.

Of note, we know very little about the relationship between specific emotional responses and the broader notion of enjoyment. That is, we know that the media are capable of evoking a wide range of emotional responses. We also know that people can enjoy the experience of feeling happy, sad, scared, or angry. But under what conditions does media-evoked emotion associate with one's sense of enjoyment? Do certain emotions generally enhance enjoyment? What moderators (e.g., gratifications sought, message-generated expectations, social environment) influence these associations? Future research might consider addressing these questions.

THEORIZING ABOUT THE INTENSITY OF EMOTIONAL RESPONSE TO MEDIA CONTENT

In addition to research that focuses on affective responses to the media, there are two additional theories that help explain, at a very general level, the intensity of the emotional reactions people have to the media they consume: excitation transfer theory and desensitization.

Excitation transfer theory (Zillmann, 1983) highlights the role of physiology in the emotional experience, arguing that the physiological arousal associated with an emotional experience decays more slowly than the associated cognitions. Therefore, if one is aroused physiologically, one's emotional response to subsequent events, including media exposure, is likely to be more intense. Thus, if one feels fright while watching a film protagonist running for her life, one will feel even more relief than one would have otherwise once she has reached safety (Oliver, 1994; Zillmann, 1980).

Desensitization, on the other hand, focuses on the dampening of the intensity of emotional experiences. Drawing from the therapeutic technique designed to help people overcome phobias (e.g., fear of spiders), media desensitization suggests that, with repeated exposure, messages that typically evoke an emotionally-based physiological response (e.g., those that contain violence) lose their capacity to do so (e.g., Carnagey, Anderson, & Bushman, 2007; Cline, Croft, & Courrier, 1973). Although a strict interpretation of desensitization focuses on physiological response, research has expanded to consider self-reported arousal along with emotional and cognitive reactions (e.g., Mullin & Linz, 1995). The concern associated with desensitization, of course, is that this emotional dampening will transfer to the real world such that people will also have reduced emotional reactions to situations that might benefit from action (e.g., offering aid to someone in need), or it may minimize the disincentive to engage in antisocial behavior (e.g., aggressive behavior; Bartholow, Sestir, & Davis, 2005).

Ultimately, both excitation transfer and desensitization have implications for the intensity of emotional arousal experienced as a result of media exposure, though the specifics in terms of the scope of these effects are remarkably unexplored. For example, we know little about whether these processes work equally well for various negative or positive emotions. Can one be desensitized to fear appeals? To "feel-good" movies? Does excitation transfer work equally well for humor compared with fright? Further, these processes are assumed to be uncontrolled, and especially in the case of desensitization, negative. But how might these processes be harnessed to positive effect (e.g., see Wilson, 1987)? To the extent emotional intensity has implications for outcomes like attention, encoding, recall, and behavior (see the following section), a more complete understanding of these processes would be of great value.

◆ Emotion as the Mechanism of Effect

Finally, there has been increasing attention to the role of emotion as a key mechanism

through which other effects might emerge. Although space precludes an extensive discussion of these issues, three such effects that represent steps along the influence continuum are highlighted here: message processing, persuasion, and aggressive behavior.

EMOTION AND MESSAGE PROCESSING

Offering a perspective on emotion and message processing rooted as strongly in communication as in psychology, Lang's (2000) limited capacity model of motivated mediated message processing (LC4MP) essentially suggests that media consumers allocate cognitive resources to the messages they choose to process. However, they only have limited cognitive capacity to do so. Their cognitive resources, then, are spread among the processing tasks of attention, encoding, storage, and retrieval, and how those resources are allocated is argued to be driven by the message's characteristics, signal properties, and motivational relevance (see Lang, Chapter 13, this volume, for a detailed model description). Drawing emotion into the equation, Lang argues that motivational activation underlies and enables emotional experiences, which in turn influence the distribution of cognitive resources. More specifically, aversive (or avoid) system activation leads to negative emotional experience, and appetitive (or approach) system activation leads to positive emotional experiences. As the level of appetitive system activation increases, relatively more resources are thought to be allocated to encoding and storage of message information. As the level of aversive system activation increases, an increase, followed by a slight decrease, in allocation to encoding is expected. Recent research has begun to test these predicted relationships (e.g., Lang, Park, Sanders-Jackson, Wilson, & Wang, 2007).

The LC4MP serves as a useful guide toward understanding the message features that stimulate the motivational systems that, in turn, impact the information attention, encoding, storage, and retrieval that underlie media messages' effects on knowledge structures and decision making. Thus, the LC4MP is poised to be a foundational model in the area of emotion and media effects. Although rooted in the dimensional perspective of emotion, it could be interesting, as research develops, to integrate a discrete emotion perspective given that some negative emotions are aversive (e.g., fear), but others are appetitive (e.g., anger). Thus, looking beyond valence could possibly enhance the explanatory power of this model.

EMOTION AND PERSUASION

Perhaps the most well-known and well-researched area of study of emotion as a moderator of media effects comes from the domain of persuasion. Most of the research here has focused on fear arousal and its effects on both message processing and persuasion-related outcomes (e.g., attitudes, behavioral intentions, and behaviors), although increasing attention is being paid to the persuasive influence of other emotional states.

Fear appeal research. The fear appeal literature has cycled through several theoretical perspectives over the past 50 years (see Nabi, 2007, for more detailed discussion), including (a) the drive model, that conceptualized fear as resembling a drive state, motivating people to adopt recommendations expected to alleviate the unpleasant state (e.g., Hovland et al., 1953); (b) the parallel processing model (PPM; Leventhal, 1970), which separated the motivational from the cognitive aspects involved in processing fear appeals, suggesting that those who respond to fear appeals by focusing on the threat (cognition) would engage in adaptive responses, whereas those responding with fear (emotion) would engage in maladaptive responses; (c) the

expectancy-value-based protection motivation theory (PMT; Rogers, 1975, 1983), which ultimately focused on four categories of thought generated in response to fear appeals—judgments of threat severity, threat susceptibility, response efficacy, and self-efficacy—and how they might combine to predict message acceptance; and (d) the extended parallel process model (EPPM; Witte, 1992), which integrated the PPM and PMT, predicting that if perceived efficacy outweighs perceived threat, danger control and adaptive change will ensue. If, however, perceived threat outweighs perceived efficacy, then fear control and maladaptive behaviors are expected.

Although meta-analyses of fear research essentially suggest that the cognitions identified in the PMT, and later the EPPM, are important to fear appeal effectiveness, no model of fear appeals has been endorsed as accurately capturing the process of fear's effects on decision making (see Mongeau, 1998; Witte & Allen, 2000). Regardless, evidence does support a positive linear relationship between fear and attitude, behavioral intention, and behavior change. Thus, to the extent message features evoke perceptions of susceptibility and severity, as well as response and self-efficacy, fear may moderate persuasive outcome, though there are still important questions about the interrelationships among these constructs that remain unanswered.

Beyond fear appeals. There is growing interest in understanding the effects of emotions other than fear in the processing of persuasive messages (see Nabi, 2007, for a more extensive discussion), and emerging models attempt to examine those processes. For example, the cognitive functional model (CFM; Nabi, 1999) attempts to explain how message-relevant negative emotions (e.g., fear, anger, sadness, guilt, disgust) affect the direction and stability of persuasive outcomes based on three constructs: emotion-driven motivated attention, motivated processing, and expectation of message reassurance. An initial test of the model (Nabi, 2002) offered support for some, though not all, of the model's propositions, but as it awaits future tests, the CFM offers insight into the process through which a range of discrete emotions, not just fear, influence message processing and outcomes.

In a similar vein, Nabi (2003, 2007) posits an emotions-as-frames model to explain the effects of more general media exposure on attitudinal and behavioral outcomes. In this model, emotions are conceptualized as frames, or perspectives, through which incoming stimuli are interpreted. The model first notes the message features likely to evoke various discrete emotions. These emotional experiences, moderated by individual differences (e.g., schema development, coping style), are predicted to influence both information accessibility and information seeking, which ultimately generate emotion-consistent decisions and action. Nabi argues that through this perspective, we may ultimately have a better understanding of the potentially central role emotions may play in understanding how a range of media messages—not just those designed to persuade—might impact attitudes and behaviors.

Notably missing from this discussion thus far, however, is research on the persuasive effect of positive emotional states. In this regard, there has been a fair amount of attention to humor, although reviews of the humor literature have concluded that though humor may enhance message attention and source liking, it is generally no more persuasive than non-humorous messages (see Weinberger & Gulas, 1992, for a more nuanced discussion).

With the increasing popularity of political satire programs, such as *The Daily Show* and *The Colbert Report,* there has been an upswing in interest in examining the process through which humor may be revealed to have persuasive effect. For example, Nabi, Moyer-Guse, and Byrne (2007) argue that humor may not have immediate persuasive effect because though audiences attend closely to the message, they discount it as a joke that is not intended to persuade, thus minimizing the message content's effects on their attitudes. However, they also posit that this type of processing may lead to a "sleeper effect" such that the persuasive effect of humor may emerge after some time has passed (see also Young, 2008). Clearly, future research would benefit from closer examination of the persuasive effect of positive emotions, like hope and pride, and the processes through which such effects might emerge.

EMOTION AND AGGRESSIVE BEHAVIOR

Although it is important to examine the effects of media messages on emotional arousal and, in turn, mental processes, most people interested in media effects are especially concerned with behavior—antisocial behavior in particular. Indeed, one of the earliest interests in media effects stemmed from concern over the potentially violence-inducing effects of film and comic book consumption. Scholarly interest in the area of media violence has yet to wane, with meta-analyses revealing a small but significant association between media exposure and antisocial behavior (e.g., Anderson & Bushman, 2001; Paik & Comstock, 1994; see Bushman, Huesmann, & Whitaker, Chapter 24, this volume).

As this research program has matured, attention to the processes through which such effects emerge has developed. Most notable is the general aggression model (GAM; Anderson & Bushman, 2002), which suggests that aggression is a function of the learning, activation, and application of aggression-related knowledge structures. Thus, exposure to violent media content can promote short-term aggressive behavior by priming aggressive cognitions, increasing arousal, and generating an aggressive (i.e., angry) affective state. Further, the GAM suggests that over time, people learn appropriate responses to the social environment. Thus, each exposure to media violence is another opportunity to learn that aggression is an appropriate way to deal with life's obstacles.

Clearly, emotions (e.g., anger, shame) play a central role in explaining the link between media exposure and aggressive behavior (see also Baumeister & Bushman, 2007). If we assume that other behavioral responses to media messages operate similarly, and recognize that emotions function to motivate behavior (e.g., Izard, 1977; Lazarus, 1991), then it is reasonable to imagine that any research on the behavioral outcomes resulting from media exposure should consider the emotions underlying those effects.

◆ Methods of Emotion and Media Effects Research

MEASUREMENT ISSUES

The validity of our conclusions regarding emotion's role in media effects is of course contingent on the quality of our measures of emotion. The vast majority of emotion and media effects studies rely on self-reported emotional experience. Although this confines the realm of study to conscious emotional experience and is constrained by respondents' abilities to understand and report their particular emotional states, self-report is accepted as a valid form of assessing felt emotions (see Parrott & Hertel, 1999). Indeed, the published literature includes several validated measures of emotion and affect, like the Positive and Negative Affect Scale (PANAS; Watson, Clark, & Tellegen, 1988), the Multiple Affective Adjective Checklist–Revised (MAAC-R; Zuckerman & Lublin, 1985), and the State-Trait Anxiety Scale (Spielberger, Gorsuch, & Lushene, 1970; see Nabi, 2007, for a more complete list). However, these measures are rarely used in full in media effects research. Rather, most studies appear to develop their own collection of items to assess the target emotion. Although this does

not constitute a fatal flaw in such research, it does make comparability across studies more difficult. Thus, as research moves forward, greater attention to consistency in measures used would be most useful.

In addition to self-report, other measures of emotion, like facial expression or physiological reactions (e.g., heart rate, eye movement, skin conductance) as well as neurophysiological assessments (e.g., EEGs, fMRI) are becoming increasingly more common. Although physiological measures generally are of little use in distinguishing among particular emotions and thus are best used by those basing their work on the dimensional approach, unique facial expressions have been associated with discrete emotions (Ekman & Friesen, 1971). Thus, emotional reactions could be assessed by coding facial expression (see Ekman & Friesen, 1978). However, although a nice complement to subjective reports of emotional experience, such techniques can be time and resource intensive. Another option, though more invasive and requiring specialized equipment, is facial electromyography (EMG), which can measure action potential or movement of facial muscles during stimulus exposure and associate such movement with specific emotions. Arguably a more reliable indicator than self-report measures or coding systems, this technique is perhaps best applied to visual stimuli. By linking video segments to EMG output, this procedure could be very helpful in identifying images associated with discrete emotions to be used in other research. Given the increasing availability and accessibility of equipment to measure physiological response, it is likely that the upcoming years will see increasing use of these and other procedures to gain insight into issues related to emotional arousal.

RESEARCH DESIGN AND ANALYSIS ISSUES

Most research on discrete emotions and media effects is confined to either surveys, in which researchers assess recalled emotional responses to media fare and associate those responses to outcomes of interest, or experimental designs, in which participants (generally students) are randomly assigned to groups in which they receive a message designed to elicit high or low levels of an emotion (sometimes moderate or control groups are included), and the various groups are compared on outcomes of interest.

Both of these approaches, though, have their limitations. With surveys, researchers are relying on respondents' abilities to accurately recall their emotional experiences, which may be highly variable, and it is also not always evident what content respondents have in mind when they complete the survey. Although experiments help address this latter issue, concerns with this approach include (a) the artificial circumstances in which data are gathered, which may constrain emotional response; (b) the representativeness of the stimuli designed to elicit the emotion of interest; (c) the lack of differentiation among various emotional states within "positive" and "negative" mood conditions; and (d) the varying levels of emotional intensity aroused in different experimental groups. Pursuant to the latter point, it is important not only for one emotion condition to elicit more of the target affect than the other conditions (e.g., fear should exceed anger within the fear condition), but also that the target emotions be at comparable levels (i.e., the degree of fear and anger should be comparable in their respective conditions). Further, interpreting results based on a more objective standard of arousal rather than relative ones within the study would help clarify what a collection of studies has to contribute to our knowledge in this area (see Nabi, 2007, for a more detailed discussion of these issues).

◆ **Limitations and Future Directions**

Although there is mounting evidence that emotions are not only important, but

arguably central to a host of media effects, there is still too little attention paid to the impact of discrete emotions in the process of media effects. This section is devoted to translating the current limitations in the examination of emotion and media effects into directions for research in the coming decade. Given that discrete emotions are argued to have adaptive purposes (e.g., Lazarus, 1991) and generate the motivation that underlies human behavior (Izard, 1977), I will focus specifically on discrete emotions and how they might help illuminate current media effects theories and behavioral outcomes.

THE ROLE OF EMOTION IN EXISTING MEDIA EFFECTS PARADIGMS

Given that media effects research tends to be rooted in psychological approaches, and in light of the cognitive revolution in the 1960s and 1970s, it is not surprising that the dominant theories of media effects that have driven the vast majority of related research since the 1970s have overwhelmingly emphasized cognition in their explanatory mechanisms. In light of the emotion "uprising" in recent years, it is appropriate for media effects scholars to consider the role of emotion in the processes of effects as delineated by some of the more frequently-referenced theories. Thus, this section focuses on four broad paradigms of media research: cultivation, social cognitive theory, social comparison theory, and perceptual biases.

Cultivation theory. Cultivation theory addresses the relationship between TV content and viewers' beliefs about social reality, primarily asserting that compared with light TV viewers, heavy viewers perceive their social environment as more similar to the world as portrayed on TV than it really is (e.g., Gerbner, Gross, Morgan, & Signorielli, 2002; see also Morgan, Chapter 5, this volume). A significant body of evidence supports this hypothesis (Morgan & Shanahan, 1996).

But with the exception of research that suggests that exposure to crime programs can cultivate fear (e.g., Romer, Jamieson, & Aday, 2003), cultivation research is remarkably silent on issues of emotion. However, not only might we consider the cultivation of emotions other than fear (e.g., joy, anger) as a result of media diets; we might also consider that emotional portrayals are particularly influential in cultivating a range of beliefs. Exemplification theory touches on this theme by arguing that emotionally-arousing exemplars are more accessible and thus more influential in judgments than nonarousing exemplars (Zillmann, 2002), although again, the focus of the supportive research is on fear. Examination of the impact of a range of emotional depictions on perceptions, along with deeper consideration of the cultivation of emotional experiences themselves, will surely enrich this long-standing thread of media effects research.

Social cognitive theory. Bandura's social cognitive theory (SCT) revolves primarily around the functions and processes of observational learning (Bandura, 1986, 2002; see also Pajares, Prestin, Chen, & Nabi, Chapter 19, this volume). That is, by observing others' behaviors, including those of media figures, one may develop rules to guide subsequent actions. Although moderated by observers' cognitive development and skills, observational (or social) learning is guided by four processes: *attention* to certain models and their behavior based on source and contextual features; *retention* of the observed behavior and its consequences; *production* of the observed behavior in appropriate contexts; and *motivation* to selectively engage in observed behaviors based on positive or negative reinforcement from one's own behavior, the observed feedback given to others, or internal incentives (e.g., self-standards). As observational learning occurs via symbolic representations, the effects are potentially long lasting, and self-efficacy is believed to be central to behavioral performance.

SCT focuses primarily on the cognitive elements of outcome expectancies and self-efficacy. However, one can easily imagine the role of emotion in these processes. For example, emotional experiences (e.g., regret, pride) might be conceptualized as relevant outcomes (i.e., positive or negative cues) that influence behavior. Also, how one *feels* about performing the behavior—not just whether one *thinks* one can perform it—may be relevant. That is, whereas self-efficacy provides motivation to engage in behavior because people believe they can do it, how they feel about that ability might be equally important. If individuals believe they can begin a program of exercise, but do not feel excited about that prospect, they may be less likely to do it. Thus, I argue that integrating emotion into SCT-based research could be both illuminating and useful.

Social comparison theory. According to Festinger's (1954) social comparison theory, people are driven to evaluate their own opinions and abilities, and when objective assessment is not possible, people compare themselves to others who are both similar on ability-related (though sometimes unrelated) attributes and are close (but not too close) in ability or opinion. Discrepancy on the target dimension then sets both the standard and the motivation for achievement. Since its initial formulation, additional motives for comparison beyond self-evaluation have emerged, including self-improvement and self-enhancement (see Wood, 1989).

Social comparison theory suggests that the gap between the actual and the desired motivates behavior. However, I argue that it is what one *feels* about that gap that influences what behaviors might result in light of perceived discrepancies. For example, if one perceives another to be more attractive than oneself and feels envious, one might denigrate the other person. If one feels hopeful, one may pursue strategies to achieve that look (e.g., dieting, plastic surgery). However, if one feels indifferent, action is unlikely. Nabi (2008) examined the emotions media consumers typically reported feeling while watching cosmetic surgery makeover programs and found that different emotional reactions (envy, hope, happiness) positively associated with social comparison. However, envy moderated the relationship between social comparison and desire for plastic surgery more so than the other affects. Thus, it would behoove future researchers to consider more seriously the role of emotion in social comparison processes.

Perceptual biases. Theories of perceived media influence focus not on how media content actually influences viewers' attitudes, beliefs, or behaviors, but rather on individuals' *perceptions* of such influence and how those perceptions, in turn, influence audience reactions (e.g., Gunther & Storey, 2003; see also Tal-Or, Tsfati & Gunther, Chapter 7, this volume). Most notable among these are the hostile media perception (e.g., Vallone, Ross, & Lepper, 1985), which suggests that individuals who are partisan on a given issue tend to perceive news coverage as biased and thus hostile (or at least unsympathetic) to their position, and the third-person effect, which refers to the general tendency for individuals to believe that others are more (negatively) influenced by the media than they are, which in turn has both attitudinal and behavioral implications (Davison, 1983). For example, if an individual believes that others are more influenced by violence in the media, he or she may be more likely to support censorship initiatives. In these contexts, as argued previously, one can imagine that it is not the perception per se that leads to the behavioral effect, but rather how one feels about that perception. That is, if people are scared by the thought that others will be negatively influenced by sex or violence on TV, they will be motivated to support censorship policies. However, if they are indifferent to their perceptions,

their behavior is unlikely to be affected (see Hwang, Pan, & Sun, 2008, for related evidence).

In sum, we have a host of media effects theories that purport to explain how the media affect attitudes and behaviors. However, they largely omit the role emotion plays in motivating the translation of thoughts into action. Were researchers to begin to incorporate emotion constructs into their theoretical investigations, the explanatory power of these (and other) models and theories would surely improve.

THE ROLE OF EMOTION IN EXPLAINING MEDIA EFFECTS-RELATED BEHAVIORS

Emotion might further illuminate media effects research by focusing not simply on how emotion influences the process of effects, but also on how it might more directly associate with behaviors of interest and the role that media exposure may play in triggering that relationship. For example, three quite popular and enduring lines of media effects research involve the effects of media exposure on viewers' body image (see Harrison, Chapter 26, this volume), sexual behavior (see Brown, Chapter 27, this volume), and violent behavior (see Bushman et al., Chapter 24, this volume). Focusing first on body image, most research attempts to explain the role of media in disordered eating behaviors by focusing on socialization, modeling, or social comparison processes. However, absent from this discussion is the recognition that eating (or not eating) can be an emotionally-driven behavior. The notion of "comfort food" or drowning one's sorrows in a tub of ice cream captures this association quite well. Thus, it is reasonable that any consideration of media's role in influencing disordered eating or other behaviors associated with body dysmorphia should consider how media messages contribute to the link between emotion and food consumption. Similarly, the positive emotions associated with sexual behavior or the anger associated with violent behavior cannot be readily disassociated. Future research would do well to assess not simply the emotions evoked by a media message but also the emotions associated with the target behaviors themselves to determine how the two might interact.

EMOTION AND THE
NEW MEDIA ENVIRONMENT

In light of the rapid development of new technologies through which media are created and displayed, it is only sensible to consider emotion's role in these phenomena. Indeed, there are numerous possibilities. First, given the wealth of information available online, examining the role of emotion in information seeking and content selection is fundamental (e.g., Nabi, 2003, 2007; Turner, Rimal, Morrison, & Kim, 2006; Valentino, Hutchings, Banks, & Davis, 2008).

Second, given the explosion of user-generated content on the Internet in venues such as YouTube, it would be interesting to consider how the emotions people experience are expressed via the content they generate. For example, it is likely that blogging could serve as a relatively productive way to vent anger and frustration, whereas excitement to express creativity may lead to the creation and posting of videos on YouTube.

Third, in the context of social networking sites, it would be worthwhile to consider how affective states (e.g., boredom, loneliness, jealousy, anxiety) influence the use of these sites. This would include paying attention to not simply how feelings motivate use, but also the feelings that result from the information and experiences gained from use. For example, as users learn about events in their friends' lives—relationship break-ups, egagements, illnesses, and so on—not only are emotions likely to shift but behaviors consistent with those emotions (e.g., offering or seeking social support) are likely to emerge.

Emotions might also explain certain online phenomena. For example, videos that "go viral," or spread rapidly to viewers, likely do so because they strike emotional chords, whether they be erotic, as in any number of celebrity sex tapes that find their way to the Internet, or amusing, as is the famed "History of Dance" YouTube video, which has been viewed nearly 100,000,000 times in two years, or Tina Fey's portrayal of Sarah Palin on *Saturday Night Live,* which was viewed over 1,200,000 times within one week of being posted. To the extent messages get attention and spread, emotion likely plays a critical role. With this in mind, it would be particularly useful to work toward understanding how message features—both content and structure—impact emotional experience.

◆ *Conclusion*

As social psychological research evolved from behaviorism to cognitivism, it was generally accepted that what we think drives our actions. In light of the increasing recognition of the centrality of emotion to the human experience, it is perhaps more fair to say that it is emotion, in conjunction with thought, that leads to action. Further, without emotional impetus, the thoughts we do have are less likely to translate into behavior. Clearly, this is a highly dynamic process in which cognitions, emotions, and behaviors influence one another over time, but in essence, this conceptualization indicates that to understand media effects processes and outcomes—whether they be rooted in thoughts, perceptions, or behaviors—we must more carefully examine the many roles that emotions may play. This includes not just considering emotions as simple outcomes of media exposure, but looking at the range of emotional experiences as the stimulus for and moderators of a far broader range of outcomes than we have considered to this point. To do so will surely improve our ability to understand

and explain the diverse and exciting ways the media impact our personal, social, and emotional lives.

◆ References

Anderson, C. A., & Bushman, B. J. (2001). Effects of violent video games on aggressive behavior, aggressive cognition, aggressive affect, physiological arousal, and prosocial behavior: A meta-analytic review of the scientific literature. *Psychological Science, 12,* 353–359.

Anderson, C. A., & Bushman, B. J. (2002). Human aggression. *Annual Review of Psychology, 53,* 27–51.

Arnold, M. B. (1960). *Emotion and personality.* New York: Columbia University Press.

Bandura, A. (1986). *Social foundations of thought and action: A social cognitive theory.* Englewood Cliffs, NJ: Prentice-Hall.

Bandura, A. (2002). Social cognitive theory of mass communication. In J. Bryant & D. Zillmann (Eds.), *Media effects: Advances in theory and research* (pp. 121–153). Mahwah, NJ: Erlbaum.

Bartholow, B. D., Sestir, M. A., & Davis, E. B. (2005). Correlates and consequences of exposure to video game violence: Hostile personality, empathy, and aggressive behavior. *Personality & Social Psychology Bulletin, 31,* 1573–1586.

Baumeister, R. F., & Bushman, B. J. (2007). Angry emotions and aggressive behaviors. In G. Steffgen & M. Gollwitzer (Eds.), *Emotions and aggressive behavior* (pp. 61–75). Ashland, OH: Hogrefe & Huber.

Boyanowsky, E. (1977). Film preferences under conditions of threat: Whetting the appetite for violence, information, or excitement? *Communication Research, 4,* 133–144.

Bryant, J., Roskos-Ewoldsen, D., & Cantor, J. (Eds.). (2003). *Communication and emotion: Essays in honor of Dolf Zillmann.* Mahwah, NJ: Erlbaum.

Cannon, W. B. (1927). The James-Lange theory of emotion: A critical examination and an alternative theory. *American Journal of Psychology, 39,* 106–124.

Cantor, J. (2002). Fright reactions to mass media. In J. Bryant & D. Zillmann (2002), *Media effects: Advances in theory and research* (2nd ed., pp. 287–306). Mahwah, NJ: Erlbaum.

Carnagey, N. L., Anderson, C. A., & Bushman, B. J. (2007). The effect of video game violence on physiological desensitization to real-life violence. *Journal of Experimental Social Psychology, 43,* 489–496.

Cline, V. B., Croft, R. G., & Courrier, S. (1973). Desensitization of children to television violence. *Journal of Personality and Social Psychology, 27,* 360–365.

Damasio, A. R. (1994). *Descartes' error: Emotion, reason, and the human brain.* New York: Brosset/Putnam.

Darwin, C. R. (1965). *The expression of the emotions in man and animals.* Chicago: University of Chicago Press. (Original work published 1872)

Davidson, R. J. (2000). Cognitive neuroscience needs affective neuroscience (and vice versa). *Brain and Cognition, 42,* 89–92.

Davison, W. P. (1983). The third-person effect in communication. *Public Opinion Quarterly, 47,* 1–15.

Ekman, P., & Friesen, W. V. (1971). Constants across cultures in the face and emotion. *Journal of Personality and Social Psychology, 17,* 124–129.

Ekman, P., & Friesen, W. V. (1978). *Facial action coding system: A technique for the measurement of facial movement.* Palo Alto, CA: Consulting Psychologists Press.

Festinger, L. (1954). A theory of social comparison processes. *Human Relations, 7,* 117–140.

Fiske, S. T., & Taylor, S. E. (1991). *Social cognition.* New York: McGraw-Hill.

Frijda, N. H. (1986). *The emotions.* New York: Cambridge University Press.

Gerbner, G., Gross, L., Morgan, M., & Signorielli, N. (2002). Growing up with television: The cultivation perspective. In J. Bryant & D. Zillmann (Eds.), *Media effects: Advances in theory and research* (pp. 43–67). Hillsdale, NJ: Erlbaum.

Gunther, A. C., & Storey, J. D. (2003). The influence of presumed influence. *Journal of Communication, 53,* 199–215.

Hovland, C. I., Janis, I. L., & Kelley, H. H. (1953). *Communication and persuasion*. New Haven, CT: Yale University Press.

Hwang, H., Pan, Z., & Sun, Y. (2008). Influence of hostile media perception on willingness to engage in discursive activities: An examination of mediating role of media indignation. *Media Psychology, 11*, 76–97.

Izard, C. E. (1977). *Human emotions*. New York: Plenum Press.

Izard, C. E. (2007). Basic emotions, natural kinds, emotion schemas, and a new paradigm. *Perspectives on Psychological Science, 2*, 260–280.

James, W. (1884). What is an emotion? *Mind, 9*, 188–205.

Knobloch, S. (2003). Mood adjustment via mass communication. *Journal of Communication, 53*, 233–250.

Lang, A. (2000). The limited capacity model of mediated message processing. *Journal of Communication, 50*(1), 46–71.

Lang, A., Park, B., Sanders-Jackson, A. N., Wilson, B. D., & Wang, Z. (2007). Cognition and emotion in TV message processing: How valence, arousing content, structural complexity, and information density affect the availability of cognitive resources. *Media Psychology, 10*, 317–338.

Lang, P. J., Greenwald, M. K., Bradley, M. M., & Hamm, A. O. (1993). Looking at pictures: Affective, facial, visceral, and behavioral reactions. *Psychophysiology, 30*, 261–273.

Lazarus, R. S. (1991). *Emotion and adaptation*. New York: Oxford University Press.

Leventhal, H. (1970). Findings and theory in the study of fear communications. In L. Berkowitz (Ed.), *Advances in experimental social psychology* (Vol. 5, pp. 119–186). New York: Academic Press.

Mongeau, P. (1998). Another look at fear-arousing persuasive appeals. In M. Allen & R. W. Preiss (Eds.), *Persuasion: Advances through meta-analysis* (pp. 53–68). Cresskill, NJ: Hampton.

Morgan, M., & Shanahan, J. (1996). Two decades of cultivation research: An appraisal and meta-analysis. In B. R. Burleson (Ed.), *Communication yearbook 20* (pp. 1–45). Newbury Park, CA: Sage.

Mullin, C. R., & Linz, D. (1995). Desensitization and resensitization to violence against women: Effects of exposure to sexually violent films on judgments of domestic violence victims. *Journal of Personality and Social Psychology, 69*, 449–459.

Nabi, R. L. (1999). A cognitive-functional model for the effects of discrete negative emotions on information processing, attitude change, and recall. *Communication Theory, 9*, 292–320.

Nabi, R. L. (2002). Anger, fear, uncertainty, and attitudes: A test of the cognitive-functional model. *Communication Monographs, 69*, 204–216.

Nabi, R. L. (2003). The framing effects of emotion: Can discrete emotions influence information recall and policy preference? *Communication Research, 30*, 224–247.

Nabi, R. L. (2007). Emotion and persuasion: A social cognitive perspective. In D. R. Roskos-Ewoldsen & J. Monahan (Eds.), *Social cognition and communication: Theories and methods* (pp. 377–398). Mahwah, NJ: Erlbaum.

Nabi, R. L. (2008). *The role of emotion in body image-related social comparison processes*. Unpublished data.

Nabi, R. L., Finnerty, K., Domschke, T., & Hull, S. (2006). Does misery love company? Exploring the therapeutic effects of TV viewing on regretted experiences. *Journal of Communication, 56*, 689–706.

Nabi, R. L., & Krcmar, M. (2004). Conceptualizing media enjoyment as attitude: Implications for mass media effects research. *Communication Theory, 14*, 288–310.

Nabi, R. L., Moyer-Guse, E., & Byrne, S. (2007). All joking aside: A serious investigation into the persuasive effect of funny social issue messages. *Communication Monographs, 74*, 29–54.

Nabi, R. L., & Wirth, W. (2008). Exploring the role of emotion in media effects: An introduction to the special issue. *Media Psychology, 11*, 1–6.

Oliver, M. B. (1994). Contributions of sexual portrayals to viewers' responses to graphic horror. *Journal of Broadcasting & Electronic Media, 38*, 1–17.

Oliver, M. B. (2003). Mood management and selective exposure. In J. Bryant, D. Roskos-Ewoldsen, & J. Cantor (Eds.), *Communication and emotion: Essays in honor of Dolf Zillmann* (pp. 85–106). Mahwah, NJ: Erlbaum.

Oliver, M. B. (2008). Tender affective states as predictors of entertainment preference. *Journal of Communication, 58,* 40–61.

Oliver, M. B., & Nabi, R. L. (2004). Special issue: Conceptualizing media enjoyment. *Media Psychology, 14.*

Ortony, A., Clore, G. L., & Collins, A. (1988). *The cognitive structure of emotions.* New York: Cambridge University Press.

Paik, H., & Comstock, G. (1994). The effects of television violence on antisocial behavior: A meta-analysis. *Communication Research, 21,* 516–546.

Parrott, W. G., & Hertel, P. (1999). Research methods in cognition and emotion. In T. Dalgleish & M. J. Power (Eds.), *Handbook of cognition and emotion* (pp. 61–81). New York: John Wiley & Sons.

Plutchik, R. (1980). *Emotion: A psychoevolutionary synthesis.* New York: Harper & Row.

Raney, A. A. (2003). Disposition-based theories of enjoyment. In J. Bryant, D. Roskos-Ewoldsen, & J. Cantor (Eds.), *Communication and emotion: Essays in honor of Dolf Zillmann* (pp. 61–84). Mahwah, NJ: Erlbaum.

Raney, A. A. (2004). Expanding disposition theory: Reconsidering character liking, moral evaluations, and enjoyment. *Communication Theory, 14,* 348–369.

Raney, A. A., & Bryant, J. (2002). Moral judgment and crime drama: An integrated theory of enjoyment. *Journal of Communication, 52,* 402–415.

Rogers, R. W. (1975). A protection motivation theory of fear appeals and attitude change. *Journal of Psychology, 91,* 93–114.

Rogers, R. W. (1983). Cognitive and physiological processes in fear appeals and attitude change: A revised theory of protection motivation. In J. T. Cacioppo & R. E. Petty (Eds.), *Social psychophysiology* (pp. 153–176). New York: Guilford.

Romer, D., Jamieson, K. H., & Aday, S. (2003). Television news and the cultivation of fear of crime. *Journal of Communication, 53,* 88–104.

Russell, J. A. (1980). The circumplex model of affect. *Journal of Personality and Social Psychology, 39,* 1161–1178.

Schacter, S., & Singer, J. (1962). Cognitive, social, and physiological determinants of emotional state. *Psychological Review, 69,* 379–399.

Scherer, K. R. (1984). On the nature and function of emotion: A component process approach. In K. R. Scherer & P. Ekman (Eds.), *Approaches to emotion* (pp. 293–318). Hillsdale, NJ: Erlbaum.

Spielberger, C. D., Gorsuch, R. L., & Lushene, R. E. (1970). *STAI Manual for the state-trait anxiety inventory.* Palo Alto, CA: Consulting Psychologists Press.

Turner, M. M., Rimal, R., Morrison, D., & Kim, H. (2006). The role of anxiety in seeking and retaining risk information: Testing the risk perception attitude framework in two studies. *Human Communication Research, 32,* 130–156.

Valentino, N. A., Hutchings, V. L., Banks, A. J., & Davis, A. K. (2008). Is a worried citizen a good citizen? Emotions, political information seeking, and learning via the Internet. *Political Psychology, 29,* 247–273.

Vallone, R. P., Ross, L., & Lepper, M. R. (1985). The hostile media phenomenon: Biased perception and perceptions of media bias in coverage of the Beirut massacre. *Journal of Personality and Social Psychology, 49,* 577–585.

Watson, D., Clark, L. A., & Tellegen, A. (1988). Development and validation of brief measures of positive and negative affect: The PANAS scales. *Journal of Personality and Social Psychology, 54,* 1063–1070.

Weaver, J. B. (2000). Personality and entertainment preferences. In D. Zillmann & P. Vorderer (Eds.), *Media entertainment: The psychology of its appeal* (pp. 235–248). Mahwah, NJ: Erlbaum.

Weinberger, M. G., & Gulas, C. S. (1992). The impact of humor in advertising: A review. *Journal of Advertising, 21,* 35–59.

Wilson, B. J. (1987). Reducing children's emotional-reactions to mass-media through rehearsed explanation and exposure to a replica of a fear object. *Human Communication Research, 14,* 3–26.

Witte, K. (1992). Putting the fear back into fear appeals: The extended parallel process model. *Communication Monographs, 59,* 329–349.

Witte, K., & Allen, M. (2000). A meta-analysis of fear appeals: Implications for effective public health campaigns. *Health Education & Behavior, 27,* 591–615.

Wood, J. (1989). Theory and research concerning social comparisons of personal attributes. *Psychological Bulletin, 106,* 231–248.

Young, D. (2008). The privileged role of the late-night joke: Exploring humor's role in disrupting argument scrutiny. *Media Psychology, 11,* 119–142.

Zillmann, D. (1980). Anatomy of suspense. In P. H. Tannenbaum (Ed.), *The entertainment functions of television* (pp. 133–163). Hillsdale, NJ: Erlbaum.

Zillmann, D. (1983). Transfer of excitation in emotional behavior. In J. T. Cacioppo & R. E. Petty (Eds.), *Social psychophysiology: A sourcebook* (pp. 215–240). New York: Guilford.

Zillmann, D. (1988). Mood management: Using entertainment to full advantage. In L. Donohew & H. E. Sypher (Eds.), *Communication, social cognition, and affect* (pp. 147–171). Hillsdale, NJ: Erlbaum.

Zillmann, D. (1991). Empathy: Affect from bearing witness to the emotions of others. In J. Bryant & D. Zillmann (Eds.), *Responding to the screen: Reception and reaction processes* (pp. 135–167). Hillsdale, NJ: Erlbaum.

Zillmann, D. (2000). Mood management in the context of selective exposure theory. *Communication Yearbook, 23,* 103–123.

Zillmann, D. (2002). Exemplification theory of media influence. In J. Bryant & D. Zillmann (Eds.), *Media effects: Advances in theory and research* (pp. 19–41). Mahwah, NJ: Erlbaum.

Zillmann, D. (2003). Exemplification theory of media influence. In J. Bryant & D. Zillmann (Eds.), *Media effects: Advances in theory and research* (pp. 19–41). Mahwah, NJ: Erlbaum.

Zuckerman, M., & Lublin, B. (1985). *Manual for the Multiple Affect Adjective Check List-Revised.* San Diego: EdITS/ Educational and Industrial Testing Service.

15

MEDIATED RELATIONSHIPS AND MEDIA EFFECTS

Parasocial Interaction and Identification

◆ Jonathan Cohen

As people read books, listen to radio, or watch movies or television, one of the common responses these texts engender is the development of feelings toward the people who occupy the texts being consumed. Whether the text is in the form of a fictional or real narrative, a game show, a reality show, or even a nonfiction book, the degree to which the people in the text elicit a response from us is a crucial factor in how we will engage with the text and the degree to which it will affect us. Our responses to people in texts (be they characters, hosts, or the subject of an account or analysis) may be short-lived and leave no lasting impression, or they may be recurring, memorable, and leave a more lasting impression. Such responses may be a simple feeling we have about the target, may increase our engagement with the text, or may involve an imagination of the target's feelings and take a more interactive form

---

Author's Note: I wish to thank my colleague Yariv Tsfati for his critical and insightful comments on earlier drafts of this chapter.

◆ 223

that can develop into a feeling of closeness between us and the target. But though our responses to people in texts may take many forms, they all possess one common characteristic in that they are all forms of human relationships that are mediated through some form of communication medium. The two most commonly used and studied concepts that describe forms of mediated relationships are parasocial relationships and identification, and these will be the focus of this chapter.

Whereas the idea of identification has deep roots in literary studies and psychoanalysis, the notion of parasocial relationships is relatively new, emerging with the invention of domestic, electronic, mass media: the radio and then television. Both concepts—identification and parasocial interaction—describe ways in which audience members connect, emotionally and cognitively, with images of people they see and hear through mass media, and can be collectively called mediated relationships. Hence, both concepts describe modes of audience involvement that play a central role in audiences' understanding and interpreting of media texts, and, as will be detailed in the following paragraphs, both concepts have played a major role in theorizing about media effects.

But though these concepts are similar in these ways, they are theoretically distinct; they describe different psychological phenomena and emerge from different intellectual histories. This chapter will attempt to trace the development of these two concepts, describe their role in the study of media effects, and provide an overview of the theories to which they are central. In addition, methodological issues relating to the study of identification and parasocial interaction will be examined, and the major theoretical questions facing research on identification and parasocial interaction will be posed.

◆ Parasocial Interaction and Parasocial Relationships

THEORETICAL DEVELOPMENT

In an innovative view of media and communication as more than a linear transmission of information, Horton and Wohl (1956), followed by Horton and Strauss (1957), drew attention to the importance of the relationship between radio and television talk show hosts and their audiences. They argued, in essence, that the social impact of mass media is not limited to the behavioral consequences of media messages, but includes the emotional impact that media personae have on our lives and how we come to relate to them. In the spirit of the Chicago School's symbolic interactionism, Horton and Wohl proposed that a symbolic relationship develops between performer and audience members who play interactional roles opposite each other (Peters & Simonson, 2004). Unlike rhetorical studies' emphasis on the importance of the messenger's ethos as a source of trust, or Lasswell and Bryson's (1948) view of the communicator as a point of origin and intent, the notion of interaction highlights the relational aspect of communication. The performer (messenger, communicator, or sender) is seen as a partner in a relationship with the audience, and this perspective focuses attention on the relational aspects of the media experience.

Noting the social impact of several broadcast stars that had achieved incredible fame (e.g., the noted success of Kate Smith in selling bonds; Merton, 1946), and the increasing personalization of media content, these early scholars realized that source credibility alone cannot explain the centrality, importance, and success of media personae. Simply, the singer Kate Smith sold war bonds not because she meant well or because she was an expert on war or on investments, but rather because of some psychological connection she was able to create with her listeners. This connection, which Horton and Wohl called a relationship, and which they saw as based on a repeated pattern of parasocial interaction, is a paradoxical relationship in that it is based on "intimacy at a distance." People come to feel intimately related to performers whom they have never met, but with whom they feel a special and close relationship. *Thus, even before it became fashionable for scholars to view media audiences as active, Horton and Wohl suggested they were interactive.*

Following the initial introduction of the concept of parasocial relationships, however, the scholars interested in parasocial interaction were functionalist scholars working within the tradition of uses and gratifications (Nordlund, 1978; Rosengren & Windahl, 1972; Rubin & Step, 2000), rather than interactionists. Uses-and-gratifications scholars saw the development of these relationships as an effect of the media, fulfilling needs for social interaction and alleviating loneliness. Rosengren and Windahl (1972) developed a theoretical argument that links needs for social interaction to various forms of relations to characters and to preferences for genres. This typology rests on defining forms of involvement with characters that include parasocial interaction as well as other types of responses to mediated characters such as identification, imitation, or attraction. These were seen as representing a complement for social interaction and as representing moderate forms of dependence on mass media for satisfying the need for social interaction. But because texts are complex and often include many characters and situations that arouse emotional responses, identification with only one character is seen by Rosengren and Windahl (1972) as very rare. Furthermore, they claim that if one identifies with a character, then through this identification he or she interacts with other characters (when the character interacts

with them). Thus, they use the term *capture* to describe what they see as the most common way viewers interact with, and become involved in, television content, and which they define as a mix of identification with one or more characters and interaction with others. Capture is understood as a form of substitute for face-to-face personal interaction, and is theorized most often as associated with consumption of narrative texts such as dramas, plays, and so forth.

But, as successive studies failed to find evidence of this compensatory role of parasocial interaction, it became clear that parasocial interaction is more than a substitute for social interaction. Despite Horton and Wohl's (1956) and Rosengren and Windahl's (1972) assumption that parasocial relationships substitute for a lack of "real" social interaction, numerous studies (e.g., Ashe & McCutcheon, 2001; Levy, 1979; Perse & Rubin, 1990; Rubin, Perse, & Powell, 1985) found no connection between deficits in social contacts (e.g., loneliness, social anxiety) and parasocial interaction. Indeed, Tsao (1996) directly tested the hypothesis that people with psychological traits associated with low sociability (e.g., anxiety, neuroticism) would develop stronger parasocial relationships, but found the opposite. Thus, parasocial interaction and relationships can be seen not as substituting for, but rather as complementing, social interaction.

Following this failure to establish parasocial relationships as a motive for media exposure, Alan Rubin and his students (e.g., Eyal & Rubin, 2003) began thinking of parasocial relationships as a form of audience activity and as evidence for instrumental and active, rather than habitual and passive, media consumption. They conceptualized parasocial relationships alternatively as a psychological effect of media exposure and as a form of psychological involvement that mediates between motives, selective exposure, and behavioral media effects. For example, Kim and Rubin

(1997) classified parasocial interaction as a media effect and found that the intensity of parasocial interaction can be predicted by media motivations and selectivity. Similarly, Rubin and Perse (1987) included parasocial interaction as an involvement outcome in their study of audience involvement with soap operas. On the other hand, Rubin and Step (2000) used parasocial interaction as a predictor of behavioral effects of talk radio, and thus as a mediator between motives and effects. More recently, however, researchers have become less interested in the functions of parasocial interaction as part of the process of media effects and returned their focus back to thinking about the nature of parasocial relationships and how they operate as relationships.

CURRENT FINDINGS ON THEIR DEVELOPMENT AND EFFECTS

Research into parasocial interaction and relationships has flourished in the past two decades. Relatively fewer studies have examined the interactions Horton and Wohl were so fascinated with, and more interest has been focused on aspects of the relationships that evolve from such interaction. Many studies have explored how parasocial relationships are similar to, and different from, social relationships. For example, the attraction of viewers to television characters was found to be based on traits that were quite similar to the traits that attract people in social relationships (Hoffner, 1996; Hoffner & Cantor, 1991; Turner, 1993). Though there are differences between male and female viewers in what they seek in male and female performers, in general the attributes follow stereotypical lines so that female performers are appreciated more for their looks whereas males are appreciated more for strength and humor. Opposite-sex characters are sought more for attractiveness than same-sex characters (Cohen, 1999;

Hoffner, 1996; Turner, 1993). From the viewers' perspective, the intensity of parasocial relationships, much like the intensity of romantic and other close social relationships, was found to be related to adult attachment patterns (Cohen, 1997; Cole & Leets, 1999).

Once parasocial relationships are formed, they tend to develop in a manner similar to social relationships. In examining soap opera characters, Perse and Rubin (1989) found that, as in social relationships, as parasocial relationships develop, viewers feel that they are more familiar with the performers. As they reported knowing performers longer and better, their uncertainty about the characters' actions was reduced and they felt that they could more confidently predict the attitudes and emotions of the characters. And when the time comes for parasocial relationships with favorite characters to end, Eyal and Cohen (2006) report that the anxiety felt by viewers can be predicted by some of the same variables that predict the levels of anxiety following relationship dissolution. Thus, many lines of similarity have been identified between social and parasocial relationships, suggesting that the two kinds of relationships follow similar patterns and rely on the same social schemas.

More recently, a series of studies have demonstrated that parasocial relationships can have effects similar to those of social relationships. Schiappa, Gregg, and Hewes (2005, 2006) tested the ability of parasocial contact with minority characters to reduce stereotyping and prejudice, and found that, like interpersonal intergroup contact, developing parasocial relationships with characters portraying minority group members on television can reduce prejudice. Furthermore, they found that this occurs under the same conditions in which social contact works to reduce intergroup tensions (Allport, 1954). These studies show that knowledge gleaned from parasocial contact is stored and processed in a manner that is similar to ways information from interpersonal contact is managed, and that it can be activated in the context of social relationships. In health communication research, parasocial relationships with spokespersons have been shown to increase persuasive effects in a manner similar to role modeling of parents, teachers, or peers in social relationships (Brown & Basil, 1995).

CONCEPTUAL ISSUES

Performers invite audience members into parasocial relationships in the hope of securing their loyalty to a show. They attempt to entice interactions by employing production techniques such as characters directly addressing the audience (Auter & Davis, 1991), using medium-range camera angles that simulate face-to-face interaction, and creating an informal atmosphere on the set that simulates friendly gatherings (Horton & Wohl, 1956). In response to such behaviors, audience members often engage in role-appropriate responses that create the sense of interaction, which over time can crystallize into patterned relationships. Readers, listeners, and viewers can develop such a strong sense that characters/performers are speaking directly to them that they sometimes talk back to the television or radio. Conceptually, a distinction exists between parasocial interaction and a parasocial relationship. Parasocial interaction is defined as the emotions, thoughts, and actions (i.e., speech) *that occur during exposure to a media performer* and that are geared toward that performer. Parasocial interaction occurs within a symbolic relationship in which performer and audience member each assume a role. Over time, interaction can become patterned and routinized, and these routines form relationships.

A relationship develops over time and across viewing opportunities (Klimmt, Hartmann, & Schramm, 2006) from repeated interactions. The imagined interactions with media performers are seen as a response to certain ways in which performers address the audience through radio, television, and, more recently, the computer screen. These responses follow patterns that are learned from social situations (Klimmt et al., 2006) and thus are integrated into one's social life and become part of one's social knowledge. By making repeated references to past programs, performers create a sense of history to relationships and open up the possibility for "inside jokes" that make repeated viewers/listeners feel that they have unique knowledge about the performer and a shared history with him or her. This sense of knowing the performers, having a close familiarity with them, and having an intimate knowledge of their lives creates the intimacy that Horton and Wohl defined, even though this sense is based on mediated interactions and physical distance.

Because such relationships are likely to increase interest in a performer and result in seeking information about this performer or trying to meet him or her, relationships are often confused with fandom, worship, and adulation. But whereas parasocial relationships develop as viewers and listeners feel closer to, and more intimate with, the performer, fandom and adulation connote a relationship defined by distance. Fans put their object of adulation on a pedestal, and imagine him or her as larger than life and psychologically distant and out of reach. And so, even though imitation may result from a strong parasocial relationship, parasocial relationships are distinct from fandom and do not necessarily lead to modeling of the performer or even a desire to imitate him or her.

Parasocial interaction is often explained as similar to interaction with friends, but it is not identical with social interaction; rather, as Horton and Wohl (1956) point out, it is based on an imagined "intimacy at a distance." In many ways, these relationships are one-sided, because even though performers are trained to behave in ways that anticipate audience responses, these anticipations can never be perfect and are understood by viewers to be impersonal. So, even if parasocial relationships make viewers feel as if they have an intimate, unique, and special bond with a performer, they know this is not the case. Most probably, audience members respond automatically, based on learned responses, to communication cues sent by the performer that make them feel as though they are in a relationship, but when they care to think about it, they are reminded that this is not a social relationship. But perhaps because most recent research has been aimed at identifying similarities between parasocial and social relationships, we know relatively little about how the textual and technological mediation that underlies parasocial relationships defines their nature, how they differ from social relationships, and how such differences shape their effects. It is toward these questions that we can expect future research to be headed.

FUTURE CONCEPTUAL DIRECTIONS

One development in the study of parasocial relationships is the burgeoning study of new technology and the interface of humans with such technology (see also the discussion of future direction later in this chapter). This research has shown that humans react to computers in a manner that is similar to their reactions within human relationships (Reeves & Naas, 1996). This suggests two advances for the study of parasocial relationships. First, it expands the scope of study from television and film to computers and Internet technologies that have become major players in media markets. Second, in the attempt to explain why humans develop relationships with nonhuman actors (or with humans they only know via technology), the study

of social presence of computers shifts some of the focus from exploring production (as Horton and Wohl did) to a focus on the ability of humans to develop imaginary relationships.

In essence, the ability of humans to develop relationships with computers shows that it is not the unique ability of television personae to act in ways that simulate social interaction that allows for parasocial relationships to develop, but rather that humans have the capacity to develop imaginary relationships even without talented simulation of face-to-face interaction. Reeves and Naas (1996) argue that mistaking human forms for real humans is a consequence of the fast-paced development of technology that has outpaced human development, and that people need to expend mental effort to distinguish images of humans from real humans because we are yet to be evolutionarily programmed to automatically distinguish images from reality. But regardless of whether one seeks a biological explanation for the development of mediated relationships, the research on social presence offers a new set of data that can be integrated into the study of parasocial relationships.

Another interesting trend that has potential to inform the study of mediated relationships is the testing of principles of interpersonal contact and relationships in the realm of mediated relationships. Examples include studies into how parasocial relationships are initiated and develop using theories of interpersonal relationship development (Cohen, 1997; Cole & Leets, 1999; Perse & Rubin, 1989), studies of how effects of mediated relationships are similar to those of social relationships (Schiappa et al., 2005), and studies of how mediated relationships end using theories of relationship breakup (Cohen, 2004). However, many other aspects of personal relationships have yet to be explored in the context of parasocial relationships, and there is good reason to believe that as such research advances, the nature of parasocial relationships will become clearer.

◆ Identification With Media Characters

If fandom is based on keeping one's idols at a psychological distance that allows being awed by them, and parasocial relationships are predicated on developing more intimate feelings toward a performer, identification involves an intense, if temporary, merging of the self with a media character (Cohen, 2006). Previous scholars have suggested a range of metaphors to describe identification, from "walking in another's shoes" (Livingstone, 1998) to "getting inside someone else's head," but all seem to agree that this unity of identity is the basis for identification. When an audience member assumes, even if but for a moment, a character's identity, and shares his or her perspective, motivations, and goals, the viewer is said to identify with that character. Identification thus involves a high level of absorption in the text and involvement with the text. As opposed to parasocial interaction, in which there is interplay between viewer and persona, when identifying, viewers become engaged in media messages and discard their role and position as viewers.

THEORETICAL DEVELOPMENT

Whereas the notion of parasocial interaction emerges from thinking about symbolic interactionism, the notion of identification stems from more psychodynamic roots. Developmental theorists tell us that the creation of an adult identity, a mature self, is an end product of a succession of temporary identifications with parents (Freud, 1940/1989) and other authority figures (Bettelheim, 1943), peers, and role models; identifications that are necessary as a result of psychological pressures that

imaginative identifications can relieve. Following Freud's writing on this topic, Adorno, Frenkel-Brunswik, Levinson, and Sanford (1950) proposed that incomplete identification with parents during childhood may lead to the development of authoritarian personality traits later in life. Thus, identification is seen at once as an escape from reality and as a necessary step toward healthy psychological development. Bettelheim also uses the notion of identification with fictional characters to explain the role of children's tales in socialization. For most psychologists, identification is a precursor to imitation, learning, and psychological development and is facilitated by relatively automatic processes and motivated by a desire to be like an admired figure.

Media scholars have examined the process of identification with more concern over its impact on how mediated texts are consumed and understood than over the behavioral consequences of identification. With recent developments in the research on media psychology, the study of identification has come to play a central role in the exploration of how people respond to media texts. Related to the notion of involvement, identification is now often studied not through its role in socialization or as an aid to persuasion, but rather as part of the process of media reception and as a component of media enjoyment and media effects. With increased research about, and understanding of, identification, the need for clearer and more refined definitions and better ways to measure identification has become more evident.

CONCEPTUALIZING IDENTIFICATION

In trying to understand and conceptualize identification, media scholars have focused on the process itself, seeing it as a process by which the identities of viewers merge temporarily and fleetingly with the identity of characters. Thus, according to our current understanding, identification is based on a series of momentary connections with a fictional character or performer (Cohen, 2006). Wilson (1993) illustrates this point when he describes the viewing of television as a constant moving in and out of identification, alternating between experiencing the story from a reader's perspective and a participant's perspective. In reality, these moves in and out of identification are far from binary. They are gradual, and as audience members move in and out of identification, they carry with them relevant knowledge and parts of identity. In turn, any insights, memories, feelings, or knowledge that we experience through our identification with mediated characters is integrated into our lives.

Oatley (1999) distinguishes between prototypes of how readers experience their meetings with characters that range from spectatorship to merging. He claims that this continuum of audience experiences is parallel to the spectrum between observation and identification. In most well-written books or well-directed films, Oatley (1999) argues, readers/viewers are meant to move from identifying with the protagonist to a view of him or her from other positions. According to Oatley, this shifting of reception positions allows for a deeper appreciation of the work, one that comes from a position that is at an optimal psychological distance of the reader from the text. In less successful texts, the reception can either be overdistanced and hence removed and limited, or it can result in an underdistanced reception involving a full identification with a character that denies the viewer the necessary critical distance that enhances pleasure. Thus, the level of identification is linked to the enjoyment of the act of reading and viewing through its relationship with the position taken by the audience member.

Identification with characters is also related to our emotional responses to a text. Taking on a character's identity entails experiencing similar feelings as those understood to be felt by the character. Thus, as opposed to a detached position that removes the viewer/reader from emotional involvement, when identifying with a character, we may feel danger when the character is afraid, and be happy or sad when the character succeeds or fails. Importantly, identification is based on empathy (feeling with) rather than sympathy (feeling for), so that there is an imaginary merging of identities and the character (and his or her feelings) is experienced by the viewer from the inside rather than from the outside. Second, a merging of identities involves adopting a character's perspective. This is a crucial component of identification because it impacts how audience members decipher the text in which the target of their identification plays a role. It is thus expected that identification is an important determinant of the interpretation process that takes place during exposure to media texts.

Identification and media reception. The role of identification in interpretation of texts has been mentioned by several scholars, though the role of identification in interpretation is yet to be fully explicated. Liebes and Katz's (1990) work on *Dallas* suggests that identification played an important role in making the lives of the viewers a frame of reference for how they talked about the program and how they understood it. By identifying with various characters in the show, viewers came to understand them better, compared their own lives to those of the characters, and used their own experience to make sense of *Dallas*. Thus, identification is seen as a component of such referential readings of a text, and, as such, it is expected to have an influence on the position viewers take vis-à-vis the text and the understanding they construct of it. In support of this claim, Cohen's (2002) study of *Ally McBeal*'s reception showed that the level of identification with the protagonist was the single most important predictor of viewers' choice of a particular interpretation of the show. It remains to be seen whether the role of identification in interpretation is a function of perspective taking or whether the correlation between identification and interpretation is a function of a more general emotional orientation toward the text and its characters.

Identification and media production. Like parasocial interaction, identification can also be promoted by creators of media texts. Texts can promote identification with characters by providing likable and coherent characters whose actions and thoughts are clear and reasonable. Using a first-person narrative (Nodelman, 1991) or subjective camera angles can also increase the feeling of being a character. Thus, by providing audience members with information that is similar to what a character is seen to "know," identification should be easier and stronger. Conversely, if viewers are privy to information hidden from the character, merging of perspectives should be more difficult. Some recent evidence (Tal-Or & Cohen, 2008) suggests that identification is more strongly related to emotional orientation toward a character than to similarity in information. If this is the case, then Lombard's (1995) finding that viewing on larger screens produced more positive reactions to characters suggests that screen size may also have an indirect effect on identification. Although research has made some progress in understanding what factors foster identification, the processes underlying the creation of identification with characters seem complex and difficult to decipher.

◆ **Measuring Parasocial Interaction and Identification**

MEASURING PARASOCIAL INTERACTION AND RELATIONSHIPS

Horton and Wohl's original work was descriptive and analytic but did not include a measurement of parasocial interaction or of strength of parasocial relationships. Levy (1979) first measured parasocial interaction with newscasters using seven items, items that tapped liking, comparison, persuasion, realism, and sympathy, all of which he saw as indicators of developing a relationship with these personae. Using four of these items, the scale had a moderate reliability of .68. Rubin et al. (1985) created a 20-item scale that was later trimmed to a 10-item scale that was somewhat more focused than Levy's conceptualization (Rubin & Perse, 1987). Versions of these scales were used across several types of mediated characters, both real (i.e., hosts and news anchors) and fictional (soap opera characters), with relative success (Rubin, Palmgreen, & Sypher, 1994). However, as theory developed and the concept of parasocial interaction became distinct from other forms of viewer-character relationships such as wishful identification (Hoffner, 1996) or identification (Cohen, 2001), it has become clear that the parasocial scale should probably not be used for fictional characters and that perhaps some of the items lack discriminant validity (e.g., items that tap realism, attraction, etc.). However, the scale has been successfully used to significantly advance our understanding of both parasocial interaction and mediated relationships.

Most research on parasocial interaction has been conducted using measures of the intensity of parasocial relationships and based on viewers' self-report. Through this research, we have learned about individual differences in how and why viewers develop these relationships. What may be a useful next step is to develop a visual content analysis protocol that would assess or predict the parasociability of performers. One study that has taken this path has shown that parasocial interaction increases when characters in a narrative directly address the audience (Auter & Davis, 1991), but this area remains underdeveloped. This finding is especially interesting because the origin of research on parasocial interaction comes from observations of the personae (Horton & Wohl, 1956), and yet no instruments have been developed to gauge the persona's behaviors that are supposed to promote parasocial responses in audiences. Though the theoretical basis for such a measure is still relatively underdeveloped, such an advance would do much to promote theory and experimental research.

MEASURING IDENTIFICATION

The concept of identification, though much older than parasocial interaction, is less developed conceptually, and, as in other cases in social sciences, the colloquial use of a term hinders the process of its scientific definition. In daily parlance, "to identify" can mean to agree (as in identifying with a cause), to imitate, to see as real, or to like a film character very much or to believe his or her acting. In the realm of media studies, the concept has taken on a more precise meaning and is contrasted with other modes of response to characters such as wishful identification (Hoffner, 1996), parasocial relationships, realism, transportation, and others (Cohen, 2006). Cohen (2001) suggested a 10-item self-report scale for identification that has several items tapping into the cognitive dimension of adopting the character's perspective and understanding the character, as well as an emotional component of sharing the character's feelings and motivations. Though this scale has not received careful attention in terms of its validity, reliability, and psychometric properties, it has now been successfully used in several studies (e.g., Chory-Assad & Cicchirillo, 2005; Ryu, Kline, & Kim, 2007).

In one of the earliest quantitative attempts at studying the role of identification in learning, Maccoby and Wilson (1957) studied the effects of identification on recall of film details. As their measure of identification (which they defined as "to

put himself in the place of"), they used three items assessing the liking of the character by viewers. Brigham and Giesbrecht (1976) studied the association between identification with Archie Bunker and racial attitudes. Though they did not describe their measure, it appears that they, too, used liking or admiration as a measure of identification. Though Feilitzen and Linn'e (1975) pointed out the distinction between identification based on similarity and wishful identification (wanting to be like), this distinction took almost two decades (Hoffner, 1996) before it was established in the literature. However, with the growing interest in transportation (Green & Brock, 2000), it has become apparent that some of the items used to measure identification may not discriminate well between these concepts (e.g., feeling part of the action, being absorbed), and that perhaps only a subset of these items may be more useful.

One of the main obstacles to a development of solid understanding of identification, and a major challenge of scholars in this area, is developing ways to validly manipulate identification in an experimental context. As suggested earlier, one way to attempt this is by manipulating the perspective or the emotional stance of the viewer toward the character. With the advance of digital video editing, it may also be possible, and potentially relatively easy, to manipulate audiovisual texts in ways that will achieve varying degrees of identification. Regardless of how such a manipulation is performed, a valid and reliable experimental procedure that will manipulate identification will serve to considerably advance theory in this area. Because identification (as well as parasocial interaction) is experienced while a person is highly absorbed in viewing television or film, it is difficult to assume that reports of these experiences rely on valid introspection and memory. Therefore, experimental methods or other forms of nonreactive measures are of crucial importance in this area.

◆ *Future Direction in the Study of Mediated Relationships*

As mentioned earlier, with the advance of new technologies, research on mediated relationships has come across new challenges and opportunities. Specifically, inquiries into new technologies have taken two new directions, both exploring the consequences of technology on audience response. One new technology that has generated several studies is video games that introduce a seemingly greater degree of audience activity and involvement. Dill and Dill (1998) argue that both identification with violent video game characters, and the effects of such games, may be more powerful than violent films or TV. This is because in video games, players choose which character they play as, and such choice provides a stronger connection with the character. In addition, rather than watching the character act, players act as the character. More recently, Hefner, Klimmt, and Vorderer (2007) argued that the interactive nature of video games allows for strong identification, and that this is a crucial reason for the enjoyment of video games. Interestingly, in a meta-analysis, Sherry (2001) found that the effects of violent video games were actually somewhat weaker than those of violent TV. Thus, questions of how interactivity and audience activity affect mediated relationships remain important questions in this area.

A second issue that has gained prominence with advances in computer-mediated communication surrounds the question of presence and its relationship with parasocial interaction. Presence is the sense that a remote communication partner or environment is present, or the illusion of nonmediation (Lombard & Ditton, 1997). Unlike the notion of parasocial interaction or identification, presence does not stress the relational aspect between the character and viewer, or the response of viewers toward characters, but rather the illusion of immediacy of the environment, both physical and social, and the self (when experienced through technology; Lee, 2004). Though it is easy to see how presence (especially social presence) could be theoretically linked to parasocial interaction and identification, little investigation linking the concepts has been conducted. The notion of presence, like that of transportation and perceived realism, remains unexplicated in its relation to forms of mediated relationships, and this remains an important future challenge to our understanding of the role of mediated relationships in media effects.

◆ *Conclusion*

Though it is premature to assess the extent to which mediated relationships account for various media effects, David Morley (1992), in writing about the identification of audiences with television characters, has speculated that "one can hardly imagine any television text having any effect whatever without that identification" (p. 209). Though he specifically mentioned identification, the same can be said about other types of mediated relationships with characters in books or film. Such responses to characters, and relationships with them, are a central component of how people engage with media, process and understand media texts, react to them, and are affected by them. Producers work hard to engage audiences with characters and performers through production techniques that determine how the text is constructed, how audience members are addressed, and how the characters are introduced. And yet, we know too little about what creates these relationships and how they develop and change.

One of the problems with the study of media effects in general is the elastic definition of the concept of effects, and nowhere is this more evident than in the study of mediated relationships. If one views an effect as any audience response or reaction that would not have occurred without exposure to media content, then emotional and cognitive responses to media characters, and certainly developing relationships with them, would be categorized as media effects. Such responses would probably fall under the category of emotional effects (Perse, 2001). However, if the definition of media effects is restricted to those consequences of media exposure that are lasting and have an impact on people's lives beyond media exposure (such as learning new behaviors, becoming aggressive, undergoing changes in attitudes or in voting or consumer choices, etc.), then one may view identification and parasocial interaction as mediators of media effects rather than as effects in and of themselves. Given the findings of much of the reviewed literature, it seems more useful to take the latter view, that mediated relationships are process variables, best conceived of as responses to media that can increase their effects, rather than as effects per se. This is because some of the most exciting findings in this area of research (e.g., the parasocial contact hypothesis; Brown & Basil, 1995; Schiappa et al., 2005) demonstrate the power of mediated relationships in mediating very meaningful media effects.

This chapter has traced the development of research on parasocial interaction and identification and its conceptual, methodological, and theoretical evolution through to the present, and with an eye to future challenges. It seems that even if one views mediated relationships as a process variable, only with further advance in our understanding of these relationships and a better theory of how they relate to other components of audience involvement will we be able to arrive at a better understanding of the effects of media on individuals and society.

◆ References

Adorno, T. W., Frenkel-Brunswik, E., Levinson, D. J., & Sanford, R. N. (1950). *The authoritarian personality.* New York: Harper & Brothers.

Allport, G. W. (1954). *The nature of prejudice.* Reading, MA: Addison-Wesley.

Ashe, D. D., & McCutcheon, L. E. (2001). Shyness, loneliness, and attitude toward celebrities. *Current Research in Social Psychology, 6,* 124–132.

Auter, P. J., & Davis, D. M. (1991). When characters speak directly to viewers: Breaking the fourth wall in television. *Journalism Quarterly, 68,* 165–171.

Bettelheim, B. (1943). Individual and mass behavior in extreme situations. *Journal of Abnormal and Social Psychology, 38,* 417–452.

Brigham, J. C., & Giesbrecht, L. W. (1976). *All in the Family:* Racial attitudes. *Journal of Communication, 26*(4), 69–74.

Brown, W. J., & Basil, M. D. (1995). Media celebrities and public health: Responses to "Magic" Johnson's HIV disclosure and its impact on AIDS risk and high-risk behaviors. *Health Communication, 7,* 345–370.

Chory-Assad, R. M., & Cicchirillo, V. (2005). Empathy and affective orientation as predictors of identification with television characters. *Communication Research Reports, 22,* 153–158.

Cohen, J. (1997). Parasocial relations and romantic attraction: Gender and dating status differences. *Journal of Broadcasting & Electronic Media, 41,* 516–529.

Cohen, J. (1999). Favorite characters of teenage viewers of Israeli serials. *Journal of Broadcasting & Electronic Media, 43,* 327–345.

Cohen, J. (2001). Defining identification: A theoretical look at the identification of audiences with media characters. *Mass Communication & Society, 4,* 245–264.

Cohen, J. (2002). Deconstructing Ally: Explaining viewers' interpretations of popular television. *Media Psychology, 4,* 253–277.

Cohen, J. (2004). Parasocial break-up from favorite television characters: The role of attachment styles and relationship intensity. *Journal of Social and Personal Relationships, 21,* 187–202.

Cohen, J. (2006). Audience identification with media characters. In J. Bryant & P. Vorderer (Eds.), *The psychology of entertainment* (pp. 183–197). Mahwah, NJ: Erlbaum.

Cole, T., & Leets, L. (1999). Attachment styles and intimate television viewing: Insecurely forming relationships in a parasocial way. *Journal of Social and Personal Relationships, 16*, 495–511.

Dill, K. E., & Dill, J. C. (1998). Video game violence: A review of the empirical literature. *Aggression and Violent Behavior, 3*, 407–428.

Eyal, K., & Cohen, J. (2006). When good friends say goodbye: A parasocial breakup study. *Journal of Broadcasting & Electronic Media, 50*, 502–523.

Eyal, K., & Rubin, A. M. (2003). Viewer aggression and homophily, identification, and parasocial relationships with television characters. *Journal of Broadcasting & Electronic Media, 47*, 77–99.

Feilitzen, C., & Linn'e, O. (1975). The effect of television on children and adolescents: Identifying with television characters. *Journal of Communication, 25*(4), 51–55.

Freud, S. (1989). *An outline of psychoanalysis* (J. Strachey, Trans.). New York: Norton. (Original work published 1940)

Green, M. C., & Brock, T. C. (2000). The role of transportation in the persuasiveness of public narratives. *Journal of Personality and Social Psychology, 79*, 701–721.

Hefner, D., Klimmt, C., & Vorderer, P. (2007). Identification with the player character as determinant of video game enjoyment. *Lecture Notes in Computer Science, 4740*, 39–48.

Hoffner, C. (1996). Children's wishful identification and parasocial interaction with favorite television characters. *Journal of Broadcasting and Electronic Media, 40*, 389–402.

Hoffner, C., & Cantor, J. (1991). Perceiving and responding to mass media characters. In J. Bryant & D. Zillmann (Eds.), *Responding to the screen: Reception and reaction processes* (pp. 63–103). Hillsdale, NJ: Erlbaum.

Horton, D., & Strauss, A. (1957). Interaction in audience-participation shows. *American Journal of Sociology, 62*, 579–587.

Horton, D., & Wohl, R. R. (1956). Mass communication and para-social interaction: Observations on intimacy at a distance. *Psychiatry, 19*, 215–229.

Kim, J., & Rubin, A. M. (1997). The variable influence of audience activity on media effects. *Communication Research, 24*, 107–135.

Klimmt, C., Hartmann, T., & Schramm, H. (2006). Parasocial interactions and relationships. In J. Bryant & P. Vorderer (Eds.), *Psychology of entertainment* (pp. 291–313). Hillsdale, NJ: Erlbaum.

Lasswell, H. D., & Bryson, L. (1948). *The communication of ideas.* New York: Harper.

Lee, K. M. (2004). Presence, explicated. *Communication Theory, 14*, 27–50.

Levy, M. R. (1979). Watching TV news as parasocial interaction. *Journal of Broadcasting, 23*, 69–80.

Liebes, T., & Katz, E. (1990). *The export of meaning: Cross-cultural readings of Dallas.* New York: Oxford University Press.

Livingstone, S. M. (1998). Relationships between media and audiences: Prospects for audience reception research. In T. Liebes & J. Curran (Eds.), *Media, ritual and identity* (pp. 237–255). London: Routledge.

Lombard, M. (1995). Direct responses to people on the screen: Television and personal space. *Communication Research, 22*, 288–324.

Lombard, M., & Ditton, T. (1997). At the heart of it all: The concept of presence. *Journal of Computer Mediated Communication, 3*(2). Retrieved March 3, 2008, from http://jcmc.indiana.edu/vol3/issue2/lombard.html

Maccoby, E. E., & Wilson, W. C. (1957). Identification and observational learning from films. *Journal of Abnormal Social Psychology, 55*, 76–87.

Merton, R. K. (1946). *Mass persuasion: The social psychology of a war bond drive.* New York: Harper.

Morley, D. (1992). *Television, audiences and cultural studies.* London: Routledge.

Nodelman, P. (1991). The eye and the I: Identification and first-person narratives in picture books. *Children's Literature, 19*, 1–30.

Nordlund, J. E. (1978). Media interaction. *Communication Research, 5*, 150–175.

Oatley, K. (1999). Meeting of minds: Dialogue, sympathy, and identification, in reading fiction. *Poetics, 26*, 439–454.

Perse, E. M. (2001). *Media effects and society.* Mahwah, NJ: Erlbaum.

Perse, E. M., & Rubin, A. M. (1990). Chronic loneliness and television use. *Journal of Broadcasting and Electronic Media, 34,* 37–53.

Perse, E., & Rubin, R. (1989). Attribution in social and parasocial relationships. *Communication Research, 16,* 59–77.

Peters, J. D., & Simonson, P. (2004). *Mass communication and American social thought: Key texts, 1919–1968.* Lanham, MD: Rowman & Littlefield.

Reeves, B., & Naas, C. (1996). *The media equation: How people treat computers and new media like real people and places.* Cambridge, UK: Cambridge University Press.

Rosengren, K. E., & Windahl, S. (1972). Mass media consumption as a functional alternative. In D. McQuail (Ed.), *Sociology of mass communications* (pp. 166–194). New York: Penguin.

Rubin, A. M., & Perse, E. M. (1987). Audience activity and soap opera involvement: A uses and effects investigation. *Human Communication Research, 14,* 246–268.

Rubin, A. M., Perse, E. M., & Powell, R. A. (1985). Loneliness, parasocial interaction, and local television news viewing. *Human Communication Research, 12,* 155–180.

Rubin, A. M., & Step, M. M. (2000). Impact of motivation, attraction, and parasocial interaction on talk radio listening. *Journal of Broadcasting & Electronic Media, 44,* 635–654.

Rubin, R. B., Palmgreen, P., & Sypher, H. E. (1994). *Communication research measures: A sourcebook:* Mahwah, NJ: Erlbaum.

Ryu, S., Kline, S., & Kim, J. (2007). Identification with television newscasters and Korean college students' voting intentions and political activities. *Asian Journal of Social Psychology, 10,* 188–197.

Schiappa, E., Gregg, P. B., & Hewes, D. E. (2005). The parasocial contact hypothesis. *Communication Monographs, 72,* 92–115.

Schiappa, E., Gregg, P. B., & Hewes, D. E. (2006). Can one TV show make a difference? Will & Grace and the parasocial contact hypothesis. *Journal of Homosexuality, 51*(4), 15–37.

Sherry, J. L. (2001). The effects of violent video games on aggression: A meta-analysis. *Human Communication Research, 27,* 409–431.

Tal-Or, N., & Cohen, J. (2008, May). *Understanding audience involvement: Conceptualizing and manipulating identification and transportation.* Paper presented at the annual conference of the International Communication Association, Montreal, Canada.

Tsao, J. (1996). Compensatory media use: An exploration of two paradigms. *Communication Studies, 47,* 89–109.

Turner, J. R. (1993). Interpersonal and psychological predictors of parasocial interaction with different television performers. *Communication Quarterly, 41,* 443–453.

Wilson, T. (1993). *Watching television: Hermeneutics, reception, and popular culture.* Cambridge, UK: Polity Press.

16

INDIVIDUAL DIFFERENCES IN MEDIA EFFECTS

◆ Marina Krcmar

With the clarity of 20–20 hindsight, the earliest media research and the related theorizing appear not only arcane, but somewhat quaint. Although they were never formally stated as such, these early theories have come to be known as "magic bullet" or "hypodermic needle" theories. According to these theories, media exerted powerful and uniform effects—across situations and populations with little possibility for variation in effects resulting from individual differences in viewers or contextual variations in the viewing situation. With decades of mass media research behind us, and a new recognition that audiences are varied and heterogeneous, we now recognize this early approach as narrow, and ultimately, somewhat fruitless. Of course variations exist.

In fact, not only have most empirical studies demonstrated these variations in effects, but recent theorizing has incorporated these differences into their models. Theories of media use such as uses and gratifications, theories of media enjoyment and interpretation such as disposition-based theories, and theories of effects such as priming, have all begun to espouse the importance of individual differences in audience members in attempting to understand media outcomes. Therefore, it is the goal of this chapter to review the recent literature on the role of personality and individual differences in media theorizing and research. Specifically, I will examine, first, several theories that have identified the importance of individual differences; and second, the role of individual differences in influencing media preference and selection, enjoyment, and interpretation of various fare; and ultimately, the responses to and effects of media.

The literature on individual differences in response to media is quite large. Consider the ways in which we can view this topic. First, various theories have attempted to include individual differences in their models. However, this undertaking is an inherently dangerous one. Ignoring individual differences leaves us with theory that is lovely, parsimonious, and, ultimately, less than statistically explanatory. Including individual differences in the model leaves the theorist in the position of selecting the most important variables while ignoring others. In this case, an honest model is likely to be a messy one, with variables outnumbering the dictum that theory be parsimonious. Therefore, as we consider various theories of individual differences, we will also recognize that they, too, can capture only part of the picture.

Second, variations exist in the ways that audiences interact with media. Here, we might think of interactions with media as occurring prior to exposure (i.e., preferences), during exposure (i.e., interpretation, enjoyment), and after exposure (i.e., effects). More specifically, individuals may vary in the *preferences* they have for various genres. There are additional variations in how audiences respond to and *interpret* media. And individual differences can moderate *effects*. Furthermore, the role of individual differences can be compounded at each stage. For example, the personality factor of sensation seeking may influence preference for violent movies. Sensation seeking may further affect how that movie is attended to, interpreted, and enjoyed by those who select it. That attention and interpretation, in turn, may dampen or exacerbate effects. Therefore, it is virtually impossible to conclusively determine how a given personality factor may operate in terms of media use.

Third, even if it were possible to conclude how, say, sensation seeking affects media throughout the stages of choice, exposure, and outcomes, there are many personality factors that influence the process. Empathy, aggressive predisposition, extraversion, openness to experience, psychoticism, and sensation seeking have all been examined in relation to media use. And, obviously, these factors may interact with each other. This further expands the available data on individual differences. Thus, in this chapter, I recognize the nearly infinite number of ways that individual differences might interact with various media fare; however, I attempt to streamline the data and organize it in a way that is concise, while recognizing the complexity of the literature.

◆ Theory and Individual Differences

Although much current media research incorporates individual difference variables into its designs, a majority of theories still focus predominantly, or solely, on how media are processed and on subsequent outcomes. As such, theories may focus on the social circumstances surrounding viewing or the internal aspects of processing or the ultimate effects, but few have as their main focus the individual differences involved. Even those theories that do consider individual difference factors do so with broad strokes. Therefore, in this section, I will present several theories that do incorporate individual difference variables, however broadly.

USES AND GRATIFICATIONS

The first step in the complex process of media use outcomes is media *preference.* The uses-and-gratifications tradition has been utilized as a framework for studying audiences' motives and preferences for media use for several decades (Rubin, 1981) and, as such, has been applied to the study of media *selection and preferences*. Unlike other mass communication paradigms that emphasize either media content or effects, uses-and-gratifications researchers focus on media use and assume users to be active, purposeful, and selective in their media choices. Understanding the media user's needs and motives is the key to predicting potential media effects. Specifically, the now classic uses-and-gratifications précis seeks to understand

> the social and psychological origins of needs which generate expectations of the mass media and other sources which lead to differential patterns of media exposure (or engagement in other activities) resulting in needs gratifications and other consequences, perhaps mostly unintended ones. (Katz, Blumler, & Gurevitch, 1974, p. 20)

Given this foundational statement, we can argue that because audiences' social and *psychological* characteristics vary, the needs that arise from those characteristics are also likely to vary. Therefore, one way that we might think of individual differences is to imagine a diverse audience where psychological traits determine needs for specific types of entertainment, with variables such as sensation seeking (Krcmar & Greene, 1999), need for cognition (Brock & Livingston, 2004), and verbal aggressiveness (Krcmar & Greene, 2005) affecting what they watch. In other words, according to the uses-and-gratifications approach, personality factors influence needs, which in turn influence viewing practices.

Because of its focus on needs and the origin of needs, uses and gratifications is perhaps uniquely situated to incorporate personality factors into research designs that use them as their basis. Although the uses-and-gratifications approach does not specify which factors affect motives or how those factors may influence motives, it tangentially makes reference to personality

factors. Therefore, the approach has been used to explain simple relationships between personality variables and selective exposure (Krcmar & Kean, 2004; Weaver, 1991b). In addition, the approach has been applied using a more detailed set of arguments. For example, Krcmar and Greene (2005) posited that individual difference variables would influence the gratifications sought by viewers. Some viewers might watch a program to be entertained; others might watch the same program to be aroused. As a result, the same program may have markedly different effects on different viewers (i.e., personality factors would moderate effects), and this might be explained by the different needs that were being fulfilled for those viewers. As such, uses and gratifications encourages personality variables into a more prominent place in media effects research.

DISPOSITION THEORY(IES)

Once viewers determine their preferences and selective exposure has occurred, the second stage in the process of media use outcomes is *evaluation and interpretation*. Viewers decide how much they enjoy the content, judge the behavior and actions of the characters, and determine if they admire them or not. Disposition-based theories, then, use as their starting point the assumption that we vary in the degree to which we positively evaluate and judge the content of different media entertainment. Furthermore, our response to these media is based on our evaluations of characters and their actions. As such, these theories have been applied to the study of media evaluation and interpretations; however, one of the primary tenets of disposition-based theories is that individual factors, such as emotional responsiveness, basal morality, and personality variables, affect our appreciation of and response to media portrayals (Raney, 2006). Therefore, disposition-based theories, perhaps more so than a majority of the current theorizing in media effects research, rely on the importance of individual difference variables in determining media outcomes.

In what way are individual differences incorporated into disposition-based theories? These theories attempt to explain why audiences enjoy various media. Emotional responses to media, attitudes toward characters, and moral judgments of their actions are based in part on the media content but rely heavily, too, on characteristics of the viewer. For example, those who scored high on measures of hyper-masculinity evaluated a fictional rape victim less sympathetically and evaluated the perpetrator to be less culpable than those who scored lower on the scale (Beaver, Gold, & Prisco, 1992). Therefore, their initial personality affected their disposition toward the characters and the actions.

Although disposition-based theories focus mostly on media enjoyment and evaluation, it is not difficult to imagine how such a theory of individual differences might be extended to include the effects and outcomes of media exposure. Whereas enjoyment of and evaluation of a violent clip may vary based on personality factors, subsequent imitation of those aggressive acts are likely to vary based on enjoyment. Disposition-based theories may offer promise as we work toward crafting media theory that is broad enough to include preferences, interpretation, and effects, as well as individual differences in those processes.

SCRIPT THEORY

Following exposure and evaluation, the third step in the process of media outcomes is "*effects*." Although the use of personality and individual difference variables in media research has now become routine, many theories of media influence and effects do not explicitly incorporate personality factors into their models. Variables are added, rather, at the methodological level, as a characteristic of the research design. Several exceptions exist, however. For example, script theory (Huesmann, 1988) proposes that

> social behavior is controlled to a great extent by programs for behavior that have been learned during a person's early development. These programs can be described as cognitive scripts that are stored in a person's memory and are used as a guide for behavior and problem solving. (p. 15)

Simply put, scripts are the activated memory structures that arise when we are put in a particular situation and must choose an action or response. If I am faced with a conflict, do I withdraw, accede, or behave in a physically aggressive manner? According to script theory, the choice that is made comes from our exposure to repetitive event sequences that are similar to the situation at hand. These become stored in memory over time so that our responses are somewhat predictable and routine. When cues from a current situation activate similar event sequences stored in memory, we are prone to enact the stored script.

The media component of script theory, of course, is that scripts can be derived from real experiences or witnessed mediated ones. Furthermore, script theory argues that psychological predispositions (e.g., aggressive predisposition, empathy) may indirectly influence which environmental scripts we attend to and store in memory and, later, which we retrieve and apply. Therefore, an explicit aspect of the theory is that individual differences in personality affect how we select, interpret, and store media messages. Aggressive behavior, for example, is activated when and if an aggressive script is stored in memory and activated due to individual experiences, witnessed aggression, and the contextual cues of the situation. However, a viewer with, for example, an aggressive predisposition is more likely to select violent media, more likely to interpret aggressive or even ambiguous acts as aggressive, and more likely to store these events once exposed to them. In this way, a personality factor such as aggressive predisposition affects the steps and processes involved in script theory.

In this section, I have explored several theories that explicitly link personality and individual differences with media exposure outcomes: uses and gratifications, disposition theories, and script theory. Each argues that individual differences, specifically personality factors, may influence how we select, interpret, and respond to media messages. Overall, a complete model of media use would incorporate individual differences into each stage, recognizing direct and indirect effects as well as the recursive nature of these relationships at each stage.

◆ Individual Difference Factors

Individual differences in media use can be seen as individual differences in needs (e.g., a greater and lesser need for cognition), differences in readiness to respond (e.g., greater or lesser empathic responding), or differences in personality traits (e.g., greater or lesser aggressive predispositions; Oliver, 2002). Although Oliver (2002) presents these differences in needs, readiness, and traits as different categories, the uses-and-gratifications approach presents them as different stages in a process. Recall that the uses-and-gratifications précis seeks to understand "the social and psychological origins of needs which generate expectations of the mass media and other sources which lead to differential patterns of media exposure" (Katz et al., 1974, p. 20). From this perspective, psychological traits drive needs, which in turn drive patterns of exposure. Therefore, I will examine individual differences in terms of a drive to fulfill needs.

Furthermore, recent theorizing suggests that the need to be entertained is, in itself, an individual difference variable with both predictive and explanatory power. Brock and Livingston (2004) developed and validated a scale that taps into individuals' desire for entertainment. The three-factor scale is made up of drive for entertainment, perceived utility of entertainment, and enjoyment of passive entertainment, and the variable is inversely related to participants' need for cognition. Therefore, it appears that not only are there individual differences in personality factors that drive needs and subsequent media use, but the drive to seek out entertainment media is itself an individual difference factor.

IN SEARCH OF AROUSAL

Research into the factors that predict media use, however, has a longer history, dating back several decades (e.g., Zillmann, 1985). One area that has received much research attention is that of violent, arousing, and thrilling media. Consider, for example, the variable of sensation seeking. Sensation seeking is defined as a biologically driven characteristic in which a person is predisposed to seek out arousing stimuli (Zuckerman, 1979). Because media are often characterized along a continuum from relaxing to highly arousing, it is clear why media scholars might explore sensation seeking as a predictor. Indeed, sensation seeking does seem to predict use of more arousing media fare. For example, Krcmar and Greene (1999) sampled adolescents and college students to test the relation between sensation seeking and exposure to violent and nonviolent television. This study found that two of the four sensation-seeking dimensions, disinhibition and experience seeking, were related to adolescents' exposure to violent television. Specifically, greater disinhibition and less experience seeking were related to exposure to violent television. Tamborini and Stiff (1987) also examined sensation seeking and found a link between the variable and exposure to horror films. In fact, exposure to media violence, pornography, horror, and other arousing stimuli has been found among high sensation seekers in a number of recent studies (Aluja-Fabregat & Torrubia-Beltri, 1998; Perse, 1996). Furthermore, sensation seeking has been found to be positively associated with exposure to realistic crime shows such as *COPS* (Krcmar & Greene, 2005).

In addition to sensation seeking, other variables associated with a need for stimulation have also been investigated. For example, the conceptualization of extraversion as a personality trait characterized by a need for external stimulation such as music or interaction with other people also suggests that it will be associated with preferences for media genres that are exciting or that have social utility. If media are stimulating or provide a means for interacting with others, we would expect extraverts to consume this media type. For example, Hall (2005) found that higher levels of extraversion were positively associated with attraction to jazz and hip hop, suggesting that upbeat, exciting music may also attract those who seek out stimulation. In addition, Weaver, Brosius, and Mundorf (1993) found that those with high levels of extraversion indicated a greater preference for sexual comedy films than did those in the low or intermediate groups. In addition, Zuckerman and Litle (1986) found extraversion to be associated with exposure to horror movies, again suggesting that the stimulating aspect of the content may be at work in attracting this personality type.

IN SEARCH OF COMFORT AND RELAXATION

Not all those who consume media want to be excited, stimulated, and aroused, however. Consider the factors that predict interest in more soothing media, or media use that is habitual. Whereas some audiences use media to be aroused, others may want merely to pass time, relax, or escape (Rubin, 1994). Which personality characteristics might be associated with exposure to these types of media? Interestingly, neuroticism has been linked to exposure to soothing media. The trait of neuroticism refers to an individual's tendency toward anxiousness. Individuals

who are high in neuroticism are thought to be more reactive than those with low levels of this trait, which means that highly neurotic individuals are more likely to be anxious, to be tense, and perhaps to dislike excessive stimulation and arousal. They may, therefore, be particularly likely to use the media to provide relief from nervousness and anxiety. For example, Weaver (2000) found that those for whom neuroticism is the predominant personality trait are more likely to watch television for passing time and relaxation motives than are those for whom other traits predominate. In addition, neuroticism has been found to be associated with a preference for informational television programs and a disinclination for more exciting fare such as comedy and adventure movies (Weaver, 1991b). Those who scored high on a scale of neuroticism were also less likely to seek out club music, including rap, R&B, and dance genres (Weaver, 2000), and somewhat more likely to use the Internet to pass time or escape (Amichae-Hamburger, Wainapel, & Fox, 2002), suggesting that the Internet may also be a source of relaxation and diversion.

IN SEARCH OF VALIDATION

Thus far, I have suggested that personality factors influence needs, which in turn influence media choices in order to ostensibly fulfill those needs. This position is consistent with the initial premise of the uses-and-gratifications approach, and indeed, those with personality factors associated with a need for stimulation tend to prefer arousing media and those personality types who are more anxious or nervous may prefer media that soothe or distract them. However, a third factor has been identified in the literature. It seems that certain genres of media content may offer violent and deviant images to those who seek validation for their own aggressive tendencies. Violent, gory, or other problematic images may resonate with them because they are consistent with their own view of the world. Furthermore, violence in media can be committed by either "good guys" or "bad guys." Therefore, viewers who enjoy the violent content may appreciate identifying with the good guy. Evidence for this line of argument comes from several studies that find an association of psychoticism, aggressive predisposition, and other related personality traits with exposure to violent images.

For example, psychoticism is a cluster of traits that includes impulsive behavior, egocentricity, and a lack of concern for social norms. Conceptualizations of this trait suggest that individuals who are high in psychoticism may prefer content that is seen as deviant or nontraditional. In fact, recent research has found that those who scored higher on a scale of psychoticism consume more media that may be perceived as transgressive, including hard-rock music (Robinson, Weaver, & Zillmann, 1996); horror movies (Weaver, 1991a; Weaver et al., 1993); violent cartoons (Aluja-Fabregat & Torrubia-Beltri, 1998); "deviant and defiant" Web sites and Internet applications (Amiel & Sargent, 2004); and, among men, X-rated films (Zuckerman & Litle, 1986). It has been found to be associated with a disinclination for tragedy films (Weaver et al., 1993) and television comedy (Weaver, 1991b), both of which tend to celebrate human emotions and empathy.

In another recent study, adolescents with disruptive behavior disorder, compared with a control group matched for age, sex, and IQ, were more interested in and watched more violent television and played more violent video games than control adolescents (Kronenberger et al., 2005). Other variables, such as verbal aggressiveness and argumentativeness, have also been positively associated with exposure to violent films, horror movies, and, to a lesser extent, real crime and violent television (Krcmar & Greene, 2005). Taken together, these findings suggest that interest in specific content, and not simply the arousing nature of the content, may be attractive to certain personality types. Regardless of the level of arousal associated with these genres, the transgressive,

hostile, or antagonistic nature of these media may fulfill a need in these individuals to be validated.

♦ *Enjoyment and Interpretation*

Once media exposure has occurred, the next step in the process is an assessment of the media content or the media exposure experience. At least two forms of assessment occur. A first assessment may best be referred to as interpretive. One might attempt to make sense of, understand, and comprehend a story, a character, or a message. Although this process may ultimately be valenced and result in a value judgment of the content (Raney, 2004), it is likely to start out as mere interpretation. A second assessment might be seen as a valenced assessment: Did I like or enjoy the content? This enjoyment may have both a cognitive and an affective component, and the media user is left with a positive or negative perception of the media. Therefore, the second stage in the process of media consumption includes both interpretation and enjoyment.

INTERPRETATION

When audiences are exposed to a particular media stimulus, it is almost a truism to say that everyone does not, in fact, see the same thing. We might refer to these differences in understanding and construal of content as *interpretive* differences. A group of viewers may see an identical clip as more or less violent, more or less humorous, or more or less biased. Furthermore, how we interpret a particular stimulus may greatly impact any subsequent effects (Potter, Pashupati, & Pekurny, 2002). The literature on interpersonal differences in interpretation of media suggests that many traits may play a role in how we make sense of the images portrayed. Although it is possible that personality itself may influence interpretation, it is more likely that the process is somewhat more complex than that. For example, Potter and colleagues

(2002) argue that individual differences in audience schemata affect interpretations of media content. Specifically, they found that individuals who were exposed to an identical clip of violence perceived varying amounts of violence, some having interpreted the clip as much more violent than others. The researchers suggest not only that these differences in interpretation exist, but that they can be explained by individual differences in personal cognitive schemata about violence and associative networks regarding violence. Extending this argument, I might suggest that personal experiences may simultaneously influence personality traits and may influence schemata regarding any number of concepts, situations, and events. As a result, the relationship between personality and interpretation may best be explained by schemata that have developed over time.

In a related argument, Bushman (1995) has suggested that individual differences in cognitive networks—resulting from differences in personal experiences—may help explain variations in priming effects. Cognitive neoassociative priming (Berkowitz, 1984) argues that memories are stored in semantically related, associative networks. When a stimulus activates or primes one node in the network, related nodes are also stimulated. In this way, cognitions, affective responses, and actions can prime other nodes in the network. Like Potter et al.'s (2002) argument regarding cognitive schemata, it is possible that personal experiences influence personality factors and associative networks that in turn may influence how media are interpreted and, as I will argue in the following paragraphs, how media affect a particular viewer.

For example, individual differences in racial attitudes may influence viewers' interpretations of crime news. Although differences in racial attitudes can certainly be characterized as an individual difference variable, it is unlikely that racism is a personality trait that is unaffected by environment. Instead, racism and schemata about race relations are likely to be developed over time through environmental

influences. In one example of this phenomenon, participants were exposed to a news story about a crime, and the perpetrator was shown to be either African American or Caucasian. Participants who scored higher on a measure of racial prejudice were more likely to evaluate the Black perpetrator negatively, but more likely to have positive evaluations of the perpetrator when he was presented as White (Peffley, Shields, & Williams, 1996).

Similarly, hypermasculinity is conceptualized as a variable that measures an endorsement of males as excessively strong, dominant, and forceful. Again, this variable is likely to be influenced by personal experience and environmental influences that in turn affect one's gender schema. In support of this argument, Beaver et al. (1992) exposed participants to a clip of a date rape scenario. They found that males who scored higher on a scale of hypermasculinity interpreted the perpetrator as less culpable and showed less sympathy for the victim. Although the authors do not present cognitive gender schemata as an explanation for their findings, the results are certainly consistent with such a position. In sum, individual differences in interpretations of media stimuli have been shown to vary along personality lines; however, it is possible that cognitive schemata may offer a fruitful explanation for links that have been found between personality and media interpretations.

LIKING AND ENJOYMENT

As we consider some of the individual differences involved in the media consumption process, it is worth noting that variations in media *use* do not necessarily parallel patterns of media enjoyment (Krcmar & Kean, 2004). This suggests that we may seek out media to fulfill certain needs, but as the uses-and-gratifications approach has argued, gratifications sought are not the same as those received (Rubin, 1994). Several good examples of this phenomenon can be seen in the study of personality and media use. For example, variables that characterize a thrill-seeking personality type who is open to novel experiences and seeks out external stimulation are sometimes associated with exposure to violent media; however, recent research suggests that these individuals may not enjoy or be satisfied by media, even of the violent or arousing variety.

In addition, despite the evidence discussed earlier suggesting that the drive to be aroused by media causes high sensation seekers to seek out thrilling media, several pieces of research (e.g., Finn, 1997; Krcmar & Greene, 1999; Weaver, 2000) have found that for some individuals who are interested in novel experiences and thrilling sensations, media do not offer satisfaction. In one case, Krcmar and Greene (1999); found that true high sensation seekers do not watch television, instead preferring real, rather than mediated, arousing stimuli. In this study, the authors looked not only at sensation seeking and media use, but also at engagement in other activities, exploring the possibility that arousing media might act as a substitute for arousing activities. The results suggested that although there is a link between sensation seeking and exposure to exciting media, true sensation seekers were actually low overall media users because they likely preferred real, not mediated, stimuli. Similarly, working from the five-factor model of personality, Finn (1997) found extraversion to be negatively associated with overall television viewership and positively with the nonmediated activities of sports spectatorship and party attendance, suggesting that once again, television may offer some fulfillment in terms of arousal or excitement, but real gratification of the need to be stimulated is more likely to come from other sources. Last, Weaver's (2000) findings support this suggestion. He found that individuals for whom extraversion was the predominant personality characteristic were less likely to watch television for companionship motives than were those for whom neuroticism or

psychoticism predominated. Taken in sum, these results suggest that television can satisfy certain needs, but for some individuals, such as extraverts seeking companionship or sensation seekers seeking arousal, gratifications must be found from real rather than mediated sources.

◆ Effects

A considerably larger body of research has examined the role of individual differences in attraction to various media than has looked at effects. As Oliver (2002) has noted, the dearth of research in this area is largely an artifact of how the research is conceptualized and conducted. Those interested in media selection are likely to look for variables that may predict selection of and exposure to various media genres. This perspective has resulted in a relatively large body of research. On the other hand, those scholars interested in the effects of media are likely to conduct experiments, where the topic of interest is often the stimulus. Participants are randomly assigned to conditions with the ultimate goal of eliminating any systematic variance resulting from factors such as personality variables. When individual differences are measured, they are often used as covariates in order to better explore the uncontaminated effect of the stimulus. Thus, research on effects has not produced as large nor as systematic a body of evidence about the role of individual difference variables in moderating effects. Nevertheless, in recent years, more attention has been paid to this important issue as scholars recognize the crucial role of moderators in exploring media effects.

AGGRESSION

Recall the argument presented earlier that suggested it is not personality per se that moderates media effects, but the cognitive associative networks that are often related to personality factors. In this case, aggressive predispositions, for example, do not in and of themselves heighten the aggression-inducing effects of violent media exposure. Rather, individuals with more aggressive predispositions may have more complex and dense cognitive associative networks about violence. Once exposed to an aggressive media, they may be more apt to have violent thoughts and behaviors activated. For example, Bushman (1995) randomly assigned participants to watch either a violent or a nonviolent film. Aggressive affect and aggressive behavior increased among those in the test group, but especially for those who scored high on a measure of trait aggression. Bushman suggested that higher levels of aggression were noted among some participants due to their more elaborate networks for aggression-related behaviors, feelings, and attitudes.

Not only is trait aggression likely to be involved in an associative network for aggression, but it is possible that other personality characteristics may also be linked to these cognitive networks. For example, psychoticism is characterized by impulsive behavior, egocentricity, and a lack of concern for social norms. In their study of media and psychoticism, Zillmann and Weaver (1997) found that males who scored higher on a measure of psychoticism were more aggressive after viewing violent programming than those who scored lower on the measure. It is possible that lack of concern for social norms and behavioral impulsivity are in some way cognitively linked with aggression. When one node in the network is activated, similar nodes are likely to be activated as well, and this may be the case especially for those with rich and complex networks.

Russell (1992) also examined the effect of media on aggression; however, the moderating variable of interest was hypermasculinity. In this study, males were randomly assigned to watch a boxing match or an exciting but nonviolent skiing competition. Results from the posttest suggested that those in the high hypermasculinity group who saw the boxing

match were significantly more aggressive than those who saw the skiing competition or those who were low on the scale. Similarly, Scharrer (2001) found that men who scored high on a measure of hypermasculinity experienced greater increases in aggression after exposure to a violent clip than those who scored low on the measure. Taken together, these findings lend further support to the notion that aggressive schemata, or perhaps aggressive cognitive associative networks, may offer an explanation for greater increases in aggression among some viewers after exposure to violent media. In fact, extensions of work by Scharrer (2005) indicated that hypermasculinity could also be affected by exposure to violent media. This suggests that hypermasculinity is not only a stable personality characteristic, but one susceptible to effects of media, perhaps helping to establish aggressive cognitive networks. Overall, then, it is possible that the personality traits discussed are in some way cognitively linked with aggression.

MEMORY AND RECALL

Memory for and recall of media content has been measured as a dependent variable in many studies, and to some extent, individual differences have been considered as potential moderators of effects. For example, those who scored high on a measure of neuroticism were more likely to recall nonviolent news stories and less likely to recall violent news stories than their low-neuroticism counterparts (Gunter & Furnham, 1986). To what extent might schema, or perhaps cognitive associative networks, shed some light on this phenomenon? If cognitive associative networks can offer an explanation for the link between individual differences and media selection, might they also offer an explanation for the moderating role of various factors in the effects literature?

How would this occur? Consider the role of cognitive associative networks in priming. A network for, say, violence, might be densely or sparsely populated for a given individual. If the network is dense, it may contain many nodes about violent scenarios, conflict resolution, characters, weapons, hostile affect, and other related issues. Activating a node for *criminal,* in such a case, might also result in an activation of many related nodes. But other characteristics may be linked in this network, as well. For example, neuroticism or fear may also be associated here, but only among those who have more densely populated networks. For those for whom aggression is a distant and sparse network, neuroticism may be unassociated. Therefore, for those with dense networks regarding violence, neuroticism may be part of the network and may consequently account for an increase in recall of violent stories among those who score high on a neuroticism measure.

Other variables have also been associated with different patterns of recall. One variable that has received a lot of attention in terms of recall is sensation seeking. As I discussed earlier, those who score higher on measures of sensation seeking tend to seek out more novel stimuli than those who score lower on this measure; however, sensation seeking has also been found to moderate the effects of messages on recall. Specifically, individuals who are higher on the sensation-seeking measure prefer exciting, fast-paced messages and, consequently, seem to recall them to a greater extent (Donohew, Palmgreen, & Duncan, 1980), especially when those messages target high-risk behaviors, as is the case with antismoking public service announcements (Palmgreen et al., 1991).

Need for cognition is also associated with greater recall because those who score higher on measures of need for cognition tend to engage in and enjoy thinking. This tendency leads people to be more motivated to pay attention to and think about messages that require thought and effort (Cacioppo & Petty, 1982). Need for cognition has been associated with a preference for more complex tasks, generation of more ideas, and more careful consideration of election campaign information (Petty, Cacioppo, & Kasmer, 1988). Need for cognition has also been linked to

media usage that suggests a willingness to invest effort. Ferguson, Chung, and Weigold (1985), for example, found that higher levels of need for cognition were linked to seeking and recalling news, and in a related study, college students who scored higher on a need-for-cognition measure were more likely to seek out and recall political news information. Therefore, need for cognition is another individual difference variable that may moderate the effect of media exposure on recall.

Neuroticism has also been found to be associated positively with recall of nonviolent news stories and negatively with recall of violent news stories (Gunter & Furnham, 1986). This finding suggests that neuroticism, a trait associated with higher levels of anxiety and fear, may interact with memory because individuals with higher levels of neuroticism may pay more attention to nonviolent news stories in order to be aware of and in control of their environment. However, because violent images can be disruptive to memory processing, especially among those with higher scores on a neuroticism measure, memory for violent stories may actually be hampered.

Ultimately, the role of personality and individual difference factors in media exposure *outcomes* may be similar to the role of these factors in *interpretations* of mass media. At the microanalytic level, cognitive associative networks about a particular topic may be more or less complex and dense for a given individual. Furthermore, the relative complexity of a network is likely to be related to an individual's personal experiences and personality traits, which are, in themselves, likely linked in meaningful ways. Ultimately, then, these networks can predict how media are interpreted by that individual and how media affect him or her. Similarly, cognitive scripts may be analytically similar to priming and associative networks in that both are thought to be cognitive networks, generated through experience, which then help guide incoming information and help establish and reinforce systems of thought and behavior. In both cases, cognitive networks and scripts, individual differences are likely to be linked to these systems and, ultimately, to media use, interpretations, and outcomes.

◆ Concluding Remarks

The last few decades of research have supported the notion that individual differences exist among media users and that these individual differences are crucial aspects of the media consumption process. Future research should incorporate individual differences into models of media use and effects, not merely as an afterthought but as an integral and primary focus of the research. In addition, researchers should explore not just the role of personality in television and film use, but the role of individual differences in the use and effects of new technologies. As new technologies emerge, it is important to study how they are used, by whom, and with what effect, all the while considering the importance of individual difference variations in each stage of the process (see, for example, Amichae-Hamburger et al., 2002). These variations become nearly infinite as differences in patterns of use lead to differences in interpretation, which in turn lead to differences in effects. Furthermore, when many individual difference variables (e.g., sensation seeking, aggressive predisposition) are considered simultaneously, potential models are even further compounded. Theory that might attempt to account for all these variables would quickly become unwieldy. Nevertheless, it remains an important goal to develop media theory that can account for differences and yet remain manageable.

What might such a theory look like? In this chapter, I have attempted to suggest parallels and links between such cognitive theories as priming and script theory. Furthermore, I have reviewed the uses-and-gratifications approach and disposition-based theories, which also include personality factors in their models. Although no attempt has been made as of yet to combine these ideas, it is possible that by using the notion of cognitive associative networks, and recognizing the importance of individual differences at each stage of the media-consumption process, a broad yet coherent model could be developed. Although it goes beyond the scope of this chapter to build such a theory, I briefly present here the main ideas. Specifically, a broad-based model of the media consumption process would recognize three stages: preference and use, enjoyment and interpretation, and effects. At each stage, cognitive associative networks would provide a basis for recognizing the importance of individual differences.

For example, prior to exposure, audiences have preferences and are motivated to use particular kinds of media and indeed other kinds of stimuli. Individual-difference factors such as sensation seeking may generate a need, which in turn may result in media use. Consider an audience member who scores high on a measure of sensation seeking. For this individual, cognitive associative networks that are related to arousal (i.e., aggression or exciting sports) may be more dense, complex, and recently activated. This phenomenon may result in greater use of exciting media. But subsequently, these densely interconnected networks may result in greater enjoyment or a positive interpretation of exciting or violent media. Last, particular media that is both enjoyed and interpreted positively by the high sensation seeker may encourage imitation of the modeled behavior, once again, because the cognitive associative networks are more likely to be activated and primed by exposure to this media. In this way, priming and cognitive associative networks may offer a very broad explanation for the role of individual differences in the media consumption process.

What would such a broad-based theory offer us? Like all good theory, it would help specify the direction of future research and establish important avenues of inquiry. It would provide direction as we embark on research at the empirical and analytic level. For example, at present, additional research is needed to isolate those variables that are most strongly related to media preference, interpretation, and effects. To date, the approach to variable selection has not been systematic, leaving us with a large but somewhat messy body of research. Once the most important individual factors have been isolated, how each of these variables operates at each stage must be established. How does neuroticism, for example, affect use, interpretation, and effects? Each stage in the process might be investigated independently, and then further investigation would explore if the relationships remained the same once the entire model was tested simultaneously. Ultimately, then, a broad-based theory, built on the notion of cognitive associative networks, might allow us to generate a more detailed and specified model of media consumption that would have explanatory and predictive power at both a micro and a macro level.

◆ References

Aluja-Fabregat, A., & Torrubia-Beltri, R. (1998). Viewing of mass media violence, perception of violence, personality and academic achievement. *Personality and Individual Differences, 25,* 973–989.

Amichae-Hamburger, Y., Wainapel, G., & Fox, S. (2002). "On the Internet no one knows I'm an introvert": Extroversion, neuroticism, and Internet interaction. *Cyberpsychology and Behavior, 5,* 125–128.

Amiel, T., & Sargent, S. L. (2004). Individual differences in Internet usage motives. *Computers in Human Behavior, 20,* 711–726.

Beaver, E. D., Gold, S. R., & Prisco, A. G. (1992). Priming macho attitudes and emotions. *Journal of Interpersonal Violence, 7,* 321–333.

Berkowitz, L. (1984). Some effects of thoughts on anti- and prosocial influences of media events: A cognitive-neoassociation analysis. *Psychological Bulletin, 95,* 410–427.

Brock, T. C., & Livingston, S. D. (2004). The need for entertainment scale. In L. J. Shrum (Ed.), *Blurring the lines: The psychology of*

entertainment media (pp. 255–274). Mahwah, NJ: Erlbaum.

Bushman, B. J. (1995). Moderating role of trait aggressiveness in the effects of violent media on aggression. *Journal of Personality and Social Psychology, 69,* 950–960.

Cacioppo, J. T., & Petty, R. E. (1982). The need for cognition. *Journal of Personality and Social Psychology, 42,* 116–131.

Donohew, L., Palmgreen, P., & Duncan, J. (1980). An activation model of information exposure. *Communication Monographs, 47,* 295–303.

Ferguson, M., Chung, M., & Weigold, M. (1985, May). *Need for cognition and the medium dependency components of reliance and exposure.* Paper presented at the annual conference of the International Communication Association, Honolulu, HI.

Finn, S. (1997). Origins of media exposure: Linking personality traits to TV, radio, print, and film use. *Communication Research, 24,* 507–529.

Gunter, B., & Furnham, A. (1986). Sex and personality differences in recall of violent and non-violent news from three presentational modalities. *Personality and Individual Differences, 7,* 829–837.

Hall, A. (2005). Audience personality and the selection of media and media genres. *Media Psychology, 7,* 377–398.

Huesmann, L. R. (1988). An information processing model for the development of aggression. *Aggressive Behavior, 14,* 13–24.

Katz, E., Blumler, J. C., & Gurevitch, M. (1974). Utilization of mass communication by the individual. In J. G. Blumler & E. Katz (Eds.), *The uses of mass communications* (pp. 19–32). Newbury Park, CA: Sage.

Krcmar, M., & Greene, K. (1999). Predicting exposure to and uses of television violence. *Journal of Communication, 49*(3), 24–45.

Krcmar, M., & Greene, K. (2005). Predicting exposure to and liking of media violence: A uses and gratifications approach. *Communication Studies, 56,* 71–93.

Krcmar, M., & Kean, L. G. (2004). Uses and gratifications of media violence: Personality correlates of viewing and liking violent genres. *Media Psychology, 7,* 399–420.

Kronenberger, W. G., Mathews, V. P., Dunn, D. W., Wang, Y., Wood, E. A., Larsen, J. J., et al. (2005). Media violence exposure in aggressive and control adolescents: Differences in self- and parent-reported exposure to violence on television and in video games. *Aggressive Behavior, 31,* 201–216.

Oliver, M. B. (2002). Individual differences in media effects. In J. Bryant & D. Zillmann (Eds.), *Media effects: Advances in theory and research* (2nd ed., pp. 507–524). Mahwah, NJ: Erlbaum.

Palmgreen, P., Donohew, L., Lorch, E. P., Rogus, M., Helm, D., & Grant, N. (1991). Sensation seeking, message sensation value, and drug use as mediators of PSA effectiveness. *Health Communication, 3,* 217–227.

Peffley, M., Shields, T., & Williams, B. (1996). The intersection of race and crime in television news stories: An experimental study. *Political Communication, 13,* 309–327.

Perse, E. M. (1996). Sensation seeking and the use of television for arousal. *Communication Reports, 9,* 37–48.

Petty, R. E., Cacioppo, J. T., & Kasmer, J. A. (1988). The role of affect in the elaboration likelihood model of persuasion. In L. Donohue, H. E. Sypher, & E. T. Higgins (Eds.), *Communication, social cognition, and affect* (pp. 117–146). Hillsdale, NJ: Erlbaum.

Potter, W. J., Pashupati, K., & Pekurny, R. G. (2002). Perceptions of television: A schema. *Media Psychology, 4,* 27–50.

Raney, A. A. (2004). Expanding disposition theory: Reconsidering character liking, moral evaluations, and enjoyment. *Communication Theory, 14,* 348–369.

Raney, A. A. (2006). The psychology of disposition-based theories of media enjoyment. In J. Bryant & P. Vorderer (Eds.), *The psychology of entertainment* (pp. 137–150). Mahwah, NJ: Erlbaum.

Robinson, T. O., Weaver, J. B., & Zillmann, D. (1996). Exploring the relation between personality and the appreciation of rock music. *Psychological Reports, 78,* 259–269.

Rubin, A. M. (1981). A multivariate analysis of *60 Minutes*: Viewing motivations. *Journalism Quarterly, 58,* 529–534.

Rubin, A. M. (1994). Media uses and effects: A uses-and-gratifications perspective. In J. Bryant & D. Zillmann (Eds.), *Media effects: Advances in theory and research* (pp. 417–436). Hillsdale, NJ: Erlbaum.

Russell, G. W. (1992). Response of the macho male to viewing a combatant sport. *Journal of Personality and Social Behavior, 7,* 631–638.

Scharrer, E. (2001). Men, muscles, and machismo: The relationship between television violence exposure and aggression and hostility in the presence of hypermasculinity. *Media Psychology, 3,* 159–188.

Scharrer, E. (2005). Hypermasculinity, aggression, and television violence: An experiment. *Media Psychology, 7,* 353–376.

Tamborini, R., & Stiff, J. (1987). Predictors of horror film attendance and appeal: An analysis of the audience for frightening films. *Communication Research, 14,* 415–436.

Weaver, J. B. (1991a). Are "slasher" horror films sexually violent? A content analysis. *Journal of Broadcasting and Electronic Media, 35,* 385–392.

Weaver, J. B. (1991b). Exploring the links between personality and media preferences. *Personality and Individual Differences, 12,* 1293–1299.

Weaver, J. B. (2000). Personality and entertainment preferences. In D. Zillmann & P. Vorderer (Eds.), *Media entertainment: The psychology of its appeal* (pp. 235–248). Mahwah, NJ: Erlbaum.

Weaver, J. B., Brosius, H. B., & Mundorf, N. (1993). Personality and movie preferences: A comparison of American and German audiences. *Personality and Individual Differences, 14,* 307–315.

Zillmann, D. (1985). The experimental exploration of gratifications from media entertainment. In D. Zillmann & J. Bryant (Eds.), *Selective exposure to communication* (pp. 225–239). Hillsdale, NJ: Erlbaum.

Zillmann, D., & Weaver, J. B. (1997). Psychoticism in the effect of prolonged exposure to gratuitous media violence on the acceptance of violence as a preferred means of conflict resolution. *Personality and Individual Differences, 22,* 613–627.

Zuckerman, M. (1979). *Sensation seeking: Beyond the optimal level of arousal.* Hillsdale, NJ: Erlbaum.

Zuckerman, M., & Litle, P. (1986). Personality and curiosity about morbid and sexual events. *Personality and Individual Differences, 7,* 49–56.

17

MEDIA USE AND THE SOCIAL ENVIRONMENT

◆ Daniel G. McDonald

M ost obvious referents to the social nature of media use are to consumption as a group activity (e.g., coviewing television, going to motion pictures in groups) or to the effects of media on groups of people (e.g., the panic ensuing the *War of the Worlds* broadcast of 1938), but even solitary use of a medium provides an audience member with information about norms, values, and other aspects of the social environment. In some ways, media content can also alter or create a social environment, as described by Palmer a century ago:

> Certain [movie theaters] . . . have become genuine social centers where neighborhood groups may be found any evening of the week; where the regulars stroll up and down between the acts and visit friends. . . . (Palmer, 1909, p. 356)

This chapter provides an overview of research related to media use and the social environment through relevant literature from the birth of mass communication research to the present. For organizational purposes, the literature is first divided into two main areas: the social environment as a factor affecting media use, and media as a factor affecting the social environment. However, much of the research has pointed toward a third area, one that suggests that media use and the social environment interact in producing many effects. Additional discussion suggests that research studying causes and effects related to media use and the social environment has been inadequate, and offers suggestions for theories and methodologies that may prove useful in studying this interaction.

◆ Social Environment Influences on Media Selection and Use

Coincident with the rise of psychology in the first third of the 20th century, early conceptions of the effects of media use were primarily concerned with the psychological aspects of motion pictures (e.g., Edwards, 1915). The popular literature and public concern partially mirrored psychological perspectives (especially in regard to what people learned from film and the role models appearing on screen), but a minor thread focused on more social aspects of the audience or audience experiences, like the typical clientele of motion picture theaters; the social configurations of those in attendance (e.g., Perry, 1923); and the social activity that occurred before, during, or after viewing (e.g., Davis, 1911; Phelan, 1919).

FAMILY AND PEER INFLUENCES ON CONTENT SELECTION

Family and peer influences on content selection have been particularly important to research on more "social" media—those that involve attendance in groups of family or friends, such as the movies, or those that involve in-home, simultaneous use by multiple members of the household, such as television throughout its history or radio during the 1930s. As each medium diffused, characteristics of each technology led to a reinterpretation of social influences. Blumer (1933), for example, focused primarily on how an individual's peers

affected selection of motion picture content, especially noting how delinquents in the "rougher" areas of town tended to prefer crime and other violent motion pictures. Blumer asserted the idea that a person associated with similar others (e.g., delinquents with delinquents), and that content choice would be congruent with the social atmosphere of the group.

As radio diffused during the first three decades of the 20th century, media researchers began studies of the effects of radio in the home, and attention turned naturally toward the family more than peers. The majority of these early studies were concerned with the effects of content preference rather than selection (Cantril & Allport, 1935), but as more and more studies indicated that preference and listening were not synonymous, it became clear that people were often listening to programs that were their second or third choice. Whether listening reflected the preferences of a dominant individual or some sort of "group mean" of selection that took everyone's preferences into account was not clear. Thus, when research attention was transferred to the home, research became more concerned with parents, children, and their interrelationships, and how those interrelationships played out in media content selection. In contrast to the motion picture research focusing on congruency of choice, power and authority within parent-child relationships seems to underlie the assumptions being made by the researchers. Early radio research by Clark (1939), for example, noted that children frequently reported that their parents had developed rules for selecting particular programs or types of programs (typically focusing on the amount of violence in the content). However, the children also reported that they often disobeyed those rules (Clark, 1939).

With the arrival of television in the 1940s and 1950s, researchers continued to investigate selection as a function of relationships within the home, but also began noting the impact of interpersonal discussion of media content on content selection (McDonagh, 1950). Although some early TV studies continued with the assumption that preference and choice were synonymous (Merrill, 1961), the limited choices available and the limited number of sets in each household led to questions of decisions about viewing, especially in the case of the interpersonal conflict that can occur when selection is between conflicting preferences. A number of attempts to uncover the process or processes involved in media selection focused on whether a group choice, a dominant individual, or some other process is the mechanism for media content selection (McDonagh, 1950).

Wand's (1968) unique approach to studying the selection of content asked viewers about specific preferences when faced with particular program choices coupled with actual viewing behavior diaries in the following week (when the same choices had to be made). She found that conflicts between family members' choices occurred about one third of the time. Conflicting preference tended to affect viewing choice in two ways: by increasing the likelihood that the parent would not view any program, and also by increasing the likelihood that a parent would view a nonpreferred program. When choice differences were between members of the same generation, coviewing tended to increase, thus increasing viewing of nonpreferred programs, but when those differences were between generations, coviewing decreased, thus increasing the probability of not viewing television. Although her data indicated that father-mother preference differences were resolved in favor of the mother's preference two thirds of the time, parent-child conflicts were resolved in favor of the child about 50% of the time. Wand noted, however, that families' self-reports were that the father's preferences were usually followed.

Lull indicated that a quasi-democratic process might operate in homes when there was disagreement over which program to view (Lull, 1982). Lull's observational study indicated that the father was less likely than other members of the family to ask others' opinions before changing channels. McDonald (1985) found that the best single predictor of program viewing was having a peer member of the family (the family member closest in age) viewing. McDonald suggested that, in the age of multiple television sets in the home, overlapping preferences with a peer was the most likely predictor of program selection. Later research by Dorr, Kovaric, and Doubleday (1989) supported the overlapping preferences explanation. In sum, when content options are nonexclusive, as in the case of multiple TV sets or multiple motion pictures to choose from, overlapping preferences among peers lead to selection reflecting a shared preference, but when content options are exclusive, power, authority, and interrelationships become more important in media selection.

INTERPERSONAL INTERACTION AND THE DEVELOPMENT OF CONTENT PREFERENCES

Parental and peer influences. While the literature described in the previous section has focused on the social environment and content selection, another stream of research has focused on how our media preferences develop. Much of the popular literature suggests the importance of peer pressure on development of media content preference, selection, and interpretation, but the academic literature suggests that home influence—the influence of parents and siblings of a close age—is at least as powerful in encouraging or discouraging the development of our preferences. This literature suggests that parental influence is typically through overt action, whereas sibling influence tends to operate through reinforcing general norms of the family viewing environment. Clark's (1939) radio study, example, devoted an entire section to parental influence on radio program preferences, content rules, and allowable listening times, all of which were intended to promote a harmonious and healthy social atmosphere such that radio listening did not interfere with homework or sleep, or make excessive violence an acceptable part of family life. A recent study by Rozin, Riklis, and Margolis (2004) found that peer content preferences had little impact on the development of individual preferences in young children, suggesting that parental influences via coviewing or household rules, or general age-related norms shared by sibling peers, might have even stronger effects than were presumed earlier because they appear to have an important long-term socialization effect. An additional study by Bagley, Salmon, and Crawford (2006) add data indicating the strength of siblings' impact on the development of viewing preferences.

These studies suggest that a number of factors in the social environment of the home lead to formation of content preference and media use patterns for children. One line of research has attempted to encapsulate many of these factors under the umbrella concept of family communication patterns (FCP; McLeod, Atkin, & Chaffee, 1972). According to the FCP framework, "concept-oriented" families focus on ideas and encourage independent development whereas "soci-oriented" families focus on the notion of obtaining harmony in the family by adherence to rules, obedience to elders, and so forth. The FCP literature has been used as a framework to study how adults and children relate to each other and to selection and use of media content. The FCP strategy for understanding the norms of interpersonal communication within a household has ~~off~~ ... t steady, stream of research ... day in interpersonal com- ... rch, and also studies of ... operate with respect to ... s aspects of media use ... 2002; Krcmar & Vieira,

Parental mediation. A related stream of research has focused on the role that parents play (either actively or passively) in steering the formation of preference and choice for their children. This line of research, known as parental mediation, is focused on whether or not an adult is able to alter a child's media consumption habits or the effects of media use. Barcus (1969) found that the most frequent type of parental control over content selection tended to be negative, either turning off the set or changing channels after the program had begun. However, he also noted a number of additional methods of formal and informal controls operating before, during, and after program viewing, such as suggesting programs, discussion of program content, explaining the content, answering questions, or forbidding future viewing of programs.

Early research in this area indicated that the mere presence of others in a viewing situation may be enough to alter the development of TV preferences, but in terms of mediating effects, a review by McLeod and his colleagues (McLeod, Fitzpatrick, Glynn, & Fallis, 1982) concluded that conversation was required. By the late 1990s, there were a number of studies with mixed results on parental mediation of television's effects on children. Some of these suggested that parental coviewing with a child could have negative effects when the content was violent or unwholesome; others suggested that coviewing served to limit or nullify effects of violent content. Nathanson (2001) conducted surveys of parents and children to examine parent and child perceptions of what occurred during coviewing. She concluded that when an adult coviews with a child, it suggests to the child that the parent approves of the content, no matter what that content involves, unless the adult makes specific comments related to disapproval. If Nathanson is correct, then that interpretation helps explain that many of the differences in conclusions between studies that found negative, rather than positive, effects of parental mediation are attributable to how the parent and child interact while coviewing.

◆ Media Effects on the Social Environment

Although interpersonal communication is one aspect of the social environment influencing the choice, uses, and effects of media content, the use of media can also influence interpersonal discussion and other aspects of the social environment. This section, then, explores the media's effect on interpersonal interaction as well as media as a social environment itself.

MEDIA USE EFFECTS ON INTERPERSONAL INTERACTION

Evidence suggests that the use of media can alter the nature and extent of interpersonal conversation and interaction in at least three ways: by limiting the amount of conversation between audience members, by providing topics or information for use in interpersonal conversation, or by affecting development of social and communication skills by providing communication role models.

Much of the literature investigating the conversation-limiting effects of media stem from the early days of television, when there was a comparison, nontelevision group readily available. Riley, Cantwell, and Ruttiger (1949) noted that in early TV homes, TV had stimulated about 15% of the families to find new interest in each other, and another 13% found new interests related to staying at home and watching with others. Despite any new interests that may have emerged, however, McDonagh (1950) found that about 60% of families reported that they were talking to each other less after obtaining a television set. Similarly, Maccoby (1951) found that 58% of respondents indicated that

there was "none or very little" talking during TV viewing; another 20% indicated that they had certain times to talk; 11% indicated that they had limited comments, typically about the program; and only 11% indicated there was quite a bit of discussion during viewing. A few decades later, a study by Brody, Stoneman, and Sanders (1980) demonstrated that families talked less when viewing than when not viewing.

While people may not talk as much while viewing television as they do when not viewing, there is also evidence that people often talk about what they have seen, heard, or read about in the media. When media content serves as a topic of discussion, it has typically been referred to as *social utility,* which reflects the idea that media content can have a certain degree of usefulness in interpersonal interaction. Dervin and Greenberg (1972), for example, found that media content provides major topics of conversation for the urban poor, with more than half indicating that they talked about TV content two or more times per week. More recently, Gehrau (2007) found that media content continues to be discussed often with family members and friends, and, surprisingly, less often with acquaintances. Typically, it was thought that media content served to help "break the ice" or develop commonalities between people. However, Gehrau found that one common use of involving family and friends in conversations about media content is to avoid conversations about personal and emotional concerns. Relatedly, though somewhat beyond the scope of this chapter, a strong line of research on the use of political media content in discussion and its effects on learning and political participation has also developed (e.g., Eveland & Thomson, 2006).

Media content is also thought to be useful in future interpersonal interactions. This idea of *communicatory utility* was described by Chaffee, McLeod, and Atkin (1971), noting in a political communication study that voters were more likely to ask for campaign information if they expected to talk about the election with friends. Anticipated interaction led to increased use of media content, which changed the level of knowledge in the social environment. Both communicatory utility and social utility have become staples of the uses-and-gratifications framework (see Rubin, Chapter 10, this volume).

Researchers have also found that media use may impact interpersonal interaction through development of social and communication skills. Zimbardo (1977) suggested that passively watching television may, over time, inhibit viewers' ability to communicate effectively because viewers aren't interacting with other people during the time spent viewing. This turn on the displacement hypothesis has not been studied in great detail. However, somewhat supporting that contention, Coats and Feldman (1995) found that school-aged children communicated emotions that were commonly displayed on television better than emotions that are uncommon on television. Infrequent viewers did not exhibit that ability. Frequent TV viewers were also better encoders of spontaneous nonverbal displays, but were worse encoders of posed displays. This suggests that TV viewing may encourage nonverbal expressiveness that is more spontaneous and less controlled, and may also indicate that heavier TV viewers may fail to actively manage information being communicated in nonverbal displays. If so, heavier TV viewers may be at a social disadvantage because what they learn from television is to react to emotional displays and to display spontaneous reactions, rather than learning to control nonverbal expression and reactions that are important in developing social interaction skills.

MEDIA AS SOCIAL ENVIRONMENT

In addition to media use affecting social interaction, media can become a part of the social environment, and thus influence a number of factors related to psychological and physical well-being. Although typically not studied in the extant research, when one person in a household is watching TV, surfing the Internet, or listening to loud music, the sounds and images are part of the home environment for all members who are within visual or hearing range, and thus influence their behaviors and interactions. For example, sleep disturbances in children have been associated with media use for nearly 100 years, and the literature suggests two different underlying causes: staying up late to watch or listen to media content (which takes away from sleep time), and listening/watching exciting material (which can alter the physiological state or dream content of viewers; Paavonen, Pennonen, Roine, Valkonen, & Lahikainen, 2006; Renshaw, Miller, & Marquis, 1933). Interestingly, Paavonen et al. found that what they referred to as passive TV viewing—viewing that occurs peripherally when others are watching TV but the child is neither the primary audience nor paying particular attention to the content—was most related to sleep disturbances. They reasoned that the child is more likely to hear and see disturbing material when he or she is not the one who is actually watching it, especially when household rules are in place regarding specific content or times for viewing (see also Anderson, 1979, for evidence that even preschoolers shift attention from various play activities to active TV viewing when peers indicate an interest in the screen).

Rosenblatt and Cunningham's (1976) study of TV viewing time and family tensions provides an example of how media behaviors of other people may interact with other household factors within the environment. The authors found a moderately strong correlation between household television time and tension in homes with large families, but a much weaker correlation in homes with fewer people.

They argued that the differential suggests that TV may be used as a coping mechanism in crowded home environments, although they also suggest that the opposite could be concluded from their data: that the unrelenting sound of the TV may increase tension in the home, and greater numbers of people increase the likelihood that the TV will be on at any given time.

If media use is a method of coping with issues in the home environment, it is most likely related to other (nonmedia) methods of coping, such as hobbies, volunteering, spending time alone, and so on. Recently, a few studies have focused on TV and music as coping outlets for dealing with various tensions in the home. Hutchinson, Baldwin, and Oh (2006) found that both TV and music listening were related to the use of active coping strategies, such as engaging in sports, volunteering, and so on, as well as passive or avoidance-based strategies, such as escape and distraction used by adolescents in times of stress. They also note that the use of active and passive coping strategies are not opposites, as most activities are a mix of the two. Further complicating our understanding of the role of television in the home environment, Verma and Larson (2002) found that when adolescents are watching TV, they report lower worry and stress, so viewing may actually reduce tension in the home rather than serve as an individual means of escape from worry. One plausible interpretation here may be that if TV viewing decreases interpersonal interaction, it may also reduce the number of arguments among family members, and so alter the level of tension in the home. This would be a very different interpretation than the traditional idea that television serves as a means of psychological escape or retreat from family tension.

Hilt and Lipschultz (2004) found, in a slight turn on the "TV as coping mechanism" literature, that when fathers spent greater time coviewing and doing other activities with children, both sons and daughters had lower levels of family conflict 5 years later. This relationship was not found for mothers. It would seem likely that, rather than any causal process operating, father coviewing is currently an indicator of closer family connections and greater time spent together as a family, whereas mother coviewing may not be as strong an indicator due to less variance in mothers' coviewing time.

Taken together, these studies suggest that, in some instances, media use may cause tension by demanding attention from those who are not particularly interested in it; in other situations, it may provide a method of coping with tension-producing situations in the home; in another possibility, it may curtail tension by altering interpersonal conflict and argument. Although we typically think of media use as an "escape" or avoidance style of dealing with tension, it appears that it may also offer other types of coping options, and may, in certain situations, reduce the level of tension in the home.

◆ Interactions Between Communication and the Social Environment

Although the outline of research presented earlier suggests direct effects of the social environment on media use and of media use on the social environment, there is reason to believe that communication interacts with the environment in producing nearly all the effects previously described in reciprocal or nonlinear relationships. Media use takes time and attention, which, by and large, is taken from other activities. That is why, as indicated earlier, much of TV time is spent not talking, rather than talking, to coviewers. Media effects occur, then, not only because of what the media do, but because of what media users do not do. In this section, we will explore two areas of probable effects and their interactive nature: emotional contagion and the role of media in health and sedentary behaviors.

EMOTIONAL CONTAGION

Hylton (1971) described a general class of media effects as "intra-audience effects"—the effects of audience members on each other through verbal and non-verbal communication. One of the earliest ideas about intra-audience effects is the notion of emotional contagion, or the processes by which people "catch" the moods of those around them. In the area of mass communication, the term was used as early as 1914 (Hamilton, 1914), but little systematic research considered the possibility that emotional contagion occurs with everyday use of the media.

Recently, work in psychology has renewed the idea that when interacting with others, people can be affected by "emotional contagion" (Hatfield, Cacioppo, & Rapson, 1992). Hatfield et al. suggest that contagion leads to convergence of emotion, and perhaps convergence in attention and behavior as well. Hatfield et al. review a large body of experimental evidence indicating that emotional contagion happens quite frequently in life.

In understanding media use and the social environment, the notion of emotional contagion should have direct relevance. How much of what we enjoy or the emotions we experience during media consumption is a product of who we are with and what they are experiencing? How much do we monitor other audience members and their reactions?

While the questions seem simple, a difficulty that arises in detecting emotional contagion effects among audience members lies in separating emotional effects of contagion from the media content's effects on the audience members. Virtually all the studies of emotional contagion in psychology use media content as a stimulus so that the "sender" is controlled. From an intra-audience perspective, though, they are studying the flow of emotions from media content displays to an audience member, and not contagion effects.

McDonald and Fredin (2001) suggest that reactions to content and reactions to others (who are also reacting to content) will be highly correlated most of the time, making it extremely difficult to separate the two components. If an audience member feels sad while viewing a scene within a video, he or she will also be susceptible to "catching" sadness from other audience members who are also feeling sad. Thus, in most cases, the effects of emotional contagion will be to amplify the emotional reactions an audience member is experiencing through viewing. However, in some instances, an audience member may be feeling a certain emotion, such as sadness, while another audience member may find the same content amusing. In that situation, audience contagion effects may suppress media contagion effects. Assessing the difference between the media contagion effect and the interpersonal contagion effect is therefore extremely difficult, but an interesting area for future exploration.

MEDIA USE, HEALTH, AND SEDENTARY BEHAVIORS

A second area of research in which there are clear interactions between the social environment and use of the media is in the area of health and sedentary behaviors. Salmon, Timperio, Telford, Carver, and Crawford (2005) showed that multiple media activities, including TV and computer use, lead to low levels of physical activity among family members.

There is a great deal of information documenting the correlation between television viewing and such factors as obesity and lack of exercise, which link to a number of diseases, such as heart disease, diabetes, and so on. Some researchers have been content to study the effects of media use (and television in particular) as a direct cause of these problems, and even to develop interventions to decrease TV time as a method of ameliorating these effects (Gorin, Raynor, Chula-Maguire, & Wing, 2006; Kronenberg et al., 2000). However, results are accumulating to suggest that TV viewing habits and preferences are part of a much more complex social environment that produces, among other behaviors, certain forms of media use. Media use within that environment reinforces the environment as well. A sedentary home environment, for example, leads to less "active" behaviors by members of the family; the lack of activity leads to choices that are more sedentary. TV and other media may fit well into that lifestyle and thus reinforce the inactive lifestyle by providing a level of continual passive entertainment (Chen & Kennedy, 2005; Gorin et al., 2006; Kronenberg et al., 2000).

As might be suggested from the earlier literature on FCP, Bagley et al. (2006) find that aspects of family structure are more important influences on a child's sedentary behaviors than is TV viewing. Higher levels of TV viewing among children are related to having a TV in the bedroom, not having rules or restrictions on viewing imposed by parents, eating meals in front of the TV, and being in a single-parent home. But boys without siblings spend more time watching TV than those with siblings, and there are significant differences in the amount of viewing per day between those with one, two, or three siblings (Bagley et al., 2006). Physical activities are similarly related to the family structure.

Feldman, Eisenberg, Neumark-Sztainer, and Story (2007) find that watching TV during family meals results in lower intakes of vegetables, higher intakes of soft drinks, and lower calcium intake levels. Despite these problems, watching TV during family meals still results in healthier intakes than not eating meals together as a family. Hesketh, Ball, Crawford, Campbell, and

Salmon (2007) find that the number and placement of TVs in the home, the frequency of eating dinner with a child in front of the TV, and rules about TV viewing are all important variables in predicting children's TV viewing, and all of these factors are related to health behaviors. The relationships between TV viewing and other activities in the home are so complex that Pahkala et al. (2006) conclude that TV viewing is not a simple linear cause of any specific behaviors or effects. Instead, the time spent with television is a product of the interactive effects of the home environment: parents, siblings, household stress, parenting roles, occupation, and income. Despite the temptation to search for or assert a simple relationship, the evidence suggests that TV time is just one part of a far more complicated nexus of relationships.

◆ Methods for Studying Media Use and the Social Environment

In this section, we will cover data collection and data analysis issues in the study of media use and the social environment. Obtaining the kind of data that can illuminate environmental processes associated with media effects is very complex and expensive, and assuming the appropriate data can be collected, the issues involved with analysis are similarly complex. In terms of data collection, perhaps the largest challenge for researchers is how to access the environment. That is, once a researcher is in a home, counting, asking questions, measuring, or timing activities is relatively easy; getting into homes is difficult, expensive, and time-consuming. For this reason, communication researchers have relied on self-report measures for much of their data. These are typically reports of the amount of time spent viewing, the amount of interpersonal discussion with a sibling or parent, a checklist of programs watched, or a list of preferred content obtained from one household or family member. However, the nature of the social environment is such that information about one member may be useful for some things, but it will not be able to explain what happens in the household, which is a system of actions and reactions from multiple members.

As such, for the most part, we are relying on data that make it nearly impossible to examine much related to the social environment. In a few areas (especially parental mediation and FCP), data have been collected on dyads (spousal or parent-child pairs). Although this situation is much preferred to single-person reports, theory in the area does not really tell us how to deal with the difficult analysis issue of discrepancies in the reports (what causes the discrepancy and what is the discrepancy's impact on what we are studying?).

An additional concern is obtaining data over time. Once we have identified the important variables for a particular research question, we cannot make inferences about causal processes unless we have data over time, so that we can test whether and how variation in one variable causes variation in another. A common problem in communication research in general, it is crucial in the area of media and the social environment because of the vast number of competing explanations for most effects. Because of the expense involved, trade-offs between the number of time points and the number of cases will inevitably be made. We need both, however. We need greater detail over time to answer questions related to growth or change processes, such as how content preferences change in relation to changes in parental or peer behaviors, what impact interpersonal discussion has on the formation of content preferences, what types of content engender particular behaviors in parent-child interaction, and how the type of content affects the child's reaction to a parent's behavior.

In terms of data analysis, although advances are being made, statistical analyses are not very conducive to studying data from dyads, much less from families or households in which every household has different numbers of members of various ages and genders, except through aggregation of some sort. Multilevel analyses, which enable simultaneous statistical analysis at the level of an individual, a peer dyad, the household, and even the community, promise hope for the future, but even these techniques are limited in their application to varying sizes and compositions of households. How much more might we know now about television and household tension, for example, if we had techniques for analyzing data that track multiple households over multiple days, and included attitudinal and behavioral data from each member of the household? We might then know how one member's media content selection might irritate another member, what the common coping mechanism for this kind of irritation would be, and how that coping might, in turn, increase family tension among other family members.

Other analysis techniques, such as bootstrapping or other resampling techniques, may prove useful in providing information relative to the norms that operate within groups of people (Bollen & Stine, 1992). Generalizing about the social environment requires a great deal of information about multiple people and their behaviors, and thus resampling techniques may prove to be the best way of obtaining estimates of how much variability certain types of group behavior may have.

◆ Unresolved Issues and Directions for Future Research

Given the limited research addressing issues related to media use, effects, and the social environment, it is not surprising that this area of research also lags in terms of its efforts to draw from theory to guide data collection or analyses. There is no lack of theory that is applicable to these issues, but communication researchers will need to apply theory or theoretical perspectives in greater detail than they have previously so that data can be collected and analyzed in a way that provides much more cogent responses to our questions. In the following paragraphs are four areas in which the successful application of theory can better inform our understanding of media use and the social environment, followed by some suggestions related to the future of this line of inquiry.

APPLICATION OF THEORETICAL PERSPECTIVES

It is something of an anomaly that, even though a great deal of our media use includes a social component, most of our theories of reaction to media content are focused on the individual rather than the group. During the past 50 years, the literature on group norms and processes has steadily accumulated evidence suggesting that people react and behave differently in groups than they do alone (Bond & Smith, 1996), and we have considerable evidence that who we are with (children with parents or other children, spouses coviewing, etc.) makes a difference in terms of effects. It seems reasonable to suppose that these effects are also evident in the behavior and emotional responses of coviewing audience members.

Also lacking in the communication literature is a general approach to media use as a social process. The literature from psychology includes a great deal of theoretical work dealing with cognition and the development of close relationships, the idea of attachment and loss, and the form and nature of attribution within relationships (Cohn & Fredrickson, 2006; Forgas & Fitness, 2008). Surely, the co-media use situation provides the opportunity to extend that work to enable us to understand what occurs when two people watch

TV or play video games together. The literature outlined earlier indicates the relevance of these perspectives (Evans, 2004; Hilt & Lipschultz, 2004) to take us beyond simple correlations and better understand the social environment of media use.

Third, sorely lacking in this research domain is the integration of perspectives related to social motivations. This might include concepts such as helping, altruism, or other similar motivational factors, as well as how the nature of content, family norms, and coviewing configurations impact learning about social skills and benefits for society. Although empathy has been studied as a precursor to some of the psychological effects of the media (Bartholow, Sestir, & Davis, 2005; Wilson, 2008), it would also seem relevant in interaction with children's use of media and parental involvement. FCPs seem especially relevant to this area.

Finally, there is voluminous literature on various aspects of social influence, the self, and social comparison (Kiviniemi, Snyder, & Johnson, 2008). However, the social nature of these factors has only been touched on lightly. Recent research on video/computer gaming offers some insight, but the great majority of that research, though recognizing the importance of the social component, focuses on the individual, or, at best, incorporates others within individual perceptions. Little attention has been focused on the social activity or social configurations that give rise to social influence effects through media use.

MULTITASKING, NEW MEDIA, AND THE SOCIAL ENVIRONMENT

Media use within the social environment is a complex system of interrelationships in which activities of one member of the household affect the activities of the other members. As communication researchers, we typically conceptualize media as a primary activity—a conceptualization that implies that other activities are minimized when media use occurs. However, recent trends, such as media multitasking, complicate these conceptualizations. Rules and patterns of media use are correlated with parental involvement and socioeconomic factors, which are correlated with mental and physical stress factors. Different media have different norms associated with them, and multiplication of media use by various multitasking members of the household can increase the complexity of the situation exponentially.

The development of a vast array of newer media technologies, many of which are portable, also adds a layer of complexity to the study of media effects as related to the social environment. Contemporary media technologies have begun to be classified into two types: social media and personal media. Social media, such as traditional TV, HDTV, large-screens, instant messaging, and online computer gaming (multiplayer or massive multiplayer), are often used in small groups, whereas personal media, such as MP3 players, personal video devices, personal DVD players, and some forms of computer games that remain single-player games, are more private forms of entertainment. However, many of these personal media are being used in social environments where it would have been impossible before (e.g., coffee shops, libraries, grocery stores), and we expect that trend to continue. Thus, these newer personal media technologies are ripe for exploration into the development of norms, social attribution, self-presentation, and any other related ideas that explore the social aspect of the environment.

Some newer technologies even establish their own social environment within media use. MP3 players with earbuds produce an aurally isolated environment; multiplayer computer games provide magical or adventurous social environments; Internet chat rooms provide images and text messages or audio that bring each users' home environment to those he or she is communicating with; and at the extreme, virtual reality devices may cut off the sight, sound, or even touch of the ordinary physical environment. In these mediated social environments, technologies will surely require their own techniques of study and data analysis for us to fully understand the audience member's experience and related effects.

In sum, the interaction between the media and the social environment is key to gaining a fuller understanding of the role media play in our lives and the effects they have on how we think, act, and communicate. To separate these aspects is to lose what is most interesting in the study of the social effects of the media. It is hoped that the upcoming decades of research will pay far greater attention to these pressing, though understudied, issues.

◆ References

Anderson, D. R. (1979, September). *Active and passive processes in children's television viewing.* Paper presented at the Annual Meeting of the American Psychological Association, New York.

Bagley, S., Salmon, J., & Crawford, D. (2006). Family structure and children's television viewing and physical activity. *Medicine & Science in Sports & Exercise, 38,* 910–918.

Barcus, F. E. (1969). Parental influence on children's television viewing. *Television Quarterly, 8*(3), 63–73.

Bartholow, B. D., Sestir, M. A., & Davis, E. B. (2005). Correlates and consequences of exposure to video game violence: Hostile personality, empathy, and aggressive behavior. *Personality and Social Psychology Bulletin, 31,* 1573–1586.

Blumer, H. (1933). *Movies and conduct.* New York: Macmillan.

Bollen, K. A., & Stine, R. A. (1992). Bootstrapping goodness-of-fit measures in structural equation models. *Sociological Methods and Research, 21,* 205–229.

Bond, R., & Smith, P. B. (1996). Culture and conformity: A meta-analysis of studies using

Asch's (1952, 1956) line judgment task. *Psychological Bulletin, 119,* 111–137.

Brody, G. H., Stoneman, Z., & Sanders, A. K. (1980). Effects of television viewing on family interactions: An observational study. *Family Relations, 29,* 216–220.

Cantril, H., & Allport, G. (1935). *The psychology of radio.* New York: Harper & Brothers.

Chaffee, S. H., McLeod, J. M., & Atkin, C. K. (1971). Parental influences on adolescent media use. *American Behavioral Scientist, 14,* 323–340.

Chen, J. L., & Kennedy, C. (2005). Cultural variations in children's coping behaviour, TV viewing time, and family functioning. *International Nursing Review, 52,* 186–195.

Clark, W. R. (1939). Radio listening activities of children. *Journal of Experimental Education, 8*(1), 44–48.

Coats, E. J., & Feldman, R. S. (1995). The role of television in the socialization of nonverbal behavioral skills. *Basic and Applied Psychology, 17,* 327–341.

Cohn, M. A., & Fredrickson, B. L. (2006). Beyond the moment: Shared ground between selective investment theory and the broaden and build theory of positive emotions. *Psychological Inquiry, 17*(1), 39–44.

Davis, M. M. (1911). *The exploitation of pleasure.* New York: Department of Child Hygiene, Russell Sage Foundation.

Dervin, B., & Greenberg, B. S. (1972). The communication environment of the urban poor. In F. G. Kline & P. J. Tichenor (Eds.), *Current perspectives in mass communication research* (pp. 195–253). Beverly Hills, CA: Sage.

Dorr, A., Kovaric, P., & Doubleday, C. (1989). Parent-child coviewing of television. *Journal of Broadcasting & Electronic Media, 33*(1), 35–51.

Edwards, R. H. (1915). *Popular amusements.* New York: Associated Press.

Evans, G. (2004). The environment of childhood poverty. *American Psychologist, 59,* 77–92.

Eveland, W. P., & Thomson, T. (2006). Is it talking, thinking or both? A lagged dependent variable model of discussion effects on political knowledge. *Journal of Communication, 56,* 523–542.

Feldman, S., Eisenberg, M. E., Neumark-Sztainer, D., & Story, M. (2007). Associations between watching TV during family meals and dietary intake among adolescents. *Journal of Nutrition Education and Behavior, 39,* 257–263.

Forgas, J. P., & Fitness, J. (2008). *Social relationships: Cognitive, affective and motivational processes.* New York: Psychology Press.

Fujioka, Y., & Austin, E. W. (2002). The relationship of family communication patterns to parental mediation styles. *Communication Research, 29,* 642–655.

Gehrau, V. (2007). *Talking about media content: Characteristics and emotional functions.* Paper presented at a meeting of the International Communication Association, San Francisco, CA.

Gorin, A., Raynor, H., Chula-Maguire, K., & Wing, R. (2006). Decreasing household television time: A pilot study of a combined behavioral and environmental intervention. *Behavioral Interventions, 21,* 273–280.

Hamilton, C. (1914). Emotional contagion in the theatre. *The Bookman, 39,* 139–147.

Hatfield, E., Cacioppo, J. T., & Rapson, R. L. (1992). Primitive emotional contagion. In M. S. Clark (Ed.), *Review of personality and social psychology* (pp. 151–178). Newbury Park, CA: Sage.

Hesketh, K., Ball, K., Crawford, D., Campbell, K., & Salmon, J. (2007). Mediators of the relationship between maternal education and children's TV viewing. *American Journal of Preventive Medicine, 33*(1), 41–47.

Hilt, M. L., & Lipschultz, J. H. (2004). Elderly Americans and the Internet: E-mail, TV news, information and entertainment websites. *Educational Gerontology, 30,* 57–72.

Hutchinson, S. L., Baldwin, C. K., & Oh, S. (2006). Adolescent coping: Exploring adolescents' leisure-based responses to stress. *Leisure Sciences, 28,* 115–131.

Hylton, C. (1971). Intra-audience effects: Observable audience response. *Journal of Communication, 21,* 253–265.

Kiviniemi, M. T., Snyder, M., & Johnson, B. C. (2008). Motivated dimension manipulating in the processing of social comparison information. *Self and Identity, 7,* 225–242.

Krcmar, M., & Vieira, E. T., Jr. (2005). Imitating life, imitating television: The effects of family and television models on children's moral reasoning. *Communication Research, 32,* 267–294.

Kronenberg, F., Pereiar, M. A., Schmitz, K. H., Arnett, D. K., Evenson, K. R., Crapo, R. O., et al. (2000). Influence of leisure time physical activity and television watching on atherosclerosis risk factors in the NHLBI family heart study. *Atherosclerosis, 153,* 433–443.

Lull, J. (1982). How families select television: A mass observational study. *Journal of Broadcasting, 26,* 801–811.

Maccoby, E. (1951). Television: Its impact on school children. *Public Opinion Quarterly, 15,* 421–443.

McDonagh, E. C. (1950). Television viewing and the family. *Sociology and Social Research, 35*(2), 113–122.

McDonald, D. G. (1985). Spousal influences on television viewing. *Communication Research, 12,* 530–545.

McDonald, D. G., & Fredin, E. S. (2001, May). *Primitive emotional contagion in coviewing.* Paper presented at a meeting of the International Communication Association, Washington, DC.

McLeod, J. M., Atkin, C. K., & Chaffee, S. H. (1972). Adolescents, parents, and television use: Self-report and other-report measures from Wisconsin sample. In G. A. Comstock & E. A. Rubinstein (Eds.), *Television and social behavior; reports and papers. A technical report to the Surgeon General's Scientific Advisory Committee on Television and Social Behavior* (Vol. 3, pp. 239–313). Washington, DC: U.S. Government Printing Office.

McLeod, J. M., Fitzpatrick, M. A., Glynn, C. J., & Fallis, S. F. (1982). Television and social relations: Family influences and consequences for interpersonal behavior. In D. Pearl, L. Bouthillet, & J. Lazar (Eds.), *Television and behavior: Ten years of scientific*

progress and implications for the eighties (DHHS Publication No. ADM 82–1196, Vol. 2, pp. 272–286). Washington, DC: U.S. Government Printing Office.

Merrill, I. R. (1961). Broadcast viewing and listening by children. *Public Opinion Quarterly, 25,* 263–276.

Nathanson, A. I. (2001). Parent and child perspectives on the presence and meaning of parental television mediation. *Journal of Broadcasting & Electronic Media, 45,* 201–220.

Paavonen, E. J., Pennonen, M., Roine, M., Valkonen, S., & Lahikainen, A. R. (2006). TV exposure associated with sleep disturbances in 5- to 6-year-old children. *Journal of Sleep Research, 15,* 154–161.

Pahkala, K., Heinonen, O. J., Lagstrom, H., Hakala, P., Sillanmaki, L., & Simell, O. (2006). Leisure time physical activity of 13-year-old adolescents. *Scandinavian Journal of Medical Science Sports, 17,* 324–330.

Palmer, L. E. (1909). The world in motion. *The Survey, 22,* 355–364.

Perry, C. E. (1923). Frequency and attendance of high-school students at the movies. *The School Review, 31*(8), 573–587.

Phelan, Rev. J. J. (1919). *Motion pictures as a phase of commercialized amusement in Toledo, Ohio.* Toledo, OH: Little Book Press.

Renshaw, S., Miller, V. L., & Marquis, D. (1933). *Children's sleep.* New York: Macmillan.

Riley, J. W., Cantwell, F. V., & Ruttiger, K. F. (1949). Some observations on the social effects of television. *Public Opinion Quarterly, 13,* 223–234.

Rosenblatt, P. C., & Cunningham, M. R. (1976). Television watching and family tensions. *Journal of Marriage and the Family, 38,* 105–111.

Rozin, P., Riklis, J., & Margolis, L. (2004). Mutual exposure or close peer relationships do not seem to foster increased similarity in food, music, or television program preferences. *Appetite, 42,* 41–48.

Salmon, J., Timperio, A., Telford, A., Carver, A., & Crawford, D. (2005). Association of family environment with children's television viewing and with low level of physical activity. *Obesity Research, 13,* 1939–1951.

Verma, S., & Larson, R. W. (2002). Television in Indian adolescents' lives: A member of the family. *Journal of Youth and Adolescence, 31,* 177–183.

Wand, B. (1968). Television viewing and family choice differences. *Public Opinion Quarterly, 32,* 84–94.

Wilson, B. J. (2008). Media and children's aggression, fear, and altruism. *Future of Children, 18,* 87–118.

Zimbardo, P. G. (1977). *Shyness.* Boston: Addison-Wesley.

PART IV

PERSUASION
AND LEARNING

18

THEORIES OF PERSUASION

◆ Daniel J. O'Keefe

Persuasion is a ubiquitous function of human communication, pursued in a variety of settings from face-to-face interaction to mass media. In the context of mass media, persuasion is most commonly pursued through advertising—for consumer products and services, for political candidates, for prosocial causes (e.g., encouraging exercise or recycling), and so forth. But other forms of mass media content can also be put to the service of persuasive ends. For instance, persuaders can engage in "media advocacy," encouraging news stories that serve their interests, as when managers of a community-wide media campaign aimed at increasing regular exercise arrange to have relevant stories appear in the local newspaper (Wallack, Woodruff, Dorfman, & Diaz, 1999, provide a practical guide to media advocacy). And persuaders can blend social influence with entertainment, as when a recurring television soap opera is used to convey information about disease prevention or population control (for an overview of such "entertainment-education" campaigns, see Singhal, Cody, Rogers, & Sabido, 2004).

Regardless of the particular vehicle for mass media persuasion (advertising, news, entertainment) and regardless of the particular medium involved, the nature of mass media persuasion can be illuminated by considering general theoretical frameworks for understanding the process of persuasion. Such frameworks can both clarify how persuasion can work and (as a natural corollary) provide guidance for effective persuasive message design. Broadly interpreted, theoretical work on persuasion dates back millennia, to classical treatments by Aristotle and Cicero. In the 20th century, the spread of mass media coincided with the rise of social scientific attention to processes of social influence. For example, in the 1950s, one of the most prominent research programs in persuasion was Carl Hovland's behaviorism-based Yale School (Hovland, Janis, & Kelley, 1953; Hovland, Lumsdaine, & Sheffield, 1949). In the ensuing years, a variety of different general theoretical perspectives on persuasion have been articulated. These can usefully be glossed as forming three broad kinds of approaches: attitude theories, voluntary action theories, and theories of persuasion proper. The purpose of this chapter is to provide an overview of these perspectives; more detailed treatments are available elsewhere (e.g., Dillard & Pfau, 2002; O'Keefe, 2002; Perloff, 2003).

◆ Attitude Theories

Persuasion involves changing people's mental states, often as a precursor to changes in their behavior. A variety of different mental states can be seen as relevant targets for persuaders, but persuasion research has especially emphasized attitude, understood as the general evaluation of an object (a product, candidate, policy, etc.). Because attitude change is often key to persuasion, theories of attitude have been mined as sources of insight into persuasion processes. Three examples of such theories are discussed here: belief-based models, functional models, and cognitive dissonance theory.

BELIEF-BASED ATTITUDE MODELS

Belief-based models of attitude describe the underlying bases of attitude as consisting of one's salient beliefs about the attitude object (e.g., beliefs about properties of the object). One common conception of how beliefs combine to yield an attitude is an "expectancy-value" image: Each belief has some associated evaluation (representing the perceived desirability of the attribute) and is held with some degree of certainty or strength (indicating the perceived likelihood that the object has the attribute). Across beliefs, these two facets of belief (the "value" of each attribute and the "expectancy" of its association with the object) jointly determine the person's overall attitude toward the object (see, e.g., Fishbein, 1967).

This image of underlying attitude structure immediately suggests a number of alternative—not mutually exclusive—strategies for attitude change. A persuader might try to add some new salient belief (of appropriate valence) about the object, change the evaluation of some existing belief, or change the strength with which some existing belief is held. Naturally, different persuasion situations will require different approaches. In one circumstance, the target audience might evaluate the outcomes of the persuader's advocated policy just as the advocate wishes, but needs to be convinced that the proposed policy will actually produce those outcomes; in another circumstance, the audience may already agree about what attributes the policy has, but disagree about the evaluation of those properties. A campaign aimed at encouraging positive attitudes toward regular exercise for cardiovascular health faces different challenges depending on whether the audience thinks their cardiovascular risk is already low (and so they don't value reducing it further) or thinks that exercise won't really reduce their risk. Thus, precampaign research can potentially yield valuable information about which beliefs are the most appropriate persuasive targets for influencing attitudes (see, e.g., Chang, 2006).

FUNCTIONAL MODELS OF ATTITUDE

Functional models of attitude are based on the insight that attitudes can serve various psychological functions, such as defending the person's self-image, organizing information about the attitude object, and expressing the person's values (e.g., Katz, 1960). A number of different schemes have been put forward that identify and elaborate these various functions, but there is no consensus yet on any one detailed analysis (see, e.g., Maio & Olson, 2000). However, one broad distinction embodied in nearly all functional attitude classifications is that between symbolic and instrumental (utilitarian) functions. Attitudes serving symbolic functions are focused on the symbolic associations of the object (what the object symbolizes or represents); attitudes serving instrumental functions are focused on the intrinsic properties of the object (appraising the object in terms of intrinsic attributes or consequences). For instance, a person's attitude toward a given automobile might serve mainly instrumental functions (and so be based on beliefs about gas mileage, luggage capacity, etc.) or mainly symbolic ones (and so be based on beliefs about what sort of personal identity is projected by driving the car, how driving the car makes one feel, etc.).

From this perspective, the key to successful persuasion is the matching of the persuasive appeal to the attitude's functional basis. For example, if an audience's attitude toward the death penalty is based largely on symbolic considerations (e.g., about what makes for a moral society), persuaders may not find it useful to advance instrumentally focused arguments about whether the death penalty does or doesn't deter crime. Studies of consumer advertising have, unsurprisingly, found that instrumentally oriented appeals (emphasizing intrinsic product qualities) are more persuasive than symbolically oriented appeals (emphasizing image-based considerations) when the audience's attitudes have an instrumental basis; by contrast, with attitudes that have a symbolic basis, symbolically oriented appeals have been found more persuasive than instrumentally oriented appeals (e.g., Shavitt, 1990).

As one might suspect, the nature of the attitude object constrains the kind of function served. Some objects (such as air conditioners or aspirin) easily accommodate only an instrumental function, others (such as class rings) only a symbolic function. But some objects (automobiles, watches, sunglasses) readily permit multiple attitude functions, with corresponding variations in what makes for effective persuasion: Different advertisements will be wanted for persons whose automobile attitudes are based on beliefs about gas mileage and frequency-of-repair records than for persons whose attitudes are based on beliefs about the image projected by driving a given car. For such multifunction-capable attitude objects, the individual-difference variable of self-monitoring can play an important role in influencing attitude function. High self-monitors are generally more concerned than are low self-monitors about the image they project; hence their attitudes are more likely to have symbolic bases and are more likely to be successfully influenced by image-oriented, rather than product-quality-oriented, persuasive appeals (e.g., DeBono & Packer, 1991; Snyder & DeBono, 1985).

COGNITIVE DISSONANCE THEORY

A number of attitude theories have been based on the general idea that people strive to arrange their cognitions (attitudes, beliefs, etc.) in psychologically (subjectively) consistent ways (e.g., balance theory; Heider, 1946; see Basil & Herr, 2006, for an application). The most influential and extensively studied consistency-based approach has been cognitive dissonance theory (Festinger, 1957; Harmon-Jones, 2002).

Dissonance theory focuses on the relationships among a person's cognitions (attitudes and beliefs). Any two cognitions might be consonant (consistent) with each other (e.g., as when a person donates money to the Red Cross and believes that the Red Cross does good work), dissonant with each other (e.g., as when a person smokes cigarettes but believes that smoking causes cancer), or irrelevant to each other (e.g., the belief that the Red Cross does good work and the belief that smoking causes cancer). Two cognitions are dissonant if the opposite of one subjectively follows from the other. For example, the belief that "smoking causes cancer" implies that one ought not smoke—and so a smoker who believes that smoking causes cancer has two dissonant cognitions (namely, "I smoke" and "smoking causes cancer").

The occurrence of two (or more) dissonant cognitions gives rise to dissonance, an uncomfortable motivational state. People try to avoid experiencing dissonance—or, failing that, seek to reduce it. Dissonance can be reduced in a variety of ways, including by adding new consonant cognitions (e.g., a smoker might come to think "smoking reduces my anxiety") or by minimizing dissonant ones ("smoking isn't really that expensive"). The amount of dissonance experienced is influenced by the relative numbers of consonant and dissonant cognitions (the larger the number of dissonant cognitions relative to consonant ones, the greater the dissonance) and by the importance of the cognitions (the more important the cancer-causing aspect of smoking is perceived to be, the more dissonance the smoker will feel).

Dissonance theory has yielded a number of persuasion-relevant applications. For example, research has found that making salient the inconsistencies between people's attitudes and their actions ("hypocrisy induction") can lead people to bring their attitudes and behaviors into alignment (e.g., Aitken, McMahon, Wearing, &

Finlayson, 1994; Stone, Aronson, Crain, Winslow, & Fried, 1994), that advocacy of a counterattitudinal viewpoint can lead people to be more accepting of that view (the classic study is Festinger & Carlsmith, 1959; for some recent applications, see Roehrig, Thompson, Brannick, & van den Berg, 2006; Stice, Shaw, Becker, & Rohde, 2008), and that having people predict whether they will perform some normatively desirable behavior can increase the likelihood of their engaging in the behavior (the "self-prophesy" effect; e.g., Spangenberg & Greenwald, 1999; Spangenberg, Sprott, Grohmann, & Smith, 2003). With respect to mass media persuasion, however, the most relevant applications of dissonance theory concern people's propensities for information exposure.

Dissonance theory suggests that people will prefer to be exposed to information that is supportive of (consistent with) their current attitudes rather than to nonsupportive information; nonsupportive information might arouse dissonance, which people generally try to avoid. This "selective exposure" hypothesis naturally raises the possibility that people might generally seek out only those media sources that confirm their prior beliefs. If there is a strong tendency to avoid nonsupportive information, then persuaders may sometimes find it difficult to obtain exposure for their messages.

The research evidence indicates, however, that a preference for supportive information is only one of a number of competing influences on information exposure—and it is not so powerful as to override other influences. For example, people are willing to seek out nonsupportive information if the information appears to be useful to them, if they are striving to be fair to all sides, or if they are simply curious (for reviews, see Cotton, 1985; D'Alessio & Allen, 2007; Frey, 1986; Smith, Fabrigar, & Norris, 2008). Thus, although the preference for supportive information may represent a challenge for mass media persuaders, it is a challenge that often can be surmounted (for example, by emphasizing the utility of the information).

◆ *Voluntary Action Theories*

The behaviors that persuaders characteristically seek to influence are voluntary actions, ones under the actor's control—buying a product, voting for a candidate, adopting a program of regular exercise, and so forth. A number of theories have aimed at identifying the factors that influence voluntary action. Because the factors influencing behavior provide natural foci for persuasive efforts, these approaches offer insight into persuasion processes.

Perhaps unsurprisingly, one factor that commonly figures in explanations of voluntary action is attitude (though sometimes in a refined form). Thus, the previously discussed attitude theories can figure as elements in, or underpinnings of, these broader models of voluntary behavior. Whereas the attitude theories discussed earlier were efforts at explaining what underpins attitudes, theories of voluntary action are aimed at explaining volitional behavior (and attitudes might be one part of such explanations).

THEORY OF REASONED ACTION

The theory of reasoned action (TRA; Fishbein & Ajzen, 1975) begins with the observation that the best single predictor of a person's voluntary action is the person's intention concerning that behavior. For example, getting people to vote for one's candidate in an election requires, at a minimum, that people *intend* to vote for the candidate. (Appropriately measured, intentions can be quite good predictors of subsequent behavior; see, e.g., Eckes & Six, 1994; Kim & Hunter, 1993.)

Hence the focus of the TRA is on factors that influence behavioral intentions. The TRA suggests that a person's behavioral

intentions are influenced jointly by two considerations. One is the person's "attitude toward the behavior" (the person's evaluation of the action in question), which is distinct from other kinds of attitude. From the perspective of the TRA, with respect to (for example) consumer purchasing, what matters is not the person's attitude toward the product, but the person's attitude toward *buying* the product. The attitude toward the product and the attitude toward the act of buying the product are related but distinguishable; for instance, a person might have a positive attitude toward an expensive automobile but (because of the cost) a negative attitude toward purchasing that automobile. The second consideration is the person's "subjective norm," the person's assessment of whether significant others (people who are important to the person) desire one's performance of the behavior. Thus the TRA depicts behavioral intentions as potentially shaped by both personal (attitudinal) and social (normative) influences.

These two factors can vary in their relative impact on intention—and this relative impact may vary from behavior to behavior and from person to person. For a given behavior or audience, attitudinal considerations may weigh more heavily than normative ones, but for a different behavior or audience, the reverse may be the case. The TRA thus provides a means for persuaders to identify useful foci for persuasive messages. For example, if adolescent tobacco use is influenced more heavily by normative than by attitudinal factors, then campaigns designed to discourage such behavior should presumably give special attention to normative considerations.

The TRA also provides an account of the determinants of these attitudinal and normative factors (that is, an account of what underlies each of these), which can supply even further direction to persuaders. One's attitude toward the behavior is described as based on one's salient beliefs about the behavior (specifically, based on the evaluation of each belief and the strength with which each belief is held, combined in an expectancy-value fashion as described previously); changing the attitudinal component thus involves adding some new salient belief or changing the strength or evaluation of existing beliefs. One's subjective norm is described as based jointly on the normative beliefs ascribed to particular important others (e.g., what I think my mother wants me to do, what I think my best friend wants me to do, and so on) and on the degree to which one is motivated to comply with that person (how much I want to do what my mother wants me to, etc.). Changing the normative component thus involves adding some new salient referent other or changing the normative belief ascribed to, or the motivation to comply with, existing referent others.

This framework provides a basis for systematically considering just which message themes should be emphasized in a persuasive campaign. For example, Booth-Butterfield and Reger (2004) used the TRA to guide their mass media campaign aimed at changing the milk consumption patterns of high-fat milk users. Because previous research had indicated that milk consumption was more strongly influenced by attitudinal than by normative considerations (e.g., Brewer, Blake, Rankin, & Douglass, 1999), the campaign's messages were aimed at influencing attitude (not the subjective norm) and indeed did produce corresponding changes in behavioral beliefs, attitudes, and intentions. (For other examples and further discussion of the TRA, see Ajzen, Albarracin, & Hornik, 2007; Fishbein & Yzer, 2003; Silk, Weiner, & Parrott, 2005.)

THEORY OF PLANNED BEHAVIOR

The theory of planned behavior (TPB; Ajzen, 1991) is an elaboration of the TRA; the TPB adds a third predictor of behavioral intentions, namely, the person's perceived control over the behavior (that is, whether the person thinks it is easy or difficult to perform the action). The merit of this addition can be seen by considering behaviors such as exercise: People might think that exercising is desirable (positive attitude toward the behavior) and that significant others think they should exercise (positive subjective norm), but believe themselves incapable of performing the behavior—expensive specialized equipment is needed but not owned, the gym is far away, exercise can't be fit into one's schedule, and so forth (negative perceived behavioral control). Plainly, in such a circumstance, reiterating the advantages of exercise is unlikely to be a successful avenue to persuasion. Instead, the perceived obstacles to behavioral performance need to be addressed. Thus, akin to the TRA, the TPB identifies potential points of emphasis for persuaders and so offers some systematic guidance for the development of effective messages. For example, Stead, Tagg, MacKintosh, and Eadie (2005) reported that the TPB was useful in designing a mass media campaign to reduce speeding in Scotland. (For other examples and further discussion of the TPB, see Armitage & Christian, 2003; Babrow, Black, & Tiffany, 1990; Hardeman et al., 2002.)

PROTECTION MOTIVATION THEORY

Whereas TRA and TPB are intended as general models of voluntary behavior, protection motivation theory (PMT) was developed to illuminate the processes behind one specific kind of behavior, namely, protective behaviors such as safer-sex practices, skin cancer prevention behaviors, and smoking cessation (Rogers, 1975; Rogers & Prentice-Dunn, 1997). PMT depicts protection motivation as a function of two factors: threat appraisal (the person's assessment of the potential threat) and coping appraisal (the person's assessment of a given "coping" response, that is, a given protective behavior).

Each of these factors, in turn, has two determinants. The determinants of threat appraisal are perceived threat severity (the perception of how bad the problem is) and perceived threat vulnerability (the perception of how likely one is to suffer the threat). The determinants of coping appraisal are perceived response efficacy (how effective the behavior is in conferring protection) and perceived self-efficacy (one's perception of one's ability to perform the behavior). Each of these underlying determinants has been found to be related to protection motivation in the expected ways; for example, as a threat is perceived to be more severe or as a protective behavior is perceived to be more effective, people are more likely to intend to adopt the protective action (e.g., Floyd, Prentice-Dunn, & Rogers, 2000; Witte & Allen, 2000).

As should be plain, PMT can offer guidance to persuaders concerning the appropriate content for persuasive messages. Messages might focus on threat severity, threat vulnerability, response efficacy, or self-efficacy (or more than one of these), but different foci will be appropriate in different circumstances. For example, guided by PMT, Pechmann, Zhao, Goldberg, and Reibling (2003) found that of seven message themes commonly found in antismoking advertisements aimed at adolescents, only three—all concerning threat severity (specifically, social disapproval risks)—dependably enhanced intentions not to smoke; messages emphasizing self-efficacy, for instance, were apparently not very effective. (For other examples and further discussion of PMT and related ideas, see McKay, Berkowitz, Blumberg, & Goldberg, 2004; McMath & Prentice-Dunn, 2005; Witte, 1998.)

STAGE MODELS OF BEHAVIORAL CHANGE

A number of stage models of behavioral change have been developed with the purpose of illuminating the processes by which persons change some recurring behavior (e.g., by quitting smoking or undertaking regular exercise). The general idea is that behavioral change involves passing through a sequence of distinct stages.

Perhaps the best-known stage model is the transtheoretical model of health behavior, so named because putatively it integrates a number of different theoretical perspectives (Prochaska, 1994; Prochaska, Redding, & Evers, 2002). It identifies a number of distinct stages in a person's adoption of a given health-related behavior such as engaging in an exercise program. In the precontemplation stage, a person is not even thinking about undertaking an exercise program anytime soon; in the contemplation stage, the person is at least seriously thinking about doing so; a person in the preparation stage is ready to change and may have undertaken planning or other preparatory action (such as signing up for a health club); in the action stage, the person has undertaken the exercise program; finally, a person who has continued to engage in exercise for some time is said to be in the maintenance stage.

The relevance of such models for understanding persuasion arises from the idea that at different stages, distinct considerations underwrite movement to the next stage, and thus different messages are appropriate for those in different stages. For example, for persons in the precontemplation stage, the persuader's challenge may be to get the audience thinking about the target behavior (i.e., moving the audience from precontemplation to contemplation). By contrast, for persons in the preparation stage, persuaders will presumably want to help the audience translate their plans and intentions into actions. Hence stage-matched interventions are expected to be more successful than mismatched interventions (e.g., Slater, 1999).

Unfortunately, a satisfactory conceptualization of the stages involved in behavioral change has proved more elusive than one might have imagined, with corresponding uncertainties about the degree to which such stage models can be used as a basis for understanding the design of effective persuasive messages (e.g., Adams & White, 2005; Bridle et al., 2005; Herzog & Blagg, 2007). At least in part, this state of affairs reflects the complex evidentiary issues attendant to stage models (Weinstein, Rothman, & Sutton, 1998), but it also surely reflects the relatively weak empirical support thus far (e.g., West, 2005).

◆ Theories of Persuasion Proper

Theories of attitude and theories of voluntary action provide insight into persuasion by clarifying the underlying mental states (beliefs, attitudes, etc.) that a persuader might want to change. But other theoretical frameworks focus on the process of persuasion itself (e.g., McGuire, 1985, 2001). Two such frameworks are discussed here: social judgment theory and the elaboration likelihood model.

SOCIAL JUDGMENT THEORY

Social judgment theory (Sherif, Sherif, & Nebergall, 1965), which grew out of a broader approach to attitudes, begins with the idea that people commonly have assessments (judgments) of the various positions that might be held on a given issue. Consider, for example, gun control, where positions might vary from one extreme (no restrictions whatsoever) to the other (no private ownership, say), with many intermediate positions possible. A given person might have one particular position as his or her most preferred view, but the person may well find some other positions also acceptable, some others objectionable, and some others neither acceptable nor unacceptable. These judgments represent the person's latitudes of

acceptance, rejection, and noncommitment (respectively) on the persuasive issue. These judgmental latitudes are said to be influenced by ego involvement (the degree to which a person's identity is related to his or her stand on the issue), such that as ego involvement increases, the size of the latitude of rejection increases and the sizes of the latitudes of acceptance and noncommitment decrease.

The judgmental latitudes are taken to be important to persuasion in two ways. First, they are said to influence the perception of what position is being advocated by a message. At least with relatively ambiguous messages, perceivers may distort what position is seen to be advocated, by perceiving the message to advocate a position either more discrepant (a "contrast effect") or less discrepant (an "assimilation effect") than it actually does. Contrast effects are most likely when the advocated view falls in the latitude of rejection; assimilation effects are more likely when the advocated view is in the latitude of acceptance. For views that fall in the latitude of noncommitment, both assimilation and contrast effects are possible (though the former are more likely). These perceptual biases reflect the anchoring effect of the perceiver's initial attitude, with some messages brought perceptually closer to the anchor (assimilation) and others pushed farther away (contrast).

Second, the perceived location of the message's advocated position is said to influence receivers' reactions to the message. Messages that are perceived to advocate positions in the latitude of acceptance or the latitude of noncommitment are likely to produce attitude change in the advocated direction; those that are seen to advocate positions in the latitude of rejection are likely to yield little or no change (or perhaps even change in the direction opposite that sought).

As should be apparent, social judgment theory emphasizes that persuaders will want to know not only a receiver's most-preferred position but also the structure of the receiver's judgmental latitudes. Since two receivers might have the same most preferred position but rather different assessments of the other available positions, effective adaptation of persuasive messages will require some attention to judgmental latitudes.

Social judgment theory is now something of a historical relic, in the sense that it is not a site of active research work; this largely reflects difficulties in the conceptualization and measurement of ego involvement. Even so, the theory's contributions—especially the ideas of judgmental latitudes and assimilation and contrast effects—continue to be found useful in guiding formative campaign research (e.g., Smith, Atkin, Martell, Allen, & Hembroff, 2006) and in illuminating political campaign communication (e.g., Diamond & Cobb, 1996).

ELABORATION LIKELIHOOD MODEL

The elaboration likelihood model (ELM) suggests that there are two fundamentally different sorts of processes underlying persuasion, represented as two broad "routes to persuasion." Which one is activated depends on the degree of "elaboration" (issue-relevant thinking) in which the receiver engages (Petty & Cacioppo, 1986; Petty & Wegener, 1999). One is the central route, in which the outcomes of persuasive efforts are the result of the receiver's thoughtful consideration of issue-relevant material (e.g., the message's arguments); when central-route processes are engaged, the quality (strength) of the message's arguments are likely to be key determinants of persuasive success. The other route to persuasion is the peripheral route, in which persuasive outcomes arise from less thoughtful processes, such as the receiver's use of some heuristic (a simplifying decision rule); for example, instead of carefully considering the arguments and evidence, a receiver might reach a conclusion based on the communicator's credibility or likeability or on the reactions of others to the message. These are not two mutually exclusive routes, but rather the prototypical forms representing the extremes of an elaboration continuum; at intermediate levels of elaboration, both central-route and peripheral-route processes may be at work (see also the heuristic-systematic model, which offers another version of a "dual-process" image of persuasion; e.g., Chaiken, 1980, 1987).

The likelihood that a receiver will engage in elaboration (issue-relevant thinking) is a joint function of factors influencing elaboration ability (such as prior background knowledge, the presence of distraction in the communication setting, and so on) and factors influencing elaboration motivation (such as receiver involvement, that is, the personal relevance of the topic). So, for example, when a topic is not involving and there is some distraction present, receivers may rely on heuristics such as the communicator's apparent expertise (and thus high-credibility communicators will be more successful than low-credibility communicators). By contrast, when the topic is personally relevant and receivers are able to attend closely to the arguments and evidence, the impact of variations in communicator expertise will diminish and the effect of argument quality variations will increase (e.g., Petty, Cacioppo, & Goldman, 1981).

The central and peripheral routes differ not only with respect to the factors influencing persuasive outcomes, but also with respect to the consequences of whatever persuasion is obtained. Persuasion achieved through central-route processes is likely to be more enduring (less likely to decay over time, more resistant to counterpersuasion) and to have greater influence on subsequent behavior than is persuasion accomplished through peripheral-route processes (see Petty & Wegener, 1999, pp. 61–63).

Because persuasion processes differ depending on the receiver's degree of elaboration, campaign planners may find it important to consider the audience's likely degree of engagement with campaign messages. For example, there may be important differences between people actively seeking health information and those who more passively scan the media environment for such information (e.g., Niederdeppe et al., 2007; Shim, Kelly, & Hornik, 2006). As the audience's degree of elaboration varies, different message formats may be optimal (e.g., Bakker, 1999). And persuaders need not assume that the audience's degree of elaboration is inevitably fixed in advance; on the contrary, messages might be designed to influence elaboration ability or motivation, as when the personal relevance of a topic is emphasized in an effort to increase elaboration motivation (for further discussion of the ELM and some research applications, see Kruglanski & Thompson, 1999; Petty, Cacioppo, Strathman, & Priester, 2005; Slater, 2002).

◆ Conclusion

A recurrent theme in theoretical treatments of persuasion is the importance of adapting persuasive messages to audiences. Different theoretical frameworks can be seen to emphasize different potential bases of adaptation. For example, functional attitude models suggest the importance of distinguishing symbolic and instrumental functional motivations; stage models emphasize identification of the audience's current stage of change; the theory of planned behavior, by specifying three distinct possible influences on intention (attitude, norm, perceived behavioral control), permits a persuader to identify the key targets for persuasion in a given circumstance; and so on.

But delivering an adapted message to an audience requires the ability to reach that audience, and in this regard developments in mass media technologies have in recent years made for some important practical challenges for mass media persuaders. This can usefully be illustrated by considering U.S. television advertising. Even as late as the mid-1980s, three big networks (ABC, CBS, NBC) dominated U.S. television, with the result that consumer advertising could reach a large number of people relatively efficiently. But the penetration of cable television has meant that television viewers are now spread across hundreds of channels (Webster, 2008)—and the size of the television audience is threatened by the growth of the Internet. Television advertisers additionally face the prospect of substantial time-shifted television viewing—with the accompanying ability to skip commercials—which has revivified practices aimed at integrating advertising and media content (such as product placement; see, e.g., Kolsky & Calder, 2008). In short, as a result of technological developments, mass media advertisers confront growing challenges of finding and engaging target audiences (see Metzger, Chapter 37, this volume).

On the other hand, new communication technologies may well afford more efficient and effective vehicles for delivering well-adapted persuasive messages to target audiences. Mass media have always provided opportunities for adaptation: Television advertising can be placed on programs that attract audiences with the desired demographic characteristics, direct mail can be targeted to particular zip codes, and so forth. But recent technological developments may enable even more finely tuned adaptation than was ever available previously. For example, cable television advertising might be addressable specifically to those customers whose past viewing habits suggest that they might be likely consumers of the advertised product, online advertising can be shaped to reflect the user's characteristics and history, interactive Web sites can provide individualized information and appeals, and so forth (for discussion and examples, see Dijkstra, 2008; Kreuter,

Farrell, Olevitch, & Brennan, 1999; Rimal & Adkins, 2003; Yardley & Nyman, 2007). Precisely because tailoring messages to target audiences will be a continuing concern for mass media persuaders, general theoretical perspectives on persuasion can serve as a continuing source of guidance and insight.

◆ References

Adams, J., & White, M. (2005). Why don't stage-based activity promotion interventions work? *Health Education Research, 20,* 237–243.

Aitken, C. K., McMahon, T. A., Wearing, A. J., & Finlayson, B. L. (1994). Residential water use: Predicting and reducing consumption. *Journal of Applied Social Psychology, 24,* 136–158.

Ajzen, I. (1991). The theory of planned behavior. *Organizational Behavior and Human Decision Processes, 50,* 179–211.

Ajzen, I., Albarracin, D., & Hornik, R. (Eds.). (2007). *Prediction and change of health behavior: Applying the reasoned action approach.* Mahwah, NJ: Erlbaum.

Armitage, C. J., & Christian, J. (Eds.). (2003). Special issue: On the theory of planned behaviour. *Current Psychology, 22,* 187–280.

Babrow, A. S., Black, D. R., & Tiffany, S. T. (1990). Beliefs, attitudes, intentions, and a smoking-cessation program: A planned behavior analysis of communication campaign development. *Health Communication, 2,* 145–163.

Bakker, A. B. (1999). Persuasive communication about AIDS prevention: Need for cognition determines the impact of message format. *AIDS Education and Prevention, 11,* 150–162.

Basil, D. Z., & Herr, P. M. (2006). Attitudinal balance and cause-related marketing: An empirical application of balance theory. *Journal of Consumer Psychology, 16,* 391–403.

Booth-Butterfield, S., & Reger, B. (2004). The message changes belief and the rest is theory: The "1% or less" milk campaign and reasoned action. *Preventive Medicine, 39,* 581–588.

Brewer, J. L., Blake, A. J., Rankin, S. A., & Douglass, L. W. (1999). Theory of reasoned action predicts milk consumption in women. *Journal of the American Dietetic Association, 99,* 39–44.

Bridle, C., Riemsma, R. P., Pattenden, J., Sowden, A. J., Mather, L., Watt, I. S., et al. (2005). Systematic review of the effectiveness of health behavior interventions based on the transtheoretical model. *Psychology and Health, 20,* 283–301.

Chaiken, S. (1980). Heuristic versus systematic information processing and the use of source versus message cues in persuasion. *Journal of Personality and Social Psychology, 39,* 752–766.

Chaiken, S. (1987). The heuristic model of persuasion. In M. P. Zanna, J. M. Olson, & C. P. Herman (Eds.), *Social influence: The Ontario symposium* (Vol. 5, pp. 3–39). Hillsdale, NJ: Erlbaum.

Chang, C. (2006). Changing smoking attitudes by strengthening weak antismoking beliefs: Taiwan as an example. *Journal of Health Communication, 11,* 769–788.

Cotton, J. L. (1985). Cognitive dissonance in selective exposure. In D. Zillmann & J. Bryant (Eds.), *Selective exposure to communication* (pp. 11–33). Hillsdale, NJ: Erlbaum.

D'Alessio, D., & Allen, M. (2007). The selective exposure hypothesis and media choice processes. In R. W. Preiss, B. M. Gayle, N. Burrell, M. Allen, & J. Bryant (Eds.), *Mass media effects research: Advances through meta-analysis* (pp. 103–118). Mahwah, NJ: Erlbaum.

DeBono, K. G., & Packer, M. (1991). The effects of advertising appeal on perceptions of product quality. *Personality and Social Psychology Bulletin, 17,* 194–200.

Diamond, G. A., & Cobb, M. D. (1996). The candidate as catastrophe: Latitude theory and the problems of political persuasion. In D. C. Mutz, P. M. Sniderman, & R. A. Brody

(Eds.), *Political persuasion and attitude change* (pp. 225–247). Ann Arbor: University of Michigan Press.

Dijkstra, A. (2008). The psychology of tailoring-ingredients in computer-tailored persuasion. *Social and Personality Psychology Compass, 2,* 765–784.

Dillard, J. P., & Pfau, M. (Eds.). (2002). *The persuasion handbook: Developments in theory and practice.* Thousand Oaks, CA: Sage.

Eckes, T., & Six, B. (1994). Fakten und fiktionen in der einstellungs-verhaltens-forschung: Eine meta-analyse [Fact and fiction in attitude-behavior research: A meta-analysis]. *Zeitschrift für Sozialpsychologie, 25,* 253–271.

Festinger, L. (1957). *A theory of cognitive dissonance.* Stanford, CA: Stanford University Press.

Festinger, L., & Carlsmith, J. M. (1959). Cognitive consequences of forced compliance. *Journal of Abnormal and Social Psychology, 58,* 203–210.

Fishbein, M. (1967). A behavior theory approach to the relations between beliefs about an object and the attitude toward the object. In M. Fishbein (Ed.), *Readings in attitude theory and measurement* (pp. 389–400). New York: Wiley.

Fishbein, M., & Ajzen, I. (1975). *Belief, attitude, intention, and behavior.* Reading, MA: Addison-Wesley.

Fishbein, M., & Yzer, M. C. (2003). Using theory to design effective health behavior interventions. *Communication Theory, 13,* 164–183.

Floyd, D. L., Prentice-Dunn, S., & Rogers, R. W. (2000). A meta-analysis of research on protection motivation theory. *Journal of Applied Social Psychology, 30,* 407–429.

Frey, D. (1986). Recent research on selective exposure to information. In L. Berkowitz (Ed.), *Advances in experimental social psychology* (Vol. 19, pp. 41–80). New York: Academic Press.

Hardeman, W., Johnson, M., Johnston, D. W., Bonetti, D., Wareham, N. J., & Kinmonth, A. L. (2002). Application of the theory of planned behaviour in behaviour change interventions: A systematic review. *Psychology and Health, 17,* 123–158.

Harmon-Jones, E. (2002). A cognitive dissonance theory perspective on persuasion. In J. P. Dillard & M. Pfau (Eds.), *The persuasion handbook: Developments in theory and practice* (pp. 99–116). Thousand Oaks, CA: Sage.

Heider, F. (1946). Attitudes and cognitive organization. *Journal of Psychology, 21,* 107–112.

Herzog, T. A., & Blagg, C. O. (2007). Are most precontemplators contemplating smoking cessation? Assessing the validity of the stages of change. *Health Psychology, 26,* 222–231.

Hovland, C. I., Janis, I. L., & Kelley, H. H. (1953). *Communication and persuasion: Psychological studies of opinion change.* New Haven, CT: Yale University Press.

Hovland, C. I., Lumsdaine, A. A., & Sheffield, F. D. (1949). *Experiments on mass communication.* Princeton, NJ: Princeton University Press.

Katz, D. (1960). The functional approach to the study of attitudes. *Public Opinion Quarterly, 24,* 163–204.

Kim, M.-S., & Hunter, J. E. (1993). Relationships among attitudes, behavioral intentions, and behavior: A meta-analysis of past research, Part 2. *Communication Research, 20,* 331–364.

Kolsky, R., & Calder, B. J. (2008). The integration of advertising and media content: Ethical and practical considerations. In B. J. Calder (Ed.), *Kellogg on advertising and media* (pp. 266–281). Hoboken, NJ: John Wiley & Sons.

Kreuter, M., Farrell, D., Olevitch, L., & Brennan, L. (1999). *Tailoring health messages: Customizing communication with computer technology.* Mahwah, NJ: Erlbaum.

Kruglanski, A. W., & Thompson, E. P. (1999). Persuasion by a single route: A view from the unimodel. *Psychological Inquiry, 10,* 83–109.

Maio, G. R., & Olson, J. M. (Eds.). (2000). *Why we evaluate: Functions of attitude.* Mahwah, NJ: Erlbaum.

McGuire, W. J. (1985). Attitudes and attitude change. In G. Lindzey & E. Aronson (Eds.),

Handbook of social psychology (3rd ed., Vol. 2, pp. 233–346). New York: Random House.

McGuire, W. J. (2001). Input and output variables currently promising for constructing persuasive communications. In R. E. Rice & C. K. Atkin (Eds.), *Public communication campaigns* (3rd ed., pp. 22–48). Thousand Oaks, CA: Sage.

McKay, D. L., Berkowitz, J. M., Blumberg, J. B., & Goldberg, J. P. (2004). Communicating cardiovascular disease risk due to elevated homocysteine levels: Using the EPPM to develop print materials. *Health Education and Behavior, 31,* 355–371.

McMath, B. F., & Prentice-Dunn, S. (2005). Protection motivation theory and skin cancer risk: The role of individual differences in responses to persuasive appeals. *Journal of Applied Social Psychology, 35,* 621–643.

Niederdeppe, J., Hornik, R. C., Kelly, B. J., Frosch, D. L., Romantan, A., Stevens, R. S., et al. (2007). Examining the dimensions of cancer-related information seeking and scanning behavior. *Health Communication, 22,* 153–167.

O'Keefe, D. J. (2002). *Persuasion: Theory and research* (2nd ed.). Thousand Oaks, CA: Sage.

Pechmann, C., Zhao, G., Goldberg, M. E., & Reibling, E. T. (2003). What to convey in antismoking advertisements for adolescents: The use of protection motivation theory to identify effective message themes. *Journal of Marketing, 67*(2), 1–18.

Perloff, R. M. (2003). *The dynamics of persuasion* (2nd ed.). Mahwah, NJ: Erlbaum.

Petty, R. E., & Cacioppo, J. T. (1986). *Communication and persuasion: Central and peripheral routes to attitude change.* New York: Springer-Verlag.

Petty, R. E., Cacioppo, J. T., & Goldman, R. (1981). Personal involvement as a determinant of argument-based persuasion. *Journal of Personality and Social Psychology, 41,* 847–855.

Petty, R. E., Cacioppo, J. T., Strathman, A. J., & Priester, J. R. (2005). To think or not to think: Exploring two routes to persuasion.

In T. C. Brock & M. C. Green (Eds.), *Persuasion: Psychological insights and perspectives* (2nd ed., pp. 81–116). Thousand Oaks, CA: Sage.

Petty, R. E., & Wegener, D. T. (1999). The elaboration likelihood model: Current status and controversies. In S. Chaiken & Y. Trope (Eds.), *Dual-process models in social psychology* (pp. 41–72). New York: Guilford.

Prochaska, J. O. (1994). Strong and weak principles for progressing from precontemplation to action on the basis of twelve problem behaviors. *Health Psychology, 13,* 47–51.

Prochaska, J. O., Redding, C. A., & Evers, K. E. (2002). The transtheoretical model and stages of change. In K. Glanz, B. K. Rimer, & F. M. Lewis (Eds.), *Health behavior and health education: Theory, research, and practice* (3rd ed., pp. 99–120). San Francisco: Jossey-Bass.

Rimal, R. N., & Adkins, D. A. (2003). Using computers to narrowcast health messages: The role of audience segmentation, targeting, and tailoring in health promotion. In T. L. Thompson, A. M. Dorsey, K. I. Miller, & R. Parrott (Eds.), *Handbook of health communication* (pp. 497–513). Mahwah, NJ: Erlbaum.

Roehrig, M., Thompson, J. K., Brannick, M., & van den Berg, P. (2006). Dissonance-based eating disorder prevention program: A preliminary dismantling investigation. *International Journal of Eating Disorders, 39,* 1–10.

Rogers, R. W. (1975). A protection motivation theory of fear appeals and attitude change. *Journal of Psychology, 91,* 93–114.

Rogers, R. W., & Prentice-Dunn, S. (1997). Protection motivation theory. In D. Gochman (Ed.), *Handbook of health behavior research: Vol. 1. Personal and social determinants* (pp. 113–132). New York: Plenum.

Shavitt, S. (1990). The role of attitude objects in attitude functions. *Journal of Experimental Social Psychology, 26,* 124–148.

Sherif, C. W., Sherif, M., & Nebergall, R. E. (1965). *Attitude and attitude change: The social judgment-involvement approach.* Philadelphia: W. B. Saunders.

Shim, M., Kelly, B., & Hornik, R. (2006). Cancer information scanning and seeking behavior is associated with knowledge, lifestyle choices, and screening. *Journal of Health Communication, 11*(March 2006 Suppl.), 157–172.

Silk, K. J., Weiner, J., & Parrott, R. L. (2005). Gene cuisine or frankenfood? The theory of reasoned action as an audience segmentation strategy for messages about genetically modified foods. *Journal of Health Communication, 10,* 751–767.

Singhal, A., Cody, M. J., Rogers, E. M., & Sabido, M. (Eds.). (2004). *Entertainment-education and social change: History, research, and practice.* Mahwah, NJ: Erlbaum.

Slater, M. D. (1999). Integrating application of media effects, persuasion, and behavior change theories to communication campaigns: A stages-of-change framework. *Health Communication, 11,* 335–354.

Slater, M. D. (2002). Involvement as goal-directed strategic processing: Extending the elaboration likelihood model. In J. P. Dillard & M. Pfau (Eds.), *The persuasion handbook: Developments in theory and practice* (pp. 175–194). Thousand Oaks, CA: Sage.

Smith, S. M., Fabrigar, L. R., & Norris, M. E. (2008). Reflecting on six decades of selective exposure research: Progress, challenges, and opportunities. *Social and Personality Psychology Compass, 2,* 464–493.

Smith, S. W., Atkin, C. K., Martell, C., Allen, R., & Hembroff, L. (2006). A social judgment theory approach to conducting formative research in a social norms campaign. *Communication Theory, 16,* 141–152.

Snyder, M., & DeBono, K. G. (1985). Appeals to image and claims about quality: Understanding the psychology of advertising. *Journal of Personality and Social Psychology, 49,* 586–597.

Spangenberg, E. R., & Greenwald, A. G. (1999). Social influence by requesting self-prophesy. *Journal of Consumer Psychology, 8,* 61–69.

Spangenberg, E. R., Sprott, D. E., Grohmann, B., & Smith, R. J. (2003). Mass-communicated prediction requests: Practical application and a cognitive dissonance explanation for self-prophesy. *Journal of Marketing, 67*(3), 47–62.

Stead, M., Tagg, S., MacKintosh, A. M., & Eadie, D. (2005). Development and evaluation of a mass media theory of planned behaviour intervention to reduce speeding. *Health Education Research, 20,* 36–50.

Stice, E., Shaw, H., Becker, C. B., & Rohde, P. (2008). Dissonance-based interventions for the prevention of eating disorders: Using persuasion principles to promote health. *Prevention Science, 9,* 114–128.

Stone, J., Aronson, E., Crain, A. L., Winslow, M. P., & Fried, C. B. (1994). Inducing hypocrisy as a means of encouraging young adults to use condoms. *Personality and Social Psychology Bulletin, 20,* 116–128.

Wallack, L., Woodruff, K., Dorfman, L., & Diaz, I. (1999). *News for a change: An advocate's guide to working with the media.* Thousand Oaks, CA: Sage.

Webster, J. G. (2008). Developments in audience measurement and research. In B. J. Calder (Ed.), *Kellogg on advertising and media* (pp. 123–138). Hoboken, NJ: John Wiley & Sons.

Weinstein, N. D., Rothman, A. J., & Sutton, S. R. (1998). Stage theories of health behavior: Conceptual and methodological issues. *Health Psychology, 17,* 290–299.

West, R. (2005). Time for a change: Putting the transtheoretical (stages of change) model to rest. *Addiction, 100,* 1036–1039.

Witte, K. (1998). Fear as motivator, fear as inhibitor: Using the extended parallel process model to explain fear appeal successes and failures. In P. A. Andersen & L. K. Guerrero (Eds.), *Handbook of communication and emotion: Research, theory, applications, and contexts* (pp. 423–450). San Diego: Academic Press.

Witte, K., & Allen, M. (2000). A meta-analysis of fear appeals: Implications for effective public health programs. *Health Education and Behavior, 27,* 591–615.

Yardley, L., & Nyman, S. R. (2007). Internet provision of tailored advice on falls prevention activities for older people: A randomized controlled evaluation. *Health Promotion International, 22,* 122–128.

19

SOCIAL COGNITIVE THEORY AND MEDIA EFFECTS

◆ Frank Pajares, Abby Prestin,
Jason Chen, and Robin L. Nabi

B andura's social cognitive theory is one of the most highly influential and widely celebrated theories in the field of social psychology. Thus, it is no surprise that its influence has extended into multiple fields, including communication and especially the study of media effects. Still, despite the enthusiasm with which media scholars have embraced social cognitive theory, its integration into media research is still in its infancy. The purpose of this chapter is, first, to lay out the historical background and basic tenets of social cognitive theory. We will then explore the ways in which media effects scholars have integrated it into their research and consider the ways in which scholars might build on the existing foundation of social cognitive theory–based media research to better illuminate media effects processes and outcomes.

◆ Historical Background

In the early 1940s, at the height of the behaviorist movement in psychology, behaviorist theories, like classical conditioning, assumed that external stimuli were the primary influence on human functioning, with internal processes serving merely to transmit behavior. Around this time, however, in a paradigmatic shift, American psychologists introduced theories of social learning that rejected behaviorist notions of associationism as the primary source of behavioral motivation in favor of drive reduction principles. Despite the appeal of these approaches, though, these theories failed to explain how individuals initiated novel behaviors or why they imitated the actions of others, even when not directly reinforced. In 1963, Bandura and Walters broadened the frontiers of traditional social learning theories with the principles of social modeling, observational learning, and vicarious reinforcement. Two decades later, Bandura (1986) advanced a model of human functioning that accorded cognitive, vicarious, self-regulatory, and self-reflective processes central roles in the process of human adaptation and change.

At this point, Bandura relabeled his theory from social learning to social "cognitive," both to distance it from contemporary social learning theories and to emphasize the role of cognition in people's capabilities to construct reality, self-regulate, encode information, and act. In social cognitive theory, people are seen as self-organizing, proactive, self-reflecting, and self-regulating rather than as simply reactive organisms shaped by environmental forces or driven by basic inner impulses. For Bandura, introspection is critical to predicting the influence of environmental factors on behavior, as introspection is the mechanism by which people make sense of their psychological processes. Social cognitive theory also diverges from theories of behavior that privilege biological factors, which tend to ignore the social and technological innovations that create environmental selection pressures for adaptation (Bussey & Bandura, 1999). Instead, social cognitive theory espouses a bidirectional influence in which evolutionary pressures alter human development such that people can create complex environmental innovations, which in turn create selection pressures for the evolution of specialized biological systems for functional consciousness, language, and symbolic communication. Thus, social cognitive theory proposes that human functioning is the product of reciprocal determinism, or the dynamic interplay of (a) personal factors (e.g., cognition, affect); (b) behavior; and (c) environmental influences, which interact to shape human behavior (Bandura, 1986).

◆ Deconstructing Social Cognitive Theory

Given the breadth of social cognitive theory and the interconnectedness among its concepts, it can often be difficult to distill into a simple explication. In this section, we discuss the four cornerstones of the theory. The first two—human agency and human capabilities—might be viewed as the foundation on which social learning may develop. The third element—vicarious learning—captures the process through which observation learning takes place, and the final element—self-efficacy—is the element that underlies the enactment of those learned behaviors.

HUMAN AGENCY

Social cognitive theory is rooted in the notion of human agency, which suggests that individuals are proactively engaged in their own development and that they are able to exercise a measure of control over their thoughts, feelings, and actions (Bandura, 1986). Agency operates through three modes. *Individual agency* is exercised when one's own influence is brought to bear on one's functioning and environment. People may also obtain desired outcomes by *proxy agency,* whereby another person secures benefits for the individual. Finally, people exercise *collective agency* when they work together to advance common interests. Additionally, agency has four core properties: intentionality, forethought, self-reactiveness, and self-reflectiveness (Bandura, 2006). *Intentionality* refers to the creation of and engagement in plans and strategies by which people realize pre-determined intentions to act. *Forethought* is the property whereby people anticipate outcomes of their actions. *Self-reactiveness* is the property whereby individuals construct and regulate the appropriate courses of action. Finally, through *self-reflectiveness*, people reflect on their capabilities, the soundness of their thoughts and actions, and the meaning of their pursuits.

HUMAN CAPABILITIES

Related to the properties of agency are the capabilities—symbolization, forethought, self-regulation, self-reflection, and vicarious learning—that provide the cognitive means by which people influence their destiny. More specifically, humans possess the capacity to symbolize, by which they extract meaning from their environment, construct guides for action, gain knowledge by reflective thought, communicate with others over distance in time and space, and store information (Bandura, 1986). Symbolization also allows people to engage in forethought, by which they plan action and anticipate its consequences. People self-reflect by meta-cognitively examining their functioning, which allows them to make sense of experiences, self-evaluate, and judge their capability to accomplish tasks. Further, this self-reflection is motivated by both the long- and short-term goals and challenges that people set (Bandura, 1986, 2001). These two types of goals work together—short-term goals provide motivation to take the incremental steps leading, over time, to the accomplishment of long-term goals. Through self-regulation, people can adjust their behavior to both set and meet their short- and long-term goals (see Zimmerman, 2000). Finally, vicarious learning, in which observations are symbolically coded and

used as guides for future action, permits individuals to learn novel behaviors without the trial and error of performing them. This capability is discussed in greater detail in the following paragraph.

VICARIOUS LEARNING

Social cognitive theory's hallmark is its articulation of the functions and processes of vicarious learning (Bandura, 1986, 2002). That is, by observing the behaviors of others, an individual can develop rules to guide his or her subsequent behavior. Observational learning is governed by the processes of attention, retention, production, and motivation. First, an individual must *attend to,* or selectively observe, the actions of a model. Attention is influenced by characteristics of the modeled behavior (e.g., complexity), the model (e.g., attractiveness, similarity), and the observer (e.g., cognitive capabilities). Observed behaviors can be reproduced only if they are *retained* in memory, a process influenced by symbolic coding, cognitive organization, rehearsal, and cognitive skills. *Production* focuses on translating the symbolic representation of the observed behavior into action. This process is influenced by representational guidance (e.g., response production, guided enactment), corrective adjustment (e.g., monitoring of enactments, feedback), and the observer's capabilities and related subskills. Finally, *motivational processes* help determine whether behaviors are enacted based on the nature of the reinforcement. Reinforcement may come from feedback generated by one's behavior, the observed feedback given to others, or internal incentives, and may differ in valence (positive or negative). Reinforcement is related to another key aspect of social cognitive theory—outcome expectancies. Outcome expectancies are the judgments of the consequences associated with a behavior. Outcomes may be physical, social, or self-evaluative in nature, and are usually associated with a positive or negative valence (Bandura, 1986, 2001).

SELF-EFFICACY

Although one might learn about possible desirable behaviors from observing others, Bandura (1997) argues that those behaviors will not be enacted unless an individual possesses the self-efficacy to do so. Self-efficacy beliefs are judgments that individuals hold about their capabilities to perform a behavior at designated levels. Importantly, Bandura argues that "people's level of motivation, affective states, and actions are based more on what they believe than on what is objectively true" (1997, p. 2). For this reason, self-efficacy beliefs are better predictors of people's accomplishments than their previous attainments, knowledge, or skills, as such beliefs are associated with goal-related effort, persistence, and resilience in the face of adversity. Self-efficacy beliefs are sensitive to contextual factors, such as the regulation of one's motivation, thought processes, affective states, actions, or environmental conditions. These beliefs are often associated with outcome expectancies. More specifically, self-efficacy helps foster the outcome one expects: confident people anticipate successful outcomes, whereas the opposite is true of those lacking confidence.

The influence of self-efficacy on the accomplishment of a task, however, does have its limits. High self-efficacy will not influence behavior when people lack the resources to undertake an activity, believe the social constraints of prejudicially structured systems will prohibit them from reaching desired outcomes, or do not value the expected outcome. Furthermore, people cannot accomplish tasks beyond their capabilities simply by believing they can; efficacy will not produce a competent performance in the absence of requisite skills. These factors notwithstanding, a wealth of research shows that self-efficacy can affect motivation, performance, and attainment across a range of fields, such as life-course development, education, health, psychopathology, athletics, business, and international affairs (Bandura, 1995, 1997; Pajares, 1997; Pajares & Urdan, 2006; Stajkovic & Luthans, 1998).

Given the importance of self-efficacy beliefs in the generation of behavior, it is important to consider how such beliefs might develop. In fact, there appear to be four sources of information that help form self-efficacy beliefs. The most influential source is *mastery experience,* in which the formation of self-efficacy beliefs is intuitive: individuals engage in activities, interpret the results of their behavior, and use their interpretations to develop beliefs about their capability to engage in subsequent activities. Outcomes interpreted as successful raise self-efficacy; those interpreted as failures lower it.

People also form self-efficacy beliefs through the *vicarious experience* of observing others perform behaviors. Social modeling exerts an especially powerful effect on self-efficacy beliefs when people observe a model similar to themselves. Observing similar others succeed can enhance individuals' beliefs about their own capabilities ("If they can do it, so can I") and motivate them to perform the task. Conversely, watching similar models fail can undermine observers' beliefs about their own capability to succeed (Schunk, 1987). Model similarity is most influential for those who are uncertain about their performance capabilities, such as those who lack task familiarity and information to use in judging their self-efficacy or those who have experienced past difficulties (Bandura, 1986; Schunk, 1987; Schunk & Meece, 2006). Of note, when people perceive the model's capability as highly divergent from their own, the influence of vicarious experience is greatly minimized.

Individuals also create and develop self-efficacy beliefs as a result of *verbal persuasion,* or the verbal judgments that others provide. Effective persuaders must cultivate other people's beliefs in their capabilities while simultaneously ensuring that the envisioned success is attainable. Although positive persuasions may encourage and empower a person, negative persuasions can defeat and weaken self-efficacy beliefs. In fact, it is usually easier to weaken self-efficacy beliefs through criticism than to strengthen such beliefs through encouragement.

Finally, people can gauge their self-efficacy by the *physiological and emotional states* (e.g., anxiety, stress, and arousal) that they experience as they contemplate an action. Strong emotional reactions to a task, like excitement or fear, provide cues about the anticipated success or failure of the outcome. Focusing on negative physiological cues, negative thoughts, and fears can not only lower self-efficacy perceptions but also trigger additional stress that contributes to an inadequate performance. Thus, one way to raise self-efficacy beliefs is to improve physical and emotional well-being and reduce negative emotional states. Further, because individuals have the capability to alter their own thinking and feelings, enhanced self-efficacy beliefs can, in turn, powerfully influence the physiological states themselves. Based on the selection, integration, interpretation, and recollection of information from these four sources of information about self-efficacy, as well as the rules employed for weighting and integrating them, self-efficacy beliefs are ultimately formed.

◆ Social Cognitive Theory and the Study of Media Effects

The capacity of humans to think abstractly or symbolically positions the media as an important source of information to facilitate observational learning and increase self-efficacy to perform given behaviors (Bandura, 2001). In turn, social cognitive theory offers a vantage point from which to examine the influence of mediated content on audiences' attitudes and behaviors

(Bandura, 2001, 2002, 2004). Drawing from the previous theoretical explication, social cognitive theory suggests that, in essence, for mediated content to positively affect audience members' behaviors, the audience must pay attention to attractive or similar models realistically performing relevant behaviors. Models engaging in positive behaviors should be positively reinforced, whereas those engaging in negative behaviors should be negatively reinforced (Austin & Meili, 1994; Bandura, 2001; Stiff, 1986). In such cases, mediated depictions of behavior may be instrumental in bringing about positive personal and social changes, although alternative pairings of behaviors and reinforcements can prove to be problematic (Bandura, 2001, 2002, 2004; Nabi & Clark, 2008). As we consider the literature on the intersection between media and social cognitive theory, it is evident that the theory has been used to explain both unintended (and usually negative) as well as intended (and usually positive) effects of media depictions. We address both in turn in the following section.

SOCIAL COGNITIVE THEORY–BASED EXAMINATIONS OF UNINTENDED MEDIA EFFECTS

Throughout much of the history of media effects research, great attention has been placed on the possible negative consequences media content might have on audiences' attitudes and behaviors (see Bryant & Zillmann, Chapter 1, this volume). Thus, it should come as no surprise, given the discussion presented earlier, that social cognitive theory would be tapped to try to explain why such behavioral effects might emerge. Given that the media landscape is populated with attractive, likable characters often engaging in risky or antisocial behaviors, it is only logical to presume that audiences might model such behaviors through the processes described earlier. Thus, social cognitive theory is often cited in media effects literature as a framework to explain such unintended and negative media effects. For example, Gidwani, Sobol, DeJong, Perrin, and Gortmaker (2002) argued that the positive correlation between television viewing and the initiation of youth smoking was a result of the rarity with which television portrays the negative consequences of smoking. Similarly, Harrison and Cantor (1997) theorized that the positive relationship between exposure to their magazines and women's drive for thinness is a function of the tendency for women's magazines to link thinness to positive consequences, thus engendering extrinsic motivation for dietary behavior. To be clear, these studies did not test social cognitive theory directly, but rather drew from its predictions to presume how it would explain the effects identified in that research.

Similarly, social cognitive theory is frequently referenced as a framework that might explain the possible effects of patterns of media depictions regarding, for example, sex or race, identified through content analyses (e.g., Aubrey, 2004; Graves, 1999; Mastro & Stern, 2003). Although its predictions are in line with the theory, these studies do not test these predictions, but rather, suggest possible effects to be tested with additional empirical work (see Nabi & Clark, 2008, for a similar critique).

Although some research efforts have been engaged to examine media effects based on the tenets of social cognitive theory, most such studies tend to focus on individual aspects of the theory rather than on all of the components necessary to establish a true test of the theory. For instance, Farrar (2006) showed study participants teenage dramas in which characters engaged in either safe sex or unprotected sex. However, positive or negative reinforcements associated with these behaviors were not included, though the author noted that the absence of punishment could potentially serve as a reward. Still other studies hoping to test social cognitive theory often measure constructs in ways that may not be fully consistent with the theory. For example, in a longitudinal study of the effects

of TV viewing on initiation of sexual intercourse among adolescents, Martino, Collins, Kanouse, Elliott, and Berry (2005) found that those who watched more sexual content on TV had higher self-efficacy related to the practice of safe sex and fewer negative expectations of engaging in sexual intercourse, both of which were positively associated with intent to initiate sex. Although on its face, it seems to be well rooted in social cognitive theory, as Nabi and Clark (2008) point out, this study tested general exposure to sexually oriented content rather than specific depictions of positive or negative consequences of sex. Thus, Martino et al.'s media measure was more consistent with what one might expect of a study grounded in cultivation theory, for which gradual, cumulative exposure is the predicted mechanism of effect (see Morgan, Chapter 5, this volume), rather than social cognitive theory.

Thus, it appears that media scholars find great utility in social cognitive theory as an explanation for unintended, negative effects of media exposure, but the research often falls short of offering rigorous tests of the processes as conceptualized by the theory. More recent empirical investigations have made efforts to offer more appropriate tests of the theory through experiments in which media content is manipulated in theoretically consistent ways, though the results have not been consistent. Eyal and Kunkel (2008) presented clips of popular teen television programs portraying either positive or negative consequences of premarital sex and found that, consistent with social cognitive theory, exposure to portrayals of negative consequences led to more negative attitudes toward the behavior and harsher moral judgments of characters who modeled that behavior. Conversely, those who viewed positive consequences of sex did not report more positive attitudes toward it. However, Nabi and Clark (2008), in their theoretical comparison of social cognitive theory and schema theory (Fiske & Taylor, 1991), manipulated depictions of one-night stands to reflect either positive or negative consequences, and found, contrary to social cognitive theory (but consistent with schema theory), that positive and negative reinforcement conditions had comparable effects on behaviorally inexperienced viewers' attitudes and behavioral intentions.

In sum, social cognitive theory is likely useful in helping to explain the unintended and negative effects of media consumption on audience behaviors. However, future research would benefit from more carefully constructed studies that pay greater attention to the operationalization of the theory's constructs.

SOCIAL COGNITIVE THEORY–BASED EXAMINATIONS OF INTENDED MEDIA EFFECTS

Given the powerful social influence of media models, scholars have not only drawn from social cognitive theory to explain unintentional effects of the media, but have also found it useful in their efforts to design messages to maximize the potential positive impact of media content through entertainment-education programming and health campaigns to promote prosocial change. This research is briefly reviewed in the following paragraphs.

Entertainment-education. Entertainment-education (E-E) is the purposeful blend of prosocial messages in entertainment programming (Singhal & Rogers, 1999). This strategy owes its effectiveness to the process of oblique persuasion by which educational or persuasive messages are "sugarcoated" in entertainment content, which lowers audiences' resistance and defenses to the embedded persuasive messages. Beginning with the earliest programs developed in Mexico in the 1980s (Sabido, 1981), E-E radio and television efforts have targeted a range of behaviors and topics, such as AIDS prevention, gender equity, condom use, sex education, and literacy, and have been

guided by social cognitive theory insights regarding the influence of social models. E-E programs typically include three types of characters from which audience members can learn: positive role models who support a prosocial value, negative role models who reject this value, and transitional models who change from negative to positive models over the course of the serial or program. Transitional characters provide particularly relevant models from which audiences can learn. Audiences may relate to the uncertainty and doubt transitional characters experience when first considering a new behavior, and can observe the characters being rewarded for their adoption of the behavior as the story progresses (Singhal & Rogers, 1999).

To encourage observational learning and behavioral modeling, E-E programming is packaged in popular media formats, such as *telenovelas* in Mexico and radio serials in South Africa, which enhance attentional processes (Singhal & Rogers, 1999). Additionally, characters are physically and psychologically attractive and often of a higher status than the target audience. The repetitive structure of serial programs, such as the *telenovelas,* encourages retention processes. These retained symbols are converted into behavior by modeling, and refined based on feedback. Finally, characters are typically rewarded for positive, prosocial behavior and punished for antisocial behavior as a means of promoting motivational processes (Nariman, 1993; Singhal & Rogers, 1999).

Many E-E efforts have proven successful (see Dittman, 2004; Rosins, 2006; Smith, 2002). For example, Rogers et al. (1999) describe the effects of a radio serial drama on the self-efficacy of poor women in Tanzania to manage their reproductive lives through family planning. Before the serials aired, many women believed reproductive processes were directed by fate, and thus not under their control. As the models in the serials demonstrated personal control over these processes, listeners were empowered to seek the services of family planning clinics (see Vaughn, Rogers, Singhal, & Swalehe, 2000).

Although the success of these programs is encouraging, E-E studies are sometimes criticized for lacking rigorous evaluations that illuminate whether specific content has led to specific effects as predicted by social cognitive theory. Most programs are evaluated with relatively general measures of audience exposure, coupled with audience surveys and content analyses of scripts and audience letters (Singhal & Rogers, 1999, 2002). Thus, questions regarding the process by which resulting behavior change may have occurred are left unanswered. Indeed, Slater and Rouner (2002) have called for greater use of laboratory experiments using E-E content to better understand the theoretical mechanisms through which E-E content alters beliefs, attitudes, and behavior (see also Moyer-Gusé & Nabi, 2008).

Health campaigns. Unlike E-E efforts, health campaigns tend to focus specifically on the concept of self-efficacy given the vast body of literature supporting the influential role it plays in health behavior change (see Bandura, 1997, and Maddux, 2002, for reviews). Scholars suggest that media can help audience members develop self-efficacy by providing them with behavior models, instruction, encouragement, and the reduction of negative affect (Bandura, 1982; Flora & Maibach, 1989). There is some evidence that this is true. A number of experimental studies have tested the effectiveness of messages building self-efficacy through vicarious experience (e.g., videos presenting step-by-step instruction, encouragement, and actors demonstrating the target behavior; see Anderson, 2000; Anderson & McMillion, 1995) and verbal persuasion (e.g., videos describing the steps of a behavior and encouraging enactment by highlighting the ease, simplicity, or familiarity of the behavior; see Anderson, 1995). These messages, along with those featured in real-world campaigns, have produced encouraging results in terms of increases in self-efficacy

and behavioral intention (Agha, 2003; Anderson, 1995, 2000; Anderson & McMillion, 1995; Maibach, Flora, & Nass, 1991; Meyerowitz & Chaiken, 1987; O'Reilly & Higgins, 1991; Ripptoe & Rogers, 1987).

In sum, research on the intentional incorporation of concepts associated with social cognitive theory into health-promoting media messages—both entertainment and campaign-based—have proven effective in generating healthy behaviors in audiences. As work progresses in this area, greater attention to assessing the process of effects will be important to establishing that the process as conceptualized by the theory is, in fact, what underlies the positive effects generated by exposure to such media content.

◆ Future Directions for Social Cognitive Theory–Based Media Research

Although social cognitive theory is frequently cited as a useful theoretical framework in the literature on media effects, the previous overview suggests that its contribution to our understanding of media effects processes has not been tapped as deeply as it could be. Social cognitive theory is rich with suggestions for media message components that could be manipulated to test not only issues related to attention and motivational processes but self-efficacy as well. Therefore, in this section, we offer some thoughts regarding variables that might be particularly useful to future media effects research, drawing from a social cognitive theory perspective.

ISSUES OF ATTENTION, IDENTIFICATION, AND MOTIVATION

As noted earlier, observational learning from media begins with audience members' attention to the media content, which is affected by source and contextual features.

Attractive, similar models are proposed to facilitate attention (Bandura, 2002), as might relevant, novel, or salient content. Each of these variables has received some attention in the literature, but as we consider elements uniquely suited to media contexts, there are some message features that are likely to be influential. For instance, Nabi and Krcmar (2004) propose that enjoyment of media could potentially associate with enhanced attention to and retention of modeled behaviors. Further, any emotionally-evocative stimulus—whether enjoyable or not—is likely to capture audience attention and increase the likelihood of retention (see Nabi, Chapter 14, this volume). Indeed, features of the media themselves, such as editing style and interactivity, are also likely to promote attention. Surely there are other media features that may serve this function, and those approaching media effects research from a social cognitive theory perspective should consider incorporating these variables into their research.

Another potentially rich area of exploration involves issues of identification and behavioral reinforcement in the modeling process. Identification refers to the extent to which an individual relates to a model and perceives the model to be similar to himself or herself, with similarity being based on a number of characteristics, including demographics, physical characteristics, personality traits, or attitudes. According to Bandura (2001), greater perceived similarity is associated with greater identification, which has been shown to increase the likelihood of observational learning (e.g., Andsager, Bemker, Choi, & Torwel, 2006; Ito, Kalyanaraman, Brown, & Miller, 2008).

Evidence suggests that identification with a character in the media, coupled with perceptions of positive outcomes of their behaviors, can boost the likelihood that audience members may model the depicted behaviors (Nabi, 2009). However, although social cognitive theory suggests that the impact of identification is contingent on the nature of behavioral reinforcement (that is, the behavior of liked characters will be modeled if they experience positive outcomes but will not be modeled if the characters experience negative outcomes), recent evidence calls this prediction into question. Nabi and Clark (2008) found that intentions to model the risky behavior of a liked character with whom viewers identified increased, even when the behavior was negatively reinforced. The authors argue that this apparently surprising outcome is to be expected when one considers that viewers approach television programming with schemas that bad things don't happen to liked characters. Thus, the value of the negative reinforcement is undermined by viewers' positive future expectations. Further, they argue that a risky behavior may be associated with positive value, despite the depiction of punishment associated with the behavior, simply because of the positive feelings the audiences have for the similar, liked character who engaged in that behavior. After all, young viewers have found similar others to be fun, intelligent, and mature (Andsager et al., 2006). Therefore, audience members may be prone to modeling the behavior of liked characters, regardless of the behavioral reinforcement depicted, given their admiration for those (often idealized) personalities. If this is the case, media characters might be well suited for modeling positive behaviors, but may not serve as useful conduits for discouraging risky behavior.

Clearly, additional research on the role of identification with media characters and the conditions under which such identification motivates or discourages behavioral modeling would be most useful. Focusing specifically on issues of behavioral reinforcement, future research should examine the match between the intended valence of behavioral reinforcements depicted in mediated content and the audience members' perception of those reinforcements. Additionally, future work should investigate the degree of negative reinforcement that may be suitable for media models to experience. Nabi and Clark (2008) suggest that negative outcomes that are more severe could discourage enactment of the behavior; however, audience members may perceive harsh outcomes to be overly dramatic, and thus too unrealistic to happen in their own lives. Examining not simply whom audiences identify with but the nature of the identification-behavioral reinforcement interaction would be most useful in determining how to best structure intervention efforts regarding risky behaviors.

REFLECTIONS ON SELF-EFFICACY

Scholars suggest that media content can help develop audience self-efficacy by providing behavior models, instruction, encouragement, and the reduction of negative affect associated with behaviors (Bandura, 1982; Flora & Maibach, 1989). However, fewer media-based campaigns are built on this proposition than might be expected. As Anderson and McMillion (1995) have noted, teaching specific behavior change techniques and encouraging confidence in those skills are "components rarely addressed in public information campaigns" (p. 341). This claim speaks to the largely untapped efficacy-boosting potential of mediated content.

The research that has examined the ways in which media messages might increase self-efficacy has focused primarily on two of the four efficacy sources—vicarious experience and verbal persuasion—while ignoring enactive mastery and physiological states. Future research, then, might explore how media can be used to encourage the development of efficacy beliefs through these processes. For example, applications of new media, such as video games that monitor and encourage individuals' exercise behavior, may be well suited to promote self-efficacy gains through enactive mastery, the strongest source of self-efficacy beliefs. Further, media might be used to manage audiences' physiological states through music,

visuals, camera angles, edits, and the like, to encourage hopeful feelings and minimize anxious ones.

Finally, we wish to note that though self-efficacy is only one of the determinants that regulate motivation, affect, and behavior according to social cognitive theory, it is often tested in isolation from other theoretical components. Therefore, those engaged in health promotion efforts, or indeed any test of social cognitive theory's predicted processes, should measure the full set of determinants posited by the theory rather than only the efficacy component. Only through more complete theoretical testing will we gain a fuller appreciation for the ways in which social cognitive theory helps to explain media effects processes and any related limitations that might exist.

SOCIAL COGNITIVE THEORY AND NEW MEDIA

Given the explosion of new media in recent years, it is only reasonable to consider what such changes in the media landscape might mean for the media-social cognitive theory relationship. According to Chafee and Metzger (2001), new media, such as the Internet, are those that "allow for a greater quantity of information transmission and retrieval, place more control over both content creation and selection in the hands of their users, and do so with less cost to the average consumer" (p. 369). The interactivity associated with virtual reality technologies and video games often leads to their inclusion under the new media umbrella as well (Biocca, 1992; Livingstone, 1999). Given the characteristics differentiating them from traditional media, new media may be better suited to meeting some of the challenges of testing social cognitive theory, such as portraying a range of behavioral reinforcements, increasing identification between the model and the target audience, and building self-efficacy.

First, new media may be less limited than traditional media in their ability to portray behavioral reinforcements. Traditional media research often requires the editing of preexisting content, such as scenes from television programs, to portray behavioral consequences, and thus the availability of content may prohibit the development of stimuli that reflect a range of outcomes. Immersive virtual environment technology (IVET), which includes both the replacement of natural sensory information with digital information and the ability to tailor that digital information in response to users' actions (Blascovich, 2001), can represent a broader range of reinforcements for a behavior. For example, Fox and Bailenson (2009) tested the capacity of IVET to encourage exercise and were able to very readily manipulate the positive outcomes (the virtual self lost weight in response to exercise) and negative outcomes (weight gain in response to lack of exercise) associated with the different behaviors. Of note, the conditions in which exercise was accompanied by reinforcements of weight loss (positive) or weight gain (negative) both encouraged more voluntary exercise than did the other experimental conditions.

Health-related video games have also demonstrated the capacity to present incremental behavioral reinforcements. For example, a game designed for diabetic children awarded game players points for regulating the diet, insulin, and blood sugar levels of a diabetic elephant character. The health of the character increased when players performed maintenance behaviors, and decreased when they failed to do so. Game play led to increased self-efficacy, improved dietary and insulin practices, and reduced diabetes-related urgent care visits (Brown et al., 1997). Similar results have been found for a health video game for children with asthma (Lieberman, 1997).

Second, though similarity between the model and target is positively associated with behavioral modeling, the current degree of similarity that traditional media can offer is often limited to categorical similarities, such as sex, ethnicity, or age. Even when matched on these characteristics, targets may not highly identify with models (Eyal & Kunkel, 2008). Additionally, even when media portrayals offer maximum similarity, such as video recordings of the target, behavioral depiction is restricted to the target's skill level in that behavioral domain (Dowrick, 1999). However, as Fox and Bailenson (2009) suggest, IVET allows for the creation of virtual reality selves (VRSs) that can be matched to a target on any number of characteristics and are able to perform skills that exceed the target's ability. Therefore, these models engender the highest level of identification without sacrificing a high level of skill. Indeed, Fox and Bailenson found that participants who saw a VRS, rather than a virtual representation of another person (VRO), believed themselves to be more similar to the model and exercised significantly more than those who saw the VRO. Although technology offering the capability to create and use realistic VRSs is not yet widely available, many mass-marketed video games are beginning to offer customizable avatars, such as the Nintendo Wii's "Mii," that may serve related functions. Research examining the effects of such avatars on identification will be most useful in understanding observational learning processes from media.

Along with virtual reality and video games, the Internet also provides the capability to deliver individualized, or "tailored," messages with customized information to an individual based on characteristics that are unique to that person and related to a behavior interest (Kreuter, Stretcher, & Glassman, 1999). Tailored materials may include depictions of models that are similar on a number of demographics or psychographics, which enhances similarity between a model and a target. Thus, there is little doubt that new media will be most helpful in creating messages that boost model identification and, in turn, allow for more precise tests of the tenets of social cognitive theory.

Finally, as noted earlier, enactive mastery and physiological feedback have been largely overlooked as methods of boosting self-efficacy in media contexts. New media, however, may be well suited to testing these approaches to boosting self-efficacy. For example, the VRS in Fox and Bailenson's (2009) study responded to the actual physical activity of participants using IVET; though self-efficacy was not measured, social cognitive theory predicts that those participants who saw VRS models positively rewarded for exercise they engendered would experience an increase in self-efficacy. Additionally, mass market games, such as Nintendo's Wii Fit, monitor audience members' performance on a number of physical activities, provide feedback to help game players adjust their performance, and offer encouragement. Thus, new media are well suited to test these elements of social cognitive theory (see Downs & Oliver, 2009, for an initial effort in this regard).

◆ Conclusion

Social cognitive theory is one of the most heavily referenced in media effects research (Bryant & Miron, 2004; Potter & Riddle, 2007), and for good reason. It offers a comprehensive understanding of how people learn behaviors in a range of contexts, including those based on media exposure. Yet, empirical research is surprisingly lax in its tests of the theory in media contexts. As this new decade of media research dawns and in light of the amazing innovations in media modalities in recent years, the timing is right for more careful tests of social cognitive theory's range of predictions in media contexts. To the extent the predictions are supported, those hoping to develop interventions based on the theory's principles can be assured their strategy is appropriate. To the extent it is determined that modifications to predictions might be necessary to accommodate unique media contexts, this too is critical information to uncover. There is no doubt that social cognitive theory will continue to be a leading theory in understanding the effects of media on behavioral learning for years to come, and by more fully considering the nuances of the theory, media research will be far better positioned to benefit from its richness.

◆ References

Agha, S. (2003). The impact of a mass media campaign on personal risk perception, perceived self-efficacy and on other behavioural predictors. *AIDS Care, 15,* 749–762.

Anderson, R. B. (1995). Cognitive appraisal of performance capability in the prevention of drunken driving: A test of self-efficacy theory. *Journal of Public Relations Research, 7,* 205–229.

Anderson, R. B. (2000). Vicarious and persuasive influences on efficacy expectations and intentions to perform breast self-examination. *Public Relations Review, 26,* 97–114.

Anderson, R. B., & McMillion, P. Y. (1995). Effects of similar and diversified modeling on African American women's efficacy expectations and intentions to perform breast self-examination. *Health Communication, 7,* 327–343.

Andsager, J. L., Bemker, V., Choi, H. L., & Torwel, V. (2006). Perceived similarity of exemplar traits and behavior: Effects on message evaluation. *Communication Research, 33,* 3–18.

Aubrey, J. S. (2004). Sex and punishment: An examination of sexual consequences and the sexual double standard in teen programming. *Sex Roles, 50,* 505–514.

Austin, E. W., & Meili, H. K. (1994). Effects of interpretations on televised alcohol portrayals on children's alcohol beliefs. *Journal of Broadcasting & Electronic Media, 38,* 417–435.

Bandura, A. (1982). Self-efficacy mechanism in human agency. *American Psychologist, 37,* 122–147.

Bandura, A. (1986). *Social foundations of thought and action: A social cognitive theory.* Englewood Cliffs, NJ: Prentice-Hall.

Bandura, A. (Ed.). (1995). *Self-efficacy in changing societies.* New York: Cambridge University Press.

Bandura, A. (1997). *Self-efficacy: The exercise of control.* New York: Freeman.

Bandura, A. (2001). Social cognitive theory of mass communication. *Media Psychology, 3,* 265–299.

Bandura, A. (2002). Growing primacy of human agency in adaptation and change in the electronic era. *European Psychologist, 7,* 1–16.

Bandura, A. (2004). Social cognitive theory for personal and social change by enabling media. In A. Singhal, M. J. Cody, E. M. Rogers, & M. Sabido (Eds.), *Entertainment-education and social change: History, research, and practice* (pp. 75–96). Mahwah, NJ: Erlbaum.

Bandura, A. (2006). Toward a psychology of human agency. *Perspectives on Psychological Science, 1,* 164–180.

Bandura, A., & Walters, R. H. (1963). *Social learning and personality development.* New York: Rinehart & Winston.

Biocca, F. (1992). Communication within virtual reality: Creating a space for research. *Journal of Communication, 42,* 5–22.

Blascovich, J. (2001). Immersive virtual environments and social behavior. *Science Briefs: Psychological Science Agenda, 14,* 8–9.

Brown, S. J., Lieberman, D. A., Gemeny, B. A., Fan, Y. C., Wilson, D. M., & Pasta, D. J. (1997). Educational video game for juvenile diabetes care: Results of a controlled trial. *Medical Informatics, 22,* 77–89.

Bryant, J., & Miron, D. (2004). Theory and research in mass communication. *Journal of Communication, 54,* 662–704.

Bussey, K., & Bandura, A. (1999). Social cognitive theory of gender development and differentiation. *Psychological Review, 106,* 676–713.

Chafee, S., & Metzger, M. J. (2001). The end of mass communication? *Mass Communication & Society, 4,* 365–379.

Dittman, M. (2004). Changing behavior through TV heroes. *Monitor on Psychology, 35*(9), 70.

Downs, E., & Oliver, M. B. (2009). *How can Wii learn from video games? Examining relationships between technological*
affordances and socio-cognitive determinants on affective and behavioral outcomes. Paper presented at the annual conference of the International Communication Association, Chicago.

Dowrick, P. W. (1999). A review of self modeling and related interventions. *Applied and Preventive Psychology, 8,* 23–39.

Eyal, K., & Kunkel, D. (2008). The effects of sex in television drama shows on emerging adults' sexual attitudes and moral judgments. *Journal of Broadcasting & Electronic Media, 52,* 161–181.

Farrar, K. M. (2006). Sexual intercourse on television: Do safe sex messages matter? *Journal of Broadcasting & Electronic Media, 50,* 635–650.

Fiske, S. T., & Taylor, S. E. (1991). *Social cognition* (2nd ed.). New York: McGraw-Hill.

Flora, J. A., & Maibach, E. W. (1989). The role of media across four levels of health promotion intervention. *Annual Review of Public Health, 10,* 181–201.

Fox, J., & Bailenson, J. N. (2009). Virtual self-modeling: The effects of vicarious reinforcement and identification on exercise behaviors. *Media Psychology, 12,* 1–25.

Gidwani, P. P., Sobol, A., DeJong, W., Perrin, J. M., & Gortmaker, S. L. (2002). Television viewing and initiation of smoking among youth. *Pediatrics, 110,* 505–508.

Graves, S. B. (1999). Television and prejudice reduction: When does television as a vicarious experience make a difference? *Journal of Social Issues, 55,* 707–725.

Harrison, K., & Cantor, J. (1997). The relationship between media consumption and eating disorders. *Journal of Communication, 47,* 40–67.

Ito, K. E., Kalyanaraman, S., Brown, J. D., & Miller, W. C. (2008). Factors affecting avatar use in a STI prevention CD-ROM. *Journal of Adolescent Health, 42,* S19.

Kreuter, M. W., Stretcher, V. J., & Glassman, B. (1999). One size does not fit all: The case for tailoring print materials. *Annals of Behavioral Medicine, 21,* 276–283.

Lieberman, D. A. (1997). Interactive video games for health promotion: Effects on knowledge, self-efficacy, social support, and health. In

R. L. Street, W. R. Gold, & T. Manning (Eds.), *Health promotion and interactive technology: Theoretical applications and future directions* (pp. 103–120). Hillsdale, NJ: Erlbaum.

Livingstone, S. (1999). New media, new audiences? *New Media and Society, 1,* 59–66.

Maddux, J. (2002). Self-efficacy: The power of believing you can. In C. R. Snyder & S. J. Lopez (Eds.), *Handbook of positive psychology* (pp. 277–287). New York: Oxford University Press.

Maibach, E. W., Flora, J. A., & Nass, C. (1991). Changes in self-efficacy and health behavior in response to a minimal contact community health campaign. *Health Communication, 3,* 1–15.

Martino, S. C., Collins, R. L., Kanouse, D. E., Elliott, M., & Berry, S. H. (2005). Social cognitive processes mediating the relationship between exposure to television's sexual content and adolescents' sexual behavior. *Journal of Personality and Social Psychology, 89,* 914–924.

Mastro, D. E., & Stern, S. R. (2003). Representations of race in television commercials: A content analysis of prime-time advertising. *Journal of Broadcasting & Electronic Media, 47,* 638–639.

Meyerowitz, B. E., & Chaiken, S. (1987). The effect of message framing on breast self-examination attitudes, intentions, and behavior. *Journal of Personality and Social Psychology, 52,* 500–510.

Moyer-Gusé, E., & Nabi, R. L. (2008, November). *Explaining the persuasive effects of entertainment education programming: An empirical comparison of three theories.* Paper presented at the 94th Annual Meeting of the National Communication Association, San Diego, CA.

Nabi, R. L. (2009). Cosmetic surgery makeover programs and intentions to undergo cosmetic enhancements: A consideration of three media effects theories. *Human Communication Research, 35*(1), 1–27.

Nabi, R. L., & Clark, S. (2008). Exploring the limits of social cognitive theory: Why negatively reinforced behaviors on TV may be modeled anyway. *Journal of Communication, 58,* 407–427.

Nabi, R. L., & Krcmar, M. (2004). Conceptualizing media enjoyment as attitude: Implications for mass media effects research. *Communication Theory, 14,* 288–310.

Nariman, H. (1993). *Soap operas for social change.* Westport, CT: Praeger.

O'Reilly, K. R., & Higgins, D. L. (1991). AIDS community demonstration projects for HIV prevention among hard-to-reach groups. *Public Health Reports, 106,* 714–720.

Pajares, F. (1997). Current directions in self-efficacy research. In M. Maehr & P. R. Pintrich (Eds.), *Advances in motivation and achievement* (Vol. 10, pp. 1–49). Greenwich, CT: JAI Press.

Pajares, F., & Urdan, T. (Eds.). (2006). *Adolescence and education: Vol. 5. Self-efficacy beliefs of adolescents.* Greenwich, CT: Information Age Publishing.

Potter, W. J., & Riddle, K. (2007). A content analysis of the media effects literature. *Journalism & Mass Communication Quarterly, 84,* 90–104.

Ripptoe, P. A., & Rogers, R. W. (1987). Effects of components of protection-motivation theory on adaptive and maladaptive coping with a health threat. *Journal of Personality and Social Psychology, 52,* 596–604.

Rogers, E. M., Vaughn, P. W., Swalehe, R. M. A., Rao, N., Svenkerud, P., & Sood, S. (1999). Effects of an entertainment-education radio soap opera on family planning behavior in Tanzania. *Studies in Family Planning, 30,* 1193–1211.

Rosins, H. (2006, June 5). Life lessons: How soap operas can change the world. *New Yorker,* 40–45.

Sabido, M. (1981). *Towards the social use of soap operas.* Mexico City: Institute for Communication Research.

Schunk, D. H. (1987). Peer models and children's behavioral change. *Review of Educational Research, 57,* 149–174.

Schunk, D. H., & Meece, J. L. (2006). Self-efficacy development in adolescence. In F. Pajares & T. Urdan (Eds.), *Self-efficacy beliefs of adolescents* (pp. 71–96). Greenwich, CT: Information Age Publishing.

Singhal, A., & Rogers, E. M. (1999). *Entertainment-education: A communication strategy for social change.* Mahwah, NJ: Erlbaum.

Singhal, A., & Rogers, E. M. (2002). A theoretical agenda for entertainment-education. *Communication Theory, 12,* 117–135.

Slater, M. D., & Rouner, D. (2002). Entertainment-education and elaboration likelihood: Understanding the process of narrative persuasion. *Communication Theory, 12,* 173–191.

Smith, D. (2002). The theory heard around the world. *Monitor on Psychology, 33*(9), 30.

Stajkovic, A. D., & Luthans, F. (1998). Self-efficacy and work-related performances: A meta-analysis. *Psychological Bulletin, 124,* 240–261.

Stiff, J. B. (1986). *Persuasive communication.* New York: Guilford.

Vaughn, P. W., Rogers, E. M., Singhal, A., & Swalehe, R. M. A. (2000). Entertainment-education and HIV/AIDS prevention: A field experiment in Tanzania. *Journal of Health Communication, 5,* 81–100.

Zimmerman, B. J. (2000). Attaining self-regulation: A social cognitive perspective. In M. Boekaerts, P. R. Pintrich, & M. Zeidner (Eds.), *Handbook of self-regulation* (pp. 13–39). San Diego: Academic Press.

20

EMERGING ISSUES IN ADVERTISING RESEARCH

◆ L. J. Shrum, Tina M. Lowrey, and Yuping Liu

Advertising is a fascinating subject. No other marketing vehicle captures the attention of consumers like advertising, although the attention it does capture tends to foster a love-hate relationship. Viewers spend sizable amounts of money on recording devices to enable them to avoid viewing ads, but at the same time schedule Super Bowl parties in which ad-watching is a planned event (Lowrey, Shrum, & McCarty, 2005).

Advertising is also a fascinating area of research, and just as ads themselves capture consumers' attention, understanding how advertising works has also captured the attention of academic research. Moreover, this research has spanned a number of disciplines, including but not limited to marketing, mass communication, various areas of psychology (e.g., social, cognitive, developmental), sociology, and political science. Although each of these disciplines may have its own idiosyncratic reason for studying the phenomenon, all are interested in documenting and explaining its effects (intended or unintended, individual or societal).

The interdisciplinary attention and interest that advertising brings has generated a voluminous amount of research. Numerous books and journals are devoted primarily to advertising-related phenomena within each of the disciplines just noted. For this reason, space constraints preclude any adequate discussion of advertising effects in general (see Petty, Briñol, & Priester, 2009, and Stewart & Pavlou, 2009, for more thorough reviews). Rather, in this chapter we discuss some of the emerging issues in advertising research, with the aim of providing a snapshot of the current theoretical and functional areas that have more recently captured research interest. The broad issues we address are product placement research, interactivity effects research, and psycholinguistics research. Although these three topics are certainly not exhaustive in terms of emerging areas of research, they provide a good cross-section of theories and methodologies that are being employed.

◆ Product Placement Research

One area of advertising research that is generating substantial interest is product placement. Product placement refers to the practice of inserting identifiable brands, brand names, or brand logos within nonmarketing media content (Balasubramanian, 1994; Lowrey et al., 2005). It is most readily identifiable with placements in films and movies, but placements in other forms of media (e.g., magazines, novels) can also occur. As McCarty (2004) details, product placement has a long history, appearing as early as the 1920s (see also Balasubramanian, Karrh, & Patwardhan, 2006), but it is only most recently that placement has been seen as an important and strategic marketing function.

Although marketers seem confident enough of the positive effects of product placement on marketing effectiveness measures, the empirical research landscape is very muddled (for reviews, see Balasubramanian et al., 2006; Bhatnagar, Aksoy, & Malkoc, 2004; Law & Braun-LaTour, 2004). Part of this is because of the difficulty in conducting both internally and externally valid research. Laboratory studies tend to suffer from the usual suspects of reasons: unnatural viewing environments, short-duration experimental stimuli, and artificial stimuli, among others. Field research, which has the potential to provide the more ecologically valid results that practitioners often prefer, suffers from lack of experimental control, which is particularly problematic because the effects of product placement are not only often subtle and transitory, but difficult to distinguish from other promotional inputs (advertising, sales promotion, publicity) that are part of the entire marketing campaign (Balasubramanian et al., 2006).

FACTORS INFLUENCING PRODUCT PLACEMENT EFFECTS

Despite the difficulties just noted, a number of factors have been shown to be important mediators and moderators of product placement effects. Some of these are execution factors, such as the prominence of the placement within the media content, the modality of the placement (visual, audio, both), and the extent to which the placement is integrated into the story. Other factors include ones that pertain to the viewers themselves, such as brand familiarity, brand preferences, and attitudes toward marketing and advertising practices in general, and product placement in particular (Balasubramanian et al., 2006). Compounding the complexity is the virtual certainty that many of these factors interact with each other.

Consider the issue of the prominence of placement in the media content. An oft-cited industry maxim is that one's product (whether in conventional ads or product placements) must be noticed, or attended to, to have an effect. Thus, one would likely predict that the more prominent a placement appears within a program, the more effective the placement. However, placements are much different from ads. Viewers have come to accept ads as necessary evils (attempts to bypass them notwithstanding) that occur between the programs they are viewing for entertainment. But what happens when the entertainment itself is altered to include a marketing message via placement? In such cases, at least when noticed, the general enjoyment of watching the program may be interrupted, and feelings of "flow" (Csikszentmihalyi, 1990) or "transportation" (Green & Brock, 2000; Green, Garst, & Brock, 2004) may diminish. Research shows that when consumers recognize a communication as a persuasive attempt, they process the information in fundamentally different ways than if they are not aware of a persuasive intent (Friestad & Wright, 1994). Thus, recognition of a persuasive attempt in the form of a product placement may induce viewers to scrutinize aspects of the placement and the placement context, to disengage from the communication, and possibly to resent the intrusion into program enjoyment (McCarty, 2004). In such cases, awareness of the product placement—which should be greater in high- than low-prominence situations—may result in more negative than positive attitudes (but would result in higher recall).

Some evidence supports this possibility. For example, when placements are more prominent because they are a major focus of a scene, increased exposure time has a positive effect on recall, but when the placements are more in the background of scenes, exposure time is unrelated to recall (Brennan, Dubas, & Babin, 1999). However, the situation becomes more complex when factors such as the extent to which the placements are integrated into the program are considered. For example, when placements are highly integrated into the program, liking for the placements is greater than when the placements are not highly integrated, but delayed recall is actually lower. In a similar manner, the obviousness of the placement has a more positive effect on liking when the placement is well integrated into the scene than when it is not (d'Astous & Chartier, 2000; see also Russell, 2002).

MEASURING PRODUCT PLACEMENT EFFECTIVENESS

The issues raised concerning execution factors such as the prominence or obviousness of the placement and possible consumer reactions to the placement bring up interesting issues regarding methods used to evaluate the effectiveness of the placements. In typical advertising research, recall is often considered a crucial measure of effectiveness and even a necessary condition for attitude change. The assumption is that recall will have a positive effect because the portrayal of the brand in the ad is invariably positive. For placements, however, this may not necessarily be the case. If, as we have speculated, certain conditions foster better recall but induce more negative attitudes (e.g., an obvious, incongruous placement that is poorly integrated), then recall measures may be unrelated or negatively related to attitude and choice measures. Consistent with this proposition, Law and Braun (2000) found that even though product placements that were central to the plot were better remembered than placements that were not central, there was no effect of centrality on product choice.

Based on the findings just discussed, it seems clear that there is often a disjunction between memory and attitude measures. In some cases, placements are recalled but attitudes are unaffected; in other cases, attitudes are positively affected in conjunction with no recall effects. These situations (particularly the latter) have led a number of researchers to make a distinction between explicit and implicit memory measures when assessing product placement effects (Auty & Lewis, 2004; Law & Braun-LaTour, 2004; Yang, Roskos-Ewoldsen, & Roskos-Ewoldsen, 2004). Examples of explicit memory measures are recognition and recall, whereas implicit measures are ones such as attitudes, beliefs, and behavior, or methods that attempt to measure accessibility effects (e.g., reaction times, word fragment completion). The latter are termed implicit memory measures because it is assumed that, at least under well-controlled experimental conditions, some notice of the product placement—even if not consciously recalled—is required for attitude change or for a concept to have been made more accessible. Thus, for example, Auty and Lewis (2004) found that product placement was positively related to product choice but showed little relation with explicit recall. In a study of placement effects in video games, Yang, Roskos-Ewoldsen, Dinu, and Arpan (2006) found that participants exhibited low levels of explicit memory measured via a recognition test, but demonstrated implicit brand memory measured via a word fragment completion task.

Although the research we have reviewed represents only a subset of product placement research, it should make clear the difficulties that this type of research presents. On the one hand, marketers for the most part want to be somewhat subtle in the placement in terms of interrupting the enjoyment of the program, but on the other hand, such subtlety makes it difficult to detect memory effects. However, as the research we have reviewed also suggests, using implicit measures of memory may be more effective in detecting subtle but potentially important effects. Clearly, the issues involved in understanding the effects of product placements are very complex, and will likely be pursued for some time to come.

◆ *Interactivity Effects Research*

Another emerging area within advertising research—interactivity—is brought forth by the fast-growing Internet media. Unlike traditional mass media, interactive online media allow consumers to actively participate in the advertising process, select the information they receive, and build an instantaneous two-way dialogue with advertisers. Consider a typical Web-browsing session where a consumer encounters an advertiser's message in the form of a banner ad.

Depending on the level of interest in the ad, the consumer can ignore the ad completely, view the ad but without taking any further action, or click on the ad to access a deeper layer of information present on the advertiser's Web site. In the last scenario, the consumer can further choose from a large amount of information on the Web site and view only the pages that are most relevant to him or her, creating in effect a customized advertising exposure. The advertiser, in the meantime, can capture all this information in the form of Web log data to gain a better understanding of the audience and to customize future advertising offerings. As can be seen in this simple scenario, interactivity can significantly alter advertising experiences as traditionally constructed.

Although interactivity can have a far-reaching impact on advertising, a theoretical understanding of interactivity and its effects on advertising has only begun to emerge in recent years. Early interactivity research dealt primarily with the definition (e.g., Rafaeli & Sudweeks, 1997), representation (e.g., Ghose & Dou, 1998), and measurement of the construct (e.g., Liu, 2003). More recently, researchers have started to focus more on understanding the effect of interactivity on advertising processes and outcomes and on identifying factors that work in conjunction with interactivity to produce persuasive outcomes (e.g., Liu & Shrum, 2009; Sicilia, Ruiz, & Munuera, 2005; Sohn, Ci, & Lee, 2007). So far, some consensus seems to have emerged from the literature, such as the multidimensional nature of interactivity and its presence in both the objective and the perceptual domain. In the meantime, controversy still remains as to whether interactivity truly facilitates persuasion (Sohn et al., 2007). This section synthesizes existing research in this area, identifies agreement as well as diverging points in the literature, and points out a few important future research questions.

WHAT IS INTERACTIVITY?

Although no common definition of interactivity exists in the advertising field, three themes have emerged from the literature: (a) interactivity is a multi-dimensional construct, (b) it can reside among different entities, and (c) it can be defined both as structural characteristics and as perception. On the multidimensional nature of interactivity, two-way communication and control have been suggested most often as the subdimensions of inter-activity (Liu, 2003; McMillan & Hwang, 2002). Two-way communication refers to the bidirectional flow of information *between* two entities, and some researchers have also added to it the speed or responsiveness of the information flow (e.g., Johnson, Bruner, & Kumar, 2006; Steuer, 1992; Sundar, Kalyanaraman, & Brown, 2003). This dimension of interactivity readily distinguishes the Internet from traditional mass media, as advertising information in those media is normally presented in one direction, from advertisers to the audience, without a direct feedback channel (Hoffman & Novak, 1996).

The control dimension of interactivity refers to the autonomy consumers have in manipulating an information flow (Ariely, 2000; Liu & Shrum, 2002; Sicilia et al., 2005). One of the earliest studies on inter-activity (Bezjian-Avery, Calder, & Iacobucci, 1998), for example, manipulated inter-activity by allowing consumers to determine the order in which they viewed a series of ads instead of being given a set order of presentation. Recently, however, researchers have questioned the inclusion of control as a dimension of interactivity, citing that control cannot be readily generalized into other media contexts (Johnson et al., 2006). The difficulty with presenting control as a separate construct, however, lies in the implicit tie between control and two-way communication. By allowing bidirectional flow of information, one assumes that each party has at least some level of control over the communication process. Therefore, it

would be difficult to tease the two apart both theoretically and empirically.

Besides the dimensional content of interactivity, it is also necessary to specify the domain within which it resides. One issue in this area is the specification of the entities between which interactivity is assumed to exist (Stromer-Galley, 2004). Three dyads have been proposed: human-human, human-message, and human-machine (Ko, Cho, & Roberts, 2005; Liu & Shrum, 2002). The first dyad comes from an interpersonal communication perspective and focuses on the parties engaged in the communication and the dynamics of information exchanged, often independent of the medium involved (e.g., Alba et al., 1997; Rafaeli & Sudweeks, 1997). The second perspective, human-message interactivity, most closely resembles studies of consumer reaction to traditional advertising and has been the main focus of advertising researchers (e.g., Ariely, 2000; Cho & Leckenby, 1999). The third dyad, human-machine interactivity, focuses on users' reactions to the technical aspects of a medium and is studied most by technology researchers whose goal is to design effective and user-friendly machines and system interfaces (e.g., Gonzalez & Kasper, 1997; Rogers, 1986).

A further distinction made in the inter-activity literature is whether interactivity is a structural characteristic of a medium/ message or a subjective experience perceived by interacting parties (Tremayne & Dunwoody, 2001). The structural perspective considers interactivity to be an innate attribute of a medium (e.g., the Internet) or a message/environment within that medium (e.g., a Web site). It is created through the design features of the medium/ environment (Fortin & Dholakia, 2005; Lohtia, Donthu, & Hershberger, 2003; Sicilia et al., 2005). The experiential perspective, in contrast, defines interactivity as it is perceived by the individuals engaged in an interaction (Liu, 2003; Liu & Shrum, 2009; McMillan & Hwang, 2002; Yadav & Varadarajan, 2005). It is a malleable experience that is affected by structural interactivity but also varies with individual and situational factors (McMillan, 2003). Both of these approaches have been studied in the advertising context.

EFFECTS OF INTERACTIVITY ON INFORMATION PROCESSING AND DECISION MAKING

Within the realm of cognitive processes, interactivity has been posited to affect consumers' cognitive involvement with and elaboration of advertising messages (Johnson et al., 2006; Liu & Shrum, 2002, 2009). The control dimension of interactivity has been most often associated with this cognitive component of ad processing. The central thesis is that an interactive message or medium increases consumers' involvement in the communication process and potentially shifts the focus of processing toward a more central route (Johnson et al., 2006; Sundar et al., 2003). The result of this process is more cognitive elaboration, better recall, and learning (Tremayne & Dunwoody, 2001). Supporting this view, Gonzalez and Kasper (1997) found that a more interactive system led to higher decision quality than a less interactive system. In another study, Sicilia et al. (2005) found that a more interactive Web site not only increases the amount of elaboration, but also leads to more favorable elaboration than a noninteractive Web site.

Interactivity is also associated with significant cognitive costs. Using the talk-aloud technique, Tremayne and Dunwoody (2001) found that user navigation of an interactive system led to more elaboration effort devoted to orientating oneself (i.e., where I am), which sometimes interfered with the rehearsal and elaboration of actual information presented by the system. The effect of this interference was confirmed in Ariely (2000), who found that the ability to control information presentation was beneficial to decision making when users' concurrent cognitive load was low but was

detrimental when cognitive load was high. This negative effect of interactivity may explain the nonlinear effect of interactivity found in previous research (Fortin & Dholakia, 2005; Sundar et al., 2003; see also Liu & Shrum, 2009). It may also explain why an interactive advertising representation led to less browsing time and lower purchase intention in Bezjian-Avery et al. (1998).

Given the double-edged effect of interactivity on cognitive processing, it is not surprising that elaboration variables (e.g., need for cognition [NFC]; Cacioppo & Petty, 1982) would moderate the effects of interactivity. However, two studies on this issue have yielded very different results. Whereas Sicilia et al. (2005) found a larger effect of interactivity on high- than low-NFC individuals, Fortin and Dholakia (2005) found the opposite to be true. This divergence in findings may be attributed to the different products that the two studies used: computers for Sicilia et al. (2005) and power surge protectors for Fortin and Dholakia (2005). Because computers are high-involvement purchases, both low-NFC and high-NFC consumers are likely already engaging in high elaboration, and high-NFC individuals may have been better able to process the large amount of information and at the same time control the information flow. The power surge protectors used by Fortin and Dholakia (2005), in contrast, represent a more moderate amount of involvement. As a result, interactivity may have led to a shift in processing focus among low-NFC individuals who would not have devoted much thinking into the issue.

INTERACTIVITY AND ATTITUDINAL OUTCOMES

Studies of interactivity effects on attitudinal outcomes can be classified into two general categories, depending on whether they focus on the structural or experiential aspect of interactivity. Studies of interactivity as a structural feature of an online ad (often in the form of a Web site) typically have used experimental methodology and either manipulated interactivity through features in experimental Web sites or used existing Web sites with varying degrees of interactivity (Coyle & Thorson, 2001; Sicilia et al., 2005). So far, this stream of research has yielded ambiguous and sometimes conflicting results. Although most studies confirmed a positive effect of interactivity on attitude (e.g., Fortin & Dholakia, 2005; Sicilia et al., 2005), quite a few studies also found no or even negative effects of interactivity on persuasive outcomes (e.g., Bezjian-Avery et al., 1998; Coyle & Thorson, 2001).

The literature reveals two potential explanations for these divergent findings. The first is that interactivity may have a curvilinear (rather than linear) effect on attitudes. The positive effect of interactivity either reaches a plateau at moderate levels (Fortin & Dholakia, 2005) or peaks at moderate levels and then turns negative as the level of interactivity continues to increase (Sundar et al., 2003). Therefore, the findings from past studies may simply have resided in different segments of this curve. Second, individual user preferences and experiences may have also contributed to the ambivalent results on interactivity effects. Sohn et al. (2007), for example, found a positive effect of interactivity on Web site attitude only when users expected the interactivity level of the Web site to be high. When users expected the interactivity level to be low, interactivity had a negative effect on attitude. Liu (2007) and Macias (2003) further suggest that the effect of interactivity may be contingent on how much consumers are ready to engage in interactive communication.

In contrast with research on structural interactivity, studies of experiential interactivity have consistently found positive effects on persuasive outcomes. The shortcoming of such research, however, is the possibility of common methods bias due to the use of self-reported measures.

Criticism of such research has even suggested that studying the effects of perceived interactivity is tautological and that researchers should examine structural interactivity instead (Sundar, 2004). More recent research, however, has started to synthesize the two types of interactivity studies by presenting experiential interactivity as a mediator between structural interactivity and persuasive outcomes (Lee, Lee, Kim, & Stout, 2004; Song & Zinkhan, 2008; Wu, 2005). These researchers argue that, although interactive mechanisms are provided to users under high-interactivity conditions, it is eventually the users' idiosyncratic use and perception of these interactive features that determine the outcome of an interaction.

FUTURE INTERACTIVITY RESEARCH

Although research on interactivity has been robust over recent years, much more work remains to be done to clarify some of the existing ambiguities. Thus far, research has focused mostly on *whether* interactivity leads to positive persuasive outcomes. Once we have a better grasp on the direction of interactivity effects, however, a much more important research question is *how* interactivity actually affects persuasion. In other words, what is the underlying process through which interactivity affects persuasion? Does interactivity affect persuasion through its impact on cognitive information processing, or is there a more affect-oriented or peripheral process that may also take place? The divergence in existing findings further suggests potential individual and situational factors that may moderate the effects of interactivity.

Existing research has paid limited attention to the actual mechanisms that are used to implement interactivity. The advertising literature, however, suggests that the executional elements of an ad, such as color (Meyers-Levy & Peracchio, 1995) and use of pictures (Miniard, Bhatla, Lord, Dickson, & Unnava, 1991), may have varying effects on persuasion depending on how they are implemented. It is reasonable to expect that interactive features that offer consumers higher control versus features that facilitate two-way communication may have differential effects on how consumers respond. Most studies thus far have focused on the control element of interactivity. More research is needed to better understand the implications of two-way communication features and to compare their effect with that of control.

As the Web moves toward the second generation, Internet technology has become more content oriented, and user-generated contents are playing an even more important role in the online media. However, because many interactivity-related studies were initiated during the early stages of the Internet, they have trailed behind the evolvement of technology and consumer behavior. For example, although interactivity has been conceptualized to reside among users (e.g., Alba et al., 1997), no research on virtual communities has explicitly incorporated the concept of interactivity, despite the central role of interaction in a virtual community. The need to adapt to fundamental changes in technology will prove challenging for interactivity researchers, given the speed of technology innovation in today's environment. On the one hand, this favors the development of fundamental and systematic theories that are independent of technology (Yadav & Varadarajan, 2005). On the other hand, certain technologies create such disruptive changes in the way people communicate that they cannot be totally ignored. Interactivity researchers should endeavor to develop an underlying theory while remaining open toward new developments in the technology field and in the ways consumers utilize technologies.

◆ Psycholinguistic Studies of Advertising and Brand Names

A third area of advertising research that has received much attention in recent years is the application of psycholinguistic theory to the study of advertising and other marketing communication tools. *Psycholinguistics* refers to the psychology of language, and research in this area investigates the mechanisms underlying language acquisition, comprehension, and use. A comprehensive review of all the research that utilizes a psycholinguistic approach is beyond the scope of this chapter, but a brief overview of recent advances in three areas will be provided: (a) the effects of syntactic complexity, in conjunction with other variables, on the persuasiveness and memorability of advertising; (b) dual-language processing of advertising among bilingual consumers; and (c) evidence for phonetic symbolism in brand names across diverse languages.

SYNTACTIC COMPLEXITY

For many years, advertising copywriters have followed the adage of KISS ("keep it simple, stupid"), but evidence has been mounting that higher levels of complexity in advertising might actually enhance memory for and attitudes toward advertising (Bradley & Meeds, 2002; Chamblee, Gilmore, Thomas, & Soldow, 1993; Lowrey, 1998; Macklin, Bruvold, & Shea, 1985). At the same time, however, other studies have reported contradictory results (e.g., Chebat, Gelinas-Chebat, Hombourger, & Woodside, 2003; Meeds & Bradley, 2007). In an effort to reconcile these conflicting findings, a *complexity continuum* has been proposed (Lowrey, 2008). The complexity continuum demonstrates how a particular passage of text can be initially placed on the continuum in terms of textual factors (primarily consisting of syntax and vocabulary), but

Complexity continuum

then shift due to extratextual factors, including advertising medium and individual difference variables (e.g., age, education, motivation). This conceptualization provides a mechanism for reconciling contradictory results in past research and shows that they are in fact complementary to one another.

To illustrate, let's say that an ad is written at a moderate syntactic complexity level. If the ad is delivered through a print medium to young, well-educated individuals who happen to be highly motivated to process the information, the ad shifts to the easier end of the complexity continuum. In contrast, if that same ad is delivered through a broadcast medium to older, less educated individuals who are not as motivated to process, the ad shifts to the more complex end of the complexity continuum. It is the interaction between the syntactic complexity, the individual, and the medium of delivery that ultimately determines memory and persuasion outcomes.

In sum, the important contribution of this framework is the recognition that complexity effects occur in the individual during the processing of advertising messages. Thus, although the objective complexity of a message is an important determinant of advertising response, it interacts with the medium and individual difference variables to determine final outcomes.

DUAL-LANGUAGE PROCESSING

Given the increasingly global business environment, there has been a recent surge in research on bilingual processing of advertising (e.g., Briley, Morris, & Simonson, 2005; Luna & Peracchio, 2001; Tavassoli & Lee, 2003). Topics investigated have included alphabetic versus logographic language processing, frame switching (the moving back and forth by bilinguals between different cultural frames), and code switching (the mixing of languages in the same utterance, as in "Oh, well, c'est la vie!"), just to name a few (for an in-depth

analysis of this literature, see Carroll, Luna, & Peracchio, 2007). For example, most past advertising research using a psycholinguistic framework has been conducted in languages that are processed verbally, using a part of short-term memory known as the phonological loop. In contrast, logographic languages (e.g., Mandarin) are processed visually, with no need to use the phonological loop (Schmitt, Pan, & Tavassoli, 1994). This is particularly important for researchers interested in phonetic symbolism, which will be discussed in more detail in the following paragraphs.

Existing findings are mixed, and much more research needs to be done to more fully understand bilingual advertising processing. The fact of the matter is that the majority of the world speaks more than one language, yet until recently, there has been a lack of research addressing this situation. Indeed, it can be quite difficult to conduct multilanguage studies, in terms of both stimulus production and data collection, but it is imperative that advertising research continue to tackle this important area.

PHONETIC SYMBOLISM

The existence of phonetic symbolism (i.e., the ability of the *sound* of a word alone to convey meaning, apart from the denotative aspects of the word) has been debated since 400 BC (Plato, 1892), and the evidence in favor of phonetic symbolism, particularly in the arena of marketing communications, has been mounting in recent years (Klink, 2000, 2003; Lowrey & Shrum, 2007; Yorkston & Menon, 2004), at least with respect to vowel sounds.

Vowels can be pronounced more toward the front of the mouth (e.g., the "ih" sound in mill) or more toward the back of the mouth (e.g., the "ah" sound in mall). In basic psycholinguistic research, both Sapir (1929) and Newman (1933) demonstrated that front vowel sounds tend to be associated with attributes such as smallness, lightness, quickness, and sharpness. In contrast, back vowel sounds tend to be associated with the opposite attributes of largeness, heaviness, slowness, and dullness. Although there are exceptions to this pattern of associations (e.g., big vs. small), the general pattern has been demonstrated across a wide variety of the world's languages (Brown, 1958; Ultan, 1978; for a review, see Shrum & Lowrey, 2007).

Recent research has shown that these effects impact the preference for brand names for specific products. Klink (2003) demonstrated that sound symbolism affected perceptions of brand attributes, which in turn impacted brand liking and perceptions of taste. Yorkston and Menon (2004) found that words with back vowel sounds—which through phonetic symbolism connote concepts such as creaminess and smoothness—were preferred as brand names for an ice cream over words with front vowel sounds. Extending these findings, Lowrey and Shrum (2007) demonstrated that this preference differs as a function of product category and its related attributes. Using nonsense words (e.g., tiddip, toddip), they showed that words with front vowel sounds—which are associated with concepts such as small, fast, quick, sharp—were preferred over words with back vowel sounds when the product category was a small convertible or a knife. However, just the opposite was the case when the product category was an SUV or hammer. In those cases, the very same words with back vowel sounds—which convey the impression of an object as large, dull, or slow—were preferred over the words with front vowel sounds. A second study that held product category constant (e.g., beer) but varied the primed attributes (name preferred for a "cool, clean, crisp-tasting beer" versus a "smooth, mellow, rich-tasting beer") produced similar results.

One of the shortcomings in the research we have described is that a vast majority of the studies have been conducted only in English, and replications in other languages would be a significant contribution. Recent research has begun to investigate whether the effects obtained also hold for languages such as French, Spanish, and Mandarin (Shrum, Lowrey, Luna, & Lerman, 2009). This research investigates potential boundary conditions such as language proficiency and processing constraints (such as articulatory suppression, which attempts to diminish use of the phonological loop). The findings suggest that phonetic symbolism is observed across languages, and is for the most part unaffected by language proficiency. However, when the transfer of phonetic information into short-term memory stores is inhibited, phonetic symbolism effects are eliminated, suggesting that phonetic symbolism effects are truly acoustic ones and not the result of some other variable.

CONCLUSION

It is clear that more research needs to be conducted in all three of these areas, but it is worth noting that findings in one of these areas have important implications for the other two. Additional factors to add to the complexity continuum may include language proficiency, language processing style, and the fit between the brand name and product attributes. The study of bilingual ad processing should be greatly impacted by implications from the complexity research as well as phonetic symbolism research that looks at additional languages. Clearly, researchers interested in phonetic symbolism have a number of potential boundary conditions to investigate ranging from language proficiency issues to processing burdens such as syntactic complexity.

◆ Conclusion

Although only a subset of emerging issues in advertising research, the general topics of product placement, interactivity, and psycholinguistics represent key areas of interest. These areas are notable because they are a departure from the mainstream topics of the last 50 years. Mainstream topics in advertising research tended to center on executional dimensions of advertising (e.g., use of humor, fear, and sympathy appeals; image vs. informational appeals; celebrity endorsers; frequency of exposure), memory issues (e.g., recall and recognition), and persuasion issues (e.g., belief and attitude change). These topics are of course still well represented in current advertising research. However, as technology has changed and consumers have the ability to interact with a medium and marketers have the ability to insert promotions digitally into a program, new areas of research necessarily are opened. With respect to persuasion, the field of psycholinguistics provides a new way of looking at the persuasiveness of communications, and shows that it is not just the denotative meaning of words we use in advertising that persuades, but that the symbolic aspects of the words we use (e.g., phonetic symbolism) and the way we use them (e.g., dual-language ads) have persuasive impact as well. As new technologies are developed, and more is learned about human cognitive processing, still newer and more exciting areas of research will surely develop.

◆ References

Alba, J., Lynch, J., Weitz, B., Janiszewski, C., Lutz, R., Sawyer, A., et al. (1997). Interactive home shopping: Consumer, retailer, and manufacturer incentives to participate in electronic marketplaces. *Journal of Marketing, 61*(3), 38–53.

Ariely, D. (2000). Controlling the information flow: Effects on consumers' decision making and preference. *Journal of Consumer Research, 27,* 233–248.

Auty, S., & Lewis, C. (2004). The "delicious paradox": Preconscious processing of product placements by children. In L. J. Shrum (Ed.), *The psychology of entertainment media: Blurring the lines between entertainment and persuasion* (pp. 117–133). Mahwah, NJ: Erlbaum.

Balasubramanian, S. K. (1994). Beyond advertising and publicity: Hybrid messages and public policy issues. *Journal of Advertising, 23*(4), 29–46.

Balasubramanian, S. K., Karrh, J. A., & Patwardhan, H. (2006). Audience response to product placements. *Journal of Advertising, 35*(3), 115–141.

Bezjian-Avery, A., Calder, B., & Iacobucci, D. (1998). New media interactive advertising vs. traditional advertising. *Journal of Advertising Research, 38*(4), 23–32.

Bhatnagar, N., Aksoy, L., & Malkoc, S. A. (2004). Embedding brands within media content: The impact of message, media, and consumer characteristics on placement efficacy. In L. J. Shrum (Ed.), *The psychology of entertainment media: Blurring the lines between entertainment and persuasion* (pp. 99–116). Mahwah, NJ: Erlbaum.

Bradley, S. D., & Meeds, R. (2002). Surface-structure transformations and advertising slogans: The case for moderate syntactic complexity. *Psychology & Marketing, 19,* 595–619.

Brennan, I., Dubas, K. M., & Babin, L. A. (1999). The influence of product-placement type and exposure time on product-placement recognition. *International Journal of Advertising, 18,* 323–337.

Briley, D. A., Morris, M. W., & Simonson, I. (2005). Biculturals and shifting strategies: The role of language and audiences in eliciting cultural styles of decision making. *Journal of Consumer Psychology, 15,* 351–362.

Brown, R. (1958). *Words and things.* New York: Free Press.

Cacioppo, J. T., & Petty, R. E. (1982). The need for cognition. *Journal of Personality and Social Psychology, 42,* 116–131.

Carroll, R., Luna, D., & Peracchio, L. A. (2007). Dual language processing of marketing communications. In T. M. Lowrey (Ed.), *Psycholinguistic phenomena in marketing communications* (pp. 221–246). Mahwah, NJ: Erlbaum.

Chamblee, R., Gilmore, R., Thomas, G., & Soldow, G. (1993). When copy complexity can help ad readership. *Journal of Advertising Research, 33*(2), 23–28.

Chebat, J.-C., Gelinas-Chebat, C., Hombourger, S., & Woodside, A. G. (2003). Testing consumers' motivation and linguistic ability as moderators of advertising readability. *Psychology & Marketing, 20,* 599–624.

Cho, C., & Leckenby, J. D. (1999). Interactivity as a measure of advertising effectiveness: Antecedents and consequences of interactivity in Web advertising. In M. S. Roberts (Ed.), *Proceedings of the 1999 conference of the American Academy of Advertising* (pp. 162–179). Gainesville: University of Florida.

Coyle, J. R., & Thorson, E. (2001). The effects of progressive levels of interactivity and vividness in Web marketing sites. *Journal of Advertising, 30*(3), 65–77.

Csikszentmihalyi, M. (1990). *Flow: The psychology of optimal experience.* New York: Harper & Row.

d'Astous, A., & Chartier, F. (2000). A study of factors affecting consumer evaluations and memory of product placements in movies. *Journal of Current Issues & Research in Advertising, 22*(2), 31–40.

Fortin, D. R., & Dholakia, R. R. (2005). Interactivity and vividness effects on social presence and involvement with a Web-based advertisement. *Journal of Business Research, 58,* 387–396.

Friestad, J., & Wright, P. (1994). The persuasion knowledge model: How people cope with persuasion attempts. *Journal of Consumer Research, 22,* 62–74.

Ghose, S., & Dou, W. (1998). Interactivity functions and their impacts on the appeal of Internet presence sites. *Journal of Advertising Research, 38*(3), 29–43.

Gonzalez, C., & Kasper, G. M. (1997). Animation in user interfaces designed for decision support systems: The effects of image abstraction, transition, and interactivity on decision quality. *Decision Sciences, 28,* 793–823.

Green, M. C., & Brock, T. C. (2000). The role of transportation in the persuasiveness of public narratives. *Journal of Personality and Social Psychology, 79,* 401–421.

Green, M. C., Garst, J., & Brock, T. C. (2004). The power of fiction: Determinants and boundaries. In L. J. Shrum (Ed.), *The psychology of entertainment media: Blurring the lines between entertainment and persuasion* (pp. 161–176). Mahwah, NJ: Erlbaum.

Hoffman, D. L., & Novak, T. P. (1996). Marketing in hypermedia computer-mediated environments: Conceptual foundations. *Journal of Marketing, 60*(3), 50–68.

Johnson, G. J., Bruner, G. C., & Kumar, A. (2006). Interactivity and its facets revisited. *Journal of Advertising, 35*(4), 35–52.

Klink, R. R. (2000). Creating brand names with meaning: The use of sound symbolism. *Marketing Letters, 11,* 5–20.

Klink, R. R. (2003). Creating meaningful brands: The relationship between brand name and brand mark. *Marketing Letters, 14,* 143–157.

Ko, H., Cho, C.-H., & Roberts, M. S. (2005). Internet uses and gratifications. *Journal of Advertising, 34*(2), 57–70.

Law, S., & Braun, K. A. (2000). I'll have what she's having: Gauging the impact of product placements on viewers. *Psychology & Marketing, 17,* 1059–1075.

Law, S., & Braun-LaTour, K. A. (2004). Product placements: How to measure their impact. In L. J. Shrum (Ed.), *The psychology of entertainment media: Blurring the lines between entertainment and persuasion* (pp. 63–78). Mahwah, NJ: Erlbaum.

Lee, S.-J., Lee, W.-N., Kim, H., & Stout, P. A. (2004). A comparison of objective characteristics and user perception of Web sites. *Journal of Interactive Advertising, 4*(2). Retrieved April 21, 2009, from http://www.jiad.org/article50

Liu, Y. (2003). Developing a scale to measure the interactivity of Web sites. *Journal of Advertising Research, 43,* 207–216.

Liu, Y. (2007). Online interaction readiness: Conceptualization and measurement. *Journal of Customer Behaviour, 6,* 283–299.

Liu, Y., & Shrum, L. J. (2002). What is interactivity and is it always such a good thing? Implications of definition, person, and situation for the influence of interactivity on advertising effectiveness. *Journal of Advertising, 31*(4), 53–64.

Liu, Y., & Shrum, L. J. (2009). A dual-process model of interactivity effects. *Journal of Advertising, 38*(2), 53–68.

Lohtia, R., Donthu, N., & Hershberger, E. K. (2003). The impact of content and design elements on banner advertising click-through rates. *Journal of Advertising Research, 43*, 410–418.

Lowrey, T. M. (1998). The effects of syntactic complexity on advertising persuasiveness. *Journal of Consumer Psychology, 7*, 187–206.

Lowrey, T. M. (2008). The case for a complexity continuum. In E. F. McQuarrie & B. J. Phillips (Eds.), *Go figure: New directions in advertising rhetoric* (pp. 159–177). Armonk, NY: M. E. Sharpe.

Lowrey, T. M., & Shrum, L. J. (2007). Phonetic symbolism and brand name preference. *Journal of Consumer Research, 34*, 406–414.

Lowrey, T. M., Shrum, L. J., & McCarty, J. A. (2005). The future of television advertising. In A. J. Kimmel (Ed.), *Marketing communication: Emerging trends and developments* (pp. 113–132). New York: Oxford University Press.

Luna, D., & Peracchio, L. A. (2001). Moderators of language effects in advertising to bilinguals: A psycholinguistics approach. *Journal of Consumer Research, 28*, 284–295.

Macias, W. (2003). A beginning look at the effects of interactivity, product involvement and Web experience on comprehension: Brand Web sites as interactive advertising. *Journal of Current Issues & Research in Advertising, 25*(2), 31–44.

Macklin, M. C., Bruvold, N. T., & Shea, C. L. (1985). Is it always as simple as "Keep it simple!"? *Journal of Advertising, 14*(4), 28–35.

McCarty, J. A. (2004). Product placement: The nature of the practice and potential avenues of inquiry. In L. J. Shrum (Ed.), *The psychology of entertainment media: Blurring the lines between entertainment and persuasion* (pp. 45–61). Mahwah, NJ: Erlbaum.

McMillan, S. J. (2003). Effects of structural and perceptual factors on attitudes toward the Website. *Journal of Advertising Research, 43*, 400–409.

McMillan, S. J., & Hwang, J.-S. (2002). Measurement of perceived interactivity: An exploration of communication, user control, and time in shaping perceptions of interactivity. *Journal of Advertising, 31*(3), 41–54.

Meeds, R., & Bradley, S. D. (2007). The role of the sentence and its importance in marketing communications. In T. M. Lowrey (Ed.), *Psycholinguistic phenomena in marketing communications* (pp. 103–118). Mahwah, NJ: Erlbaum.

Meyers-Levy, J., & Peracchio, L. A. (1995). Understanding the effects of color: How the correspondence between available and required resources affects attitudes. *Journal of Consumer Research, 22*, 121–138.

Miniard, P. W., Bhatla, S., Lord, K. R., Dickson, P. R., & Unnava, H. R. (1991). Picture-based persuasion processes and the moderating role of involvement. *Journal of Consumer Research, 18*, 92–107.

Newman, S. S. (1933). Further experiments in phonetic symbolism. *American Journal of Psychology, 45*, 53–75.

Petty, R. E., Briñol, P., & Priester, J. R. (2009). Mass media attitude change: Implications of the elaboration likelihood model of persuasion. In J. Bryant & M. B. Oliver (Eds.), *Media effects: Advances in theory and research* (3rd ed., pp. 125–164). New York: Routledge.

Plato. (1892). Cratylus. In B. Jowett (Ed.), *The dialogues of Plato* (Vol. 1, pp. 253–289). Oxford: Clarendon.

Rafaeli, S., & Sudweeks, F. (1997). Networked interactivity. *Journal of Computer-Mediated Communication, 2*(4). Retrieved April 21, 2009, from http://jcmc.indiana.edu/vol2/issue4/rafaeli.sudweeks.html

Rogers, E. M. (1986). *Communication technology: The new media in society.* New York: Free Press.

Russell, C. A. (2002). Investigating the effectiveness of product placements in television shows: The role of modality and plot connection congruence on brand name memory and attitude. *Journal of Consumer Research, 29,* 306–318.

Sapir, E. (1929). A study in phonetic symbolism. *Journal of Experimental Psychology, 12,* 225–239.

Schmitt, B. H., Pan, Y., & Tavassoli, N. T. (1994). Language and consumer memory: The impact of linguistic differences between Chinese and English. *Journal of Consumer Research, 21,* 419–431.

Shrum, L. J., & Lowrey, T. M. (2007). Sounds convey meaning: The implications of phonetic symbolism for brand name construction. In T. M. Lowrey (Ed.), *Psycholinguistic phenomena in marketing communications* (pp. 39–58). Mahwah, NJ: Erlbaum.

Shrum, L. J., Lowrey, T. M., Luna, D., & Lerman, D. *(2009). Processes and generalizations for phonetic symbolism effects on brand name preference.* Manuscript submitted for publication.

Sicilia, M., Ruiz, S., & Munuera, J. L. (2005). Effects of interactivity in a Web site: The moderating effects of need for cognition. *Journal of Advertising, 34*(3), 31–45.

Sohn, D., Ci, C., & Lee, B.-K. (2007). The moderating effects of expectation on the patterns of the interactivity-attitude relationship. *Journal of Advertising, 36*(3), 109–119.

Song, J. H., & Zinkhan, G. M. (2008). Determinants of perceived Web site interactivity. *Journal of Marketing, 72*(2), 99–113.

Steuer, J. (1992). Defining virtual reality: Dimensions determining telepresence. *Journal of Communication, 42*(4), 73–93.

Stewart, D. W., & Pavlou, P. A. (2009). The effects of media on marketing communications. In J. Bryant & M. B. Oliver (Eds.), *Media effects: Advances in theory and research* (3rd ed., pp. 362–401). New York: Routledge.

Stromer-Galley, J. (2004). Interactivity-as-product and interactivity-as-process. *Information Society, 20,* 391–394.

Sundar, S. S. (2004). Theorizing interactivity's effects. *Information Society, 20,* 385–389.

Sundar, S. S., Kalyanaraman, S., & Brown, J. (2003). Explicating Web site interactivity: Impression formation effects in political campaign sites. *Communication Research, 30,* 30–59.

Tavassoli, N. T., & Lee, Y. H. (2003). The differential interaction of auditory and visual advertising elements with Chinese and English. *Journal of Marketing Research, 40,* 468–480.

Tremayne, M., & Dunwoody, S. (2001). Interactivity, information processing, and learning on the World Wide Web. *Science Communication, 23,* 111–134.

Ultan, R. (1978). Size-sound symbolism. In J. H. Greenberg, C. A. Ferguson, & E. A. Moravcsik (Eds.), *Universals of human language: Vol. 2. Phonology* (pp. 525–568). Stanford, CA: Stanford University Press.

Wu, G. (2005). The mediating role of perceived interactivity in the effect of actual interactivity on attitude toward the Website. *Journal of Interactive Advertising, 5*(2), 45–60.

Yadav, M., & Varadarajan, R. (2005). Interactivity in the electronic marketplace: An exposition of the concept and implications for research. *Journal of the Academy of Marketing Science, 33,* 585–603.

Yang, M., Roskos-Ewoldsen, B., & Roskos-Ewoldsen, D. R. (2004). Mental models for brand placements. In L. J. Shrum (Ed.), *The psychology of entertainment media: Blurring the lines between entertainment and persuasion* (pp. 45–61). Mahwah, NJ: Erlbaum.

Yang, M., Roskos-Ewoldsen, D. R., Dinu, L., & Arpan, L. M. (2006). The effectiveness of "in-game" advertising. *Journal of Advertising, 35*(4), 143–152.

Yorkston, E. A., & Menon, G. (2004). A sound idea: Phonetic effects of brand names on consumer judgments. *Journal of Consumer Research, 31,* 43–51.

21

MEDIA EFFECTS AND POPULATION HEALTH

◆ K. Viswanath, Sherrie Flynt Wallington, and Kelly D. Blake

◆ *Overview*

For good or ill, media have been ascribed a great deal of power in influencing both individual health and that of the larger population by shaping some of the critical antecedents to health behaviors, including health cognitions and beliefs at the individual level and the public agenda and social groups at the institutional and societal levels (Viswanath, Ramanadhan, & Kontos, 2007). The belief in the media's power to influence individual and population health stems in part from the immense amount of time people of different age-groups spend with the media. American adults and teens are estimated to spend approximately 3,518 hours per year consuming media (65 days of TV, 41 days of radio, a little over a week on the Internet, a week with daily newspapers, and a week with recorded music; U.S. Census Bureau, 2007). This

Authors' Note: This research has been supported by funding from the National Institutes of Health to the authors (U01 CA 114644-03S1; 5R25CA057711-14; 5R01CA128994) and funding by the Dana-Farber Harvard Cancer Center to Dr. Viswanath.

◆ 313

substantial exposure to mass media makes it a potentially leading source of health-related information (Viswanath, 2006).

In fact, media serve several functions in the realm of health: informational (awareness and knowledge), instrumental (enabling action), communal (bringing people together, generating social capital), and social control (legitimizing or delegitimizing certain health behaviors; Viswanath, 2006). Given media's wide-ranging influence across multiple levels of society, this chapter will provide a selective review of media's influence on both individual and population health. We start with a brief historical overview of health and media, followed by a review of some popular individual-level theories and approaches. Next, we discuss the impact of media on health at the macrosocial level, including our recent work on health and communication inequalities. These will be followed by a discussion of campaign exemplars, methodological challenges and opportunities, and the role of new media technologies in health.

◆ Health and Media: A Historical Context

Mass media are now a staple of public health interventions and will undoubtedly continue to be influential in the 21st century. Our conventional definitions of mass media, however, are under scrutiny because of the revolution in communication technologies that has resulted in a variety of information delivery systems, the fragmentation of mass audiences, and the horizontal and vertical integration of communication and telecommunication industries. Thus, we take an expansive view of the mass media, defining them as organizations that are structured to create or gather, generate, and disseminate news, information, and entertainment through different channels, such as print, radio, television, the Internet, and, more recently, new technologies like personal digital assistants and smart phones (Viswanath et al., 2007).

The use of mass media for health promotion and disease prevention can be traced to early public health campaigns promoting hygiene and immunization in the 18th and 19th centuries (Paisley, 1989), to persuasion studies during and after World War II (Hovland, Lumsdaine, & Sheffield, 1949; Lazarsfeld, Berelson, & Gaudet, 1948), and through to the development of communication campaigns in the 1970s (Hornik, 1988). Early campaign literature reflected pessimism about the effectiveness of such campaigns (Hyman & Sheatsley, 1947; Lazarsfeld et al., 1948). However, later examinations (Becker, McCombs, & McLeod, 1975; Chaffee & Hochheimer, 1985) shifted in this sentiment as a wider body of communication research demonstrated stronger effects of the media as well as a more sophisticated understanding of the conditions under which such effects may or may not occur. Although research has documented the long history of media use in strategic health efforts, theoretical and methodological challenges also have clearly been identified, including inadequate message exposure, meager funding, poor conceptualization, and inappropriate research design, among others (Hornik, 2002; Salmon & Atkin, 2003).

A substantial shift in thinking about the media's role in health occurred in the 1970s and 1980s in light of major community-based interventions and campaigns, especially the cardiovascular disease prevention campaigns in Minnesota; Stanford, California; Pawtucket, Rhode Island; and North Karelia, Finland (Blackburn, 1983; Farquhar et al., 1985; Finnegan & Viswanath, 2002). Public health professionals began to look to the field of health promotion and disease prevention, including health communication, and question whether health communication programs, particularly with a mass media presence, could be used to advance public health goals, given the clear association between lifestyle and chronic disease outcomes (Institute of Medicine, 2002; U.S. Department of Health & Human Services [HHS], 2000).

The emergence of mass media use in support of public health has also led to more sophisticated lines of research that examine varying consequences of media exposure—both intended and unintended—based on both incidental exposure to and purposive use of media at both individual and institutional levels (Bryant & Zillmann, 1994; Hornik, 2002; Randolph & Viswanath, 2004). Here it is important to note that despite the media's utility in promoting health messages, the media can have unintended effects by widening inequalities (Tichenor, Donohue, & Olien, 1970; Viswanath, 2006) and perpetuating a plethora of individual and public health concerns, including unsafe sexual behaviors among adolescents and young adults; violent and aggressive behavior; unhealthy diet and physical activity; alcohol consumption; and tobacco use, including smoking initiation among adolescents (National Cancer Institute, 2008; see also Bushman, Huesmann, & Whitaker, Chapter 24, this volume; Cho & Salmon, 2007; Harrison, Chapter 26, this volume). Substantial attention has also been given to the unintended consequences of mass media messages and campaigns specifically, whereby significant adverse associations have been documented regarding nutrition beliefs (Clark & Tiggemann, 2008) and smoking initiation (Charlesworth & Glantz, 2005).

Regarding intentional effects, the intended goals of public health media campaigns are to increase public knowledge on a particular topic; promote some specific action, such as wearing a bicycle helmet or fastening a seatbelt; or stop some unhealthy behavior, such as smoking (Randolph & Viswanath, 2004). Substantial theory and research on developing effective media messages and interventions to achieve these goals exist in the literature as discussed in the following section.

♦ Individual-Level Theoretical Frameworks and Approaches

Students of health behavior have paid careful attention to important antecedents to health behaviors. In fact, there is an arsenal of individual-level theories and approaches from psychology and communication that inform how psychosocial determinants, such as health cognitions; emotions (e.g., fear); and the beliefs, motivations, and perceptions of others influence individual health behaviors. Frameworks, such as social cognitive theory, the theory of reasoned action, the health belief model, the extended parallel process model, and the transtheoretical model, are useful in understanding why people do what they do (Glanz, Rimer, & Viswanath, 2008). Other approaches, such as social marketing, message tailoring, and entertainment education, provide insight and strategies for the design of messages that are suitable for addressing different problems and reaching particular groups.

INDIVIDUAL-LEVEL THEORIES: WHY PEOPLE DO WHAT THEY DO

Social cognitive theory (SCT), one of the more frequently used theoretical frameworks in health interventions, proposes that human behavior is a dynamic product of three sets of factors: personal, behavioral, and environmental (Bandura, 1994). SCT takes an "agentic" perspective, arguing that even though environment influences behavior, human beings, with their capacity for self-reflection, self-regulation, and goal setting, can also alter their environment, a process characterized as "reciprocal determinism." A key characteristic of SCT is the focus on the human capacity for observational learning and behavioral modeling with media as an important source of learning (see Pajares, Prestin, Chen, & Nabi, Chapter 19, this volume).

SCT is a complex model, and the full model is rarely tested, but its most notable contribution is the construct of *self-efficacy,* or the belief that one can perform a recommended or desired action. Self-efficacy is believed to be a key factor underlying behavioral enactment, and thus has been widely used in media studies of health (Glanz et al., 2008). For example, recently Peng (2008) used SCT to explore a new concept—mediated enactive experience—to understand the effects of game playing on self-efficacy in the context of a health promotion role-playing game. Results demonstrated that a mediated enactive experience afforded by game playing was more effective than a mediated observational experience provided by game watching in influencing self-efficacy. Other SCT and media/health applications have explored eating behaviors (Storey, Neumark-Sztainer, & French, 2002), smoking, drinking, and drug use (Stern, 2005).

Another theory that has been frequently used to guide the development of several media and health interventions is the health belief model (HBM; Rosenstock, 1974), which suggests that health prevention behavior is influenced by the individual's perceptions of the threat posed by a health problem (e.g., susceptibility and severity), the benefits of avoiding the threat, and the factors influencing the decision to act (e.g., barriers, cues to action, and self-efficacy). For example, Paskett et al. (1999) implemented the HBM as part of an overall strategy to design a range of messages to increase breast and cervical cancer screening among low-income women age 40 and older. The resulting messages led to an increase in regular use of mammography and an improvement in screening rates in the intervention city. HBM studies have focused on other health topics as well, including HIV/AIDS (Tenkorang, Rajulton, & Maticka-Tyndale, 2009) and vaccinations (Larson, Bergman, Heidrich, Alvin, & Schneeweiss, 1982).

The theory of reasoned action (TRA); its later variant, the theory of planned behavior; and the most recent iteration, the integrated model of behavior change, seek to understand the relationship between attitudes and behavior, as well as to provide a methodology for content development of health messages (Ajzen & Fishbein, 1980; Fishbein & Ajzen, 1981; Fishbein & Cappella, 2006; Montaño & Kasprzyk, 2008). According to these theories, a crucial antecedent to behavior change is the intention to perform that behavior. Intention, in turn, is influenced by attitudes toward the behavior, normative beliefs about the behavior, and self-efficacy. These antecedents to behavioral intention are, in turn, influenced by underlying beliefs: attitude beliefs about the consequences of performing a certain behavior and the evaluation of those consequences. Numerous studies have documented the associations among these variables, including Booth-Butterfield and Reger (2004), who, in their "1% or less" milk campaign targeting high-fat (whole and 2%) milk users, used TRA constructs in surveys conducted immediately before and after a 6-week mass media campaign. Findings revealed significant and predicted changes in participants' behavioral beliefs, attitudes, and intentions, though not subjective norms. TRA has been applied to numerous health contexts, including violence prevention (Meyer, Roberto, Boster, & Roberto, 2004) and parenting and drug prevention behaviors (Stephenson, Quick, Atkinson, & Tschida, 2005).

Compared with the previous models, the extended parallel process model (EPPM; Witte, 1992) focuses more on affect, proposing that health risk messages initiate two cognitive appraisals: threat and efficacy. The stronger a threat is perceived to be, the greater the aroused fear. People then appraise the efficacy of the recommended response. Witte argues that the combination of the levels of perceived threat and efficacy will determine whether adaptive or maladaptive health behavior occurs. Although meta-analyses have failed to support the predicted interaction between threat and efficacy (e.g., Witte & Allen,

2000), the EPPM represents the latest model in a long-standing tradition of fear appeal research that supports the effectiveness of fear on promoting health outcomes (see Nabi, Chapter 14, this volume).

Finally, the transtheoretical model (TTM; Prochaska & DiClemente, 1983) is a widely applied framework that focuses on targeting particular groups at their particular stage in the behavior change process. TTM characterizes change as a process involving progress through six stages (Prochaska, Redding, & Evers, 2002): (1) *precontemplation*—the individual is unaware of the problem or has not thought seriously about change; (2) *contemplation*—the individual is seriously thinking about a change (in the near future); (3) *preparation*—the individual is planning to take action and is making final adjustments before changing behavior; (4) *action*—the individual implements some specific action plan to overtly modify behavior and surroundings; (5) *maintenance*—the individual continues with desirable actions (repeating the periodic recommended steps while struggling to prevent lapses and relapse); and (6) *termination*—the individual has zero temptation and full ability to resist relapse. TTM studies evolved from research on smoking cessation (Prochaska, DiClemente, Velicer, & Rossi, 1993) to include a range of hard-to-change health behaviors like alcohol addiction (Carbonari & DiClemente, 2000) and regular exercise (Sarkin, Johnson, Prochaska, & Prochaska, 2001), and research generally suggests that the targeted message approach recommended by the TTM is more successful than more general message distribution strategies.

DESIGNING MESSAGES FOR INDIVIDUALS AND GROUPS

Although mass media campaigns are successful at targeting broad groups of audiences segmented on their demographic or psychological characteristics, another approach tailors interventions and information to individuals' situations. According to Kreuter, Lezin, Kreuter, and Green (1998), tailoring involves any combination of information and behavior change strategies intended to reach one specific person based on characteristics that are unique to that person, related to the outcome of interest, and derived from individual assessment. For example, Strecher et al. (1994) conducted sophisticated computer-based tailoring of messages targeting individual adult cigarette smokers from a cohort of family practice patients. Results suggested that tailored health letters were more effective than generic letters among moderate-to-light smokers 4 and 6 months after exposure. Tailoring communication programs have been used successfully in other smoking cessation studies (Strecher et al., 1994) as well as with fruit and vegetable interventions (Resnicow et al., 2008). The development and widespread adoption of technologies, such as cell phones, the Internet, and personal digital assistants (PDAs), have made this intervention approach more feasible then it may have been previously.

Another approach to developing more targeted messages is social marketing, which uses a variety of communication methods, including mass media campaigns, to increase awareness of various health risks to elicit desired behavior change (Storey, Saffitz, & Rimon, 2008). Kotler and Roberto (1989) define social marketing as a program-planning process that promotes the voluntary behavior of target audiences by offering benefits they want, reducing barriers they are concerned about, and using persuasion to motivate their participation in program activity. Social marketers further apply marketing's "four Ps": product (behavior the target audience must change), price (perceived physical, social, and psychological costs of suggested behavioral change), promotion (how the product or behavior can be represented or packaged), and place (availability of information or products related to recommended behavioral change).

Rimal and Creel (2008) adopted a social marketing perspective to analyze the various components of a Radio Diaries program designed to reduce stigma surrounding HIV/AIDS in Malawi in terms of three of the four Ps: product (stigma reduction), place (radio), and promotion (the program itself). Findings revealed that those with less education and knowledge were more likely to believe that persons living with HIV should be isolated from others. Although exposure to the Radio Diaries program did not directly reduce stigma, a significant interaction suggested that those with high levels of efficacy were influenced by different degrees of program exposure. Social marketing-based studies have focused on a range of health issues, including cardiovascular disease (Rocella, 2002) and binge drinking (Brower, Ceglarek, & Crowley, 2001).

Finally, another approach to structuring and delivering health intervention messages is entertainment education (EE), also referred to as *infotainment* (Kaiser Family Foundation, 2004a). EE is a way of informing the public about a social issue or concern by incorporating an educational message into popular entertainment content in order to raise awareness, increase knowledge, create favorable attitudes, and, ultimately, motivate people to take socially responsible action in their own lives (Singhal & Rogers, 1999) through stories with a persuasive twist (Slater & Rouner, 2002). For example, one recent EE effort involved embedding a health storyline in the top-rated program *Grey's Anatomy* to promote the progress that has been made around HIV-positive mothers and transmission during pregnancy (Kaiser Family Foundation, 2008). The study revealed that the audience's awareness of this information increased, and further, that viewers indicated that they had tried to find more information about a health issue or had spoken with a doctor or other health care professional because of something they saw on the show. EE strategies have been applied in a variety of ways and have

introduced a number of social and health issues in entertainment programming, including substance abuse, immunization, teenage pregnancy, HIV/AIDS, cancer, and other diseases (Singhal & Rogers, 2004).

These theories and approaches offer serviceable frameworks that can be used during the various stages of application of media (i.e., planning, implementing, and evaluating) to promote health behavior change or deter unhealthy lifestyles. They can be used to guide the search for why individuals are or are not following public health and medical advice, to pinpoint what practitioners need to know before developing and organizing a media intervention program, and to provide insight into how to shape program and media strategies to reach and influence particular individuals (Glanz et al., 2008).

◆ Social/Structural Effects of Media on Individual Health

Although the individual-level approach to health behavior change has provided fertile terrain from which to develop health interventions, it has not been adequate to explain health patterns at societal levels. Thus, we now shift our focus to macrolevel theories, from mass communication and social epidemiology literatures. One key assumption of the macrosocial approach is that individual-level health outcomes are shaped not only by individual cognitions and affect but also by factors external to the individual (i.e., social determinants of health). These areas of research emphasize the importance of structural, social, and community influences on health behavior and outcomes. Social determinants of health impact disease outcomes and health-related quality of life either directly (e.g., via environmental exposures) or indirectly, via opportunity structures that enable or constrain one's ability to participate in health-enhancing activities (Berkman & Kawachi, 2000). Social determinants of health include, but are not limited to, structural aspects of neighborhoods, poverty, income inequality, racism and discrimination, gender inequality, occupational hazards and job strain, health care policy, public health policy, social cohesion, and communication inequality (Berkman & Kawachi, 2000; Viswanath, 2006).

The social epidemiological approach parallels the structural approach in communication studies, which emphasizes social and structural influences to explain differential exposure to media and the effects of that exposure at group and community levels (Tichenor, Donohue, & Olien, 1980), including differential health effects across population subgroups (Viswanath, 2006). Successful media strategies at both the individual and social/structural levels require an acknowledgment of social determinants of health, as well as strategic communications to address those determinants either through targeting individuals or, at the macro level, with solutions that directly address social/environmental determinants. Focusing on the latter, social policies to ameliorate adverse social determinants of health require that issues and their alternatives achieve a level of salience and legitimacy and that public health problems be simultaneously on the public agenda and the policy agenda. Media play a critical role in agenda setting (discussed in the following paragraphs). In fact, some scholars suggest that health communication strategies should use the mass media as tools to pressure policymakers for social change and to reframe public debate on the attribution of key public health problems and their solutions (Dorfman, Wallack, & Woodruff, 2005).

Various media effects theories capture the social/structural influences of media on health, including cultivation theory, agenda setting, the knowledge gap hypothesis, and communication inequality. Beginning with cultivation theory, Gerbner and colleagues (Gerbner, Gross, Morgan, & Signorielli, 1980) argued that TV has emerged as the primary agent of socialization, competing with parents and religion, and that heavy TV viewing cultivates viewers' worldviews such that they buy into the "television reality" (see Morgan, Chapter 5, this volume). In one of the earliest reports to examine the significance of television and health behaviors (Pearl, Bouthilet, & Lazar, 1982), Gerbner et al. documented the unhealthy nutritional consequences of the unrelenting exposure of young children to TV. More recently, some studies have raised questions about TV's role in contributing to obesity, though these studies are not without methodological flaws (Clocksin, Watson, & Ransdell, 2002).

Similar to cultivation, agenda-setting theory uses multiple levels of analysis to examine the links between (a) issues portrayed in the media and the public's priorities (public agenda setting), (b) media coverage and its influence on the legislative agenda of policy-making bodies (policy agenda setting), and (c) antecedents such as institutional roles and processes that influence the selection of issues and content covered in the media (media agenda setting) (Kosicki, 1993). A recent example of a study of media agenda setting explored how occupational practices of health and medical science journalists may influence the media agenda and, in turn, the public and policy agendas (Viswanath et al., 2008). Another study examined the news media's influence on public awareness about chronic kidney disease (CKD) and the public policy agenda by assessing the extent and manner in which Australian TV news and newspapers covered CKD prevention and early detection (Tong, Chapman, Sainsbury, & Craig, 2008). Findings revealed that the media primarily focused on lifestyle causes and solutions. They argue that extending news media coverage to include nonlifestyle causes and consequences could help influence health policies and public awareness to improve CKD prevention and early detection.

Taking a somewhat different tack, the knowledge gap hypothesis focuses on the differential impact of the media on members of different socioeconomic status (SES) groups (Tichenor et al., 1970; Viswanath & Finnegan, 1996). Tichenor et al. argued that population segments with higher SES tend to acquire information from the media at a faster rate than do segments with lower status. Thus, the gap in knowledge between these segments tends to increase, rather than decrease, over time. Applied to health, these differences in information acquisition, or knowledge gaps, can lead to inequalities in information acquisition from health campaigns and consequent actions and health behaviors (Freimuth, 1990; Ribisl, Winkleby, Fortmann, & Flora, 1998; Viswanath et al., 2007; Winkleby & Cubbin, 2004).

More recent work in health communication has drawn further attention to inequalities in communication and how they may contribute to inequalities in health, linking the social epidemiological approach with the structural approach in mass communication (Viswanath, 2006). Communication inequality is defined as the differences among social groups in their ability to generate, disseminate, and use information at the macro level and to access, process, and act on information at the individual level. There are several dimensions to communication inequality: (a) access to and use of information channels and services, (b) attention to and processing of health information, and (c) capacity and ability to act on information provided. Figure 21.1 illustrates the structural influence model of health communication (Viswanath et al., 2007), an emerging framework that posits a connection between social determinants and health outcomes through a range of mass and interpersonal communication factors.

The argument is that social determinants, such as social class or neighborhoods, moderated by factors such as social networks, influence mass and interpersonal communication outcomes, including access to and use of media, information seeking, and processing and capacity to act on information, which in turn may influence health outcomes. Disparities in health communication outcomes stemming from social determinants may potentially lead to disparate health outcomes, such as risky behaviors, morbidity, and mortality. Recent studies have begun to use the model to explain, for example, differential effects on information seeking among cancer survivors (Ramanadhan & Viswanath, 2006),

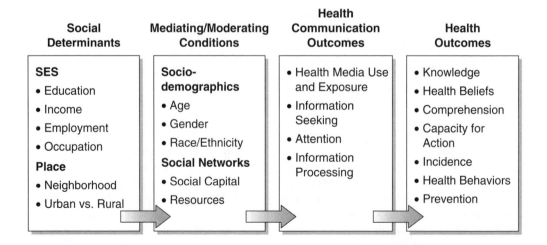

Figure 21.1 Structural Influence Model of Health Communication

channel preferences for health information (Blake, Flynt Wallington, & Viswanath, in press), and knowledge of smoking risks and skin cancer (Viswanath, Breen, et al., 2006). Clearly, the social/structural, along with the individual-level, variables are all critical to the development of successful public health interventions.

◆ Media and Public Health Campaigns

Because of their reach and appeal, mass media campaigns have become major tools in health promotion and disease prevention (Hornik, 2002). After reviewing literature on media campaigns over two decades, Randolph and Viswanath (2004) identified several components of successful public health media campaigns. First is the campaign sponsors' successful manipulation of the information environment to ensure sufficient audience exposure to the campaigns' messages. Indeed, exposure has been identified as one of the critical antecedents to campaign effects (Hornik, 2002). Campaigns are also most successful when, in addition to ensuring adequate exposure levels and audience-relevant content, campaign sponsors work to create concomitant structural conditions, such as sustained access to free or low-cost screening services or products (e.g., condoms, sunscreen), which allow the target audience to act on the promoted recommendations (Alstead et al., 1999; Black, Yamada, & Mann, 2002; Detweiler, Bedell, Salovey, Pronin, & Rothman, 1999). These are often referred to as multipronged or multifaceted campaigns, where communication is one of many strategies being implemented.

The literature describes several exemplary public health media campaigns that have successfully integrated these strategies. We draw attention to two examples to foster further thought regarding the integral role that the mass media play in the public health landscape. The *truth*® campaign and the *5 A Day for Better Health Program* represent exemplary mass media applications that contain multiple, well-designed message modalities coupled with high levels of exposure (Farrelly et al., 2002; Hornik, 2002) and that also meet most of the conditions identified by Randolph and Viswanath (2004) for successful public health campaigns.

truth®. The *truth*® campaign is a national tobacco countermarketing campaign, sponsored by the American Legacy Foundation, targeting youth ages 12 to 17. It uses multiple message modalities to draw attention to the tobacco industry's youth-specific marketing strategies. The campaign's core strategy draws upon the best practices in youth marketing and plays to the edgy and rebellious nature of youths, especially their desire to take control of their own lives. The campaign incorporates facts about the effects of tobacco consumption and the tobacco industry's marketing techniques in a manner that exposes the industry's youth-targeting tactics. The campaign may be best known for its controversial television commercial featuring youths placing body bags in front of a tobacco company building (Farrelly et al., 2002). The *truth*® campaign used paid television, print advertising, promotional items (e.g., T-shirts, stickers, etc.), edgy street marketing, and a Web site to expose the tobacco industry's youth-specific marketing strategies. By garnering ongoing input from its target audience and by investing in large media buys to ensure targeted, repeated message exposure, the campaign has successfully reduced youth smoking prevalence. In the first evaluation of this campaign, Farrelly et al. reported that the campaign accelerated the decline in youth smoking rates between 2000 and 2002 by 22%, translating into approximately 300,000 fewer youth smokers.

5 A Day for Better Health Program. The *5 A Day* program grew out of a cancer control program started in California in the late 1980s with support from the National Cancer Institute (NCI) and grew into a national nutrition education and disease prevention program led first by NCI and then by the Centers for Disease Control and Prevention (5 A Day, 2008). The program represents one of the nation's largest public-private nutrition education initiatives, working to increase Americans' fruit and vegetable consumption. (As nutritional epidemiology has progressed, the program's message has been adapted to reflect the HHS/USDA updated recommendations of seven servings per day for women and nine servings per day for men.) The program used several media channels and strategies (e.g., a mass media campaign, a retail point-of-purchase program, and community and research components), and message frames were culturally sensitive, tailored, and simple to account for the short attention span of many consumers for whom past nutrition messages may have been too complex (Havas et al., 1995). Evaluations have shown that awareness of the recommendation to eat five or more servings of fruit and vegetables each day increased from 22% in 1992 to 40% in 2002, and fruit and vegetable consumption increased by half a serving between 1992 and 1996 (5 A Day, 2008).

◆ Methodological Challenges in Health and Media Studies

Research examining the effects of media on health (and nonhealth) outcomes presents several methodological challenges and opportunities. Public health campaign and other health communication messages enter a crowded media environment with messages from many competing sources (Randolph & Viswanath, 2004). Thus, perhaps the greatest methodological challenge is measuring exposure to those health messages. Measuring exposure is essential in assessing communication campaign interventions given it is often cited as an explanation for campaign success or failure (Hornik, 2002). Indeed, media exposure measurement generally is becoming an increasing focus of researchers and clinicians, given the growing concern around the significant associations between media exposure and a variety of health risk behaviors in adults, children, and adolescents (Brown et al., 2006).

Considering the powerful influence of media exposure on both healthy and unhealthy behaviors, concerns about how to best measure exposure persist. Most exposure is assessed not at the audience or individual level, but by estimation based on the number of times the message was aired or printed and by the approximate audience size for each media channel used (see Roskos-Ewoldsen, 2008). However, investigators have also studied both direct and indirect individual media exposure measures. Standard direct measures of exposure are time spent with the media, recent exposure to media, and message discrimination. Indirect measures of exposure include attention to messages, or an individual's reliance on different media for different kinds of information. However, in general, many media exposure studies are fraught with challenges given the contemporary and changing media landscape, with the proliferation of media types, specialized media, and audience fragmentation. Thus, more systematic measures and frameworks are needed to measure media exposure accurately and consistently, particularly among those populations at greatest risk (Althaus & Tewksbury, 2007).

Further, some researchers have argued that merely measuring audience exposure falls short of measuring a message's influence because the link between the message and the audience has not been ascertained (see Potter, Chapter 2, this volume). Procedures to measure message discrimination, attention, recall, and recognition have been proposed to enhance the validity of research purporting to speak to health message effects (Clarke & Kline, 1974).

Yet another challenge to media and health research is that research designs often are not appropriate to assess message exposure and consequent effects because of, among other problems, a lack of adequate controls and cross-sectional study designs (Hornik, 2002). Further, the high expectations of media campaigns' impact on health, some argue, is unreasonable (Fishbein, 1996), and usually based on simple if not simplistic stimulus-response models, an assumption that is at odds with real-world conditions. Standard research designs such as randomized control trials are not adequate to capture media effects in health. Given these challenges, researchers have recently called for use of the "total weight of evidence" approach to better specify the impact of mass media on public health (NCI, 2008).

◆ The Impact of New Media Environments

As alluded to previously, this chapter would be incomplete were we not to discuss the effect of the new media environment on communication regarding public health. The convergence of media (i.e., computers, telephones, television, radio, video, print, cell phones, iPods, CD-ROMs, and audio) coupled with the diffusion of the Internet has created a nearly ubiquitous networked communication infrastructure (Robinson, Patrick, Eng, & Gustafson, 1998). As a result, these converging new media facilitate access to a plethora of health information and support services, thereby extending the reach of health communication efforts. Compared with traditional mass media, interactive media may have several advantages for health communication efforts. These include (1) improved access to personalized and tailored health information; (2) on-demand access to health information, support, and services; (3) enhanced ability to distribute materials widely and

rapidly to update content; (4) just-in-time expert decision support; and (5) greater health information choices for consumers (Rice & Katz, 2001).

Although some researchers view these new media as tools to improve the health and medical knowledge of and the service provided to consumers, others warn of the perils and potential dangers of these new technologies, such as the potential to harm consumers by bringing medical information that is overwhelmingly extensive, incomplete, or misleading (Bodenheimer & Grumbach, 2003), leading to potential frustration and confusion (Arora et al., 2008). Other scholars highlight such issues as security concerns, distrust of the quality of information, the potential for commercial interests to influence media content, physician ambivalence to the Internet because of poor quality of some information, disarray of current health care information systems, lack of resources for Web development in health care organizations, low literacy levels, and communication inequalities (Mittman & Cain, 2001). Thus, future research would do well to continue to focus on these barriers and concerns as well as differential access to new media technologies among various socioeconomic groups.

The digital divide, known as the perceived gap between those who have access to the latest information technologies and those who do not (DiMaggio, Hargittai, Neuman, & Robinson, 2001), still evokes a great deal of concern. Although differences in access to and use of traditional mass media have declined, differences still persist with digital media (i.e., satellite television, Internet) that involve recurring expenditures, like subscription fees. In general, more educated and higher-income groups have more access to these information resources compared with lower socioeconomic groups, thus contributing to knowledge gaps between population subgroups. If communication inequality is to be adequately addressed to ensure sufficient health information exposure for groups who experience a disproportionate disease burden, media campaigns must be supported by additional services, programs, resources, and sustained leadership designed to reach and appeal to all populations (Viswanath & Krueter, 2007).

◆ Concluding Thoughts

In our daily lives, we are immersed in mass media, and media effects can be powerful. The following question, then, remains: How can we successfully garner the power of the mass media to equalize health knowledge, beliefs, and behaviors across social boundaries while simultaneously blunting the media's negative effects? A clearer understanding of the range of mass media delivery channels; the changing and converging media environment; the communication inequalities that exist; social, institutional, cultural, and policy influences; and new and existing theoretical and methodological frameworks are all necessary to understand the complex influence of mass media on population health. Addressing these issues, both in study and in practice, will undoubtedly help researchers and health professionals harness the best practices of communication and the mass media to improve individual and population health.

◆ References

Ajzen, I., & Fishbein, M. (1980). *Understanding attitudes and predicting social behavior.* Englewood Cliffs, NJ: Prentice-Hall.

Alstead, M., Campsmith, M., Halley, C. S., Hartfield, K., Goldbaum, G., & Wood, R. W. (1999). Developing, implementing, and evaluating a condom promotion program targeting sexually active adolescents. *AIDS Education and Prevention, 11*(6), 497–512.

Althaus, S., & Tewksbury, D. (2007). *Toward a new generation of media use measures for the ANES.* American National Election Studies Pilot Study Report, No. nes011903. Retrieved June 30, 2009, from http://www.electionstudies.org/resources/papers/Pilot2006/nes011903.pdf

Arora, N. K., Hess, B. W., Rimer, B. K., Viswanath, K., Clayman, M., & Croyle, R. T. (2008). Frustrated and confused: The American public rates its cancer-related information seeking experiences. *Journal of General Internal Medicine, 23*(3), 223–228.

Bandura, A. (1994). Social cognitive theory of mass communication. In J. Bryant & D. Zillmann (Eds.), *Media effects: Advances in theory and research* (pp. 61–90). Hillsdale, NJ: Erlbaum.

Becker, L., McCombs, M., & McLeod, J. (1975). The development of political cognitions. In S. Chaffee (Ed.), *Political communication* (pp. 21–63). Beverly Hills, CA: Sage.

Berkman, L., & Kawachi, I. (2000). Social cohesion, social capital, and health. In L. Berkman & I. Kawachi (Eds.), *Social epidemiology* (pp. 174–190). New York: Oxford University Press.

Black, M. E., Yamada, J., & Mann, V. (2002). A systematic literature review of the effectiveness of community-based strategies to increase cervical cancer screening. *Canadian Journal of Public Health, 93*(5), 386–393.

Blackburn, H. (1983). Research and demonstration projects in community cardiovascular disease prevention. *Journal of Public Health Policy, 4*(4), 398–421.

Blake, K. D., Flynt Wallington, S., & Viswanath, K. (in press). Health communication channel preferences by class, race, and place. In G. Kreps (Ed.), *Health communication: Building the evidence base in cancer control.* New Jersey: Hampton Press.

Bodenheimer, T., & Grumbach, K. (2003). Electronic technology: A spark to revitalize primary care? *Journal of the American Medical Association, 290*(2), 259–264.

Booth-Butterfield, S., & Reger, B. (2004). The message changes belief and the rest is theory: The "1% or less" milk campaign and reasoned action. *Prevention Medicine, 39*(3), 581–588.

Brower, A., Ceglarek, S., & Crowley, S. (2001). *A matter of degree: Quarterly report to the Robert Wood Johnson Foundation*. Madison: University of Wisconsin.

Brown, J. D., L'Engle, K. L., Pardun, C. J., Guo, G., Kennevay, K., & Jackson, C. (2006). Sexy media matter: Exposure to sexual content in music, movies, television, and magazines predicts Black and White adolescents' sexual behavior. *Pediatrics, 117*(4), 1018–1027.

Bryant, J., & Zillmann, D. (Eds.). (1994). *Media effects: Advances in theory and research*. Hillsdale, NJ: Erlbaum.

Bushman, B. J., & Huesmann, L. R. (2001). Effects of televised violence on aggression. In D. Singer & J. Singer (Eds.), *Handbook of children and the media* (pp. 225–268). Thousand Oaks, CA: Sage.

Cabral, R. J., Cotton, D., & Gelen, A. C. (2004). Application of the transtheoretical model for HIV prevention in a facility-based and a community-level behavioral intervention research study. *Health Promotion Practice, 5*(2), 199–207.

Carbonari, J. P., & DiClemente, C. C. (2000). Using transtheoretical model profiles to differentiate levels of alcohol abstinence. *Journal of Consulting and Clinical Psychology, 68*(5), 810–817.

Chaffee, S. H., & Hochheimer, J. L. (1985). The beginnings of political communication research in the United States: Origins of the "limited effects" model. In E. M. Rogers & F. Balle (Eds.), *The media revolution in America and in Western Europe* (pp. 267–296). Norwood, NJ: Ablex.

Charlesworth, A., & Glantz, S. A. (2005). Smoking in the movies increases adolescent smoking: A review. *Pediatrics, 116*(6), 1516–1528.

Cho, H., & Salmon, C. T. (2007). Unintended effects of health communication campaigns. *Journal of Communication, 57*, 293–317.

Clark, L., & Tiggemann, M. (2008). Sociocultural and individual psychological predictors of body image in young girls: A prospective study. *Developmental Psychology, 44*(4), 1124–1134.

Clarke, P., & Kline, F. G. (1974). Media effects reconsidered: Some new strategies for communication research. *Communication Research, 1*, 224–240.

Clocksin, B. D., Watson, D. L., & Ransdell, L. (2002). Understanding adolescent obesity and media use: Implications for future research. *Quest, 54*(4), 259–276.

Detweiler, J. B., Bedell, B. T., Salovey, P., Pronin, E., & Rothman, A. J. (1999). Message framing and sunscreen use: Gain-framed messages motivate beach-goers. *Health Psychology, 18*(2), 189–196.

DiMaggio, P. E., Hargittai, E., Neuman, W. R., & Robinson, J. P. (2001). Social implications of the Internet. *Annual Review of Sociology, 27*, 307–336.

Dorfman, L., Wallack, L., & Woodruff, K. (2005). More than a message: Framing public health advocacy to change corporate practices. *Health Education & Behavior, 32*(3), 320–336.

Farquhar, J. W., Fortmann, S. P., Maccoby, N., Haskell, W. L., Williams, P. T., Flora, J. A., et al. (1985). The Stanford Five-City Project: Design and methods. *American Journal of Epidemiology, 122*(2), 323–334.

Farrelly, M. C., Healton, C. G., Davis, K. C., Messeri, P., Hersey, J. C., & Haviland, M. L. (2002). Getting to the truth: Evaluating national tobacco countermarketing campaigns. *American Journal of Public Health, 92*, 901–907.

Finnegan, J. R., & Viswanath, K. (2002). Communication theory and health behavior change: The media studies framework. In K. Glanz, B. Rimer, & F. M. Lewis (Eds.), *Health behavior and health education* (pp. 361–388). San Francisco: Jossey-Bass.

Fishbein, M. (1996). Editorial: Great expectations or do we ask too much from community-level interventions? *American Journal of Public Health, 86*(8), 1075–1076.

Fishbein, M., & Ajzen, I. (1981). Attitudes and voting behavior: An application of the theory of reasoned action. In G. M. Stephenson & J. M. Davis (Eds.), *Progress in applied social psychology* (pp. 95–125). London: Wiley.

Fishbein, M., & Cappella, J. N. (2006). The role of theory in developing effective health communications. *Journal of Communication, 56*(Suppl. 1), S1–S17.

5 A Day. (2008). The 5 a day for better health campaign. Retrieved June 15, 2008, from http://www.5aday.gov

Freimuth, V. S. (1990). The chronically uninformed: Closing the knowledge gap in health. In E. B. Roy & L. Donohew (Eds.), *Communication and health: Systems and applications* (pp. 173–174). Hillsdale, NJ: Erlbaum.

Gerbner, G., Gross, L., Morgan, M., & Signorielli, N. (1980). The "mainstreaming" of America: Violence profile No. 11. *Journal of Communication, 30,* 10–29.

Glanz, K., Rimer, B. K., & Viswanath, K. (Eds.). (2008). *Health behavior and health education: Theory, research, and practice.* San Francisco: John Wiley & Sons.

Havas, S., Heimendinger, J., Damron, D., Nicklas, T. A., Cowan, A., Beresford, S. A., et al. (1995). 5 A Day for better health: Nine community research projects to increase fruit and vegetable consumption. *Public Health Reports, 110*(1), 68–79.

Hornik, R. C. (1988). *Development communication.* New York: Longman.

Hornik, R. C. (2002). Public health communication: Making sense of contradictory evidence. In R. C. Hornik (Ed.), *Public health communication: Evidence for behavior change* (pp. 1–21). Mahwah, NJ: Erlbaum.

Hovland, C., Lumsdaine, A., & Sheffield, F. (1949). *Experiences on mass communication.* Princeton, NJ: Princeton University Press.

Hyman, H., & Sheatsley, P. (1947). Some reasons why information campaigns fail. *Public Opinion Quarterly, 11,* 412–423.

Institute of Medicine. (2002). *Committee on communication for behavior change in the 21st century: Improving the health of diverse populations: Speaking of health: Assessing health communication strategies for diverse populations.* Washington, DC: National Academies Press.

Kaiser Family Foundation. (2004a). *Entertainment education and health in the United States: Issue brief.* Retrieved September 18, 2008, from http://www.Kff.org

Kaiser Family Foundation. (2004b). *Survey of African Americans about HIV/AIDS media campaigns.* Retrieved September 18, 2008, from http://www.Kff.org

Kaiser Family Foundation. (2008). *Television as a health education: A case study of Grey's Anatomy.* Retrieved October 30, 2008, from http://www.Kff.org

Kosicki, G. M. (1993). Problems and opportunities in agenda-setting research. *Journal of Communication, 43*(2), 100–127.

Kotler, P., & Roberto, E. L. (1989). *Social marketing strategies for changing public behavior.* New York: Free Press.

Kreuter, M., Lezin, N., Kreuter, M., & Green, L. (1998). *Community health promotion ideas that work: A field-book for practitioners.* Sudbury, MA: Jones & Bartlett.

Kreuter, M. W., Farrell, D., Olevitch, L., & Brennan, L. (2000). What is tailored communication? In J. Bryant & D. Zillmann (Eds.), *Tailoring health messages: Customizing communication with computer technology* (pp. 1–23). Mahwah, NJ: Erlbaum.

Larson, E. B., Bergman, J., Heidrich, F., Alvin, B. L., & Schneeweiss, R. (1982). Do postcard reminders improve influenza compliance? A prospective trial of different postcard "cues." *Medical Care, 20,* 639–648.

Lazarsfeld, P., Berelson, B., & Gaudet, H. (1948). *The people's choice.* New York: Columbia University Press.

McQuail, D. (1979). The influence and effects of mass media. In M. Janowitz & P. M. Hirsch (Eds.), *Reader in public opinion and mass communication* (pp. 261–285). New York: Free Press.

Meyer, G., Roberto, A. J., Boster, F. J., & Roberto, H. L. (2004). Assessing the *Get Real About Violence* curriculum: Process and outcome evaluation results and implications. *Health Communication, 16*(4), 451–474.

Mittman, R., & Cain, M. (2001). The future of the Internet in health care. In R. E. Rice & J. E. Katz (Eds.), *The Internet and health communication* (pp. 47–73). Thousand Oaks, CA: Sage.

Montaño, D. E., & Kasprzyk, D. (2008). Theory of reasoned action, theory of planned behavior, and the integrated behavioral model. In K. Glanz, B. K. Rimer, & K. Viswanath (Eds.), *Health behavior and health education: Theory, research, and practice* (pp. 67–92). San Francisco: John Wiley & Sons.

National Cancer Institute. (2008). *The role of the media in promoting and reducing tobacco use* [Tobacco Control Monograph, No. 19]. Bethesda, MD: U.S. Department of Health and Human Services, National Institutes of Health, National Cancer Institute. NIH Pub. No. 07-6242.

Paisley, W. (1989). Public communication campaigns: The American experience. In R. E. Rice & C. K. Atkin (Eds.), *Public communication campaigns* (pp. 15–38). Newbury Park, CA: Sage.

Paskett, E. D., Tatum, C. M., D'Agostino, R., Rushing, J., Velez, R., Michielutte, R., et al. (1999). Community-based interventions to improve breast and cervical cancer screening: Results of the Forsyth County Cancer Screening (FoCaS) Project. *Cancer Epidemiology, Biomarkers & Prevention, 8*(5), 453–459.

Pearl, D., Bouthilet, L., & Lazar, J. (1982). *Television and behavior: Ten years of scientific progress and implications for the eighties* (Vol. 1). Washington, DC: Government Printing Office.

Peng, W. (2008). The mediational role of identification in the relationship between experience mode and self-efficacy: Enactive role-playing versus passive observation. *Cyberpsychology & Behavior, 11*(6), 649–652.

Prochaska, J. O., & DiClemente, C. C. (1983). Stages and processes of self-change of smoking: Toward an integrative model of change. *Journal of Consulting and Clinical Psychology, 51,* 390–395.

Prochaska, J. O., DiClemente, C. C., Velicer, W. E., & Rossi, J. S. (1993). Standardized, individualized, interactive, and personalized self-help programs for smoking cessation. *Health Psychology, 12*(5), 399–405.

Prochaska, J. O., Redding, C. A., & Evers, K. (2002). The transtheoretical model and stages of change. In K. Glanz, B. K. Rimer, & F. M. Lewis (Eds.), *Health behavior and health education: Theory, research, and practice* (3rd ed., pp. 99–120). San Francisco: Jossey-Bass.

Ramanadhan, S., & Viswanath, K. (2006). Health and the information nonseeker: A profile. *Health Communication, 20*(2), 131–139.

Randolph, W., & Viswanath, K. (2004). Lessons learned from public health mass media campaigns: Marketing health in a crowded media world. *Annual Review of Public Health, 25,* 419–438.

Resnicow, K., Davis, R. E., Zhang, G., Konkel, J., Strecher, V. J., Shaikh, A. R., et al. (2008). Tailoring a fruit and vegetable intervention on novel motivational constructs: Results of a randomized study. *Annals of Behavioral Medicine, 35*(2), 159–169.

Ribisl, K. M., Winkleby, M. A., Fortmann, S. P., & Flora, J. A. (1998). The interplay of socioeconomic status and ethnicity on Hispanic and White men's cardiovascular disease risk and health communication patterns. *Health Education Research, 13*(3), 407–417.

Rice, R. E., & Atkin, C. (Eds.). (1989). *Public communication campaigns.* Newbury Park, CA: Sage.

Rice, R. E., & Katz, J. E. (Eds.). (2001). *The Internet and health communication: Experiences and expectations.* Thousand Oaks, CA: Sage.

Rimal, R. N., & Creel, A. H. (2008). Applying social marketing principles to understand the effects of the radio diaries program in reducing HIV/AIDS stigma in Malawi. *Health Marketing Quarterly, 25*(1/2), 119–146.

Robinson, T. N., Patrick, K., Eng, T. R., & Gustafson, D. (1998). An evidence-based approach to interactive health communication: A challenge to medicine in the information age. *Journal of the American Medical Association, 280,* 1264–1269.

Rocella, E. J. (2002). The contributions of public health education toward the reduction of cardiovascular disease mortality: Experiences from the National High Blood Pressure Education Program. In R. C. Hornik (Ed.), *Public health communication: Evidence for behavior change* (pp. 73–84). Mahwah, NJ: Erlbaum.

Rosenstock, I. M. (1974). Historical origins of the health belief model. *Health Education Monographs, 2*(4), 354–386.

Roskos-Ewoldsen, D. R. (Ed.). (2008). *Communication Methods and Measures* [Entire Journal].

Salmon, C., & Atkin, C. (2003). Media campaigns for health promotion. In T. Thompson, A. Dorsey, K. Miller, & R. Parrott (Eds.),

Handbook of health communication (pp. 449–472). Hillsdale, NJ: Erlbaum.

Sarkin, J. A., Johnson, S. S., Prochaska, J. O., & Prochaska, J. M. (2001). Applying the transtheoretical model to regular moderate exercise in an overweight population: Validation of a stages of change measure. *Preventive Medicine, 33*, 462–469.

Singhal, A., & Rogers, E. (1999). *Entertainment-education: A communication strategy for social change.* Mahwah, NJ: Erlbaum.

Singhal, A., & Rogers, E. M. (2004). The status of entertainment–education worldwide. In A. Singhal, M. J. Cody, E. N. Rogers, & M. Sabido (Eds.), *Entertainment–education and social change* (pp. 3–20). Mahwah, NJ: Erlbaum.

Slater, M. D., & Rouner, D. (2002). Entertainment-education and elaboration likelihood: Understanding the processing of narrative persuasion. *Communication Theory, 12*(2), 173–191.

Stephenson, M. T., Quick, B. L., Atkinson, J., & Tschida, D. A. (2005). Authoritative parenting and drug prevention practices: Implications for antidrug ads for parents. *Health Communication, 17*(3), 301–321.

Stern, S. R. (2005). Messages from teens on the big screen: Smoking, drinking, and drug use in teen-centered films. *Journal of Health Communication, 10*(4), 331–346.

Storey, J. D., Saffitz, G. B., & Rimon, J. G. (2008). Social marketing. In K. Glanz, B. K. Rimer, & K. Viswanath (Eds.), *Health behavior and health education: Theory, research, and practice* (pp. 435–464). San Francisco: John Wiley & Sons.

Storey, M., Neumark-Sztainer, D., & French, S. (2002). Individual and environmental influences on adolescent eating behaviors. *Journal of the American Dietetic Association, 102*(3 Suppl.), S40–S51.

Strecher, V. J., Kreuter, M. W., Den Boer, D. J., Kobrin, S., Hospers, H. J., & Skinner, C. S. (1994). The effects of computer-tailored smoking cessation messages in family practice settings. *Journal of Family Practice, 39*(3), 262–270.

Tenkorang, E. Y., Rajulton, F., & Maticka-Tyndale, E. (2009). Perceived risks of HIV/AIDS and first sexual intercourse among youth in Cape Town, South Africa. *AIDS and Behavior, 13*(2), 234–245.

Tichenor, P. J., Donohue, G. A., & Olien, C. N. (1970). Mass media flow and differential growth in knowledge. *Public Opinion Quarterly, 34*, 158–170.

Tichenor, P. J., Donohue, G. A., & Olien, C. N. (1980). *Community conflict and the press.* Newbury Park, CA: Sage.

Tong, A., Chapman, S., Sainsbury, P., & Craig, J. C. (2008). An analysis of media coverage on the prevention and early detection of CKD in Australia. *American Journal of Kidney Diseases, 52*(1), 159–170.

U.S. Census Bureau. (2007). *Statistical abstract of the United States.* Retrieved June 30, 2008, from http://www.census.Gov/prod/www/statistical-abstract.html

U.S. Department of Health and Human Services. (2000). *Healthy people 2010: With understanding and improving health and objectives for improving health.* Washington, DC: U.S. Government Printing Office.

Viswanath, K. (2006). Public communication and its role in reducing and eliminating health disparities. In G. Thompson, F. Mitchell, & M. Williams (Eds.), *Examining the health disparities research plan of the National Institutes of Health: Unfinished business* (pp. 215–233). Washington, DC: National Academies Press.

Viswanath, K., Blake, K., Meissner, H. I., Saiontz, N. G., Mull, C., Freeman, C. S., et al. (2008). Occupational practices and the making of health news: A national survey of U.S. health and medical science journalists. *Journal of Health Communication, 13*(8), 759–777.

Viswanath, K., Breen, N., Meissner, H., Moser, R. P., Hesse, B., Steele, W. R., et al. (2006). Cancer knowledge and disparities in the information age. *Journal of Health Communication, 11*(Suppl. 1), 1–17.

Viswanath, K., & Finnegan, J. R. (1996). The knowledge gap hypothesis: Twenty-five years later. In B. Burleson (Ed.), *Communication yearbook 19* (pp. 187–227). Thousand Oaks, CA: Sage.

Viswanath, K., & Kreuter, M. W. (2007). Health disparities, communication inequalities, and eHealth: A commentary. *American Journal of Preventive Medicine, 32*(5), S131–S133.

Viswanath, K., Ramanadhan, S., & Kontos, E. Z. (2007). Mass media and population health: A macrosocial view. In S. E. Galea (Ed.), *Macrosocial determinants of population health* (pp. 275–294). New York: Springer.

Viswanath, K., Randolph, W., & Finnegan, J. R. (2006). Connecting the dots between social capital and public health outcomes: The role of communication and community pluralism. *American Journal of Public Health, 96*(8), 1456–1461.

Winkleby, M. A., & Cubbin, C. (2004). Changing patterns in health behaviors and risk factors related to chronic diseases, 1990–2000. *American Journal of Health Promotion, 19*(1), 10–27.

Witte, K. (1992). Putting the fear back into fear appeals: The extended parallel process model. *Communication Monographs, 59*, 329–349.

Witte, K., & Allen, M. (2000). A meta-analysis of fear appeals: Implications for effective public health campaigns. *Health Education & Behavior, 27*, 591–615.

22

EDUCATIONAL TELEVISION

◆ Marie-Louise Mares

Whtat do children learn when they watch educational television? The simple answer suggested by the research reviewed in this chapter is that they often learn a lot. The more complex answer is that there also appear to be important developmental changes—in content, in parental encouragement to watch, in interest and attention, and in the effects of viewing.

The research discussed in this chapter has an added significance given the ongoing evolution of the Federal Communications Commission's (FCC's) position on educational programming. The 1996 Federal Communications Commission processing guideline indicated that broadcast stations that aired 3 hours of children's educational/informative (E/I) television per week could receive expedited renewal of their license. To be considered educational, either programs could include traditional curriculum-related content such as math, science, or history, or they could focus on meeting the "social/emotional needs" of children (FCC, 2007). The FCC has not issued explicit guidelines about what constitutes an educational program, nor does it require that producers provide any evidence that viewers learn from watching their E/I programs. To a large degree, it is up to the academic community to conduct and present research that would enable informed decisions about what should and should not count as informative.

◆ The Youngest Audience

At the time of writing this chapter, the question of whether infants can learn from audiovisual content is the newest, hottest topic in research on educational programming. In effect, there are two questions—whether children under 2 years of age learn from viewing (hence whether it is meaningful to speak of educational media for them), and whether viewing audiovisual content actually harms them. As early as the 1970s and 1980s, research suggested that children under age 2 were exposed to television for almost 2 hours a day (Anderson, Lorch, Field, Collins, & Nathan, 1986; Hollenbeck, 1978), and there were some anecdotes of toddlers repeating phrases such as "Coke is it" from commercials (Lemish & Rice, 1986). However, there was virtually no programming specifically targeted to this group, so infants were "watching" either adult programming or programs, such as *Sesame Street,* that were intended for older children. An early study by Anderson and Levin (1976) on visual attention to *Sesame Street* found that children under 2 spent less than 30% of the time looking at the television screen, often sitting with their backs to the screen. In consequence, few media effects researchers examined whether infants were learning from watching TV programming, because they did not seem to be watching in any real sense.

With the advent of infant-oriented DVDs (e.g., Baby Einstein and Baby Genius) and programming such as *Teletubbies,* the question of whether infants can learn from media content became more pressing. In response to the sudden boom in infant-oriented content, the American Academy of Pediatrics (1999) recommended that children under age 2 spend no time with television, DVDs, or computer programs, acknowledging that they were making this recommendation in the absence of research about the possible harm or benefits of media use in infancy.

Research suggests that many parents do not comply with this guideline. In a recent phone survey of 1,009 parents, 40% of 3-month-old infants were reportedly watching television or DVDs regularly, and those that did watched for an average of an hour per day. Among 2-year-olds, about 90% watched television or DVDs regularly, and those that did were reportedly watching for an average of approximately 1.5 hours per day (Zimmerman, Christakis, & Meltzoff, 2007). In addition, recent research has reported much higher levels of infants' visual attention to television than in the early Anderson and Levin study (Linebarger & Walker, 2005; Valkenburg & Vroone, 2004).

Why might the American Academy of Pediatrics expect there to be negative rather than positive effects of viewing? Various hypotheses have been put forward about possible effects. One has to do with time displacement—perhaps if infants and toddlers are watching television, they are spending less time doing other things that are more critical to development. For example, research suggests that when the television is on, young children are less focused in their play (Evans, Pempek, Kirkorian, Frankenfield, & Anderson, 2004) and parents are less responsive to their children (Tanimura, Okuma, & Kyoshima, 2007). Thus, having the television on may disrupt internal and interpersonal processes that foster development. Yet another possible route for negative effects is that the sorts of programs that catch infants' attention may offer inappropriate linguistic models or overly stimulating events and cause confusion among their young viewers.

Two widely publicized longitudinal studies reported that early viewing of television was associated with negative cognitive outcomes. In one, viewing before age 3 was associated with greater probability that the parents would subsequently report that the child had attention problems at age 7 (Christakis, Zimmerman, DiGiuseppe, & McCarty, 2004). In the second, viewing before age 3 was associated with poorer performance on tests of reading recognition and comprehension and short-term memory capacity at ages 6 and 7 (Zimmerman & Christakis, 2005). However, these studies were based on data gathered before the advent of infant-oriented programming, and they did not differentiate between types of content viewed. Moreover, they did not control for children's initial levels of cognitive development. Thus, the results based on these early data are consistent with at least two interpretations. One is that infant viewing of age-inappropriate programming (the only thing available at the time the data were gathered) was detrimental to their development. The second is that families with less-developed children may have been more likely to encourage those children to watch television. Both scenarios make sense, but there is some prior support for the second possibility. In a study by Rice, Huston, Truglio, and Wright (1990), parental encouragement to view *Sesame Street* was associated with children having lower vocabulary scores, even though viewing itself was positively associated with vocabulary.

Two further studies include specific measures of what content the children watched and contain data gathered more recently, when infant-oriented programming was available. Linebarger and Walker (2005) conducted a longitudinal study of 51 infants beginning when the children were 6 months old. The parents reported that the babies' first interest in viewing was, on average, at around 9 months of age. By 30 months old, children were watching about 9.3 hours of television per week, most of which could be classified as educational. What were the relationships between viewing and language production? On average, parents reported that their children could produce about 438 words by 30 months, but heavy viewing was associated with approximately 8 fewer words. More important, the

relationship between time spent viewing and vocabulary depended on the specific program viewed—*Barney & Friends, Teletubbies,* and *Sesame Street* were associated with parental reports of between 8 and 12 fewer words; *Dora the Explorer, Blue's Clues, Arthur,* and *Clifford* were associated with reports of 8 to 14 more words. Much the same relationships were observed when the researchers measured the children's language production during play sessions. In particular, the researchers noted that children who were heavy viewers of *Teletubbies* (in which anthropomorphic characters emit shrieks and squeaks and one-word utterances) tended to also rely on vocalizations and one-word utterances. Overall, though, these were not huge effects (either positive or negative).

In the second study, Zimmerman et al. (2007) surveyed 1,008 parents of children aged 2 to 24 months about their children's media use and also asked a set of standardized questions about their child's linguistic development. The authors reported that parental reports of their children's language skills were strongly negatively predicted by the child's viewing of baby DVDs/videos. Time spent viewing educational programs, movies, non-educational programs, or grown-up TV was unrelated to language scores. Interestingly, those children who had no media exposure at all had marginally lower language scores than those who had at least some media exposure.

Taken together, these studies suggest that there is no single effect of viewing in infancy; if there is an effect, it varies by what is viewed, with differences even within the genre of "educational" content. However, all of these correlational studies are open to questions about self-selection (e.g., perhaps children with less advanced language find it more enjoyable to watch programs such as *Teletubbies*). Even if the results are not attributable to selection, it remains unclear what characteristics of each of these programs was causing the positive or negative effects. For that, as Linebarger and Walker (2005) point out, experiments are needed.

A rapidly expanding set of experimental research suggests that children under age 2 *can* learn from audiovisual representations, but they do not learn as well as from live interactions (Anderson & Pempek, 2005, have referred to this as a "video deficit"). In various studies, 12-month-olds to 3-year-olds were less able to imitate novel actions seen on a video than the same actions demonstrated (in exactly the same way) by an experimenter (e.g., Barr & Hayne, 1999; Hayne, Herbert, & Simcock, 2003). Performance in the video conditions was only equivalent when the video was twice as long and had more repetitions of the actions than the live condition (Barr, Muentener, Garcia, Fujimoto, & Chavez, 2007). In other studies, 2- and 3-year-old children watched an experimenter hide a toy and then had to retrieve it. Those who had watched over a live video monitor showed more difficulty retrieving the toy than those who had watched the same actions through a window (Schmitt & Anderson, 2002; Troseth, 2003; Troseth & DeLoache, 1998). Kuhl, Tsao, and Liu (2003) exposed 9-month-old infants to Mandarin Chinese via live speakers, audiovisual DVDs, or audio-only DVDs for twelve 25-minute sessions over the period of a month. Those infants who watched a live speaker maintained their ability to detect the phonetic contrasts present in Mandarin, but the other children did not. The video deficit even appears to extend to children's recognition of themselves: in a series of studies, children were less likely to notice a sticker on their head or on their leg if they saw themselves on a video monitor rather than in a mirror, even when the image was the same size and the video image was reversed in the same way as a mirror image (Suddendorf, Simcock, & Nielsen, 2006).

Various explanations have been put forward for this deficit: that infants have trouble translating from the smaller images on-screen to the larger reality, or relating television's two-dimensional representations to the three-dimensional world around them (Schmitt & Anderson, 2002). However, research by Schmidt, Crawley-Davis, and Anderson (2007) found that controlling for these features does not eliminate infants' difficulty learning from video. Troseth, Saylor, and Archer (2006) suggested, rather, that infants learn that video/television content is not interactive in the way that other sources of information (such as parents) are. Because of this, they (in effect) dismiss the content as irrelevant to the world around them. To test this, Troseth et al. (2006) had 2-year-olds interact with an adult on-screen via live-circuit television. After a set of initial interactions in which the adult on-screen asked the child questions and responded to the answers, the children were as able to follow the adult's instructions about where to retrieve a toy as those who interacted face-to-face with an adult.

In addition to the lack of socially contingent interaction when watching audiovisual content, research by Krcmar, Grela, and Lin (2007) suggests that regular television programming may have other features that make learning difficult for infant viewers. In their study, Krcmar et al. examined whether children aged 15 to 24 months would learn new words from a live adult speaker, from a videotape of the speaker, or from the same words inserted in a segment from *Teletubbies*. Consistent with the prior video deficit findings, children learned the words best when they paid attention to a live speaker, and learned fewer words from the video of the adult. However, they learned still less from the segment of *Teletubbies*, particularly if they were under 22 months or had low initial vocabulary scores. The authors suggested that the amount of visual and auditory stimulation in the *Teletubbies* segment was too taxing for infant viewers.

Summary. It seems fairly uncontroversial that infants learn best from social interactions. By extension, it seems clear that replacing such interactions with extensive viewing of audio-visual content is unlikely to produce an infant Einstein, however much parents might wish it to be so. However, it is *unclear* that much harm is done by small amounts of exposure, despite the forceful conclusions of some authors (Strasburger, 2007). At the moment, there appear to be some programs that offer poor linguistic role models for children under age 2, some that may have no effect, and some that may help language learning. Future research needs to examine the interplay between children's linguistic and cognitive development and the specific linguistic features of the content. Ideally, research would also begin to consider other outcomes besides language development.

♦ **Early Childhood**

Given that *Sesame Street* is targeted at preschoolers, and given that it was one of the first and most successful educational programs, it is not surprising that the majority of research on educational television has focused on the effects of this program on preschool viewers. To anticipate a little, the conclusions of research about *Sesame Street* and other educational programs are markedly different from those of research on infants. Overall, the findings suggest that there are positive, enduring effects (across a variety of cognitive and social domains) of preschoolers' exposure to age-appropriate educational content.

There are numerous expert reviews of the early research on *Sesame Street*. The interested reader is referred to a review by Fisch, Truglio, and Cole (1999), as well as articles by Anderson (1998) and Huston and Wright (1998). Rather than attempting to reproduce the quality and quantity of their discussion, only a few key points are covered here.

There have been three clusters of criticisms leveled at *Sesame Street,* each of which was, in essence, a theory about the effects of using television to educate young children. The first was related to the form of television, and of *Sesame Street* in particular. The suggestion was that learning from television would be so easy and enjoyable that children would be spoiled for the regular classroom, and that the rapid cuts and edits and other visual characteristics of the program would reduce children's ability to concentrate and persist in tasks requiring extended reflection (e.g., Healy, 1990; Winn, 1977). The second was an argument that television viewing (even of educational programming) would displace other, more intellectually valuable activities so that the net effect of viewing would be negative (e.g., Valkenburg & van der Voort, 1994; Williams, 1986). The third was a form of the knowledge gap hypothesis—perhaps middle-class families would be most prone to encourage their children to watch educational programming, hence the positive effects of viewing would be stronger for middle-class viewers than for lower-income families, and the gap between advantaged and disadvantaged children would be widened rather than narrowed (e.g., Cook et al., 1975). Obviously not all of these could be correct since some posit positive outcomes and some posit negative outcomes of viewing. In fact, the results of three major longitudinal studies and a national survey suggest that none of these criticisms were supported by data.

In the first longitudinal study, Rice et al. (1990) repeatedly assessed 326 children (aged 3 or 5 at the beginning of the study) over the course of 2 years. Among the younger cohort, greater viewing of *Sesame Street* was associated with higher vocabulary scores at the end of the study, even after controlling for initial vocabulary scores and various family characteristics. Viewing of noneducational children's programming or general audience programming were both unrelated to vocabulary scores. For the older cohort, amount of viewing of *Sesame Street* when they were age 5 was unrelated to their vocabulary when they were age 7.

In the second study, Wright et al. (2001) followed 182 children from low- to moderate-income families for 3 years (i.e., age 2 until age 5; age 4 until age 7). As with the previous study, there were positive associations between viewing educational TV content at 2 and 3 years of age and subsequent academic performance (correlations ranged from .21 to .32), even after controlling for family characteristics and initial ability. Thus, contrary to the argument that educational programming would spoil children for school, those children who watched such programming when they were 2 or 3 actually did better than those who did not watch. In contrast, viewing educational content at ages 4 to 7 was not associated with achievement, presumably because watching *Sesame Street* and similar programs at those ages did not provide enough new, stimulating content to cause subsequent positive effects. For both cohorts, viewing general-audience programs was associated with poorer subsequent achievement: The effects of viewing depended on the content (educational vs. not).

It is also worth noting that there were bidirectional effects: Children with good skills at age 5 selected more child-audience informative programs and fewer cartoons at ages 6 and 7. Children with lower skills at age 3 shifted to viewing more general-audience programs by ages 4 and 5. Thus, educational content may appeal more to those who are already somewhat more academically engaged, and may wind up helping them to become even more involved and successful. To the extent that there was a knowledge gap effect, it was not related to social class but rather to initial ability.

The third longitudinal study suggested that early viewing choices can set up trajectories that endure long past the initial effects of learning letters and numbers. Anderson, Huston, Schmitt, Linebarger, and Wright (2001) recontacted 570 adolescents whose childhood viewing patterns had been measured approximately 10 years earlier. There were numerous, sometimes complicated, results from this large data set. Most relevant here were the positive relationships between early viewing of *Sesame Street* and subsequent high school science grades, time spent reading books for leisure, and attitudes toward achievement. For boys (but not girls), there were additional positive associations for English grades, overall GPA, and level of difficulty of math classes taken in high school. Early viewing of other educational programs did not predict grades, but early viewing of *Mister Rogers' Neighborhood* (a program emphasizing imagination) predicted adolescent creativity scores. In addition, males who had watched more child informative programming (not specifically *Sesame Street* or *Mister Rogers' Neighborhood*) in childhood had lower self-reports of aggression in adolescence. The authors concluded that these patterns (together with their findings of negative effects of early viewing of violence) indicated that the content of viewing mattered: Even within the genre of educational programming, there were different associations with specific programs.

Finally, the results of a 1993 National Household Education Survey (with a national sample of 10,888 children) did not support the idea that *Sesame Street* increased the knowledge gap between social classes. The majority of children from all social classes watched the program and, in fact, the positive correlations between exposure to *Sesame Street* and emerging literacy and numeracy were stronger (rather than weaker) for low-income families than for more affluent families (Zill, 2001).

What about the effects of other educational programs? As noted earlier, childhood exposure to *Mister Rogers' Neighborhood* was positively associated with adolescent creativity scores (Anderson et al., 2001). A series of field experiments also suggested other positive effects of watching *Mister Rogers' Neighborhood*, particularly when the program was watched in preschool and accompanied by other materials and activities that elaborated on the prosocial content (Friedrich & Stein, 1975; Friedrich-Cofer, Huston-Stein, Kipnis, Susman, & Clewett, 1979). In one study, Friedrich and Stein (1973) reported that children who were randomly assigned to view *Mister Rogers' Neighborhood* in preschool persisted longer at tasks than those assigned to watch other programs, were more likely to obey rules, and were more likely to delay gratification without protest. Moreover, the program did not appear to be merely reinforcing positive behavior among children who were already predisposed to act prosocially; the effects on playground behavior were strongest among children from low-SES backgrounds who were initially less prosocial.

Taken together, the early research suggested that viewing of educational programming in the preschool years was associated with positive academic and social outcomes. There is less research on more recent programs for preschool children. An exception is a longitudinal study by Anderson et al. (2000) of the effects of watching *Blue's Clues,* a preschool series designed to encourage problem solving and thinking skills. Children who were regular viewers of the program throughout the 2 years of the research were compared with those who had virtually no exposure to that particular program. Although the two sets of children had equivalent scores on a variety of problem-solving measures at the beginning of the study, the *Blue's Clues* group scored increasingly better than the nonviewing group over the course of the 2 years. There was also some indication that the program's emphasis on viewers "helping" the main characters solve puzzles may have fostered positive behavior: By the end of the study, children in the *Blue's Clues* group were rated slightly more positively on various aspects of social behavior by their caregivers.

Summary. In contrast to the research on infants, studies of preschool children's learning from educational television typically find positive effects, in both cognitive and social domains, and these effects are often enduring. However, much of the research has focused on *Sesame Street* and *Mister Rogers' Neighborhood*. There are numerous newer educational programs for this age-group and very few studies of the effects of watching them.

◆ *Grade School and Beyond*

After children enter school, the picture changes quite substantially. To preview briefly, there is some indication that as children grow older, they are less likely to watch programming that is explicitly educational. Perhaps because of this, there are no educational programs for school-aged children that are analogous to *Sesame Street* or *Mister Rogers' Neighborhood*— watched by the vast majority of children and on the air for many years. In turn, the result appears to be that there is far less research about the long-term effects on school-aged children of exposure to educational programming.

Huston and Wright (1998) noted that it is easier to attract preschoolers to watch educational programming than older children. There are, of course, exceptions— *Ghostwriter, The Magic School Bus, Beakman's World,* and *Wishbone* were all highly popular series for older children— but none of these have endured for great lengths of time. Survey results (e.g., Rideout & Hamel, 2006; Rideout, Roberts, & Foehr, 2005; Schmitt, 2000) suggest that parents of preschool children are more likely to actively steer their children toward educational programming than parents of children aged 8 and older. In fact, parents of 8- to 18-year-olds typically had no television-related rules for their children, apart from requiring that children get their homework or chores done first.

Left thus to themselves, school-aged children appear to be less likely to watch educational content than noneducational content. A study by Calvert and Kotler (2003) suggests that when school-aged children do watch educational programming, the most popular programs tend to be those that resemble entertainment programming, focusing on social-emotional themes played out with fictional characters rather than teaching traditional curriculum-related content. As children (particularly boys) in their sample grew older throughout the course of the study, they were less and less likely to report watching educational programs.

The tendency not to watch curriculum-based television content may reflect something of a vicious cycle. Both Jordan (1996) and Mitroff (2003) noted that television producers and network executives strongly believe that school-aged children do not want to watch educational content. Because of this, stations tend to air academic-based programs at relatively low-viewing times and tend not to bother promoting them heavily (Anderson, 2003; Jordan, 2003). Moreover, the lineup of educational programming is in constant flux, with programs going on and off the air (Jordan, 2003). Thus, it is possible that school-aged children would be more likely to watch high-quality educational programming if it were consistently available during prime viewing hours.

In addition, though, it is also possible that there is some genuine disinclination on the part of children; having spent approximately 7 hours a day in school plus more time for homework, they may not want any additional education. Krcmar

and Albada (2000) investigated whether the mere fact of being told that content was educational would affect children's responses. They compared children's enjoyment, attention, and recall of a short educational clip that was shown either with or without an E/I label, and with or without adult explanation of the label. Among the 5- to 7-year-olds, there was little effect of condition. Among the 8- to 11-year-olds, the responses were mixed, but there was some indication that attention and liking decreased with the presence of the E/I label, particularly when the meaning of the label was made explicit.

Given all of the above, it is not surprising that many producers have opted to meet the E/I requirement by airing stories that teach social lessons. Content analyses of broadcast networks' educational offerings that aired in Philadelphia from 1989 to 2000 found that the majority focused on prosocial lessons such as the importance of getting along with others, being honest, overcoming prejudice, or feeling good about oneself (Jordan, 2004; Jordan, Schmitt, & Woodard, 2001). Such programs can potentially appeal to a broad age range. In contrast, programs that teach traditional educational material such as math or reading can only plausibly target a very narrow age range.

Unfortunately, there is a dearth of experimental or correlational research on the effectiveness of the current crop of socioemotional programs for school-aged children. Given their prevalence and relative popularity, it would be helpful to know whether, and under what conditions, such programs are effective. When broadcast stations describe the lessons taught by their socioemotional E/I programs, their claims are typically vague and ambitious. For example, the Fox affiliate in Madison, Wisconsin, described *Sabrina,* an animated series about a witch, as helping 9- to 12-year-olds "learn what it takes to become a truly good human being."

Calvert and Kotler (2003) reported that the second- to sixth-grade children in their study remembered lessons from socio-emotional educational content better than lessons from curriculum-based content. However, the children's answers about lessons learned from specific episodes were coded for clarity and length, but were not actually compared with the content of the episodes. Moreover, it is unclear whether children might not report learning the same sorts of lessons from general-audience programs (*American Idol* teaches me to stick with my dreams, etc.). Without knowing that these E/I programs foster prosocial behavior and attitudes in a way that general audience programs do not, it is hard be sure of the value of such programs.

What do school-aged children learn from watching curriculum-based, academic programming? Most of the research has consisted of evaluative or summative studies conducted by the Children's Television Workshop, and most of it has only examined what children learn when they watch a specific program in the classroom, not what they learn from self-selected exposure at home. The results of these experiments (comparing groups who watch in the classroom with those who do not watch) generally find that children learn at least some of the intended material. Thus, children (particularly girls) who watched *3-2-1 Contact* showed more understanding of the science topics presented than those who did not watch, as did children in other studies who watched *Cro*, *Bill Nye the Science Guy*, or *The Magic School Bus* (Fisch, 2004). Similarly, fifth graders who watched *Square One TV* were better able to engage in mathematical problem solving than those who did not (Hall, Esty, & Fisch, 1990). Similar effects were also found for other math-based programs such as *Cyberchase* and *Infinity Factory*. Uchikoshi (2005, 2006) examined the effects of *Arthur* and *Between the Lions* on the narrative skills of children whose parents did not speak

English. Extensive classroom exposure over the course of a year resulted in learning of the specific skills emphasized in each of the programs.

In some studies, ceiling and floor effects demonstrated the importance of targeting programs to narrow age ranges. For example, Linebarger, Kosanic, Greenwood, and Doku (2004) studied the effects of viewing a literacy-based program called *Between the Lions*. They found that learning occurred primarily among those who were at the optimal level of readiness for the content—not overly familiar with the concepts (e.g., first-grade children) and not completely unfamiliar with them either (e.g., kindergartners who scored very low on initial reading ability).

The few studies that have examined the effects of self-selected viewing at home have generally found much weaker effects than in the classroom. *The Electric Company* helped children who were struggling with reading, but only if they watched the program in school as part of the classroom activities (Ball & Bogatz, 1973). *Freestyle* helped encourage more egalitarian gender role beliefs, but primarily when the program was watched and discussed in school (Johnston & Ettema, 1982).

These studies, although suggestive, are not enough to answer important questions about the possible effects of viewing educational programming at home. Are the charges that were initially leveled at *Sesame Street*—that viewing displaces more useful activities, or that viewing educational programming creates a knowledge gap between haves and have-nots—more accurate for school-aged children? We don't know, because we don't have the relevant research that compares the effects of watching educational and noneducational programs at home for this age-group. However, a series of surveys conducted by the Kaiser Family Foundation provide some tentative answers about displacement. The results of teen time-use diaries indicated that heavy viewers (of overall TV, not specifically educational television) spent no less time doing homework, helping their parents, or doing chores, and spent only 7 fewer minutes a day reading for leisure (Rideout et al., 2005). Thus, it seems unlikely that watching educational programming would somehow have *more* pernicious displacement effects.

What about the knowledge gap? Fisch (2004) reported that classroom exposure to *Infinity Factory* (a math-based program for 8- to 11-year-olds that focused on African Americans and Latinos) improved the math scores of White children more than the scores of minority children. It seems plausible that this gap might be even larger if children were left to decide whether they wanted to watch it.

Perhaps counterintuitively, some research suggests that overall television viewing may actually shrink the achievement gap. Fetler's (1984) analyses of math and reading scores in California suggested that for children of low-education parents, achievement was higher among those who watched substantial amounts of television than those who watched less. Morgan (1980) reported that for children with low and moderate scores on IQ tests, achievement was higher among those who watched 3 to 5 hours a day than those who watched less. Comstock and Paik (1991) noted that among children who were non-native speakers of English, more viewing was associated with higher academic performance than less viewing.

This is not to argue against Anderson et al.'s (2000) claim that content matters. The results of the various studies cited in this chapter clearly suggest that content does matter. However, even without knowing the specific content viewed, it appears that television viewing can be somewhat beneficial, particularly in the absence of more educational external resources. Research by Neuman and Celano (2001) on the amount and quality of reading material available in four neighborhoods in Philadelphia provides compelling evidence

that poorer children grow up in environments where the likelihood of encountering printed words or stories is far lower than for children in more affluent neighborhoods. Similarly, research by Jordan (2005) on the media use in preschools and among families in poorer neighborhoods suggested that the books available to children were generally of low quality and were often age inappropriate. Under such circumstances, it is not surprising that television viewing would offer at least some useful content that is unavailable elsewhere.

Summary. There have been numerous educational programs for school-aged children that have aired over the years that were successful at teaching children educational content when viewed in the classroom. However, recent research suggests that producers often focus on creating programs with socioemotional messages given their (possibly somewhat justified) fear that school-aged children prefer not to watch educational content in their leisure time. There is little research about the effectiveness of these types of programs.

◆ Further Directions

One possibility suggested by the previous paragraphs is that a primary function of educational television targeted toward school-aged children could be to provide teachers with tools to use in the classroom. That is, if school-aged children are unlikely to watch educational programming at home but research suggests that viewing in the classroom teaches children more than they would get from only having regular classroom content, then perhaps children should watch educational programs at school. Of course, this is not to advocate wholesale replacement of regular classroom activities with television viewing, but perhaps there is more of a place for television in the classroom than has been traditionally granted it. That way, programs could be appropriately targeted to a narrow age/developmental stage, but seen by a wide audience. Moreover, widespread classroom exposure would reduce the possibility that such programs would primarily be seen by a privileged and motivated few.

In addition, research on educational media has much less to say about the effects of children's use of computers than about television. Although there has been a growing body of qualitative work on the ways in which children learn to negotiate their way through games (e.g., Oliver & Pelletier, 2006) or to express themselves on message boards (Polack, 2006), there is relatively little systematic research on more traditional curricular effects. In part, this reflects the fragmentation of content offered by computers. Current studies of educational effects of computers tend to focus on specific programs that are unique to that particular study and are not in wide use. In fact, although there are Web sites that have become immensely popular with children, there is no equivalent of *Sesame Street* or the Nick Jr. lineup. That is, there are no educational Web sites or programs that are consistently regarded by parents as beneficial and are extensively used by large numbers of children. This may change as television production companies such as Sesame Workshop are working to develop their Web sites into more substantial educational offerings. The research that will emerge from these efforts should provide an intriguing examination of medium effects as well as revive questions about access, learning, and the knowledge gap.

◆ In Conclusion . . .

Here, at the end of the chapter, it seems very vivid how many people have worked long and hard to do good things for children via television. Revisiting the formative and evaluative research on programs such as *Freestyle* or *3-2-1 Contact*, it is hard not to be moved by the dedication and effort involved in making such programs. Similarly, it is very compelling to read Mitroff (2003) as she ponders how to balance the need for commercial viability with the genuine desire to educate and illuminate children. Then there is what Anderson (himself a prime exemplar) has called "a small but dedicated band" of researchers who have spent most of their careers documenting those instances where television has had positive educational effects and helping to figure out the failures (Anderson & Pempek, 2005). It became clear in writing this chapter how much more there is to know, and how interesting and worthwhile it is to try to find the answers.

◆ *References*

American Academy of Pediatrics. (1999). Policy statement. *Pediatrics, 104,* 341–343.

Anderson, D. R. (1998). Educational television is not an oxymoron. *Annals of the American Academy of Political and Social Science, 557,* 24–38.

Anderson, D. R. (2003). The Children's Television Act: A public policy that benefits children. *Journal of Applied Developmental Psychology, 24,* 337–340.

Anderson, D. R., Bryant, J., Wilder, A., Santomero, A., Williams, M., & Crawley, A. M. (2000). Researching *Blue's Clues:* Viewing behavior and impact. *Media Psychology, 2,* 179–194.

Anderson, D. R., Huston, A. C., Schmitt, K. L., Linebarger, D. L., & Wright, J. (2001). Early childhood television viewing and adolescent behavior: The recontact study. *Monographs of the Society for Research in Child Development, 66*(1), vii–147.

Anderson, D. R., & Levin, S. R. (1976). Young children's attention to *Sesame Street. Child Development, 47,* 806–811.

Anderson, D. R., Lorch, E. P., Field, D. E., Collins, P. A., & Nathan, J. G. (1986). Television viewing at home: Age trends in visual attention and time with TV. *Child Development, 57,* 1024–1033.

Anderson, D. R., & Pempek, T. A. (2005). Television and very young children. *American Behavioral Scientist, 48,* 505–532.

Ball, S., & Bogatz, G. A. (1973). *Reading with television: A follow-up evaluation of* The Electric Company. Princeton, NJ: Educational Testing Service.

Barr, R., & Hayne, H. (1999). Developmental changes in imitation from television during infancy. *Child Development, 70,* 1067–1081.

Barr, R., Muentener, P., Garcia, A., Fujimoto, M., & Chavez, V. (2007). The effect of repetition on imitation from television during infancy. *Developmental Psychobiology, 10,* 196–207.

Calvert, S. L., & Kotler, J. A. (2003). Lessons from children's television: The impact of the Children's Television Act on children's learning. *Journal of Applied Developmental Psychology, 24,* 275–335.

Christakis, D. A., Zimmerman, F. J., DiGiuseppe, D. L., & McCarty, C. A. (2004). Early television exposure and subsequent attentional problems in children. *Pediatrics, 113,* 708–713.

Comstock, G., & Paik, H. J. (1991). *Television and the American child.* New York: Academic Press.

Cook, T. D., Appleton, H., Connor, R. F., Shaffer, A., Tamkin, G., & Weber, S. (1975). Sesame Street *revisited.* New York: Russell Sage Foundation.

Evans, M. K., Pempek, T. A., Kirkorian, H. L., Frankenfield, A. E., & Anderson, D. R. (2004, May). *The impact of background television on the complexity of play.* Paper presented at the 14th Biennial International Conference on Infant Studies, Chicago.

Federal Communications Commission. (2007). *FCC consumer facts: Children's educational television.* Retrieved October 2, 2007, from http://www.fcc.gov/cgb/consumerfacts/childtv.html

Fetler, M. (1984). Television viewing and school achievement. *Journal of Communication, 34,* 104–118.

Fisch, S. M. (2004). *Children's learning from educational television.* Mahwah, NJ: Erlbaum.

Fisch, S. M., Truglio, R. T., & Cole, C. F. (1999). The impact of *Sesame Street* on preschool children: A review and synthesis of thirty years' of research. *Media Psychology, 1,* 165–190.

Friedrich, L., & Stein, A. H. (1973). Aggressive and prosocial television programs and the natural behavior of preschool children. *Monographs of the Society for Research in Child Development, 38*(4, Serial No. 151).

Friedrich, L., & Stein, A. H. (1975). Prosocial television and young children: The effects of verbal labeling and role playing on learning and behavior. *Child Development, 46,* 27–38.

Friedrich-Cofer, L. K., Huston-Stein, A., Kipnis, D. M., Susman, E. J., & Clewett, A. S. (1979). Environmental enhancement of prosocial television content: Effect on interpersonal behavior, imaginative play, and self-regulation in a natural setting. *Developmental Psychology, 15,* 637–646.

Hall, E. R., Esty, E. T., & Fisch, S. M. (1990). Television and children's problem-solving behavior: A synopsis of an evaluation of the effects of *Square One TV. Journal of Mathematical Behavior, 9,* 161–174.

Hayne, H., Herbert, J., & Simcock, G. (2003). Imitation from television by 24- and 30-month-olds. *Developmental Science, 6,* 254–261.

Healy, J. M. (1990). *Endangered minds: Why our children don't think.* New York: Simon & Schuster.

Hollenbeck, A. R. (1978). Television viewing patterns of families with young infants. *Journal of Social Psychology, 105,* 259–264.

Huston, A. C., & Wright, J. C. (1998). Television and the information and educational needs of children. *Annals of the American Academy of Political and Social Science, 557,* 9–23.

Johnston, J., & Ettema, J. S. (1982). *Positive images: Breaking stereotypes with children's television.* Beverly Hills, CA: Sage.

Jordan, A. B. (1996). *The state of children's television: An examination of quantity, quality, and industry beliefs* (Report No. 2). Philadelphia: University of Pennsylvania, Annenberg Public Policy Center.

Jordan, A. B. (2003). Children remember prosocial program lessons but how much are they learning? *Journal of Applied Developmental Psychology, 24,* 341–345.

Jordan, A. B. (2004). The three-hour rule and educational television for children. *Popular Communication, 2,* 103–118.

Jordan, A. B. (2005). Learning to use books and television: An exploratory study in the ecological perspective. *American Behavioral Scientist, 48,* 523–538.

Jordan, A. B., Schmitt, K. L., &Woodard, E. H. (2001). Developmental implications of commercial broadcasters' educational offerings. *Journal of Applied Developmental Psychology, 22,* 87–101.

Krcmar, M., & Albada, K. F. (2000). The effect of an educational/informational rating on children's attraction to and learning from an educational program. *Journal of Broadcasting & Electronic Media, 44,* 674–689.

Krcmar, M., Grela, B., & Lin, K. (2007). Can toddlers learn vocabulary from television? An experimental approach. *Media Psychology, 10,* 41–63.

Kuhl, P. K., Tsao, F. M., & Liu, H. M. (2003). Foreign-language experience in infancy: Effects of short-term exposure and social interaction on phonetic learning. *Proceedings of the National Academy of Sciences of the United States of America (PNAS), 100,* 9096–9101.

Lemish, D., & Rice, M. L. (1986). Television as a talking picture book: A prop for language acquisition. *Journal of Child Language, 13,* 251–274.

Linebarger, D. L., Kosanic, A. Z., Greenwood, C. R., & Doku, N. S. (2004). Effects of viewing the television program *Between the Lions* on the emergent literacy skills of young children. *Journal of Educational Psychology, 96,* 297–308.

Linebarger, D. L., & Walker, D. (2005). Infants' and toddlers' television viewing and language outcomes. *American Behavioral Scientist, 48,* 624–645.

Mitroff, D. (2003). On the horns of a dilemma. *Journal of Applied Developmental Psychology, 24,* 355–361.

Morgan, M. (1980). Television viewing and reading: Does more equal better? *Journal of Communication, 30,* 159–165.

Neuman, S. B., & Celano, D. (2001). Access to print in low-income and middle-income communities: An ecological study of four neighborhoods. *Reading Research Quarterly, 36,* 8–26.

Oliver, M., & Pelletier, C. (2006). Activity theory and learning from digital games: Developing an analytic methodology. In D. Buckingham & R. Willett (Eds.), *Digital generations: Children, young people, and new media* (pp. 67–88). New York: Erlbaum.

Polack, M. (2006). It's a guURL thing: Community versus commodity in a girl-focused netspace. In D. Buckingham & R. Willett (Eds.), *Digital generations: Children, young people, and new media* (pp. 177–192). New York: Erlbaum.

Rice, M. L., Huston, A. C., Truglio, R., & Wright, J. C. (1990). Words from *Sesame Street:* Learning vocabulary while viewing. *Developmental Psychology, 26,* 421–428.

Rideout, V. J., & Hamel, E. (2006). *The media family: Electronic media in the lives of infants, toddlers, preschoolers and their parents* (Kaiser Family Foundation report). Retrieved May 4, 2009, from www.kff.org

Rideout, V., Roberts, D. F., & Foehr, U. G. (2005). *Generation M: Media in the lives of 8–18 year-olds. Executive summary* (Kaiser Family Foundation report). Retrieved May 4, 2009, from www.kff.org

Schmidt, M. E., Crawley-Davis, A. M., & Anderson, D. R. (2007). Two-year-olds' object retrieval based on television: Testing a perceptual account. *Media Psychology, 9,* 389–409.

Schmitt, K. (2000). *Public policy, family rules and children's media use in the home* (Report No. 35). Philadelphia: University of Pennsylvania, Annenberg Public Policy Center.

Schmitt, K. L., & Anderson, D. R. (2002). Television and reality: Toddlers' use of visual information from video to guide behavior. *Media Psychology, 4,* 51–76.

Strasburger, V. C. (2007). First do no harm: Why have parents and pediatricians missed the boat on children and media? *Journal of Pediatrics, 151,* 334–336.

Suddendorf, T., Simcock, G., & Nielsen, M. (2006). Visual self-recognition in mirrors and live videos: Evidence for a developmental asynchrony. *Cognitive Development, 22,* 185–196.

Tanimura, M., Okuma, K., & Kyoshima, K. (2007). Television viewing, reduced parental utterance, and delayed speech development in infants and young children. *Archives of Pediatric and Adolescent Medicine, 161,* 618–619.

Troseth, G. L. (2003). TV guide: Two-year-old children learn to use video as a source of information. *Developmental Psychology, 39,* 140–150.

Troseth, G. L., & DeLoache, J. S. (1998). The medium can obscure the message: Young children's understanding of video. *Child Development, 69,* 950–965.

Troseth, G. L., Saylor, M. M., & Archer, A. H. (2006). Young children's use of video as a source of socially relevant information. *Child Development, 77,* 786–799.

Uchikoshi, Y. (2005). Narrative development in bilingual kindergarteners: Can *Arthur* help? *Developmental Psychology, 41,* 464–478.

Uchikoshi, Y. (2006). Early reading in bilingual kindergarteners: Can educational television help? *Scientific Studies of Reading, 10,* 89–120.

Valkenburg, P. M., & van der Voort, T. H. A. (1994). Influence of TV on daydreaming and creative imagination: A review of research. *Psychological Bulletin, 116,* 316–339.

Valkenburg, P. M., & Vroone, M. (2004). Developmental changes in infants' and toddlers' attention to television entertainment. *Communication Research, 31,* 288–311.

Williams, M. E., & Hall, E. (1994). Creating educational television programs that are relevant to the lives of children. *Youth & Society, 26,* 243–255.

Williams, T. M. (Ed.). (1986). *The impact of television: A natural experiment in three communities.* Orlando, FL: Academic Press.

Winn, M. (1977). *The plug-in drug.* New York: Penguin.

Wright, J. C., Huston, A. C., Murphy, K. C., St. Peters, M., Pinon, M., Scantlin, R., et al. (2001). The relations of early television viewing to school readiness and vocabulary of children from low-income families: The Early Window project. *Child Development, 72,* 1347–1367.

Zill, N. (2001). Does *Sesame Street* enhance school readiness? Evidence from a national survey of children. In S. M. Fisch & R. T. Truglio (Eds.), *"G" is for growing: Thirty years of research on children and* Sesame Street (pp. 115–130). Mahwah, NJ: Erlbaum.

Zimmerman, F. J., & Christakis, D. A. (2005). Children's television viewing and cognitive outcomes. *Archives of Pediatric and Adolescent Medicine, 159,* 619–625.

Zimmerman, F. J., Christakis, D. A., & Meltzoff, A. N. (2007). Television and DVD/video viewing in children younger than 2 years. *Archives of Pediatric and Adolescent Medicine, 161,* 473–479.

23

MEDIA LITERACY

◆ W. James Potter and Sahara Byrne

I t is our purpose in this chapter to review the literature of media literacy effects studies, particularly those empirical studies that test the effectiveness of interventions. To fulfill this purpose, we first explain how we chose the focus of this review. Then we present an analysis of the two main components of the media literacy intervention literature—formal interventions and natural interventions. Finally, we provide a critique of this literature.

DELINEATING THIS REVIEW

There is great variety in the way media literacy has been conceptualized. For example, in a symposium on media literacy published in the *Journal of Communication,* Brown (1998) observed, "The term media literacy means many things to many people" (p. 44). Hobbs (1998) concluded that "at present, media literacy is still an umbrella concept, with a wide spectrum of different educational philosophies, theories, frameworks, practices, settings, methods, goals, and outcomes" (p. 27). And Zettl (1998) said, "Surprisingly, the plethora of available articles, books, classroom materials, and information on the internet dealing with media literacy does not seem to help very much in answering the question, 'What is media literacy?'" (p. 81). In the years since the publication of this symposium, little has changed to indicate a consensus on what media literacy is (Potter, 2004).

Given the wide variety of conceptualizations for media literacy, it follows that there would be a wide variety of conceptualizations of media literacy *effects*. However, scholars rarely write about mass media effects, preferring instead to sketch out general goals, such as fostering an empowered citizenry (Hobbs, 1998; Lewis & Jhally, 1998). Other media literacy scholars write about the importance of creating or strengthening skills of critical thinking (Silverblatt & Eliceiri, 1997) or other cognitive skills (Hobbs, 1998; Potter, 2004). Although this broad literature has been valuable in stimulating thinking about media literacy and providing a useful vision for what media literacy can be, relatively few studies have moved toward elaborating in detail what a media literacy effect is. Those studies that have done so are referred to as formal intervention studies in this chapter. This chapter must narrow its focus from all conceptualizations about what media literacy effects could be or should be, because that is too large a literature for one chapter to review. Instead, we will focus our attention on the studies in the mass media intervention literature. These are empirical studies that have identified a particular media effect and then tested treatments to determine which treatments are successful in preventing or reducing that effect.

COMMONALITIES

The studies in media literacy intervention literature share a handful of important commonalities. These include three assumptions that underlie these studies as well as four design characteristics.

As for assumptions, the studies in this literature assume that the mass media are continually exerting all kinds of direct and indirect influences on individuals and society. These influences can immediately trigger manifest effects—cognitively, attitudinally, affectively, physiologically, and/or behaviorally—during an exposure to a media message or gradually build up over time in the shaping and reinforcing of knowledge structures, beliefs, and habits. A second assumption is that many of these naturally occurring effects are negative, that is, they are harmful to individuals, or at least not useful to the individual in a positive or constructive way. Third, it is assumed that we can construct interventions that can help people avoid these negative effects in their everyday lives. Building on these assumptions, we define a media literacy effect as a *counternegative effect*. This means that a media literacy effect is, in essence, the removal of—or the empowering of individuals to avoid—a naturally occurring negative effect that results wholly or in part from the influence of messages from the mass media.

The studies in this media literacy effects literature each exhibit four design characteristics. They have a clearly identified agent, target, treatment, and outcome (Potter & Byrne, 2007). The agent is the person or vehicle that is delivering the lessons. Usually, this is a researcher, teacher, or parent, but media literacy interventions are also delivered via media messages such as films (Linz, Fuson, & Donnerstein, 1990) and campaigns. The target of the intervention is the person who is receiving the media literacy intervention. The most common targets of media literacy intervention studies are children, but the need for adult media literacy (especially that of parents, teachers, and doctors) has become a recent point of debate (Rich & Bar-on, 2001). The treatment is the content and design of the intervention. For example, some scholars and practitioners focus on teaching participants media production skills (Banerjee & Greene, 2006), whereas others view media literacy as a set of critical viewing skills that can change a viewer's perspective during exposure (Potter, 2004; Vande Berg, Wenner, & Gronbeck, 2004). Finally, the outcome is some aspect of the target that should change as a result of the intervention, such as a cognition, attitude, emotion, or behavior.

◆ *Formal Interventions*

A major part of the intervention literature includes studies that have been designed by researchers to assess the value of providing media literacy skills, broadly defined, to individuals. These studies examine how the acquisition of these skills affects individuals' attitudes, beliefs, behaviors, and cognitive structures. Researchers usually develop a lesson that is designed to help targets (typically children) learn how to avoid naturally occurring negative media effects or to reshape that media influence into a positive effect, and then run an experiment to test the effectiveness of the intervention (or interventions) against a control group that does not experience the intervention. However, assessments of how media literacy skills lead to media effects also occur through correlational studies (Nathanson, 1999), focus groups (Cohen, 2002), qualitative interviews (Moore, DeChillo, Nicholson, Genovese, & Sladen, 2000), and participant observations (Bragg, 2002). We will analyze this assessment literature first by content, then by the theoretically proposed process of mitigation.

CONTENT

Violence. The content area that has enjoyed the most empirical attention is media violence, with more than 25 published assessments of interventions attempting to lower aggressive responses to violent media messages (see Cantor & Wilson, 2003, for a comprehensive review). Some of these interventions are more successful than others, and several studies have documented a "boomerang effect," or an increase in the aggressive attitudes of individuals who participated in certain interventions (Byrne, 2009; Byrne & Hart, 2009; Byrne, Linz, & Potter, in press; Cantor & Wilson, 2003).

Advertising and health. Close behind violence as a topic of intervention studies is advertising, with at least 15 published studies that examine the effectiveness of various interventions in reducing the potentially negative effects of viewing commercial advertising. Scholars investigating this area tend to focus on preventing unhealthy attitudes and behaviors resulting from exposure to advertisements (Austin & Johnson, 1997; Banerjee & Greene, 2006; Elliot et al., 2006; Pinkleton, Austin, Cohen, Miller, & Fitzgerald, 2007).

In fact, there has been a recent surge in media literacy efforts to mitigate health-related effects of media. In addition to those related to advertising, scholars have also recently investigated the role of entertainment content in promoting poor body image (Choma, Foster, & Radford, 2007; Evans et al., 2006; Nathanson & Botta, 2003).

Unfortunately, interventions in the context of health and advertising can result in a similarly ineffective pattern as those intending to reduce media-induced violence (Irving & Berel, 2001; McVey & Davis, 2002; Neumark-Sztainer, Sherwood, Coller, & Hannan, 2000). One explanation is that the interventions function to elicit deeper processing of unhealthy images, leading to an increase in body image disturbance (Nathanson & Botta, 2003).

Other areas. Other research areas have received considerably less attention from media literacy scholars compared with those mentioned previously. Researchers have designed and tested interventions that have targeted media-induced stereotypes. These interventions have focused on reducing viewers' stereotypes relating to age (Cohen, 2002), gender roles (Nathanson, Wilson, McGee, & Sebastian, 2002; Steinke et al., 2007), and race (Ramasubramanian & Oliver, 2007). The findings are mixed, with some studies resulting in less positive evaluations of stereotypical content and less acceptance of stereotypical attitudes (Nathanson et al., 2002), whereas other interventions fail to achieve this goal (Steinke et al., 2007) or even backfire (Ramasubramanian & Oliver, 2007).

Sexual content, in addition, has been cited as a rich area of great potential by many (Brown, 2000; Durham, 1999; Merskin, 2004), but few have investigated the effect of media literacy or critical viewing skills empirically (see Linz et al., 1990; Nathanson, 2001b, 2002, for successful exceptions). Perhaps this is because most media literacy efforts tend to be biased toward targeting children and adolescents instead of adults (Potter, 2004), and certain challenges arise when investigators undertake studies about sexuality and related behaviors with children.

Scary programs have also been proposed as one area where media literacy skills might help the well-being of viewers (Bar-on et al., 2001), but, perhaps for similar reasons, few have directly investigated this potential. Findings are mixed in the few studies that have attempted to mitigate fear responses to the media. Interventions may have positive effects on older rather than younger children (Cantor & Wilson, 1984) and may actually function to produce anxiety in individuals exposed to an intervention that is not followed by a scary media message (Slone & Shoshani, 2006).

Turning to news programming, the limited work to date in this area has resulted in reducing some anxiety-producing effects, as mentioned in Slone and Shoshani (2006), and been shown to increase political efficacy and discussion of politics (Chaffee, Morduchowicz, & Galperin, 1997). Not surprisingly, recent articles on the effects of technology have argued for the impending necessity of media literacy skills (Olson & Pollard, 2004; Thoman & Jolls, 2004). We should expect to see some empirical follow-ups to these suggestions.

MITIGATION PROCESSES

In this section, we analyze the experimental intervention literature along the dimension of how an intervention exerts its influence on mitigating a negative effect. That is, we examine what the researchers regard as the way in which the intervention disrupts the usually occurring process that leads to a negative effect.

Information processing. The majority of media literacy interventions are designed around the idea that active and/or critical processing while viewing media inhibits negative effects. Although Potter (2004) proposed a formal theory to delineate this process, it is more common to see it described in a general way (Gonzales, Glik, Davoudi, & Ang, 2004; Irving & Berel, 2001; McVey & Davis, 2002; Moore et al., 2000; Slone & Shoshani, 2006). Interventions structured with this broad approach often result in unsuccessful or mixed results (Irving & Berel, 2001; McVey & Davis, 2002; Slone & Shoshani, 2006).

Other scholars have designed media literacy interventions with a more specific information-processing perspective. Successful interventions have resulted from studies by interrupting media processing through providing specific decentration tasks (Leyens, Cisneros, & Hossay, 1976; Vooijs & van der Voort, 1993), tailoring to developmental processing limitations (Nathanson, 2004), and attempting to alter the formation of cognitive scripts during viewing (Rosenkoetter, Rosenkoetter, Ozretich, & Acock, 2004).

Persuasion. Although not mutually exclusive from an information-processing perspective, several formal theories of persuasion have been applied to media literacy interventions. There is a broad range of approaches. One framework argues that media literacy lessons serve to inoculate targets (i.e., McGuire, 1964) against forthcoming media messages. Research applying inoculation theory to interventions has mixed results, with some successfully inducing resistance to unhealthy media messages (Banerjee & Greene, 2006) and others with mixed results, or the opposite result (Doolittle,

1980; Wilksch, Tiggemann, & Wade, 2006). Media literacy interventions that encourage viewers to adopt healthy attitudes in order to remain cognitively consistent with the elements of the intervention have documented success, particularly when participants are provided with the opportunity to publicly demonstrate a prosocial attitude (Byrne, 2009; Huesmann, Eron, Klein, Brice, & Fischer, 1983; Linz et al., 1990) or provide new information that is inconsistent with previous attitudes (Vooijs & van der Voort, 1993). Other theories of persuasion that have been rarely applied, but have successfully interrupted the media effect in question, are social judgment theory (Austin et al., 2002); the social influence model (Gonzales et al., 2004); and specifically targeting certain audiences, like sensation seekers (Helme, Donohew, Baier, & Zittleman, 2007) or other at-risk groups, through social comparison (Lew, Mann, Myers, Taylor, & Bower, 2007).

Social cognition. Several interventions have been constructed according to social cognitive theory (Bandura, 1986). Interventions with this framework are usually designed to increase efficacy to change behavior (Evans et al., 2006) or to draw awareness to the negative consequences of antisocial behavior (Neumark-Sztainer et al., 2000; Ramasubramanian & Oliver, 2007; Rosenkoetter et al., 2004; Vooijs & van der Voort, 1993). In particular, researchers have focused on altering identification and involvement with characters that engage in antisocial behavior (Nathanson & Cantor, 2000). Others have applied the closely related message interpretation process (MIP) model, to change how viewers identify with media characters (Austin & Johnson, 1997; Austin, Pinkleton, & Funabiki, 2007; Pinkleton et al., 2007). With few exceptions (Neumark-Sztainer et al., 2000; Ramasubramanian & Oliver, 2007), interventions adopting a social cognitive or MIP approach have succeeded in mitigating the media effect in question.

◆ Natural Interventions

Natural interventions are those that are motivated, planned, and delivered by people in the target's everyday lives, not usually by scholars or researchers. The agents of these interventions need not be experts; to the contrary, they are typically parents or caregivers who are concerned about protecting their targets—typically children. Also, the interventions themselves are often not constructed from theory or an awareness of any particulars from the media effects literature; instead, they are constructed from everyday logic that suggests what might be useful in protecting targets. With this type of study, researchers observe naturally occurring interventions in the targets' own environments. Sometimes these "observations" are not made by the researchers but are gathered through a survey questionnaire; in this case, the observations are those of the targets themselves or of their agents (typically parents and teachers).

A useful way to organize all these natural interventions is to use the scheme developed by Valkenburg, Krcmar, Peeters, and Marseille (1999), who argued that there are three types of natural interventions, which they labeled "restrictive mediation," "social co-viewing," and "instructive mediation."

RESTRICTIVE INTERVENTION

Restrictive invention is when an authority figure, such as a parent, prohibits the target from using certain media or sets rules that limit exposure to media (see Nathanson, 2001a, for a review of this research). Research has shown mixed support for the effectiveness of this type of intervention. For example, Desmond, Singer, Singer, Calam, and Colimore (1985) argued that it has been found to be a useful technique. In contrast, Nathanson (2002) found that restrictive intervention was related to less positive attitudes toward parents, more positive attitudes toward the content, and more viewing of the content with friends. This appears to be opposite of what parents intend as an outcome of using this strategy. Nathanson wrote, "Unfortunately, parents' good intentions in using restrictive intervention may actually contribute to the harmful outcomes parents wished to prevent in the first place" (p. 221).

SOCIAL COVIEWING

Social coviewing is a technique where parents and children simply watch television together. Most research studies find that this technique is relatively rare. For example, Lawrence and Wozniak (1989) found that most viewing is solitary and that when children do view with a family member, it is usually a sibling. Also, when coviewing with parents and children does occur, it is usually with older children who are likely to watch shows the adults also like (Dorr, Kovaric, & Doubleday, 1989). Among children 7 and older, 95% never watch TV with their parents, and even among children 2 to 7, 81% never watch with their parents (Rideout, Foehr, Roberts, & Brodie, 1999).

Coviewing, like restrictive intervention, has had mixed results in the research literature. Coviewing has also been found to be associated with negative outcomes such as coming to believe that television characters are like real-world people (Messaris & Kerr, 1984) and learning aggression from violent television (Nathanson, 1999). However, coviewing has been shown to have positive outcomes such as increasing the learning of educational content (Salomon, 1977).

INSTRUCTIONAL INTERVENTION

Instructional intervention is not one technique but itself is an umbrella term for many techniques, usually verbal, that parents use when viewing with their children. Messaris (1982) explained that typically parents who use instructional intervention will discuss the reality status of programs, make critical comments about the behavior of characters their children witness on television, and provide supplemental information about topics introduced by the television messages.

Instructional intervention is rare. Several studies have found that there is generally no dialogue when a parent and child are viewing together (Austin, 1993a, 1993b; Himmelweit, Oppenheim, & Vince, 1958). Likewise, a Gallup poll indicated that when parents and a child are viewing television and some offensive material comes on the screen, parents are seven times more likely to ignore it by quickly changing the channel than to discuss the offending content with their child (Austin, 1993a, 1993b).

Instructional intervention techniques have been found useful in helping children reduce unwanted effects from viewing television (Austin, 1993a, 1993b; Nathanson & Cantor, 2000; Nathanson & Yang, 2003). There is also evidence that instructional intervention works better than more punitive techniques (Desmond et al., 1985; Singer, Singer, & Rapaczynski, 1984). Children who experience instructional intervention in general are less vulnerable to negative effects of all kinds—cognitive (Austin, 1993a, 1993b; Desmond et al., 1985), attitudinal (Austin, 1993a; Nathanson & Botta, 2003), affective (Cantor, 2001; Hoffner, 1997), and behavioral (Nathanson, 1999; Nathanson & Cantor, 2000; Reid, 1979).

The effectiveness of instructional interventions has been found to vary by the agents of instruction. For example, Nathanson (2001a) reported that instructional mediation produced stronger effects when delivered by peers than by parents; however, these effects were negative rather than positive. She found that peer mediation led to more positive orientations toward antisocial television, which in turn led to greater aggression. Of course, the intention of parental mediation is to inhibit negative media effects, but peer mediation facilitates harmful outcomes.

The success of intervention techniques is also tied to the type of person who is the target. For example, Nathanson and Yang (2003) demonstrate that certain techniques work well with younger children (5 to 8). Also, some techniques work better with one gender (Nathanson & Cantor, 2000).

Finally, the effectiveness of instructional interventions varies by the particular techniques used. Interventions work better when parents are more active during television viewing (Austin, 1993a, 1993b). Also, parents need to use noncognitive as well as cognitive strategies (Cantor, 2001). Role modeling has been found to be a successful technique. For example, Austin and Meili (1995) found that children use their emotion and logic to develop expectations about alcohol use in the real world when they see alcohol used by characters on television. When children rely on both real life and televised sources of information, they are more likely to develop skepticism about television portrayals of alcohol use than when they rely on parents as primary sources of information and behavioral modeling.

SUMMARY OF NATURAL INTERVENTIONS

In reviewing this literature several years ago, Nathanson (2001a) showed the complexity inherent in natural interventions. Her conclusions still stand. Some techniques work whereas others do not; some work with certain kinds of parents or certain kinds of children; and the effects are varied, ranging from cognitions (learning about television messages), to attitudes (developing skepticism for ads and news), to perceptions (of television reality), to behaviors (including aggression, viewing habits, and response to advertising).

◆ Critique

Now that we have analyzed the media literacy intervention literature, we will make three critical observations about what needs to be done in the future. These observations focus scholarly attention on the use of theory, the need to map the phenomenon, and the overall utility of the general literature on mass media effects.

USE OF THEORY

A serious shortcoming of this literature is that less than half of the published assessments of media literacy interventions that we reviewed for this chapter acknowledged a theoretical mechanism driving the media effect under investigation. Media literacy intervention studies that do acknowledge a theory typically cite social cognitive theory (Austin et al., 2007; Austin & Johnson, 1997; Nathanson, 1999; Pinkleton et al., 2007; Rosenkoetter et al., 2004; Vooijs & Van der Voort, 1993), desensitization (Linz et al., 1990; Slone & Shoshani, 2006; Vooijs & van der Voort, 1993), or cultivation theory (Austin & Johnson, 1997; Nathanson, 1999; Slone & Shoshani, 2006).

Although social cognitive theory, desensitization, and cultivation are the most prevalent in media literacy studies, there are other media effects mechanisms that have been given attention. These include priming, accessibility, and schema or script activation (Moore et al., 2000; Nathanson et al., 2002; Ramasubramanian & Oliver, 2007; Rosenkoetter et al., 2004), the elaboration likelihood model (Slater & Rouner, 2002), social norms (Elliot et al., 2006; Ramasubramanian & Oliver, 2007), disposition theory (Wilksch et al., 2006), displacement (Kline, 2005), and uses and gratifications (Nathanson, 2001a). Many theoretical mechanisms for media effects have been ignored altogether by media literacy scholars. To our knowledge, there have been no explicit attempts to mitigate framing effects, agenda setting, the third-person effect, media dependency, medium theory, diffusion, or issues related to limited capacity (see related chapters in this book).

It is interesting to note that whereas many social science theoretical mechanisms have been tested and found useful for explaining effects, most of the media literacy literature ignores these mechanisms. Furthermore, there is little evidence of systematic programmatic lines of research based on any of these mechanisms. These characteristics seriously limit the growth of our understanding about media literacy effects.

SUCCESSFUL MAPPING

Now that we have a clearer picture of the theories that media literacy scholars apply to their work, either from the effects perspective or the mitigation perspective, it is worth noting that very few studies map these two conceptualizations onto one another. That is, rarely do media literacy scholars identify a media effects process and then argue, within the constructs and propositions of the theory, how to interrupt this process with a media literacy intervention. There are a few stellar exceptions to this rule. For example, Austin et al. (2002) wished to mitigate the original predictions of their MIP model and, therefore, specifically designed media literacy interventions that moderated emotional and logic-driven responses to media messages through reducing antisocial learning and moderating character identification. Similarly, Rosenkoetter et al. (2004) directly attempted to disrupt social learning and script building by challenging the rewards and consequences portrayed in media messages. Ramasubramanian and Oliver (2007) took a mixed-theory approach, suggesting that the most useful

way to interrupt a priming effect is by drawing on social cognitive theory. Specifically, they proposed that an authority figure can point out negative consequences to viewers before the antisocial cognitions are activated. Nathanson (2001a) proposed that, according to uses and gratifications, children who view with a negative orientation toward the messages, such as parental negative mediations, will be less susceptible to negative effects. Lew et al. (2007) explicitly intervened in social comparison processes that result in viewing idealized images.

CRITICAL ANALYSIS OF GENERAL MEDIA EFFECTS LITERATURE

The general literature on mass media effects is fairly large, consisting of perhaps as many as 10,000 empirical studies (Potter & Riddle, 2007). Although this literature has high value in *suggesting* where vulnerabilities may exist in different kinds of targets, it offers relatively low value in prescribing the power of various elements that reduce naturally occurring negative media effects. In this critique, we argue that there are four characteristics of the mass media effects literature that limit its usefulness in helping construct media literacy interventions.

First, there is little calibration of the relative strength or prevalence of negative mass media effects. The mass media effects literature is overflowing with studies that have found a relationship between some form of media message and some kind of effect, but it is not likely that all of these effects are equally important. Such a calibration is important for media literacy interventions so that we can know where our limited efforts are likely to make the most impact.

Another facet of calibrating media influence is the issue of prevalence, that is, how many people experience an influence (prevalence in population) and how often people experience the influence (prevalence in time). Until we can do this well, we will not have much ability to focus the attention of the public on their risks of media exposures. As of now, we have identified a long list of effects that have been linked with various kinds of media exposure, that is, our list of "yes" effects is very long. If we simply present this to the public, we will scare many people with the length of the list and turn off others with the apparent range of effects. It is rather like the health community giving us a list of harms to our health that includes not taking a vitamin, smoking, having sex with someone who is HIV-positive, and getting too little sleep once in a while. We need to develop more of a sense of the power of media influence across the entire range of effects. Until we can do this, we cannot target our policy and educational efforts well.

Second, there is little calibration of the importance of different factors in bringing about any negative effect. We need to move beyond the reporting of whether or not a particular media message can be linked to a particular effect; we already have a good deal of information of this nature. Our challenge now is to examine *how strongly* particular patterns of media exposure are related to each particular effect. With limited resources, we cannot afford to design weak interventions when the well-being of children or other vulnerable targets is at stake.

Third, there is little attention to inter-actions among factors. It is not enough to identify what the most important influ-ences are on a particular effect; we also need to know how those influences work together. Media messages are not simple, monolithic stimuli; they are complex. And those complex elements interact variously with the constellation of factors that make up a target's personality. We need to develop a much better understanding about which factors are the most powerful in these interactions. It is not sufficient to calibrate the relative power across all

relevant factors of influence; we also need to know the nature of how these factors work together.

Fourth, and perhaps most serious as a limitation of the mass media effects literature, is that there is much more of a focus on comparisons across group means than a focus on how a person's vulner-ability to negative effects changes over time. Thus, experimental participants with an unusual sensitivity to a particular effect get averaged in with participants who have little or no sensitivity to that effect. However, from a media literacy perspective, these "unusual sensitivities" are important because they deserve the most attention when designing interventions.

Summarizing the main points of this critique, our research field has developed a long list of effects that have been linked to media exposures. Also, we have generated an inventory of particular factors about the media messages, audience members, and situations that have been found related to those effects. However, we have little idea—other than our intuitive opinions—about which of these many effects are the most serious or the most widespread. Also, we have little sense about which factors are the most impor-tant influences and how those factors work together in bringing about media effects. And most limiting, we are focused on conducting research that compares means across groups statistically rather than comparing changes in an individual's vulnerability over time as sets of influences change (for a more detailed explication of these criticisms, see Potter, 2009).

◆ *Conclusion*

Mass media literacy effects is a very important area for scholarship. We have made a begin-ning by identifying some negative effects of media exposure on vulnerable targets, especially children. And we have begun to build an understanding about which interventions do not work as planned, as well as which interventions have promise. We have much more work to do in building knowledge about which targets are most vulnerable to which effects. We also have a great deal more work to do in translating the findings of the general mass media effects literatures into interventions that have the potential to build greater media literacy.

Media literacy will only increase in importance as new media become available and are adopted widely, especially the so-called new media and new technologies. The interactive nature provided by computers in the areas of social networking and game playing offer a greater potential for negative effects (such as addiction and invasion of privacy) as well as positive effects (such as simulations to teach processes and the offering of a much wider range of information to a much wider range of people). As parents, policymakers, and institutions become increasingly concerned about guiding people away from potentially negative effects and toward the benefits of positive effects, they will need media literacy scholars to provide them with a range of interventions that have been demonstrated to provide more good than harm.

◆ References

Austin, E. W. (1993a). Exploring the effects of active parental mediation of television content. *Journal of Broadcasting & Electronic Media, 37,* 147–158.

Austin, E. W. (1993b). The importance of perspective in parent-child interpretations of family communication patterns. *Journalism Quarterly, 70,* 558–568.

Austin, E. W., & Johnson, K. K. (1997). Effects of general and alcohol-specific media literacy training on children's decision making about alcohol. *Journal of Health Communication, 2,* 17–42.

Austin, E. W., & Meili, H. K. (1995). Effects of interpretations of television alcohol portrayals on children's alcohol beliefs. *Journal of Broadcasting & Electronic Media, 39,* 417–435.

Austin, E. W., Miller, A. C. R., Silva, J., Guerra, P., Geisler, N., Gamboa, L., et al. (2002). The effects of increased cognitive involvement on college students' interpretations of magazine advertisements for alcohol. *Communication Research, 29,* 155–179.

Austin, E. W., Pinkleton, B. E., & Funabiki, R. P. (2007). The desirability paradox in the effects of media literacy training. *Communication Research, 34,* 483–506.

Bandura, A. (1986). *Social foundations of thought and action: A social cognitive theory.* Englewood Cliffs, NJ: Prentice Hall.

Banerjee, S. C., & Greene, K. (2006). Analysis versus production: Adolescent cognitive and attitudinal responses to antismoking interventions. *Journal of Communication, 56,* 773–794.

Bar-on, M. E., Broughton, D. D., Buttross, S., Corrigan, S., Gedissman, A., de Rivas, M. R. G., et al. (2001). Media violence. *Pediatrics, 108,* 1222–1226.

Bragg, S. (2002). Wrestling in woolly gloves: Not just being critically media literate. *Journal of Popular Film and Television, 30,* 41–51.

Brown, J. A. (1998). Media literacy perspectives. *Journal of Communication, 48*(1), 44–57.

Brown, J. D. (2000). Adolescents' sexual media diets. *Journal of Adolescent Health, 27*(2), 35–40.

Byrne, S. (2009). Media literacy interventions: What makes them boom or boomerang? *Communication Education, 58,* 1–14.

Byrne, S., & Hart, P. S. (2009). The "boomerang" effect: A synthesis of findings and a preliminary theoretical framework. In C. Beck (Ed.), *Communication yearbook 33* (pp. 3–37). Mahwah, NJ: Erlbaum.

Byrne, S., Linz, D., & Potter, W. J. (in press). A test of competing cognitive explanations for the boomerang effect in response to the deliberate disruption of media-induced aggression. *Media Psychology.*

Cantor, J. (2001). The media and children's fears, anxieties, and perceptions of danger. In D. G. Singer & J. L. Singer (Eds.), *Handbook of children and the media* (pp. 207–221). Thousand Oaks, CA: Sage.

Cantor, J., & Wilson, B. J. (1984). Modifying fear responses to mass media in preschool and elementary school children. *Journal of Broadcasting & Electronic Media, 28,* 431–443.

Cantor, J., & Wilson, B. J. (2003). Media and violence: Intervention strategies for reducing aggression. *Media Psychology, 5,* 363–403.

Chaffee, S., Morduchowicz, R., & Galperin, H. (1997). Education for democracy in Argentina: Effects of a newspaper-in-school program. *International Journal of Public Opinion Research, 9,* 313–335.

Choma, B. L., Foster, M. D., & Radford, E. (2007). Use of objectification theory to examine the effects of a media literacy intervention on women. *Sex Roles, 56,* 581–590.

Cohen, H. L. (2002). Developing media literacy skills to challenge television's portrayal of older women. *Educational Gerontology, 28,* 599–620.

Desmond, R. J., Singer, J. L., Singer, D. G., Calam, R., & Colimore, K. (1985). Family mediation patterns and television viewing: Young children's use and grasp of the medium. *Human Communication Research, 11,* 461–480.

Doolittle, J. C. (1980). Immunizing children against possible antisocial effects of viewing television violence: A curricular intervention. *Perceptual & Motor Skills, 51,* 498.

Dorr, A., Kovaric, P., & Doubleday, C. (1989). Parent-child coviewing of television. *Journal of Broadcasting & Electronic Media, 33,* 35–51.

Durham, M. G. (1999). Girls, media, and the negotiation of sexuality: A study of race, class, and gender in adolescent peer groups. *Journalism & Mass Communication Quarterly, 76,* 193–216.

Elliot, D. L., Moe, E. L., Goldberg, L., DeFrancesco, C. A., Durham, M. B., & Hix-Small, H. (2006). Definition and outcome of a curriculum to prevent disordered eating and body-shaping drug use. *Journal of School Health, 76,* 67–73.

Evans, A. E., Dave, J., Tanner, A., Duhe, S., Condrasky, M., Wilson, D., et al. (2006). Changing the home nutrition environment: Effects of a nutrition and media literacy pilot intervention. *Family & Community Health, 29,* 43–54.

Gonzales, R., Glik, D., Davoudi, M., & Ang, A. (2004). Media literacy and public health: Integrating theory, research, and practice for tobacco control. *American Behavioral Scientist, 48,* 189–201.

Helme, D. W., Donohew, R. L., Baier, M., & Zittleman, L. (2007). A classroom-administered simulation of a television campaign on adolescent smoking: Testing an activation model of information exposure. *Journal of Health Communication, 12,* 399–415.

Himmelweit, H. T., Oppenheim, A., & Vince, P. (1958). *Television and the child.* London: Oxford University Press.

Hobbs, R. (1998). The seven great debates in the media literacy movement. *Journal of Communication, 48,* 16–32.

Hoffner, C. (1997). Children's emotional reactions to a scary film: The role of prior outcome information and coping style. *Human Communication Research, 23,* 323–341.

Huesmann, L. R., Eron, L. D., Klein, R., Brice, P., & Fischer, P. (1983). Mitigating the imitation of aggressive behaviors by changing children's attitudes about media violence. *Journal of Personality & Social Psychology, 44,* 899–910.

Irving, L. M., & Berel, S. R. (2001). Comparison of media-literacy programs to strengthen college women's resistance to media images. *Psychology of Women Quarterly, 25,* 103–111.

Kline, S. (2005). Countering children's sedentary lifestyles: An evaluative study of a media-risk education approach. *Childhood: A Global Journal of Child Research, 12,* 239–258.

Lawrence, F., & Wozniak, P. (1989). Children's television viewing with family members. *Psychological Reports, 65,* 395–400.

Lew, A. M., Mann, T., Myers, H., Taylor, S., & Bower, J. (2007). Thin-ideal media and women's body dissatisfaction: Prevention using downward social comparisons on non-appearance dimensions. *Sex Roles, 57,* 543–556.

Lewis, J., & Jhally, S. (1998). The struggle over media literacy. *Journal of Communication, 48*(1), 109–112.

Leyens, J. P., Cisneros, T., & Hossay, J. F. (1976). Decentration as a means for reducing aggression after exposure to violent stimuli. *European Journal of Social Psychology, 6,* 459–473.

Linz, D., Fuson, I. A., & Donnerstein, E. (1990). Mitigating the negative effects of sexually violent mass communications through preexposure briefings. *Communication Research, 17,* 641–674.

McGuire, W. J. (1964). Inducing resistance to persuasion: Some contemporary approaches. In L. Berkowitz (Ed.), *Advances in experimental social psychology* (Vol. 1, pp. 191–229). New York: Academic Press.

McVey, G. L., & Davis, R. (2002). A program to promote positive body image: A 1-year follow-up evaluation. *Journal of Early Adolescence, 22,* 96–108.

Merskin, D. (2004). Reviving Lolita? A media literacy examination of sexual portrayals of girls in fashion advertising. *American Behavioral Scientist, 48,* 119–129.

Messaris, P. (1982). Parents, children, and television. In G. Gumpert & R. Cathcart (Eds.), *Inter/Media* (2nd ed., pp. 580–598). New York: Oxford University Press.

Messaris, P., & Kerr, D. (1984). TV-related mother-child interaction and children's perceptions of TV characters. *Journalism Quarterly, 61,* 662–666.

Moore, J., DeChillo, N., Nicholson, B., Genovese, A., & Sladen, S. (2000). Flashpoint: An innovative media literacy intervention for high-risk adolescents. *Juvenile and Family Court Journal, 51*(2), 23–34.

Nathanson, A. I. (1999). Identifying and explaining the relationship between parental mediation and children's aggression. *Communication Research, 26,* 124–143.

Nathanson, A. I. (2001a). Mediation of children's television viewing: Working toward conceptual clarity and common understanding. In W. B. Gudykunst (Ed.), *Communication yearbook 25* (pp. 115–151). Mahwah, NJ: Erlbaum.

Nathanson, A. I. (2001b). Parents versus peers: Exploring the significance of peer mediation of antisocial television. *Communication Research, 28,* 251–274.

Nathanson, A. I. (2002). The unintended effects of parental mediation of television on adolescents. *Media Psychology, 4,* 207–230.

Nathanson, A. I. (2004). Factual and evaluative approaches to modifying children's responses to violent television. *Journal of Communication, 54,* 321–336.

Nathanson, A. I., & Botta, R. A. (2003). Shaping the effects of television on adolescents' body image disturbance: The role of parental mediation. *Communication Research, 30,* 304–331.

Nathanson, A. I., & Cantor, J. (2000). Reducing the aggression-promoting effect of violent cartoons by increasing children's fictional involvement with the victim: A study of active mediation. *Journal of Broadcasting & Electronic Media, 44,* 94–109.

Nathanson, A. I., Wilson, B. J., McGee, J., & Sebastian, M. (2002). Counteracting the effects of female stereotypes on television via active mediation. *Journal of Communication, 52,* 922–937.

Nathanson, A. I., & Yang, M.-S. (2003). The effects of mediation content and form on children's responses to violent television. *Human Communication Research, 29,* 111–134.

Neumark-Sztainer, D., Sherwood, N. E., Coller, T., & Hannan, P. J. (2000). Primary prevention of disordered eating among preadolescent girls: Feasibility and short-term effect of a community-based intervention. *Journal of the American Dietetic Association, 100,* 1466–1473.

Olson, S. R., & Pollard, T. (2004). The muse pixeliope: Digitalization and media literacy education. *American Behavioral Scientist, 48,* 248–255.

Pinkleton, B. E., Austin, E. W., Cohen, M., Miller, A., & Fitzgerald, E. (2007). A statewide evaluation of the effectiveness of media literacy training to prevent tobacco use among adolescents. *Health Communication, 21,* 23–34.

Potter, W. J. (2004). *Theory of media literacy: A cognitive approach.* Thousand Oaks, CA: Sage.

Potter, W. J. (2009). *Arguing for a general framework for mass media theory and research.* Thousand Oaks, CA: Sage.

Potter, W. J., & Byrne, S. (2007). What are media literacy effects? In S. R. Mazzarella (Ed.), *20 questions about youth and the media.* New York: Peter Lang.

Potter, W. J., & Riddle, K. (2007). A content analysis of the media effects literature. *Journalism & Mass Communication Quarterly, 84,* 90–104.

Ramasubramanian, S., & Oliver, M. B. (2007). Activating and suppressing hostile and benevolent racism: Evidence for comparative media stereotyping. *Media Psychology, 9,* 623–646.

Reid, L. N. (1979). Viewing rules as mediating factors in children's responses to commercials. *Journal of Broadcasting, 23,* 15–26.

Rich, M., & Bar-on, M. (2001). Child health in the information age: Media education of pediatricians. *Pediatrics, 107,* 156–162.

Rideout, V. J., Foehr, U. G., Roberts, D. F., & Brodie, M. (1999). *Kids & media @ the new millennium.* Menlo Park, CA: Kaiser Foundation.

Rosenkoetter, L. I., Rosenkoetter, S. E., Ozretich, R. A., & Acock, A. C. (2004). Mitigating the harmful effects of violent television. *Journal of Applied Developmental Psychology, 25,* 25–47.

Salomon, G. (1977). Effects of encouraging Israeli mothers to co-observe Sesame Street with their five-year-olds. *Child Development, 48,* 1146–1151.

Silverblatt, A., & Eliceiri, E. M. E. (1997). *Dictionary of media literacy.* Westport, CT: Greenwood Press.

Singer, J. L., Singer, D. G., & Rapaczynski, W. S. (1984). Family patterns and television viewing as predictors of children's beliefs and aggression. *Journal of Communication, 34*(2), 73–89.

Slater, M. D., & Rouner, D. (2002). Entertainment-education and elaboration likelihood: Understanding the processing of narrative persuasion. *Communication Theory, 12,* 173–191.

Slone, M., & Shoshani, A. (2006). Evaluation of preparatory measures for coping with anxiety raised by media coverage of terrorism. *Journal of Counseling Psychology, 53,* 535–542.

Steinke, J., Lapinski, M. K., Crocker, N., Zietsman-Thomas, A., Williams, Y., Evergreen, S. H., et al. (2007). Assessing media influences on middle school-aged children's perceptions of women in science using the Draw-A-Scientist Test (DAST). *Science Communication, 29,* 35–64.

Thoman, E., & Jolls, T. (2004). Media literacy: A national priority for a changing world. *American Behavioral Scientist, 48,* 18–29.

Valkenburg, P. M., Krcmar, M., Peeters, A. L., & Marseille, N. M. (1999). Developing a scale to assess three styles of television mediation: "restrictive mediation," "instructive mediation," and "social coviewing." *Journal of Broadcasting & Electronic Media, 43,* 52–66.

Vande Berg, L. R., Wenner, L. A., & Gronbeck, B. E. (2004). Media literacy and television criticism: Enabling an informed and engaged citizenry. *American Behavioral Scientist, 48,* 219–228.

Vooijs, M. W., & van der Voort, T. H. A. (1993). Learning about television violence: The impact of a critical viewing curriculum on children's attitudinal judgments of crime series. *Journal of Research and Development in Education, 26,* 133–142.

Wilksch, S. M., Tiggemann, M., & Wade, T. D. (2006). Impact of interactive school-based media literacy lessons for reducing internalization of media ideals in young adolescent girls and boys. *International Journal of Eating Disorders, 39,* 385–393.

Zettl, H. (1998). Contextual media aesthetics as the basis for media literacy. *Journal of Communication, 48*(1), 81–95.

PART V

CONTENT
AND AUDIENCES

24

VIOLENT MEDIA EFFECTS

◆ Brad J. Bushman, L. Rowell Huesmann, and Jodi L. Whitaker

Times have not become more violent. They have just become more televised.

—Marilyn Manson (1999), "I Don't Like the Media but the Media Likes Me"

Consuming media has become a full-time job for most children—they spend about 40 hours per week doing it (Roberts, Foehr, & Rideout, 2005). There is plenty of violence in the media. For example, about 60% of television programs contain violence (e.g., National Television Violence Study, 1998), and about 90% of video games contain violence (e.g., Children Now, 2001). Children are exposed to about 10,000 violent crimes in the media each year (Signorielli, Gerbner, & Morgan, 1995).

Parents, policymakers, and other members of society might wonder what impact exposure to violent media has on those who consume it. The purpose of this chapter is to review scientific research on violent media effects. In this chapter, we divide the effects that observing media violence has on the viewer into three categories that we name, respectively, (1) the *aggressor* effect—the more violent media you consume, the more aggressive you become; (2) the *fear-of-victimization* effect—the more violent media you consume, the more afraid you are of becoming a victim of violence; and (3) the *conscience-numbing* effect—the more violent media you consume, the less you care about others being victimized. Similar psychological processes underlie all three of these effects, and we will discuss those processes as well.

◆ Violent Media Effects

THE AGGRESSOR EFFECT

More than five decades of scientific data lead to the irrefutable conclusion that exposure to violent media increases aggression. About 300 studies involving about 50,000 subjects have been conducted on this topic and reviewed and meta-analyzed multiple times (Anderson & Bushman, 2002a; Bushman & Huesmann, 2006; Paik & Comstock, 1994). The results from Anderson and Bushman's meta-analysis (2002a) are depicted in Figure 24.1 for the different types of methodologies researchers have used. Experimental studies have shown that exposure to media violence *causes* people to behave more aggressively immediately afterward. Experimental studies typically expose participants to violent media for relatively short amounts of time (usually about 15–30 minutes) before measuring aggressive thoughts, feelings, and most important, behaviors. For example, research has shown that exposure

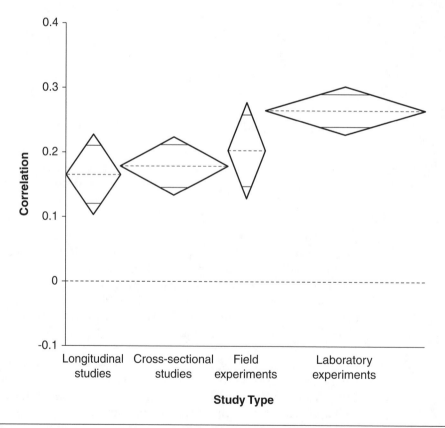

Figure 24.1   Effect of Violent Media on Aggression for Different Types of Studies

Source: Based on 287 studies involving 51,597 subjects (Anderson & Bushman, 2002a).

Note: Middle bars are average correlations. Outer bars are 95% confidence intervals. Diamonds are proportional to the number of studies.

to violent media immediately makes people more willing to give others painful electric shocks (Geen & O'Neal, 1969) and loud noise blasts (Bartholow & Anderson, 2002), and makes young children and adolescents more likely to attack each other physically (Josephson, 1987).

Experimental studies have been criticized for their somewhat artificial nature (for reviews and rebuttals of these criticisms, see Anderson, Lindsay, & Bushman, 1999), but field experiments have produced similar results in more realistic settings. For example, delinquent boys who were shown violent films every night for five nights were more likely than those shown nonviolent films to get into fights with other boys (Leyens, Parke, Camino, & Berkowitz, 1975) or display higher levels of verbal aggression (Sebastian, Parke, Berkowitz, & West, 1978). Similar effects have been found with nondelinquent children who saw a single episode of a violent children's television program (Boyatzis, Matillo, & Nesbitt, 1995).

However, it is not so much the immediate effects of media violence that are of concern, but rather the aggregated long-term effects. Longitudinal studies offer evidence of a relationship between exposure to violent television as a child and aggressive and violent behavior many years later as an adult. Children who have a heavy diet of violent television are more likely to behave aggressively later in life. For example, in one longitudinal study, children exposed to violent media at ages 8 to 10 were significantly more aggressive 15 years later as young adults (Huesmann, Moise-Titus, Podolski, & Eron, 2003). Importantly, this study also found that aggression as a child was unrelated to exposure to violent media as a young adult, effectively ruling out the possibility that this relationship is merely a result of more aggressive children consuming more violent media.

Longitudinal studies have also demonstrated that exposure to violent media is related to serious aggressive behavior.

For example, the amount of violent media consumed is related to aggressive behavior in adolescents (e.g., fighting) in high school students (McLeod, Atken, & Chaffee, 1972). Similarly, men who watched violent media during childhood are nearly twice as likely to have assaulted their spouses 15 years later and significantly more likely to have been arrested for a crime (Huesmann et al., 2003). Adolescent males from a high-risk sample who were high media violence viewers in middle childhood were recently found to be 18% more likely to have threatened or used a knife or a gun on someone in the last year (Huesmann et al., 2007).

Although the majority of studies to date have focused on violent television and movies, the same general pattern of effects appears to be present after exposure to different forms of media, including violent music (Anderson, Carnagey, & Eubanks, 2003; Johnson, Jackson, & Gatto, 1995) and violent video games (Konijn, Nije Bijvank, & Bushman, 2007). In fact, recent theorizing (Bushman & Huesmann, 2006) and empirical research (Polman, Orobio de Castro, & van Aken, 2008) suggest that the effects of violent video games are stronger than the effects of passive visual media. Each research method has its own strengths and weaknesses. Yet across the different methods, there is a convergence of evidence (see Figure 24.1). Scientists call this convergence "triangulation." Regardless of the method used, the conclusion is the same: Exposure to violent media increases aggression and violence.

Of course violent media is not the only risk factor for violent and aggressive behavior, or even the most important risk factor, yet it is an important risk factor that cannot be dismissed as "trivial" or "inconsequential." Although the typical effect size for exposure to violent media is relatively small by conventional standards (Cohen, 1977) and is therefore dismissed by some critics, this "small effect" translates into significant consequences for society as a whole, which may be a better standard to measure the magnitude of the effect (Abelson, 1985; Yeaton & Sechrest, 1981). For example, the U.S. Surgeon General's Report on youth violence found that violent media is as large a risk factor for youth violence as other well-known factors such as poverty, substance abuse, and bad parenting (Anderson, Berkowitz, et al., 2003; U.S. Department of Health and Human Services, 2001).

THE FEAR-OF-VICTIMIZATION EFFECT

Research has shown that heavy TV viewers (defined as at least 4 hours per day) are more fearful about becoming victims of violence, are more distrustful of others, and are more likely to perceive the world as a dangerous, mean, and hostile place than are light TV viewers (e.g., Gerbner & Gross, 1976, 1981). For example, in one study, television exposure was predictive of fear of crime, whereas actual exposure to crime was not (Van den Bulck, 2004). A similar but stronger relationship has been reported between watching television news and fear of crime (Romer, Jamieson, & Aday, 2003). Like the *aggressor* effect, this *fear-of-victimization* effect seems to begin early in childhood, with even 7- to 11-year-olds displaying this pattern (Peterson & Zill, 1981).

In general, the fear-of-victimization effect only seems to apply when people are evaluating unfamiliar environments. Although violent media make people more afraid of crime in their city and increase their estimates of the prevalence of crime in general, they have relatively little impact on people's feelings of fear in their own neighborhood (Heath & Petraitis, 1987; Hughes, 1980; Sparks & Ogles, 1990). This suggests that the fear-of-victimization effect may be related to the availability heuristic (Tversky & Kahneman, 1973). The *availability heuristic* is the tendency to judge the frequency or likelihood of an event by the ease with

which relevant instances come to mind. People make evaluations based on salient or noticeable information, and when people have relatively little firsthand experience with an environment, they may draw upon television as an additional source of information.

THE CONSCIENCE-NUMBING EFFECT

People who consume a lot of violent media become less sympathetic to victims of violence. In one study, people who played violent video games assigned less harsh penalties to criminals than those who played a nonviolent game (Deselms & Altman, 2003). People exposed to violent media also perceive victims as less injured (Linz, Donnerstein, & Adams, 1989) and display less empathy toward them (Linz, Donnerstein, & Penrod, 1988). The *conscience-numbing effect* appears to be an enduring one. Even several days after watching violent, sexually explicit scenes, men still displayed an increased tolerance to aggression directed toward women (Malamuth & Check, 1981; Mullin & Linz, 1995).

The reduced empathy for victims of violence causes people to become less willing to help a victim of violence in the real world (Drabman & Thomas, 1974, 1976; Molitor & Hirsch, 1994). Children in these studies who had been exposed to violent programs were less willing to intervene when they saw two younger children fighting. Adults are also less helpful to those in need after exposure to violent media (Bushman & Anderson, 2009). One reason why people may become more tolerant of violence and less sympathetic toward violence victims is because they become desensitized to it over time. Consistent with this interpretation, research has shown that after consuming violent media, people are less physiologically aroused by real depictions of violence (Carnagey, Anderson, &

Bushman, 2007; Cline, Croft, & Courrier, 1973; Thomas, 1982).

The effects of violent video games on children's empathy toward victims are of particular concern. Feeling empathy requires taking the perspective of the victim, whereas violent video games encourage players to take the perspective of the aggressor. Whereas in at least some television and video depictions of violence, the viewer has the choice of taking the perspective of the aggressor or victim, in most violent video games, the player is forced into taking the perspective of the aggressor. Thus, playing violent video games may have a particularly strong effect on diminishing the empathy the player feels for the victim (Bushman & Anderson, 2009; Funk, Baldacci, Pasold, & Baumgardner, 2004). This conscience-numbing effect of media violence is a process that contributes to the aggressor effects described previously.

◆ *Why Do People Deny Media Effects?*

Although the scientific evidence shows that violent media effects are undeniable, many people still deny these effects. There are at least four reasons why.

First, people may think, "I (or other people I know) watch a lot of violent shows and I've never killed anyone. Furthermore, I never heard of anyone watching a lot of violence and then murdering someone. Therefore, media violence has no effect." This fallacious reasoning is a good example of how the availability heuristic coupled with the *base rate problem* (Kahneman & Tversky, 1973) distort reasoning. People have great difficulty judging influences on events when the base rate probability of the event is very low. It is not surprising that people who consume violent media have not killed anyone because very few people kill anyone. For example, fewer than 6 people per 100,000 are murdered each year in the United States (U.S. Federal Bureau of Investigation, 2008). It is very difficult to predict rare events, such as murder, using exposure to violent media or any other factor. However, murder is the most salient violent event to most people; so when they don't have "available" in memory cases of people viewing media violence and then murdering, they ignore the base rate of murder and conclude that media violence has no effect. They do this despite the fact that one can predict less extreme and more common violent behaviors from media violence viewing. For example, in one 15-year longitudinal study (Huesmann et al., 2003), heavy viewers of violent TV shows in first and third grade were three times more likely to be convicted of criminal behavior by the time they were in their twenties. They were also more likely to have abused their spouses and assaulted other people at least once in the past year.

Second, researchers have also found that people believe the media have a much stronger effect on others than on themselves. This effect is very robust and is called the *third-person effect* (Davison, 1983; Innes & Zeitz, 1988; Perloff, 1999). The consequence of this psychological effect is that people may often agree that media violence has a bad effect on some people, but not on themselves, their own children, or other children who are "brought up like mine." This thinking may then lead to a denial of the overall importance of the effects from a public health standpoint.

Third, the entertainment industry frequently claims that violent media do not increase aggression (Bushman & Anderson, 2001). Even though the public may recognize that making such claims is in the economic self-interest of the entertainment industry, the repetition of the claims of no effects still seems to have an effect. In 1972, the U.S. Surgeon General issued a warning about the harmful effects of TV violence. Since then, the scientific evidence has grown even stronger (see Figure 24.2). But an analysis of over 600 news reports shows that over time, news stories are more likely to deny the harmful effect of media violence (see Figure 24.2). Most Americans aren't even aware that the U.S. Surgeon General issued a warning about TV violence. Perhaps this is because most Americans get their information from the mass media. The entertainment industry is probably reluctant to admit that they are marketing a harmful product, much like the tobacco industry was reluctant to admit that they were marketing a harmful product.

Fourth, people do not understand psychological processes as well as they understand biological processes. If you see a violent video game player assault another person, it is difficult to know the direct cause of the assault. Was it playing violent video games for hours on end, or was it something else? The psychological process by which playing violent video games produces this result is not as intuitive to most people as are biological processes. People are probably more accepting of the idea that smoking causes lung cancer, for example, because it is much easier to grasp the idea that smoke going into the lungs damages cells and starts tumor growth.

These processes combine to create an atmosphere in which not only nonexpert journalists but also scholars who have not done research in the area write articles and books arguing that there are no effects (see Huesmann & Taylor, 2003). However, the vast majority of social scientists working in the area now accept that media violence poses a danger to society (Murray, 1998).

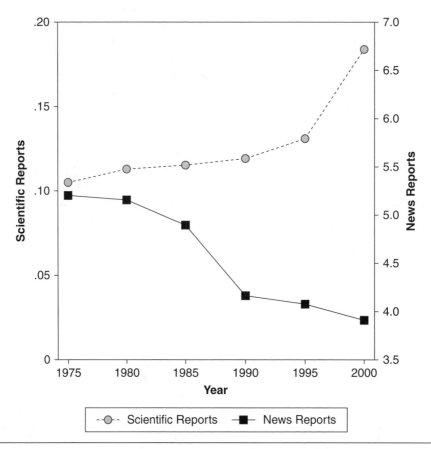

Figure 24.2 Conservative Scientific (Lower Boundary of 99.9% Confidence Interval) Versus News Reports of the Effect of Media Violence on Aggression

Source: Anderson & Bushman (2002b).

◆ Moderators of Violent Media Effects

Although research has shown that violent media can produce aggressor, victim, and conscience-numbing effects, there are a number of important moderators of these effects. One is age. As we discuss in the following paragraphs, different psychological processes are responsible for short-term and long-term effects of media violence. Although the short-term effects of media violence can be detected in any age viewer, children are most at risk for experiencing the longer-term changes in social cognitions that control behavior over time. Children have less well developed neurological and emotional systems and less well developed personalities that can more easily be changed by repeated exposure to violence. Consequently, younger children appear to be particularly vulnerable to the long-term effects of violence (Eron, Huesmann, Lefkowitz, & Walder, 1972; Huesmann et al., 2003; Paik & Comstock, 1994).

Another important moderator is exactly how the violence is depicted in the media. Media that glamorize violence may have a particularly strong influence on the aggressor and conscience-numbing effects (Bushman & Huesmann, 2001). In contrast, the fear-of-victimization effect may be constrained to media that children believe have an informative role about the world around them, such as television news. Whether someone is more likely to become an aggressor or a victim may also depend on whom they identify with: the perpetrators of violence, or their victims. However, for practical purposes, the sheer amount and variety of violence children are exposed to make it likely that all children are vulnerable to these effects in varying degrees.

Also, *who* consumes violent media is important. A number of individual differences put some people at greater risk than others. One key individual difference is trait aggressiveness. People who score high in trait aggressiveness behave more aggressively after being exposed to violent media than those low in trait aggressiveness (Bushman, 1995; Josephson, 1987). However, these findings represent trait differences at a single point in time in an experimental setting. Exposure to media violence increases trait aggressiveness, which in turn increases the likelihood of aggressive behavior (Anderson, Berkowitz, et al., 2003). This suggests that the short-term effects of violent media observed in experimental research may become increasingly pronounced within individuals as they are repeatedly exposed to violence. Additionally, there is some evidence that in the long run, more aggressive individuals turn to exposing themselves more to violent media for social comparison motivations (Huesmann et al., 2003). This leads to a "downward spiral" into greater levels of aggression (Slater, Henry, Swaim, & Anderson, 2003).

Some studies have found that males are more influenced by media violence than are females (Eron et al., 1972), but these effects are inconsistent; other researchers find little difference between males and females (Huesmann et al., 2003). This inconsistency may be a result of different measures of aggression (Anderson, Carnagey, & Flanagan, 2004) or different gender norms in the sample populations, or changes in gender norms over time. Longitudinal studies have shown that gender differences in aggression have decreased over time, probably because aggressive female models are becoming more common in the media and because it has become more socially acceptable for females to behave aggressively. One clear difference is that the combination of exposure to sex *plus* violence appears to be particularly potent in males. In one study, college students watched movies portraying violence, sex and violence, or neither sex nor violence (Donnerstein & Berkowitz, 1981). Men exposed to both sex and violence were more aggressive toward a female who provoked them than were men exposed to only violence or men exposed to no sex or violence.

◆ Why Do Violent Media Increase Aggression?

The psychological processes that underlie media-related aggression can be divided into those that produce more immediate, but transient, short-term effects on behavior, and those that produce more delayed, but enduring, long-term effects on behavior (Bushman & Huesmann, 2006; Huesmann, 1988, 1997; Huesmann & Kirwil, 2007).

EXPLAINING SHORT-TERM VIOLENT MEDIA EFFECTS

Research shows that short-term increases in children's aggressive behavior following the observation of violence are mainly due to three psychological processes: (1) the priming of already existing aggressive behavioral scripts, aggressive cognitions, or angry emotional reactions; (2) simple mimicking of aggressive scripts; and (3) changes in emotional arousal stimulated by the observation of violence. In films and plays, scripts tell actors what to say and do. In memory, scripts define situations and guide behavior: The person first selects a script from memory to represent the situation and then assumes a role in the script. Scripts can be learned by direct experience or by observing others, including media characters.

Priming. Neuroscientists and cognitive psychologists posit that the human mind acts as an associative network that consists of nodes and links. The nodes represent concepts, and the links represent associations among concepts. Thoughts, feelings, and behavioral tendencies are linked together in memory. Exposure to a stimulus can activate or prime concepts in memory (Fiske & Taylor, 1984). The activation produced by an observed stimulus spreads along network links to associated concepts as well. Thus, exposure to a stimulus can prime related concepts, ideas, and emotions in a person's memory, even without the person being aware of it (e.g., Bargh & Pietromonaco, 1982). For example, exposure to a weapon can increase aggressive thoughts and behaviors (Berkowitz & LePage, 1967).

Mimicry. Human and primate young have an innate tendency to mimic whomever they observe (e.g., Hurley & Chatter, 2004; Meltzoff & Moore, 2000). Neuroscientists have discovered "mirror neurons" in primates that seem to promote such mimicry and longer-term imitation (Rizzolati, Fadiga, Gallese, & Fogassi, 1996). The immediate "mimicry" of aggressive behaviors does not require a complex cognitive representation of the observed act, but only a simple "mirror" representation of the aggressive behavior. Consequently, children who observe (in the media or in the environment around them) others doing a specific aggressive behavior are more likely to do the same aggressive behavior immediately after observing it (Bandura, 1997). Theoretically, the more similar children think they and the observed model are, the more readily mimicry will take place, but the mimicry mechanism is so powerful that even fantasy characters can be imitated by young children. Children under about age 7 cannot tell the difference between reality and fantasy (e.g., Davies, 1997).

Arousal and excitation transfer. Observed violence often consists of action-packed scenes that increase physiological arousal (e.g., heart rate, blood pressure). There are two possible reasons why arousal may increase aggression in the short run. First, high arousal generated by exposure to violence makes any dominant response tendency more likely to be carried out in the short run. Consequently, the individual with aggressive tendencies behaves even more aggressively (e.g., Geen & O'Neal, 1969). Second, when an individual is highly aroused by viewing violence, a mild specific emotion (e.g., mild anger) experienced sometime later may be "felt" as more severe (e.g., intense anger) than otherwise because some of the emotional response stimulated by the violent media presentation is misattributed as due to the provocation. This process is called *excitation transfer* (Bryant & Zillmann, 1979; Zillmann, Bryant, & Comisky, 1981).

EXPLAINING LONG-TERM VIOLENT MEDIA EFFECTS

Research shows that long-term increases in aggressive behavior are mainly due to two psychological processes: (1) observational learning, and (2) activation and desensitization of emotional processes.

Observational learning. By *observational learning* we mean the process through which behavioral scripts, world schemas, and normative beliefs become encoded in a person's mind simply as a consequence of observing others (Huesmann, 1988, 1997). Observational learning is a powerful extension of imitation in which logical induction and abstraction are used to encode complex representations in memory. For example, extensive observation of violence biases children's world schemas toward "hostility," and they then attribute more hostility to others' actions (e.g., Dodge, 1985), which in turn increases the likelihood of aggression (e.g., Dodge, Pettit, & Bates, 1995). Similarly, through repeated observation of aggressive role models in the media and in the real world, children develop normative beliefs that aggression is appropriate, and they acquire social scripts for how to behave aggressively. Whereas short-term mimicry requires only one exposure to an observed behavior, long-term observational learning usually requires repeated exposures. The more the child's attention is riveted on the observed behavior, the fewer the number of repetitions needed. However, numerous other factors besides attention affect the extent of observational learning. For example, the more the child identifies with the observed models, and the more the observed scripts for behavior are rewarded and are portrayed as appropriate, the more firmly the scripts will be encoded in memory. Similarly, if the world schemas and normative beliefs that a child acquires through observing others (again, in real life and in the media) lead to valuable outcomes for the child, they will become more firmly encoded and more resistant to change (Huesmann & Guerra, 1997).

Activation and desensitization of emotional processes. The long-term effects of exposure to violence also involve the vicarious conditioning of emotional reactions. Through classical conditioning, fear or anger can become linked with specific stimuli after only a few exposures (e.g., Cantor, 1998). These emotions influence behavior in social settings away from the media source through stimulus generalization. An individual may then react with inappropriate fear or anger in a novel situation similar to one that he or she has observed in the media. Repeated exposure to emotionally arousing media or video games can also lead to habituation of certain natural emotional reactions. This process is often called *desensitization,* and it has been used to explain a reduction in distress-related physiological reactivity to media portrayals of violence. Indeed, violent scenes do become less arousing over time (Cline et al., 1973), and brief exposure to media violence can reduce physiological reactions to real-world violence (Thomas, Horton, Lippincott, & Drabman, 1977). Behaviors observed by the viewer that might seem unusual at first begin to seem more normative after repeated presentations. For example, most humans seem to have an innate negative emotional response to observing blood and violence, as evidenced by increased physiological arousal, and self-reports of discomfort that often accompany such exposure. However, with repeated exposure, this negative emotional response habituates, and individuals become "desensitized." As a result, these individuals can then think about and plan proactive aggressive acts without experiencing negative affect.

◆ Reducing Violent Media Effects

The U.S. government has been involved in the TV violence debate since the 1950s. In 1972, the Surgeon General concluded that TV violence was harmful to children and issued his famous warning about it (Steinfeld, 1972). However, it took almost 25 years for the legislature to actually do something about the problem. In 1996, the Telecommunications Act was passed and signed into law. This act mandated that new television sets be manufactured with a V-chip that allows parents to block out TV programs with objectionable content. This act also mandated that TV programs be rated or labeled to provide information that can be read by the V-chip. When the V-chip is activated by a special code inserted by broadcasters into the TV signal, it scrambles the reception of the incoming picture. One problem with the V-chip is that some parents have difficulty with modern technology and cannot program it. A bigger problem, however, concerns the rating system adopted. Within a year of passage of the 1996 Telecommunications Act, the TV industry announced a new age-based rating system that is similar to the movie rating system used by the Motion Picture Association of America (e.g., "TV-14, Parents Strongly Cautioned . . . many parents would find this program unsuitable for children under 14"). Some violent programs also contain a warning label (e.g., "Due to some violent content, viewer discretion is advised"). Research has shown

that such labels just make violent media "forbidden fruits" that attract young audiences (Bushman & Cantor, 2003; Nije Bijvank, Konijn, Bushman, & Roelofsma, in press). It is somewhat ironic that although labels can increase the attractiveness of violent TV programs, the TV industry can claim that it is attempting to be more responsible and proactive about the potentially harmful effects of TV violence.

Sitting a child in front of a TV set or video game console can buy the parent time—a precious commodity to any parent, especially single parents. However, a TV program or video game is often a shoddy baby-sitter, especially when the content is not monitored. Parents are in the best position to counteract the harmful effects of violent media on their child. The primary media exposure a child experiences occurs in the home. Media habits are established early in life and are quite persistent over time. The harmful effects of violent media are also greatest for young children. Thus, the parent should take an active role in counteracting the potentially harmful effects of media violence.

Training for parents includes informing them of the negative effects that media violence can have on their child, and teaching them how to counteract these negative effects. Parents should teach their child how to be a critical media consumer. Previous research has shown that teaching children critical TV viewing skills can make them less susceptible to the harmful effects of TV violence (e.g., Abelman & Courtright, 1983; Eron, 1982; Watkins, Sprafkin, Gadow, & Sadetsky, 1988). Unfortunately, very few parents (about 10%) do this.

◆ Conclusions and Future Directions

Exposure to media violence increases the risk of anyone behaving more aggressively in the short run. The effects will be larger for people who already have aggressive scripts that can be primed by the violence or who have poorer emotion regulation, but the increase in risk is universal. Habitual exposure to media violence also increases the risk of younger viewers developing into more habitually aggressive adolescents and adults regardless of how aggressive they were initially. Violent media have other effects too, such as increasing the fear of victimization and numbing people to the pain and suffering of others. The processes that produce these effects are now fairly well understood. Still, there are a number of unknowns that deserve further exploration.

Near the top of this list would be how the effects vary for different kinds of mass media, including new emerging media. Theorizing leads us to believe that video games should have even larger effects than passive visual media, and some research has shown this (e.g., Polman et al., 2008), but more research needs to be carried out to establish this fact. In particular, little is known about the effects of massively multiplayer online role-playing games (MMORPGs). Similarly, much more research is needed on the effects of even newer mass media. For example, what are the consequences of the exponential growth and use of Web sites to tell personal stories and present personal videos? How many of these presentations are violent, and what effect do they have? What about the growing use of "smart phones" to play videos and send material to others? Certainly, theory gives us reasons to be concerned about all of these and particularly about their long-term effects on children and adolescents.

Another promising area for future research is the investigation of individual difference moderators and internal mediators of the effects of observing violence or playing violent games. Clearly, some people seem to be more susceptible to influence than others, but it has been hard to pin down the characteristics that produce such differences. Whereas already-more-aggressive children seem more susceptible to short-term effects (as theory would predict), even initially nonaggressive children seem susceptible to long-term influences. Are individual differences in emotion regulation or other arousability important? Are changes in arousal mediating some of the effects? Fortunately, new advances in brain imaging and neuroscience are likely to make it easier to investigate the role of individual differences in physiology as both moderators and mediators. However, we also need to attend more to the moderating role of individual differences in socialization by parents and peers in the process. These kinds of investigations are also likely to lead to better insights for interventions to reduce the effects of media violence on individuals.

In his book *Civilization and Its Discontents,* Sigmund Freud (1930/1961) argued that children do not have to learn how to behave aggressively. Instead, they have to learn how to restrain their aggressive impulses. One of the main functions of society is to curb aggressive behavior. Virtually every society has laws against violent acts such as murder, assault, and rape. It is somewhat ironic, therefore, that many societies tolerate and even encourage the use of graphic forms of violent entertainment. In ancient Rome, it was gladiators killing each other or animals in a coliseum. Today, it is gamers "killing" enemies in a virtual world. In either case, violent forms of entertainment make us less civilized and contribute to a more violent and less peaceful society.

◆ References

Abelman, R., & Courtright, J. A. (1983). Television literacy: Amplifying the cognitive level effects of television's prosocial fare through curriculum intervention.

Journal of Research and Development in Education, 17, 46–57.

Abelson, R. P. (1985). A variance explanation paradox: When a little is a lot. *Psychological Bulletin, 97,* 128–132.

Anderson, C. A., Berkowitz, L., Donnerstein, E., Huesmann, R. L., Johnson, J. D., Linz, D., et al. (2003). The influence of media violence on youth. *Psychological Science in the Public Interest, 4,* 81–110.

Anderson, C. A., & Bushman, B. J. (2001). Effects of violent video games on aggressive behavior, aggressive cognition, aggressive affect, physiological arousal, and prosocial behavior: A meta-analytic review of the scientific literature. *Psychological Science, 12,* 353–359.

Anderson, C. A., & Bushman, B. J. (2002a). Media violence and societal violence. *Science, 295,* 2377–2378.

Anderson, C. A., & Bushman, B. J. (2002b). Media violence and the American public revisited. *American Psychologist, 57,* 448–450.

Anderson, C. A., Carnagey, N. L., & Eubanks, J. (2003). Exposure to violent media: The effects of songs with violent lyrics on aggressive thoughts and feelings. *Journal of Personality & Social Psychology, 84,* 960–971.

Anderson, C. A., Carnagey, N. L., & Flanagan, M. (2004). Violent video games: Specific effects of violent content on aggressive thoughts and behavior. *Advances in Experimental Social Psychology, 36,* 199–249.

Anderson, C. A., Lindsay, J. J., & Bushman, B. J. (1999). Research in the psychological laboratory: Truth or triviality? *Current Directions in Psychological Science, 8,* 3–9.

Bandura, A. (1997). *Social learning theory.* New York: Prentice Hall.

Bargh, J. A., & Pietromonaco, P. (1982). Automatic information processing and social perception: The influence of trait information presented outside of conscious awareness on impression formation. *Journal of Personality and Social Psychology, 43,* 437–449.

Bartholow, B. D., & Anderson, C. A. (2002). Effects of violent video games on aggressive behavior: Potential sex differences. *Journal of Experimental Social Psychology, 38,* 283–290.

Berkowitz, L., & LePage, A. (1967). Weapons as aggression-eliciting stimuli. *Journal of Personality and Social Psychology, 7,* 202–207.

Boyatzis, C. J., Matillo, G. M., & Nesbitt, K. M. (1995). Effects of the "Mighty Morphin Power Rangers" on children's aggression with peers. *Child Study Journal, 25,* 45–55.

Bryant, J., & Zillmann, D. (1979). Effect of intensification of annoyance through unrelated residual excitation on substantially delayed hostile behavior. *Journal of Experimental Social Psychology, 15,* 470–480.

Bushman, B. J. (1995). Moderating role of trait aggressiveness in the effects of violent media on aggression. *Journal of Personality and Social Psychology, 69,* 950–960.

Bushman, B. J., & Anderson, C. A. (2001). Media violence and the American public: Scientific facts versus media misinformation. *American Psychologist, 56,* 477–489.

Bushman, B. J., & Anderson, C. A. (2009). Comfortably numb: Desensitizing effects of violent media on helping others. *Psychological Science, 21*(3), 273–277.

Bushman, B. J., & Cantor, J. (2003). Media ratings for violence and sex: Implications for policy makers and parents. *American Psychologist, 58,* 130–141.

Bushman, B. J., & Huesmann, L. R. (2001). Effects of televised violence on aggression. In D. Singer & J. Singer (Eds.), Handbook of children and the media (pp. 223–254). Thousand Oaks, CA: Sage.

Bushman, B. J., & Huesmann, L. R. (2006). Short-term and long-term effects of violent media on aggression in children and adults. *Archives of Pediatrics & Adolescent Medicine, 160,* 348–352.

Cantor, J. (1998). *"Mommy, I'm scared": How TV and movies frighten children and what we can do to protect them.* San Diego: Harvest/Harcourt.

Carnagey, N. L., Anderson, C. A., & Bushman, B. J. (2007). The effect of video game violence on physiological desensitization to real life violence. *Journal of Experimental Social Psychology, 43,* 489–496.

Children Now. (2001). *Children and the media.* Retrieved July 1, 2001, from http://www.childrennow.org

Cline, V. B., Croft, R. G., & Courrier, S. (1973). Desensitization of children to television violence. *Journal of Personality and Social Psychology, 27,* 360–365.

Cohen, J. (1977). *Statistical power analysis for the behavioral sciences* (Rev. ed.). Hillsdale, NJ: Erlbaum.

Davies, M. M. (1997). *Fake, fact, and fantasy: Children's interpretations of television reality.* Mahwah, NJ: Erlbaum.

Davison, W. P. (1983). The third-person effect in communication. *Public Opinion Quarterly, 47,* 1–15.

Deselms, J. L., & Altman, J. D. (2003). Immediate and prolonged effects of videogame violence. *Journal of Applied Social Psychology, 33,* 1553–1563.

Dodge, K. A. (1985). Attributional bias in aggressive children. In P. C. Kendall (Ed.), *Advances in cognitive-behavioral research and therapy* (Vol. 4, pp. 73–110). San Diego: Academic Press.

Dodge, K. A., Pettit, G. S., & Bates, J. E. (1995). Social information-processing patterns partially mediate the effect of early physical abuse on later conduct problems. *Journal of Abnormal Psychology, 104,* 632–643.

Donnerstein, E., & Berkowitz, L. (1981). Victim reactions in aggressive erotic films as a factor in violence against women. *Journal of Personality and Social Psychology, 41,* 710–724.

Drabman, R. S., & Thomas, M. H. (1974). Does media violence increase children's tolerance of real-life aggression? *Developmental Psychology, 10,* 418–421.

Drabman, R. S., & Thomas, M. H. (1976). Does watching violence on television cause apathy? *Pediatrics, 57,* 329–331.

Eron, L. D. (1982). Parent-child interaction, television violence, and aggression of children. *American Psychologist, 37,* 197–211.

Eron, L. D., Huesmann, L. R., Lefkowitz, M. M., & Walder, L. O. (1972). Does television violence cause aggression? *American Psychologist, 27,* 253–263.

Fiske, S. T., & Taylor, S. E. (1984). *Social cognition.* Reading, MA: Addison-Wesley.

Freud, S. (1961). *Civilization and its discontents* (standard ed.). London: Norton. (Original work published 1930)

Funk, J. B., Baldacci, H. B., Pasold, T., & Baumgardner, J. (2004). Violence exposure in real-life, video games, television, movies, and the Internet: Is there desensitization? *Journal of Adolescence, 27,* 23–39.

Geen, R. G., & O'Neal, E. C. (1969). Activation of cue-elicited aggression by general arousal. *Journal of Personality and Social Psychology, 11,* 289–292.

Gerbner, G., & Gross, L. (1976). Living with television: The violence profile. *Journal of Communication, 26,* 172–199.

Gerbner, G., & Gross, L. (1981). The violent face of television and its lessons. In E. I. Palmer & A. Dorr (Eds.), *Children and the faces of television: Teaching, violence, selling* (pp. 149–162). New York: Academic Press.

Heath, L., & Petraitis, J. (1987). Television viewing and fear of crime: Where is the mean world? *Basic and Applied Social Psychology, 8,* 97–123.

Huesmann, L. R. (1988). An information processing model for the development of aggression. *Aggressive Behavior, 14,* 13–24.

Huesmann, L. R. (1997). Observational learning of violent behavior: Social and biosocial processes (pp. 69–88). In A. Raine, P. A. Brennen, D. P. Farrington, & S. A. Mednick (Eds.), *Biosocial bases of violence.* London: Plenum.

Huesmann, L. R., Boxer, P., Bushman, B., Johnson, T., Moceri, D., & O'Brien, M. (2007, November). *The relation between exposure to video violence in childhood and engagement in violence and delinquency during adolescence.* Paper presented at meetings of the American Society for Criminology, Atlanta, GA.

Huesmann, L. R., & Guerra, N. (1997). Children's normative beliefs about aggression and aggressive behavior. *Journal of Personality and Social Psychology, 72*(2), 408–419.

Huesmann, L. R., & Kirwil, L. (2007). Why observing violence increases the risk of violent behavior in the observer. In D. J. Flannery, A. T. Vazsonyi, & I. D. Waldman (Eds.), *The Cambridge handbook of violent behavior and aggression* (pp. 545–570). Cambridge, UK: Cambridge University Press.

Huesmann, L. R., Moise-Titus, J., Podolski, C. L., & Eron, L. D. (2003). Longitudinal relations between children's exposure to TV violence and their aggressive and violent behavior in young adulthood: 1977–1992. *Developmental Psychology, 39*, 201–221.

Huesmann, L. R., & Taylor, L. D. (2003). The case against the case against media violence (pp. 107–130). In D. Gentile (Ed.), *Media violence and children*. Westport, CT: Greenwood Press.

Hughes, M. (1980). The fruits of cultivation analysis: A reexamination of the effects of television watching on fear of victimization, alienation, and the approval of violence. *Public Opinion Quarterly, 44*(3), 287–302.

Hurley, S., & Chatter, N. (2004). *Perspectives on imitation: From cognitive neuroscience to social science*. Cambridge, MA: MIT Press.

Innes, J. M., & Zeitz, H. (1988). The public's view of the impact of the mass media: A test of the "third person" effect. *European Journal of Social Psychology, 18*, 457–463.

Johnson, J. D., Jackson, L. A., & Gatto, L. (1995). Violent attitudes and deferred academic aspirations: Deleterious effects of exposure to rap music. *Basic and Applied Social Psychology, 16*, 27–41.

Josephson, W. L. (1987). Television violence and children's aggression: Testing the priming, social script, and disinhibition predictions. *Journal of Personality and Social Psychology, 53*, 882–890.

Kahneman, D., & Tversky, A. (1973). On the psychology of prediction. *Psychological Review, 80*, 237–251.

Konijn, E. A., Nije Bijvank, M., & Bushman, B. J. (2007). I wish I were a warrior: The role of wishful identification in effects of violent video games on aggression in adolescent boys. *Developmental Psychology, 43*, 1038–1044.

Leyens, J. P., Parke, R. D., Camino, L., & Berkowitz, L. (1975). Effects of movie violence on aggression in a field setting as a function of group dominance and cohesion.

Journal of Personality & Social Psychology, 32, 346–360.

Linz, D. G., Donnerstein, E., & Adams, S. M. (1989). Physiological desensitization and judgments about female victims of violence. *Human Communication Research, 15*, 509–522.

Linz, D. G., Donnerstein, E., & Penrod, S. (1988). Effects of long-term exposure to violent and sexually degrading depictions of women. *Journal of Personality and Social Psychology, 55*, 758–768.

Malamuth, N. M., & Check, J. V. P. (1981). The effects of mass media exposure on acceptance of violence against women. *Journal of Research in Personality, 15*, 436–446.

Manson, M. (1999). *I don't like the media, but the media likes me*. Retrieved March 3, 2008, from http://www.quotationspage.com/quote/33585.html

McLeod, J. M., Atkin, C. K., & Chaffee, S. H. (1972). Adolescents, parents, and television use: Adolescent self-report measures from Maryland and Wisconsin samples. In G. A. Comstock & E. A. Rubinstein (Eds.), *Television and social behavior: A technical report to the Surgeon General's Scientific Advisory Committee on Television and Social Behavior: Vol. 3. Television and adolescent aggressiveness* (DHEW Publication No. HSM 72-9058, pp. 173–238). Washington, DC: U.S. Government Printing Office.

Meltzoff, A. N., & Moore, M. K. (2000). Imitation of facial and manual gestures by human neonates: Resolving the debate about early imitation. In D. Muir & A. Slater (Eds.), *Infant development: The essential readings* (pp. 167–181). Malden, MA: Blackwell.

Molitor, F., & Hirsch, K. W. (1994). Children's toleration of real-life aggression after exposure to media violence: A replication of the Drabman and Thomas studies. *Child Study Journal, 24*, 191–207.

Mullin, C. R., & Linz, D. (1995). Desensitization and resensitization to violence against women: Effects of exposure to sexually violent films on judgments of domestic violence victims. *Journal of Personality and Social Psychology, 69,* 449–459.

Murray, J. P. (1998). Studying television violence: A research agenda for the 21st century. In J. K. Asamen & G. L. Berry (Eds.), *Research paradigms, television, and social behavior* (pp. 369–410). Thousand Oaks, CA: Sage.

National Television Violence Study. (1998). *National television violence study* (Vol. 3). Santa Barbara: The Center for Communication and Social Policy, University of California, Santa Barbara.

Nije Bijvank, M., Konijn, E. A., Bushman, B. J., & Roelofsma, P. H. M. P. (2009). Age and content labels make video games forbidden fruit for youth. *Pediatrics, 123,* 870–876.

Paik, H., & Comstock, G. (1994). The effects of television violence on antisocial behavior: A meta-analysis. *Communication Research, 21,* 516–546.

Perloff, R. M. (1999). The third-person effect: A critical review and synthesis. *Media Psychology, 1,* 353–378.

Peterson, J. L., & Zill, N. (1981). Television viewing in the United States and children's intellectual, social, and emotional development. *Television and Children, 2,* 21–28.

Polman, H., Orobio de Castro, B., & van Aken, M. (2008). Experimental study of the differential effects of playing versus watching violent video games on children's aggressive behavior. *Aggressive Behavior, 34,* 256–264.

Rizzolati, G., Fadiga, L., Gallese, V., & Fogassi, L. (1996). Premotor cortex and the recognition of motor actions. *Cognitive Brain Research, 3,* 131–141.

Roberts, D., Foehr, U., & Rideout, V. (2005). *Generation M: Media in the lives of 8–18 year-olds.* Menlo Park, CA: Kaiser Family Foundation. Retrieved May 4, 2009, from www.kff.org

Roberts, D. F., Foehr, U. G., Rideout, V., & Brodie, M. (1999). *Kids and media @ the new millennium.* Menlo Park, CA: Kaiser Family Foundation.

Romer, D., Jamieson, K. H., & Aday, S. (2003). Television news and the cultivation of fear of crime. *Journal of Communication, 53,* 88–104.

Sebastian, R. J., Parke, R. D., Berkowitz, L., & West, S. G. (1978). Film violence and verbal aggression: A naturalistic study. *Journal of Communication, 28, 157,* 164–171.

Signorielli, N., Gerbner, G., & Morgan, M. (1995). Violence on television: The cultural indicators project. *Journal of Broadcasting and Electronic Media, 39,* 278–283.

Slater, M. D., Henry, K. L., Swaim, R. C., & Anderson, L. L. (2003). Violent media content and aggressiveness in adolescents: A downward spiral model. *Communication Research, 30,* 713–736.

Sparks, G. G., & Ogles R. M. (1990). The difference between fear-of-victimization and the probability of being victimized: Implications for cultivation. *Journal of Broadcast Electronic Media, 34,* 351–358.

Steinfeld, J. (1972). *Statement in hearings before Subcommittee on Communications of Committee on Commerce* (United States Senate, Serial #92-52, pp. 25–27). Washington, DC: United States Government.

Thomas, M. H. (1982). Physiological arousal, exposure to a relatively lengthy aggressive film, and aggressive behavior. *Journal of Research in Personality, 16,* 72–81.

Thomas, M. H., Horton, R. W., Lippincott, E. C., & Drabman, R. S. (1977). Desensitization to portrayals of real life aggression as a function of television violence. *Journal of Personality and Social Psychology, 35,* 450–458.

Tversky, A., & Kahneman, D. (1973). Availability: A heuristic for judging frequency and probability. *Cognitive Psychology, 5,* 207–232.

U.S. Department of Health and Human Services. (2001). *Youth violence: A report of the Surgeon General.* Rockville, MD: U.S. Government Printing Office.

U.S. Federal Bureau of Investigation. (2008). *Uniform crime reports.* Washington, DC: U.S. Government Printing Office.

Van den Bulck, J. (2004). Research note: The relationship between television fiction and fear of crime: An empirical comparison of three causal explanations. *European Journal of Communication, 19,* 239–248.

Watkins, L. T., Sprafkin, J., Gadow, K. D., & Sadetsky, I. (1988). Effects of a critical viewing skills curriculum on elementary school children's knowledge and attitudes about television. *Journal of Educational Research, 81,* 165–170.

Yeaton, W., & Sechrest, L. (1981). Meaningful measures of effect. *Journal of Consulting and Clinical Psychology, 49,* 766–767.

Zillmann, D., Bryant, J., & Comisky, P. W. (1981). Excitation and hedonic valence in the effect of erotica on motivated inter-male aggression. *European Journal of Social Psychology, 11,* 233–252.

25

RACIAL/ETHNIC STEREOTYPING AND THE MEDIA

◆ Dana E. Mastro

Stereotypes are an inherent feature of human cognitive processing (Operario & Fiske, 2003). Although a variety of reasons have been offered as to why this may be the case, the most notable among these link stereotypes to operations related to managing demands on cognitive capacity, serving self-enhancement needs, and (more generally) performing a host of environmental functions (Hamilton & Sherman, 1994; Hilton & von Hippel, 1996; Tajfel & Turner, 1986). Yet, despite these differing rationales regarding the *why* of stereotyping, there is little disagreement that people, indeed, engage in stereotypic thinking. What is particularly notable about this near consensus on the inevitability of stereotyping (see Lepore & Brown, 1999, for a divergent view) is the emphasis placed on the media's role in this process.

Media images are assumed to contribute substantially to the construction and maintenance of stereotypes (see Mackie, Hamilton, Susskind, & Rosselli, 1996), including those pertaining to race/ethnicity; however, almost no empirical attention has been devoted to this assertion. Instead, the lion's share of media effects research has concentrated on outcomes associated with activating racial/ethnic cognitions based on media use. Although this work is to be applauded for advancing our awareness of how exposure to media messages can influence a number of cognitive and motivational outcomes, understanding the ways media use may shape the development and structure of stereotypic notions is equally critical. Accordingly, to fully appreciate the unique function of media exposure in issues related to stereotypes and stereotyping, the following must be considered: (a) formation and cognitive representation of stereotypes, (b) activation of these representations, and (c) application of strategies within and beyond the media environment. To this end, this chapter highlights the existing media-based stereotyping research in each of these domains. The most prominent theoretical and empirical contributions in each area alongside conspicuous lacunae are addressed.

◆ Conceptualizing Stereotypes and the Media

What are stereotypes? Most agree that stereotypes can be characterized as the beliefs, expectations, and theories one holds about groups in society (irrespective of accuracy or valence) that influence information processing and guide judgments about and behaviors toward groups and their members (Hamilton & Sherman, 1994; Hilton & von Hippel, 1996). The manner in which stereotypes are formed and represented in memory, however, is a matter of some debate. As advances in new technologies enhance our understanding of cognitive neuroscience and related cognitive processes, the need for theorizing in this area may become altogether obsolete. Still, until such time, awareness of the assumptions and implications of the prominent models of stereotype formation and representation can only serve to better structure our understanding of how media messages may shape consumers' stereotypes about race/ethnicity.

STEREOTYPE REPRESENTATION AND FORMATION

Representation. The way stereotypes are represented in memory speaks directly to

the issue of how individuals understand and evaluate different groups. Although competing theories of cognitive representation offer distinct assertions regarding such operations, there are generalities that can be extracted from among the most recognized models such as schemata, prototypes, and exemplars, among others. When taken together, this research suggests that knowledge about groups and group members can be represented in memory as linked sets of features, attributes, beliefs, behaviors, traits, values, places, objects, emotions, evaluations, and so on, that vary in representativeness in a particular domain (Hamilton & Sherman, 1994; Hilton & von Hippel, 1996; Operario & Fiske, 2003; Roskos-Ewoldsen, Davies, & Roskos-Ewoldsen, 2004). These may be generalized abstractions (e.g., prototypes, schemata) or concrete instances (e.g., exemplars) that are used as a basis for making social judgments. They may emerge from socialization processes in real-world or mediated contexts. Moreover, the media's ability to generate and shape these cognitive structures is stronger when consumers' real-world experiences with the target group are limited (Hawkins & Pingree, 1990). Of course, there is no assumption that these are veridical representations. Are gay men really more fashionable than straight men? Are Whites indeed less rhythmic than Latinos? It is tough to shake these notions—whether or not legitimate.

Formation. The next question becomes, when and why might stereotypes be formed based on media exposure? The prevailing media-based frameworks that speak to this issue are cultivation theory (see Morgan, Chapter 5, this volume) and framing (see Shah, McLeod, Gotlieb, & Lee, Chapter 6, this volume). To be fair, these theories' premises are more squarely centered on issues related to socialization and priming, respectively. Nonetheless, their tenets address the manner in which media consumption can lead to the formation of stereotypes about race/ethnicity. Before any such discussion, however, it is important to note that stereotypes are not inherently negative, as they can serve important cognitive and social functions. What is seen as potentially problematic is the fact that media messages offer little in the way of comprehensive explanations for portrayals and instead merely link groups with both desirable and undesirable characterizations. Work in the domains of both cultivation theory and media framing addresses this issue.

Generally speaking, framing focuses on the ways media may shape audience members' conceptualizations of reality by placing attention on particular issues/topics (and certain aspects of those issues), thereby increasing their accessibility in processing subsequent information (Entman, 2007; Scheufele, 1999). From a more macro level perspective, cultivation theory emphasizes the role of media as a socializing agent, such that the more consumers attend to the media's messages, the more their perceptions are reflective of the media version of reality (Gerbner, Gross, Morgan, Signorielli, & Shanahan, 2002; Shrum, 2002). Both theories maintain that through consumption of the implicit and explicit messages about race/ethnicity that are offered in the media's texts and images, audience members develop a media-formulated understanding of race-based issues and related judgments. Thus, when taken together, these theories suggest that media messages provide consumers with the sets of features to be associated with different groups, including normative behaviors, traits, values, attitudes, demographic compositions, and the like. Additionally, these depictions situate groups, both geographically and hierarchically, such that different races/ethnicities become tied to features such as physical locations and status-based positions. When it comes to status, for example, content analyses have revealed that television news disproportionately associates African Americans with criminal activity and depicts these individuals as threatening, disheveled, and in restraints

(Dixon & Linz, 2000; Entman, 1994). Moreover, when excessive force is required to control a criminal on prime-time entertainment television, odds are that the perpetrator is African American and the officer is White (Mastro & Robinson, 2000).

It should also be stated that although media representations of race/ethnicity are argued to be relatively stable across genres and media types, the features inherent to particular content types (e.g., TV sitcom vs. crime drama vs. news) are also recognized for their influence (Armstrong, Neuendorf, & Brentar, 1992). For example, increased exposure to entertainment programming, such as sitcoms, has been found to be associated with more favorable views about African Americans' socioeconomic status (Armstrong et al., 1992) and educational attainment (Busselle & Crandall, 2002). Alternatively, exposure to dramatic programs has been linked to less favorable perceptions about the educational achievement of African Americans (Busselle & Crandall, 2002). Elevated levels of news exposure, whether televised (Armstrong et al., 1992; Dixon, 2007) or in print (Vergeer, Lubbers, & Scheepers, 2000), have been shown to predict stereotypic and unfavorable views about minority group's socioeconomic status, criminality, and threatening nature. In light of this research, it appears that both overall media consumption and idiosyncratic usage patterns would each be expected to contribute to audience members' racial/ethnic cognitions.

In an attempt to provide greater clarity into the cognitive processes that may govern these content-specific outcomes, researchers have integrated insights from the mental modeling literature into the cultivation approach (Mastro, Behm-Morawitz, & Ortiz, 2007). Mental models are cognitive devices that allow individuals to construct malleable versions of knowledge that incorporate subjective and objective components into a single mental representation (Zwann & Radvansky, 1998). When applied to media, mental models allow consumers to make sense of the content of media messages by integrating the constant stream of information provided both verbally and pictorially into a comprehensible knowledge structure. The work in this area has revealed that both perceptions about the attributes associated with portrayals of Latinos in the media and the amount of exposure to these messages contribute to the construction of stereotypes about Latino criminality, intelligence, and work ethic. These findings are meaningful, as they indicate that alongside the explicit messages offered about race/ethnicity in the media, assessments of the perceived or implicit content may be equally important in understanding the effects on stereotype development. Simply put, what we *perceive* in media content may be just as important as what and how much we consume.

It should additionally be noted that social cognitive theory (see Pajares, Prestin, Chen, & Nabi, Chapter 19, this volume) offers a detailed account of the process of learning from media content, which could be applied to understanding stereotype formation. This comprehensive framework integrates specific aspects of media content (including features, such as message repetition and simplicity, as well as motivations, like positive/negative reinforcements in the content) with particular characteristics of the viewing audience (e.g., cognitive ability, past reinforcement, character identification) as well as the social environment to address the mechanisms through which media may influence consumers (Bandura, 2002).

To date, however, the three studies that have applied the theory's assumptions to acquiring race-related cognitions tested only the reinforcement-based aspects (i.e., motivation) of the model (Fujioka, 1999; Tan, Fujioka, & Lucht, 1997; Tan, Fujioka, & Tan, 2000). As such, processes related to attention to the message, retention of the message, and cognitive rehearsal have largely been ignored. Nonetheless, the existing research in this area sheds light on the social-cognitive components associated with media and stereotyping. In particular, this work has focused on the degree to which exposure to positive versus negative portrayals of race (as a proxy for rewarding versus punishing messages) influences stereotype development (Fujioka, 1999; Tan et al., 1997; Tan et al., 2000). Although the findings are not entirely consistent, in the main the data indicate that among Whites, exposure to negative portrayals leads to more unfavorable perceptions of African Americans in terms of attributes such as intelligence, work ethic, and welfare status (Fujioka, 1999; Tan et al., 2000) and more negative views of Native Americans in terms of wealth (Tan et al., 1997). On the other hand, exposure to positive images predicts more positive stereotypes about African Americans among Japanese sojourners (Fujioka, 1999) and more favorable perceptions about Native Americans among Whites (Tan et al., 1997). It is important to note that Tan et al. as well as Fujioka also have assessed the influence of total media consumption on the development of stereotypes. Consistently, their results indicate that positive/negative portrayals better explain stereotype formation than does the cultivation-based measure of overall exposure.

When taken together, these findings implicate media exposure in the formation and development of racial/ethnic stereotypes. Yet, the specific mechanisms underlying this process remain poorly explicated. It can be assumed, however, that any feature of the media that prompts differentiation between racial/ethnic groups (regardless of real differences) can provide the foundation for developing stereotypes (Mackie et al., 1996). Thus, to the extent that racial/ethnic minority groups are represented in the media, content analytic research can provide an account of the discrepancies in characterizations that may provoke the formation of stereotypes.

MEDIA DEPICTIONS
OF RACE AND ETHNICITY

The bulk of the content analytic research on depictions of race/ethnicity in the media has focused on television portrayals, including entertainment programming, commercials, and news. Given that the work in this area has been comprehensively reviewed elsewhere (see Mastro, 2009), only a composite sketch of racial/ethnic characterizations in the media will be detailed here. What has been repeatedly confirmed in these investigations is that for a number of years, African Americans and White Americans have been presented at rates that meet or exceed their proportions of the U.S. population. This is not the case for Asian Americans, Latino Americans, or Native Americans, who are all seen in the media at levels well below their proportions of U.S. society. Numeric parity is meaningful as the sheer frequency of images of different groups conveys information about the value and vitality of the group in society (Harwood & Roy, 2005). However, the quality of images is equally critical, as the particular messages communicated about race/ethnicity in the media shape the characteristics that become associated with these groups.

When the nature and variety of roles are considered, distinct differences emerge based on race/ethnicity (Mastro, 2009). With regard to White Americans, they can be seen in an assortment of roles representing the gamut of possible portrayals (although this is less true when assessed by gender). In addition, they are more likely than their racial/ethnic counterparts to be in positions of prestige or authority. Latinos, on the other hand, are depicted in a fairly limited set of roles, often revolving around themes of sexuality, criminality, subservience, or intellectual ineptitude. For African Americans, representations vary dramatically based on the type of media. In entertainment programming the images are generally evenhanded.

The same cannot be said for depictions in the news. Here, African Americans are disproportionately presented as menacing criminals compared with real-world arrest reports as well as with their racial/ethnic peers on the news. Due to the scarcity of roles for Asian Americans and Native Americans, little can be established about the manner in which these groups are characterized. The analyses that have been conducted suggest that Asian Americans are most often seen as minor and non-recurring characters, but in high-status positions (Children Now, 2004). Native Americans, when shown, are presented as spiritual, as social problems, or as warriors (Fryberg, 2003).

With relatively rich data regarding the characterizations of racial/ethnic groups in the media and abundant theorizing on how these images may infiltrate consumers' cognitions, one might think that equivalent efforts have been made to document the effects of exposure on the development of stereotypes. As the present review illustrates, this has not been the case. Instead, investigators have aligned their research (whether explicitly or not) with one or a combination of assertions from cognitive models of stereotype representation and looked for outcomes consistent with their assumptions as verification—most often in the domain of media priming.

◆ Stereotype Activation

The vast majority of research examining the effects of exposure to media depictions of racial/ethnic stereotypes on audience members has utilized a priming approach (see Roskos-Ewoldsen & Roskos-Ewoldsen, Chapter 12, this volume, for a review of media priming). In this context, priming refers to the process through which information activated by media consumption is used to interpret incoming messages and guide subsequent judgments (Roskos-Ewoldsen,

Roskos-Ewoldsen, & Dillman Carpentier, 2002). In addition to influencing ongoing perceptions, priming also facilitates stereotype maintenance by inhibiting the accessibility of alternate constructs and determining how perceivers store information for later use (Hilton & von Hippel, 1996). Once consciously or unconsciously triggered by media exposure, stereotypic constructs become both prescriptive and self-sustaining. Accordingly, even a single exposure, in both the short and long term (Smith, Stewart, & Buttram, 1992), can influence real-world racial/ ethnic judgments (Dixon, 2006, 2007; Givens & Monahan, 2005), prompt negative affective responses to minorities (Gilliam & Iyengar, 2000; Mendelberg, 1997), and direct intergroup behaviors and outcomes (Fryberg, 2003; Mastro, 2003). Indeed, more than a decade of experimental research offers evidence for these assertions.

PRIMING CRIME

When considering that depictions of race are often unfavorably and disproportionately linked with crime and deviance, it is appropriate that the bulk of the priming research has focused on crime-related outcomes. Peffley, Shields, and Williams (1996) examined the extent to which exposure to news coverage intersecting race and crime influenced race-based judgments. Their results revealed that after only a brief exposure, White respondents (particularly those who endorsed negative stereotypes about African Americans) judged an African American (vs. White) suspect more unfavorably in terms of determinations of guilt, allocations of prison sentence, and estimations of potential to repeat the behavior. Similarly, Johnson, Adams, Hall, and Ashburn (1997) examined the role of exposure to violent media information on judgments of African Americans. Their results showed that priming racialized depictions of crime generated more dispositional judgments

when the target suspect was African American and more situational attributions when the suspect was White.

Parallel outcomes emerge in studies of more blatantly prejudicial responses. Findings from Oliver, Jackson, Moses, and Dangerfield (2004), as well as Dixon and Maddox (2005), suggest that criminality is stereotypically and erroneously linked to overt physical attributes of African Americans, such as skin tone and Afrocentric features. In particular, Oliver et al.'s (2004) data establish a link between exposure to crime news and misperceptions regarding the Afrocentric qualities of the individual depicted in the media. Their results revealed that these attributes were deemed more pronounced when viewers were exposed to a violent crime story (vs. nonstereotype and noncrime stereotype story). Further, data from Dixon and Maddox (2005) indicate that exposure to darker-complected African American perpetrators (compared with Whites) generated greater concern and compassion for the victim. In aggregate, these findings plainly establish that exposure to media content that characterizes minorities as criminal has a deleterious effect on subsequent race-based judgments.

PRIMING AND
SOCIAL JUDGMENTS

Alongside prompting the more overtly stereotypic responses noted earlier, media priming has also been linked to more nuanced race-related outcomes (Abraham & Appiah, 2006). For example, when abstractions are linked with undesirable out-group characterizations (or desirable in-group characterizations) in either mediated or real-world messages, out-group stereotypes are subtly transmitted because abstract statements are perceived as person/ group specific, dispositional, and stable (Gorham, 2006; Maass, Corvino, & Arcuri, 1994; Maass, Salvi, Arcuri, & Semin, 1989).

Inconspicuous stereotype-based associations also can be seen in the misidentification of target individuals akin to racial profiling (Oliver & Fonash, 2002), but are most often reflected in research on race-coded issues such as welfare and crime (Gilliam, 1999; Valentino, 1999). This work has repeatedly demonstrated that activating race-coded topics not only guides responses in a manner consistent with the specific prime (e.g., crime) but also directs judgments along racial/ethnic lines (Gilliam, 1999; Valentino, 1999). For example, Valentino's (1999) examination of the effects of exposure to crime in television news on evaluations of presidential candidates revealed that support for the Democratic presidential candidate was particularly low when those depicted in the news stories were minorities, whereas the Republican candidate's support was high, despite the fact that the news content was unrelated to the candidates. Valentino argues that these results are illustrative of the activation of existing perceptions that Democrats are "soft" on crime and supportive of minorities, thus resulting in the unfavorable evaluations (see also Ford, 1997).

PRIMING PROSOCIAL OUTCOMES

Although the greater portion of the priming research has focused on identifying the potentially harmful effects of exposure to media stereotypes, this is not to say that more auspicious outcomes are improbable. In fact, Bodenhausen, Schwarz, Bless, and Wanke (1995) as well as Power, Murphy, and Coover (1996) each demonstrate that exposure to positive counterstereotypes in the media can produce constructive and compassionate race-based judgments. Bodenhausen et al. examined the effects of exposure to well-known African American media exemplars on Whites' racial attitudes. Their data suggest that viewing positive media exemplars not only generates more favorable attitudes toward out-group races but also promotes more sympathetic responses toward discrimination as a social problem. Power et al.'s (1996) work offers comparable results, revealing that exposure to positive counterstereotypes of African Americans in the news yields more favorable evaluations of African Americans among White audience members (compared with a control condition).

Despite the value and contribution of the findings in this domain, priming alone addresses only a portion of the relationship between media and stereotypes. What must also be examined is the extent to which media messages additionally promote group-based processing leading to intergroup outcomes such as favoring one's own group over others' groups and utilizing these group comparisons to maintain and enhance self-concept and self-esteem.

◆ Stereotypes and Intergroup Processes

At its core, stereotyping is an issue of intergroup dynamics. Despite the obvious nature of this statement, researchers have only recently begun to apply the assumptions from intergroup theories to phenomena related to media and stereotyping. Most prominent within this burgeoning area of inquiry is the research utilizing social identity theory (Tajfel & Turner, 1986) and self-categorization theory (Turner, 1987). These theories suggest that individuals' self-concept is derived in part from their group memberships. Because these groups play an important role in self-evaluation (varying based on the salience and importance of the particular group membership), individuals utilize group-based comparisons to provide a comparative advantage for their in-group. Thus, when taken together, social identity theory and self-categorization theory offer a conceptual framework for understanding how media exposure may contribute to stereotyping and discrimination by promoting biased intergroup comparisons that ultimately serve the esteem needs of dominant group members. That said, it should not be assumed that these frameworks' assumptions apply only to majority group members. Rather, these theories offer insights into which subgroups of audience members are more likely to engage in intergroup behaviors and what features of media content may provoke these outcomes (Harwood & Roy, 2005; Reid, Giles, & Harwood, 2005).

SOCIAL IDENTITY AND RACIAL MAJORITY GROUPS

Experimental tests of these models' assumptions in the context of media have met with fairly consistent support in application to majority group (e.g., White) exposure to minority group representations. Among Whites, exposure to stereotypical media representations of race/ethnicity appears to encourage race-based social comparisons, which advantage the in-group and serve identity needs, particularly among consumers who are high in racial identification (Mastro, 2003). That is, viewing unfavorable characterizations of minorities in the media provokes negative, stereotypical responses among White consumers (particularly highly race-identified Whites), which, in turn, boosts these viewers' self-concept by offering a comparison that advantages their in-group (i.e., Whites).

Further, when contextual features of the media content (e.g., message ambiguity) obscure the threat of appearing racist (i.e., aversive racism), the potential for intergroup bias is enhanced (Mastro, Behm-Morawitz, & Kopacz, 2008). Certainly, stereotypic responses to media content are likely to manifest based on exposure to overtly negative depictions of out-group races/ethnicities; however, such outcomes appear to emerge even more so when the media content offers protection from the perception of racial bias. Specifically, experimental evidence relatively consistently suggests that White consumers' racially driven responses to media, especially among those highly identified with their race, are more pronounced when the content of the media message offers sufficient ambiguity for the response to be deemed unrelated to race. Here again, this ability to privilege one's in-group through advantageous comparisons with a mediated out-group seems to aid in esteem maintenance.

Alongside identifying routes to straightforward stereotyping and discrimination, these identity-based perspectives additionally provide insights into the features of media content that may discourage such biases and promote more favorable intergroup outcomes. This research suggests that media depictions of race/ethnicity that accommodate White identity and dominant value systems (Coover & Godbold, 1998; Mastro, Tamborini, & Hullett, 2005), as well as encourage racial harmony (Coover, 2001), are likely to elicit the most favorable out-group evaluations and promote out-group social attraction. Moreover, long-term exposure to appealing characterizations of underrepresented groups appears to promote positive changes in beliefs about and prejudicial attitudes toward such groups among majority group consumers (Schiappa, Gregg, & Hewes, 2005).

SOCIAL IDENTITY AND RACIAL/ETHNIC MINORITY GROUPS

The assumptions underlying social identity-based approaches to media are applicable not only to majority groups. This same identity-based perspective can help explain how minority groups respond to unfavorable depictions of their in-group and negotiate the effects on the self. As Harwood and Roy (2005) assert, "people are creatively dealing with the media in ways that make their personal viewing profile considerably more supportive of their group identity than it would be otherwise" (p. 195). This claim finds empirical support in the works of Abrams and Giles (2007) and Fujioka (2005), which reveal that minority and majority groups differentially select, avoid, process, and retain media offerings—all in an effort to manage group identity needs.

Despite efforts among underrepresented groups to mitigate the potentially harmful effects of consuming stereotypical images of one's in-group in mass media offerings, research demonstrates that exposure can nonetheless damage self-concept and -esteem. In her research examining the impact of exposure to Native American mascots on Native American consumers, Fryberg (2003) found evidence that these images (e.g., Chief Wahoo) negatively affected audience members' self-esteem and beliefs about community efficacy. Comparable results were obtained in research on Latino Americans (Rivadeneyra, Ward, & Gordon, 2007). This work indicates that increasing exposure to mainstream media (including TV, film, music, and magazines) has a detrimental effect on Latinos' self-esteem along a number of dimensions. Generally speaking, this effect was determined to be more pronounced among consumers high in ethnic identification and among those who actively engaged with the content.

RACE-RELATED POLICY REASONING

No research in the domain of media and stereotyping offers more straightforward implications than the work examining the effects of news exposure on political decision making and policy reasoning—in terms of both the individual effects and the broader societal consequences. The theoretical frameworks used to examine these relationships are varied. Although social cognitive models

(Tan et al., 2000), as well as traditional stereotyping frameworks (Mendelberg, 1997; Pan & Kosicki, 1996), have been employed, more recent efforts have tapped into features of social identity-based models (Mastro & Kopacz, 2006; Richardson, 2005). In aggregate, the results from this small body of work reveal that race-related policy preferences are affected, in part, by media consumption. Indeed, both a single exposure (Mendelberg, 1997; Richardson, 2005) and use over time (Mastro & Kopacz, 2006; Pan & Kosicki, 1996; Tan et al., 2000) are found to meaningfully influence political decisions ranging from preferences for candidates and parties to positions on policies such as affirmative action.

This research additionally points to a number of factors that contribute to this process. First, the characteristics of the media messages themselves are critical, as unfavorable content yields unsympathetic policy outcomes. However, the definition of "unfavorable" looks to be more a matter of conformity to group identity-based norms (e.g., the character speaks and behaves in a particular way; Mastro & Kopacz, 2006; Richardson, 2005) than it is a reflection of the concrete, objective features associated with the message (e.g., the character is a good guy vs. bad guy). Indeed, although exposure to outright stereotypes in the media can promote biased political decisions, this relationship is better explained when images are understood in terms of the embodiment of (or deviation from) dominant norms and ideals (Mastro & Kopacz, 2006). Moreover, constructive media messages appear to indirectly increase support for race-related policies by weakening the link between racial attitudes and unfavorable positions toward such programs (Richardson, 2005). Second, attributes of the consumer also play a significant role. It seems that the motivation underlying consumers' media usage patterns, such as seeking information-oriented media (Pan & Kosicki, 1996), as well as consumers' existing racial/ethnic attitudes (Mendelberg, 1997), each enhance the influence of negative racial/ethnic media messages on subsequent policy decisions.

Despite the relative consistency of the findings in the domain of policy reasoning, numerous questions remain regarding the mechanisms underlying these processes and the contingencies to these effects. Given the profound social implications of this research, it is disappointing that so few studies have been devoted to this area of inquiry.

◆ Where Do We Go From Here?

Whether in terms of formation, application, or perpetuation, mass media appear to play a meaningful role in stereotyping processes. From the perspective of shared reality theory, this is not unexpected (Hardin & Higgins, 1996). This theory suggests that reality is a function of social verification, maintained based on a dynamic process of shared experience. Accordingly, media messages have the potential to play a significant role in this process by both establishing and broadening audience members' range of unifying experiences. In fact, Hardin and Higgins (1996) argue that the features of media content, in conjunction with the attributes of audience members, together create a common version of what race/ethnicity represents in U.S. society. In defining, reinforcing, and transmitting messages about race/ethnicity, they contend, the mass media verify and legitimize their own messages, moving the subjective into the objective and superseding individual experience. Although the research noted in this chapter offers meaningful evidence in support of this assertion, the full range of implications has only begun to be examined. This may be due, in part, to the challenges inherent to race-based research but also reflects the fact that the multifaceted nature of our new media environment has largely been overlooked.

METHODOLOGICAL CHALLENGES TO RESEARCH ON RACE/ETHNICITY

It is important to note that research in the domain of media and racial/ethnic stereotyping comes with intrinsic challenges. First, isolating race-related media effects can be an arduous undertaking given the small—but meaningful—influence of the media relative to other social influences. Certainly, decades of research in social psychology underscores the important role played by family, friends, and real-world contact in shaping race-related attitudes, beliefs, and behaviors. Still, as the work addressed in this chapter documents, the media's effect on this process is not inconsequential. In part, the difficulty associated with measuring media-based, race-related outcomes comes from participants' attempts to avoid biases (stemming from real or perceived racially driven influences) in their responses (see Dovidio & Gaertner, 2000, and Wegener & Petty, 1995, for reviews). Although such factors contribute to a complex research environment, innovative methodological approaches have emerged to address some of the challenges. Among the most notable of these approaches is the work utilizing the Implicit Association Test (IAT).

The IAT is a computer-based program that measures the relative strength of association between a target (e.g., African American and Caucasian standardized faces) and an evaluative concept (positive and negative words) using millisecond-sensitive response latencies in a series of timed tests, pairing, in this example, faces and words (Greenwald, Nosek, & Banaji, 2003). The assumption here (supported by empirical evidence) is that the stronger the association between the target and the evaluative concept, the faster the two can be paired together during the computer trials. Faster pairings, then, are considered to be an indication of implicit or automatic attitudes toward that group. Accordingly, a more rapid association between "good" and "White" compared with "good" and "African American" is interpreted as a bias favoring Whites. Measuring racial cognitions in this manner could potentially open the door for media researchers to tap into attitudes and beliefs that audience members may otherwise be reluctant or unable to reveal.

CONSIDERATIONS FOR OUR NEW MEDIA ENVIRONMENT

Also critical to examine is the extent to which the unique features of new media technologies (e.g., increased interactivity), as well as the enhanced production and consumption opportunities of our new media environment, can be utilized to promote more prosocial racial/ethnic outcomes. Currently, it is not clear that the environment provided by new technologies, such as video games, is any more promising than that offered in more traditional media. A content analysis of top-selling video games found that the vast majority of video game characters (65%) were White (Glaubke, Miller, Parker, & Espejo, 2001). Moreover, these White characters were most often the game's protagonist (87%). In games designed expressly for children, only White characters were depicted. Thus, it looks as though new media may be reproducing many of the same stereotype-based patterns as those found in traditional media like television.

Ignoring these content limitations for the moment, the features distinctive to interaction with new media technologies, like flow and presence (Tamborini & Skalski, 2006), actually suggest cause for (cautious) optimism. To illustrate, those in a state of flow (Csikszentmihalyi, 1990) while playing video games (e.g., immersed, in control, less consciousness of the passage of time, self-identity decreases to be later reinforced) may, in fact, experience the optimal conditions for positive parasocial contact, which could ultimately improve race-based attitudes and behaviors given the appropriate video game offerings. Such outcomes could only be achieved, however, if scholars were to (a) generate research that would help explicate the nature of ideal, parasocial relationships and (b) encourage game producers to provide more diverse and wholesome video game environments.

Another particularly promising aspect of the new media environment is the opportunity for consumers to both create and disseminate original media products via the Web and venues such as YouTube. These opportunities suggest that the Internet may provide an environment in which users can find images and subject matter that support their identity needs, even among underrepresented or marginalized groups. Indeed, given adequate access, Internet users can find images of, discussions from, and content addressing similar or like-minded others—on any imaginable dimension of interest. Still, users must be vigilant when utilizing this content, as alongside the potential to encounter respectable messages regarding one's group comes the risk of being confronted with highly incendiary race-related content. In fact, if research on the online experiences of adolescents is any example, the anonymity offered on the Web may actually enhance expressions of racial enmity. Tynes, Reynolds, and Greenfield (2004) analyzed racial/ethnic communication in both monitored and unmonitored popular adolescent chat rooms. They found that nearly all (97%) of these adolescents' online discussions contained at least one racial expression (positive, negative, or neutral), with approximately 59% of adolescents in unmonitored chat rooms exposed to negative racial remarks. Thus, inasmuch as diverse groups may find similar others in the vast offerings online, so too can those harboring racially antagonistic views.

This is not to say, however, that the outlook is bleak. Instead, it underscores the need for focused, programmatic research into both the prosocial and antisocial effects of exposure to racial/ethnic representations in mass media. Paramount among such efforts is greater attention to identifying how media messages create and shape the stereotypes consumers hold about different racial/ethnic groups. To illustrate, if media stereotypes are stored in a manner consistent with prototype-based models, subsequent stereotyping will be based on comparisons with general category attributes (Hilton & von Hippel, 1996; Operario & Fiske, 2003). Accordingly, stereotyping will be strongest when real-world contact is lacking. To alter stereotypes stored in this way, beliefs about the typical or average group member must be changed. On the other hand, if stereotypes emanating from media messages are stored as exemplars, ensuing stereotyping should be based on comparisons with the concrete features associated with the exemplar. Consequently, stereotyping will be strongest when perceivers have undeveloped attitudes about the target and when multiple exemplars of the target group are accessible (Operario & Fiske, 2003). From this perspective, stereotyping can be reduced when counterstereotypic exemplars are presented. Of course, each cognitive model of stereotype structure offers insights into these issues. Thus, researchers interested in confronting the issue of media and stereotyping can only benefit from directing more concerted efforts at understanding the cognitive nature of media-based stereotypes. Elucidating these cognitive mechanisms opens the door to (a) enhancing the positive effects of exposure to constructive images, (b) diminishing the negative outcomes associated with consuming unfavorable characterizations, and (c) changing stereotypes altogether.

◆ References

Abraham, L., & Appiah, O. (2006). Framing news stories: The role of visual imagery in priming racial stereotypes. *Howard Journal of Communications, 17,* 183–203.

Abrams, J., & Giles, H. (2007). Ethnic identity gratifications selection and avoidance by African Americans: A group vitality and social identity perspective. *Media Psychology, 9,* 115–134.

Armstrong, G., Neuendorf, K., & Brentar, J. (1992). TV entertainment, news, and racial perceptions of college students. *Journal of Communication, 42,* 153–176.

Bandura, A. (2002). Social cognitive theory of mass communication. In J. Bryant & D. Zillmann (Eds.), *Media effects: Advances in theory and research* (pp. 121–153). Hillsdale, NJ: Erlbaum.

Bodenhausen, G., Schwarz, N., Bless, H., & Wanke, M. (1995). Effects of atypical exemplars on racial beliefs: Enlightened racism or generalized appraisals? *Journal of Experimental Social Psychology, 31,* 48–63.

Busselle, R., & Crandall, H. (2002). Television viewing and perceptions about race differences in socioeconomic success. *Journal of Broadcasting & Electronic Media, 46,* 256–282.

Children Now. (2004). *Fall colors, 2003–2004: Prime time diversity report.* Oakland, CA: Children Now.

Coover, G. (2001). Television and social identity: Race representation as "White" accommodation. *Journal of Broadcasting and Electronic Media, 45,* 413–431.

Coover, G., & Godbold, L. (1998). Convergence between racial and political identities: Boundary erasure or aversive racism? *Communication Research, 25,* 669–688.

Csikszentmihalyi, M. (1990). *Flow: The psychology of optimal experience.* New York: Harper Collins.

Dixon, T. (2006). Psychological reactions to crime news portrayals of Black criminals: Understanding the moderating roles of prior news viewing and stereotype endorsement. *Communication Monographs, 73,* 162–187.

Dixon, T. (2007). Black criminals and White officers: The effects of racially misrepresenting law breakers and law defenders on television news. *Media Psychology, 10,* 270–291.

Dixon, T., & Linz, D. (2000). Overrepresentation and underrepresentation of African

Americans and Latinos as lawbreakers on television news. *Journal of Communication, 50,* 131–154.

Dixon, T., & Maddox, K. (2005). Skin tone, crime news, and social reality judgments: Priming the stereotype of the dark and dangerous Black criminal. *Journal of Applied Social Psychology, 35,* 1555–1570.

Dovidio, J. F., & Gaertner, S. L. (2000). Aversive racism and selection decisions: 1989 and 1999. *Psychological Science, 11,* 315–319.

Entman, R. (1994). African Americans according to TV news. *Media Studies Journal, 8,* 29–38.

Entman, R. (2007). Framing bias: Media in the distribution of power. *Journal of Communication, 57,* 163–173.

Ford, T. (1997). Effects of stereotypical television portrayals of African-Americans on person perception. *Social Psychology Quarterly, 60,* 266–278.

Fryberg, S. (2003). Really? You don't look like an American Indian: Social representations and social group identities. *Dissertation Abstracts International.*

Fujioka, Y. (1999). Television portrayals and African-American stereotypes: Examination of television effects when direct contact is lacking. *Journalism & Mass Communication Quarterly, 76,* 52–75.

Fujioka, Y. (2005). Emotional TV viewing and minority audience: How Mexican Americans process and evaluate TV news about ingroup members. *Communication Research, 32,* 566–593.

Gerbner, G., Gross, L., Morgan, M., Signorielli, N., & Shanahan, J. (2002). Growing up with television: Cultivation processes. In J. Bryant & D. Zillmann (Eds.), *Media effects: Advances in theory and research* (pp. 43–68). Hillsdale, NJ: Erlbaum.

Gilliam, F. D. (1999). The "welfare queen" experiment. *Nieman Reports,* 49–52.

Gilliam, F., & Iyengar, S. (2000). Prime suspects: The influence of local television news on the viewing public. *American Journal of Political Science, 44,* 560–573.

Givens, S., & Monahan, J. (2005). Priming mammies, jezebels, and other controlling images: An examination of the influence of mediated stereotypes on perceptions of an African American woman. *Media Psychology, 7,* 87–106.

Glaubke, C., Miller, P., Parker, M., & Espejo, E. (2001). *Fair play? Violence, gender, and race in video games.* Oakland, CA: Children Now.

Gorham, B. (2006). News media's relationship with stereotyping: The linguistic intergroup bias in response to crime news. *Journal of Communication, 56,* 289–308.

Greenwald, A., Nosek, B., & Banaji, M. (2003). Understanding and using the Implicit Association Test: I. An improved algorithm. *Journal of Personality and Social Psychology, 85,* 197–216.

Hamilton, D., & Sherman, J. (1994). Stereotypes. In R. Wyer & T. Srull (Eds.), *Handbook of social cognition* (2nd ed.). Hillsdale, NJ: Erlbaum.

Hardin, C. D., & Higgins, E. T. (1996). Shared reality: How social verification makes the subjective objective. In R. M. Sorrentino & E. T. Higgins (Eds.), *Handbook of motivation and cognition* (Vol. 3, pp. 28–84). New York: Guilford Press.

Harwood, J., & Roy, A. (2005). Social identity theory and mass communication research. In J. Harwood & H. Giles (Eds.), *Intergroup communication* (pp. 189–211). New York: Peter Lang.

Hawkins, R., & Pingree, S. (1990). Divergent psychological processes in constructing social reality from mass media content. In N. Signorielli & M. Morgan (Eds.), *Cultivation analysis: New directions in media effects research* (pp. 35–50). Newbury Park, CA: Sage.

Hilton, J., & Von Hippel, W. (1996). Stereotypes. *Annual Review of Psychology, 47,* 237–271.

Johnson, J. D., Adams, M. S., Hall, W., & Ashburn, L. (1997). Race, media, and violence: Differential racial effects of exposure to violent news stories. *Basic and Applied Social Psychology, 19,* 81–90.

Lepore, L., & Brown, R. (1999). Exploring automatic stereotype activation: A challenge to the inevitability of prejudice. In D. Abrams & M. Hogg (Eds.), *Social identity and social cognition.* Malden, MA: Blackwell.

Maass, A., Corvino, G., & Arcuri, L. (1994). Linguistic intergroup bias and the mass media. *Revue de Psychologie Sociale, 1,* 31–43.

Maass, A., Salvi, D., Arcuri, L., & Semin, G. (1989). Language use in intergroup contexts: The linguistic intergroup bias. *Journal of Personality and Social Psychology, 57*(6), 981–993.

Mackie, D., Hamilton, D., Susskind, J., & Rosselli, F. (1996). Social psychological foundations of stereotype formation. In C. Macrae, C. Stangor, & M. Hewstone (Eds.), *Stereotypes and stereotyping.* London, UK: Guilford Press.

Mastro, D. (2003). A social identity approach to understanding the impact of television messages. *Communication Monographs, 70,* 98–113.

Mastro, D. (2009). Effects of racial and ethnic stereotyping. In J. Bryant & M. B. Oliver (Eds.), *Media effects: Advances in theory and research* (3rd ed., pp. 325-341). Hillsdale, NJ: Erlbaum.

Mastro, D., Behm-Morawitz, E., & Kopacz, M. (2008). Exposure to TV portrayals of Latinos: The implications of aversive racism and social identity theory. *Human Communication Research, 34,* 1–27.

Mastro, D., Behm-Morawitz, E., & Ortiz, M. (2007). The cultivation of social perceptions of Latinos: A mental models approach. *Media Psychology, 9,* 1–19.

Mastro, D., & Kopacz, M. (2006). Media representations of race, prototypicality, and policy reasoning: An application of self-categorization theory. *Journal of Broadcasting & Electronic Media, 50,* 305–322.

Mastro, D., & Robinson, A. (2000). Cops and crooks: Images of minorities on primetime television. *Journal of Criminal Justice, 28,* 385–396.

Mastro, D., Tamborini, R., & Hullett, C. (2005). Linking media to prototype activation and subsequent celebrity attraction: An application of self-categorization theory. *Communication Research, 32,* 323–348.

Mendelberg, T. (1997). Executing Hortons: Racial crime in the 1988 presidential campaign. *Public Opinion Quarterly, 61,* 134–157.

Oliver, M. B., & Fonash, D. (2002). Race and crime in the news: Whites' identification and misidentification of violent and nonviolent criminal suspects. *Media Psychology, 4,* 137–156.

Oliver, M. B., Jackson, R., II, Moses, N., & Dangerfield, C. (2004). The face of crime: Viewers' memory of race-related facial features of individuals pictured in the news. *Journal of Communication, 54,* 88–104.

Operario, D., & Fiske, S. (2003). Stereotypes: Content, structures, processes, and context. In R. Brown & S. Gaertner (Eds.), *Blackwell handbook of social psychology: Intergroup processes.* Malden, MA: Blackwell.

Pan, Z., & Kosicki, G. M. (1996). Assessing news media influences on the formation of Whites' racial policy preferences. *Communication Research, 23,* 147–178.

Peffley, M., Shields, T., & Williams, B. (1996). The intersection of race and crime in television news stories: An experimental study. *Political Communication, 13,* 309–327.

Power, J., Murphy, S., & Coover, G. (1996). Priming prejudice: How stereotypes and counter-stereotypes influence attribution of responsibility and credibility among ingroups and outgroups. *Human Communication Research, 23,* 36–58.

Reid, S., Giles, H., & Harwood, J. (2005). A self-categorization perspective on communication and intergroup relations. In J. Harwood & H. Giles (Eds.), *Intergroup communication* (pp. 241–263). New York: Peter Lang.

Richardson, J. (2005). Switching social identities: The influence of editorial framing on reader attitudes toward affirmative action and African Americans. *Communication Research, 32,* 503–528.

Rivadeneyra, R., Ward, L. M., & Gordon, M. (2007). Distorted reflections: Media exposure and Latino adolescents' conception of self. *Media Psychology, 9,* 261–290.

Roskos-Ewoldsen, B., Davies, J., & Roskos-Ewoldsen, D. (2004). Implications of the mental models approach for cultivation theory. *Communications, 29,* 345–363.

Roskos-Ewoldsen, D. R., Roskos-Ewoldsen, B., & Dillman Carpentier, F. R. (2002). Media priming: A synthesis. In B. Jennings & D. Zillmann (Eds.), *Media effects: Advances in theory and research* (2nd ed., pp. 97–120). Hillsdale, NJ: Erlbaum.

Scheufele, D. (1999). Framing as a theory of media effects. *Journal of Communication, 49,* 103–122.

Schiappa, E., Gregg, P. B., & Hewes, D. E. (2005). The parasocial contact hypothesis. *Communication Monographs, 72,* 92–115.

Shrum, L. J. (2002). Media consumption and perceptions of social reality: Effects and underlying processes. In J. Bryant & D. Zillmann (Eds.), *Media effects: Advances in theory and research* (2nd ed.). Mahwah, NJ: Erlbaum.

Smith, E., Stewart, T., & Buttram, R. (1992). Inferring a trait from a behavior has long-term, highly specific effects. *Journal of Personality & Social Psychology, 62,* 753–759.

Tajfel, H., & Turner, J. (1986). The social identity theory of intergroup behavior. In S. Worchel & W. Austin (Eds.), *The psychology of intergroup relations* (2nd ed., pp. 7–24). Chicago: Nelson-Hall.

Tamborini, R., & Skalski, P. (2006). The role of presence in the experience of electronic games. In P. Vorderer & J. Bryant (Eds.), *Playing video games: Motivations, responses, and consequences.* Mahwah, NJ: Erlbaum.

Tan, A., Fujioka, Y., & Lucht, N. (1997). Native American stereotypes, TV portrayals, and personal contact. *Journalism & Mass Communication Quarterly, 74,* 265–284.

Tan, A., Fujioka, Y., & Tan, G. (2000). Television use, stereotypes of African Americans and opinions on affirmative action: An effective model of policy reasoning. *Communication Monographs, 67,* 362–371.

Turner, J. (1987). A self-categorization theory. In J. Turner, M. Hogg, P. Oakes, S. Reicher, & M. Wetherell (Eds.), *Rediscovering the social group: A self-categorization theory* (pp. 42–67). Oxford, UK: Basil Blackwell.

Tynes, B., Reynolds, L., & Greenfield, P. (2004). Adolescence, race and ethnicity on the Internet: A comparison of discourse in monitored vs. unmonitored chat rooms. *Journal of Applied Developmental Psychology, 25,* 667–684.

Valentino, N. A. (1999). Crime news and the priming of racial attitudes during evaluations of the president. *Public Opinion Quarterly, 63,* 293–320.

Vergeer, M., Lubbers, M., & Scheepers, P. (2000). Exposure to newspapers and attitudes toward ethnic minorities: A longitudinal analysis. *Howard Journal of Communication, 11,* 127–143.

Wegener, D., & Petty, R. (1995). Flexible correction processes in social judgment: The role of naïve theories in corrections for perceived bias. *Journal of Personality and Social Psychology, 68,* 36–51.

Zwaan, R. A., & Radvansky, G. A. (1998). Situation models in language comprehension and memory. *Psychological Bulletin, 123,* 162–185.

MEDIA AND THE BODY

◆ Kristen Harrison

♦ *Historical Context: Underweight Overrepresented*

OVERVIEW

The possibility that exposure to electronic and print media depicting the ideal human body might influence audience members' satisfaction with their own bodies began to pique researchers' interest in the last quarter of the 20th century. A meta-analysis (Groesz, Levine, & Murnen, 2002) of experiments on this topic identified the publication date of the first such experiment as 1979 (Tan, 1979). Following the death of popular musical artist Karen Carpenter from anorexia nervosa in 1983, public interest in the sociocultural factors that drive people toward self-starvation initiated an upswing in research within fields as diverse as communication, marketing, medicine, psychology, sociology, nursing, nutrition, kinesiology, and others. Since the early 1990s, there has been an explosion of theory and research advancing our understanding of media effects on body image and disordered eating (see Grabe, Ward, & Hyde, 2008). Few media effects research areas have gained so much momentum in so little time.

This chapter introduces readers to scholarship on this topic by summarizing key concepts, theoretical approaches, methodological approaches, research findings, and outstanding research issues. The primary focus is traditional media (e.g., television and magazines), but emerging scholarship on new media is also covered. Key outcomes include body image, disordered eating, and, in the final section of the chapter, obesity.

IDEAL-BODY MEDIA CONTENT

Because a genuine understanding of media effects is facilitated by knowledge about the media content that produces these effects, the chapter begins with an overview of content-analytic research on media body ideals. The recent surge in effects research on this topic seems justified by content analyses reporting how ubiquitous the lean body ideal is and how much leaner it has become over the past 50 years. The earliest analyses of media body ideals concerned *Playboy* playmates and Miss America Pageant contestants from the 1950s through the 1970s (Garner, Garfinkel, Schwartz, & Thompson, 1980) and the 1970s through the 1990s (Spitzer, Henderson, & Zivian, 1999). These studies together document significant declines in body size over time. For instance, Spitzer et al. (1999) analyzed data from 1977 to 1996, converting playmates' heights and weights to body mass index (BMI). The Centers for Disease Control and Prevention (2006) define a BMI of 18.5 to 25 as optimal for health, and a BMI below 18.5 as predictive of anorexia nervosa. Spitzer and colleagues found that playmates' average BMIs ranged from 17.91 to 18.40, whereas pageant winners' BMIs declined from 19.35 in the 1950s to 18.06 in the 1980s. Thus was offered some of the first content-analytic evidence that the female body ideal in the media had become excessively thin during the second half of the 20th century.

Assorted content analyses of modern body ideals in print and electronic media document similar trends and support the conclusion that "thin is in." Greenberg, Eastin, Hofschire, Lachlan, and Brownell (2003) coded the body sizes of 1,018 major characters on prime-time television during the 1999–2000 season and found that whereas approximately 5% of U.S. women and 2% of U.S. men are underweight, over 30% of female characters and 12% of male characters were underweight. The overrepresentation of thinness in the media sends the message that a thin body is good, right, and normative. Adding weight to this message are depictions of fatness as bad, wrong, and non-normative. Greenberg et al. (2003) also found that, compared with 51% of U.S. women and 59% of U.S. men, only 13% of female characters and 24% of male characters were overweight. Compared with thinner characters, fatter characters were depicted with more negative personality and social attributes and fewer romantic and positive social interactions. Additional research shows that thinner female characters are more likely to receive praise (Fouts & Burggraf, 1999) and fatter female characters to be insulted (Fouts & Burggraf, 2000).

These content analyses document the prevalence of the thin body ideal and the various ways its merits are communicated through the media. Not surprisingly, studies measuring the effects of this ideal have become more numerous in recent years. The next section of this chapter conceptualizes the audience within this line of research and identifies some of the key theoretical emphases of studies concerned with the effects of exposure to media body ideals.

◆ Key Concepts

CONCEPTUALIZATION OF CONSTRUCTS

Ideal-body media. In one of the earliest surveys linking media exposure to disordered eating, Harrison and Cantor (1997) used the term *thinness depicting and promoting media* to describe media that display and idealize the lean body ideal. For the purposes of this chapter, the term *ideal-body media* indicates the same construct. Both slender female bodies and muscular, defined male bodies represent this lean body ideal. Notably, some studies (e.g., Harrison & Hefner, 2006) have measured general media exposure rather than exposure to ideal-body media specifically, but given the content-analytic research described earlier, it seems that the thin ideal has become so pervasive in the media that it might be argued that general media exposure *is* ideal-body media exposure.

Body image. Most of the research on ideal-body media effects concerns body image. At its most basic, body image is "the picture of our own body which we form in our own mind" (Schilder, 1935, p. 11). In modern research, "body image" is usually defined more narrowly as *body image disturbance,* which is a maladaptive response to the body image itself (Stewart & Williamson, 2004). Such responses often include distortions, such as an underweight girl's conviction that she is fat, and negative evaluations, such as discontent with the body's features or its weight or shape (Botta, 2000). Recent research indicates that 40% to 60% of adolescent girls and women are dissatisfied with some aspect of their appearance (Thompson, 2004), and that boys and men are becoming increasingly dissatisfied with theirs (Cafri, Strauss, & Thompson, 2002).

Disordered eating. A smaller number of studies have gone beyond body image to explore disordered eating as an outcome. The two types of eating disorders most frequently studied in connection with the media are anorexia nervosa and bulimia nervosa, both characterized by a strong drive for thinness. Anorexia is marked by the routine and deliberate refusal to maintain the minimum normal weight for one's age, sex, and height, along with a loss of 15% of expected weight, whereas bulimia is marked by recurrent binging followed by purging via vomiting, diuretics, laxatives, or exercise (American Psychiatric Association, 2000). Notably, most research linking media exposure to these behaviors does not measure eating disorders *per se* (that is, the clinically established conditions), but rather *disordered eating* (that is, the drives and behaviors closely associated with these conditions).

CONCEPTUALIZATION OF THE AUDIENCE

The primary object of investigation in research on this topic is the independent contribution of media exposure to the development and maintenance of body image disturbance and disordered eating among audience members (who, in most studies, are young, female, and White). In spite of this unidirectional conceptualization, most researchers recognize that the real-world relationship between media and the body is cyclical because people with body image disturbance and eating disorders actively, selectively, and enthusiastically seek out thin-ideal media (Thomsen, McCoy, Gustafson, & Williams, 2002). Moreover, an inclination to question or critique the ideal-body depictions in these media does not necessarily confer protection from harmful effects of exposure on body image. Research suggests that attributes that might be expected to produce resistance to ideal-body portrayals, such as low adherence to the attractive ideal (Thornton & Maurice, 1997), low self-objectification (Monro & Huon, 2005), and the absence of existing eating disorders (Irving, 1990), in fact do little to reduce effects (Grabe et al., 2008). On the other hand, people who are already dissatisfied with their bodies are especially vulnerable to negative effects (Posavac, Posavac, & Posavac, 1998) and, ironically, are among the most avid users of ideal-body media (Thomsen et al., 2002), perhaps because they believe these media are the key to self-transformation. The end result is a challenging situation in which those audience members who stand to be harmed most by ideal-body media content are in fact its biggest fans.

◆ *Theoretical Emphases*

Most media-body research is built on the assumption that the viewer observes and evaluates characters' and models' bodies and, subsequently, observes and evaluates his or her own body, resulting in dissatisfaction and the motivation to change. Beyond this assumption, studies relying on different theoretical approaches emphasize different key constructs and processes. The theoretical approaches described in the following paragraphs are categorized by emphasis on perceptions of rewards associated with attainment of the ideal, perceptions of the self in relation to the ideal, and emotional responses to the ideal and their direct effect on eating.

PERCEIVED REWARDS OF ATTAINING THE IDEAL

The process of social learning or modeling outlined in *social cognitive theory* (Bandura, 2002; Pajares, Prestin, Chen, & Nabi, Chapter 19, this volume) has been invoked to explain why people change their eating and exercise behaviors in response to media depictions. The core process of modeling the thin body ideal involves attention to the ideal and the behaviors associated with its attainment; retention of these behaviors in memory; efforts and capacities to reproduce these behaviors (and confidence in this ability, also called self-efficacy); and, finally, motivation to reproduce the retained behaviors. If a certain set of behaviors or ideals is consistently associated with rewards, social cognitive theory predicts that exposure to such portrayals will increase motivation to perform the behaviors thought to generate those rewards. Because the thin ideal is prevalent in both print and electronic media, and is associated with positive attributes and outcomes whereas fatness is ridiculed (Fouts & Burggraf, 1999, 2000), audience members are given many

incentives to attain the thin bodies they see displayed in the media. In recognition of this, several authors have proposed that modeling mechanisms underlie much of the correlation between exposure to idealized depictions of thinness in entertainment media and disordered eating (e.g., Dittmar, Halliwell, & Ive, 2006; Harrison, 2001). Although dieting behaviors are rarely explicitly portrayed in thin-ideal entertainment media, it is common knowledge that dieting produces weight loss. Thus, viewers who wish to emulate the slight frame of a television character know that they need to eat less to achieve this goal, whether or not they have seen the character dieting on-screen. When eating behaviors *are* explicitly portrayed, direct modeling occurs as well, as evidenced by research on food preferences following exposure to food advertising (Chernin, 2008).

PERCEPTIONS OF SELF VERSUS THE IDEAL

Social cognitive theory does not require that audience members personally embrace a depicted ideal to be motivated to attain it. Internalization of the ideal is not necessary for modeling to occur. Therefore, ideal-body media portrayals may lead viewers to take a rather utilitarian view of dieting (e.g., "I like my body as it is, but what I see on TV suggests that I'll get more positive attention if I'm 10 pounds thinner, so pass the diet soda"). In contrast, the theoretical approaches that emphasize perceptions of the self versus media figures rely heavily on a construct called *thin-ideal internalization*. Thin-ideal internalization, which reflects the degree to which a person consciously accepts the thin body ideal as his or her own personal standard, is considered a major risk factor in the development of disordered eating (Thompson, Heinberg, Altabe, & Tantleff-Dunn, 1999). Studies demonstrating positive correlations among media exposure, a drive for thinness, and disordered eating (e.g., Hargreaves & Tiggemann, 2003) have been interpreted as evidence that media exposure fosters internalization of the thin ideal, and that this internalization increases the risk of disordered eating. The following theoretical approaches all involve the concept of thin-ideal internalization, with varying degrees of explicitness, in their explanations of media effects on body image and disordered eating.

Cultivation. Cultivation theory (Gerbner, Gross, Morgan, Signorielli, & Shanahan, 2002; Morgan, Chapter 5, this volume) offers an explanation for how the thin body ideal in the media may come to be perceived as ubiquitous, normal, personally desirable, and achievable. According to the cultivation model, systematic exposure to television's messages over time leads to the formation of a worldview that is consistent with the world of television. Because the ultrathin body ideal is so prevalent on television, especially for female characters, and because it is portrayed so positively (that is, within a thin-is-good contextual frame), cultivation theory supports the prediction that more avid viewers are more likely to find extreme thinness normative and attractive. In support of this model, research has shown that television viewing among grade-school boys is correlated with a tendency to ascribe negative attributes to fat girls (Harrison, 2000), and among college women is correlated with the idealization of the "curvaceously thin" body type commonly depicted on television (Harrison, 2003).

Social comparison. Perhaps the most popular theory in work on media and body image is social comparison theory (Festinger, 1954). This theory holds that people are driven to evaluate themselves via comparisons to reasonably similar targets. "Upward" comparisons (in which the target of comparison is judged to be superior) in particular can lead to negative self-evaluations and motivate behavioral change aimed at increasing similarity to the target. Supporting research

reveals that ideal-body media exposure predicts poor body image, disordered eating, and endorsement of the thin ideal most acutely among audience members who regularly compare their own bodies with those of media personalities, and who have already internalized the thin body ideal (e.g., Botta, 1999; Tiggemann, 2005).

EMOTIONAL RESPONSES AND THEIR DIRECT EFFECT ON EATING

Eating disorders have a pronounced affective/emotional component (American Psychiatric Association, 2000) that is often overlooked within more rational choice models of behavior adoption and modification. Eating disorders have been conceptualized as methods of coping with noxious emotions, particularly agitation and dejection, which, according to *self-discrepancy theory* (Higgins, 1987), are activated when information in the environment reminds individuals that who they think they are fails to match who they want to be or think they ought to be (Strauman, Vookles, Berenstein, Chaiken, & Higgins, 1991). Such discrepancies can be activated by media exposure (Harrison, 2001) and are associated with an increased risk of disordered eating. Specifically, anorexic behavior tends to follow from agitation, bulimic behavior from dejection (Strauman et al., 1991). Thus, environmental stimuli (media or other) that give rise to feelings of agitation or dejection via self-discrepancy activation should facilitate patterns of disordered eating. Supporting research by Harrison (2001) showed that agitation and dejection rose significantly among self-discrepant adolescents following exposure to ideal-body television, whereas nondiscrepant adolescents displayed little emotional response.

In media-body research, the theoretical emphasis invoked by the researcher frequently influences the methodological approach of the study. The next section summarizes three key methodological approaches—experiments, cross-sectional surveys, and longitudinal surveys—and the research findings these types of studies have generated.

◆ Key Methodological Approaches and Research Findings

KEY METHODOLOGICAL APPROACHES

Experiments. The typical experiment on body image randomly assigns participants (usually adolescents or college women) to view a set of idealized images (usually still photographs or videos), then complete a set of body image measures. A meta-analysis of 25 experiments on women's body satisfaction by Groesz et al. (2002) revealed an average effect size of $d = -.31$, representing reduced body satisfaction among those in treatment conditions. Although experimental research on boys and men is less abundant, television portrayals of the muscular male body ideal have been shown in experiments (e.g., Agliata & Tantleff-Dunn, 2004) to produce significant increases in depression and muscle dissatisfaction. In contrast, little experimental research measures disordered eating because eating disorders are ongoing patterns of behavior that cannot be reliably measured in the lab. However, some experimental research (e.g., Harrison, Taylor, & Marske, 2006) has employed observations of eating behavior after exposure to ideal-body slides and demonstrated changes in eating that could become part of a pathological pattern of eating if repeated daily. Other experimental research has explored disordered eating outside the laboratory as an outcome of prolonged ideal-body magazine exposure. Stice, Spangler, and Agras (2001) assigned adolescent girls to receive a subscription to *Seventeen* and tracked them, along with a control group, for 15 months. The subscription was associated with a modest but significant increase in bulimic symptoms among girls who reported low levels of social support. This study suggests that social support could provide protection against the effects of media body ideals in at least one type of fashion magazine.

Cross-sectional surveys. This type of study generally measures self-reported media exposure, body image, and disordered eating with the aim of analyzing correlations among these variables. Most studies reveal small to moderate positive correlations between exposure to ideal-body television and magazines and variables such as a drive for thinness, body dissatisfaction, and body shame (for a review, see Levine & Harrison, 2003). Some studies go further to measure the role of cognitive processing during exposure. Botta (1999) reported that body image processing (e.g., thinking about how one's body compares with the bodies of television characters) was a stronger predictor of body dissatisfaction and a drive for thinness than was mere exposure, a finding consistent with social comparison theory. One of the earliest cross-sectional surveys linking media exposure with disordered eating (Stice, Schupak-Neuberg, Shaw, & Stein, 1994) tested a cross-sectional path model investigating the relationship between college women's media exposure (a composite measure of various magazine and television genres) and disordered eating. Media exposure predicted disordered eating both directly ($\beta = .30$) and indirectly through a chain of variables including gender-role endorsement, ideal-body internalization, and body dissatisfaction.

Longitudinal surveys. The few longitudinal studies on media exposure and body image reveal modest but durable long-term correlations among children. For prepubescent girls, viewing of appearance-focused television programs was followed by a decrease in appearance satisfaction after a year

(Dohnt & Tiggemann, 2006), and overall television exposure was followed after a year by a tendency to choose a thinner ideal adult body shape (Harrison & Hefner, 2006). Meanwhile, for prepubescent boys, exposure to video gaming magazines was followed one year later by an increased drive for muscularity (Harrison & Bond, 2007). One of the most compelling longitudinal studies on disordered eating concerned changes among adolescent girls in the Polynesian island of Fiji after the introduction of television in 1995 (Becker, Burwell, Gilman, Herzog, & Hamburg, 2002). In this study, disordered eating was significantly more prevalent 3 years after television's introduction than 1 month after (19% versus 8%), and vomiting to control weight increased from an incidence of zero to 7%. Qualitative interviews revealed that 77% of girls studied felt pressured by television to lose weight, with a primary motivation being to emulate a Western television personality.

KEY RESEARCH FINDINGS

Given the multitude of ways media exposure has been defined, manipulated, and measured by researchers from various fields exploring the media-body connection, it is difficult to assemble a coherent "big picture" of effects from reading the literature. Fortunately, an additional methodological approach—the meta-analysis—can be used to generate a wide-angle view of effects. Grabe et al. (2008) recently provided such a view with a meta-analysis of 141 studies (80 experimental and 61 correlational) representing a total of 15,047 research participants. Effect sizes for body dissatisfaction, thin-ideal internalization, and eating behaviors and beliefs about eating ranged from $d = -.28$ to $-.39$, representing moderate effects in the direction of decreased satisfaction with the body and increased eating pathology. For thin-ideal internalization as the outcome, effect sizes were larger for

adolescents ($d = -.42$) than adults ($d = -.31$), and about equal for television ($d = -.39$), magazines ($d = -.33$), and generalized media ($d = -.33$). For eating behaviors and beliefs about eating as the outcome, effect sizes were larger for adults ($d = -.35$) than for adolescents ($d = -.20$), and effects for generalized media ($d = -.50$) were larger than those for television ($d = -.29$) and magazines ($d = -.26$). The average effect size was larger in correlational ($d = -.42$) than in experimental ($d = -.21$) studies when internalization was the outcome, but smaller in correlational ($d = -.28$) than experimental ($d = -.36$) studies when eating beliefs and behaviors were the outcomes. Age, medium, and study design were not tested as moderators for body dissatisfaction as the outcome. Unfortunately, there were too few studies involving boys and men to examine effect size by gender, an omission that underscores the need to include males in future media-body research.

Several conclusions may be drawn on the basis of the Grabe et al. (2008) meta-analysis. For girls and young women, both print and electronic media encourage body dissatisfaction, a drive for thinness, and disordered eating. Effects are moderate but consistent and robust across both correlational and experimental studies. Moreover, longitudinal research on children between the ages of 5 and 10 (e.g., Dohnt & Tiggemann, 2006; Moriarty & Harrison, 2008) is consistent with these conclusions and suggests that media exposure can produce effects that last.

To date, experimental, cross-sectional, and longitudinal studies on the media-body link have mostly measured exposure to traditional media like television and magazines. What is still unknown is the extent to which *new media* and media technologies, such as the Internet, video games, and digital retouching technology, can affect body image and disordered eating. The next section of this chapter addresses this issue.

◆ New Media and the Body

THE INTERNET

There are few content analyses of body ideals on the Internet, but one study suggests that Internet body ideals in advertisements are similar to those in traditional media (Owen & Laurel-Seller, 2000). However, Internet body ideals depart somewhat from traditional media ideals on pro-anorexia or "pro-ana" Web sites and in pro-eating-disorder video material featured on YouTube.com and similar sites. These sites offer resources for people who view disordered eating as a lifestyle choice. A textual content analysis of 12 pro-ana sites by Norris, Boydell, Pinhas, and Katzman (2006) revealed themes of control, success, perfection, sacrifice, transformation, and revolution, transmitted through elements like religious icons and metaphors (e.g., the "Ana Psalm and Creed") and "thinspirational" imagery such as photographs of extremely thin girls and women, many of which were digitally retouched to accentuate protruding bones. In a small pilot study of the effects of exposure to such sites, Bardone-Cone and Cass (2006) assigned college women to view a typical pro-ana site, a women's fashion site, or a home décor site. Those who viewed the pro-ana site experienced increased negative affect and perceived weight, and decreased self-esteem and perceived attractiveness to men. More research with larger samples will be needed to further assess the harmful health effects of pro-eating-disorder sites and videos.

VIDEO GAMES

To date, most research on the representation of bodies in video games examines behavioral attributes like violence and sexuality rather than body shape and size. Notably, such research shows that females are much more likely than males to be scantily clad and featured in sexually provocative poses (Dill & Thill, 2007). Thus it seems important to study body shape and size among video game characters, as characters designed to be perceived as sexually attractive would likely feature highly gender-stereotyped bodies (e.g., the "skinny-yet-busty" body ideal; Harrison, 2003). The practice of "embodying" such characters during play could encourage body-specific social comparisons between player and character(s), even among players not predisposed to such comparisons. Moreover, exposure to video game body ideals of the opposite sex could lead to intolerance of deviation from that ideal in others, as suggested by one study showing that video game exposure among 10- to 13-year-olds predicted increased stigmatization of obesity (Latner, Rosewall, & Simmonds, 2007).

DIGITAL RETOUCHING TECHNOLOGY

As children age, they grow better at distinguishing fantasy from reality (McKenna & Ossoff, 1998), so a Barbie doll has little effect on the body ideals of an older child, who knows it is artificial (Dittmar et al., 2006). Yet modern technology can be used to alter or create images imperceptibly, blurring the distinction between fantasy and fact. Longitudinal research linking video gaming magazine exposure with a stronger drive for muscularity than was predicted by exposure to photorealistic genres (i.e., sports, fitness, and fashion magazines; Harrison & Bond, 2007) suggests that media body ideals can be artificial and still have an impact. Moreover, research on young women shows that knowledge that digital manipulation has occurred does not reduce effects (Bissell, 2006). More research is needed to determine how and to what extent recognition of artificiality moderates effects, as well as the extent to which even obviously distorted or unrealistic images (e.g., modern advertisements that digitally force real models' bodies into doll-like proportions) can lead to social comparisons and foster negative self-assessments.

◆ Outstanding Issues

Over the past 20 years, we have learned much about media effects on body image and disordered eating, yet many of the mechanisms underlying these effects remain poorly understood, especially as they interact with developmental and social processes and contexts. Three sets of outstanding issues—maturational, health, and social—warrant special attention.

MATURATIONAL ISSUES

Although thin-ideal internalization has been documented among children (Sands & Wardle, 2003), research calls into question the idea that thin-ideal internalization *necessarily* mediates the relationship between media exposure and disordered eating early in life. Studies on prepubescent children show that media exposure only marginally predicts thin-ideal internalization, yet robustly predicts disordered eating (Harrison, 2000; Harrison & Hefner, 2006; Sands & Wardle, 2003). How is it possible that media exposure could encourage disordered eating without encouraging the internalization of a thin body ideal? One possibility is that modeling of media dieting behaviors, such as those depicted in food advertisements, is the primary route of effects for young children, and that as they age, processes of social comparison, cultivation, and self-discrepancy activation become more important. Thus, young children's prodieting behaviors and attitudes may be more in line with a desire to mimic "glamorous" adult behaviors in the media than to meet some personal ideal. In any case, further research is needed to determine the point in

development when thin-ideal internalization assumes its role as a key mediator in the media-body relationship.

HEALTH ISSUES

Research on media body ideals is largely concerned with anorexia and bulimia as effects, yet body image disturbance need not lead to eating disorders to be harmful. Smoking (Neumark-Sztainer, Paxton, Hannan, Haines, & Story, 2006) and anabolic steroid use (Brower, Blow, & Hill, 1994) among adolescents are both increased by body image disturbance. Another health issue is the need to determine who is most vulnerable genetically to the effects of environmental stimuli like media because eating disorders appear to be at least partially heritable (Bulik et al., 2003).

Last, the risks young people will take to maintain a slim frame, like cosmetic surgery and off-label prescription drug use, are worthy of systematic investigation. Cosmetic surgery, like all surgery, comes with attendant risks, emotional as well as physical. Epidemiological research links breast augmentation surgery with twice the expected rate of suicide among surgical patients compared with the general population (Sarwer, Brown, & Evans, 2007), though the causal nature of the relationship between elective cosmetic surgery and psychopathology is unclear. Research on media exposure and attitudes toward cosmetic surgery has shown that among college women, overall television exposure correlated with endorsement of liposuction and breast surgery as acceptable ways to alter the shape of the body (Harrison, 2003), and exposure to televised cosmetic surgery makeover programs predicted an increased desire for invasive cosmetic procedures (Nabi, 2009). Young people will also take risks to attain the thin ideal that are *not* sanctioned by the medical establishment. Anecdotal reports gathered by this chapter's author point to a pattern among college students of ingesting benzodiazepines before drinking with the intent of becoming inebriated on fewer drinks and therefore saving calories. Clearly, research on the health outcomes associated with the thin body ideal must go beyond disordered eating if it is to comprehensively catalog the full array of outcomes influenced by this ideal.

SOCIAL ISSUES

The drug-mixing scenario described in the previous paragraph illustrates the importance of considering media effects within a social context. Most research on media and body image assumes direct effects of ideal-body content. However, adolescent girls interviewed by Milkie (1999) reported that they personally resisted emulating the media ideal but felt pressured to lose weight to impress their friends, whom they believed "bought into" that ideal. Presumptions about the media's influence on others may exert their own influence on the person doing the presuming (i.e., the "influence of presumed influence," Gunther & Storey, 2003; Tal-Or, Tsfati, & Gunther, Chapter 7, this volume). Supporting research on the presumed influence of ideal-body media on significant others shows that this presumption may play as important a role as direct exposure does in predicting body dissatisfaction and disordered eating (Park, 2005).

◆ Obesity

A chapter summarizing media effects on eating and weight imbalance would be remiss were it to omit discussion of obesity. Occasionally, the high rate of childhood obesity in the United States is presented as "evidence" that media exposure cannot contribute to excessive dieting because if it did, U.S. children would be getting thinner, not fatter. This attitude reveals misconceptions that pathological undereating and overeating are opposites rather than related patterns of eating disturbance (American Psychiatric Association, 2000), and that media cannot somehow encourage both. In fact, research on excessive dieting identifies unhealthful weight control as one of the risk factors of obesity. Prospective research shows that unhealthful weight control in childhood and adolescence increases the subsequent risk not only of eating disorders but of overeating and obesity, even for youngsters who were thin at baseline (Neumark-Sztainer, Wall, et al., 2006). It seems that a childhood deviation on *either* side of that elusive fulcrum known as "balanced eating" increases the risk of obesity later in life.

So, does media exposure encourage overeating and weight gain? The answer appears to be yes. One observational study showed that for each additional hour of television viewed, children's daily calories increased by 167 (Weicha et al., 2006). Video game playing has also been linked to weight gain (Vandewater, Shim, & Caplovitz, 2004). Media portrayals of obesity are not flattering (Greenberg et al., 2003), so effects are not likely to be produced by modeling or social comparison processes. Some other set of processes must explain the media-obesity relationship. Based on their review of research findings, Jordan and Robinson (2008) advanced four causal mechanisms: (1) lower resting metabolism, (2) displacement of physical activity, (3) food advertising leading to greater intake, and (4) eating while viewing leading to greater intake. Support is relatively weak for lower metabolism (e.g., Dietz, Bandini, Morelli, Peers, & Ching, 1994; Klesges, Shelton, & Klesges, 1993) and displacement of physical activity (Neumark-Sztainer, Story, Hannan, Tharp, & Rex, 2003). Much stronger support emerges for advertising as obesogenic via encouragement of greater caloric intake (Institute of Medicine, 2006). Last, few studies have investigated actual eating behaviors during viewing, but one study shows that people eat more in front of a television that is turned on than turned off (Blass et al., 2006).

The family media context seems to matter as well. The majority of American children over 8 years of age have televisions in their bedrooms (Rideout, Roberts, & Foehr, 2005). Among preschool children, a television in the bedroom has been associated with a 31% increase in the risk of becoming overweight (Dennison, Erb, & Jenkins, 2002). Moreover, children with televisions in their rooms are able to view at night, disrupting sleep. Sleep displacement and poor quality sleep have been associated with increased obesity (Gangwisch, Malaspina, Boden-Albala, & Heymsfield, 2005), so late-night media use could contribute to obesity independently of obesogenic media content.

In the continuing quest to understand media and marketing effects on obesity, researchers are branching out into contextual levels beyond family, such as community (e.g., by exploring food marketing discrepancies in neighborhoods; Short, Guthman, & Raskin, 2007). Research is still needed at the cellular level (e.g., studies of media effects on biological processes) and the cultural level (e.g., studies of collective beliefs about obesogenic foods as comforting and rewarding). To obtain a wide-angle picture of media effects on obesity, researchers will need to continue studying media effects within a wide array of social and biological contexts.

◆ Conclusion

This chapter has linked media exposure to weight disturbance of both types (underweight and overweight) via different sets of mechanisms. The ability to maintain a healthy, balanced diet and body size is essential for vitality and well-being. That media exposure may hinder this ability should be of concern to all stakeholders in the health of the public, especially its youngest constituents. A summary of research-based suggestions for strategies to solve the problems of media effects on body image, disordered eating, and obesity is beyond the scope of this chapter. However, most intervention work suggests that alternative sources of information are essential to offset the power of media messages. Parental and peer social support can make teens more resistant to the influence of ideal-body media (Stice et al., 2001), and it is well known that parents who stock their kitchens with healthy foods will have healthier children than those who do not. However, responsibility for children's weight status should not fall solely on the shoulders of parents. Media producers and advertisers should be encouraged to seriously reexamine their current equation of beauty with extremely low body fat in light of evidence that this ideal can be harmful to the public. With collaborative efforts on the part of concerned citizens and conscientious corporations, a society of individuals who value a balanced physique and eat for strength and health is achievable.

◆ References

Agliata, D., & Tantleff-Dunn, S. (2004). The impact of media exposure on males' body image. *Journal of Social and Clinical Psychology, 23*(1), 7–22.

American Psychiatric Association. (2000). *Diagnostic and statistical manual of mental disorders* (4th ed., text revision). Washington, DC: Author.

Bandura, A. (2002). Social cognitive theory of mass communication. In J. Bryant & D. Zillmann (Eds.), *Media effects: Advances in theory and research* (pp. 121–154). Mahwah, NJ: Erlbaum.

Bardone-Cone, A. M., & Cass, K. M. (2006). Investigating the impact of pro-anorexia Websites: A pilot study. *European Eating Disorders Review, 14,* 256–262.

Becker, A. E., Burwell, R. A., Gilman, S. E., Herzog, D. B., & Hamburg, P. (2002). Eating behaviors and attitudes following prolonged exposure to television among ethnic Fijian adolescent girls. *British Journal of Psychiatry, 180*(6), 509–514.

Bissell, K. L. (2006). Skinny like you: Visual literacy, digital manipulation, and young women's drive to be thin. *SIMILE: Studies in Media and Information Literacy Education, 6*(1), 1–14.

Blass, E. M., Anderson, D. R., Kirkorian, H. L., Pempek, T. A., Price, I., & Koleini, M. F. (2006). On the road to obesity: Television viewing increases intake of high-density foods. *Physiology and Behavior, 88,* 597–604.

Botta, R. A. (1999). Television images and adolescent girls' body image disturbance. *Journal of Communication, 49*(2), 22–41.

Botta, R. A. (2000). The mirror of television: A comparison of Black and White adolescents' body image. *Journal of Communication, 50*(3), 144–159.

Brower, K. J., Blow, F. C., & Hill, E. M. (1994). Risk factors for anabolic-androgenic steroid use in men. *Journal of Psychiatric Research, 28*(4), 369–380.

Bulik, C. M., Devlin, B., Bacanu, S. A., Thornton, L., Klump, K. L., Fichter, M. M., et al. (2003). Significant linkage on chromosome 10p in families with bulimia nervosa. *American Journal of Human Genetics, 72*(1), 200–207.

Cafri, G., Strauss, J., & Thompson, J. K. (2002). Male body image: Satisfaction and its relationship to psychological functioning using the somatomorphic matrix. *International Journal of Men's Health, 1,* 215–231.

Centers for Disease Control and Prevention. (2006). *BMI—Body mass index: About BMI for adults.* Retrieved October 16, 2006, from http://www.cdc.gov/nccdphp/dnpa/bmi/adult_BMI/about_adult_BMI.htm

Chernin, A. (2008). The effects of food marketing on children's preferences: Testing the moderating roles of age and gender. *Annals of the American Academy of Political and Social Science, 615*(1), 102–118.

Dennison, B. A., Erb, T. A., & Jenkins, P. L. (2002). Television viewing and television in bedroom associated with overweight risk among low-income preschool children. *Pediatrics, 109,* 1028–1035.

Dietz, W. H., Bandini, L. G., Morelli, J. A., Peers, K. F., & Ching, P. L. (1994). Effect of sedentary activities on resting metabolic rate. *American Journal of Clinical Nutrition, 59, 556–559.*

Dill, K. E., & Thill, K. P. (2007). Video game characters and the socialization of gender roles: Young people's perceptions mirror sexist media depictions. *Sex Roles, 57*(11–12), 851–864.

Dittmar, H., Halliwell, E., & Ive, S. (2006). Does Barbie make girls want to be thin? The effect of experimental exposure to images of dolls on the body image of 5–8-year-old girls. *Developmental Psychology, 42*(2), 283–292.

Dohnt, H., & Tiggemann, M. (2006). The contribution of peer and media influences to the development of body satisfaction and self-esteem in young girls: A prospective study. *Developmental Psychology, 42*(5), 929–936.

Festinger, L. (1954). A theory of social comparison processes. *Human Relations, 7,* 117–140.

Fouts, G., & Burggraf, K. (1999). Television situation comedies: Female body images and verbal reinforcements. *Sex Roles, 40*(5/6), 473–481.

Fouts, G., & Burggraf, K. (2000). Television situation comedies: Female weight, male negative comments, and audience reactions. *Sex Roles, 42*(9–10), 925–932.

Gangwisch, J. E., Malaspina, D., Boden-Albala, B., & Heymsfield, S. B. (2005). Inadequate sleep as a risk factor for obesity: Analyses of the NHANES I. *Sleep, 28*(10), 1289–1296.

Garner, D. M., Garfinkel, P. E., Schwartz, D., & Thompson, M. (1980). Cultural expectations of thinness in women. *Psychological Reports, 47*(2), 483–491.

Gerbner, G., Gross, L., Morgan, M., Signorielli, N., & Shanahan, J. (2002). Growing up with television: The cultivation process. In J. Bryant & D. Zillmann (Eds.), *Media effects: Advances in theory and research* (pp. 43–68). Mahwah, NJ: Erlbaum.

Grabe, S., Ward, L. M., & Hyde, J. S. (2008). The role of the media in body image concerns among women: A meta-analysis of experimental and correlational studies. *Psychological Bulletin, 134*(3), 460–476.

Greenberg, B. S., Eastin, M., Hofschire, L., Lachlan, K., & Brownell, K. D. (2003).

Portrayals of overweight and obese individuals on commercial television. *American Journal of Public Health, 93*(8), 1342–1348.

Groesz, L. M., Levine, M. P., & Murnen, S. K. (2002). The effect of experimental presentation of thin media images on body satisfaction: A meta-analytic review. *International Journal of Eating Disorders, 31,* 1–16.

Gunther, A. C., & Storey, J. D. (2003). The influence of presumed influence. *Journal of Communication, 53*(2), 199–215.

Hargreaves, D., & Tiggemann, M. (2003). Longer-term implications of responsiveness to "thin ideal" television: Support for a cumulative hypothesis of body image disturbance? *European Eating Disorders Review, 11,* 465–477.

Harrison, K. (2000). Television viewing, fat stereotyping, body shape standards, and eating disorder symptomatology in grade school children. *Communication Research, 27*(5), 617–640.

Harrison, K. (2001). Ourselves, our bodies: Thin-ideal media, self-discrepancies, and eating disorder symptomatology in adolescents. *Journal of Social and Clinical Psychology, 20*(3), 289–323.

Harrison, K. (2003). Television viewers' ideal body proportions: The case of the curvaceously thin woman. *Sex Roles, 48,* 255–264.

Harrison, K., & Bond, B. J. (2007). Gaming magazines and the drive for muscularity in preadolescent boys: A longitudinal examination. *Body Image, 4,* 269–277.

Harrison, K., & Cantor, J. (1997). The relationship between media consumption and eating disorders. *Journal of Communication, 47*(1), 40–66.

Harrison, K., & Hefner, V. (2006). Media exposure, current and future body ideals, and disordered eating among preadolescent girls: A longitudinal panel study. *Journal of Youth and Adolescence, 35*(2), 146–156.

Harrison, K., Taylor, L. D., & Marske, A. L. (2006). Women's and men's eating behavior following exposure to ideal-body images and text. *Communication Research, 33*(6), 507–529.

Higgins, E. T. (1987). Self-discrepancy: A theory relating self and affect. *Psychological Review, 94,* 319–340.

Institute of Medicine (IOM) Committee on Food Marketing and the Diets of Children and Youth, and Food and Nutrition Board. (2006). *Food marketing to children and youth: Threat or opportunity?* Washington, DC: National Academies Press.

Irving, L. M. (1990). Mirror images: Effects of the standard of beauty on the self- and body esteem of women exhibiting varying levels of bulimic symptoms. *Journal of Social and Clinical Psychology, 9*(2), 230–242.

Jordan, A. B., & Robinson, T. N. (2008). Children, television viewing, and weight status: Summary and recommendations from an expert panel meeting. *Annals of the American Academy of Political and Social Science, 615,* 119–132.

Klesges, R. C., Shelton, M. L., & Klesges, L. M. (1993). Effects of television on metabolic rate: Potential implications for childhood obesity. *Pediatrics, 91,* 281–286.

Latner, J. D., Rosewall, J. K., & Simmonds, M. B. (2007). Childhood obesity stigma: Association with television, videogame, and magazine exposure. *Body Image, 4*(2), 147–155.

Levine, M. P., & Harrison, K. (2003). Media's role in the perpetuation and prevention of negative body image and disordered eating. In J. K. Thompson (Ed.), *Handbook of eating disorders and obesity* (pp. 695–717). New York: Wiley.

McKenna, M. W., & Ossoff, E. P. (1998). Age differences in children's comprehension of a popular television program. *Child Study Journal, 28*(1), 53–68.

Milkie, M. (1999). Social comparisons, reflected appraisals, and mass media: The impact of pervasive beauty images on Black and White girls' self-concepts. *Social Psychology Quarterly, 62*(2), 190–210.

Monro, F., & Huon, G. (2005). Media-portrayed idealized images, body shame, and appearance anxiety. *International Journal of Eating Disorders, 38,* 85–90.

Moriarty, C. M., & Harrison, K. (2008). Television exposure and disordered eating among children: A longitudinal panel study. *Journal of Communication, 58*(2), 361–381.

Nabi, R. L. (2009). Cosmetic surgery makeover programs and intentions to undergo cosmetic enhancements: A consideration of three models of media effects. *Human Communication Research, 35*, 1–27.

Neumark-Sztainer, D., Paxton, S. J., Hannan, P. J., Haines, J., & Story, M. (2006). Does body satisfaction matter? Five-year longitudinal associations between body satisfaction and health behaviors in adolescent females and males. *Journal of Adolescent Health, 39*(2), 244–251.

Neumark-Sztainer, D., Story, M., Hannan, P. J., Tharp, T., & Rex, J. (2003). Factors associated with changes in physical activity: A cohort study of inactive adolescent girls. *Archives of Pediatrics and Adolescent Medicine, 157*, 803–810.

Neumark-Sztainer, D., Wall, M., Guo, J., Story, M., Haines, J., & Eisenberg, M. (2006). Obesity, disordered eating, and eating disorders in a longitudinal study of adolescents: How do dieters fare 5 years later? *Journal of the American Dietetic Association, 106*(4), 568.

Norris, M. L., Boydell, K. M., Pinhas, L., & Katzman, D. K. (2006). Ana and the Internet: A review of pro-anorexia Websites. *International Journal of Eating Disorders, 39*(6), 443–447.

Owen, P. R., & Laurel-Seller, E. (2000). Weight and shape ideals: Thin is dangerously in. *Journal of Applied Social Psychology, 30*, 979–990.

Park, S. Y. (2005). The influence of presumed media influence on women's desire to be thin. *Communication Research, 32*(5), 594–614.

Posavac, H., Posavac, S., & Posavac, E. (1998). Exposure to media images of female attractiveness and concern with body weight among young women. *Sex Roles, 38*, 187–201.

Rideout, V. J., Roberts, D. F., & Foehr, U. G. (2005). *Generation M: Media in the lives of 8–18 year-olds: Executive summary*. Menlo Park, CA: Kaiser Family Foundation.

Sands, E. R., & Wardle, J. (2003). Internalization of ideal body shapes in 9–12-year-old girls. *International Journal of Eating Disorders, 33*, 193–204.

Sarwer, D. B., Brown, G. K., & Evans, D. L. (2007). Cosmetic breast augmentation and suicide. *American Journal of Psychiatry, 164*, 1006–1013.

Schilder, P. (1935). *The image and appearance of the human body*. New York: International Universities Press.

Short, A., Guthman, J., & Raskin, R. (2007). Food deserts, oases, or mirages? *Journal of Planning Education and Research, 26*(3), 352–364.

Spitzer, B. L., Henderson, K. A., & Zivian, M. T. (1999). Gender differences in population versus media body sizes: A comparison over four decades. *Sex Roles, 40*(7–8), 545–565.

Stewart, T. M., & Williamson, D. A. (2004). Assessment of body image disturbances. In J. K. Thompson (Ed.), *Handbook of eating disorders and obesity* (pp. 495–514). Hoboken, NJ: Wiley.

Stice, E., Schupak-Neuberg, E., Shaw, H. E., & Stein, R. I. (1994). Relation of media exposure to eating disorder symptomatology: An examination of mediating mechanisms. *Journal of Abnormal Psychology, 103*(4), 836–840.

Stice, E., Spangler, D., & Agras, W. S. (2001). Exposure to media-portrayed thin-ideal images adversely affects vulnerable girls: A longitudinal experiment. *Journal of Social and Clinical Psychology, 20*(3), 270–288.

Strauman, T. J., Vookles, J., Berenstein, V., Chaiken, S., & Higgins, E. T. (1991). Self-discrepancies and vulnerability to body dissatisfaction and disordered eating. *Journal of Personality and Social Psychology, 61*, 946–956.

Tan, A. S. (1979). TV beauty ads and role expectations of adolescent female viewers. *Journalism Quarterly, 56*(2), 283–288.

Thompson, J. K. (2004). Eating disorders and obesity: Definitions, prevalence, and associated features. In J. K. Thompson (Ed.), *Handbook of eating disorders and obesity* (pp. xiii–xix). Hoboken, NJ: Wiley.

Thompson, J. K., Heinberg, L., Altabe, M., & Tantleff-Dunn, S. (1999). *Exacting beauty: Theory, assessment, and treatment of body image disturbance*. Washington, DC: American Psychological Association.

Thomsen, S. R., McCoy, J. K., Gustafson, R. L., & Williams, M. (2002). Motivations for reading beauty and fashion magazines and anorexic risk in college-age women. *Media Psychology, 4*(2), 113–135.

Thornton, B., & Maurice, J. (1997). Physique contrast effect: Adverse impact of idealized body images for women. *Sex Roles, 37,* 433–439.

Tiggemann, M. (2005). Television and adolescent body image: The role of program content and viewing motivation. *Journal of Social & Clinical Psychology, 24*(3), 361–381.

Vandewater, E. A., Shim, M., & Caplovitz, A. G. (2004). Linking obesity and activity level with children's television and video game use. *Journal of Adolescence, 27,* 71–85.

Weicha, J. L., Peterson, K. E., Ludwig, D. S., Jim, J., Sobol, A., & Gortmaker, S. L. (2006). When children eat what they watch: Impact of television viewing on dietary intake in youth. *Archives of Pediatrics and Adolescent Medicine, 160,* 436–442.

27

MEDIA AND SEXUALITY

◆ Jane D. Brown

Sex is more exciting on the screen and between the pages than between the sheets.

—Andy Warhol (1975, p. 44)

For mass communication effects researchers, the pervasiveness and apparent appeal of sexual media content raises questions about how "sex on the screen and between the pages" might be influencing sexual socialization and real-life sexual behavior. Do young people develop unrealistic expectations of what real sex will be like from reading *Cosmo* and *Maxim*, watching TV shows such as *Sex and the City*, gossiping about celebrity pregnancies online, or listening to songs with titles such as "Touch My Body" and "Sensual Seduction"? Do the glamorous depictions of sex and lack of negative consequences hasten initiation of sexual behavior?

Sexual socialization is "the process by which knowledge, attitudes, and values about sexuality are acquired" (Ward, 2003, p. 348). In an era of "abstinence only" sex education in schools and religious institutions (Santelli et al., 2006) and embarrassed parents who don't

---

Author's Note: Many thanks to UNC-CH doctoral student Sheila Rose Peuchaud, who contributed to the development of this chapter.

know what to say to their children, the media may play an important role as young people learn about sex and sexuality. In one national survey of U.S. teens (15–19 years old), the media and friends far outranked parents or schools as sources of information about birth control (Kaiser Family Foundation, 2004); more than 40% of young people say they have changed their behavior because of health information they found online (Ybarra & Suman, 2008). Given that peers' as well as parents' attitudes about sex may also be shaped by the media, understanding more about the role media play in sexual socialization is important.

A growing body of media effects research has focused on the frequency and kind of sexual content in mainstream media, and some experimental and longitudinal studies are telling us more about the effects of exposure to sexual content on young media consumers' sexual lives. The purpose of this chapter is to provide an overview of current research, to highlight some promising new avenues of research, and to pose some challenges for the next generation of scholars. I focus primarily on the effects sexual content may have on adolescents and young adults, rather than older adults, because adolescence and young adulthood is when learning about sexual norms and the adoption of patterns of sexual behavior are most salient. Some developmental scholars have proposed that between about 18 and 25 years of age, young people in industrialized countries are experiencing a new life stage known as "emerging adulthood" (Arnett & Tanner, 2006). Spurred by increased access to higher education for women, the need for more education to access good careers, and higher housing costs, many young people are waiting longer than ever before to get married and to start their own families. Pubertal onset occurs around age 11 for boys and age 10 for girls (Sun et al., 2002), whereas the average age at first marriage is 25 for women in the United States and 27 for

men (U.S. Census Bureau, 2005a, 2005b). Such a long period between the onset of puberty and first marriage affects patterns of sexual behavior and the potential impact of the media on sexual socialization even into early adulthood.

Although a great deal of work has been done on the effects of pornography and sexually explicit content on adults (Zillmann & Bryant, 1989), very little has been conducted in the era of Internet porn, or with younger viewers, so I focus here primarily on the potential of mainstream media, such as television, music, movies, and magazines, and nonpornographic Internet content to affect the sexual socialization of adolescents and emerging adults. Although we suspect the new media technologies, such as text messaging on cell phones, blogs, and social networking sites such as MySpace and Facebook, are also important in the sexual lives of young people, we currently know very little from scientific research about their use or effects.

◆ Risky Sexual Behavior

Many adolescents and emerging adults engage in sexual behaviors that put them at risk for unwanted pregnancies and sexually transmitted diseases. In the United States in 2005, according to the U.S. Centers for Disease Control, 47% of high school students had had sexual intercourse, and 14% had already had four or more sex partners. More than half of both males and females aged 15 to 19 had engaged in oral sex with someone of the opposite sex. About half of young people have had sexual intercourse by the time they reach 18 years of age, and almost all have by 25 years old; very few wait until they are married (Lefkowitz & Gillen, 2006). Condoms and other forms of contraception are often not used during initial sexual encounters and often are used only inconsistently thereafter. The U.S. Centers for Disease Control and Prevention reported in

2008 that one quarter of all teen girls—and 48% of African American teen girls—were infected with at least one sexually transmitted infection. According to the National Campaign to Prevent Teen and Unplanned Pregnancy (2005), women in their twenties experience 1.5 million unplanned pregnancies annually, and the children born to these women show significantly more negative health, cognitive, and social outcomes than children born to women who planned their pregnancies. It is important to note that in other developed countries, such as the Netherlands, France, and Germany, young people do not suffer such negative sexual health outcomes, apparently due to more comprehensive and early sex education, access to confidential health care services, and a cultural expectation that young people can and will be responsible for their sexual behavior (Feijoo, 2001).

◆ *Media and Sexual Socialization*

Previous research on the impact of the media on sexual beliefs and behaviors typically has begun with analyses of content that address what kind of sexual imagery and information is available, with what frequency, to which audiences. Numerous analyses, both quantitative and qualitative, have been conducted, especially on prime-time television and specific TV genres such as soap operas and music videos. Teen girl magazines, popular music, movies, and movie previews have also been studied, but not as thoroughly as television (Stern & Brown, 2008). Comparatively little has been written about the sexual content on popular radio channels, in video games, in premium cable television programming, or on the Internet, although such media include sexual content and are popular among young people (Roberts & Foehr, 2004).

A number of studies have taken the next step beyond content analysis to assess the relationship between exposure to sexual content and sexual beliefs and behaviors in small, usually nonrepresentative samples, and a few experimental studies that have manipulated exposure to specific kinds of sexual media content have been conducted. Excellent comprehensive reviews of this research are available (e.g., Escobar-Chaves et al., 2005). Since 2004, the results of some larger-scale longitudinal surveys also have been published that provide further evidence of a connection between exposure to sexual content in the media and young people's sexual behavior. Thus, at this point, the evidence of effects is accumulating, but much remains to be done to establish under what circumstances and for which young people the media are important sexual socialization agents. Here I briefly review what is known about sexual content with some illustrative recent content studies. Then I turn to the most recent studies of effects and offer suggestions for future studies.

◆ *Sexual Content in the Media*

Drawing on a comprehensive review of studies of sexual content in the media, Ward (2003) identified six consistent patterns in talk about and depictions of sexual behavior across the media young people attend to in the United States, and increasingly around the world. Recent content analyses suggest the patterns remain.

(1) *Sexual content is more likely to be verbal innuendo or jokes than graphic visual depictions, and visual depictions are "mostly precursory (e.g., flirting, kissing)"* (Ward, 2003, p. 351). In an extensive analysis of the sexual content across television channels frequently watched by U.S. adolescents in 2001, for example, Fisher, Hill, Grube, and Gruber (2004) found that more than 80% of the 1,276 shows analyzed included sexual content, but only about 4% depicted sexual intercourse. The

majority of the sexual content was coded as physical flirting or kissing and touching. In another content analysis conducted in 2001 across four media (television, as well as music, movies, and magazines) used frequently by early (12–14 years old) adolescents, Pardun, L'Engle, and Brown (2005) found that "body exposure" (e.g., cleavage, bare buttocks) and the depiction of romantic relationships accounted for two thirds of all the sexual content coded. Sexual innuendos, defined as "gestures or exchanges meant to arouse sexual interest," occurred in 12% of the sexual content; about 7% of the sexual content included mention or depiction of sexual intercourse.

(2) *Most sexual activity in the media occurs outside of marital relationships.* Cope-Farrar and Kunkel (2002), in an extensive analysis of sexual content on television, found that 70% of programs (77% of prime-time programs) portrayed sexual behavior or talk, and more than three fourths (79%) of the depictions involved characters who were not married to each other. Two years later, 15% of scenes depicting sexual intercourse involved characters who had just met—up from 7% in 2002 (Kaiser Family Foundation, 2005).

(3) *Contraception or the physical consequences (such as pregnancy or sexually transmitted infections) of sexual activity are rarely discussed or depicted.* We might characterize this pattern of portrayals as the missing three Cs of sexual health—commitment, contraception, and consequences. Only about 10% of sexual scenes in television programs popular among teens in 2005 contained a sexual precaution message (Kaiser Family Foundation, 2005). In the Pardun et al. (2005) content analysis of four media, less than 1% of the sexual content contained discussion or depiction of sexual consequences or contraception. A subsequent qualitative analysis found that even the rare sexual health messages tended to reinforce the stereotypes that males are obsessed with sex and sexual performance

and it is up to females to prevent undesired outcomes such as pregnancy or sexually transmitted diseases (Hust, Brown, & L'Engle, 2008).

(4) *The quantity of different kinds of sexual content vary within and across television genres, as well as across media.* Prime-time television programming, for example, typically contains more visually explicit sexual activity, whereas talk shows contain more graphic and personal sexual discussion. Programs most viewed by teens have unusually high sexual content compared with prime-time programs in general or television overall (Hetsroni, 2007). In the analysis of four media, music lyric lines contained dramatically more sexual content (40%) than scenes in movies (12%); or on television (11%); or in the headlines, pictures, and paragraphs in magazines (8%; Pardun et al., 2005).

(5) *Women's bodies are more frequently sexually objectified than men's.* In magazines, gender roles are constructed along traditional lines, emphasizing the need for women to please their partners by enhancing their own beauty and sexual availability (Ward, 2003). One analysis of 151 movie previews found that more than one half included at least one sexual scene, and females were much more likely than males to be portrayed as sexual (Oliver & Kalyanaraman, 2005). Perry (2004, p. 175) argued that women of color, in particular, are portrayed as scantily clad commodities "not unlike the luxury cars, Rolex watches, and platinum and diamond medallions" also featured in hip hop videos. In her qualitative study of the sexual scripts found on 14- to 17-year-old Black girls' home pages, Stokes (2007) found that the girls often defined their own sexuality in terms that reproduced oppressive stereotypes, such as "downass chick" and "pimpette," that focused on their partners' needs and mirrored the hip hop video depictions Perry described. The girls who reported listening only to rap music reproduced the most sexualized

scripts on their home pages, whereas those who presented themselves with "virgin" or "resister" scripts reported the broadest musical tastes.

(6) *Sexual references are increasing over time in some media.* Most of the media young people attend to include more sexual depictions and discussion than they used to. Based on a review of studies of sexual content in the movies, music, and television programs popular among adolescents since the 1950s, Stern and Brown (2008, p. 335) concluded,

> There is little question that sexual behaviors have become more frequent and explicit across all media with each passing decade. Images that would have been censored in the 1950s became increasingly common in the 1980s, and, by 2005, were mainstream. Romance and courtship—practices that used only to hint at sexuality—have received shorter and shorter shrift as media producers vie for the lucrative youth market, which is presumed to be sexually curious and easily bored. In consequence, content that might have shocked a 15-year-old in the 1960s might not even earn a second glance from a contemporary teenager, who encounters such imagery daily from an array of media sources.

◆ Beyond Content to Possible Effects

A growing body of studies has documented the media's ability to transmit information about sex, shape attitudes and perceptions of sexual norms, and encourage sexual activity. Some of the classic media effects theories, including cultivation theory, social cognitive theory, and information processing theory, have been used to explain the media's effects on sexual knowledge, attitudes, and behaviors. The theories predict that the media influence consumers' perceptions of social behavior and social reality, cultivate

cultural norms (Gerbner, 1998), and offer young people "scripts" for sexual behavior that they might not be able to observe elsewhere (Gagnon & Simon, 1973). Social cognitive theory (Bandura, 1986) proposes that individuals learn about appropriate and inappropriate behavior by observing which behaviors are rewarded or punished, and that the media provide compelling models for observation. Special attention typically is more likely paid to models who are perceived as attractive, powerful, or similar to the observer. Cultivation theory holds that television's portrayal of the world is unrealistic, but that frequent exposure to televised portrayals will result in a view of the world more in line with the unrealistic TV portrayal than with reality. Information-processing theory suggests that recurring portrayals will be more readily accessible from memory and that behavioral scripts seen in the media will help guide behavior in novel situations (Shrum, 2001). Taken together, these theories help explain how the media's depiction of sexuality and sexual interaction might influence young media consumers' *beliefs* about the acceptability and prevalence of sexual behaviors, their *expectations* about who does what to whom with what consequences, and ultimately, their own sexual *behaviors.*

In the late 1990s, with encouragement from Congress, the U.S. National Institutes of Health issued a call for proposals for further investigation of the effects of the media on adolescents' sexual behavior. These NIH-funded longitudinal studies provide the most compelling evidence to date that early exposure to sexual content on television and in other teen-oriented media, such as music, movies, and magazines, "hastens" initiation of sexual intercourse. Although each study varied in design, sample, and measures, the first publications from each of the studies supported the hypothesis that exposure to sexual content on television (Ashby, Arcari, & Edmonson, 2006; Collins et al., 2004), sexually degrading music (e.g., lyrics that portray men as sexually insatiable and women as valuable solely as sex objects; Martino, Collins, Kanouse, Elliott, & Berry, 2006), and a "sexual media diet" across four media (music, movies, television, and magazines; Brown et al., 2006) is related to subsequent sexual behavior. In each study, many of the possible alternative explanations for the relationship, such as demographics, extent of connection or closeness with parents, school, religion, sensation seeking, and self-esteem, were included, and the media variables still predicted sexual behavior 1 to 2 years later. The Ashby et al. study found a link between amount of time spent television viewing and sexual behavior, although the other studies found that overall exposure was less predictive than more specific measures of exposure to sexual content.

Such studies take us closer to establishing the causal sequence of media's effects because they measure adolescents' media use and sexual behavior over time and in teens' natural media-use settings, while controlling for alternative explanations. We will learn more as the findings of the other large studies become available. A number of important theoretical and methodological questions remain, however.

◆ Theoretical Challenges: Who, When, and How?

We still know relatively little about how the process works, for whom, and under what circumstances. As we learn more about the media's role in adolescents' sexual socialization, it is increasingly clear that this is a complicated process in which selection, attention, interpretation, and sometimes even resistance to media content as well as other contextual factors are important. Social-demographic identities, such as gender and race/ethnicity, personality characteristics, and other socialization

contexts, affect which media are selected, which content receives attention, and to what extent it is incorporated into a teen's everyday life and sense of sexual self (Steele & Brown, 1995). Media use and effects do not occur in isolation and are affected by the young person's family and peer configuration and interactions, as well as their existing beliefs about sexual behavior. Martino et al. (2006), for example, found that the relationship between exposure to TV sexual content and initiation of sexual intercourse was mediated by perceived peer norms, as well as by sexual self-efficacy and negative outcome expectancies. Further study of these and other potential mediators and moderators of the relationship between media exposure and teen sexual behavior would be helpful both in theoretical understanding of the process of sexual media effects and also in designing media interventions for sexual health.

◆ Key Moderators: Gender and Race/Ethnicity

One of the core developmental tasks of adolescence is developing a sense of self in relation to others and the culture. The digital revolution has resulted in an amazing array of channels of television, movies, and music that are increasingly accessible to even young children on portable devices such as laptop computers and cell phones, and increasingly in the privacy of their own bedrooms (Roberts & Foehr, 2004). Gender and race/ethnicity are two key components of identity that affect both which media content is chosen and how it is interpreted.

From early on, it is as if boys and girls live in different media worlds (Roe, 1998), as girls tend to choose more relationship-oriented content and boys choose sports and action-adventure. Boys are much more likely to attend to pornography on the Internet than girls (Peter & Valkenburg, 2006) and play more video and online games, whereas girls spend more time on social networking sites creating content and commenting on others' postings (*Teens and Social Media,* 2007). So males and females may be getting very different views of sexuality from the media content they choose.

Ward (2003) concluded that males' sexual beliefs are less affected by television programming than are females', but this may be because young men don't find typical dramatic television programming very interesting. Some relatively new genres, such as reality dating shows *Elimidate, Blind Date,* and *Dismissed,* appear to be attracting more male interest, however, and may be affecting young men's sexual beliefs. In one study, college males were found to watch reality dating shows almost as frequently as females, and said they watched to learn about dating and because the shows were entertaining. Frequent viewers of both sexes were more likely than those who didn't view as often to believe in a sexual double standard, that relationships are adversarial, that men are sex driven, that dating is a game, and that appearance is important in dating (Zurbriggen & Morgan, 2006).

Race also affects media selection and use. One analysis of the television shows watched by a large sample of adolescents found that Black and White and male and female adolescents had only 4 of a list of 150 current television shows in common. The majority of Black teens, both boys and girls, regularly watched shows that featured Black casts, whereas White girls and boys rarely watched shows with Black casts and tended to choose gender-stereotypical fare (Brown & Pardun, 2004).

Although Collins et al.'s (2004) study of exposure to sexual content on television found similar patterns of effects for Blacks and Whites, Brown et al. (2006) found that for Black teens, the strength of the link between media exposure at 12 to 14 years and sexual behavior 2 years later disappeared when perceptions of parental expectations and peers' sexual behavior were taken into account. Brown et al. speculated that the effect of the media may occur earlier for Black children both because Blacks on average reach sexual maturity earlier than Whites, and because the media that Blacks attend to is more sexual than the media White teens typically use. Peer and parental influences may also be different for Black and White youth.

Such factors as gender, race, and other socialization influences need to be taken into account in future studies. Given the currently high rates of teen pregnancy among Hispanic youth in the United States—51% of Latinas become pregnant at least once between the ages of 15 and 19, compared with 34% of all American teens (National Campaign to Prevent Teen and Unplanned Pregnancy, 2005)—it is important to learn more about the media as sexual socialization agents in their lives as well.

What About New Media?

The new, more interactive media tools such as chat rooms, blogs, social networking sites, and even text messaging provide a much more interactive and user-driven media environment in which young people may project their emerging sexual selves and interact sexually with people they may never meet in real life. Although we know relatively little about how sexual life in these new media environments may play out, early research suggests both benefits and risks. On the one hand, studies show that many teens use the Internet for finding sexual health information (Borzekowski & Rickert, 2001). But sexual health sites for teens have addressed only some topics, and have not optimized the potential for interactivity and customization as effectively as they might (Noar, Clark, Cole, & Lustria, 2006). Some Internet-based sexual health interventions have provided teens with the information and skills necessary to prevent pregnancy and sexually transmitted diseases (e.g. Roberto et al., 2007). And even text messaging is being used as a sexual health tool. The San Francisco Department of Public Health used a text-messaging service, SexInfo, to answer queries such as "what to do if a condom broke," and "if you think you're pregnant" (Levine, McCright, Dobkin, Woodruff, & Klausner, 2008).

On the other hand, the openness of the Internet has increased concerns about unwanted exposure to pornography, online sexual harassment, and young people taking sexual risks with people they meet online. In a nationally representative survey of youth Internet users in 2005, one fifth reported being harassed online, primarily by being asked to send sexual pictures of themselves (Mitchell, Finkelhor, & Wolak, 2007). More than half (59%) of college students reported in another survey that they had received unwanted pornography; 10% to 15% said they had been harassed, primarily by strangers, in e-mail and via instant messaging (Finn, 2004).

◆ Methodological Challenges

If we think about a young person's sexual development from a socioecological perspective (Bronfenbrenner, 1977), it is clear that media are only one of a number of possible contexts in which he or she may learn about norms and expectations for sexual behavior. Most young people are learning about sex in a mixture of ways. Some are able to talk with their parents about sex, some adhere to religious principles, some get sex education at school, and some rely on their friends. In fact, the media are a rather distant context in relation to parents, friends, and schools for most young people. It may be most appropriate, however, to think of the media as permeating all these other contexts, especially as the new, more portable media find their way into every young person's pocket or purse. Youths' interactions with

their friends, parents, and school both influence and are influenced by media use. These other contexts are also influenced by mass media depictions of sexual behavior and affect attention to and interpretation of media content, so it is difficult if not impossible to assess the unique influence of the media with traditional survey research designs.

The selectivity and complexity of typical media use has led some methodologists to argue that the standard longitudinal survey research design is inappropriate for establishing media as the cause of unhealthy behaviors, even though it is the prototype for epidemiological research (Oakes, 2006). In media research, a true "control" group that has not been exposed to some media content rarely exists, and it is impossible to fully account for all other possible factors that might influence either media selection or sexual behavior. Given these inherent problems, it may be most profitable both theoretically and practically to put more energy into conducting interventions that focus on factors that may decrease the potentially negative effects of the media on youth than to continue to mount studies that cannot fully control for differential selection. Ideally, interventions would be set up as randomized field experiments in which exposure to media can be controlled and measured. Such interventions would still be useful in testing effects hypotheses, but would take a solution-oriented rather than problem-oriented approach by manipulating exposure to media that might reduce rather than encourage sexual risk behavior (Robinson & Sirard, 2005).

◆ The Potential of Interventions for Sexual Health

The media have been used effectively to promote sexual and reproductive health in other countries for decades (Singhal & Rogers, 1999). The media may be especially useful for teaching young people about sexual and reproductive health practices, for precisely the same reasons they are influential in promoting sexually risky behaviors. Teens may find using the media a less embarrassing way to learn about sex than talking with a parent or other adult, and messages can be presented in the media teens use frequently by media characters they admire and wish to emulate. A few media-based campaigns in the United States do suggest that the media could be used in the promotion of sexual health and pregnancy prevention. Few of these have been set up as field experiments or evaluated systematically, however.

Three kinds of media-based interventions that could result in positive sexual health outcomes for young people are worth pursuing: sexual health media campaigns, entertainment-education, and media literacy education. Each of these kinds of interventions should be looking for ways to use the interactivity and customization possibilities of new media such as blogs, social networking sites, text messaging, and videos on cell phones. Some already are incorporating the new media.

Sexual health media campaigns. In 2002, MTV and Advocates for Youth sponsored a year-long campaign focused on HIV/AIDS, other sexually transmitted diseases (STDs), and unintended pregnancy. The campaign included special programming and public service announcements (PSAs), as well as a comprehensive sexual health Web site for youth. A survey in 2003 of MTV viewers (16–24 years old) found that of those who had seen the campaign, three fourths were more likely to take a relationship seriously, and were more likely to use a condom if having sex. Two thirds said they were more likely to talk to a boyfriend or girlfriend about safer sex and were more likely to wait to have sex (Kaiser Family Foundation, 2003).

A more localized campaign, the Two-City Safer Sex Campaign conducted in two cities in Kentucky and Tennessee, targeted high sensation-seeking and impulsive decision-making at-risk young adults with intense, emotional, and fast-paced televised PSAs. The PSAs aired on shows popular with the target audience for more than a year. Evaluations showed a significant increase in condom-use self-efficacy as well as condom use, with no changes in the comparison city that didn't get the ads. It was estimated that the campaign caused a 13% increase in safer sex acts (Zimmerman et al., 2007).

From evaluations of other sexual health-related media interventions such as these, it is clear that to be effective, media campaigns must reach target audiences with clear messages and be sustained over time. Stimulation of interpersonal communication and access to health services also will increase desired outcomes (Noar, 2006).

ENTERTAINMENT-EDUCATION

In a number of countries around the world, embedding sexual health messages in entertainment content also has been found to be effective in persuading young adult audiences to seek and use contraceptives, to limit the size of their families, and to postpone sexual behavior (Singhal & Rogers, 1999). The advantage of entertainment-education over traditional media campaigns is that the complexity that surrounds sexual issues (relationships, values, love, parents, regret) can be explored in more depth, with more nuance, and often in a narrative form that is more compelling than traditional mass media campaigns that rely on PSAs (Green, 2006). In the United States, the technique also has been effective, but more limited, given the difficulty of working with a highly commercialized media free from government control. Two groups (the Kaiser Family Foundation in partnership with Advocates for Youth, and the and Unplanned National Campaign to Prevent Teen and Unplanned Pregnancy) have been most effective in working with the entertainment media to get responsible sexual health messages into media content that adolescents or their parents see.

Since the mid-1990s, for example, the National Campaign to Prevent Teen and Unplanned Pregnancy has generated pregnancy-prevention-related programming that has reached more than 300 million teens and parents on all six TV networks and top cable outlets, in national magazines, and on leading Web sites. The Campaign encouraged media producers to explore the motivations behind adolescents' decisions either to wait to have sex or to use protection if they do have sex, and to get teens to engage in conversation about their own decision making. The Campaign also developed innovative ways of increasing the teen audience's involvement with the material. After one episode of a show and a PSA that promoted the Campaign's Web site, viewers were encouraged to answer questions online that challenged them to relate what happened in the show to their own lives. The Campaign learned that regular viewers care a lot about what their favorite characters do, and when these "superpeers" begin dealing with sex and pregnancy, viewers react and talk about it.

Rigorous evaluation of the effectiveness of such efforts in the United States has been sparse, but promising. One evaluation found that exposure to a 3-minute discussion on the television program *ER* increased viewers' awareness of emergency contraception 17 percentage points, and a one-minute discussion of HPV (human papilloma virus) increased viewers' awareness 23 percentage points. The show also stimulated viewers to talk with friends and family about the topics (Brodie et al., 2001). An experiment with college students found that young women who saw episodes of popular television shows with depictions of condoms held more favorable attitudes toward condoms than women who saw shows that depicted sexual intercourse but no condoms (Farrar, 2006). Research has shown that entertainment-education efforts are more successful if the messages are simple, presented by characters and on shows that young people like, and are frequent and sustained over time (Keller & Brown, 2002).

MEDIA LITERACY

Media literacy education is a relatively new approach to helping young people make good decisions about their health. Media literacy typically focuses on increasing awareness of how media are produced and packaged with the assumption that young people who are more critical of what they see and hear will be less likely to engage in the unhealthy behavior promoted in the media. In the United States, two national organizations advance media education training, networking, and information exchange through professional conferences and listservs: National Association for Media Literacy (NAMLE) and Action Coalition for Media Education (ACME).

Although only a few media literacy curricula have focused on sexual health issues, evaluations have established that media literacy training increases critical thinking about the media and/or affects attitudes about health issues such as alcohol and tobacco use, body image, and violence. Studies have found that even one media literacy training session can increase early adolescents' skepticism toward advertising (Primack, Gold, Land, & Fine, 2006), and that taking a more emotional rather than only a fact-based approach may be most effective with middle schoolers (Austin, Chen, Pinkleton, & Johnson, 2006). Similar media literacy interventions focused on the norms of sexual behavior presented in the media may be helpful in reducing the impact of the media's sexual portrayals on adolescents (Pinkleton, Austin, Cohen, Chen, & Fitzgerald, 2008).

◆ Conclusions

A growing body of rigorously conducted studies suggests that the media play an important role in the sexual development of adolescents and emerging adults. Although much of the work has focused primarily on content, an increasing number of studies have established that exposure to sexual content is related to sexual beliefs as well as behaviors. Recent longitudinal panel studies provide further evidence that exposure to sexual content in the media may encourage young people to engage in sexual activities earlier than they might have otherwise.

Much research remains to be done, however. We still know relatively little about the intervening mechanisms in the connection between exposure and effects, and we have only begun to sort out the extent to which effects occur similarly or differently for males and females, and for different racial/ethnic groups. Very few experimental studies have been conducted, especially with non-college students, which would be helpful in learning more about which kinds of portrayals are most compelling.

Given the inherent difficulties in studying sexual issues, especially in younger populations, and the clear public health issues, it could be worthwhile to spend more time and resources in the future on interventions designed to ameliorate the negative effects and enhance potentially positive effects of sexual content in the media. Evaluations of the few media campaigns, entertainment-education, and media literacy efforts that have focused on sexual health have been promising. In the process of conducting such campaigns, we could learn more about the effects of sexual media content as well as make a positive difference in the sexual lives of young people.

It is also clear that in the future, we must focus more attention on new forms of media. Most of the research on sexual effects of the media conducted thus far has focused almost exclusively on television. Although television remains an important medium in the lives of young people, all kinds of media are converging onto mobile, 24–7 accessible screens. Selectivity will become an even bigger methodological issue than it has been in the past, given that audiences can now create idiosyncratic media diets that may or may not include different kinds of sexual content. Social networking sites add another dimension to the mix as young people are receiving constant feedback and comment on everything they are doing and viewing. The increased access to more sexually explicit content on the Internet, and effects on adolescents' sexual interest and behavior (e.g., Brown & L'Engle, 2009; Peter & Valkenburg, 2008) is also worthy of more scholarly attention. We have much more to learn about the role of the media in the sexual socialization of young people.

◆ References

Arnett, J. J., & Tanner, J. L. (2006). *Emerging adults in America: Coming of age in the 21st century*. Washington, DC: American Psychological Association.

Ashby, S. L., Arcari, C. M., & Edmonson, M. B. (2006). Television viewing and risk of sexual initiation by young adolescents. *Archives of Pediatrics & Adolescent Medicine, 160*, 375–380.

Austin, E. A., Chen, Y.-C., Pinkleton, B. E., & Johnson, J. Q. (2006). Benefits and costs of Channel One in a middle school setting and the role of media-literacy training. *Pediatrics, 117*, 423–433.

Bandura, A. (1986). *Social foundations of thought and action*. Englewood Cliffs, NJ: Prentice Hall.

Borzekowski, D. L. G., & Rickert, V. I. (2001). Adolescent cybersurfing for health information: A new resource that crosses barriers. *Archives of Pediatric and Adolescent Medicine, 155*, 813–817.

Brodie, M., Foehr, U., Rideout, V., Baer, N., Miller, C., Flournoy, R., et al. (2001). Communicating health information through the entertainment media. *Health Affairs, 20*(1), 192–199.

Bronfenbrenner, U. (1977). Toward an experimental ecology of human development. *American Psychologist, 32,* 513–531.

Brown, J. D., & L'Engle, K. L. (2009). X-rated: Sexual attitudes and behaviors associated with U.S. early adolescents' exposure to sexually explicit media. *Communication Research, 36,* 129–151.

Brown, J. D., L'Engle, K. L., Pardun, C. J., Guo, G., Kenneavy, K., & Jackson, C. (2006). Sexy media matter: Exposure to sexual content in music, movies, television, and magazines predicts Black and White adolescents' sexual behavior. *Pediatrics, 117,* 1018–1027.

Brown, J. D., & Pardun, C. J. (2004). Little in common: Racial and gender differences in adolescents' television diets. *Journal of Broadcasting & Electronic Media, 48,* 266–278.

Centers for Disease Control and Prevention, National Center for HIV/AIDS, Viral Hepatitis, STD and TB Prevention. (2008). *Nationally representative CDC study finds 1 in 4 teenage girls has a sexually transmitted disease.* Retrieved March 27, 2008, from http://www.cdc.gov/stdconference/2008/media/release-11march2008.htm

Collins, R. L., Elliott, M. N., Berry, S. H., Kanouse, D. E., Kunkel, D., & Hunter, S. B. (2004). Watching sex on television predicts adolescent initiation of sexual behavior. *Pediatrics, 114,* e280–e289.

Cope-Farrar, K. M., & Kunkel, D. (2002). Sexual messages in teens' favorite prime-time television programs. In J. D. Brown, J. R. Steele, & K. Walsh-Childers (Eds.), *Sexual teens, sexual media: Investigating media's influence on adolescent sexuality* (pp. 59–69). Mahwah, NJ: Erlbaum.

Escobar-Chaves, S. L., Tortolero, S., Markham, C., Low, B., Eitel, P., & Thickstun, P. (2005). Impact of the media on adolescent sexual attitudes and behavior. *Pediatrics, 116,* 297–331.

Farrar, K. M. (2006). Sexual intercourse on television: Do safe sex messages matter? *Journal of Broadcasting & Electronic Media, 50,* 635–650.

Feijoo, A. N. (2001). *Adolescent sexual health in Europe and the U.S.: Why the difference?* Washington, DC: Advocates for Youth.

Finn, J. (2004). A survey of online harassment at a university campus. *Journal of Interpersonal Violence, 19,* 468–483.

Fisher, D. A., Hill, D. L., Grube, J. W., & Gruber, E. L. (2004). Sex on American television: An analysis across program genres and network types. *Journal of Broadcasting & Electronic Media, 48,* 529–553.

Gagnon, J. H., & Simon, W. (1973). *Sexual conduct: The social sources of human sexuality.* Chicago: Aldine.

Gerbner, G. (1998). Cultivation analysis: An overview. *Mass Communication & Society, 1,* 175–194.

Green, M. C. (2006). Narratives and cancer communication. *Journal of Communication, 56,* S163–S183.

Hetsroni, A. (2007). Three decades of sexual content on prime-time network programming: A longitudinal meta-analytic review. *Journal of Communication, 57,* 318–348.

Hust, S., Brown, J. D., & L'Engle, K. (2008). Boys will be boys and girls better be prepared: An analysis of the rare sexual health messages in young adolescents' media. *Mass Communication and Society, 11,* 1–21.

Kaiser Family Foundation. (2003). *National Survey of Teens and Young Adults on Sexual Health Public Education Campaigns: Toplines.* Menlo Park, CA: The Foundation. Retrieved July 23, 2008, from http://www.kaisernetwork.org

Kaiser Family Foundation. (2004). *Seventeen Magazine and Kaiser Family Foundation Release Survey of Teens About Birth Control and Protection: Toplines.* Menlo Park, CA: The Foundation. Retrieved July, 25, 2008, from http://www.kff.org

Kaiser Family Foundation. (2005). *Sex on TV 4.* Menlo Park, CA: The Foundation.

Keller, S. N., & Brown, J. D. (2002). Media interventions to promote responsible sexual behavior. *Journal of Sex Research, 39,* 67–72.

Lefkowitz, E., & Gillen, M. (2006). Sex is not just a normal part of life: Sexuality in emerging adulthood. In J. J. Arnett & J. L. Tanner (Eds.), *Emerging adults in America: Coming of age in the 21st century* (pp. 235–256). Washington, DC: American Psychological Association.

Levine, D., McCright, J., Dobkin, L., Woodruff, A., & Klausner, J. (2008). SexInfo: A sexual health text messaging service for San Francisco youth. *American Journal of Public Health, 98,* 393–395.

Martino, S. C., Collins, R. L., Kanouse, D. E., Elliott, M., & Berry, S. H. (2006). Social cognitive processes mediating the relationship between exposure to television's sexual content and adolescents' sexual behavior. *Journal of Personality and Social Psychology, 89,* 914–924.

Mitchell, K. J., Finkelhor, D., & Wolak, J. (2007). Online requests for sexual pictures from youth: Risk factors and incident characteristics. *Journal of Adolescent Health, 41,* 196–203.

National Campaign to Prevent Teen and Unplanned Pregnancy. (2005). *Fact sheet: Teen pregnancy and childbearing among Latinos in the United States.* Washington, DC: Author.

Noar, S. (2006). A 10-year retrospective of research in health mass media campaigns: Where do we go from here? *Journal of Health Communication, 11,* 21–42.

Noar, S., Clark, A., Cole, C., & Lustria, M. (2006). Review of interactive safer sex Web sites: Practice and potential. *Health Communication, 20,* 233–241.

Oakes, J. M. (2006). *The effect of media on children: A methodological assessment from a social pathologist.* Background paper prepared for Workshop on Media Research and Methods. Washington, DC: Board on Children, Youth, and Families, National Research Council and Institute of Medicine. Available at http://www.bocyf.org/030206.html

Oliver, M. B., & Kalyanaraman, S. (2005). Using sex to sell movies: A content analysis of movie trailers. In T. Reichert & J. Lambiase (Eds.), *Sex in consumer culture: The erotic content of media and advertising* (pp. 15–32). Hillsdale, NJ: Erlbaum.

Pardun, C. J., L'Engle, K., & Brown, J. D. (2005). Linking exposure to outcomes: Early adolescents' consumption of sexual content in six media. *Mass Communication and Society, 8,* 75–91.

Perry, I. (2004). *Prophets of the hood.* Durham, NC: Duke University Press.

Peter, J., & Valkenburg, P. M. (2006). Adolescents' exposure to sexually explicit material on the Internet. *Communication Research, 33*(2), 178–204.

Peter, J., & Valkenburg, P. M. (2008). Adolescents' exposure to sexually explicit Internet material and sexual preoccupancy: A three-wave panel study. *Media Psychology, 11,* 207–234.

Pinkleton, B. E., Austin, E. W., Cohen, M., Chen, Y., & Fitzgerald, E. (2008). The value of a peer-led media literacy curriculum for adolescent sex education. *Health Communication, 23*(5), 462–472.

Primack, B. A., Gold, M. A., Land, S. R., & Fine, M. J. (2006). Association of cigarette smoking and media literacy about smoking among adolescents. *Journal of Adolescent Health, 39,* 465–472.

Roberto, A., Zimmerman, R., Carlyle, K., Abner, E., Cupp, P., & Hansen, G. (2007). The effects of a computer-based pregnancy, STD, and HIV prevention intervention: A nine-school trial. *Health Communication, 21*(2), 115–124.

Roberts, D., & Foehr, U. G. (2004). *Kids and media in America.* Oxford, UK: Oxford University Press.

Robinson, T. N., & Sirard, J. R. (2005). Preventing childhood obesity: A solution-oriented research paradigm. *American Journal of Preventive Medicine, 28,* 194–201.

Roe, K. (1998). Boys will be boys and girls will be girls: Changes in children's media use. *Communications, 23,* 5–25.

Santelli, J., Ott, M. A., Lyon, M., Rogers, J., Summers, D., & Schleifer, R. (2006). Abstinence and abstinence-only education: A review of U.S. policies and programs. *Journal of Adolescent Health, 38,* 72–81.

Shrum, L. J. (2001). Processing strategy moderates the cultivation effect. *Human Communication Research, 27,* 94–120.

Singhal, A., & Rogers, E. M. (1999). *Entertainment-education: A communication strategy for social change.* Mahwah, NJ: Erlbaum.

Steele, J. R., & Brown, J. D. (1995). Adolescent room culture: Studying media in the context of everyday life. *Journal of Youth and Adolescence, 24,* 551–576.

Stern, S., & Brown, J. D. (2008). From twin beds to sex at your fingertips: Teen sexuality in movies, music, television and the Internet, 1950–2005. In P. E. Jamieson & D. Romer (Eds.), *The changing portrayal of adolescents in the media since 1950* (pp. 313–343). Oxford, UK: Oxford University Press.

Stokes, C. E. (2007). Representin' in cyberspace: Sexual scripts, self-definition, and hip hop culture in Black American adolescent girls' home pages. *Culture, Health & Sexuality, 9,* 169–184.

Sun, S. S., Schubert, C. M., Chumlea, W. C., Roche, A. F., Kulin, H. E., Lee, P. A., et al. (2002). National estimates of the timing of sexual maturation and racial differences among U.S. children. *Pediatrics, 110,* 911–919.

Teens and social media: The use of social media gains a greater foothold in teen life as they embrace the conversational nature of interactive online media. (2007, December 19). Pew Internet & American Life Project. Retrieved July 10, 2008, from http://pew internet.org/PPF/r/230/report_display.asp

U.S. Census Bureau, 2005 American Community Survey. (2005a). *Median age at first marriage for men* (Publication No. R1204). Retrieved March 27, 2008, from http:// factfinder.census.gov

U.S. Census Bureau, 2005 American Community Survey. (2005b). *Median age at first marriage for women* (Publication No. R1205). Retrieved March 27, 2008, from http:// factfinder.census.gov

Ward, L. M. (2003). Understanding the role of entertainment media in the sexual socialization of American youth: A review of empirical research. *Developmental Review, 33,* 347–388.

Warhol, A. (1975). *The philosophy of Andy Warhol: From A to B and back again.* New York: Harcourt Brace Jovanovich.

Ybarra, M. L., & Suman, M. (2008). Reasons, assessments, and actions taken: Sex and age differences in uses of Internet health information. *Health Education Research, 23,* 512–521.

Zillmann, D., & Bryant, J. (Eds.). (1989). *Pornography: Research advances and policy considerations.* Hillsdale, NJ: Erlbaum.

Zimmerman, R. S., Palmgreen, P. M., Noar, S. M., Lustria, M. L. A., Hung-Yi, L., & Horsewski, M. L. (2007). Effects of a televised two-city safer sex media campaign targeting high-sensation-seeking and impulsive-decision-making young adults. *Health Education & Behavior, 34,* 810–826.

Zurbriggen, E. L., & Morgan, E. M. (2006). Who wants to marry a millionaire? Reality dating television programs, attitudes toward sex, and sexual behaviors. *Sex Roles, 54,* 1–17.

28

PERCEPTIONS OF MEDIA REALISM AND REALITY TV

◆ Alice E. Hall

A udiences' perceptions of media realism have been proposed as contributors to a wide range of media effects. However, the pattern of findings within the literature is complex and often inconsistent. For example, some studies have found realism perceptions of mass media content to associate with a variety of presumed outcomes of media exposure, including aggressive behavior (Atkin, 1983; Huesmann, Lagerspetz, & Eron, 1984); violence prevalence perceptions (Potter, 1986); and attitudes related to romance, dating, and sex (Ferris, Smith, Greenberg, & Smith, 2007; Peter & Valkenburg, 2006). However, other studies have failed to find evidence of such associations (Bandura, Ross, & Ross, 1963; Eggermont, 2004; Hawkins & Pingree, 1980; Ward & Rivadeneyra, 1999). Inconsistencies such as these suggest that there are substantive gaps in our current understanding of the role perceived realism plays in audiences' responses to media texts. This chapter reviews previous research on this topic, first describing how audiences' judgments of media realism have been conceptualized and measured, and then summarizing research regarding the antecedents and implications of realism perceptions. It goes on to describe the cognitive processes through which media realism judgments are made and then focuses on research relating to a specific type of media that is a particularly provocative exemplar of some of the issues relating to audiences' evaluations of media realism—reality

TV. Finally, suggestions for future research are advanced.

◆ What Is Perceived Media Realism?

Despite being the subject of a great deal of interest, perceived media realism is difficult to define. It has been treated in a variety of ways in the empirical literature, and there is no consensus regarding how it is best conceptualized or measured. This chapter takes a relatively broad view of the subject, defining perceived media realism as the way media content is seen by the audience to relate to the real world. It should be noted that media texts can portray the world with varying levels of accuracy or fidelity. A film that portrays a World War II battle being fought with rifles and tanks, for example, is more faithful to the historical record than one that includes crossbows. However, though a text's degree of objective fidelity can inform audiences' judgments of its level of realism, it does not determine them. Indeed, audience members routinely vary in their judgments of how closely a specific text's portrayal matches the true nature of its subject (e.g., Gunther & Liebhart, 2006; Press, 1989). Thus, audience members' subjective perceptions of media realism are distinct from the objective relationship between a media portrayal and its subject.

CONCEPTUALIZING REALISM PERCEPTIONS

Two features of media realism judgments are particularly central to interpreting the extant research (see Busselle & Greenberg, 2000, for a more detailed review). One feature is the point in the interpretive process at which a realism judgment is made. Audiences can make retrospective judgments by thinking back to material they have previously seen and evaluating the realism of what they recall. However, they may also craft online judgments of media realism by consciously or unconsciously monitoring how the content of the text relates to their understandings of the world as they interpret that text (Busselle & Bilandzic, 2008; Shapiro & Chock, 2003).

The second important feature of realism judgments is the way in which perceived realism is conceptualized, that is, what is thought to make a text "realistic." Scholars have defined a host of standards with which media texts could be compared when audience members make realism judgments. It sometimes feels as if there are as many conceptualizations of what would make a media text realistic as there are studies of the subject. However, two general ways of defining realism judgments have tended to emerge in slightly different forms and under various names throughout the literature: (1) realism as factuality, or the degree to which a text is understood to accurately portray specific real-world events or people, and (2) realism as real-world similarity, or whether what is portrayed in a text is like what the audience would expect to find in the real world. In terms of factuality, viewers' perceptions of this form of realism may vary both across individuals (i.e., disagreements about whether the footage of the moon landing was staged or not) and different media texts (i.e., a memoir vs. a novel). This conceptualization implies that audiences inevitably discount fiction as make-believe, and thus not "real."

In contrast, real-world similarity allows fiction to be judged as quite realistic provided it is consistent with what the audience member believes the real world to be like. Busselle and Greenberg (2000) identified four ways in which media have been conceptualized as having the potential to be seen as similar to real life: (1) *possibility*, or whether something portrayed in the media could occur in the real world; (2) *probability*, or the likelihood that something in the media would occur in the real world; (3) *identity*, or the extent to which audience members involve themselves in the representation; and (4) *utility,* or how much something in the media is useful to the audience. To these could be added two other similarity criteria that have been addressed in recent research: (5) *visual persuasiveness,* or the degree to which a text looks real or creates a compelling visual illusion (Hall, 2003); and (6) *narrative realism,* or the extent to which events within a media story are well explained and coherent with each other (Busselle & Bilandzic, 2008).

It is not always clear which of these criteria are the most salient to audience members. However, there is evidence that possibility and probability or typicality are the biggest contributors to general, retrospective judgments of the entertainment-oriented narrative media that have been the most frequent subject of study. Open-ended interviews with audience members about what they mean when they describe TV programming or movies as realistic have found that plausibility and probability tend to be the criteria volunteered most readily (Dorr, 1983; Hall, 2003). Furthermore, in a series of experimental studies, Shapiro and Chock (2003, 2004) found that stories whose outcomes were judged to be more likely or typical tended to be rated as more "like real life."

MEASURING PERCEIVED REALISM

Realism perceptions have been considered as contributors to media effects by researchers working from several different theoretical perspectives. This work has tended to employ one of two methodologies. A substantial number of experimental studies have manipulated audiences' factual realism perceptions and then measured effect outcomes. A larger body of work has measured naturally occurring variation in audiences' realism judgments and then evaluated whether these measures are associated with effects of interest. However, to interpret this research, one needs to consider the ways that perceived realism has typically been measured.

Memory-based measures seem to be the most common means of evaluating audiences' perceptions of media realism in the quantitative studies published on this topic. Respondents are typically invited to think back either to a specific text that they have already seen or to a body of texts, such as television programming in general or crime programs, and then rate the realism of the material on a closed-ended scale (Busselle & Greenberg, 2000). The types of realism judgments measured by these scales differ in their conceptualization of realism. Some scholars have used multidimensional scales designed to distinguish between factual realism and real-world similarity perceptions (e.g., Hawkins, 1977; Wright, Huston, Reitz, & Piemyat, 1994). Some of these scales make further distinctions between types of real-world similarity perceptions (e.g., Potter, 1986). However, many studies employ generally worded survey items designed to measure real-world similarity perceptions, but do not specify the type of similarity judgment respondents are being asked to make (e.g., Elliott & Slater, 1980; Huesmann et al., 1984; Shapiro & Chock, 2003). For example, Rubin's Perceived Realism Scale includes items that ask whether the material "presents things as they really are in life" and "lets me see how other people live" (Rubin, 1981; Rubin & Perse, 1987; Rubin, Perse, & Powell, 1985).

CORRELATES OF REALISM PERCEPTIONS

It is also important to investigate the correlates of realism perceptions to determine the specific characteristics of media texts and attributes of audiences that may influence these perceptions. One textual characteristic that can contribute to at least some types of realism perceptions is a text's genre. Genres are often partially defined by a text's ostensible purpose and by the way its source claims the content relates to real-world events. News, documentaries, and fiction films, for example, each imply different kinds of truth claims (Hill, 2007). Audiences, therefore, may take a text's apparent genre into account when making some types of realism judgments. For example, Atkin (1983) found that video footage was rated as more "real" when it was said to be from a news story rather than a feature film. Huston et al. (1995) and Huston, Wright, Fitch, Wroblewski, and Piemyat (1997) found that manipulating the labels and the genre markers of television programs (e.g., the use of voice-over) affected retrospective judgments of the program's factual realism and real-world similarity (see also Pouliot & Cowen, 2007). As discussed in more detail in the following paragraphs, a text's perceived genre may also affect realism judgments indirectly by shaping the attributes of the text that audience members attend to or by affecting the way in which the text is processed.

Age is the audience characteristic that has perhaps been most frequently examined as a potential contributor to perceptions of the realism of audiovisual media such as TV programming. Children's abilities to make different types of realism judgments about TV programming develop in different ways. Children under the age of 4 cannot consistently distinguish between an image of something and the thing itself, which makes them susceptible to errors such as believing that a person on TV can hear something happening in the room in which the TV is located (Flavell, Flavell, Green, & Korfmacher, 1990). Very young children, therefore, are likely to see all TV content as factually real. Once children are able to understand that what is portrayed on the screen is an image, they refine their understandings of how TV programs are constructed by, for example, developing the knowledge that many people on television are actors playing a scripted role (Wright et al., 1994). Studies of children (Hawkins, 1977) and teenagers (Potter, 1992) have found evaluations of factual realism of television tend to decline as the age of the respondent increases. Young

people also develop the ability to make real-world similarity judgments, but these perceptions do not necessarily decrease as children get older (Dorr, Kovaric, & Doubleday, 1990; Hawkins, 1977; Wright et al., 1994). Rather, their judgments seem to get more complex as they learn to consider a wider range of criteria (Dorr, 1983).

Finally, other research, most often based on the uses-and-gratifications (U&G) perspective (see Rubin, Chapter 10, this volume), has investigated individual differences in adults' perceptions of real-world similarity. The evidence suggests that real-world similarity perceptions of television are associated with an engaged viewing orientation and with a variety of viewing motives, including viewing for information, arousal, entertainment, and social interaction (Haridakis & Rubin, 2003; Perse, 1986; Rubin & Perse, 1987; Rubin et al., 1985).

◆ Perceived Realism and Media Influence

One of the primary reasons researchers are interested in the notion of perceived realism is because it is thought to contribute to the effects that might result from media exposure. Researchers working from several theoretical perspectives, including cultivation theory (see Morgan, Chapter 5, this volume), social cognitive theory (see Pajares, Prestin, Chen, & Nabi, Chapter 19, this volume), and arousal theory, have considered this view.

EXPERIMENTAL STUDIES

Many of the earliest investigations of media realism were experimental studies that sought to determine whether believing images of media violence were factually real would enhance viewers' tendencies to behave aggressively afterward. For example, Berkowitz and Alioto (1973) showed participants segments from a war documentary and told them either that it was footage that had been shot by a war correspondent or that it was a scene portraying a Hollywood reenactment. Participants who were told they were watching footage of actual violence showed greater tendencies toward aggression than those who were told they were watching staged violence (see also Atkin, 1983; Thomas & Tell, 1974). Similarly, Geen (1975) found that participants who viewed violent video footage labeled as real tended to score higher on physiological measures indicative of arousal than those who watched footage labeled as fiction (see also Reeves & Vega, 2006). This work suggests that viewers' belief in the actuality of emotionally charged images may increase their level of physiological arousal relative to images that are believed to portray actors playing out scripted scenes. This research is consistent with excitation transfer theory (Zillmann, 1991), which suggests that heightened arousal will intensify audience members' emotional responses to other stimuli after viewing. If those emotions are frustration and anger, this may increase aggressive behavior. There is evidence, therefore, that if images or brief video segments of highly charged content are believed to be factually real, it can intensify viewers' level of arousal and any short-term effects that may follow from that arousal.

However, there is little evidence that belief in a media text's factual realism enhances the influence of different types of texts or moderates media influence on outcomes other than short-term arousal and immediate aggressive tendencies. Experimental studies that have manipulated perceptions of the factuality of longer stimulus material or more mundane subject matter suggest that factual realism does not systematically enhance viewers' discrete emotional reactions (Huston et al., 1995; Pouliot & Cowen, 2007). Furthermore, perceiving something as factually unrealistic does not insulate audiences from the effect of stories on their attitudes and beliefs. For example, Green and Brock (2000) investigated the

impact of narratives on audiences' attitudes regarding social issues by asking participants to read short stories and then measuring their attitudes on related topics. Although the stories were found to influence the readers' attitudes, those effects were not moderated by whether the stories were labeled as true or as fiction. That is, readers did not seem to discount the fiction narratives when integrating the content of the stories into their beliefs about the world (see also Strange & Leung, 1999).

CORRELATIONAL ANALYSES

The possibility that perceived realism may be a potential moderator of media effects has also been investigated through correlational analyses involving audience members' self-reports of perceived realism. For example, cultivation researchers have repeatedly predicted that television content that is believed to be realistic is more likely to be integrated into viewers' worldviews, and thus is more likely to shape their attitudes. However, empirical studies have failed to find strong, consistent evidence that perceptions of either television's factual realism or its real-world similarity moderate the effect of exposure on either first-order cultivation estimates or mean world perceptions (Hawkins & Pingree, 1980; Potter, 1986).

Researchers working within the social cognitive theory paradigm or similar models have also speculated that real-world similarity perceptions may moderate the influence of media models on audience members' behaviors and attitudes. Although the mechanism is not always specified, the general idea is that media models that are perceived as realistic are more likely to be seen as relevant to real-world situations. Thus realistic behaviors (provided they are positively depicted) are more likely to be accepted or adopted than unrealistic behaviors. Again, there is not strong, consistent empirical evidence that realism perceptions moderate these sorts of effects (Eggermont, 2004; Ferris et al., 2007; Reeves, 1978).

However, several studies have found real-world similarity perceptions directly associate with feelings, attitudes, beliefs, or behaviors that are consistent with the media content consumed. Retrospective evaluations of the real-world similarity of TV programming have been found to associate with cultivation estimates (Perse, 1986), aggressive behavior (Haridakis & Rubin, 2003; Huesmann et al., 1984), and views of men as sex driven and of women as sex objects (Ferris et al., 2007). In one of the few studies in this area that has considered a medium other than TV, Peter and Valkenburg (2006) found that perceptions that sexual material on the Internet was realistic seemed to mediate the effects of exposure on adolescent viewers' attitudes about sex.

These associations, however, are difficult to interpret for several reasons. First, the pattern of associations often varies in unpredicted and unexplained ways. Not only are there inconsistencies in findings across studies, as noted in the opening of this chapter, but there are also unexplained inconsistencies within single studies (e.g., Busselle, 2001; Rubin, Perse, & Taylor, 1988; Weiss & Wilson, 1998). For example, Ward and Rivadeneyra (1999) found perceptions of the realism of relationship-themed situation comedies to be associated with females' estimates of their male peers' sexual behavior, but not with estimates of female peers' behavior or with their own attitudes. Realism was also not associated with any of the male participants' judgments. Second, the nature and causal direction of these relationships is often difficult to determine. It is not always clear whether realism contributes to the attitudes and perceptions, whether the attitudes and perceptions shape the realism judgments, or whether both kinds of variables are the product of an uncontrolled third variable or a more general mindset or orientation.

In summary, the perceived actuality of brief images of vivid subject matter may be associated with increased arousal effects. However, there is little evidence that the perceived factual realism of longer material systematically affects the intensity of audience members' discrete emotions or the likelihood that their attitudes will shift as the result of reading a compelling story. The pattern of research findings relating to real-world similarity judgments is more complicated. This form of realism perception does not seem to consistently moderate the effects of media exposure, although perceptions of media content as similar to real life have been found to modestly associate with a variety of behaviors and attitudes that are consistent with that content. However, the nature of these direct associations has not been clearly established, and there is unexplained variability across outcomes and types of viewers. Perceived realism, therefore, does not seem to be uniformly associated with a greater match between media content and audience members' attitudes or behavior. Although the notion that realism perceptions contribute to media effects holds intuitive appeal, the paucity of consistent findings in comparison to the volume of research that has addressed this issue is discouraging. It suggests that if perceived realism does play wider roles in media effects, they are often subtle and indirect.

One of the limitations of the research on this topic is that it is something of a patchwork. Perceived realism is often of secondary interest in studies that are focused on developing a particular theory or testing media effects on a particular outcome. Even studies dealing with similar variables are often so different in the way the concepts are operationalized and how the relationships between them are modeled that it is difficult to determine what accounts for inconsistencies in their findings. This makes it difficult to generalize from specific studies to other contexts or to determine which findings represent real relationships and which are significant by chance.

To get a clearer grasp of if and when realism judgments make a difference to media effects, researchers need to address the topic more systematically. One way of doing so is to step back and conceptualize more clearly when and how realism judgments are made. These conceptualizations can be applied to models of media influence in order to craft more precise and theory-driven investigations into the roles that realism perceptions may play.

◆ Mechanisms of Evaluating Media Realism

Research in social and cognitive psychology provides insight into these processes. One of the most important implications of this work to the study of perceived realism is that there is not one single process through which realism judgments can be made, but rather several. Audience members are likely to evaluate media realism differently, for example, depending on whether the judgment is made retrospectively or online. However, models of each of these types of realism judgments are informed by the principle that humans have a limited pool of cognitive resources with which to make sense of what they encounter in the world, including media texts.

RETROSPECTIVE JUDGMENTS

The limited cognitive capacity perspective suggests that when audience members make retrospective evaluations of media realism, such as the memory-based judgments measured in most survey studies, they are unlikely to make a systematic or comprehensive search of all available information. Rather, they will tend to rely on the information that is most readily accessible. What comes to mind most easily, therefore, is likely to have the greatest influence on these judgments. There are a variety of factors that can shape the accessibility of examples or information in memory, including the frequency with which a concept has been activated and how recently it has been activated (Higgins, 2000; Higgins & King, 1981).

This has both methodological and conceptual implications for the study of perceived realism. First, it suggests that when audiences are evaluating the realism of a body of texts, such as television programming as a whole, each text will not be equally weighed in the evaluation. Material that has been encountered frequently or recently is likely to have the greatest influence on realism evaluations. This model also suggests that retrospective evaluations are subject to priming effects (Busselle, 2003).

ONLINE JUDGMENTS

The research on online processing that is most relevant to the largest amount of research on perceived realism focuses on audiences' interpretations of narratives. Studies of perceived realism have tended to deal either with television, which is dominated by narrative-oriented content, or with specific narrative films or programs. Emerging perspectives in this area suggest that audience members do not evaluate the realism of mediated stories as much as notice when something is unrealistic. Much of this work is based on the premise, first developed by Spinoza and applied to cognitive psychology by scholars such as Gilbert (e.g., Gilbert, Krull, & Malone, 1990) and Gerrig (e.g., Gerrig, 1993), that accepting propositions as true and real is essentially the human default cognitive mode. If these principles are applied to the interpretation of media narratives, they suggest that interpreting a story implies at least initial belief. Discounting something as untrue or dismissing it as fiction requires additional cognitive effort. Audiences can, of course, do this readily if they are prompted to do so. If movie viewers are interrupted while watching an action film and asked about what they are seeing on the screen, they are likely to note that most of what is happening is unrealistic. However, when audiences are left to their own devices, models of narrative comprehension suggest that they not only will tend to lack a positive motive to expend these cognitive resources, but will also have a disincentive to do so. Green and Brock's (2000) narrative transportation model proposes that audiences who are highly engaged in a narrative experience a sense of transportation, in which their attention is absorbed by the story, they feel strong emotions about the story's characters and events, and they become less aware of their physical surroundings. Transportation is conceptualized as an enjoyable state that audience members seek out (Green, Brock, & Kaufman, 2004).

This has several implications for online processing of media realism. One is that narrative audiences will tend to engage in the construction of the story rather than in actively seeking out discrepancies between the real world and the world portrayed in that story. Furthermore, since noticing these discrepancies tends to interfere with audience members' sense of the flow of the narrative and reduces their enjoyment of the text, they are unlikely to be motivated to make these judgments. Transportation, therefore, is thought to be associated with a reduction in audience members' capacity and motivation to question a story's authenticity (Green, 2004; Green & Brock, 2000). Readers who report greater transportation into written narratives tend to identify fewer "false notes" in the stories (Green & Brock, 2000) and to report higher retrospective evaluations of their real-world similarity (Green, 2004). Also, television viewers' critical judgments of audiovisual narratives have been found to be negatively associated both with transportation and with retrospective judgments of real-world similarity (Quintero-Johnson & Busselle, 2004; Wilson & Busselle, 2004). This model suggests that failing to judge a story as unrealistic is a marker of an enjoyable, engaged form of processing in which audience members are immersed in the construction of the story (Busselle & Bilandzic, 2008).

This model raises the question of what can lead audiences to flag a story as unrealistic. Busselle and Bilandzic (2008)

argue that the trigger is not necessarily elements of a story that are discordant with the audience members' own experience, or even with their more general perceptions of what the world is like. Rather, they argue that audience members are most likely to notice something that violates the narrative realism of the story, that is, something that is unexplained or inconsistent within the world of the narrative itself and interferes with their ability to construct the narrative. A story's genre or factuality may be relevant to these forms of online judgments, but not because the fictional material is automatically discounted. Rather, understandings of the nature of the text inform audience members of the standards to which the story should be held and of the type of previous knowledge that can be called upon to facilitate interpretation (Busselle & Bilandzic, 2008; Green, Garst, & Brock, 2004). If the story has a real-world setting, some kinds of inconsistencies between the story world and the real world may lead viewers to critique the realism of the text because their understandings of real-world situations and behavior have been used in constructing the narrative world. However, in many cases, these inconsistencies will not interfere with an audience member's experience of a story as realistic. For example, viewers of a science fiction movie may be unfazed by the introduction of elements, such as starships and ray-guns, that are inconsistent with what they know to exist in the actual world. Because these elements are allowed for by their expectations of this type of text, they can be readily integrated into their understanding of the story world.

The view that understanding a story to be fictional functions as a cue that frees audiences from expecting it to directly correspond with real-world experience or to be factually true also implies that material that is marked as nonfiction may be held to expectations of factual realism. Many kinds of texts, including news, documentaries, and reality programs, claim to be factually real. The processes through which audiences evaluate the realism claims of specific nonfiction materials have been subject to less attention than fiction, at least within the literature dealing with perceived realism. However, these judgments are not necessarily simple or straightforward. Audiences do not uniformly discount the realism of fiction nor do they uniformly accept the realism of nonfiction. There is room for considerable variation in perceptions of texts' factuality or how accurately they portray the true nature of their "real" subjects. Nonfiction texts can also vary in different types of perceived real-world similarity, further complicating these judgments (Shapiro & Chock, 2003). This suggests that audiences may have to balance multiple, potentially conflicting criteria when evaluating these texts.

A genre that illustrates the complexity of audiences' judgments of nonfiction is reality television (or reality TV). As is the case with other narratives, realism perceptions of these programs seem to be associated with specific ways of processing or engaging with the material. However, the nature of the association seems to differ. Whereas transportation or engagement with fiction narratives seem to depend on a lack of critical realism judgments, some forms of engaging with reality programs seem to be based on suspicion of certain elements of the programs' realism.

◆ Reality TV

Reality TV is as a distinct genre made up of entertainment-oriented programs that feature nonprofessional actors playing themselves whose words and behavior are presented as being unscripted (Hall, 2006; Hill, 2005; Nabi, Biely, Morgan, & Stitt, 2003). The programs' content often combines elements of a variety of different genres. Many of the formal features are similar to those of documentaries (i.e., direct address to the camera by the cast members). Although most of the programs have a narrative line, many also have

elements of a game, such as "challenges" and "eliminations." Reality TV's popularity with viewers, low production costs, affinity with product placement, and more limited reliance on writers and actors have helped to make it appealing to the television industry. The genre has become a prominent and well-entrenched part of TV programming across the globe. At the start of the 2007–2008 television season, every U.S. broadcast network had multiple reality programs in their prime-time lineup (Metacritic.com, 2007). A 2001 survey found that 45% of U.S. adults and 70% of 18- to 24-year-olds reported watching reality programs (Gardyn, 2001). In Britain, 70% of adults reported watching the genre at least occasionally (Hill, 2002).

The programs have also been the subject of considerable scholarly interest. Researchers have examined the content patterns of reality programs (Cavender, 1998; Oliver, 1994) as well as the correlates of audiences' exposure to and enjoyment of the programs (Nabi et al., 2003; Nabi, Stitt, Halford, & Finnerty, 2006; Oliver & Armstrong, 1995; Papacharissi & Mendelson, 2007; Reiss & Wiltz, 2004). In addition, several studies have considered the potential effects of viewing reality programs. Exposure to particular types of programs has been found to be associated with perspectives that are consistent with the programs' content in areas including perceptions of crime prevalence (Oliver & Armstrong, 1998), views of law enforcement (Eschholz, Blackwell, Gertz, & Chiricos, 2002), expectations regarding romantic relationships (Ferris et al., 2007), and perceptions of body image (Kubic & Chory, 2007). There is modest evidence that perceptions of the realism of these programs may be associated with the stronger endorsement of media-consistent attitudes (Ferris et al., 2007; Oliver & Armstrong, 1998). However, as is the case with studies of perceived realism and media effects more generally, the causal direction of these associations is difficult to determine.

IS REALITY TV REAL?

The way audiences perceive the realism of these shows is complex. As the genre label indicates, the programs claim a certain type of authenticity that seems to inform viewers' responses. Viewers seem to distinguish reality programs from other shows and to define them as a group in part because of their ambiguous factual status somewhere between the real and the fictional (Hall, 2006; Hill, 2007; Nabi et al., 2003).

Interviews and surveys of viewers have repeatedly indicated that one of the draws of these programs is that they promise the opportunity to observe real people. Nabi et al. (2003) found that viewers tended to indicate that they enjoyed watching real people rather than actors, the unscripted nature of the programs, and the fact that people on the shows had something at stake. In a later study, Nabi et al. (2006) found that feeling that one was getting a peek into others' lives was associated with enjoyment of reality TV and tended to distinguish the appeal of reality programs from fiction ones. In investigations of the British version of Big Brother, both Hill (2002) and Jones (2003) found that watching the nonprofessional cast members was an important part of the appeal.

However, interviews and surveys also consistently indicate that reality TV viewers do not accept at face value the implicit claim that the shows are real. Viewers are aware that the settings and situations can be contrived, know that the people and stories featured on the shows are carefully selected, and often suspect that the events presented on the shows are staged or manipulated by producers (Andrejevic, 2004; Hall, 2006; Lundy, Ruth, & Park, 2008). Nabi et al. (2003) found that viewers generally failed to endorse the notion that the programs were "real" and tended to feel that the behavior of people on reality programs was affected by the presence of the cameras. Hill's (2002, 2005) interviews suggest that viewers tend to believe that reality TV cast members routinely modify their behavior for the cameras. These studies suggest that audiences are drawn to the programs because they promise the opportunity to see real people. At the same time, audiences tend to be well aware that many aspects of the programs are highly contrived.

INTERPRETING REALITY TV

The potential complexity of the way in which the programs relate to their subjects can allow audience members to engage with the programs in ways that would not be possible if the programs' reality status were less ambiguous. Hill (2002, 2005) argues, for example, that one of the primary ways audiences engage with long-form competition programs such as Survivor and Big Brother is by monitoring the cast for moments when their artifice breaks down and they reveal their "real" selves. Her work suggests that viewers engage in an ongoing assessment of when the cast members are being true to themselves and when they are pretending to be something other than who they really are (see also Andrejevic, 2004; Jones, 2003). Hall (in press) examined the relationships between reality program viewers' evaluations of several textual characteristics that can contribute to realism judgments, including the cast members' typicality and perceptions of various aspects of the programs' actuality, along with measures of involvement and enjoyment. She found that involvement in a show was associated with perceptions that it was realistic in some ways (i.e., that the cast was representative) and unrealistic in others. Believing that the producers manipulated what the viewer saw was positively associated with cognitive involvement. Involvement, in turn, was associated with enjoyment. Thus, reality TV viewers seem to be interested in watching because the cast members are real or authentic, but they seem to become engaged in watching, in part, because the presentation of the cast is often manipulated or insincere.

◆ *Directions for*
Further Research

Despite the considerable amount of research on perceived realism in the existing literature, there are several areas that continue to cry out for further investigation. First, although the issue has often been studied, findings concerning perceived realism's role in media effects are contradictory and muddled. There is little clear evidence that perceived realism has a systematic influence on anything other than short-term arousal outcomes. One way forward would be to target research more specifically by taking into account the processes through which different types of realism judgments are made. Although the work of cognitive and social psychologists suggests models of both retrospective and online realism judgment processes, these models have rarely been applied to the investigation of realism and media effects.

Failing to take into account the mechanisms through which realism judgments are made has contributed to a lack of precision in the investigation of this topic. For example, much of the work on the implications of both perceived factual realism and real-world similarity has operationalized these variables as retrospective judgments in that perceived realism is evaluated through memory-based survey measures. However, the proposed mechanisms of many of the most-often-studied media effects theories suggest that the effects are driven, at least in part, by the way media content is processed or encoded. For example, the mechanisms of social cognitive theory predict that interpretation and encoding processes, such as attention and retention, shape learning effects. What individuals attend to in the media and how they construct the meaning of what they see is thought to shape what they learn (see also Busselle, Ryabovolova, & Wilson, 2004; Roskos-Ewoldsen, Davies, & Roskos-Ewoldsen, 2004; Shrum, 2004). However, the retrospective judgments that are measured in surveys do not directly tap into these processes (Busselle et al., 2004).

Taking cognitive models into account would give researchers a better chance of identifying when and how realism perceptions have consequences. It may also help researchers determine, once and for all, when perceived realism essentially makes no difference or when these perceptions are merely markers of more fundamental attributes, such as engagement (Busselle & Bilandzic, 2008) or a general critical orientation (Pingree, 1978), that more directly shape media effects. Media researchers should seek to ground their predictions in tested models of how audiences judge realism and how media effects occur. They should also ensure that the methods and measures through which they are investigating these effects are consistent with the mechanism through which realism is thought to make a difference.

Developing clearer understandings of how realism is judged is even more important when one considers the ways that mass communication messages are changing. For example, it is increasingly common for texts to combine characteristics of both fiction and nonfiction genres. Reality TV, which combines elements of game shows, documentaries, and soap operas, is perhaps the most visible example of this. Others include documentaries that use re-creations and fiction narratives that employ the textual markers of documentaries or of found footage (i.e., *The Blair Witch Project, Best in Show*). Furthermore, the traditional associations of nonfiction television content with serious or educational purposes and fiction with entertainment are continuing to blur as nonfiction genres, such as reality programs, documentaries, and political talk shows, become increasingly entertainment oriented.

However, even as media forms have converged and shifted, research on the way audiences judge the match between a mediated portrayal and the word itself has remained largely compartmentalized. This makes it more difficult to understand how audience members may evaluate the realism of new or hybrid genres. Work on media realism is focused on narrative entertainment media, whereas work on nonfiction media tends to focus on issues of credibility or accuracy. Research into digital games investigates players' experiential sense that content is real through the concept of presence. Incorporating these varied approaches into a more comprehensive conceptualization of perceived media realism would give researchers additional tools to keep up with the shifting nature of media texts and to evaluate the implications of these changes.

It has been argued that the convergence of media forms and the development of new media have the potential to profoundly change the ways audiences think about media realism in general. Hill (2007), for example, has suggested that viewers' distrust of the realism of popular reality programs may transfer to their evaluations of more traditional nonfiction genres, such as news and documentaries (see also Corner, 2002). Viewers may become more cautious about trusting any form of media content to accurately represent the world. Alternatively, they may abandon efforts to evaluate the factual realism of many texts entirely and instead judge these programs solely in terms of whether they provide an engaging experience. However, there has been relatively little applied, empirical research on these issues. This is something that should be on the research agenda.

Finally, it is time to consider media other than television. For decades, television has been the most ubiquitous medium of modern life. This is unlikely to be the case for much longer, and for many young people, it is unlikely to be the case now. Audiences now have a wide range of options, including Internet content and video games. Increasingly, the stories and images that make up our symbolic world will come from sources other than broadcast and cable television. These new materials differ from older media content in several key ways. One is that much of this material is short and self-contained. Rather than

watching a 30-minute sitcom or a 90-minute movie, viewers may watch a series of 2- to 5-minute clips on YouTube. The most consistent evidence that perceptions of factual realism influence outcomes has been in relation to brief clips of visual material. However, factuality is particularly difficult to evaluate on the Web. Scholars should consider how audiences evaluate the realism of this material, as well as whether these evaluations make a difference in terms of viewer responses.

New media are also distinguished by their level of interactivity. In the case of video games, for example, players do not merely construct a mental representation of a narrative. They construct the narrative, albeit within the constraints provided by the game's programmers. Questions this raises include whether the greater control that users have over the content increases their sense of the material as realistic and, if so, whether it does so in a way that differs from audiences' feelings of immersion in traditional narratives.

Perceived media realism is a concept that has long intrigued scholars. Recent shifts in media content and in the development of new technologies suggest exciting new avenues for further research in this area. However, to move the field forward, researchers need to be more aware of the processes through which realism judgments are made so that they can be more precise in their examination of the roles that the judgments may play in media reception. Furthermore, to stay relevant, this area of study needs to widen the type of media and media content that it considers.

◆ References

Andrejevic, M. (2004). *Reality TV: The work of being watched*. Lanham, MD: Rowman & Littlefield.

Atkin, C. (1983). Effects of realistic TV violence versus fictional violence on aggression. *Journalism Quarterly, 60,* 615–621.

Bandura, A., Ross, D., & Ross, A. (1963). Imitation of film-mediated aggressive models. *Journal of Abnormal and Social Psychology, 66*, 3–11.

Berkowitz, L., & Alioto, J. T. (1973). The meaning of an observed event as a determinant of its aggressive consequences. *Journal of Personality and Social Psychology, 28*, 206–217.

Busselle, R. W. (2001). Television exposure, perceived realism, and exemplar accessibility in the social judgment process. *Media Psychology, 3*, 43–67.

Busselle, R. W. (2003). Television realism measures: The influence of program salience on global judgments. *Communication Research Reports, 20*, 367–375.

Busselle, R. W., & Bilandzic, H. (2008). Fictionality and perceived realism in experiencing stories. *Communication Theory, 18*, 255–280.

Busselle, R. W., & Greenberg, B. S. (2000). The nature of television realism judgments: A reevaluation of their conceptualization and measurement. *Mass Communication and Society, 3*, 249–268.

Busselle, R., Ryabovolova, A., & Wilson, B. (2004). Ruining a good story: Cultivation, perceived realism and narrative. *Communications: The European Journal of Communication Research, 29*, 365–378.

Cavender, G. (1998). In "The shadow of shadows": Television reality crime programming. In M. Fishman & G. Cavender (Eds.), *Entertaining crime: Television reality programs* (pp. 79–94). New York: Aldine de Gruyter.

Corner, J. (2002). Performing the real: Documentary diversions. *Television and New Media, 3*, 255–269.

Dorr, A. (1983). No shortcuts to judging reality. In J. Bryant & D. R. Anderson (Eds.), *Children's understanding of television: Research on attention and comprehension* (pp. 199–220). New York: Academic Press.

Dorr, A., Kovaric, P., & Doubleday, C. (1990). Age and content influences on children's perceptions of the realism of television families. *Journal of Broadcasting and Electronic Media, 34*, 377–397.

Eggermont, S. (2004). Television viewing, perceived similarity, and adolescents' expectations of a romantic partner. *Journal of Broadcasting and Electronic Media, 48*, 244–265.

Elliott, W. R., & Slater, D. (1980). Exposure, experience, and perceived TV reality for adolescents. *Journalism Quarterly, 57*, 409–414, 431.

Eschholz, S., Blackwell, B. S., Gertz, M., & Chiricos, T. (2002). Race and attitudes toward the police: Assessing the effects of watching "reality" police programs. *Journal of Criminal Justice, 30*, 327–341.

Ferris, A. L., Smith, S. W., Greenberg, B. S., & Smith, S. L. (2007). The content of reality dating shows and viewer perceptions of dating. *Journal of Communication, 57*, 490–510.

Flavell, J. H., Flavell, E. R., Green, F. L., & Korfmacher, J. E. (1990). Do young children think of television images as pictures or real objects? *Journal of Broadcasting and Electronic Media, 34*, 399–414.

Gardyn, R. (2001, September). The tribe has spoken. *American Demographics, 23*(9), 34–40.

Geen, R. G. (1975). The meaning of observed violence: Real vs. fictional violence and consequent effects on aggression and emotional arousal. *Journal of Research in Personality, 9*, 270–281.

Gerrig, R. J. (1993). *Experiencing narrative worlds: On the psychological activities of reading.* New Haven, CT: Yale University Press.

Gilbert, D. T., Krull, D. S., & Malone, P. S. (1990). Unbelieving the unbelievable: Some problems with the rejection of false information. *Journal of Personality and Social Psychology, 59*, 601–613.

Green, M. C. (2004). Transportation into narrative worlds: The role of prior knowledge and perceived realism. *Discourse Processes, 38*, 247–266.

Green, M. C., & Brock, T. C. (2000). The role of transportation in the persuasiveness of public narratives. *Journal of Personality and Social Psychology, 79*, 701–721.

Green, M. C., Brock, T. C., & Kaufman, G. E. (2004). Understanding media enjoyment: The role of transportation into narrative worlds. *Communication Theory, 14*, 311–327.

Green, M. C., Garst, J., & Brock, T. C. (2004). The power of fiction: Determinants and boundaries. In L. J. Shrum (Ed.), *The psychology of entertainment media: Blurring the lines between entertainment and persuasion* (pp. 161–176). Mahwah, NJ: Erlbaum.

Gunther, A. C., & Liebhart, J. L. (2006). Broad reach or biased source? Decomposing the hostile media effect. *Journal of Communication, 56,* 449–466.

Hall, A. (2003). Reading realism: Audiences' perceptions of the reality of mass media texts. *Journal of Communication, 53,* 624–641.

Hall, A. (2006). Viewers' perceptions of reality programs. *Communication Quarterly, 54,* 191–214.

Hall, A. (in press). Perceptions of the authenticity of reality programs and their relationships to audience involvement, enjoyment, and perceived learning. *Journal of Broadcasting and Electronic Media.*

Haridakis, P. M., & Rubin, A. M. (2003). Motivation for watching television violence and viewer aggression. *Mass Communication and Society, 6,* 29–56.

Hawkins, R. P. (1977). The dimensional structure of children's perceptions of television reality. *Communication Research, 4,* 299–320.

Hawkins, R. P., & Pingree, S. (1980). Some processes in the cultivation effect. *Communication Research, 7,* 193–226.

Higgins, E. T. (2000). Social cognition: Learning about what matters in the world. *European Journal of Social Psychology, 30,* 3–39.

Higgins, E. T., & King, G. (1981). Accessibility of social constructs: Information-processing consequences of individual and contextual variability. In N. Cantor & J. F. Kihlstrom (Eds.), *Personality, cognition, and social interaction* (pp. 69–121). Hillsdale, NJ: Erlbaum.

Hill, A. (2002). *Big Brother:* The real audience. *Television and New Media, 3,* 323–340.

Hill, A. (2005). *Reality TV: Audiences and popular factual television.* New York: Routledge.

Hill, A. (2007). *Restyling factual TV: Audiences and news, documentary and reality genres.* New York: Routledge.

Huesmann, L. R., Lagerspetz, K., & Eron, L. D. (1984). Intervening variables in the TV violence-aggression relation: Evidence from two countries. *Developmental Psychology, 5,* 746–775.

Huston, A. C., Wright, J. C., Alvarez, M., Truglio, R., Fitch, M., & Piemyat, S. (1995). Perceived television reality and children's emotional and cognitive responses to its social content. *Journal of Applied Developmental Psychology, 16,* 231–251.

Huston, A. C., Wright, J. C., Fitch, M., Wroblewski, R., & Piemyat, S. (1997). Effects of documentary and fictional television formats on children's acquisition of schemata for unfamiliar occupations. *Journal of Applied Developmental Psychology, 18,* 562–585.

Jones, J. M. (2003). Show your real face. *New Media and Society, 5,* 400–421.

Kubick, K. N., & Chory, R. M. (2007). Exposure to television makeover programs and perceptions of self. *Communication Research Reports, 24,* 283–292.

Lundy, L. K., Ruth, A. M., & Park, T. D. (2008). Simply irresistible: Reality TV consumption patterns. *Communication Quarterly,* 208–225.

Metacritic.com. (2007, June 18). *Fall 2007 television season.* Retrieved February 25, 2008, from http://www.metacritic.com/tv/seasons/2007fall/networks.shtml

Nabi, R. L., Biely, E. N., Morgan, S. J., & Stitt, C. R. (2003). Reality-based television programming and the psychology of its appeal. *Media Psychology, 5,* 303–330.

Nabi, R. L., Stitt, C. R., Halford, J., & Finnerty, K. L. (2006). Emotional and cognitive predictors of the enjoyment of reality-based and fictional programming: An elaboration of the uses and gratifications perspective. *Media Psychology, 8,* 421–447.

Oliver, M. B. (1994). Portrayals of crime, race, and aggression in "reality-based" police shows: A content analysis. *Journal of Broadcasting and Electronic Media, 38,* 179–192.

Oliver, M. B., & Armstrong, G. B. (1995). Predictors of viewing and enjoyment of reality-based and fictional crime shows. *Journalism and Mass Communication Quarterly, 73,* 559–570.

Oliver, M. B., & Armstrong, G. B. (1998). The color of crime: Perceptions of Caucasians' and African-Americans' involvement in crime. In M. Fishman & G. Cavender (Eds.), *Entertaining crime: Television reality programs* (pp. 19–35). New York: Aldine de Gruyter.

Papacharissi, Z., & Mendelson, A. L. (2007). An exploratory study of reality appeal: Uses and gratifications of reality TV shows. *Journal of Broadcasting and Electronic Media, 51,* 355–370.

Perse, E. M. (1986). Soap opera viewing patterns of college students and cultivation. *Journal of Broadcasting and Electronic Media, 30,* 175–193.

Peter, J., & Valkenburg, P. M. (2006). Adolescents' exposure to sexually explicit online material and recreational attitudes toward sex. *Journal of Communication, 56,* 639–661.

Pingree, S. (1978). The effects on nonsexist television commercials and perceptions of reality on children's attitudes about women. *Psychology of Women Quarterly, 2,* 262–277.

Potter, W. J. (1986). Perceived reality and the cultivation hypothesis. *Journal of Broadcasting and Electronic Media, 30,* 159–174.

Potter, W. J. (1992). How do adolescents' perceptions of television reality change over time. *Journalism Quarterly, 69,* 392–405.

Pouliot, L., & Cowen, P. S. (2007). Does perceived realism really matter in media effects. *Media Psychology, 9,* 241–259.

Press, A. (1989). Class and gender in the hegemonic process: Class differences in women's perceptions of television realism and identification with television characters. *Media, Culture, and Society, 11,* 229–251.

Quintero-Johnson, J., & Busselle, R. (2004, August). *Thinking while viewing: The influence of thoughts about a program on transportation and perceived realism.* Paper presented at the meeting of the Association for Education in Journalism and Mass Communication, Toronto, Canada.

Reeves, B. (1978). Perceived TV reality as a predictor of children's social behavior. *Journalism Quarterly, 55,* 682–689, 695.

Reeves, B., & Vega, V. (2006, June). *Priming arousal responses to media with labels of reality and fantasy.* Paper presented at the

meeting of the International Communication Association, Dresden, Germany.

Reiss, S., & Wiltz, J. (2004). Why people watch reality TV. *Media Psychology, 6,* 363–378.

Roskos-Ewoldsen, B., Davies, J., & Roskos-Ewoldsen, D. R. (2004). Implications of the mental models approach for cultivation theory. *Communications: The European Journal of Communication Research, 29,* 345–363.

Rubin, A. M. (1981). An examination of television viewing motivations. *Communication Research, 8,* 141–165.

Rubin, A. M., & Perse, E. M. (1987). Audience activity and soap opera involvement: A uses and effects investigation. *Human Communication Research, 14,* 246–268.

Rubin, A. M., Perse, E. M., & Powell, R. A. (1985). Loneliness, parasocial interaction, and local television news viewing. *Human Communication Research, 12,* 156–180.

Rubin, A. M., Perse, E. M., & Taylor, D. S. (1988). A methodological examination of cultivation. *Communication Research, 15,* 107–134.

Shapiro, M. A., & Chock, T. M. (2003). Psychological processes in perceiving reality. *Media Psychology, 5,* 163–198.

Shapiro, M. A., & Chock, T. M. (2004). Media dependency and perceived reality. *Journal of Broadcasting and Electronic Media, 48,* 675–695.

Shrum, L. J. (2004). The cognitive processes underlying cultivation effects are a function of whether the judgments are online or memory-based. *Communications: The European Journal of Communication Research, 29,* 327–344.

Strange, J. J., & Leung, C. C. (1999). How anecdotal accounts in news and in fiction can influence judgments of a social problem's urgency, causes, and cures. *Personality and Social Psychology Bulletin, 25,* 436–449.

Thomas, M. H., & Tell, P. M. (1974). Effects of viewing real versus fantasy violence upon interpersonal aggression. *Journal of Research in Personality, 8,* 153–160.

Ward, L. M., & Rivadeneyra, R. (1999). Contributions of entertainment television to adolescents' sexual attitudes and expectations: The role of viewing amount versus viewer involvement. *Journal of Sex Research, 36,* 237–249.

Weiss, A. J., & Wilson, B. J. (1998). Children's cognitive and emotional responses to the portrayal of negative emotions in family-formatted situation comedies. *Human Communication Research, 24,* 584–609.

Wilson, B., & Busselle, R. (2004, May). *Transportation into the narrative and perceptions of media realism.* Paper presented at the meeting of the International Communication Association, New Orleans, LA.

Wright, J. C., Huston, A. C., Reitz, A. L., & Piemyat, S. (1994). Young children's perceptions of television reality determinates and developmental differences. *Developmental Psychology, 30,* 229–239.

Zillmann, D. (1991). Television viewing and physiological arousal. In J. Bryant & D. Zillmann (Eds.), *Responding to the screen: Reception and reaction processes* (pp. 103–133). Hillsdale, NJ: Erlbaum.

29

THE EFFECTS OF VIEWING TELEVISED SPORTS

◆ Arthur A. Raney

On February 3, 2008, an estimated 97.5 million Americans tuned in to watch Eli Manning lead his underdog New York Giants to victory over the previously unbeaten and heavily favored New England Patriots in Super Bowl XLII. Only one show in U.S. television history garnered a larger audience: the 1983 final episode of the long-running dramedy *M*A*S*H*. In fact, 9 of the 15 most watched programs of all time, and all of the top-10 most watched shows since 2000, are sporting events. Further, no BBC program has ever drawn more viewers than the 1966 FIFA World Cup final between England and West Germany. Perhaps it goes without saying, but sports and media are truly a match made in entertainment heaven.

Although the appeal of sports media is indisputable, the effects of viewing the contests have been fodder for scientific exploration and academic speculation for decades. Of course, the term *sports media* may be applied to a variety of contents: live sporting events; media promotion, as well as print and electronic news coverage of those specific events; print and electronic commentary about the participants, the coaches, the leagues, and the bodies that govern them; the media promotion of the athletes, teams, and leagues; fan-to-fan discussions; fantasy leagues and digital games that simulate the games and leagues; and fictional accounts of all of these. Scholars have indeed trained their analytic gaze on the psychological and sociological impacts of these various sports media aspects over the past several decades. Unfortunately, space constraints do not allow us to investigate all of these research threads in the current chapter.

With that stated, the specific focus of this chapter will be the potential individual-level effects from viewing live sports broadcasts, primarily on television. Further, I will limit the discussion (as much as possible) to studies that attempt to identify the causal relationship between live sports television consumption and viewer effects. Therefore, examinations employing an experimental methodology will primarily be offered as evidence, although a reliance on some correlational studies will be necessary to provide context in some cases. Also, most studies described in the following paragraphs specifically focused on viewers of televised sports; a few, though, relied on in-stadium spectators. Although I readily acknowledge the differences between the two viewing environments, I have attempted to ensure that the observed effects could just as reasonably have resulted from television viewing as in-stadium spectatorship. Finally, as I alluded to previously, the area boasts a broad tradition, with scholars from many disciplines, theoretical perspectives, and methodological approaches all attempting to better understand the sports-media relationship. What I attempt to present here is just a portion of a much larger whole.

As this volume attests, the scholarly record of television viewing effects is quite extensive, and surely the wisdom gained from that record can be applied to televised sports. However, the nature of live sports programming differentiates it from other forms of entertainment media. For instance, live sporting events are just that—live (with a 5–10 second delay). Although television's foundation was built on live broadcasts, their presence on the entertainment landscape today is limited to a weekend sketch comedy offering, a handful of awards shows, and the intermittent final episode of a (so-called) reality program. But live sporting events are the true reality programs, with the spontaneity, unpredictability, suspense, and surprise longed for in other forms of entertainment, without the need to suspend disbelief. Further accentuating the live quality of sports is the constant threat of success, failure, and injury to the performers, as well as (for some) the fear of losing part of the estimated $380 billion dollars illegally wagered on sports in the United States every year (American Gaming Association, 2008).

Further, live sporting events are among the remaining few truly periodic media offerings. In our current era of midseason replacements and delayed premieres, live sporting events continue to offer viewers a consistent programming schedule—from year to year, season to season, month to month, and even day to day—that promotes a unique brand of appointment viewing. But perhaps most important, sports teams and athletes engender unparalleled partisanship and rooting among viewers. Harry Potter emulators, Trekkies, and *American Idol* fanatics notwithstanding, most non-sports media fanship is fleeting. By and large (my apologies to Brooklyn Dodgers, Baltimore Colts, and Vancouver Grizzlies fans), sports teams and their fan bases are seemingly timeless, with team allegiances passed from one generation to another.

It is these distinctive programming characteristics that lead consumers back to the couch, beer and hot dog in hand, time and time again. Additionally, it is these characteristics that can potentially lead to distinctive effects on viewers that can be emotional, cognitive, or social in nature. What follows is a summary of those effects.

◆ Effects of Viewing Televised Sports

ENJOYMENT

The primary motivation for millions of viewers to tune in and watch televised sports, at least according to survey results (e.g., Gantz, 1981; Wenner & Gantz, 1998), is for entertainment or enjoyment. As the burgeoning field of entertainment theory confirms, we now study entertainment *as a media effect* (see Zillmann & Bryant, 1994). As a result, enjoyment—that is, the pleasure derived from consuming media entertainment—has become the focus of increased scholarly attention. Entertainment theorists generally agree on several enjoyment-related issues (see Oliver, Chapter 11, this volume). For instance, enjoyment is experienced primarily as an emotional response to media, through the activation of neurotransmitters associated with pleasure and pain in the limbic areas of the brain. Further, enjoyment is thought to be a judgment rendered through the interaction of user, content, and environmental variables. Therefore, the judgment or evaluation of enjoyment is seen as a process.

Disposition-based effects on enjoyment. The leading entertainment theory explaining the enjoyment process is affective disposition theory (ADT; see Raney, 2006, for a recent overview). The disposition theory of sports spectatorship (Zillmann, Bryant, & Sapolsky, 1989; Zillmann & Paulus, 1993) is an application of the general principals of ADT to better understand how and why people enjoy mediated sporting events. At the crux of the theory are the intense emotional attachments (i.e., affective dispositions) that viewers form toward athletes and teams. The theory posits that a viewer's affiliation with a team falls along a continuum of affect, from intense disliking through indifference to intense liking. The reader is surely familiar with rabid sports fans, whose team allegiances are literally worn on their coat sleeves, as well as on their toboggans, car bumpers, and front lawns, and even their caskets. The love that those fans hold for their favorite teams is typically only rivaled in intensity by the enmity they hold toward a bitter rival. As the disposition theory of sports spectatorship contends, these passions

hold the key to the enjoyment of sporting contests.

According to the theory, the enjoyment of viewing a sporting event is a function of the outcome of the contest in relation to the strength and valence of the dispositions held toward the competitors. Specifically, enjoyment increases the more the viewer favors the winning team or dislikes the losing one. Conversely, enjoyment decreases the more the winning team is disliked or the more the losing team is loved by the viewer. In fact, Zillmann and his colleagues have postulated that maximum enjoyment from viewing sports should be experienced when an intensely liked team defeats an intensely disliked team. In contrast, maximum disappointment or negative enjoyment should be experienced when a hated rival defeats your beloved team.

As is the case with the more general ADT, support for the disposition theory of sports spectatorship is widespread. In two of the earliest studies, Zillmann et al. (1989) demonstrated the basic principles of the theory with examinations of professional American football (hereafter, just *football*) and Olympic basketball. In the first, viewers holding either a positive, neutral, or negative disposition toward two professional teams rated their enjoyment of a live televised game between the two squads. As predicted, those with a positive disposition toward the victorious team enjoyed the game more than those who disliked the team and more than those who liked the losing one. Further, enjoyment was greatest for those viewers who really liked the winning team and really disliked the losing team, whereas enjoyment was least for those viewers who liked the losing team and disliked the winning team.

In the second study, students at Indiana University rated their enjoyment of each play in a portion of the 1976 men's gold medal basketball game between the United States and Yugoslavia. As expected, the American students (who purportedly favored the U.S. squad) reported greater enjoyment when the U.S. team scored and less enjoyment when Yugoslavia scored. Additionally, it was observed that the highest enjoyment ratings were found on scoring plays involving two U.S. players who had previously attended and competed for Indiana University. The researchers concluded that the participants held the most positive dispositions toward the two alumni; therefore, enjoyment was highest on plays in which they scored. Additional support for the basic tenets of the disposition theory of sports spectatorship has been reported with college football (Raney & Kinnally, 2006, 2007), college basketball (Peterson & Raney, 2008), tennis (Tüzünkan, 2007), and professional wrestling (Tamborini & Lachlan, 2004).

To my knowledge, only one study has attempted to empirically examine the Zillmann et al. (1989) proposal of maximum sports enjoyment coming from seeing a beloved team defeat a bitter rival, and minimum enjoyment coming from the converse. Without rigging the outcome of games (which is of course illegal), the most ecologically valid way to examine this proposition is to measure enjoyment of several rivalry contests in hopes of finding an obliging team that wins one and loses another. That is just what my students and I did. Specifically, more than 1,100 viewers rated their enjoyment of eight televised Florida State University (FSU) football games over the course of the 2003 season (Raney & Kinnally, 2006).

FSU is a perennial top-25 team with two hated in-state rivals: the University of Florida and the University of Miami. Our season-long rivalry ratings consistently confirmed that these two teams were disliked more than all other opponents. Fortunately for us (but not for the team), FSU beat the former and lost to the latter; so, at least theoretically, we had the situations which should have generated maximum and minimum enjoyment. As expected, across the eight games, one was enjoyed significantly more than all the others: the thrilling 38–34

victory over the then #11-ranked and hated Florida Gators. Therefore, we found initial support for the maximum-enjoyment proposition. And, as expected, we found that one game was enjoyed significantly less than all others. Unexpectedly, though, that game was a late-season 26–10 loss to unranked Clemson University—a team that fans consistently rated as a midrange rival—and not the 22–14 loss to rival Miami earlier in the season. Rather than undermine the minimum-enjoyment proposition, which we think is still quite reasonable all things being equal, these findings highlight the complexity of the sports enjoyment process. Although team affiliations (in relation to the contest outcomes) are exceedingly important to enjoyment, they are not the sole determinants. In this case, additional factors such as expectations of a win (FSU was heavily favored against Clemson) and potential for a loss (Miami was ranked #2 in the country when FSU played them) surely affected the ultimate evaluation of enjoyment. This was not the first study to illuminate such complexities; over the years, scholars have identified several other game and viewer factors that influence the enjoyment of live televised sports contests.

Effect of drama and suspense perceptions on enjoyment. Historically, sporting contests have been described as high drama (cf. Bentham, 1802/1931). This is reasonable given that conflict and competition—particularly between emotionally involving participants—are at the heart of the activity. Within the enjoyment process, drama plays an important role: The more the perceived drama (which is primarily experienced as suspense by the viewer), the greater the potential enjoyment. This formula, of course, is not unique to sports but is found in most forms of entertainment fare (see Vorderer, Wulff, & Friedrichsen, 1996). However, even a cursory view of today's sports coverage reveals that producers and directors capitalize on and draw attention to this feature, relying heavily on "bitter conflict" between teams to construct the narrative of sports (Bryant, Comisky, & Zillmann, 1977).

Previous research validates the perceived-drama-increases-enjoyment formula, especially when the drama is hyped by the announcers. Owens and Bryant (1998) found that commentary provided by a home-team radio announcer can indeed add to the level of perceived suspense experienced by listeners rooting for the home team. Further, Comisky and his collaborators (Comisky, Bryant, & Zillmann, 1977) demonstrated the effect of dramatic commentary on enjoyment when they showed participants hockey action, either with or without conflict-highlighting commentary. Viewers who watched the game with the commentary perceived it to be more intense and more enjoyable than those who saw the same action without the commentary. Extending this research, Bryant, Brown, Comisky, and Zillmann (1982) demonstrated that the way announcers frame a contest (rather than just the way they describe the play) can greatly impact a viewer's experience. The researchers created three versions of a tennis match between players described by the commentators as best friends, bitter enemies, or having no prior relationship. Although the on-the-court action was identical in all three conditions, participants viewing the players-as-enemies version described the action as more enjoyable than participants viewing the other two versions.

Commentators may highlight and dramatize the suspense inherent in the games, but to do so, the contests themselves must contain actual suspenseful moments, which certainly they do. A few studies have looked at the way game features affect perceptions of suspense and enjoyment. Operationalizing suspense as an inverse function of the final point differential between two teams—specifically, the closer the final score, the higher the suspense—Gan and her colleagues (Gan, Tuggle,

Mitrook, Coussement, & Zillmann, 1997) demonstrated the relationship between suspense and enjoyment. As predicted, enjoyment was highest for males who viewed the closest (and thus most suspenseful) NCAA men's basketball tournament games. Peterson and Raney (2008) recently added a bit more nuance to our understanding of suspense's role in sports enjoyment with a replication of the Gan et al. (1997) study. Relying on a host of additional game features now available through new media technology, the researchers demonstrated how the cumulative time (in seconds) that a NCAA men's basketball tournament game score was extremely close is a powerful measure of perceived suspense and predictor of overall enjoyment. Similarly, Knobloch-Westerwick and colleagues (Knobloch-Westerwick, David, Eastin, Tamborini, & Greenwood, 2008) demonstrated the complexity and unfolding nature of suspense and affect as a predictor of enjoyment in an intercollegiate football game between two heated rivals.

Finally, one study has manipulated both commentary and in-game action to examine the impact of suspense on enjoyment. Bryant, Rockwell, and Owens (1994) professionally recorded, edited, and provided commentary for a high school football game. Suspense was manipulated through play-by-play announcing (e.g., emphasis on the importance of the game on the playoff picture for each team) and play selection (e.g., unsuccessful and dull plays versus successful and scoring plays), resulting in high and low suspenseful conditions. As expected, viewers of the more suspenseful version reported greater enjoyment, along with more anxiety in relation to the game outcome.

Effects of the presence and perceptions of violence on enjoyment. The appeal of media violence is well documented (see Goldstein, 1989). However, as Young noted, "the concept of *sports violence* is elusive" (2000, p. 382). At some points in the literature, it is called just that: sports violence (cf. Gunter, 2006). Elsewhere, Zillmann and his colleagues have used the more benign term *roughness* (1989, p. 268). Smith (1983) classified player action as brutal body contact, borderline violence, quasi-criminal violence, and criminal violence. Unfortunately, all of these terms have their limitations when applied to sports play (cf. Young, 2000). Moreover, because otherwise violent acts are sanctioned and encouraged, and fulfill such a central role in some sports, perhaps we should be concerned with the extent to which viewers *perceive* the action to be violent.

Despite this problem with operationalization, scholars have consistently shown that violence plays a role in the appeal and enjoyment of televised sports contests. In general, males appear to be drawn to combative sports more than females, and they often report that enjoyment increases the more violent, active, and dangerous they perceive the sport to be (Sargent, Zillmann, & Weaver, 1998). However, Sargent et al. also found that men and women combined favored violent team sports significantly more than all other types; Bryant and his colleagues (Bryant, Zillmann, & Raney, 1998) reported a similar pattern. In fact, in one study, among a host of salient characteristics (e.g., violence, risk, artistry, action) found in each event, violence received the highest enjoyment ratings across all sports on television (Bryant et al., 1998).

With regard to the effects of viewing sports violence, the research record suggests an impact on enjoyment. In one of the earliest studies, Goldstein and Arms (1971) reported that sports containing violence—specifically a college football rivalry game—can excite an audience, leading to increased enjoyment. Additionally, Bryant, Comisky, and Zillmann (1981) coded professional football plays as containing low, intermediate, or high levels of violence, and had participants rate each play for enjoyment. A consistent pattern emerged: Enjoyment increased with the degree of violence, with the relationship being particularly strong for male viewers. Raney and Depalma (2006) also reported that viewers watching clips from a violent sport (i.e., boxing) enjoyed their experience more than viewers of a nonviolent sport (e.g., baseball); this trend was particularly pronounced for males and self-reported sports fans. DeNeui and Sachau (1996) sought to predict spectator enjoyment using a variety of statistics from 16 hockey matches. They found the number of penalty minutes assessed—clearly an indicator of aggressive or violent play—to be the only significant predictor of reported enjoyment. Finally, in a study of intercollegiate football contests, Raney and Kinnally (2007) reported that television viewers perceived games between two heated rivals to be more violent than non-rivalry games, with games won by the favored team being seen as more violent than those lost. Also, viewers perceiving high levels of violence reported greater enjoyment than those who perceived low levels of violence, regardless of rivalry level.

As noted earlier, announcers can impact viewers' perceptions of the games, and this is certainly the case with perceptions of violence. In the Comisky et al. (1977) study of normal or unusually rough hockey play either with or without commentary, the researchers found that normal play accompanied by conflict-centered commentary was perceived to be more intense and violent than identical action without commentary. In the same study, rough play without commentary was perceived as less rough than the same action with commentary. Additionally, Sullivan (1991) analyzed reactions to portions of a televised college basketball game featuring one particularly aggressive team and an in-game fight; participants viewed game clips with either highly dramatic, neutral, or no commentary. Announcer effects on perceptions of violence were found: Viewers who heard the neutral commentary were more tolerant of the fight than viewers who saw the game with no commentary.

AROUSAL AND MOOD

Surely in the pursuit of enjoyment, many fans report tuning in to live sports to escape boredom and experience stimulation. Viewers consistently describe the activity as exciting and arousing (e.g., Wann, Melnick, Russell, & Pease, 2001), and able to "get me psyched up" (e.g., Gantz, 1981) or "pumped up" (e.g., Wann, 1995). Thus, it should come as no surprise that the research record clearly demonstrates that sports viewing can lead to increased physiological arousal and affective engagement. For instance, Hillman and his colleagues reported that ardent fans self-reported greater arousal after viewing team-relevant photos (of both winning and losing) as compared with team-irrelevant photos (Hillmann, Cuthbert, Bradley, & Lang, 2004). The self-reports were consistent with physiological measures, with smaller startle probe-P3 reflexes, increased positive slow cortical potentials, and greater skin conductance responses observed in reaction to photos featuring the favored team. These findings mirror those reported in a previous study examining the reactions of sports fans to (only) positive or pleasant sports pictures (Hillmann et al., 2000).

If such reactions can be elicited by sports photos, then the arousal impact of viewing live action is surely great. In fact, such feelings are experienced even before the game starts: Wann, Schrader, and Adamson (1998) demonstrated that sports fans—especially ardent fans of a particular team—experience increased somatic anxiety in the days leading up to an important game. With regard to game play itself, one team of scholars found an increase in testosterone levels (typically associated with sexual arousal) in saliva samples of male fans following a televised World Cup soccer match featuring two international rivals (Bernhardt, Dabbs, Fielden, & Lutter, 1998). In fact, it appears that for some, the in-game stress becomes so great and the arousal so unpleasant that even the most loyal fans may be forced to remove themselves from the viewing environment for a period of time (Eastman & Riggs, 1994).

Changes in mood state have also been observed during the viewing of live sports, primarily for fans who have a strong (positive or negative) attachment to one or both of the contestants (Sloan, 1979). Not unexpectedly, Schwarz and colleagues demonstrated that viewers of a televised win by the German national soccer squad reported increased positive mood (as well as greater satisfaction with their lives) within the first 30 minutes following the game. Conversely, viewers reported being in a more negative mood state after watching the team play to a 0–0 tie (Schwarz, Strack, Kommer, & Wagner, 1987). Similarly, fans of a winning college football team reported more positive mood (i.e., euphoria) compared with fans of the losing team immediately following a televised rivalry game; the losing fans reported significantly more tension than their counterparts (Schweitzer, Zillmann, Weaver, & Luttrell, 1992). Other studies have demonstrated an increase in aggressive mood following exposure to hockey and professional wrestling (Arms, Russell, & Sandilands, 1979), as well as increased negative mood states following professional wrestling (Raney & Depalma, 2006).

LEARNING

Despite the extended discussion of sports viewing for the sake of pleasure and arousal, an additional effect of consuming live sports is quite cognitive in nature: knowledge acquisition. In fact, fans consistently report that learning about teams and players is one of the most important motivations for viewing sports (Gantz, 1981; Wenner & Gantz, 1998). A great deal of social capital is flaunted and spent on the playground, around the water cooler, in the bar, and in chat rooms when fans rattle off the latest sports stat, trivia, or rumor. In fact, the universal language of sports arguably transcends social status, education, and occupation (Lever, 1983). More so, as opposed to politics or religion, sports discussions often offer a welcomed opportunity for friendly disagreements with friends and strangers (Karp & Yoels, 1990). Much of the training for these conversations occurs during television viewing of both games and sports news, during which endless commentary and countless statistical, historical, and trivial sports facts are communicated.

Whereas the previous paragraph centered on the sports-smart-getting-smarter effect, it should be noted that an additional effect of sports viewing is the learning about sports by novices, in particular (historically) females and nonsports fans. By and large, individuals motivated to view sports for this reason report a desire to become more knowledgeable so that they can enjoy sports viewing with a loved one. At times, this strategy is seen as noble, with the learned other encouraging and facilitating the learning. At other times, however, an elitist or privileged position is taken by the learned other, with such attempts viewed with much skepticism and contempt.

SOCIAL INTERACTION

Another effect of—or motivation for, depending on how you look at it—viewing sports on television is social interaction. Sports programming allows for more communicative behaviors between viewers than most television content (Wenner & Gantz, 1998), whether viewing takes place at home with friends or at a sports bar with complete strangers (Eastman & Land, 1997). In fact, social interaction seems to affect the overall entertainment experience as viewers report enjoying sports programming more when they can talk with friends about the game (Gantz, 1981).

Televised sports offer unique experiences for interactions among family members; in truth, sports are one of the few remaining family coviewing television experiences. As alluded to, females have historically reported a greater likelihood than males to view sports on television for family reasons (Gantz & Wenner, 1991; Wann et al., 2001), a finding that remains when level of sports interest is held constant. As a result, it is not surprising that females tend to be less involved than males in the actual viewing, often completing household tasks during the course of the game (Gantz & Wenner, 1991). Despite this, sports television leads to relatively few conflicts between married couples. Females, more so than males, report that sports viewing actually plays a positive role in the marriage relationship (Gantz, Wenner, Carrico, & Knorr, 1995).

Outside the home, another social effect of sports viewing is found: a communicative experience between strangers called the *sports encounter* (Melnick, 1993). Live sports viewing provides strangers interesting and legitimate opportunities to interact. However, unlike similar opportunities (e.g., air travel), sports encounters carry a set of assumptions: an assumed level of knowledge, an assumed set of shared behaviors and motivations, an assumed commitment to and enthusiasm about sports, and an assumed understanding of time boundaries during which a conversation can take place (e.g., during time-outs, halftime, and commercials, but not during the actual play). With these assumptions intuitively agreed on, participants in legitimate sports encounters understand that the conversational topic will be restricted to the current game, the teams, the sport, or perhaps sports in general. To stray from this accepted set of topics is to violate the implicit terms of the social arrangement. However, as noted previously, as long as participants abide by these assumptions, sports encounters may be one of the few forms of public discourse that allow for friendly disagreements. Understandably, then, viewers find solace and enjoyment in the social interactions afforded through and because of sports viewing.

SELF-ESTEEM AND SOCIAL IDENTITY

Another socially oriented effect of televised sports viewing involves strategic self-esteem maintenance and self-presentation, where viewers often seek to minimize the perceived psychological distance between themselves and winning teams. This phenomenon is referred to as basking in the reflected glory (or BIRGing) of a team's success (Cialdini et al., 1976).

Kimble and Cooper (1992) found that fans can, in fact, experience feelings of vicarious achievement through being a fan of a successful sports team. Viewers can use those affiliations with successful teams, for instance, to help them feel better about themselves. Basketball fans who watched their favored team win reported greater confidence in their own abilities to perform various social, mental, and motor tasks than fans viewing a loss by their favored team (Hirt, Zillmann, Erickson, & Kennedy, 1992). Additional studies have reported similar findings (Madrigal, 1995; Owens & Bryant, 1998).

Similarly, viewers seek to outwardly align themselves with winning teams to improve their perception of their own public image. In other words, according to the BIRGing literature, some sports fans appear to assume that being readily identified with a winning team will result in others perceiving them as winners themselves. Several image-maintenance strategies in relation to sports viewing have been identified in the literature. For one, Cialdini and his associates found that a higher percentage of college students wore university-identifying clothing on Mondays following a football victory than following a defeat. Also, in telephone interviews, students were more likely to describe the game using the pronoun "we"

when referring to the team after a victory than after a defeat (Cialdini et al., 1976). Additional studies lend further support to the BIRGing phenomenon (Cialdini & Richardson, 1980; Snyder, Higgins, & Stucky, 1983). Perhaps not surprisingly, Wann and Branscombe (1990a) found that ardent fans were more likely to BIRG than fans with low team identification.

Conversely, when a favored team fails, fans will often seek to distance or disassociate themselves from the team through a process known as cutting off reflected failure (or CORFing; Snyder, Lassegard, & Ford, 1986). In doing so, of course, the fans seek to minimize harm to their self-image in the social environment. However, one group of researchers suggests that this tendency is greater among less-identified (or "fair-weather") fans than among those with strong team affiliations (Wann & Branscombe, 1990a). Thus, the interaction between team affiliation and game outcome that is so important in the enjoyment equation outlined earlier has far-reaching and meaningful impacts on self-esteem and image-maintenance practices.

AGGRESSIVE BEHAVIOR

As I noted previously, the violence inherent in sports is one (perhaps major) reason for their appeal. Of course, the question must be asked: Can viewing sports violence lead to increased real-world aggression? The answer to this question is a bit complicated, with the evidence pointing to a definite "maybe."

One way that sports viewing can potentially lead to aggressive behaviors is through the activation and increased salience of aggressive thoughts. And the effect seems to be quite powerful. For instance, just the reading of names of aggressive sports in a text has been shown to elicit more hostile thoughts than reading the names of nonaggressive sports (Wann & Branscombe, 1990b). Further, male spectators of a college football rivalry reported greater hostility after the game than before, regardless of whether their favored team won or lost (Goldstein & Arms, 1971). As noted previously, however, team identification surely compounds these effects, especially in relation to game outcome. Males and females who identified themselves as ardent fans of a college basketball team reported being more verbally aggressive toward the officials during a loss than their nonfan counterparts (Wann, Carlson, & Schrader, 1999). Similar findings have been reported with other sports as well (e.g., Branscombe & Wann, 1994; Wann et al., 2001). Admittedly, these studies analyzed the responses of game attendees, but it is reasonable to assume that similar effects can be found in mediated settings as well.

One line of inquiry that supported the sports violence–real-world aggression link actually did not have sports as a key focus (e.g., Berkowitz, 1965; Berkowitz & Geen, 1966). The work on aggressive cues and media priming effects conducted by Leonard Berkowitz and his colleagues often used a filmed (though fictitious) boxing match as a stimulus (see Roskos-Ewoldsen & Roskos-Ewoldsen, Chapter 12, this volume, for more details on media priming). Repeatedly, the researchers showed that an angered or irritated person who viewed the boxing match was more likely to display aggression (i.e., presumably delivering increased levels of electrical shock) toward others than those not viewing the match.

But the research reporting increased hostile thoughts and behaviors in experimental settings after sports viewing does not unquestionably establish the causal relationship between viewing sports violence and increased real-world aggression. Researchers have attempted to find a relationship between professional football and homicide rates (e.g., Miller, Heath, Molcan, & Dugoni, 1990; Phillips, 1983), child abuse (Drake & Pandey, 1996), battery against women (White, Katz, &

Scarborough, 1992), marital discord (Hettich, 2001), and domestic violence (Gantz, Bradley, & Wang, 2006), as well as between major boxing matches and homicides (Phillips & Hensley, 1984). Few have demonstrated a link, and where correlations do exist they are weak and typically nonlinear (e.g., Gantz et al., 2006) or heavily scrutinized (e.g., Phillips, 1983; Phillips & Hensley, 1984). But still, we have all seen the mass fights in soccer stadiums around the world. We have watched the news reports of riots after championship wins. Surely, a link must exist, and of course from a theoretical perspective it does.

The learning of aggressive behaviors in a mediated setting, like those found in many televised sports, has been empirically demonstrated countless times (see Pajares, Prestin, Chen, & Nabi, Chapter 19, this volume, and Bushman, Huesmann, & Whitaker, Chapter 24, this volume). Moreover, sports contain many contextual features—liked perpetrators being rewarded for committing sanctioned and justified acts of violence that result in minimal consequences—that have been identified as potential disinhibitors of real-world aggression. Thus, to postulate that viewers can learn to act aggressively from watching sports violence seems reasonable. Frustration brought on by a favored team losing might result in an aggressive response (Miller, 1941), especially if the game included violence (or aggressive cues; Berkowitz, 1989). Further, as was noted earlier, sports violence can lead to hostile thoughts, and perhaps more importantly increased levels of arousal. According to excitation transfer theory, if a subsequent stimulus elicits anger or hostility in the viewer, then the residual excitation from the sports action may compound one's emotional experience, theoretically creating a setting more likely to result in aggressive behaviors. Partner these with group contagion, alcohol, crowds, and noise, and the recipe for social aggression seems high (see Wann et al., 2001). And surely we have seen the end results, as mentioned before. High-profile examples of sports-related aggression aside, the direct and unique contribution of live sports viewing to personal aggression is difficult to measure. But the culture of aggression that pervades sports (and arguably, society) at all levels—from soccer moms yelling at referees to baseball fathers killing umpires, from professional basketball players beating their spouses to them attacking spectators in the stands, from high school athletes being arrested for rape to professional athletes being arrested for murder—is most certainly influenced and perpetuated by the violence, sanctioned or not, found in the games themselves. Continuing to tease out the unique influence of media in that cycle will be the work of scholars for decades to come.

◆ *Concluding Thoughts*

The nature of live televised sports and the emotional stake that viewers have in the outcomes based on team affiliations make the potential effects quite diverse and distinct. At the same time, the unique qualities of the action—especially when it comes to the way viewers actually *perceive* the play—complicate the study of media sports. In the preceding paragraphs, I have attempted to outline the breadth of sports media effects from live television viewing. I trust that the reader can see that, despite this breadth, many more avenues of inquiry exist.

Moreover, a new arena for sports media effects studies has emerged, as live sporting events are finding a home on newer media technologies. Professional baseball games have been streamed in real time on MLB.com since 2002; CBS began live streaming of NCAA men's basketball tournament games the same year. Many major college athletic programs have started doing the same, especially for non-revenue-generating sports. With new cellular technologies, these events can be watched and enjoyed literally from anywhere. Additionally, sports titles constitute 17% of the U.S. video game market (Entertainment Software Association, 2008), generating more than $1.2 billion in sales (Doty, 2005). These games, of course, allow you to virtually participate in all forms of simulated live sports action, from alpine skiing to wakeboarding. Further, the nearly $2 billion online fantasy sports industry in the U.S. (Dahle, 2008) now gives fans the opportunity to simulate the managing of live team sports events, redefining sports fanship as fantasy players must negotiate rooting for their favorite teams and their virtual ones (which might include an athlete from a hated rival). With the emergence of these newer media technologies, the landscape for research endeavors is quickly expanding.

The place of sports in our entertainment society is indisputable. As noted, the effects from consuming sports media are surely varied and complex and will only continue to be so in the digital era. With this in mind, I encourage the next generation of scholars not to ignore but to embrace these significant media texts and to further investigate their role in and impact on society.

◆ *References*

American Gaming Association. (2008). *Industry issues detail: Sports wagering.* Retrieved February 27, 2008, from http://www.american gaming.org/Industry/factsheets/issues_detail .cfv?id=16

Arms, R. L., Russell, G. W., & Sandilands, M. L. (1979). Effects of viewing aggressive sports on the hostility of spectators. *Social Psychology Quarterly, 42,* 275–279.

Bentham, J. (1931). *The theory of legislation.* London: Kegan Paul. (Original work published 1802)

Berkowitz, L. (1965). Some aspects of observed aggression. *Journal of Personality and Social Psychology, 2,* 359–369.

Berkowitz, L. (1989). Frustration-aggression hypothesis: Examination and reformulation. *Psychological Bulletin, 106,* 59–73.

Berkowitz, L., & Geen, R. G. (1966). Film violence and the cue properties of available targets. *Journal of Personality and Social Psychology, 3,* 525–530.

Bernhardt, P. C., Dabbs, J. M., Fielden, J. A., & Lutter, C. D. (1998). Testosterone changes during vicarious experiences of winning and losing among fans at sporting events. *Physiology and Behaviors, 18,* 263–268.

Branscombe, N. R., & Wann, D. L. (1994). Collective self-esteem consequences of out-group derogation when a valued social identity is on trial. *European Journal of Social Psychology, 24,* 641–657.

Bryant, J., Brown, D., Comisky, P. W., & Zillmann, D. (1982). Sports and spectators: Commentary and appreciation. *Journal of Communication, 32,* 109–119.

Bryant, J., Comisky, P., & Zillmann, D. (1977). Drama in sports commentary. *Journal of Communication, 27,* 140–149.

Bryant, J., Comisky, P., & Zillmann, D. (1981). The appeal of rough-and-tumble play in televised professional football. *Communication Quarterly, 29,* 256–262.

Bryant, J., Rockwell, S. C., & Owens, J. W. (1994). "Buzzer beaters" and "barn burners": The effects on enjoyment of watching the game go "down to the wire." *Journal of Sport & Social Issues, 18,* 326–339.

Bryant, J., Zillmann, D., & Raney, A. A. (1998). Violence and the enjoyment of mediated sport. In L. A. Wenner (Ed.), *MediaSport* (pp. 252–265). London: Routledge.

Cialdini, R. B., Borden, R. J., Thorne, A., Walker, M. R., Freeman, S., & Sloan, L. R. (1976). Basking in reflected glory: Three (football) field studies. *Journal of Personality and Social Psychology, 34,* 366–375.

Cialdini, R. B., & Richardson, K. D. (1980). Two indirect tactics of image management: Basking and blasting. *Journal of Personality and Social Psychology, 39,* 406–415.

Comisky, P., Bryant, J., & Zillmann, D. (1977). Commentary as a substitute for action. *Journal of Communication, 27,* 150–153.

Dahle, S. (2008, April 2). *Fantasy sports become big business.* ABC News. Retreived April 10, 2008, from http://www.abcnews.go.com

DeNeui, D. L., & Sachau, D. A. (1996). Spectator enjoyment of aggression in intercollegiate hockey games. *Journal of Sport and Social Issues, 20,* 69–77.

Doty, C. (2005, January 24). Most wanted: Drilling down/sports video games. *New York Times.* Retrieved April 10, 2008, from http://nytimes.com

Drake, B., & Pandey, S. (1996). Do child abuse rates increase on those days on which professional sporting events are held? *Journal of Family Violence, 11,* 205–218.

Eastman, S. T., & Land, A. (1997). The best of both worlds: Sports fans find good seats at the bar. *Journal of Sports & Social Issues, 21,* 156–178.

Eastman, S. T., & Riggs, K. E. (1994). Televised sports and ritual: Fan experiences. *Sociology of Sport Journal, 11,* 149–174.

Entertainment Software Association. (2008). Facts and research: Sales and genre data. Retrieved April 10, 2008, from http://www.theesa.com

Gan, S.-L., Tuggle, C. A., Mitrook, M. A., Coussement, S. H., & Zillmann, D. (1997). The thrill of a close game: Who enjoys it and who doesn't? *Journal of Sport & Social Issues, 21,* 53–64.

Gantz, W. (1981). An exploration of viewing motives and behaviors associated with television sports. *Journal of Broadcasting, 25,* 263–275.

Gantz, W., Bradley, S. D., & Wang, Z. (2006). Televised NFL games, the family, and domestic violence. In A. A. Raney & J. Bryant (Eds.), *Handbook of sports and media* (pp. 365–382). Mahwah, NJ: Erlbaum.

Gantz, W., & Wenner, L. A. (1991). Men, women, and sports: Audience experiences and effects. *Journal of Broadcasting & Electronic Media, 35,* 233–243.

Gantz, W., Wenner, L. A., Carrico, C., & Knorr, M. (1995). Televised sports and marital relationships. *Sociology of Sport Journal, 12,* 306–323.

Goldstein, J. H. (Ed.). (1989). *Why we watch: The attractions of violent programming.* New York: Oxford University Press.

Goldstein, J. H., & Arms, R. L. (1971). Effects of observing athletic contests on hostility. *Sociometry, 34,* 83–90.

Gunter, B. (2006). Sport, violence, and the media. In A. A. Raney & J. Bryant (Eds.), *Handbook of sports and media* (pp. 353–364). Mahwah, NJ: Erlbaum.

Hettich, R. R. (2001). The relationship between viewing violent sports on television and negative marital interactions. *Dissertation Abstracts International Part B: Science & Engineering, 62*(4-B), 2059.

Hillmann, C., Cuthbert, B., Bradley, M., & Lang, P. (2004). Motivated engagement to appetitive and aversive fanship cues: Psychophysiological responses of rival sports fans. *Journal of Sports & Exercise Psychology, 26,* 338–351.

Hillmann, C., Cuthbert, B., Curaugh, J., Schupp, H., Bradley, M., & Lang, P. (2000). Psychophysiological responses of identified sports fans. *Motivation and Emotion, 24,* 13–28.

Hirt, E. R., Zillmann, D., Erickson, G. A., & Kennedy, C. (1992). Costs and benefits of allegiance: Changes in fans' self-ascribed competencies after team victory versus defeat. *Journal of Personality and Social Psychology, 63,* 724–738.

Karp, D. A., & Yoels, W. C. (1990). Sport and urban life. *Journal of Sports & Social Issues, 14,* 77–102.

Kimble, C. E., & Cooper, B. P. (1992). Association and disassociation by football fans. *Perceptual and Motor Skills, 75,* 303–309.

Knobloch-Westerwick, S., David, P., Eastin, M., Tamborini, R., & Greenwood, D. (2008, May). *Sports spectators' suspense: Affect and uncertainty in sports entertainment.* Paper presented at the annual meeting of the International Communication Association, Montreal, Canada.

Lever, J. (1983). *Soccer madness.* Chicago: University of Chicago Press.

Madrigal, R. (1995). Cognitive and affective determinants of fan satisfaction with sporting event attendance. *Journal of Leisure Research, 27,* 205–227.

Melnick, M. J. (1993). Searching for sociability in the stands: A theory of sports spectating. *Journal of Sports Management, 7,* 44–60.

Miller, N. E. (1941). The frustration-aggression hypothesis. *Psychological Review, 48,* 337–342.

Miller, T. Q., Heath, L., Molcan, J. R., & Dugoni, B. L. (1990). Imitative violence in the real world: A reanalysis of homicide rates following championship prize fights. *Aggressive Behavior, 17,* 121–134.

Owens, J. B., & Bryant, J. (1998, July). *The effects of a hometeam ("homer") announcer and color commentator on audience perceptions and enjoyment of a sports contest.* Paper presented at the annual meeting of the International Communication Association, Jerusalem, Israel.

Peterson, E., & Raney, A. A. (2008). Exploring the complexity of suspense as a predictor of mediated sports enjoyment. *Journal of Broadcasting & Electronic Media, 52*(4), 544-562.

Phillips, D. P. (1983). The impact of mass media violence on U.S. homicides. *American Sociological Review, 48,* 560–568.

Phillips, D. P., & Hensley, J. E. (1984). When violence is rewarded or punished: The impact of mass media stories on homicide. *Journal of Communication, 34,* 101–116.

Raney, A. A. (2006). Why we watch and enjoy mediated sports. In A. A. Raney & J. Bryant (Eds.), *Handbook of sports and media* (pp. 313–329). Mahwah, NJ: Erlbaum.

Raney, A. A., & Depalma, A. (2006). The effect of viewing varying levels of aggressive sports programming on enjoyment, mood, and perceived violence. *Mass Communication and Society, 9,* 321–338.

Raney, A. A., & Kinnally, W. (2006, June). *The thrill of victory and the agony of defeat? The complexity of enjoyment in rivalry game wins and losses.* Paper presented at the annual meeting of the International Communication Conference, Dresden, Germany.

Raney, A. A., & Kinnally, W. (2007, May). *Examining perceived violence in and enjoyment of televised rivalry sports contests.* Paper presented at the annual meeting of the International Communication Association, San Francisco, CA.

Sargent, S. L., Zillmann, D., & Weaver, J. B. (1998). The gender gap in the enjoyment of televised sports. *Journal of Sports & Social Issues, 22,* 46–64.

Schwarz, N., Strack, F., Kommer, D., & Wagner, D. (1987). Soccer, rooms, and the quality of your life: Mood effects on judgments of satisfaction with life in general and with specific domains. *European Journal of Social Psychology, 7,* 69–79.

Schweitzer, K., Zillmann, D., Weaver, J. B., & Luttrell, E. S. (1992). Perception of threatening events in the emotional aftermath of a televised college football game. *Journal of Broadcasting & Electronic Media, 36,* 75–82.

Sloan, L. R. (1979). The function and impact of sports for fans: A review of theory and contemporary research. In J. H. Goldstein (Ed.), *Sports, games, and play: Social and psychological viewpoints* (pp. 219–262). Hillsdale, NJ: Erlbaum.

Smith, G. J. (1988). The noble sports fan. *Journal of Sport & Social Issues, 12,* 54–65.

Smith, M. (1983). *Violence and sport.* Toronto: Butterworths.

Snyder, C. R., Higgins, R. L., & Stucky, R. J. (1983). *Excuses: Masquerades in search of grace.* New York: Wiley-Interscience.

Snyder, C. R., Lassegard, M., & Ford, C. E. (1986). Distancing after group success and failure: Basking in reflected glory and cutting off reflected failure. *Journal of Personality and Social Psychology, 51,* 382–388.

Sullivan, D. B. (1991). Commentary and viewer perception of player hostility: Adding punch to televised sport. *Journal of Broadcasting & Electronic Media, 35,* 487–504.

Tamborini, R., & Lachlan, K. (2004, May). *Disposition toward perpetrator, motives for violence, and attitudes toward aggression: An examination of shifts in latitudes of acceptance.* Paper presented at the annual

meeting of the International Communication Association, New Orleans, LA.

Tüzünkan, F. (2007). *The role of morality and physical attractiveness of athletes on disposition formation.* Unpublished doctoral dissertation, Florida State University.

Vorderer, P., Wulff, H. J., & Friedrichsen, M. (1996). *Suspense: Conceptualizations, theoretical analyses, and empirical explorations.* Mahwah, NJ: Erlbaum.

Wann, D. L. (1995). Preliminary validation of the Sports Fan Motivational Scale. *Journal of Sport & Social Issues, 19,* 377–396.

Wann, D. L., & Branscombe, N. R. (1990a). Die-hard and fair-weather fans: Effects of identification on BIRGing and CORFing tendencies. *Journal of Sport & Social Issues, 14,* 103–117.

Wann, D. L., & Branscombe, N. R. (1990b). Person perception when aggressive or non-aggressive sports are primed. *Aggressive Behavior, 16,* 27–32.

Wann, D. L., Carlson, J. D., & Schrader, M. P. (1999). The impact of team identification on the hostile and instrumental verbal aggression of sport spectators. *Journal of Social Behavior and Personality, 14,* 279–286.

Wann, D. L., Melnick, M. J., Russell, G. W., & Pease, D. G. (2001). *Sports fans: The psychology and social impact of spectators.* New York: Routledge.

Wann, D. L., Schrader, M. P., & Adamson, D. R. (1998). The cognitive and somatic anxiety of sport spectators. *Journal of Sport Behavior, 21,* 322–337.

Wenner, L. A., & Gantz, W. (1998). Watching sports on television: Audience experience, gender, fanship, and marriage. In L. A. Wenner (Ed.), *MediaSport* (pp. 233–251). London: Routledge.

White, G. F., Katz, J., & Scarborough, K. E. (1992). The impact of professional football games upon violent assaults on women. *Violence and Victims, 7,* 157–171.

Young, K. M. (2000). Sport and violence. In J. Coakley & E. Dunning (Eds.), *Handbook of sport studies* (pp. 382–407). Thousand Oaks, CA: Sage.

Zillmann, D., & Bryant, J. (1994). Entertainment as media effect. In J. Bryant & D. Zillmann (Eds.), *Media effects: Advances in theory and research* (pp. 437–462). Hillsdale, NJ: Erlbaum.

Zillmann, D., Bryant, J., & Sapolsky, B. (1989). Enjoyment from sports spectatorship. In J. H. Goldstein (Ed.), *Sports, games, and play:* *Social and psychological viewpoints* (2nd ed., pp. 241–278). Hillsdale, NJ: Erlbaum.

Zillmann, D., & Paulus, P. B. (1993). Spectators: Reactions to sports events and effects on athletic performance. In R. N. Singer, M. Murphey, & L. K. Tennant (Eds.), *Handbook of research on sports psychology* (pp. 600–619). New York: Macmillan.

30

DIGITAL GAMES

◆ Peter Vorderer and Ute Ritterfeld

This chapter aims to conceptualize and systematize the past decade's theoretical and empirical work on digital games.[1] We focus on the social scientific perspective, with special consideration for advances in communication science and media psychology theories and research. Therefore, we do not cover the history of (developing) digital games (e.g., Lowood, 2006), their content (cf. B. Smith, 2006; S. Smith, 2006), design (Moore, 2007), meaning, or philosophy (cf. Jahn-Sudmann & Stockmann, 2008). Rather this chapter highlights their use by and impact on players, as well as their appeal around the globe. We call this research area "playing digital games" to emphasize this particular point of view. We begin with a brief overview of the prevalence and types of digital games and their users (though these numbers are changing rapidly) to demonstrate the relevance of digital games for modern life and modern societies, and as a topic of research within our own disciplines. Next, we divide the "playing digital games" research into two subareas: (a) individual processes that precede the individual playing activity ("preexposure") and (b) processes that follow using digital games ("postexposure"). The latter processes include the many various effects of playing digital games and have received the most attention, both within academia and in the public discourse. Therefore, we further distinguish between two domains of research within postexposure processes. The first concerns games that users select for entertainment purposes but that often may have detrimental effects on those users.

The second examines the more recently developed types of games that are meant to be educational (often called "serious games").

Who is playing? According to the latest numbers of the U.S.-based Entertainment Software Association (Entertainment Software Association, 2008), 69% of heads of U.S. households play computer and video games (referring to an almost obsolete distinction between games that are played on a computer in contrast to those that are played on a Playstation, Xbox, Wii, or other console). The average game buyer (again, in the U.S.) is 40 years old, and the average game player age is 33, where 28.2% are under 18 years; 47.6% are between 18 and 49 years old; and 24.2% are 50 years and older. Players in the United States spend between 7 and 8 hours (men play an average of 7.6 and women an average of 7.4 hours) per week on this activity, with currently 44% of the most frequent players stating that they play online (Entertainment Software Association, 2008).

Although usage of digital games elsewhere may differ somewhat from that in the United States (e.g., due to a greater popularity of the Playstation in Asia than in the U.S.), the overall trend seems clear: Playing digital (computer, console, online) games has become a major leisure-time activity for boys, girls, men, and women—at least in industrialized and wealthy nations around the world. The use of digital games is not restricted to only a particular group of people, nor are children and adolescents the only ones who spend time playing digital games (for an overview, see Vorderer & Bryant, 2006).

No doubt, this development will affect not only individuals who regularly use those games but also societies at large. Digital games have already changed the way people communicate and socialize, entertain themselves and learn, work and play, trade and negotiate, teach and understand. These daily life experiences are likely to change further, as new forms and applications of digital gaming emerge. Nevertheless, treatment of these issues by academic disciplines such as communication science and media psychology do not yet reflect digital games' individual and societal importance. Only a few edited volumes covering various aspects of people playing digital games have been published (e.g., Raessens & Goldstein, 2005; Vorderer & Bryant, 2006), as well as a few others that focus on rather narrow topics, such as learning through digital games (cf. Gee, 2003, 2007; Ritterfeld, Cody, & Vorderer, in press b). Although some volumes are written in languages other than English (e.g., in German: Kaminski & Lorber, 2006; Quandt, Wimmer, & Wolling, 2008; von Salisch, Kristen, & Oppl, 2007), most of the work is still published in mainstream communication journals (e.g., *Journal of Communication, Human Communication Research, Media Psychology*). Consequently, the published research emphasizes empirical (mainly experimental) work about the interest in playing digital games and about the effects of playing them, rather than theory building. In fact, most of the theories applied to explain interest in games and the effects of playing them have been incorporated into and applied to this topic from other areas of communication research and media psychology (e.g., mood management theory, affective disposition theory; cf. Bryant & Davies, 2006). Only a few scholars (e.g., Klimmt, 2003) have introduced new theoretical conceptualizations that account for the interactive nature of digital game play, perhaps because this approach diverges from those traditionally used to explain the use of noninteractive media, for example, watching TV.

◆ Preexposure

Theoretical approaches that focus on the situation *before* an individual player decides to play and the factors that determine media selection for an upcoming session typically try to explain *why* somebody plays digital games. These perspectives assume that understanding the situation players come from can explain why they play and why they select the games they do. These attempts, at least in communication research and media psychology, include reference to the personalities (e.g., Hartmann & Klimmt, 2006) of and the gratifications sought by players (Sherry, Lucas, Greenberg, & Lachlan, 2006), players' evolutionary history (Ohler & Nieding, 2006), and players' intrinsic motivation (Raney, Smith, & Baker, 2006).

The uses-and-gratifications perspective posits that specific game genres, or even individual games, can provide gratifications that a user seeks to a greater or lesser degree. The player selects these genres or games as a result (cf. Sherry, 2001; Sherry et al., 2006). Game play can satisfy specific psychological motives such as *sensation seeking* (Slater, 2003), *competition/challenge* (Vorderer, Hartmann, & Klimmt, 2006), and *interest in experiencing presence* (Tamborini & Skalski, 2006). The ability of certain games to satisfy these motives has been used to explain users' selection of games. More generally, players' interest may be a result of the games' appeal to needs humans have developed as an evolutionary advantage, which may no longer be evolutionarily adaptive but still encourage this particular behavior (Ohler & Nieding, 2006).

The most prominent example of such a motivational approach, however, has been the application of affective disposition theory, that is, considering digital game play to be a form of selective exposure. This perspective considers the selection of game playing in general, as well as the selection of a specific game, to follow some psychological regularities. The most prominent theory has been called "mood management" within communication research (Bryant & Davies, 2006; Raney et al., 2006), whereas nonacademic contexts often refer to the phenomenon as "escapism." These concepts differ in their theoretical complexity, specificity, and empirical utility. For example, the concept of escapism has had a long history in

disciplines other than communication (e.g., in the humanities) and outside academia, but it is not based on any well-defined theoretical assumptions, nor does the concept have much remarkable empirical support. Although mood management seems to reduce the complexity of a media user's decision process to a single dimension (i.e., choosing a media product that promises to enhance one's mood), its empirical support is overwhelming. The more inclusive concept behind mood management is "selective exposure," which claims that the selection of specific media content follows mood management. To date, the selective exposure research seems to be the most differentiated, best specified, and most empirically supported. Hence, its application on the selection of digital games is among the most promising (cf. Bryant & Davies, 2006).

However, newer theoretical advancements have attempted to surpass mood management theory in explaining the appeal of recently developed entertaining products such as digital games. One such approach emphasizes the fact that media products like games are interactive (i.e., they are used in an interactive way) and therefore provide users with novel modes of entertainment (Vorderer, 2000). Klimmt (2003), for example, has pointed out that a player's individual entertainment experience needs to be described and explained on various levels simultaneously, as users can feel differently at the same time because they are able to have simultaneous yet distinct experiences while playing. According to this model, "effectance," "suspense," "pride through achievement," and an "improved self-image through identification with a game character" belong to the most important, yet diverse, modes of experience. Klimmt argues that the entertainment experience a game provides is a dynamic and complex product of these possibly divergent responses.

This argument is consistent with other, newer perspectives that describe entertainment experiences by pointing out that they usually serve *various* functions at the same time:

Media offerings, or more precisely situations that include the use of media offerings, are entertaining if they satisfy a user's need to maintain physiological and psychological balance. Successful homeostatic regulation causes pleasure, whereas sensory stimulation is unpleasant if it fosters severe imbalance. Comprehension and resolution of cognitive incongruencies are likely to result in positive affect, whereas a lack of cognitive challenges, or incongruencies that are overly complex, create aversion or disinterest. The user's involvement in the media offering triggers both positive and negative primary emotions. (Vorderer & Hartmann, 2009, pp. 544–545)

This conceptualization distinguishes between the mechanisms assumed necessary to elicit homeostatic regulation, and other processes just described as "mood regulation" or "mood management." These two lines of theorizing have developed independently from each other. The latter has been studied mainly in communication science and in media psychology and was applied particularly to entertainment experiences of media users by referring to the term *pleasure* (cf. Bryant & Vorderer, 2006, for an overview). The inclusion of "meta-emotions" as part of this experience has recently advanced this approach. Incorporating meta-emotions, the approach suggests that media users are not only entertained by content they are exposed to; they also enjoy the ongoing chain of their own primary affective responses. The meta-emotion rests on the appreciation of both the continuing chain of sensory stimulation and the primary emotions stimulated by the present environment, *and* is maintained by the mood-regulating user throughout a certain episode (cf. Bartsch, Vorderer, Mangold, & Viehoff, 2008).

In contrast, the first line of research has roots in the psychology of perception and art, a tradition systematized by Berlyne (1974) and recently advanced by Silvia (2005, 2006), more often referring to terms

like *comprehension* or *interest*. Taken together, media users' motivation to become entertained with digital games can be conceptualized as a *combination* of their need to manage and regulate their moods (where pleasure seems to be the ultimate goal) and to *also* and *simultaneously* elicit and experience various affects by exposing themselves to challenges that will provide understanding and resolution (a goal that could best be described by the word "comprehension").

The difference between entertainment experiences in the context of digital games and those felt in other media environments (e.g., in front of a TV) could be that comprehension is more important than pleasure when playing a digital game than it is when watching TV (or playing a game more for mood management than for the challenge it can provide). Alternatively, it seems likely that pleasure is more important than comprehension for selecting a TV show. These two components of entertainment seeking via homeostatic regulation (both physiological and psychological balance) produce *enjoyment* (as an outcome of this balance). As theoretical constructs, they provide a possible explanation for why people approach and use digital games (and other media formats).

However, some recent publications in entertainment theory have expressed concern that much of what has been described as the core of the entertainment experience reduces the complexity of this experience to rather immediate, lower-order functions of exposure (Oliver, 2008, in press; Oliver & Raney, 2008; Vorderer, Klimmt, & Ritterfeld, 2004). According to their reasoning, another component or dimension to the experience of entertainment—one that tries to go beyond immediate enjoyment—seems to be missing, and that is *appreciation* (e.g., Oliver, 2008, in press). We believe that the best way to conceptualize this dimension is through self-determination theory (Deci & Ryan, 1985; Ryan & Deci, 2000) and to claim that all entertainment experiences should be considered in light of both the immediate but lower-level functions of homeostatic regulation (enjoyment) *and* the less immediate, higher-order goals, such as *autonomy, competence,* and *relatedness.* Vorderer, Steen, and Chan (2006) have already pointed out that these global motives, and entertainment products, which are able to satisfy these needs, can provide explanations for media users' interest in entertainment programs. While watching TV, for example, viewers can feel autonomous (they aren't forced to watch), competent (the programs don't overwhelm them), and related (to coviewers but also to those who appear in the media). But when playing a digital game, these experiences are even more pronounced (Ryan, Rigby, & Przybylski, 2006), which makes games one of the most appropriate media to satisfy these needs. In accordance with conceptualizations by Oliver (2008, in press), we propose to call this dimension of entertainment seeking "appreciation."

How do enjoyment and appreciation go together? It seems as if both can be achieved at the same time, if someone is embedded in an entertainment context. However, enjoyment seeking as a motive seems to be not only more immediate and context specific, but also easier to satisfy via a given entertainment product or situation. These situations are basically what entertainment research has already successfully studied, particularly in the tradition of Zillmann and his collaborators (e.g., Bryant, Roskos-Ewoldsen, & Cantor, 2003). Appreciation, in contrast, is broader, more cross-situational, and applicable to many different human activities. Therefore, it should be affected but not fundamentally altered by a specific media experience. In other words, although a game player can satisfy his or her need for enjoyment by playing a specific game, the need for appreciation, in contrast, depends on the experience of autonomy, competence, and relatedness, all of which can also be felt while playing, but will not be completely satisfied (see Figure 30.1).

This two-level model of entertainment motivation allows us to derive a number

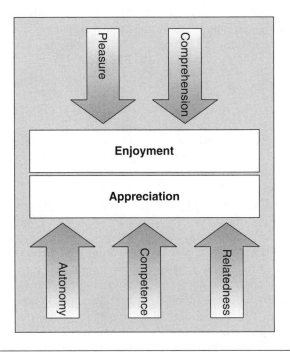

Figure 30.1   A Two-Level Model of Entertainment Motivation

of meaningful empirical questions: What happens if a specific game can only satisfy some of the player's needs and interests, and does it make a difference whether those needs that are or that are not satisfied are conceptualized on the same level? Can the satisfaction of one goal compensate for the nonsatisfaction of another goal, and does it matter whether these goals are on the same level? Would players rather compromise their higher-order or lower-order needs, and how does this depend on the person or on the situation?

◆ Postexposure

The study of what follows a user's interaction with a digital game (e.g., the effects or consequences of playing) has become two separate lines of research, and it is interesting to note that the two lines seldom intersect. It's *either* about the detrimental *or* about the positive (i.e., the educational) effects of playing. First, we briefly overview findings about the detrimental effects of digital games. Subsequently we turn to what often has been called "serious gaming," that is, the topic of learning, education, and change through game-play.

Entertainment games and violence. In terms of the detrimental effects, a well-established field of research has investigated the effects of playing primarily entertaining games and those that contain violence or seem to trivialize violent content, in particular. Nearly all of this research follows one of three or four theoretical paradigms (cf. Lee & Peng, 2006; Weber, Ritterfeld, & Kostygina, 2006). The first is Bandura's social cognitive theory (Bandura, 2001), which has not only become the most prominent theory of media effects in most areas of communication but has also influenced many scholars' attempts to explain how, when, and why a digital game player learns to become violent—if the game's violence is explicitly justified (Funk & Buchman, 1996). Next is

Zillmann's excitation transfer theory (1988), which aggression research and entertainment research have applied broadly. The theory describes the transfer of residual excitation from one exposure to media content as intensifying the individual's subsequent response to new content either additional media content or a situation following the initial exposure (cf., e.g., Calvert & Tan, 1994). Third, the study of "cognitive priming" in social psychology has found a number of applications in media research as well, particularly for the study of effects of exposure to violent media content. This perspective suggests that exposure to violent content or playing violent games increases the accessibility of individuals' aggressive cognitions, which ultimately will result in more aggressive behaviors (due to the cognitions' increased accessibility and salience), even in a wholly separate social context (Anderson & Dill, 2000). A fourth line of research follows communication research's own cultivation approach (cf. Gerbner, Gross, Morgan, Signorielli, & Shanahan, 2002), which we will not elaborate on because it has not yet been applied to digital games, despite the fact that it seems to be a very promising perspective, particularly for this sort of problem (cf. van Mierlo & van den Bulck, 2004).

Anderson and his collaborators (Anderson & Bushman, 2001; Anderson & Dill, 2000) have tried to integrate these theoretical perspectives, and they have proposed the general aggression model (GAM). Today, the GAM is seen as the most important model to explain both short- and long-term effects of playing violent games (and those of exposure to other types of media content as well). These effects include changes in media users' thinking (cognitions), feeling (affects), and acting (behavior), and imply alterations in their physiological arousal, aggressive attitudes, hostility biases, and desensitization. The personality of a player of violent digital games also changes over time, which can lead to changes in his or her social and media environments and the selection of even more violent content. This ultimately results in a downward spiral of violence as aggressive behaviors are consistently reinforced (Lee & Peng, 2006; Slater, Henry, Swaim, & Anderson, 2003).

Regarding empirical evidence of the negative effects of digital game playing, researchers are in a rather comfortable situation of having access to three meta-analyses, all published in the past few years, that focus on this very topic (Anderson, 2004; Anderson & Bushman, 2001; Sherry, 2001). Anderson and Bushman's (2001) early analysis involved 33 independent tests and a total of more than 3,000 participants. The relation between digital game violence and aggressive behavior revealed an effect size ($r = .19$) that was positive and significant but rather small. It was bigger for aggressive cognitions ($r = .27$) than for aggressive affects ($r = .18$). Sherry (2001) covered 25 independent studies and found an effect size even smaller ($r = .15$), with more than 2,700 subjects included. It is important to note that Sherry also identified the strongest relationship between the effect sizes and the year a game was released, that is, the more recently a game was released, the more intensive its negative effects. However, the relation between aggression and playing time was negative, that is, the more time players spend with the digital game, the smaller the effects. Finally, Anderson (2004) provided the most recent meta-analysis, expanding his initial study by including more than 5,000 participants. The previously claimed connection between violence and aggressive behavior was reconfirmed ($r = .20$). More interestingly, this time he distinguished between "best practice" and "non-best practice" studies (based on their methodological rigor) and showed that the less rigorous studies showed smaller effect sizes than the more rigorous ones ($r = .26$).

Given these results, it is hard to doubt the potentially detrimental effects of playing violent digital games. Nevertheless, three main questions that are important for a more general verdict about games remain unanswered: First, it becomes clear that the existing literature on the effects of playing violent games has focused on the effects of the *content* of games. Lee and Peng (2006) have proposed that researchers also focus on the media *forms*, given that forms such as size, fidelity, and cuts influence media effects (cf. Reeves & Nass, 1996). Second, there is lack of research on how players *understand* games (Lee & Peng, 2006; Weber et al., 2006). Most studies have implied that the effects of games on their users are rather direct and immediate, and occur without mental elaborations on the user's part. This is similar to studying the impact of a literary text by counting the number of words the text contains but ignoring how readers interpret and make meaning from the text. Although this perspective conforms to other traditions of the media effects literature such as TV research, the approach is no longer justifiable. Finally, longitudinal studies on the effects of playing games are still necessary and lacking. Most effects will only materialize over time, and one could argue that the long-term effects on adolescents (e.g., on their psychological development) or on society are the most important ones. Of course, long-term effects are also the most difficult and costly to study. This fact might explain the present lack of results available from long-term studies, but it doesn't excuse it any longer.

Serious games for learning. The term *serious games* emerged through the attempt of educators, trainers, and advocates to utilize the motivational potential of digital games for serious purposes. The implicit or explicit understanding was that the success of entertainment games gives proof that (some of those) games offer a unique set of features that elicit deliberate and enduring gaming. As motivating someone for deliberate practice defines one of the biggest challenges in education, these features were supposed to be harvested in an educational setting (Gee, 2003, 2007).

The U.S. military was one of the first agencies to recognize the inherent potential of games and to invest significant funds for new developments, which have been tremendously successful (e.g., *America's Army*). At the same time, education for children within and outside the curriculum was targeted by less economically powerful agencies such as schools, museums, or small companies devoted to enriching learning experiences for children and adolescents. Their attempts resulted in much less sophisticated games that often did not fulfill the promise of an engaging learning experience (Shen, Wang, & Ritterfeld, in press).

Over the last few years, another area for serious games emerged with only a few applications in the beginning but growing to become one of the highly successful and recognized serious games domains: games for health promotion. Such games target all age-groups and a wide range of health areas, including games for prevention, attitude or behavior change, or posttreatment care. Some of those games are high-profile developments (e.g., *Re-Mission* by Hope Lab) that can even compete with entertainment games in terms of technical capacities, game play, and aesthetics (Shen et al., in press).

Ratan and Ritterfeld (in press) created a database of all self-acclaimed serious games in 2007 and found that more than half of all those games were devoted to academic education, whereas health games account for roughly 10% and military games for about 5% of serious games. A somewhat higher distribution (15%) was observed for the fourth of five clusters, that is, games for social change, whereas the fifth cluster, games for occupational training, received about 10% of all counts. Games for social change are those that intend to increase awareness about social and political issues and may also develop social participation (e.g., *Darfur Is Dying*). Companies may create games for occupational training to facilitate internal communication or to specifically address

professional skills such as medical care, accounting, or law practice (e.g., *Objection*). It can be assumed that the prevalence of this cluster is underestimated due to a lack of publicity of within-company developments.

Thus, serious games are recognized as such because they have been developed with the intention of a serious impact, that is, the ambition to elicit the desired effects without having unintended, negative effects (cf. Ritterfeld et al., in press b). The targeted intention is hereby defined by the agency that develops or commissions the game design. However, this intention is by no means equivalent to a serious effect. Strictly speaking, serious games are all games that are considered serious by some agency without taking into account whether the implied promise of a well-intended effect does hold true. No doubt, the seriousness of the built-in intentions can be criticized. For example, so-called marketing games may be serious games because their primary purpose is not entertainment. However, their objective to increase consumption may cause one to question the acclaimed seriousness (Ratan & Ritterfeld, in press). More important, the overlap between intended impacts and those achieved requires empirical research. An impressive number of effect studies have been conducted on serious games over the last decade, demonstrating the potential effectiveness of the medium (for an overview, see Durkin, 2006; Lee & Peng, 2006; Lieberman, 2006; Ritterfeld & Weber, 2006). However, these studies all suffer from a lack of generalizability (Watt, in press). As the nature of digital games is interactive, the game play is different in each single situation (Klimmt, Vorderer, & Ritterfeld, 2007). Consequently, the term *serious games* should be replaced by the concept of serious gaming, as Jenkins et al. (in press) recently proposed.

However, if serious gaming is the ultimate goal, the well-established dichotomy of serious versus entertainment games becomes obsolete: Serious gaming may be the result of playing a game that was designed with a serious purpose. But serious gaming may as well be caused by entertainment games (Ritterfeld, in press). Many commercial games that were developed from an entertainment perspective contain possibilities for educational experiences (Ritterfeld & Weber, 2006), either because they depict detailed and accurate content (e.g., history or science) or because they require sensory, cognitive (e.g., spatial navigation), or even social skills that may be cultivated over time.

Ratan and Ritterfeld (in press) identified four underlying psychological mechanisms embedded in serious games: skill practice, knowledge gain through exploration, cognition, and social problem solving. According to their database, skill practice is the primary mechanism for the majority of all serious games. Practice is undoubtedly important for learning. Nevertheless, this finding implies that most of these games do not target more sophisticated, deeper learning. In this respect, the potential of digital games is not yet fully exploited. It is therefore not surprising that most of these skill-focused games that have been shown to effectively facilitate learning are not deliberately selected or deliberately played over a longer period of time by their users, but are often only prescribed by a research team instead. In some studies, incentives were even given to impose the necessary game play, which in turn triggered extrinsic motivation only (e.g., Moore, Rosenberg, & Coleman, 2005). In those cases, the expectation to harvest the potential for intrinsically motivating game play in digital games is clearly not fulfilled.

The main assumption in *entertainment-education* models is the successful blending of both (entertaining and educational) game play experiences (Ritterfeld & Weber, 2006; Wang & Singhal, in press). It is hereby suggested that entertainment makes a manifold contribution on game selection and persistence of game play. As indicated previously, the deliberate selection of a game (in contrast to its prescribed use), as well as enduring and repeated gaming, will provide the motivational basis for sustained skill practice, content processing, or problem solving and, consequently, result in deeper learning. One of the main challenges posed for entertainment education in game play is how to sustain enjoyment despite an enrichment of content. Shen et al. (in press) have already pointed to the potentially paradoxical effects of prescribing a joyful experience. Moreover, the context of game play may significantly interfere with game play experiences: People may not be willing to choose serious gaming if it competes with other leisure activities. In the school context, however, games may be a welcome alternative to more traditional pedagogy.

Wang, Shen, and Ritterfeld (in press) conducted a comprehensive analysis of game elements that accounted for enjoyment and identified five clusters, which they labeled the "Big Five in game play enjoyment." These clusters encompass technological capacity, game design, aesthetic presentation, game play entertainment experience, and narrativity. Empirical data derived from content analyses of game reviews was used to identify a hierarchy of thresholds in game enjoyment. Whereas visual and auditory technological capacity and game design define the primary threshold of games to be enjoyed at all, aesthetics are necessary for a decent game. "Super fun games" fulfill both of these two thresholds, but add an additional dimension in providing social experiences, interesting characters, and compelling storylines. Although most of the serious games on the market do not yet provide the complex quality necessary for true enjoyment, preliminary data suggest that—depending on budget and effort— they can be developed (Shen et al., in press). Such games would use entertainment features for more than motivational prompts or gratifications, but would blend the entertainment with the education experience. As a result, learning unfolds its potential rather incidentally, and the effects may vary significantly between players. Consequently, it is the responsibility of future effects studies to go beyond the effects of a particular serious game and to investigate more closely the mechanisms that scaffold learning.

◆ Concluding Comments

This short overview about "playing digital games" has aimed to very briefly conceptualize the various research developments we have observed over the past few years. As far as psychological processes are concerned that occur before players expose themselves to games, we believe that advancements in our scientific disciplines can be found rather on the theoretical than on the empirical level. We are optimistic, though, that this achievement will also lead to more systematic data–based explorations and hypothesis testing in the very near future. In respect to effects of playing digital games, we have identified a new research perspective and agenda that will hopefully complete our overall picture of what such games can and will do to players. Although there still is a need to study the various detrimental effects of playing entertaining games (including those that only occur over longer periods of time), it is time to also consider the great potential that games may have for learning and teaching. A general and one-sided verdict about the general impact of games on users will be shortsighted if it does not take into account that games can always be both a curse and a blessing to individuals and to society at large. Which of the two possible effects prevails is not only a matter of producing the appropriate games, but also of understanding the user and the fascination a game can have for him or her.

◆ Note

1. We use *digital game* as a generic term encompassing computer, video, or handheld games played on any platform, online or offline.

◆ References

Anderson, C. A. (2004). An update on the effects of playing violent video games. *Journal of Adolescence, 27,* 113–122.

Anderson, C. A., & Bushman, B. J. (2001). Effects of violent video games on aggressive behavior, aggressive cognition, aggressive affect, physiological arousal, and prosocial behavior: A meta-analytic review of the scientific literature. *Psychological Science, 12,* 353–359.

Anderson, C. A., & Dill, K. E. (2000). Video games and aggressive thoughts, feelings, and behavior in the laboratory and in life. *Journal of Personality and Social Psychology, 78,* 772–790.

Bandura, A. (2001). Social cognitive theory of mass communication. *Media Psychology, 3,* 265–299.

Bartsch, A., Vorderer, P., Mangold, R., & Viehoff, R. (2008). Appraisal of emotions in media use: Towards a process model of meta-emotion and emotion regulation. *Media Psychology, 11,* 7–27.

Berlyne, D. E. (1974). *The new experimental aesthetics: Steps toward an objective psychology of aesthetic appreciation.* Washington, DC: Hemisphere.

Bryant, J., & Davies, J. (2006). Selective exposure to video games. In P. Vorderer & J. Bryant (Eds.), *Playing video games; Motives, responses, and consequences* (pp. 181–194). Mahwah, NJ: Erlbaum.

Bryant, J., Roskos-Ewoldsen, D., & Cantor, J. (Eds.). (2003). *Communication and emotion: Essays in honor of Dolf Zillmann.* Mahwah, NJ: Erlbaum.

Bryant, J., & Vorderer, P. (Eds.). (2006). *Psychology of entertainment.* Mahwah, NJ: Erlbaum.

Calvert, S., & Tan, S. L. (1994). Impact of virtual reality on young adults' physiological arousal and aggressive thoughts: Interaction versus observation. *Journal of Applied Developmental Psychology, 15,* 125–139.

Deci, E. L., & Ryan, R. M. (1985). *Intrinsic motivation and self-determination in human behavior.* New York: Plenum.

Durkin, K. (2006). Game playing and adolescents' development. In P. Vorderer & J. Bryant (Eds.), *Playing video games: Motives, responses, and consequences* (pp. 415–428). Mahwah, NJ: Erlbaum.

Entertainment Software Association. (2008). Retrieved April 2008 from http://www .theesa.com/facts/pdfs/ESA_EF_2008.pdf

Funk, J. B., & Buchman, D. D. (1996). Playing violent video games and adolescent self-concept. *Journal of Communication, 46*, 19–32.

Gee, J. P. (2003). *What digital games have to teach us about learning and literacy.* New York: Palgrave Macmillan.

Gee, J. P. (2007). *Good digital games and good learning.* New York: Lang.

Gerbner, G., Gross, L., Morgan, M., Signorielli, N., & Shanahan, J. (2002). Growing up with television: Cultivation processes. In J. Bryant & D. Zillmann (Eds.), *Media effects: Advances in theory and research* (pp. 43–68). Mahwah, NJ: Erlbaum.

Hartmann, T., & Klimmt, C. (2006). The influence of personality factors on computer game choice. In P. Vorderer & J. Bryant (Eds.), *Playing video games: Motives, responses, and consequences* (pp. 115–131). Mahwah, NJ: Erlbaum.

Jahn-Sudmann, A., & Stockmann, R. (Eds.). (2008). *Computer games as a sociocultural phenomenon: Games without frontiers. War without tears.* New York: Palgrave Macmillan.

Jenkins, H., Camper, B., Chisholm, A., Grigsby, N., Klopfer, E., Osterweil, S., et al. (in press). From serious games to serious gaming. In U. Ritterfeld, M. Cody, & P. Vorderer (Eds.), *Serious games: Mechanisms and effects.* New York: Routledge/LEA.

Kaminski, W., & Lorber, M. (Eds.). (2006). *Computerspiele und soziale Wirklichkeit.* Munich: Kopaed.

Klimmt, C. (2003). Dimensions and determinants of the enjoyment of playing digital games: A three-level model. In M. Copier & J. Raessens (Eds.), *Level up: Digital Games Research Conference* (pp. 246–257). Utrecht: Faculty of Arts, Utrecht University.

Klimmt, C., Vorderer, P., & Ritterfeld, U. (2007). Interactivity and generalizability: New media,

new challenges? *Communication Methods and Measures, 1*(3), 169–179.

Lee, K. M., & Peng, W. (2006). What do we know about social and psychological effects of computer games? A comprehensive review of the current literature. In P. Vorderer & J. Bryant (Eds.), *Playing video games: Motives, responses, and consequences* (pp. 325–345). Mahwah, NJ: Erlbaum.

Lieberman, D. A. (2006). What can we learn from playing interactive games? In P. Vorderer & J. Bryant (Eds.), *Playing video games: Motives, responses, and consequences* (pp. 379–397). Mahwah, NJ: Erlbaum.

Lowood, H. (2006). A brief biography of computer games. In P. Vorderer & J. Bryant (Eds.), *Playing video games: Motives, responses, and consequences* (pp. 25–41). Mahwah, NJ: Erlbaum.

Moore, D. R., Rosenberg, J. F., & Coleman, J. S. (2005). Discrimination training of phonemic contrasts enhances phonological processing in mainstream school children. *Brain and Language, 94*, 72–85.

Moore, M. M. (2007). *Game design and development: Introduction to the game industry.* Upper Saddle River, NJ: Pearson Education.

Ohler, P., & Nieding, G. (2006). Why play? An evolutionary perspective. In P. Vorderer & J. Bryant (Eds.), *Playing video games: Motives, responses, and consequences* (pp. 101–113). Mahwah, NJ: Erlbaum.

Oliver, M. B. (2008). Tender affective states as predictors of entertainment preference. *Journal of Communication, 58*, 40–61.

Oliver, M. B. (in press). Affect as a predictor of entertainment choice: The utility of looking beyond pleasure. In T. Hartmann (Ed.), *Media choice: A theoretical and empirical overview.* New York: Routledge.

Oliver, M. B., & Raney, A. A. (2008, May). *Development of hedonic and eudaimonic measures of entertainment motivations: The role of affective and cognitive gratifications.* Paper presented at the annual meeting of the International Communication Association, Montréal.

Quandt, T., Wimmer, J., & Wolling, J. (Eds.). (2008). *Die Computerspieler: Studien zur*

Nutzung von Computergames. Wiesbaden: Verlag für Sozialwissenschaften.

Raessens, J., & Goldstein, J. (Eds.). (2005). *Handbook of computer game studies*. Cambridge, MA: MIT Press.

Raney, A. A., Smith, J. K., & Baker, K. (2006). Adolescents and the appeal of video games. In P. Vorderer & J. Bryant (Eds.), *Playing video games: Motives, responses, and consequences* (pp. 165–179). Mahwah, NJ: Erlbaum.

Ratan, R., & Ritterfeld, U. (in press). Towards a psychological classification of serious games. In U. Ritterfeld, M. Cody, & P. Vorderer (Eds.), *Serious games: Mechanisms and effects*. New York: Routledge/LEA.

Reeves, B., & Nass, C. (1996). *The media equation*. New York: Cambridge University Press.

Ritterfeld, U. (in press). Identity construction and emotion regulation in digital gaming. In U. Ritterfeld, M. Cody, & P. Vorderer (Eds.), *Serious games: Mechanisms and effects*. NewYork: Routledge/LEA.

Ritterfeld, U., Cody, M., & Vorderer, P. (Eds.). (in press a). *Serious games: Mechanisms and effects*. New York: Routledge/LEA.

Ritterfeld, U., Cody, M., & Vorderer, P. (in press b). Serious games: Promises, challenges, and limitations. In U. Ritterfeld, M. Cody, & P. Vorderer (Eds.), *Serious games: Mechanisms and effects*. New York: Routledge/LEA.

Ritterfeld, U., & Weber, R. (2006). Digital games for entertainment and education. In P. Vorderer & J. Bryant (Eds.), *Playing video games: Motives, responses, and consequences* (pp. 399–413). Mahwah, NJ: Erlbaum.

Ryan, R. M., & Deci, E. L. (2000). Self-determination theory and the facilitation of intrinsic motivations, social development, and well-being. *American Psychologist, 1*, 68–78.

Ryan, R. M., Rigby, C. S., & Przybylski, A. (2006). The motivational pull of video games: A self-determination theory approach. *Motivation and Emotion, 30*, 347–363.

Shen, C., Wang, H., & Ritterfeld, U. (in press). Serious games and seriously fun games: Can they be one and the same? In U. Ritterfeld, M. Cody, & P. Vorderer (Eds.), *Serious games: Mechanisms and effects*. New York: Routledge/LEA.

Sherry, J. L. (2001). Toward an etiology of media use motivations: The role of temperament in media use. *Communication Monographs, 68*, 274–288.

Sherry, J. L., Lucas, K., Greenberg, B. S., & Lachlan, K. (2006). Video game uses and gratifications as predictors of use and game preference. In P. Vorderer & J. Bryant (Eds.), *Playing video games: Motives, responses, and consequences* (pp. 213–224). Mahwah, NJ: Erlbaum.

Silvia, P. J. (2005). Emotional responses to art: From collation and arousal to cognition and emotion. *Review of General Psychology, 9*(4), 342–357.

Silvia, P. J. (2006). *Exploring the psychology of interest*. Oxford: Oxford University Press.

Slater, M. (2003). Alienation, aggression, and sensation seeking as predictors of adolescent use of violent film, computer, and Website content. *Journal of Communication, 53*(1), 105–121.

Slater, M. D., Henry, K. L., Swaim, R. C., & Anderson, L. L. (2003). Violent media content aggressiveness in adolescents. *Communication Research, 30*(6), 713–736.

Smith, B. P. (2006). The (computer) games people play. In P. Vorderer & J. Bryant (Eds.), *Playing video games: Motives, responses, and consequences* (pp. 43–56). Mahwah, NJ: Erlbaum.

Smith, S. (2006). Perps, pimps, and provocative clothing: Examining negative content patterns in video games. In P. Vorderer & J. Bryant (Eds.), *Playing video games: Motives, responses, and consequences* (pp. 57–75). Mahwah, NJ: Erlbaum.

Tamborini, R., & Skalski, P. (2006). The role of presence in the experience of electronic games. In P. Vorderer & J. Bryant (Eds.), *Playing video games: Motives, responses, and consequences* (pp. 225–240). Mahwah, NJ: Erlbaum.

van Mierlo, J., & van den Bulck, J. (2004). Benchmarking the cultivation approach to video game effects: A comparison of the correlates of TV viewing and game play. *Journal of Adolescence, 27*, 97–111.

von Salisch, M., Kristen, A., & Oppl, C. (2007). *Computerspiele mit und ohne Gewalt: Auswahl und Wirkung bei Kindern.* Stuttgart: Kohlhammer.

Vorderer, P. (2000). Interactive entertainment and beyond. In D. Zillmann & P. Vorderer (Eds.), *Media entertainment: The psychology of its appeal* (pp. 21–36). Mahwah, NJ: Erlbaum.

Vorderer, P., & Bryant, J. (Eds.). (2006). *Playing video games: Motives, responses, and consequences.* Mahwah, NJ: Erlbaum.

Vorderer, P., & Hartmann, T. (2009). Entertainment and enjoyment as media effects. In J. Bryant & M. B. Oliver (Eds.), *Media effects: Advances in theory and research* (pp. 532–550). New York: Routledge.

Vorderer, P., Hartmann, T., & Klimmt, C. (2006). Explaining the enjoyment of playing video games: The role of competition. In D. Marinelli (Ed.), *ICEC conference proceedings 2003: Essays on the future of interactive entertainment* (pp. 107–120). Pittsburgh, PA: Carnegie Mellon University Press.

Vorderer, P., Klimmt, C., & Ritterfeld, U. (2004). Enjoyment: At the heart of media entertainment. *Communication Theory, 14*(4), 388–408.

Vorderer, P., Steen, F. F., & Chan, E. (2006). Motivation. In J. Bryant & P. Vorderer (Eds.), *Psychology of entertainment* (pp. 3–18). Mahwah, NJ: Erlbaum.

Wang, H., Shen, C., & Ritterfeld, U. (in press). Enjoyment in games. In U. Ritterfeld, M. Cody, & P. Vorderer (Eds.), *Serious games: Mechanisms and effects.* New York: Routledge/LEA.

Wang, H., & Singhal, A. (in press). Entertainment education through digital games. In U. Ritterfeld, M. Cody, & P. Vorderer (Eds.), *Serious games: Mechanisms and effects.* New York: Routledge/LEA.

Watt, J. (in press). Improving methodology in serious games research with elaborated theory. In U. Ritterfeld, M. Cody, & P. Vorderer (Eds.), *Serious games: Mechanisms and effects.* New York: Routledge/LEA.

Weber, R., Ritterfeld, U., & Kostygina, A. (2006). Aggression and violence as effects of playing violent video games? In P. Vorderer & J. Bryant (Eds.), *Playing video games: Motives, responses, and consequences* (pp. 347–361). Mahwah, NJ: Erlbaum.

Zillmann, D. (1988). Cognition-excitation interdependencies in aggressive behavior. *Aggressive Behavior, 14,* 51–64.

31

CHILDREN AND ADOLESCENTS

Distinctive Audiences of Media Content

◆ Barbara J. Wilson and Kristin L. Drogos

American children today are immersed in a world of electronic gadgets. It is not uncommon to see them with a cell phone in their hand, texting a friend, while at the same time listening to music on an iPod. In fact, the average age at which children begin using electronic devices has declined from 8.1 years in 2005 to 6.7 years in 2007 (NPD Group, 2007). Today, over half of teens own a portable MP3 player (54%), whereas only 13% of 35- to 54-year-olds do (Ipsos Insight, 2006). By 2010, 81% of youth between ages 5 and 24 will own a cell phone (Holson, 2008).

Children also have tremendous access to media in the home. The average child in the United States lives in a household with three television sets, three VCR/DVD players, three radios, three CD players, two video game consoles, and a personal computer (Roberts, Foehr, & Rideout, 2005). Much of this equipment eventually migrates to the child's bedroom. Indeed, a full 68% of children between the ages of 8 and 18 have a television set in their room (Roberts et al., 2005).

The purpose of this chapter is to overview what we know about media and youth today. The focus is how young people interact with the media, how they interpret media content, and how they respond emotionally, cognitively, and behaviorally to media messages. Other chapters in this volume also touch on topics that are pertinent to children and teens (Bushman, Huesmann, & Whitaker, Chapter 24; Mares, Chapter 22), so we try not to duplicate such material in our overview. We begin by outlining a few generalizations we can draw about youth and media from decades of research on this broad topic. We then describe several areas of research that are receiving substantial attention in the first decade of the 21st century. We conclude by outlining some directions for future research.

◆ Well-Established Generalizations About Youth and Media

CHILDREN SPEND A GREAT DEAL OF TIME WITH MEDIA

The typical school-aged child in this country spends about 6 hours each day in the classroom and another 9 hours sleeping. That leaves roughly 9 hours for all other activities. Two thirds of that time, approximately 6½ hours a day, is spent with the media (Roberts et al., 2005). As a comparison, youth spend only about 1 hour a day engaged in physical activity, 50 minutes doing homework, and 30 minutes doing chores. In spite of the growing popularity of interactive technologies, the bulk of their media time still is spent with traditional screen media such as television, movies, and videotapes/ DVDs (Roberts et al., 2005). Screen media exposure declines somewhat with age, especially during adolescence, as exposure to audio media (i.e., listening to music) increases.

A look at children's bedrooms offers additional evidence of the centrality of media in their lives. According to a national study of over 2,000 8- to 18-year-olds, a full 68% have a television in their room and another 37% have cable or satellite

television (Roberts et al., 2005). Not surprisingly, those with a TV set in the bedroom spend almost 1½ hours more per day watching television than do those without a set in their room.

Recent research indicates that media are penetrating the lives of even younger-aged children. A national study of 1,051 parents of babies and toddlers found that children this age (0–6 years) use screen media for an average of just under 2 hours a day (Rideout & Hamel, 2006), roughly the same amount of time they spend playing outdoors. Most of this media time is spent watching television. Moreover, 29% of 2- to 3-year-olds and 43% of 4- to 6-year-olds in this country have a television set in their bedroom (Rideout & Hamel, 2006).

Although the sheer amount of time youth devote to media each day has not increased in the last 5 years (Roberts et al., 2005), the way in which they use media has. One trend is that young people increasingly are "media multitasking" (Roberts et al., 2005), or using more than one medium at the same time. In fact, in 1999, youth spent about 16% of their media time multitasking with more than one device, whereas by 2005 they spent 26% of their time multitasking.

Clearly, American children live media-centric lives. Their homes and even their bedrooms are saturated with electronic devices, they are targeted consumers for products ranging from leap pads to cell phones to MP3 players, and they spend what amounts to a full-time job across 7 days a week with some form of media (Roberts et al., 2005), often using more than one device at a time.

DEVELOPMENTAL THEORY IS CRUCIAL IN UNDERSTANDING MEDIA IMPACT

Early research on children and media typically involved a single age-group or, if multiple ages were included, the goal was to test the generalizability of the results. Much of this work was based on social learning theory, which focused on behavioral imitation of media content, with little attention to how children comprehended or interpreted such messages. Since the 1970s, researchers increasingly have adopted a cognitive model of childhood, one that recognizes the child as an active processor of media content (Pecora, 2007). Today, dozens of studies demonstrate that children at different levels of development or maturation respond to the same media message in distinct yet predictable ways (see Calvert & Wilson, 2008).

Several influential theories of cognitive development have been used by media scholars to explain and predict childhood responding. Piaget (1950) argued that children's thinking undergoes qualitative changes that can be characterized by distinct stages of development (i.e., sensorimotor, approximately 0–2 years of age; preoperational, 2–7 years; concrete operational, 7–11 years; formal operational, 11 years and older). Researchers have used these stages to predict developmental differences in children's comprehension of a television narrative (Mares, 2006), fright reactions to media content (Cantor & Sparks, 1984), and responses to advertising (Stutts & Hunnicutt, 1987). Because development is often more uneven and domain specific than a stage approach suggests, recent theories of information processing have focused instead on the schemas, strategies, and rules that children acquire with maturation (Flavell, Miller, & Miller, 2002). Development, according to these models, consists of both qualitative and quantitative changes in cognitive skills such as selective attention, encoding, and information retrieval.

Regardless of which theoretical approach is adopted, most research indicates that there are marked differences in cognitive processing between early childhood (roughly 2–7 years of age) and late childhood (8–12 years), and between late childhood

and adolescence (13–17 years). Some of the cognitive characteristics that are most relevant for young people's interactions with the media are described in the following paragraphs.

Characteristics of early childhood cognition. Young children pay close attention to immediately perceptible or salient attributes in a situation, a characteristic that has been called *perceptual boundedness* (Springer, 2001). For example, preschoolers typically group objects together based on perceptual qualities such as color and shape, whereas older children focus more on conceptual properties such as the functions that objects share (Tversky, 1985). With regard to the media, younger children pay more attention to highly salient formal features in a program, such as animation, sound effects, and lively music, whereas older children's attention is more selective and oriented to meaningful cues in the plot (Schmitt, Anderson, & Collins, 1999). Younger children also are more likely to focus on a character's appearance than on his or her motives (Hoffner & Cantor, 1985), and they remember a character's behavior, especially if it is aggressive, more than other elements in the plot (McKenna & Ossoff, 1998). Finally, young children are likely to be most frightened by strong visual images in a scary program (Cantor, 2002) or news story (Smith & Wilson, 2002). All of these patterns can be explained by perceptual boundedness or dependency.

Another characteristic of younger children is that they have difficulty distinguishing fantasy from reality (Dorr, 1983). Toddlers frequently talk to the television and wave at characters, showing little understanding of the boundary between TV and the real world (Jaglom & Gardner, 1981). By late preschool, children begin using terms like *real* and *not real*, but their understanding of these concepts is fragile and based on striking violations of physical reality (Wright, Huston, Reitz, & Piemyat, 1994). Thus, younger children may say that a character is not real, but their fears typically are centered on fantasy creatures such as witches and ghosts (Cantor, 2002). Their inability to distinguish between appearance and reality also means that they are more trusting of advertising (Robertson & Rossiter, 1974).

Younger children's thinking has also been described as egocentric (Piaget, 1950), which means that they have difficulty considering the perspective of others. Because of their difficulty in role taking, preschoolers and younger elementary schoolers are less likely to empathize with media characters (Wilson & Cantor, 1985) and less likely to recognize and think about the motives of advertisers (Faber, Perloff, & Hawkins, 1982).

Characteristics of late childhood cognition. As children move into the later elementary school years, they increasingly are able to look beyond the surface and consider more subtle and conceptual information in a story (Mares, 2006). So, for example, in retelling a violent program, children under the age of 7 are likely to focus on a character's aggressive behavior, whereas older children are more likely to discuss the character's motives (Collins, Berndt, & Hess, 1974). Older children also are more likely than younger children to mention a character's emotional reactions when describing a story or plot (Trabasso, Secco, & van den Broek, 1984). There is no doubt that older children still can be misled by appearances (Hoffner & Cantor, 1985), but they also are attuned to less salient information concerning a character's motives, intentions, and inner thoughts (van den Broek, 1989).

During late childhood, children also show an increasing ability to link story events together and draw causal and time-order inferences (Collins, Wellman, Keniston, & Westby, 1978). Thus, older children can incorporate information across scenes and even across episodes to make sense of the plot (van den Broek, 1989).

Older children also exhibit a more sophisticated understanding of reality and

fantasy in the media (McKenna & Ossoff, 1998). They are able to consider multiple cues such as genre, production techniques, and even the purpose of the program in making reality judgments (Wright et al., 1994). More important, they routinely compare media to the real world, judging depicted events as realistic only if they could *possibly* occur in real life (Dorr, 1983). Because of this orientation toward realism, older children are more likely to be frightened by fictional programs and even by the news than by fantasy portrayals (see Cantor, 2002).

Late childhood is also a time when children engage in forms of role taking or imagining themselves in other people's situations. Hence, they are capable of strong identification with media characters (Hoffner, 1996) and of sharing characters' emotions (Wilson & Cantor, 1985).

Characteristics of adolescent cognition. In many ways, adolescents' cognitive skills reflect increasing levels of abstraction. For instance, when making reality-fantasy judgments about the media, they are more likely to focus on the *plausibility* than on the mere possibility that depicted events could occur in the real world (Dorr, 1983). Consequently, they are less likely than older elementary schoolers to be frightened of child kidnapping cases profiled in the news (Wilson, Martins, & Marske, 2005), presumably because teens recognize that such events actually are rare. Adolescents' abstract thinking also helps them to extract the theme or moral lesson in a program, something those under 12 often have difficulty doing (Rosenkoetter, 1999).

Adolescents also become increasingly capable of using formal logic and hypothetical reasoning (Byrnes, 2003). Thus, compared with older children, teens should be better able to anticipate various outcomes of a story, critique the logical and causal structure of different messages, and even consider the meaning behind the message.

Another skill that characterizes adolescence is metacognition, or the ability to think about one's own thought processes (Flavell et al., 2002). As children move into the teenage years, they become increasingly aware of how the human mind works (Friedman, 2007), and they are better able to monitor and regulate their own thought processes (Flavell et al., 2002). Compared with children under age 12, then, adolescents should be more conscious of how they are responding to an arousing program, of what strategies they are using to search the Web, and of how much cognitive effort is needed to engage in different media-related activities. Such ideas await empirical testing.

Despite these cognitive advances, there are still significant changes in brain development that occur during adolescence (Kuhn, 2006). Much of this growth occurs in the frontal cortex region of the brain, which is involved in regulating behavior and emotion (Sowell et al., 2002). Reflective of this development, younger adolescents typically exhibit less control and more risk taking than their older counterparts do (Gardner & Steinberg, 2005). For example, when compared with older teens, younger teens are more likely to play with their identity when communicating with others online (Valkenburg, Schouten, & Peter, 2005) and to talk with strangers on the Internet (Peter, Valkenburg, & Schouten, 2006).

CONTENT MATTERS MORE THAN SHEER EXPOSURE

In a recent national poll, 57% of parents said they were concerned about their children spending too much time with the media (Common Sense Media, 2007). Parents of older children (11–16 years of age) expressed more worry than did parents of younger children (under age 11). Somewhat surprisingly, parents reported greater concern about their children over-using media than smoking, drinking, or engaging in sexual behavior.

Undoubtedly, parents are reacting to the long, uninterrupted hours that today's youth can spend glued to computer screens, personal DVD players, and even the television. Yet research demonstrates that the content of media messages varies a great deal across channels, genres, Web sites, and even video games, so that *what* the child is doing with media may be more crucial than how much time is spent. For example, a child who watches an hour of superhero cartoons will witness an average of 28 violent incidents, whereas a child who watches a magazine-formatted program such as *Sesame Street* or *Blue's Clues* will be exposed to fewer than 2 violent incidents during this same 60-minute period (Wilson et al., 2002). Likewise, styles of music vary substantially in terms of violent content and drug use (Jones, 1997), and genres of television programming vary in their degree of sexual content (Eyal, Kunkel, Biely, & Finnerty, 2007).

Consistent with such content distinctions, studies show that children's selective media habits often matter more than the sheer amount of time they spend with the media (see Wilson, 2008). For example, a study of infants and toddlers found that overall television viewing at an early age had little impact on language development two years later, but that viewing of particular programs such as *Dragon Tales* and *Dora the Explorer* produced higher vocabularies and expressive language scores (Linebarger & Walker, 2005). Similarly, a 3-year longitudinal study of 182 preschoolers found that those who watched educational programs such as *Sesame Street* subsequently performed better on a variety of academic tests involving reading, math, vocabulary, and school readiness than did infrequent viewers (Wright, Huston, Scantlin, & Kotler, 2001). In contrast, frequent preschool viewing of general audience programming and even cartoons had no such positive effect, and in some cases actually diminished academic performance over time.

Particular types of media content influence emotional responses as well. A random sample survey found that children's fear of being kidnapped was positively related to the amount of television news they viewed but not more generally to how much television they watched (Wilson et al., 2005).

Even among adolescents, content matters. A recent study found that exposure to televised music videos and to pro wrestling, both of which combine sexual content and violence, was associated with increased acceptance of date rape among seventh- and eighth-grade boys (Kaestle, Halpern, & Brown, 2007). Yet overall television viewing was unrelated to such attitudes.

Such findings raise questions about the utility of perspectives like cultivation theory that make assumptions about the uniformity of messages in the media (Gerbner, Gross, Morgan, Signorielli, & Shanahan, 2002). This type of supposition may have been valid decades ago when there were fewer channels, fewer genres, and few technologies from which young people could choose. But today, a young child who spends a great deal of time watching educational TV and reading will have a significantly different media experience than one who watches endless cartoons and plays violent video games.

CHILDREN LEARN FROM MEDIA

It may seem obvious to make the claim that children learn from the media. Advertisers spend millions of dollars targeting youth because children learn brand loyalty from commercials (Robinson, Borzekowski, Matheson, & Kraemer, 2007). Still, public concern has focused mostly on the negative or harmful learning that can occur, and far less attention has been paid to the positive potential of the media. On the negative side, there is substantial evidence that cumulative exposure to both television violence (Paik & Comstock, 1994) and video game violence (Anderson & Bushman, 2001) contributes to aggressive attitudes and behaviors in youth (see Bushman, Huesmann, & Whitaker, Chapter 24, in this volume). According to

an information-processing perspective, repeated exposure to violence in the media encourages the learning of scripts or mental routines involving aggression that then become activated when a child encounters ambiguous or challenging social situations (Huesmann, 1998).

Exposure to media violence also can lead to desensitization. Surveys have documented a link between heavy exposure to media violence and children's acceptance or tolerance of aggression as a problem-solving tactic (e.g., Funk, Baldacci, Pasold, & Baumgardner, 2004). In addition, there is experimental evidence that exposure to fictional violence can reduce children's willingness to intervene in real-life aggressive altercations (Molitor & Hirsch, 1994).

Children also can learn fear from the media (see Cantor, 2002). Some of these fright responses are transitory, but others can persist for long periods. One study found that 90% of college students could describe an intense, long-lasting fear response from seeing a TV program or movie as a child (Harrison & Cantor, 1999). Moreover, 25% of these students reported that the fear had persisted into adulthood. On occasion, media can contribute to more serious emotional challenges, such as posttraumatic stress disorder (PTSD). For example, heavy viewing of news coverage of the Oklahoma City bombing (Pfefferbaum et al., 2000) and the September 11th terrorist attacks (Otto et al., 2007) has been linked to PTSD symptoms in children.

Stereotypes can be learned from the media as well. Despite calls for more positive representations of various groups in the media, stereotypes related to gender (Aubrey & Harrison, 2004) and to race (Bramlett-Solomon & Roeder, 2008) abound in the messages that children see on television. There is far less evidence on the impact of these misrepresentations, but correlational data reveal that children who are heavy viewers of television possess more stereotyped attitudes about other groups (see Greenberg & Mastro, 2008). Once again, however, content matters. Exposure to positive portrayals of race and ethnicity, especially those commonly found on educational television, can increase children's acceptance of people from other racial and ethnic groups (Gorn, Goldberg, & Kanungo, 1976).

Other types of prosocial attitudes and behaviors can be learned from the media as well. For example, children can learn helping behaviors from watching such behaviors modeled on television (Sprafkin, Liebert, & Poulos, 1975). A recent meta-analysis revealed that exposure to prosocial television programs can also enhance children's positive interactions with others, such as being friendly and cooperative (Mares & Woodard, 2005).

Finally, children can learn cognitive skills from the media. Research shows that early exposure to *Sesame Street* predicts subsequent increases in reading and math skills as well as increased readiness for school as children approach elementary school (Wright et al., 2001). Furthermore, watching *Sesame Street* in preschool has been linked to higher grades and more leisure reading in high school, even after statistically controlling for parental education, birth order, sex, and geographic location (Huston, Anderson, Wright, Linebarger, & Schmitt, 2001).

There is little doubt, then, that children learn from the media. Some of what they acquire can be positive and useful, and some of what they discover can be detrimental to their emotional and social well-being (Wilson, 2008). The challenge is to help them make wise media choices and to prepare them for coping with what they are likely to encounter, as discussed in the following paragraphs.

FAMILIES CAN MAKE A DIFFERENCE

Parents and other family members have a substantial influence on children's media experiences. For one thing, parents model

and thereby influence how much time children spend with the media (Barradas, Fulton, Blanck, & Huhman, 2007). Family habits are telling: 51% of American children report that they live in homes where the television set is turned on "most of the time" and another 63% report that the TV is usually on during meals (Roberts et al., 2005).

Parents also can exert active involvement in their children's media experiences by explaining content and teaching children to be critical of certain types of messages. Research shows that this type of active mediation can bolster children's learning from educational programming (Reiser, Tessmer, & Phelps, 1984), decrease their susceptibility to advertising (Buijzen, 2007), and reduce their fright reactions to media (see Cantor & Wilson, 1988). Teaching children to think about the victim in a violent cartoon can change their interpretations of television violence (Nathanson & Cantor, 2000).

Parental mediation with adolescents is a bit more complicated. One study found that teens who reported high parental restriction regarding the media had less positive attitudes toward their parents, had more positive attitudes toward violent and sexual content in the media, and were more likely to view such content with friends (Nathanson, 2002). On the other hand, other forms of parental involvement can be beneficial. A recent survey of 518 adolescents found that parental monitoring of Internet behavior (e.g., placing computer in open area) and open parent-child communication were associated with less likelihood of teens engaging in disapproved Internet behaviors such as visiting forbidden sites and talking with strangers online (Cottrell et al., 2007).

Most of the research to date is on parental influence. Yet there is evidence that children spend more of their media time with siblings than with parents (Roberts, 2000). One experiment found that compared with watching alone, preschoolers who watched a frightening program with an older sibling were less scared and liked the program more (Wilson & Weiss, 1993). Yet watching with an older sibling interfered with preschoolers' comprehension of the plot. Future studies should explore the impact of sharing media experiences with different-aged siblings.

◆ Current Topics of Interest

ADVERTISING AND MARKETING TO YOUTH

Children and adolescents today have a great deal more of their own money to spend than did youth of past generations, and advertisers recognize the growing influence youth have on consumer spending in the family (McNeal, 2007). Moreover, marketing efforts are targeting younger and younger audiences, as evidenced by the "cradle-to-grave" efforts to establish brand loyalty. Parents can buy Baby Gap clothes for their infants, LeapPad computers for their toddlers, and Disney cell phones for their young children. Advertising even has permeated many American schools (Palmer & Carpenter, 2006). Indeed, critics argue that we are witnessing the commercialization of childhood in the 21st century (Linn, 2004).

Young children certainly pay attention to advertising (Schmitt, Wolf, & Anderson, 2003) and to brand names (Valkenburg & Buijzen, 2005). Yet preschoolers have difficulty discriminating advertising content from programming, and until about 8 years of age, children do not fully understand the selling intent of commercials (Kunkel et al., 2004). One recent study of low-income, predominantly African American children found that selling intent was not understood well before age 11 (Batada & Borzekowski, 2008). Because of such cognitive vulnerability, many have argued that advertising to young children is unfair (Kunkel et al., 2004).

Nevertheless, the ability to recognize and understand commercial intent does not necessarily make a child immune to persuasion. Experimental (Chernin, 2008) and correlational research (Buijzen & Valkenburg, 2000) demonstrates that exposure to advertising increases children's desire for products, and age does not necessarily moderate this impact (Chernin, 2008). Part of the problem is that older children are not yet capable of spontaneously retrieving and applying their knowledge and growing skepticism while watching commercials (Buijzen, 2007). Adolescents, on the other hand, routinely are more critical of advertising (Boush, Friestad, & Rose, 1994), although they too can be influenced by commercials.

There are unintended effects of advertising on youth as well. For example, extensive exposure to advertising can cause parent-child conflict (Stoneman & Brody, 1981) and is positively associated with materialistic attitudes in children (Buijzen & Valkenburg, 2003) and in teens (Moschis & Moore, 1982). Much of the evidence for materialism is correlational, however, so it may be that youth who value possessions and money are seeking out commercial messages.

Newer marketing strategies are emerging each year, and several are likely to challenge even the most discerning child (Calvert, 2008). For example, popular characters such as Harry Potter are being marketed in a highly integrated fashion across different media. Advertisers also are arranging to have their products placed in storylines in movies, popular television programs, and video games. In addition, advertisers are experimenting with viral marketing, which involves creating a "buzz" about certain products among consumers who are considered trendsetters (Calvert, 2008). Finally, numerous Web sites are targeting children, many of which encourage young users to play games, join contests, and register to win prizes. As an example, the highly popular Webkinz site invites children to enter a virtual world where they can name and adopt the Webkinz stuffed animals they have purchased. Future studies need to explore the impact of these types of tactics, which blur the distinctions between commercial and entertainment content, on children's cognitive and emotional responses to advertising.

MEDIA AND CHILDREN'S PHYSICAL HEALTH

Obesity has reached epidemic proportions in the United States, and youth are part of the problem. According to body mass index (BMI) statistics, 16% of American children between the ages of 6 and 19 are considered obese and another 16% are overweight and at risk for becoming obese (Ogden et al., 2006). Childhood obesity is associated with significant health risks, including type 2 diabetes and hypertension (Daniels, 2006). In addition, being overweight as a child is a strong predictor of adult obesity (Anderson & Butcher, 2006). There are numerous and complementary causes of childhood obesity, including factors related to heredity, diet, and exercise (Anderson & Butcher, 2006). In addition, critics have charged that children's media use is a culprit.

Several studies have found a correlation between heavy television viewing and children's weight, even after statistically controlling for demographic factors (see Jordan & Robinson, 2008). Furthermore, longitudinal research indicates that children who watch a great deal of television are at greater risk of becoming overweight several years later than are those who watch less television (Henderson, 2007). The most convincing data come from experiments with randomly assigned groups. In one recent study, children who were encouraged to reduce time with screen media (i.e., TV, computers) showed a significant reduction in BMI and in food intake compared with a no-treatment control group (Epstein et al., 2008).

There are at least four possible explanations for the observed relationship between

screen media use and obesity (Jordan & Robinson, 2008). First, watching television and playing video games may lower energy expenditure, even compared with simply resting. Second, spending time with screen media may displace more physically active leisure behaviors. Third, children may eat more while sitting in front of the screen. Fourth, exposure to food advertising, especially on television, may lead children to eat unhealthy foods.

The evidence is strongest for the two explanations involving food (Jordan & Robinson, 2008). Regarding the third explanation, research shows that children who regularly eat in front of the television are less likely to eat vegetables, more likely to eat pizza and snacks, and more likely to consume caffeine than are children who do not eat in front of the screen (Coon, Goldberg, Rogers, & Tucker, 2001). These relationships hold up even controlling for the child's age and sex, parental income and education, parental knowledge of nutrition, and maternal employment outside the home.

Related to the fourth explanation, most of the commercials on television that are targeted to children are for snacks, fast foods, and sugared cereals (Gantz, Schwartz, Angelini, & Rideout, 2007). One recent study analyzed the nutritional breakdown of foods advertised to children and found that there were few health-related messages in the ads, most of the eating involved snacking instead of sitting down for a meal, and most of the featured foods were high in sugar and low in nutrients (Harrison & Marske, 2005). Even brief exposure to food commercials can cause children to prefer advertised products over other choices (Borzekowski & Robinson, 2001). Moreover, survey research indicates that heavy exposure to television during childhood is associated with higher consumption of both junk foods and fast foods (Dixon, Scully, Wakefield, White, & Crawford, 2007). Finally, one study found that eating high-calorie foods was related more strongly to watching food advertising than to watching television in general (Buijzen, Schuurman, & Bomhof, 2008), again supporting the idea that the content of media messages is crucial. Clearly, there is a need for studies that track children's media habits, particularly their exposure to commercials, over time.

INFANTS AND MEDIA

Media products for infants and toddlers began appearing in the marketplace in the late 1990s, starting with video series like "Baby Einstein." Now, there is an explosion of products targeting the youngest consumers, including video game consoles like the V.Smile Baby and handheld games like the Leapster. There is even a 24-hour television channel called BabyFirstTV, which features more than 40 programs tailored specifically to infants.

Partly in response to such products, the American Academy of Pediatrics (AAP) issued a policy statement in 1999 that urged parents to avoid all television viewing for children less than 2 years of age (AAP, 1999). The AAP recommended that young children instead engage in more interactive activities with parents and caregivers that foster brain development and social skills.

Mares, in Chapter 22 of this volume, provides a cogent review of the limited research on the educational impact of media on babies. We know that infants and young toddlers do watch television and videos despite the AAP recommendations (Rideout & Hamel, 2006). There is also evidence suggesting that the impact of viewing, especially on language acquisition, depends on what types of programs infants watch (Linebarger & Walker, 2005). Furthermore, a growing body of research indicates that up until about 2½ years of age, children learn better from live demonstrations than from audiovisual presentations of the same material (see Barr, 2008). This "video deficit" may be due to a host of factors, including young children's difficulty grappling with multiple representations

of objects and events (Wartella & Robb, 2007). Far more research is needed on what babies learn from educational media products and how these mediated experiences affect brain development.

It is also possible that inadvertent exposure to screen media impacts young babies. Indeed, the television is turned on as background in many American households with children (56%; Roberts et al., 2005). In one study, a majority of mothers reported that the TV was frequently on when their infants played in a room (Masur & Flynn, 2008). Such constant exposure to screen media might interfere with other activities that are crucial for infant development. One experiment found that 12- to 36-month-old children spent less time playing with novel toys when a television in the room was turned on than when it was off (Evans, Pempek, Kirkorian, Frankenfield, & Anderson, 2004). Furthermore, parents interact less with young children when a television is on in the room (Brody, Stoneman, & Sanders, 1980). Thus, even when in the background, the presence of screen media may disrupt social interaction and play, both of which are vital for younger children's development.

ONLINE COMMUNICATION AND ADOLESCENCE

An overwhelming majority of adolescents (93%) use the Internet for social and communicative purposes (Lenhart, Madden, Macgill, & Smith, 2007). They create and share content such as pictures, chat with friends, and interact with others (Lenhart et al., 2007). Over half (55%) of America's youth ages 12 to 17 have a social networking profile (Lenhart et al., 2007). In fact, most teens report using multiple applications of the Internet (e.g., instant messaging, social networking sites) as well as other communication media at the same time (e.g., cell phones; Lenhart et al., 2007). Because of such intense adoption of and devotion to online activities among teens, there is a great deal of parental anxiety about the impact of the Internet on youth.

Early studies found that heavy Internet use was negatively associated with psychological well-being among adolescents (Kraut et al., 1998). However, recent research indicates that *what* teens do online matters. Instant messaging (IM) among teens is typically nonanonymous communication between friends, whereas chat in public chat rooms tends to be anonymous and with unacquainted partners (Valkenburg & Peter, 2007b). In a large survey of teens, Valkenburg and Peter (2007a) found that IM was positively related to time spent with existing friends. Moreover, the quality of a teen's friendships mediated the positive relationship found between time spent with IM and adolescent well-being. In other words, online communication stimulates friendships and, in turn, seems to enhance social well-being for most teens.

Yet not all teens reach out to friends online. Some adolescents turn to the Internet to interact with strangers (Peter et al., 2006). These teens tend to be younger (12–14 years old), they spend more time in public chat rooms than their peers do, and they report using online communication for social compensation motives (e.g., "to feel less shy"; Peter et al., 2006). Still, relatively few teens chat exclusively or more often with strangers than friends (Peter et al., 2006). Future studies should explore the nature of teen messages online as well as the impact of online communication on social development and on family relationships.

ELECTRONIC BULLYING

Because teens spend so much time with electronic devices, such technology is sometimes used as a vehicle for harassment. In a national study of over 900 12- to 17-year-olds, about one third of the teens reported that they had been the target of threatening activities online, including receiving an aggressive text message or e-mail, having a picture or private communication posted without permission, or having a rumor about them spread online (Lenhart, 2007). Older girls and those who use social network sites like MySpace and Facebook were more likely to report having been bullied. Yet nearly 70% of these teens reported that bullying still occurs more frequently *offline* than online. There appears to be some overlap between physical bullying at school and online bullying away from school, although some youth report being victims of only online harassment (Ybarra, Diener-West, & Leaf, 2007).

Similar to physical bullying, online victimization is associated with a range of psychosocial problems for youth, including depression, delinquent behavior, and substance abuse (Mitchell, Ybarra, & Finkelhor, 2007). In one recent study, youth who reported being harassed online were more likely to have skipped school and to have carried a weapon to school in the last 30 days, even after controlling for sex, age, race, income, and Internet use (Ybarra et al., 2007).

Some issues pertain uniquely to electronic forms of bullying. Unlike face-to-face aggression, electronic aggression allows perpetrators to remain anonymous. One recent study found that nearly half of the middle schoolers who had been electronically harassed did not know the identity of the perpetrator (Kowalski & Limber, 2007). In addition, unlike school bullying, there is no place to escape or feel safe when victimized electronically, which can occur 24 hours a day. Clearly, we need more studies of this insidious form of electronic communication.

◆ Directions for the Future

Children's interactions with media are well integrated into their daily activities, especially as electronic devices become more portable and personalized. As researchers, we need to ratchet up our scientific approaches to better capture youths' pervasive mediated experiences. We have several broad suggestions. First, researchers need to pay more attention to children's overall media diets in assessing impact. Scholars have tended to explore one medium at a time, overlooking the fact that children utilize multiple media simultaneously and often experience particular types of content (e.g., violence) across different media platforms. Second, we need valid and sensitive measures of media exposure. How do we operationalize constant cell phone use? How do we capture media in the background? Third, we need more longitudinal studies that track changes in attitudes and behaviors over time, as a function of early media use. Admittedly, this type of research is expensive, but it is crucial for sorting out the causal impact of media on development, in relation to other factors. Finally, the two ends of the continuum of youth deserve more attention—infancy and adolescence. Studying how infants respond to the media will require more sensitive, nonverbal measures. Studying adolescents will require us to expand our models of cognitive development as well as to incorporate issues related to puberty, identity, and peer groups. Broadening our theoretical and methodological approaches will help us elucidate the complex role of media during infancy, childhood, and adolescence.

◆ **References**

American Academy of Pediatrics Committee on Public Education. (1999). Media education. *Pediatrics, 104*, 341–343.

Anderson, C. A., & Bushman, B. J. (2001). Effects of violent video games on aggressive behavior, aggressive cognition, aggressive affect, physiological arousal, and prosocial behavior: A meta-analytic review of the scientific literature. *Psychological Science, 12*, 353–359.

Anderson, P. M., & Butcher, K. F. (2006). Childhood obesity: Trends and potential causes. *The Future of Children, 16*, 19–45.

Aubrey, J. S., & Harrison, K. (2004). The gender-role content of children's favorite television programs and its links to their gender-related perceptions. *Media Psychology, 6*, 111–146.

Barr, R. (2008). Attention to and learning from media during infancy in early childhood. In S. L. Calvert & B. J. Wilson (Eds.), *Handbook of children, media, and development*. Boston: Wiley-Blackwell.

Barradas, D., Fulton, J., Blanck, H., & Huhman, M. (2007). Parental influences of youth television viewing. *Journal of Pediatrics, 151*, 369–373.

Batada, A., & Borzekowski, D. (2008). SNAP! CRACKLE! WHAT? Recognition of cereal advertisements and understanding of commercials' persuasive intent among urban, minority children in the U.S. *Journal of Children and Media, 2*, 19–36.

Borzekowski, D., & Robinson, T. N. (2001). The 30-second effect: An experiment revealing the impact of television commercials on food preference of preschoolers. *Journal of the American Dietetic Association, 101*, 42–46.

Boush, D. M., Friestad, M., & Rose, G. M. (1994). Adolescent skepticism toward TV advertising and knowledge of advertiser tactics. *Journal of Consumer Research, 21*, 165–175.

Bramlett-Solomon, S., & Roeder, Y. (2008). Looking at race in children's television: Analysis of Nickelodeon commercials. *Journal of Children and Media, 2*, 56–66.

Brody, G. H., Stoneman, Z., & Sanders, A. K. (1980). Effects of television viewing on family interactions: An observational study. *Family Relations, 29*, 216–220.

Buijzen, M. (2007). Reducing children's susceptibility to commercials: Mechanisms of factual and evaluative advertising interventions. *Media Psychology, 9*, 411–430.

Buijzen, M., Schuurman, J., & Bomhof, E. (2008). Associations between children's television advertising exposure and their food consumption patterns: A household diary-survey study. *Appetite, 50*, 231–239.

Buijzen, M., & Valkenburg, P. (2000). The impact of television advertising on children's

Christmas wishes. *Journal of Broadcasting & Electronic Media, 44,* 456–470.

Buijzen, M., & Valkenburg, P. M. (2003). The unintended effects of television advertising. *Communication Research, 30,* 483–503.

Byrnes, J. P. (2003). Cognitive development during adolescence. In G. R. Adams & M. D. Berzonsky (Eds.), *Blackwell handbook of adolescence* (pp. 227–247). Malden, MA: Blackwell.

Calvert, S. (2008). Children as consumers: Advertising and marketing. *The Future of Children, 18,* 205–234.

Calvert, S. L., & Wilson, B. J. (Eds.). (2008). *Handbook of children, media, and development.* Boston: Wiley-Blackwell.

Cantor, J. (2002). The media and children's fears, anxieties, and perceptions of danger. In D. S. Singer & J. Singer (Eds.), *Handbook of children and the media* (pp. 207–221). Thousand Oaks, CA: Sage.

Cantor, J., & Sparks, G. G. (1984). Children's fear responses to mass media: Testing some Piagetian predictions. *Journal of Communication, 34,* 90–103.

Cantor, J., & Wilson, B. J. (1988). Helping children cope with frightening media presentations. *Current Psychology: Research and Reviews, 7,* 58–75.

Chernin, A. (2008). The effects of food marketing on children's preferences: Testing the moderating roles of age and gender. *The Annals of the American Academy of Political and Social Science, 615,* 101–118.

Collins, W. A., Berndt, T. J., & Hess, V. L. (1974). Observational learning of motives and consequences for television aggression: A developmental study. *Child Development, 45,* 799–802.

Collins, W. A., Wellman, H., Keniston, A. H., & Westby, S. D. (1978). Age-related aspects of comprehension and inference from a televised dramatic narrative. *Child Development, 49,* 389–399.

Common Sense Media. (2007, February 5). *Parents say their #1 health concern is overuse of the media, even more than drinking or smoking.* Retrieved May 3, 2009, from http://www.commonsensemedia.org/about-us/news/press-releases/health-concern-overuse-media

Coon, K. A., Goldberg, J., Rogers, B. L., & Tucker, K. L. (2001). Relationships between use of television during meals and children's food consumption patterns. *Pediatrics, 107,* e7.

Cottrell, S. A., Branstetter, S., Cottrell, L., Harris, C. V., Rishel, C., & Stanton, B. F. (2007). Development and validation of a parental monitoring instrument: Measuring how parents monitor adolescents' activities and risk behaviors. *Family Journal, 15,* 328–335.

Daniels, S. R. (2006). The consequences of childhood overweight and obesity. *Future of Children, 16,* 47–67.

Dixon, H. G., Scully, M. L., Wakefield, M. A., White, V. M., & Crawford, D. A. (2007). The effects of television advertisements for junk food versus nutritious food on children's food attitudes and preferences. *Social Science & Medicine, 65,* 1311–1323.

Dorr, A. (1983). No shortcuts to judging reality. In J. Bryant & D. R. Anderson (Eds.), *Children's understanding of television: Research on attention and comprehension* (pp. 199–220). New York: Academic Press.

Epstein, L. H., Roemmich, J. N., Robinson, J. L., Paluch, R. A., Winiewicz, D. D., Fuerch, J. H., et al. (2008). A randomized trial of the effects of reducing television viewing and computer use on body mass index in young children. *Archives of Pediatrics & Adolescent Medicine, 162,* 239–245.

Evans, M. K., Pempek, T. A., Kirkorian, H. L., Frankenfield, A. E., & Anderson, D. R. (2004, May). *The impact of background television on the complexity of play.* Paper presented at the 14th Biennial International Conference on Infant Studies, Chicago.

Eyal, K., Kunkel, D., Biely, E. N., & Finnerty, K. L. (2007). Sexual socialization messages on television programs most popular among teens. *Journal of Broadcasting & Electronic Media, 51,* 316–336.

Faber, R. J., Perloff, R. M., & Hawkins, R. P. (1982). Antecedents of children's comprehension of television advertising. *Journal of Broadcasting, 26,* 575–584.

Flavell, J. H., Miller, P. H., & Miller, S. A. (2002). *Cognitive development* (4th ed.). Englewood Cliffs, NJ: Prentice-Hall.

Friedman, W. J. (2007). The development of temporal metamemory. *Child Development, 78,* 1472–1491.

Funk, J. B., Baldacci, H. B., Pasold, T., & Baumgardner, J. (2004). Violence exposure in real-life, video games, television, movies, and the Internet: Is there desensitization? *Journal of Adolescence, 27,* 23–39.

Gantz, W., Schwartz, N., Angelini, J. R., & Rideout, V. (2007). *Food for thought: Television food advertising to children in the United States.* Menlo Park, CA: Henry J. Kaiser Family Foundation.

Gardner, M., & Steinberg, L. (2005). Peer influence on risk taking, risk preference, and risky decision making in adolescence and adulthood: An experimental study. *Developmental Psychology, 41,* 625–635.

Gerbner, G., Gross, L., Morgan, M., Signorielli, N., & Shanahan, J. (2002). Growing up with television: The cultivation perspective. In J. Bryant & D. Zillmann (Eds.), *Media effects: Advances in theory and research* (pp. 43–68). Hillsdale, NJ: Erlbaum.

Gorn, G. J., Goldberg, M. E., & Kanungo, R. N. (1976). The role of education television in changing the intergroup attitudes of children. *Child Development, 47,* 277–280.

Greenberg, B. S., & Mastro, D. E. (2008). Children, race, ethnicity, and media. In S. L. Calvert & B. J. Wilson (Eds.), *Handbook of children, media, and development* (pp. 74–97). Boston: Wiley-Blackwell.

Gross, E. F., Juvonen, J., & Gable, S. L. (2002). Internet use and well-being in adolescence. *Journal of Social Issues, 58,* 75–90.

Harrison, K., & Cantor, J. (1999). Tales from the screen: Enduring fright reactions to scary media. *Media Psychology, 1*(2), 97–116.

Harrison, K., & Marske, A. (2005). Nutritional content of foods advertised during the television programs children most watch. *American Journal of Public Health, 95,* 1568–1574.

Henderson, V. (2007). Longitudinal associations between television viewing and body mass index among White and Black girls. *Journal of Adolescent Health, 41,* 544–550.

Hoffner, C. (1996). Children's wishful identification and parasocial interaction with favorite television characters. *Journal of Broadcasting and Electronic Media, 40,* 389–402.

Hoffner, C., & Cantor, J. (1985). Developmental differences in responses to a television character's appearance. *Developmental Psychology, 21,* 1065–1074.

Holson, L. M. (2008, March 9). Text generation gap: U R 2 old (JK). *New York Times Online.* Retrieved March 13, 2008, from http://www.nytimes.com/2008/03/09/business/09cell.html

Huesmann, L. R. (1998). The role of social information processing and cognitive schema in the acquisition and maintenance of habitual aggressive behavior. In R. G. Geen & E. Donnerstein (Eds.), *Human aggression: Theories, research, and implications for policy* (pp. 73–109). New York: Academic Press.

Huston, A. C., Anderson, D. R., Wright, J. C., Linebarger, D. L., & Schmitt, K. L. (2001). *Sesame Street* viewers as adolescents: The recontact study. In S. M. Fisch & R. T. Truglio (Eds.), *"G" is for growing* (pp. 97–115). Mahwah, NJ: Erlbaum.

Ipsos Insight. (2006, June 29). *Portable MP3 player ownership reaches new high* [Press release]. Retrieved March 20, 2008, from http://www.ipsosna.com/news/pressrelease.cfm?id=3124

Jaglom, L. M., & Gardner, H. (1981). The preschool television viewer as anthropologist. *New Directions for Child and Adolescent Development, 13,* 9–30.

Jones, K. (1997). Are rap videos more violent? Style differences and the prevalence of sex and violence in the age of MTV. *Howard Journal of Communication, 8,* 343–356.

Jordan, A. B., & Robinson, T. N. (2008). Children, television viewing, and weight status: Summary and recommendations from an expert panel meeting. *The Annals of the American Academy of Political and Social Science, 615,* 119–132.

Kaestle, C. E., Halpern, C. T., & Brown, J. D. (2007). Music videos, pro wrestling, and acceptance of date rape among middle school males and females: An exploratory analysis. *Journal of Adolescent Health, 70,* 185–187.

Kowalski, R. M., & Limber, S. P. (2007). Electronic bullying among middle school students. *Journal of Adolescent Health, 41,* S22–S30.

Kraut, R., Patterson, M., Lundmark, V., Kiesler, S., Mukopadhyay, T., & Scherlis, W. (1998). Internet paradox: A social technology that reduces social involvement and psychological well-being? *American Psychologist, 53,* 1017–1031.

Kuhn, D. (2006). Do cognitive changes accompany developments in the adolescent brain? *Perspectives on Psychological Science, 1*(1), 59–67.

Kunkel, D., Wilcox, B. L., Cantor, J., Palmer, E., Linn, S., & Dowrick, P. (2004). *The report of the APA task force on advertising and children.* Washington, DC: American Psychological Association.

Lenhart, A. (2007). *Cyberbullying and online teens.* Washington, DC: Pew Internet & American Life Project. Retrieved May 12, 2008, from http://www.pewinternet.org/pdfs/PIP%20Cyberbullying%20Memo.pdf

Lenhart, A., Madden, M., Macgill, A. R., & Smith, A. (2007). *Teens and social media.* Washington, DC: Pew Internet & American Life Project. Retrieved May 5, 2008, from http://www.pewinternet.org/~/media//Files/Reports/2007/PIP_Teens_Social_Media_Final.pdf.pdf

Linebarger, D. L., & Walker, D. (2005). Infants' and toddlers' television viewing and language outcomes. *American Behavioral Scientist, 48,* 624–645.

Linn, S. (2004). *Consuming kids: The hostile takeover of childhood.* New York: New Press.

Mares, M. A. (2006). Repetition increases children's comprehension of television content—up to a point. *Communication Monographs, 73,* 216–241.

Mares, M., & Woodard, E. (2005). Positive effects of television on children's social interactions: A meta-analysis. *Media Psychology, 7,* 301–322.

Masur, E. F., & Flynn, V. (2008). Infant and mother-infant play and the presence of the television. *Journal of Applied Developmental Psychology, 29,* 76–83.

McKenna, M., & Ossoff, E. (1998). Age differences in children's comprehension of a popular television program. *Child Study Journal, 28,* 53–68.

McNeal, J. U. (2007). *On becoming a consumer: Development of consumer behavior patterns in childhood.* Burlington, MA: Butterworth-Heinemann.

Mitchell, K. J., Ybarra, M., & Finkelhor, D. (2007). The relative importance of online victimization in understanding depression, delinquency, and substance abuse. *Child Maltreatment, 12,* 314–324.

Molitor, F., & Hirsch, K. W. (1994). Children's toleration of real-life aggression after exposure to media violence: A replication of the Drabman and Thomas studies. *Child Study Journal, 24,* 191–207.

Moschis, G. P., & Moore, R. L. (1982). A longitudinal study of television advertising effects. *Journal of Consumer Research, 9,* 279–286.

Nathanson, A. I. (2002). The unintended effects of parental mediation of antisocial television on adolescents. *Media Psychology, 4,* 207–230.

Nathanson, A., & Cantor, J. (2000). Reducing the aggression-promoting effect of violent cartoons by increasing children's fictional involvement with the victim: A study of active mediation. *Journal of Broadcasting & Electronic Media, 44,* 125–142.

NPD Group. (2007, June 7). *Children are becoming exposed to and adopting electronic devices at earlier ages* [Press release]. Retrieved March 20, 2008, from http://www.npd.com/press/releases/press_070605.html

Ogden, C. L., Carroll, M. D., Curtin, L. R., McDowell, M. A., Tabak, C. J., & Flegal, K. M. (2006). Prevalence of overweight and obesity in the United States. *Journal of the American Medical Association, 295,* 1549–1555.

Otto, M., Henin, A., Hirshfeld-Becker, D., Pollack, M. H., Biederman, J., & Rosenbaum, J. F. (2007). Posttraumatic stress disorder symptoms following media exposure to tragic events: Impact of 9/11 on children at risk for anxiety disorders. *Journal of Anxiety Disorders, 21,* 888–902.

Paik, H. J., & Comstock, G. (1994). The effects of television violence on antisocial behavior: A meta-analysis. *Communication Research, 21,* 516–546.

Palmer, E. L., & Carpenter, C. F. (2006). Food and beverage marketing to children and youth: Trends and issues. *Media Psychology, 8,* 165–190.

Pecora, N. (2007). The changing nature of children's television: Fifty years of research. In N. Pecora, J. P. Murray, & E. A. Wartella (Eds.), *Children and television: Fifty years of research* (pp. 1–40). Mahwah, NJ: Erlbaum.

Peter, J., Valkenburg, P. M., & Schouten, A. P. (2006). Characteristics and motives of adolescents talking with strangers on the Internet. *CyberPsychology & Behavior, 9,* 526–530.

Pfefferbaum, B., Seale, T. W., McDonald, N. B., Brandt, E. N., Jr., Rainwater, S. M., Maynard, B. T., et al. (2000). Posttraumatic stress two years after the Oklahoma City bombing in youths geographically distant from the explosion. *Psychiatry, 63,* 358–370.

Piaget, J. (1950). *The psychology of intelligence.* New York: International Universities Press.

Reiser, R. A., Tessmer, M. A., & Phelps, P. C. (1984). Adult-child interaction in children's learning from *Sesame Street. Educational Communication & Technology Journal, 32,* 217–223.

Rideout, V., & Hamel, E. (2006). *The media family: Electronic media in the lives of infants, toddlers, preschoolers and their parents.* Palo Alto, CA: Kaiser Family Foundation.

Roberts, D. F. (2000). Media and youth: Access, exposure, and privatization. *Journal of Adolescent Health, 27S,* 8–14.

Roberts, D. F., Foehr, U. G., & Rideout, V. (2005). *Generation M: Media in the lives of 8–18 year-olds.* Palo Alto, CA: Kaiser Family Foundation.

Robertson, T. S., & Rossiter, J. R. (1974). Children and commercial persuasion: An attribution theory analysis. *Journal of Consumer Research (pre-1986), 1,* 13–20.

Robinson, T. N., Borzekowski, D. L. G., Matheson, D. M., & Kraemer, H. C. (2007). Effects of fast food branding on young children's taste preference. *Archives of Pediatrics & Adolescent Medicine, 161,* 792–797.

Rosenkoetter, L. I. (1999). The television situation comedy and children's prosocial behavior. *Journal of Applied Social Psychology, 29,* 979–993.

Schmitt, K. L., Anderson, D. R., & Collins, P. A. (1999). Form and content: Looking at visual features of television. *Developmental Psychology, 35,* 1156–1167.

Schmitt, K. L., Wolf, K. D., & Anderson, D. R. (2003). Viewing the viewers: Viewing behaviors by children and adults during television programs and commercials. *Journal of Communication, 53,* 265–281.

Smith, S. L., & Wilson, B. J. (2002). Children's comprehension of and fright reactions to television news. *Media Psychology, 4,* 1–26.

Sowell, E. R., Thompson, P. M., Peterson, B. S., Mattson, S. N., Welcome, S. E., Henkenius, A. L., et al. (2002). Mapping cortical gray matter asymmetry patterns in adolescents with heavy prenatal alcohol exposure. *Neuroimage, 17,* 1807–1819.

Sprafkin, J., Liebert, R., & Poulos, R. (1975). Effect of a prosocial televised example on children's helping. *Journal of Experimental Child Psychology, 20,* 119–126.

Springer, K. (2001). Perceptual boundedness and perceptual support in conceptual development. *Psychological Review, 108,* 691–708.

Stoneman, Z., & Brody, G. H. (1981). The indirect impact of child-oriented advertisement on mother-child interactions. *Journal of Applied Developmental Psychology, 2,* 369–376.

Stutts, M. A., & Hunnicutt, G. G. (1987). Can young children understand disclaimers in television commercials? *Journal of Advertising, 16,* 41–46.

Trabasso, T., Secco, T., & van den Broek, P. (1984). Causal cohesion and story coherence. In H. Mandl, N. L. Stein, & T. Trabasso (Eds.), *Learning and comprehension of text* (pp. 83–111). Hillsdale, NJ: Erlbaum.

Tversky, B. (1985). The development of taxonomic organization of named and pictured categories. *Developmental Psychology, 21,* 1111–1119.

Valkenburg, P. M., & Buijzen, M. (2005). Identifying determinants of young children's brand awareness: Television, parents and peers. *Journal of Applied Developmental Psychology, 26,* 456–468.

Valkenburg, P. M., & Peter, J. (2007a). Online communication and adolescent well-being: Testing the stimulation versus the displacement hypothesis. *Journal of Computer-Mediated Communication, 12,* 1169–1182.

Valkenburg, P. M., & Peter, J. (2007b). Preadolescents' and adolescents' online communication and their closeness to friends. *Developmental Psychology, 43,* 267–277.

Valkenburg, P. M., Schouten, A. P., & Peter, J. (2005). Adolescents' identity experiments on the Internet. *New Media & Society, 7,* 383–402.

van den Broek, P. (1989). Causal reasoning and inference making in judging the importance of story statements. *Child Development, 60,* 286–297.

Wartella, E., & Robb, M. (2007). Young children, new media. *Journal of Children and Media, 1,* 35–44.

Wilson, B. J. (2008). Media and children's aggression, fear, and altruism. *The Future of Children, 18,* 87–118.

Wilson, B. J., & Cantor, J. (1985). Developmental differences in empathy with a television protagonist's fear. *Journal of Experimental Child Psychology, 39,* 284–299.

Wilson, B. J., Martins, N., & Marske, A. L. (2005). Children's and parents' fright reactions to kidnapping stories in the news. *Communication Monographs, 72,* 46–70.

Wilson, B. J., Smith, S. L., Potter, W. J., Kunkel, D., Linz, D., Colvin, C., et al. (2002). Violence in children's television programming: Assessing the risks. *Journal of Communication, 52,* 5–35.

Wilson, B. J., & Weiss, A. J. (1993). The effects of sibling coviewing on preschoolers' reactions to a suspenseful movie scene. *Communication Research, 20,* 214–248.

Wright, J. C., Huston, A. C., Reitz, A. L., & Piemyat, S. (1994). Young children's perceptions of television reality: Determinants and developmental differences. *Developmental Psychology, 30,* 229–239.

Wright, J. C., Huston, A. C., Scantlin, R., & Kotler, J. (2001). The Early Window project: *Sesame Street* prepares children for school. In N. S. M. Fisch & R. T. Truglio (Eds.), *"G" is for "growing": Thirty years of research on children and Sesame Street* (pp. 97–114). Mahwah, NJ: Erlbaum.

Ybarra, M. L., Diener-West, M., & Leaf, P. J. (2007). Examining the overlap in Internet harassment and school bullying: Implications for school intervention. *Journal of Adolescent Health, 41,* S42–S50.

PART VI

MEDIUM ISSUES

32

DIFFUSION OF INNOVATIONS

Theoretical Extensions

◆ Ronald E. Rice

◆ *Brief Overview and History of*
Diffusion of Innovations Theory

D iffusion of innovations (DOI) theory (Rogers, 2003) is probably the most cited, summarized, and applied of all communication theories. By 2003, there were already over 5,000 publications in this area (Rogers, 2004), and a search for "diffusion of innovations" in June 2008 found 29,000 citations in Google Scholar. *Diffusion* is the process through which an innovation (an idea, product, technology, process, or service) spreads (more or less rapidly, in more or less the same form) through mass and digital media, interpersonal and network communication, over time, through a social system, with a wide variety of consequences. Underlying the components of the diffusion process is the extent to which various actions, perceptions, communication processes and sources, and social norms and structures sufficiently reduce the potential adopter's *uncertainty* regarding the innovation. Figure 32.1 organizes the main components and their relationships in DOI theory.

Media and interpersonal *communication* and the wider *social system* both affect all aspects of these components. An individual in a social system may become aware of an innovation through mass or digital

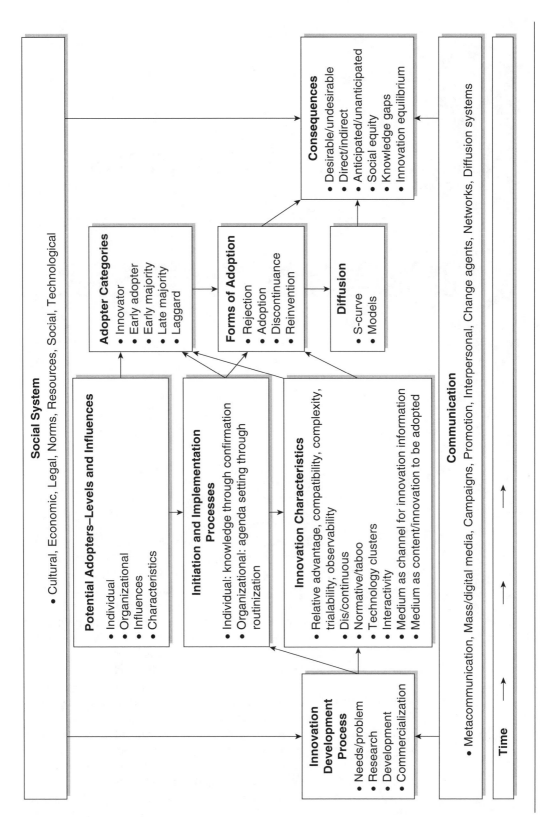

Figure 32.1 Main Components of Diffusion of Innovations Theory

media and individually choose to adopt it, or may be persuaded through interpersonal communication by influential peers. Unequal social structures, regulatory policies, and industry trends highly constrain what kinds of innovations are available and to whom.

During the *innovation development process,* actors ranging from individual entrepreneurs and collaborative users through governmental agencies and corporations attempt to identify needs and/or problems, conduct research on the ways to solve those problems, develop the innovation, and commercialize or otherwise promote it. *Potential adopters* may be individuals, groups, communities, organizations, governments, and so on, and may be affected by higher-level prior adoption decisions. The characteristics of and influences on these potential adopters affect their adoption perceptions and behaviors. These potential adopters must go through an *innovation-decision process,* consisting of first *initiation* and then *implementation* subprocesses.

During these processes, potential adopters develop perceptions of the *innovation characteristics,* which are influenced by peers, change agents, mass media portrayals, social norms, the kinds of innovation information needed, initial experiences, and, in some cases, the adoption by others. A particularly intriguing aspect of this theory relevant to media effects is that a medium can be a channel for communication about an innovation, but also an innovation itself (Rice, 1987).

The characteristics and social contexts of the potential adopters, the stage and outcomes of the initiation and implementation processes, and the perceived innovation characteristics influence one's *adoption category* (innovators, early adopters, early majority, late majority, and laggards). The initiation and implementation processes, the innovation characteristics, and one's adoption category all influence the timing, extent, and *form of the adoption.*

The timing and form of adoption in turn affect and constitute the rate of *diffusion of the innovation* throughout the social system. To the extent that the adoption times are normally distributed (the basis for the five adopter categories), the cumulative number of adopters over time is the well-known *S-shaped diffusion curve. Adoption* is an individual or organizational action (emphasizing the adopter's perspective), while *diffusion* is the spread over time of the innovation (emphasizing the supplier's, market's, and society's perspective). The innovation's diffusion through the social system generates various individual and social *consequences.*

Many of the foundations of DOI theory were developed at the beginning of the 20th century. Gabriel Tarde argued that what he called "imitation" was the basic source of social change, and he developed now-familiar concepts such as the diffusion S-curve, opinion leaders, and compatibility. Georg Simmel emphasized social influence on innovation through the role of the "stranger" who brings new ideas into a social system, heterophily, cosmopoliteness, and social networks. Early on, Rogers (1962) synthesized what had been separate, though converging, disciplinary approaches to diffusion in his *Diffusion of Innovations.* He particularly emphasized the role of the classic Ryan and Gross (1943) hybrid seed corn study through Iowa State University, which integrated and clarified many of the concepts within a primarily quantitative framework that established the DOI paradigm (Rogers, 2003, 2004).

The two-step flow model (Katz & Lazarsfeld, 1955/2005) highlighted the role of opinion leaders in filtering, interpreting, and diffusing mass media messages. Also influential was Coleman, Katz, and Menzel's (1966) analysis of physicians' adoption of prescribing the antibiotic tetracycline. By analyzing data about the doctors' individual backgrounds, their communication networks with the other doctors, and the local pharmacies' records of when the doctors first prescribed the new drug for their patients, they established the importance of communication networks in influencing individual adoption and thus the rate of diffusion throughout the social system.

The following sections briefly discuss some central issues and theoretical extensions of each of the DOI model's components, ending with some critiques of DOI.

◆ Communication and the Diffusion Process

All components of the diffusion model are potentially influenced by communication activities, from mass, digital, and local media, to interpersonal and change agent interactions (Kotler & Roberto, 1989, p. 127).

MASS AND DIGITAL MEDIA

The mass media play a central role in diffusing new ideas throughout a social system, especially in generating awareness of the innovation and providing information for opinion leaders to filter and discuss with their social system members. We may consider several mass media theories, alternate conceptualizations of mass media, and the growing importance of digital media as relevant to DOI theory.

News diffusion and agenda setting. The diffusion of news (e.g., about explosions, assassinations, celebrity gossip) was a central and early focus of mass media (DeFleur, 1987) and communication-oriented diffusion research (Rogers, 2003), and this persists as a central topic of media effects research (Lim & Kim, 2007; Perse, 2001; see also Allport & Postman, 1947). More specifically, agenda-setting research (see Shah McLeod, Gotlieb, & Lee, Chapter 6, this volume) may be conceptualized as a special case of the study of news diffusion, as it analyzes how social issues that become part of the mass media agenda,

through frequent and highlighted coverage, in turn, are raised higher on the public's agenda (McCombs & Shaw, 1972). *Bandwagon* and *underdog* effects of media coverage of opinion polls on voting are other forms of agenda-setting diffusion effects, especially for political non-elites (Perse, 2001).

Communication campaigns. A second major area of media effects research is the study and implementation of programs intended to change knowledge, attitudes, and behaviors at both the individual and social level through well-designed and evaluated communication-based interventions, or communication campaigns (Rice & Atkin, 2001). This research field overlaps with DOI in that campaign goals include diffusing information and practices throughout a social system over time, through mass, interpersonal, and social network communication. Rogers (2003) particularly highlights the successes of using mass media in edu-entertainment campaigns in fostering improved health, agricultural productivity, economic development, and prosocial norms in less developed countries.

Local media. Traditional definitions of "mass media" may unnecessarily limit our understanding of how media influence diffusion processes. Lin and Burt (1975) found that in underdeveloped areas, mass media and local media (announcers, leaflets, educational and government offices) are predicted by different demographic factors and have different influences on participation in adoption. For example, people who used local media more tended not to own radios and were well integrated into the local communication network.

Digital media. Digital media (e-mail, Internet, mobile phones, etc.) have also been considered for how they affect DOI, as well as how they themselves are diffused and adopted. Initially, because of their asynchronous and text-based nature, new media were not considered to be successful channels for innovative ideas, which supposedly require contextualization and interpretation through face-to-face communication. However, it quickly became clear that given their ability to overcome the traditional communication and mass media barriers of time and location via asynchronous sending and receiving, Internet and mobile communication allow for message tailoring, two-way interaction, searching, and sharing of knowledge among unknown others, greatly expanding the opportunities for the diffusion of new ideas (Rice, 1987; Rice & Webster, 2002). Communication research about information diffusion is especially relevant in the Internet era, where rumors and inaccurate or dangerous political or health information can spread nearly instantaneously, and be both reinforced and challenged in blogs, discussion lists, personal Web pages, etc. (Bordia & DiFonzo, 2004; Rice, 2001; Walker & Gibbons, 2006).

INTERPERSONAL COMMUNICATION AND SOCIAL NETWORKS

Interpersonal communication is particularly important in reducing uncertainty about an innovation as potential adopters turn to similar, trusted, or close—that is, *homophilous*—others for insights, interpretations, attitudes, and experiences, especially during the persuasion and decision-making phases (Rogers, 2003). A major influence on normative acceptance of an innovation is the social system's *opinion leaders* and the extent to which potential adopters communicate with them (Coleman, Katz, & Menzel, 1966). Similar to the *change agent,* who represents the organization or agency sponsoring the innovation and who works with opinion leaders and other clients to develop an understanding of the costs and benefits of the innovation, the *technology champion* in organizational contexts plays a significant interpersonal role in influencing the adoption of new organizational media (Howell & Higgins, 1990).

More specifically, one's location in a social system's *communication network* strongly affects the speed and extent of information/adoption diffusion (Valente, 2005). Weak ties—infrequent communication with those who are not close—provide exposure to new ideas and information (Granovetter, 1973). Frequent social or physical exposure to salient others is then crucial for reducing uncertainty about the innovation, fostering supportive social norms, and persuading potential adopters (Rice, 1993b). Now, social networking Web sites enable rapid diffusion of information and norms (Wang, Carley, Zeng, & Mao, 2007). The importance of interpersonal communication networks in combination with targeted media messages on DOI has been popularized through concepts such as the tipping point (Gladwell, 2000; related to a *critical mass* of adopters, Markus, 1987) and new product "buzz" (Rosen, 2000).

Network influences also provide explanations for how initial minority views about innovations generate widespread diffusion. Once innovators and those who may have more resources or can obtain early benefits adopt, then those with higher *network adoption* thresholds will be more open to adoption (Valente, 2005). *Bounded normative influence* explains how a minority, through network centrality, persuasiveness, consistency, confidence, commitment, and difficulty of expelling deviants, may succeed in establishing their norm as a majority norm, especially if the majority is not well articulated, is ambiguous, misperceives the situation, or has low commitment (Kincaid, 2004).

◆ Social System(s) and the Diffusion Process

Social system conditions include economics, network cooperation, power relations, governmental policies, competition/cooperation, and standardization (Andriessen,

1994). O'Callaghan (1998) emphasized that individual organizations rarely adopt an innovation in isolation from the surrounding industry. Diffusion of a technology throughout an industry can change organizational and industry perceptions of the innovation through increased knowledge of the technology, applications, benefits, and reduced risk, as well as develop positive network externalities of supporting innovations, which in turn influence later adaptations and likelihood of adoption by other organizations. Historical analyses of technological innovations clearly reveal the wide range of prior developments, path dependencies, and actor networks fostering or constraining an innovation (e.g., Aikat, 2001; Sedman, 1998; Streeter, 1996).

A theoretical approach to understanding the complex social, technological, and economic context of DOI is *mediamorphosis,* or "the transformation of communication media, usually brought about by the complex interplay of perceived needs, competitive and political pressures, and social and technological innovations" (Fidler, 1997, p. xv). In the case of media innovations, these include, for example (Fidler, 1997; Winston, 1998), (1) competition (e.g., between radio and TV); (2) new opportunities and needs fostered by other innovations (e.g., the development of stereo audio recordings stimulating the advantage of FM over AM radio); (3) regulation and technical standards (e.g., changes in copyright and cross-ownership criteria; Rice, 2008a); and (4) economic factors (e.g., microprocessor chip costs). More general theoretical approaches to the evolution, diffusion, shaping, and application of technological innovations include social construction of technology, co-construction of technology, sociotechnical systems theory, and path dependence.

◆ *The Innovation Development Process*

Many of the social systems approaches may be seen as explaining general contexts for,

as well as specific aspects of, the innovation development process. Understanding this process is the goal of a vast realm of studies on research and development, technology and innovation management, technology transfer, entrepreneurship, marketing/ promotion, financing, licensing/patents/ copyrights, and so on. However, Rogers (2003) recommends greater attention to how the social system fosters and constrains both the initial development of innovations and their form and features before adopters even become aware of the innovation.

Scientific and technical communication among researchers, both within and across organizations, through media (such as specialist journals and online discussion lists) and interpersonal networks (gatekeepers, conferences, local professional networks) is a central topic of R&D and organizational innovation research (e.g., Rice, 1987). Diffusing the innovation beyond the initial innovators and early adopters is a particularly risky and difficult process, especially for discontinuous technology innovations, as discussed later in this chapter.

◆ *Potential Adopters: Levels and Influences*

INDIVIDUAL CHARACTERISTICS AND INFLUENCES

Innovativeness is conceptualized as relative earliness in adopting an innovation and being receptive to new ideas independent of others' influence (Lin, 1998). It can be categorized into two types: *inherent* innovativeness (tendencies or drives) and *actualized* innovativeness (behaviors). Innovativeness is positively related to other individual characteristics such as SES, and to earlier adoption (Rogers, 2003), and has been shown to moderate the relationship between perceived innovation attributes and adoption decisions (Agarwal & Prasad, 1998).

Adoption may also be influenced by other individual factors, such as media use (though research is not consistent), technology ownership/experience/expertise, demographics (age), personality (such as dogmatism), obstacles to innovation (access), and needs and expected gratifications (entertainment). Other factors include task characteristics (interdependency, equivocality), contexts (other users, situational constraints), technical (standards, technological literacy), social influences (peers, status), communication competence, mental models (blogs as journalism or opinion), and user attitudes (expected benefits, costs; Andriessen, 1994; James, Wotring, & Forrest, 1995; Jeffres & Atkin, 1996; Lin, 2002; Rice, 1987; Rice & Webster, 2002). Indeed, individual demographic and access factors capture most of the factors representing the *digital divide* (markedly differential adoption of the Internet) in the United States (Katz & Rice, 2002), although these factors combine somewhat differently to explain adoption patterns for the Internet and mobile phones (Rice & Katz, 2003). Recently, there have also been some notable attempts to integrate individual characteristics within a range of theoretical perspectives to better understand their role in the adoption, use, and diffusion of communication/information technologies (see Rice & Webster, 2002; Van den Hooff, Groot, & de Jonge, 2005).

ORGANIZATIONAL CHARACTERISTICS AND INFLUENCES

In many cases, organizations (in the DOI model, broadly meaning any collectivity of people, including departments, organizations, communities, states, etc.) must adopt an innovation (which may include technical standards or underlying infrastructure) before individual members have the possibility (whether by choice or requirement) of also adopting the innovation (what is called a *contingent* adoption decision).

Organizational characteristics, such as size, formality, complexity, centralization, and slack resources, also influence innovation adoption. In the media industry, because digital information can be easily distributed, repackaged, and cross-promoted, organizational characteristics, such as vertical and horizontal integration, can both foster innovation (multiplatform programming) and stifle it (excessive copyrights, suppressed independent production; Rice, 2008a). An *innovative organizational culture* is characterized by the ability to manage its environments, a proactive support of appropriate human activity, pragmatic assessments of truth, medium-length time horizons, an assumption that people are generally good and capable of improvement, a positive view of individualism and diversity, support for participation appropriate to the type of innovation, and diverse but connected subcultures (Schein, 1994).

◆ *Initiation and Implementation Processes at the Individual and Organizational Level*

Because of the need to reduce their uncertainty about an innovation, both individuals and organizations must go through several phases before making the decision and then integrating the innovation into regular use. For individuals, these phases include knowledge/awareness, persuasion decision, implementation, and confirmation. For organizations, they include agenda setting, matching, redefining, clarifying, and routinization. The first three individual phases and the first two organizational phases are more generally considered *initiation* processes (and are arguably the foci of some media effects research), whereas the latter individual and organizational phases are considered *implementation* processes (Rogers, 2003; Wirsan & Muller, 2006). These phases are not necessarily sequential, as experiences and decisions in one phase may require returning to an earlier phase.

O'Callaghan (1998) felt that the organizational adoption process is perhaps the least useful part of the DOI model because it provides no insight into the often extremely time-consuming, risky, and often unsuccessful *technology implementation process* (Andriessen, 1994; Cooper & Zmud, 1990; Johnson & Rice, 1987). His more comprehensive diffusion process model included (1) preexisting organizational and environmental context, (2) technology assessment, (3) planning and adoption decision, (4) usage or internal diffusion, and (5) organizational changes (1998, p. 399). Andriessen's (1994) organizational-level diffusion of innovation model included (1) creation in the industry (research and development), (2) transfer to the organization (diffusion often requiring adoption by a cluster of organizations, then adoption within a particular organization), and (3) introduction into the organization (design/implementation and incorporation, within different contexts).

◆ Innovation Characteristics

The likelihood and form of adoption are influenced by how potential adopters perceive the primary *innovation characteristics* of relative advantage, complexity, trialability, compatibility, and observability/communicability. Other central characteristics include *ease of use* and *usefulness,* central concepts in the technology acceptance model (TAM), which is typically applied to understanding the adoption of information technologies in organizational settings (Venkatesh, Morris, Davis, & Davis, 2003). Moore and Benbasat's (1991) review of information systems research concluded that relative advantage (similar to perceived usefulness), compatibility, and complexity (similar to perceived ease of use) had the most consistent influences on adoption. Fidler (1997) added another innovation attribute: *bridges of familiarity.* These include links to the past, whereby new media initially incorporate (and may be limited by) both technological and social forms from prior media, though these then are elaborated, transformed, and replaced over time. Bridges of familiarity also include metaphors, whereby both media messages and design elements provide ways of understanding and contextualizing new media characteristics through familiar metaphors, such as computer "desktops" or early TV programs replicating radio shows (see Jensen, 1990, for a discussion of how responses to media that are new at the time, such as radio and TV, take the form of one of four general metaphors).

Vishwanath and Goldhaber (2003) developed an integrated TAM/DOI model specifically to predict possible intention of adoption by mobile phone *nonadopters* (there were many more of those in 2002!). The interesting approach here was using perceived innovation attributes as *mediators* between typical TAM and DOI influences. The model almost perfectly fit the data, showing that demographics influenced communication factors, such as media use, new media ownership, and change agent contact (sales representatives and friends), which in turn differentially affected perceptions of relative disadvantages, perceived complexity, lack of observability, and perceived incompatibility, which in turn fostered a negative attitude toward using mobile phones, leading to decreased behavioral intention. Rice and Webster's (2002) integrated model also portrayed innovation attributes as mediators between exogenous influences and adoption, diffusion, and use of new media.

Other distinctions among innovation characteristics include *incremental* versus *radical/discontinuous, administrative* versus *technological, process* versus *product,* and *content* versus *role/process* (Robertson, 1971; Schein, 1994). For example, HDTV is a radical innovation because it requires discontinuous changes in technical standards, program production, and TV sets, and allows new content in the form of digital information used for tracking, retrieving, and reprocessing of program content. However, the actual viewing experience and program content may change only incrementally. Further, a new medium may be perceived by a potential adopter as fitting into an acceptable *technology cluster,* conceptualized as either the extent to which technologies similar to the innovation have already been adopted by the individual, or as interrelated components of a technological innovation (LaRose & Atkin, 1992; Lin, 2002).

As noted earlier, with respect to DOI, media (mass and digital) are unique in that they may be channels for information and influence about an innovation, as well as innovations to be diffused and communicated about, and in some cases both in the same study (Rice, 1987). For example, Rice (1993a) found that peer influence in organizational settings about perceptions of social presence in various media was a significant factor only about the newest medium (desktop video conferencing) and then only when communicated through that medium itself.

◆ *Adopter Categories*

Although adopter categories have traditionally been divided into the five groups described earlier (innovator, early adopter, early majority, late majority, and laggard), recent research has explored alternative ways of grouping potential adopters. For example, Lin (1998) created *nonadopter, likely adopter,* and *adopter* groups, which were statistically distinguished by many of the usual new media predictors (such as demographics, innovativeness, less TV viewing, and other communication technology adoption). Von Hippel (1986) introduced the distinctive category of *lead users,* who contribute to product concept and design and foreshadow the needs of the general marketplace, and thus are especially relevant during the innovation development

process. Another newer distinction is between *innovators*—those who make their decision to adopt independently based on their innovativeness and awareness of the innovation through media—and *imitators*—those influenced by the nature and timing of others' adoption (O'Callaghan, 1998). This distinction is the basis for the Bass diffusion model, described in the following section.

Finally, a pragmatic extension to the traditional adopter categories is the concept of a *chasm* between early and later adopters, relevant for discontinuous (primarily technological) innovations (Moore, 2002). Firms must *cross the chasm* from an early market dominated by a few *visionary* customers (innovators and early adopters) who are interested in the sophisticated technology features or the status of early adoption, to a mainstream market dominated largely by *pragmatists* (early majority) and *conservatives* (late majority), who look for value, maintenance of ongoing practices, and ongoing vendor support.

◆ *Forms of Adoption*

The concept of adoption is more complex than a simple binary use/no use. Adoption may involve *purchase, usage, acceptance, resistance, discontinuance, avoidance,* or *reinvention/adaptation.* At-risk audiences may well adopt the knowledge and attitudes promoted by a communication campaign, but not alter their practices. Organizational adoption of a new medium, such as shared online calendars, may require usage but not gain acceptance (Hiltz & Johnson, 1989). An innovation, once adopted, may later be discontinued, such as when a newer technology achieves *critical mass* (the number of users sufficient to stimulate and justify adoption by other members of the social system; Kraut, Rice, Cool, & Fish, 1998; Markus, 1987). Fidler (1997), for example, provided a detailed analysis of the eventual diffusion failure of teletext, after several national trials and services.

One particularly interesting form of adoption is *reinvention,* or the adaptation of an innovation after adoption (Hays, 1996; Johnson & Rice, 1987), which includes the development of new features and applications of the initial innovation. The telephone and the mobile phone, for example, are exceptionally rich contexts for reinvention with a constantly changing diversity of bundled services and features. Such reinventions pose considerable challenge to the traditional adoption/diffusion model of a dichotomous adoption of a fixed innovation (LaRose & Atkin, 1992; Wirth, von Pape, & Karnowski, 2008).

There are many mass media, sociological, and organizational theories potentially applicable to understanding reinvention (Wirth et al., 2008). *Uses-and-gratifications* theory emphasizes the active choice and reinvention by users in selecting and applying media (Blumler & Katz, 1974; Rubin, Chapter 10, this volume). Sociological approaches such as *domestication* (Silverstone & Haddon, 1996) and *social shaping of technology* (Lievrouw & Livingstone, 2002; MacKenzie & Wajcman, 1999) show how adopters can project their own interpretations and derive their own meanings about both mass media (TV use in the home) and new media (mobile phone use by teenagers) to make them more useful and meaningful. *Frame analysis* has been used by Ling (2004) to analyze mobile phone use. Because social norms lag behind technological diffusion, people apply current *normative frames* to try to make sense of, and understand how to use, this malleable and changing medium. Studies of adoption of information/ communication technologies in organizations apply the concept of *adaptive/ technology structuration* (e.g., Majchrzak, Rice, Malhotra, King, & Ba, 2000; Poole & DeSanctis, 1990). A related concept as applied to reinvention in new media is *metacontrol,* the negotiation of the

shaping of user control options—an unintended consequence of converging digital media resulting in detailed personalization of a new medium (Kilker, 2003).

◆ Diffusion of an Innovation Through a Social System Over Time

The traditional DOI theory largely focuses on predicting adoption by individuals or organizations, rather than diffusion per se. *Diffusion* is the cumulative number of adopters over time, and may be represented through different visual curves and statistical models, taking into account factors such as supplier marketing, environmental influences, market capacity, competition, and so on (Wirsan & Muller, 2006). Kotler and Roberto (1989, p. 120) described three kinds of diffusion curves. The *rapid penetration* model identifies the likely percentage of total adopters from the population (say, 40%) over time, and the percentage of remaining adopters likely to adopt in each time period, leading to the ceiling adoption level. The *gradual penetration* diffusion model is the typical S-curve (central to the DOI theory), with a normal distribution of adopters in each time period, using the standard adopter categories, with an initial adoption rate, a rapid *take-up* portion, and a leveling off to the maximum adoption percentage. The *contagion-like,* or Bass (1969), diffusion model takes into account the separate influences of media and of prior adopters on nonadopters. Showing that the Bass diffusion model nicely fits data about U.S. radio, TV, cable, VCR, and home computer use, Dimmick and Wang (2005) proposed that such media are adopted to the extent that adopters anticipate deriving various gratification utilities before adopting the medium. Applying a diffusion approach to agenda setting, Fan (1988) compared time-series analysis of computergenerated content analyses of media coverage with time-series analysis of opinion poll results about various issues, essentially showing the influence of media content on the subsequent diffusion of public agenda issues over time.

Due to the Internet and digital markets, the diffusion curve has been extended both temporally and conceptually, resulting in what Anderson (2006) called the "long tail." Storage, search, retrieval, and distribution costs of digital information are nearing zero. Potential adopters can access a Web site providing media products and content from around the world. Collaborative filtering and recommender software can introduce people to otherwise unknown, but appropriate, products. Thus, companies or individuals can now maintain inventories of, and make money from, otherwise obscure and niche products. All of these factors extend the right side of the diffusion curve along the full length of the "long tail," often leading to even more total adopters than associated with media "hits" and "best sellers," and making media content (books, music, art) available that otherwise would have been removed from physical inventory.

◆ *Consequences of Innovation Adoption and Diffusion*

The implementation and diffusion literature provides many frameworks for identifying and evaluating the direct/indirect, short-term/long-term, intended/unintended, and positive/negative social consequences of innovation adoption (O'Callaghan, 1998; Rice, 2008b; Tenner, 1997). Perhaps those that have received the most attention are those that involve the negative or unintended consequences of diffusion. Like the unintended consequences of media campaigns, such as boomerang effects where at-risk audiences develop greater awareness of or more positive attitudes toward, or engage more in, the risky behavior (such as youth drug use; Hornik et al., 2003), innovation diffusion may also backfire, spreading too quickly for a social system to adapt, creating disequilibrium and dysfunctional feedback loops (especially in complex technological and biological systems; Tenner, 1997).

In addition, as Rogers (2003) has claimed, without proactive policies and diffusion strategies, innovations in general tend to *increase* socioeconomic inequalities. This point is supported by research on the knowledge gap hypothesis, which highlights how, for example, the diffusion of educational information through the media may raise knowledge levels of children overall, but will benefit those who are already higher in socioeconomic status (SES), further widening the knowledge gap (Tichenor, Donohue, & Olien, 1970).

The adoption and diffusion of media itself has significant economic consequences, both as *factors affecting the adoption* (the technology and service), and as *outcomes*, such as increased distribution of information about production and purchasing of goods and services (Dimmick & Wang, 2005). Economic aspects of media structures (such as concentration of media outlets and ownership by nonmedia corporations) affect the diffusion of information about the media itself and its content (such as controversial topics, critiques of the media organization or its owners, or new reporting resources; Rice, 2008a).

◆ *Critiques and Conclusion*

DOI theory has been criticized on a number of grounds. Rogers (2003), for example, has noted several biases in the theory, including the *pro-innovation* and the *individual blame* biases. Other, more recent, challenges focus on the need to broaden the scope of diffusion research to consider all the factors leading up to public access to the innovation, and involving relevant communities in any diffusion efforts (Kreps & Hider, 2004). Cooper (1998) emphasized the need to consider multiple dimensions of innovations, each of which may be associated with somewhat different influences and adoption processes. Rogers (2003) also suggested the need for a much wider array of methodologies than the traditional cross-sectional survey employed, in which only a single innovation is examined from the adopters' perspective, using recall data from relatively late in the diffusion process. Newer methodological approaches might include panel studies for causal analysis, point-of-adoption data collection, archival records, quasi-experimental field studies, technological forecasting, network analysis, and qualitative evidence (Klopfenstein, 1989; Valente, 2005).

The diffusion of innovations theory is a complex and comprehensive interdisciplinary framework for understanding how new ideas diffuse (or not) through a social system. Central to the process is the role of mass and digital media, in combination with interpersonal communication and social networks, in reducing the potential adopter's uncertainty. I hope this chapter has served as a means to appreciate not only the richness of the theory but also the unique role of media as both the channel for communicating and providing information about an innovation, and also (especially with digital media) an innovation itself.

◆ References

Agarwal, R., & Prasad, J. (1998). The antecedents and consequents of user perceptions in information technology adoption. *Decision Support Systems, 22,* 15–29.

Aikat, D. (2001). Pioneers of the early digital era: Innovative ideas that shaped computing in 1833–1945. *Convergence: Journal of Research Into New Media Technologies, 7*(4), 52–81.

Allport, G. W., & Postman, L. J. (1947). *The psychology of rumor.* New York: Holt, Rinehart & Winston.

Anderson, C. (2006). *The long tail: Why the future of business is selling less of more.* NY: Hyperion.

Andriessen, J. H. E. (1994). Conditions for successful adoption and implementation of telematics in user organizations. In J. H. E. Andriessen & R. Roe (Eds.), *Telematics and work* (pp. 411–439). Hillsdale, NJ: Erlbaum.

Bass, F. M. (1969). A new product growth for model consumer durables. *Management Science, 15*(5), 215–227.

Blumler, J. G., & Katz, E. (1974). (Eds.). *The uses of mass communications: Current perspectives in gratifications research.* Beverly Hills, CA: Sage.

Bordia, P., & DiFonzo, N. (2004). Problem solving in social interactions on the Internet: Rumor as social cognition. *Social Psychology Quarterly, 67,* 33–49.

Coleman, J. S., Katz, E., & Menzel, H. (1966). *Medical innovation: A diffusion study.* New York: Bobbs-Merrill.

Cooper, J. R. (1998). A multidimensional approach to the adoption of innovation. *Management Decision, 36*(8), 493–502.

Cooper, R., & Zmud, R. (1990). Information technology implementation research: A technological diffusion approach. *Management Science, 36*(2), 123–139.

DeFleur, M. L. (1987). The growth and decline of research on the diffusion of news, 1945–1985. *Communication Research, 14,* 109–130.

Dimmick, J., & Wang, T. (2005). Toward an economic theory of media diffusion based on the parameters of the logistic growth equation. *Journal of Media Economics, 18*(4), 233–246.

Fan, D. P. (1988). *Predictions of public opinion from the mass media.* New York: Greenwood Press.

Fidler, R. (1997). *Mediamorphosis: Understanding new media.* Thousand Oaks, CA: Pine Forge Press.

Gladwell, M. (2000). *The tipping point: How little things can make a big difference.* New York: Little, Brown & Co.

Granovetter, M. (1973). The strength of weak ties. *American Journal of Sociology, 78,* 1360–1380.

Hays, S. P. (1996). Influences on reinvention during the diffusion of innovations. *Political Research Quarterly, 43*(3), 631–650.

Hiltz, S. R., & Johnson, K. (1989). Measuring acceptance of computer-mediated communication systems. *Journal of the American Society for Information Science, 40*(6), 386–397.

Hornik, R., Maklan, D., Cadell, D., Barmada, C. H., Jacobsohn, L., Prado, A., et al. (2003). *Evaluation of the National Youth Anti-Drug Media Campaign: Fifth semi-annual report of findings.* Washington, DC: Report by Westat to Office of National Drug Control Policy, National Youth Anti-Drug Campaign.

Howell, J. M., & Higgins, C. A. (1990). Champions of technological innovation. *Administrative Science Quarterly, 35,* 317–341.

James, M. L., Wotring, C. E., & Forrest, E. J. (1995). An exploratory study of the perceived benefits of electronic bulletin board use and their impact on other communication activities. *Journal of Broadcasting and Electronic Media, 39,* 30–50.

Jeffres, L. W., & Atkin, D. (1996). Predicting use of technologies for consumer and communication needs. *Journal of Broadcasting & Electronic Media, 40,* 315–330.

Jensen, J. (1990). *Redeeming modernity: Contradictions in media criticism.* Thousand Oaks, CA: Sage.

Johnson, B., & Rice, R. E. (1987). *Managing organizational innovation: The evolution from word processing to office information systems.* New York: Columbia University Press.

Katz, E., & Lazarsfeld, P. F. (2005). *Personal influence: The part played by people in the flow of mass communication* (Rev. ed.). New Brunswick, NJ: Transaction Publishers. (Original work published 1955)

Katz, J. E., & Rice, R. E. (2002). *Social consequences of Internet use: Access, involvement and interaction.* Cambridge, MA: MIT Press.

Kilker, J. (2003). Shaping convergence media: "Meta-control" and the domestication of DVD and Web technologies. *Convergence: The International Journal of Research Into New Media Technologies, 9*(3), 20–39.

Kincaid, D. L. (2004). From innovation to social norm: Bounded influence. *Journal of Health Communication, 9*(6), 37–57.

Klopfenstein, B. C. (1989). Problems and potential of forecasting the adoption of new media. In J. Salvaggio & J. Bryant (Eds.), *Media use in the Information Age: Emerging patterns of adoption and consumer use* (pp. 21–41). Hillsdale, NJ: Erlbaum.

Kotler, P., & Roberto, E. L. (1989). *Social marketing: Strategies for changing public behavior.* NY: Free Press.

Kraut, R., Rice, R. E., Cool, C., & Fish, R. (1998). Varieties of social influence: The role of utility and norms in the success of a new communication medium. *Organization Science, 9*(4), 437–453.

Kreps, G. L., & Hider, M. (2004). Forty years of diffusion of innovations: Utility and value in public health. *Journal of Health Communication, 9*(6), 3–11.

LaRose, R., & Atkin, D. (1992). Audiotext and the re-invention of the telephone as a mass medium. *Journalism Quarterly, 69,* 413–421.

Lievrouw, L., & Livingstone, S. (Eds.). (2002). *Handbook of new media: Social shaping and social consequences.* London: Sage.

Lim, T.-S., & Kim, S. Y. (2007). Many faces of media effects. In R. Preiss, B. M. Gayle, N. Burrell, M. Allen, & J. Bryant (Eds.), *Mass media effects research: Advances through meta-analysis* (pp. 315–325). Mahwah, NJ: Erlbaum.

Lin, C. A. (1998). Exploring personal computer adoption dynamics. *Journal of Broadcasting & Electronic Media, 42,* 95–112.

Lin, C. A. (2002). Perceived gratifications of online media service use among potential users. *Telematics and Informatics, 19*(1), 3–19.

Lin, N., & Burt, R. S. (1975). Differential effects of information channels in the process of innovation diffusion. *Social Forces, 54*(1), 256–274.

Ling, R. (2004). *The mobile connection: The cell phone's impact on society.* San Francisco: Morgan Kaufmann.

MacKenzie, D., & Wajcman, J. (Eds.). (1999). *The social shaping of technology* (2nd ed.). McGraw-Hill Education.

Majchrzak, A., Rice, R., Malhotra, A., King, N., & Ba, S. (2000). Technology adaptation:

The case of computer-supported inter-organizational virtual teams. *MIS Quarterly, 24*(4), 569–600.

Markus, M. L. (1987). Toward a "critical mass" theory of interactive media, universal access, interdependence and diffusion. *Communication Research, 14*(5), 491–511.

McCombs, M. E., & Shaw, D. L. (1972). The agenda-setting function of the mass media. *Public Opinion Quarterly, 36*(2), 176–187.

Moore, G. A. (2002). *Crossing the chasm: Marketing and selling disruptive products to mainstream customers.* New York: Collins Business Essentials.

Moore, G. C., & Benbasat, I. (1991). Development of an instrument to measure the perceptions of adopting an information technology innovation. *Information Systems Research, 2,* 192–222.

O'Callaghan, R. (1998). Technology diffusion and organizational transformation: An integrative framework. In T. Larsen & E. McGuire (Eds.), *Information systems innovation and diffusion: Issues and directions* (pp. 390–410). Hershey, PA: Idea Group.

Perse, E. M. (2001). *Media effects and society.* Mahwah, NJ: Erlbaum.

Poole, M. S., & DeSanctis, G. (1990). Understanding the use of group decision support systems: The theory of adaptive structuration. In J. Fulk & C. Steinfield (Eds.), *Organizations and communication technology* (pp. 173–193). Beverly Hills, CA: Sage.

Rice, R. E. (1987). Computer-mediated communication and organizational innovation. *Journal of Communication, 37*(4), 65–94.

Rice, R. E. (1993a). Media appropriateness: Using social presence theory to compare traditional and new organizational media. *Human Communication Research, 19*(4), 451–484.

Rice, R. E. (1993b). Using network concepts to clarify sources and mechanisms of social influence. In W. Richards, Jr., & G. Barnett (Eds.), *Progress in communication sciences: Advances in communication network analysis* (pp. 43–62). Norwood, NJ: Ablex.

Rice, R. E. (2001). The Internet and health communication: A framework of experiences. In R. E. Rice & J. E. Katz (Eds.), *The Internet and health communication: Expectations and experiences* (pp. 5–46). Thousand Oaks, CA: Sage.

Rice, R. E. (2008a). *Media ownership: Research and regulation.* Cresskill, NJ: Hampton Press.

Rice, R. E. (2008b). Unusual routines: Organizational (non)sensemaking. *Journal of Communication, 58*(1), 1–19.

Rice, R. E., & Atkin, C. (2001). *Public communication campaigns* (3rd ed.). Thousand Oaks, CA: Sage.

Rice, R. E., & Katz, J. E. (2003). Comparing Internet and mobile phone usage: Digital divides of usage, adoption, and dropouts. *Telecommunications Policy, 27*(8/9), 597–623.

Rice, R. E., & Webster, J. (2002). Adoption, diffusion and use of new media in organizational settings. In C. Lin & D. Atkin (Eds.), *Communication technology and society* (pp. 191–227). Cresskill, NJ: Hampton Press.

Robertson, T. S. (1971). *Innovative behaviour and communication.* New York: Holt.

Rogers, E. M. (1962). *Diffusion of innovations.* Glencoe, IL: Free Press.

Rogers, E. M. (2003). *Diffusion of innovations* (5th ed.). New York: Free Press.

Rogers, E. M. (2004). A prospective and retrospective look at the diffusion model. *Journal of Health Communication, 9*(6), 13–19.

Rosen, E. (2000). *The anatomy of buzz: How to create word-of-mouth marketing.* New York: Random House.

Ryan, B., & Gross, N. (1943). The diffusion of hybrid seed corn in two Iowa communities. *Rural Sociology, 8,* 15–24.

Schein, E. (1994). Innovative cultures and organizations. In T. Allen & M. Scott-Morton (Eds.), *Information technology and the corporation of the 1990s: Research studies* (pp. 125–146). New York: Oxford University Press.

Sedman, D. (1998). Market parameters, marketing hype, and technical standards: The introduction of DVD. *Journal of Media Economics, 11*(1), 49–58.

Silverstone, R., & Haddon, L. (1996). Design and the domestication of information and communication technologies: Technical change and everyday life. In R. Silverstone & R. Mansell (Eds.), *Communication by design: The politics of information and communication technologies* (pp. 44–74). Oxford, UK: Oxford University Press.

Streeter, T. (1996). *Selling the air: A critique of the policy of commercial broadcasting in the United States.* Chicago: University of Chicago Press.

Tenner, E. (1997). *Why things bite back: Technology and the revenge of unintended consequences.* New York: Vintage.

Tichenor, P. J., Donohue, G. A., & Olien, C. N. (1970). Mass media flow and differential growth in knowledge. *Public Opinion Quarterly, 34,* 159–170.

Valente, T. W. (2005). Network models and methods for studying the diffusion of innovations. In P. Carrington, J. Scott, & S. Wasserman (Eds.), *Models and methods in social network analysis* (pp. 98–116). Cambridge, UK: Cambridge University Press.

Van den Hooff, B., Groot, J., & de Jonge, S. (2005). Situational influences on the use of communication technologies: A meta-analysis and exploratory study. *Journal of Business Communication, 42*(1), 4–27.

Venkatesh, V., Morris, M. G., Davis, G. B., & Davis, F. D. (2003). User acceptance of information technology: Toward a unified view. *MIS Quarterly, 27*(3), 425–478.

Vishwanath, A., & Goldhaber, G. M. (2003). An examination of the factors contributing to adoption decisions among late diffused technology products. *New Media Society, 5,* 547–572.

von Hippel, E. (1986). Lead users: A source of novel product concepts. *Management Science, 32*(7), 791–805.

Walker, W. R., & Gibbons, J. A. (2006). Rumor mongering as a collective coping strategy for traumatic public events: Evidence from face to face interactions and rumors on the Internet. *International Journal of Cognitive Technology, 11,* 31–35.

Wang, F.-Y., Carley, K. M., Zeng, D., & Mao, W. (2007). Social computing: From social informatics to social intelligence. *IEEE Intelligent Systems, 22*(2), 79–83.

Winston, B. (1998). *Media technology and society: A history: from the telegraph to the Internet.* London: Routledge.

Wirsan, J., & Muller, C. (2006). Applicability and assessment of adoption and diffusion models: Review of the models of Bass, Milling and Maier, Rogers and Frambach and Schillewaert. *International Journal of Enterprise Network Management, 1*(1), 62–78.

Wirth, W., von Pape, T., & Karnowski, V. (2008). An integrative model of mobile phone appropriation. *Journal of Computer Mediated Communication, 13*(3), 593–617. Retrieved April 2009 from http://www3.interscience .wiley.com/cgi-bin/fulltext/119414158/ HTMLSTART

33

DISPLACEMENT EFFECTS

◆ Jennings Bryant and Wes Fondren

According to conventional wisdom, time is a limited resource. Every hour has 60 minutes; every day, 24 hours. So what happens when 2 hours of new activity enter one's daily schedule? Most likely, some other activity gets displaced. The supply is the same, but with new demands. In displacement theory, the core assertion is that media consumption will displace some other activity or activities, such as exercise or social interaction, or even shift time from one medium to another. This is often referred to as the displacement hypothesis.[1]

Concerns about displacement effects become most evident at the introduction of a new medium. A new demand is placed on the same old time supply. Accordingly, "speculations about the death of old media in the face of new communication technologies are widespread" (Nguyen & Western, 2006, p. 2). Speculation about these ultimate displacement effects (i.e., "death") is rampant. However, as will be seen throughout this chapter, systematic theoretical explication and empirical investigation to support such claims is less than overwhelming.

In the 20th century, no medium was as broadly and quickly adopted as television (Carey, 1993), and accordingly, no medium has been as heavily investigated for displacement effects as television. As reflected in this chapter, the majority of all displacement research is focused on television viewing, primarily by children, although a burgeoning literature is increasingly addressing displacement effects of the Internet, video games, text messaging, and other mobile media.

This chapter will briefly survey the historical roots of displacement theory, address the major assumptions of the theory, and attempt to answer the question, "What exactly is being displaced?" Then we will briefly identify some of the many challenges to the future of displacement research in the emerging digital environment.

◆ The Roots of Displacement Theory

When the first prehistoric cave dwellers finished their delicious meal of rack of Brontosaurus and turned to the canvas of the cave wall to scratch out the saga of the tribal kill, undoubtedly some of their peers immediately decried their artistic efforts by bemoaning the time their creative efforts displaced from the traditional oral means of telling the story of the hunt. Many millennia later, about 5,000 years ago, when the Babylonians and Assyrians began to write on clay tablets (e.g., Chiera, 1938), it is almost certain that the cave-petrography guild accused these early tableteers of sounding the death knell of cave art. We have no extant historical evidence to support either claim, but we do know that in about 370 BCE, Plato expressed fear that the written word would supplant time and effort devoted to the spoken word (Perloff, 2002).

Jumping to early scientific attempts to examine displacement, traces of displacement effects can be seen as early as the late 1920s in the Payne Fund studies on the impact of cinema on children, but displacement research had begun in earnest by the mid-20th century. In the early 1950s, interviews were conducted with 379 mothers in Cambridge, Massachusetts, to compare the behavior of children who watched television with those who did not (Maccoby, 1954). Although methodological problems plagued the study, the results indicated a great need for—and rich potential of—further research. Even at this early stage in the adoption of television, the median

estimation by mothers of viewers was that their children devoted 1½ hours to television each day.

In the mid-1950s, Himmelweit, Oppenheim, and Vince (1958) performed the first empirical study on changes in how children spent their time once broadcast television was introduced in England. Four thousand children ages 10 to 14 were included in the study, organized into pairs, one non-viewer and one viewer, and matched as well by other criteria (e.g., age, gender, intelligence). Similarly, by the late 1950s, Schramm, Lyle, and Parker (1961) were undertaking a comparable study of 5,000 children in the United States and Canada. Although the two studies were conducted independently and in different countries, both revealed remarkably similar findings. Children appeared to use television viewing to replace other, lighter forms of recreation, such as reading comic books and listening to radio, but not to replace more serious enterprises like homework and reading books. Out of their study findings, Himmelweit et al. developed three principles of displacement that were also later supported by the findings of the Schramm et al. study: functional similarity, transformation, and marginal fringe activities. Neuman (1995), in her review of the two studies, added a fourth principle, physical and psychological proximity.

◆ Principles of Displacement

FUNCTIONAL SIMILARITY

If two media perform the same function, the medium that best satisfies the given need typically will be selected. The degree of satisfaction could be based on an array of criteria, such as the amount of effort required to meet the need or the amount of pleasure derived from the process. Himmelweit et al. (1958) referred to this relationship as "functionally equivalent." For example, remember that researchers had found that children tended to replace comic book reading with television viewing (Himmelweit et al., 1958; Schramm et al., 1961). Both activities can serve the function of entertainment. The moving images and sounds provided by television, however, supply more detailed and robust information with less effort on the child's part. The same is true when comparing television with radio. Television not only provides the soundtrack, but also requires less imaginative work. Assumptions about the passivity of the television viewer are apparent in these early studies. This assumption would be challenged in the coming years, as will be discussed in greater detail later in the chapter.

The preference for television was not just based on vividness and reduced cognitive work; simplified physical activity also played a role. Walking to a friend's house for social interaction, or a trip to the playground or theater, now had to compete with a stream of freely broadcast television programs delivered into the comfort of one's own living room. The cinema was particularly hard hit by the direct competition. Neuman (1995) blamed the functional similarity between movies and television for the 56% drop in weekly cinema attendance in America between 1946 and 1955. The silver screen might have been more captivating, but television was more convenient.

TRANSFORMATION

Himmelweit et al. (1958) posited that in light of functional similarity, for the displaced medium to survive, its function must change. When a dominant new medium like television was introduced, functionally similar media had to adapt to survive, which generally required them to develop new functions. An excellent example of transformation is how radio adjusted to the firestorm of television's rapid adoption. No longer able to successfully compete head-to-head with television in formats like game shows, dramas, and comedies, radio

instead focused on niche musical tastes, news, and traffic reports. Later researchers (Jeffres, Atkin, & Neuendorf, 1995; Krugman, 1985) would extend the concept of transformation by stating that a key element in a preexisting medium's survival is getting consumers to alter their understanding of the medium's function. A successful transformation is not merely finding a new function, but also changing the users' perceptions. Radio stations managed to persuade listeners that radio could also enhance other tasks. Radio moved from being the centerpiece of Saturday evenings, families gathered in singular focus around a radio drama, to being background entertainment while cleaning house or driving. In losing prime time, radio gained time shared with other activities.

MARGINAL FRINGE ACTIVITIES

The Himmelweit et al. (1958) and Schramm et al. (1961) studies found that another type of activity displaced by television viewing was actually not necessarily any activity at all—free time. Unstructured play and leisure time lost out to the attraction of television. With increasing frequency, having nothing to do meant having time to watch television. True to the displacement hypothesis, the studies found that regular television viewing was linked with reduced leisure time for children. This led Himmelweit et al. (1958) to speculate that "fringe" activities, defined as ones not measured by time, were more likely to be replaced. A later study (Brown, Cramond, & Wilde, 1974) appeared to find contradictory evidence that suggested structured time is displaced more often than is unstructured time. The studies may be in closer agreement than first appears, because the divergence primarily seems to highlight the difficulties of trying to measure unstructured time.

A survey of 700 participants by Roberts, Foehr, and Rideout (2005) seemed to clarify the situation. These investigators found that younger children reported watching more television than did older kids. When including all forms of video exposure, 15- to 18-year-olds watched an hour a day less than did 8- to 10-year-olds, and three quarters of an hour less than did 11- to 14-year-olds, and both sets of comparisons between mean scores were found to be statistically significant. One viable explanation put forth is that as children get older, they have increased structured time (e.g., after-school jobs, athletics, dating), thereby providing support for the original marginal fringe activities hypothesis.

PHYSICAL AND PSYCHOLOGICAL PROXIMITY

When two competing activities occupy the same physical space, the one that provides greater satisfaction will most often be selected. For example, if a child has a television and a radio in the same room, more times than not the television will be selected. Furu (1971) surveyed 3,000 children in Japan about their degree of television and print media usage. Television viewers performed fewer household chores and less homework compared with children who did not watch television, suggesting that being in proximity to a television creates a competition for time that favors television viewing. Furu explained the findings by stating that television was more satisfying to children than work, and that the key variable was accessibility. Consistent with Furu's claim, he found that heavy television viewing correlated negatively with academic achievement.

Although the three studies (Furu, 1971; Himmelweit et al., 1958; Schramm et al., 1961) are early milestones in displacement research, conceptual and methodological differences confound direct comparisons. Are household chores unstructured activities if time is not measured? If homework is neither functionally similar nor fringe activity, why was it displaced in the Furu study? Clearly a need remained for

increased sophistication and refinement in investigating displacement.

◆ Conceptual Refinement

Williams (1986) attempted to more clearly define displacement concepts and move beyond a simple notion of one activity replacing another by examining the nature and degree of displacement effects, as well as by attempting to discover which groups were most affected. She introduced the purpose of this investigation as follows: "In particular, the displacement hypothesis requires considerable refinement. We must ask not only *whether* displacement occurs but more specifically *for whom* and *what* is displaced" (p. 10). Moreover, she indicated that displacement effects might not always be detrimental: "In some circumstances, the effect may be positive, in others, negative" (p. 10). What followed Williams's ambitious statement of purpose was a classic set of field investigations that included a two-tiered rollout of multiple television stations in three Canadian towns. In Phase 1, the town called "Notel" received no television channels, "Unitel" received one, and "Multitel" received four. Two years later, Phase 2 brought one channel to Notel, two channels to Unitel, and Multitel continued with four channels. The results supported earlier findings in that some children's leisure time decreased as the presence of television increased. But unlike functional similarity, Williams and Handford (1986) found that whereas television use displaced some of the young people's participation in sports and community activities with more similar but competing activities such as television viewing and reading, available time was often divided, rather than television viewing dominantly displacing other activities. The Williams (1986) investigation, as impressive as it was, did not provide all the answers regarding displacement effects. In fact, it has been viewed as a clarion call for further investigations into displacement (Bryant & Bryant, 2003).

◆ *Displacement Variables—What Gives?*

Since the displacement hypothesis centers on one activity replacing another, a logical question is, "What gives?" What gets less time to make room for two new hours of television viewing, for example? In seeking to answer this question, assumptions often are made about the nature of displacement. In the majority of displacement research, especially in the early days, the effects were assumed to be negative. This is apparent in the types of variables chosen to examine (e.g., homework, exercise, reading, etc.), which are typically activities of value. Often the concern is that something valuable is being replaced by an activity of lesser value or even harm. Does academic achievement decline with heavy television viewing? It is far less common to see variables that reflect the assumption of a positive effect. Does after-school television viewing diminish opportunities for bullying? Would access to a large video library reduce commonly reported feelings of loneliness for latchkey children? Could providing game consoles in inner city clubs decrease gang violence?

The predominate assumption of negativity in displacement research is ironic considering the origins of mass entertainment. In ancient Rome, vast structures, like the Colosseum and amphitheaters, were created to entertain the masses for free. One of the main reasons for such extensive undertakings was to give the large numbers of unemployed or partially employed people an activity to fill their free time (Ibrahim, 1979; Kraus, 1971; Zillmann, 2000). Mass entertainment originally displaced crime and discontentment. Displacement, in general, was perceived to have a positive effect.

As displacement theory grew more sophisticated, along with advancements in research methods and statistical tools, the assumption of negative effects was challenged. Research questions were crafted and variables selected that considered the potentially positive, or even neutral, outcomes of displacement. The following section examines displacement research through the lens of the variables being investigated, while also looking at the assumptions of positive and negative effects. The following review will focus on three areas in which researchers have sought to answer the question, "What is being displaced?" namely, social interaction, physical activity, and cognitive development.

SOCIAL INTERACTION

In television's early days, it appeared that television viewing rarely involved social interaction for most children; therefore, fears emerged that social development would be stunted due to heavy viewing habits. Even the relationships within the nuclear family were feared to be at risk. Concerns over damaging effects on the family and children's social growth became, and still are, the impetus for much of the displacement research. Testifying before a congressional subcommittee in 1955, communication research pioneer Paul Lazarsfeld stated the pressing need for studies to produce "ideas as to how the average family can create an atmosphere which will compete with television" (Lazarsfeld, 1955, p. 247). The negative social assumptions can be seen in the belief that without action, the average family would lose out to television. Forty-four years after Lazarsfeld's testimony, the American Academy of Pediatrics called for the elimination or significant reduction in the amount of television viewing for young children based on the assumption that it displaces family interaction (Hogan et al., 1999).

Research has shown that concern is not without merit. Two studies, Williams (1986) in Canada and Mutz, Roberts, and Vuuren (1993) in South Africa, found that when television access was introduced into a town, social interaction among children decreased as television viewing increased.

The Mutz et al. (1993) study was conducted over a 6-year period, which provided additional data as to how viewers adjusted over time. Once the novelty of television dissipated, television viewing declined, but social activity and other media usage never returned to the pretelevision levels. These data suggest that displacement effects may not be symmetrical, but may be long term.

What about parents who watch television with their children? Could a social bond be formed that leads to more familial interaction and time relating? A recent study of 1,712 children younger than 13 years of age found that time spent watching television, both viewing with a parent and alone, negatively correlated with time spent with parents in other activities (Vandewater, Bickham, & Lee, 2006). Television time displaced other family time, even with a parent coviewing. There were similar findings regarding time spent with siblings.

A difficulty with assessing whether television displaces children's social activity is that all television viewing is not the same. Viewing Saturday-morning cartoons typically differs greatly from viewing prime-time crime dramas. Perse (2001) recognized the classification of displacement effects as being content irrelevant, but she rightly stated that first it must be determined whether the effects actually are content irrelevant. If one media experience replaces another, is it possible to divorce the content from the experience? One study (Huston, Wright, Marquis, & Green, 1999) found a negative correlation between television viewing and social interaction, but only for entertainment television. Increased educational television was not related to changes in social interaction. These results suggest that it may be inaccurate or even naive to view displacement effects as being content irrelevant. Although the focus is often on what is being missed out on (e.g., social interaction), we must also look at what is filling the new space.

The arrival of a new medium often triggers attention about displacement effects.

As the Internet has grown in popularity with adolescents, so have concerns that online interaction is displacing face-to-face social interaction. There is little evidence so far to support concerns about distorted social development due to online social activity. Several studies found that online interaction actually augmented social relationships among adolescents and college students, rather than replacing them (Bryant, Sanders-Jackson, & Smallwood, 2006; Ellison, Steinfield, & Lampe, 2007; Valkenburg & Peter, 2007). Little is yet known about the long-term effects of highly popular online social networks, however.

PHYSICAL ACTIVITY

Television viewing often requires little or no physical exertion. It is hypothesized that if watching television displaces routine physical activity (e.g., sports, exercise, play time)—and early research supported that notion (Williams & Handford, 1986)—then weight gain and related health risks are more likely. In order to investigate the amount of energy expended while watching television, researchers (Klesges, Shelton, & Klesges, 1993) measured the metabolic rate of 31 children, 15 of whom were obese. Measurements were taken while each child was sitting still for 25 minutes and while watching the television show *Wonder Years* for 25 minutes. The order of events varied. A within-subjects comparison showed that energy expenditures significantly dropped for both groups of children while watching television when compared with normal resting rates.

Although television viewing is a low-exertion task, for the displacement hypothesis to be valid, more strenuous activity would have to be replaced by viewing. One study (Lumeng, Rahnama, Appugliese, Kaciroti, & Bradley, 2006) in 10 U.S. cities examined the impact of daily television exposure on young children beginning at 36 months of age through 54 months of age. The children were exposed to 2 or more hours of television per day during awake time. When controlling for variables such as income-needs ratio, race, and hours of nonparental care, results revealed the younger television viewers were 2.92 times more likely to be overweight compared national averages. In a study of a national sample of 746 adolescents, 10 to 15 years of age (Gortmaker et al., 1996), research showed a 4.6 times greater chance of being overweight if the participant watched 5 or more hours of television a day, compared with adolescents who watched 2 hours or less. After controlling for several covariates, researchers concluded that more than 60% of overweight incidence in adolescence nationally could be directly linked to excessive television viewing.

Children are not the only population at risk. Two studies examined the relationship between watching television and risk of obesity and type 2 diabetes (Hu et al., 2001; Hu, Li, Colditz, Willett, & Manson, 2003). One study examined males (Hu et al., 2001), the other females (Hu et al., 2003). The study of males was a 10-year biannual survey of 37,918 respondents aged 40 to 75, in which health and lifestyle information were reported, including weekly hours of television viewing. The results revealed a significant association between time spent watching television and type 2 diabetes. A significant positive trend between viewing and weight gain was also found. The study of 50,277 females rendered similar significant results. Research presents a compelling case that watching television is linked to weight gain across the life span, supporting the displacement theory.

COGNITIVE DEVELOPMENT

It is often assumed that television viewing is a cognitively passive act. A common concern is that trading a cognitively active task, like reading, for a supposedly passive task, like watching television, will be detrimental to a child's cognitive development. All the major studies of the 1950s through the 1970s included some index of time spent

reading, obviously out of fear that television would displace reading (for a review of literacy displacement research, see Neuman, 1995). Seeking to understand television's impact on literacy and cognitive development is still a major focus of displacement research.

For example, Koolstra and van der Voort (1996) sought to understand how television viewing affected children's leisure reading as opposed to required reading. Researchers surveyed 1,050 Dutch elementary school children annually for 3 years regarding television-viewing and book-reading habits. Structural equation modeling was used to analyze the data in an effort to show a causal relationship, which had eluded past correlation research (Neuman, 1995). Results indicated television viewing led to a temporary decline in comic reading and a sustained decline in book reading. Researchers concluded that increased television viewing yielded decreases in both children's attitude toward reading and children's ability to concentrate when reading. Ennemoser and Schneider (2007) compared reading skills with the amount of television children viewed. Three hundred and thirty-two German elementary school children were tested each year for 4 years to measure reading speed and comprehension. Results revealed that heavy television viewers trailed behind light and moderate viewers. The findings showed that by the end of the 4-year period there was at least a one-grade-level reading-skill differential between heavy viewers and light viewers. Interestingly, total viewing time was negatively correlated to reading achievement, but the association was limited to entertainment programming and not educational programming. It appears that the displacement effect of television viewing, by degree and content, is related to weaker reading abilities. The negative assumption of displacement is supported, but does educational television viewing have a positive displacement effect?

In the 1980s, two studies were conducted regarding television-viewing habits of preschoolers, one study in Kansas (Huston,

Wright, Rice, Kerkman, & St. Peters, 1990) and one in Massachusetts (Anderson, Field, Collins, Lorch, & Nathan, 1985). Fifteen and 18 years later, respectively, researchers returned to gather follow-up information about academic achievement, behavior, and numerous other variables (Anderson, Huston, Schmitt, Linebarger, & Wright, 2001). High school students with high viewing habits of educational (informative) television as preschoolers scored significantly higher in course grades, had higher academic and leadership achievements, spent more time leisure book reading, and participated in more service activities, compared with their cohort group that had low educational viewing as preschoolers. Sixty-two variables were statistically significant either favorably for the high educational viewing group or unfavorably for the low educational viewing group. These extensive findings show a multifaceted association between academic achievement, cognitive development, and exposure to educational programming as a preschooler, or a lack of exposure. The results indicate that viewing educational content relates to a positive displacement effect on preschoolers in the long term.

As can be seen in the areas of social interaction, physical activity, and cognitive development, displacement theory has moved from simple quid pro quo hypotheses to providing insight into the complicated, interwoven relationships between variables. And yet, many questions remain about displacement theory, and numerous underlying assumptions still need investigating.

◆ *The Future of Displacement Theory: Plurality in the Era of Multitasking and Convergence*

CONSIDERING CONTENT

In light of current research, it is difficult to comprehend how displacement theory could continue to be viewed as content irrelevant (Perse, 2001). Instead, it seems more reasonable to consider activity displacement in light of what makes up the activity (e.g., content, medium, environment, etc.), which is what much of the recent research has done. Yet the temptation still exists to ignore content. For example, the most compelling argument for content-irrelevant displacement effects may be television viewing and weight gain. The sedentary nature of watching television lowers metabolic rates and is often associated with multiple hours of daily physical inactivity. It appears that activity is exchanged for inactivity and weight gain follows. But is it really content irrelevant? Researchers testing metabolic rates (Klesges et al., 1993) intentionally selected mild media fare in order to avoid arousal that would increase metabolism. Many types of content (e.g., action, pornography, suspense) increase sympathetic activation system responses, which increase heart rate and energy expenditure (for an explanation of excitation and media use, see Bryant & Miron, 2003; Lang, Potter, & Bolls, 2009).

Media content produces more than just physiological effects; it frequently influences behavior. Two content analyses of television shows, one popular with children (Harrison & Marske, 2005), and the other with the general market (Henderson & Kelly, 2005), both discovered the prevalence of advertisements for high-calorie foods, like fast food and soft drinks. Gorn and Goldberg (1982) showed one group of children at a summer camp 4.5 minutes of high-calorie food commercials during a 30-minute cartoon, and they repeated that treatment every day for 2 weeks. Results showed that children who viewed the high-calorie food commercials selected candy and sweets at snack times significantly more often than did children in the control groups. In unrestricted viewing (Hu et al., 2001), how many more minutes of high-calorie food commercials are heavy viewers (5 or more hours of television per day) exposed to than are light viewers?

There is good reason to believe that media content matters significantly in activity choices. Displacement research in the future will need to continue and extend the trend of incorporating content variables in studies. One of the strengths of displacement theory is that it can support and be supported by many other theories. Displacement can fit well alongside cultivation theory, or agenda setting, or framing, or many other theories. In fact, it may help explain the processes or effects typically involved in other theoretical models, ultimately improving their utility. The irony is that displacement theory does not need to displace other theories, but rather it can serve complementary purposes. It may be that this functional plurality of theories best helps researchers understand the complexity of variables and effects of media choices.

SHARED MEDIA SPACE

Perse (2001) stated that one of the faulty assumptions of the displacement hypothesis is that people use only one medium at a time. In reality, media are often experienced simultaneously. Maybe a person accesses the Internet while the television plays in the background or listens to music while reading. Himmelweit et al.'s (1958) principle of transformation posits that media have to find new functions to coexist. Within today's media environment, that is an everyday story. Nowadays, the family SUV comes equipped with one or more DVD players to entertain passengers. Where movies were once an event to be experienced at a theater, a movie can now fill down time during a long trip, or maybe just a short trip to school and back. Moreover, in the era of convergence, movies that were designed and produced to be seen in theaters are now watched on televisions, on computer screens (delivered by DVDs or via the Internet), or on iPods

and cell phones. Those exemplar cases only scratch the surface of the complexity of our modern media-use environment.

The openness to view media as serving secondary and tertiary purposes, along with increased media availability, has led to a glut of media exposure. In a report by the Kaiser Family Foundation (Foehr, 2006), findings from a major survey revealed that 81% of young people use more than one medium at a time during a typical week. Sixty-two percent reported performing another task when reading was their primary activity, and 24% reported using other media "most of the time" while they were watching television. The study also found that "light" media multitasking young people were exposed to an average of more than 6½ hours of media a day; "heavy" multitaskers experienced almost 12.82 hours of media a day. In another Kaiser Family Foundation report (Rideout, Roberts, & Foehr, 2005), 61% of students reported using media or talking on the phone at least some of the time while doing homework. The report referred to 8- to 18-year-olds as "Generation M" due to their heavy media use. The evidence suggests that this label could mean both "Generation Media" and "Generation Multitaskers."

It appears that rather than one medium displacing another, with ever-increasing frequency, media are sharing time slots. This poses interesting and difficult challenges in displacement research. For example, how does an investigator determine when media-use time is actually being shared, or if multiple but intermittent moments of displacement are taking place within the multitasking experience? We began this chapter with the claims that (a) each day has only 24 hours, and (b) doing one thing displaces doing another. With media multitasking, for today's and tomorrow's generations, at some level those claims may no longer be valid. If multiple, overlapping media usage is disaggregated and disambiguated, it is feasible that some media junkies may use more than 24 hours of media in one day (although they obviously still cannot use media for more than 24 hours per day).

Now the question becomes, in this present era and presumably beyond, as we time-share multiple converged media, what *really* gets displaced and replaced? Is it merely time? Or is that which is lost a type of mental processing? Is it linear, rational thought? Is it quality of human interaction? Such questions go far beyond the issue of whether consuming medium A supplants the pursuit of leisure-time hobbies versus the pursuit of knowledge. More important, perhaps, almost none of these more complex displacement questions have been the subject of rigorous theory construction, nor have they been subjected to systematic empirical investigation. In other words, many of the big questions of displacement theory and effects have yet to be asked, and the final word in displacement effects has yet to be spoken or published.

◆ Note

1. Although the focus of this chapter is on *time* displacement, it should be noted that a quite different theoretical and empirical approach to media displacement and replacement effects takes an *economic* perspective. Anchored by McCombs's (1972) principle of relative constancy, the thrust of this argument is, "in spite of the increasing complexity of mass communications with the advent of new media, *the pattern of economic support has been relatively constant and more closely related to the general economy* than to the various changes and trends taking place within the mass media field itself" (McCombs, 1972, p. 5). In other words, the relative constancy principle alleged that the media industries and their products account for a relatively fixed share of the national economic pie, and what one medium (typically a newer medium) gains is subtracted from prior expenditures on older media. The basis for this thesis was a major study on consumer and advertiser expenditures nationally, using aggregate data from the United States from 1929 through 1968. McCombs's basic hypothesis was strongly supported. However, in recent years, even a cursory study of national economic data from the U.S. Department of Commerce would reveal that the average individual and household media budgets (or, more specifically, the *media entertainment* budget) is occupying an ever-increasing portion of overall consumer dollars. In light of such trends, updated research on the principle of relative constancy is sorely needed.

◆ References

Anderson, D. R., Field, D. E., Collins, P. A., Lorch, E. P., & Nathan, J. G. (1985). Estimates of young children's time with television: A methodological comparison of parent reports with time-lapse video home observation. *Child Development, 56,* 1345–1357.

Anderson, D. R., Huston, A. C., Schmitt, K. L., Linebarger, D. L., & Wright, J. C. (2001). Early childhood television viewing and adolescent behavior: The reconnect study. *Monographs of the Society for Research in Child Development, 66,* 1–145.

Brown, J. R., Cramond, J. K., & Wilde, R. J. (1974). Displacement effects of television and the child's functional orientation to the media. In J. G. Blumer & E. Ktaz (Eds.), *The uses of mass communication* (pp. 93–112). Beverly Hills, CA: Sage.

Bryant, J., & Miron, D. (2003). Excitation-transfer theory and three-factor theory of emotion. In J. Bryant, D. Roskos-Ewoldsen, & J. Cantor (Eds.), *Communication and emotion: Essays in honor of Dolf Zillmann* (pp. 31–59). Mahwah, NJ: Erlbaum.

Bryant, J. A., & Bryant, J. (2003). Effects of entertainment televisual media on children. In E. L. Palmer & B. M. Young (Eds.), *The faces of televisual media* (2nd ed., pp. 195–217). Mahwah, NJ: Erlbaum.

Bryant, J. A., Sanders-Jackson, A., & Smallwood, A. M. K. (2006). IMing, text messaging, and adolescent social networks. *Journal of Computer-Mediated Communication, 11,* 577–592.

Carey, J. (1993). Looking back to the future: How communication technologies enter American households. In J. V. Pavlik & E. E. Dennis (Eds.), *Demystifying media technology* (pp. 32–39). Mountain View, CA: Mayfield.

Chiera, E. (1938). *They wrote on clay: The Babylonian tablets speak today.* Chicago: University of Chicago Press.

Ellison, N. B., Steinfield, C., & Lampe, C. (2007). The benefits of Facebook "friends": Social capital and college students' use of online social network sites. *Journal of Computer-Mediated Communication, 12,* 1143–1168.

Ennemoser, M., & Schneider, W. (2007). Relations of television viewing and reading development: Finding from a 4-year longitudinal study. *Journal of Educational Psychology, 99,* 349–368.

Foehr, U. G. (2006). *Media multitasking among American youth: Prevalence, predictors and pairings.* Menlo Park, CA: Kaiser Family Foundation.

Furu, T. (1971). *The function of television for children and adolescents.* Rutland, VT: Charles E. Tuttle.

Gorn, G. J., & Goldberg, M. E. (1982). Behavioral evidence of the effects of televised food messages on children. *Journal of Consumer Research, 9,* 200–205.

Gortmaker, S. L., Must, A., Sobol, A. M., Peterson, K., Colditz, G. A., & Dietz, W. H. (1996). Television viewing as a cause of increasing obesity among children in the United States, 1986–1990. *Archives of Pediatric & Adolescent Medicine, 150,* 356–362.

Harrison, K., & Marske, A. L. (2005). Nutritional content of foods advertised during the television programs children watch most. *American Journal of Public Health, 95,* 1568–1575.

Henderson, V. R., & Kelly, B. (2005). Food advertising in the age of obesity: Content analysis of food advertising on general market and African American television. *Journal of Nutrition Education and Behavior, 37,* 191–196.

Himmelweit, H. T., Oppenheim, A. N., & Vince, P. (1958). *Television and the child: An empirical study of the effect of television on the young.* London, New York: Published for the Nuffield Foundation by the Oxford University Press.

Hogan, M., Bar-on, M., Beard, L., Corrigan, S., Gedissman, A., Palumbo, F., et al. (1999). Media education. *Pediatrics, 104,* 341–343.

Hu, F. B., Leitzmann, M. F., Stampfer, M. J., Colditz, G. A., Willett, W. C., & Rimm, E. B. (2001). Physical activity and television watching in relation to risk for type 2 diabetes mellitus in men. *Archives of Internal Medicine, 161,* 1542–1548.

Hu, F. B., Li, T. Y., Colditz, G. A., Willett, W. C., & Manson, J. E. (2003). Television watching and other sedentary behaviors in relation to risk of obesity and type 2 diabetes mellitus in women. *Journal of the American Medical Association, 289,* 1785–1791.

Huston, A. C., Wright, J. C., Marquis, J., & Green, S. (1999). How young children spend their time: Television and other activities. *Developmental Psychology, 35,* 912–925.

Huston, A. C., Wright, J. C., Rice, M. L., Kerkman, D., & St. Peters, M. (1990). The development of television viewing patterns in early childhood: A longitudinal investigation. *Developmental Psychology, 26,* 409–420.

Ibrahim, H. (1979). Leisure in the ancient world. In H. Ibrahim & J. S. Shivers (Eds.), *Leisure: Emergence and expansion* (pp. 45–77). Los Alamitos, CA: Hwong.

Jeffres, L., Atkin, D., & Neuendorf, K. (1995). The impact of new and traditional media on college student leisure preferences. *World Communication, 24,* 67–73.

Klesges, R. C., Shelton, M. L., & Klesges, L. M. (1993). Effects of television on metabolic rate: Potential implications for childhood obesity. *Pediatrics, 91,* 281–285.

Koolstra, C. M., & van der Voort, T. H. A. (1996). Longitudinal effects of television on children's leisure-time reading. *Human Communication Research, 23,* 4–35.

Kraus, R. (1971). *Recreation and leisure in modern society.* New York: Appleton-Century-Crofts.

Krugman, D. (1985). Evaluating the audiences of the new media. *Journal of Advertising, 14*(4), 14–19.

Lang, A., Potter, R. F., & Bolls, P. (2009). Where psychophysiology meets the media: Taking the effects out of mass media research. In J. Bryant & M. B. Oliver (Eds.), *Media effects: Advances in theory and research* (3rd ed., pp. 185–206). New York: Routledge.

Lazarsfeld, P. (1955). Why is so little known about the effects of television on children and what can be done? *Public Opinion Quarterly, 19,* 243–251.

Lumeng, J. C., Rahnama, S., Appugliese, D., Kaciroti, N., & Bradley, R. H. (2006). Television exposure and overweight risk in preschoolers. *Archives of Pediatric & Adolescent Medicine, 160,* 417–422.

Maccoby, E. E. (1954). Why do children watch television? *Public Opinion Quarterly, 18,* 239–244.

McCombs, M. (1972). *Mass media in the marketplace.* Thousand Oaks, CA: Sage.

Mutz, D. C., Roberts, D. F., & Vuuren, D. P. (1993). Reconsidering the displacement hypothesis: Television's influence on children's time use. *Communication Research, 20,* 51–75.

Neuman, S. B. (1995). *Literacy in the television age: The myth of the TV effect* (2nd ed.). Norwood, NJ: Ablex.

Nguyen, A., & Western, M. (2006). The complementary relationship between the Internet and traditional mass media: The case of online news and information. *Information Research, 11*(3), 1–19.

Perloff, R. M. (2002). The third-person effect. In J. Bryant & D. Zillmann (Eds.), *Media effects: Advances in theory and research* (2nd ed., pp. 489–506). Mahwah, NJ: Erlbaum.

Perse, E. M. (2001). *Media effects and society.* Mahwah, NJ: Erlbaum.

Putnam, R. D. (1995). Tuning in, tuning out: The strange disappearance of social capital in America. *PS: Political Science & Politics, 28,* 664–683.

Rideout, V., Roberts, D. F., & Foehr, U. G. (2005). *Generation M: Media in the lives of 8–18 year-olds.* Menlo Park, CA: Kaiser Family Foundation.

Roberts, D. F., Foehr, U. G., & Rideout, V. (2005). *Generation M: Media in the lives of 8–18 year-olds* (Kaiser Family Foundation study). Menlo Park, CA: Kaiser Family Foundation.

Schramm, W. L., Lyle, J., & Parker, E. B. (1961). *Television in the lives of our children.* Stanford, CA: Stanford University Press.

U.S. Bureau of the Census. (1975). *Historical statistics of the United States, colonial times to 1970.* Washington, DC: U.S. Government Printing Office.

Valkenburg, P. M., & Peter, J. (2007). Online communication and adolescent well-being: Testing the stimulation versus the displacement hypothesis. *Journal of Computer-Mediated Communication, 12,* 1169–1182.

Vandewater, E. A., Bickham, D. S., & Lee, J. H. (2006). Time well spent? Relating television use to children's free-time activities. *Pediatrics, 117*(2), e181–e191.

Williams, T. M. (1986). Background and overview. In T. M. Williams (Ed.), *The impact of television* (pp. 1–36). Orlando, FL: Academic Press.

Williams, T. M., & Handford, G. (1986). Television and other leisure activities. In T. M. Williams (Ed.), *The impact of television* (pp. 143–213). Orlando, FL: Academic Press.

Zillmann, D. (2000). The coming of media entertainment. In D. Zillmann & P. Vorderer (Eds.), *Media entertainment: The psychology of its appeal* (pp. 1–20). Mahwah, NJ: Erlbaum.

34

MEDIUM THEORY

An Alternative to the Dominant Paradigm of Media Effects

◆ Joshua Meyrowitz

W hen printing first spread through Western Europe in the late 15th century, it was tightly controlled by the Church and Crown. An analyst who looked at this situation through the most common approach to "media effects"—with a focus on the influence of media content and medium control—would likely have predicted that the long-term impact of the printing press on Western Europe would be to increase religiosity and strengthen the authority of monarchs. Evidence to support this view was plentiful in the early era of printing. Indeed, many of those who first tried to use the new medium to question religious or monarchal authority were severely punished, sometimes even put to death. Yet, most historians and other observers would now agree that the ultimate influence of the spread of printing and literacy was in direct opposition to the thrust of early printed content and the desires of the medium's first masters. In the long run, printing helped to secularize society through the spread of scientific learning and also

Author's Note: Thanks to Renée Carpenter and Peter Schmidt for their comments and suggestions.

undermined the authority of monarchs by supporting the development of constitutional systems, where widely available printed documents literally constituted the shared conceptions and laws of each nation.

To observe these types of potential media effects—whether in the past, present, or future—one needs to shift the focus from the content of media as the prime source of influence and look to the nature and capacities of each medium itself. A key question is: How do the characteristics of each medium differ from those of other means of communication? To ask such a question is not to argue that a medium can have influence without any content, nor is it to argue that a medium's features magically "determine" the medium's impact on passive humans. Rather, the exploration of the features that distinguish one medium from another is compatible with the assumptions that the same or similar content often has different effects in different media, that new means of communication afford new possibilities that human beings creatively exploit for both old and new purposes, and that people actively develop new forms of content and new ways of interacting to match the potentialities and constraints of new media.

Printing, for example, differed dramatically from handwritten manuscripts in that it allowed for relatively inexpensive, rapid, and widespread sharing of identical texts. Printing facilitated a shift from a focus on copying and preserving existing "authoritative" documents to a focus on broad distribution. Printing made possible more sophisticated means of organizing, searching, and citing written material with such innovations as page numbers, tables of contents, and indexes (in place of identifying scribal content by a name for a whole manuscript or, at best, by chapter and verse). Broad distribution and new forms of organizing writings increased interaction among authors who referenced and critiqued each other. And such interaction led to incremental improvements in texts and in knowledge through many new books and through corrected and expanded editions of older volumes. All told, these and other contrasts between handwritten manuscripts and printed books were differences that made a difference in political, religious, and intellectual life.

Medium theory is a special type of media study that focuses on such characteristics of each medium and on how each medium (or each *type* of media) is physically, socially, and psychologically distinct from other media. Medium theorists, for example, look both at how the Internet is different from television and at how television and the Internet (as two forms of electronic media) differ from books and newspapers (two forms of print media). Medium theory also compares and contrasts each medium with unmediated face-to-face interaction. The term *medium theory* was coined in the 1980s (Meyrowitz, 1985, p. 16) to give a unifying name to scholarship in a variety of fields, including political economy, literature, anthropology, history, the classics, religion, and communication. The singular "medium" is used in the name of the theory to distinguish this perspective from more generic "media theory" by calling attention to the special focus on the particular characteristics of each medium. Medium theory is closely related to the field of "media ecology" (cf. Lum, 2006; Strate, 2006). This chapter describes the types of differences among media that medium theory explores, the history of medium theory, subgenres of medium theory, micro- versus macrolevel medium theory, and the critiques and limitations of medium theory.

◆ Medium Characteristics

In comparing and contrasting different communication technologies, medium theorists attempt to identify the characteristics of media and how those characteristics may have an influence on human interactions, institutions, and social structure. Such characteristics of media include

- *the type of sensory information* the medium is able and unable to transmit (e.g., visual, aural, tactile, olfactory, etc.) and whether the medium is *uni-* or *multisensory;*

- the *form or forms* of information conveyed by the medium within each sense (e.g., the dots and dashes of abstract Morse code contrasted with speech, as two distinct types of sound; or ideograph vs. photograph vs. written word, as three distinct types of visual information);

- the *degree of verisimilitude between the medium form and "reality"* (e.g., one may mistake a radio voice for a real person in the next room, but rarely does one mistake a TV image for a live visitor in the house, and yet, the TV images of people certainly look more like real persons than do written descriptions of them);

- whether the medium offers *unidirectional versus bidirectional versus multidirectional communication;*

- whether exchanges through the medium are *sequential or simultaneous* (as in the difference between the telephone, with its overlapping utterances, and the turn-taking in CB radio);

- the *degree and type of control the users have over reception and transmission* (e.g., the fixed speed and sequence of a TV news broadcast as opposed to readers' freedom to jump around in a newspaper or create their own paths through Internet news via hyperlink options);

- the *physical requirements for using the medium* (such as whether one has to touch the medium, remain in a fixed location, look in a certain direction, and so forth) and what other mediated and unmediated activities can and cannot be done easily at the same time (e.g., while many people drive or make love while listening to music, television watching and computer keyboarding are generally considered less compatible with those activities);

- the *degree and type of human intervention/manipulation that is necessary or possible in creating a message* (as in the difference between snapping the shutter of an automatic camera and painting an oil portrait, or the different range of manipulations possible with digital photography contrasted with a chemical photo darkroom);

- *the scope and nature of dissemination* of the medium (e.g., the question of how many people in different locations can experience the same message at the same time);

- the medium's *durability* (how long the medium or its messages last) and *portability* (how easily the medium and its messages can be transported over great distances);

- *the relative ease or difficulty of learning to code and decode messages in the medium,* including the issue of whether one tends to learn to use the medium all at once (as seems to be more true of radio and TV than of most other media) or in stages (as is typical with literacy) and the issue of the *ratio of coding/decoding complexity* (e.g., learning to *watch* an animated cartoon is much simpler than learning to *produce* an animated cartoon, but listening and speaking over the telephone are on a relatively equal plane of difficulty); and

- all the ways in which *media physically interact with each other* (e.g., a letter can be "sent"—actually, just reproduced—by a fax machine over phone lines, but a videotape would have to be physically transported from one place to another unless its content is first digitized for electronic transmission, and while one can easily place text on a computer screen, one cannot as simply put a computer screen in a book).

By focusing on these and other differences among media, medium theorists argue that media, far from being passive channels for transmitting information from one environment to another, are themselves distinct communication environments. As a type of environment, each medium tends to encourage certain types of interaction while discouraging others.

◆ The History of Medium Theory

Medium theory has ancient roots. A medium theory perspective is implicit in the Ten Commandments, which suggested that the medium through which God was portrayed made a difference. Graven images and idols were forbidden in favor of worship of an abstract, imageless god.

Perhaps the first explicit medium theory was articulated by Socrates (469–399 BC), who, as a master of oral discourse, looked at the spread of writing with a suspicious and critical eye. Writing, he recognized, was not just another way of speaking. Writing, Socrates said, would lead to forgetfulness, because writers and readers would no longer need to rely on their memories. In addition, writing diminished dialogue, since a reader could not ask a text a question or directly influence the thoughts of the writer. Moreover, while something spoken was typically tailored to the specific abilities, interests, and concerns of those present, something written was imprecise communication that might or might not be understandable or of interest to those whom it eventually reached. Although these critiques may at first seem odd and humorous to the modern mind, a few moments' reflection suggests that Socrates was perhaps a more perceptive

analyst of some of the effects of writing than those born into cultures where widespread writing and reading have been taken for granted. Few literate people can display the feats of memory that anthropologists have discovered among extant oral cultures, and the lack of writer-reader dialogue in manuscripts and printed books is obvious upon reflection. (Even a written-down conversation is static and excludes the reader.)

Socrates, however, was better at seeing how writing was different from the oral interactions he treasured than he was at seeing what writing could facilitate that did not yet exist, including extended treatises and arguments too complex even for their own writers to memorize, let alone share with any large number of people through conversation. Moreover, what Socrates disparaged as texts composed for no one in particular, is now praised by writing teachers who encourage children to write in an "objective tone." Although Socrates was correct about the basic differences between speech and writing, he missed the fact that the values he imposed on the distinctions would later come to be reversed: The book would come to be seen as the facilitator and repository of all sophisticated science, philosophy, and literature, while conversation was often seen as too "personal," ephemeral, and idiosyncratic. (These relative values have been in flux again in the electronic age.) Socrates was unable, of course, to see the distant future of more spontaneous and interactive forms of writing in e-mail, instant messaging, text messaging, and blogging and reader responses. One wonders if the wise Socrates could anticipate the irony that his own medium theory is now remembered primarily because his best student, Plato, wrote it down in the *Phaedrus*.

Until the mid-20th century, most other medium theory appeared in bits and pieces, often buried within different primary concerns. In the mid-15th century, Johannes Gutenberg boasted of the ways in which his invention of movable type bypassed the power of the Church's scribes. In the early 16th century, religious reformer Martin Luther and his protégés consciously exploited the unique features of printing for the first mass-mediated publicity campaign for the Protestant Reformation. A perspective akin to medium theory was implicit in the birth of the field of sociology in the 19th century, which recognized that the impact of industrialization could not be reduced to the products that were produced (the "content") but had to be gauged instead in the ways that changes in means of production (the "medium") altered the structure of institutions and social relations and led to dramatic changes in rural and urban life. Yet, sociology's founders were often blind to the similarly transformational role of communication media. Indeed, they mostly overlooked the prior role that the printing press based on movable type had played for several centuries as the prototype of standardization, interchangeable parts, and mechanized production—as well as being the mass production machine that made possible the widespread sharing of the plans for new forms of making goods and organizing social life.

In the early 20th century, Patrick Geddes (1904) moved toward medium theory by studying the interrelationships between natural and built environments. Geddes's disciple Lewis Mumford (1934) advanced that project into the heart of medium theory in his analyses of the impact of printing and other technologies, as well as the broader myths and influences of "the machine." In the 1930s, gestalt theorist and film enthusiast Rudolf Arnheim (1957) developed a form of medium theory as a response to those who claimed that movies could not be an art form because they merely involve the mechanical reproduction of reality. Arnheim's *materialtheorie* argued that scientific and artistic descriptions of reality are shaped as much by the peculiarities of the medium used as by the reality being portrayed.

Full-scale medium theory arose in the era of radio and with the birth of television. In the 1940s, Canadian political economist Harold Innis realized that his prior studies of the ways in which natural and human-made waterways affected the flow of the fur trade and other staples were, in effect, studies of communication media. That insight led Innis (1950, 1951) to write two books, *Empire and Communications* and *The Bias of Communication*. In these dense works, Innis extended principles of economic monopolies to the study of information monopolies from early Mesopotamia and Egypt to the British Empire and the Nazis, rewriting the history of civilization as the history of communication media and their influences.

Before his death in 1952, Innis influenced the thinking of his University of Toronto colleague Marshall McLuhan, a professor of literature. McLuhan's (1962, 1964) aphoristic and pun-filled style, combined with his bold claims (he preferred to call them "probes") and his lack of respect for what he characterized as print-inspired separations between disciplines, helped to make him the most famous—and infamous—of medium theorists. Building on Innis, McLuhan argued that the spread of literacy and printing enhanced individuality, gave oral people an eye for an ear, detribalized society and created isolated "points of view," encouraged cause-and-effect thinking, and fostered belief in linear "progress." Electronic media, McLuhan argued, were reversing many of these trends, retribalizing society, minimizing the gap between action and reaction, and imploding the world into a "global village" of greater interconnection. McLuhan criticized the content-obsessed focus of most media research with his oft-quoted, and usually misunderstood, pun, "The *medium* is the message," by which he meant that many significant and pervasive social influences derive more from the nature of the medium employed than from the particular messages sent through it. McLuhan's message resonated well enough with media gatekeepers for him to become famous through TV and print exposure. At the same time, McLuhan incurred the wrath of many writers and scholars through his argument that television and other electronic media were having a major, and not necessarily bad, influence on the culture and that such changes were diminishing the significance of literacy-inspired modes of thought and social organization. McLuhan's reputation declined dramatically in the late 1970s and 1980s, only to be revived from the mid-1990s onward, as the spread of globalization, the dramatic impact of the World Wide Web, other media developments, and cultural trends seemed to match his descriptions of how an electronic era and the "age of information" differed from "print culture."

Innis and McLuhan are unique in terms of the scope of their claims and the breadth of history and culture that they attempt to analyze within their frameworks. Other theorists, however, have added texture to medium theory by exploring narrower topics in greater depth. Various aspects of the shift from orality to literacy have been explored by J. C. Carothers (1959), Jack Goody and Ian Watt (1963), Eric Havelock (1963, 1976), Robert Logan (1986), and Walter Ong (1982). These works suggest that orality and literacy foster different definitions of "knowledge" and encourage different conceptions of the individual, modes of consciousness, and social organization.

The significance of the shift from script to print has been explored by H. J. Chaytor (1945) and Elizabeth Eisenstein (1979). Chaytor argues that what is often thought of merely as the "mechanization" of writing created a new sense of "authorship" and intellectual property, reshaped literary style, fostered the growth of nationalistic feelings, and altered the psychological interaction of words and thought. Eisenstein's masterful study supports many of Chaytor's themes and also presents extensive evidence and

argument that the printing press revolutionized Western Europe by facilitating the Protestant Reformation and the growth of modern science.

The influences of electronic media have been explored by numerous scholars. Ong (1967), for example, analyzes how the "primary orality" of preliterate societies compares and contrasts with the "secondary orality" of electronic media. He explores the spiritual and psychological significance of the return of "the word" in electronic form. Daniel Boorstin (1973) compares and contrasts political revolutions with technological revolutions and describes how electronic media make experience "repeatable," "mass-produce the moment," and, along with other technological inventions, "level" time and space and alter conceptions of nationality, history, and progress. Joshua Meyrowitz (1985) analyzes how electronic media tend to reshape the social roles of print culture by fostering more shared patterns of access to social information, making the dividing line between public and private behaviors more permeable, and undermining the link between physical place and social "place." Manuel Castells (1996) explores how electronic media facilitate the global dominance of a form of connection—the network—that could previously exist only on a smaller scale. Mark Poster (2006) analyzes the structure and the social and cultural influences of the new relations between humans and information machines. Rich Ling (2008) explores how mobile communication alters social spheres and reshapes the patterns of social cohesion.

The current era of hypermediation has created a milieu of enhanced appreciation for, and study of, medium theory. The growth of the World Wide Web, mobile telephones, Wi-Fi, video surveillance technologies, virtual communities, radio frequency identification (RFID) tags, global positioning systems (GPS), social networking Web sites, blogs, and many other mediated environments has led to broader acceptance of the basic medium theory premise: that such media must be looked at as creating new social settings, settings whose influence on the structure of social life cannot be reduced to the content of the messages transmitted through them. Medium theory helps us to understand some of the ways in which the technologies we create tend to re-create us.

◆ Subgenres of Medium Theory

Even without any direct collaboration, many medium theorists share a common view of general communication history, such as epochal differences between oral and literate societies, that printing was much more than mechanized writing, and that the electronic era is dramatically different from the print era. At the same time, medium theory can be divided into various subgenres based on different foci and concepts. A key concept in Innis's medium theory, for example, is the distinction between "time-biased" and "space-biased" media. The characteristics of a time-biased medium (such as stone hieroglyphics) allow it to last for a very long time, while the characteristics of a space-biased medium (such as papyrus) allow it to move over great distances. Innis sees such "media biases" as tied to a culture's ability to maintain stability over long periods of time or to control large areas of territory. Innis's medium theory also explores how these and other characteristics of media tend to encourage or undermine "knowledge monopolies." Central tenets in McLuhan's medium theory include the idea that media are extensions of the human senses and that changes in media alter the ratio of the senses transforming the nature of humans' self-perceptions and their interactions with each other and the outside world. In the shift from the circular world of oral sound to the visual world of writing and then print, for example, McLuhan sees a move from round huts and villages and a focus on cycles of nature toward straight-line architecture, gridlike cities, and a one-thing-at-a-time and one-thing-after-another linear philosophy that

mimicked the lines of text on a printed page. Meyrowitz has developed a "role-system" medium theory that begins with the argument that a society's typical stages of socialization, types of group identity, and levels of hierarchy are dependent on certain patterns of access (and restrictions of access) to social information. Role-system medium theory suggests that changes in media foster the restructuring of social roles by altering the balance of what different types of people know *about* each other and *relative to* each other. Ronald Deibert's (1997) "ecological holism" medium theory eschews the notion of "inherent effects" of any medium, focusing instead on the ways in which preexisting trends are either favored or not favored by the new communication environment. Deibert explores how the "chance fitness" with a new medium tends to bring some existing ideas and social forces from the margins of society to the center.

◆ Microlevel Versus Macrolevel Medium Theory

Medium theory can also be divided into microlevel and macrolevel approaches. In microlevel medium theory, the focus is on the use of one medium or type of media for a particular purpose in a specific situation. Microlevel medium questions, for example, might explore the intended and unintended consequences of employing one medium over others (and over face-to-face communication) for such activities as applying for a job, initiating or ending a romantic relationship, communicating with one's employees or supervisor, teaching a course, commanding troops, staying in touch with one's relatives or neighbors, promoting a product or a political candidate, and so forth. Macrolevel medium theory, however, looks at broader issues, such as how the widespread use of a new medium, when added to the existing matrix of media and face-to-face interaction, may influence many dimensions of social life within societies and globally. Macrolevel medium theory explores how changes in media may subtly or not so subtly reshape social roles, social institutions, conceptions of time and space, thinking patterns, architecture, urban design, interactions among cultures, and social structure in general.

In microlevel medium theory, the different characteristics of various media are seen as interacting with an individual's or group's communication style and the nature of the specific task at hand. A medium theorist, for example, would argue that there is a significant difference between choosing a telephone conversation over a textual medium to end an intimate relationship. On the phone, the words we speak are typically upstaged by our emotional vocal overtones, and we are interrupted by the words and sounds of the other person. Also, discourse on the telephone is often hesitant and rambling (or incredibly off-putting if read from a text), and a speaker cannot "erase" what he or she has said to that moment to revise the message invisibly or to begin anew. For many people, using a telephone to end a close relationship entails paradoxical communication: the telephone conversation maintains an intimate and fluidly bidirectional bond (for at least the length of the call), even as one is supposedly trying to dissolve it. (Telephone calls, however, often function well for *renegotiating* the terms of an intimate relationship, since they combine highly interactive, intimate talking with barriers to sight and touch.) For these reasons, perhaps, our culture is familiar with the "Dear John letter," but not the "Dear John telephone call." A letter writer can revise a letter until it has a formal and polished form. There are no emotional vocalizations; only words are conveyed. The letter writer can state a position without any interruption or immediate response from the other party. Newer media add new options for establishing, maintaining, and breaking off intimate relationships, with different features for each. E-mail, instant messaging, and text messaging lie somewhere in between

telephone calls and letters. These media allow users some letter-like opportunities to craft, edit, and time the delivery of messages, and yet they retain telephone-like characteristics of speed and nearly simultaneous bidirectionality.

Individuals' personalities and inclinations—combined with cultural and subcultural differences, generational styles, and relational context—influence the choice of medium and the ways in which selected media are used for particular purposes. Yet, people cannot create channels of interaction not afforded by the selected medium (a father is able to sing a lullaby to a child over the phone but not in a text message), nor can they obliterate the channels that are in play (one is rarely successful in asking someone to ignore one's tone of voice over the telephone and focus solely on the words spoken). The medium is part of the overall message.

On the macro, societal, and global levels, medium theorists who study the telephone would ask different types of questions, such as: How has the use of the telephone altered the texture of social relationships in general? How has the phone affected the speed, style, and degree of formality of business interactions? How does use of the telephone change the frequency and function of personal letter writing (potentially complicating biographers' research tasks, as old forms of correspondence diminish)? How has the telephone affected social hierarchies by changing the typical patterns of who can easily interact directly with whom? Has the telephone fostered the development of virtual "neighborhoods" and "communities" by extending the range and customization options for frequent conversational partners while also weakening ties in physically defined locales, including the home? Similar questions could be asked about the explosion in use of e-mail, which has led to changes in the frequency and function of letters, faxes, and telephone calls. Medium theorists would also examine the subtler, yet significant, distinctions between landline telephone interactions and mobile phone conversations in terms of sound quality, reliability of the connection, degree of mobility, conceptions of phone etiquette and privacy, and other significant differences. For example, since calls to a mobile phone generally reach an individual (regardless of where he or she is), rather than reaching a location (regardless of who is there), mobile phones tend to bypass many social mediators (such as parents, spouses, roommates, receptionists, and coworkers) who once monitored wired phone contacts.

Micro- and macrolevel medium theory issues are obviously related to each other. A microlevel medium study of political style, for example, might ask how a candidate for public office alters the content and tone of her speeches when a video camera and microphone are present. Related macrolevel questions include how electronic media have reshaped political styles in general, changed the range of viable political candidates by shifting the general criteria that the public uses to judge public figures, and perhaps changed the overall status and credibility that leaders in general hold in the eyes of the public.

Macrolevel medium theory is usually more provocative and controversial than microlevel medium theory, both because it makes grander claims and because it is less subject to empirical investigation through typical observational or experimental methods (Meyrowitz, 1994). Macrolevel medium theory is also quite distinct from the dominant "media effects" approach of studying the potential imitative and persuasive impact of media content. Millions of dollars, for example, have been spent over the last decades studying what is perhaps the most popular media research question: Do children imitate the violence and other antisocial behaviors they watch on TV or experience through other media, such as movies and video games? Macrolevel medium analysis, in contrast, is more likely to ask broader questions about how different types of media create different forms of experience for children and different patterns of access to information about the outside world. The role-system form of medium theory, as one example, suggests that the more overlap there is in what children know about adults, and compared with adults, the more difficult it is to maintain sharp child-adult role distinctions. Because children learn to read in stages, adults can use books to stagger children's access to information about the adult world. Different sets of information can be created for children of different ages based on "reading level." (To this day, many children's books have a code on the back cover, such as "4:2," meaning fourth grade, second month.) Moreover, each book is a discrete object that can be made accessible to children or restricted from them. Indeed, a parent can be in the same room with a child and yet be reading a book or newspaper the content of which is not accessible to the child. Similarly, children of different ages in the same room can be separated into different "stages" of literate information.

Television is completely different on all these counts. Because it presents its information in image and voice, TV does not have clear levels of viewing difficulty; many top-rated shows among children have been programs designed for adults. Many different types of programs come through the same object—the TV set—making it difficult to control which content is or is not accessible to children. And parents have difficulty censoring children's access to television without censoring their own TV viewing or making certain that children are not in the same room. The resulting "effects" of television cannot be seen merely by studying media content. An advice book for parents that suggests what subjects to discuss with or hide from young children is effective in controlling children's access to information not because of the messages alone, but also because of the restrictive nature of the book as a medium. A television program with the same content presents a paradoxical situation: on TV, hundreds of thousands of children who are not yet able or likely to read an adult advice book can listen in, hearing about those things that parents are considering keeping secret from them, and learning the biggest secret of all—the "secret of secrecy," that is, that adults conspire about what to tell and not tell children. Television exposure, in general, contrasts with children's books that once presented children with an image of all-knowing, calm, cool, and collected adults. With television, parents are generally unable to hide the fact that adults engage in irrational behavior and violence; commit crimes; and have doubts, fears, and anxieties. As a result of all these features of the medium, television routinely exposes children to aspects of adult life that parents over several centuries tried to keep hidden from young children.

Medium theory, therefore, looks not just at how children may imitate the content and characters they are exposed to through television, but how the whole structure of adult-child interactions may change. In a television (and now an Internet) culture, children know more about many types of social behavior than they did through book-controlled socialization. Because adult life in general is now more exposed to children, parents, teachers, and other adults have great difficulty convincingly pretending for children that they always behave maturely and usually know best. The result is much more than a change in the particular behaviors of children; we have seen a transformation in the very cultural meanings of "childhood" and "adulthood." The claim that television could foster such changes is supported by the fact that modern conceptions of childhood and adulthood did not develop in Western cultures until the spread of printing and literacy-based education (Meyrowitz, 1985, pp. 226–267).

The contrast between medium theory and the typical media effects approach is equally stark with respect to other popular research topics. A large body of feminist research, for example, has focused on concerns that women and young girls would imitate the sexist behavior in the media content that dominated early television and persists in many TV programs, movies, and other media. Early television, within this dominant view, was a powerful and sexist force that served the patriarchal interests of keeping women in their place as housewives and mothers. Yet, as with the alternative arguments about the impact of printing at the start of this chapter, medium theorists would point out that the actual behavioral outcomes seem to contradict the typical claims. The first generation of female viewers to grow up watching television has not been known for wanting to stay in the kitchen or nursery; indeed, they have pushed hard for gender integration of the spheres that were once limited primarily to men. Medium theory would explain this outcome by arguing, again, that the major impact of a medium comes not from imitation of, or persuasion by, its messages, but in how it alters the boundaries of social experience. At the height of print culture, the Victorians lauded the notion of "separate spheres" for men and women, and this view was strong in middle-class American life at the dawn of the TV era. There was the public, male realm of rationality and suppressed emotion, work and accomplishments; and there was the private, female sphere of emotion, home, and childrearing. Men and women were not supposed to dwell in, or even know that much about, the other's sphere. Although the content of early television projected this worldview, the characteristics of the medium undermined the continuity of such gender distinctions among its viewers.

Unlike etiquette books and other literature written for each gender, television exposed similar behaviors and locations to all viewers. Although most of the *characters* in early TV existed in their separate gender spheres, the *viewers* were allowed to see into the settings of "the other." Television exposed young girls and homebound women to all those realms of the culture—business, government, courtrooms, war, and so forth—that men used to tell women "not to worry your pretty little head about." Such exposure would be unlikely to make female viewers satisfied with their traditional roles, since there is nothing more frustrating than being shown the activities and places that you are told are not meant for you. Rather than female viewers being relatively passive recipients of content for their imitation or persuasion, they apparently actively *used* the content to make sense of the gendered society and then to reimagine more inclusive roles for themselves in it. Television's images and voices demystified men and their behaviors for women viewers, making the male world and its roles seem less mysterious and inaccessible. Conversely, television close-ups made it difficult for male viewers to ignore the emotional dimensions and consequences of public actions. Television revealed the sweat on the brow, tears welling up in the eyes of leaders, voices cracking with emotion. Television also exposed male and female viewers to the strategies that each gender traditionally used to "manage" the other, thereby making it more difficult to use such techniques successfully in real life. Such macrolevel medium theory argues that the potential changes encouraged by media cannot be seen clearly by studying media content alone. Indeed, often the shifts in long-term behaviors are in opposition to initial content, such as in changes in concepts of appropriate male and female roles. Within this view, television, in spite of early sexist content (and perhaps even more so because of it), has encouraged gender blending, with more career-oriented women and more family oriented men. Again, the plausibility of this argument is reinforced by the fact that distinctions between male and female roles in Western cultures increased with the spread of printing, literacy, and literacy-based education (Meyrowitz, 1985, pp. 187–225).

◆ Critiques and Limitations of Medium Theory

The most common critique of medium theory is that it is a form of "technological determinism" that ignores human agency. Yet, a close reading of most medium theory demonstrates that it argues for a probabilistic, rather than a deterministic, model. Even McLuhan (McLuhan & Fiore, 1967), whose bold, declarative statements led him to be dismissed by many as a determinist, argued, "There is absolutely no inevitability as long as there is a willingness to contemplate what is happening" (p. 25). McLuhan's colleague Edmund Carpenter (2001), who edited the journal *Explorations* with McLuhan in the 1950s, summarizes their approach as studying the ways in which "each medium is a unique soil. That soil doesn't guarantee which plants will grow there, but it influences which plants blossom or wilt there" (p. 239). Paul Levinson (1997) prefers the notion of a "soft determinism" that "entails an interplay between the information technology making something possible" and human "decision and planning" shaping the use and impact of the technology (p. 4). Walter Ong (1986) avoids simple deterministic arguments, describing instead a technological "relationism" in which a medium that "grows to more than a marginal status" tends to interact in "a bewildering variety of ways" with social and intellectual practices and forms (p. 36).

Because medium theory implicitly or explicitly critiques the content-based focus of most other types of media theory and research, it often has the complementary weakness: it tends to pay insufficient attention to how the effects of media are modulated by variations in their content, control, and use, including the wide range of meanings that audiences bring to and take out of media texts. Medium theory also usually ignores the impact of manipulations of production variables (such as TV shot framing, camera angles, selective focus, and so forth), which influence audience members' perceptions of, and relationships with, characters and events (Meyrowitz, 1998). Additionally, most medium theory tends to analyze existing forms of media rather than charting the sociopolitical and economic forces that usually shape and limit the invention, design, and uses of media. Medium theory tends to ignore, for example, the economic and political interests of state and corporate elites that encouraged the development of television as a unidirectional form of mass communication for the selling of products and ideologies, rather than as an interactive community medium. Most medium theory also offers few insights into how we can resist and counter dominant cultural narratives that permeate most of the media in a society, including the highly selective "stories" that are told across mainstream media to shape public perceptions of "enemies" and war. Thus, while role-system medium theory argues that television has allowed children to share much of the information aimed at adults, it tends to ignore the fact that the news presented to adults in corporate-controlled media typically conveys narratives of good and evil that are as simplistic as a child's bedtime story. More recent medium theory, however, has been sensitive to the power of media propaganda and to the ways in which new media create opportunities for bypassing traditional "disinformation systems" (Meyrowitz, 2006).

In focusing on how new media may reshape existing societies, medium theory tends to give less attention to the ways in which significant variations among cultures (e.g., differing perceptions of time, space, nature, human relations, and human-technology interactions) may differentially shape the use of media. Additionally, even though medium theorists examine media as types of "environments," surprisingly few medium theorists explore the ways in which "advances" in technology often lead to the depletion of natural resources and an increase in toxic environmental waste, or how the benefit/burden ratio of the "information age" is experienced differently by people in different countries and economic strata.

However, in specializing in the study of the unintended communication consequences of new media, medium theory has the potential for insightful analysis of the ways in which technologies such as the Internet, mobile phones, camcorders, and GPS equipment have been embraced by third-world and other activists to protest and undermine the neoliberal agendas that fostered the development of these technologies in the first place.

◆ Conclusion: Enhancing the Media Studies Toolkit

As noted in the introduction to this chapter, the potential of print to undermine the power of monarchs and the dominance of the Church did not manifest itself immediately. Indeed, to this day, millions of people still worship earthly and heavenly kings and are indifferent to, or dismissive of, the findings of science. Moreover, the uses that people have made of print over the centuries, as well as the reactions that people have had to printed material, are so varied as to defy easy summary. Thus, the significant "medium effects" analyzed in this chapter remain complex and partial.

We also must not forget that in the short term, those who printed the "wrong" material often suffered severe consequences. In 1584, for example, William Carter printed a pro-Catholic pamphlet in Protestant-ruled England and was hanged. Had a medium theory analysis of the liberating potential of printing been presented at Carter's funeral, it would have provided only cold comfort to the relatives of the executed man. More appropriate responses would have been outrage at the injustice of the hanging and commitment to collective social action to fight for greater freedom of expression. A parallel response in the present time would be to work toward greater media democracy with limits on the corporate control over our technologies, rather than relying solely on the "characteristics" of new media to do that work for us. Thus, although medium theory offers a unique and valuable insight into the power of printing and other media, the history of printing also suggests the need to consider multiple approaches to studying and actively responding to media effects.

In short, medium theory is a valuable addition to the toolkit that scholars can use to explore what media do to us and for us. As with most other major approaches to media, however, medium theory offers important insights and has significant blind spots (Meyrowitz, 2008). Medium theory is best conceived of as a crucial complement to, rather than as a replacement for, the media effects tradition and other forms of media study.

◆ References

Arnheim, R. (1957). *Film as art.* Berkeley: University of California Press.

Boorstin, D. J. (1973). *The Americans: The democratic experience.* New York: Random House.

Carothers, J. C. (1959). Culture, psychiatry and the written word. *Psychiatry, 22,* 307–320.

Carpenter, E. (2001). That not-so-silent sea [historical appendix]. In D. Theall, *The virtual Marshall McLuhan* (pp. 236–261). Montreal: McGill–Queens University Press.

Castells, M. (1996). *The rise of the network society.* Oxford, UK: Blackwell.

Chaytor, H. J. (1945). *From script to print: An introduction to medieval vernacular literature.* Cambridge, England: W. Heffer & Sons.

Deibert, R. (1997). *Parchment, printing, and hypermedia: Communication in world order transformation.* New York: Columbia University Press.

Eisenstein, E. (1979). *The printing press as an agent of change: Communications and cultural transformations in early-modern Europe* (Vols. 1 & 2). Cambridge, UK: Cambridge University Press.

Geddes, P. (1904). *City development: A study of parks, gardens, and culture-institutes.* Edinburgh, Scotland: Geddes.

Goody, J., & Watt, I. (1963). The consequences of literacy. *Comparative Studies in Society and History, 5,* 304–345.

Havelock, E. A. (1963). *Preface to Plato.* Cambridge, MA: Harvard University Press.

Havelock, E. A. (1976). *Origins of western literacy.* Toronto: Ontario Institute for Studies in Education.

Innis, H. A. (1950). *Empire and communications.* London: Oxford University Press.

Innis, H. A. (1951). *The bias of communication.* Toronto: University of Toronto Press.

Levinson, P. (1997). *The soft edge: A natural history and future of the information revolution.* London: Routledge.

Ling, R. (2008). *New tech, new ties: How mobile communication is reshaping social cohesion.* Cambridge, MA: MIT Press.

Logan, R. K. (1986). *The alphabet effect.* New York: William Morrow.

Lum, C. M. K. (Ed.). (2006). *Perspectives on culture, technology and communication: The media ecology tradition.* Cresskill, NJ: Hampton Press.

McLuhan, M. (1962). *The Gutenberg galaxy: The making of typographic man.* Toronto: University of Toronto Press.

McLuhan, M. (1964). *Understanding media: The extensions of man.* Toronto: University of Toronto Press.

McLuhan, M., & Fiore, Q. (1967). *The medium is the massage: An inventory of effects.* New York: Bantam Books.

Meyrowitz, J. (1985). *No sense of place: The impact of electronic media on social behavior.* New York: Oxford University Press.

Meyrowitz, J. (1994). Medium theory. In D. Crowley & D. Mitchell (Eds.), *Communication theory today* (pp. 50–77). Cambridge, UK: Polity Press.

Meyrowitz, J. (1998). Multiple media literacies. *Journal of Communication, 48*(1), 96–108.

Meyrowitz, J. (2006). American homogenization and fragmentation: The influence of new information systems and disinformation systems. In W. Uricchio & S. Kinnebrock (Eds.), *Media cultures* (pp. 153–186). Heidelberg: Universitätsverlag.

Meyrowitz, J. (2008). Power, pleasure, patterns: Intersecting narratives of media influence. *Journal of Communication, 58,* 641–663.

Mumford, L. (1934). *Technics and civilization.* New York: Harcourt Brace.

Ong, W. J. (1967). *The presence of the word: Some prolegomena for cultural and religious history.* New Haven, CT: Yale University Press.

Ong, W. J. (1982). *Orality and literacy: The technologizing of the word.* London: Methuen.

Ong, W. J. (1986). Writing is a technology that restructures thought. In G. Baumann (Ed.), *The written word: Literacy in transition* (pp. 23–50). New York: Oxford University Press.

Poster, M. (2006). *Information please: Culture and politics in the age of digital machines.* Durham, NC: Duke University Press.

Strate, L. (2006). *Echoes and reflections: On media ecology as a field of study.* Cresskill, NJ: Hampton Press.

35

THE EVOLUTION OF MEDIA SYSTEM DEPENDENCY THEORY

◆ Sandra J. Ball-Rokeach
and Joo-Young Jung

I n this chapter, we first situate how media system dependency (MSD) theory grew out of the issues and debates surrounding prevailing theories of media effects. Following this contextual discussion, we proceed to examine the development of the theory over three decades—the 1970s, the 1980s, and the 1990s. We conclude the chapter by discussing the profound changes in the media system that prompted substantial expansion of MSD theory in the form of communication infrastructure theory.

◆ Questions, Challenges, and Ideas That Prompted MSD Theory

In the late 1960s and early 1970s, media effects theories tended to address processes that operated at either a macro (societal or cultural) or a micro (individual) level of analysis. Macro theories, such as cultivation (Gerbner & Gross, 1976) and cultural imperialism (Schiller, 1973), tended to emphasize the power of media production systems to shape people's beliefs and behavior. The dominant micro theory of this era, uses and gratifications (Katz, Blumer, & Gurevitch, 1973–1974), tended to emphasize the power of media consumers to make what they

◆ 531

will of media messages. These contrasting positions can be described as powerful media/weak audience (macro positioning) and weak media/powerful audience (micro positioning), respectively.

Neither of these positionings, however, seemed adequate as a full account of media effects. Instead of developing theories that posit powerful media/weak audience or weak media/powerful audience, it seemed more important to follow the classical theory tradition of identifying the conditions under which media do *or* do not have powerful effects. In the turbulent times of the 1960s and early 1970s, media messages did not seem to go unchallenged by consumers, nor did media consumers seem able to construct their social and personal realities independent of the media.

Ball-Rokeach, who developed MSD theory, also began to question the idea that media power rests upon its power to persuade. This had been an important assumption in the thick literature on persuasion and attitude change that began in World War II (Hovland, 1948; Stouffer, Suchman, DeVinney, Star, & Williams, 1949) and continued through the subsequent decades to this day (Perloff, 2007). The persuasion frame suggests that the key focus is to identify the best combination of message and audience characteristics for persuasion to be most likely to occur.

Questioning the persuasion frame led Ball-Rokeach to make a major shift away from regarding media as a persuasion system to regarding media as *an information system*. Once this fundamental shift in thinking occurred, all kinds of new possibilities opened up. By conceiving of the media as an information system, (1) it directed attention to a relationship between producers and consumers where producers control scarce information resources, and consumers utilize those resources to make sense of, and act meaningfully in, their personal and social environs; (2) it was possible to examine all media products for their potential information value, crossing entertainment and news genres; (3) it

encouraged viewing media consumers as active processors of media resources, not passive receptors, thus incorporating the active audience perspective that had developed in uses and gratifications without asserting anarchical audience interpretive freedoms; (4) it allowed the possibility that some media effects were intentional and others were not; and (5) it encouraged a multilevel analysis made possible by the ecological notion of a dependency relationship.

◆ *The Emergence of the Concept of a MSD Relationship*

Probably the most novel and difficult aspect of MSD theory to grasp is the ecological conception of a dependency relationship that crosses levels of analysis from media producers (macro) to media consumers (micro). This central concept derives from power-dependency theory (Emerson, 1962) in which power is conceived to reside in other actors' having to access resources that you control, not in the resources per se. If you control resources that others do not have to access, then your resources create no power. The basic point of the first MSD paper (Ball-Rokeach, 1974) was that we can understand media effects as the outcome of dependency relations where consumers require access to information resources controlled by the media system to achieve their everyday goals, whereas the media system does not really require access to resources controlled by any one consumer in order to achieve its economic and political goals.

Most media effects theories focus on the attributes or characteristics of messages or audience members. The simplest way to distinguish between such attributional thinking and MSD ecological thinking is that the focus in ecological thinking is on the characteristics of relationships (e.g., intensity, scope), not on the attributes of the actors. Thus, it is a mistake to speak of "dependent audience members," making dependency a characteristic of individual consumers. Attention has to focus on how media resources are implicated in the everyday ways that people develop relations with the media to attain their understanding, orientation, and play goals (Ball-Rokeach, 1985).

This way of framing the issue resonated with a time when people were connecting with the media to try to make sense of a world that was full of change, conflict, ambiguity, and threat, a world very much like the one we have as this chapter is being written. The media system was an essential information system in efforts to understand faraway wars, domestic civil strife, emergent cultural forms, economic conditions, and all the other things that people care about or need to know in order to orient to their world. Of course, people differed in their goal priorities and thus differed in the scope and intensity of their MSD relations. For example, political activists were more likely to connect with media telling political stories than people who were not so engaged and, thus, activists were more likely to evidence media effects on their political beliefs and behaviors.

With the foregoing as context, we move to look more closely at the stages of development of MSD theory. We bring into the discussion exemplar research efforts that advanced the theory in each stage.

◆ MSD Theory in the 1970s

The first published formulation of MSD theory appeared in the mid-1970s (Ball-Rokeach & DeFleur, 1976). Emile Durkheim's (1933/1964) classical argument that mass media were essential to the development of a modern society was extended to suggest that we need to understand the media as a system that is central to the functioning of personal *and* social life. We could not understand media effects on individuals or groups without understanding media system roles in society. These roles were largely informational. This might be most easily understood by imagining that you wake up in the morning to find that all media have vanished—everything from television to the Internet. What personal goals would be impossible or very difficult for you to attain? Of course, the early development of MSD theory was three decades prior to the emergence of the Internet, but the general point is that basic goals could not be achieved without the presence of media system resources. The political and economic systems would be in chaos, as would the lives of everyday people and communities.

When societies go through periods of rapid social change, as was the case in the late 1960s and 1970s, the societal role of the media system becomes even more central. This is because neither people nor social systems can simply assume that the world they knew yesterday is the same as the world they are in today. Basic requirements of understanding the world around you and figuring out how to act in that world require constant updating through the media system's capacities to gather, process, and disseminate information contained in both news and entertainment genres. Thus, the process of media effects is initiated by media control over scarce and prized information resources—gathering, processing, and dissemination—that must be accessed in order for the larger social system, as well as members of the media audiences, to achieve a range of goals (e.g., building shared understandings to guide social action). The more exclusive the media system's control over these resources, and the more essential it is to have access to these resources to achieve goals, the more likely it is that there will be media effects. Cognitive, affective, and behavioral effects follow from the playing out of this process where both social systems (macro) and individuals (micro) develop MSD relations to achieve their goals. For example, electoral campaigns would be impossible to conduct without access to media resources, and the media-political system dependency relation means that voters, too, must go to the media to stay on top of political campaigns.

The process, however, is not linear or one-way. Media must also have access to resources controlled by other agents in order to achieve their economic and organizational goals. The legislative/ regulatory resources of the political system and the advertising revenues of the economic system, for example, are essential to the survival of media systems in the U.S. context. Thus, symmetrical or balanced dependency relations can exist at the macro level between media and other systems. As hinted at earlier, the relationship is asymmetric when it comes to dependency relations at the micro level. As individuals, we control few, if any, resources that the media must access to thrive. Only when media systems aggregate individuals into audience segments do we see the audience, en masse, controlling the scarce and prized resource of our attention or consumption of media products. Over time, there is a feedback loop whereby changes in the audiences' tastes or media consumption patterns feed back through marketers or pollsters to influence media production decisions. For example, when the Vietnam War became a hotly contested issue and moved up to a top position of the public discourse agenda, media organizations invested more staff and financial resources in war coverage.

◆ MSD *Theory in the 1980s*

The 1980s was a period of conceptual elaboration and early empirical assessment of the theory (Ball-Rokeach, 1985; Ball-Rokeach, Rokeach, & Grube, 1984; Becker & Whitney, 1980; Hirschburg, Dillman, & Ball-Rokeach, 1986; Manross, 1987; Turner & Paz, 1986). One way to clarify the ecological notion of a dependency relation was to inquire more specifically into the *origins* of individuals' media system dependency relations. The origins can be classified into four categories, starting at the bottom of Figure 35.1 and moving upward, going from micro (*individuals*) to meso (*interpersonal networks*) to macro conditions (*social environment* and *media system activity*) and macro relationships (*structural dependency relations*).

INDIVIDUALS

We start with *personal goals*, the all-important question of which goals motivate the formation of individuals' dependency relations with the media. One challenge was to develop a typology of goals that captures the range of individuals' motivations and allows for individual variation at the same time. Individual variations in goals motivating media dependency relations, we argue, are an important reason why some individuals may, and others may not, exhibit media effects on their beliefs, feelings, and behavior, even when they consume the same media content. The typology, influenced by others' efforts, especially those of Katz and his colleagues (Katz, Gurevitch, & Haas, 1973), is presented in Table 35.1.

We argue that there are three main goals that motivate media dependency relations: understanding, orientation, and play. Further, we see both social and personal dimensions for each goal type. Understanding the social world around you is a social understanding goal, and understanding yourself is a personal goal. Figuring out how to interact with others is the social side of orientation and figuring out what actions you want to take is the personal side. When the presence of other people is an important part of your consumption of media entertainment, you are engaging in social play, but when the presence of others is not a concern, you are exhibiting the solitary or personal side of play. Individuals vary considerably in which media they choose to attain these

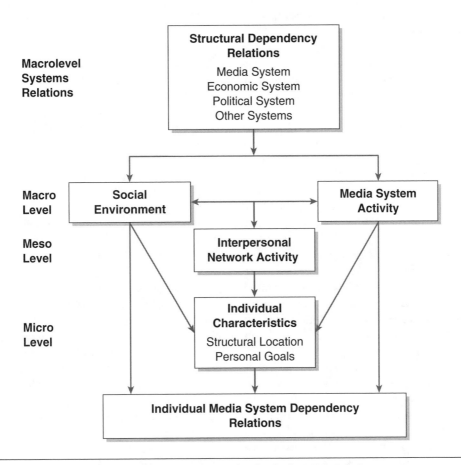

Figure 35.1 1980s: Elaboration on the Origins of Individuals' MSD Relations

Source: Adapted from Ball-Rokeach (1985, p. 499).

Table 35.1 Typology of Goals Engendering MSD Relations Among Individuals

Understanding	*Orientation*	*Play*
Social	Interaction	Social
Self	Action	Solitary

goals. For example, though television was the dominant medium in the 1980s, there were still many people who preferred newspapers to television to attain their social understanding goals. Similarly, some people regularly attained their social play goals by going to the movies or listening to music on the radio or cassette players. Further, any one media exposure can be motivated by more than one goal. For example, the edutainment literature (Singhal & Rogers, 2002) tells us that entertainment/play goals can be combined with self-understanding goals where people learn new ways of behaving from media models.

In terms of media effects, it is important to know what goals are motivating people's media exposure. For example, in an early study, Ball-Rokeach et al. (1984) used conventional advertising techniques to create a specific kind of audience for a half-hour television program. They wanted viewers with strong MSD relations with television with the goals of social and self-understanding because these were the people most likely to relate to the program in a way that would maximize the likelihood of media effects. The experimental treatments they had embedded in the program were designed to activate viewers to examine their beliefs about equality and environmentalism. The self-confrontation method the researchers were using relied on people's willingness to process the information presented in the program in a self-relevant way. Thus, viewers who came to the program with understanding motivations were more likely to be open to confronting their own race, gender, and environmental beliefs. The effort to constitute this type of audience was successful and, as a result, the experimental treatments were effective.

Apart from goals, another important difference between individuals is their *structural location* in the information environment (see Figure 35.1). Some individuals have access to information systems that can serve as alternatives to the media, and others do not. For example, when it comes to health, some people are linked into knowledgeable networks of doctors and other health professionals, whereas others do not have access to the resources of this alternative information system of experts. For those whose main resources of health-related information are the media, their dependency on media is likely to be more intense than those who have alternative resources for health information.

INTERPERSONAL NETWORKS

As we move from the micro level of individuals to the meso level of interpersonal networks (see Figure 35.1), we see an important elaboration of MSD theory as interpersonal networks are seen to play critical roles in other media effects theories, such as the classical two-step flow model (Katz, 1957). In MSD theory, interpersonal networks can either enhance or limit media effects. Media stories often stimulate interpersonal conversations. Sometimes these conversations may challenge the premises of the media story or filter the meaning of the story such that it ultimately conforms to the social network's attitudes and norms. On other occasions, especially when the story is on a topic about which the network has no firmly established beliefs, interpersonal conversations may reinforce the meaning as conveyed by the media. MSD theory thus embraces the importance of interpersonal networks, but departs from the more conventional idea that these networks operate largely to limit media effects.

SOCIAL ENVIRONMENT AND MEDIA SYSTEM ACTIVITY

Media effects are especially likely when there is ambiguity or threat in people's *social environments* and when the *media system is activated* to address that ambiguity and threat (see Figure 35.1). This is particularly likely when the media's information resources are exclusive. *Exclusivity* is an important dimension in this context as the media are more likely to have effects when they are the sole information system people can access than when people have other options.

Everyday examples of the exclusivity of media abound as we try to understand and act in a rapidly changing world marked by social conflicts—from making economic or employment decisions to staying on top of youth culture and finding ways to express ourselves and play in a tense social world. The media system has the information resources that people so often need to construct understandings of their social worlds. Further, on those rare occasions when natural disasters occur, the importance of these information resources becomes crystal clear. This was the case when residents in eastern Washington were searching for information to figure out the best ways to react to the Mount St. Helens volcanic eruption, an event outside the experience of all but a few experts (Hirschburg et al., 1986).

STRUCTURAL DEPENDENCY RELATIONS

The interaction of social environments, media system activity, interpersonal networks, and individual characteristics (structural location and personal goals) are all seen to take place in the macro context of *structural dependency relations* between the media and other social systems. This is where the MSD relations of the media with political, economic, and other systems come into play in the effects process. Put most briefly, these relations relate most strongly to media production processes, or what content the media do and do not produce. Examples include restrictions on war coverage, government secrecy laws and practices, or production of cheap reality shows in the face of economic pressures. The influence of these macro MSD relations is complex and requires in-depth case studies to track. For example, sources of local news have declined in the past few decades, thus making it hard for people to sustain MSD relations to stay on top of what is happening in their local residential communities. The reasons for this decline lie at the macrolevel issues of disinvestment in newspapers, locally oriented radio, and other local media. The result is that we have to discover new local media or create our own local news

through interpersonal discourse (Ball-Rokeach, Kim, & Matei, 2001).

◆ MSD Theory in the 1990s

Perhaps it is appropriate that an ecological theory evolves over time and becomes more complex in the process. Figure 35.2 highlights three elaborations of MSD theory that occurred in the 1990s: (1) specification of the dimensions of MSD relations, (2) development of the idea that interpersonal networks can be seen to have MSD relations, and (3) incorporation of explicit connections between media production and consumption.

DIMENSIONS OF MSD RELATIONS

The most commonly discussed dimensions or characteristics of MSD relations are *structure, intensity,* and *goal scope.* Structure, or "the degree of asymmetry in control over dependency engendering resources," is seen as variable only at the macro level and invariant at the micro level (Ball-Rokeach, 1998, p. 19). Thus, relations between the media and other social systems can vary between symmetry and asymmetry, while the relationship between the media system and individuals is mostly asymmetric.

The structure of the dependency relation between the media system and the political system in the United States is an example of a symmetrical macro relation. The political system could not operate without access to the resources of the media system. It could not have elections, for example. The media system could not operate without the First Amendment guarantees, tariff controls, regulatory resources, and other legislative resources controlled by the political system. In other countries, the relationship between the media and political systems may be asymmetric. This

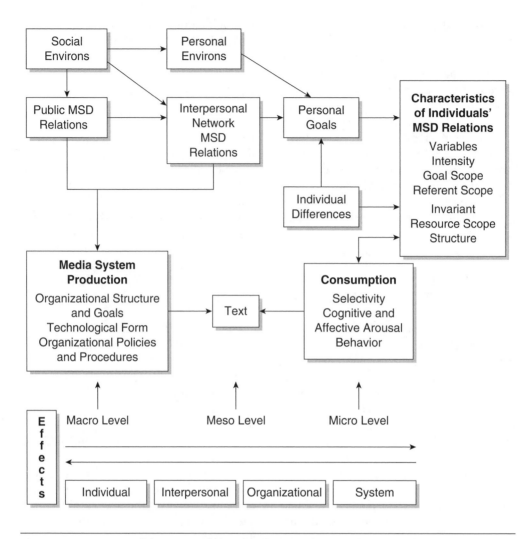

Figure 35.2   1990s: Elaboration of Mesolevel Dependency Relations and Cross-Level
Interactions

Source: Adapted from Ball-Rokeach (1998, p. 18).

would be the case where the media system is run by the government or operates without "free press" protections (Halpern, 1994; Pitts, 2000).

At the individual, or micro, level, the primary dimensions along which dependency relations vary are intensity and goal scope. *Intensity* refers to both the importance of the goal(s) that motivate(s) the MSD relation and the exclusivity of media resources for goal attainment. Intensity is usually measured by asking people how

helpful a medium is in their efforts to attain understanding (social or self), orientation (interaction or action), or play (social or solitary) goals. *Goal scope* is the number of goals that motivate a MSD relation. For example, Loges (1994) found that the more people perceived threat in their environments, the more intense their MSD relations. He did not, however, find that the scope of goals implicated in people's MSD relations increased with perceptions of threat. Referent scope, or the number of media implicated in a dependency relation, and resource scope, the number of media information resources implicated in a relation, are not included in this discussion as they have not been included in empirical tests.

INTERPERSONAL NETWORKS HAVE MSD RELATIONS, TOO

As MSD theory developed, it became clear that a broader conception of the role of interpersonal networks in the effects process was emerging. Interpersonal networks not only played a discursive role in media effects; they could also be said to have their own MSD relations. For example, groups, as well as individuals, experience ambiguity when they do not have the information resources they need to make sense of social conflicts, new environmental threats, and rapid social changes. In these circumstances, the media system becomes a, if not the, shared source of information. Another example is a threatening economic crisis where friendship, family, or coworker networks do not know how serious the crisis is, nor how to respond (e.g., should they take their money out of the bank or leave it in?). In such cases, people in these networks experience intense MSD relations *as a group* where they share or pool the information they get from media.

FLESHING OUT BRIDGES BETWEEN LEVELS OF ANALYSIS

From a theory-building point of view, the result of incorporating the MSD relations of interpersonal networks into the model was to flesh out the meso links between macro and micro MSD relations. In other words, the MSD relations of interpersonal networks are the critical link between the structural, system-level MSD relations that affect the production process and the micro MSD relations that affect individuals' consumption of media messages. These are intermediate and moderating relations that play a fundamental role in the effects process.

Viewed more as discourse creators than buffers, interpersonal networks require access to media system resources, but the outcome of their MSD relations is not fully predictable. The same conditions that affect the intensity and goal scope of individuals' MSD relations are likely to affect the intensity and goal scope of interpersonal network MSD relations; namely, the degree of ambiguity and threat and the rate of social change and social conflict in the social environment. The discourse agenda of interpersonal networks is more likely to be affected by the media in times of ambiguity, threat, change, and conflict than in times of stable and secure social environs. In unstable, problematic times, the text that is created by interpersonal networks will often be shaped by media texts. More broadly speaking, the construction of social reality is not a macro-, meso-, or microeffects phenomenon; rather, it is a product of ecological relationships among these levels of analysis. Individuals' social realities are not formed in a vacuum; they emerge from relationships with interpersonal networks and the media. Interpersonal network social realities are not formed in a vacuum, either; they emerge from relationships between the members and relationships with the media.

◆ Challenges to MSD Theory: Critics and Changing Times

Several challenges and criticisms have been directed at MSD, some of which have resulted in some interesting developments to the theory, as discussed in greater detail in the following paragraphs. First, in MSD's early days, scholars such as Rubin and Windahl (1986) contended that there was little, if any, difference between MSD theory and uses and gratifications (U&G) at the micro or individual level of analysis. So, basically, the criticism was, "what's new?" Ball-Rokeach (1998) was written, in part, to delineate the differences between the two approaches, the key differences of which are noted here. To start, the theories have different origins. U&G theory grew out of social psychological approaches to perception, attitudes, and diffusion (e.g., the two-step flow model). MSD theory grew out of a social psychological theory of power, power-dependency theory (Emerson, 1962), and classical ecology theory from sociology (Hawley, 1950). As a result, U&G theory focused largely on individual (micro) and interpersonal (meso) levels of analysis, whereas MSD sought to bring together the micro, meso, and macro levels of analysis into an ecology of MSD relations. The focus in U&G is on consumption of media, while the MSD ecology of relations joins concerns for both production (the macro MSD relations) and consumption (the micro and meso MSD relations).

One more concrete way to grasp the differences is to ask where the action is in the effects process. In U&G theory, the action is largely in the individuals' and the interpersonal networks' capacities to reconstruct media messages to gratify their needs. In MSD, the action is in the relationships between goals and media information resources—how media information resources are implicated in individuals' and interpersonal networks' attempts to attain understanding, orientation, and play goals. The social environs are key in MSD theory, but are not a central concern of U&G theory. Thus, there is a heavy emphasis in MSD on the difficulty individuals and interpersonal networks have in making sense of (and acting in) an ambiguous and threatening world marked by social change and social conflict without having access to media information resources. The consumers of media in U&G are not contextualized in these environments; thus, media consumers seem more in charge of how they are going to "use" media messages for their own purposes.

Another difference relates to the use of the term *needs*, in U&G theory as opposed to the term *goals* in MSD theory. Needs are *attributes* of individuals, whereas goals insinuate the social settings in which individuals and groups go about establishing everyday *relationships* (including MSD relations). The final key difference we consider here is that the two approaches have different conceptions of the media system. In U&G theory, the media are seen largely as "text creators." In MSD theory, the media system is seen as an information system central to the conduct of personal and social life (see Ball-Rokeach, 1998, for a more detailed discussion of these issues).

A second significant criticism of MSD research was raised by Halpern (1994), who argued that MSD research failed to include the exclusivity dimension of intensity in research. He was working at a time when the Chilean political system was authoritarian and controlled the mainstream media system. He found that Chileans' political perceptions, even when profound distrust of the media existed, were still influenced by the mainstream media. This was because the few and small oppositional media could not duplicate the range and reach of information resources controlled by the mainstream media. Halpern concluded that the media's degree of exclusivity of information sources was a meaningful dimension that influenced people's progovernmental political perceptions. Thus, Halpern's study is one of only a few empirical works that has demonstrated the importance of the exclusivity dimension in people's MSD relations.

Probably the most serious criticism of MSD theory came not from other scholars, but from the realities of a changing media environment. The development of MSD theory began in an era when three TV networks (ABC, NBC, and CBS), along with a few "prestigious" national newspapers (*New York Times, Washington Post,* and the *Los Angeles Times*), dominated both media discourse and media effects research. Indeed, this situation had been relatively stable since the widespread diffusion of television in the late 1950s. The Internet had not yet been introduced into popular use, and cable television was still struggling. Thus, it made sense to talk about a "media system" because most people knew what that meant. As time went on, however, the introduction of new digital and satellite technologies disrupted the stability of the system to the point where, today, the phrase "media system" does not have a consensual meaning. We cannot talk about a stable media production system, as it is changing rapidly with the merger of new and old media forms. Because the "media system" addressed in the MSD theory mainly concerns the macrolevel mainstream media, it does not accommodate well the evolving new media technologies. That is, MSD theory does not actively address the ways in which new communication technologies are incorporated into the existing media system. Communication infrastructure theory, which is articulated in the following section, however, does actively incorporate various new and old media in its framework.

MSD theory is still employed by researchers (Boer & Velthuijsen, 2001; Jung, Kim, Lin, & Cheong, 2005; Matsaganis & Payne, 2005; Morton & Duck, 2000), but most of these works address micro dependency relations with respect to a particular media form (e.g., television or Internet platforms). Further, the blurring of media forms makes the study of media effects increasingly problematic. For example, conventional television programs may be received in a living room or as a podcast. Newspapers are scurrying to become online media. Social network Internet sites blur the once-clear distinction between interpersonal and mass communication. All of these changes and more pose a challenge to the media effects theorist and researcher. Oddly enough, it may be more accurate to talk about the effects of an evolving media system that joins old and new media than it is to talk about this or that media form. This would be consistent with the overall thrust of MSD theory with its emphasis upon the societal role of media

as information systems that are sensitive to the requirements of an evolving society—the move from modern to global social forms.

◆ From MSD to Communication Infrastructure Theory

We conclude this chapter with a brief overview of a theory that emerged at the turn of the 21st century, communication infrastructure theory (CIT). It has roots in MSD theory, but takes on a more grounded, less national, and less media-centric focus. We will briefly summarize the major components of this theory and, in the process, indicate how most of them evolved from MSD theory. Put most briefly, the movement from MSD theory to CIT is a movement from a theory of media effects to a theory of communication effects where media become part of a larger storytelling system. The purpose of the theory changes from trying to understand media effects *per se* to trying to understand how the media in concert with other communication agents have effects on the quality of personal, family, and community life. Further, the media in CIT are more broadly defined compared with the media in MSD theory. The media not only include macrolevel mainstream media, but also mesolevel community or ethnic media, as well as new communication technologies.

The communication infrastructure is defined as a *storytelling system* set in its *communication action context* (Ball-Rokeach et al., 2001). The mass media are part of this system, but *mainstream media* are distinguished from what we call *geo-ethnic media* in terms of what they tell stories about (the storytelling referent) and their imagined audiences. Mainstream media tell stories about large geographic units (cities, nations, etc.) and imagine their audience as all the people contained in those units. Geo-ethnic media may be traditional media or new media, but the important thing is that they are directed to a particular ethnic group or a particular local community/ neighborhood (Kim, Jung, & Ball-Rokeach, 2006). Thus, mass media are macrolevel storytellers while geo-ethnic media are mesolevel storytellers. Added to this are the interpersonal networks that are conceived as microlevel storytellers as they tell stories about the shared lives of people in a community. The multilevel nature of MSD thinking as well as the bringing together of media and interpersonal network actors is reflected in this conception of a storytelling system.

Before we consider the communication action context, we need to introduce the *storytelling network*. This network is based in a community such that mass media are not major actors. The storytelling network consists of two mesolevel actors—geo-ethnic media and community organizations—and one microlevel storyteller—residents, as they are constituted in interpersonal networks (see Figure 35.2). The ecological focus on relationships in MSD theory is carried forward in CIT—the critical concern is not the separate activities of each of these storytellers, but the *strength of their relationships* with each other. For example, the initial effects focus in CIT was on how strong communities with civically engaged citizens are imagined and constructed through communication. The basic hypothesis is that when each of these storytellers *prompts the others* to tell stories about their community, residents become civically engaged because they can imagine themselves as a community (Ball-Rokeach et al., 2001; Kim & Ball-Rokeach, 2006). If the geo-ethnic media tell stories about how a community organization is trying to improve a local park, for example, then residents who are connected to those media may talk about the story with neighbors over the proverbial backyard fence. This may encourage residents to meet and greet each other at the park and develop relationships with each other and a sense of belonging. All communities are constructed or imagined through storytelling (Anderson, 2006). The

demands of 21st-century life, however, make it hard, if not impossible, for people to carry the burden of *storytelling community* on their own; they need the media and organizational storytellers to sustain them. The central role of the media in civil society as conceived in MSD theory is maintained in CIT, but the media of interest change from mass media to geo-ethnic media, and these media are conceived as key storytellers in a larger storytelling network.

The *communication action context* is an extension of the social environs component in MSD theory. In MSD, the focus is on the degree of ambiguity and threat and the larger conditions of social change and social conflict. In CIT, the focus is on all the features of the communication environment that affect the capacity of the storytelling network to function. The context varies along a dimension of openness to closedness, where an open context is one that encourages neighborhood storytelling and a closed context discourages such storytelling. For example, cultural tensions or unsafe streets discourage people from meeting and greeting each other, whereas a resource-rich environment with safe parks, good libraries, well-stocked grocery stores, and strong schools encourages people to gather together and develop community pride. This context also affects the kinds of stories that media tell and the success of community organization outreach efforts. Thus, the effect of the social environs on people's dependency relations in MSD theory is transformed to a more concrete examination of how the communication environment affects the strength of the storytelling network.

A final link that we consider between MSD theory and CIT is the conception of the individual and interpersonal networks as having understanding, orientation, and play goals that motivate them to establish relationships with information systems. This conception was, in many respects, the starting point for the development of MSD theory and, thus, brings us full circle to CIT.

In MSD theory, the primary information system considered is the mass media. In CIT, information systems are conceived in more narrative form as storytellers. Media are central communication agents, but they are differentiated in their functions: mainstream media having a broad reach (macro) and geo-ethnic media having a community reach (meso). Moreover, media are not separated out as a single storyteller, but rather are seen as being integrated with other storytellers (community organizations and interpersonal networks) in storytelling networks that, when there is a conducive communication environment, can operate to fulfill understanding, orientation, and play goals. This shift in positioning of the media reflects an attempt to capture a new world where there is not one dominant media system and a world in which new media allow us to bring together stories that are produced by communicators, large and small. Indeed, Internet-based media can be seen as a storytelling system that crosses or joins macro (e.g., national news sites), meso (ethnic community or community organization sites), and micro (e.g., social network sites) storytellers.

We conclude this discussion with the observation that media effects theories are challenged to adapt to the evolving media and communication world. In our view, it is not enough to apply the same theories that applied in the 1970s media world to the media world of the 21st century. In a sense, we are in a parallel situation to that of journalism and journalists. Journalism is in a chaotic state, midstream in the process of change that challenges common understandings of how journalism is practiced and the culture that drives those practices. This is not to say that we throw our established theories out the window, as parts of them are likely to survive the changing media world. It is to say that, just as MSD theory evolved into CIT, our theories need to reflect the changing phenomenological realities of media production and consumption.

◆ **References**

Anderson, B. (2006). *Imagined communities.* London, New York: Verson.

Ball-Rokeach, S. J. (1974). *The information perspective.* Paper presented at the Annual Meeting of the American Sociological Association, Montreal.

Ball-Rokeach, S. J. (1985). The origins of individual media-system dependency: A sociological framework. *Communication Research, 12,* 485–510.

Ball-Rokeach, S. J. (1998). A theory of media power and a theory of media use: Different stories, questions, and ways of thinking. *Mass Communication & Society, 1*(1/2), 5–40.

Ball-Rokeach, S. J., & DeFleur, M. L. (1976). A dependency model of mass media effects. *Communication Research, 3*(1), 3–21.

Ball-Rokeach, S. J., Kim, Y.-C., & Matei, S. (2001). Storytelling neighborhood: Paths to belonging in diverse urban environments. *Communication Research, 28*(4), 392–428.

Ball-Rokeach, S. J., Rokeach, M., & Grube, J. W. (1984). *The great American values test: Influencing behavior and belief through television.* New York: Free Press.

Becker, L. B., & Whitney, D. C. (1980). Effects of media dependencies: Audience assessment of government. *Communication Research, 7,* 95–120.

Boer, C. D., & Velthuijsen, A. S. (2001). Participation in conversations about the news. *International Journal of Public Opinion, 13*(2), 140–158.

Durkheim, E. (1964). *The division of labor in society* (G. Simpson, Trans.). New York: Free Press of Glencoe. (Original work published 1933)

Emerson, R. M. (1962). Power-dependence relations. *American Sociological Review, 27,* 31–41.

Gerbner, G., & Gross, L. (1976). Living with television: The violence profile. *Journal of Communication, 26,* 173–199.

Halpern, P. (1994). Media dependency and political perceptions in the authoritarian political system. *Journal of Communication, 44*(4), 39–52.

Hawley, A. H. (1950). *Human ecology: A theory of community structure.* New York: Ronald Press.

Hirschburg, P. L., Dillman, D. A., & Ball-Rokeach, S. J. (1986). Media system dependency theory: Responses to the eruption of Mount St. Helens. In S. J. Ball-Rokeach & M. G. Cantor (Eds.), *Media, audience, and social structure* (pp. 117–126). Newbury Park, CA: Sage.

Hovland, C. I. (1948). Psychology of the communicative process. In W. Schramm (Ed.), *Communications in modern society* (pp. 59–65). Urbana: University of Illinois Press.

Jung, J.-Y., Kim, Y.-C., Lin, W.-Y., & Cheong, P. H. (2005). The influence of social environment on Internet connectedness of adolescents in Seoul, Singapore and Taipei. *New Media & Society, 7*(1), 64–88.

Katz, E. (1957). The two-step flow of communication: An up-to-date report. *Public Opinion Quarterly, 21*(1), 61–78.

Katz, E., Blumer, J. G., & Gurevitch, M. (1973–1974). Uses and gratifications research. *Public Opinion Quarterly, 37*(4), 509–523.

Katz, E., Gurevitch, M., & Haas, H. (1973). On the use of mass media for important things. *American Sociological Review, 38,* 164–181.

Kim, Y. C., & Ball-Rokeach, S. J. (2006). Civic engagement from a communication infrastructure perspective. *Communication Theory, 16*(2), 173–197.

Kim, Y.-C., Jung, J.-Y., & Ball-Rokeach, S. J. (2006). "Geo-ethnicity" and neighborhood engagement: A communication infrastructure perspective. *Political Communication, 23*(4), 421–441.

Loges, W. E. (1994). Canaries in the coal mine: Perceptions of threat and media system dependency relations. *Communication Research, 21*(1), 5–23.

Manross, G. G. (1987). *Confirming media effects in voting behavior: A media dependency perspective.* Unpublished PhD dissertation, University of Southern California, Los Angeles.

Matsaganis, M. D., & Payne, J. G. (2005). Agenda setting in a culture of fear: The lasting effects of September 11 on American politics and journalism. *American Behavioral Scientist, 49*(3), 379–392.

Morton, T. A., & Duck, J. M. (2000). Social identity and media dependency in the gay community: The prediction of safe sex attitudes. *Communication Research, 27*(4), 38–61.

Perloff, R. M. (2007). *The dynamics of persuasion: Communication and attitudes in the 21st century* (3rd ed.). Hillsdale, NJ: Erlbaum.

Pitts, G. (2000). Democracy and press freedom in Zambia: Attitudes of members of Parliament toward media and media regulation. *Communication Law and Policy, 5*(2), 269–294.

Rubin, A. M., & Windahl, S. (1986). The uses and dependency model of mass communication. *Critical Studies in Mass Communication, 3*(2), 184–199.

Schiller, H. J. (1973). *Communication and cultural domination.* White Plains, NY: International Arts and Sciences Press.

Singhal, A., & Rogers, E. M. (2002). A theoretical agenda for entertainment-education. *Communication Theory, 12*(2), 117–135.

Stouffer, S. A., Suchman, E. A., DeVinney, L. C., Star, S. A., & Williams, R. M., Jr. (1949). *Studies in social psychology in World War II: The American soldier: Vol. 1. Adjustment during army life.* Princeton, NJ: Princeton University Press.

Turner, R. H., & Paz, D. H. (1986). The mass media in earthquake warning. In S. J. Ball-Rokeach & M. G. Cantor (Eds.), *Media, audience, and social structure* (pp. 99–115). Newbury Park, CA: Sage.

36

MEDIA EFFECTS 2.0

Social and Psychological Effects of Communication Technologies

◆ S. Shyam Sundar

The term *media effects* is somewhat of a misnomer because the vast majority of research in this tradition investigates effects of *content* delivered by mass media rather than effects of the media technologies themselves. But that is changing in the new era of media effects research. Revolutions in communication technology in the last two decades have brought to the fore the important role of media hardware and software in shaping receivers' reception, perception, and experience of content, echoing the theoretical claim of media ecologists (e.g., McLuhan, 1964) that the arrival of any new media technology unalterably modifies the scope and nature of human psychology by ushering in systemic changes.

In the last quarter of the 20th century, experimental social scientists were beginning to find that computer-based technologies were indeed altering the social psychology of organizational and interpersonal communications (Kiesler, Siegel, & McGuire, 1984; Short, Williams, & Christie, 1976). Mass communication scholars likewise started factoring technological aspects into their study of content uses and effects (e.g., Salvaggio & Bryant, 1989). Some media effects scholars, like Zillmann (1994), wondered whether advancements in communication technology altered our reception of media content. Others, like Reeves and Nass (1996), explicitly investigated how features relating to form and structure of the medium affected our responses to media content. The concept of "medium" was not an uninteresting channel between senders and receivers anymore. Effects researchers began to view it as a veritable repository of relevant variables with significant potential for social and psychological impact.

This chapter discusses four such classes of variables. It begins by delineating issues involved in applying the media effects approach to the study of technology. It then covers research pertaining to *modality* and *agency* (concepts that are analogous to "channel" and "source" elements in transmission models of mass communication via traditional media). Next, it covers research pertaining to *interactivity* and *navigability,* which are technological variables unique to newer media. Along the way, this chapter highlights principles about the effects of these variables on individuals, outlines theoretical and methodological issues in studying them, and identifies future directions for research on the psychological aspects of media technologies.

◆ Media Effects Approach to the Study of Communication Technology

Message variables constitute the starting point for most traditional media effects studies. The independent variable (i.e., causal factor) in a media effects study is a message attribute or content feature, such as the type of appeals used in an advertisement (rational versus emotional), the type of source delivering a piece of news (credible versus noncredible), the genre of programming (comedy versus tragedy), and so on. The dependent variables (i.e., effect or outcome considerations) span a whole host of psychological variables, ranging from attention and perception to memory and

conation that underlie acquisition of knowledge, formation of attitudes, and execution of behaviors.

The effects tradition is driven by a focus on independent variables. Scholars frequently identify themselves and characterize their work in terms of the message genres governing their independent variables (e.g., violence researcher, entertainment scholar), and chapters in media effects textbooks are often organized along similar lines (e.g., effects of political communication, effects of horror). Effects-based technology research borrows from this tradition and treats noncontent technological aspects of the mass medium as independent variables. Thus, whereas traditional media effects researchers view technology as a constant, technology researchers keep message content a constant while varying structural aspects of the technology. This means that content is not confounded with variations in technology, and technology is studied in terms of its constituent parts rather than as a whole.

Unlike traditional technology studies that employ a user-centered or object-centered approach (wherein the effects of a given technology are studied as a whole; e.g., the effects of telephone or the effects of television), the media effects paradigm suggests a variable-centered approach, which seeks to study technologies in terms of the specific variables that they embody (Nass & Mason, 1990). A given technology possesses a number of psychologically relevant variables, and different technologies may assume different values on these variables, though some may share the same value on certain variables. For example, television technology and computer technology share the same value, "visual," on the variable "presentation mode" but the two differ on a number of other variables, such as input device (the value for television is "remote control" whereas for computer it is "keyboard") and screen size. The variable-centered approach helps us pinpoint which psychological effect is predicted by what value on which variable. Therefore, if a given psychological effect is attributable solely to a technology's value on the "presentation mode" variable, then we should see no differences between televisions and computers on that outcome. However, if the effect is linearly related to the "screen size" variable such that greater size increases the magnitude of the effect, then that effect would be more pronounced among television viewers than among computer users.

By employing the variable-centered approach, we can not only isolate psychological effects of key technological variables, but also study the effects of combinations of these variables. In a dynamic and constantly evolving environment such as the Web, it is less useful to study the effects of the technology as a whole because it does not help us predict the psychosocial impact of future extensions or innovations in this technology. For example, if we found that news gathered from the Web leads to greater learning of new information compared with news gathered via television, the object-centered approach can tell us only that the two media differ on the dependent variable, learning. It can neither tell us why nor identify the precise cause, that is, the independent variable(s) on which the two media differ. The variable-centered approach, on the other hand, allows researchers to attribute the learning differences between the two media to one or more specific features, such as interactivity or navigability. If we know from this approach that it is indeed interactivity that is driving the learning difference, we will be able to make a number of specific predictions about future changes in both media technologies (e.g., a more interactive television will narrow the gap in learning between the two media).

As noted earlier, the effects tradition is driven mostly by independent variables. The dependent variables are broadly conceptualized as any psychological effect of interest in a given context. In a similar vein, if we apply the effects approach to the study of Web-based mass communication, the dependent variables could be *any* and *every* psychological effect of interest, depending on the context. For example, a study involving interactivity of a political candidate's Web site will focus on dependent variables relating to impression formation, whereas a study about interactivity effects of a distance-education Web site will have dependent measures relating to memory and learning.

The flexibility offered by this approach in allowing contextual specification of dependent variables opens the door for far-reaching discovery about the role of communication technology in a number of psychological domains. A preoccupation with independent variables allows us to look beyond the computer medium as a box and perform a rigorous study of the *processes* by which technology affects individuals because it disaggregates the technological black box in psychologically meaningful terms (Reeves, 1989). That said, there is a difference between specifying technological variables in user terms (e.g., modalities that aid touch vs. modalities that aid gaze) and *defining* them in eye-of-the-beholder terms (e.g., an interface is interactive only when it is perceived as such by the user). Technology researchers are particularly susceptible to the latter tendency given that technological variables are conceptualized as affordances (or action possibilities) subject to user perceptions (rather than as products delivered to users). The media effects approach helps reduce this problem by requiring that technological variables be operationally defined in objective, ontological terms so that they are susceptible to experimental manipulation (O'Keefe, 2003), with the perceptual component measured among study participants either as a check on the manipulation or as a mediator.

Just as message variables constitute the starting point for traditional media effects research, medium-related structural variables drive technology research (Sundar, 2004). Aside from modality and agency, which enjoy a strong presence in traditional media and have attracted considerable scholarly attention even before the advent of computer-based media, there are a number of new technological variables identified by scholars in the subdiscipline. Interactivity is one that appears on most people's lists, as do multimedia and hypertextuality (e.g., Newhagen & Rafaeli, 1996). Multimedia is a particular instantiation of the modality variable, and hypertextuality, or the interlinking of information through hypertext that defines the essential structure of the Web, is part of the broader variable of navigability (Sundar, 2008a). Thus, the four variables of modality, agency, interactivity, and navigability are discussed in this chapter. They are each treated as a technological "affordance" (Gibson, 1977; Norman, 1999), meaning that their underlying technical attributes will be ignored in favor of their objective functionalities that visually suggest "action possibilities," with the extent of their use being dependent on the subjective interpretation of those functionalities by users.

◆ *Modality*

Modality is defined as both a method of presentation (e.g., audio, picture) via media and the particular human sense (hearing, sight) that is best able to perceive that presentation method. More broadly, each modality is associated with its unique perceptual representation in the human cognitive system. For example, newer modalities, such as animation (e.g., animated graphic), help us perceive motion in addition to vision. Historically, a given mass medium has been distinguished by its delivery mechanism or modality—newspapers predominantly use textual mode, radio uses audio mode, and so on. Therefore, a study of differences between any two mass media would mean an investigation of differences due to the unique modalities of these two media. The arrival of any new medium is typically greeted by researchers with a comparison to older media. In keeping with this practice, scholars in the 1990s compared the effects of Web content to those of identical content in older media such as newspapers, radio, and television (Tewksbury & Althaus, 2000; Sundar, Narayan, Obregon, & Uppal, 1998). However, increasing digitalization of traditional media has complicated such comparisons. Historically distinct media have been rendered indistinct by trends in convergence of media production, presentation, and consumption. Most newspaper articles, radio shows, and television programs are available on the Internet and can be accessed through a computer. Differences in delivery mechanisms or modalities (print, audio, video), which tended to define older media, are not quite applicable to digital media because they are not exclusively tied to one modality.

In modern media, modality is not a constant but a variable. Not only do computer-based media feature a number of modalities; they also allow users to switch back and forth between various modalities and combinations of modalities. Modality is therefore an "affordance" of media technology, suggestive of action possibilities and subject to the imagination of the user.

Communication research on modality started in the heyday of television because audiovisual media were the first to offer more than one modality. Guided by theories in cognitive psychology, such as "separate streams" and "dual coding," which tended to treat different modalities as impacting different cognitive subsystems (verbal, visual), media effects researchers hypothesized greater memory for content that is delivered through multiple modalities (Sundar, 2000). Whereas some focused on the nature of the affordance made possible by multimodality, such as semantic overlap in content across modalities (van der Molen & Klijn, 2004) or greater number of retrieval cues available, others have focused on user exploitation of the affordance, such as rehearsal and elaboration. But, as Lang (1995) noted, redundancy in content between audio and video modalities does not guarantee superior memory, and she suggested that multiple modalities can overload the human information processing system by commanding more resources for encoding incoming information at the cost of storing them.

This serves as a good illustration of the role of modality as a technological *affordance* rather than as just another independent variable—user factors, including cognitive reception, are critically important in determining the direction of its effects. For example, Eveland and Dunwoody (2002) found that Web users learned more compared with their print-using counterparts if they elaborated more, but learned less if they engaged in selective scanning. Further, research with multimedia Web sites has shown that the particular combination of modalities on an interface is more important than the sheer number of modalities (Sundar, 2000). Among the theoretical explanations for such findings are the aforementioned possibility of cognitive load (imposed by additional modalities), disorientation (caused by having to toggle between modalities), distraction (caused by a particularly attention-grabbing modality), and overwriting (of content from one modality by subsequent content from another modality).

Such theoretical concerns stand in contrast to previously mentioned theoretical positions such as dual coding, which hold that different modalities are encoded by different systems (text verbally and images visually). By that logic, newer modalities such as animation may benefit from both verbal and visual coding, resulting in a net gain of information from multiple modalities. As Rieber (1991) argues, moving images not only enable visual coding of the image itself but also verbal coding of the relationships implied by the trajectory of motion in the image. Indeed, animated images on Web sites and online advertisements have been associated with stronger content memory compared with still images across a number of studies (e.g., Lang, Borse, Wise, & David, 2002; Li & Bukovac, 1999). Furthermore, animated ads have been known to elicit higher arousal (Heo & Sundar, 2000),

stronger orienting responses (Lang et al., 2002), and faster click-throughs (Li & Bukovac, 1999) than static ads, especially among those who are low on product involvement (Cho, 2003). They are also more likely to aid the persuasion function. Motion effect and distinctiveness theories address the superior attention-getting potential of animation whereas bioinformation theory of emotion, excitation transfer, limited capacity, and vividness propositions have been used to hypothesize the effects of animation (and related modalities such as pop-up windows) on higher-order outcomes such as content memory and impression formation (see Sundar & Kalyanaraman, 2004, for an overview). It is clear that certain new modalities, by affording new means of representing content, are able to evoke meaningful cognitive responses.

In general, effects of a given modality are premised on the degree of its *sensory richness*, evident from its ability to enhance presentation vividness and user feelings of presence in a mediated environment. For example, modalities that feature dynamic motion are often referred to as "rich media" because they promise users a richer experience of content (e.g., Appiah, 2006; Li, Daugherty, & Biocca, 2002), which means greater amount and depth of sensory exchanges between the user and the interface, or what Reeves and Nass (2000) call "perceptual bandwidth." Motion is a primitive cue, and an interface that induces the perception of motion can profoundly dictate subsequent psychological processing and action (Reeves & Nass, 1996).

Another key perceptual cue that can contribute to sensory richness is display size, which has consequences for arousal, memory, and a sense of presence. The notion of "presence," or the "perceptual illusion of non-mediation" (Lombard & Ditton, 1997), has pervaded modality research ever since Steuer (1992) operationally defined modalities in terms of sensory breadth (number of senses engaged by a modality) and sensory depth (resolution within each perceptual channel). Text scores lowest and virtual reality highest along his vividness continuum, with higher levels predicting greater "telepresence," or the illusion of being transported to the mediated environment. Coyle and Thorson (2001) found that vividness, operationalized as animation and presence of audio in Web marketing sites, led to a greater sense of telepresence as well as more positive and enduring attitudes toward the site (see also Li et al., 2002). Sundar (2008a) calls this the "being there" heuristic, which leads users to factor the authenticity and intensity of their media experience in later evaluations, including those pertaining to the presence they felt during the interaction. In his MAIN model framework, users' perceptual experience with digital media is shaped by a variety of heuristics triggered by cues embedded in particular modalities—cues such as realism, coolness, novelty, intrusiveness, and distraction.

In sum, modality is a key technological variable that significantly determines user interaction with media, and affects both processing and perception of mediated content. Different modalities carry different levels of user engagement with the medium, as indexed by both physiological and cognitive indicators, and therefore hold important implications for information processing. Moreover, combinations of modalities are cognitively as well as perceptually significant, with both positive and negative effects. By deploying newer modalities, such as animation and virtual reality, digital technologies profoundly shape the range and scope of our media experiences. Future research will probably focus on theoretical mechanisms that attempt to reconcile the positive cognitive effects of richer modalities with their negative effects. With the rapid growth and adoption of mobile media, the importance of sensory richness as a mediator of modality effects on user experience is likely to be questioned. The degree to which the degradation of sensory richness (caused by small screens and private audio) will be overcome by the affordance of mobility remains an open question for future research.

◆ Agency

Agency is a complex variable of modern media. It refers to the different types of sourcing afforded by new communication technologies. All models of mediated communication begin with a sender or source. In fact, one of the earlier and best-known programs of media effects research, led by Yale psychologist Carl Hovland, investigated the role of media source in fostering message acceptance. Since then, hundreds of source effects studies have examined a range of source characteristics, including credibility, attractiveness, and ideological similarity (Wilson & Sherrell, 1993). Together, these studies have documented the extent to which communication source perception can mediate receivers' cognitive and behavioral responses to media messages (e.g., Basil, 1996). Whereas traditional media have capitalized on this by ascribing importance to brands (*The New York Times*, CNN) and personalities (Walter Cronkite, Oprah) that serve as sources of mass communication, computer-based media afford a greater variety of sourcing—not simply by allowing users to choose from a larger variety of sources, but also by offering nonhuman sources and by enabling users themselves to serve as sources of communication.

Sundar and Nass (2001) attempted to make sense out of the confusing array of sourcing possibilities in online media by proposing a typology of four distinct communication sources that distinguish between nonhuman and professional gatekeeper sources as well as between sender and receiver sources: (1) *Visible source* refers to the sender in traditional communication models (e.g., an evening news anchorperson or the editorial staff of a news organization as signified by its masthead/logo); (2) *Technological source* refers to the computer itself or some interface element or software product that sifts through information and selects a subset of it for user consumption; (3) *Self as source* refers to interfaces that allow the individual user to act as gatekeeper of content, as in customized portals (e.g., myYahoo.com); and (4) *Audience as source* refers to any situation that highlights the usage patterns of the collective audience as a heuristic offered to users for determining the relative worth of different pieces of information (e.g., indicators of what others bought on Amazon.com or opinions of callers on radio call-in shows). These four sources map onto the basic elements of sender, channel, and receiver in traditional engineering flow models of communication, thereby calling into question the distinctions between these elements that were inspired by traditional mass media.

There are plenty of examples of visible sources online as in the logo of a Web site, like WebMD.com. Users often assign agency to such sources, just as in traditional mass media, and the influence of such sources on users is similar, as theorized and demonstrated by source-credibility researchers. The more intriguing type of source is the technological one. Over 15 years of research has shown that users tend to automatically assign agency to the medium itself, as evident from the social responses that individuals show to computers and televisions (Reeves & Nass, 1996). Users appear to mindlessly apply social rules of human-human interaction (such as politeness norms, reciprocity, and gender stereotypes) to human-computer interaction because they orient toward the computer as an autonomous source (Sundar & Nass, 2000). The increasing use of interface agents on a variety of Internet sites capitalizes on this tendency, with many of them being anthropomorphized to boost the source signal. Studies have shown that anthropomorphic agents and robots serve to increase social presence and influence users' emotional responses as well as attitudes toward the agent (Lee, Peng, Jin, & Yan,

2006), the site hosting the agent (Nowak, 2004), and other content on the site (Choi, Miracle, & Biocca, 2001). Attributions to the entire medium (e.g., "I got this off the Internet") would also constitute assignment of agency to technological source.

Aside from agency being located in the medium, communication receivers are now able to serve as sources on a variety of sites, from blogs and news sites to e-commerce and social networking sites (i.e., self as source). Web 2.0 technology is often dubbed "social media" in reference to its ability to involve users collectively as contributors of content. Many sites allow users to assert their agency by choosing or designing avatars to represent themselves, and research has demonstrated that avatars tend to increase one's social presence in the environment (Bailenson, Blascovich, Beall, & Loomis, 2003) and aid persuasion (e.g., Holzwarth, Janiszewski, & Neumann, 2006). This speaks to the powerful appeal of customization, which is strongly associated with positive attitudes toward the site (Kalyanaraman & Sundar, 2006). In his agency model of customization, Sundar (2008b) identifies the interface's ability to let the user assume agency as the critical mediator between technological affordances, such as interactivity, and psychological outcomes. Self-agency imbues the user with a strong sense of identity as well as control and involvement, which predict attitudes, behaviors, and cognitions, respectively.

In the fourth and final category, audience as source, the audience as a collective is given agency, in the form of metrics on e-commerce sites (e.g., number of stars given to a hotel) and online news sites (e.g., most e-mailed stories of the day). Studies have shown that users are particularly influenced by other-agency in their ratings of news stories (Knobloch-Westerwick, Sharma, Hansen, & Alter, 2005) and attitudes and intentions toward products, a tendency that is fully mediated by bandwagon perceptions (Sundar, Oeldorf-Hirsch, & Xu, 2008).

With the exponential growth of intelligent applications and user-generated content, all four types of sources are quite prevalent on the Web, and, as it turns out, user perceptions of online content are shaped by which of these sources is assigned agency by the user during a given interaction. Sundar and Nass (2001) found that when a news story was said to be selected by a computer, study participants rated it higher in quality than when it was ostensibly chosen by news editors. But they rated the quality (and other attributes, such as liking of story and its newsworthiness) even higher when the attributed source was "other users." One interpretation of these findings treats sources as peripheral cues, positing that different sources trigger different heuristics (or mental shortcuts) that shape the way the story is read and evaluated. Whereas technological source cues the machine heuristic (leading to an expectation and perception of objectivity in selection), news editors (or visible sources) cue the expertise heuristic, "other users" cue the bandwagon heuristic, and "self as source" cues the own-ness heuristic (Sundar, 2008b; Sundar, Knobloch-Westerwick, & Hastall, 2007).

In sum, the agency affordance of modern media technologies taps into an innate human need for both sourcing the information we receive and exerting one's influence over the nature of communication. Digital media have challenged the authority of professional sources as the gatekeepers of content by introducing technologies that assign agency to users as well as the machine. Avatars and interface agents have come to symbolize the user and the machine, respectively, with a sense of agency and anthropomorphism serving as critical concepts for a theoretical understanding of the psychological importance of agency. Depending on who or what is assigned agency, user stance toward media is likely to be different, resulting in differential perception and processing of media content en route to differential attitudes and conations, with implications for learning,

persuasion, and a host of related outcomes. Future research is likely to assess the effects on these outcomes of competing agency in online media as well as the cumulative or biasing effect of the multiple layers of agents that exist in modern media.

◆ Interactivity

The concept of interactivity lies at the heart of Media Effects 2.0 in that it challenges the linearity of traditional theoretical models of media effects and further calls into question the assumption of a passive audience. Interactivity has been variously conceptualized over the years, from the extent to which an interface allows users to modify "the form and content of a mediated environment in real-time" (Steuer, 1992, p. 84) to the sheer number of interaction-generating functions offered by the interface (Sundar, Kalyanaraman, & Brown, 2003). Interactivity has been equated with the provision of choice to users; control over information flow and speed; responsiveness; dialogue facilitation; and a host of similar, but subtly different, meanings (see Bucy & Tao, 2007; Kiousis, 2002; and Sundar et al., 2003, for some recent explications). Debates about definition, locus, and unit of interactivity (Bucy, 2004; Rafaeli & Ariel, 2007) have served to highlight the fact that it is unlike any of the traditional causal variables used in effects research, and have led to an ecumenical view of interactivity as a true affordance with both technological and psychological facets. Sundar and Bellur (in press) have called for conceptualizing and labeling these facets distinctly (*available interactivity* vs. *perceived interactivity*) so that they lend themselves to linear effects–type investigations wherein the ontological component is entered in the model as the independent variable and the perceptual component as the mediator of psychological dependent variables (Bucy & Tao, 2007).

That said, several studies have shown a direct effect of variations in structural aspects of interactivity even without involving the perceptual component, although the nature of such relationships is not altogether straightforward. For instance, McMillan, Hwang, and Lee (2003) found that attitudes toward a hotel Web site were poorer when it had a lot of interactive features. Sundar et al. (2003) qualified this by discovering a curvilinear effect—users' appraisal of a political candidate's Web site was more positive when it was moderately interactive than when it was noninteractive or highly interactive.

Other studies have shown variations in effects depending on the locus of interactivity (i.e., interactivity of the site as a whole vs. interactivity in particular content domains, such as ads). Coyle and Thorson (2001) found that while interactivity enhanced telepresence in Web marketing sites, it did not affect product attitudes, whereas Sundar and Kim (2005) found that greater interactivity within online advertisements led to more positive attitudes toward products. Most of these main effects of interactivity on attitudes are qualified by significant interactions involving both manipulated and user-based moderators. For example, Sundar and Kim found that when interactivity was high, respondents were relatively invulnerable to peripheral cues, such as animation. This, along with the significant mediation of perceived product involvement, led Sundar (2007) to conclude that interactivity results in closer scrutiny of content. If the content is good, then it leads to positive outcomes. But if it is not, as is the case with much Internet (and experiment) content, then the effect is negative. However, it should be noted that interactivity itself could be a "peripheral cue," with its sheer presence influencing the attitudes of low-involvement users more positively than those of high-involvement users.

When it comes to actually using the interactive feature, the story of interactivity effects can be quite different. For example,

Vorderer, Knobloch, and Schramm (2001) found that the ability to influence the plot of a movie significantly improved the entertainment experience for viewers with high cognitive capacity, but the opposite was true for those with low cognitive capacity. Likewise, Tremayne and Dunwoody (2001) found that user Web experience interacted with structural interactivity on a Web site such that veterans were more likely than novices to elaborate on the scientific information presented under conditions of high, rather than low, interactivity. It appears, then, that the direction of the interaction effect depends on whether the user actually uses the interactivity affordance or simply notices its presence on the interface.

Clearly, effects of interactivity are quite complex, encouraging serious consideration of trait moderators and perceptual mediators (Bucy & Tao, 2007). In addition to methodological complexity, greater theoretical specification is needed. Sundar (2007) has proposed a model of interactivity effects whereby different aspects of the affordance affect user engagement through different mechanisms. Whereas "modality interactivity" operates by varying the range of perceptual experiences, "source interactivity" cues a sense of customization, and "message interactivity" builds contingency in user interactions with the medium. User engagement with content is a critical mediator arising from the actual use of the interactive features. Sometimes, the mere presence of interactive features, such as choice, responsiveness, and telepresence, carry rich meanings for users and cue cognitive heuristics (Sundar, 2008a), without the user engaging the affordance. Thus, in keeping with the two-way notion of communication engendered by it, the concept of interactivity has invited effects scholars to step back from media determinism and consider user factors more rigorously. Not only is the definition of interactivity contingent upon user interpretation; the psychological effects of interactive tools in modern media technologies, too, are critically dependent on the nature and extent of user engagement with those tools.

The proliferation of interactive media tools has served to integrate interpersonal communication in otherwise mass communication venues (e.g., chat functions on e-commerce Web sites), but paradoxically has led to a greater divide between interpersonal and mass communication scholars in their conceptions of the definition and locus of interactivity. Whereas interpersonal scholars (who study computer-mediated communication between dyads and groups) tend to adopt a message-centered definition of interactivity by focusing on the process of contingent message exchange (Rafaeli & Ariel, 2007), media scholars tend to view it either as a technological affordance that offers opportunities for interaction (e.g., Sundar et al., 2003) or as a psychological construct dependent on subjective determination of the level of interaction by users (e.g., McMillan & Hwang, 2002). In the previous example of a chat feature on a Web site, interpersonal scholars would concern themselves with the degree of contingency or threadedness between messages in any given exchange between human interactants, whereas media scholars would focus on the ability of the technology to allow idiosyncratic interaction with the site. This ability, it is predicted, has the potential to significantly alter users' engagement with content on the site and therefore determine its psychological effects (Sundar, 2007).

Research on interactivity has moved beyond the concept explication phase, with scholars now paying attention to theoretical mechanisms by which interactivity affects the dynamics of communication. These mechanisms bear testing in the future by including user traits as moderators and user perceptions as mediators in experimental studies. With more research, we will learn whether interactivity effects are domain specific and verify whether the effects of interactivity are contingent upon its locus

(e.g., whether findings about Web site interactivity are applicable to interactive news stories). We will also see an emphasis on behavioral outcomes (e.g., what user actions are prompted by which kinds of interactivity) shedding light into the activity engendered by interactivity.

◆ Navigability

The navigability affordance refers to the tools on the interface that suggest or aid user movement through the media space under consideration. Unlike traditional media, the Web is a space that can be infinitely organized and idiosyncratically traversed. Metaphors such as "cyberspace" and "information superhighway" emphasize the spatial aspect of this medium, thus bringing architectural and interior-design considerations to the creation, production, and dissemination of mass communication. Conventional wisdom is that navigational aids, such as hyperlinks and site maps, enhance users' flexibility in accessing and organizing knowledge from a wide variety of sources on the Web. Attendant technologies, such as cookies, log files, and history commands on Web browsers, facilitate precise recording of such user activity. Therefore, it becomes possible for us to systematically study the complexity of human navigation during online communication. Navigation recording tools offer us the Web equivalent of recording every channel-changing activity on every television set of every household in the country, as opposed to inferring national TV viewing patterns based on a relatively small sample of households outfitted with the Nielsen box.

While our colleagues in information science and technology have extensively explored the effectiveness of various navigability tools, such as menu formats and link types, upon information-seeking behaviors, effects scholars have studied perceptual and cognitive outcomes. For example, likening the nonlinear structure of the Web to the associative network view of human memory, Eveland and Dunwoody (2002) found that learning from this medium positively correlated with elaboration, or the act of connecting new bits of information to related information. More specifically, hyperlinks within a narrative on the Web are believed to make users wonder about the relationship between the link and the main site content. Nonlinear linking strategies increase knowledge structure density (interconnectedness of information), whereas linear designs promote factual learning (Eveland, Cortese, Park, & Dunwoody, 2004).

In addition to site structure, interface features, such as the level of customization, can affect user navigation. Kalyanaraman and Sundar (2006) found that higher levels of customization were associated with more frequent returns to the home/main page as well as a decreased use of the "edit" and "search" functions and lower overall site visitations. Aside from customization inhibiting navigation, the clear implication for the designer is that a main page with personal identity is a "landmark" (i.e., an architecturally significant navigability cue).

It should be noted, though, that traditional print media, such as newspapers and magazines, also feature navigability cues in the form of headlines, size of photographs, and so forth, but newer media tend not to have such features of professional journalistic presentation unless they are Web sites of traditional print and broadcast media companies. The vast majority of news obtained via Web sites, cell phones, e-mails, and other online means carry little, if any, variations in their size to suggest prominence of one story over another. Physiological findings by Wise, Bolls, and Schaefer (2008) suggest that when faced with a large, compared with a small, menu of online news items, there is a greater allocation of cognitive resources, indicating decision stress. Therefore, navigability cues are especially important in online media. As Sundar, Knobloch-Westerwick, et al. (2007) found, "online news cues," such as those supplied by Google News (source of the lead, recency of the upload, number of related articles on the news event), do significantly aid user perceptions of credibility and newsworthiness of underlying news stories.

A simple cause-and-effect mechanism governs much navigability research. Navigability tools (e.g., menus) or metrics (e.g., number of related articles) provided by the technology are independent variables that affect user perceptions about underlying content, and these perceptions in turn dictate their navigation behaviors. That is, "navigability" is a media affordance whereas "navigation" is user behavior. Much work remains to be done in bridging the two. Sundar (2008a) offers a number of heuristics, such as browsing, play, scaffolding, and similarity, that might be triggered by navigability cues on a media interface and serve to determine user navigation. Another approach might be to examine the impact of these cues on users' construal of the media space (see Wirth et al., 2007).

The larger implication of navigability is one of space and motion. Most digital media, from cell phones to TVs to games, are rife with tools that encourage us to think of media as spaces in which we can move about. As the few existing studies demonstrate, user navigation in these spaces is patterned and predictable, generally as a function of navigational aids and cues embedded in the structure and functionality of online sites. Therefore, the next generation of effects research will likely focus on the theoretical mechanisms (such as selective exposure and knowledge acquisition) by which navigability affordances in media contribute to perceptions, uses, and effects of traversing these spaces.

◆ Conclusion

Modality, agency, interactivity, and navigability are but four species of variables embedded in most recent media technologies. As evident from the current review, their effects are investigated in a manner similar to the way message variables are studied in media effects experiments. Aspects of the technology (e.g., pop-up vs. banner; user as source vs. other users as source; high vs. low interactivity; linear vs. nonlinear hyperlinking) are systematically varied and isolated through controlled experiments in order to determine their effects on reception, processing, perception, and reactions to content. Given that "message" is the basic commodity in any mass communication transaction, outcomes pertain to user processing of messages, but the causal variables are technology centered rather than message based. Even though the methods used are old, relying mostly on psychological experiments, it should be clear from the foregoing discussion that a new wave of research has emerged in mass communication over the last two decades, signaling the importance of technological factors in explaining significant variance in outcome variables of interest to media effects researchers.

That said, research examining media technologies is characterized by two principal methodological challenges: (1) operationalizing technological independent variables as "affordances"; and (2) keeping media content constant when these affordances are engaged by study participants. Given that an affordance is an action possibility perceived by the user, care must be taken not to ignore the objective existence of a particular functionality offered by the technology in favor of a purely perceptual notion of that functionality because the latter is subject to user skills. That is, variations in perceived navigability, for example, should not be construed as variations in actual navigability offered by an interface. Norman (1999) suggests a separation between "real affordances" (invariant properties of the system) and "perceived affordances" (what the user perceives as being possible to do with the system). We could adopt this distinction in media effects by treating the former as manipulated

independent variables and the latter as measured mediators. The second challenge is that of keeping content constant when the manipulated technological variables allow for idiosyncratic construction of content. For example, in a study that manipulates interactivity, participants in the high-interactivity condition are more likely to individualize content according to their personal preferences compared with their counterparts in the low-interactivity condition, resulting in content variations across the two conditions that would confound the technological manipulation. In response, Klimmt, Vorderer, and Ritterfeld (2007) suggest recording and statistically accounting for such content variations to help us isolate the unique contribution, if any, of the technological factors on dependent variables, and also estimate the degree of overlap between real and perceived affordances.

In sum, developments in Internet technology and a spate of innovations in media interfaces have persuaded scholars to consider medium-related factors in explaining the effects of media content on individuals. Under Media Effects 2.0, technology is not incidental to content effects; it is integral. Furthermore, it is not conceptualized as a black box but as a bundle of affordances. Each affordance generates ontological as well as psychological variables for empirical testing with "users," not audience members. Users, in turn, are affected perceptually by the sheer presence of an affordance and experientially when they engage it for information and entertainment needs. Technology research from a media effects perspective explains more of the variance on traditional effect outcomes by not only introducing new concepts (e.g., interactivity) but also challenging us to rethink old concepts, such as source. It helps build theories about media in addition to providing new, ecologically valid operationalizations for testing theories in psychology. Many psychologists use media to present their stimuli without explicitly accounting for the role played by the medium itself. Given rapid advances in technologies, media are not windows any more into a world of well-controlled psychological stimuli, but a veritable suite of devices enabling users to enter those stimuli and interact with them. By taking seriously the structural elements in media, we will be able not only to test theoretical propositions from psychology (e.g., limited capacity, cognitive load, distinctiveness, excitation transfer, elaboration likelihood, knowledge-structure density), but also to develop and test media theories (e.g., media richness, media equation, interactivity effects, MAIN model, agency model of customization, spatial situation model of presence) about the role played by current and future technologies in shaping uses and effects of mass communication in the 21st century.

◆ **References**

Appiah, O. (2006). Rich media, poor media: The impact of audio/video vs. text/picture testimonial ads on browsers' evaluations of commercial Web sites and online products. *Journal of Current Issues and Research in Advertising, 28*(1), 73–86.

Bailenson, J. N., Blascovich, J., Beall, A. C., & Loomis, J. M. (2003). Interpersonal distance in immersive virtual environments. *Personality and Social Psychology Bulletin, 29,* 819–833.

Basil, M. D. (1996). Identification as a mediator of celebrity effects. *Journal of Broadcasting & Electronic Media, 40,* 478–495.

Bucy, E. P. (2004). Interactivity in society: Locating an elusive concept. *The Information Society, 20*(5), 373–383.

Bucy, E. P., & Tao, C. C. (2007). The mediated moderation model of interactivity. *Media Psychology, 9*(3), 647–672.

Cho, C. H. (2003). Factors influencing clicking of banner ads on the WWW. *CyberPsychology & Behavior, 6*(2), 201–215.

Choi, Y. K., Miracle, G. E., & Biocca, F. (2001). The effects of anthropomorphic agents on advertising effectiveness and the mediating role of presence. *Journal of Interactive Advertising, 2*(1), 3–21.

Coyle, J. R., & Thorson, E. (2001). The effects of progressive levels of interactivity and vividness in Web marketing sites. *Journal of Advertising, 30*(3), 65–77.

Eveland, W. P., Cortese, J., Park, H., & Dunwoody, S. (2004). How Web site organization influences free recall, factual knowledge, and knowledge structure. *Human Communication Research, 30,* 208–233.

Eveland, W. P., & Dunwoody, S. (2002). An investigation of elaboration and selective scanning as mediators of learning from the Web versus print. *Journal of Broadcasting & Electronic Media, 46*(1), 34–53.

Gibson, J. J. (1977). The theory of affordances. In R. Shaw & J. Bransford (Eds.), *Perceiving, acting and knowing: Toward an ecological psychology.* Hillsdale, NJ: Erlbaum.

Heo, N., & Sundar, S. S. (2000). *Visual orientation and memory for Web advertising: A study of animation and position effects.* Paper presented at the 50th annual convention of the International Communication Association, Acapulco, Mexico.

Holzwarth, M., Janiszewski, C., & Neumann, M. M. (2006). The influence of avatars on online consumer shopping behavior. *Journal of Marketing, 70,* 19–36.

Kalyanaraman, S., & Sundar, S. S. (2006). The psychological appeal of personalized content in Web portals: Does customization affect attitudes and behavior? *Journal of Communication, 56,* 110–132.

Kiesler, S., Siegel, J., & McGuire, T. W. (1984). Social psychological aspects of computer-mediated communication. *American Psychologist, 39*(10), 1123–1134.

Kiousis, S. (2002). Interactivity: A concept explication. *New Media & Society, 4*(3), 355–383.

Klimmt, C., Vorderer, P., & Ritterfeld, U. (2007). Interactivity and generalizability: New media, new challenges. *Communication Methods and Measures, 1*(3), 169–179.

Knobloch-Westerwick, S., Sharma, N., Hansen, D. L., & Alter, S. (2005). Impact of popularity indications on readers' selective exposure to online news. *Journal of Broadcasting and Electronic Media, 49*(3), 296–313.

Lang, A. (1995). Defining audio/video redundancy from a limited-capacity information processing perspective. *Communication Research, 22*(1), 86–115.

Lang, A., Borse, J., Wise, K., & David, P. (2002). Captured by the World Wide Web: Orienting to structural and content features of computer-presented information. *Communication Research, 29*(3), 215–245.

Lee, K. M., Peng, W., Jin, S. A., & Yan, C. (2006). Can robots manifest personality? An empirical test of personality recognition, social responses, and social presence in human-robot interaction. *Journal of Communication, 56*(4), 754–772.

Li, H., & Bukovac, J. L. (1999). Cognitive impact of banner ad characteristics: An experimental study. *Journalism and Mass Communication Quarterly, 76*(2), 341–353.

Li, H., Daugherty, T., & Biocca, F. (2002). Impact of 3-D advertising on product knowledge, brand attitude, and purchase intention: The mediating role of presence. *Journal of Advertising, 31*(3), 43–58.

Lombard, M., & Ditton, T. (1997). At the heart of it all: The concept of presence. *Journal of Computer-Mediated Communication, 3*(2). Retrieved November 6, 2008, from http://jcmc.indiana.edu/vol3/issue2/lombard.html

McLuhan, M. (1964). *Understanding media*. New York: Signet.

McMillan, S. J., & Hwang, J. S. (2002). Measures of perceived interactivity: An exploration of the role of direction of communication, user control, and time in shaping perceptions of interactivity. *Journal of Advertising, 31*(3), 29–43.

McMillan, S. J., Hwang, J. S., & Lee, G. (2003). Effects of structural and perceptual factors on attitudes toward the Website. *Journal of Advertising Research, 43*(4), 400–410.

Nass, C., & Mason, L. (1990). On the study of technology and task: A variable-based approach. In J. Fulk & C. Steinfield (Eds.), *Organizations and communication technology* (pp. 46–67). Newbury Park, CA: Sage.

Newhagen, J. E., & Rafaeli, S. (1996). Why communication researchers should study the Internet: A dialogue. *Journal of Communication, 46*(1), 4–13.

Norman, D. A. (1999). Affordance, conventions, and design. *Interactions, 6*(3), 38–41.

Nowak, K. (2004). *The influence of anthropomorphic agents on attitudes toward the Website: A test of two mediating routes.* Paper presented at the International Communication Association, New Orleans, LA.

O'Keefe, D. J. (2003). Message properties, mediating states, and manipulation checks: Claims, evidence, and data analysis in experimental persuasive message effects research. *Communication Theory, 13,* 251–274.

Rafaeli, S., & Ariel, Y. (2007). Assessing interactivity in computer-mediated research. In A. N. Joinson, K. Y. A. McKenna, T. Postmes, & U. D. Rieps (Eds.), *Oxford handbook of Internet psychology* (pp. 71–88): Oxford University Press.

Reeves, B. (1989). Theories about news and theories about cognition: Arguments for a more radical separation. *American Behavioral Scientist, 33,* 191–198.

Reeves, B., & Nass, C. (1996). *The media equation: How people treat computers, television, and new media like real people and places.* New York: Cambridge University Press.

Reeves, B., & Nass, C. (2000). Perceptual user interfaces: Perceptual bandwidth. *Communications of the ACM, 43*(3), 65–70.

Rieber, L. P. (1991). Animation, incidental learning, and continuing motivation. *Journal of Educational Psychology, 83*(3), 318–328.

Salvaggio, J. L., & Bryant, J. (Eds.). (1989). *Media use in the information age: Emerging patterns of adoption and consumer use.* Hillsdale, NJ: Erlbaum.

Short, J., Williams, E., & Christie, B. (1976). *The social psychology of telecommunications.* London: John Wiley & Sons.

Steuer, J. (1992). Defining virtual reality: Dimensions determining telepresence. *Journal of Communication, 42*(4), 73–93.

Sundar, S. S. (2000). Multimedia effects on processing and perception of online news: A study of picture, audio, and video downloads. *Journalism and Mass Communication Quarterly, 77*(3), 480–499.

Sundar, S. S. (2004). Theorizing interactivity's effects. *The Information Society, 20,* 385–389.

Sundar, S. S. (2007). Social psychology of interactivity in human-Website interaction. In A. N. Joinson, K. Y. A. McKenna, T. Postmes, & U.-D. Reips (Eds.), *The Oxford handbook of Internet psychology* (pp. 89–104). Oxford, UK: Oxford University Press.

Sundar, S. S. (2008a). The MAIN model: A heuristic approach to understanding technology effects on credibility. In M. J. Metzger & A. J. Flanagin (Eds.), *Digital media, youth, and credibility* (pp. 72–100). Cambridge, MA: MIT Press.

Sundar, S. S. (2008b). Self as source: Agency and customization in interactive media. In E. Konijn, S. Utz, M. Tanis, & S. Barnes (Eds.), *Mediated interpersonal communication.* New York: Routledge.

Sundar, S. S., & Bellur, S. (in press). Concept explication in the Internet age: The case of political interactivity. In E. P. Bucy & R. L. Holbert (Eds.), *Sourcebook for political communication research: Methods, measures, and analytical techniques.* New York: Routledge.

Sundar, S. S., Edwards, H. H., Hu, Y., & Stavrositu, C. (2007). Blogging for better health: Putting the "public" back in public health. In M. Tremayne (Ed.), *Blogging, citizenship, and the future of media.* New York: Routledge.

Sundar, S. S., & Kalyanaraman, S. (2004). Arousal, memory, and impression-formation effects of animation speed in Web advertising. *Journal of Advertising, 33*(1), 7–17.

Sundar, S. S., Kalyanaraman, S., & Brown, J. (2003). Explicating Web site interactivity: Impression formation effects in political campaign sites. *Communication Research, 30*(1), 30–59.

Sundar, S. S., & Kim, J. (2005). Interactivity and persuasion: Influencing attitudes with information and involvement. *Journal of Interactive Advertising, 5*(2), 6–29.

Sundar, S. S., Knobloch-Westerwick, S., & Hastall, M. R. (2007). News cues: Information scent and cognitive heuristics. *Journal of the American Society for Information Science and Technology, 58*(3), 366–378.

Sundar, S. S., Narayan, S., Obregon, R., & Uppal, C. (1998). Does Web advertising work? Memory for print vs. online media. *Journalism and Mass Communication Quarterly, 75*(4), 822–835.

Sundar, S. S., & Nass, C. (2000). Source orientation in human-computer interaction: Programmer, networker, or independent social actor. *Communication Research, 27*(6), 683–703.

Sundar, S. S., & Nass, C. (2001). Conceptualizing sources in online news. *Journal of Communication, 51*(1), 52–72.

Sundar, S. S., Oeldorf-Hirsch, A., & Xu, Q. (2008). *The bandwagon effect of collaborative filtering technology.* Proceedings of the Conference on Human Factors in Computing Systems (ACM SIGCHI), Florence, Italy.

Tewksbury, D., & Althaus, S. L. (2000). Differences in knowledge acquisition among readers of the paper and online versions of a national newspaper. *Journalism and Mass Communication Quarterly, 77*(3), 457–479.

Tremayne, M., & Dunwoody, S. (2001). Interactivity, information processing, and learning on the World Wide Web. *Science Communication, 23*(2), 111–134.

van der Molen, J. H. W., & Klijn, M. E. (2004). Recall of television versus print news: Retesting the semantic overlap hypothesis. *Journal of Broadcasting & Electronic Media, 48*(1), 89–107.

Vorderer, P., Knobloch, S., & Schramm, H. (2001). Does entertainment suffer from interactivity? The impact of watching an interactive TV movie on viewers' experience of entertainment. *Media Psychology, 3*(4), 343–363.

Wilson, E., & Sherrell, D. (1993). Source effects in communication and persuasion research: A meta-analysis of effect size. *Journal of the Academy of Marketing Science, 21*(2), 101–112.

Wirth, W., Hartmann, T., Böcking, S., Vorderer, P., Klimmt, C., Schramm, H., et al. (2007). A process model of the formation of spatial presence experiences. *Media Psychology, 9,* 493–525.

Wise, K., Bolls, P. D., & Schaefer, S. R. (2008). Choosing and reading online news: How available choice affects cognitive processing. *Journal of Broadcasting & Electronic Media, 52*(1), 69–85.

Zillmann, D. (1994). Cognitive and affective adaptation to advancing communication technology. In P. Zoche (Ed.), *Herausforderungen für die Informationstechnik* (pp. 416–428). Heidelberg: Physica-Verlag.

37

THE STUDY OF MEDIA
EFFECTS IN THE ERA OF
INTERNET COMMUNICATION

◆ Miriam J. Metzger

As the realization set in during the final years of the 20th century that the Internet was the next significant medium of communication, many began to speculate about the effects this new medium was having, or would likely have, on both individuals and society. Like most communication media before it, including print, the telephone, film, and broadcasting, initial predictions were that the Internet would be the harbinger of profound changes reaching across all levels of the social spectrum. Calls to research the impending effects of "the Internet" were made in both the popular press and scholarly journals (see, for example, Newhagen & Rafaeli's winter 1996 special issue of the *Journal of Communication* on "The Net").

Few realized at the time, however, that to speak of "Internet effects" is as unproductive as speaking of "television effects." To be sure, we have very few theories of "television effects," although many theories of the effects of specific types of television uses and content, including violence, sex, stereotypical portrayals of minorities, news, and so on, have been developed and applied in useful ways. A common misunderstanding in the early days of Internet research, although it still persists today to some degree, was that the Internet is an undifferentiated entity (Walther, Gay, & Hancock, 2005).

Conceptualizing "the Internet as mass medium" (Morris & Ogan, 1996) reflects this early thinking.

As media researchers, we must be much clearer in how we talk about, and study, the "effects of the Internet." The Internet is less a mass medium than it is a conduit for mass, as well as other forms of, communication. Walther et al. (2005) write that "Internet use is too broad a category to assess systematically or sensitively potential impacts of various communication channels for which the Internet is a conduit" (p. 650). We need to talk instead about the effects that *various uses* of the Internet have on users, as well as the effects of *specific forms* of online content and *particular applications*. At the same time, we must also realize that different Internet uses, content, and applications may produce various or even contradictory effects at both social and individual levels of analysis (McKenna & Bargh, 2000; Solomon, 1990). Moreover, rather than talking about the effects of the Internet as a mass medium, this perspective allows us to talk about the effects that the Internet as a means of message delivery has on mass, as well as other forms of, communication. As such, scholars "need to refocus research on the Internet as *media* rather than *medium*" (Walther et al., 2005, p. 651, emphasis added).

This chapter examines what the shift in the channel of communication from traditional media to networked digital media means for media effects theory. It does so by first considering what *is* and *is not* new about new media. It then focuses on how similarities and differences between new and traditional media affect existing media effects theories, and finally the chapter offers ideas about future media effects theorizing in the era of Internet communication.

◆ Differences and Similarities in Traditional and New Media

An important argument made in this chapter is that the Internet has not changed, nor is it likely to change, *everything* about the media. Although this notion may seem obvious, it is oddly absent in many theorists' prognostications about the Internet. Certainly some things have changed. The major media *channel* or *conduit* of communication (i.e., the means of message delivery) is changing from analog to digital, from print and broadcast/cable to the Internet. However, older forms of mass communication will likely persist as well. Similarly, some media *content* has changed, but not all. For example, although blogs offer new possibilities for news content, the story content of the online edition of the *New York Times* differs only slightly if at all from its print version (Li, 2006). More and more broadcast content is being moved online too, often with little or no modification. Finally, some aspects of the *audience* have changed, such as the time audiences apportion to traditional media, as well as their ability to participate in content creation, while other aspects of audiences have not changed, including the basic psychology underlying people's motivations for media use.

Analyses of the differences between old and new media structures and audiences have been fashionable in the research literature, and several inventories of these differences have been proposed by scholars in recent years (Chaffee & Metzger, 2001; Eveland, 2003; Kaye & Medoff, 2001; Lieberman, 2001; Newhagen & Rafaeli, 1996; Silverstone, 1999; Solomon, 1990). Across these scholars, the following differences emerge as the most widely cited and the most enduring over the short history of the Internet: *interactivity, diversity of content, audience control and selectivity, personalization, media convergence, the structure or organization of information,* and *global reach*. Each of these differences has implications for a number of media effects theories. Two other newly emerging differences between more recent and traditional mass media forms that may have important implications for media effects researchers in the near future are *media portability* and *audience social connectivity*. After these differences are elaborated, the chapter will discuss their consequences for theorizing about media effects in the Internet era.

INTERACTIVITY

Scholars generally argue that Internet-based communication allows for more interactivity on the part of users compared with most traditional mass media, particularly print and broadcasting. Although interactivity has been defined in many ways, in the context of mass communication it most commonly refers to the degree to which communication over a medium is two-way rather than one-way (see Bucy, 2004, for a review). Inherent in this definition is the idea that interactivity allows greater audience participation in mass (i.e., one-to-many) communication. The current trend toward social computing and user-generated content enabled by "Web 2.0" applications, such as blogs or YouTube.com, illustrates this nicely. These applications open possibilities for audiences to affect media content, thus reversing the flow of effects typically examined in our field. The potential for greater audience activity afforded by interactivity, in terms of both media content creation and audience members' degree of control over the communication exchange, is related to the next two differences between traditional and new media to be examined.

DIVERSITY OF CONTENT AND VIEWPOINTS

The range of content available over the Internet is unsurpassed by any mass medium with regard to its sheer volume, as well as the fact that the Internet as a channel of communication is "multimodal," allowing textual, audio, and visual means of information conveyance across individuals, groups, and organizations. It has been estimated that the Web currently has about 281 exabytes of information and that number will increase ten-fold in the next 5 years (Williams, 2008). The Internet offers media audiences easy access to a much wider array of information and information sources, including non-elite and geographically distant sources and media outlets, compared with its mass media predecessors. Consequently, the Internet provides audiences no coherent set of messages, but rather offers a multitude of content across Web sites that include many viewpoints, in contrast to some accounts of traditional newspapers and television. This has implications for effects theories based on the media providing audiences with a consistent set of messages (e.g., cultivation theory) or viewpoints (e.g., agenda-setting theory), as discussed later.

AUDIENCE SELECTIVITY AND CONTROL

The combination of increased interactivity and diversity of content means that audiences can both be more selective about and exert more control over the media content they are exposed to. New media audiences play a greater role as gatekeepers both because they have more choices as receivers of media content, and because they can filter, produce, and distribute information to themselves or others more easily (e.g., via blogs and other types of user-generated content). Moreover, digital video recorders (DVRs) and other devices allow users to time shift their media exposure in new ways. As Shaw and Hamm (1997) argue, digital information technologies allow for a shifting of media control from the center (i.e., a few dominant mainstream media institutions) to the periphery (i.e., millions of geographically dispersed individual users).

Selectivity challenges media effects theories that assume audiences are exposed to the same messages at approximately the same time, including agenda-setting and cultivation theories, as well as notions of "media events" (Dayan & Katz, 1992), such as the famous television miniseries of the 1970s and 1980s like *Roots* or *The Day After* (Chaffee & Metzger, 2001). With DVRs, even live televised events may not be experienced on the same simultaneous mass scale.

Greater selectivity and user control also have implications for media effects theories that assume there is a lack of alternatives to mainstream media viewpoints, such as agenda–setting and framing. For example, the abundance of information online facilitates the possibility that audiences will be exposed to competing agendas or frames, rather than the narrow set of agendas and frames supplied by mainstream news media outlets in broadcast television and newspapers. However, greater selectivity and control on the part of audiences might work against this, as people may be more likely to filter out frames or perspectives that are inconsistent with their own social or political views. Bennett and Iyengar (2008), in fact, argue that such biased selection of content will result in less attitude *change* and more attitude *reinforcement* effects of the media.

PERSONALIZATION OF THE MEDIA EXPERIENCE

Just as users can tailor their own content exposure using digital media, media organizations can use networked communication technologies to collect information about individual audience members and then tailor or customize content for them. This trend is perhaps most advanced in the advertising industry, although news and entertainment media organizations are also developing methods to use the Internet to deliver personalized content. Some have described this as a shift from "broadcasting" to "narrowcasting" (Massey, 2004), which is further evidenced by the change in focus from general-appeal to special-appeal television programming. As with selectivity, personalization problematizes the notion

that mass media audiences of the future will be exposed to the same content, which is the bedrock of several media effects theories. Concern about the impacts of personalized content have led to new theorizing about the media's effects on social fragmentation and attitude polarization (e.g., Bennett & Iyengar, 2008; Sunstein, 2001; Turow, 1998).

MEDIA CONVERGENCE

Media convergence reflects the idea that the technological boundaries between previously distinct forms of communication and media are blurred as a result of digitization, video compression, broadband, and multimedia technologies. Indeed, newer media forms have been heralded for their ability to transmit messages via multiple modes (audio, visual, textual, etc.), as well as their capacity for carrying one-to-one, one-to-few, one-to-many, and many-to-many communication. Moreover, the Internet's ability to convey interpersonal, group, organizational, and mass communication has caused some researchers to rethink definitions of "mass" compared with other forms of communication, and presents challenges to theorizing about communication carried by digital media. As new technologies blur the line between mass and interpersonal communication, models based on either mass media or face-to-face contexts may not work to explain the impacts new media may have (Morris & Ogan, 1996). Nonetheless, the combination of personalized media content and media convergence offered by digital media (i.e., sending customized messages to audience members via multiple mass *and* interpersonal channels) presents intriguing possibilities for fresh models of media persuasion.

MESSAGE STRUCTURE

Newhagen and Rafaeli (1996) were among the first to point out that a core difference between traditional and newer forms of mass media lies in the way messages are organized for audiences in terms of their linear structure. Newer media, they say, offer more *hypertextuality,* which is the degree to which media narratives may be received in nonlinear versus linear ways. The fact that different users may not follow the same path in a hypertext document presents challenges similar to those discussed earlier under personalization and audience selectivity/control for theories of media effects that presume all audience members for a particular text, program, or film view the same content and thus receive the same message. Differences in message structure and degree of audience control between traditional and newer media have also prompted recent theorizing about the impacts of new media on learning. Eveland and Dunwoody (2001), for example, find significant differences in learning due to the nonlinear information organization schemes in Web environments versus the more linear message structures of traditional mass media formats.

GLOBAL REACH

Although traditional mass media, such as newspapers and television, were able to transcend the boundaries of space that had limited prior forms of communication to a relatively small geographical radius, most mass media were still bound to particular locations and regions until fairly recently. For example, terrestrial radio and TV broadcasters operated on regional or national levels due to limitations on how far spectrum signals can travel through the air. Newspapers, too, were typically tied to a particular region or nation because delivery to distant locations in the pre-Internet age was cost prohibitive for all but the largest publishers. By increasing efficacy and lowering the cost of information delivery, the Internet has expanded the market for traditional media to global proportions to an extent never before realized, and to a greater number of information producers

than ever before in history.

To date, theorizing about the impact of these enlarged markets for mass media products via satellites and global syndication of television programming has focused on cultural imperialism, leaving questions raised by Internet-based communication largely ignored. Specifically, as the Internet opens even more possibilities for distribution of media content around the world and allows for greater interactivity between information producers and receivers, could this increase cross-cultural dialogue and collaboration and, thus, foster better cross-cultural understanding? Will increasingly globalized markets affect the type or variety of media content that is likely to be produced as media firms seek to appeal to culturally diverse audiences around the world? How will media firms that must compete in the global market cut through the abundance of media choices available to capture consumers' limited attention? One strategy might be producing more sensationalized content, while another strategy might be to increase experimentation and innovation in both media content and format. In any case, media globalization facilitated by interactive digital technologies begs the question of the effects that the newly resulting forms and formats of media content might have at the cultural and global levels on media audiences, as well as on media firms and industries themselves.

MEDIA PORTABILITY

New communication technologies are increasingly bringing a new era of media mobility, including in portability of media content both across time, such as time shifting television content using VCRs and now DVRs, and across space. Wireless technologies in particular allow for media content that was previously tied to specific locations (particularly television and cable) to be experienced in a wider array of physical and social spaces than before. The "mobile revolution" is only just beginning, but it does bring the issue of *context* to the fore in media effects research.

Although media effects researchers generally focus on the impact of media content (e.g., violence, sexual content) as the independent variable, wireless digital technologies may call more attention to the media context or experience of using media as a contributor to media effects (see McDonald, Chapter 17, this volume). To be sure, researchers have examined contextual effects of traditional media (e.g., studies of the impact of coviewing; effects of time displacement on interpersonal communication and association; see Bryant & Fondren, Chapter 33, this volume, and Wilson & Drogos, Chapter 31, this volume), but they have done so to a far less extent than content-based effect studies. However, wireless Internet communication may change audience habits, patterns, and places of traditional mass media consumption. For example, notions of television as a domestic medium and the family as the primary consumption unit for television will need rethinking as hand-held digital technologies move usage of television and other video content outside the home and to places besides the living room (Bryant & Miron, 2004; Grindstaff & Turow, 2006). These changes wrought by technology challenge media effects researchers to reconsider the circumstances of media use as a central variable in the effects process.

SOCIAL CONNECTIVITY OF THE AUDIENCE

Although mass media audiences have always been embedded in social networks and often experience media content within social groups (such as the family), networked digital media extend the social reach of audience members significantly, particularly in terms enabling direct social interaction between audience members. Also, while audiences of television, print, and film can and do discuss mass media content via other communication channels (e.g., by talking to one another about a news story or television program in person, by phone, or through e-mail), audiences of new media can engage each other without venturing outside the medium through which they experience the content (e.g., when online news consumers interact with each other via the newspaper's blog). This encourages social connectivity in theory as it reduces the effort for audience members to discuss and comment on media content delivered online. YouTube's "comments and suggestions" feature is a good example of this capability. Social computing in its myriad forms (e.g., blogs, wikis, feedback, recommender and rating systems, and so on) furthers this idea and could be considered a new form of interactivity that centers on exchange between individual audience members rather than between a receiver of mass media content and the media institution that produced that content, as in previous conceptualizations of interactivity. New media's ability to extend social connectivity among their audiences is important because the social interaction surrounding mass media exposure can influence viewers' interpretations of media content and, thus, how that content may affect them.

◆ Theorizing About New Media Effects

Differences in both the structure and audience usage of new versus traditional forms of mass communication, such as those outlined previously, have prompted calls for entirely new models and modes of thinking about media effects. In some ways, this is a curious position because, in nearly all cases, the differences between traditional and newer media discussed in this chapter are not absolute, but rather are a matter of degree (Eveland, 2003). For example, print is portable and can achieve global reach, although not as easily or instantly as Internet-based communication; cable television offers a greater diversity of content than broadcast television, although less diversity than the Internet; and VCRs did provide television viewers some ability to customize their communication experiences. Also, it is not yet clear whether audiences will use new media in fundamentally different ways than they used "older" media. For example, while new media have the potential to increase audience activity via greater opportunities for interactivity, selectivity, and user control, some evidence suggests that audience members will not necessarily take full advantage of these capabilities (Neuman, 1991). Thus, theories of effects may not be justified in assuming new media audiences will be more active in the future.

This suggests that before throwing the baby out with the bathwater, media researchers should consider carefully what has and has not changed about the media that could impact their theories of media effects. In some cases, new theoretical models will be called for; in other cases, older models may still be appropriate; but in most cases, researchers will likely need to adjust existing models in light of differences in new media structures, characteristics, and audiences to appropriately understand the effects of media today. The result will be more useful and enduring models of effects that fit the media landscape as it changes through time as a result of technological development (see Eveland, 2003, for a similar argument).

As a starting point for theorizing effects processes in the future, the remainder of this chapter will discuss how new media challenge some of the core theories of media effects in the mass communication literature, it will review existing studies that have applied each theory to Internet contexts, and it will suggest some opportunities for further research in each domain. It focuses on agenda setting, cultivation, the spiral of silence, and communication campaigns not only because these are core paradigms of media effects research, but also because each of these theories or approaches rests on the assumption of mass exposure to relatively

uniform content via the media (Blumler & Kavanagh, 1999), an assumption that is significantly undermined by the features of new media discussed earlier.

AGENDA SETTING

The agenda-setting effect of the mass media is premised on the notions that news audiences have a limited array of sources from which to get public affairs information, and that the news media present a relatively uniform agenda of issues at any given time (Chaffee & Metzger, 2001). The explosion in the amount and diversity of Internet-based news information in recent years seriously weakens the first assumption, and the ability of audiences to be more selective and to customize their exposure to issues undermines the second assumption (see also Bennett & Iyengar, 2008). Research, in fact, shows that online news consumers select different issues to read than do print news consumers, choosing to follow their own issue priorities instead of those selected by professional gatekeepers (Althaus & Tewksbury, 2002). Moreover, studies find that audiences of Internet-based news expose themselves to a narrower agenda of issues according to personal interests than do consumers of print news (Schoenbach, de Waal, & Lauf, 2005; Tewksbury, 2003). These findings have led to claims that, because there is no longer a consistent media agenda that audiences are attending to *en masse*, and as more alternatives to mainstream news appear online, the media will no longer have the power to set the public agenda (Chaffee & Metzger, 2001; Shaw & Hamm, 1997).

So, does this mean that agenda setting theory must be thrown out? Perhaps not. Takeshita (2006) argues that despite the abundance of news outlets available via the Internet, there is little evidence that the majority of people are availing themselves of the plethora of choices, and instead typically use online versions of traditional media news outlets. He concludes from this that agenda-setting effects are likely to survive into the Internet age. Supporting his position, a few studies have found that agenda setting follows theoretical predictions in the online environment, whereby the public agenda is influenced by Internet-based media such as candidate Web sites and alternative progressive online news services (Ku, Kaid, & Pfau, 2003; Song, 2007).

New media may, however, force changes to some tenets of agenda setting theory, as well as the methods used to measure the media and public agendas. For example, the increased interactivity and social connectivity afforded by the Internet have produced a new type of news, namely blogs. News and political blogs written by citizens constitute a form of public agenda that may be influenced by traditional media (and thus follow the typical pattern of media-to-public agenda setting), but may also significantly complicate the agenda-setting process. For example, some studies find that while the traditional news media set the agenda for online discussions (Lee, Lancendorfer, & Lee, 2005; Roberts, Wanta, & Dzwo, 2002), others find that the blog agenda does not match the mainstream news media agenda (Delwiche, 2005). Wallsten (2007) examined the agenda-setting power of blogs and mainstream media and found that the relationship was complex. In some cases, there was no relationship between the blog and mainstream media agendas, but in most cases the influence was bidirectional. This suggests that, in some instances, a reversal of the typical media-to-public agenda-setting process took place whereby the public (blog) agenda set the mainstream media agenda.

Blogs also have the capacity to cut traditional media out of the agenda setting equation, as do other social computing technologies that enable citizens to connect directly and, thus, set each other's agendas. Social media may enable individuals to increasingly take their cues from each other

rather than from mainstream media (Mermingas, 2006). Supporting this, a study of collaborative filtering of news found that people are more likely to select and spend time reading stories that are recommended by other news consumers than stories that have no social recommendations (Knobloch-Westerwick, Sharma, Hansen, & Alter, 2005). Other interesting and related questions revolve around issues such as, To what extent do bloggers set other bloggers' agendas? Will social networking sites facilitate this type of agenda setting, too? These forms of public-to-public agenda setting enabled by Internet-based media offer new possibilities for agenda setting theory and research.

The challenges new media bring to agenda setting open up several avenues for theoretical development. Perhaps the first questions for agenda-setting researchers to pursue are whether agenda-setting effects will be weaker overall for mainstream media as the media agenda and, thus, the public agenda fragment due to increased news choice and user selectivity. Will agenda setting be stronger for alternative media as people act as their own gatekeepers and pay attention to just the issues that interest them? And what does the fact that people tend to selectively attend to soft news more often than hard news (Althaus & Tewksbury, 2002) mean for general political knowledge and civic engagement?

Agenda setting theory may also need to place more emphasis on the power of the public agenda to set the policy agenda in the future. As people customize their news exposure to narrower, special interest topics via new media, they may have more power to set the policy agenda directly, without the help of mainstream media. An intriguing question is whether online political interest groups, such as MoveOn.org, or social networking sites will enable the public to bypass mainstream media to help set the policy agenda. Indeed, as people self-select, learn about, and identify strongly with particular issues online, they may be more motivated to act on those issues (Bimber,

Stohl, & Flanagin, 2008). At the same time, the portability and social connectivity of new media can help connect politically motivated individuals and inform them about when and how to act on issues. On-the-spot organizing enabled by new media may help complete the media agenda–public issue knowledge–political action causal chain. In this way, new media may tell people not only what issues to think about, but how and when to act on those issues as well.

CULTIVATION THEORY

Cultivation theory shares some of its assumptions with agenda setting in that it presumes traditional mass media (i.e., television in this case) are the primary source for information and entertainment for most people, and that they present a relatively uniform set of messages on various topics (e.g., violence). A number of scholars have questioned whether these assumptions, and thus whether the theory itself, can withstand recent changes in the media landscape toward increased content diversity and audience selectivity (Chaffee & Metzger, 2001; Williams, 2006). Indeed, an early study by Perse, Ferguson, and McLeod (1994) found reduced cultivation effects among owners of media technologies that enable greater selectivity and control (VCRs and cable) compared with traditional broadcasting.

Chaffee and Metzger (2001), however, argue that although cultivation to a single mainstream view (e.g., of a mean and scary world) may be less possible with new media, cultivation processes may still be at play. They contend that, "as many worldviews are disseminated through the new media, cultivation theory may shift toward a vision in which individuals are cultivated to specialized worldviews of their own choosing" (p. 376). As people select media content based on their own interests and points of view, this content may cultivate or shape their perceptions of social reality toward the themes or mechanisms of

storytelling typical of that selected content (Hawkins & Pingree, 1982; Segrin & Nabi, 2002). Chaffee and Metzger further suggest that cultivation effects in this environment may be stronger than with television because of *resonance,* or when media content reinforces viewers' preexisting realities. Because users of new media have a greater ability to select content of their own choosing, or even create their own content, it is possible that they will gravitate toward content that conforms to their own attitudes, biases, or perspectives online. Sunstein (2001) and others fear that this may result in social fragmentation and attitude polarization on a larger scale than was possible before the Internet.

Williams (2006) agrees that cultivation effects may be stronger in new media environments, although for different reasons. He focuses on the question of whether violent online video games cultivate fears about crime and violence in players. He argues that the highly interactive and participatory nature of online video game play results in a more involving and immersive media experience than television, and thus might serve to heighten cultivation effects. He also notes that many online games are a site of social interaction for players, and so these games must be understood as a convergence of mass and interpersonal communication. Interactions between players can reinforce or contest the violent messages and themes in the games and so can influence cultivation effects.

Only a few studies have examined cultivation effects of video games, and findings are mixed. While some have found little evidence of cultivation (Ivory & Kalyanaraman, 2007; Van Mierlo & Van den Bulck, 2004), others have found a connection between video game usage and cultivation effects, including fear of crime and violence (Williams, 2006) and aggressive feelings (Persky & Blascovich, 2007). Interestingly, the studies where effects were found involved violent video games played in immersive virtual environments rather than other video game formats, which suggests that cultivation processes may be most evident in digital environments that are involving and highly participatory. This raises questions about other types of virtual worlds and communities that people participate in online (e.g., *World of Warcraft, Second Life*). Although *Second Life* might not contain large amounts of violence, there may be other beliefs that could be cultivated within that online environment, including, for example, beliefs about interpersonal norms or relationship expectations. For many people, blogs and social networking sites (SNS), such as Facebook and MySpace, constitute online "worlds" through which they receive a great deal of their social and political information. While these are not "entertainment" media in the traditional sense, the degree to which SNS might cultivate certain beliefs about social relationships, including views about identity, friendship, self-disclosure, relationship formation and maintenance, popularity, politics, and privacy, could be interesting subjects of future cultivation-based research.

THE SPIRAL OF SILENCE

The theory of the spiral of silence makes several assumptions that are difficult to sustain in the new media environment. First, the theory assumes little content diversity in the media in terms of alternative viewpoints. Second, it assumes audiences have little control or ability to select media content that varies from the views espoused by mainstream media. This culminates in the theoretical prediction that if audience members do not agree with mainstream media views, they will avoid expressing their own views for fear of social isolation. However, as Shaw and Hamm (1997) and others argue, the Internet provides access to a much wider array of opinion, and thus audience members do not necessarily live in isolation

if they hold views at variance with those circulated in the mass media.

Slater (2007) also says that by increasing audience members' ability to access information that reflects their own views, the Internet invalidates many of the premises of the original theory. He offers instead a "spirals of selectivity model" that says when people who do not identify with the values expressed by mainstream media select other content that affirms their views, this may lead to reinforcement spirals that foster increased identification with values outside the mainstream. He suggests that

> a more contemporary version of the spiral of silence, then, might be concerned rather with the degree to which religious, political, or lifestyle subcultures perceive that their values and concerns are reflected in mainstream media content or political and social discourse. Such perception may influence the degree of openness or closure to outside influence, as well as feelings of personal alienation or connection and the degree of willingness to engage in political processes and debate. (p. 297)

Reinforcement spirals may also lead to other effects, including, for example, political attitude polarization and social fragmentation, as people surround themselves with consonant viewpoints and have fewer collective media experiences by virtue of exposing themselves to specialized media content (Bennett & Iyengar, 2008; Shaw & Hamm, 1997; Sunstein, 2001).

It would appear, then, that the spiral of silence in its original form may have little predictive power in the new media environment due to the increased diversity of content, audience control and selectivity, interactivity, and social connectivity, as well as the anonymity afforded by the Internet. However, there is reason to theorize a spiral of silence within certain online social contexts. Social networking environments that are designed to help people form new relationships, for example, Facebook and LinkedIn, may be key sites in which to examine the spiral of silence because of the fear of isolation that would likely result from appearing unpopular or otherwise socially undesirable within these networks. Indeed, studies of Facebook users show that political preferences are among the least-disclosed types of personal information (Gross & Acquisti, 2005), which could be due to a fear of losing friend or professional contact requests. Interestingly, almost no work has been done on the spiral of silence in these and other online contexts (though see Lee, Choi, & Lee, 2004).

COMMUNICATION CAMPAIGNS

The Internet's capacity for interactivity, diversity of content, audience control and selectivity, personalization, media convergence, global reach, portability, and social connectivity all have important implications for persuasion-based media effects, such as communication campaigns research. Research on communication campaigns has been active in examining how new media extend and alter mechanisms of persuasion to produce media effects. Rice and Atkin (2009), for example, discuss how interactivity and personalized feedback in Internet-based communication campaigns increase motivation and self-efficacy to adhere to campaign objectives because of greater message relevance, attention, and processing. Personalized information and messages tailored to the needs of individual audience members via Internet-based technology have been shown to increase communication campaign effectiveness in many instances (see Kreuter, Farrell, Olevitch, & Brennan, 2000).

Communication campaigns are also more effective when several forms of communication are used to reach audiences and when peer-to-peer communication augments media-based messages (Rice & Atkin, 2009). The multimedia capabilities of the Internet (via media convergence) can be used by audiences to learn about a topic from many channels and may facilitate immediate and sustained interpersonal communication surrounding mediated campaign messages. The social connectivity of new media may also promote interpersonal communication about the campaign, which could in turn increase campaign effectiveness via persuasion based on networks of trusted peers. The portability, relative low cost, and global reach of mobile phones and Internet-based communication may also help spread campaign messages and provide feedback and support to campaign targets at any time, wherever they are located (Rice & Atkin, 2009). For these reasons, the persuasive capacity of new media campaigns may be greater than that of traditional media campaigns.

On the other hand, the diversity of content and audience selectivity in the digital media environment may work against the persuasive objectives of communication campaigns. The irony is that while digital media make it easier to reach larger audiences, the sheer amount of information available challenges communication campaign designers to capture audience members' attention through all the informational clutter available today (Rice & Atkin, 2009). Indeed, this is becoming the key problem for all communicators in the new media environment. Technical problems and lingering digital divide issues also pose hurdles for communication campaigns and other persuasion-based media effects models in the online environment.

◆ Measuring Exposure in the Age of New Media

A fundamental challenge that cuts across all the theories discussed in the previous sections is how to measure exposure to media content in the future. Theories such as agenda setting and cultivation rely on content analyses to reveal consistencies in mainstream media messages, such as what is "the" news agenda or what are the themes of storytelling used in entertainment media. But simple content analyses to determine the consistent message(s) in the media will not work well in the Internet age. First, there are far too many "channels" to monitor in the digital realm (Chaffee & Metzger, 2001). Second, assumptions that nearly everyone is tuning to the same channels will become less tenable over time, except in special cases (Bennett & Iyengar, 2008). Third, as audiences generate their own content, in blogs or multiplayer online video games, for example, media content will come as much from fellow users as it does from media organizations (Williams, 2006). Content analyses of the number of violent incidents per hour or percentages of mentions of a news issue that do not factor the social interactions between audience members into users' media exposure may provide inaccurate accounts of the content that audiences are actually exposed to.

Together, this suggests that much more detailed and precise measurement of exactly where audiences get their information and entertainment content from will be needed to determine the extent the media still set the public's agenda, or the degree to which users' exposure to specific content cultivates their worldviews. The typical "hours of media use" measures will not suffice to uncover effects in the new media age, and self-reports of media exposure may be unreliable as users jump from one media source to another via a jumble of hyperlinks or digital devices. Ironically, digital technologies can actually help researchers get these precise estimates of audience exposure to certain content through page visit and clickstream data, which have the added advantage of being captured relatively unobtrusively. In any case, media measurement in the future must respond to changes in the media environment by becoming more flexible, more portable, and less device specific as people time shift, produce, and transfer media content across a multitude of delivery platforms.

Moreover, self-selection of media content based on political preferences will require a different approach to both conceptualizing and measuring media effects. Not only will it be more difficult to detect evidence of attitude change as people select information that reinforces their preexisting beliefs, but researchers will need to develop methods to disentangle the confounded and reciprocal effects of media exposure on political attitudes in survey research (Bennett & Iyengar, 2008). For example, Bennett and Iyengar argue that it will be important to offer research participants the ability to self-select media content in order to enhance the generalizability of findings from experimental media effects research to the real world. In all cases, measuring media exposure and any effects of that exposure is a much more complex task in the new media environment.

◆ Conclusion

The extent to which new media challenge existing theories of media effects depends largely on whether the theory hypothesizes effects due to the content or the system of message delivery, and the degree to which those two things interact. For example, effects theories that rest on outdated assumptions about mass media structures and how those structures impact audiences face an uncertain future (e.g., agenda setting). Theories that posit effects of the media are due to basic and enduring aspects of human psychology, information processing, and physiology will likely be relatively unaffected by changes in communication technologies (e.g., media information processing theories, excitation transfer theory, the third-person effect, catharsis).

Of course, many theories fall in between these extremes in the sense of being affected, but not completely undermined, by the characteristics and capabilities of new media. Mood management theory, for example, is not fundamentally altered as a result of the Internet, and indeed, increased content diversity and audience control may bolster its theoretical tenets (see Mastro, Eastin, & Tamborini, 2002). The central claim of Bandura's social cognitive theory—that audiences learn from observing media models—also may be enhanced due to the participatory nature of Internet use. Not only do players of violent video games observe aggression by their favorite characters, but players direct that aggression themselves. In this way, video games combine social learning with learning-by-doing, which may increase media effects. Desensitization is another theory that is touched, but not completely altered, by the appearance of interactive media. Again, as video game players enact violence rather than just view it passively on television, desensitization processes could be accelerated. In short, theories whose effects rest on audience choice, control, and direct participation will be enhanced rather than undermined by new media that feature these characteristics.

Ironically, then, this chapter ends where it began, with the argument that while the Internet has changed a lot about the media, it does not change everything with regard to media effects theory. Rather than discarding everything that has been learned about the effects of the media, as some have suggested, media effects researchers should apply existing models to the new media environment with careful consideration to how aspects of the new environment affect theoretical assumptions about the media and audiences. As discussed earlier, we need to more fully incorporate new media attributes and affordances into our theories of media effects (Eveland, 2003; Sundar, Chapter 36, this volume).

We also need to broaden the scope of our inquiry. To be sure, the Internet has produced some revolutionary effects that are not captured by the typical perspectives, methods, and theories used in our field, which tend to center on media content. For example, the Internet has caused sweeping and profound changes in media regulation, law, and policy due to the breakdown of the public interest model of broadcasting; it has had powerful economic effects on certain markets and industries, including traditional media industries themselves, as well as many others; it has created important societal-level effects such as mobilizing collective action in new ways around the globe and altering individuals' sense of social connectivity, place, and power. The challenge will be to figure out how to theorize, quantify, measure, and research these institutional and macrolevel (new) media effects in a way that connects to our core disciplinary roots and concerns. This will also require media effects researchers to stretch beyond social-psychological theory when looking for evidence of "Internet effects."

Gone are the days of journal articles and special issues that aim to convince the field that we should study the Internet (e.g., Newhagen & Rafaeli, 1996). The Internet is becoming integrated into our media landscape and also into our research. However, theory about the effects of the Internet has been slower to respond (Walther et al., 2005). This chapter suggests that new media theorists do not have to start from scratch in most cases, and urges researchers to think about how new and old media converge or diverge in theoretically important ways. Ideally, this chapter will help researchers more carefully consider how they theorize about media effects in the Internet age and provide some useful guidance for how to proceed in that endeavor.

◆ References

Althaus, S. L., & Tewksbury, D. (2002). Agenda setting and the "new" news: Patterns of issue importance among readers of the paper and online version of the *New York Times*. *Communication Research*, 29(2), 180–207.

Bennett, W. L., & Iyengar, S. (2008). A new era of minimal effects? The changing foundations of political communication. *Journal of Communication, 58,* 707–731.

Bimber, B., Stohl, C., & Flanagin, A. J. (2008). Technological change and the shifting nature of political organization. In A. Chadwick & P. N. Howard (Eds.), *Handbook of Internet and politics* (pp. 72–85). New York: Routledge.

Blumler, J. G., & Kavanagh, D. (1999). The third age of political communication: Influences and features. *Political Communication, 16,* 209–230.

Bryant, J., & Miron, D. (2004). Theory and research in mass communication. *Journal of Communication, 54*(4), 662–704.

Bucy, E. (2004). Interactivity in society: Locating an elusive concept. *The Information Society, 20,* 373–383.

Chaffee, S. H., & Metzger, M. J. (2001). The end of mass communication? *Mass Communication & Society, 4*(4), 365–379.

Dayan, D., & Katz, E. (1992). *Media events: The live broadcasting of history.* Harvard University Press.

Delwiche, A. (2005). Agenda-setting, opinion leadership, and the world of Web logs. *First Monday, 10*(12). Retrieved March 2, 2008, from http://www.firstmonday.org/issues/issue10_12/delwiche/index.html

Eveland, W. P. (2003). A "mix of attributes" approach to the study of media effects and new communication technologies. *Journal of Communication, 53*(3), 395–410.

Eveland, W. P., & Dunwoody, S. (2001). User control and structural isomorphism or disorientation and cognitive load? Learning from the Web versus print. *Communication Research, 28,* 48–78.

Grindstaff, L., & Turow, J. (2006). Video cultures: Television sociology in the "New TV" age. *Annual Review of Sociology, 32,* 103–125.

Gross, R., & Acquisti, A. (2005, November 7). *Information revelation and privacy in online social networks (the Facebook case).* ACM Workshop on Privacy in the Electronic Society (WPES). Retrieved January 25, 2008, from http://www.heinz.cmu.edu/~acquisti/papers/privacy-facebook-gross-acquisti.pdf

Hawkins, R. P., & Pingree, S. (1982). Television's influence on constructions of social reality. In D. Pearl, L. Bouthilet, & J. Lazar (Eds.), *Television and behavior: Ten years of scientific progress and implications for the eighties* (pp. 224–247). Washington, DC: U.S. Government Printing Office.

Ivory, J. D., & Kalyanaraman, S. (2007). The effects of technological advancement and violent content in video games on players' feelings of presence, involvement, physiological arousal, and aggression. *Journal of Communication, 57*(3), 532–555.

Kaye, B. K., & Medoff, N. J. (2001). *The World Wide Web: A mass communication perspective.* Mountain View, CA: Mayfield.

Knobloch-Westerwick, S., Sharma, N., Hansen, D. L., & Alter, S. (2005). Impact of popularity indications on readers' selective exposure to online news. *Journal of Broadcasting & Electronic Media, 49*(3), 296–313.

Kreuter, M., Farrell, D., Olevitch, L., & Brennan, L. (2000). *Tailoring health messages: Customizing communication with computer technology.* Mahwah, NJ: Erlbaum.

Ku, G., Kaid, L. L., & Pfau, M. (2003). The impact of Web site campaigning on traditional news media and public information processing. *Journalism & Mass Communication Quarterly, 80*(3), 528–547.

Lee, B., Lancendorfer, K. M., & Lee, K. J. (2005). Agenda-setting and the Internet: The intermedia influence of Internet bulletin boards on newspaper coverage of the 2000 general election in South Korea. *Asian Journal of Communication, 15*(1), 57–71.

Lee, J. H., Choi, Y. J., & Lee, C. (2004, May 27). *The spiral of silence in online discussions.* Paper presented at the annual meeting of the International Communication Association, New Orleans, LA.

Li, X. (2006). News of priority issues in print vs. Internet newspapers. In X. Li (Ed.), *Internet newspapers: Making of a mainstream medium* (pp. 261–281). Mahwah, NJ: Erlbaum.

Lieberman, D. A. (2001). Using interactive media in communication campaigns for children and adolescents. In R. E. Rice & C. K. Atkin (Eds.), *Public communication campaigns* (3rd ed., pp. 373–388). Thousand Oaks, CA: Sage.

Massey, K. (2004). *Narrowcasting*. The Museum of Broadcast communications. Retrieved March 23, 2008, from http://www.museum.tv/archives/etv/N/htmlN/narrowcasting/narrowcasting.htm

Mastro, D. E., Eastin, M. S., & Tamborini, R. (2002). Internet search behaviors and mood alterations: A selective exposure approach. *Media Psychology, 4,* 157–172.

McKenna, K., & Bargh, J. A. (2000). Plan 9 from cyberspace: The implications of the Internet for personality and social psychology. *Personality and Social Psychology Review, 4*(1), 57–76.

Mermingas, D. (2006, March 14). New media's effect on the value of a viewer. *Hollywood Reporter.* Retrieved March 27, 2008, from http://www.hollywoodreporter.com/hr/search/article_display.jsp?vnu_content_id=1002157837

Morris, M., & Ogan, C. (1996). The Internet as mass medium. *Journal of Communication, 46*(1), 39–50.

Neuman, R. W. (1991). *The future of the mass audience.* New York: Cambridge University Press.

Newhagen, J. E., & Rafaeli, S. (1996). Why communication researchers should study the Internet: A dialogue. *Journal of Communication, 46*(1).

Perse, E. M., Ferguson, D. A., & McLeod, D. M. (1994). Cultivation in the newer media environment. *Communication Research, 21,* 79–104.

Persky, S., & Blascovich, J. (2007). Immersive virtual environments versus traditional platforms: Effects of violent and nonviolent video game play. *Media Psychology, 10*(1), 135–156.

Rice, R. E., & Atkin, C. K. (2009). Public communication campaigns: Theoretical principles and practical applications. In J. Bryant & M. B. Oliver (Eds.), *Media effects: Advances in theory and research* (3rd ed., pp. 436-468). Hillsdale, NJ: Erlbaum.

Roberts, M., Wanta, W., & Dzwo, T. (2002). Agenda setting and issue salience online. *Communication Research, 29*(40), 452–465.

Schoenbach, K., de Waal, E., & Lauf, E. (2005). Online and print newspapers: Their impact on the extent of the perceived public agenda. *European Journal of Communication, 20*(2), 245–258.

Segrin, C., & Nabi, R. L. (2002). Does television viewing cultivate unrealistic expectations about marriage? *Journal of Communication, 52,* 247–263.

Shaw, D. L., & Hamm, B. J. (1997). Agendas for a public union for private communities? How individuals are using media to reshape American society. In M. McCombs, D. L. Shaw, & D. Weaver (Eds.), *Communication and democracy: Exploring the intellectual frontiers in agenda-setting theory* (pp. 209–230). Mahwah, NJ: Erlbaum.

Silverstone, R. (1999). What's new about new media? *New Media & Society, 1*(1), 10–12.

Slater, M. D. (2007). Reinforcing spirals: The mutual influence of media selectivity and media effects and their impact on individual behavior and social identity. *Communication Theory, 17*(3), 281–303.

Solomon, G. (1990). Cognitive effects with and of computer technology. *Communication Research, 17*(1), 26–44.

Song, Y. (2007). Internet news media and issue development: A case study on the roles of independent online news services as agenda-builders for anti-U.S. protests in South Korea. *New Media & Society, 9*(1), 71–92.

Sunstein, C. (2001). *Republic.com.* Princeton, NJ: Princeton University Press.

Takeshita, T. (2006). Current critical problems in agenda-setting research. *International Journal of Public Opinion Research, 18*(3), 275–296.

Tewksbury, D. (2003). What do Americans really want to know? Tracking the behavior of news readers on the Internet. *Journal of Communication, 53*(4), 694–710.

Turow, J. (1998). *Breaking up America: Advertisers and the new media world.* Chicago: University of Chicago Press.

Van Mierlo, J., & Van den Bulck, J. (2004). Benchmarking the cultivation approach to video game effects: A comparison of the correlates of TV viewing and game play. *Journal of Adolescence, 27,* 97–111.

Wallsten, K. (2007). Agenda setting and the blogosphere: An analysis of the relationship between mainstream media and political blogs. *Review of Policy Research, 24*(6), 567–582.

Walther, J. B., Gay, G., & Hancock, J. T. (2005). How do communication and technology researchers study the Internet? *Journal of Communication, 55*(3), 632–657.

Williams, D. (2006). Virtual cultivation: Online worlds, offline perceptions. *Journal of Communication, 56*(1), 69–87.

Williams, I. (2008). *Digital universe set to expand.* Retrieved March 16, 2008, from http://www.vnunet.com/vnunet/news/2211903/digital-universe-continues-explode

AUTHOR INDEX

Abelman, R., 370
Abelson, R. P., 364
Abner, E., 416
Abraham, L., 187, 382
Abrams, J., 385
Abu-Lughod, L., 61
Acock, A. C., 348, 349, 351, 352
Acquisti, A., 571
Adams, J., 276
Adams, J. T., 132
Adams, M. S., 382
Adams, S. M., 364
Adamson, D. R., 445
Aday, S., 215, 364
Adkins, D. A., 279
Adorno, T. W., 229
Agarwal, R., 494
Agha, S., 290
Agliata, D., 398
Agras, W. S., 398, 403
Aikat, D., 494
Aitken, C. K., 272
Ajzen, I., 44, 45,
    107, 273, 274, 316
Aksoy, L., 300
Alba, J., 303, 306
Albada, K. F., 338
Albarracin, D., 274
Alger, D. E., 121
Alioto, J. T., 426
Allen, M., 15, 35, 47,
    211, 272, 275, 316
Allen, R., 277

Allport, G. W., 226, 252, 492
Alstead, M., 321
Altabe, M., 396
Alter, S., 164, 551, 568
Althaus, S. L., 116, 118, 124, 185,
    322, 548, 567, 568
Altman, J. D., 364
Aluja-Fabregat, A., 163, 241, 243
Alvarez, M., 426, 427
Alvin, B. L., 316
Amichae-Hamburger, Y., 242, 248
Amiel, T., 243
Anderson, B., 542
Anderson, C. A., 181, 182, 183,
    210, 212, 362, 363, 364,
    365, 367, 460, 461, 474, 499
Anderson, D. R., 24, 77, 256, 332,
    334, 335, 336, 337, 338, 340,
    402, 471, 475, 476, 478, 512
Anderson, J. A., 54, 56, 57, 58
Anderson, J. D., 105
Anderson, J. R., 92
Anderson, L. L., 367, 461
Anderson, P. M., 477
Anderson, R. B., 290, 292
Andrejevic, M., 432
Andriessen, J. H. E., 493, 495, 496
Andsager, J. L., 105, 291
Ang, A., 348, 349
Ang, I., 61, 136, 139
Angelini, J. R., 201, 477
Appiah, O., 187, 382, 549
Appleton, H., 335

Appugliese, D., 510
Arcari, C. M., 413
Archer, A. H., 334
Arcuri, L., 382
Ariel, Y., 552, 554
Ariely, D., 303, 304
Armitage, C. J., 274
Arms, R. L., 444, 445, 448
Armstrong, C. B., 154
Armstrong, C. L., 90, 91
Armstrong, G., 379
Armstrong, G. B., 431
Arnett, D. K., 259
Arnett, J. J., 410
Arnheim, R., 521
Arnold, M. B., 206
Aronson, E., 272
Arora, N. K., 323
Arpan, L. M., 181, 301, 302
Ashburn, L., 382
Ashby, S. L., 413
Ashe, D. D., 225
Atkin, C. K., 254, 255, 277, 314, 363, 423,
    426, 427, 492, 571
Atkin, D., 495, 497, 498, 507
Atkinson, J., 316
Atkinson, P., 54
Atwood, L. E., 106
Aubrey, J. S., 288, 474
Aust, C. F., 164
Austin, E. A., 418
Austin, E. W., 254, 287,
    347, 349, 350, 351, 352, 418
Auter, P. J., 227, 231
Auty, S., 301, 302

Ba, S., 498
Babin, L. A., 301
Babrow, A. S., 44, 274
Bacanu, S. A., 401
Baer, N., 418
Bagley, S., 254, 259
Baier, M., 349
Bailenson, J. N., 293, 294, 551
Baker, K., 457
Bakker, A. B., 278
Balasubramanian, S. K., 300
Baldacci, H. B., 365, 474
Baldwin, C. K., 257
Ball, K., 259
Ball, S., 339
Ball-Rokeach, S. J., 152, 154, 532, 533,
    534, 535, 536, 537, 538, 540, 541, 542
Banaji, M., 386
Bandini, L. G., 402

Bandura, A., 215, 284, 285, 286, 287, 290,
    291, 292, 315, 349, 368, 380, 396,
    413, 423, 460
Banerjee, S. C., 346, 347, 348
Banks, A. J., 217
Barcus, F. E., 254
Bardone-Cone, A. M., 400
Bargh, J. A., 179, 180, 368, 562
Barker, C., 91
Barmada, C. H., 46
Barmada, D. H., 499
Barnard, P. J., 186
Bar-On, M. E., 346, 348, 509
Baron, R. M., 90
Barr, R., 334, 478
Barradas, D., 475
Barsch, A., 165
Bartels, L. M., 116
Bartholow, B. D., 183, 210, 261, 363
Bartsch, A., 169, 458
Basil, D. Z., 271
Basil, M. D., 152, 199, 227, 234, 550
Batada, A., 476
Bates, J. E., 369
Bateson, G., 85
Bauer, R., 19, 20
Baum, M. A., 117
Baumeister, R. F., 213
Baumgardner, J., 365, 474
Bavelas, J. B., 55
Bayley, O., 64
Baym, G., 123, 137
Beach, L. R., 102
Beall, A. C., 551
Beard, L., 509
Beaver, E. D., 240, 244
Bechenham, A., 139
Becker, A. E., 399
Becker, C. B., 272
Becker, L. B., 147, 314, 534
Beckmann, N. M., 90, 91, 117
Bedell, B. T., 321
Behm-Morawitz, E., 379, 384
Bell, T., 85
Bellur, S., 552
Beltz, C., 64
Bemker, V., 291
Benbasat, I., 496
Benjamin, A. J., Jr., 183
Bennett, C., 40
Bennett, L. L. M., 119
Bennett, S. E., 119
Bennett, W. L., 114, 115, 124,
    564, 567, 570, 572
Ben-Porath, E., 124

Bentham, J., 442
Berel, S. R., 347, 348
Berelson, B., 12, 115, 149, 314
Berenstein, v., 397
Beresford, S. A., 322
Bergman, J., 316
Berkman, L., 318, 319
Berkowitz, J. M., 275
Berkowitz, L., 181, 182, 184, 244,
        363, 364, 367, 368, 426, 448
Berlyne, D. E., 458
Berndt, T. J., 472
Bernhardt, P. C., 445
Berntson, G. G., 196
Berry, S. H., 288, 413, 414, 415
Berry, W. D., 45
Bettelheim, B., 229
Bezjian-Avery, A., 303, 304, 305
Bhatla, S., 306
Bhatnagar, N., 300
Bickham, D. S., 510
Biederman, J., 474
Biely, E. N., 431, 432, 473
Bilandzic, H., 167, 424, 425, 430, 433
Bimber, B., 124, 568
Biocca, F. A., 21, 292, 549, 550, 551
Bischel, J., 185
Bissell, K. L., 400
Biswas, R., 164
Black, D. R., 274
Black, M. E., 321
Blackburn, H., 314
Blackwell, B. S., 431
Blagg, C. O., 276
Blair, L. V., 89
Blake, A. J., 274
Blake, K. D., 319, 321
Blanck, H., 475
Blascovich, J., 293, 551, 569
Blass, E. M., 402
Bless, H., 383
Blitz, C. L., 45
Blow, F. C., 401
Bluemke, M., 183
Blumberg, J. B., 275
Blumer, H., 20, 56, 133, 252
Blumler, J. G., 20, 121, 148, 149,
        150, 162, 239, 241, 498, 531, 567
Blut, D., 186
Bobo, J., 139
Bock, K., 85
Böcking, S., 555
Boden-Albala, B., 403
Bodenhausen, G., 383
Bodenheimer, T., 323

Boer, C. D., 541
Bogatz, G. A., 339
Boiarsky, G., 36
Bollen, K. A., 260
Bolls, P. D., 117, 196,
        198, 199, 200, 512, 555
Bolt, D., 107
Bomhof, E., 478
Bond, B. J., 399, 400
Bond, R. N., 180, 261
Bonds-Raacke, J., 170
Bonetti, D., 274
Boorstin, D. J., 522
Booth-Butterfield, S., 274, 316
Borchers, H., 136
Borden, R. J., 447
Bordia, P., 493
Born, M., 14
Borse, J., 196, 549
Borzekowski, D., 476, 477
Borzekowski, D. L., 415
Borzekowski, D. L. B., 107
Borzekowski, D. L. G., 474
Boster, F. J., 316
Botan, C. H., 35
Botta, R. A., 347, 350, 395, 397, 398
Boush, D. M., 476
Bouthilet, L., 319
Bower, J., 349
Boxer, P., 363
Boyanowsky, E., 208
Boyatzis, C. J., 363
Boydell, K. M., 400
Boyle, M. P., 90, 91
Bracken, C. C., 24
Bradley, M. M., 196, 200, 206, 445
Bradley, R. H., 510
Bradley, S. D., 196, 197,
        200, 201, 202, 306, 448
Bragg, S., 347
Bramlett-Solomon, S., 474
Brandt, E. N., Jr., 474
Brannick, M., 272
Brannon, L., 93
Branscombe, N. R., 447, 448
Branstetter, S., 475
Braun, K. A., 301
Braun-LaTour, K. A., 300, 301
Breen, N., 321
Brennan, I., 301
Brennan, L., 279, 571
Brentar, J., 379
Brewer, J. L., 274
Brewer, P. R., 89, 90, 91
Brice, P., 349

Bridle, C., 276
Brigham, J. C., 232
Briley, D. A., 307
Briñol, P., 300
Brock, T. C., 26, 167, 168,
    232, 239, 301, 427, 430
Brodie, M., 350, 418
Brody, G. H., 255, 476, 478
Bronfenbrenner, U., 416
Brosius, H. B., 118, 120, 122, 242, 243
Broughton, D. D., 348
Brower, A., 318
Brower, K. J., 401
Brown, D., 443
Brown, G. K., 401
Brown, J., 303, 304, 305, 552, 553, 554
Brown, J. A., 345
Brown, J. D., 64, 101, 291, 322, 348,
    411, 412, 413, 414, 415, 418, 419, 474
Brown, J. R., 149, 507
Brown, R., 308, 377
Brown, S. J., 293
Brown, W. J., 152, 227, 234
Brownell, K. D., 394
Brundidge, J. S., 103
Bruner, G. C., 303, 304
Bruner, J., 92
Bruntz, G. G., 11
Bruvold, N. T., 306
Bryant, J., 1, 10, 13, 15, 20, 35, 39, 47, 48,
    69, 100, 109, 161, 163, 164, 166, 207,
    209, 294, 315, 337, 340, 369, 410, 441,
    442, 443, 444, 447, 456, 457, 458, 459,
    508, 512, 545, 566
Bryant, J. A., 508, 510
Bryson, L., 224
Buchanan, M., 105
Buchman, D. D., 460
Buckingham, D., 136
Bucy, E. P., 117, 552, 553, 563
Buhr, T. A., 90, 91, 117
Buijzen, M., 475, 476, 478
Bukovac, J. L., 549
Bulik, C. M., 401
Burggraf, K., 394, 396
Burke, K., 24
Burrell, N., 15, 35, 47
Burt, R. S., 492
Burwell, R. A., 399
Bushman, B. J., 181, 182, 183, 210, 212, 213,
    244, 246, 362, 363, 364, 365, 367, 368,
    370, 460, 461, 474
Busselle, R. W., 167, 379, 424, 425, 428,
    429, 430, 433

Bussey, K., 284
Butcher, K. F., 477
Butsch, R., 21, 132
Buttram, R., 382
Buttross, S., 348
Byrne, S., 103, 212, 346, 347, 349
Byrnes, J. P., 472

Cacioppo, J. T., 42, 122, 168, 196, 247, 258,
    277, 278, 304
Cadell, D., 499
Cafri, G., 395
Cain, M., 323
Calam, R., 349, 350
Calder, B., 303, 304, 305
Calvert, S. L., 338, 339, 460, 471, 476
Camboa, L., 349
Cameron, G. T., 46
Camino, L., 363
Campbell, D. T., 37, 38, 42
Campbell, J. D., 168
Campbell, K., 259
Campsmith, M., 321
Cannon, W. B., 206
Cantor, J., 164, 166, 207, 208, 226, 288,
    347, 348, 349, 350, 351, 369, 370, 394,
    459, 471, 472, 474, 475, 476
Cantril, H., 20, 188, 252
Cantwell, F. V., 255
Caplan, S. E., 154
Caplovitz, A. G., 402
Cappella, J. N., 2, 86, 88, 89, 91, 114, 118,
    119, 316
Carbonari, J. P., 317
Carey, J., 505
Carley, K. M., 493
Carlsmith, J. M., 272
Carlson, J. D., 448
Carlyle, K., 416
Carnagey, N. L., 183, 210, 363, 364, 367
Carothers, J. C., 522
Carpenter, C. F., 476
Carpenter, E., 527
Carpentier, F. R. D., 178, 185
Carragee, K. M., 61
Carrico, C., 446
Carroll, M. D., 477
Carroll, R., 307
Carver, A., 258
Cass, K. M., 400
Castells, M., 16, 522
Cavender, G., 431
Ceglarek, S., 318
Celano, D., 340

Centerwall, B. S., 15, 40
Chaffee, S. H., 46, 116, 120, 254, 255, 292, 314, 348, 363, 562, 564, 567, 569, 572
Chaiken, S., 122, 277, 290, 397
Chamblee, R., 306
Chan, E., 459
Chang, C., 270
Chang, S., 44
Chapman, S., 319
Charlesworth, A., 315
Charters, W. W., 133
Chartier, F., 301
Chartier, R., 132, 139, 140
Chatter, N., 368
Chavez, V., 334
Chaytor, H. J., 522
Chebat, J.-C., 306
Check, J. V. P., 364
Chen, G. M., 155
Chen, J. L., 259
Chen, Y., 418
Chen, Y.-C., 418
Cheong, P. H., 541
Chernin, A., 396, 476
Chia, S., 107
Chiera, E., 506
Ching, P. K., 402
Chiricos, T., 431
Chmielewiski, D. C., 138
Cho, C., 154, 303
Cho, C.-H., 303, 549
Cho, H., 315
Cho, J., 40, 90, 91, 93
Chock, T. M., 424, 425, 431
Choi, H. L., 291
Choi, Y. J., 571
Choi, Y. K., 551
Choma, B. L., 347
Chong, D., 86, 88, 89, 122
Chory-Assad, R. M., 183, 232
Chory, R. M., 431
Christakis, D. A., 332, 333
Christian, J., 274
Christie, B., 545
Chula-Maguire, K., 259
Chumlea, W. C., 410
Chung, M., 247
Ci, C., 302, 305
Cialdini, R. B., 447
Cicchirillo, V., 232
Cietz, W. H., 511
Cisneros, T., 348
Clark, A., 415
Clark, L., 315

Clark, L. A., 213
Clark, S., 287, 288, 291, 292
Clark, W. R., 252, 253
Clarke, J., 85
Clarke, P., 322
Clawson, R. A., 89, 90, 91, 94
Clayman, M., 323
Clewett, A. S., 337
Clifford, R., 139
Cline, V. B., 210, 365, 369
Clocksin, B. D., 319
Clore, G. L., 206
Coats, E. J., 256
Cobb, M. D., 277
Cody, M. J., 269, 456, 462
Cohen, A. A., 21, 24
Cohen, B., 117
Cohen, H. L., 347
Cohen, J., 101, 102, 106, 107, 109, 226, 228, 229, 230, 231, 232, 363
Cohen, M., 347, 349, 351, 418
Cohn, M. A., 261
Colditz, G. A., 511, 512
Cole, C. F., 335, 415
Cole, T., 226, 228
Coleman, J. S., 463, 491, 493
Colimore, K., 349, 350
Coller, T., 347, 349
Collins, A., 206
Collins, P. A., 332, 471, 512
Collins, R. L., 288, 413, 414, 415
Collins, W. A., 472
Comisky, P. W., 369, 443, 444
Comstock, A., 133
Comstock, G., 212, 340, 367, 474
Condrasky, M., 347, 349
Connor, R. F., 335
Converse, P. E., 119, 122
Conway, J. C., 153
Cook, D. T., 135
Cook, F. L., 106, 118
Cook, T. D., 37, 38, 43, 335
Cook, T. E., 121
Cool, C., 497
Coon, K. A., 477
Cooper, B. P., 447
Cooper, J. R., 499
Cooper, R., 496
Coover, G., 383, 384
Cope-Farrar, K. M., 412
Cornell, D. P., 101
Corner, J., 22, 434
Corrigan, S., 348, 509
Cortese, J., 117, 555

Corvino, G., 382
Cotton, J. L., 272
Cottrell, L., 475
Cottrell, S. A., 475
Courrier, S., 210, 365, 369
Courtright, J. A., 152, 370
Coussement, S. H., 443
Cowan, A., 322
Cowen, P. S., 426, 427
Coyle, J. R., 305, 550, 553
Crabe, M. E., 24
Craig, J. C., 319
Craig, K., 137
Crain, A. L., 272
Cramond, J. K., 507
Crandall, H., 379
Crapo, R. O., 259
Crawford, D. A., 254, 258, 259, 477
Crawley, A. M., 337, 340
Crawley-Davis, A. M., 334
Creel, A. H., 318
Crigler, A. N., 121
Critcher, C., 85
Crocker, N., 347
Croft, R. G., 210, 365, 369
Crowley, S., 318
Croyle, R. T., 323
Csikszentmihalyi, M., 24, 26, 301, 387
Cubbin, C., 320
Cummins, R. G., 35, 48
Cunningham, M. R., 256
Cunningham, S., 139
Cupp, P., 416
Curraugh, J., 445
Curtin, L. R., 477
Cuthbert, B., 445
Czilli, E. J., 117

Dabbs, J. M., 445
D'Agostino, R., 316
Dahle, S., 449
Dale, E., 133
D'Alessio, D., 272
Damasio, A. R., 206
Damron, D., 322
Dangerfield, C., 382
Daniels, S. R., 477
Danielson, W. A., 151
Dansereau, F., 40
Darwin, C. R., 206
d'Astous, A., 301
Daugherty, T., 549, 550
Dave, J., 347, 349
David, P., 104, 196, 443, 549

Davidson, R. J., 206
Davies, J., 183, 378, 433, 456, 457
Davies, M. M., 368
Davis, A. K., 217
Davis, D. M., 227, 231
Davis, E. B., 210, 261
Davis, F. D., 496
Davis, G. B., 496
Davis, K. C., 321
Davis, M. M., 252
Davis, R. E., 124, 317, 347, 348
Davison, W. P., 100, 105, 106, 216, 365
Davoudi, M., 348, 349
Dayan, D., 564
Dearing, J. W., 44, 84
DeBono, K. G., 271
De Certeau, M., 15
DeChillo, N., 347, 351
Deci, E. L., 168, 458
DeClemente, C. C., 317
DeCoster, J., 182
DeFao, J., 135
DeFleur, M. L., 19, 152, 492, 533
DeFrancesco, C. A., 351
Deibert, R., 523
DeJong, W., 288
Delli Carpini, M. X. D., 123
DeLoache, J. S., 334
Delwiche, A., 94, 568
Den Boer, D. J., 317
De Neui, D. L., 444
DeNeve, K. M., 181, 182
Dennison, B. A., 403
Depalma, A., 444, 445
de Rivas, M. R. G., 348
Dervin, B., 255
DeSanctis, G., 498
Deselms, J. L., 364
Desmond, R. J., 349, 350
Detenber, B. H., 87, 89, 91, 100, 102, 104
Detweiler, J. B., 321
Deuser, W. E., 181, 182
DeVellis, R. F., 47
Devinitz, V., 100
DeVinney, L. C., 532
Devlin, B., 401
de Vreese, C. H., 91, 117
de Wall, E., 567
Dholakia, R. R., 303, 304, 305
Diamond, G. A., 277
Diao, F., 196
Diaz, I., 269
Dickson, P. R., 306
DiClemente, C. C., 317

Diener-West, M., 479
Dietz, W. H., 402
DiFonzo, N., 493
DiGiuseppe, D. L., 332
Dijkstra, A., 278
Dill, J. C., 233
Dill, K. E., 233, 400, 460
Dillard, J. P., 94, 107, 109, 270
Dillman Carentier, F. R., 382
Dillman, D. A., 534, 537
DiMaggio, P. E., 323
Dimmick, J., 498, 499
Dinu, L., 301, 302
Dittman, M., 289
Dittmar, H., 396, 400
Ditton, T., 549
Ditton, T. B., 24, 233
Dixon, H. G., 477
Dixon, T., 382
Dixon, T. L., 187, 379, 382
Dobkin, L., 416
Dodge, K. A., 369
Dohnt, H., 399
Doku, N. S., 339
Doll, J., 154
Dominick, J. R., 35
Domke, D., 84, 85, 86, 87,
    88, 89, 91, 93, 94, 187
Domschke, T., 164, 208
Donnerstein, E., 346, 348,
    349, 351, 364, 367
Donohew, L., 247
Donohew, R. L., 349
Donohue, G. A., 116, 315, 319, 320, 499
Donthu, N., 303
Doolittle, J. C., 348
Doppelt, J. C., 106
Dorfman, L., 269, 319
Dorr, A., 253, 350, 425, 426, 471, 472
Doty, C., 449
Dou, W., 302
Doubleday, C., 253, 350, 426
Douglas, K. M., 102
Douglass, L. W., 274
Dovidio, J. F., 386
Downing, J., 64
Downs, A., 44
Downs, E., 294
Dowrich, P. W., 293, 476
Drabman, R. S., 364, 369
Drake, B., 448
Drew, D., 116
Driscoll, P. D., 105
Druckman, D., 102, 104

Druckman, J. N., 86, 88, 89, 90,
    91, 93, 120, 122
Dubas, K. M., 301
Duck, J. M., 101, 541
Dugoni, B. L., 448
Duhe, S., 347, 349
Duncan, J., 247
Dunn, D. W., 243
Dunwoody, S., 117, 303, 304,
    549, 553, 555, 565
Dupagne, M., 100, 101
Durham, M. B., 351
Durham, M. G., 348
Durkheim, E., 533
Durkin, K., 462
Dykers, C. R., 64
Dzwo, T., 568

Eadie, D., 274
Eagly, A., 122
Eastin, M. S., 153, 170, 394, 402, 443, 573
Eastman, S. T., 445, 446
Eckes, T., 273
Eco, U., 136
Edmonson, M. B., 413
Edwards, H. H., 88, 90
Edwards, R. H., 252
Eggermont, S., 423, 427
Eisenberg, M., 402
Eisenberg, M. E., 259
Eisenstein, E., 522
Eitel, P., 411
Ekman, P., 213
Elder, T. Y., 102
Elesges, L. M., 510
Eliceiri, E. M. E., 346
Elliot, D. L., 351
Elliott, M., 288, 414
Elliott, M. N., 413, 415
Elliott, P., 148
Elliott, R., 61
Elliott, W. R., 425
Ellison, N. B., 510
Embretson, S. E., 47
Emerson, R. M., 532, 540
Eng, T. R., 323
Ennemoser, M., 511
Eno, C., 182
Entman, R. M., 84, 85, 86, 119, 379
Epstein, L. H., 477
Erb, T. A., 403
Erber, M. W., 164
Erber, R., 164
Erickson, G. A., 447

Eron, L. D., 15, 349, 363, 365, 367, 370, 423, 425, 428
Eschholz, S., 431
Escobar-Chaves, S. L., 411
Espejo, E., 387
Estrada, G., 85
Esty, E. T., 339
Ettema, J. S., 19, 106, 339
Eubanks, J., 363
Eulau, H., 40
Evans, A. E., 347, 349
Evans, D. L., 401
Evans, G., 261
Evans, J. St B. T., 29
Evans, M. K., 332, 478
Eveland, W. P., Jr., 45, 100, 102, 104, 105, 116, 117, 155, 255, 549, 555, 562, 565, 566, 567, 573
Evenson, K. R., 259
Evergreen, S. H., 347
Evers, K. E., 275, 317
Eyal, K., 225, 226, 288, 293, 473

Faber, R. J., 85, 103, 105, 472
Fabrigar, L. R., 272
Fadiga, L., 368
Fairchild, A. J., 45
Fallis, S. F., 254
Fan, D. P., 85, 87, 89, 94, 498
Fan, Y. C., 293
Farquhar, J. W., 314
Farquhar, L. K., 153
Farrar, K. M., 288, 418
Farrell, D., 279, 571
Farrelly, M. C., 321
Fazio, R. H., 44, 180, 189
Feijoo, A. N., 411
Feilden, J. A., 445
Feilitzen, C., 232
Feldman, L., 120
Feldman, R. S., 256
Feldman, S., 259
Fenton, E., 115
Ferguson, D. A., 163, 569
Ferguson, M., 247
Fernandez-Ardevol, M., 16
Ferris, A. L., 423, 427, 428, 431
Festinger, L., 215, 272, 397
Fetler, M., 340
Fichter, M. M., 401
Fidler, R., 494, 496, 497
Field, D. E., 332, 512
Findahl, O., 117
Fine, M. J., 418

Finkelhor, D., 416, 479
Finkel, S. E., 116
Finlayson, B. L., 272
Finn, J., 416
Finn, S., 152, 245
Finnegan, J. R., 314, 320
Finnerty, K. L., 152, 164, 208, 431, 432, 473
Fiore, Q., 527
Firotto, V., 29
Fischer, M. M. J., 58
Fischer, P., 349
Fisch, S. M., 335, 339, 340
Fish, R., 497
Fishbein, M., 36, 44, 45, 46, 107, 270, 273, 274, 316, 323
Fisher, B. A., 148
Fisher, D. A., 411
Fiske, J., 137
Fiske, S., 377, 378, 388
Fiske, S. T., 206, 288, 368
Fitch, M., 426, 427
Fitness, J., 261
Fitzgerald, E., 347, 349, 418
Fitzpatrick, M. A., 254
Flaherty, L. M., 153
Flanagan, M., 367
Flanagin, A. J., 569
Flavell, E. R., 426
Flavell, J. H., 426, 471, 473
Flegal, K. M., 477
Flickinger, R. S., 119
Flora, J. A., 290, 292, 314, 320
Flournoy, R., 418
Floyd, D. L., 275
Floyd, K., 154
Flynn, V., 478
Flynt Wallington, S., 321
Foehr, U. G., 135, 337, 340, 350, 361, 403, 411, 414, 418, 469, 470, 475, 478, 507, 513
Fogassi, L., 368
Fonash, D., 383
Ford, C. E., 447
Ford, T., 383
Ford, V. L., 46
Forgas, J. P., 261
Forman, H. J., 133
Forrest, E. J., 495
Fortin, D. R., 303, 304, 305
Fortmann, S. P., 32, 314, 320
Foss, K. A., 36
Foster, M. D., 347
Foucault, M., 131
Fouts, G., 394, 396

Fowler, E. F., 94
Fox, J. A., 117, 293, 294
Fox, S., 242, 248
Frankenfield, A. E., 332, 478
Frazier, P., 168
Fredin, E. S., 258
Fredrickson, B. L., 261
Freedman, J. L., 20, 40
Freeman, C. S., 319
Freeman, S., 447
Freimuth, V. S., 320
French, S., 316
Frenkel-Brunswik, E., 229
Freud, S., 229, 371
Frey, D., 272
Frey, L. R., 35
Friderich-Cofer, L. K., 337
Fried, C. B., 272
Friedman, W. J., 473
Friedrich, L., 337
Friedricksen, M., 442
Friedson, E., 19
Friesen, W. V., 213
Friestad, J., 301
Friestad, M., 476
Frijda, N. H., 206
Fritz, M. S., 45
Frosch, D. L., 278
Fryberg, S., 381, 382, 385
Fuerch, J. H., 477
Fujimoto, M., 334
Fujioka, Y., 254, 380, 385
Fulton, J., 475
Funabiki, R. P., 349, 351
Fung, R., 139
Funk, J. B., 365, 460, 474
Furnham, A., 246, 247
Furu, T., 508
Fuson, L. A., 346, 348, 349, 351

Gadow, K. D., 370
Gaertner, S. L., 386
Gagnon, J. H., 413
Gallese, V., 368
Galperin, H., 348
Gamboa, L., 349, 352
Gamson, W. A., 89, 121
Gan, S.-L., 443
Gangwisch, J. E., 403
Gantz, W., 441, 445, 446, 448, 477
García, A., 334
Garcia Canclini, N., 136, 139
Gardner, H., 471
Gardner, M., 473

Gardner, W. L., 196
Gardyn, R., 431
Garfinkel, H., 134, 137
Garfinkel, P. E., 394
Garner, D. M., 394
Garst, J., 26, 301, 430
Gatto, L., 363
Gaudet, H., 12, 115, 188, 314
Gaudiosi, J., 137
Gauntlett, D., 22
Gavassoli, N. T., 307
Gay, G., 561, 562, 573
Gayle, B. M., 15, 35, 47
Geddes, P., 521
Gedissman, A., 348, 509
Gee, J. P., 456, 461
Geen, R. G., 363, 369, 427, 448
Geertz, C., 55
Gehrau, V., 255
Geiger, S., 21, 198
Geisler, N., 349, 352
Gelinas-Chebat, C., 306
Gemeny, B. A., 293
Genvese, A., 347
Gerbner, G., 25, 69, 70, 71, 74,
    75, 76, 214, 319, 361, 364,
    379, 397, 413, 460, 474, 531
Gerrig, R. J., 429
Gertz, M., 431
Ghanem, S. I., 83
Ghose, S., 302
Gibbons, J. A., 493
Gibson, J. J., 548
Gibson, R., 164
Gidwani, P. P., 288
Giesbrecht, L. W., 232
Gilbert, D. T., 182, 429
Gil de Zuniga, H., 90, 91, 93
Giles, H., 384, 385
Gillen, M., 410
Gillespie, M., 61, 139
Gilliam, F., 382, 383
Gilman, S. E., 399
Gilmore, R., 306
Gitlin, T., 84, 85
Givens, S., 382
Gladwell, M., 493
Glantz, S. A., 315
Glanz, K., 315, 316, 318
Glassman, B., 293
Glaubke, C., 387
Glik, D., 348, 349
Glynn, C. J., 119, 254
Godbold, L., 384

Goetz, E. G., 118
Goffman, E., 85
Gold, M. A., 418
Gold, S. R., 240, 244
Goldberg, J., 477
Goldberg, J. P., 275
Goldberg, L., 351
Goldberg, M. E., 275, 475, 512
Goldhaber, G. M., 496
Goldman, R., 277
Goldstein, J., 456
Goldstein, J. H., 443, 444, 448
Goldstein, K. M., 94
Gonzales, R., 348, 349
Gonzalez, C., 303, 304
Gonzenbach, W. J., 47
Goody, J., 522
Gordon, M., 385
Gordon, M. T., 106, 118
Gorham, B., 382
Gorin, A., 259
Gorn, G. J., 475, 512
Gorr, M. B., 153
Gorsuch, R. L., 213
Gortmaker, S. L., 288, 402, 511
Gotlieb, M. R., 91
Grabe, M. E., 117
Grabe, S., 393, 395, 399
Graber, D. A., 85, 122
Graham, S., 178, 179, 180
Granger, C. W. J., 43
Granovetter, M., 493
Grant, A. E., 154
Grant, N., 247
Grant, S. C., 180
Graves, S. B., 288
Gray, A., 22
Green, D. P., 89
Green, F. L., 426
Green, L., 317
Green, M. C., 26, 167, 168,
    232, 301, 417, 427, 430
Green, S., 510
Greenberg, B. S., 255, 394, 402, 423,
    424, 425, 427, 428, 431, 457, 474
Greene, K., 239, 241, 242, 243, 245,
    346, 347, 348
Greenfield, P., 387
Greenwald, A., 386
Greenwald, A. G., 154, 272
Greenwald, M. K., 206
Greenwood, C. R., 339
Greenwood, D., 443
Gregg, P. B., 226, 228, 234, 384

Grela, B., 334
Grimes, T., 199
Grindstaff, L., 566
Groesz, L. M., 393, 398
Grohmann, B., 272
Gronbeck, B. E., 346
Groot J., 495
Gross, K., 90, 91
Gross, L., 69, 74, 75, 76, 214, 319, 364,
    379, 397, 460, 474, 531
Gross, N., 491
Gross, R., 571
Grube, J. W., 411, 534, 536
Gruber, E. L., 411
Grumbach, K., 323
Guadano, R., 182
Guerra, N., 369
Guerra, P., 349, 352
Gulas, C. S., 212
Gunter, B., 117, 246, 247, 444
Gunther, A. C., 101, 103, 105, 106, 107,
    216, 402, 424
Guo, G., 322, 414, 415
Guo, S., 402
Gurevitch, M., 20, 121, 149, 150, 162,
    239, 241, 531, 534
Gustafson, D., 323
Gustafson, R. L., 395
Guthman, J., 403

Haas, H., 150, 162, 534
Habermas, J., 113
Haddon, L., 498
Hagstrom, A. E., 64
Haines, J., 401, 402
Hakala, P., 259
Hale, M., 94
Halford, J., 152, 431, 432
Hall, A., 242, 425, 431, 432
Hall, E. R., 339
Hall, S., 20, 22, 28, 29, 48, 58, 85, 136
Hall, W., 382
Hallin, D., 119
Halliwell, E., 396, 400
Halpern, C. T., 474
Halpern, P., 538, 540
Hamburg, P., 399
Hamel, E., 470, 478
Hamel, F., 337
Hamilton, C., 258
Hamilton, D., 377, 378, 380
Hamilton, M. A., 43
Hamm, A. O., 206
Hamm, B. J., 563, 567, 570

Hammersley, M., 54
Hancock, J. T., 561, 562, 573
Handford, G., 508, 510
Hannan, P. J., 347, 349, 401, 402
Hansen, C. H., 186
Hansen, D. L., 551, 568
Hansen, G., 416
Hansen, G. J., 185, 186
Hansen, R. D., 186
Hardeman, W., 274
Hardin, C. D., 386
Hargittai, E., 323
Hargreaves, D., 397
Haridakis, P. M., 154, 155, 426, 428
Harmon-Jones, E., 272
Harris, C. V., 475
Harris, R. J., 11, 13
Harrison, K., 152, 288, 394, 395, 397, 398, 399, 400, 401, 474, 477, 512
Hartley, J., 135, 139
Hartmann, T., 227, 457, 458, 555
Hart, P. S., 347
Hart, W. B., 84
Harwood, J., 381, 384
Haskell, W. L., 314
Hastall, M. R., 552, 555
Hatfield, E., 258
Hauser, P. M., 133
Havas, S., 322
Havelock, E. A., 522
Haviland, M. L., 321
Hawkins, R. P., 378, 423, 425, 426, 427, 472, 569
Hawley, A. H., 540
Hayes, A. F., 39, 40, 42, 45, 46, 119
Hayne, H., 334
Hays, S. P., 498
Hayward, S., 15
Healton, C. G., 321
Healy, J. M., 335
Hearn, G., 151
Heath, L., 364, 448
Hebdige, D., 136
Hefner, D., 233, 399, 401
Hefner, V., 395
Heider, F., 100, 271
Heidrich, F., 316
Heimendinger, J., 322
Heinberg, L., 396
Heinonen, O. J., 259
Heins, M., 133
Helm, D., 247
Helme, D. W., 349
Hembroff, L., 277

Henderson, K. A., 394
Henderson, V. R., 477, 512
Henin, A., 474
Henkenius, A. L., 473
Henry, K. L., 367, 461
Hensley, J. E., 448
Heo, N., 549
Herbert, J., 334
Herrr, P. M., 271
Hersey, J. C., 321
Hershberger, E. K., 303
Hertel, P., 213
Herzog, D. B., 39
Herzog, H., 56, 149, 162, 188
Herzog, T. A., 276
Hesketh, K., 259
Hess, B. W., 323
Hess, V. K., 185
Hess, V. L., 472
Hesse, B., 321
Hessler, R. M., 64
Hetsroni, A., 412
Hettich, R. R., 448
Hewes, D. E., 226, 228, 234, 384
Heymsfield, S. B., 403
Hezel, R. T., 164
Hider, M., 499
Higgins, C. A., 493
Higgins, D. L., 290
Higgins, E. T., 92, 93, 179, 180, 386, 397, 429
Higgins, R. L., 447
Hill, A., 426, 431, 432, 434
Hill, D. L., 411
Hill, E. M., 401
Hill, J., 185
Hill, T. G., 95, 185
Hillback, E., 90, 91, 93
Hillmann, C., 445
Hilt, M. L., 257, 261
Hilton, J., 282, 377, 378, 388
Hiltz, S. R., 497
Himmelweit, H. T., 350, 506, 507, 508, 513
Hindus, D., 64
Hirsch, K. W., 364, 474
Hirsch, P., 75
Hirschburg, P. L., 534, 537
Hirshfeld-Becker, D., 474
Hirt, E. R., 447
Hix-Small, H., 351
Hobbs, R., 345, 346
Hochheimer, J. L., 314
Hodge, B., 136
Hoffman, D. L., 303

Hoffman, K., 185
Hoffner, C., 105, 226, 231, 232,
    350, 471, 472
Hofschire, L., 394, 402
Hofstetter, C. R., 114
Hogan, M., 509
Hogg, M. A., 101, 102
Hoijer, B., 59, 117
Holbert, R. L., 36, 45, 119, 123, 185, 186
Holbrook, R. A., 95, 185
Hollenbeck, A. R., 332
Holson, L. M., 469
Holzwarth, M., 551
Hombourger, S., 306
Hornik, R. C., 36, 38, 43, 46, 48, 274, 278,
    314, 315, 321, 322, 323, 499
Horrigan, J., 171
Horsewski, M. L., 417
Horton, D., 152, 224, 225, 226, 227, 232
Horton, R. W., 369
Hospers, H. J., 317
Hossay, J. F., 348
Hovland, C. I., 12, 207, 211, 270, 314, 532
Howell, J. M., 493
Hu, F. B., 511, 512
Hubbs, L. A., 105
Hudley, C., 178, 179, 180
Huesmann, L. R., 15, 240,
    349, 362, 363, 364, 365, 366,
    367, 368, 369, 423, 425, 428, 474
Hughes, M., 75, 364
Huh, J., 108
Huhman, M., 475
Hull, S., 164, 208
Hullett, C., 384
Hullett, C. R., 36
Hume, D., 37
Hung-Yi, L., 417
Hunnicutt, G. G., 471
Hunter, J. E., 273
Hunter, S. B., 413, 415
Huon, G., 395
Hurley, R. J., 102
Hurley, S., 368
Hust, S., 412
Huston, A. C., 333, 335, 336, 337, 415, 426,
    427, 471, 472, 473, 475, 510, 511, 512
Huston-Stein, A., 337
Hutchings, V. L., 118, 217
Hutchins, R. M., 113
Hutchinson, S. L., 257
Hwa, A. P., 101
Hwang, H., 91, 216
Hwang, J.-S., 303

Hwang, J. S., 553, 554
Hyde, J. S., 393, 395, 399
Hylton, C., 258
Hyman, H., 314
Hyun, K., 124

Iacobucci, D., 303, 304, 305
Ibrahim, H., 509
Innes, J. M., 365
Innis, H. A., 521
Intons-Peterson, M. J., 186
Irving, L. M., 347, 348
Ito, K. E., 291
Ive, S., 396, 400
Ivory, J. D., 569
Iyengar, S., 83, 84, 86, 88, 89, 90, 94, 114,
    118, 122, 184, 382, 564, 567, 570, 572
Izard, C. E., 206, 213, 214

Jackson, C., 322, 414, 415
Jackson, L. A., 363
Jackson, R. H., 382
Jackson-Beeck, M., 74
Jacobsohn, L., 499
Jahn-Sudmann, A., 455
James, M. L., 495
James, W., 206
Jamieson, K. H., 86, 88, 89, 91, 114, 118,
    119, 215, 364
Janis, I. L., 207, 211, 270
Janiszewski, C., 303, 306, 551
Jasperson, A. E., 85
Jefferson, T., 85
Jeffres, L. W., 495, 507
Jeffries-Fox, S., 74
Jenkins, H., 62, 63, 137
Jenkins, P. L., 403
Jensen, J., 496
Jensen, J. D., 102
Jensen, K. B., 59, 60, 63
Jeong, J., 124
Jhally, S., 346
Jim, J., 402
Jin, S. A., 551
Johnson, B., 496, 498
Johnson, B. C., 261
Johnson, G. J., 303, 304
Johnson, J. D., 363, 367, 382
Johnson, J. Q., 418
Johnson, K., 497
Johnson, K. K., 347, 349, 351
Johnson, M., 274
Johnson, M. A., 104
Johnson, S. S., 317

Johnson, T., 363
Johnson, T. J., 153
Johnston, D. D., 163
Johnston, D. W., 274
Johnston, J., 339
Jolls, T., 348
Jones, D. A., 124
Jones, J., 117, 123
Jones, J. M., 432
Jones, K., 473
Jonge, S., 495
Jordan, A. B., 62, 338, 340, 402, 477
Josephson, W. L., 180, 181,
    182, 183, 363, 367
Judd, C. M., 93
Jung, J.-Y., 541, 542
Just, M. R., 121

Kaciroti, N., 510
Kaestle, C. E., 474
Kahneman, D., 86, 87, 88, 364, 365
Kaid, L. L., 568
Kaiser, S. B., 135
Kaler, M., 168
Kalyanaraman, S., 291, 303, 304, 305, 412,
    549, 551, 552, 553, 554, 555, 569
Kamhawi, R., 35
Kamigaki, S. K., 105
Kaminski, W., 456
Kanouse, D. E., 288, 413, 414, 415
Kanungo, R. N., 475
Kao, C. F., 168
Kaozman, D. K., 400
Kaplan, M., 94
Kardes, F. F., 180
Karnowski, V., 498
Karp, D. A., 446
Karrh, J. A., 300
Kasmer, J. A., 247
Kasper, G. M., 303, 304
Kasprzyk, D., 316
Kates, S. M., 63
Katz, D., 271
Katz, E., 20, 41, 60, 120, 121, 148, 149, 150,
    162, 230, 239, 241, 491, 493, 498, 531,
    534, 536, 564
Katz, J., 448
Katz, J. E., 323, 495
Kaufman, G. E., 168, 430
Kavanagh, D., 567
Kawachi, I., 318, 319
Kawahara, K., 117, 198
Kaye, B. K., 153, 562
Kean, L. G., 153, 239, 244

Keefe, T., 36
Keeter, S., 123
Keller, S. N., 418
Kelley, H. H., 207, 211, 270
Kelly, B. J., 278, 512
Keniston, A. H., 472
Kenneavy, K., 414, 415
Kennedy, C., 259, 447
Kennevay, K., 322
Kenny, D. A., 90
Kepplinger, H. M., 118
Kerkman, D., 512
Kern, M., 121
Kerr, D., 350
Keum, H., 90, 91, 93
Kiesler, S., 479, 545
Kilker, J., 498
Kim, C., 155
Kim, H., 217, 305
Kim, J., 152, 186, 225, 232, 553
Kim, M.-S., 273
Kim, S. Y., 492
Kim, Y.-C., 537, 541, 542
Kim, Y. M., 117, 118, 185, 186
Kimble, C. E., 447
Kincaid, D. L., 493
Kinder, D. R., 84, 86, 88,
    90, 91, 93, 118, 184
King, G., 429
King, N., 498
Kinmonth, A. L., 274
Kinnally, W., 442, 444
Kiousis, S., 22, 23, 84, 552
Kipnis, D. M., 337
Kirkorian, H. L., 332, 402, 478
Kirwil, L., 368
Kittross, J. M., 134
Kitzinger, J., 19
Kiviniemi, M. T., 261
Klapper, J. T., 12, 20, 115, 148, 149
Klausner, J., 416
Klein, R., 349
Klesges, L. M., 402, 512
Klesges, R. C., 402, 510, 512
Klijn, M. E., 548
Klimmt, C., 165, 171, 227, 233, 456, 457,
    458, 462, 555, 556
Kline, F. G., 322
Kline, S., 135, 138, 232, 351
Klinger, M., 178, 179, 180, 183, 185
Klink, R. R., 307, 308
Klopfenstein, B. C., 500
Klump, K. L., 401
Knobloch, S., 164, 167, 171, 208, 553

Knobloch-Westerwick, S., 164, 443, 551, 552, 555, 568
Knorr, M., 446
Ko, H., 154, 303
Kobrin, S., 317
Koleini, M. F., 402
Koloen, G., 117
Kommer, D., 445
Konijn, E. A., 363, 370
Konkel, J., 317
Kontos, E. Z., 313, 314, 320
Koolstra, C. M., 30, 511
Kopacz, M., 379, 384, 385
Korfmacher, J. E., 426
Koruth, J., 199, 201
Kosanic, A. Z., 339
Kosicki, G. M., 83, 84, 85, 86, 91, 93, 94, 319, 385
Kostygina, A., 460, 461
Kotler, J. A., 338, 339, 473, 475
Kotler, P., 317, 492, 498
Kovach, B., 124
Kovaric, P., 253, 350, 426
Kowalczyk, L., 105
Kowalski, R. M., 479
Kraemer, H. C., 474
Kraidy, M. M., 62
Kraus, R., 509
Kraut, R., 479, 497
Krcmar, M., 153, 164, 165, 167, 209, 239, 241, 242, 243, 244, 245, 254, 291, 334, 338, 349
Kreps, G. L., 35, 499
Kreuter, M., 317
Kreuter, M., 278, 317, 571
Kreuter, M. W., 293, 317, 324
Kreutzner, G., 136
Kristen, A., 456
Kronenberg, F., 259
Kronenberger, W. G., 243
Krosnick, J. A., 86, 93, 184, 185
Kruglanski, A. W., 278
Krugman, D. M., 46, 507
Krugman, H. E., 151
Krull, D. S., 429
Krygowski, W., 186
Ku, G., 568
Kubey, R. W., 22, 23, 24
Kubic, K. N., 431
Kuhl, P. K., 334
Kuhn, D., 473
Kulin, H. E., 410
Kumar, A., 303, 304
Kunda, Z., 48

Kunkel, D., 288, 293, 412, 413, 415, 473, 476
Kurita, S., 201
Kushner, D., 138
Kwak, N., 45, 89, 91, 116, 119
Kyoshima, K., 332

Lachlan, K., 394, 442, 457
Lagerspetz, K., 423, 425, 428
Lahikainen, A. R., 256
Lampe, C., 510
Lancendorfer, K. M., 568
Land, A., 446
Land, S. R., 418
Lang, A., 117, 193, 194, 196, 197, 198, 199, 200, 201, 202, 207, 210, 512, 548, 549
Lang, G., 56
Lang, G. E., 118
Lang, K., 56, 118
Lang, P., 445
Lang, P. J., 196, 206
Langteau, R., 108
Lanstrom, H., 259
La Pastina, A. C., 61
Lapinski, M. K., 347
LaRose, R., 153, 497, 498
Larsen, J. J., 243
Larson, E. B., 316
Larson, R. W., 257
Lassegard, M., 447
Lasswell, H. D., 11, 149, 224
Latner, J. D., 400
Latour, B., 140
Lauf, E., 567
Laurel-Seller, E., 400
Lavine, H., 122
Law, S., 300, 301
Lawrence, F., 350
Lazar, J., 319
Lazarsfeld, P. F., 12, 20, 41, 100, 115, 116, 120, 121, 149, 162, 314, 491, 509
Lazarus, R. S., 206, 213, 214
Leaf, P. J., 479
Le Bon, G., 132
Leckenby, J. D., 303
Leduc, N., 64
Lee, B., 568
Lee, B.-K., 302, 305
Lee, C., 571
Lee, G., 553
Lee, H. F., 166
Lee, J. H., 510, 571
Lee, J. K., 124
Lee, K. J., 568

Lee, K. M., 233, 460, 461, 462, 551
Lee, N. J., 94
Lee, P. A., 410
Lee, S., 201
Lee, S.-J., 305
Lee, W.-N., 305
Lee, Y. H., 307
Leets, L., 226, 228
Leff, D. R., 106, 118
Lefkowitz, E., 410
Lefkowitz, M. M., 367
Legrenzi, P., 29
Leitzmann, M. F., 511, 512
Leman, D., 308
Lemish, D., 58, 151, 332
Lenart, S., 120
L'Engle, K. L., 322, 412, 414, 415, 419
Lenhart, A., 478, 479
Lenoir, T., 137
LePage, A., 368
Lepore, L., 377
Lepper, M. R., 114, 121, 216
Leung, C. C., 427
Leventhal, H., 211
Lever, J., 446
Levin, I. P., 90
Levin, S. R., 332
Levine, D., 416
Levine, M. P., 393, 398
Levine, T. R., 36
Levinson, D. J., 229
Levinson, P., 527
Levitt, G., 154
Levy, M. R., 116, 225, 231
Lew, A. M., 349, 352
Lewis, C., 301, 302
Lewis, J., 135, 139, 346
Leyens, J. P., 348, 363
Lezin, N., 317
Li, H., 549, 550
Li, T. Y., 511
Li, X., 562
Lieberman, D. A., 293, 462, 562
Liebert, R., 475
Liebes, T., 60, 230
Liebhart, J. L., 107, 424
Lievrouw, L., 498
Lim, T.-S., 492
Limber, S. P., 479
Lin, C. A., 150, 151, 152, 153,
    161, 494, 495, 497
Lin, K., 334
Lin, N., 492
Lin, W.-Y., 541

Lindlof, T. R., 54, 55
Lindsay, J. J., 363
Linebarger, D. L., 332, 333, 334, 336, 337,
    339, 473, 475, 478, 512
Ling, C., 185
Ling, R., 498, 522
Linn'e, O., 232
Linn, S., 476
Linz, D., 210, 346, 347, 348, 349, 351, 364,
    367, 379
Lippincott, E. C., 369
Lippmann, W., 11, 14
Lipschultz, J. H., 257, 261
Litle, P., 163, 242, 243
Littlejohn, S. W., 36
Liu, H. M., 334
Liu, Y., 302, 303, 304, 305
Livingstone, S. M., 23, 61, 62, 229, 292, 498
Livingston, S. D., 115, 239, 241
Lodge, M., 122
Loebell, H., 85
Loechner, J., 138
Logan, G. D., 180
Logan, R. K., 522
Loges, W. E., 538
Lohtia, R., 303
Lombard, M., 24, 231, 233, 549
Lombardi, W. J., 179, 180
Long, M., 36
Loomis, J. M., 551
Lorber, M., 456
Lorch, E. P., 247, 332, 512
Lord, C. G., 121
Lord, K. R., 306
Lotz, A. D., 63
Low, B., 411
Lowery, S. A., 19
Lowood, H., 455
Lowrey, T. M., 299, 300, 306, 307, 308
Lowry, D. T., 35
Lubbers, M., 379
Lublin, B., 213
Lucas, K., 457
Lucht, N., 380
Ludwig, D. S., 402
Lull, J., 57, 58, 253, 254
Lum, C. M. K., 518
Lumeng, J. C., 510
Lumsdaine, A. A., 270, 314
Luna, D., 307, 308
Lundmark, V., 479
Lundy, L. K., 432
Lushene, R. E., 213
Lustria, M. L. A., 415, 417

Luthans, F., 286
Luther, M., 521
Lutter, C. D., 445
Luttrell, E. S., 445
Lutz, R., 303
Lyle, J., 506, 507, 508
Lynch, J., 303, 306
Lyon, M., 409

Ma, E. K., 139
Maass, A., 382
Maccoby, E. E., 232, 255, 506
Maccoby, N., 314
Macgill, A. R., 478
Macias, W., 305
MacKenzie, D., 498
Mackie, D., 377, 380
MacKinnon, D. P., 45
MacKintosh, A. M., 274
Macklin, M. C., 306
Madden, M., 478
Maddox, K., 382
Maddux, J., 290
Madrigal, R., 447
Maher, T. M., 83
Mailbach, E. W., 290, 292
Mainwaring, S. D., 64
Maio, G. R., 271
Majchrzak, A., 498
Maklan, D. M., 46, 499
Malamuth, N. M., 364
Malaspina, D., 403
Malhotra, A., 498
Malinowski, B., 55
Malkoc, S. A., 300
Malone, P. S., 429
Mangold, R., 165, 458
Manguel, A., 133, 135
Mankekar, P., 139
Mann, T., 349, 352
Mann, V., 321
Manross, G. G., 534
Manson, J. E., 511
Mao, W., 493
Marcus, G. E., 58
Mares, M. A., 471, 472, 475
Mares, M.-L., 16
Mares, M. L., 164
Margolis, L., 254
Markham, C., 411
Markus, M. L., 493, 497
Marlow, M. L., 103
Marquis, D., 256
~uis, J., 510

Marseille, N. M., 349
Marske, A. L., 398, 472, 474, 477, 512
Martell, C., 277
Martin, L. L., 101
Martin, P. S., 124
Martino, S. C., 288, 414
Martins, N., 472, 474
Mason, L., 546
Massey, K., 564
Mastro, D. E., 170, 288,
    379, 381, 382, 384, 385, 474, 573
Masur, E. F., 478
Matei, S., 537, 541, 542
Mather, L., 276
Matheson, D. M., 474
Mathews, V. P., 243
Maticka-Tyndale, E., 316
Matillo, G. M., 363
Matsaganis, M. D., 541
Mattelart, A., 138
Mattson, S. N., 473
Maurice, J., 395
Maxwell, R., 139
May, M. A., 133
Mayer, V., 61, 62
Maynard, B. T., 474
Mazzarella, S. R., 135
McCarty, C. A., 332
McCarty, J. A., 299, 300, 301
McCombs, M., 314
McCombs, M. E., 83, 84, 85, 118, 492
McCoy, J. K., 395
McCoy, K., 187
McCright, J., 416
McCutcheon, L. E., 225
McDonagh, E. C., 253, 255
McDonald, D. G., 253, 258
McDonald, N. B., 474
McDowell, M. A., 477
McGee, J., 347, 351
McGraw, K. M., 122, 185
McGuire, T. W., 545
McGuire, W. J., 83, 121, 276, 348
McKay, D. L., 275
McKearney White, C., 46
McKenna, K., 562
McKenna, M., 471, 472
McKenna, M. W., 400
McLeod, D. M., 87, 89, 90, 91, 92, 93, 94,
    100, 102, 104, 105, 569
McLeod, J., 314
McLeod, J. M., 39, 41, 147, 254, 255, 363
McLuhan, M., 13, 521, 527, 545
McMahon, T. A., 272

McMath, B. F., 275
McMillan, S. J., 303, 304, 553, 554
McMillion, P. Y., 290, 292
McNeal, J. U., 476
McPhee, W. N., 115
McQuail, D., 19, 21, 23, 149
McVey, G. L., 347, 348
Meadowcroft, J. M., 164
Medoff, N. J., 164, 562
Meece, J. L., 286
Meeds, R., 153, 306
Meier, B. P., 183, 189
Meili, H. K., 287, 351
Meirick, P. C., 101
Meissner, H. I., 319, 321
Melnick, M. J., 445, 446, 448, 449
Meltzoff, A. N., 332, 333, 368
Mendelberg, T., 382, 385, 386
Mendelsohn, A. L., 431
Mendelsohn, M., 93
Menon, G., 307, 308
Menzel, H., 491, 493
Mermingas, D., 568
Merrill, I. R., 253
Merskin, D., 348
Merton, R. K., 20, 100, 116, 121, 224
Messaris, P., 350
Messeri, P., 321
Metzger, M. J., 292, 562, 564, 567, 569, 572
Meyer, G., 316
Meyer, T. P., 57, 58
Meyerowitz, B. E., 290
Meyers-Levy, J., 306
Meyrowitz, J., 518, 522, 525,
    526, 527, 528, 529
Michelle, C., 61
Michels, R., 132
Michielutte, R., 316
Milkie, M. A., 107, 402
Mill, J. S., 37
Miller, A., 347, 349
Miller, A. C. R., 349, 352
Miller, C., 418
Miller, D., 22
Miller, J. M., 184, 185
Miller, M. M., 154
Miller, N. E., 448
Miller, P., 387
Miller, P. H., 471, 473
Miller, S. A., 471, 473
Miller, T., 133, 136
Miller, T. Q., 448
Miller, V. L., 256
Miller, W. C., 291

Miniard, P. W., 306
Miracle, G. E., 551
Miron, D., 1, 13, 69, 100, 109, 166, 294,
    512, 566
Mitchell, A. M., 133
Mitchell, K. J., 416, 479
Mitrock, M. A., 443
Mitroff, D., 338
Mittman, R., 323
Moceri, D., 363
Moe, E. L., 351
Moise-Titus, J., 363, 365, 367
Molcan, J. R., 448
Molitor, F., 364, 474
Monahan, J., 382
Mondak, J., 122
Mongeau, P. A., 109, 211
Monro, F., 395
Montaño, D. E., 316
Moore, D. R., 463
Moore, G. A., 497
Moore, G. C., 496
Moore, J., 347, 351
Moore, M. K., 368
Moore, M. M., 455
Moore, R. L., 476
Moores, S., 58
Morahan-Martin, J., 153, 154
Morduchowicz, R., 348
Morelli, J. A., 402
Morgan, E. M., 415
Morgan, M., 69, 70, 71, 74, 75, 76, 77, 80,
    214, 319, 340, 361, 379, 397, 460, 474
Morgan, S. J., 431, 432
Morgan, S. L., 37
Moriarty, C. M., 399
Morley, D., 15, 21, 58, 59, 60, 61, 136, 233
Morris, M., 562, 564
Morris, M. G., 496
Morris, M. W., 307
Morrison, D., 217
Morrison, G., 104
Morton, T. A., 541
Mosca, G., 132
Moschis, G. P., 476
Mosco, V., 134
Moser, R. P., 321
Moses, N., 382
Moy, P., 106, 185
Moyer-Gusé, E., 212, 290
Muentener, P., 334
Mukopadhyay, T., 479
Mull, C., 319
Muller, C., 495, 498

Mullin, B., 101
Mullin, C. R., 210, 364
Mumford, L., 521
Mundorf, N., 242, 243
Mundy, P., 101
Munuera, J. L., 302, 303, 304, 305
Murnen, S. K., 393, 398
Murphy, K. C., 336
Murphy, P. D., 62
Murphy, S., 383
Murray, J. P., 366
Must, A., 511
Mutz, D. C., 101, 107, 119, 124, 509, 510
Myers, H., 349, 352

Naas, C., 228
Nabi, R. L., 2, 36, 48, 91, 94, 152, 164, 165,
    167, 192, 207, 208, 209, 211, 212, 213,
    214, 216, 217, 287, 288, 290, 291, 292,
    401, 431, 432, 569
Naficy, H., 139
Nah, S., 91
Narayan, S., 548
Nass, C., 290, 461, 546, 549, 550, 551, 552
Nathan, J. G., 332, 512
Nathanson, A. I., 100, 102, 105, 254, 347,
    348, 349, 350, 351, 352, 475
Nebergall, R. E., 276
Nelson, K. R., 88, 90, 91, 93, 120
Nelson, T. E., 88, 89, 90, 91, 94
Nesbitt, K. M., 363
Neuendorf, K., 379, 507
Neumann, M. M., 551
Neuman, R. W., 567
Neuman, S. B., 340, 506, 507, 511
Neuman, W. R., 323
Neumark-Sztainer, D., 259, 316, 347, 349,
    401, 402
Newhagen, J. E., 21, 548, 561, 562, 564, 573
Newman, S. S., 307
Nguyen, A., 505
Nicholson, B., 347, 351
Nicklas, T. A., 322
Nieborg, D. B., 137
Niederdeppe, J., 278
Nieding, G., 457
Nielsen, M., 334
Nightingale, V., 23
Nije Bijvank, M., 363, 370
Niven, D., 114
Noar, S. M., 415, 417
Noble, G., 24
Nodelman, P., 231
Noelle-Neumann, E., 100, 107, 119

Nordlund, J. E., 225
Norman, D. A., 548, 556
Norris, M. E., 272
Norris, M. L., 400
Norris, P., 119
Nosek, B., 386
Novak, T. P., 303
Nowak, K., 551
Nwosu, P., 155
Nyman, S. R., 279

Oakes, J. M., 416
Oakes, P. J., 102
Oatley, K., 230
Obregon, R., 548
O'Brien, M., 363
O'Callaghan, R., 494, 496, 497, 499
Oeldorf-Hirsch, A., 551
Ogan, C., 562, 564
Ogden, C. L., 477
Ogles, R. M., 364
Oh, S., 257
Ohler, P., 457
Ohman, A., 195
Oishi, S., 168
Okdie, B., 182
O'Keefe, D. J., 45, 270, 547
Okuma, K., 332
Olevitch, L., 279, 571
Olien, C. N., 116, 315, 319, 320, 499
Oliver, M. B., 152, 163, 167, 168, 169,
    186, 207, 208, 209, 241, 245, 294,
    341, 347, 349, 351, 352, 382, 383,
    412, 431, 458, 459
Olson, J. M., 271
Olson, M. A., 189
Olson, S. R., 348
O'Neal, E. C., 363, 368
Ong, W. J., 522, 527
Onwumechili, C., 155
Operario, D., 377, 378, 388
Oppenheim, A. N.,
    350, 506, 507, 508, 513
Oppl, C., 456
O'Reilly, K. R., 290
Orobio de Castro, B., 363, 371
Ortony, A., 206
Ossoff, E. P., 400, 471, 472
Ott, M. A., 409
Otten, S., 179
Otto, M., 474
Owen, P. R., 400
Owens, J. B., 443, 447
Owens, J. W., 443

Oxley, Z. M., 89, 90, 91, 94
Ozretich, R. A., 348, 349, 351, 352

Paavonen, E. J., 256
Pacanowsky, M., 58
Packer, M., 271
Pahkala, K., 259
Paik, H. J., 212, 340, 367, 474
Paisley, W., 314
Pajares, F., 286
Palmer, E. L., 476
Palmer, L. E., 251
Palmgreen, P. M., 20, 46, 148, 231, 247, 417
Paluch, R. A., 477
Palumbo, F., 509
Pan, Y., 307
Pan, Z., 39, 41, 84, 85, 91, 93, 94, 216, 385
Pandey, S., 448
Papacharissi, Z., 153, 154, 431
Parameswaran, R., 62
Pardun, C. J., 322, 412, 414, 415
Pareto, V., 132
Park, B., 201, 210
Park, H., 117, 555
Park, S. Y., 402
Park, T. D., 432
Parke, R. D., 363
Parker, E. B., 506, 507, 508
Parker, M., 387
Parkin, F., 136
Parks, M. R., 153, 154
Parrott, R. L., 274
Parrott, W. G., 213
Pashler, H. E., 22
Pashupati, K., 243, 244
Paskett, E. D., 316
Pasold, T., 365, 474
Pasta, D. J., 293
Patrick, K., 323
Pattenden, J., 276
Patterson, M., 479
Patterson, T. E., 114
Patwardhan, H., 300
Paul, B., 100
Paulus, P. B., 441
Pavlou, P. A., 300
Paxton, S. J., 401
Payne, J. G., 541
Paz, D. H., 534
Pearce, K. J., 153
Pearl, D., 319
Pearl, J., 36, 37
Pease, D. G., 445, 446
Pechmann, C., 275

Pecora, N., 470
Peers, K. F., 402
Peeters, A. L., 349
Peffley, M., 244, 382
Pekurny, R. G., 243, 244
Pelletier, C., 341
Pelliccio, A., 64
Pempek, T. A., 332, 334, 402, 478
Peng, W., 316, 460, 461, 462, 551
Pennonen, M., 256
Penrod, S., 364
Peracchio, L. A., 306, 307
Pereiar, M. A., 259
Perloff, R. M., 9, 101, 102, 107, 270,
    365, 472, 506, 532
Perrin, J., 288
Perry, C. E., 252
Perry, D. K., 14, 15
Perry, I., 412
Perse, E. M., 10, 13, 100, 151, 152, 153, 163,
    225, 226, 228, 231, 234, 241, 425, 426,
    428, 492, 510, 512, 513, 569
Persky, S., 569
Peter, J., 414, 419, 423, 428, 473, 479, 510
Peters, J. D., 224
Peters, M. D., 84
Peterson, B. S., 473
Peterson, C. R., 102
Peterson, E., 442, 443
Peterson, J. L., 364
Peterson, K., 511
Peterson, K. E., 402
Peterson, T., 100
Petraitis, J., 364
Pettit, G. S., 369
Petty, R. E., 42, 122, 168, 247, 277, 278,
    300, 304, 386
Pfau, M., 270, 568
Pfefferbaum, B., 474
Phalen, P. F., 19, 23
Phelan, Rev. J. J., 252
Phelps, P. C., 475
Phillips, D. P., 448
Phillips, J. G., 154
Philo, G., 22
Piaget, J., 471, 472
Piemyat, S., 425, 426, 427, 471, 472
Pietromonaco, P., 368
Pingree, S., 378, 423, 427, 433, 569
Pinhas, L., 400
Pinkleton, B. E., 347, 349, 351, 418
Pinon, M., 336
Pitts, G., 538
Plato, 307

Plutarch, 132
Plutchik, R., 206
Podolski, C. L., 363, 365, 367
Polack, M., 341
Pollack, M. H., 474
Pollard, T., 348
Polman, H., 363, 371
Pool, M. M., 30
Poole, M. S., 498
Popkin, S. L., 122
Popper, K. R., 37
Pornsakulvanich, V., 154
Posavac, E., 395
Posavac, H., 395
Posavac, S., 395
Poster, M., 522
Postman, L. J., 492
Postman, N., 161
Postrel, V., 137
Potter, R. F., 117, 195, 198, 199,
    200, 201, 512
Potter, W. J., 1, 24, 29, 35, 46, 75, 152, 181,
    243, 244, 294, 345, 346, 347, 348, 352,
    353, 423, 425, 426, 427
Pouliot, L., 426, 427
Poulos, R., 475
Powell, M., 64
Powell, M. C., 180
Powell, R. A., 152, 153,
    225, 231, 425, 426
Power, J., 383
Power, M., 137
Power, P., 22, 23
Powers, E., 89, 91, 117
Prado, A., 499
Prasad, J., 494
Preacher, K. J., 45
Preiss, R. W., 15, 35, 47
Prentice-Dunn, S., 274, 275
Press, A. L., 60
Price, I., 402
Price, V., 40, 84, 86, 89, 91, 93, 101, 116,
    117, 118, 120, 122, 184, 185
Priester, J. R., 278, 300
Primack, B. A., 418
Prior, M., 124
Prisco, A. G., 240, 244
Prochaska, J. M., 317
Prochaska, J. O., 275, 317
Pronin, E., 321
Protess, D. L., 106, 118
Przybylski, A., 459
Pufendorf, S., 132
Putnam, R., 119

Qiu, J., 16
Quick, B. L., 316
Quintero-Johnson, J., 430

Raacke, J., 170
Radford, E., 347
Radvansky, G. A., 379
Radway, D. J., 21, 60
Radway, J., 59, 136
Raessens, J., 456
Rafaeli, S., 302, 303, 548, 552, 554,
    561, 562, 564, 573
Rahnama, S., 510
Rainwater, S. M., 474
Rajulton, F., 316
Ramanadhan, S., 313, 314, 320
Ramasubramanian, S., 186, 347, 349,
    351, 352
Randolph, W., 315, 321, 322
Raney, A. A., 166, 168, 169, 209, 239, 243,
    441, 442, 443, 444, 445, 457, 458
Rankin, S. A., 274
Ransdell, L., 319
Rao, N., 289
Rapaczynski, W. S., 350
Rapson, R. L., 258
Rasewall, J. K., 400
Raskin, R., 403
Ratan, R., 462, 463
Raynor, H., 259
Redding, C. A., 275, 317
Reese, S. D., 86, 114, 124, 154
Reeves, B., 228, 427, 461,
    546, 547, 549, 551
Reger, B., 274, 316
Reibling, E. T., 275
Reich, R. D., 24
Reicher, S. D., 102
Reid, L. N., 350
Reid, S., 384
Reid, S. A., 102
Reise, S. P., 47
Reiser, R. A., 475
Reiss, S., 163, 431
Reitz, A. L., 425, 426, 471, 472
Renshaw, S., 256
Resnicow, K., 317
Rex, J., 402
Reynolds, L., 387
Rhee, J. W., 87, 88, 89
Rhine, S. E., 119
Rhodes, N., 181, 185
Ribisl, K. M., 320
Rice, M. L., 332, 333, 335, 512

Rice, R. E., 323, 491, 492, 493, 494, 495, 496, 497, 498, 499, 571
Rich, M., 346
Richardson, J. D., 89, 385
Richardson, K. D., 447
Rickert, V. I., 415
Riddle, K., 1, 35, 294, 352
Rideout, V. J., 135, 337, 340, 350, 361, 403, 418, 469, 470, 475, 477, 478, 507, 513
Rieber, L. P., 549
Riegner, C., 48
Riemsma, R. P., 276
Riffe, D., 164
Rigby, C. S., 459
Riggs, K. E., 139, 445
Riklis, J., 254
Riley, J. W., 255
Rimal, R. N., 40, 217, 279, 318
Rimer, B. K., 315, 316, 318, 323
Rimm, E. B., 511, 512
Rimon, J. G., 317
Ripptoe, P. A., 290
Rishel, C., 475
Rissolati, G., 368
Ritchie, L. D., 40
Ritson, M., 61
Ritterfeld, U., 165, 171, 456, 458, 460, 461, 462, 463, 556
Rivadeneyra, R., 385, 423, 428
Robb, M., 478
Roberto, A. J., 316, 416
Roberto, E. L., 317, 492, 498
Roberto, H. L., 316
Roberts, B., 85
Roberts, D. F., 135, 337, 340, 350, 361, 403, 411, 414, 469, 470, 475, 478, 507, 509, 510, 513
Roberts, L. D., 153
Roberts, M. S., 154, 303, 568
Robertson, T. S., 472, 496
Robinson, A., 379
Robinson, J. L., 477
Robinson, J. P., 116, 120, 323
Robinson, M. D., 183, 189
Robinson, M. J., 119
Robinson, T. N., 323, 402, 416, 474, 477
Robinson, T. O., 243
Rocella, E. J., 318
Roche, A. F., 410
Roe, K., 414
Roeder, Y., 474
Roehrig, M., 272
Roelofsma, P. H. M. P., 370
Roemmich, J. N., 477

Rogers, B. L., 477
Rogers, E. M., 41, 44, 84, 155, 188, 269, 289, 290, 303, 318, 416, 417, 489, 491, 492, 493, 494, 495, 499, 500, 535
Rogers, J., 409
Rogers, R. W., 211, 274, 275, 290
Rogus, M., 247
Rohde, P., 272
Roine, M., 256
Rojas, H., 90, 91, 93, 103, 105
Rokeach, M., 534, 536
Romantan, A., 278
Romer, D., 215, 364
Rose, G. M., 476
Rosen, E., 493
Rosen, J., 124
Rosenbaum, J. F., 474
Rosenberg, J. F., 463
Rosenblatt, P. C., 256
Rosengren, K. E., 20, 59, 147, 148, 149, 154, 225
Rosenkoetter, L. I., 472
Rosenkoetter, L. L., 348, 349, 351, 352
Rosenkoetter, S. E., 348, 349, 351, 352
Rosenstiel, T., 124
Rosenstock, I. M., 316
Roser, C., 151
Rosins, H., 289
Roskos-Ewoldsen, B. B., 178, 179, 180, 183, 185, 186, 188, 378, 382, 433
Roskos-Ewoldsen, D. R., 2, 44, 93, 178, 179, 180, 181, 182, 183, 185, 207, 301, 302, 322, 378, 381, 433, 459
Roskwell, S. C., 443
Ross, A., 423
Ross, D., 423
Ross, F., 104
Ross, L., 114, 121, 216
Ross, S. M., 63
Rosselli, F., 377, 380
Rossi, J. S., 317
Rossiter, J. R., 472
Rothman, A. J., 276, 321
Rouner, D., 290, 318, 351
Roy, A., 381, 384
Rozin, P., 254
Rubin, A. M., 21, 148, 150, 151, 152, 153, 154, 155, 162, 225, 226, 228, 231, 239, 242, 244, 425, 426, 428, 539
Rubin, R. B., 46, 153, 154
Rucinski, D., 103
Ruggiero, T. E., 155, 163
Ruiz, S., 302, 303, 304, 305
Rushing, J., 316

Russell, G. W., 246, 445, 446, 448, 449
Russell, J. A., 206
Ruth, A. M., 432
Rutigliano, L., 124
Ruttiger, K. F., 255
Ryabovolova, A., 433
Ryan, B., 491
Ryan, R. M., 168, 458
Ryu, S., 232

Sabido, M., 269, 289
Sachau, D. A., 444
Sadetsky, I., 370
Saffitz, G. B., 317
Sahin, V., 117
Sainsbury, P., 319
Saiontz, N. G., 319
Salmon, C. T., 103, 151, 314, 315
Salmon, J., 254, 258, 259
Salomon, G., 21, 24, 350
Salovey, P., 321
Salvaggio, J. L., 545
Salvi, D., 382
Salwen, M. B., 100, 101, 105
Sanbonmatsu, D. M., 180
Sanders, A. K., 255, 478
Sanders, L. M., 90, 91
Sanders-Jackson, A. N., 201, 210, 510
Sandilands, M. L., 445
Sands, E. R., 401
Sanford, R. N., 229
Santelli, J., 409
Santomero, A., 337, 340
Sapir, E., 307
Sapolsky, B. S., 166, 441, 442, 444
Sargent, S. L., 243, 444
Sarkin, J. A., 317
Sarwer, D. B., 401
Sawyer, A., 303
Saylor, M. M., 334
Sayre, B., 91, 94
Scantlin, R., 336, 473, 475
Scarborough, K. E., 448
Scealy, M., 154
Schacter, S., 206
Schaefer, S. R., 555
Scharrer, E., 103, 104, 246
Scheepers, P., 379
Schein, E., 495, 496
Scherer, K. R., 206
Scherlis, W., 479
Scheufele, D. A., 44, 120, 184, 185
Schiappa, E., 226, 228, 234, 384
Schilder, P., 395

Schiller, H. I., 138
Schiller, H. J., 531
Schleifer, R., 409
Schleuder, J., 116
Schmidt, M. E., 334
Schmierbach, M. G., 89, 90, 91
Schmitt, B. H., 307
Schmitt, K., 337
Schmitt, K. L., 24, 334, 336, 337, 338,
    471, 475, 476, 512
Schmitz, K. H., 259
Schneeweiss, R., 316
Schneider, W., 511
Schoenbach, K., 567
Schoening, G. T., 57
Schooler, C., 151
Schouten, A. P., 473, 479
Schrader, M. P., 445, 448
Schramm, H., 227, 553, 555
Schramm, W., 19, 35, 171
Schramm, W. L., 506, 507, 508
Schubert, C. M., 410
Schumacher, P., 153, 154
Schunk, D. H., 286
Schupak-Neuberg, E., 398
Schupp, H., 445
Schuurman, J., 478
Schwartz, D., 394
Schwartz, N., 477
Schwarz, N., 383, 445
Schweitzer, K., 445
Scully, M. L., 477
Seale, T. W., 474
Sears, D., 20
Sebastian, M., 347, 351
Sebastian, R. J., 363
Secco, T., 472
Sechrest, L., 364
Sedman, D., 494
Segrin, C., 569
Seiter, E., 60, 136, 139
Semetko, H. A., 91, 117
Semin, G., 382
Sestir, M. A., 210, 261
Sey, A., 16
Shaffer, A., 335
Shah, D. V., 45, 84, 85, 86, 87, 88, 89, 90,
    91, 92, 93, 94, 103, 105, 119
Shaikh, A. R., 317
Shanahan, J., 69, 70, 75, 79, 119, 185,
    214, 379, 397, 460, 474
Shao, G., 170
Shapiro, M. A., 424, 425, 431
Sharma, N., 551, 568

Shavitt, S., 271
Shaw, D. L., 83, 84, 118, 492, 563, 567, 570
Shaw, H., 272
Shaw, H. E., 398
Shea, C. L., 306
Sheafer, T., 109, 185
Sheatsley, P., 314
Sheffield, F., 314
Sheffield, F. D., 270
Shelton, M. L., 402, 510, 512
Shen, C., 462, 463
Shen, F., 88, 89, 90, 91, 93
Shen, L., 94, 109
Sherif, C. W., 276
Sherif, M., 276
Sherman, J., 377, 378
Sherrell, D., 550
Sherry, J. L., 169, 233, 457, 461
Sherwood, N. E., 347, 349
Shields, T., 244, 382
Shiffrin, R. M., 22
Shim, M., 278, 402
Shin, M., 197, 201
Shirley, M., 186
Shively, J., 139
Shoemaker, P. J., 86, 114, 151
Shoham, M. D., 103
Short, A., 403
Short, J., 545
Shoshani, A., 348, 351
Shrum, L. J., 25, 79, 299, 300, 302, 303, 304, 307, 308, 413, 433
Shuttleworth, F. K., 133
Sicilia, M., 302, 303, 304, 305
Siegel, J., 545
Signorielli, N., 69, 74, 75, 76, 214, 319, 361, 379, 397, 460, 474
Silk, K. J., 274
Sillanmaki, L., 259
Silva, J., 349, 352
Silverblatt, A., 346
Silverstone, R., 498, 562
Silvia, P. J., 458
Simcock, G., 334
Simell, O., 259
Simmonds, M. B., 400
Simon, A., 83, 89, 184
Simon, W., 413
Simonson, I., 307
Simonson, P., 224
Singer, D. G., 349, 350
Singer, J., 206
Singer, J. L., 349, 350
Singer, M. J., 169

Singhal, A., 269, 289, 290, 318, 416, 417, 463, 535
Sirard, J. R., 416
Six, B., 273
Sjoberg, U., 153
Skalski, P., 387, 457
Skinner, C. S., 317
Slade, C., 139
Sladen, S., 347
Slater, D., 425
Slater, M. D., 36, 39, 40, 46, 275, 278, 290, 318, 351, 367, 461, 570
Sloan, L. R., 445, 447
Sloan, W. D., 10
Slone, M., 348, 351
Slothuus, R., 90
Smallwood, A. M. K., 510
Smith, A., 478
Smith, B. P., 455
Smith, D., 289
Smith, E., 382
Smith, J. K., 457
Smith, M., 444
Smith, P. B., 261
Smith, R. J., 272
Smith, S., 455
Smith, S. L., 423, 427, 428, 431, 471
Smith, S. M., 90, 272
Smith, S. W., 277, 423, 427, 428, 431
Smythe, D., 138
Sniderman, P. M., 89, 91
Snyder, C. R., 447
Snyder, L. B., 39, 40, 43, 118
Snyder, M., 261, 271
Sobol, A. M., 288, 402, 511
Socrates, 520
Sohn, D., 302, 305
Soldow, G., 306
Solomon, G., 562
Song, J. H., 305
Song, Y., 568
Sood, S., 289
Southwell, B. G., 46
Sowden, A. J., 276
Sowell, E. R., 473
Spangenberg, E. R., 272
Spangler, D., 398, 403
Sparks, G. G., 364, 471
Sparks, J. V., Jr., 200, 201
Spielberger, C. D., 213
Spitzer, B. L., 394
Sprafkin, J., 370, 475
Springer, K., 471
Sprott, D. E., 272

Stack, S., 132
Staiger, J., 15, 133, 134
Stajkovic, A. D., 286
Stampfer, M. J., 511, 512
Stanton, B. F., 475
Stanton, F., 20
Stapel, D. A., 179
Stapel, L., 36
Star, S. A., 532
Starker, S., 10
Stead, M., 274
Steams, P. N., 133
Steele, J. R., 64, 414
Steele, W. R., 321
Steen, F. F., 459
Steger, M. F., 168
Stein, A. H., 337
Steinberg, L., 473
Steinfeld, J., 370
Steinfield, C., 510
Steinke, J., 347
Step, M. M., 152, 225, 226
Stephenson, M. T., 36, 45, 316
Stern, S., 411, 412, 413
Stern, S. R., 288, 316
Steuer, J., 303, 549, 552
Stevens, R. S., 278
Stevenson, R., 154
Stewart, D. W., 300
Stewart, T., 382
Stice, E., 398, 403
Stiff, J. B., 109, 241, 287
Stinchcombe, A. L., 37
Stine, E., 272
Stine, R. A., 260
Stipp, H., 166
Stitt, C. R., 152, 431, 432
Stockmann, R., 455
Stohl, C., 569
Stokes, C. E., 412
Stone, J., 272
Stoneman, Z., 255, 476, 478
Storey, J. D., 105, 106, 216, 402
Storey, M., 316, 317
Story, M., 259, 401, 402
Stouffer, S. A., 532
Stout, D. A., 63
Stout, P. A., 305
St. Peters, M., 336, 512
Strack, F., 445
Strange, J. J., 427
Strasburger, V. C., 335
Strate, L., 518
Strathman, A. J., 278

Strauman, T. J., 397
Strauss, A., 224
Strauss, J., 395
Strecher, V. J., 317
Streeter, T., 494
Stretcher, V. J., 293
Strickwerda, M., 198
Strizhakova, Y., 164, 167
Stroh, P., 122
Stromer-Galley, J., 303
Stroud, N. J., 121
Stryker, J. E., 40, 45, 46
Stucky, R. J., 447
Stutts, M. A., 471
Suchman, E. A., 532
Suddendorf, T., 334
Sudweeks, F., 302, 303
Sullivan, D. B., 444
Suman, M., 410
Summers, D., 409
Sumner, J., 198
Sun, S. S., 154, 155, 410
Sun, Y., 216
Sundar, S. S., 196, 303, 304, 305, 547, 548,
    549, 550, 551, 552, 553, 554, 555
Sunstein, C., 564, 569, 570
Susman, E. J., 337
Susskind, J., 377, 380
Sutton, R. M., 102
Sutton, S. R., 276
Svenderud, P., 289
Swaim, R. C., 367, 461
Swalehe, R. M. A., 289, 290
Sypher, H. E., 46, 231

Tabak, C. J., 477
Tagg, S., 274
Tajfel, H., 107, 377, 383
Takeshita, T., 567
Tal-Or, N., 101, 102, 104, 231
Tamborini, R., 166, 170, 183, 241,
    384, 387, 442, 443, 457, 573
Tamking, G., 335
Tan, A., 380, 385
Tan, A. S., 393
Tan, G., 380, 385
Tan, S. L., 460
Tanimura, M., 332
Tanner, A., 347, 349
Tanner, J. L., 410
Tantleff-Dunn, S., 396, 398
Tao, C. C., 552, 553
Tatum, C. M., 316
Tavassoli, N. T., 307

Taylor, B. C., 54
Taylor, D. S., 152, 155, 428
Taylor, L. D., 365, 398
Taylor, S. E., 101, 206, 288, 349, 352, 368
Teasdale, J. D., 186
Teggemann, M., 315
Telford, A., 258
Tell, P. M., 427
Tellegen, A., 213
Tenkorang, E. Y., 316
Tenner, E., 499
Terry, D. J., 101
Tesser, A., 101
Tessmer, M. A., 475
Tewksbury, D., 84, 86, 89, 91, 93,
        106, 116, 117, 118, 121, 122,
        124, 184, 185, 322, 548, 567, 568
Tharp, T., 402
Theriault, S. M., 89, 91
Thickstun, P., 411
Thill, K. P., 400
Thoman, E., 348
Thomas, G., 306
Thomas, L., 186
Thomas, M. H., 364, 365, 369, 427
Thompson, C., 137
Thompson, E. P., 278
Thompson, J. B., 25, 53
Thompson, J. K., 272, 395, 396
Thompson, M., 394
Thompson, P. M., 473
Thompson, S., 10, 35, 39
Thomsen, S. R., 395
Thomson, T., 255
Thorne, A., 447
Thornton, B., 395
Thornton, L., 401
Thorson, E., 198, 305, 550, 553
Tichenor, P. J., 116, 315, 319, 320, 499
Tidwell, L. C., 154
Tiffany, S. T., 274
Tiggemann, M., 349, 351, 397, 399
Timperio, A., 258
Tong, A., 319
Torres, M., 187
Torrubia-Beltri, R., 163, 241, 243
Tortolero, S., 411
Torwel, V., 291
Tota, M. E., 180
Trabasso, T., 472
Trapnell, P. D., 168
Traudt, P. J., 57
Tremayne, M., 303, 304
Tripp, D., 136

Troseth, G. L., 334
Truglio, R. T., 333, 335, 426, 427
Truhillo, N., 54
Tsao, F. M., 334
Tsao, J., 225
Tschida, D. A., 316
Tsfati, Y., 101, 102, 104, 106, 107, 109
Tuchman, G., 85
Tucker, K. L., 477
Tuggle, C. A., 443
Turner, J., 377, 383
Turner, J. C., 102, 107
Turner, J. R., 226
Turner, M. M., 217
Turner, R. H., 534
Turow, J., 564, 566
Turse, N., 137
Tüzünkan, F., 442
Tversky, A., 86, 87, 88, 364, 365, 471
Tyler, T. R., 100, 118
Tynes, B., 387

Uchikoshi, Y., 339
Ultan, R., 308
Unnava, H. R., 306
Uppal, C., 548
Urdan, T., 286

Vail, R. G., 109
Vale, W., 64
Valente, T. W., 493, 500
Valentino, N. A., 90, 91, 117, 118, 217, 383
Valkenburg, P. M., 91, 117, 332, 335, 349,
        414, 419, 423, 428, 473, 476, 479, 510
Valkonen, S., 256
Vallone, R. P., 114, 121, 216
van Aken, M., 363, 371
Vande Bergt, L. R., 346
van den Berg, P., 272
van den Broek, P., 472
Van den Bulck, J., 364, 460, 569
Van den Hooff, B., 495
van der Molen, J. H. W., 548
van der Voort, T. H. A., 30, 335,
        348, 349, 351, 511
Vandewater, E. A., 402, 510
VanLear, A., 42, 44
VanLear, C. A., 42
van Mierlo, J., 460, 569
Varadarajan, R., 303, 306
Vaughn, P. W., 289, 290
Veenstra, A. S., 91, 94
Vega, V., 427
Velez, R., 316

Velicer, W., 317
Velthuijsen, A. S., 541
Venkatesh, V., 496
Vergeer, M., 379
Verma, S., 257
Viehoff, R., 165, 458
Vieira, E. T., Jr., 254
Vince, P., 350, 506, 507, 508, 513
Vishak, J., 117
Vishwanath, A., 496
Viswanath, K., 313, 314, 315, 316, 318, 319,
    320, 321, 322, 323, 324
Von Hippel, E., 497
von Hippel, W., 377, 378, 382, 388
von Pape, T., 498
von Salisch, M., 456
Vooijs, M. W., 348, 349, 351
Vookles, J., 397
Vorderer, P., 165, 169, 171, 233, 442, 456,
    457, 458, 459, 462, 553, 555, 556
Vroone, M., 332
Vuuren, D. P., 509, 510

Wackman, D. B., 84, 85, 86, 88, 91, 93
Wade, T. D., 349, 351
Wagner, D., 445
Wainapel, G., 242, 248
Wajcmam, J., 498
Wakefield, M. A., 477
Walder, L. O., 367
Walker, A., 139
Walker, D., 332, 333, 334, 473, 478
Walker, M. R., 447
Walker, W. R., 493
Wall, M., 402
Wallack, L., 269, 319
Wallas, G., 132
Wallsten, K., 568
Walther, J. B., 154, 561, 562, 573
Wand, B., 253
Wang, F.-Y., 493
Wang, H., 463
Wang, T., 498, 499
Wang, W., 243, 462
Wang, Z., 201, 202, 210, 448
Wanke, M., 383
Wann, D. L., 445, 446, 447, 448, 449
Wanta, W., 568
Ward, L. M., 385, 393, 395, 399,
    409, 411, 412, 415, 423, 428
Wardle, J., 401
Wareham, N. J., 274
Wartella, E., 2, 134, 478
Waterman, A. S., 168

Watkins, L. T., 370
Watson, D. L., 213, 319
Watt, I. S., 276, 522
Watt, J. H., 42, 118
Watts, M., 85, 87, 89, 94
Wearing, A. J., 272
Weaver, D. L., 35, 83, 84, 116
Weaver, J. B., 209, 239, 242, 243, 245, 246,
    444, 445
Weber, R., 166, 460, 461, 462, 463
Weber, S., 335
Webster, J. G., 19, 23, 54, 278, 493, 495, 496
Wegener, D. T., 277, 386
Weicha, J. L., 402
Weigold, M., 247
Weimann, G., 120, 185
Weinberger, M. G., 212
Weiner, J., 274
Weinstein, N. D., 276
Weis, D. S., 106
Weisbach, K., 167
Weiss, A. J., 428, 476
Weitz, B., 303, 306
Welcome, S. E., 473
Wellman, H., 472
Wenner, L. A., 20, 148, 346, 441, 445, 446
West, D. M., 121
West, R., 276
West, S. G., 363
Westby, S. D., 472
Western, M., 505
Wetherell, M. S., 102
White, A. B., 64
White, C., 58
White, G. F., 448
White, H. A., 101, 105
White, I. K., 118
White, M., 276
White, R. A., 54, 59
White, V. M., 477
Whitney, D. C., 19, 534
Wilcox, B. L., 476
Wilcox, D. F., 113
Wilde, R. J., 507
Wilder, A., 337, 340
Wilkowski, B. M., 183, 189
Wilksch, S. M., 349, 351
Willett, W. C., 511, 512
Williams, B. A., 123, 244, 382
Williams, D., 569, 572
Williams, E., 545
Williams, I., 563
Williams, M., 56, 337, 340, 395
Williams, P. T., 314

Williams, R. M., Jr., 532
Williams, T. M., 335, 508, 509, 510
Williams, Y., 347
Wilson, B. D., 201, 210, 430, 433
Wilson, B. J., 210, 261, 347, 348, 351, 428,
    471, 472, 473, 474, 475, 476
Wilson, D. M., 293, 347, 349
Wilson, E., 550
Wilson, T., 230
Wilson, W. C., 232
Wiltz, J., 163, 431
Wimmer, R. D., 35
Windahl, S., 151, 152, 154, 225, 539
Wing, R., 259
Winiewicz, D. D., 477
Winkleby, M. A., 320
Winn, M., 335
Winocur, R., 139
Winship, C., 37
Winslow, M. P., 272
Winston, B., 494
Wirsan, J., 495, 498
Wirth, W., 207, 498, 555
Wise, K., 196, 549, 555
Witment, B. G., 169
Witte, K., 45, 211, 275, 316
Wohl, R. R., 152, 224, 225, 226, 227, 232
Wolak, J., 416
Wolf, K. D., 476
Wolf, M. A., 58
Wolfradt, U., 154
Wood, E. A., 243
Wood, J., 215
Wood, R. W., 321
Woodard, E. H., 16, 338, 475
Woodruff, A., 416
Woodruff, K., 269, 319
Woodside, A. G., 306
Woolf, K. D., 24
Wotring, C. E., 495
Wozniak, P., 350
Wrath, E.-M., 136
Wright, C. R., 19, 149
Wright, J. C., 333, 335, 336, 337, 425, 426,
    427, 471, 472, 473, 475, 510, 512
Wright, P., 301
Wroblewski, R., 426
Wu, G., 305
Wulff, H. J., 442

Xu, Q., 551

Yadav, M., 303, 306
Yamada, J., 321

Yammarino, F. J., 40
Yan, C., 551
Yan, J., 118
Yang, M., 301, 302
Yang, M.-S., 350, 351
Yanovitzky, I., 38, 40, 41, 42,
    43, 44, 45, 48
Yardley, L., 279
Ybarra, M. L., 410, 479
Yeaton, W., 364
Yegiyan, N., 197, 202
Yoels, W. C., 446
Yorkson, E. A., 307, 308
Youn, S., 103
Young, D., 212
Young, K. M., 443, 444
Yu, H. J., 185
Yzer, M. C., 274

Zaichkowsky, J. L., 151
Zaller, J., 86, 116, 122
Zanutto, E., 38, 48
Zeitz, H., 365
Zeng, D., 493
Zenos, M. A., 185
Zettl, H., 345
Zhang, G., 317
Zhao, G., 275
Zhao, X., 117
Zhou, S., 117
Zhu, J., 118
Zietsman-Thomas, A., 347
Zill, N., 336, 364
Zillmann, D., 20, 47, 122, 163,
    164, 166, 167, 169, 207, 209,
    215, 241, 243, 246, 315, 369,
    410, 427, 441, 442, 443, 444,
    445, 447, 509, 545
Zimbardo, P. G., 256
Zimmerman, B. J., 285
Zimmerman, F. J., 332, 333
Zimmerman, R. S., 45,
    416, 417
Zinkhan, G. M., 305
Zittleman, L., 349
Zivian, M. T., 394
Zmud, R., 496
Zubric, J., 89, 91
Zuckerman, M., 163, 213, 241,
    242, 243
Zumbach, J., 183
Zurbriggen, E. L., 415
Zwann, R. A., 379
Zyvatkauskas, C., 132

SUBJECT INDEX

Achievement gap, 340
Action for Children's
     Television, 135
Action Coalition for Media
     Education (ACME), 418
Active audiences, 12, 20, 22, 23,
     47–48, 121, 150–151
Actor-observer attribution
     bias, 103
Adolescents, 11
  abstract thinking and, 472
  adolescent cognition,
       characteristics of, 472–473
  advertising/marketing campaigns
       and, 476–477
  aggressive behavior, violent
       media and, 243, 363–364
  anti-smoking messages and,
       275, 288, 321
  body image and, 397, 402
  cognitive allocation, exposure
       state and, 30–31
  developmental theory, media
       impact and, 472–473
  early educational television
       exposure and, 336–337
  electronic bullying, 479
  family-based media experiences
       and, 475–476
  formal logic/hypothetical
       reasoning and, 472
  future research directions
       on, 480

media content vs. viewing time
     and, 473–474
media use, displacement effects
     and, 510
media use patterns and, 15–16,
     243, 252, 253–255, 470
metacognitive skill and,
     472–473
online communication
     and, 478–479
parental mediation with, 475
racial/ethnic communication
     and, 387
self-discrepant adolescents, 397
sensation need,
     violent/nonviolent media
     and, 241
sexual activity among,
     288, 410–411, 413–414
sexually transmitted diseases
     and, 411, 416
stress levels, media use and, 257
teen pregnancy,
     318, 410–411, 415
See also Children; Displacement
     effects; Educational
     television; Family groups;
     Sexual media messages
Adopters/adoption. See Diffusion
     of innovations (DOI) theory
Advertising, 11, 16
  body ideals and, 400–401
  digital retouching and, 400–401

instrumentally vs. symbolically
    oriented appeals and, 271
media literacy interventions and, 347
obesity-media relationship and, 477–478
prescription drug advertising, 108
public service advertising, 275
Web advertising, 79, 400, 476–477, 549
youth audience and, 476–477
See also Advertising research;
    Marketing; Persuasion theories;
    Persuasive messages
Advertising research, 299–300
alphabetic vs. logographic language
    processing and, 307
attitudinal outcomes and,
    301–302, 304–305
boundary conditions and, 308
code switching and, 307
complexity continuum and, 306–307
dual-language processing and, 307
information processing/decision making,
    interactivity and, 304–305
interactivity, definition of, 303–304
interactivity effects research, 302–306
memory function and, 301–302, 306
persuasive outcomes, factors in, 302, 309
phonetic symbolism and, 307–308
phonological loop and, 307, 308
product placement effectiveness,
    measurement of, 301–302
product placement effects, factors in,
    300–301
product placement research, 300–306
psycholinguistics studies of
    advertising/brand names, 306–308, 309
syntactic complexity, advertising copy
    and, 306–307
See also Advertising
Advocacy messages, 269, 276–277, 289–290
Advocates for Youth, 417
Affect. *See* Affective disposition
    theory (ADT); Emotions
Affective disposition theory (ADT), 441, 457
Affirmative action policy, 385
Agency concept, 284–285
collective agency, 284–285
communication technologies effects
    and, 550–552
core properties of, 285
forethought and, 285
health behaviors and, 315–316
human capabilities and, 285
individual agency, 284
intentionality and, 285

proxy agency, 284
self-reactiveness and, 285
self-reflectiveness and, 285
See also Social cognitive theory (SCT)
Agenda setting model, 13, 41, 44, 69, 83
controversy and, 85
first level agenda setting, 85
framing and, 83–84, 85–86
future research topics on, 94–95
Internet-based information/communication
    and, 567–569
message processing model and,
    92–93, 92 (figure)
news reporting and, 117–118, 492
population health, media influences on, 319
priming and, 84, 86
psychological processes and, 84
salience transfer and, 84
second level agenda setting, 85
See also Framing effects; Priming effects
Aggressiveness:
early educational television
    exposure and, 336
emotions and, 212–213
generalized aggression model and,
    212–213
predisposition for, 212–213, 242–243, 246
script theory and, 240–241
televised sports viewing and, 447–449
validation, search for, 242–243
See also Media violence;
    Priming effects; Violence
Aggressor effect, 361, 362–364, 362 (figure)
Ally McBeal, 230
American Academy of Pediatrics (AAP), 15,
    332, 478
American Idol, 72, 339
American Medical Association (AMA), 15
American Psychological Association (APA), 15
American Revolution, 10
America's Army, 137, 462
Animation, 549, 550
Anorexia nervosa, 395, 400, 401–402
Antisocial behaviors, 212–213, 287–288
    See also Aggressiveness;
        Media violence; Violence
Arousal/excitation transfer, 368–369
Arousal need, 241–242, 245, 349
Atomistic fallacy, 40
Attentional state, 24–25, 30 (table), 31
issue-attention cycle, 44
vicarious learning and, 285, 290–291
See also Audiences; Exposure to messages;
    Media exposure model

Attention deficit hyperactivity disorder
(ADHD), 16
Attitude theories, 270
attitude change, strategies for, 270
belief-based attitude models, 270
cognitive dissonance theory and, 271–273
counterattitudinal view, advocacy of, 272
functional models of attitude, 271
hypocrisy induction and, 272
self-monitoring variable and, 271
self-prophesy effect and, 272
See also Attitudinal effects;
    Persuasion theories; Social cognitive
    theory (SCT); Theory of planned
    behavior (TPB); Theory of reasoned
    action (TRA); Voluntary action theories
Attitudinal effects, 12, 13–14, 15, 42
attitude activation, 178–179
attitude-behavior link and, 109
entertainment-education programming
    and, 289–290
framing and, 91
interactivity, attitudinal outcomes
    and, 304–305
product placement and, 301–302
racial attitudes, interpretive function
    and, 244
See also Attitude theories
Audiences, 19
active audiences, 12, 20, 22, 23, 47–48,
    121, 150–151
collaborative studies of, 63–64
community, text usage and, 63
contemporary qualitative research on,
    61–63
contextual factors, influence of, 61–62
cultural/social groupings of, 21
cultural studies' conceptualization of,
    135–137, 140
decoding process and, 27–29, 58–59, 63
diasporic communities, syncretic cultures of
    reception and, 139
ethnographic research on, 54–58, 62
exposure/attention to media messages and,
    21–22, 23, 48
flow, state of, 26, 167
historic approach to, 19–21
individual difference factors and, 20, 22–23
intra-audience effects, emotional
    contagion and, 258
issue-attention cycle and, 44
limited media effects model and, 20
mass audience, propaganda effects and, 20
meaning, locus of, 22–23, 54

media effects, inoculation against, 11
media effects, sense extension theory of, 13
media impact, message interpretation
    and, 12, 15
media industry discourse and, 61
media messages, polysemic nature of, 20–21
news media, influence of, 11
news reporting, audience for, 121
news reporting, perceptions of issues
    and, 117–119
opinion leaders, message interpretation
    and, 20
passive audiences, 20, 22, 23, 47
qualitative audience studies, history
    of, 56–63
reception analysis research and, 59–61
receptive activity and, 25, 53–54
screen theory, text-spectator relations
    and, 58–59
semiotic democracy and, 60–61
spiral of silence and, 107, 119, 570–571
suspension of disbelief and, 26
sustainer/supporter role of media and, 12
talk-back radio and, 139
two-step flow model and, 20
typologies of, 23
user-controlled/on-demand media and,
    62–63
vulnerability of, 11, 20, 22
See also Causation; Mass communication;
    Mass media; Media effects; Media
    exposure model; Parasocial
    interaction/identification; Presumed
    media influence; Social environment;
    Uses and gratifications model
Automatic attention, 21–22
Automatic processing state,
    25–26, 30 (table), 31
Availability heuristic, 364

Baby Einstein, 332
Baby Genius, 332
Barney & Friends, 333
Behavioral change. *See* Attitude theories;
    Population health; Stage models of
    behavioral change; Theory of planned
    behavior (TPB); Theory of reasoned
    action (TRA); Voluntary action theories
Behavioral effects, 12, 13, 15
attitude-behavior link, 109
entertainment-education programming
    and, 289–290
framing and, 91
intended media effects and, 289–290

moral panics and, 22
unintended media effects and, 287–289
See also Presumed media influence;
Social cognitive theory (SCT)
Belief-based attitudes, 270
health belief model and, 316
self-efficacy beliefs, 286–287
See also Attitude theories
Bias:
actor-observer attribution bias, 103
correction, methods for, 48
disconfirmation bias, 121
group-level effects and, 42
judgmental heuristics and, 122
negativity bias, 196, 201–202
news biases, 114–115
perceptual biases, 216
time-biased vs. space-biased media, 523
See also Racial/ethnic stereotyping
Bill Nye the Science Guy, 339
Bill of Rights, 10
Blogs, 63, 415, 522, 563, 566, 568
Blue's Clues, 337
Body image, 107, 393
attainment of ideal body,
perceived rewards of, 396
body mass index and, 394
cosmetic surgery and, 401
cultivation theory and, 397
definition of, 395
digital retouching technology
and, 400–401
disordered eating and, 395, 396–397, 400
emotional responses,
eating behavior and, 397
health issues and, 401–402
historical context, underweight bodies
and, 393, 394
ideal-body media, audience for, 395
ideal-body media content and, 394–395
internalization of thin-ideal and,
396–397, 401
Internet body ideals, 400
maturational issues and, 401
media messages/emotions and, 216
new media technologies and, 400–401
obesity and, 402–403
research findings on, 399
research methodologies and, 398–399
self-discrepancy theory and, 397
self vs. ideal, perceptions of, 396–397
social cognitive theory and, 396–397
social comparison theory and, 397
social issues and, 402

thin-ideal depicting/promoting media
and, 394, 395
video game body images, 400
women's magazine copy and, 288
See also Sexual media messages
Body mass index (BMI), 394, 477
Boundary conditions, 308
Brands. *See* Advertising research;
Product placement research
Bridges of familiarity, 496
Built environments, 521
Bulimia nervosa, 395, 401–402
Bullying, 479
Bureau of Applied Social Research
(Columbia University), 12

Capture, 225
Causation, 14–15, 20
active audience conception and, 47–48
agency/manipulation and, 37, 38
causal chains, complexity of, 44–46
causal inference, requirements for, 37
causal inference, threats to validity
of, 37, 40–42
causal laws, empirical observation and,
37–38
challenges to causal inference, 39–48
counterfactual approach to, 37–38
cross-level theorizing and, 41
deterministic perspective, 14, 38, 39
ecological fallacy and, 40–41
effects tradition theories and, 36
experimental designs and, 38
fallacy of composition and, 40
fallacy of confusing cause and
effect, 42–43
fallacy of ignoring the future and, 43
fallacy of ignoring the past and, 43
fallacy of nonreciprocal causation and, 45
fallacy of the secular trend and, 43
fallacy of wrong causal process and, 44–45
fallacy of the wrong level and, 41
fallacy of the wrong timing and, 44
Granger causality test and, 43
group-level effects, bias and, 42
issue-attention cycle and, 44
media effects, multilevel nature of, 39–42
media effects research and, 36, 38–42
multiple-level analysis and, 41–42
naturally occurring regularities in, 38, 39
probabilistic-causality perspective
and, 14, 39
sampling methodology and, 41–42
social scientific perspective and, 36–38

third variable fallacy and, 45
See also Quantitative methods
Censorship, 10
Centers for Disease Control and Prevention, 322, 394, 410
Centre for Contemporary Cultural Studies (University of Birmingham), 58
Chat rooms, 63, 137, 387, 415, 446
Chicago School, 224
Children, 11, 12, 469–470
    advertising/marketing campaigns and, 476–477
    cognitive skill development and, 475, 511–512
    developmental theory, media impact and, 470–472
    early childhood cognition, characteristics of, 471–472
    egocentric cognition and, 472
    emotions, communication of, 256
    family-based media experiences and, 475–476
    fright reactions to media, 208–209, 474
    future research directions on, 479–480
    infants, media exposure and, 332, 333–335, 478
    late childhood cognition, characteristics of, 472
    learning from media content and, 474–475
    media content vs. viewing time and, 473–474
    media multitasking and, 470
    media use patterns and, 15–16, 252, 253–255, 469, 470
    obesity-media relationship and, 402–403, 477–478, 510–511
    parental mediation with, 475
    physical health, media effects and, 477–478
    prosocial attitudes/behaviors, media exposure and, 475
    reality vs. fantasy and, 368, 471–472
    role-taking/imagining and, 472
    sedentary behaviors of, 259, 477
    sleep disturbances, media use and, 256
    social skill development and, 510
    stereotyping by, 474–475
    television programming, protections from, 135
    television viewing, displacement effects and, 332, 335, 339–340, 509–510
    video deficit and, 334, 478
    See also Adolescents; Displacement effects; Educational television; Family groups

Children's Television Workshop, 339
Civic engagement, 119
Civil society, 132
    new media as, 137
    risks to, 134–135
Cognitive dissonance theory, 271–273
Cognitive effects, 12, 14, 15, 44
    attentional state and, 24–25
    cognitive allocation, exposure state and, 30–31
    cognitive gender schemata and, 244
    cultivation hypothesis and, 25–26
    framing/priming processes and, 86, 91, 178, 181–182
    media violence and, 181
    suspension of disbelief, 26
    transported state and, 26–27, 167–168
    See also Advertising research; Persuasion theories; Social cognitive theory (SCT)
Cognitive functional model (CFM), 211–212
Cognitive representation, 378
Colbert Report, The, 212
Collective agency, 284–285
Comfort food, 216
Comfort need, 242
Commercial content, 10
    See also Advertising; Advertising research; Product placement research
Common assumptions, 56, 71
Communication infrastructure theory (CIT), 541–543
    communication action context and, 541–543
    geo-ethnic media and, 541
    mainstream media and, 541
    media system dependency theory and, 542–543
    storytelling system and, 541–542
Communication technologies effects, 545–546
    affordances of media technology and, 548, 556
    agency variable and, 550–552
    animation, motion effect/distinctiveness theories and, 549, 550
    being-there heuristic and, 550
    communication sources, receiver perceptions and, 550–552
    contextual specification of variables and, 547
    dual coding and, 548, 549
    human information processing system and, 548–549
    independent variables and, 546, 547
    interactivity concept and, 552–554

interpersonal communication, mass
communication venues and, 554
medium-related structural variables
and, 547–548, 556
modality variable and, 548–550
navigability through media space and,
554–555
psychological domains and, 547, 548,
553–554, 556–557
research, media effects approach to,
546–548
research, methodological challenges in,
556–557
sensory richness and, 549–550
social domains and, 550–552, 554
variable-centered approach and, 546–547
See also Computer-mediated
communication (CMC); Internet;
Technology
Communicatory utility, 255–256
Compensatory principal, 121–122
Computer games, 16
See also Digital games; Games; Video games
Computer-mediated
communication (CMC), 148
adaptive/technology structuration and, 498
individual dispositions and, 154
parasocial relationships and, 228, 233
presence, sense of, 233
See also Communication technologies
effects; Internet; Technology
Comstock Law, 133
Conscience-numbing effect, 362, 364–365
Constructivism:
experience, interpretation of, 55–56
intersubjective agreement, common
understanding and, 56
meaning construction, 28 (table),
29, 31, 54, 121
news reporting, political meaning
construction and, 121
reality and, 55–56
researcher-researched roles and, 62
science, brute data and, 56
See also Ethnography; Qualitative methods
Construct validity, 46–47
Controlled attention, 21, 22
Controversy, 85
Coping mechanisms, 257, 274–275, 397
Corporations:
collective consciousness and, 78
communication technologies,
adaptive/technology
structuration and, 498

diffusion of innovation and, 495
discontinuous innovation,
chasm concept and, 497
early advertising campaigns, 11
information monopolies/economic
monopolies and, 521
innovative organizational culture and, 495
media democracy and, 528
media structures, economic aspects of, 499
technology implementation
process and, 496
Web advertising and, 79, 400,
476–477, 549
See also Advertising;
Advertising research; Marketing
Court of the Star Chamber, 10
Crime news/shows, 242, 244, 252, 382
Crime-related outcomes, 382
Cross-sectional surveys, 398
Cues, 94
Cultivation analysis, 69–70
audience activity and, 77–78
conceptual framework of, 70–71
critiques/refinements of, 75–77
cross-cultural/international comparative
analysis, 80
cultivation relationships, variability in, 74
Cultural Indicators paradigm and,
70–71, 75
early findings of, 74–75
future trends in, 79–80
heavy vs. light television viewing
and, 73–74
mainstreaming pattern and, 75–77,
76 (figure)
mass-cultural process and, 70, 71, 72
message system analysis and, 73, 74
message system data, symbolic
transformation of, 74–75
message systems, roles of, 70, 71, 72
methodology of, 73–74
new media environment and, 78–79, 80
real-world vs. TV-world statistics and, 74
survey methods and, 69, 73
symbolic cultural environment and,
70, 74–75
See also Cultivation theory; Television
Cultivation theory, 15, 25–26, 69
cross-level links and, 41
emotion, issue of, 214–215
new media environment and, 78–79, 80,
569–570
population health, media influences on, 319
sexual media messages and, 413–414

storytelling concept and, 71–72
supportive evidence for, 75–76
thin-body ideal and, 397
See also Cultivation analysis
Cultural Indicators paradigm, 70–71, 75
Cultural studies, 131
audience, conceptualization of,
135–137, 140
audience meaning making and,
134, 136–137
audience power/vulnerability, 134–135
audience studies, non-radical nature of, 138
communication studies,
development of, 134
conservative concerns and, 132, 133–135
crowd/mob, anxieties about, 132, 133
diasporic communities, syncretic cultures of
reception and, 139
dominant norms/expressions and, 136–137
encoding/decoding processes, locus of
power and, 136–137
future research topics in, 138–140
Generation M and, 135
ideal-typical reasoning, fallacy of, 135
mass literacy, gendered reactions to, 133
media effects research,
meta-criticism of, 132–135
movies, potential to corrupt and, 133–134
newly literate publics,
manipulation of, 132–133
psy-function concept and,
131–132, 133, 135
Cultures:
ethnographic research, cross-cultural
encounters and, 62
iterative media effects and, 15
language usage and, 22
media effects, sense extension theory of, 13
media messages, polysemic nature of, 20–21
message systems and, 70
news consumption and, 121
oral cultures, memory skill and, 520
storytelling and, 71–72
uprooted populations, 11
See also Cultivation analysis;
Cultural studies; Material culture
analysis; Racial/ethnic stereotyping
Cyberspace, 554

*Daily Show With Jon Stewart,
The*, 72, 117, 123, 212
Data:
aggregated data, 40, 41, 42
bias, correction of, 48

brute data, reality construction and, 56
environmental processes data, 259–260
longitudinal data, 43, 45
message system data, 74
multilevel data, 45
popular culture artifacts, 64
unstructured data and, 54–55
Decoding. *See* Audience; Meaning;
Media exposure model
Democracy, 60–61, 113, 132, 139, 528
Dependency model, 152
Desensitization, 209–210, 460
Deterministic perspective, 14, 38, 39
Diffusion of innovations (DOI) theory,
41, 489
adopters of innovations and, 494–495, 497
adoption/diffusion, consequences of, 499
adoption, forms of, 497–498
bounded normative influence and, 493
bridges of familiarity and, 496
communication campaigns and, 492
communication, diffusion process and, 489,
491, 492–493
contingent adoption decision and, 495
critique of, 499–500
digital divide and, 495
digital media and, 492–493
discontinuous innovations, chasm concept
and, 497
history/overview of, 489–492, 490 (figure)
imitators vs. innovators and, 497
individual adopters and, 494–495
information diffusion and, 493
initiation/implementation processes and,
495–496, 499
innovation characteristics, form/likelihood
of adoption and, 496–497
innovation development process and, 494
innovativeness and, 494
Internet, diffusion curve and, 499
interpersonal communication, social
networks and, 493
lead users and, 497
local media and, 492
mass media and, 492–493
mediamorphosis and, 494
models of diffusion process and,
498–499
network adoption thresholds and, 493
news diffusion, agenda setting and, 492
opinion leaders and, 491, 493
organizational adopters and, 495
reinvention process and, 498
scientific/technical communication and, 494

social systems, diffusion process and,
493–494, 498–499
socioeconomic inequalities and, 499
technology acceptance model and, 496
technology clusters and, 497
two-step flow model and, 491–492
See also Displacement effects
Digital divide, 323–324, 495
Digital games, 455–456
affective disposition theory and, 457
appreciation dimension and, 458, 459
cognitive priming perspective and, 460
entertainment-education models and,
463–464
entertainment experiences and, 457–459
escapism and, 457
excitation transfer theory and, 460
general affective aggression model and,
460–461
health promotion games, 462
leisure-time activity of, 456
military recruitment and, 137, 462
mood management theory and, 457
players of, 456
postexposure stage and, 460–464
preexposure stage and, 456–460
research on, 456
self-determination theory and, 458–459
serious learning games and, 461–464
social cognitive theory and, 460
social/political issues and, 462
two-level model of entertainment
motivation and, 459–460,
459 (figure)
uses-and-gratifications perspective and, 457
violent content, negative effects of, 460–461
Digital media technologies, 61, 62, 79, 414,
492–493, 570
See also Digital games; Internet
Dimensional emotion theory, 200
Displacement effects, 505–506
cognitive skill development and, 511–512
displacement theory, conceptual refinement
of, 508
displacement theory, future of, 512–514
displacement theory, historic roots of, 506
functional similarity principle and, 506–507
marginal fringe activities and, 507–508
media content, relevance of, 512–513
new media, introduction of, 505
physical activity, limitations on, 510–511
physical/psychological proximity and, 508
principles of, 506–508
shared media space and, 513–514

social/communication skill development
and, 256, 509–510
time displacement and, 332, 335, 339–340
transformation concept and, 507
variables in, 509–512
See also Educational television;
Televised sports; Television
Disposition theories, 166, 239–240
Domestication, 498
Dora the Explorer, 333, 473
Drip/drench model, 15
Drive model of fear, 211
Dual-processing models, 122

Eating behaviors, 216
disordered eating, 393, 395,
396–397, 400
emotional responses and, 397
health issues and, 401–402
Internet sites and, 400
maturational issues and, 401
modeling of, 396
obesity-media relationship, 402–403,
477–478
thin-ideal internalization and, 401
See also Body image; Obesity
Ecological fallacy, 40–41
Ecological holism medium theory, 523
Educational television, 331
achievement gap and, 340
bidirectional effects of, 336
ceiling/floor effects,
narrow targeting and, 339
classroom experience,
adaptation to, 335, 336
concentration/extended
reflection, reduction in, 335
curriculum-based content and, 338, 339
displacement effects of, 511–512
early childhood and, 335–337
English limited children and, 339, 340
future directions in, 340–341
grade school and beyond, 337–340
guidelines for viewing of, 332
infant development and, 333–335
infant-oriented content, 332, 333
internal/interpersonal processes,
disruption of, 332
knowledge gap hypothesis and,
335, 339, 340
language development/use and,
333, 335–336
live interactions, learning progress
and, 334–335

negative cognitive outcomes and,
    332–333, 335
new media technology and, 341
positive cognitive outcomes of, 336–337
socioeconomic status and,
    335, 336, 337, 340
socioemotional content and, 338–339
time displacement issue and,
    332, 335, 339–340
video deficit and, 334
vocabulary development and, 335–336
youngest audience and, 332–335
See also Adolescents; Children; Television
Education-entertainment (E-E) programming,
    289–290, 318, 417–418, 463–464, 492
Elaboration likelihood model (ELM), 15, 122,
    277–278
Electric Company, The, 339
Electronic bullying, 479
Emotional contagion, 258
Emotions, 12, 14, 15, 205
    affect-based response to media, 208–209
    aggressive behavior and, 212–213
    child fright response and, 208–209
    cognitive functional model and, 211–212
    cultivation theory and, 214–215
    desensitization and, 209–210
    eating behaviors and, 216, 397
    emotion, definitions of, 206
    emotions-as-frames model and, 212
    enjoyment response, 209, 230, 240, 244
    excitation transfer theory and,
        209, 210, 427
    facial electromyography measure and, 213
    fear appeal research and, 211
    future research trends and, 214–217
    generalized aggression model and, 212–213
    intensity of emotional response
        to media, 209–210
    limitations in emotion-media effects
        research, 214–217
    measures of, 200, 201–202
    media effects paradigms and, 214–216
    media effects-related behaviors and,
        216–217
    media exposure, emotion-based outcome of,
        208–210
    media research, history of emotion in,
        206–207
    media selection, emotion as impetus
        for, 207–208
    message processing and, 210–211
    mood management/adjustment and,
        207–208

mood optimization and, 208
    moral judgments/empathy and, 209
    motivational activation and, 199–200
    negativity bias and, 196, 201–202
    new media environment and, 217
    parasocial interaction/identification
        and, 152, 230
    perceptual biases and, 216
    persuasion and, 211–212
    positivity offset and, 201–202
    research design/analysis issues and,
        213–214
    research measurement issues and, 213
    self-discrepancy theory and, 397
    self-efficacy beliefs and, 287
    social cognitive theory and, 215
    social comparison theory and, 215–216
Encoding process, 194–195
Enjoyment response, 209
    identification and, 230
    individual differences and, 240, 244–245
    televised sports and, 440–444
    See also Entertainment content
Entertainment content, 10, 16, 117, 149,
    161–162
    comedy, 164, 166
    displacement effects and, 509
    disposition theory, enjoyment
        concept and, 166
    enjoyment of, 165–167, 168, 169, 209, 230
    entertainment-education programming,
        289–290
    excitation transfer model and, 166
    hedonic motivations vs. eudaimonic
        motivations and, 168–169
    immoral behaviors, capacity for enjoyment
        and, 166
    individuals' desire/need for, 241–243
    infotainment, 72, 117, 123, 124
    interactivity component and, 170–171
    meaningfulness, gratification and, 168–169
    media entertainment research,
        future of, 169–171
    mood management model and, 163–164
    narrative depictions, enjoyment
        and, 165–166
    product placement and, 301
    technological innovation and, 169, 170–171
    tragic content and, 167, 169
    transportation/engagement experiences and,
        167–168
    two-level model of entertainment
        motivation and, 459–460, 459 (figure)
    uses and gratification model and, 162–163

viewer mobility and, 171
See also Digital games;
    Parasocial interaction/identification;
    Televised sports
Entertainment-education (E-E) programming,
    289–290, 318, 417–418, 463–464, 492
Entertainment Software Association, 170
Entertainment Tracking System, 135
Espionage Act of 1917, 10
Ethnic stereotypes. *See* Racial/ethnic
    stereotyping
Ethnography, 54–55
    constructed reality and, 55–56
    contemporary rediscovery of, 61–62
    cross-cultural encounters and, 62
    family studies and, 57–58
    native viewpoint and, 55
    social action approach and, 57
    telenovelas and, 61
    unstructured data and, 54, 55
    verstehen/empathetic understanding and, 55
    See also Qualitative methods
Eudaimonic motivations, 168–169, 208
Excitation transfer theory, 13, 166,
    209, 210, 368–369, 427, 460
Expectancy-value image, 270
Experimental research designs, 38, 43, 46,
    57, 398
Exposure to messages, 21
    attention and, 21–22
    automatic attention, 21–22
    consciousness, continuum of, 22
    conscious/unconscious exposure, 23
    construct validity and, 46–47
    controlled attention and, 21, 22
    definition of, 22
    new media age, exposure measures and,
        571–572
    selective exposure hypothesis, 272
    stereotype formation and, 378–380
    See also Audiences; Media exposure model
Extended parallel process model (EPPM),
    45, 211, 316–317

Face validity, 25
Facebook, 571
Facial electromyography (EMG), 200, 213
Fallacy of composition, 40
Fallacy of confusing cause and effect, 42–43
Fallacy of ignoring the future, 43
Fallacy of ignoring the past, 43
Fallacy of nonreciprocal causation, 45
Fallacy of the secular trend, 43
Fallacy of the wrong causal process, 44–45

Fallacy of the wrong level, 41
Fallacy of the wrong timing, 44
Family communication patterns (FCP),
    254, 259
Family groups, 11
    ethnographic study of, 57–58
    family environment, media use and, 256
    family tensions, household television
        viewing and, 256–257
    instructional intervention technique
        and, 350–351
    media selection/use and, 252–253
    obesity and, 402–403
    parental mediation, media selection and,
        252, 254, 260, 338, 370, 475–476
    quasi-democratic process and, 253
    restrictive intervention technique and,
        349–350
    sedentary behaviors and, 259
    social coviewing technique and, 350, 510
    televised sports and, 446
    See also Adolescents; Children;
        Displacement effects; Educational
        television; Social environment
Fandom, 229, 395, 447
Fear appeal research, 211
    decision making, fear effects on, 211
    drive model and, 211
    extended parallel process model and, 211
    parallel processing model and, 211
    persuasive outcomes and, 211
    protection motivation theory and, 211
    See also Emotions
Fear-of-victimization effect, 361–362, 364
Federal Communications
    Commission (FCC), 331
*Federal Communications
    Commission v. Pacifica* (1978), 133
Fieldwork methods, 54, 58, 62
    textual analysis, Internet use and, 63
    See also Qualitative methods
Film. *See* Movies
Filtering task, 27, 28 (table), 30 (table)
5 A Day for Better Health Program, 321–322
Five-factor model of personality, 245
Flow, 26, 167
Focus group interviews, 55, 56, 60
Forethought, 285
Framing effects, 44, 83
    adoption/reinvention of
        innovations and, 498
    agenda setting and, 83–84
    audience cognitions and, 90–91
    cognitive process outcomes and, 91

context-specific vs. context-transcendent frames, 88
contextual moderators and, 91, 94
counterframes, 91
cross-frame shifts and, 89–90
cues and, 94
definition of, 85–86
ethical frames, 88–89
experimental orientation, precision vs. realism approaches and, 87–88
frame competition and, 89
framing effects research examples, 88–89
free speech frame, 89
future research topics on, 93–95
hybrid research designs/blended approaches and, 89–90
immigration issues and, 187
issue frame, 89
message processing model and, 92–93, 92 (figure), 94
moderators of, 90–91
muted framing effects and, 89
news reporting and, 114, 117, 118–119
precision-specific research example, 88
precision-transcendent research example, 88–89
priming process and, 86
public aid frame, 88, 91
public order values frame, 89
realism-specific research example, 89
realism-transcendent research example, 89
research approaches to, 86–90
source credibility and, 91
stereotype formation and, 379
strategy frame, 89
strict work frame, 88, 91
See also Agenda setting model; Priming effects
Freedom of the press, 10
Free speech issue, 89, 528
French Revolution, 10
Functional similarity principle, 506–507

Games:
America's Army recruiting game, 137, 462
body images and, 400
health promotion, self-efficacy and, 316
health-related video games, 293, 462
massively multiplayer online role-playing games, 371
serious learning games, 461–464

video games, 16, 27, 169, 181, 182, 233, 364, 365, 400, 569–570
See also Digital games
Gender differences:
aggressive response to media violence and, 367–368
interpretive function and, 244
sexual objectification and, 412–413
See also Body image; Individual differences; Sexual media messages
General affective aggression model (GAAM), 182–183, 460–461
General aggression model (GAM), 212–213
General Social Survey (GSS), 73, 80
Generation M, 135
Geo-ethnic media, 541
Ghostwriter, 337
Globalization, 61
cultivation analysis and, 80
Internet reach and, 565
storytelling and, 71–72
Global positioning systems (GPS), 522
Glocalization, 80
Golden Age of media effects research, 13
Google News, 555
Google Scholar database, 100
Gradual penetration diffusion model, 498
Granger causality test, 43
Gratification:
entertainment content and, 168–169, 171
See also Uses and gratifications model
Grey's Anatomy, 72
Group dynamics, 107
Groups:
ecological fallacy and, 40–41
fallacy of composition and, 40
group-level factors, 40–41, 42
two-step flow model and, 41
See also Cultures; Family groups; Social environment; Social systems
Gulf War coverage, 184, 185, 186
Gun control persuasion, 276

Health belief model (HBM), 316
Health communication models, 15
expectancy-value image and, 270
health campaigns and, 290, 292, 314–315, 321–322
health-related video games, 293
media literacy interventions and, 347, 418
parasocial relationships and, 227
sexual health interventions, 416–418
smoking messages, 107, 272, 275, 288

structural influence model, 320, 320 (figure)
See also Health impacts; Population health
Health impacts, 12
emotions, eating behaviors and, 216
media use patterns and, 15–16
physical activity limitations, 510–511
sedentary behaviors, media use and,
258–259
thin-body ideal and, 401–402
transtheoretical model of
health behavior and, 275
See also Obesity; Physiological effects;
Population health
Hedonistic concerns, 163, 164, 168, 207, 208
Heuristic-systematic model, 122
Horror films, 163, 207, 241, 242, 243
Hostility, 16
Human agency. *See* Agency concept
Humor, 164, 166, 212
Hydraulic model of political priming,
185–186
Hypermasculinity, 244, 246
Hypermediated environments, 522–523, 528
See also Communication technologies
effects; Internet; Technology
Hypertextuality, 548, 565
Hypocrisy induction, 272
Hypodermic needle/magic bullet models,
11, 21, 121, 237

I-thou dialectic, 58
Ideal body. *See* Body image
Identification theory, 229
See also Parasocial interaction/identification
Immersive virtual environment
technology (IVET), 293
Implicit Association Test (IAT), 386–387
Individual agency, 284
Individual-differences, 12, 20, 237–238
aggressive predisposition and, 212–213,
242–243, 245–246
arousal/sensation, search for,
241–242, 245, 247, 248
cognition need, complex approaches to
media and, 247
cognitive associative networks and,
246–247, 248
cognitive gender schemata, 244
comfort/relaxation, search for, 242
cultivation effects and, 41
disposition theories, media
evaluation/interpretation and, 239–240
ecological fallacy and, 40–41
effects research and, 245–248

enjoyment, valenced assessment and,
244–245
entertainment needs and, 241–243
extraversion, 242, 245
factors in, 241
fallacy of composition and, 40
future research topics in, 248–249
group-level properties and, 40–41, 42
hypermasculinity, 244, 246
interpretive assessment and, 243–244, 247
magic bullet/hypodermic needle
models and, 237
meaning construction process and, 22–23
media preferences/selection and, 238–239,
243, 248
memory/recall functions and, 246–248
neuroticism, soothing media and,
242, 245, 246, 247
new technologies, emergence of, 248
psychoticism, transgressive media
and, 243, 246
schema activation and, 93, 244, 246–247
script theory and, 240–241, 247
theoretical foundations of, 238–241, 248
two-step flow model and, 41
uses and gratifications model and, 152–153,
163, 238–239, 241, 244–245
validation, search for, 242–243
See also Audiences
Industrialization, 11
Industrial Revolution, 132
Infinity Factory, 339, 340
Influence. *See* Media effects; Presumed media
influence; Third-person perception (TPP)
Information content, 10, 16
dual-processing models of information
processing, 122
framing and, 85–86
judgmental heuristics, information
processing and, 122
media literacy intervention and, 348
message processing model and, 92–93, 92
(figure)
online vs. memory-based news processing,
122–123
preference for, 242
structural information biases, 114–115
See also Limited capacity model
of motivated mediated message
processing (LC4MP); Meaning;
Media exposure model
Information introduced (II) measure, 201
Information monopolies, 521, 523, 528
Information societies, 16, 528

Information superhighway, 554
Infotainment programs, 72, 117, 123, 124, 318, 417–418
Innovations, 1, 2
    adopters of, 494–495
    characteristics of, 496–497
    innovation development process, 494
    mediamorphosis, 494
    movable type, printed word and, 9–10, 520–521
    See also Diffusion of innovations (DOI) theory; Technology
Inoculation theory, 348
Instant messaging (IM), 479
Institute for Propaganda Analysis (IPA), 11
Institutional process analysis, 70, 71
    collective consciousness and, 78
    See also Corporations
Instructional intervention technique, 350–351
Integrated model of behavior change, 316
Intentionality, 285
    behavior change and, 316
    risky behaviors, imitation of, 291
    unintended media effects, 287–289
    See also Agency; Attitude theories; Social cognitive theory; Voluntary action theories
Interactivity effects research, 302
    attitudinal outcomes and, 304–305
    cognitive costs of interactivity, 304
    dyads of interactivity, 303
    experiential perspective and, 303–304, 305
    future topics for, 305–306
    implementation of interactivity, mechanisms of, 305–306
    interactivity, definition of, 303–304
    need for cognition and, 302
    persuasion and, 305
    structural perspective and, 303, 304
    two-way communication/control and, 303, 306
    See also Advertising research
International Communication Association, 2
Internet, 16, 561–562
    adolescent online communication and, 478–479
    advertising and, 79, 400, 476–477, 549
    agenda setting model and, 567–569
    audience selectivity/control and, 563–564, 565, 570
    blogs, 63, 415, 522, 563, 566, 568
    body ideals on, 400
    bullying and, 479
    chat rooms and, 63, 137, 387, 415, 446

    communication campaigns and, 571
    context of media experiences and, 566
    cultivation theory and, 569–570
    diffusion of innovations and, 499
    digital downloading and, 79
    displacement effects and, 510
    diversion/relaxation and, 242
    diversity of content/viewpoints and, 563, 571
    eating disorders and, 400
    emotions, role of, 217
    entertainment content and, 170
    exposure to media content, measurement of, 571–572
    global reach of, 565, 566
    Google Scholar database, 100
    hypermediation age and, 522–523, 528, 564
    hypertextuality and, 565
    individualized/tailored messages and, 293, 564
    information exchange, trust and, 119
    instant messaging and, 479
    interactivity and, 302, 306, 563, 570
    interpersonal interaction and, 153–154
    market testing and, 138
    massively multiplayer online role-playing games, 371
    media convergence and, 564
    media dependency and, 154–155
    message structure and, 564–565
    military recruitment tools, 137, 462
    mood management theory, surfing behavior and, 170
    new media effects theories and, 566–571
    online news consumption, 116, 124
    online news information processing, 122–123
    personalized media experience and, 564
    pornography on, 416
    portability of new media and, 565–566
    public postings, observation of, 63
    resonance factor and, 569
    sexual harassment and, 416
    sexual health sites, 415–416
    social connectivity and, 566, 570
    social networking sites, 217, 415, 568, 571
    spiral of silence theory and, 570–571
    streaming content, 78, 170
    television viewing and, 79
    text messaging, 416
    traditional vs. new media and, 562–566, 572–573

user-controlled on-demand media,
62–63, 170, 564
user-generated content on, 217, 306
virtual communities and, 63
virtual worlds, 27, 63, 169, 371, 522, 524
YouTube, 217, 387, 400, 563, 566
See also Communication technologies
effects; Computer-mediated
communication (CMC); Technology
Interpersonal interaction. *See* Diffusion of
innovations (DOI) theory; Internet;
Parasocial interaction/identification;
Social networks; Social systems
Interpretation. *See* Audiences; Individual
differences; Meaning; Message
interpretation process (MIP) model
Interview methods, 56, 59–60, 64
Isolation, 11
Issue-attention cycle, 44

Judgment:
judgmental heuristics, 122
moral judgment, 240
realism judgments, 424–425, 428–429
retrospective judgments, 429
See also Social judgment;
Social judgment theory

Kaiser Family Foundation, 513
KISS (keep it simple, stupid), 306
Knowledge gap, 41
diffusion of innovations and, 499
educational television and, 335, 339, 340
news reporting and, 116
population health, media influences on,
319–320
See also Cognitive effects
Knowledge monopolies, 521, 523, 528

Limited capacity model of motivated
mediated message processing (LC4MP),
122, 193–194
appetitive system activation
and, 196, 197, 200
assumption of, 194
aversive system activation
and, 196–197, 200
cognitive effort and, 199
cognitive overload and, 197–198
controlled resource allocation and, 195
emotion, message processing and, 210–211
emotions, measures of, 200
encoding, assessment of, 200
encoding process and, 194–195, 196, 197

future directions of, 202
human motivated information processing
system and, 194–198, 202, 210–211
information introduced measure and, 201
information processing, definition of, 195
media types and, 198
media user, measurement of, 201–202
message structure/content,
measurement of, 201
motivational activation, emotional
experience and, 199–200
motivationally relevant stimuli
and, 196–197, 201
orienting-eliciting structural features
measure and, 201
orienting response, automatic
resource allocation and, 195–196
phasic analysis of heart rate and, 199
resource allocation and, 195–196,
197, 198–199, 210
retrieval, assessment of, 200
retrieval of information and, 195
retrospective evaluations and, 429
secondary task reaction time assessment
method and, 199
storage, assessment of, 200
storage of information and, 195
variables in, 198–202
Limited effects model, 12, 20
news, political persuasion and, 115–116
priming and, 188
LinkedIn, 571
Literacy:
concentrated attention to messages and, 24
early history of, 9–10
See also Media literacy research
Logographic language processing, 307
Longitudinal surveys, 398–399

Magic bullet/hypodermic needle models,
11, 20, 121, 237
Magic School Bus, The, 337, 339
Mainstreaming pattern, 75–77, 76 (figure)
Mainstream media, 541, 568
Marketing:
active audiences and, 137
four "Ps" of, 317
media-obesity relationship
and, 402–403
new technologies/genres, marketing
techniques and, 134–135
psychographic profiles and, 137–138
social marketing methods, 317–318
symbolic world and, 72

youth audience and, 476–477
See also Advertising; Advertising research
Mass behavior concept, 11
Mass communication, 10
   academic discipline of, 12
   communication revolution and, 16
   framing process and, 86
   institutional/cultural qualities of, 71
   mediamorphosis and, 494
   qualitative research methods and, 56–57
   traditional functions of, 16
   See also Communication technologies
         effects; Internet; Mass media; Media
         effects; Media effects research; Medium
         theory; Social environment
Mass media:
   active audience,
         self-determination/influence of, 12
   audiences, historic approach to, 19–21
   audience vulnerability, mass behavior
         concept and, 11
   broadcast personalities, illusionary
         relationships and, 152
   bullet/hypodermic needle
         theories and, 11, 20
   functions of, 149
   future of, 16
   meaning construction process and, 22–23
   medium-specific effects of, 13
   moral panics and, 22, 131
   subversive messages, 11
   sustainer/supporter role of, 12
   See also Audiences; Mass communication;
         Media effects; Social environment
Massively multiplayer online role-playing
      games (MMORPGs), 371
Mastery experience, 286, 294
Material culture analysis, 56
Meaning:
   decoding process, closed/open codes and,
         27–29
   eudaimonic motivations, 168–169
   faulty meaning, 22
   locus of, 22
   meaning assessment task, 27–29
   meaning construction and,
         28 (table), 29, 31, 54, 121
   meaning matching and, 28 (table), 29, 31
   news reporting, meaning
         construction and, 121
   symbolic meaning, 285
   See also Audiences; Individual differences
Measurement approaches, 15
Media ecology, 518

Media effects, 1–3
   attitudinal effects, 12, 13–14, 15
   audience vulnerability, mass behavior
         concept and, 11
   behavioral effects, 12, 13, 15
   bullet/hypodermic needle theories of, 11
   change and, 12
   cognitive effects, 12, 14, 15
   communication effects, historic
         interest in, 9–11
   conceptualizations of, 13–16
   cultivation hypothesis and, 15
   definition of, 4, 13–14
   drip/drench model of, 15
   dynamic process of, 42–44
   early scientific study of, 11–12
   emotional effects, 12, 14, 15
   health communication models and, 15
   holistic models of, 15
   intended media effects, 289–290
   issue-attention cycle and, 44
   limited effect model and, 12, 20
   media reception theory and, 15
   mediating/mitigating factors in, 15
   medium-specific effects, 13
   moderate-to-powerful effects model,
         13, 15–16
   multilevel nature of, 39–42
   opinion leaders, message interpretation
         and, 12, 20
   physiological effects, 12, 14, 15
   powerful effects model and, 11, 12
   probabilistic-causality perspective and, 14
   process/precursors of effects and, 15, 42–44
   social/psychological impact, 10, 11
   stalactite/stalagmite model of, 15
   stimulus-response models and, 10
   time element in, 42–44
   two-step flow model and, 20, 41, 120, 491
   unintended media effects, 287–289
   written word, ascendancy of, 9–10
   written word, censorship/suppression of, 10
   See also Audiences; Causation;
         Communication technologies effects;
         Mass communication; Mass media;
         Media effects research; Media exposure
         model; Medium theory; Presumed
         media influence; Quantitative methods
Media effects research, 1
   academe, structural issues within, 2
   active audience,
         self-determination/influence of, 12
   aggregated research data, 15
   causal inference, challenges to, 39–48

causation/explanation, controlled
    experiments and, 38–39
conceptual issues in, 2
conceptualizations of media effects
    and, 13–16
early scientific research, 11–12
Golden Age of, 13
limited effects model and, 12, 20
mass behavior, concept of, 11
mass communication, discipline of, 12–13
medium/culture-specific effects, 13
methodology of, 2
moderate-to-powerful effects model and, 13
modern media study and, 2–3
opinion leaders, message
    interpretation and, 12, 20
phenomenistic approach to, 12
powerful effects model and, 11, 12
problem-based research and, 2
process, illumination of, 2
propaganda analysis and, 11
public opinion research, 11
recent trends in, 15–16
reorientation of, 2, 12–13
sense extension theory, 13
technological/content innovations and, 2
theoretical foundations of, 1–2
See also Mass media; Media effects;
    Qualitative methods; Quantitative
    methods
Media exposure model,
    23–24, 29, 30 (table)
attentional state and, 24–25, 31
automatic processing state and, 25–26, 31
cognitive allocations,
    exposure states and, 30–31
construct validity and, 46–47
cultivation hypothesis and, 25–26
decoding process, closed/open
    codes and, 27–29, 58
exposure experiences, measurement of, 31
exposure experiences,
    qualitative differences in, 24
exposure states and, 24–27, 29–30,
    30 (table)
exposure tasks and, 27–29
filtering task and,
    27, 28 (table), 30 (table)
meaning assessment task and, 27–29,
    28 (table), 30 (table), 31
meaning construction process and, 29, 31
meaning matching process and, 29, 31
self-reflexive state and, 27
suspension of disbelief and, 26

transported state and, 26–27
See also Audiences;
    Exposure to messages; Media effects
Media literacy research, 345
content area research and, 347–348
critique of, 351–353
formal interventions, media literacy skills
    development and, 347–349
information processing and, 348
inoculation theory and, 348
instructional intervention and, 350–351
intervention construction, mass media
    effects literature and, 352–353
intervention research assumptions, 346
intervention research design
    characteristics, 346
literacy intervention studies,
    commonalities among, 346
mapping, media effects process/media
    literacy intervention and, 352
media literacy, conceptualization
    of, 345–346
mitigation processes research, 348–349
natural interventions and, 349–351
new media technologies and, 354
persuasion theories and, 348–349
restrictive intervention and, 349–350
social cognition framework and, 349
social coviewing technique, 350
theoretical foundation,
    shortcomings in, 351–352
violent media messages and, 347
Media multitasking, 470
Media realism, 423–424
audience age and, 426
correlational analyses of, 427–429
engaged processing and, 430
evaluation mechanisms for, 429–431
experimental studies of, 426–427
factuality and, 424, 430, 431
future research directions in, 433–434
genres and, 425–426, 430, 431
narrative realism, evaluations of, 430–431
new media technology and, 434
online judgments and, 429–430
perceived media realism, definition of,
    424–426
perceived realism, measurement of, 425
perceived realism, media effects and,
    426–429
realism judgment and, 424–425, 428–429
realism perceptions,
    correlates of, 425–426
reality television and, 431–432

real-world similarity and, 424–425,
    426, 427–428
retrospective judgments and, 429
transported state and, 430
uses-and-gratifications perspective and, 426
Media reception theory, 15
Media system dependency (MSD) theory, 531
  challenges to, 539–541
  communication infrastructure
      theory and, 541–543
  individuals and, 534–536,
      535 (figure, table)
  interpersonal networks and, 536, 539
  levels of analysis, bridges between, 539
  media system dependency relations,
      dimensions of, 537–539
  media system dependency relationship
      concept and, 532–533
  1970s theory, 533–534
  1980s theory, 534–537
  1990s theory, 537–539, 538 (figure)
  origins of, 531–532, 533
  social environment, media system activity
      and, 536–537
  structural dependency relations and, 537
Media violence, 12, 16
  aggressive predispositions and,
      212–213, 242–243, 246
  antisocial behavior, generalized
      aggression model and, 212–213
  behavior disordered youth and, 243
  consumption rationale for, 163
  hypermasculinity and, 244, 246
  identification with, 233
  individuals' need for, 241–242
  media literacy interventions and, 347
  priming effects and, 181–182
  probabilistic-causality perspective and, 14
  symbolic violence, power/social
      control and, 75
  validation, search for, 242–243
  verbal aggression/argumentativeness
      and, 243
  See also Media violence effects; Violence
Media violence effects, 361–362
  aggregated long-term effects, 363
  aggressive responses, mechanisms of,
      368–370
  aggressor effect, 361, 362–364, 362 (figure)
  arousal, excitation transfer and, 368–369
  availability heuristic and, 364
  classical conditioning, stimulus
      generalization and, 369
  conscience-numbing effect, 362, 364–365

cross-media effects, 363
denial of, 365–366, 366 (figure)
desensitization effect, 364, 369–370
emotional processes,
    activation/desensitization of, 369–370
empathy, lack of, 364, 365
fear-of-victimization effect, 361–362, 364
future directions for, 371
gender differences in aggression and,
    367–368
long-term effects, 369–370
mimicry, mirror neurons and, 368
moderators of, 367–368
new media technology and, 371
observational learning and, 369
parent education and, 370
priming, associative networks and, 368
reduction of, 370, 371
serious aggressive behavior and, 363–364
short-term effects, 368–369
third-person effect and, 365
violent video games and, 364, 365
See also Media violence; Violence
Mediamorphosis, 494
Mediated environments, 522–523
  See also Computer-mediated
      communication (CMC); Internet
Mediated relationships. *See* Parasocial
    interaction/identification
Mediation relationship, 45–46, 350–351
Medium theory, 517–518
  academic disciplines, print-inspired
      separations between, 521
  critiques/limitations of, 527–528
  ecological holism medium theory, 523
  electronic media effects and,
      521, 522–523, 525
  feminist research, gender-role topics and,
      526–527
  history of, 520–523
  hypermediated environments and,
      522–523, 528
  knowledge monopolies and, 521, 523
  materialtheorie argument and, 521
  media ecology field and, 518
  medium characteristics and, 518–520,
      524–525
  medium as message and, 521–522
  micro-level vs. macro-level
      medium theory, 523–527
  natural environments/built environments,
      relationships between, 521
  political style, electronic
      media and, 525

printed word and, 517–518,
520–521, 522, 523, 528
role-system medium theory, 523, 525, 528
spoken vs. written word and, 520, 523, 524
subgenres of, 523
technological determinism, human agency
and, 527
television, introduction of, 521
television programming/viewing and,
525–527
time-biased vs. space-biased media and, 523
transformational role, communication
media and, 521, 523
Memory:
advertising complexity and, 306
cued recall measures, 200
early childhood television viewing and, 333
encoded information, storage of, 195, 200,
246–247
free recall techniques, 200
memory-based news processing, 122–123
multiple modalities and, 548–549
network models of, 184
oral cultures and, 520
perceived realism, measurement of, 425
phonological loop, 307
product placement and, 301–302
retrieval of information,
195, 200, 247
scripts and, 240
stereotype priming model and, 187
stereotype representation and, 378
vicarious learning and, 285
Mental health, 16
Mental models, 379–380
Message interpretation process (MIP) model,
349, 352
Message processing model, 92–93, 92 (figure)
Message processing. *See* Limited capacity
model of motivated mediated message
processing (LC4MP); Message
interpretation process (MIP) model;
Message processing model
Message system analysis, 70–71, 72
content, dimensions of, 73
storytelling, symbolic functions in, 73
See also Cultivation analysis
Meta-analysis, 15
Metacontrol concept, 498
Mimicry, 368
Mirror neurons, 368
Miss America Pageants, 394
Mister Rogers' Neighborhood, 336, 337
Mobile network society, 16, 62, 565

Mobile telephones, 371, 495, 496, 498,
522, 555
Moderate-to-powerful media effects,
13, 15–16
Monopolization, 116, 521, 523, 528
Mood adjustment theory, 208
Mood management model, 15
absorbing potential and, 163
adjustment of mood and, 164
arousing potential of media and, 163
behavioral affinity and, 163, 164
calming content and, 164
comedies, viewing of, 164
entertainment selection and, 163–164
gender differences, entertainment
selections and, 164
hedonic valence and, 163
hedonistic concerns and, 163, 164,
207, 208
media characteristics and, 163–164
musical selections and, 164
negative mood states and, 163–164,
169, 208
refinements of, 164
See also Emotions;
Entertainment content
Mood management theory (MMT), 207–208
Moral judgment, 240
Moral panics, 22, 131
Motion Picture Association of America, 370
Motion pictures. *See* Movies
Motivated mediated message processing.
See Limited capacity model of motivated
mediated message processing (LC4MP)
Motivational Activation Measure
(MAM), 201
Movable type, 9–10, 520–521
MoveOn.org, 568
Movies, 12
aggressive predispositions and, 246
horror films, 163, 207, 241, 242, 243
interactivity and, 171
materialtheorie argument and, 521
potential to corrupt and, 133–134
rating system for, 370
selection of, peer influence and, 252
suspense films, 166
verbal aggression/argumentativeness
and, 243
See also Parasocial
interaction/identification
MTV, 417
Multiple Affective Adjective Checklist-Revised
(MAAX-R), 213

National Association for Media Literacy
    Education (NAMLE), 418
National Campaign to Prevent Teen
    and Unplanned Pregnancy,
    411, 415, 417, 418
National Cancer Institute (NCI), 322
National Household Education Survey, 336
National Institutes of Health, 413
National Television Violence Study, 361
Native viewpoint, 55
Need for cognition (NFC), 304
Neoassociationistic model, 181–182
Network society, 16, 20, 21, 62, 565
Neuroticism, 242
News media:
    alternative information sources,
        72, 117, 123, 124
    controversy and, 85
    issue-attention cycle and, 44
    learning from news, news media differences
        and, 116–117
    newscasters, parasocial
        relationships with, 153
    propaganda, audience perceptions and, 11
    selective exposure and, 124
    spiral of silence theory and, 107
    traditional media functions and, 16
    See also Agenda setting model;
        Framing; Newspapers;
        News reporting; Print media
Newspapers, 9, 10
    censorship/suppression of, 10
    freedom of the press, 10
    motives for reading, 149
    newly literate publics and, 133
    online versions of, 116, 124
    public opinion and, 10
    sensationalized reporting and, 10
    trust and, 119
    See also News media;
        News reporting; Print media
News reporting, 113–114
    agenda setting effect and, 117–118, 492
    audience, conceptualization of, 121
    biases in the news, 114–115
    canalization and, 116
    compensatory principal and, 121–122
    contemporary news environment and,
        123–124
    dual-processing models of information
        processing and, 122
    fear of victimization and, 364
    framing effect and, 114, 117, 118–119
    Gulf War coverage, 184, 185, 186

impact of, 115–120, 120
individual neuroticism, recall of news
    stories and, 247
infotainment and, 72, 117, 123, 124
Israeli settlements, 107
issues, perceptions of, 117–119
judgmental heuristics, information
    processing and, 122
knowledge gaps and, 116
Ku Klux Klan activity, 89
learning from news coverage, 116–117, 120
limited capacity theory and, 122
limited effects model and, 115–116
mass communication/interpersonal
    communication, interplay of, 120
monopolization and, 116
news construction, phenomena in, 114
news-politics interactions, research
    on, 120–123
news processing, theoretical approaches to,
    121–123
objectivity, normalization and, 115
online vs. memory-based processing and,
    122–123
opinion leaders, two-step flow and, 120
Philadelphia mayoral election, 89
political coverage, priming effects and,
    183–186
political engagement goal and, 119
political partisan bias and, 114, 123
political persuasion and, 115–116
posttraumatic stress disorder and, 474
priming effect and, 118
public opinion, perceived climate of, 119
racial attitudes and, 244
racial stereotypes and, 187
soft news outlets and, 117
story features and, 117
structural information biases and, 114–115
supplementation and, 116
trust in news and, 119, 123
various media, learning from, 116–117
videomalaise hypothesis and, 119
violence, reporting of, 365–366,
    366 (figure)
welfare reform, 88
See also News media; Newspapers
New York Society for the Suppression of
    Vice, 133
Nielsen/NetRatings reports, 79
Nintendo Wii, 293, 294
Norms, 40, 100
    bounded normative influence, 493
    compliance reactions, 107

defiance reactions, 107–108
in-group/out-group norms, 102
normative beliefs, behavior change and, 316
normative influence and, 107–108
spiral of silence theory and, 107
Novel stimuli. *See* Sensation need

Obesity, 16, 258, 319
body mass index, 394, 477
childhood obesity, 402–403, 477–478
physical activity, limitations on, 510–511
Observational learning. *See* Vicarious learning
Opinion leaders, 12, 20, 115, 120, 491, 493
Oral histories, 60
Organizations. *See* Corporations
Orienting-eliciting structural features (OESF)
measure, 201

Parallel processing mode (PPM), 211
Parasocial interaction/identification,
152, 153, 223–224
audience activity and, 225–226
automatic/learned responses and, 228
capture, media content and, 225
computer-mediated communication,
presence and, 233
conceptual issues in, 227–228
current research findings on, 226–227
deficits in social contacts and, 225
emotional responses to media and, 230
enjoyment of media consumption and, 230
fandom and, 229
future research topics in, 228–229, 233
identification, audience experience of,
229–231, 232
identification, definition of, 232
identification, theoretical
foundations of, 229
inside jokes, role of, 227
intimacy at a distance and, 225, 227–228
measurement of, 231–232
media characters, identification with,
229–231
media production, identification and, 231
media reception/interpretation,
identification and, 230–231
merging identities and, 230
parasocial interaction, definition of, 227
persuasion and, 227
repeated pattern of interaction and, 227
social relationships, comparison
with, 226–227
symbolic interactionism and, 224
theoretical foundation of, 224–226

trust, development of, 224
uses and gratifications tradition and, 225
wishful identification and, 231, 232
Parents Television Council, 135
Parent-Teachers Association, 15
Participant observation, 56
future of, 64
media ethnography and, 56–58
social action approach and, 57
See also Ethnography
Passive audiences, 20, 22, 23, 47, 77, 132
Pay-per-view (PPV), 78
Payne Fund studies, 12, 56, 133
Peer influences, 11, 252, 253–254, 497
Perceptions. *See* Audience; News reporting;
Perceptual biases; Presumed media
influence; Third-person perception (TPP)
Perceptual biases, 216
Personality traits. *See* Individual differences
Persuasion theories, 269–270
adaptation of persuasive messages and, 278
attitude change strategies and, 270
attitude theories and, 270–273
belief-based attitude models, 270
cognitive dissonance theory and, 271–273
elaboration likelihood model and, 277–278
expectancy-value image and, 270
functional models of attitude and, 271
media literacy interventions and, 348–349
new communication technologies and, 278
persuasion process theories, 276–278
protection motivation theory and, 274–275
selective exposure hypothesis and, 272
social judgment theory and, 276–277
stage models of behavioral change and,
275–276
theory of planned behavior and, 274
theory of reasoned action and, 273–274
voluntary action theories and, 273–276
See also Persuasive messages
Persuasive messages, 71, 78
adaptation of, 278
advertising research and, 302, 309
advocacy messages, 269, 276–277
attitude-behavior link and, 109
cognitive functional model and,
211–212
contrast vs. assimilation effects and, 276
dual-processing models and, 122
emotion and, 211–212
fear appeal research and, 211
fear effects and, 211
humor and, 212
interactivity and, 305

news reporting, compensatory principal
    and, 121–122
other-than-fear emotions and, 211–212
parasocial relationships and, 227
political persuasion, 115–116
product placement and, 301
public service content, 269
self-efficacy beliefs, verbal
    persuasion and, 286–287
See also Persuasion theories
Phasic analysis of heart rate, 199
Phenomenistic approach, 12, 148–149
Phonetic symbolism, 307–308
Phonological loop, 307, 308
Physical activity, 258–259, 510–511
Physiological effects, 12, 14, 15
    emotions, eating behaviors and, 216
    media use patterns and, 15–16
    physiological state,
        self-efficacy beliefs and, 287, 294
    sedentary behaviors and, 258–259
    televised sports and, 445
    See also Health impacts; Obesity
Planned behavior. *See* Theory of planned
    behavior (TPB)
Playboy magazine, 394
Playstation, 456
Podcasts, 63
Policy. *See* Public policy
Politics, 113, 114
    agenda setting effect and, 117–118
    alternative sources of
        information on, 123
    campaign messages, audience engagement
        with, 278
    contemporary news environment and,
        123–124
    dual-processing model of information
        processing and, 122
    hydraulic model of political priming,
        185–186
    limited capacity theory, simplifying
        heuristics and, 122
    mass communication/interpersonal
        communication, interplay of, 120
    media content, communicatory utility and,
        255–256
    news processing, theoretical approaches
        to, 121–123
    news reporting, political partisan bias, 114
    online vs. memory-based processing and,
        122–123
    political coverage, priming effects and,
        183–186

political engagement, journalistic practice
    and, 119
political information, diffusion of, 116
political persuasion, news content and,
    115–116
race-related policy reasoning and, 385–386
Popular culture, 56, 64, 134–135
Population health, 313–314
    agenda-setting theory and, 319
    cancer prevention, 316, 318, 321–322
    chronic disease prevention,
        314–315, 319, 322
    communication inequalities and, 320–321
    cultivation theory and, 319
    entertainment-education
        programming and, 318
    extended parallel process model
        and, 316–317
    5 A Day for Better Health Program,
        321–322
    health belief model and, 316
    health-media relationship, historical context
        of, 314–315
    health/media studies, methodological
        challenges in, 322–323
    HIV/AIDS programs, 316, 318
    hygiene promotion, 314
    immunization promotion, 314, 318
    individual health, social/structural media
        effects on, 318–321
    individual-level theoretical frameworks,
        315–318
    knowledge gap hypothesis and, 319–320
    low-fat milk campaign, 316
    message design, individuals/groups and,
        317–318
    multipronged/multifaceted campaigns, 321
    new media environments, impact
        of, 323–324
    public health media campaigns,
        314–315, 321–322
    Radio Diaries program and, 318
    smoking messaging and,
        107, 272, 275, 288, 317, 321
    social cognitive theory, agentic perspective
        and, 315–316
    social determinants of health and, 318–321
    social epidemiological approach and, 319
    social marketing methods and, 317–318
    structural influence model of health
        communication, 320, 320 (figure)
    tailored communication programs and, 317
    teen pregnancy, 318, 410–411, 415
    theory of reasoned action and, 316

transtheoretical model and, 317
truth® campaign, 321
  See also Health communication models;
    Health impacts; Obesity
Pornography, 16, 241, 414, 416
Positive and Negative
  Affect Scale (PANAS), 213
Post Office moralist, 133
Power distribution, 53–54
  media selection/use and, 252
  symbolic violence,
    power/social control and, 75
  See also Media system
    dependency (MSD) theory
Powerful effects model, 11, 12
Press. *See* Agenda setting model; Framing;
  News media; Newspapers; News
  reporting; Print media
Presumed media influence, 99
  behavioral reactions, factors in, 108
  behavioral response to, 104–108
  cognitive explanations for, 102–104
  compliance reactions to, 107
  coordination reactions to, 105–106
  defiance reactions to, 107–108
  motivational explanations
    for, 100–102, 103–104
  normative influence and, 107–108
  perceptions of media impact,
    reactions to, 99–100
  perceptions of media influence,
    explanations of, 100–104
  prevention reactions to, 105
  social norms, enforcement of, 100
  third-person effects and, 100–104
  See also Third-person perception (TPP)
Priming effects, 44, 84, 86, 177–178
  aggression priming, limitations/future
    directions for, 182–183
  aggression priming models
    and, 181–183, 368
  ambiguous situations and, 179, 180
  behavior data and, 180, 181–182
  characteristics of, 179–180
  chronically accessible concepts and, 180
  cognitive associative networks
    and, 246–247
  cognitive origins of priming,
    178, 181–182
  concepts at rest, accessibility of, 179–180
  construct accessibility/applicability and, 118
  deliberative processing and, 184–185
  dissipation over time of, 179, 188
  future research trends in, 189

general affective aggression model and,
    182–183
hydraulic model of political priming and,
    185–186
large effects, potential for, 188
limited effects model and, 188
measurement of, 180–181
message processing model and,
    92–93, 92 (figure)
moderators of, 183
neoassociationistic model and, 181–182
network models of memory and, 184
news reporting and, 118
operationalization of priming, judgment of
    ambiguous events and, 180
political coverage/Presidential evaluations
    and, 183–186
political priming, limitations/future
    directions for, 185–186
political priming, models of, 184–186
priming, definition of, 178–179
rape myths and, 186–187
reaction time data and, 180–181, 185
stereotype priming, limitations/future
    directions for, 187–188
stereotype priming models and,
    178, 186–188, 381–383
strength of primes and, 179
technological innovation and, 189
television violence and, 181, 183
  See also Agenda setting model;
    Framing effects
Print media, 9–10
  academic disciplines, print-inspired
    separation of, 521
  censorship and, 10
  media effects research,
    public awareness of, 13
  press freedoms and, 10
  printed word, 517–518,
    520–521, 522, 523, 528
  social systems, upheaval in, 10
  See also News media; Newspapers;
    Parasocial interaction/identification
Prior knowledge, 103
Probabilistic-causality perspective, 14, 39
Product placement research, 300
  attitude measures and, 301–302
  entertainment content and, 301
  persuasive messages and, 301
  product placement effectiveness,
    measurement of, 301–302
  product placement effects,
    factors in, 300–301

recall and, 301–302, 306
See also Advertising research; Interactivity
    effects research
Propaganda, 10, 11
    early television research and, 71
    public opinion and, 20
Propensity score models, 48
Prospect theory, 87
Protection motivation theory (PMT),
    211, 274–275
Protestant Reformation literature,
    10, 521, 522
Protocol analysis, 56
Proxy agency, 284
Psychological communication perspective.
    See Communication technologies effects;
    Uses and gratifications model
Psychoticism, 243
Psy-function concept, 131–132, 133, 135
Public affairs information, 114, 116, 117
    news reporting, public opinion climate
        and, 119
    political messages, limited capacity theory
        and, 122
    public knowledge of, 123
    television public affairs programming, 119
Public health. *See* Health communication
    models; Health impacts; Population health
Public information campaigns, 275, 288, 290,
    292, 417–418
Public opinion, 10, 11, 40
    collective opinion, media source of, 119
    coverage of issues and, 85
    issue-attention cycle and, 44
    judgmental heuristics and, 122
    message interpretation,
        media impact and, 12
    news reporting, perceived public opinion
        and, 119
    opinion leaders and, 12, 20,
        115, 120, 491, 493
    propaganda, powerful effects of, 20
    television programming planning and, 138
Public policy, 16, 40, 319
    public agenda, power of, 568–569
    race-related policy reasoning and, 385–386
    See also Politics; Public opinion
Public relations, 11
Publishing history, 9–10

Qualitative methods, 53–54
    audience-as-agent, meaning
        construction and, 54
    audience decoding process and, 58–59

audience studies, history of, 56–63
collaborative audience studies and, 63–64
communication technologies and,
    61, 62, 64
constructivism and, 55–56
contemporary audience research, 61–63
contextual factors' influence, study
    of, 61–62
definition of qualitative methodology,
    54–56
ethnographic research and, 54–62
fieldwork methods, 54, 58, 62, 63
focus group interviews, 55, 56, 60
future trends in, 63–64
I-thou dialectic and, 58
interpretive purposes of, 55–56
interview method, 56, 59–60, 64
material culture analysis, 56
measurement instruments and, 57
media landscape transformation and, 62–63
native viewpoint and, 55
oral histories, 60
participant observation, 56, 57–58, 64
popular culture artifacts and, 64
power differences and, 62
protocol analysis, 56
reactivity effects, researcher
    involvement and, 58
reception analysis research, 59–61
screen theory, text-spectator
    relations and, 58–59
semiotic democracy and, 60–61
social action media theory and, 57
symbolic interactionism and, 57
taken-for-granted knowledge,
    questioning of, 56, 57
theoretical inferences, sociohistorical
    particularity of, 56
uses and gratifications theory and, 57
verstehen/empathetic understanding and, 55
webs of significance and, 55
See also Quantitative methods
Quantitative methods, 35–36
    active audience conception and, 47–48
    aggregated data and, 40, 41, 42
    causal chains, complexity of, 44–46
    causation/explanation, media effects
        research and, 38–39
    causation/explanation, social science
        research and, 36–38
    cause-effect relationship and, 36
    challenges to causal inference and, 39–48
    construct measurement,
        problems with, 46–47

cross-level theorizing and, 41
cross-sectional designs and, 43
ecological fallacy and, 40–41
experimental designs and, 38, 43, 46, 57
fallacy of composition and, 40
fallacy of confusing cause and
    effect and, 42–43
fallacy of ignoring the future and, 43
fallacy of ignoring the past and, 43
fallacy of nonreciprocal causation and, 45
fallacy of the secular trend and, 43
fallacy of wrong causal process and, 44–45
fallacy of the wrong level and, 41
fallacy of the wrong timing and, 44
Granger causality test and, 43
group-level effects, bias and, 42
interrupted time-series designs and, 43
media effects, dynamic process of, 42–44
media effects, multilevel
    phenomena of, 39–42
mediation relationships and, 45–46
multilevel modeling and, 41–42
statistical inference and, 38
structural equation modeling and, 45
third variable fallacy and, 45
two-step flow model and, 41
type I/type II errors and, 43
See also Causation; Media effects research;
    Qualitative methods

Racial/ethnic stereotyping, 187, 232, 244
    activation of stereotypes and, 381–383
    content-specific outcomes and, 379–380
    crime, race-based judgments
        and, 82, 244, 382
    cross-media effects and, 379
    dominant culture/race and, 380, 381, 382
    framing effects and, 379
    intergroup processes and, 383–386
    mental models and, 379–380
    new media environment and, 387–388
    policy reasoning and, 385–386
    priming approach to, 381–383
    prosocial outcomes and, 383, 387
    race-ethnicity, media depictions of, 381
    racial/ethnic majority groups,
        social identity and, 384
    racial/ethnic minority groups, social identity
        and, 384–385
    racial profiling, 383
    real-world contact and, 388
    reduction of, 388
    research, methodological challenges of,
        386–387

shared reality theory and, 386
    social cognitive theory and, 380
    social identity-based approaches
        and, 383–385
    social judgments and, 382–383
    stereotype formation,
        media exposure and, 378–380
    stereotype representation and, 378
    See also Stereotyping
Racial profiling, 383
Radio, 25
    entertainment-education programming,
        289–290
    family influence and, 252
    quiz shows, 162
    soap operas, 149, 162
    talk-back radio, 139
    television, introduction of, 507, 521
    War of the Worlds broadcast, 188, 251
    See also Parasocial interaction/identification
Radio Diaries program, 318
Radio frequency identification (RFID)
    tags, 522
Rape, 186–187, 244
Rapid penetration diffusion model, 498
Reality:
    constructivism and, 55–56
    materialtheorie argument and, 521
    science, value-laden pursuit of, 56
    shared reality theory, 386
    storytelling and, 71–72
    See also Cultivation analysis; Media
        realism; Reality television
Reality television, 80, 163, 431
    interpretation of, 432
    nonprofessional cast members on, 431, 432
    perceptions of reality and, 432
    See also Media realism;
        Reality; Television
Reasoned action. *See* Theory of reasoned
    action; Voluntary action theories
Reception analysis research:
    contextual factors, influence of, 61–62
    diasporic communities, syncretic cultures of
        reception and, 139
    ethnographic research, 59–61
    See also Audience; Qualitative methods
Receptive activity, 25, 53–54
Regina v. Hicklin (1868), 133
Reinforcement spirals, 570
Reinvention process, 498
Relationships. *See* Internet; Parasocial
    interaction/identification; Social
    networks; Social systems

Relaxation need, 242
Resource distribution, 54
  assessment of, 199
  cognitive effort and, 199
  controlled resource allocation, 195
  limited capacity model of motivated
    mediated message processing and,
    195–196, 197, 198–199
  orienting response, automatic resource
    allocation and, 195–196
Restrictive intervention technique, 349–350
Risk behaviors, 291–292, 320, 349
  sexual behavior, 410–411
  teen pregnancy and, 318, 410–411, 415
  See also Aggressiveness; Violence
Role-system medium theory,
  523, 525, 528

Salience transfer, 84
Schema theory, 288–289
Schemata, 93, 244, 378
Scientific communication, 494
Screen theory of text-spectator
  relations, 58–59
Script theory, 240–241, 247, 351, 352
Second Life, 63
Secondary task reaction time (STRT), 199
Secular trend, 43
Sedentary behaviors, 258–259
Sedition Act of 1798, 10
Sedition Act of 1918, 10
Selective exposure hypothesis, 272
Self-categorization theory, 102, 383–384
Self-determination theory, 458–459
Self-discrepancy theory, 397
Self-efficacy beliefs, 286–287, 292
  behavior change techniques and, 292
  enactive mastery/physiological
    feedback and, 294
  health campaigns and, 290, 292, 316
  mastery experience and, 286, 294
  physiological/emotional states and, 287
  verbal persuasion and, 286–287
  vicarious experience and, 286
  See also Social cognitive theory (SCT)
Self-enhancement motivation, 101, 103
Self-esteem:
  group-based processing,
    group comparisons and, 383
  interchangeability studies and, 104
  pro-eating-disorder Web sites and, 400
  stereotypical images and, 385
  televised sports viewing and, 447
  See also Body image

Self-prophesy effect, 272
Self-reactiveness, 285
Self-reflectiveness, 168, 285
Self-reflexiveness, 27, 30 (table)
Self-regulation, 285
Semiotic democracy, 60–61
Sensation need, 241–242, 245, 349
Sense extension theory, 13
Sesame Street, 332, 333, 335, 336,
  337, 339, 341, 473, 475
Seventeen magazine, 398
Sexual media messages, 107, 409
  campaign against, 133
  content analysis, sexual content patterns
    and, 411–413
  contraception and, 412
  cultivation theory and, 413–414
  entertainment-education messages and,
    417–418
  extra-marital relationships and, 412
  gender as moderator of, 414–415
  health/precaution messages and, 412
  media effects process, theoretical challenges
    and, 414
  media literacy interventions and, 348, 418
  new media technology and, 414, 415–416
  objectification of bodies and, 412–413
  physical consequences of sex and, 412
  pornography, 16, 241, 414, 416
  precursory/coded content, 411–412
  quantity of sexual content and, 412, 413
  race-ethnicity as moderators of, 414, 415
  research, methodological challenges in, 416
  risky sexual behavior, 410–411
  sexual health interventions,
    potential for, 416–418
  sexual health media campaigns, 417
  sexual socialization and, 409–410, 411, 415
  social cognitive theory and, 413–414
  superpeers and, 418
  teenage dramas and, 288
Shared media space, 513–514
Shared reality theory, 386
Smart phones, 371
Smoking messages, 107, 272, 275, 288,
  317, 321
Soap operas, 149, 162, 166, 226, 269
Social action media theory, 57
Social capital, 54, 119, 445–446
Social cognitive theory (SCT), 215, 283
  admired characters, behavioral imitation
    and, 291
  agency concept and, 284–285
  attention to media content and, 290–291

behavioral reinforcement, modeling process
    and, 291–292
behavior-reward mechanisms and, 396
bi-directional evolutionary
    pressures and, 284
deconstruction of, 284–287
entertainment-education
    programming and, 289–290
entertainment games, violence and, 460
future directions for, 290–294
health behaviors and, 315–316
historical background of, 283–284
human capabilities, shaping
    destiny and, 285
identification, modeling process
    and, 291–292
individual aspects of, 288
individual agency and, 284
intended media effects and, 289–290
internalization of ideal and, 396–397
mastery experience and, 286, 294
media effects research and, 287–290
media literacy interventions and, 349
metacognition, forethought and, 285
new media, theory testing and, 292–294
outcome expectancies and, 285–286
physiological feedback and, 294
proxy agency, 284
reinforcement and, 285–286
self-efficacy beliefs and, 286–287, 292, 293
self-reflection and, 285
self-regulation and, 285
sexual media messages and, 413–414
stereotyping and, 380
symbolization and, 285
unintended media effects and, 287–289
vicarious learning and, 285–286, 290–291
Social comparison theory, 215–216
    body image and, 216, 397
    media literacy interventions and, 349
    upward comparisons, 397
Social coviewing technique, 350, 510
Social distance corollary, 101
Social environment, 251–252
    communication-social environment
        interactions, 257–259
    communicatory utility,
        media content and, 255–256
    conversation-limiting
        media effects and, 255
    coping mechanism, media use and, 257
    emotional contagion and, 258
    family communication
        patterns and, 254, 259

family environment, peripheral media
    consumption and, 256, 261
family/parental influences and, 252–255
family tensions, household media use and,
    256–257
future research, issues/directions
    for, 260–262
interpersonal interaction, content
    preferences and, 253–255
intra-audience effects and, 258
media effects on, 255–257
media selection/use, influences on, 252–255
media as social environment, 256–257
media use, interpersonal interaction and,
    255–256
multitasking trend and, 262
newer media technologies and, 262
nonverbal communication skills, media
    viewing and, 256
parental mediation, media selection and,
    252, 254, 260
peer influences and, 252, 253–254
preferences for media content, 252–255
research methods, media use-environment
    studies and, 259–260
sedentary behaviors/health, media use and,
    258–259
social/communication skill development
    and, 256
social shaping of technology and, 498
social utility effect, topics for conversation
    and, 255–256
theoretical perspectives, application of, 261
See also Audiences; Communication
    technologies effects; Social networks;
    Social systems
Social identity theory, 107, 383
    racial/ethnic majority groups and, 384
    racial/ethnic minority groups
        and, 384–385
    televised sports viewing and, 447
    See also Social cognitive theory (SCT);
        Social environment
Social influence model, 349
Social judgment, 378, 382–383
Social judgment theory, 276–277, 349
Social learning theories, 284, 396
Social marketing methods, 317–318
Social networking Web sites,
    217, 415, 568, 571
Social networks, 16, 120, 217, 320, 493, 536
    See also Communication technologies effects;
        Parasocial interaction/identification;
        Social environment; Social systems

Social science research:
    causation/causal inference and, 36–38
    computer-based technologies, social
        psychological effects and, 545–546
    news processing, 117–119
Social Sciences Citation Index, 100
Social systems:
    common sense/taken-for-granted
        knowledge and, 56
    cultivation effects and, 41
    hypermediated environments and, 522–523
    information societies and, 16
    innovation diffusion process and, 493–494,
        498–499
    knowledge, status-based
        differences and, 116
    mass behavior, concept of, 11
    media messages, polysemic nature of, 20–21
    media use patterns and, 15–16
    mobile network society and, 16
    network society and, 16, 20, 21
    printed word, exposure to, 10, 11
    real communities, dense features of, 63
    social constraints, 15
    subversive messages, inoculation against, 11
    urbanization/industrialization of, 11
    See also Parasocial interaction/identification;
        Social environment; Social networks
Social trust, 119
Social utility, 255–256
Social verification, 386
Socialization process, 378
    book-controlled socialization, 526
    sexual socialization, 409–410, 411, 415
    See also Social environment; Social
        influence model
Socioeconomic status (SES), 116, 320,
    320 (figure), 323, 335, 337, 499
Sopranos, The, 72, 166
Speech effects, 9, 520
Spiral of silence theory, 107, 119,
    567, 570–571
Sports. *See* Televised sports
Stage models of behavioral change, 275–276
Stalactite/stalagmite model, 15
State-Trait Anxiety Scale, 213
Stereotyping:
    cross-media influences and, 379
    framing effects and, 379
    immigration issues, framing and, 187
    intergroup processes and, 383–386
    media literacy interventions and, 347
    media priming and, 178, 186–188, 377–378
    mental models and, 379–380

    parasocial relationships and, 226–227
    positive depictions, priming and, 188
    priming models and, 381–383
    rape myths and, 186–187
    sexuality, oppressive stereotypes
        of, 412–413
    social cognitive theory and, 380
    stereotype, definition of, 378
    stereotype formation, media exposure and,
        378–380
    stereotype priming, models of, 187
    stereotype representation, 378
    See also Racial/ethnic stereotyping
Stimulus-response models, 10, 38, 44
Storytelling, 71–72
    communication infrastructure
        theory and, 541–542
    tragedy and, 167, 169
    transportation, concept of, 167–168
Structural equation modeling (SEM), 15, 45
Structural influence model of health
    communication, 320, 320 (figure)
Subversive messages, 11
Survey methods, 69, 73
Suspension of disbelief, 26
Symbolic interactionism, 57, 224
Symbolic meaning, 285
    phonetic symbolism, 307–308
    See also Meaning

Taken-for-granted knowledge, 56, 57, 71
Technical communication, 494
Technology, 1, 2
    adaptive/technology structuration
        and, 498
    body image and, 400–401
    cultivation theory, new media environment
        and, 78–79
    digital divide and, 323–324
    digital media technologies,
        61, 62, 79, 414, 492–493
    digital retouching technology, 400–401
    emotion's role in, 217
    entertainment content and, 169, 170–171
    future mass communication and, 16
    health-related video games, 293
    hypermediation trend and, 522–523, 528
    immersive virtual environment
        technology, 293
    individualized/tailored messages and, 293
    metacontrol concept and, 498
    mobile network society and, 16, 62
    movable type, printed word and, 9–10
    news environment and, 123

Nintendo Wii, 293, 294
on-demand content delivery and, 62
priming effects and, 189
social shaping of technology, 498
technological fragmentation, individual
    choice/initiative and, 152
user-generated content, 217
virtual reality selves, 293
virtual representation of other, 293
wireless communication, 16
See also Communication technologies
    effects; Computer-mediated
    communication (CMC); Diffusion of
    innovations (DOI) theory; Internet;
    Parasocial interaction/identification
Technology acceptance model (TAM), 496
Technology implementation process, 496
Teen pregnancy, 318, 410–411, 415
Telecommunications Act of 1996, 370
Telenovelas, 61, 139
Teletubbies, 332, 333, 334
Televised sports, 439–440
    aggressive behavior and, 447–449
    announcer effects and, 443, 444
    disposition-based effects on enjoyment, 441
    drama/suspense perceptions, enjoyment and,
        442–443
    enjoyment outcomes and, 440–444
    knowledge acquisition and, 445–446
    newer media technology and, 449
    physiological arousal/affective engagement
        and, 445
    self-esteem/social identity and, 447
    social capital and, 445–446
    social interaction and, 446–447
    sports encounter and, 446
    violence presence/perceptions, enjoyment
        and, 443–444
Television:
    age-based rating system for, 370
    audience, exposure to content and, 21, 24
    automatic processing state and, 24, 25
    broadcast personalities, illusionary
        relationships and, 152, 153
    digital interactive television, 137
    digital media environment and, 78–79
    early research on, 71
    family influence and, 252–253
    heavy vs. light viewing of, 73–74
    informational programming, 242
    mainstreaming pattern and,
        75–77, 76 (figure)
    mealtime viewing and, 259
    message systems and, 72

political affairs information and, 119
psychographic profiles and, 137–138
public affairs programming, 119
social action approach to, 57
storytelling and, 71–72
V-chip and, 370
videomalaise hypothesis and, 119
viewing, rationale for, 149–150, 153
violence, priming effects and, 181–182, 183
See also Cultivation analysis; Cultivation
    theory; Displacement effects;
    Educational television; Individual
    differences; Media violence; Obesity;
    Parasocial interaction/identification;
    Reality television; Social environment;
    Televised sports
Theoretical paradigms, 1–2
Theory of planned behavior (TPB), 274, 316
Theory of reasoned action (TRA),
    45, 107, 273–274, 316
Third-person perception (TPP), 100
    actor-observer attribution bias and, 103
    behavioral response and, 104–108
    cognitive explanations for, 102–104
    control of life events and, 102
    coordination reactions and, 105–106
    future research topics on, 108–109
    impression management motives and, 102
    in-group/out-group norms and, 102
    media violence, perception of, 365
    message relevance and, 102
    motivational explanations for,
        100–102, 103–104
    normative influence and, 107–108
    perceived exposure and, 102
    prevention reactions and, 105
    prior knowledge,
        schemata/stereotypes and, 103
    reality constraints and, 103
    self-enhancement motivation and, 101, 103
    social distance corollary and, 101
    susceptibility to influence and, 103, 104
    See also Presumed media influence
Third variable fallacy, 45
Threat. *See* Fear appeal research; Health belief
    model (HBM); Protection motivation
    theory (PMT)
3-2-1 Contact, 339, 341
Time displacement issue, 332, 335, 339–340
Transformation concept, 507, 521
Transported state, 26–27, 30 (table),
    167–168, 430
Transtheoretical model (TTM), 317
Trust and media, 119, 123, 224, 364

truth® campaign, 321
Truth-seeking, 168–169
24, 166
Two-level model of entertainment motivation,
    459–460, 459 (figure)
Two-step flow model, 20, 41, 120, 491

Urbanization, 11
USA PATRIOT Act of 2001, 10
User-generated communication,
    16, 217, 306
Uses and dependency model, 152
Uses and gratifications model, 13, 20,
    57, 69, 147–148, 239
  audience choice/initiative and, 148–149
  communication motivation, newer media
      and, 153–154
  communication orientations and, 151–152
  core elements of, 150–153
  digital games and, 457
  emerging communication
      technologies and, 150
  foundational assumptions of, 148
  individual differences/choice and, 152–153,
      163, 238–239, 241
  individual dispositions, computer-mediated
      communication and, 154
  instrumental orientation, content-focus
      of, 151–152
  Internet use, motives for, 153–154, 163
  media content, satisfaction with, 151, 152
  media dependency and, 154–155
  media entertainment and, 162–163
  media functions and, 149
  media motives, audience attitudes and, 150
  media preferences/selection and, 239
  media realism and, 426
  motivated audience behavior/involvement
      and, 150–151
  newer media environment and, 153–155
  news consumption and, 121, 153
  parasocial interactions and, 152, 225
  personal communication/mediated
      communication, interface of, 152
  phenomenistic approach and, 148–149
  radio/newspapers, appeal of, 149
  reality-based vs. fictional programming
      and, 152
  reinvention and, 498
  research foundations of, 148, 149–150
  ritualized orientation,
      medium-focus of, 151
  television viewing, rationale for,
      149–150, 162

V-chip, 370
Validation need, 242–243
Validity:
  causal inference, threats to validity
      of, 37, 40–42
  construct validity, 46–47
  ecological fallacy and, 40–41
  face validity, 25
  fallacy of composition and, 40
  fallacy of confusing cause and
      effect and, 42–43
  fallacy of ignoring the future and, 43
  fallacy of ignoring the past and, 43
  fallacy of nonreciprocal causation and, 45
  fallacy of the secular trend and, 43
  fallacy of wrong causal process and, 44–45
  fallacy of the wrong level and, 41
  fallacy of the wrong timing and, 44
  third variable fallacy and, 45
Verstehen, 55
Vicarious learning, 285–286
  attention to modeled actions
      and, 285, 290–291
  motivational processes and, 285
  production of symbolic
      representation and, 285
  retained memories and, 285
  self-efficacy beliefs and, 286
  See also Social cognitive theory (SCT)
Victimization, 361–362, 364
Video deficit, 334, 478
Video games, 16, 27, 169, 181, 182,
    233, 293, 364, 365, 400, 569–570
Video surveillance technologies, 522
Videomalaise hypothesis, 119
Violence:
  behavior disordered youth and, 243
  digital entertainment games
      and, 460–461
  general affective aggression model and, 182
  neoassociationistic model and, 181–182
  prevention of, 316
  priming effects and, 181–182
  psy-function concept and, 131–132
  symbolic violence, power/social control
      and, 75
  televised sports and, 443–444, 447–449
  violent video games, 233, 569–570
  See also Media violence;
      Media violence effects
Virtual reality selves (VRSs), 293
Virtual representation of
    other (VRO), 293
Virtual worlds, 27, 63, 169, 371, 522, 524

Voluntary action theories, 273
    protection motivation theory, 274–275
    stage models of behavioral change, 275–276
    theory of planned behavior, 274
    theory of reasoned action, 273–274
    See also Attitude theories;
        Persuasion theories
Voting, 13, 84, 91
Vulnerability, 11, 20, 22, 75, 134–135

War of the Worlds broadcast, 188, 251
Welfare reform, 88, 91

Wireless communication, 16
World War I, 10, 11
Written word, 9–10
    attempted suppression of, 10
    printed word, 517–518,
        520–521, 522, 523, 528
    social systems, upheaval in, 10
    spoken vs. written word,
        520, 523, 524
    See also Media effects; Print media

YouTube, 217, 387, 400, 563, 566

ABOUT THE CONTRIBUTORS

Sandra J. Ball-Rokeach (PhD, University of Washington, 1968) is a Professor of Communication and Sociology at the Annenberg School for Communication at the University of Southern California. She is Principal Investigator of the Metamorphosis Project (www.metamorph.org), which is an in-depth inquiry into the transformation of urban community under the forces of globalization, new communication technologies, and population diversity.

Kelly D. Blake (ScD, Harvard School of Public Health) is a research assistant at the Dana-Farber Cancer Institute and a cancer prevention fellow with the Harvard Education Program in Cancer Prevention and Control. Her research interests include health policy, risk communication, and media studies, specifically looking at how information access gaps contribute to health disparities in underserved populations. She was formerly a science writer and editor in the Division of Cancer Control and Population Sciences at the National Cancer Institute, National Institutes of Health.

Jane D. Brown (PhD, University of Wisconsin–Madison, 1978) is the James L. Knight Professor in the School of Journalism and Mass Communication at the University of North Carolina at Chapel Hill. Dr. Brown's research focuses on the effects of the media on adolescents' health. She recently completed an NIH-funded longitudinal study of the effects of the media on adolescents' sexual behavior, and is a member of a team of U.S. and Chinese scholars collaborating on research and communication campaigns to prevent the spread of HIV in China. Dr. Brown's books include *Sexual Teens* and *Sexual Media*, and she was associate editor of the *Encyclopedia of Children, Adolescents, and the Media*. Her research has been published in adolescent as well as communication journals, including the *Journal of Adolescent Health*, *Pediatrics*, and *Communication Research*.

Jennings Bryant (PhD, Indiana University, 1974) is CIS Distinguished Research Professor, holder of the Reagan Endowed Chair of Broadcasting, and Associate Dean for Graduate Studies and Research in the College of Communication & Information Sciences at the University of Alabama. He received the university's Blackmon-Moody Outstanding Professor Award for 2000 and was President of the International Communication Association in 2002–2003. His primary research interests are in entertainment theory, mass communication theory, media effects, and media and children.

Brad J. Bushman (PhD, University of Missouri, 1989) is a Professor of Communication Studies and Psychology at the University of Michigan. He has been studying violent media effects for over 20 years. He has authored over 100 scientific publications. His research has been published in the top scientific journals (e.g., *Science*) and has been featured on television (e.g., ABC News *20/20*, Discovery Channel), on radio (e.g., NPR, BBC), in magazines (e.g., *Newsweek, American Scientist*), and in newspapers (e.g., *New York Times, Wall Street Journal*).

Sahara Byrne (PhD, University of California, Santa Barbara, 2007) is an Assistant Professor of Communication at Cornell University. Her research examines message disruption processes. Her specific interests are in understanding when and why messages backfire, especially strategies to prevent negative effects of the media on children.

Jason Chen (MAT, Emory University, 2004) is a third-year doctoral student at Emory University, where he earned his MAT in secondary science education and his BS as a double major in biology and educational studies. His research interests include implicit theories of ability, science self-efficacy beliefs, and epistemological beliefs about the nature of science.

Jonathan Cohen (PhD, University of Southern California, 1995) is a Senior Lecturer at the Department of Communication, University of Haifa in Israel. His research and teaching focus on the relationships audiences develop with media characters, media effects, and perceptions of media influence. He has published more than 30 articles, chapters, and research reports on these and related topics. During his career, he has been awarded several national research grants and has received top-paper awards at international conferences. He currently serves on the editorial boards of *Journal of Communication* and *Media Psychology*.

Kristin L. Drogos (MA, University of Illinois, 2006) is currently a doctoral student in the Department of Communication at the University of Illinois at Urbana-Champaign. Her research focuses on youth and media, particularly the impact of new communication technologies on adolescents. During her graduate career, she has coauthored three top papers presented at national and international conferences.

Lauren Feldman (PhD, University of Pennsylvania, 2008) is Assistant Professor of Public Communication in the School of Communication at American University. Her research on the processing and effects of news has been supported by grants from the Carnegie-Knight Task Force on Journalism and published in several journals, including *Political Communication* and *Communication Research*.

Wes Fondren (PhD, University of Alabama, 2009) is an Assistant Professor of Communication at Coastal Carolina University. His research interests and teaching focus are on media effects; communication and technology; and children, family, and media. Before returning to graduate school, he was the director of technology for a group of 35 newspapers and 40 news Web sites.

Melissa R. Gotlieb (MA, University of Wisconsin, 2007) is a doctoral student in the School of Journalism and Mass Communication at the University of Wisconsin–Madison. Her research interests are broadly centered on understanding media effects on perceptions, attitudes, and behaviors, and the role of individual differences and predispositions in fostering a more active and critical consumption of media.

Kathryn Greene (PhD, University of Georgia, 1992) is an Associate Professor of Communication at Rutgers University. Her research and teaching focus on health communication and decision making. Specifically, she studies relational influences on health disclosure and messages targeting adolescent risk-taking decision making. Dr. Greene has published one book and more than 60 chapters and articles. During her career, her research has received numerous top-paper awards at national and international conferences.

Albert C. Gunther (PhD, Stanford University, 1987) is a Professor and Director of Graduate Studies in the Department of Life Sciences Communication at the University of Wisconsin–Madison. His research interests focus on the psychology of the mass media audience—often in the context of scientific controversies or public health. Gunther has published in most major communication journals and has received funding from numerous sources, including the USDA, NSF, NIH, and Robert Wood Johnson Foundation.

Alice E. Hall (PhD, University of Pennsylvania, 2001) is an Associate Professor of Communication at the University of Missouri–St. Louis. Her research focuses on media realism and the factors that contribute to individual differences in the ways audience members select and interpret entertainment media.

Kristen Harrison (PhD, University of Wisconsin, 1997) is an Associate Professor of Communication and Nutritional Sciences at the University of Illinois. Her scholarship concerns mass media and child/adolescent body image, disordered eating, and nutritional knowledge. She has published widely in communication, psychology, and public health. Her recent work has been supported by grants from the William T. Grant Foundation, the Illinois Council on Food and Agriculture Research, and the Illinois Department of Human Services.

L. Rowell Huesmann is Amos N. Tversky Collegiate Professor of Psychology and Communication Studies at the University of Michigan and Director of the Research Center for Group Dynamics at Michigan's Institute for Social Research. Huesmann's research focuses on the psychological foundations of aggressive behavior and, in particular, on how violence in the mass media and video games influences the development of aggressive and violent behavior. Huesmann has authored over 100 scientific articles and books, including *Growing Up to Be Violent, Television and the Aggressive Child,* and *Aggressive Behavior.* He is editor of the international journal *Aggressive Behavior* and was the 2005 recipient of the American Psychological Association's award for *Distinguished Lifetime Contributions to Media Psychology.*

Joo-Young Jung (PhD, University of Southern California, 2003) is an Associate Professor of Communication at International Christian University in Tokyo, Japan. Her research focuses on the impact of sociocultural factors on the use of communication technology, particularly the issues of the digital divide, Internet connectedness, and the influence of cultural differences in using the Internet and mobile phones. Jung's work has been published in outlets such as *Communication Research, Political Communication,* and *New Media and Society.* Her chapter in this volume is based, in part, on her analysis in her doctoral dissertation, *Internet Connectedness and Its Social Origins: An Ecological*

Approach to Communication Media and Social Inequality.

Marina Krcmar (PhD, University of Wisconsin–Madison, 1995) is an Associate Professor at Wake Forest University. Her research focuses on children, adolescents, and the media. Her current research examines the effect of violent video games on adolescents and the effect of videos targeting infants (e.g., Baby Einstein) on preverbal children. Her research has appeared in *Journal of Communication, Human Communication Research, Media Psychology, Communication Research,* and other journals. Her book *Living Without the Screen* was recently published by Routledge. She is on the editorial board of *Media Psychology* and the *Journal of Broadcasting & Electronic Media.*

Annie Lang (PhD, University of Wisconsin–Madison, 1987) is a Professor of Telecommunications and Cognitive Science at Indiana University Bloomington. Her research focuses on the dynamic interaction between media content and structure and the motivated human information processing system. During her career, she has published extensively in this area. Much of her research has been funded by the National Institute of Drug Abuse, for which she gives thanks. She is currently serving as an editor of *Media Psychology* and has served or is serving on the editorial boards of many other communication journals, including *Journal of Broadcasting and Electronic Media, Journal of Communication, Human Communication Research,* and *Communication Research,* and has been elected a Fellow of the International Communication Association.

Nam-Jin Lee (MA, University of Wisconsin, 2003) is a doctoral candidate in the School of Journalism and Mass Communication at the University of Wisconsin–Madison. His main research areas include media framing, public deliberation, and public opinion. He is particularly interested in the cognitive

and communicative activities that underlie democratic deliberation and how the quality and quantity of mediated political communication and talk facilitate or constrain this process.

Thomas R. Lindlof (PhD, University of Texas, 1980) is Professor of Telecommunications at the University of Kentucky. Lindlof's research and teaching focus on media and culture, audience studies, and interpretive research methods. He has recently served as editor of the *Journal of Broadcasting & Electronic Media.* His latest books are *Hollywood Under Siege: Martin Scorsese, the Religious Right, and the Culture* Wars and the third edition of *Qualitative Communication Research Methods,* with Bryan C. Taylor.

Yuping Liu (PhD, Rutgers University, 2002) is Associate Professor of Marketing and E. V. Williams Faculty Fellow at Old Dominion University. Her research focuses on the intersection among marketing, technology, and psychology. Her main research areas include Internet marketing and customer relationship management. Her research has appeared in *Journal of Marketing, Journal of Advertising, Journal of Advertising Research, Journal of Customer Behaviour,* and *Business Horizons.*

Tina M. Lowrey (PhD, University of Illinois, 1992) is Professor of Marketing at the University of Texas at San Antonio. Her main research interests include psycholinguistic analyses of advertising, and gift giving and ritualistic consumption. Her work has appeared in such journals as *Journal of Consumer Research, Journal of Consumer Psychology,* and *Journal of Advertising,* as well as numerous edited books. She is editor of *Psycholinguistic Phenomena in Marketing Communications* and *Brick & Mortar Shopping in the 21st Century.* She is a member of the *Journal of Consumer Psychology, Journal of Advertising, Media Psychology,* and *Psychology & Marketing* editorial boards.

Marie-Louise Mares (PhD, University of Wisconsin–Madison, 1994) is an Associate Professor in the Department of Communication Arts at the University of Wisconsin–Madison. Her research and teaching focus on developmental changes in media effects and the use of media for educational and prosocial ends. Her work has been published in journals such as *Communication Monographs, Human Communication Research,* and *Media Psychology.*

Dana E. Mastro (PhD, Michigan State University, 2000) is an Associate Professor in the Department of Communication at the University of Arizona. Her research documents depictions of race/ethnicity in the media (Latinos, in particular) and assesses the extent to which exposure influences stereotyping and racial/ethnic cognitions as well as a variety of intergroup and identity-based outcomes. She has published her research in journals such as *Human Communication Research, Communication Research, Media Psychology,* and *Communication Monographs.*

Daniel G. McDonald (PhD, University of Wisconsin, 1983) is a Professor of Communication at the Ohio State University. Throughout his career, Professor McDonald has concentrated on social aspects of the audience and intra-audience effects. Most recently, he has been researching the social nature of the media experience and studying the blend of interpersonal and mass communication processes. He has published more than 30 journal articles and book chapters.

Douglas M. McLeod (PhD, University of Minnesota, 1989) is a Professor of Journalism and Mass Communication at the University of Wisconsin–Madison. His research focuses on social conflicts and the cognitive effects of the mass media. He has examined the antecedents and consequences of media coverage of both domestic and international conflicts, including social protests. He also researches how news coverage shapes knowledge and public opinion, including framing and priming effects.

Miriam J. Metzger (PhD, Annenberg School for Communication at the University of Southern California, 1997) is currently an Associate Professor in the Department of Communication at University of California, Santa Barbara. Her research interests include the social uses and effects of traditional and emerging communication technologies. She is the author of *Digital Media, Credibility, and Youth,* published by MIT Press, as well as numerous articles in the field of communication.

Joshua Meyrowitz (PhD, New York University, 1979) is a Professor of Communication at the University of New Hampshire. His research and teaching areas include media theory and critical analysis of news. He is the author of *No Sense of Place,* an award-winning book on the impact of electronic media on society. He has published over 90 articles and book chapters and has won numerous awards for his teaching and research.

Toby Miller (PhD, Murdoch University, 1992) chairs the Department of Media & Cultural Studies at the University of California, Riverside. He is the author and editor of over 30 books and hundreds of journal articles and book chapters, and edits *Television & New Media* and *Social Identities.* His work has been translated into Chinese, Swedish, Spanish, German, and Japanese, and he is regularly interviewed by the *bourgeois* media about disappointingly trivial matters.

Michael Morgan (PhD, University of Pennsylvania, 1980) is a Professor in the Department of Communication at the University of Massachusetts Amherst. He has authored or coauthored over 100 national and international scholarly articles and book chapters on the effects of television on images of violence, sex roles, aging, health, science, academic achievement, political orientations, the family, and other issues. He was a Fulbright Research Scholar in Argentina and has received the University of Massachusetts Distinguished Teaching Award.

Robin L. Nabi (PhD, Annenberg School for Communication, University of Pennsylvania, 1998) is an Associate Professor of Communication at the University of California, Santa Barbara. Her research interests focus on discrete emotions' influence on message processing and decision making in response to media messages that concern health or social issues. Her work has appeared in numerous communication journals, and she has served on several editorial boards, as the Chair of the Mass Communication Division of the International Communication Association, and as a coeditor of *Media Psychology*.

Daniel J. O'Keefe (PhD, University of Illinois at Urbana-Champaign, 1976) is a Professor of Communication Studies at Northwestern University. He has been a faculty member at the University of Michigan, Pennsylvania State University, and the University of Illinois at Urbana-Champaign. His research focuses on persuasion and argumentation. His work has received numerous awards, including the International Communication Association's Best Article Award, the National Communication Association's Charles Woolbert Research Award, its Golden Anniversary Monograph Award, its Rhetorical and Communication Theory Division Distinguished Scholar Award, and its Health Communication Division Distinguished Article Award, as well as the International Society for the Study of Argumentation's Distinguished Scholar Award and the American Forensic Association's Daniel Rohrer Memorial Research Award.

Mary Beth Oliver (PhD, University of Wisconsin–Madison, 1991) is a Professor in and Codirector of the Media Effects Research Lab in the College of Communications at Penn State University. Her research and teaching focus on media effects, with an emphasis on media entertainment, media and emotion, and media and social cognition. She was a Fulbright Research Scholar in New Zealand and served as Chair of the Mass Communication Division of the National Communication Association. She is coeditor with Jennings Bryant of *Media Effects, Advances in Theory and Research* (3rd ed.), and is former coeditor of *Media Psychology*, former associate editor of the *Journal of Communication* and *Communication Theory*, and former book-review editor for the *Journal of Communication*.

Frank Pajares was Winship Distinguished Research Professor at Emory University. His research focused on motivation and self-efficacy in educational contexts. He served on six editorial boards, was a Fellow of the American Psychological Association, coeditor of the book series *Adolescence and Education,* and associate editor of the *Journal of Educational Psychology*. He had published six books, including *Self-Efficacy Beliefs of Adolescents*. Professor Pajares passed away on January 14, 2009.

W. James Potter (PhD, Indiana University, 1979; PhD, Florida State University, 1981) is a Professor in the Department of Communication at the University of California at Santa Barbara, where he teaches courses in media literacy, media content, and media effects. He is the author of numerous scholarly articles, book chapters, and 15 books, including *Theory of Media Literacy: A Cognitive Approach, The 11 Myths of Media Violence, Arguing for a General Framework for Mass Media Scholarship, An Analysis of Thinking and Research About Qualitative Methods,* and the forthcoming *Media Literacy* (5th ed.).

Abby Prestin (MA, University of California, Santa Barbara, 2008) is a doctoral student at the University of California, Santa Barbara. Her research interests are situated in the area of health communication. Within this context, she focuses on the ways in which emotion research and theory can inform the design of media messages promoting the performance of health behaviors, as well as the ways in which individuals cope with their own or a loved one's chronic illness.

Vincent Price (PhD, Stanford University, 1987) is Associate Provost at the University of Pennsylvania, where he is also Steven H. Chaffee Professor of Communication and Political Science. He was formerly Chair of the Department of Communication Studies at the University of Michigan and editor-in-chief of *Public Opinion Quarterly.* He has written extensively on mass communication and public opinion, social influence processes, and political communication. His work has been translated and published in a half-dozen languages.

Arthur A. Raney (PhD, University of Alabama, 1998) is an Associate Professor at Florida State University. His research centers on the enjoyment of entertainment content such as drama, sports, and digital games, as well as the role that factors such as moral judgment and cognitive schemata play in media enjoyment. His writings have been published in various anthologies as well as journals, including *Journal of Communication, Media Psychology,* and *Communication Theory.* He is the lead editor of *Handbook of Sports and Media.*

Ronald E. Rice (PhD, Stanford, 1982) is the Arthur N. Rupe Chair in the Social Effects of Mass Communication in the Department of Communication at the University of California, Santa Barbara. He has coauthored/edited *Media Ownership, The Internet and Health Care, Social Consequences of Internet Use, The Internet and Health Communication, Accessing and Browsing Information and Communication, Public Communication Campaigns* (three editions), *Research Methods and the New Media, Managing Organizational Innovation,* and *The New Media.*

Ute Ritterfeld (PhD, Technical University of Berlin, 1995) is Professor of Media Psychology at the VU University Amsterdam and Cofounder of the Center for Advanced Media Research Amsterdam (CAMeRA@VU). Her research and teaching focus on educational usage of (entertaining) media in the area of health and science communication with a special emphasis on youth and the elderly. Ritterfeld is currently coediting the *Journal of Media Psychology.*

Beverly Roskos-Ewoldsen (PhD, Indiana University, 1989) is an Associate Dean in the College of Arts & Sciences and an Associate Professor of Psychology at the University of Alabama. She teaches courses in perception, visual-spatial cognition, and statistics. Her research interests involve visual-spatial cognition, especially individual and group differences in the comprehension, representation, and use of visual and spatial information. Her recent research includes comprehension of the media and wayfinding in real and virtual environments.

David R. Roskos-Ewoldsen (PhD, Indiana University, 1990) is a Professor in the School of Communication at the Ohio State University. He teaches courses on media psychology, attitudes and persuasion, and research methods. His research involves attitude and norm accessibility and media psychology with an emphasis on the dynamic relationship between the media, culture, and cognitive processes. He is the founding coeditor of the journal *Media Psychology* and founding editor of *Communication Methods & Measures.*

Alan M. Rubin (PhD, University of Illinois at Urbana-Champaign) is Emeritus Professor and Emeritus Director of Communication Studies at Kent State University. His research interests include the uses and effects of traditional and newer communication media. He is past editor of the *Journal of Communication* and the *Journal of Broadcasting & Electronic Media,* coauthor of *Communication Research: Strategies and Sources,* associate editor of *Communication Research Measures,* and coauthor of *Communication Research Measures II.* Besides publishing numerous articles, books, and chapters, he has given lectures and presentations in a dozen countries. He is a Fellow of the International Communication Association and recipient of the Broadcast Education Association's Distinguished Scholar Award.

Dhavan V. Shah (PhD, University of Minnesota, 1999) is Maier-Bascom Professor of Journalism and Mass Communication and Political Science at the University of Wisconsin–Madison. His research focuses on the capacity of mass and interpersonal communication, particularly the Internet, to encourage civic engagement; the influence of news framing, cueing, and priming on cognitive complexity, social judgment, and public opinion; and the correspondence between media use and the intersection of consumer and civic culture, particularly the politics of consumption.

L. J. Shrum (PhD, University of Illinois at Urbana-Champaign, 1992) is Professor and Chair of Marketing at the University of Texas at San Antonio. His primary area of research investigates the psychological processes underlying media effects, particularly the role of media information in the construction of values, attitudes, and beliefs. Other areas of research include psycholinguistics, impulsive consumption, and culture, and their relation to consumer behavior. This work has appeared in such journals as *Journal of Personality and Social Psychology, Journal of Consumer Research, Journal of Consumer Psychology, Personality and Social Psychology Bulletin, Human Communication Research, Public Opinion Quarterly,* and *Journal of Advertising,* as well as numerous edited books. He recently edited *The Psychology of Entertainment Media: Blurring the Lines Between Entertainment and Persuasion.* He currently serves on the editorial

boards of *Journal of Consumer Psychology, Human Communication Research, Communication Research,* and *Communication Monographs.*

S. Shyam Sundar (PhD, Stanford University, 1995) is Professor and Founding Director of the Media Effects Research Laboratory at Penn State University's College of Communications. His research investigates the effects of technological variables in user responses to Web content. Sundar has been identified as the most published author of Internet-related research in communication during the medium's first decade, and currently serves as Chair of the Communication & Technology Division of the International Communication Association. He is on visiting assignment at Sungkyunkwan University in Seoul, South Korea, as a WCU (World Class University) professor in the Department of Interaction Science.

Nurit Tal-Or (PhD, University of Haifa, 2001) is a Lecturer in the Department of Communication at the University of Haifa, Israel. Her research and teaching focus on media psychology and interpersonal communication.

Yariv Tsfati (PhD, University of Pennsylvania, 2001) is a Senior Lecturer in the Department of Communication, University of Haifa, Israel. His research and teaching focus on trust in media, the third-person effect, and campaign effects. His research has been funded by the Israel Science Foundation, the German-Israel Foundation, and other institutes. He currently serves as Vice-Chair of the Political Communication Division of the International Communication Association.

K. Viswanath (PhD, University of Minnesota, 1990) is a faculty member in the Department of Society, Human Development, and Health at the Harvard School of Public Health (HSPH), and in the Division of Population Sciences at the Dana-Farber Cancer Institute. He is the Director of the Health Communication Core of the Dana-Farber/Harvard Cancer Center (DFHCC), founding Director of Enhancing

Communications for Health Outcomes Laboratory at DFHCC, and the Chair of the Steering Committee of the Health Communication Concentration at HSPH. His research interests include communication and social change in health with a particular focus on communication inequalities and health disparities, and the sociology of health journalism. His most recent work examined the impact of communication inequalities in health in the domains of tobacco use and cancer survivorship, social capital and health, the digital divide, and occupational practices of health journalists. His research is funded by the National Institutes of Health, the Centers for Disease Control and Prevention, and the Lance Armstrong Foundation, among others. He has edited three books and published more than 80 papers and book chapters. He was also the editor of the Social and Behavioral Sciences section of the *International Encyclopedia of Communication*.

Peter Vorderer (PhD, Technical University of Berlin, 1992) is Professor of Communication Science and Scientific Director of the Center for Advanced Media Research Amsterdam (CAMeRA), both at the VU University Amsterdam, the Netherlands. He specializes in media use and media effects research with a focus on media entertainment and digital games. He has served as editor of *Zeitschrift für Medienpsychologie* and *Media Psychology*.

Sherrie Flynt Wallington (PhD, Howard University, 2006) is an Assistant Professor of Oncology at the Lombardi Comprehensive Center, Georgetown University Medical Center. She recently completed her postdoctoral fellowship with the Harvard School of Public Health and the Dana-Farber Cancer Institute. Her research focuses on communication inequalities and health disparities. She has a particular interest in cancer information-seeking patterns and barriers and new media technologies in the dissemination of cancer information, particularly among minority and underserved populations.

Jodi L. Whitaker is a graduate student in social psychology at the University of Michigan. Her research focuses on media effects, aggression, and cultural differences in emotion and media effects. She is an editorial assistant for *Personality and Social Psychology Bulletin*.

Barbara J. Wilson (PhD, University of Wisconsin–Madison, 1985) is the Kathryn Lee Baynes Dallenbach Professor and Vice Provost of the University of Illinois at Urbana-Champaign. Her research focuses on the social and psychological effects of the media on youth. She is coauthor of *Children, Adolescents, and the Media* (2nd ed.) and three book volumes of the *National Television Violence Study*. She also coedited *The Handbook of Children, Media, and Development*. In 2008, she was named a Fellow of the International Communication Association.

Itzhak Yanovitzky (PhD, University of Pennsylvania, 2000) is an Associate Professor of Communication at Rutgers University. His research program in the area of health communication explores the strategic use of mass and interpersonal communication to influence individual and social change. He has published numerous articles and book chapters about methodological issues in communication research, including such topics such causal inference, time-series analysis, and propensity score methods.

Dolf Zillmann (PhD, University of Pennsylvania, 1969) is Professor Emeritus of Communication and Psychology at the University of Alabama, where he was Senior Associate Dean for Graduate Studies and Research in the College of Communication & Information Sciences from 1989 to 2001. He received the University's Burnam Distinguished Professor Award in 2001. His primary research interests are in media psychology, media effects, entertainment theory, and mass communication theory.